Formation of Government Contracts

Third Edition

Formation of Government Contracts
third edition

John Cibinic, Jr.
Ralph C. Nash, Jr.

The George Washington University
WASHINGTON DC

LAW SCHOOL

GOVERNMENT CONTRACTS PROGRAM

Library of Congress Catalog Card Number: 98-70436
casebound ISBN 0-935165-41-X
perfectbound ISBN 0-935165-42-8

PREFACE

In 1960 the National Law Center of The George Washington University decided to establish a special program devoted to research and teaching in the field of Government procurement. We named it the Government Contracts Program and began to teach a series of continuing education courses and to publish in the field. In the early years, we devoted our attention to publishing a casebook on the law, *Federal Procurement Law*, and a series of monographs. The University was highly supportive in establishing two tenured positions on the law faculty devoted to work in the field of Government procurement. We were fortunate to hold those positions for thirty years, enabling us to accomplish the work that we have done.

By 1980 it was clear that our publications were being used by many business people as well as lawyers and that our courses were being heavily attended by contracting officers and corporate contract managers. To assist these people in performing their jobs, we embarked on a project to publish a series of textbooks in the field. *Formation of Government Contracts*, published in 1982, was the second of this series. After the enactment of the Competition in Contracting Act and the issuance of the *Federal Acquisition Regulation* in 1984, it became clear that a revision was necessary. Hence, the second edition of *Formation of Government Contracts* was published in 1986. It has been a best seller, with more than 20,000 copies sold in the ensuing years.

The passage of the Federal Acquisition Streamlining Act in 1994 and the Clinger-Cohen Act in 1996 made such significant changes in the Government contracting process that it was clear that a third edition was needed. It was ready for publication early in 1997 but we decided to wait until Part 15 of the *Federal Acquisition Regulation* was rewritten. This has enabled us to include all of the current statutes and regulations as well as the cases into the early part of 1998.

The book integrates the three sources of the rules of the formation of Government contracts — statutes, regulations and cases — into a single work. It is long because these rules are detailed and complex. We have attempted to assist our readers in dealing with the length of the book by providing a Subject Index. We also suggest that readers become familiar with the topics covered in each chapter. We believe that the maximum benefit can be gained from the book by becoming intimately familiar with each chapter and learning to use the book as an initial source of information when a contract formation problem is encountered.

Finally, this book would not have been possible without the able assistance of a large number of people. The primary credit goes to Karen R. O'Brien, Director of Publications of the Government Contracts Program. She managed the entire effort of turning out the third edition and did a large amount of the detailed work on it as well. She was assisted by Deborah Brissman and Claude Hooker. Student research assistants who contributed substantial research and writing were: Andrea Anderson, Jessica L. Atkins, Michael C. Boteler, Robert Busby, Jr., Mary E. Carney, Bethany DuPont, James C. Jacobus, Peter F. Jazayeri, Michael J. Martin, Hae Sung Nam, Kristin L. Peters, Steven A. Pozefsky, Stacy Rantala, Agnes Rodriguez, Margaret N. Rosenfeld, Sarah E. Shaw, Joseph P. Shereda, and Jason D. Smith. We would also like to thank Susan Knight who created the index, and Terry Elaine Miller who offered many helpful suggestions for improvement of the book.

Washington, D.C. — John Cibinic, Jr.
February — Ralph C. Nash, Jr.

ABOUT THE AUTHORS

John Cibinic, Jr. is Professor Emeritus at The George Washington University Law School where he taught from 1963 to 1993. From 1966 to 1974, he was Director of the Government Contracts Program. A respected spokesman in the field of Government contracts, Professor Cibinic conducts seminars and conferences on Government contracts for professionals in Government and corporations, and for lawyers. He also serves as a consultant to Government agencies, private corporations, and law firms. He was vice-chairman of the Cost and Pricing Committee of the Public Contract Section of the American Bar Association. Professor Cibinic has coauthored several books, including *Administration of Government Contracts*, *Cost-Reimbursement Contracting*, *Competitive Negotiation: The Source Selection Process*, and *Construction Contracting*. He received an A.B. from the University of Pittsburgh and a J.D. from The George Washington University. Together, Professors Cibinic and Nash coauthor the *Nash & Cibinic Report*, published monthly by Federal Publications, Inc.

Ralph C. Nash, Jr. is a widely recognized author and lecturer in the Government contracts field. He taught at the George Washington University Law School from 1960 to 1993, retiring to become Professor Emeritus. In 1960, he founded the University's Government Contracts Program and served as its Director from 1960 to 1966 and from 1979 to 1984. In addition to teaching, he does consulting work for Government agencies, private corporations, and law firms. He is a member of the Public Contract Section of the American Bar Association, is a member of the Procurement Round Table, and is a Fellow and serves on the Board of Advisors of the National Contract Management Association. He was a member of the DOD Advisory Panel on Streamlining and Codifying Acquisition Laws (Section 800 Panel). Professor Nash is the author of *Government Contract Changes* and the coauthor of several texts, including *Administration of Government Contracts*, *Cost-Reimbursement Contracting*, *Competitive Negotiation: The Source Selection Process*, *Construction Contracting*, and *Patents and Technical Data*. He received an A.B. from Princeton University and a J.D. from The George Washington University.

SUMMARY TABLE OF CONTENTS

[illegible]Y TABLE OF CONTENTS

CONTENTS

CHAPTER 1

BASIC PRINCIPLES OF FEDERAL PROCUREMENT

This book covers contracts of *executive branch agencies* for the *procurement* of goods and services where the Government is acting in the role of a buyer. While procurement is a major form of contracting activity of the Federal Government, it is only one of several types of contracting in which the Government engages. Other types of contractual arrangements include sales of personal property, purchases and sales of real property, grants, cooperative agreements, and employment contracts. Many of the legal principles and general rules applicable to these nonprocurement transactions are the same as those applied to procurement. Thus, many statutes, regulations, and decisions involving these principles and general rules will apply to both procurement and nonprocurement transactions. However, this book does not cover the detailed rules that apply to these nonprocurement transactions.

Procurement of goods and services by the United States Government is a unique form of activity dominated by numerous specialized rules. These rules arise out of the nature of the Government as a contracting party and the distinctive forms and procedures used in the procurement process. The rules governing this process are contained in statutes, regulations, and decisions, many of which are designed to protect the public's interest while assuring fair treatment to those who deal with the Government. Most of these rules are of general application but some apply only to specific agencies. In addition, procurement is conducted under the general rules governing all contracts entered into by the Federal Government. This general rule structure is exemplified by the basic principles of contract law discussed in Chapter 2.

This chapter covers issues that are fundamental to the federal procurement process. The first section illustrates the role of procurement in the operation of the Government by examining the variety of Government organizations that procure goods and services and the statutes and regulations that cover this area. It also describes the different types of contractual transactions in which the Government engages in order to show the relationship of procurement to other transactions. The next three sections consider how the special nature of the Government as a contracting party is recognized by legal principles aimed at protecting the public from unauthorized or improper activity. This consideration starts with an examination of the statutes and regulations that control the procurement activities of Government agencies and the methods of oversight used to assure compliance with these authorities. The next two sections analyze the special rules that apply to the authority of individual Government personnel as well as the binding nature of the activities of contractor personnel. The chapter concludes with a survey of the standards of conduct required of those representing or dealing with the Government.

I. TRANSACTIONS AND AGENCIES

Procurement is an essential element of the operation of almost every organization within the executive branch. To achieve a full understanding of the procurement process, it is necessary to see the relationship of procurement to the other types of contractual transactions carried out by these agencies. To understand the full scope of the procurement process, one must be aware of the variety of agencies within that branch of the Government and the statutes and regulations that govern the procurement activities of these agencies.

A. Transactions

As noted earlier, procurement is only one of a number of contractual transactions in which the Government regularly engages. Thus, procurement has a large number of special rules, and it also shares in general rules applicable to all contractual transactions of the Federal Government. These general rules of contract law, discussed in detail in Chapter 2, are most frequently found in judicial decisions where fundamental contract law issues are raised. Similarly, statutes and regulations dealing with litigation against the Federal Government or with socioeconomic policies are often broadly applicable to contracts regardless of the nature of the transaction. In contrast, statutes and regulations dealing with contracting procedures are usually more specific in their application and may affect only particular types of transactions. However, here too there is a large degree of commonality in the rule structure. Many of the procedural rules developed for one type of activity have been adopted for others. Since procurement contracts have attracted the greatest degree of statutory and regulatory attention, the procurement rules are often used as models for rules in other types of contracting. Thus, while the discussion in this book is directed specifically to procurement contracts, some of the cases cited as precedent have involved other types of Government contracts, and some of the procurement rules have application to other types of contracts.

The major categories of Government transactions utilizing contractual agreements are:

(1) Procurement of goods and services,

(2) Purchase of real property,

(3) Sale of real or personal property,

(4) Grants, cooperative agreements, cooperative research and development agreements, and "other agreements," and

(5) Employment of personnel.

Ordinarily, each of these transactions can be readily distinguished from the others. However, there can be a significant overlap between procurement transactions and other types of contractual arrangements. This section first discusses the types of transactions that are considered to be procurement of goods and services and the statutes and regulations applying to those contracts. It then considers the other types of Government contracts and analyzes their relationship to procurement contracts.

1. Procurement (Acquisition)

Government procurement, or "acquisition" as it is called in the Federal Acquisition Regulation (FAR), involves contracting for goods and services. The following guidance on the use of procurement contracts is provided at 31 U.S.C. § 6303:

> An executive agency shall use a procurement contract as the legal instrument reflecting a relationship between the United States Government and a State, a local government, or other recipient when —

(1) the principal purpose of the instrument is to acquire (by purchase, lease, or barter) property or services for the direct benefit or use of the United States Government; or

(2) the agency decides in a specific instance that the use of a procurement contract is appropriate.

The provision requiring that procurement be for the direct benefit and use of the United States Government has not been applied literally. For example, in *Civic Action Inst.*, 61 Comp. Gen. 637 (B-206372), 82-2 CPD ¶ 270, the Comptroller General held that if the instrument required performance, procurement was appropriate even though the performance was being acquired for others.

While this statute mentions only property and services, other statutes may be more specific. In addition, the regulations contain a detailed description of the types of services included. FAR 2.101 defines acquisition as "acquiring by contract with appropriated funds of supplies or services (including construction) by and for the use of the Federal Government through purchase or lease."

The major categories of procurement are:

(1) supplies,

(2) construction,

(3) services,

(4) research and development, and

(5) rental of real property.

Within each of these major categories are numerous specialized types of procurement. The classification of the procurement is extremely important for purposes of funding, types of contracts to be used, applicability of contract clauses, and coverage of socioeconomic provisions. See FAR 52.300 providing a matrix of solicitation provisions and contract clauses for specific types of procurement.

a. Personal Property (Supplies)

FAR 2.101 defines "supplies" as follows:

> "Supplies" means all property except land or interest in land. It includes (but is not limited to) public works, buildings, and facilities; ships, floating equipment, and vessels of every character, type, and description, together with parts and accessories; aircraft and aircraft parts, accessories, and equipment; machine tools; and the alteration or installation of any of the foregoing.

This definition of "supplies" is much more expansive than the meaning otherwise used in the FAR and is somewhat confusing. For example, contracts for the construction or repair of buildings and other permanent improvements to land are considered to be construction contracts not supply contracts, FAR Part 36. However, contracts for the "construction" of ships are considered to be supply contracts, FAR 36.102. Nevertheless, some construction rules may be applied to contracts for work on ships. See, for example, *Southwest Marine, Inc.*, 64 Comp. Gen. 714 (B-218875.2), 85-2 CPD ¶ 104 (Miller Act performance and payment bonds applicable to ship conversion contract).

There are special rules and procedures governing the acquisition of certain types of supplies. For example, "major systems" are governed by OMB Circular A-109 and FAR Part 34. Detailed guidance on such procurements is contained in DOD Directives 5000.1 and DOD Regulation 5000.2-R. NASA Guidance is contained in NASA Management Instruction 7100.14.

For many years there were special rules governing the acquisition of automatic data processing equipment in the Brooks Act, 40 U.S.C. § 759. However, this Act was repealed by Section 5101 of the Clinger-Cohen Act of 1996, and a new Information Technology Management Reform Act of 1996 was substituted. The special rules in this Act are implemented in FAR Part 39.

b. Construction

FAR 36.102 contains the following definition of "construction":

> "Construction" means construction, alteration, or repair (including dredging, excavating, and painting) of buildings, structures, or other real prop-

> erty. For purposes of this definition, the terms "buildings, structures, or other real property" include but are not limited to improvements of all types, such as bridges, dams, plants, highways, parkways, streets, subways, tunnels, sewers, mains, power lines, cemeteries, pumping stations, railways, airport facilities, terminals, docks, piers, wharves, ways, lighthouses, buoys, jetties, breakwaters, levees, canals, and channels. Construction does not include the manufacture, production, furnishing, construction, alteration, repair, processing, or assembling of vessels, aircraft, or other kinds of personal property.

Construction contracts are unique because they generally involve improvements to Government-owned property. Special rules governing these contracts are contained in FAR Part 36.

The Clinger-Cohen Act of 1996 adds 10 U.S.C. § 2305a and 41 U.S.C. § 253m, permitting the acquisition of construction using a special two-phase design-build selection procedure. This procedure may be used when there will be significant costs in competing for the award. See FAR Subpart 36.3.

In order to provide protection for subcontractors, suppliers, and laborers, the Miller Act, 40 U.S.C. § 270a, requires that performance and payment bonds be obtained for all construction contracts for fixed prices over $100,000, 40 U.S.C. § 270d-1. The Act also requires that the FAR contain payment protection on contracts from $25,000 to $100,000. See FAR 28.102. Bid guarantees are normally used when performance and payment bonds are required, FAR 28.101.

c. Services

FAR 37.101 defines a "service contract" as follows:

> "Service contract" means a contract that directly engages the time and effort of a contractor whose primary purpose is to perform an identifiable task rather than to furnish an end item of supply. A service contract may be either a nonpersonal or personal contract. It can also cover services performed by either professional or nonprofessional personnel whether on an individual or organizational basis. Some of the areas in which service contracts are found include the following:
>
> (a) Maintenance, overhaul, repair, servicing, rehabilitation, salvage, modernization, or modification of supplies, systems, or equipment.

(b) Routine recurring maintenance of real property.

(c) Housekeeping and base services.

(d) Advisory and assistance services.

(e) Operation of Government-owned equipment, facilities, and systems.

(f) Communications services.

(g) Architect—Engineering (see Subpart 36.6).

(h) Transportation and related services (see Part 47).

(i) Research and development (see Part 35).

Several types of services contracts are the subject of special statutory authorizations or procedures that supplement the general procurement statutes and regulations One type of services contract is architect-engineer (A-E) services. A-E services contracts are generally subject to the procurement statutes and regulations but are to be acquired under special negotiation procedures prescribed by the Brooks Architect-Engineering Act, 40 U.S.C. § 541 et seq. See Chapter 7 for a discussion of these procedures. Other types of services contracts are discussed below.

(1) Transportation and Travel Services

Transportation and travel services may be acquired under procurement contracts subject to the procurement statutes and FAR Part 47, or under Government bills of lading, travel requests, and other such documents under the provisions of the Transportation Act of 1940, 49 U.S.C. § 10721. Services procured under the Transportation Act are not subject to procurement statutes and regulations, FAR 47.000(a)(2). See *Petchem Inc.*, 65 Comp. Gen. 328 (B-220902), 86-1 CPD ¶ 179. 40 U.S.C. § 481 makes the General Services Administration (GSA) responsible for prescribing policies and methods of procurement and supply for transportation and travel services and authorizes the Administrator of GSA to enter into contracts on behalf of executive agencies. These statutes are implemented in the Federal Property Management Regulations (FPMR). 41 C.F.R § 101-40 deals with Transportation and Traffic Management, and 41 C.F.R. § 101-7 incorporates the Federal Travel Regulations Handbook by reference.

41 C.F.R. § 101-40.109-3 makes GSA transportation contracts mandatory on executive agencies. In addition to travel and transportation contracts, the GSA also enters into no-cost-no-fee travel management services contracts for use by executive agencies. The solicitation and award of such contracts are covered by the procurement statutes and regulations, *T.V. Travel, Inc.*, 65 Comp. Gen. 109 (B-218198.6), 85-2 CPD ¶ 640.

(2) Public Utility Services

The GSA Administrator is authorized under 40 U.S.C. § 481(a) to acquire "public utility services" for the use of executive agencies. However, the Department of Defense (DOD) and the Department of Energy (DOE) have independent authority to procure utility services, and other agencies may obtain such authority by delegation from the GSA, FAR 41.103. Contracts for utility services are subject to FAR Part 41 and may be made for periods not exceeding 10 years.

"Utility service" is not defined at 40 U.S.C. § 481(a), but FAR 41.101 contains the following definition:

> "Utility service" means a service such as furnishing electricity, natural or manufactured gas, water, sewage, thermal energy, chilled water, steam, hot water, or high temperature hot water. The application of part 41 to other services (e.g., rubbish removal, snow removal) may be appropriate when the acquisition is not subject to the Service Contract of 1965 (see 37.107).

Additionally, in *GSA Procurement of Equip. under 40 U.S.C. § 481(a)(3)*, 62 Comp. Gen. 569 (B-208422) (1983), the Comptroller General found that a procurement of telephone equipment and related installation and maintenance services from a nontariffed supplier was a procurement of public utility services. The supplier of such services need not be a "regulated, monopolistic public utility" in order for the services to be classified as a public utility service subject to 40 U.S.C. § 481(a), 45 Comp. Gen. 59 (B-155725) (1965).

Even though a service may fit the definition of a "public utility," FAR Part 41 procedures may not apply. See FAR 41.102(b) for utilities that are exempted from these procedures. See also DFARS Subpart 239.74.

Utility services above the simplified acquisition threshold must be acquired by a bilateral written contract regardless of whether rates or terms or conditions of service are fixed or adjusted by a regulatory body, FAR 41.201(b). If a utility supplier refuses to execute a contract, the agency is required to obtain a written refusal signed by an official of the supplier. This document, along with statements of the reasons for the refusal and the record of negotiations, are to be sent to the GSA, FAR 41.202(c). Unless urgent and compelling circumstances exist, the contracting officer must notify the GSA prior to acquiring utility services. After such notification, the agency may proceed with the acquisition and pay for utility services under the provisions of 31 U.S.C. § 1501(a)(8). When public utility services are being acquired by procurement contract, they are subject to the competition requirements of the procurement statutes, *R.C.A. Alaska Communications, Inc.*, Comp. Gen. Dec. B-178442, 74-1 CPD ¶ 336.

(3) Advisory and Assistance Services

Contracts for advisory and assistance services have been subject to special scrutiny and oversight because these services are closely related to inherent governmental functions. See Chapter 3 for a discussion of inherently governmental functions. These contracts are subject to FAR Subpart 37.2. FAR 37.201 contains the following definition of advisory and assistance services:

> "Advisory and assistance services" means those services provided under contract by nongovernmental sources to support or improve: organizational policy development; decision-making; management and administration; program and/or project management and administration; or R&D activities.

FAR 37.203(a) permits the use of advisory and assistance services "to help managers achieve maximum effectiveness or economy in their operations." However, FAR 37.203(c) prohibits contracting for advisory and assistance services:

> (1) Used in performing work of a policy, decision-making, or managerial nature which is the direct responsibility of agency officials;
>
> (2) Used to bypass or undermine personnel ceilings, pay limitations, or competitive employment procedures;
>
> (3) Contracted for on a preferential basis to former Government employees;

(4) Used under any circumstances specifically to aid in influencing or enacting legislation;

(5) Used to obtain professional or technical advice which is readily available within the agency or another Federal agency.

Concern over the possible improper use of advisory and assistance services has resulted in the imposition of numerous management controls. OFPP Policy Letter 93-1 deals with management oversight of service contracting and incorporates many provisions of rescinded OMB Circular A-120, and OFPP Policy Letter 89-1 provides detailed guidance on conflicts of interest.

(4) CONCESSION CONTRACTS

The Government often obtains services under concession contracts. Under these arrangements, fees are charged to the public and the Government obtains the services or provides the services to recipients at no cost to the Government. See, for example, *Systems Planning Corp.*, Comp. Gen. Dec. B-244697.4, 92-1 CPD ¶ 516 (operation of Securities Exchange Commission Lost and Stolen Securities Program) and *Ann Riley & Assocs.*, Comp. Gen. Dec. B-241309-2, 91-1 CPD ¶ 142 (stenographic services at public hearing). Although no public funds are expended under these contracts, they are considered procurement and the procurement statutes are applicable if the Government receives a benefit from the transaction. The benefit may be one received by the Government or it may be the discharge of an obligation of the Government. See *Total Med. Management, Inc. v. United States*, 104 F.3d 1314 (Fed. Cir. 1997), which involved a Memorandum of Understanding (MOU) between the Government and a health care provider. The court stated at 1320:

> Finally, the government argues that, if contracts, the MOUs are not subject to the Contract Disputes Act, 41 U.S.C. § 602(a), because they are not procurement contracts for the benefit of the government. The government argues that the MOUs are solely for the benefit of the military dependents who receive the medical care. We reject this argument since it is clear that the government has legal obligations to military dependents and benefits by obtaining said dependents' care at a reduced cost.

The determination of whether a sufficient benefit is received by the Government is done on a case-by-case basis. See *Bararossa Reiseservice*

GmbH, 66 Comp. Gen. 474 (B-225641), 87-1 CPD ¶ 529 (agreement providing for official travel services subject to procurement rules and agreement only for unofficial travel not subject to procurement rules). In *Maritime Global Bank Group*, Comp. Gen. Dec. B-272552, 96-2 CPD ¶ 62, the Comptroller General dismissed a protest against the Navy's execution of an agreement with a bank for the provision of on-base services. In its reasoning, the Comptroller General stated:

> Where a concession or similar type of transaction results in a benefit to the government, the transaction is one for the procurement of property or services, and is thus subject to our bid protest jurisdiction; whether the performance of the business opportunity in question relates to the advancement of the agency's mission depends, in turn, upon whether the agency's workload will be reduced or whether the effort is somehow rendered, either directly or indirectly, in support of the agency's mission requirements. Thus, for example, our Office has assumed jurisdiction over a protest against the award of a photocopy concession to provide copying services paid for by the public, where the services in question are a part of the agency's mission requirement of furnishing copies of documents to the public. *West Coast Copy, Inc.*; *Pacific Photocopy and Research Servs.*, B-254044; B-254044.2, Nov. 16, 1993, 93-2 CPD ¶ 283. Similarly, we have found jurisdiction where the agency was granting a concession for providing initial haircuts to new recruits at an Air Force base because the record reasonably established that receiving an initial haircut was an important aspect of the training experience, the provision of which was integral to the agency's mission. *Gino Morena Enters.*, 66 Comp. Gen. 231 (1987), 87-1 CPD ¶ 121, *aff'd on recon*, B-224235.2, May 13, 1987, 87-1 CPD ¶ 501. We also have found jurisdiction where the government receives a benefit in connection with the transaction, even where the benefit is not, strictly speaking, related to fulfilling the agency's mission. *See Americable Int'l, Inc.*, B-225570.2, July 20, 1987, 87-2 CPD ¶ 64 (agreement requiring cable television service provider to furnish free cable television services to all Navy ships and duty rooms on base confers benefit on government).
>
> On the other hand, where any benefit to the government is speculative or contingent, we have found jurisdiction lacking, and have declined to consider the merits of the protest, even though earmarks of a procurement were present. *See North Florida Shipyards, Inc.*, B-243575, May 3, 1991, 91-1 CPD ¶ 434 (although solicitation for the lease of a drydock facility by the Navy to a private concern required offerors to submit a capital maintenance plan with their offers, the agency was not obligated to obtain the services under the terms of the contract, and thus any procurement aspect of the transaction was merely speculative).

Here, the Comptroller General found no benefit to the agency sufficient to establish jurisdiction. The Comptroller General pointed out that the services were for the direct benefit of Navy personnel, not the Navy. Moreover, Navy personnel were not required to use the services and the bank was not required to provide such services.

The fact that the agency receives compensation from a concessionaire does not convert a concession contract into a procurement contract. See, e.g., *Good Food Serv., Inc.*, Comp. Gen. Dec. B-253161, 93-2 CPD ¶ 107; and *YRT Servs. Corp. v. United States*, 28 Fed. Cl. 366 (1993). The *YRT* case involved a concession by the National Park Service executed under specific statutory authority providing for such concessions, The National Park Systems Concessions Policy Act of 1965, 16 U.S.C. § 20 et seq. Even though a concession contract is not subject to procurement rules, modifications of the contract could be subject to the procurement if they provide for the expenditure of public funds. See *Yosemite Park & Curry Co. v. United States*, 217 Cl. Ct. 360, 582 F.2d 582 (1978).

d. Research and Development

Research and development is a specialized form of service contracting dealt with in FAR Part 35. Most agencies also have a separate appropriation for research and development contracts — requiring that this work be segregated from other types of work. FAR 35.001 contains definitions of applied research and basic research and development. DFARS 235.001 contains definitions of subcategories of these types of effort. FAR 35.002 contains the following statement of general principles applicable to contracting for research and development:

> The primary purpose of contracted R&D programs is to advance scientific and technical knowledge and apply that knowledge to the extent necessary to achieve agency and national goals. Unlike contracts for supplies and services, most R&D contracts are directed toward objectives for which the work or methods cannot be precisely described in advance. It is difficult to judge the probabilities of success or required effort for technical approaches, some of which offer little or no early assurance of full success. The contracting process shall be used to encourage the best sources from the scientific and industrial community to become involved in the program and must provide an environment in which the work can be pursued with reasonable flexibility and minimum administrative burden.

There are a number of techniques used to acquire research and development in addition to the standard negotiation technique. Basic research may be procured through broad agency announcements, 10 U.S.C. § 2302(2)(B) and 41 U.S.C. § 259(b)(2). Contracts for research and development may also be awarded on the basis of unsolicited proposals. In addition, all major agencies must use a designated percentage of their research and development funds in awards of research contracts to small businesses, 15 U.S.C. § 638. See Chapter 7 for a discussion of procedures followed when broad agency announcements are used to obtain research contracts.

e. Rental of Real Property

The rental of real property is also subject to procurement rules. See *Forman v. United States*, 767 F.2d 875 (Fed. Cir. 1985), holding that the exclusion in the Office of Federal Procurement Policy Act, 41 U.S.C. § 401 et seq., of contracts for the acquisition of "real property in being" does not apply to the acquisition of "new" as opposed to "existing" leases. General authority for leasing real property for the Federal Government is vested in the GSA, e.g., 40 U.S.C. § 490(h)(1) and 40 U.S.C. § 490 note. The GSA has, in turn, delegated authority for leasing of certain types of property and location to other agencies, 41 C.F.R. § 101-18.104. Limitations on the use of this delegated authority are contained in 41 C.F.R. § 101-18.104-1(a), as follows:

> The authority granted in and pursuant to this subpart shall be exercised in accordance with the requirements and limitations of the Federal Property and Administrative Services Act of 1949, as amended; the Budget Enforcement Act of 1990 and OBM Bulletin 91-02, Part B; Federal Property Management Regulations, subchapter D, those authorities listed in § 101-18.001; and other applicable laws and regulations, including the General Services Administration Acquisition Regulation (GSAR), the Competition in Contracting Act (CICA), and other OMB requirements.

GSAR Part 570 prescribes procedures for leasing real property, including build-lease arrangements. In *Aerolease Long Beach & Satsuma Inv. Co. v. United States*, 31 Fed. Cl. 342, *aff'd*, 39 F.3d 1198 (Fed. Cir. 1994), the court dealt with a provision of the GSAR that conflicted with a FAR provision. The court held that, in the absence of an authorized deviation (none was present in this case), the GSAR provision was invalid.

2. Other Contractual Arrangements

There are numerous other types of contractual relationships in which the Federal Government engages. The major nonprocurement transactions and their relationship to procurement are discussed in this section.

a. Purchase of Real Property

The purchase of real property is not covered by the procurement statutes. See 10 U.S.C. § 2303(a), stating that the Armed Services Procurement Act (ASPA) applies to the procurement of "all property (other than land)," and 40 U.S.C. § 471, stating that the Federal Property and Administrative Services Act (FPASA) applies to the procurement of "personal property." In addition, the FAR system applies to the procurement of "property other than real property in being," 41 U.S.C. § 405(a)(1). 41 U.S.C. § 14 provides that "[n]o land shall be purchased on account of the United States, except under a law authorizing such purchase."

b. Sale of Property

Article IV, Section 3, Clause 2 of the Constitution gives Congress the exclusive authority to dispose of Federal Government property. See, e.g., *Royal Indemn. Co. v. United States*, 313 U.S. 289 (1941). 40 U.S.C. § 484 et seq. Grants this authority to the GSA Administrator, who may delegate this authority to other agencies. The statute is implemented by the Federal Property Management Regulations, 41 C.F.R. § 101, and by subsidiary agency regulations such as the Defense Utilization and Disposal Manual, DOD Manual 4160.21-M. In addition to this general authority, specific statutory authority to dispose of property is granted to some agencies. See, for example, 16 U.S.C. § 477 granting the Secretary of Agriculture authority to sell timber from the national forests. The FAR does not apply to the sale of property, *Sandia Die & Cartridge Co.*, Comp. Gen. Dec. B-218011, 85-1 CPD ¶ 308.

There can be considerable overlap between a property disposal contract and a procurement contract. In some cases, work that would ordinarily be accomplished under a procurement contract may be made a part of the property disposal contract. For example, 16 U.S.C. § 535 gives the Secretary of Agriculture authority to provide for the acquisition, construction, and maintenance of roads within and near national forests by placing requirements on purchasers of national forest timber. The Miller Act, 40 U.S.C. § 270a, has been held not to apply to road construction under such contracts, *Keller v. United States*, No. 2356 (D. Mont. 1975). On the other hand, contracts for the "dismantling, demolition, or removal of improvements" are considered service contracts as provided under FAR Subpart 37.3. Under FAR 37.303(a)(2), such contracts may require the contractor to pay the Government for the right to salvage and remove materials resulting from the dismantling or demolition of operations. In a similar vein, the Secretary of Labor, in regulations promulgated under the Service Contract Act, found that while timber sale contracts generally do not constitute service contracts, contracts for the removal of diseased or dead timber would be service contracts under the Act, 29 C.F.R. § 4.111 and § 4.131.

c. *Grants and Cooperative Agreements*

Grants and cooperative agreements are used when the Federal Government intends to provide assistance or support to private organizations or to State and local governments. A grant without any contractual obligations on the part of the recipient may be characterized as a gift. See *Alabama v. Schmidt*, 232 U.S. 168 (1914) (Alabama had no contractual obligation to use land granted by Congress for public schools); *King County, Wash. v. Seattle School Dist. No. 1*, 263 U.S. 361 (1923) (congressional intent that grant money be used for public schools is not a requirement that grant money be used for public schools); and *Madison County Bd. of Educ. v. Illinois Cent. R.R. Co.*, 939 F.2d 292 (1991) (grant of land for public schools was a gift and not an honorary trust arrangement). However, most grants now require the recipient to use the funds or property only for specified purposes, 42 Comp. Gen. 289 (B-149441) (1962). Such grants are contractual agreements but are not procurement contracts, *Thermalon Indus., Ltd. v. United States*, 34 Fed. Cl. 411 (1995). Compare *Trauma Serv. Group, Ltd. v. United States*, 33 Fed. Cl. 426 (1995), holding that a cooperative agreement for shared health services under 10 U.S.C. § 1096 in which the Government made no promise to compensate the recipient was not a contract, and *D.R. Smalley & Sons, Inc. v. United States*, 178 Ct. Cl. 593, 372 F.2d 505, *cert. denied*, 389 U.S. 835 (1967), holding that a highway contractor with a state using federal highway grant funds could not sue the Federal Government because the state was not an agent of the Federal Government and such grants are "in reality gifts or gratuities."

Unlike procurement contracts, which agencies have the inherent authority to use in carrying out authorized activities, assistance agreements require that an agency have specific statutory authority for their use, *Federal Facility Contributions to Capital Costs of Sewage Treatment Projects*, 59 Comp. Gen. 1 (B-194912) (1979). Many agencies have such statutory authority. See, for example, 10 U.S.C. § 2358(b) (DOD may perform research and development by "contract, cooperative agreement, or grant"); 15 U.S.C. § 638 (agencies may award "funding agreements" — contracts, grants or cooperative agreements — to small businesses to carry out the SBIR program); 42 U.S.C. § 2473(d)(5) (NASA may enter into and perform such contracts, leases, cooperative agreements, or other transactions as may be necessary); 42 U.S.C. § 7256 (DOE may enter into and perform such contracts, leases, cooperative agreements, or other similar transactions). Although there is no overall grant procedural statute, individual statutes authorizing assistance programs often contain procedural and other requirements. See, for example, 7 U.S.C. § 450i(b) establishing the Department of Agriculture Research Grant Program (implemented in 7 C.F.R. Part 3200), and the National Science Foundation Act of 1950, 42 U.S.C. § 1871. See also 42 U.S.C. § 7274d (DOE may award grants for training); and 42 U.S.C. § 2486d (NASA may award grants to assist any space grant and fellowship program).

Neither grants nor cooperative agreements are governed by the procurement statutes or the FAR, *Trauma Serv. Group, Ltd. v. United States*, 33 Fed. Cl. 426 (1995). However, there are a few statutes and a number of regulations that govern these assistance agreements. Provisions concerning the disposition of patent rights in "funding agreements" (grants, cooperative agreements, and procurement contracts) with small businesses and nonprofit organizations are specified in 35 U.S.C. § 200 et seq. These provisions are implemented by the Department of Commerce in 37 C.F.R. Part 401. Broad guidance for assistance agreements is contained in OMB Circular A-102, Grants and Cooperative Agreements with State and Local Governments, 59 Fed. Reg. 52224 (1994), amended, 62 Fed. Reg. 45934 (1997); Grants Management Common Rule, 60 Fed. Reg. 19638 (1995); and OMB Circular A-110, Uniform Administrative Requirements for Grants and Agreements with Institutions of Higher Education, Hospitals and Nonprofit Organizations, 58 Fed. Reg. 62992 (1993), amended, 62 Fed. Reg. 45934 (1997). In addition, cost allowability for assistance agreements (as well as procurement contracts) is covered by OMB Circulars A-21, Cost Principles for Educational Institutions, 58 Fed. Reg. 39996 (1993), amended, 62 Fed. Reg. 45934 (1997); A-87, Cost Principles for State and Local Governments, 60

Fed. Reg. 26484 (1995), amended, 62 Fed. Reg. 45934 (1997); and A-122, Cost Principles for Non-Profit Organizations, 52 Fed. Reg. 19788 (1987), amended, 62 Fed. Reg. 45934 (1997). A few agencies have issued guidance on grants and cooperative agreements. See, for example, NASA Grant and Cooperative Agreement Handbook, 14 C.F.R. Part 1260.

Whether an assistance agreement takes the form of a grant or a cooperative agreement depends upon the Government's degree of involvement in the activity being supported, *Xcavators, Inc.*, 59 Comp. Gen. 758 (B-198297), 80-2 CPD ¶ 229. The following guidance on the use of grants is provided at 31 U.S.C. § 6304:

> An executive agency shall use a grant agreement as the legal instrument reflecting a relationship between the United States Government and a State, a local government, or other recipient when —
>
> (1) the principal purpose of the relationship is to transfer a thing of value to the State or local government or other recipient to carry out a public purpose of support or stimulation authorized by a law of the United States instead of acquiring (by purchase, lease, or barter) property or services for the direct benefit or use of the United States Government; and
>
> (2) substantial involvement *is not expected* between the executive agency and the State, local government, or other recipient when carrying out the activity contemplated in the agreement (emphasis added).

The conditions for use of cooperative agreements are specified in 31 U.S.C. § 6305 as follows:

> An executive agency shall use a cooperative agreement as the legal instrument reflecting a relationship between the United States Government and a State, a local government, or other recipient when —
>
> (1) the principal purpose of the relationship is to transfer a thing of value to the State, local government, or other recipient to carry out a public purpose of support or stimulation authorized by a law of the United States instead of acquiring (by purchase, lease, or barter) property or services for the direct benefit or use of the United States Government; and
>
> (2) substantial involvement *is expected* between the executive agency and the State, local government, or other recipient when carrying out the activity contemplated in the agreement (emphasis added).

FAR 35.003(a) implements this statute by stating that "[g]rants or cooperative agreements should be used when the principal purpose of the transaction is to stimulate or support research and development for [a] public purpose [other than acquisition of supplies or services for the direct benefit or use of the Federal Government]." An agency may not avoid compliance with the procurement rules by using a cooperative agreement when a contract is the proper vehicle, 67 Comp. Gen. 13 (B-227084.5) (1987), *recons. denied*, Comp. Gen. Dec. B-227084.6, Dec. 19, 1988, *Unpub.* (procurement contract rather than cooperative agreement should be used to obtain services of operation of a facility); *R&R Enters.*, IBCA 2417, 89-2 BCA ¶ 21,708 (agreement to run a concession is a contract, not a cooperative agreement); Comp. Gen. Dec. B-257430, Sept. 12, 1994, *Unpub.* (arrangement to conduct a survey was a procurement contract, not an "assistance relationship"). The distinction in these cases is between procuring services and providing assistance, with the cases holding that an arrangement to obtain services, even when other parties pay for them, will require the use of a procurement contract, *West Coast Copy, Inc.*, Comp. Gen. Dec. B-254044, 93-2 CPD ¶ 283. Compare *Montana Human Rights Comm'n*, HUDBCA 90-5305-C8, 91-2 BCA ¶ 23,993, holding that a cooperative agreement was properly used in an arrangement where the federal agency assisted a state in developing a complaint resolution process.

A recipient of a grant or cooperative agreement is not in a position to dictate an agency's choice of the instrument and is not liable to the Government if the agency makes the wrong choice, Comp. Gen. Dec. B-198846, Feb. 24, 1981, *Unpub.* (grant); *Protection Agency*, Comp. Gen. Dec. B-262110, 97-1 CPD ¶ 131 (cooperative agreement).

The distinction between procuring services and providing assistance is most obscure when an agency provides funds to support basic or applied research. In that situation, some agencies use grants while other agencies use procurement contracts. NASA provides guidance on the appropriate choice of award instruments for basic or applied research at 14 C.F.R. § 1260.302(h).

One of the purposes of the Federal Grant and Agreement Act was to "encourage competition in making grants and cooperative agreements," 31 U.S.C. § 6301. However, there is no overall statutory requirement for competition in such awards, *Burgos & Assocs.*, 58 Comp. Gen. 785 (B-194140), 79-2 CPD ¶ 194, and the Comptroller General will not consider protests that improper procedures have been used to award grants or cooperative agreements, *Sprint Communications Co.*, Comp. Gen. Dec. B-256586, 94-1 CPD ¶ 300 (protest will only consider whether procurement contract should have been used and whether there was a conflict of interest). In some cases, individual statutes require competition, e.g., 7 U.S.C. § 450i(b).

d. Other Transactions

Several major agencies have the authority to enter into "other transactions" that are neither procurement contracts, grants, nor cooperative agreements. See 10 U.S.C. § 2371(a), stating:

> Additional Forms of Transactions Authorized.—The Secretary of Defense and the Secretary of each military department may enter into transactions (other than contracts, cooperative agreements, and grants) under the authority of this subsection in carrying out basic, applied, and advanced research projects. The authority of this subsection is in addition to the authority provided in section 2358 of this title to use contracts, cooperative agreements, and grants in carrying out such projects.

Section 804 of the 1997 National Defense Authorization Act, P.L. 104-201, extends this authority to September 30, 1999, to "prototype projects that are directly relevant to weapons or weapon systems to be acquired or developed by the Department of Defense."

NASA has similar authority. See 42 U.S.C. § 2473, stating that the Administrator is authorized

> to enter into and perform such contracts, leases, cooperative agreements, or other transactions as may be necessary in the conduct of its work and on such terms as it may deem appropriate, with any agency or instrumentality of the United States, or with any State, Territory, or possession, or with any political subdivision thereof, or with any person, firm, association, corporation, or educational institution.

The DOE also has this type of authority with regard to its nonnuclear research, development, demonstration, and commercial application program. See 42 U.S.C. § 13541.

These agencies can use this other-transactions authority for any type of work within the scope of the statutory delegation. See, however, *Energy*

Conversion Devices, Inc., Comp. Gen. Dec. B-260514, 95-2 CPD ¶ 121, where the Comptroller General denied a protest that a procurement contract should have been used in lieu of a DOD other transaction on the grounds that the principal purpose of the agreement was to stimulate and support the development of new manufacturing technology not to acquire services. The discussion in this decision indicates that the Comptroller General might rule that the other-transactions authority could not be properly used if the agency was merely procuring services. Such a ruling would appear to be in conflict with the express statutory provisions.

When an agency uses its other-transactions authority, it need not comply with the procurement statutes, the FAR, or the statutes and regulations applying to grants and cooperative agreements. However, it will be required to comply with any other statute that applies to contractual transactions in general. To make this determination, the terms of each statute must be analyzed closely. There is no uniform guidance as to which statutes apply to these other transactions.

e. Cooperative Research and Development Agreements

Another form of contract is the cooperative research and development agreement (CRADA). The Federal Technology Transfer Act (FTTA), 15 U.S.C. § 3710a(d), defines a CRADA as follows:

> (1) [T]he term "cooperative research and development agreement" means any agreement between one or more Federal laboratories and one or more non-Federal parties under which the Government, through its laboratories, provides personnel, services, facilities, equipment, intellectual property, or other resources with or without reimbursement (but not funds to non-Federal parties) and the non-Federal parties provide funds, personnel, services, facilities, equipment, intellectual property, or other resources toward the conduct of specified research or development efforts which are consistent with the missions of the laboratory; except that such term does not include a procurement contract or cooperative agreement as those terms are used in sections 6303, 6304, and 6305 of title 31, United States Code;

15 U.S.C. § 3710a authorizes the directors of federal laboratories to enter into CRADAs. The purpose of these CRADAs is to "transfer federally owned or originated technology to State and local governments and to the private sector," 15 U.S.C. § 3710a(1). To accomplish this purpose, the Act

permits federal laboratories to provide any resources *except federal funds* to the parties entering into CRADAs. The other parties can, and generally do, provide funding to support the work of the laboratory. Agencies with the authority to enter into other transactions could enter into an agreement similar to a CRADA and provide federal funds as part of the arrangement.

A CRADA cannot be awarded when a procurement contract is the proper instrument, *Chem Serv., Inc. v. Environmental Monitoring Sys. Lab.*, 12 F.3d 1256 (3d Cir. 1993). The Comptroller General will only consider protests to the award of CRADAs if there is an allegation that a procurement contract should have been used or that there is a conflict of interest, *Management Dev. Group*, 64 Comp. Gen. 669 (B-219245), 85-2 CPD ¶ 34. In *Spire Corp.*, Comp. Gen. Dec. B-258267, 94-2 CPD ¶ 257, the Comptroller gave the following guidance as to how this issue would be decided:

> The FTTA sets forth specific requirements for using a CRADA which are different from the more general requirements for using a cooperative agreement specified in the FGCA. As a general matter, CRADAs under the FTTA may only be used where the purpose of the agreement is to transfer technology from a federal laboratory to a nonfederal entity for the purpose of conducting specified scientific research or development work in collaboration with the nonfederal entity. 15 U.S.C. §§ 3702, 3710a(c)(2) (1988). Given the more specific requirements under the FTTA, the terms of that statute would be the basis for determining whether a CRADA was appropriate here. It follows that the agency's actions would have to be shown to be impermissible under the terms of the FTTA in order for our Office to object to the agency's use of a CRADA.

CRADAs are not subject to the procurement statutes, the FAR, the statutes and regulations governing grants and cooperative agreements, or the statutes governing "other transactions." Furthermore, there is no Government-wide regulatory guidance and very little agency-wide guidance on the use of CRADAs. Thus, each agency is free to follow its own procedures. As with the case of "other transactions," other statutes pertaining to contracting by the Federal Government must be carefully analyzed to determine if they apply to CRADAs.

f. Employment Contracts

The employment of individuals by the Federal Government is accomplished pursuant to civil service laws. See generally 5 U.S.C. § 2101 et seq.

However, services may be acquired under a procurement contract, *either from an individual or an organization*, as long as an employer-employee relationship is not established between the Government and the persons performing the services, *Sunbelt Properties, Inc.*, Comp. Gen. Dec. B-249469, 92-2 CPD ¶ 353. In addition, 5 U.S.C. § 3109 permits agencies to "procure by contract the temporary (not in excess of one year) or intermittent services of experts or consultants" when authorized by an appropriation or other statute. FAR 37.104(f) requires the contracting officer to coordinate with the appropriate personnel office prior to entering into "personal services" contracts with individual experts or consultants. In this regard, FAR 37.104(b) states that personal services contracts shall not be awarded unless specifically authorized by statute.

An employer-employee relationship may be created when the Government hires and supervises an individual or when the Government controls and supervises a service contractor's employees. The FAR confuses the issue of whether an arrangement is that of employer-employee or independent contractor by equating personal services with the employer-employee relationship. See FAR 37.101, which states:

> "Personal services contract" means a contract that, by its express terms or as administered, makes the contractor personnel appear, in effect, Government employees (see 37.104).

The Comptroller General also uses the term "personal services" at times to describe an employer-employee relationship. See *Cerberonics, Inc.*, Comp. Gen. Dec. B-192161, 78-2 CPD ¶ 354, where the Comptroller, relying on an Armed Services Procurement Regulation provision, stated, "[A] personal services contract is the procuring of services by contract in such manner that the contractor or his employees are in effect employees of the Government"; and *Computer Sciences Corp.*, Comp. Gen. Dec. B-210800, 84-1 CPD ¶ 422, stating that "personal services may not be obtained on a contractual basis."

It is possible to require the services of a particular individual and yet have an independent contractor relationship. See, for example, *Payment by Nat'l Mediation Bd. to A. Robert Lowry, Inc.*, Comp. Gen. Dec. B-217468, June 25, 1985, *Unpub.*, which involved a contract for the personal services of an individual to act as an independent-contractor neutral arbitrator. In other cases, a contract for the personal services of an individual might be subject to Government supervision. See *Lynn Francis Jones*, 63 Comp. Gen. 507 (B-214432) (1984), where the Comptroller stated at 509:

> In view of the purely personal nature of the services provided to the Army by Mr. Jones as an individual and of the contract provision for Government supervision over the services rendered by Mr. Jones, we regard the contract as establishing an employer-employee relationship between him and the Government rather than an independent contractor relationship. See 26 Comp. Gen. 188 (1946), 27 Comp. Gen. 46 (1947) and 53 Comp. Gen. 542 (1974).

This discussion of personal services contracts would indicate that the term as used by the FAR and interpreted by the Comptroller General, refers to a service contract where an improper employer-employee relationship is created, but does not preclude contracting for the services of a specific individual as an independent contractor.

It is also improper for the Federal Government to, in effect, hire employees through the creation of an employer-employee relationship between the Government and a contractor's employees in a procurement contract, *United States Advisory Comm'n on Pub. Diplomacy*, 61 Comp. Gen. 69 (B-202159), 81-2 CPD ¶ 404. FAR 37.104 contains the following guidance for determining when an employer-employee relationship is created under a service contract:

> (1) An employer-employee relationship under a service contract occurs when, as a result of (i) the contract's terms or (ii) the manner of its administration during performance, contractor personnel are subject to the relatively continuous supervision and control of a Government officer or employee. However, giving an order for a specific article or service, with the right to reject the finished product or result, is not the type of supervision or control that converts an individual who is an independent contractor (such as a contractor employee) into a Government employee.
>
> (2) Each contract arrangement must be judged in the light of its own facts and circumstances, the key question always being: Will the Government exercise relatively continuous supervision and control over the contractor personnel performing the contract? The sporadic, unauthorized supervision of only one of a large number of contractor employees might reasonably be considered not relevant, while relatively continuous Government supervision of a substantial number of contractor employees would have to be taken strongly into account.

FAR 37.104(d) contains additional guidance on this issue:

> The following descriptive elements should be used as a guide in assessing whether or not a proposed contract is personal in nature:
>
> (1) Performance on site.
>
> (2) Principal tools and equipment furnished by the Government.
>
> (3) Services are applied directly to the integral effort of agencies or an organizational subpart in furtherance of assigned function or mission.
>
> (4) Comparable services, meeting comparable needs, are performed in the same or similar agencies using civil service personnel.
>
> (5) The need for the type of service provided can reasonably be expected to last beyond 1 year.
>
> (6) The inherent nature of the service, or the manner in which it is provided, reasonably requires directly or indirectly, Government direction or supervision of contractor employees in order to —
>
> (i) Adequately protect the Government's interest;
>
> (ii) Retain control of the function involved; or
>
> (iii) Retain full personal responsibility for the function supported in a duly authorized Federal officer or employee.

In *Lodge 1858, AFGE v. Webb*, 580 F.2d 496 (D.C. Cir.), *cert. denied*, 439 U.S. 927 (1978), the court held that *supervision* is the all-important factor in determining whether services are being performed under an employment arrangement or under an independent contractor relationship. The court recognized that either actual supervision or the contractual right to supervise could create an employer-employee relationship. Supervision was defined as "control of the individual workman's physical conduct." In this case, the service contracts were held not to violate the proscription because the Government did not directly control the contractor's employees since all Government orders were made through the contractor's management. The court discussed all the FAR factors and held that it was not necessary for all the factors to be present; the critical item is supervision. See also *Hines v. United States*, 60 F.3d 1442 (9th Cir. 1995) (contractual right of Postal

Service to screen driving records of independent contractor's employees is not supervision); *Minority Communications, Inc.*, Comp. Gen. Dec. B-228230.2, 88-1 CPD ¶ 88 (fact that Government approval is required for contractor to substitute employees for those identified in proposal does not constitute supervision even though contractor's traditional management prerogatives are infringed); and *Work Sys. Design, Inc.*, Comp. Gen. Dec. B-213451, 84-2 CPD ¶ 226 (failure of contract to specify details of work direction does not create employer-employee relationship if written technical instructions are given to contractor's management). By referring to the employer-employee relationship as one of personal services, the FAR provisions divert attention from the most critical factor, that of supervision.

B. Agencies Covered by Procurement Statutes

The terms "Government" and "Federal Government" are used extensively in statutes, regulations, and in this book to refer to the United States in its contractual dealings. However, contracts are not made by the United States generally but are entered into by individual organizations in all three branches of the Government. These numerous organizations are varied in nature, ranging from old-line departments to recently formed corporations. Some have very large procurement budgets and procurement organizations with thousands of employees while others perform a modest amount of contracting with a small number of personnel engaged in such activity. **Figure 1-1** contains the Organization Chart of the United States Government depicting the major governmental units. While there is a small amount of procurement carried out by the legislative branch and the judicial branch, the vast majority of all procurement is done by the executive branch of the Government.

1. Statutes Governing Procurement

Congress has not adopted one procurement statute for the entire Government. The two major statutes covering most Government procurement are the Armed Services Procurement Act (ASPA), 10 U.S.C. § 2302 et seq., and the Federal Property and Administrative Services Act (FPASA), 41 U.S.C. § 251 et seq. The ASPA was passed in 1948, and the FPASA, which was modeled after the ASPA, was enacted in 1949. Through the

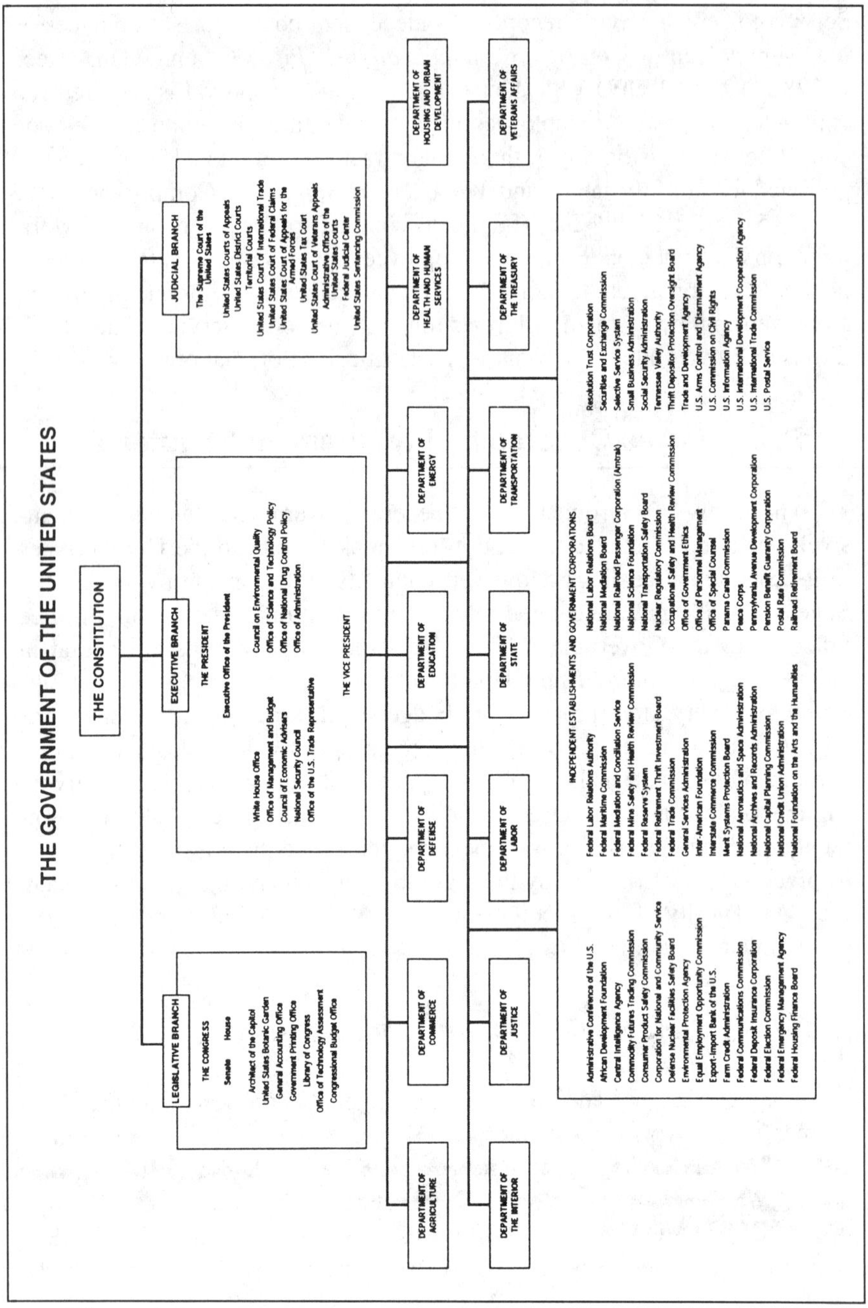
THE GOVERNMENT OF THE UNITED STATES
THE CONSTITUTION
LEGISLATIVE BRANCH
THE CONGRESS
Senate House
Architect of the Capitol
United States Botanic Garden
General Accounting Office
Government Printing Office
Library of Congress
Office of Technology Assessment
Congressional Budget Office
EXECUTIVE BRANCH
THE PRESIDENT
Executive Office of the President
White House Office
Office of Management and Budget
Council of Economic Advisers
National Security Council
Office of the U.S. Trade Representative
Council on Environmental Quality
Office of Science and Technology Policy
Office of National Drug Control Policy
Office of Administration
THE VICE PRESIDENT
JUDICIAL BRANCH
The Supreme Court of the United States
United States Courts of Appeals
United States District Courts
Territorial Courts
United States Court of International Trade
United States Court of Federal Claims
United States Court of Appeals for the Armed Forces
United States Tax Court
United States Court of Veterans Appeals
Administrative Office of the United States Courts
Federal Judicial Center
United States Sentencing Commission
DEPARTMENT OF AGRICULTURE
DEPARTMENT OF COMMERCE
DEPARTMENT OF DEFENSE
DEPARTMENT OF EDUCATION
DEPARTMENT OF ENERGY
DEPARTMENT OF HEALTH AND HUMAN SERVICES
DEPARTMENT OF HOUSING AND URBAN DEVELOPMENT
DEPARTMENT OF THE INTERIOR
DEPARTMENT OF JUSTICE
DEPARTMENT OF LABOR
DEPARTMENT OF STATE
DEPARTMENT OF TRANSPORTATION
DEPARTMENT OF THE TREASURY
DEPARTMENT OF VETERANS AFFAIRS
INDEPENDENT ESTABLISHMENTS AND GOVERNMENT CORPORATIONS
Administrative Conference of the U.S.
African Development Foundation
Central Intelligence Agency
Commodity Futures Trading Commission
Consumer Product Safety Commission
Corporation for National and Community Service
Defense Nuclear Facilities Safety Board
Environmental Protection Agency
Equal Employment Opportunity Commission
Export-Import Bank of the U.S.
Farm Credit Administration
Federal Communications Commission
Federal Deposit Insurance Corporation
Federal Election Commission
Federal Emergency Management Agency
Federal Housing Finance Board
Federal Labor Relations Authority
Federal Maritime Commission
Federal Mediation and Conciliation Service
Federal Mine Safety and Health Review Commission
Federal Reserve System
Federal Retirement Thrift Investment Board
Federal Trade Commission
General Services Administration
Inter-American Foundation
Interstate Commerce Commission
Merit Systems Protection Board
National Aeronautics and Space Administration
National Archives and Records Administration
National Capital Planning Commission
National Credit Union Administration
National Foundation on the Arts and the Humanities
National Labor Relations Board
National Mediation Board
National Railroad Passenger Corporation (Amtrak)
National Science Foundation
National Transportation Safety Board
Nuclear Regulatory Commission
Occupational Safety and Health Review Commission
Office of Government Ethics
Office of Personnel Management
Office of Special Counsel
Panama Canal Commission
Peace Corps
Pennsylvania Avenue Development Corporation
Pension Benefit Guaranty Corporation
Postal Rate Commission
Railroad Retirement Board
Resolution Trust Corporation
Securities and Exchange Commission
Selective Service System
Small Business Administration
Social Security Administration
Tennessee Valley Authority
Thrift Depositor Protection Oversight Board
Trade and Development Agency
U.S. Arms Control and Disarmament Agency
U.S. Commission on Civil Rights
U.S. Information Agency
U.S. International Development Cooperation Agency
U.S. International Trade Commission
U.S. Postal Service

Figure 1-1

years, the ASPA was modified extensively, but the FPASA was not. Then, in 1984, through the Competition in Contracting Act (CICA), P.L. 98-369, Congress made these two statutes almost identical. However, changes were subsequently made to both Acts with the result that over the next decade, the two statutes again diverged. The Federal Acquisition Streamlining Act of 1994 (FASA), P.L. 103-355, again brought the two statutes into closer conformity. The Clinger-Cohen Act of 1996, P.L. 104-106, retains this conformity by amending both statutes in most cases.

There are a few minor agencies not covered by either of these two statutes, most of which conduct their procurement under Revised Statutes 3709 and 3710, 41 U.S.C. § 5 and 41 U.S.C. § 8, respectively. There are also several agencies, most notably the Postal Service and the Federal Aviation Administration, which have been specifically authorized to conduct their procurement without following the major procurement statutes. Finally, there is an overriding statute, the Office of Federal Procurement Policy Act (OFPPA), 41 U.S.C. § 401 et seq., that contains a number of procurement rules covering almost all Government agencies. The problems inherent in this unnecessarily complex and burdensome statutory scheme were recognized in the President's Blue Ribbon Commission on Defense Management, *A Quest for Excellence — Final Report to the President* (June 1986), which states at 55, "[W]e recommend that Congress work with the Administration to recodify federal laws governing procurement in a single, consistent, and greatly simplified procurement statute." However, there has been no significant effort to enact a single procurement statute for the entire Federal Government.

There are also numerous statutes that have an impact on the procurement process because they govern the internal workings of the Government. A number of these statutes are listed in **Figure 1-2**. One of the confusing elements of these statutes is that they use different terms to describe the agencies that they cover.

In addition, procurement rules may be found in statutes creating an agency or in funding statutes. As a result, the specific rules that apply to procurements must be determined agency by agency. This section examines the coverage of the four major procurement statutes.

ORGANIZATIONAL TERMINOLOGY OF THE FEDERAL GOVERNMENT

Statute or Regulation	Organizational Element	Definition
40 U.S.C. § 703 Public Buildings, Property, and Works	Federal Government	Includes the legislative, executive, and judicial branches of the Government of the United States, and the government of the District of Columbia
31 U.S.C. § 101 Money and Finance	Agency	A department, agency, or instrumentality of the United States Government
40 U.S.C. § 472 Public Buildings, Property, and Works*	Federal Agency	Any executive agency or any establishment in the legislative or judicial branch of the Government (except the Senate, the House of Representatives, and the Architect of the Capitol and any activities under its direction)
40 U.S.C. § 472 Public Buildings, Property, and Works*	Executive Agency	Any executive department or independent establishment in the executive branch of the Government including any wholly owned Government corporations
5 U.S.C § 101 Government Organization and Employees	Executive Departments	Departments of State, the Treasury, Defense, Justice, the Interior, Agriculture, Commerce, Labor, HHS, HUD, Transportation, Energy, Education, and Veterans Affairs
5 U.S.C. § 102 Government Organization and Employees	Military Departments	Departments of the Army, Navy, and Air Force
5 U.S.C. § 103 Government Organization and Employees	Government Corporations	A corporation owned or controlled by the Government of the United States (Government-controlled corporation does not include a corporation owned by the Government of the United States)
5 U.S.C. § 104 Government Organization and Employees	Independent Establishment	An establishment in the executive branch (other than the United States Postal Service or the Postal Rate Commission) that is not an executive department, military department, Government corporation, or part thereof, or part of an independent establishment and the General Accounting Office

*FAR 2.101 contains substantially the same *definitions*.

Figure 1-2

a. *Armed Services Procurement Act*

The applicability of the ASPA is specified at 10 U.S.C. § 2303 as follows:

> (a) This chapter applies to the procurement by any of the following agencies, for its use or otherwise, of all property (other than land) and all services for which payment is to be made from appropriated funds:
>
> (1) The Department of Defense.
>
> (2) The Department of the Army.
>
> (3) The Department of the Navy.
>
> (4) The Department of the Air Force.
>
> (5) The Coast Guard.
>
> (6) The National Aeronautics and Space Administration.

When a provision states that it is to be implemented by "the head of an agency," all of the agencies listed above are covered. However, some sections and paragraphs call for implementation by "the Secretary of Defense." In those cases, the provisions apply only to defense agencies, including the military services, but not to the Coast Guard and NASA.

b. *Federal Property and Administrative Services Act*

41 U.S.C. § 252 makes the FPASA applicable to procurements of "executive agencies" except for procurements by the following:

(1) Agencies covered by the Armed Services Procurement Act,

(2) Agencies whose procurements are made inapplicable by 40 U.S.C. § 474, and

(3) Agencies whose procurements are excepted by "any other law."

In order to ascertain the coverage of the FPASA, it is necessary to determine whether the contracting organization is an executive agency and whether it comes under one of the exemptions. The following material considers the meaning of the term "executive agency" and the breadth of the exemptions under 40 U.S.C. § 474 and those under "any other law."

(1) Executive Agency

The term "executive agency" is defined in 40 U.S.C. § 472 as follows:

> (a) The term "executive agency" means any executive department or independent establishment in the executive branch of the Government, including any wholly owned Government corporation.

Organizations other than the departments, establishments, and corporations listed in **Figure 1-1** can also be considered to be executive agencies if they perform procurement functions for the executive agencies. However, the mere fact that the Government provides funding for the operation of an organization will not make that agency a federal instrumentality, *United States v. Orleans*, 425 U.S. 807 (1976). The total factual circumstances surrounding the creation of the organization must be considered in determining whether it constitutes an executive agency under a particular statute, *Motor Coach Indus., Inc. v. Dole*, 725 F.2d 958 (4th Cir. 1984). In that case, the Federal Aviation Agency required a trust to be formed by airlines for purposes of receiving airport landing fees due to the United States and using those fees for the purchase of buses for passenger transportation to the airport. All the employees of the trust were airline personnel. However, the court held that the trust was an executive agency and that the FPASA applied to its purchases, stating at 964-65:

> Whether a trust becomes a public instrumentality must be determined by analyzing the total factual circumstances surrounding its creation. See, e.g., *United States v. Orleans*, 425 U.S. 807, 815, 96 S. Ct. 1971, 1976, 48 L.Ed.2d 390 (1976) (whether an agency acts as an instrumentality of the government depends on the day-to-day supervision over its operations by the government); *Lewis v. United States*, 680 F.2d 1239, 1240 (9th Cir. 1982) (degree of control, source of finances, and public character of the agency's mission are important criteria for determining whether the entity is governmental in nature); *Federal Reserve Bank of St. Louis v. Metrocentre Improvement District No. 1*, 657 F.2d 183, 185 (8th Cir. 1981) (the governmental or private character of the agency's function is important in determining whether it is a governmental instrumentality). We must consider, at a minimum, the purposes for which the trust was established; the public or private character of the entity spearheading the trust's creation; the iden-

> tity of the trust's beneficiary and administrators; the degree of control exercised by the public agency over disbursements and other details of administration; and the method by which the trust is funded.
>
> The Trust was established at the urging of the FAA to accomplish an objective it had long sought — improved public access to Dulles Airport. The documents governing the Trust not only made the FAA the sole beneficiary, but gave the agency a prominent, if not exclusive, role in the Trust's administration. The FAA established the airlines' contribution formula, monitored collections with its own staff, exercised final approval power over disbursements, and participated in every phase of the decision to award Eagle the bus contract.

An organization may be considered to be an executive agency for purposes of the procurement statutes but not a federal agency under other statutes. See *Flight Int'l Group, Inc. v. Federal Reserve Bank of Chicago*, 583 F. Supp. 674, *vacated because of parties' settlement*, 597 F. Supp. 462 (N.D. Ga. 1984), where procurement by a Federal Reserve Bank was found to be governed by the FPASA. The court noted that 40 U.S.C. § 472 does not explicitly define an independent establishment, and it therefore applied the definition of that term contained in 5 U.S.C. § 104 and deemed the Federal Reserve Bank an executive agency subject to the FPASA. The court observed that the Board of Governors of the Federal Reserve System, the members of which are appointed by the President, is listed among the "Independent Establishments and Government Corporations" under the executive branch in *The United States Government Organization Manual.* See also *Dorsey v. Federal Reserve Bank of St. Louis*, 451 F. Supp. 683 (N.D. Mo. 1978), where a bank was held to be an executive agency for purposes of application of Title VII of the Civil Rights Act. Compare *Lewis v. United States*, 680 F.2d 1239 (9th Cir. 1982) (Federal Reserve Board does not exercise sufficient control over member banks to have bank be considered a federal agency for purposes of the Federal Tort Claims Act); *Mendrala v. Crown Mortgage Co.*, 955 F.2d 1132 (7th Cir. 1992) (Federal Home Loan Mortgage Corporation can be a federal agency for other purposes — estoppel); and *Lee Constr. Co. v. Federal Reserve Bank of Richmond*, 558 F. Supp. 165 (D. Md. 1982) (court held, without analysis, that a Federal Reserve Bank was neither a federal agency nor an executive agency under 40 U.S.C. § 472(a) or (b) and that the 40 U.S.C. § 484 restrictions on disposal of surplus Government property did not apply).

Even an Article I court may be considered an executive agency under the FPASA, despite its being listed within the judicial branch in **Figure 1-1**.

Article I courts include the United States Court of Federal Claims, the United States Court of Military Appeals, the United States Court of Veterans Appeals, and the United States Tax Court.

(2) 40 U.S.C. § 474 EXEMPTIONS

41 U.S.C. § 252 provides that the FPASA need not be followed by an executive agency when it "is made inapplicable pursuant to [40 U.S.C. § 474]." However, 40 U.S.C. § 474 does not explicitly grant exemptions. It provides that "[n]othing in this Act shall impair or affect any authority of . . ." and then lists 21 organizations whose transactions are totally or partially subject to its coverage. It is not clear whether this provision is intended to grant exemptions to the organizations listed or is merely supportive of exemption authority independently granted by some other statute. In addition, some of the exemptions have limited application. See, for example, 40 U.S.C. § 474(14) exempting the Federal Aviation Agency only from property disposal provisions, *Motor Coach Indus., Inc. v. Dole*, 725 F.2d 958 (4th Cir. 1984).

(3) ANY OTHER LAW

The phrase "any other law" used in 41 U.S.C. § 252 has been interpreted to require that the statute relied upon for exemption contain "express terms" exempting the procurements from 41 U.S.C. § 251 through § 260 before the agency will be exempted. See *Andrus v. Glover Constr. Co.*, 446 U.S. 608 (1980), where the Court held that the Buy Indian Act, which authorizes the Secretary of the Interior to purchase "the products of Indian industry . . . in open market," does not authorize an exemption from the FPASA. The express terms exemption is apparently satisfied by 39 U.S.C. § 410(a), which states that "no Federal law dealing with public or Federal contracts . . . shall apply to the exercise of the powers of the Postal Service." The intent of Congress to exempt the Postal Service from the FPASA seems evident, even though the FPASA is not specifically mentioned. A clear exemption is contained in P.L. 104-50, stating that after April 1, 1996, the Federal Aviation Administration will not be subject to a list of statutes including the FPASA, the OFPPA, 41 U.S.C. § 252 et seq., and the Small Business Act, 15 U.S.C. § 631 et seq. Less clear is the statutory language applicable to the Tennessee Valley Authority (TVA), 16 U.S.C. § 831h(b), and the Bonneville Power Administration, 16 U.S.C. § 832a(f). These statutes permit the head of each organization to enter into contracts "upon such terms and conditions and in such manner as he may deem necessary." In *Inryco, Inc. v. Tennessee Valley Auth.*, 471 F. Supp. 59 (D. Tenn. 1978), the court held that 41 U.S.C. § 253 did not apply to TVA projects and cited the predecessor TVA statute, 16 U.S.C. § 831h(b), and 40 U.S.C. § 474(12) in support of its decision.

When a statute does contain the proper express terms exemption from the FPASA, the court will scrutinize the action taken under the statute to assure that the statute is not being invoked in order to circumvent the FPASA provisions. See *Chem Serv., Inc. v. Environmental Monitoring Sys. Lab.*, 12 F.3d 1256 (3d Cir. 1993), where the court found that although the Federal Technology Transfer Act (FTTA) explicitly allowed research and development agreements without following the FPASA provisions, an agreement made under the FTTA that manifested the features of a traditional procurement contract had improperly bypassed the FPASA provisions.

c. Revised Statutes 3709 and 3710

These basic procurement statutes originally applied to all Government agencies. They are presently codified in 41 U.S.C. § 5 and § 8, and apply to procurement by "federal agencies" when the ASPA and the FPASA do not apply, 41 U.S.C. § 252(a). Thus, unless otherwise excepted, they apply to procurement by all Government organizations not within the executive branch. Exemptions from 41 U.S.C. § 5 do not necessarily exempt an agency from other procurement statutes. For example, the Buy American Act, 41 U.S.C. § 10, provides that "[n]otwithstanding any other provision of law . . . only such unmanufactured articles, materials, and supplies as having been mined or produced in the United States, and only such manufactured articles, materials, and supplies as have been manufactured in the United States . . . shall be acquired for public use."

d. Office of Federal Procurement Policy Act

The OFPPA, 41 U.S.C. § 401 et seq., also applies to "executive agencies," which are defined in 41 U.S.C. § 403(1), as follows:

> [T]he term "executive agency" means —
>
> (A) an executive department specified in section 101 of title 5, United States Code;

(B) a military department specified in section 102 of such title;

(C) an independent establishment as defined in section 104(1) of such title; and

(D) a wholly owned Government corporation fully subject to the provisions of chapter 91 of title 31, United States Code.

This Act creates the Office of Federal Procurement Policy (OFPP) in the Office of Management and Budget (OMB) and gives its Administrator broad powers to "provide overall direction of procurement policy and leadership in the development of procurement systems of the executive agencies," 41 U.S.C. § 405(a). It also contains a number of sections applicable to all "executive agencies," 41 U.S.C. §§ 414, 416–419, 422–23, and 425–32. These sections have been added to the statute periodically when Congress enacts a provision applicable to the entire executive branch without amending both the ASPA and the FPASA.

2. Federal Acquisition Regulation System

Although Congress has not enacted a single statute covering all agencies, it has provided that a *single regulation* be promulgated in this area, 41 U.S.C. § 405. This regulation is known as the Federal Acquisition Regulation (FAR). It is written by the Federal Acquisition Regulatory Council, with membership established by 41 U.S.C. § 421(b) as follows:

(1) The Council shall consist of the Administrator for Federal Procurement Policy and —

(A) the Secretary of Defense;

(B) the Administrator of National Aeronautics and Space; and

(C) the Administrator of General Services.

The FAR is issued under the statutory authority of the Secretary of Defense, the Administrator of NASA, and the Administrator of GSA. See 41 U.S.C. § 421(c), stating:

(1) Subject to the provisions of [41 U.S.C. § 405], the General Services Administration, the Department of Defense, and the National Aeronautics

> and Space Administration, pursuant to their respective authorities under title III of the Federal Property and Administrative Services Act of 1949 (41 U.S.C. § 251 et seq.), chapters 4 and 137 of title 10, United States Code, and the National Aeronautics and Space Act of 1958 (42 U.S.C. § 2451 et seq.), shall jointly issue and maintain in accordance with subsection (f) of this section a single Government-wide procurement regulation, to be known as the "Federal Acquisition Regulation."

All of the major agencies with procurement functions issue supplementary regulations to implement the FAR. However, these FAR Supplements are required to be limited in scope in accordance with 41 U.S.C. § 421(c), as follows:

> (2) Any other regulations relating to procurement issued by an executive agency shall be limited to (A) regulations essential to implement Government-wide policies within the agency, and (B) additional policies and procedures required to satisfy the specific and unique needs of the agency.

The Administrator of the OFPP has the authority to rescind, revise, or deny promulgation of any regulation that does not meet these standards, 41 U.S.C. § 421(c)(5). The Administrator also has the authority to issue regulations if the three designated agencies do not issue necessary regulations in a timely manner, 41 U.S.C. § 405(b). However, these reserve powers have not been used, as the promulgation of the FAR has been achieved in a collegial manner.

The FAR and its many supplements are known as the "FAR system." **Figure 1-3** depicts this system, and **Figure 1-4** contains a listing of the agency supplemental regulations. The FAR became effective April 1, 1984.

II. CONTRACTING POWERS

Although the Constitution does not expressly refer to contracts, the United States Government has the inherent power to use procurement contracts in carrying out its duties and exercising its powers, *United States v. Maurice*, 26 F. Cas. 1211 (No. 15747) (C.C.D. Va. 1823). This contracting power is shared by the legislative and executive branches of the Government. The executive branch, which has the constitutional power to execute the laws, enters into contracts. Congress, which is granted the power to make the laws and appropriate money, enacts statutes which authorize programs or activities and provide funds for their accomplishment.

Statutes delegate power to the Government agencies. In addition, they often contain requirements to be followed when contracts are used. Thus, statutes serve two purposes in the Government contracting process. They are the principal means of authorizing and funding programs that are implemented, in whole or in part, by contracting with private parties. At the same time, they are used to place *limitations* on the way in which those contracting powers are exercised.

Statutes are supplemented by regulations that contain detailed procedures to be used in awarding contracts and that require the use of specified terms and conditions. When promulgated pursuant to statutory authority, regulations take on the status of law. Together, statutes and regulations are of supreme importance because the Government can be contractually bound only through the proper exercise of validly conferred powers.

However, statutes and regulations are not self-enforcing. Control over the day-to-day activities of a Government agency is usually vested in the head of the agency, who normally has great discretion in making contracts to carry out Government programs. In most cases, these delegated powers are performed properly. However, differences of opinion often arise in interpreting statutes and regulations that may result in an improper use of power. In addition, whether by inadvertence or design, there are numerous instances where an agency's contracting activity violates statutory or regulatory authority. Congress uses a number of oversight techniques to give reasonable assurance that the contracting powers are properly exercised.

This section discusses the statutory mechanisms that Congress uses to delegate powers and to provide funding to the Government agencies; the degree of control that various statutes and regulations have over the contracting process; and the techniques used to oversee Government agencies in the contracting process.

A. Congressional Delegation of Power

The primary means that Congress uses to delegate power to the executive branch is the enactment of laws establishing new programs and the

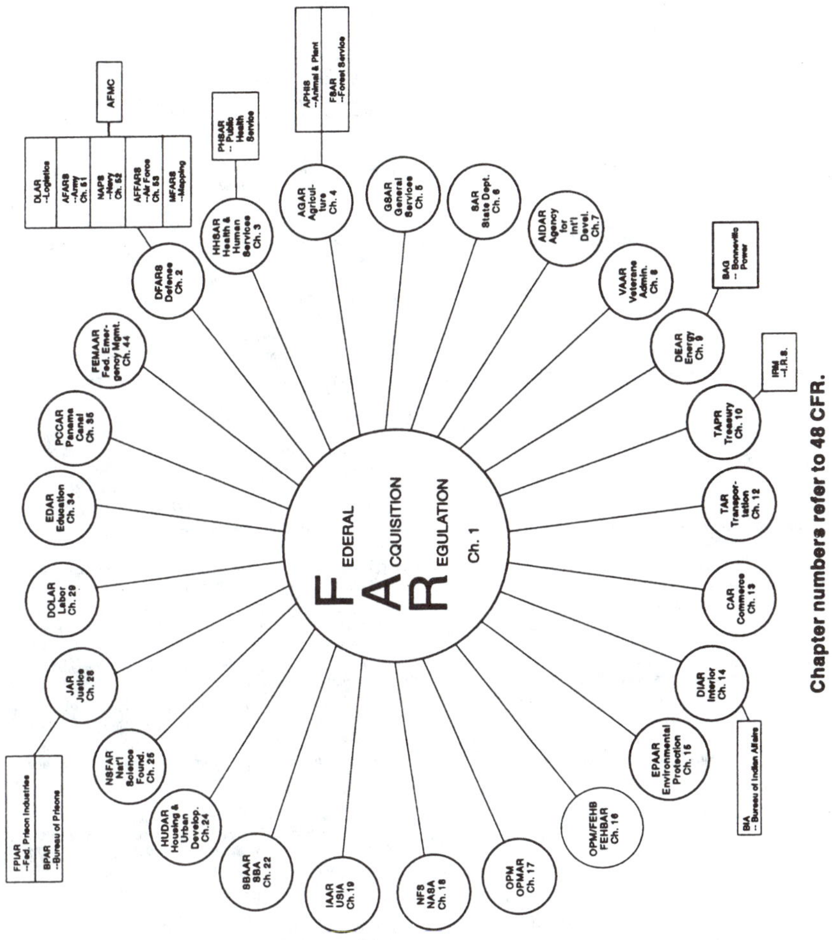
F EDERAL
A CQUISITION
R EGULATION
Ch. 1
DFARS Defense Ch. 2
DLAR --Logistics
AFARS --Army Ch. 51
NAPS --Navy Ch. 52
AFFARS --Air Force Ch. 53
MFARS --Mapping
AFMC
HHSAR Health & Human Services Ch. 3
PHSAR -- Public Health Service
AGAR Agricul-ture Ch. 4
APHIS --Animal & Plant
FSAR --Forest Service
GSAR General Services Ch. 5
SAR State Dept. Ch. 6
AIDAR Agency for Int'l Devel. Ch.7
VAAR Veterans Admin. Ch. 8
DEAR Energy Ch. 9
BAG -- Bonneville Power
TAPR Treasury Ch. 10
IRM --I.R.S.
TAR Transpor-tation Ch. 12
CAR Commerce Ch. 13
DIAR Interior Ch. 14
BIA -- Bureau of Indian Affairs
EPAAR Environmental Protection Ch. 15
OPM/FEHB FEHBAR Ch. 16
OPM OPMAR Ch. 17
NFS NASA Ch. 18
IAAR USIA Ch. 19
SBAAR SBA Ch. 22
HUDAR Housing & Urban Develop. Ch. 24
NSFAR Nat'l Science Found. Ch. 25
JAR Justice Ch. 28
FPIAR --Fed. Prison Industries
BPAR --Bureau of Prisons
DOLAR Labor Ch. 29
EDAR Education Ch. 34
PCCAR Panama Canal Ch. 35
FEMAAR Fed. Emer-gency Mgmt. Ch. 44
Chapter numbers refer to 48 CFR.

Figure 1-3

Principal Federal Agency Acquisition Regulations
(Compiled by David W. Bertoni, Nathan S. Tash, and Lori M. Jensen, research sssistants)

Abbrevia-ted Title	Proper Title	Citation	Published By
AGAR	Agricultural Acquisition Regulations	48 CFR 4	U.S. Department of Agriculture; Office of Operations; Procurement Division; 14th and Independence Ave. N.W.; Washington, D.C. 20250. (202) 720-3037
APHIS Directives	Animal and Plant Health Inspection Service Directives		APHIS; Administrative Services Division; Procurement and Property; U.S. Department of Agriculture. (202) 720-3037
FSAR	Forest Service Acquisition Regulations		FS; Administration; Procurement and Property Staff; Department of Agriculture. (202) 235-3329
AIDAR	Agency for International Development Acquisition Regulation	48 CFR 7	Agency for International Development; Office of Procurement; 320 21st Street, N.W.; Washington, D.C. 20623. (703) 875-1150
CAR	Commerce Acquisition Regulation	48 CFR 13	Office of Procurement Management; U.S. Department of Commerce; 14th and Constitution Ave., N.W.; Washington, D.C. 20623. (703) 482-4167
DEAR	Department of Energy Acquisition Regulations	48 CFR 9: CCH, Vol 7	Department of Energy; Office of Procurement Assistance and Program Management; Office of Policy; Washington, D.C. 20585. (202) 586-8182
EFARS	U.S. Army Corps of Engineers		U.S. Army Corps of Engineers; Principal Assistant Responsible for Contracting; 20 Massachusetts Ave., N.W.; Washington, D.C. 20314. (202) 761-0566
BAG	Bonneville Power Acquisition Guide		General Accounting Section–DKTC; Bonneville Power Administration; P.O. Box 3621; Portland, Oregon 97208.
DFARS	Defense Federal Acquisition Regulations Supplement	48 CFR 2: CCH, Vol 5	Defense Acquisition Regulations Council; The Pentagon; Washington, D.C. 20301. (703) 604-5929
NAPS	Navy Acquisition Regulations Supplement	48 CFR 52: CCH, Vol 6	Navy Department; Deputy for Acquisition and Business Management; The Pentagon; Washington, D.C. 20350-1000. (703) 602-2338
AFARS	Army FAR Supplement	48 CFR 51: CCH, Vol 6	Army Department, Office of Procurement Policy; The Pentagon; Washington, D.C. 20310-1504. (703) 697-9982
SBAFAR	Small Business Admin. Acquisition Regulations	48 CFR 22	Small Business Administration; 409 3rd St. S.W.; Washington, D.C. 20416
AFFARS	Air Force FAR Supplement	48 CFR 53	Air Force Department; Assistant for FAR System; The Pentagon; Washington, D.C. 20330. (703) 697-9441
MFARS	Defense Mapping Agency FAR Supplement		Defense Mapping Agency; Procurement and Contracts Directorate; 8613 Lee Highway; Fairfax, Virginia 22031-2137. (703) 285-9147
DLAR	Defense Logistics Acquisition Regulation	CCH, Vol 6	Defense Logistics Agency; Executive Director; Procurement; Cameron Station; Alexandria, Virginia 22314. (703) 274-6401
DIAR	Department of the Interior Acquisition Regulation	48 CFR 14	U.S. Department of the Interior; Office of Acquisition and Property Management; 18th and C Streets, N.W.; Washington, D.C. 20240. (202) 208-3668
	Bureau of Indian Affairs Acquisition Regulation		Department of the Interior; Bureau of Indian Affairs; Contracts and Grants Administration Staff; 1951 Constitution Ave., N.W.; Washington, D.C. 20245. (202) 208-2825
DOLAR	Department of Labor Acquisition Regulation	48 CFR 29	U.S. Department of Labor; Directorate of Administration and Procurement Programs; Procurement and Grant Policy Div.; 200 Constitution Ave., N.W.; Washington, D.C. 20210. (202) 219-9174
EDAR	Education Department Acquisition Regulation	48 CFR 34	Department of Education; Grants and Contract Services; Acquisition Policy Branch; 400 Maryland Ave., S.W.; Washington, D.C. 20202. (202) 708-8266
EPAAR	Environmental Protection Agency Acquisition Regulation	48 CFR 15: CCH, Vol 7	Office of Acquisition Management; Environmental Protection Agency; 401 M Street, S.W.; Washington, D.C. 20460. (202) 260-5020
FEMAAR	Federal Emergency Management Agency Acquisition Regulation	48 CFR 44	Office of Acquisition Management; Federal Emergency Management Agency; 500 C Street, S.W.; Washington, D.C. 20472. (202) 646-3743
GSAR	General Services Acquisition Regulation	48 CFR 5: CCH, Vol 7	Office of General Services Administration Acquisition Policy and Regulations; Office of Acquisition Policy; 18th and F Streets, N.W.; Washington, D.C. 20405. (202) 501-1043

Figure 1-4 (cont'd on next page)

Principal Federal Agency Acquisition Regulations
(Compiled by David W. Bertoni, Nathan S. Tash, and Lori M. Jensen, research sssistants)

Abbreviated Title	Proper Title	Citation	Published By
HHSAR	Health and Human Services Acquisition Regulation	48 CFR 3	Office of Grants and Acquisition Management; 200 Independence Ave., S.W.; Washington, D.C. 20201. (202) 690-7079
PHSAR	Public Health Service Acquisition Regulation	48 CFR 3 Appendix A	Public Health Service; Office of Resource Management; Division of Grants and Contracts; Room 17A-39; Parklawn Building; 5800 Fishers Lane; Rockville, Maryland 20867. (301) 443-6630
HUDAR	Housing and Urban Development Acquisition Regulation	48 CFR 24	Office of Procurement and Contracts; Department of Housing and Urban Development; 451 7th Street, S.W.; Washington, D.C. 20410. (202) 708-0294
IAAR	Information Agency Acquisition Regulation	48 CFR 19	Office of Contracts Policy and Procedures Staff; U.S. Information Agency; 301 4th Street, S.W.; Washington, D.C. 20547. (202) 205-5404
JAR	Justice Acquisition Regulation	48 CFR 28	Department of Justice; Justice Management Division; Procurement Executive; 10th & Constitution Ave., N.W.; Washington, D.C. 20530. (202) 514-6868
	Federal Prison Industries Acquisition Regulation		Federal Prison Industries; 320 1st Street, N.W.; Washington, D.C. 20534. (202) 307-3250
BPAR	Bureau of Prisons Acquisition Regulation		Bureau of Prisons; Room 618 Property Management and Procurement Office; 320 1st Street, N.W.; Washington, D.C. 20634. (202) 307-3198
	FBI Procurement and Property Management Handbook		FBI; Ninth Street and Pennsylvania Ave., N.W.; Washington, D.C. 20535; Administrative Services Div. (202) 324-3514
	U.S. Marshals Service Manual		600 Army Navy Drive; Arlington, Virginia. (202) 307-9065
	U.S. Marshals Service Contract and Policy Procedures Manual		
NFS	National Aeronautics and Space Administration FAR Supplement	48 CFR 18; CCH, Vol 7	Office of Procurement; NASA Headquarters; 300 E Street, S.W.; Washington, D.C. 20546. (202) 358-2090
NSFAR	National Science Foundation Administration FAR Supplement	48 CFR 25	Division of Grants and Contracts; Policy Office; National Science Foundation; 4201 Wilson Blvd.; Arlington, Virginia 22230. (703) 306-1234
TAPR	Treasury Acquisition Procurement Regulation	48 CFR 10	Department of the Treasury; Office of Procurement; Treasury Bldg. Annex; Pennsylvania Ave. and Madison Place, N.W.; Washington, D.C. 20220. (202) 622-0520
FEHBAR	Federal Employees Health Benefits Acquisition Regulation	48 CFR 16	Retirement and Insurance Policy; 1900 E Street, N.W., Room 4351; Washington, D.C. 20415. (202) 606-0788
DOSAR	Department of State Acquisition Regulation	48 CFR 6 (proposed)	Office of the Procurement Executive; Room 202, SA-6; U.S. Department of State; Washington, D.C. 20520. (703) 875-7046
IRM	Internal Revenue Manual		IRS PM:S: FMC; 1111 Constitution Ave., Washington, D.C. 20324. (202) 535-4795
TAR	Department of Transportation Acquisition Regulation	48 CFR 12	Office of Acquisition and Grant Management; Department of Transportation; 400 7th Street; Washington, D.C. 20590. (202) 366-4285
VAAR	Veterans Administration Acquisition Regulation	48 CFR 8	Department of Veterans Affairs; Office of Acquisition and Material Management; 810 Vermont Ave., N.W.; Washington, D.C. 20420. (202) 233-3808
OPMAR	Office of Personnel Mgmt. Acquisition Regulation Supplement	48 CFR 17	Office of Personnel Management; Office of Procurement and Administrative Services; 1900 E Street, N.W.; Room 1466; Washington, D.C. 20415. (202) 606-2200
SSAR	Social Security Acquisition Regulation	48 CFR 23	Social Security Administration; Division of Policy and Information Management; Office of Acquisition and Grants; 1710 Gwynn Oak Ave.; Baltimore, Maryland 21207. (410) 965-9540.

NOTES:

1. *If no citation is given, regulations must be obtained from the particular agency.*
2. *Telephone number of FAR Secretariat in the GSA is (202) 523-4755.*
3. *Various commands and agencies of the Army, Navy, and Air Force have also issued acquisition regulations. See DFARS for a complete listing of the commands and agencies.*
4. *APHIS, FSAR, MFARS, and EFARS are internal procurement manuals.*

Figure 1-4 (cont'd from previous page)

appropriation of funds to pay for these programs. This activity occurs each year in the "budget and appropriations" process of the Federal Government. This process is controlled by the Congressional Budget and Impoundment Control Act of 1974, 2 U.S.C. § 621 et seq., and various sections of Title 31. See also the GAO, *Principles of Federal Appropriations Law* (2d ed., 1991) (www.gao.gov/special.pubs/publist.htm).

This section first considers the legal requirements for congressional appropriations before contracts can be awarded. It then reviews the budget and appropriations process which is the primary means of conferring contracting power. Finally, it summarizes the manner that appropriations law impacts the contracting process.

1. Need for Congressional Appropriation

Congress exerts authority over the contracting process through the use of its constitutional powers. Article 1, Section 9, Clause 7, of the Constitution provides that "[n]o money shall be drawn from the Treasury, but in Consequence of Appropriations made by Law." This provision of the Constitution prohibits any *payments* by agencies unless funds have been approved by Congress. Congress has extended this control mechanism by restricting Government agencies from *obligating funds* unless there is existing congressional authority. This proposition is embodied in the Anti-Deficiency Act, 31 U.S.C. § 1341(a), which states as follows:

> (1) An officer or employee of the United States Government or of the District of Columbia government may not —
>
> (A) make or authorize an expenditure or obligation exceeding an amount available in an appropriation or fund for the expenditure or obligation; or
>
> (B) involve either government in a contract or obligation for the payment of money before an appropriation is made unless authorized by law.

In the contracting process the signing of a contract legally obligates the funds necessary to carry out the contract. Thus, Government agencies cannot make *payments* under a contract or *enter into* a contract unless Congress has given them proper authority.

In order to obligate the Government by contract, the agency must have received sufficient funds in an existing appropriations statute to cover the obligation, or there must be some other statute by which Congress specifically empowers an agency to make contracts without regard to the need for appropriations. The authority inherent in both types of statutes is called "budget authority." See 2 U.S.C. § 622(2), which states:

> The term "budget authority" means the authority provided by Federal law to incur financial obligations, as follows:
>
> (i) provisions of law that make funds available for obligation and expenditure (other than borrowing authority), including the authority to obligate and expend the proceeds of offsetting receipts and collections;
>
> (ii) borrowing authority, which means authority granted to a Federal entity to borrow and obligate and expend the borrowed funds, including through the issuance of promissory notes or other monetary credits;
>
> (iii) contract authority, which means the making of funds available for obligation but not for expenditure; and
>
> (iv) offsetting receipts and collections as negative budget authority, and the reduction thereof as positive budget authority.

The first form of budget authority defined in 2 U.S.C. § 622(2) is an appropriation. Congress allows agencies to incur obligations and make payments for obligations through appropriations. Appropriations are the most common forms of budget authority. They give agencies the power to enter into and pay for contracts. This type of budget authority will be discussed in more detail in subsequent sections.

"Borrowing authority" can also apply to contracts. Borrowing authority allows Government agencies to incur obligations and liquidate these obligations out of borrowed funds. Agencies with borrowing authority can enter into contracts and make payments with borrowed monies. See, for example, Comp. Gen. Dec. B-223857, Feb. 27, 1987, *Unpub.* (Commodity Credit Corporation violated the Anti-Deficiency Act because it had used all funds available from its borrowing authority but still had contractual obligations). Borrowing authority may consist of the authority to borrow from the Treasury, authority to borrow directly from the public, authority to borrow from the Federal Financing Bank, or a combination, *Principles of Federal Appropriations Law* 2-6 (2d ed., 1991). However, since direct appropriations provides more congressional control than borrowing authority, the Congressional Budget Act requires new borrowing authority to be limited to the extent or amounts provided in appropriations acts, 2 U.S.C. § 651(a).

"Contract authority," referred to at 2 U.S.C. § 622(2)(iii), is found in statutes authorizing contracts without regard to appropriations. See, for example, *People's Bank & Trust Co. v. United States*, 11 Cl. Ct. 554 (1987) (court found "contract authority" in applicable statutes and regulations governing FmHA); *New York Airways, Inc. v. United States*, 177 Ct. Cl. 800, 369 F.2d 743 (1966) (although Congress did not grant appropriations, Government was not relieved of contractual obligation because appropriations restrictions did not apply to 49 U.S.C. § 1376(c) giving contract authority). 31 U.S.C. § 1301(d) provides that for a law to be construed to authorize a contract for payment of money in excess of an appropriation, it must specifically state that such a contract may be made. Like borrowing authority, 2 U.S.C. § 651(a) also restricts the use of new "contract authority" in future statutes by providing that it will be out of order for either house to consider any bill, resolution, conference report, or amendment that provides "new spending authority" beyond the amount of the appropriations of that fiscal year.

Another form of budget authority, which is characterized as offsetting collections in 2 U.S.C. § 622(2), is a revolving fund. Revolving funds allow Government corporations and offices to generate income as well as expend money. Agencies are allowed to conduct public or intragovernmental transactions which generate income. Specific statutory authority allows these agencies to deposit the income in an appropriation or fund account. The agency is then permitted to make use of such income to finance continued operations. See *Principles of Federal Appropriations Law* 2-8 (2d ed., 1991). For an example of a revolving fund, see 31 U.S.C. § 5142, which establishes such a fund for the Bureau of Engraving and Printing.

2. Budget and Appropriations Process

The budget and appropriations process is the involved means that the Federal Government arrives at the annual budget that supports its varied programs. The "budget and appropriations" process has three phases: the budgetary phase, the authorization phase, and the appropriations phase.

a. Budgetary Phase

The budgetary phase of the process begins with the administrative process of budget preparation and review. Agencies gather information through reviews of current operations, program objectives and future plans. This, along with information from other federal departments, is used to prepare the President's budget, which must be submitted on or before the first Monday in February for the fiscal year starting the following October 1. See 2 U.S.C. § 631; *Principles of Federal Appropriations Law* 1-15 (2d ed., 1991).

Upon receipt of the President's budget, the Budget Committees of the House of Representatives and the Senate begin work on a budget resolution which packages the entire federal budget for the following year. By February 15, the Congressional Budget Office must submit a budget report to the Budget Committees, and within 10 days of that date all other congressional committees with oversight over agency programs are required to submit their views and estimates to the Budget Committees. Then the Senate Budget Committee reports a concurrent resolution on the budget, and by April 15, Congress is required to complete action on the concurrent resolution. After the concurrent resolution is passed, annual authorization and appropriation bills can be considered, 2 U.S.C. § 631.

b. Authorization of Appropriations

The next phase in the process is the authorization of appropriations. Before an appropriations statute is passed there usually must be some separate statute authorizing the program or activity that is the subject of the appropriation. Although there is no general statutory provision to this effect, House of Representatives Rule XXI(2) prohibits the reporting out of general appropriations unless the proposed expenditures were "previously authorized by law." In addition, Congress has required annual authorizations for some agencies. See, for example 42 U.S.C. § 7270 (DOE); 10 U.S.C. § 114 (DOD); and 42 U.S.C § 2460 (NASA). The Comptroller General, using the authority granted by 31 U.S.C. § 1112(c)(1), has defined "authorizing" legislation. See *A Glossary of Terms Used in the Federal Budget Process* (Exposure Draft) (GAO/AFMD-2.1.1) (Jan. 1993), defining the term at 17:

> Substantive legislation that sets up or continues the operation of a federal program or agency either indefinitely or for a specific period of time or sanctions a particular type of obligation or expenditure within a program.
>
> Authorizing legislation is normally a prerequisite for appropriations. It may place a limit on the amount of budget authority to be included in appropriation acts or it may authorize the appropriation of "such sums as may be necessary."

Under this definition the authorization for an appropriation may be the organic act that established the agency, a separate statute establishing a particular program, or the annual authorization statutes required for some agencies. The purpose of these authorizations is to ensure that the legislative committees with oversight of specific agencies retain control over the programs that these agencies undertake.

While annual authorization statutes specify definite appropriation limits, other authorization statutes may be indefinite in amount. Amounts established in definite authorization statutes are not binding on Congress in passing an appropriations act. Congress can appropriate a greater amount, 36 Comp. Gen. 240 (B-128902) (1956), or a lesser amount, 53 Comp. Gen. 695 (B-180517) (1974). When the amount appropriated is greater than that authorized, the intent to fund the program at the higher level must be clear, 64 Comp. Gen. 282 (B-214172) (1985). In 36 Comp. Gen. 240 (B-128902) (1956), the Comptroller General stated that the expenditure of excess funds without such clear intent would constitute a violation of the Anti-Deficiency Act — reasoning that the excess amounts were not available for obligation.

Annual authorization statutes usually contain a number of provisions governing the procurement process. See, for example, the National Defense Authorization Act for Fiscal Year 1995, P.L. 103-337, Title VIII.

c. Appropriations Statutes

The final stage of the process is the passage of the annual appropriations statutes. In order to ensure that funds are available to operate the Government in the fiscal year beginning on October 1, all appropriations acts should be enacted by September 30. There are 13 appropriations statutes, as follows:

- Departments of Commerce, Justice, and State, the Judiciary, and related agencies
- Department of Defense
- Department of the Interior and related agencies
- Departments of Labor, Health and Human Services, and Education and related agencies
- Department of Transportation and related agencies
- Department of the Treasury, Postal Service, and general government
- Departments of Veterans Affairs and Housing and Urban Development and independent agencies
- District of Columbia
- Energy and water development
- Foreign operations, export financing, and related programs
- Legislative branch
- Military construction
- Rural development, Department of Agriculture, and related agencies

Appropriations being considered by either house of Congress in the absence of an authorization statute are subject to being ruled out of order. However, if the point of order is not raised and the appropriation is passed, it would appear that the impropriety was waived by Congress. See, however, *Atchison, Topeka & Santa Fe Ry. Co. v. Callaway*, 382 F. Supp. 610 (D.D.C. 1974), holding that the failure to raise a point of order would not cure the invalidity of an appropriation passed in the absence of an authorizing statute.

Most agencies have separate appropriations for functions such as operation and maintenance, procurement, construction, and research and development. A typical functional breakdown for the DOD is set forth in the DOD Appropriations Act, 1996, P.L. 104-61, as follows:

Title I	Military Personnel
Title II	Operation and Maintenance
Title III	Procurement
Title IV	Research, Development, Test and Evaluation
Title V	Revolving and Management Funds
Title VI	Other Department of Defense Programs
Title VII	Related Agencies

Such appropriations can be, and sometimes are, further divided so that specific amounts are allocated to particular programs, such as the construction of individual buildings, or to separate subcomponents of an agency, such as a bureau, command, or administration within a department.

Each of these statutes may contain numerous special sections, called "riders," directing certain contractual actions or limiting the use of the appropriation for specified purposes. See, for example, the DOD Appropriations Act, 1996, P.L. 104-61, § 8010 ("None of the funds provided in this Act shall be available to initiate (1) a multiyear contract that employs economic quantity procurement in excess of $20,000,000 in any one year of the contract or that includes an unfunded contingent liability in excess of $20,000,000"); the Department of Transportation and Related Agencies Appropriations Act, 1996, P.L. 104-50, § 309 ("The expenditure of any appropriation under this Act for any consulting service through procurement contract pursuant to section 3109 of title 5, United States Code, shall be limited to those contracts where such expenditures are a matter of public record and available for public inspection"); and the Treasury, Postal Service, and General Government Appropriations Act, 1996, P.L. 104-52 § 517 ("If it has been finally determined by a court or Federal agency that any person intentionally affixed a label bearing a 'Made in America' inscription . . . [and such product] is not made in the United States, such person shall be ineligible to receive any contract or subcontract made with funds provided pursuant to this Act").

3. *Appropriations Law As It Affects the Contracting Process*

The same means by which Congress delegates power to the executive branch — appropriations and authorizations — also enables Congress to limit that power. Thus, appropriations law is an important part of the contracting process.

This section first reviews the rules determining the scope of each appropriation. It then considers the requirements that contracts be made only for purposes covered by an appropriation. Finally it addresses the rule that contracts may be entered into only during the time that the appropriation is available for obligation.

a. Scope of Appropriations

Appropriations are made for *designated purposes* during *specified fiscal years*. Thus, in entering into a contract, an agency must determine if an appropriation covers the activity being procured and if the appropriated funds may be used at the time the contract is formed. This determination is based on an analysis of the appropriations act. An appropriations act is defined in *A Glossary of Terms Used in the Federal Budget Process* (Exposure Draft) (GAO/AFMD-2.1.1) (Jan. 1993) at 16:

> A statute, under the jurisdiction of the House and Senate Committees on Appropriations, that generally provides authorization for Federal agencies to incur obligations and to make payments out of the Treasury for specified purposes. . . . An appropriation act generally follows enactment of authorizing legislation unless the authorizing legislation provides budget authority.

For a law to be construed as an appropriation, 31 U.S.C. § 1301(d) requires that "the law specifically states that an appropriation is made."

Appropriations acts are not substantive law. Thus, the mere appropriation of money for a program does not mean that other laws applicable to the program may be ignored. In *Tennessee Valley Auth. v. Hill*, 437 U.S. 153 (1978), the Court ruled that the unspecified inclusion of funds to construct a dam did not constitute a repeal by implication of the Endangered Species

Act, which had previously been held by the Supreme Court to prohibit construction of the dam.

b. Purpose of Appropriations

31 U.S.C. § 1301(a) states that "[a]ppropriations shall be applied only to the objects for which the appropriations were made except as otherwise provided by law." In other words, appropriations may be used only for the purpose for which they were appropriated. Thus, Congress has limited the Government agencies' expenditure of appropriated funds by denying the agencies the power to use funds for a purpose beyond that which the appropriations act allows. Agencies have considerable discretion in incurring all expenses reasonably necessary to carry out the purpose of the appropriation, Comp. Gen. Dec. B-252467, June 3, 1994, *Unpub.*, but they are not authorized to use appropriated funds (1) for purposes that do not bear a logical relationship to the appropriation, (2) for purposes that are prohibited by law, or (3) from a general appropriation for an item that is specifically covered in another appropriation, Comp. Gen. Dec. B-230304, Mar. 18, 1988, *Unpub.* See also Comp. Gen. Dec. B-254666, Nov. 18, 1993, *Unpub.*; 67 Comp. Gen. 276 (B-226132) (1988). If two or more appropriations are available for the same purpose, the agency may choose between appropriations; once the choice is made, however, the agency must continue to use that appropriation, Comp. Gen. Dec. B-235086, Apr. 24, 1991, *Unpub.*; 67 Comp. Gen. 276 (B-226132) (1988).

The determination of the purposes covered by an appropriation is largely a question of determining the intent of Congress in making the appropriation. In interpreting the meaning of an appropriation, the Comptroller General relies primarily on the statutory language itself. The fact that a program has been specifically presented to the congressional committee during budget hearings will be considered by the Comptroller, 35 Comp. Gen. 220 (B-124672) (1955), but the mere inclusion of an item in a budget justification does not enlarge the purpose of the appropriation where such an expenditure is otherwise expressly prohibited by law, 26 Comp. Gen. 545 (B-62700) (1947). Similarly, a limitation expressed in the legislative history will not restrict the use of the funds in a broadly worded appropriation, Comp. Gen. Dec. B-258000, Aug. 31, 1994, *Unpub.* In *LTV Aerospace Corp.*, 55 Comp. Gen. 307 (B-183851), 75-2 CPD ¶ 203, the Comptroller General considered whether statements from the Congressional Conference Report on an appropriations act indicating that certain funds could only be used for a specified purpose imposed a legal restriction on the use of such funds. In determining that the Navy was not required to spend the funds in accordance with the Conference Report restriction, the Comptroller General noted at 325-26:

> To be binding as a matter of law, an intention to so restrict the legal availability of the funds provided would have to be expressed in the statute. However, if the issue is whether a particular aircraft is in fact a "military aircraft," as that term is used in the statute, resort to legislative history is required.
>
> * * *
>
> As observed above, this does not mean agencies are free to ignore clearly expressed legislative history applicable to the use of appropriated funds. They ignore such expressions of intent at the peril of strained relations with the Congress. The executive branch — as the Navy has recognized — has a practical duty to abide by such expressions. This duty, however, must be understood to fall short of a statutory requirement giving rise to a legal infraction where there is a failure to carry out that duty.

See also *Forest Serv.*, Comp. Gen. Dec. B-231711, Mar. 28, 1989, *Unpub.* (congressional committee's recommendation that a specific dollar amount be used for liquidating the debt of prior fiscal year was not binding because Congress did not impose the requirement in the appropriations act); *Newport News Shipbuilding & Dry Dock Co.*, 55 Comp. Gen. 812 (B-184830), 76-1 CPD ¶ 136 (specific dollar amount for one ship in an appropriations committee report did not limit the amount the procuring agency could obligate for that ship out of an appropriation covering two ships).

Executive agencies have a measure of flexibility so that they can make adjustments for unforeseen developments or changed circumstances. Congress grants this flexibility by appropriating funds in lump sum amounts. Such an appropriation is a *general purpose appropriation* — one appropriation made for a group of objects necessary for the performance of a broad function. The great majority of appropriations presently used for the procurement of supplies, services, research and development, ships, aircraft, and missiles are general purpose appropriations. Appropriations are also made for the accomplishment of a single object. Such appropriations are *specific purpose appropriations*.

Congress may stipulate, by statute, that certain types of appropriations only be authorized via specific purpose appropriations. For example, 41 U.S.C. § 12, states:

> No contract shall be entered into for the erection, repair, or furnishing of any public building, or for any public improvement which shall bind the Government to pay a larger sum of money than the amount in the Treasury appropriated for the specific purpose.

This statute has been interpreted as imposing a special rule prohibiting the construction of public buildings or improvements unless appropriations specifically provide for the item, 38 Comp. Gen. 758 (B-138598) (1959) (appropriation for "necessary expenses" not broad enough to include the cost of construction for building alterations nor definite enough to comply with 41 U.S.C. § 12 requiring specific authorization for such work). In referring to this statute, the Comptroller General has stated that expenditures for such projects must "be authorized by specific appropriations," 42 Comp. Gen. 212 (B-146728) (1962). The use of the words "specific appropriations" is misleading, however, since the statute appears to require no more than a reference in an appropriations act or its legislative history that indicates that congressional authority for a project has, in fact, been granted. For example, in 38 Comp. Gen. 392 (B-137094) (1958) the Comptroller General denied a request to construct a special building for hydrostatic testing, painting, and maintaining helium tank cars under an appropriation designated for "acquiring and developing helium properties." In the absence of any legislative history establishing a congressional intent to attribute a broadened meaning to those general terms, the Comptroller concluded that the necessary express statutory authority was lacking. With respect to the definitions of the terms "public building" and "public improvement," the Comptroller General has uniformly held that any structure in the form of a building not clearly of a temporary character qualifies as a public building or public improvement, 42 Comp. Gen. 212 (B-146728) (1962).

"Riders" on appropriations acts, whether for general or specific purpose, frequently impose explicit statutory restrictions that are binding on the agency. See Comp. Gen. Dec. B-254086, May 2, 1994, *Unpub.* (Section 9047 of fiscal year 1993 DOD Appropriations Act prohibited the DOD from using funds to implement consolidation plans for data processing centers without submitting a report to appropriation committees); and Comp. Gen. Dec. B-251481.4, Sept. 30, 1994, *Unpub.* (Section 207 of the Legislative Branch Appropriation Act prohibited executive agencies from using appropriated funds to procure duplicating services from any source except the Government Printing Office). However, since annual appropriations acts are, by their nature, nonpermanent legislation, there is a presumption that legislative riders in annual appropriations are effective only for that fiscal year, 70 Comp. Gen. 351 (B-242142) (1991). A provision in an appropriations act may not be construed as permanent legislation unless the language or nature of the provision expresses a clear intent of Congress to make the provision permanent, Comp. Gen. Dec. B-230110, Apr. 11, 1988, *Unpub.* The principal means of establishing permanence is to include "words of futurity" in the provision of the appropriations act, Comp. Gen. Dec. B-230110, Apr. 11, 1988, *Unpub.* Other indications of permanence are if the provision is general in nature and bears no relation to the objects of the appropriations acts or if the provision would be meaningless if it were not interpreted to be a permanent legislation, 65 Comp. Gen. 588 (B-222097) (1986).

31 U.S.C. § 1532 also ensures that appropriations are only used for the purposes covered by the appropriations act. This statute specifically prohibits transfer between appropriations unless specifically authorized by statute. See also 70 Comp. Gen. 592 (B-238024) (1991); 33 Comp. Gen. 216 (B-117393) (1953). However, the shifting of funds between objects in a lump sum appropriation is not a transfer but a *reprogramming*. Reprogramming is a nonstatutory accommodation between Government agencies and legislative committees. See *Principles of Federal Appropriations Law* 2-25 (2d ed., 1991). However, failure to follow reprogramming procedures will not justify cancellation of a contract entered into as a result of the shifting of funds, *LTV Aerospace Corp.*, 55 Comp. Gen. 307 (B-183851), 75-2 CPD ¶ 203. Furthermore, the denial of approval for reprogramming from one program element to another does not prohibit the agency from using other funds within the same program element, 65 Comp. Gen. 360 (B-220113) (1986).

c. *Obligation of Appropriations*

Congress controls the expenditure of public funds by restricting the time in which appropriations may be used to incur *obligations*. For procurement transactions, 31 U.S.C. § 1501(a) provides that "[a]n amount shall be recorded as an obligation of the United States Government only when supported by documentary evidence." This would normally require a properly executed, written contractual document. However, the obligation arises when the Government incurs a liability even though the documentary evidence is not yet available to support its recordation, 38 Comp. Gen. 81 (B-114876) (1958). Thus, if the Government acts in a way that legally binds it under contract-law concepts, an obligation may have occurred.

In addition to the Anti-Deficiency Act preclusion of obligations not supported by appropriations or contract authority, 31 U.S.C. § 1517 requires an *apportionment* before an appropriation may be obligated. An apportionment is a distribution of appropriated funds made by the President through the OMB to executive agencies. Apportionments are made by time periods, usually quarters, and by activities to maintain control over the rate of obligation and expenditure of funds.

(1) Time for Obligation

The time when obligations may be made depends upon the type of appropriation. Basically, three types of appropriations are used. These are *annual appropriations*, *multiple-year appropriations*, and *no-year appropriations*. If an obligation is properly incurred during the period of availability of the appropriated funds, the appropriation will be available for *expenditure* to pay for the incurred obligation during the five subsequent fiscal years, 31 U.S.C. § 1552. Thereafter, the appropriation is canceled and the money is no longer available for expenditure — even if it was properly obligated before such cancellation.

Annual appropriations may be obligated only in the specified fiscal year. Under an annual appropriation, if no obligation is made during the year for which the money was appropriated, the appropriation is said to "expire" and is no longer available for obligation. However, as discussed below, it will still be available to fund some additional contractual activities under contracts that were entered into during the fiscal year. Multiple-year appropriations are governed by the same principles except that they are available for obligation for a specified number of years rather than a single year. No-year appropriations are available for obligation until completely obligated and are not limited by time.

(2) Bona Fide Needs Rule

Another limitation on obligation of annual appropriations is the "bona fide needs" rule, based on 31 U.S.C. § 1502(a), which states:

> The balance of an appropriation or fund limited for obligation to a definite period is available only for payment of expenses properly incurred during the period of availability or to complete contracts properly made within that period of availability and obligated consistent with section 1501 of this title. However, the appropriation or fund is not available for expenditure for a period beyond the period otherwise authorized by law.

Thus, annual funds may be used only to fulfill the *bona fide needs* of the fiscal year for which the funds were appropriated. Agencies cannot obligate an annual appropriation for the needs of prior or subsequent years, Comp. Gen. Dec. B-229873, Nov. 29, 1988, *Unpub.* See Comp. Gen. Dec. B-235678, July 30, 1990, *Unpub.*; Comp. Gen. Dec. B-226801, Mar. 2, 1988, *Unpub.* The Comptroller General recognizes that a need may arise and be contracted for in one fiscal year but that deliveries may not occur until the following or subsequent fiscal years because of necessary lead time. Thus, articles procured with annual funds do not have to be delivered or used in that fiscal year, so long as the need for the articles arose during the fiscal year, *U.S. Geological Survey*, Comp. Gen. Dec. B-226198, July 21, 1987, *Unpub.* In addition, annual funds may be used to replenish stock for future use, Comp. Gen. Dec. B-251706, Aug. 17, 1994, *Unpub.*; 21 Comp. Gen. 1159 (A-44006) (1941). However, if too long a period exists between contract award and delivery, especially for items that will be available on the open market at the time needed for use, the contract will not be considered as having fulfilled the needs of the fiscal year for which the funds were appropriated, 38 Comp. Gen. 628 (B-138574) (1959) (excessively long period to satisfy need where the units were ordered in April 1958 but would not be delivered until the later part of fiscal year 1960). But see 70 Comp. Gen. 296 (B-238940) (1991), where the agency was permitted to charge fiscal year 1989 appropriations for the cost of a training course scheduled to begin the first day of fiscal year 1990 because the two-week period between procurement and performance was not excessive.

Services that extend beyond the fiscal year may only be procured with annual funds to the extent they are nonseverable. The Comptroller General defined severable and nonseverable services in Comp. Gen. Dec. B-240264, Feb. 7, 1994, *Unpub.*, stating that services are severable if they can be divided into components that independently meet a separate need of the Government. If the services constitute a specific, entire job with a defined end product that cannot be feasibly subdivided for separate performance, then they are nonseverable. Services that are nonseverable should be charged to the year when the need for the services was identified and the contract awarded, even though performance may extend beyond the fiscal year, Comp. Gen. Dec. B-240264, Feb. 7, 1994, *Unpub.*; 71 Comp. Gen. 428 (B-241415) (1992). See also 60 Comp. Gen. 452 (B-174226) (1981); 50 Comp. Gen. 589 (B-171457) (1971). However, if the services are severable and continuous in nature, they must be charged to the appropriation current when the services are rendered, *Acumenics Research & Technology, Inc.*, Comp. Gen. Dec. B-224702, 87-2 CPD ¶ 128; 60 Comp. Gen. 219 (B-198574) (1981).

In order to facilitate the procurement of severable services, Congress has created statutory exceptions to the bona fide needs rule that authorize contracts covering periods that do not correspond to the fiscal year. The DOD has authority to contract for certain types of services for 12-month periods beginning at any time during the fiscal year and to charge the appropriation current when the contract is made for the full 12 months of services, 10 U.S.C. § 2410a. NASA has similar authority, 42 U.S.C. § 2459a.

The bona fide needs rule applies to all types of procurement in which Congress has limited the period of availability of funds. See 64 Comp. Gen. 163 (B-215825) (1984), where the Comptroller General applied it to prohibit procurement of sixth and seventh year needs on a multiyear program Congress had authorized for five years. Thus, it also applies to multiple-year appropriations, Comp. Gen. Dec. B-235678, July 30, 1990, *Unpub.*; 68 Comp. Gen. 170 (B-232024) (1989). But it has been held not to apply to no-year appropriations, 43 Comp. Gen. 657 (B-152766) (1964). See 67 Comp. Gen. 553 (B-208637.2) (1988); Comp. Gen. Dec. B-226922, May 21, 1987, *Unpub.*

(3) Contract Modifications

When performance of contracts continues beyond the fiscal year of an annual or multiple-year appropriation, the question arises as to which fiscal year's appropriation is chargeable for changes and modifications. Generally, contract modifications that are found to be within the scope of the original contract are considered bona fide needs of the fiscal year when the original contract was made. Thus, the funds used on the original contract have been properly used to fund changes issued under the Changes clause, 23 Comp. Gen. 943 (B-41903) (1944), overruns on cost-reimbursement contracts under the Limitation of Cost clause, 59 Comp. Gen. 518 (B-195732) (1980), and price adjustments under an Economic Price Adjustment, Price Redetermination or Incentive Price Revision clause, 34 Comp. Gen. 418 (B-121982) (1955). This rule is premised on the theory that these clauses do not create new liabilities but simply make existing ones certain. Modifications that are not within the scope of such clauses must use appropriations current at the time of the modification. Thus, a modification adding quantities of items procured under a contract was required to use current-year funds because it was not within the scope of the contract, Comp. Gen. Dec. B-207433, Sept. 16, 1979, *Unpub.* (funds available from downward price reduction could not be used in subsequent fiscal year to buy additional quantities even though their need had been identified in year contract was issued); Comp. Gen. Dec. B-257617, Apr. 18, 1995, *Unpub.* (funds available from downward price adjustment could not be used in subsequent fiscal year to buy additional quantities on indefinite-quantity contract).

In some cases, modifications arguably within the scope of the contract are not considered bona fide needs of the year in which the original agreement was made, and any price adjustments arising out of these modifications must be charged to a later year's appropriation, 59 Comp. Gen. 518 (B-195732) (1980). Letter contracts and contracts containing "cost of limitation" clauses are examples in which price adjustments must be charged to the later-year appropriations. In *Environmental Protection Agency*, 61 Comp. Gen. 609 (B-195732), 82-2 CPD ¶ 491, the Comptroller General held that discretionary cost increases in cost-reimbursement contracts that exceed contractually stipulated ceilings set forth in "limitation of cost" clauses and that are not based on an antecedent liability enforceable by the contractor are properly chargeable to funds available when the increase was granted. The Comptroller General reasoned at 612:

> [I]t would not be reasonable to require that amounts for cost increases beyond the contract's ceiling . . . be reserved. There is no way to estimate the anticipated amount of such increases or the need for them in any future years and it would therefore be difficult to consider them as bona fide needs of an earlier year.

The same reasoning was used for letter contract conversions. In *Obligating Letter Contracts*, Comp. Gen. Dec. B-197274, 84-1 CPD ¶ 90, the Comptroller General held that the maximum liability that may be incurred under the letter contract is chargeable to the year's appropriation current when the letter contract was made, and the amount of the definitized contract is chargeable to the year's appropriation current when the contract was definitized. The Comptroller General equated letter contracts to cases in which there is a cost increase that exceeds contractually stipulated ceilings and that is not based on antecedent liability enforceable by the contractor. In both cases, the Government is not legally liable beyond the amount set forth in the original contract until the Government and contractor agree on the modifications.

It is also improper to use current-year funds to finance a contract that has been awarded in violation of the Anti-Deficiency Act. See 55 Comp. Gen. 768 (B-132900) (1976), stating at 773-74:

> The purpose of [31 U.S.C. § 1502(a)] is to restrict the use of annual appropriations to expenditures required for the service of the particular fiscal year for which they were made. *See* 42 Comp. Gen. 272, 275 (1962). We have long held, consistent with the above statute, as well as 31 U.S.C. [§ 1341(a)] and 41 U.S.C. § 1, that a claim against a fixed year appropriation, when otherwise proper, is chargeable to the appropriation for the fiscal year in which the liability was incurred. *See, e.g.*, 18 Comp. Gen. 363, 365 (1938); 50 Comp. Gen. 589 (1971). The same rule requires, of course, that all liabilities and expenditures attributable to contracts made under the instant 3-year procurement appropriations remain chargeable to those appropriations.
>
> As we understand the proposal, the prior year contracts under which the funds were originally obligated, would not be canceled. Rather, only the source of funding those obligations would be changed, so that current year funds would be used to pay for performance already contracted for in previous years. Under these circumstances, 31 U.S.C. [§1502(a)] would preclude the use of current appropriations to fund these prior year contracts since such transactions would constitute neither "the payment of expenses properly incurred" nor "the fulfillment of contracts properly made" in fiscal year 1976.

(4) CONTINGENT OR INDEFINITE LIABILITIES

Where the Government's liability is not definite in amount, there is a question as to the proper amount to be obligated. A strict interpretation of the Anti-Deficiency Act would require agencies to obligate an amount sufficient to cover the total possible liability. However, neither the Comptroller General nor the House Committee on Appropriations has read the Act so strictly. See 34 Comp. Gen. 418 (B-121982) (1955) permitting a substantial amount of flexibility in determining the amount to be recorded as obligations for contracts involving liabilities that are indefinite in amount. In this decision, the Comptroller General, commenting on a proposed DOD directive, discussed the Government's policy with respect to obligations recorded for contracts that provide for price redetermination or revision. For fixed-price contracts with escalation or price redetermination provisions, there would be no objection to an agency's obligating only the fixed-price stated in the contract. In the case of a contract with an incentive clause, the target or billing price should be recorded as an obligation; the agency would be required, however, to safeguard against the possibility of violating the Anti-Deficiency Act by administratively reserving sufficient funds to cover at least the excess of estimated increases over decreases. Under contracts authorizing variations in quantities to be delivered, the same method could be followed (with the recorded obligation limited to the price of the quantity specified) providing that the agency reserve an amount estimated to be sufficient to cover any variations. In the case of letter contracts, letters of intent, and amendments thereto, the amount stated as the maximum liability under such agreements would be required to be recorded as the Government's obligation. Under all of these situations, the amount recorded as the original obligation is to be increased or decreased to reflect price revisions at the time such revisions are made. See also 55 Comp. Gen. 812 (B-184830) (1976). In such cases, an administrative reserve, called a *commitment*, may be made of the estimated amount of liability. See DOD Directive 7220.9-M, Oct. 1983. There are no uniform procedures governing the use of commitments. The decision to commit funds is made on a contract-by-contract basis depending on the likelihood of an underobligation of funds, the amount of money available in the appropriation, and the need for flexibility in administering the appropriation.

When the Government's liability under a contract is contingent on some future event that is not certain to occur, there is considerable controversy as to the proper treatment. In 37 Comp. Gen. 691 (B-114876) (1958), the Comptroller General ruled that claims made under the Changed Conditions clauses of several excavation contracts that were denied by the contracting officer did not require obligation because they were contingent liabilities. At the same time the Comptroller General agreed with the agency involved that amounts to cover these contingent liabilities should be administratively reserved. However, the Comptroller General has stated that, absent specific statutory authority, indemnity provisions that subject the United States to contingent and undetermined liabilities and contain no limitations contravene the Anti-Deficiency Act, 62 Comp. Gen. 361 (B-201072), 83-1 CPD ¶ 501. In response to this decision the standard Insurance — Liability to

Third Persons clause in FAR 52.228-7, which makes the Government liable for claims of third parties not compensated by the contractor's insurance, was amended to include the following paragraph:

> (d) The Government's liability under paragraph (c) of this clause is subject to the availability of appropriated funds at the time a contingency occurs. Nothing in this contract shall be construed as implying that the Congress will, at a later date, appropriate funds sufficient to meet deficiencies.

The last sentence of this provision was included to overcome criticisms that indemnity provisions may create "coercive deficiencies." See *Project Stormfury*, 59 Comp. Gen. 369 (B-198206) (1980), where the Comptroller stated that an agreement that is solely contingent on Congress passing an appropriation for its fulfillment may not violate the letter of the Act but violates its spirit; it could be considered a coercive deficiency in that Congress has little choice in such a situation. The Comptroller has continued to object to "open-ended indemnification agreements," Comp. Gen. Dec. B-260063, June 30, 1995, *Unpub.*; Comp. Gen. Dec. B-242146, Aug. 16, 1991, *Unpub.* See *Hercules, Inc. v. United States*, 116 S. Ct. 981 (1996) recognizing those cases.

Even if the amount is determinable, a clause subjecting the Government to a contingent liability could violate the statute. See *Federal Data Corp.*, 60 Comp. Gen. 584 (B-194709), 81-2 CPD ¶ 28, where the agency was found to have violated the Anti-Deficiency Act by obligating only the rental payments but agreeing to be liable for the full price of the item in case of loss. The Comptroller General stated at 590:

> Agreements to assume the risk of loss for contractor-owned equipment have often been disapproved by our Office on the basis of 31 U.S.C. § [1341] and 41 U.S.C. § 11 (1976), for the reason that such agreements could subject the United States to a contingent liability in an indeterminate amount which could exceed the available appropriation. See 54 Comp. Gen. 824, *supra*. Here, the agency only obligates a sum sufficient to meet the monthly payments required by the [lease-purchase] for the current fiscal year. Any loss which might occur during the first 2 years of the [lease-purchase] would exceed that amount and therefore unobligated funds must be available in the appropriation to cover such a contingency. While in this case the agency's maximum liability is determinable, the amount of a loss could be such as to exceed the unobligated portion of the appropriation.

The Government may possess statutory authority, which is the equivalent of contract authority, to include indemnification agreements in certain instances. For example, 10 U.S.C. § 2354 permits indemnification for research and development activity, and the Price-Anderson Act, 42 U.S.C. § 2210, covers nuclear risks. In addition, Exec. Order No. 11610, 36 Fed. Reg. 13755 (1971), uses P.L. 85-804 to permit heads of specified agencies to indemnify contractors from risks arising from unusually hazardous or nuclear activity. See FAR 50.403.

B. Control and Oversight of Procurement

There are a number of techniques that Congress and the executive agencies use to control and oversee the conduct of procurement. The primary techniques for control are the limitations on the exercise of contracting power contained in statutes and regulations. One of the major methods of overseeing compliance with these requirements is the contract award litigation process discussed in Chapter 11. In addition, organizations in both legislative and executive branches review whether procurement of authorized programs has been carried out in accordance with laws and regulations. The following material discusses the proper roles of the executive and legislative branches with respect to procurement and considers the major techniques used to control and oversee the process.

1. Executive Branch

The primary method of control of procurement in the executive branch is through the promulgation of regulations. The major executive branch oversight of procurement is conducted by Inspectors General.

a. Regulations

Rules affecting contracting are promulgated in a number of different types of regulations. Executive orders, issued by the President, OMB Circulars, and OFPP Policy Letters deal with matters having broad application throughout the executive branch. These regulations may be published to implement statutes or may be based upon executive branch policies. Another type of regulation affecting procurement is issued by an agency with oversight of a specific Government program or policy. For example, the Department of Labor has issued regulations in Volume 29 of the Code of

Federal Regulations under the Davis-Bacon Act, 40 U.S.C. § 276(a) (29 C.F.R. Part 5), and the Service Contract Act, 41 U.S.C. §§ 351–58 (29 C.F.R. Part 4).

The most important regulations governing procurement are the regulations in the FAR system, discussed earlier. When these regulations use the term "shall," they are binding on contracting agencies, FAR 2.101. However, if the regulations are less specific regarding an issue, an agency has the discretion to take action. FAR 1.102 contains a "statement of guiding principles" for the FAR system, and FAR 1.102(d) states:

> The role of each member of the Acquisition Team is to exercise personal initiative and sound business judgment in providing the best value product or service to meet the customer's needs. In exercising initiative, Government members of the Acquisition Team may assume if a specific strategy, practice, policy or procedure is in the best interests of the Government and is not addressed in the FAR nor prohibited by law (statute or case law), Executive order or other regulation, that the strategy, practice, policy or procedure is a permissible exercise of authority.

Many regulations regarding procurement are required to be posted for notice and an opportunity for comment before taking effect. 41 U.S.C. § 418b requires notice and an opportunity for public comment prior to publication of procurement policies, regulations, procedures, or forms having a "significant effect beyond the internal operating procedures of the agency" or a "significant cost or administrative impact on contractors or offerors." Thus, final regulations in the FAR system may not take effect until 60 days after publication in the *Federal Register*. However, procurement policies, regulations, procedures, or forms may take effect earlier than 60 days after the publication date when there are compelling circumstances for the earlier effective date, but in no circumstances can the effective date be less than 30 days after the publication date. If the prepromulgation notice is impracticable, the agency head may issue a temporary regulation with public comment invited before final promulgation.

The legal status of a specific provision in a regulation is a subject of great uncertainty. The provision may be found to be an "interpretative" or "housekeeping" rule. Such rules are intended as instructions to Government personnel or to indicate the agency's interpretation of a statute. Other provisions may be found to be "substantive" or "legislative" rules that implement a statute. Either type of regulation may serve as notice of limitations on the authority of Government employees or as an aid in determining the intention of the contracting parties. However, regulations will have the "force and effect of law" only if authorized by Congress, *Chrysler Corp. v. Brown*, 441 U.S. 281 (1979). There is not complete agreement as to the nature and extent of the required congressional authorization. *G.L. Christian & Assocs. v. United States*, 160 Ct. Cl. 1, 312 F.2d 418, *reh'g denied*, 160 Ct. Cl. 58, 320 F.2d 345, *cert. denied*, 375 U.S. 954 (1963), is the leading case for the proposition that provisions in procurement regulations that do not implement specific statutes may have the force and effect of law. In finding that an Armed Services Procurement Regulation (ASPR) provision mandating inclusion of a Termination for Convenience of the Government clause in defense contracts had the force and effect of law even though there was no specific statutory authority for such provision, the court looked to the general authority of the agency to issue procurement regulations and then considered the importance of the Government policy. More recently, the focus has been on finding a nexus between the regulatory provision and specific statutory authority rather than on the importance of the policy. In *Liberty Mut. Ins. Co. v. Friedman*, 639 F.2d 164 (4th Cir. 1981), the court considered the congressional authority required to support Exec. Order No. 11246 and its implementing regulations, stating at 169:

> A congressional grant of legislative authority need not be specific in order to sustain the validity of regulations promulgated pursuant to the grant, but a court must "reasonably be able to conclude that the grant of authority contemplates the regulations issued." [*Chrysler Corp. v. Brown*, 441 U.S. 281] at 308, 99 S. Ct. at 721. Our examination of the possible statutory sources of congressional authorization for Executive Order 11,246 convinces us that none of the statutes reasonably contemplates that Liberty, as a provider of workers' compensation insurance to government contractors, may be required to comply with Executive Order 11,246. We conclude therefore that none of the cited statutes authorize the action taken by defendants.

The court went on to hold that the delegation of general procurement power by Congress to the executive branch by the FPASA, 40 U.S.C. § 471 et seq., would support regulations not specifically authorized only to the extent that they were adopted to further the congressional purpose of achieving an "economical and efficient system" of procurement. The court rejected the "proposition that equal employment goals themselves, reflecting important national policies, validate the use of procurement power" to impose affirmative action requirements on an insurer. In doing so, it disagreed with *United*

States v. New Orleans Pub. Serv., Inc., 553 F.2d 459 (5th Cir. 1977), *vacated & remanded on other grounds*, 436 U.S. 942 (1978), to the extent that the case held that no nexus between the purpose of the congressional act and the provision of a regulation was required. In *Matter of Gary Aircraft Corp.*, 698 F.2d 775 (5th Cir.), *cert. denied*, 464 U.S. 820 (1983), the court held that the Disputes clause mandated by the ASPR did not have the force and effect of law because the clause was not specifically authorized by the Armed Services Procurement Act. Though the Contract Disputes Act of 1978 statutorily mandates the inclusion of a Disputes clause, it did not apply to this case because it was not in effect at the time of the contracts. The court did not discuss the general authority of the Secretary of Defense to draft regulations contained in 10 U.S.C. § 2202; neither was there discussion of the efficiency and economy nexus found necessary in the *Liberty Mutual* case. Arguably, the Disputes clause with its remedial provisions would satisfy this requirement. In *AFL-CIO v. Kahn*, 618 F.2d 784 (D.C. Cir.), *cert. denied*, 443 U.S. 915 (1979), the court upheld the requirement for Government contractors to certify compliance with "voluntary" wage and price guidelines under Exec. Order No. 12092. It found that the executive order's predominant objective of containing procurement costs furnished the required nexus to the procurement Act's criteria of efficiency and economy. However, in *Chamber of Commerce v. Reich*, 74 F.3d 1322 (D.C. Cir. 1996), the court held that the President did not have authority under the FPASA to issue an executive order authorizing the Secretary of Labor to disqualify employers with federal contracts exceeding $100,000 that hire permanent replacement workers during a lawful economic strike. In distinguishing *Kahn*, the court stated at 1322:

> [T]he President, even under the Procurement Act, does not have unlimited authority to make decisions he believes will likely result in savings to the government. We cautioned that our decisions did not "write a blank check for the President to fill in at his will. The procurement power must be exercised consistently with the structure and purposes of the statute that delegates that power." Despite our expansive reasoning [in *Kahn*] upholding President Carter's Executive Order, we stressed the importance of the "nexus between the wage and price standards and likely savings to the government."

The court found that the executive order was not rationally related to the statutory objective of providing an economical and efficient system of federal procurement but, rather, was premised on labor relations policy.

Thus, the court held that the executive order was preempted by the National Labor Relations Act.

In order for a regulation to affect legal relations, the contractor must have actual or constructive notice of the regulation. Constructive notice occurs when regulations have been published in the *Federal Register*, *Federal Crop Ins. Corp. v. Merrill*, 332 U.S. 380 (1947). The Freedom of Information Act, 5 U.S.C. § 552(a)(1), precludes constructive notice for matters "required to be published in the *Federal Register* and not so published," stating:

> Except to the extent that a person has actual and timely notice of the terms thereof, a person may not in any manner . . . be adversely affected by a matter required to be published in the *Federal Register* and not so published.

It also provides that "substantive rules" must be published in the *Federal Register*. Thus, for a regulation to have the force and effect of law either it must be published in the *Federal Register* or the affected person must have actual notice. As provided at 5 U.S.C. § 552(a)(2)(C), "administrative staff manuals and instructions to staff that affect a member of the public" need only be made available for public inspection or copies offered for sale.

Contractors have been held to have notice of regulations not published in the *Federal Register* even though there was no actual notice. In *Planning Research Corp.*, 55 Comp. Gen. 911 (B-184926), 76-1 CPD ¶ 202, the contractor was held to have constructive notice of the contents of an agency manual that was incorporated in the contract by reference. The agency manual, though not published, was available for public inspection, as required by Section 552(a)(2)(C). See also *Timber Access Indus. Co. v. United States*, 213 Ct. Cl. 648, 553 F.2d 1250 (1977), where the plaintiff was held to have had actual and timely notice of regulations contained in an unpublished Forest Service Manual and was therefore bound by the terms of the manual.

b. Inspectors General

Under the Inspector General Act of 1978, 5 U.S.C. App. § 2, Inspectors General have been established in the following departments and agencies:

> Agency for International Development, Agriculture, Commerce, Community Services Administration, Defense, Education, Environmental Protection Agency, General Services Administration, Housing & Urban Development, Interior, Labor, NASA, Small Business Administration, State, Transportation, Veterans Affairs, United States Information Agency

The Inspectors General have broad investigative powers, and their investigations are required to be free of agency influence, 5 U.S.C. App. § 3(a). They may make such investigations as they consider to be necessary or desirable. They have access to all records relating to any agency's programs and operations, 5 U.S.C. App. § 6(a)(1), and may issue subpoenas for "all information, documents, reports, answers, records, accounts, papers, and other data and documentary evidence necessary in the performance" of their duties, 5 U.S.C. App. § 6(a)(4). In *United States v. Iannone*, 610 F.2d 943 (D.C. Cir. 1979), the court held that this subpoena power relates to documents only and cannot be used to compel oral testimony.

Inspectors General have the following broad duties and responsibilities, as set forth at 5 U.S.C. App. § 4(a):

> It shall be the duty and responsibility of each Inspector General, with respect to the establishment within which his Office is established —
>
> (1) to provide policy direction for and to conduct, supervise, and coordinate audits and investigations relating to the programs and operations of such establishment;
>
> (2) to review existing and proposed legislation and regulations relating to programs and operations of such establishment and to make recommendations in the semiannual reports required by section 5(a) concerning the impact of such legislation or regulations on the economy and efficiency in the administration of programs and operations administered or financed by such establishment or the prevention and detection of fraud and abuse in such programs and operations;
>
> (3) to recommend policies for, and to conduct, supervise, or coordinate other activities carried out or financed by such establishment for the purpose of promoting economy and efficiency in the administration of, or preventing and detecting fraud and abuse in, its programs and operations;
>
> (4) to recommend policies for, and to conduct, supervise, or coordinate relationships between such establishment and other Federal agencies, State and local governmental agencies, and nongovernmental entities with respect

to (A) all matters relating to the promotion of economy and efficiency in the administration of, or the prevention and detection of fraud and abuse in, programs and operations administered or financed by such establishment, or (B) the identification and prosecution of participants in such fraud or abuse; and

(5) to keep the head of such establishment and the Congress fully and currently informed, by means of the reports required by section 5 and otherwise, concerning fraud and other serious problems, abuses, and deficiencies relating to the administration of programs and operations administered or financed by such establishment, to recommend corrective action concerning such problems, abuses, and deficiencies, and to report on the progress made in implementing such corrective action.

In addition, 5 U.S.C. App. § 5(a) requires the submission of semiannual reports to the head of the agency who, in turn, is required to submit the report to the appropriate congressional committees. The reports are required to contain the following information:

(1) a description of significant problems, abuses, and deficiencies relating to the administration of programs and operations of such establishment disclosed by such activities during the reporting period;

(2) a description of the recommendations for corrective action made by the Office during the reporting period with respect to significant problems, abuses, or deficiencies identified pursuant to paragraph (1);

(3) an identification of each significant recommendation described in previous semiannual reports on which corrective action has not been completed;

(4) a summary of matters referred to prosecutive authorities and the prosecutions and convictions which have resulted;

(5) a summary of each report made to the head of the establishment under section 6(b)(2) during the reporting period; and

(6) a listing of each audit report completed by the Office during the reporting period.

Limitations on the scope of the DOD Inspector General's investigative and reporting roles for classified and other sensitive matters are contained in 5 U.S.C. App. § 8.

2. Legislative Branch

Congressional control over the procurement function is manifested in requirements and limitations included in procurement statutes, authorization acts, appropriations acts, and other statutes. Oversight of the procurement function by the legislative branch is conducted by Congress itself and by its agent, the Comptroller General of the United States, the head of the General Accounting Office.

a. Congressional Oversight

Among the principal means of congressional oversight are the investigations and hearings of its committees. Oversight of general procurement matters is largely carried out by the Governmental Affairs Committee in the Senate, by the Government Reform and Oversight Committee in the House of Representatives, and by the Small Business Committees of both houses of Congress. However, each legislative committee of Congress with authority over the programs of a procuring agency, such as the Senate Armed Services Committee and the House National Security Committee (formerly, the House Armed Services Committee), monitors the procurement practices of that agency, and the Appropriations Committees are quite active in reviewing selective procurement policies. Even when these congressional committees do not formally adopt statutory language establishing binding procurement rules, their views are normally given great respect by agencies in formulating contracting policies. Failure of the agencies to follow the "recommendations" of committees often leads to additional statutory requirements or limitations.

Historically, there have been a number of cases where Congress authorized a program and appropriated funds but the executive agency failed or refused to carry out the program or delayed or reduced the scope of the program. Such actions have been called *impoundments*. In litigation over impoundments, it was held that the executive branch had no inherent authority to refuse to allot funds where Congress had mandated their use. See, e.g., *Train v. City of N.Y.*, 420 U.S. 35 (1975), and *Train v. Campaign Clean Water, Inc.*, 420 U.S. 136 (1975), holding that there was a clear statutory interest and direction for the funds to be obligated in those cases. In response to increased litigation and political controversy over such impoundments, Congress passed the Congressional Budget and Impoundment Control Act of 1974, 2 U.S.C. § 681 et seq. The Act divides impoundments into *rescissions*, which cancel previously granted budget authority still unused and available for obligation, and *deferrals*, which delay the obligation or expenditure of budget authority. For a rescission to take place, the President must send a message to Congress requesting rescission of budget authority and must obtain a rescinding bill. If both houses of Congress do not pass a rescinding bill within 45 days of continuous session after the message is received, the funds must be made available for obligation. The President can defer funds by sending a special deferral message to Congress; if either house passes a simple resolution disapproving the deferral, funds must be made available for obligation. If there is no disapproval the deferral remains in effect for the remainder of the fiscal year, at which time funds must be released or a new message sent. Although a number of separation of powers issues were raised by the Act, it stipulates that it shall not be construed as "asserting or conceding the constitutional powers or limitations of either Congress or the President," 2 U.S.C. § 681(1). The executive branch has, for the most part, complied with the Act. However, in *City of New Haven v. United States*, 634 F. Supp. 1449 (D.D.C. 1986), the court held that the one House veto provision on deferrals violated the Constitution's separation of powers under the holding of *Immigration & Naturalization Serv. v. Chadha*, 462 U.S. 919 (1983). As a result the court held that the deferral authority under the Act could not be used by the executive branch to defer the expenditure and issued an injunction ordering that the funds be made available. The court refused to decide the question of the President's authority to impound independently of the Act because the Act had been relied upon to defer the spending. It has been held that the Act does not require the application of some part of the funds in a lump sum appropriation to all of the objects for which it is appropriated so long as all of the funds in the appropriation are obligated, *International Union, United Automobile, Aerospace & Agricultural Implement Workers v. Donovan*, 746 F.2d 855 (D.C. Cir. 1984), *cert. denied*, 474 U.S. 825 (1985). The court reasoned that the only clear statutory intent and directive in a lump sum appropriation is to obligate all of the funds.

Another example of congressional retention of power over implementation of statutes after they have been enacted into law was present in the statute creating the Cost Accounting Standards Board (CASB), 50 U.S.C. App. § 2168. The board was granted authority to promulgate regulations and cost accounting standards but was established as an agent of the Congress, independent of the executive branch, 50 U.S.C. § 2168(a). In addition, the Comptroller General was designated as the Chairman of the Board with the authority to appoint all of its members. The constitutionality of the CASB's rulemaking power was open to question in view of *Buckley v. Valeo*, 424 U.S. 1 (1976). In that case, dealing with the Federal Election Commission, the Court stated that rule-making is an administrative function and can be carried out only by persons appointed in compliance with Article II, Section 2, Clause 2 of the Constitution. The CASB did not meet this appointment criteria. See *Bowsher v. Synar*, 478 U.S. 714 (1986), holding that the Comptroller General was an agent of Congress. These constitutional issues were resolved when the CASB was reestablished by 41 U.S.C. § 422 with membership composed entirely of members of the executive branch and members of the public.

b. Comptroller General

The Comptroller General of the United States and the General Accounting Office (GAO), headed by the Comptroller General, have been given a prominent role in the oversight of Government procurement and procurement-related functions. The office and the organization were created by the Budget and Accounting Act of 1921, 42 Stat. 20, to provide Congress with a continuing review of the Government's financial affairs. When originally established, the GAO was given a number of responsibilities previously performed in the Treasury Department. The Act gave the office additional auditing functions, and from time to time, Congress has given new responsibilities to the Comptroller General. Currently, the Comptroller audits Government agencies and their contractors, decides contract award controversies and other procurement-related disputes, settles claims, finally settles Government financial accounts, and prescribes executive agency accounting principles.

In *Bowsher v. Synar*, 478 U.S. 714 (1986), the Court, in an opinion of five justices, held that since the Comptroller General is under the control of Congress, it violates the separation of powers doctrine of the Constitution for the Comptroller General to perform the executive functions of establishing a final estimate of expenditures and revenues. Thus, the Gramm-Rudman-Hollings Act, 2 U.S.C. § 901 et seq., was held unconstitutional. A concurring opinion agreed that the Comptroller General and the GAO were part of the legislative branch but disagreed with the conclusion that the functions being performed by the Comptroller under the Act were executive functions. However, it held the Act to be unconstitutional under *Immigration & Naturalization Serv. v. Chadha*, 462 U.S. 919 (1983), because Congress could not delegate such a fundamental power to formulate national policy to an individual agent of Congress.

The Comptroller General's procurement-related functions that are clearly legislative would be constitutional to the extent that they do not delegate to the Comptroller General powers that must be exercised by Congress itself. Clearly within this category of powers would be the broad investigative and audit powers of the Comptroller. These powers include the investigation of all matters relating to the receipt, disbursement, and use of public money, 31 U.S.C. § 712; the auditing of the financial transactions of each Government agency, 31 U.S.C. § 3523; and the evaluation of programs and activities of Government agencies, 31 U.S.C. § 717. In the performance of this audit function, the Comptroller has access to all Government records, and each agency is required to supply information the Comptroller General requires concerning audit of the agency, 31 U.S.C. § 716. This statute also grants the Comptroller General subpoena power to compel the production of documents. In addition, the Comptroller has the right to audit directly the pertinent books and records of contractors that are awarded negotiated contracts, 10 U.S.C. § 2313(b) and 41 U.S.C. § 254(c). Thus, these substantial oversight powers are preserved.

The Comptroller General's functions that are executive are of questionable validity under *Bowsher*. Such functions would include the power to settle all claims of or against the United States, 31 U.S.C. § 3702. However, the Comptroller General has rarely used this power in significant procurement actions. Similarly, the Comptroller's authority to collect or compromise claims due to the United States, 31 U.S.C. § 3711, would appear to be an executive function.

The Comptroller General has been granted numerous powers dealing with the financial accounts to be maintained by executive agencies and the liability of Government certifying and disbursing officers for losses or improper disbursement of funds. See, for example, 31 U.S.C. § 3511 (prescription of agency accounting principles); 31 U.S.C. § 3512 (review and approval of agency accounting systems); 31 U.S.C. § 3526(a) (settlement of financial accounts conclusive on executive agencies); and 31 U.S.C. § 3527 (relief of accountable officers for losses). These would also appear to be executive powers.

One of the most effective control and oversight techniques used by the Comptroller General is the power to give advance decisions to certifying or disbursing officers involving payments or vouchers, 31 U.S.C. § 3529. Such decisions are almost always respected by agencies because they indicate how the Comptroller will rule when reviewing financial accounts if payment is made. However, as a matter of law, these decisions are advisory only and are binding only upon the Comptroller General, 31 U.S.C. § 3526(b). See *Greene County Planning Bd. v. Federal Power Comm'n*, 559 F.2d 1227 (2d Cir. 1976), *cert. denied*, 434 U.S. 1086 (1978). Thus, this provision would not appear to be constitutionally offensive. However, it might lose its effectiveness if the Comptroller General's power to disallow accounts under 31 U.S.C. § 3526(a) were held to be an unconstitutional delegation of executive powers.

The most significant use of the 31 U.S.C. § 3529 advance decision power in the past was in the area of contract award controversies. Although the statute mentions only decisions requested by certifying or disbursing officers, the Comptroller General agreed to give such advance decisions at the request of disappointed bidders and other parties who had an interest in a procurement. The Comptroller General's power in the contract award controversy area was formally authorized by the Competition in Contracting Act, P.L. 98-369, 31 U.S.C. § 3551 et seq. In *Ameron, Inc. v. United States Army Corps of Eng'rs*, 787 F.2d 875 (3d Cir. 1986), this statute was held not to violate the Constitution on the grounds that congressional removal powers did not make the Comptroller General "an agent of Congress for the purposes of this case." The court did not directly address the question of whether the statutory powers granted to the Comptroller General were executive in nature. In view of the Supreme Court's holding in *Bowsher v. Synar*, the *Ameron* case can no longer be cited in support of the constitutionality of the statute. Whether the Comptroller General's powers under the Act are executive in nature and therefore an unconstitutional delegation remains to be decided. The entire subject of contract award controversies is discussed in detail in Chapter 11.

The Comptroller General also has significant powers under the Congressional Budget and Impoundment Control Act of 1974, 2 U.S.C. § 681 et seq. The Act makes the Comptroller General a key figure in impoundment. The Comptroller General:

1. receives and reviews all deferral or rescission messages and informs Congress of the findings,

2. reports any executive withholding of funds where the executive has not sent a message to Congress,

3. reports to Congress if it is determined that a presidential deferral should be classed as a rescission, and

4. has authority to bring suit to require that budget authority be made available.

It would appear that these responsibilities are not executive branch functions.

C. Contracts Varying from Statutory or Regulatory Requirements

Government agencies quite frequently use procedures or enter into contracts that, either intentionally or inadvertently, vary from the requirements of statutes or regulations. Some variations from the controls imposed by the applicable statutes and regulations are authorized since the need for flexibility is frequently recognized by provisions permitting *waiver* or *deviation*. However, without a waiver or deviation, the failure to follow precisely the prescribed procedures may result in an unauthorized transaction. Where no waiver or deviation is permitted, the failure to comply with the statute or regulation will also result in an unauthorized transaction. The following section discusses waiver and deviation procedures and the effect of noncompliance.

1. Deviations and Waivers

The commonly used terminology describes departures from regulations as "deviations" and from statutes as "waivers." The procedures for deviating from regulations and waiving statutory requirements are generally strictly enforced.

a. Deviations from Regulations

Authority and procedures for obtaining deviations from the regulations in the interest of providing some flexibility in the system are contained in FAR Subpart 1.4. FAR 1.402 states:

> Unless precluded by law, executive order, or regulation, deviations from the FAR may be granted as specified in this subpart when necessary to meet the specific needs and requirements of each agency. The development and testing of new techniques and methods of acquisition should not be stifled simply because such action would require a FAR deviation. The fact that deviation authority is required should not, of itself, deter agencies in their development and testing of new techniques and acquisition methods. Refer to 31.101 for instructions concerning deviations pertaining to the subject matter of Part 31, Contract Cost Principles and Procedures. Deviations are not authorized with respect to Part 99. Refer to 99-201-5 for instructions concerning waivers pertaining to Cost Accounting Standards.

The authority to approve deviations varies, based upon the agencies involved and whether the deviation is requested for an individual contract or for more than one contract or contractor. See, for example, DFARS Subpart 201.4. There is no similar deviation procedure for other executive branch regulations such as executive orders, OMB circulars, and OFPP policy letters.

Deviations are effective only if they are granted by the designated official. In *G.L. Christian & Assocs. v. United States*, 160 Ct. Cl. 1, 312 F.2d 418, *reh'g denied*, 160 Ct. Cl. 58, 320 F.2d 345, *cert. denied*, 375 U.S. 954 (1963), the court refused to find that a proper deviation had been obtained when an Assistant Secretary of Defense approved the omission of a required clause from a contract. The court held that the deviation was only authorized if it was granted by an official with authority to grant a deviation, stating at 70:

> The Armed Services Procurement Regulations contemplated a specific mechanism for receiving permission to deviate from required forms or articles. . . . There is no proof, or offer to prove, that this mechanism was used. It is said, however, that the general agreement of the Assistant Secretary of Defense (Properties and Installations) with the Federal Housing Commissioner upon a number of forms, including a form of housing contract, constituted sufficient permission to eliminate the termination-for-convenience clause. Here, too, there is lacking any proof that this particular Assistant Secretary was empowered to approve alterations in articles mandatorily required by the ASPR. More importantly, we are not persuaded that a conscious decision was made, at the appropriate level in the Defense Department, to eliminate the required termination article and thus to subject the Government to the full common-law measures of damages (including unearned profits).

See also *McDonnell Douglas Corp. v. United States*, 229 Ct. Cl. 323, 670 F.2d 156 (1982), holding that deviation from the precise wording of a prescribed clause without obtaining approval pursuant to the regulations was beyond the authority of the contracting officer. In *Whittaker Corp.*, ASBCA 18422, 81-1 BCA ¶ 15,055, the board refused to find that a deviation was required when, after award of the contract, the contracting officer entered into a modification giving a board of contract appeals jurisdiction over a claim specifically excluded from jurisdiction by a mandatory contract clause. The board noted that the Government received consideration for the modification and that the "granting of such a waiver was well within the ambit of the contracting officer's authority to administer the contract." The impact of the board's decision is that while the contracting officer had no authority to modify or exclude the clause without a deviation when the contract was formed, such authority existed during contract administration.

b. Waiver of Statutory Requirements

In the absence of a specific statutory provision granting such authority, Government officials do not have the authority to waive statutory requirements, *M-R-S Mfg. Co. v. United States*, 203 Ct. Cl. 551, 492 F.2d 835 (1974) (requirements of the Truth in Negotiations Act not waivable by the contracting officer); *Harry L. Lowe & Assocs.*, 53 Comp. Gen. 620 (B-178307), 74-1 CPD ¶ 96 (requirement for a valid ICC operating authority for interstate motor transportation services cannot be waived by a Government agency). However, Congress has provided such authority in a significant number of statutes. For example, see 41 U.S.C. § 10a (heads of agencies may waive the requirements of the Buy American Act upon determination that the cost of compliance is unreasonable or application is inconsistent with the public interest); 40 U.S.C. § 270a(b) (contracting officers may waive Miller Act bond requirements with respect to as much of the work as is to be performed in a foreign country if it is impracticable for the contractor to furnish such bonds); 40 U.S.C. § 270e (department secretaries may waive the Miller Act bond requirements with respect to cost type contracts for construction of public buildings and procurement of certain material and supplies for the Army, Navy, Air Force, and Coast Guard); 40 U.S.C. § 481 (Secretary of Defense may exempt the DOD from certain procurement methods and policies prescribed by the GSA unless the President directs otherwise); 41 U.S.C. § 40 (Secretary of Labor may provide exemptions from wage and hour requirements of the Walsh-Healey Act and the President may suspend certain sections of the Act upon judgment that such action would be in the public interest); 40 U.S.C. § 331 (Secretary of Labor may provide exemptions from the Contract Work Hours and Safety Standards Act); 41 U.S.C. § 353(b) (Secretary of Labor may provide exemptions from the Service Contract Act of 1965); 40 U.S.C. § 276a-5 (the President may suspend the provisions of the Davis-Bacon Act in the event of a national emergency); 46 U.S.C. § 1241(b) (the President or the Secretary of Defense may temporarily waive requirements of the Cargo Preference Act upon declaration that an emergency exists justifying such action); 10 U.S.C. § 2306a(b)(1)(B) and 41 U.S.C. § 254b(b)(1)(B) (agency heads may waive requirement for cost or pricing data in exceptional cases).

A judicially forged exception to the requirement for specific statutory authority for a Government official to waive a statute has been applied to the Assignment of Claims Act, 41 U.S.C. § 15. This statute states that any prohibited assignment "shall cause the annulment of the contract." In *Tuftco Corp. v. United States*, 222 Ct. Cl. 277, 614 F.2d 740 (1980), the court held that a contracting officer possessed the necessary authority to waive the statute. This seemingly controverts not only conventional concepts of sources of authority, but also the specific policies inherent in the Act.

2. Unauthorized Variations

When unauthorized procedures or terms and conditions are used, a variety of consequences may follow. In some cases, the Government may be permitted to avoid the contract. In other instances, the contract may be rewritten to add a mandatory clause or exclude a prohibited clause. Finally, the contractor may be able to require the Government to abide by mandatory procedures.

a. Contract Avoidance

The most drastic consequence of a contract made in violation of a statute or a regulation with the force and effect of law is that the Government has the right to avoid the contract. Such contracts have been variously described as "void ab initio," *Trilon Educ. Corp. v. United States*, 217 Ct. Cl. 266, 578 F.2d 1356, *aff'd*, 217 Ct. Cl. 284 (1978); "invalid," *Prestex Inc. v. United States*, 162 Ct. Cl. 620, 320 F.2d 367 (1963); or "illegal," *Alabama Rural Fire Ins. Co. v. United States*, 215 Ct. Cl. 442, 572 F.2d 727 (1978). Government avoidance is limited to clear-cut violations of statutes or regulations, *John Reiner & Co. v. United States*, 163 Ct. Cl. 381, 325

F.2d 438 (1963), *cert. denied*, 377 U.S. 931 (1964). In *Reiner*, the court held that an improper "cancellation" should be treated as a termination for the convenience of the Government, stating that the "binding stamp of nullity" should only be imposed when the illegality is "plain." In *United States v. Amdahl Corp.*, 786 F.2d 387 (Fed. Cir. 1986), the court stated that in determining whether an award is "plainly or palpably illegal," consideration should be given to whether a statute or regulation was violated because of some action or statement by the contractor or if the contractor was on direct notice that the procedures followed violated such rules. See *Total Med. Management, Inc. v. United States*, 104 F.3d 1314 (Fed. Cir. 1997), where the court held the contract to be void because it was in direct conflict with governing regulations and the contractor knew that those regulations were controlling. See also *American Tel. & Tel. Co. v. United States*, 124 F.3d 1471 (Fed. Cir. 1997), where the court affirmed the Court of Federal Claims holding that the contract was invalid because the Under Secretary of Defense had not "determined in writing" that realistic pricing can occur in accordance with the requirements of Section 8118 of the 1988 Fiscal Year Department of Defense Appropriations Act, Pub. L. 100-202. In affirming, the court rejected the Government's argument that the contract did not involve a "major system" as defined by the DOD under another statute and adopted by DOD for Section 8118 purposes. The Federal Circuit also rejected the Government's argument that the contract was valid because "a restriction on the availability of funding is not tantamount to a lack of authority to contract." The court stated at 1494–95:

> The Court of Federal Claims concluded that § 8118's requirement for a written determination upholding the pricing integrity of a fixed-price development contract operates as a constraint on the contracting process intended for the protection of both Government and contractor. We agree with the Court of Federal Claims on this point, and affirm its conclusion. The congressional purpose is abundantly clear: "None of the funds provided . . . may be obligated or expended for [certain] fixed price-type contracts." Department of Defense Appropriations Act, Pub. L. No. 100-202, § 8118, 101 Stat. 1329, 1329–84 (1987). The attempt by the Navy to obligate or expend funds for a contract not properly authorized by Congress is ineffective to either commit or make use of federal dollars. *See*, *Office of Personnel Management v. Richmond*, 496 U.S. 414, 424, 427-28 (1990). The Government's attempt to contract fails. No valid contract was or could be entered into in face of the express congressional prohibition. *See*, e.g., 31 U.S.C. § 1341 (1994) ("Limitations on expending and obligating amounts" (the "Anti-deficiency Act").).

Following avoidance, the contractor may not recover under the contract. Further, the contractor may be denied any compensation if fraud or other criminal conduct of the contractor was involved, *K & R Eng'g Co. v. United States*, 222 Ct. Cl. 340, 616 F.2d 469 (1980) (contractor not entitled to payments due for completed work on contracts involving a violation of the conflict of interest statute, 18 U.S.C. § 208, and Government entitled to recover amounts already paid), or if the Government received no benefit from the contractor's efforts, *Prestex Inc. v. United States*, 162 Ct. Cl. 620, 320 F.2d 367 (1963) (Government permitted to reject a shipment of supplies that conformed to the contract but not to the IFB).

However, where there has been no criminal conduct and the Government has received a benefit from the contractor's performance, the contractor has been permitted to recover the value of the benefit conferred. See *United States v. Amdahl Corp.*, 786 F.2d 387 (Fed. Cir. 1986), where the court stated at 393:

> [I]n many circumstances it would violate good conscience to impose upon the contractor all economic loss from having entered an illegal contract. Where a benefit has been conferred by the contractor on the government in the form of goods or services, which it accepted, a contractor may recover at least on a quantum valebant or quantum meruit basis for the value of the conforming goods or services received by the government prior to the rescission of the contract for invalidity. The contractor is not compensated under the contract, but rather under an implied-in-fact contract.
>
> * * *
>
> Even though a contract be unenforceable against the Government, because not properly advertised, not authorized, or for some other reason, it is only fair and just that the Government pay for goods delivered or services rendered and accepted under it. In certain limited fact situations, therefore, the courts will grant relief of a quasi-contractual nature when the Government elects to rescind an invalid contract. No one would deny that ordinary principles of equity and justice preclude the United States from retaining the services, materials, and benefits and at the same time refusing to pay for them on the ground that the contracting officer's promise was unauthorized, or unenforceable for some other reason. However, the basic fact of legal significance charging the Government with liability in these situations is its retention of benefits in the form of goods or services.

See also *New York Mail & Newspaper Transp. Co. v. United States*, 139 Ct. Cl. 751, 154 F. Supp. 271, *cert. denied*, 355 U.S. 904 (1957) (contract "null and void" for violating the advertising statute, but contractor entitled to recover for the value of services rendered to the date of avoidance not limited to quantum meruit); and *Urban Data Sys., Inc. v. United States*, 699 F.2d 1147 (Fed. Cir. 1983) (contract invalid for violation of cost-plus-a-percentage-of-cost prohibition, but recovery permitted on quantum valebant basis).

b. *Inclusion or Exclusion of Clause*

A statute or a regulation with the force and effect of law may also impact the contract language to which the parties agreed. Thus, if a mandatory clause is required to be included in the contract, the contract will be read to include it even though it is not physically incorporated in the document, *G.L. Christian & Assocs. v. United States*, 160 Ct. Cl. 1, 312 F.2d 418, *reh'g denied*, 160 Ct. Cl. 58, 320 F.2d 345, *cert. denied*, 375 U.S. 954 (1963) (Termination for the Convenience of the Government clause); *Santa Fe — Andover Oil Co.*, ASBCA 35256, 88-2 BCA ¶ 20,607 (Disputes clause); *Bromley Contracting Co.*, DOTCAB 1284, 84-2 BCA ¶ 17,233 (Payment of Interest on Contractors' Claims clause); *Dayron Corp.*, ASBCA 24919, 84-1 BCA ¶ 17,213 (Government Property clause); *Benjamin P. Garcia*, ASBCA 18035, 73-2 BCA ¶ 10,196 (Equal Opportunity clause). Similarly, if a certain clause is prohibited, it will be read out of the contract even though it is physically present, *Charles Beseler Co.*, ASBCA 22669, 78-2 BCA ¶ 13,483 (Value Engineering clause). In the early application of this rule, it was held to apply only to clauses that contained significant procurement policies, *Chamberlain Mfg. Co.*, ASBCA 18103, 74-1 BCA ¶ 10,368 (Government Property clause). Subsequently, cases appeared to apply the rule to all mandatory clauses without analyzing whether they contained significant policies. See, for example, *Balimoy Mfg. Co.*, ASBCA 43768, 93-1 BCA ¶ 25,437 (First Article Approval clause); *Rodgers Constr., Inc.*, IBCA 2777, 92-1 BCA ¶ 24,503 (Assignment of Claims clause); *M.E. McGeary Co.*, ASBCA 36788, 90-1 BCA ¶ 22,512 (Disputes Concerning labor Standards clause); and *Fireman's Fund Ins. Co.*, ASBCA 38284, 91-1 BCA ¶ 23,439 (Dispute clause). Some later cases did, however, analyze whether the mandatory clause contained significant policies. See, for example, *Miller's Moving Co.*, ASBCA 42114, 92-1 BCA ¶ 24,707 (the board incorporated the Services Contract Act provisions in a contract because the Act was an "obligatory congressional enactment"); and *H&R*

Machinists Co., ASBCA 38440, 91-1 BCA ¶ 23,373 (the board incorporated the Default clause in the contract because it implemented "fundamental procurement policy").

Other cases incorporated a mandatory clause without discussion, but did deal with more significant issues. See, for example, *Technical & Management Servs. Corp.*, ASBCA 39999, 93-2 BCA ¶ 25,681 (Limitation of Price and Contractor Obligation clause); *Telesec Library Servs.*, ASBCA ¶ 42968, 92-1 BCA ¶ 24,650 (Fair Standards Act and Service Contract Act — Price Adjustment clause); and *OFEGRO*, HUDBCA 88-3410-C7, 91-3 BCA ¶ 24,206 (Default clause).

In 1993, the Federal Circuit announced that the rule applied when the clause contained a significant procurement policy *or* when it was written to "benefit or protect the party seeking incorporation," *General Eng'g & Mach. Works v. O'Keefe*, 991 F.2d 775 (Fed. Cir. 1993). See *Rehabilitation Servs.*, ASBCA 47085, 96-2 BCA ¶ 28,324, where the board incorporated a Government Furnished Property clause in the contract because it was a "mandatory contract clause that expresses a significant and deeply ingrained strand of public procurement policy." But see *Computing Application Software Technology, Inc.*, ASBCA 47554, 96-1 BCA ¶ 28,204, where the board refused to incorporate a mandatory NASA Government Furnished Property clause placing the risk of loss on the contractor. The board stated that this clause had the opposite effect of the standard FAR clause and that it was to be used in the special circumstance of contracts for the repair or modification of Government property. The board found that this was such a narrow category of contracts that it was not covered by the FAR provisions on Government property and therefore it was not "fundamental policy."

There are cases subsequent to the *General Engineering* decision incorporating clauses into a contract without a discussion of whether they expressed significant policy. See, for example, *Alta Constr. Co.*, PSBCA 1463, 94-3 BCA ¶ 27,961 (the Postal Service board read regulatory language into the Termination for Convenience clause that was placed in the contract); *C&J Assocs. v. VA Med. Ctr.*, VABCA 3892, 95-2 BCA ¶ 27,834 (the Department of Veterans Affairs board incorporated a Termination of Convenience clause in a purchase order but refused to incorporate a Default clause because it was not mandatory); *GAI Consultants, Inc.*, ENGBCA 6030, 95-2 BCA ¶ 27,620 (the GSBCA incorporated the correct Changes clause in a contract for archeological investigation); and *Unit Data Servs. Corp. v. Department of Veterans Affairs*, GSBCA 10775-P-R, 93-3 BCA

¶ 25,964 (the GSBCA incorporated a clause requiring small business set-aside contractor to perform at least 50 percent of the work with its own employees).

If the statute or regulation is not mandatory with respect to the use of a clause, this rule will not apply. See *Professional Servs. Unified, Inc.*, ASBCA 48883, 96-1 BCA ¶ 28,073, where the board held that a contracting officer had correctly interpreted the FAR in using a "Federal, State and Local Taxes" clause which did not provide for price adjustments for subsequent tax increases. The board found that the clause giving price adjustments was to be used only in noncompetitive procurements and the procurement at issue was competitive. See also *Shawn K. Chistensen*, AGBCA 95-188-R, 95-2 BCA ¶ 27,724 (Differing Site Conditions clause); *Jamsar, Inc.*, GSBCA 4396, 76-2 BCA ¶ 12,053 (Changes clause in building services contract); *Jacqueline Howell, Ltd.*, ASBCA 27026, 82-2 BCA ¶ 16,086 (Liquidated Damages clause); *Palmer & Sicard, Inc.*, ASBCA 23485, 81-1 BCA ¶ 15,029 (Government Delay of Work clause); *Muncie Gear Works, Inc.*, ASBCA 16153, 72-1 BCA ¶ 9429 (Duty-Free Entry clause).

3. Contractor Benefit

These rules involving statutes and regulations have been used primarily for the benefit of the Government. However, statutes and regulations have been used by contractors as well, *American Tel. & Tel. Co. v. United States*, 124 F.3d 1471 (Fed. Cir. 1997). In *Fletcher v. United States*, 183 Ct. Cl. 1, 392 F.2d 266 (1968), the court held that regulations that are intended to define or state the rights of a class of persons are presumably intended for the benefit of those persons. Such regulations can be asserted for a contractor's benefit, *Moran Bros., Inc. v. United States*, 171 Ct. Cl. 245, 346 F.2d 590 (1965) (Atomic Energy Commission procurement regulation that permitted appeals within 60 days had the effect of law, and appeal was timely even though it exceeded the 30-day limit included in the contract); 47 Comp. Gen. 457 (B-162272) (1968) (mandatory Government liability for insurance premiums read into the contract); *Bethlehem Steel Corp. v. United States*, 191 Ct. Cl. 141, 423 F.2d 300 (1970) (regulation prescribing technique for determining the profit for defense contractors used for the benefit of contractors); *Chris Berg, Inc. v. United States*, 192 Ct. Cl. 176, 426 F.2d 314 (1970) (ASPR provision giving contractors the right to correct clerical mistakes in bids binding on the Government).

III. AUTHORITY OF GOVERNMENT PERSONNEL

The formation or modification of a Government contract may involve many Government and contractor personnel with varying degrees of authority. Specialists representing both parties engage in activities such as cost and price analysis, technical review, preaward surveys, negotiation, and preparation of contract documents. Accountants, attorneys, auditors, engineers, and other specialists may represent both parties. The ultimate aim of their activity is the creation of a legally enforceable agreement. In the vast majority of the cases, this goal is achieved. However, legal problems concerning the authority of these personnel are frequently encountered — most often when the Government refuses to recognize an alleged contractual agreement on the grounds that the contractor has dealt with an unauthorized agent. Contractors occasionally raise the same defenses, but with much less success. This section considers the legal principles relevant to determining the authority of Government personnel, the consequences of dealing with unauthorized personnel, and the effect of notice of limitations on authority. A later section examines a number of the same principles as applied to contractor personnel.

The fundamental rule regarding Government personnel is that the Government is not bound by unauthorized acts of its officers or agents, *Wilber Nat'l Bank v. United States*, 294 U.S. 120 (1935). The Government has taken advantage of this rule by allocating the major grant of contractual authority to *a special and limited class of employees* called *contracting officers*. Contracting officers have the sole authority to legally bind the Government to contracts and contract modifications, FAR 1.601. However, they are frequently not involved in the day-to-day activities that occur in the contract formation process. In some agencies, the designated contracting officer may be an active participant in the steps leading to signature of a contract, while in others, the contracting officer's role may be only to sign the document. Thus, during the formation process, a contractor may deal primarily with Government personnel bearing titles such as contract specialist, contract negotiator, cost analyst, project manager, engineer, contracting officer's representative, auditor, and attorney. In many cases, those personnel who are not contracting officers may be delegated authority to perform specific functions even though the general grant of contractual authority is made only to contracting officers. Additionally, the authority of contracting officers may range from full authority, regardless of the nature and size of the transaction (plenary authority), to authority to perform only a limited class of contractual activities described by type and dollar amount. This fragmentation of authority in the contracting process has created difficult legal problems.

A. Actual Authority Required

In private agency law, an employer will be bound by an employee under the legal theory of *apparent authority* if the employer has permitted the employee to assume authority or has held out the employee as possessing authority. See *Restatement, Second, Agency* § 8. Recognizing the importance of effective Government control over the conduct of its agents, the boards and courts have rejected the apparent-authority rule, holding that *actual authority* is required to bind the Government. See *Federal Crop Ins. Corp. v. Merrill*, 332 U.S. 380 (1947), where the Court stated at 383:

> Whatever the form in which the Government functions, anyone entering into an arrangement with the Government takes the risk of having accurately ascertained that he who purports to act for the Government stays within the bounds of his authority. The scope of this authority may be explicitly defined by Congress or be limited by delegated legislation, properly exercised through the rule-making power. And this is so even though, as here, the agent himself may have been unaware of the limitations upon his authority. See, e.g., *Utah Power & Light Co. v. United States*, 243 U.S. 389, 409 (1917); *United States v. Stewart*, 311 U.S. 60 (1940).

For cases where Government employees with apparent authority were found to have no actual authority, see *Jascourt v. United States*, 207 Ct. Cl. 955, *cert. denied*, 423 U.S. 1032 (1975) (Government not bound by the actions of the Deputy Assistant Secretary of Labor for Labor Relations, or the Director of the Division of Public Employees, since neither official had the authority to enter into a contract); *Housing Corp. v. United States*, 199 Ct. Cl. 705, 468 F.2d 922 (1972) (HUD Secretary's unauthorized signature would not bind Government as a third party responsible for costly changes); *Byrne Org., Inc. v. United States*, 152 Ct. Cl. 578, 287 F.2d 582 (1961) ("letters of intent" issued by director and chief administrative officer of the National Capital Sesquicentennial Commission not binding on the Government); and *Gordon Woodroffe Corp. v. United States*, 122 Ct. Cl. 723, 104 F. Supp. 984 (1952) (special assistant to State Department coordinator for aid to Greece and Turkey had no authority to purchase equipment).

The fact that an official appears to be a superior of a contracting officer does not establish the authority of that official. See *Inter-Tribal Council of Nev., Inc.*, IBCA 1234-12-78, 83-1 BCA ¶ 16,433, stating at 81,745-46:

> The facts that the Assistant Area Director for Education was the "boss" for Area education matters, . . . that the CO sought his approval for a contract budget modification, . . . and that he was named as the "contact person" for negotiations for an upcoming contract . . . are irrelevant in this context. The best that can be said about them is that they are probative of the fact and conclusion that the Assistant Area Director had *apparent* authority here, which we have already noted is insufficient authority for [the contractor's] reliance under the *Federal Crop Insurance* rule. The reason for excepting the Government from the rule of apparent authority generally applicable to private contracts has been oft-stated as grounded in the difference between protecting the public treasury, a public right or a public interest on the one hand, and protecting private concerns on the other. *Federal Crop Insurance Corp. v. Merrill, supra* at 385, and *Utah Power & Light Co. v. United States*, 243 U.S. 389, 37 S. Ct. 387, 391 (1917). Also, the Government practice of specifically designating only one person, the CO, as having exclusive actual authority for dealing with the administration of a contract avoids the chaos and lack of protection for those Government interests which would result if a contractor were allowed to rely on the authority of any one of dozens or potentially hundreds of Government "agents" who might have some relationship with the contract. See *Dresser Industries, Inc. v. United States*, [596 F.2d 1231, 1237 (5th Cir. 1979)].

See also *Henry Burge & Alvin White*, PSBCA 2431, 89-3 BCA ¶ 21,910, where a project manager was held to have no authority to relax the specifications. Compare *Zoubi v. United States*, 25 Cl. Ct. 581 (1992), where an "acting program director" was held to have authority to contract for services because he was responsible for obtaining such services and had obtained them in the past.

On the working level, personnel with official-sounding titles such as contract specialist, negotiator, and administrator work for contracting officers and handle the day-to-day contracting activity of the Government, but such personnel generally do not have authority to order additional work or to commit the Government by virtue of their position. In, the board stated at 29,525–26: *General Elec. Co.*, ASBCA 11990, 67-1 BCA ¶ 6377, *rev'd on other grounds*, 188 Ct. Cl. 620, 412 F.2d 1215 (1969)

> [The contract specialist's] only function was to serve as contact point between the Government and [the contractor]. He can be considered little

> more than a messenger. There is no evidence that he was delegated any power to bind the Government; on the contrary the testimony establishes that he was delegated no authority to bind the Government. No authority to bind the Government for additional funds by demanding the report notwithstanding the funding situation can be implied from [his] position.

See also *Mil-Spec Contractors, Inc. v. United States*, 835 F.2d 865 (Fed. Cir. 1987) (Government not bound by alleged oral agreement by contract negotiator); and *Precision Standards, Inc.*, ASBCA 41375, 96-2 BCA ¶ 28,461 (contract administrator working for ACO had no authority to waive delivery schedule). In *Kahaluu Constr. Co.*, ASBCA 33248, 90-2 BCA ¶ 22,663, the Government argued that a binding agreement had been reached on a "Board on Changes Report" signed by a contractor's representative and Government members of the board. However, the board found that neither the Government members nor the contractor's representatives had authority to bind their respective parties.

B. Delegation of Authority

The contracting authority in each agency flows from the head of the agency to contracting officers. See FAR 1.601, stating:

> [A]uthority and responsibility to contract for authorized supplies and services are vested in the agency head. The agency head may establish contracting activities and delegate broad authority to manage the agency's contracting functions to heads of such contracting activities. Contracts may be entered into and signed on behalf of the Government only by contracting officers. In some agencies, a relatively small number of high level officials are designated contracting officers solely by virtue of their positions. Contracting officers below the level of a head of a contracting activity shall be selected and appointed under 1.603.

This regulation recognizes two types of officials with contracting officer authority. At the upper level of the agency, in secretarial positions or as head of a contracting activity, officials have contracting authority "by virtue of their positions." These officials are not required to meet the qualification requirements for appointment and generally do not act as contracting officers except on special matters. Yet they have full authority to act as contracting officers. Below these officials are the *designated contracting officers*, appointed in accordance with the regulations discussed below.

Each agency is authorized to delegate contracting officer authority in accordance with its own procedures. See FAR 1.603-1, stating that the agency shall

> establish and maintain a procurement career management program and a system for the selection, appointment, and termination of appointment of contracting officers. Agency heads or their designees may select and appoint contracting officers and terminate their appointments.

Thus, agency heads may appoint contracting officers or may delegate this authority. In some agencies authority has been delegated to appoint subsidiary contracting officers or other representatives. FAR 1.602-1(a) requires clear instructions in the appointment document, as follows:

> Contracting officers may bind the Government only to the extent of the authority delegated to them. Contracting officers shall receive from the appointing authority (see 1.603-1) clear instructions in writing regarding the limits of their authority. Information on the limits of contracting officers' authority shall be readily available to the public and agency personnel.

The term "contracting officer" is used to describe those individuals with the authority to execute contractual documents that bind the Government and to sign determinations and findings and other internal documents. FAR 2.101 contains the following definition:

> "Contracting Officer" means a person with the authority to enter into, administer, and/or terminate contracts and make related determinations and findings. The term includes certain authorized representatives of the contracting officer acting within the limits of their authority as delegated by the contracting officer. "Administrative contracting officer (ACO)" refers to a contracting officer who is administering contracts. "Termination contracting officer (TCO)" refers to a contracting officer who is settling terminated contracts. A single contracting officer may be responsible for duties in any or all of these areas. Reference in this regulation to administrative contracting officer or termination contracting officer does not (a) require that a duty be performed at a particular office or activity or (b) restrict in any way a contracting officer in the performance of any duty properly assigned.

The first sentence of this FAR definition refers to the official who has been designated as a contracting officer. However, the second sentence creates confusion by stating that *the term includes* any "authorized representative" of the contracting officer. This broad definition of contracting officer is also included in the Definitions clause in FAR 52.202-1.

The inclusion of "authorized representatives" within the definition of contracting officer is very misleading, because formally designated contracting officers will normally have a much broader grant of authority than authorized representatives. In addition, not all representatives are appointed in the same manner or with the same degree of authority. The following discussion explores the method of appointment and stated scope of authority of three categories of Government employees — designated contracting officers, contracting officer representatives, and other employees with contractual duties.

1. Designated Contracting Officers

FAR 1.603-3 calls for the appointment of designated contracting officers *by name* using the Certificate of Appointment, Standard Form 1402. In addition, each agency is required to establish a system that ensures that each designated contracting officer is fully qualified by experience and training. The following guidance for selection criteria is given in FAR 1.603-2:

> In selecting contracting officers, the appointing official shall consider the complexity and dollar value of the acquisitions to be assigned and the candidate's experience, training, education, business acumen, judgment, character, and reputation. Examples of selection criteria include —
>
> (a) Experience in Government contracting and administration, commercial purchasing, or related fields;
>
> (b) Education or special training in business administration, law, accounting, engineering, or related fields;
>
> (c) Knowledge of acquisition policies and procedures, including this and other applicable regulations;
>
> (d) Specialized knowledge in the particular assigned field of contracting; and
>
> (e) Satisfactory completion of acquisition training courses.

More precise and demanding requirements have been called for in recent years. See, for example, Exec. Order No. 12931, 59 Fed. Reg. 52387 (1994), requiring heads of agencies to:

(h) Establish career education programs for procurement professionals, including requirements for successful completion of educational requirements or mandatory training for entry level positions and for promotion to higher level positions, in order to ensure a highly qualified procurement work force.

See also the Office of Personnel Management Standard for GS-1102 (the series for contracting professionals), which contains educational or experience requirements. A number of agencies have adopted higher standards for their contracting officers. See DFARS 201.603-2, imposing the following requirements on contracting officers in the DOD:

(1) Pursuant to 10 U.S.C. 1724, beginning October 1, 1993, in order to qualify to serve as a contracting officer with authority to award or administer contracts for amounts above the small purchase threshold in FAR 13.000, a person must —

(i) Have completed all mandatory contracting courses required for a contracting officer at the grade level, or in the position within the grade of the General Schedule in which the person is serving;

(ii) Have at least two years' experience in a contracting position;

(iii) Have —

(A) Received a baccalaureate degree from an accredited educational institution;

(B) Completed at least 24 semester credit hours, or equivalent, of study from an accredited institution of higher education in any of the following disciplines: accounting, business finance, law, contracts, purchasing, economics, industrial management, marketing, quantitative methods, and organization and management; or

(C) Passed an examination considered to demonstrate skills, knowledge, or abilities comparable to that of an individual who has completed at least 24 semester credit hours, or equivalent, of study from an accredited institution of higher education in any of the disciplines in paragraph (1)(iii)(B) of this subsection; and

(iv) Meet such additional requirements, based on the dollar value and complexity of the contracts awarded or administered in the position as may be established by the Secretary of Defense.

(2) The requirements in 201.603-2(1)(iii) do not apply to any employee who, as of October 1, 1991, had at least 10 years' experience in acquisition positions, in comparable positions in other government agencies or the private sector, or in similar positions in which the individual obtained experience directly relevant to the field of contracting.

a. *Internal Limitations on Authority*

In each agency there are one or more contracting officers with plenary authority. Even these contracting officers, however, may be subject to internal regulations governing how that authority is exercised, and the contractor is responsible for being aware of any regulations made known to it through publication or otherwise, *Federal Crop Ins. Corp. v. Merrill*, 332 U.S. 380 (1947). In *Porter v. United States*, 204 Ct. Cl. 355, 496 F.2d 583 (1974), *cert. denied*, 420 U.S. 1004 (1975), published regulations delegated authority to the high commissioner and the director of the Office of Territories to contract for shipping services "on behalf of the Trust Territory of the Pacific Islands." The contractor was deemed to have notice that these officials were acting for the Trust Territory government and had no authority to bind the United States. In contrast, the contractor is not bound by limitations in unpublished regulations. See *NI Indus., Inc. v. United States*, 841 F.2d 1104 (Fed. Cir. 1988) (contractor not bound by limitations set forth in unpublished value engineering change proposal rule); *A-1 Garbage Disposal & Trash Serv.*, ASBCA 30623, 89-1 BCA ¶ 21,323 (contractor not bound by unpublished regulation of Small Business Administration); and *New England Tank Indus. of N.H., Inc.*, ASBCA 26474, 88-1 BCA ¶ 20,395, *vacated & remanded on other grounds*, 861 F.2d 685 (Fed. Cir. 1988) (Government bound to modification signed by contracting officer even though unpublished regulation prohibited agreement). See also *Devil's Lake Sioux Tribe*, IBCA 1953, 88-1 BCA ¶ 20,320, where the board held that the contractor was not bound by a published regulation that was so vague and ambiguous that it could not be understood by a typical contractor. However, if the contractor is aware of the unpublished regulation, it will be bound by the limitations contained therein. See *D.M. Summers, Inc.*, VABCA 2750, 89-3 BCA ¶ 22,123 (contractor could not recover for lost work because it had actual knowledge of changes in internal agency regulations that reduced the requirements of the contract). In *LDG Timber Enters., Inc. v. Glickman*, 114 F.3d 1140 (Fed. Cir. 1997), the court held that the Government had the burden of proving that an internal regulation barred a contracting officer from taking normal action within his or her authority.

b. Functional Contracting Officers

In the DOD, different types of contracting officers perform different functions. Contracting officers that award contracts are known as procuring contracting officers (PCOs); contracting officers that administer contracts are known as administrative contracting officers (ACOs); and contracting officers that handle contract terminations are known as terminating contracting officers (TCOs). In most other agencies, there is no such fragmentation of authority, with the result that the contracting officers who award contracts usually retain authority to administer them. There may be additional specialized contracting officers with limited scopes of authority, such as corporate administrative contracting officers (CACOs).

FAR 1.603-3 requires that limitations on authority be included in the certificate of appointment of each contracting officer and that contractors be responsible for ascertaining the limits of authority of contracting officers. See, for example, *Strick Corp.*, ASBCA 15921, 73-2 BCA ¶ 10,077 (modification not binding because ACO had no authority to sign it); and *Atlantic, Gulf & Pac. Co.*, ASBCA 13533, 72-1 BCA ¶ 9415 (termination settlement not binding because TCO acted beyond authority). However, such limitations on authority will not control if they are neither published nor communicated to the contractor. See *Texas Instruments, Inc. v. United States*, 922 F.2d 810 (Fed. Cir. 1990) (Government bound by ACO signature on agreement even though internal regulations required internal approvals).

c. Specific Designation by Contract

There is also a difference in the way contracting officer authority is distributed relative to supply versus construction contracts. In construction contracts, the contractor can generally expect to be informed of a single named individual who has authority to bind the Government. There is usually no designation of ACOs; the field functions relating to the day-to-day administration of the contract are performed through contracting officer representatives. In supply contracts, there is usually no designation of a single person to serve as contracting officer. Thus, any employee of the agency who has been properly designated a contracting officer may act on any contract of the agency, provided that he or she is acting within the limits of this authority. This procedure gives the agency much greater internal operating flexibility, but it creates difficulties for contractors in ascertaining the authority of the person with whom they are dealing.

d. Dollar Limitations on Authority

There are frequently various tiers of contracting officers with decreasing amounts of authority given to each succeeding lower tier. This practice is particularly prevalent in supply contracting. At the top may be the contracting officer who signed the contract and has full ("plenary") authority within the agency. Below may be a contracting officer with authority to sign contracts and changes up to $500,000 in value, and another step down may be a contracting officer with authority to sign changes up to $25,000. The contractor must know this internal structure and be aware of the personnel and organizational changes that occur within the agency in order to determine whether a particular employee has authority at any given time. Since, as a general rule, no notice is given to contractors of such personnel or organizational changes, this task is a difficult one for the contractor that does not deal with the agency regularly.

Contractors must ascertain the monetary limitations on the authority of subsidiary contracting officers. See *Edwards v. United States*, 22 Cl. Ct. 411 (1991) (Government not bound when contracting officer agreed to modification above dollar limitation for agreements without approval of higher authority); *OAO Corp. v. United States*, 17 Cl. Ct. 91 (1989) (Government not bound by "handshake" of contracting officer when approval of higher authority required; however, court did find an implied-in-fact contract); and *Danac, Inc.*, ASBCA 30227, 90-3 BCA ¶ 23,246 (Government would not have been bound by a settlement agreement above dollar limitation in contract, without approval of higher authority as provided for in contracting officer's warrant).

2. Authorized Representatives

A considerable degree of confusion surrounds the term "authorized representative." One source of the confusion is the regulatory definition of contracting officer, discussed above, which defines the term to include "the authorized representatives of the contracting officer acting within the limits of their authority," FAR 2.101. However, authorized representatives traditionally have *a much narrower scope of authority* than those specifically appointed as contracting officers, and it should be clear that authorized representatives *do not have the authority to sign contracts or contract modifications*. See *Essen Mall Properties v. United States*, 21 Cl. Ct. 430 (1990), rejecting the argument that an authorized representative had the full authority of a contracting officer because of the regulatory definition.

Further confusion results from the varying methods used by contracting officers to appoint representatives — with some representatives being formally designated as contracting officer representatives (CORs), and other representatives merely being assigned functions to be performed in the procurement process without specific use of the term "authorized representative" in their selection or appointment. For this reason, these two types of representatives are discussed separately.

a. *Formally Designated Representatives*

There are a number of formally designated representatives who act on behalf of the Government — primarily during contract administration. Depending upon the agency involved, these representatives may bear the title of contracting officer representative (COR), contracting officer technical representative (COTR), Government technical representative (GTR), or Government technical evaluator (GTE). Although their responsibilities vary, an OFPP memorandum on Government-wide Guidance on Contract Administration (1991) states that the principal responsibilities of COTRs are as follows:

> (1) Inspecting and accepting or rejecting work performed under the contract. It is important that the COTR alerts the contracting officer immediately when it is discovered that the contractor is not performing adequately. Since the COTR is most often a member of the project office, the COTR should not assume the role of advising the contractor on how to resolve deficiencies in performance or to presume that given enough time the contractor will take corrective actions.
>
> (2) Representing the government in technical phases of the work. The COTR is responsible for the technical administration of the contract and will advise the contractor on all technical matters relating to the contract. The COTR will also interpret technical directives having a bearing on the contractor's performance.

For guidance on best practices in contract administration for COTRs, see *A Guide to Best Practices for Contract Administration* (OFPP, Oct. 1994).

There is no guidance in the FAR as to the method of appointing these representatives except for the statement in the definition. Thus, one must look to the subsidiary regulations in each agency to determine the method of appointment. Generally, such regulations provide that appointment will be in writing, either by a separate letter or by designation in the contract, and that each contractor affected should receive notice of the appointment. The OFPP memorandum on Government-wide Guidance on Contract Administration indicates that a separate designation must be issued for each contract. The OFPP memorandum also states that "[t]he delegated responsibilities of the COTR shall not be redelegated to others. A COTR cannot inherit authority of another COTR who previously held that position." Authority delegated to representatives is always much narrower than that possessed by the contracting officer. See, for example, the Department of Interior Regulation, DIAR 1401.670, which provides:

> 1401.670-1 General.
>
> A contracting officer may select and appoint an individual to act as an authorized representative in the administration of a contract based on the technical, professional and administrative qualifications of the individual.
>
> 1401.670-2 Appointment.
>
> > (a) Contracting officers' representatives shall be appointed in writing by the contracting officer. The appointment shall state the scope and limitations of authority (see 1401.670-3) and identify the contract(s) which the representative will administer.
> >
> > (b) Changes in the scope or limitations of authority shall be made by written amendments to the existing appointment or by issuance of a new appointment.
> >
> > (c) A copy of the appointment shall be promptly forwarded to the contractor after issuance by the contracting officer.
>
> 1401.670-3 Limitations.
>
> Each appointment of a contracting officers' representative made by the contracting officer shall clearly state that the representative is not authorized under any circumstances to —
>
> > (a) Award, agree to, or execute any contract, contract modification, or notice of intent;

(b) Obligate, in any way, the payment of money by the Government;

(c) Make a final decision on any contract matter which is subject to the clause at FAR 52.233-1, Disputes; or

(d) Terminate, for any cause, the contractor's right to proceed.

The DOD uses the following Contracting Officer's Representative clause in DFARS 252.201-7000 to alert its contractors that CORs may be appointed:

> (a) *Definition. Contracting officer's representative* means an individual designated in accordance with subsection 201.602-2 of the Defense Federal Acquisition Regulation Supplement and authorized in writing by the contracting officer to perform specific technical and administrative functions.
>
> (b) If the Contracting Officer designates a contracting officer's representative (COR), the Contractor will receive a copy of the written designation. It will specify the extent of the COR's authority to act on behalf of the contracting officer. The COR is not authorized to make any commitments or changes that will affect price, quality, quantity, delivery, or any other term or condition of the contract.

Limitations on authority of CORs or COTRs that have been communicated to the contractor are binding on the contractor. See, for example, *Construction Equip. Lease Co. v. United States*, 26 Cl. Ct. 341 (1992) (COR technical project officer had no authority to change contract in face of explicit language in appointment letter); (project manager acting as authorized *Essen Mall Properties v. United States*, 21 Cl. Ct. 430 (1990) representative had no authority to bind Government agency to contract); *David W.E. Cabell*, VABCA 3402, 93-2 BCA ¶ 25,598 (COR had no authority to interpret an unambiguous contract in a manner that leads to additional compensation); *HTC Indus., Inc.*, ASBCA 40562, 93-1 BCA ¶ 25,560, *recons. denied*, 93-2 BCA ¶ 25,701, *aff'd*, 22 F.3d 1103 (Fed. Cir. 1994) (COTR had no authority to order contractor to continue performance while he sought additional funding in view of the specific language in the contract); and *Carothers & Carothers Co.*, ENGBCA 4015, 88-3 BCA ¶ 21,162 (COR had no authority to issue major change). On the other hand, the Government may be bound by the actions of a COR or COTR acting within the scope of his or her authority, even if additional work is called for. See *Oliver Eng'g Servs.*, DOTBCA 2549, 94-3 BCA ¶ 27,203 (providing faulty technical information within scope of COTR's duties); *Hudson Contracting, Inc.*, ASBCA 41023, 94-1 BCA ¶ 26,466 (making Government property available to contractor within authority of COR); *Diversified Marine Tech, Inc.*, DOTBCA 2455, 93-2 BCA ¶ 25,720 (granting permission to perform work within scope of COR's delegation when, as the Government representative at the site, he was the most logical person to act); *MJW Enters., Inc.*, ENGBCA 5813, 93-1 BCA ¶ 25,405 (interpretation of vague specification within scope of COR's authority); and *Farr Bros., Inc.*, ASBCA 42658, 92-2 BCA ¶ 24,991 (COR had authority to order work suspension).

b. Other Representatives

The vast majority of personnel involved in the contract formation process are designated neither as contracting officers nor CORs. Many of these personnel are organizationally separate specialists, such as attorneys, auditors, or engineers, from whom the contracting officer is required to request advice, FAR 1.602-2(c). These same personnel may receive information from contractors and may, in the course of their duties, participate in discussions or negotiations. Thus, their role may be seen as independent Government representatives or as informally recognized representatives of the contracting officer. Other Government personnel, such as auditors or procurement specialists, often are assigned responsibilities in the contract formation process without formal designation as CORs. The regulations in this area do not clearly delineate the authority of these personnel and generally do not require specific written designation as CORs.

The absence of formal delegation as a "representative" has not prevented the courts and boards of contract appeals from finding that these personnel are authorized representatives of the contracting officer. See, for example, *Cessna Aircraft Co.*, ASBCA 37726, 95-1 BCA ¶ 27,373 (Government "evaluators" had authority to issue technical directions that changed contract because their direction was reportedly followed by COTR and contracting officer); *Zoubi v. United States*, 25 Cl. Ct. 581 (1992) (program director had authority to enter into a contract for interpreter services because his job carried with it an implied authorization to obtain all necessary personnel); *H. Landau & Co. v. United States*, 886 F.2d 322 (Fed. Cir. 1989) (employees with contract administration authority held to bind the Government when they stated that Government would guarantee payment for materials); *Walter Straga*, ASBCA 26134, 83-2 BCA ¶ 16,611 (project manager considered by board to be proper official to respond to technical inquiries and "was a representative of the contracting officer"); and *Contractors Equip. Rental Co.*, ASBCA 13052, 70-1 BCA ¶ 8183 (statement by contracting officer that official was "the man to satisfy" and deferral to him for equipment needs held "tantamount to a delegation de facto" as contracting officer's authorized representative).

When a contractor is expressly informed of limitations on the authority of these representatives, the contractor is generally unable to recover for unauthorized acts. Such notifications are often contained in letters to contractors or in contract clauses. One standard clause containing such an express statement is the Inspection of Construction clause in FAR 52.246-12, which states:

> (d) The presence or absence of a Government inspector does not relieve the Contractor from any contract requirement, nor is the inspector authorized to change any term or condition of the specification without the Contracting Officer's written authorization.

For cases denying relief based on this language, see *DeKonty Corp.*, ASBCA 32140, 89-2 BCA ¶ 21,586; *Commercial Contractors, Inc.*, ASBCA 30675, 88-3 BCA ¶ 20,877; and *Allen's of Fla., Inc.*, ASBCA 14656, 71-1 BCA ¶ 8646. For a rare case where the Government was held liable in the face of this clause, see *Townsco Contracting Co.*, ASBCA 13742, 71-2 BCA ¶ 8962, where a Government inspector gave the contractor faulty direction.

Similar contract language has been used to deny relief to contractors. See, for example, *Woodcraft Corp. v. United States*, 146 Ct. Cl. 101, 173 F. Supp. 613 (1959) (contract contained a clause advising the contractor that "[t]he Inspector has no authority to advise or direct a contractor to use a particular method of production"); *Crow & Sutton Assocs.*, ASBCA 44392, 93-1 BCA ¶ 25,503 (contract contained two agency clauses warning that inspectors had no authority to order changes); and *Inez Kaiser & Assocs.*, ASBCA 22212, 88-2 BCA ¶ 20,732 (contract stated that only the contracting officer could order changes).

Letters limiting the authority of representatives generally have the same result. See *Franchi Realty Trust v. General Servs. Admin.*, GSBCA 11149, 92-3 BCA ¶ 25,180; and *F.H. Antrim Constr. Co.*, IBCA 882-12-70, 71-2 BCA ¶ 8983.

C. Dealing with Personnel Lacking Full Contractual Authority

As previously indicated, the vast majority of Government personnel with whom a contractor deals do not possess full contractual authority; this does not mean, however, that dealings with such unauthorized personnel are without legal significance. This section considers several of the theories used to bind the Government when the contractor has dealt with personnel possessing less than full authority to bind the Government. The first of these theories is implied authority, where no authority has been specifically granted; the second is contracting officer ratification of the unauthorized act or statement; and the third is imputation of knowledge of unauthorized representatives to contracting officers.

1. Implied Authority

While "apparent authority" will not be sufficient to bind the Government, the boards and courts have frequently granted contractors relief on the basis of "implied authority." The implied authority cases primarily involve determining what delegations would mean under a "reasonable person" standard. Thus, precise written delegations leave little room for implication of authority, while broad general delegations provide a greater opportunity for finding implied authority, *DOT Sys., Inc.*, DOTCAB 1208, 82-2 BCA ¶ 15,817. Most of the cases finding implied authority have involved delegations by contracting officers to project managers, engineers, inspectors, and other personnel involved in contract administration. Although the principle of implied authority is not necessarily inapplicable to designated contracting officers, the nature of the Certificate of Appointment and pertinent regulations leave relatively little room for its application, *Strick Corp.*, ASBCA 15921, 73-2 BCA ¶ 10,077.

To find implied authority, there must have been some authority delegated. See *California Sand & Gravel, Inc. v. United States*, 22 Cl. Ct. 19 (1990), *aff'd*, 937 F.2d 624 (Fed. Cir. 1991), where the Claims Court stated at 27:

> [A] person with some limited actual authority impliedly may have broader authority. However, a person with no actual authority may not gain actual authority though the court-made rule of implied actual authority. Specifically, the court may not substitute itself unconditionally for the executive in

> granting authority to an unauthorized person. The most the court can do is interpret the limited authority of an authorized person in a broader manner than ordinarily would be the case.

Thus, Government employees with no authority to act in the contracting process have no authority to bind the Government even in an emergency situation, *City of El Centro v. United States*, 922 F.2d 816 (Fed. Cir. 1990), *cert. denied*, 501 U.S. 1230 (1991). In that case, border patrol agents had agreed to pay for hospital services for illegal aliens injured in a high-speed chase. The court held that the agents could not bind the Government because they had no semblance of contracting officer authority. Compare *Sigma Constr. Co.*, ASBCA 37040, 91-2 BCA ¶ 23,926, where a contract administrator was held to have authority to bind the Government in an emergency situation.

Authority to bind the Government is generally implied when such authority is considered to be an integral part of the duties assigned to a Government employee, *H. Landau & Co. v. United States*, 886 F.2d 322 (Fed. Cir. 1989). In *DOT Sys., Inc.*, DOTCAB 1208, 82-2 BCA ¶ 15,817, the board stated at 78,386:

> [T]he fact that the COTR had neither actual nor apparent authority to bind the Government does not necessarily preclude the granting of relief under the circumstances as here exist. Rather, such authority may be implied when considered an integral part of specific duties assigned to a government employee. *Urban Pathfinders, Inc.*, ASBCA No. 23134, 79-1 BCA ¶ 13,709; *Contractors Equipment Rental Co.*, ASBCA No. 13052, 70-1 BCA ¶ 8183. In view of the specific duties assigned to the COTR, and the circumstances surrounding his directives regarding the arrangement of the exhibits, we find the COTR was clothed with the requisite implied authority to bind the government to a constructive change under the terms of the contract.

See also *Jordan & Nobles Constr. Co.*, GSBCA 8349, 91-1 BCA ¶ 23,659, where implied delegation of authority was found. The board noted at 118,511-12:

> [The Government] argues that the on-site representative lacked the authority to make a change to the contract. The authority of officials subordinate to the contracting officer is derived from the facts of each case, based on the words of the contract and the conduct of the parties during the contract administration. *Stephenson Assocs., Inc.*, GSBCA Nos. 6573, 6815, 86-3

> BCA ¶ 19,071 at 96,325-26. Here, by the admission of the contracting officer, the on-site representative had the authority to determine whether supplies met contract requirements and to direct [the contractor's] work under the contract.

Similarly, inspectors with authority to accept or reject the work have been held to bind the Government when they ordered minor adjustment to the work, *Construction Foresite, Inc.*, ASBCA 42350, 93-1 BCA ¶ 25,515; improperly rejected the work, *Gonzales Custom Painting, Inc.*, ASBCA 39527, 90-3 BCA ¶ 22,950; ordered extra work in the course of contract administration, *Gricoski Detective Agency*, GSBCA 8901, 90-3 BCA ¶ 23,131; or prescribed additional testing procedures, *Switlik Parachute Co.*, ASBCA 17920, 74-2 BCA ¶ 10,970. See also *WRB Corp. v. United States*, 183 Ct. Cl. 409 (1968) (authority to inspect, reject, and require replacement implied authority to "order" constructive change); *Urban Pathfinders, Inc.*, ASBCA 23134, 79-1 BCA ¶ 13,709 (project officer with authority to certify vouchers, receive progress reports, perform inspections, and accept work, held to have the implied authority to issue a change order where immediate action was required); *Tasker Indus., Inc.*, DOTCAB 71-22, 75-2 BCA ¶ 11,372 (authority to issue engineering interpretations or to reject end product, erroneously exercised, amounted to constructive change even though contractor was on notice that representative was not authorized to "order" any changes); and *Cameo Curtains, Inc.*, ASBCA 3574, 58-2 BCA ¶ 2051 (inspector authorized to reject work had implied authority to change work through improper rejection).

It has been held that a contractor is not obligated to appeal to the contracting officer if a representative with such implied authority erroneously construes the contract, *WRB Corp. v. United States*, 183 Ct. Cl. 409 (1968). However, prudent contract administration demands that contractors bring to the attention of the contracting officer any interpretation or instruction issued by an official who lacks formal contracting authority, rather than rely on the implied authority doctrine. See *Singer Co. v. United States*, 215 Ct. Cl. 281, 568 F.2d 695 (1977), denying a constructive-change claim based upon interpretations issued by a technical coordinating group where the contractor was aware that the group lacked formal contracting officer authority but failed to bring the interpretations to the attention of the contracting officer. See also *United Food Servs., Inc. v. United States*, 19 Cl. Ct. 539 (1990), *aff'd*, 928 F.2d 411 (Fed. Cir. 1991) (mess sergeant had no authority to order extra work); *AAA Eng'g & Drafting, Inc.*, ASBCA 44605, 96-1 BCA ¶ 28,182 (inspector had no authority to order change);

P.J. Dick Inc. v. General Servs. Admin., GSBCA 12033, 95-2 BCA ¶ 27,739 (resident engineer had no authority to approve overtime work); *J.S. Alberici Constr. Co.*, GSBCA 10977, 91-3 BCA ¶ 24,204 (architect had no authority to order corrections of defective work); *RMTC Sys.*, AGBCA 88-198-1, 91-2 BCA ¶ 23,873 (shipment before purchase order in response to an unauthorized request did not form a contract). Such action is particularly necessary when the contract contains a clause informing the contractor of the limited authority of Government personnel, *Brand S Roofing*, ASBCA 24688, 82-1 BCA ¶ 15,513 (Designation of Technical Representative clause); *W.W. Wilkinson, Inc.*, ASBCA 23031, 80-2 BCA ¶ 14,749 (Government Inspectors clause).

2. *Ratification*

Ratification is the adoption of an unauthorized act resulting in the act being given effect as if originally authorized, *Restatement, Second, Agency* § 82. In Government contracting, representatives' unauthorized actions may subsequently be ratified by those with authority to bind the Government. If the ratifying Government official has actual or constructive knowledge of a representative's unauthorized act and expressly or impliedly adopts the act, ratification will be found, *Williams v. United States*, 130 Ct. Cl. 435, 127 F. Supp. 617, *cert. denied*, 349 U.S. 938 (1955). See also *Moran Bros. Co. v. United States*, 39 Ct. Cl. 486 (1904) ("[I]f upon a full knowledge of the facts, the superior officer ratifies and confirms the action of his subordinate, is not that in law equivalent to an express authority in the subordinate at the time he ordered the performance of the labor?").

a. *Authority to Ratify*

In general, the authority to ratify has been considered to be an integral part of an agent's authority without the need for specific statutory or regulatory coverage. For many years, the procurement regulations contained no specific ratification provisions. However, the Government was held bound on the basis of ratifications without reference to regulatory authorities, *Michael Guth*, ASBCA 22663, 80-2 BCA ¶ 14,572; *Norwood Precision Prods.*, ASBCA 24083, 80-1 BCA ¶ 14,405.

In the 1970s and 1980s, agency regulations began to provide for ratification of unauthorized acts and to specify how such ratifications should be handled. Finally, in 1988, the following Government-wide guidance was added to FAR 1.602-3:

> (b) *Policy.*
>
> > (1) Agencies should take positive action to preclude, to the maximum extent possible, the need for ratification actions. Although procedures are provided in this section for use in those cases where the ratification of an unauthorized commitment is necessary, these procedures may not be used in a manner that encourages such commitments being made by Government personnel.
> >
> > (2) Subject to the limitations in paragraph (c) of this subsection, the head of the contracting activity, unless a higher level official is designated by the agency, may ratify an unauthorized commitment.
> >
> > (3) The ratification authority in subparagraph (b)(2) of this subsection may be delegated in accordance with agency procedures, but in no case shall the authority be delegated below the level of chief of the contracting office.
> >
> > (4) Agencies should process unauthorized commitments using the ratification authority of this subsection instead of referring such actions to the General Accounting Office for resolution. (See 1.602-3(d).)
> >
> > (5) Unauthorized commitments that would involve claims subject to resolution under the Contract Disputes Act of 1978 should be processed in accordance with Subpart 33.2, Disputes and Appeals.
>
> (c) *Limitations.* The authority in subparagraph (b)(2) of this subsection may be exercised only when —
>
> > (1) Supplies or services have been provided to and accepted by the Government, or the Government otherwise has obtained or will obtain a benefit resulting from performance of the unauthorized commitment;
> >
> > (2) The ratifying official has the authority to enter into a contractual commitment;
> >
> > (3) The resulting contract would otherwise have been proper if made by an appropriate contracting officer;
> >
> > (4) The contracting officer reviewing the unauthorized commitment determines the price to be fair and reasonable;

(5) The contracting officer recommends payment and legal counsel concurs in the recommendation, unless agency procedures expressly do not require such concurrence;

(6) Funds are available and were available at the time the unauthorized commitment was made; and

(7) The ratification is in accordance with any other limitations prescribed under agency procedures.

While these procedures are quite explicit, they have not prevented a finding of implied ratification. See *Reliable Disposal Co.*, ASBCA 40100, 91-2 BCA ¶ 23,895, where three contracting officers supported a request to pay the contractor for extra work but did not follow the FAR procedures. The board found that the failure to follow the FAR was not a bar to a finding of implied ratification. See also *Tripod, Inc.*, ASBCA 21305, 89-1 BCA ¶ 21,305 (contracting officer's knowledge of the contractor's complaints and review of inspection reports evidenced implied ratification); *Tri-West Contractors, Inc.*, AGBCA 95-200-1, 97-1 BCA ¶ 28,662 (contracting officer's acquiescence in proceeding with the work that was not in accordance with the specifications effectively ratified the deviation). For a similar ruling under prior regulations, see *Driftwood of Ala.*, GSBCA 5429, 81-2 BCA ¶ 15,169. Compare *Fish & Wildlife Serv.*, Comp. Gen. Dec. B-208730, 83-1 CPD ¶ 75, where ratification regulations were specifically invoked to support a finding of ratification.

Ratification also requires that the ratifying official be authorized to delegate contracting officer authority. Where a statute required an official to act "in his discretion," he was not authorized merely to adopt the acts of his representative, 22 Comp. Gen. 1083 (B-33769) (1943).

Boards and courts do not possess the authority to ratify; they may only determine whether a ratification has occurred. They have recommended, however, that ratification authority be liberally exercised in cases where an injustice would result if the Government did not become bound. See *Globe Indem. Co. v. United States*, 102 Ct. Cl. 21 (1944), *cert. denied*, 324 U.S. 852 (1945), where the court stated at 38:

> The head of the department, or his duly authorized agent, of course, could have ratified these unauthorized acts, and in our opinion should have done so, since the work was necessary and for [the Government's] benefit, but he did not do so, and we are powerless to do it for him.

From this case two lessons are to be drawn: (1) contracting officers and heads of departments should exercise the great powers conferred on them by these contracts to do equity; they should not feel under obligation to take advantage of technicalities, where to do so would defeat justice; (2) contractors must study their contracts and insist on compliance with their terms; before relying on any promise they should ascertain that it is made by a person having authority to make it.

b. Authority to Perform or Authorize Acts Being Ratified

The ratifying official must have the power to perform or authorize the unauthorized act. See 22 Comp Gen. 1083 (B-33769) (1943). Thus, an official lacking the authority to enter into contracts cannot ratify an agreement, *Consortium Venture Corp. v. United States*, 5 Cl. Ct. 47 (1984); *Western Contract Furnishers*, PSBCA 317, 76-2 BCA ¶ 12,216. Similarly, illegal actions cannot be ratified because officials lack the authority to enter into illegal agreements. In *Trio Mach. Works, Inc.*, NASABCA 480-6, 82-1 BCA ¶ 15,465, *recons. denied*, 82-2 BCA ¶ 15,968, an alleged agreement between the contractor and a representative — whereby the contractor, for keeping a modification under a certain dollar amount, was to receive preferred treatment in future contract awards — was illegal and beyond the contracting officer's ratification authority. Similarly, where an agency purchased spark plugs on a sole source basis in violation of statutes requiring formal advertising, the Assistant Secretary of War could not subsequently ratify the transaction by classifying the spark plugs as an experimental item subject to negotiated procurement, 15 Comp. Gen. 618 (A-66806) (1936).

Proper authority to ratify was found in *Romac, Inc.*, ASBCA 41150, 91-2 BCA ¶ 23,918 (officer in charge of construction could order additional work); *Fish & Wildlife Serv.*, Comp. Gen. Dec. B-208730, 83-1 CPD ¶ 75 (acting director of Fish and Wildlife Service had authority to issue a split procurement); *Mil-Pak Co.*, GSBCA 5849, 83-1 BCA ¶ 16,482 (contracting officer had authority to issue a change order); and *W. Southard Jones, Inc.*, ASBCA 6321, 61-2 BCA ¶ 3182 (contracting officer had authority to alter contract).

Under these rules, ratification normally requires action or inaction by a specific individual having the requisite authority to ratify the previously unauthorized act. However, some cases have found ratification without identifying such a specific individual (known as "institutional ratification"). In *Silverman v. United States*, 230 Ct. Cl. 701, 679 F.2d 865 (1982), the court found that the agency ratified the agreement by accepting the benefits flowing from the unauthorized official's promise. See also *Rapp v. United States*, 2 Cl. Ct. 694 (1983), where the court found ratification where a Government auctioneer's authority to extend the winning bidder's period of payment was in dispute: "[I]f any question remains as to the auctioneer's authority, it is rendered moot by the Customs Service's ratification of the announcement." Compare *City of El Centro v. United States*, 922 F.2d 816 (Fed. Cir. 1990), *cert. denied*, 501 U.S. 1230 (1991), where the Federal Circuit reversed a finding of institutional ratification by the Claims Court (16 Cl. Ct. 500 (1989)). See also *Choe-Kelly, Inc.*, ASBCA 43481, 94-1 BCA ¶ 26,431, refusing to apply the institutional ratification logic. Although the decision in *City of El Centro* seemed to indicate that institutional ratification was no longer a viable doctrine, recently, in *Janowsky v. United States*, __ F.3d __ (Fed. Cir. 1998) , the Federal Circuit found that the Court of Federal Claims erred when it dismissed Janowskys' implied-in-fact contract claim without considering whether the agency ratified the proposed contract with the Janowskys by receiving the benefits from a sting operation.

c. Knowledge of Unauthorized Acts

A prerequisite to ratification is the ratifying official's knowledge, either actual or constructive, of the facts affecting the unauthorized action. In *United States v. Beebe*, 180 U.S. 343 (1901), the Court stated at 354:

> Where an agent has acted without authority and it is claimed that the principal has thereafter ratified his act, such ratification can only be based upon a full knowledge of all the facts upon which the unauthorized action was taken. This is as true in the case of the Government as in that of an individual. Knowledge is necessary in any event. Story on Agency, 9th ed. sec. 239, notes 1 and 2. If there be want of it, though such want arises from the neglect of the principal, no ratification can be based upon any act of his. Knowledge of the facts is the essential element of ratification, and must be shown or such facts proved that its existence is a necessary inference from them.

See *California Sand & Gravel, Inc. v. United States*, 22 Cl. Ct. 19 (1990), *aff'd*, 937 F.2d 624 (Fed. Cir. 1991), holding that there could be no ratification without "full knowledge of all facts" pertinent to the unauthorized commitment; *Durocher Dock & Dredge, Inc.*, ENGBCA 5768, 91-3 BCA

¶ 24,145, where ratification was denied because the contracting officer, as the only official with authority to ratify, had no knowledge of the events; and *Tymshare*, PSBCA 206, 76-2 BCA ¶ 12,218, where there was no ratification of an unauthorized representative's agreement because the authorized official neither knew nor should have known of the unauthorized agreement.

The ratifying official may obtain actual knowledge from various sources, *Mick DeWall Constr.*, PSBCA 2580, 91-1 BCA ¶ 23,510 (contracting officer received notice in claim that COR had agreed to modification); *Brown Constr. Co.*, ASBCA 22648, 79-1 BCA ¶ 13,745 (contracting officer participated in a preconstruction conference where a representative stated that construction policy required a contract change); *Globe Constr. Co.*, GSBCA 2197, 67-2 BCA ¶ 6478 (contracting officer received notice of prior actions from his representative and through the contractor's formal claim for additional compensation).

A ratifying official may also gain knowledge constructively. Constructive notice was found in *Williams v. United States*, 130 Ct. Cl. 435, 127 F. Supp. 617, *cert. denied*, 349 U.S. 938 (1955), where an unauthorized Air Force officer and the contractor agreed that the contractor could use the Air Force's asphalt plant in return for seal coating the base's roads. The base contracting officer was held to have constructive knowledge of the agreement because the roads were wholly within the base where he was located.

Imputed knowledge from representatives may also serve as constructive knowledge of a ratifying official. See, for example, *W. Southard Jones, Inc.*, ASBCA 6321, 61-2 BCA ¶ 3182, where base technical personnel knew that the contractor's performance did not conform to contract drawings. This knowledge was imputed to the contracting officer, who frequently met with the base engineer and discussed projects at the base. When the relationship between two persons creates a presumption that one would have informed the other of certain events, the boards may impute the knowledge of one to the other, *Leiden Corp.*, ASBCA 26136, 83-2 BCA ¶ 16,612. In *Southwestern Sheet Metal Works, Inc.*, ASBCA 22748, 79-1 BCA ¶ 13,744, *recons. denied*, 79-2 BCA ¶ 13,949, inspectors functioned as the contracting officer's "eyes and ears"; hence, the contracting officer had actual or constructive knowledge of the inspector's directive changing contract terms, where the inspector lacked authority to issue such a change.

d. Adoption of Unauthorized Acts

The contractor must show that an authorized official has adopted the unauthorized action, either expressly, by conduct, or by silence. In *DBA Sys., Inc.*, NASABCA 481-5, 82-1 BCA ¶ 15,468, ratification did not occur because the contracting officer "consistently and expressly disavowed the purported funding agreement and likewise did nothing which, by implication, could be reasonably interpreted as his concurrence with [his representative's] belief that the overrun should be funded." See also *Prestex Inc. v. United States*, 162 Ct. Cl. 620, 320 F.2d 367 (1963) (upon learning of deviations from specifications, the Government repudiated the contract, never having accepted or used the product, so that no ratification of deviations existed).

An express adoption of an unauthorized act clearly establishes ratification, *Fish & Wildlife Serv.*, Comp. Gen. Dec. B-208730, 83-1 CPD ¶ 75 (authorized official signed a document expressing his intent to ratify the unauthorized act); *Globe Constr. Co.*, GSBCA 2197, 67-2 BCA ¶ 6478 (contracting officer stated that his subordinate's prior action had been done "within his authority").

An authorized official's adoption of an unauthorized act may result from conduct, *Boeing Computer Servs.*, ASBCA 42674, 94-3 BCA ¶ 27,114 (acceptance of user manual containing procedure modifying the contract specifications); *T.W. Cole*, PSBCA 3076, 92-3 BCA ¶ 25,091 (acceptance of work with knowledge of order to modify it); *Henry Burge & Alvin White*, PSBCA 2431, 89-3 BCA ¶ 21,910 (acceptance of work with knowledge of modification); *Norwood Precision Prods.*, ASBCA 24083, 80-1 BCA ¶ 14,405 (payment for products accepted after a default termination indicated the official's adoption of the inspector's unauthorized acceptance); *Mil-Pak Co.*, GSBCA 5849, 83-1 BCA ¶ 16,482 (contracting officer ratified a "change order by unilaterally fixing the amount of the equitable adjustment"). But see *Metcalf & Assocs.*, GSBCA 3190, 72-2 BCA ¶ 9516, where the board held that a contracting officer's award of compensation to a contractor for certain changes directed by unauthorized representatives did not constitute a ratification but was an attempt at settlement not binding upon the Government.

Silence or inaction may also constitute adoption by an authorized official. See *KRW, Inc.*, DOTBCA 2572, 94-1 BCA ¶ 26,435 (contracting officer acquiesced in alteration of work product); *HFS, Inc.*, ASBCA 43748,

92-3 BCA ¶ 25,198 (contracting officer took no action on letter describing the order for extra work); *Gricoski Detective Agency*, GSBCA 8901, 90-3 BCA ¶ 23,131 (total inaction after letter was sent to contracting officer describing an order to change the method of performance); *Lox Equip. Co.*, ASBCA 8985, 1964 BCA ¶ 4463 (failure of contracting officer "to take effective action to correct the situation" adopted his inspector's directives); *Michael Guth*, ASBCA 22663, 80-2 BCA ¶ 14,572 (contracting officer affirmed by not questioning a manager's interpretation of liability provisions); *Brown Constr. Co.*, ASBCA 22648, 79-1 BCA ¶ 13,745 (contracting officer silent when unauthorized official prohibited the use of contract-designated plywood); and *Triangle Elec. Mfg. Co.*, ASBCA 15995, 74-2 BCA ¶ 10,783 (contracting officer's silence regarding representatives' interpretation "was conduct amounting to consent to the performance of such duties").

Acquiescence has been premised on the ratifying official's constructive notice coupled with silence. See *Williams v. United States*, 130 Ct. Cl. 435, 127 F. Supp. 617, *cert. denied*, 349 U.S. 938 (1955); *Southwestern Sheet Metal Works, Inc.*, ASBCA 22748, 79-1 BCA ¶ 13,744, *recons. denied*, 79-2 BCA ¶ 13,949; and *W. Southard Jones, Inc.*, ASBCA 6321, 61-2 BCA ¶ 3182.

e. *Ratification and Quantum Meruit*

The Comptroller General has often held that ratification by authorized officials is required before he will approve payment to persons conferring a benefit on the Government. In discussing recovery under quantum meruit or quantum valebant theories, the Comptroller General in *Acme, Inc.*, Comp. Gen. Dec. B-182584, 74-2 CPD ¶ 310, stated:

> Before a right to payment under such basis may be recognized it must be shown that the Government has received a benefit, and that the unauthorized goods or services were expressly or impliedly ratified by authorized contracting officials.

See *Checker Van Lines*, Comp. Gen. Dec. B-206542, 82-2 CPD ¶ 219 (obligation of funds beyond a 180-day period was statutorily prohibited; therefore, ratification could not support the requisite implied-in-fact contract for recovery); and Comp. Gen. Dec. B-164087, July 1, 1968, *Unpub.* (no basis for quantum meruit recovery where the authorized contracting officials were not aware of the project director's action and immediate action was taken to curtail such activity when it became known). See also *Equal Employment Opportunity Comm'n*, Comp. Gen. Dec. B-207492, 82-2 CPD ¶ 112 (failure of authorized representatives to curtail contractor's activities constituted adoption); *Mathews Furniture Co.*, Comp. Gen. Dec. B-195123, 79-2 CPD ¶ 131 (acquiescence by an authorized official determined from his negotiations seeking a settlement); *Defense Mapping Agency*, Comp. Gen. Dec. B-183915, 75-2 CPD ¶ 15 (recommendation for payment); and *INTASA, Inc.*, Comp. Gen. Dec. B-180876, 74-1 CPD ¶ 148 (unauthorized notice to proceed affirmed by intention to formalize a contract and recommendation for payment).

Ratification has been found even after the authorized contracting officer refused to adopt the unauthorized act. In *Acme, Inc.*, Comp. Gen. Dec. B-182584, 74-2 CPD ¶ 310, an officer exceeded his authority by soliciting informal quotations. The authorized contracting officer found that the work was necessary, the Government benefited, and the contractor performed in good faith at a reasonable price, but the contracting officer refused to ratify the procurement. However, payment was recommended by the director of fiscal management. The Comptroller General inferred an implied ratification from the contracting officer's determination that the work performed was in the best interest of the Government and from the director's recommendation for payment. Similarly, authorized contracting officers refused to ratify an unauthorized order for a contractor to conduct training sessions in *Singer Co.*, Comp. Gen. Dec. B-183878, 75-1 CPD ¶ 406, "primarily because the officials had no basis to determine if the price was reasonable." Implied ratification was inferred "from the issuance of a contract for a subsequent identical training session" to be conducted by the contractor. See also *Maintenance Serv. & Sales Corp.*, 70 Comp. Gen. 664 (B-242019) (1991), where the contracting officer refused to ratify and took no action, but the Comptroller General granted relief under quantum meruit.

3. Knowledge Imputed to Authorized Personnel

In many cases it is important to determine whether the contracting officer or other authorized representative has knowledge of certain facts. Such knowledge may be important because the contract requires that information be furnished to the authorized person or that notice be given of events such as delays or constructive changes. In other situations, the legal significance of statements or acts of an authorized person depends upon whether the person was in possession of specific knowledge. Almost all instances of imputed knowledge arise in the contract administration process, but the legal principles are equally applicable to contract formation.

The authorized person is held to have knowledge under the common-law concept that a principal is charged with knowledge that an agent has a duty to deliver to the principal, *Restatement, Second, Agency* § 272. In applying this rule to Government contracts, the courts and boards have imputed knowledge to contracting officers and other authorized persons when the nature of the relationship between the authorized person and the representative establishes a presumption that the authorized person would be informed. Thus, knowledge of a claim based upon nondisclosure of information by the Government was imputed in *Cryo-Sonics, Inc.*, ASBCA 11483, 66-2 BCA ¶ 5890 (information known to a Government engineer was imputed to the Government negotiators). See also *J.A. Jones Constr. Co. v. United States*, 182 Ct. Cl. 615, 390 F.2d 886 (1968). In most cases involving imputed knowledge, the unauthorized representative possesses actual knowledge obtained within the scope of his or her duties. In *Xplo Corp.*, DOTCAB 1250, 86-2 BCA ¶ 18,863, the board noted at 95,110:

> The COTR, as the Contracting Officer's authorized representative, had a duty to communicate [the contractor's] notice of problems to the Contracting Officer and therefore knowledge of [those problems] will be imputed to the Contracting Officer.

See also *KRW, Inc.*, DOTBCA 2572, 94-1 BCA ¶ 26,435, where the board not only imputed the COTR's notice to the contracting officer but further stated that, upon receipt of notice, it is incumbent upon the contracting officer to "make some response."

Two cases have held a contracting officer to have imputed knowledge although only constructive knowledge on the part of the representatives was demonstrated, *Inet Power*, NASABCA 566-23, 68-1 BCA ¶ 7020, and *W. Southard Jones, Inc.*, ASBCA 6321, 61-2 BCA ¶ 3182.

Constructive notice to a representative has been expressly rejected in cases involving cost or pricing data. Because of the contractor's affirmative duty to submit such data, knowledge would not be imputed to the Government if auditors lack actual knowledge. See *Libby Welding Co.*, ASBCA 15084, 73-1 BCA ¶ 9859 (contractor listed costs twice on bill that auditors overlooked and imputation held improper); and *Sylvania Elec. Prods., Inc.*,

ASBCA 13622, 70-2 BCA ¶ 8387, *aff'd*, 202 Ct. Cl. 16, 479 F.2d 1342 (1973) (auditors did not cross-check data and therefore failed to uncover a material cost error, but absent auditors' actual knowledge, the contracting officer was not charged with knowledge).

a. Technical Representatives

Knowledge of information related to technical details of performance is imputed to the authorized person when such knowledge is in the possession of the Government's technical representatives, *U.S. Federal Eng'g & Mfg., Inc.*, ASBCA 19909, 75-2 BCA ¶ 11,578 (Government project engineer "was not only the person responsible for inspection and acceptance of the job but also the most significant contact the contractor had with the Government"). Finding that the contracting officer was uninformed both of the required additional work and of the fact that it was to be performed, the board stated at 55,298-99:

> The fact that the contracting officer did not have actual knowledge of the additions to be made to the device does not insulate the Government from the consequences that actual knowledge would impose. His various representatives are his eyes and ears (if not his voice) and their knowledge is treated for all intents and purposes as his.

See also *Glenda R. Whitaker*, PSBCA 3443, 94-2 BCA ¶ 26,643 (knowledge of contractor's protests, having been communicated to those authorized by the contracting officer to administer the contract, may be imputed to the contracting officer); *Walter Straga*, ASBCA 26134, 83-2 BCA ¶ 16,611 (project manager's knowledge that the contractor's interpretation of the drawings differed from his own imputed to contracting officer); *Carl J. Bonidie, Inc.*, ASBCA 25769, 82-2 BCA ¶ 15,818 (Changes clause notice requirement was satisfied by knowledge of base civil engineer, whose recommendations apparently determined the contracting officer's contractual decisions); *Singleton Contracting Corp.*, IBCA 1413-12-80, 81-2 BCA ¶ 15,269 (COTR's knowledge of potential claim imputed to contracting officer); *Powers Regulator Co.*, GSBCA 4668, 80-2 BCA ¶ 14,463 (presumption that the representative would inform the contracting officer arose from the complex technical issues that required the contracting officer's reliance on the representative's technical expertise); *Piland Corp.*, ASBCA 22560, 78-2 BCA ¶ 13,227 (knowledge was imputed to the contracting officer in order to satisfy the Suspension of Work clause notice requirements); *Burn Constr. Co.*, IBCA 1042-9-74, 78-2 BCA ¶ 13,405

(Government engineer lacked authority to make changes, but knowledge imputed because he was charged with administering the contract); and *W. Southard Jones, Inc.*, ASBCA 6321, 61-2 BCA ¶ 3182 (knowledge imputed upon presumption that "the Base engineer and contracting officer met not infrequently about projects").

Not all information possessed by a technical representative will be imputed, as the information may not be the type that technical representatives would be presumed to convey to a contracting officer. In *A.L. Constr. Co.*, NASABCA 178-1, 78-2 BCA ¶ 13,284, a project engineer who was not authorized to change the contract had actual knowledge of the contractor's installation of vents. Since it was unclear at the time of the extra performance that a claim would result, the board found that the project engineer's failure to object to the contractor's installation of the vents was not a constructive order to proceed by an unauthorized representative, and the knowledge of the contractor's actions did not constitute constructive notice to the contracting officer. Additionally, in *Franchi Realty Trust v. General Servs. Admin.*, GSBCA 11149, 92-3 BCA ¶ 25,180, a directive by a Drug Enforcement Administration (DEA) representative concerning the construction of new DEA offices was not imputed to the contracting officer. The board stated at 125,483-84:

> Of course, the actions of the DEA employee might be found to be binding if there was a showing that a "responsible officer" (authorized contracting officer) "knew or should have known of the situation" such that knowledge of the DEA employee's could be imputed to the contracting officer so as to bind the Government. . . . [H]owever, there simply is no basis to find that a contracting officer knew or had reason to know [of the situation]. . . . Under the circumstances, we can find neither actual nor implied notice of the subject change.

In *United States v. Hanna Nickel Smelting Co.*, 253 F. Supp. 784 (D. Ore. 1966), *aff'd on other grounds*, 400 F.2d 944 (9th Cir. 1968), an engineer "was instructed to maintain surveillance of purchase orders and paid vouchers to assure that funds are charged against the proper account." Finding knowledge of the contractor's accounting system imputable through others, the court made no determination of the engineer's duties, noting at 794:

> Whether [the engineer's] duties can be interpreted to include meaningful reporting on the Company's accounting practices, since he was not a trained accountant, is not free from doubt.

b. Inspectors

Information obtained by inspectors and pertinent to their duties has been imputed to the contracting officer, *Polan Indus., Inc.*, ASBCA 3996, 58-2 BCA ¶ 1982. See *Raby Hillside Drilling, Inc.*, AGBCA 75-101, 78-1 BCA ¶ 13,026 (knowledge of inspectors who daily administer a contract on the site must be imputed to the contracting officer); *Peters Mach. Co.*, ASBCA 21857, 78-1 BCA ¶ 12,865 (inspector's knowledge of deviation imputed to the contracting officer); *Hartford Accident & Indemnity Co.*, IBCA 1139-1-77, 77-2 BCA ¶ 12,604 (field inspector "was the representative of the Government on the job"); and *Gresham & Co. v. United States*, 200 Ct. Cl. 97, 470 F.2d 542 (1972) (contracting officer could not reject nonconforming items because his quality assurance representatives had known of the deviations). See also *Hudson Contracting, Inc.*, ASBCA 41023, 94-1 BCA ¶ 26,466, where the board upheld a Government inspector's oral agreement for the furnishing of Government property in return for the contractor providing equipment and an operator for unrelated Government work. The board found that the Government project manager, with authority to provide the Government property involved, had imputed knowledge of the agreement "by virtue of [his] supervision of the inspector . . . [and his] extensive day-to-day involvement in the progress of the contract."

Not all relationships between contracting officers and inspectors are sufficiently close to raise the presumption that the contracting officer would be informed of relevant facts. In *Canadian Commercial Corp.*, ASBCA 17187, 76-2 BCA ¶ 12,145, *recons. denied*, 77-2 BCA ¶ 12,758, an inspector's knowledge of design defects was not imputable to the contracting officer because "close contact between the resident Canadian inspector and the [Government's] contract administration or technical personnel" was not established. Further, the contractor knew the inspector lacked authority to make design changes and that such changes were within the contracting officer's discretion. The presumption that the inspector would act as the contracting officer's informant was held improper.

c. Administrative and Clerical Personnel

Whether knowledge possessed by administrative and clerical personnel will be imputed to authorized representatives depends upon the nature of their relationship with the contracting officer. In *Precision Prods.*, ASBCA 25280, 82-2 BCA ¶ 15,981, Government representatives responsible for administering the contract "were the eyes and ears of the contracting officer," and their knowledge was therefore imputed to the contracting officer. Similarly, in *KRW, Inc.*, DOTBCA 2572, 94-1 BCA ¶ 26,435, a contract administrator's knowledge was imputed to the contracting officer because the contractor had been directed to send reports to the contract administrator. However, the relationship between an airman, who knew of the contractor's causes of delay, and the contracting officer was not sufficient to establish a presumption that the information would be reported, *M.J. Newsom*, ASBCA 9799, 1964 BCA ¶ 4444. The board noted that the airman's "status with respect to the contracting officer remains undetermined."

d. Auditors

Since auditors are expected to convey information to the contracting officer, information related to the audit function will be imputed. In *Chrysler Corp.*, ASBCA 17259, 75-1 BCA ¶ 11,236, *recons. denied*, 76-1 BCA ¶ 11,665, Army Audit Agency knowledge of the contractor's accrual account and the manner in which it operated was imputed to the contracting officer. Similarly, in *E-Systems, Inc.*, ASBCA 18877, 76-1 BCA ¶ 11,797, where the Defense Contract Audit Agency was aware of the contractor's pooling and allocation of material costs, this information was imputed to the contracting officer. See also *United States v. Hanna Nickel Smelting Co.*, 253 F. Supp. 784 (D. Ore. 1966), *aff'd on other grounds*, 400 F.2d 944 (9th Cir. 1968) (contractor's accounting practices regarding allocation of capital items known by auditors); and *Western Elec. Co.*, ASBCA 21294, 79-1 BCA ¶ 13,550.

IV. GOVERNMENT BOUND BY AUTHORIZED AGENTS

Since the Government can act only through its agents and employees, it is clear that it will be bound when authorized agents carry out their duties properly. However, Government personnel cannot be expected to act only in ways favorable to the United States. Whether resulting from mistakes, negligence, or poor judgment, their statements, acts, or omissions are sometimes contrary to the Government's best interests. This may become evident from later reflection or subsequent events, or it may be determined by the agents' advisers, superiors, or successors. In such cases, attempts may be made to avoid the consequences by repudiating or countermanding the agents' acts. There are two major concepts that are invoked to prevent the Government from disowning authorized agents' acts or agreements, thereby making them binding on the Government. The first concept is finality, the second is estoppel.

A. Finality

The actions of a Government employee acting within the scope of his or her employment are the actions of the Government itself, and as with any contracting party, once the Government has taken the final step toward committing a contractual act, it is bound by it. Once an authorized representative enters into a contract not even Congress has the authority to abrogate it, *United States v. Winstar Corp.*, 116. S. Ct. 2432 (1996).

1. Sources of Finality

Finality of contractual acts may attach as a result of either the application of a legal rule or a provision of the contract that is interpreted as providing that finality attaches to a decision or action of a Government agent. The clearest example of a legal rule creating finality occurs in the contract formation process where the normal binding effect of the acceptance of an offer is applied to the Government. This rule of contract law states that at the time an offer is accepted, a binding contract is formed. See *United States v. Purcell Envelope Co.*, 249 U.S. 313 (1919), where the Court held that the Government was bound when the Postmaster General accepted the offer of a company in a formally advertised procurement. Similarly, the Government will be bound if an authorized official enters into a contract modification adjusting the price after a change has been ordered, *Liberty Coat Co.*, ASBCA 4119, 57-2 BCA ¶ 1576. See also *Airmotive Eng'g Corp.*, ASBCA 15235, 71-2 BCA ¶ 8988, where the board held that the Government was bound when a contracting officer entered into a contract amendment modifying the price to reflect the adoption of a value engineering proposal.

The most direct example of a contract clause providing for finality is the Disputes clause, which makes decisions of contracting officers final. The Government was held bound by such decisions in *Bell Helicopter Co.*, ASBCA 17776, 74-1 BCA ¶ 10,411. Another such clause is the Inspection clause, which states that Government acceptance of work will be final, with certain exceptions. In *C.H. McQuagge v. United States*, 197 F. Supp. 460 (W.D. La. 1961), the contracting officer had issued a certificate of final acceptance despite the knowledge of the Government that the concrete used in airport taxiways did not measure up to the specifications. The court found the acceptance final and conclusive, stating at 468:

> In a case such as this, the government can only act through those to whom it has delegated authority to make decisions. It was within the discretion of the Contracting Officers to determine whether the work was acceptable to the government, and final acceptance by such officers was subject to being opened or questioned only upon evidence of collusion, fraud, or obvious error.

See also *Mil-Spec Contractors, Inc. v. United States*, 835 F.2d 865 (Fed. Cir. 1987); *S.E.R., Jobs for Progress, Inc. v. United States*, 759 F.2d 1 (Fed. Cir. 1985); *Walsky Constr. Co.*, ASBCA 19875, 77-1 BCA ¶ 12,388; *Conrad Weihnacht Constr., Inc.*, ASBCA 20767, 76-2 BCA ¶ 11,963; and *Genuine Motor Parts of Pa., Inc.*, ASBCA 19063, 76-1 BCA ¶ 11,860.

Finality has also been found when the Government acts under contract clauses that do not expressly state that the action is "final." One such clause that has been interpreted as creating finality is the Allowable Cost, Fixed Fee and Payment clause. See *Chrysler Corp.*, ASBCA 17259, 75-1 BCA ¶ 11,236, *recons. denied*, 76-1 BCA ¶ 11,665, holding that this clause should be interpreted to bar the Government from contesting payments after final payment on the contract has been made. In *Bell Aircraft Corp. v. United States*, 120 Ct. Cl. 398, 100 F. Supp. 661 (1951), the court held that approval and payment of invoices under a cost-reimbursement contract was binding on the Government at the time the payment was made. The same result was reached in *United States v. Mason & Hanger Co.*, 260 U.S. 323 (1922), and *Leeds & Northrup Co. v. United States*, 101 F. Supp. 999 (E.D. Pa. 1951). Finality was also found when a contracting officer made a decision to fund an overrun under the Limitation of Cost clause, *General Elec. Co. v. United States*, 188 Ct. Cl. 620, 412 F.2d 1215, *mot. for reh'g denied*, 189 Ct. Cl. 116, 416 F.2d 1320 (1969).

Finality has been found in a few instances where the act of the Government was not communicated to the contractor at the time the act was taken. In *General Elec. Co. v. United States*, 188 Ct. Cl. 620, 412 F.2d 1215, *mot. for reh'g denied*, 189 Ct. Cl. 116, 416 F.2d 1320 (1969), the court found a final decision because the contracting officer had signed an internal memorandum stating that an overrun would be funded, even though this contracting officer's decision was not communicated to the contractor. The same result was reached in *Texas Instruments, Inc. v. United States*, 922 F.2d 810 (Fed. Cir. 1990), where an ACO had signed a price negotiation memorandum (PNM) agreeing to a negotiated settlement of a claim. The court found that this was a final decision, stating at 813-14:

> Under *General Electric*, the law presumes that when an ACO acquainted with the underlying facts signs an internal document, such as the PNM, that she has decided to express a definite opinion on the merits of the claim in the absence of contrary testimony or evidence. Such contrary evidence or testimony is lacking here.

These cases indicate that the Government will be bound during contract administration by the doctrine of finality whenever an authorized employee signs a document or takes an action that is properly construed as resolving the issue at hand.

A variety of other actions and determinations by Government officials may also be final and binding on the Government. For example, a determination by a contracting officer that the contractor's labor cost estimating technique was not defective was final and binding on the Government and could not be revoked or overruled by his successor, *Bell Helicopter Co.*, ASBCA 17776, 74-1 BCA ¶ 10,411. In *Southern Waldrip & Harvick Co. v. United States*, 167 Ct. Cl. 488, 334 F.2d 245 (1964), the court held that the chief of engineers could not overrule a finding of the contracting officer that a telegraphic bid modification had been timely received. The instructions to bidders had stated that a determination of timeliness of modifications would rest with the contracting officer. These instructions constituted an agreement between the Government and the contractor and left the chief of engineers without authority to determine timeliness independently.

2. Authority Required

For the action to be binding and final, the Government employee must be acting within his or her authority. See *Trevco Eng'g & Sales*, VACAB 1021, 73-2 BCA ¶ 10,096, where the board found that an inspector had not been delegated the authority to make final acceptance. See also Comp. Gen. Dec. B-170360, Apr. 6, 1971, *Unpub.*, stating that an award by a contracting officer to the second low bidder could be overruled by his superiors, because the contracting officer had no authority to make a valid award to anyone but the low responsible bidder; and 35 Comp. Gen. 63 (B-120714) (1955), stating that no finality attaches to payment contrary to the cost-plus-a-percentage-of-cost prohibition. Acts of unauthorized representatives that are ratified by an authorized official are also accorded finality, *Tucker & Assocs. Contracting, Inc.*, IBCA 1468-6-81, 83-1 BCA ¶ 16,140.

3. Government Bound by Prejudicial Decisions

The Government is bound by the acts of its authorized representatives, even if their decisions are the result of poor judgment that is injurious to the Government. In *Liberty Coat Co.*, ASBCA 4119, 57-2 BCA ¶ 1576, the contracting officer issued findings and determinations that certain changes reduced the contractor's costs and adjusted the contract price accordingly. A successor contracting officer issued new determinations and findings on the same changes and greatly increased the reductions in price. In ruling for the contractor that the original contracting officer's decision was binding, the board stated at 5671-72:

> The Government makes no allegation of mutual mistake and, while admitting that it has no other evidence of fraud or collusion, argues that we are required to draw such an inference from the gross disparity between the equitable adjustments agreed to by the original contracting officer and the "correct and equitable adjustment for the deviation[s]" as found by the successor contracting officer. Assuming for the purposes of decision on [the contractor's] motion, the validity of the successor contracting officer's determination of "correct and equitable" price adjustments, in the absence of even a scintilla of other evidence of fraud and collusion, we think the proper inference is that, relying on erroneous advice of his price analysts, the original contracting officer made a bad bargain. We are not aware of any authorities, nor has counsel invited our attention to any, holding that an agreement is vitiated by this fact alone.
>
> The Government seeks to distinguish these cases from our prior holdings on the ground that in their determination the Board did not consider its present argument that the original contracting officer acted "outside the bounds of his authority" in agreeing to allegedly grossly inadequate price adjustments. Under the terms of the standard "Changes" article of these contracts, and procurement regulations, the contracting officer had clear authority to make changes in the specifications of the contracts. Upon doing so he was specifically charged with the responsibility of determining whether the change caused "an increase or decrease in the cost of . . . this contract . . . ," and,

> upon such a determination, the clause continues, "an equitable adjustment shall be made in the contract price . . . and the contract shall be modified in writing accordingly." The Government's argument, reduced to its lowest common denominator, is that while the contracting officer had authority to make a good bargain, he had no authority to make a bad one. We are unable to accept such an argument. It confuses the contracting officer's authority to act with the judgment displayed by him in performing the act. It seeks to measure authority by the results obtained upon its exercise. Counsel has not cited, and we have been unable to find, any cases supporting this method of measuring authority.

See also *Chrysler Corp.*, ASBCA 17259, 75-1 BCA ¶ 11,236, *recons. denied*, 76-1 BCA ¶ 11,665. While it cannot be said that the Government "authorizes" its agents to make mistakes or to commit torts, it is liable for the agent's action if it is within the scope of his or her authority. See *Cooke v. United States*, 91 U.S. (1 Otto) 389 (1875), where the Court stated at 398:

> Laches is not imputable to the government, in its character as sovereign, by those subject to its dominion. Still a government may suffer loss through the negligence of its officers. If it comes down from its position of sovereignty, and enters the domain of commerce, it submits itself to the same laws that govern individuals there. Thus, if it becomes the holder of a bill of exchange, it must use the same diligence to charge the drawers and indorsers that is required of individuals; and, if it fails in this, its claim upon the parties is lost. Generally, in respect to all the commercial business of the government, if an officer specially charged with the performance of any duty, and authorized to represent the government in that behalf, neglects that duty, and loss ensues, the government must bear the consequences of his neglect. But this cannot happen until the officer specially charged with the duty, if there be one, has acted, or ought to have acted. As the government can only act through its officers, it may select for its work whomsoever it will; but it must have some representative authorized to act in all the emergencies of its commercial transactions. If it fails in this, it fails in the performance of its own duties, and must be charged with the consequences that follow such omissions in the commercial world.

See also *Rockwell Int'l Corp.*, EBCA C-9509187, 97-1 BCA ¶ 28,814 (Government bound by provisions of settlement agreement entered into by Department of Justice and accepted by court); *Honeywell Fed. Sys., Inc.*, ASBCA 39974, 92-2 BCA ¶ 24,966 (Government bound by contracting officer's determination that cost or pricing data not required because contractor met commercial item exemption); *Sterling Millwrights, Inc. v. United States*, 26 Cl. Ct. 49 (1992) (Government bound where contracting officer made progress payments with full knowledge of costs included therein); *Summit Contractors*, AGBCA 81-252-1, 86-1 BCA ¶ 18,632 (Government bound by contract modification favorable to contractor); and *United States v. Hadden*, 192 F.2d 327 (6th Cir. 1951) (Government could not recover mistaken payments made to contractor's creditors). Of course, the Government will not be bound by a bad decision of an employee who lacks authority, *Winn-Senter Constr. Co. v. United States*, 110 Ct. Cl. 34, 75 F. Supp. 255 (1948) (absent special circumstances, Government agent has no authority to order contractor to increase wages and agree to Government reimbursement).

B. Equitable Estoppel

Equitable estoppel is a concept that prohibits a party from escaping liability for statements, actions, or inactions if it has been relied on by the other party. It has traditionally been thought that two prerequisites exist for estopping the Government: (1) the Government's representative must have been acting within the scope of his or her authority, and (2) the Government must be acting in its proprietary capacity rather than its sovereign capacity, *United States v. Georgia-Pacific Co.*, 421 F.2d 92 (9th Cir. 1970). The Supreme Court has altered the focus of the first prerequisite to the requirement that the act of the Government must be one that is not barred by statute or published regulation, *OPM v. Richmond*, 496 U.S. 414, *reh'g denied*, 497 U.S. 1046 (1990). Once these threshold requirements are met, the normal common-law rules of estoppel apply. Thus, the Government can be estopped based on its actions in the contracting process. See *Burnside-Ott Aviation Training Ctr., Inc. v. United States*, 985 F.2d 1574 (Fed. Cir. 1993), stating at 1581:

> The Claims Court improperly relied on *Richmond* to conclude that Burnside-Ott's equitable estoppel claim is barred as a matter of law. In particular, the Claims Court erred in concluding that *Richmond* stands for the proposition that equitable estoppel will not lie against the government for any monetary claim. The *Richmond* holding is not so broad. *Richmond* is limited to "claim(s) for the payment of money from the Public Treasury *contrary to a statutory appropriation.*" 496 U.S. at 424 (emphasis added). Indeed, because the Supreme Court's analysis in *Richmond* is based entirely on the Appropriations Clause of the Constitution, Article 1, Section 9, Clause 7, which provides that "No Money shall be drawn from the Treasury, but in Consequence of Appropriations made by Law," its holding must be limited to claims of entitlement contrary to statutory appropriations.

> Burnside-Ott's assertion of a right to payment of money from the Public Treasury, however, is not based upon a statutory entitlement. Burnside-Ott's assertion is instead based upon its contract with the Navy. Nor does Burnside-Ott claim entitlement contrary to statutory eligibility criteria, as did Richmond. Thus, neither the holding nor analysis in *Richmond* is applicable in this case, and Burnside-Ott's equitable estoppel claim is not barred as a matter of law because of *Richmond.* Equitable estoppel may or may not apply in this case depending on facts yet to be established.

In *Emeco Indus. v. United States*, 202 Ct. Cl. 1006, 485 F.2d 652 (1973), the court required that four elements be established before estoppel is invoked:

> (1) The party to be estopped must know the facts; (2) he must intend that his conduct shall be acted on or must so act that the party asserting the estoppel has a right to believe it is so intended; (3) the latter must be ignorant of the true facts; and (4) he must rely on the former's conduct to his injury.

Additionally, the contractor may have to show affirmative misconduct by the Government, *Howard v. United States*, 23 Cl. Ct. 432 (1991).

When the official is acting within the scope of delegated authority and the actions are not prohibited by statute or regulation, estoppel will be found even though the action is based upon *a mistaken interpretation* of the Government's obligations, *USA Petroleum Corp. v. United States*, 821 F.2d 622 (Fed. Cir. 1987); *Portmann v. United States*, 674 F.2d 1155 (7th Cir. 1982); *Broad Ave. Laundry & Tailoring v. United States*, 231 Ct. Cl. 1, 681 F.2d 746 (1982). Note, however, that *Broad Avenue Laundry* is questionable precedent since the contracting officer's statement was contrary to a published regulation. In *Kozak Micro Sys., Inc.*, GSBCA 10519, 91-1 BCA ¶ 23,342, *recons. denied*, 91-1 BCA ¶ 23,593, the board stated that where Government representatives acting within their scope of authority make statements to contractors that result in factual interpretations not consistent with the contract or its provisions, and the recipients of these statements can prove the elements of estoppel, the Government cannot act contrary to its representations.

Because estoppel accomplishes the same result as finality, the two concepts are often confused. However, there are two important differences between finality and estoppel. Estoppel requires *detrimental reliance* by the party who seeks to invoke it, while reliance is not an element of finality. The other difference is that the statement or action leading to finality is by its very nature contractually binding upon the Government through the operation of legal principles such as offer and acceptance, acceptance of goods, etc. The Government is held bound by estoppel, however, because it would be *unfair* not to do so even though the statement, action, or inaction would not be contractually binding. Thus, the Government has been estopped through its course of conduct as well as through its verbal representations. See *Peninsular ChemResearch, Inc.*, ASBCA 14384, 71-2 BCA ¶ 9066 (Government required to accept results of accounting method it previously approved by implication); and *Litton Sys., Inc. v. United States*, 196 Ct. Cl. 133, 449 F.2d 392 (1971) (Government's knowledge of, acquiescence to, and approval of contractor's accounting system precluded retroactive disallowance of cost).

The Supreme Court's ruling in *Heckler v. Community Servs. of Crawford County, Inc.*, 467 U.S. 51 (1984), casts doubt as to the validity of reliance on oral advice as the basis for asserting estoppel against the Government. The Court stated at 65:

> The appropriateness of respondent's reliance is further undermined because the advice it received from Travelers was oral. It is not merely the possibility of fraud that undermines our confidence in the reliability of official action that is not confirmed or evidenced by a written instrument. Written advice, like a written judicial opinion, requires its author to reflect about the nature of the advice that is given to the citizen, and subjects that advice to the possibility of review, criticism, and reexamination. The necessity for ensuring that governmental agents stay within the lawful scope of their authority, and that those who seek public funds act with scrupulous exactitude, argues strongly for the conclusion that an estoppel cannot be erected on the basis of the oral advice that underlay respondent's cost reports.

See also *Eastern Marine, Inc.*, Comp. Gen. Dec. B-213945, 84-1 CPD ¶ 343, where a claim of estoppel against the Government could not be based upon advice, allegedly received during a telephone conversation, that was in direct conflict with the provisions in the RFP.

1. Government Not Estopped by Unauthorized Actions

The Government will not be estopped by the unauthorized actions of its representatives, *United States v. Georgia-Pacific Co.*, 421 F.2d 92 (9th Cir. 1970). Frequently, the lack of authority results from the action being contrary to statutory requirements. In such cases, courts will construe authority narrowly, *Schweiker v. Hansen*, 450 U.S. 785 (1981) (all courts have a duty to observe conditions defined by Congress for charging the public treasury); *OPM v. Richmond*, 496 U.S. 414, *reh'g denied*, 497 U.S. 1046 (1990) (Government cannot be bound by payment contravening explicit statutory limitation). Similarly, in *Singer Co.*, ASBCA 17604, 75-2 BCA ¶ 11,401, *aff'd*, 217 Ct. Cl. 225, 576 F.2d 905 (1978), the contractor submitted cost or pricing data that the Government representative knew were not current. Since the Government official had no authority to waive the requirements of the Truth in Negotiations Act, 10 U.S.C. § 2306a, the Government could not be estopped from obtaining a price reduction. The board stated at 54,288:

> In the appeal before us, no Government representative had authority to waive the statutory requirement of disclosure of accurate, complete and current data. We need not further discuss the application of estoppel since it fails at a threshold question. We note parenthetically that a far different case would exist had [the contractor] fully disclosed its data in relation to its proposal and the Government then, for whatever reason, failed to make use of the data in the negotiation process. *Muncie Gear Works, Inc.*, ASBCA No. 18184, [75-2 BCA ¶ 11,380]; *Levinson Steel Co.*, ASBCA No. 16520, 73-2 BCA ¶ 10,116.

The same rule applies when the employee is acting contrary to delegated authority, *Atlantic Gulf & Pac. Co. of Manila v. United States*, 207 Ct. Cl. 995 (1975) (no estoppel to disavow settlement agreement negotiated without required advance approval).

Other cases finding no estoppel because of lack of authority include *Essen Mall Properties v. United States*, 21 Cl. Ct. 430 (1990) (Postal Service negotiator lacked implied authority to bind Postal Service); *Lance Dickinson & Co.*, ASBCA 36408, 89-3 BCA ¶ 22,198, *recons. denied*, 90-1 BCA ¶ 22,511 (no implied contract where contractor knew that Government employee lacked authority to contract); *Aetna Casualty & Surety Co. v. United States*, 208 Ct. Cl. 515, 526 F.2d 1127 (1975), *cert. denied*, 425 U.S. 973 (1976) (Government not estopped from recovering illegal payment); *California-Pacific Utilities Co. v. United States*, 194 Ct. Cl. 703 (1971) (no authority to include indemnity provision in contract); *Fansteel Metallurgical Corp. v. United States*, 145 Ct. Cl. 496, 172 F. Supp. 268 (1959) (unauthorized overpayment does not bind Government); and *Carroll Beaver*, Comp. Gen. Dec. B-184130, 75-2 CPD ¶ 14 (Government not bound to rental exceeding maximum authorized amount). See *Toyo Menka*

Kaisha, Ltd. v. United States, 220 Ct. Cl. 210, 597 F.2d 1371 (1979), where the court held that the Government was not estopped to deny the validity of a contract since the contracting officer was not authorized to make an award on a nonresponsive bid. The Comptroller General has consistently held that, even with contractor's detrimental reliance in formulating its bid, "erroneous advice or contract actions of Government officials do not estop an agency from rejecting a nonresponsive bid when required to do so by law," *International Waste Indus.*, Comp. Gen. Dec. B-210500.2, 83-1 CPD ¶ 652. See also *International Med. Indus., Inc.*, 62 Comp. Gen. 31 (B-208235), 82-2 CPD ¶ 386.

In *Urban Data Sys., Inc. v. United States*, 699 F.2d 1147 (Fed. Cir. 1983), a small business contract contained a cost-plus-percentage-of-cost pricing clause at the Government's insistence. Because agents lack the authority to compensate contractors under such a clause, the Government was not estopped to deny its validity. Urban was entitled to compensation, however, under quantum valebant.

2. Sovereign Capacity Exception

It has been stated that the Government will not be estopped from performing sovereign acts, *United States v. Georgia-Pacific Co.*, 421 F.2d 92 (9th Cir. 1970). In *United States v. Lazy FC Ranch*, 481 F.2d 985 (9th Cir. 1973), the court considered both the questions of lack of authority and actions within the Government's sovereign capacity. Citing *Georgia-Pacific, Moser v. United States*, 341 U.S. 41 (1951), *Brandt v. Hickel*, 427 F.2d 53 (9th Cir. 1970), and *Schuster v. C.I.R.*, 312 F.2d 311 (9th Cir. 1962), the court stated at 989:

> The *Moser-Brandt-Schuster* line of cases establish the proposition that estoppel is available as a defense against the government if the government's wrongful conduct threatens to work a serious injustice and if the public's interest would not be unduly damaged by the imposition of estoppel. *Gestuvo v. District Dir. of I.N.S.*, 337 F. Supp. 1093 (C.D. Cal. 1971). This proposition is true even if the government is acting in a capacity that has traditionally been described as sovereign (as distinguished from proprietary) although we may be more reluctant to estop the government when it is acting in this capacity. See *Georgia-Pacific, supra.*

This case rejects the sovereign-capacity exception and also appears to reject the rule that the Government is not estopped by unauthorized acts. However, the court found that "the agency's published regulations arguably permitted" the action taken by the Government's representatives. The Supreme Court has not ruled on whether estoppel lies against the Government when the Government acted in its sovereign capacity. In *Schweiker v. Hansen*, 450 U.S. 785 (1981), the Court referred to *Lazy FC Ranch* in a footnote, stating, "We do not need to consider the correctness of these cases."

3. Reliance

Reasonable reliance by the contractor is an essential element of estoppel, *California-Pacific Utilities Co. v. United States*, 194 Ct. Cl. 703 (1971). In this case, the court held that the contractor could not claim reliance on an alleged agreement to include an indemnification clause in a permit when it had notice that the Government official who allegedly agreed to include the clause did not have authority to do so. See *Diamond v. Federal Emergency Management Agency*, 689 F. Supp. 163 (E.D.N.Y. 1988) (reliance in contradiction of policy provision was unreasonable).

Reliance cannot occur when the contractor's action took place *before* the Government act that is alleged to have created the estoppel. Thus, in *Rockwell Int'l Corp.*, ASBCA 20304, 76-2 BCA ¶ 12,131, no reliance was found because the contractor changed its accounting system before the Government acted. See *Codex Corp.*, ASBCA 17983, 75-2 BCA ¶ 11,554, *remanded on other grounds*, 226 Ct. Cl. 693 (1981) (costs were incurred before action by contracting officer). Estoppel was also denied in *Blount, Inc.*, VABCA 3719, 95-2 BCA ¶ 27,874, where the board found that although the subcontractor probably relied on the VA review finding that its system appeared to meet the specification requirements, there was no detrimental reliance by the prime contractor. The board outlined three factors leading to this conclusion at 139,059:

> The first factor is that Blount [the prime contractor] included the SBS [the subcontractor] quote as a part of its (MHS) bid to the VA *before* the VA's notification to SBS that, in effect, the Bavis product was a functionally equivalent system. The second factor against detrimental reliance is that Blount also signed the subcontract which it proffered to SBS *before* the VA's favorable evaluation of the Bavis system. Finally, the VA awarded the contract to Blount *before* the agency had even communicated its evaluation of the Bavis system to SBS. Thus, Blount, the only party to this contract with the Government, had already committed itself to furnish and install an MHS system which met the VA's specifications by the time of

the VA's Bavis evaluation. Blount could not possibly have relied on the later actions by the VA in this respect.

The contractor must prove that it actually relied on the Government statement or act. In *Mountain Plains Educ. & Economic Dev. Program, Inc.*, ASBCA 21714, 78-1 BCA ¶ 13,083, the Government was not estopped to deny the reasonableness of payments under employment contracts where the contractor could not show that it relied upon the contracting officer's concurrence in the validity of the proposed payments. See *Snowbird Indus., Inc.*, ASBCA 33027, 89-3 BCA ¶ 22,065 (no reliance where contractor did not know of Government act alleged to create estoppel); *Meridian Inc.*, PSBCA 2203, 89-2 BCA ¶ 21,648 (no evidence that contractor action occurred because of Government act); *Baifield Indus., Div. of A-T-O, Inc.*, ASBCA 19025, 75-1 BCA ¶ 11,245 (no indication that contractor would have altered actions if Government had made demand earlier); and *General Sec. Servs. Corp. v. General Servs. Admin.*, GSBCA 11381, 92-2 BCA ¶ 24,897 (no reliance on an alleged Government waiver of the specification was found because the contractor did not indicate in negotiations that it was relying on the waiver).

4. Injury

Injury is essential to estoppel. The contractor must establish that its reliance has placed it in a worse position than it would have been in otherwise, *Chula Vista City School Dist. v. Bennett*, 824 F.2d 1573 (Fed. Cir. 1987), *cert. denied*, 484 U.S. 1042 (1988). See also *Grigor E. Atoian v. General Servs. Admin.*, GSBCA 12765, 95-1 BCA ¶ 27,444 (contractor's delay in filing claim in reliance on advice from Government employee caused no loss or harm to contractor); *Okaw Indus., Inc.*, ASBCA 17863, 75-1 BCA ¶ 11,321, *recons. denied*, 75-2 BCA ¶ 11,571 (no injury to contractor from disallowance of settlement); *Simmonds Precision Prods., Inc.*, ASBCA 18110, 74-1 BCA ¶ 10,472 (Government not estopped from assessing liquidated damages after two years absent proof of prejudice from delay); and *General Dynamics Corp.*, ASBCA 13868, 69-2 BCA ¶ 8044 (contractor not deprived of recovery of allocable costs by retroactive change of accounting system).

5. Waiver

Closely related to and sometimes used interchangeably with estoppel is the concept of waiver — the relinquishment of a legal right. See *American Nat'l Bank & Trust Co. v. United States*, 23 Cl. Ct. 542 (1991); *Branch Banking & Trust Co. v. United States*, 120 Ct. Cl. 72, 98 F. Supp. 757, *cert. denied*, 342 U.S. 893 (1951); and Comp. Gen. Dec. B-174410, June 30, 1972, *Unpub.* As with estoppel, the Government will be bound by a waiver if the contractor relies upon it to its detriment, *De Vito v. United States*, 188 Ct. Cl. 979, 413 F.2d 1147 (1969). However, a waiver may be retracted if it is not supported by consideration or if the contractor has not relied upon the waiver to its detriment, *Mark Dunning Indus.*, ASBCA 29599, 86-1 BCA ¶ 18,521.

The term "waiver" is frequently used in connection with the Government's failure to promptly terminate a delinquent contractor when that contractor has relied on the Government's failure to terminate by continuing performance or preparation for performance with the Government's knowledge and express or implied consent. In such cases, the Government will have waived its right to terminate the contractor for default. In *Freeway Ford Truck Sales, Inc. v. General Servs. Admin.*, GSBCA 10662, 93-3 BCA ¶ 26,019, a default termination was held to be improper despite the contractor's late delivery. The board found that the Government had waived its right to terminate by allowing the contractor to continue with production. In *Marci Enters., Inc. v. General Servs. Admin.*, GSBCA 12197, 94-1 BCA ¶ 26,563, the board held that the Government improperly terminated the contract, stating that the Government had waived the delivery date by telling the contractor to delay the shipment for inspection and by continuing to encourage the contractor to correct the deficiencies. See also *Applied Companies*, ASBCA 43210, 94-2 BCA ¶ 26,837 (Government waived delivery date by rescheduling a date for witnessing the first article test and approving engineering change proposals after the contract delivery date); *Vista Scientific Corp.*, ASBCA 25974, 87-1 BCA ¶ 19,603 (Government waived completion date by encouraging and participating in contractor's efforts to fulfill contract after due date); and *S.T. Research Corp.*, ASBCA 39600, 92-2 BCA ¶ 24,838 (Government waived right to terminate where the contracting officer told the contractor to continue and proposed a new delivery schedule).

The Government's acceptance of a nonspecification performance under a prior or current contract may give rise to a constructive waiver of specifications. The Court of Federal Claims explained the concept of constructive waiver of specifications in *Miller Elevator Co. v. United States*, 30 Fed. Cl. 662 (1994), at 687:

> While the constructive waiver of specifications incorporates estoppel theories into the legal doctrine of waiver, the theory finds basis in any certain interpretation given to a contract specification by the contracting parties. Once the parties continue performance under the interpretation, one party may not later seek to enforce a contrary interpretation, even if the former interpretation results in the constructive waiver of specifications.

The Court of Federal Claims has adopted a four-part test for constructive waiver. In *Hannon Elec. Co. v. United States*, 31 Fed. Cl. 135 (1994), the court stated at 147 that to establish a constructive waiver of specifications, the contractor must show that:

> (1) The [contracting officer] had notice that the work differed from the contract requirements. (2) Action or inaction of the [contracting officer] indicated that the non-specification performance was acceptable. (3) The contractor relied on the [contracting officer's] action or inaction. (4) It would be unfair to permit the Government to retract the waiver.

In *Gresham & Co. v. United States*, 200 Ct. Cl. 97, 470 F.2d 542 (1972), the contract called for dishwashers with automatic detergent dispensers. The Government had accepted dishwashers without automatic dispensers in the previous 21 contracts. The Court of Claims held that the Government's knowing acceptance of nonspecification dishwashers effectively removed the specification requirement in question. In *Hannon Elec.*, however, the contractor disregarded the contract's size requirements for load banks (electrical testing devices) and built larger, nonspecification load banks. Unbeknownst to the contractor, the Government discovered that the load banks were too large before they were completed. Because the contractor was unaware of the Government's knowledge of the deviation, it could not have relied on the Government's alleged acquiescence. Therefore, the contractor's constructive waiver defense failed.

Acceptance of a small number of deviating performances will not constitute waiver, *Western States Constr. Co.*, ASBCA 37611, 92-1 BCA ¶ 24,418 (waiver on only two prior contracts — one with another contractor); *Kvaas Constr. Co.*, ASBCA 45965, 94-1 BCA ¶ 26,513 (waiver on four prior contracts). Waiver can also occur on a single contract. See *General Motors Corp.,* ASBCA 15807, 72-1 BCA ¶ 9405, where the Government was held to have waived the reliability requirement by knowingly authorizing the contractor to proceed with production despite nonconformity with reliability criteria; and *Walsky Constr. Co.*, ASBCA 36940, 90-2 BCA ¶ 22,934, where waiver was found when the contracting officer permitted seal coating of a road at temperatures below the specified minimum.

6. Estoppel Improperly Used

In numerous cases involving finality of action, the boards and courts have unnecessarily used the term estoppel in holding that the Government is bound. This, of course, has led to confusion because it has been the operation of the legal principle involved (acceptance of offer or goods, interpretation of contract, etc.) rather than the doctrine of equitable estoppel that has bound the Government. See *H & M Moving, Inc. v. United States*, 204 Ct. Cl. 696, 499 F.2d 660 (1974) (ambiguous term construed in contractor's favor); *Emeco Indus. v. United States*, 202 Ct. Cl. 1006, 485 F.2d 652 (1973) (implied-in-fact contract existed based upon Government's actions); *Dana Corp. v. United States*, 200 Ct. Cl. 200, 470 F.2d 1032 (1972) (contractor's offer accepted); *Gresham & Co. v. United States*, 200 Ct. Cl. 97, 470 F.2d 542 (1972) (ambiguous term construed in contractor's favor based upon similar interpretation by Government representative); *Manloading & Management Assocs. v. United States*, 198 Ct. Cl. 628, 461 F.2d 1299 (1972) (oral agreement at bidder's conference not precluded by parol evidence rule); *Mercury Mach. & Mfg. Co.*, ASBCA 20068, 76-1 BCA ¶ 11,809; *Fink Sanitary Serv., Inc.*, 53 Comp. Gen. 502 (B-179040), 74-1 CPD ¶ 36; and *Unidynamics/St. Louis, Inc.*, ASBCA 17592, 73-2 BCA ¶ 10,360.

A good example of the confusion that exists in the use of the term "estoppel" is *Lockheed Shipbuilding & Constr. Co.*, ASBCA 18460, 75-1 BCA ¶ 11,246, *recons. denied*, 75-2 BCA ¶ 11,566. This controversial case involved broad multicontract, multiservice negotiations between Deputy Secretary of Defense Packard and the contractor whereby an overall settlement plan was negotiated. Pursuant to these negotiations, the contractor agreed to assume a fixed loss of $2 million under its C-5A contracts with the Air Force and to accept a $62 million settlement on its Navy contracts. The board held that Deputy Secretary Packard had impliedly assured the contractor that the $62 million settlement would be approved by "higher authorities" in the Navy, as required by regulations. Although the overall agreement between Deputy Secretary Packard and the contractor appeared to have all the elements of an enforceable contract, the board used the doctrine of estoppel to hold that the Navy higher authorities could not refuse to approve the $62 million settlement.

Another example of misuse of the estoppel doctrine is found in *LDG Timber Enters., Inc.*, AGBCA 91-213-1, 95-2 BCA ¶ 27,906, where the board held the Government was not estopped by a letter from the contracting officer granting a time extension. The board reasoned the contractor had not proved that it relied on the letter. In reversing this decision, the Federal Circuit held that the estoppel analysis was misused because the Government was bound by the *promise* in the letter in accordance with "ordinary contract principles," *LDG Timber Enters., Inc. v. Glickman*, 114 F.3d 1140 (Fed. Cir. 1997).

V. SUITS AGAINST GOVERNMENT EMPLOYEES

Suits against Government officers, employees, or agents are either of two types. First is the suit, almost always for monetary damages, that seeks to obtain relief directly from the officer, employee, or agent. The second seeks *relief from the Government* by a suit against the employee, officer, or agent in his or her official capacity. Such suits were the normal means of seeking injunctive relief against the Government prior to 1976.

Both types of litigation may be subject to some form of "immunity" defense. Suits against the individual personally will invariably be challenged on the ground that the employee is entitled to the *personal immunity* that attaches to public employees. In suits against the officer or employee in his or her official capacity, the Government may move for dismissal if it has not waived its *sovereign immunity* from such suits. Such suits are no longer necessary because 5 U.S.C. § 702, as amended in 1976, P.L. 94-574, 90 Stat. 2721, permits such suits to be filed directly against the "United States" in order to obtain injunctive relief against adverse agency action. Thus, the only necessity of naming the employee in such suits is to specify who should be enjoined in the event the plaintiff prevails. This section considers the first type of suit against Government employees — those attempting to obtain monetary relief against the employees personally.

Traditionally, Government employees were *immune from personal suit* when acting within the scope of their authority. The courts have recognized the necessity of protecting the freedom of federal officers and employees to exercise the discretion that is required for the proper execution of their duties by prohibiting suits against such employees in their personal capacity. In *Ove Gustavsson Contracting Co. v. Floete*, 299 F.2d 655 (2d Cir. 1962), *cert. denied*, 374 U.S. 827 (1963), a contractor brought suit against federal employees in their private capacities, seeking damages for alleged intentional and malicious falsification of progress reports filed with the Government. Affirming the district court's grant of summary judgment for the Government employees, the court stated at 658:

> [O]fficials of the federal Government are not personally liable for alleged torts based upon acts, done within the scope of their duties, which necessarily involved the exercise of a judgment or discretion which public policy requires be made without fear of personal liability.

This type of immunity has been referred to as *absolute immunity*.

When the Government officer or employee is charged with violating a person's *constitutional rights*, a *qualified immunity* rather than an absolute immunity will be invoked. In *Scheuer v. Rhodes*, 416 U.S. 232 (1974), involving a suit under 42 U.S.C. § 1983 against the governor of Ohio and other high state officials for killing four demonstrators, the Court ruled that state officials could claim only a "qualified immunity." Thus, they would be immune only to the extent that the acts were within the scope of their duties, that they were done with a good faith belief that they were correct, and that such belief was reasonable in light of the facts as they existed at the time of the acts.

The Supreme Court extended this rule to Federal Government employees in *Butz v. Economou*, 438 U.S. 478 (1978), when violations of constitutional rights were alleged. Absolute immunity for constitutional violations was held to apply only to "those exceptional situations where it is demonstrated that absolute immunity is essential for the conduct of the public business." Subsequently, the Court has indicated that absolute immunity for constitutional violations is to be accorded to legislators and judges in their legislative and judicial capacities, respectively, to prosecutors and similar officials of executive agencies, and to executive officers engaged in adjudicative functions. Other federal officials who seek absolute exemption from personal liability for unconstitutional conduct must bear the burden of showing that public policy requires an exemption of that scope based on their functions, not merely their positions. See *Harlow v. Fitzgerald*, 457 U.S. 800 (1982).

In *Harlow*, senior presidential aides and advisers were charged with violating Fitzgerald's constitutional and statutory rights. The Court held that absolute immunity is not "an incident of the office of every presidential subordinate based in the White House." However, an official would be entitled to absolute immunity for constitutional violations by showing (1) "that the responsibilities of his office embraced a function so sensitive as to require a total shield from liability," and (2) "that he was discharging the protected function when performing the act for which liability is asserted." With respect to qualified immunity, the Court stated that it would not apply if the official "knew or reasonably should have known that the action he took within his sphere of official responsibility would violate the constitutional rights of the [plaintiff], or if he took the action with malicious intention to cause a deprivation of constitutional rights or other injury," further stating that "government officials performing discretionary functions generally are shielded from liability for civil damages insofar as their conduct does not violate clearly established statutory or constitutional rights of which a reasonable person would have known." The judge is to determine the threshold question of whether a clearly established law existed at the time of the action of which the Government employee "knew or should have known."

The Supreme Court placed another limitation on absolute immunity in *Westfall v. Erwin*, 484 U.S. 292 (1988). There, the Court ruled that absolute immunity would be granted only if the act were discretionary in nature. Thus, not all acts of high-level officials would necessarily be subject to absolute immunity. The Court also described at 295–96 the following policy reasons as supporting such immunity:

> The purpose of such official immunity is not to protect an erring official, but to insulate the decision making process from the harassment of prospective litigation. The provision of immunity rests on the view that the threat of liability will make federal officials unduly timid in carrying out their official duties, and that effective government will be promoted if officials are freed of the costs of vexatious and often frivolous damages suits. . . . This Court always has recognized, however, that official immunity comes at a great cost. An injured party with an otherwise meritorious tort claim is denied compensation simply because he had the misfortune to

> be injured by a federal official. Moreover, absolute immunity contravenes the basic tenet that individuals be held accountable for their wrongful conduct. We therefore have held that absolute immunity for federal officials is justified only when "the contributions of immunity to effective government in particular contexts outweighs the perhaps recurring harm to individual citizens." *Doe v. McMillan*, [412 U.S. 306, 320 (1973)].

In response to the Court's decision in *Westfall*, Congress enacted the Federal Employees Liability Reform and Tort Compensation Act of 1988, P.L. 100-694, which contained the following statement:

> It is the purpose of this Act to protect Federal employees from personal liability for common law torts committed within the scope of their employment, while providing persons injured by the common law torts with an appropriate remedy against the United States.

To achieve this purpose, the Act amended the Federal Torts Claims Act (FTCA), 28 U.S.C. § 1346(b) and § 2671 et seq., to restore the immunity that the Supreme Court had taken away in *Westfall*. The Act restored absolute immunity for suits for money damages when common-law torts are alleged and did not make the immunity dependent upon the discretionary nature of the employee's duties. In such cases, only the Government may be sued. See 28 U.S.C. § 2679(b).

As a result, Government employees have absolute immunity from suits for monetary compensation unless such suit is based on (1) an act totally outside of the scope of their employment, or (2) an act that deprives a person of his or her constitutional rights and the employee is not a member of the class of employees that has absolute immunity. The Supreme Court has held that this immunity applies even "when an FTCA exception precludes recovery against the Government," *United States v. Smith*, 499 U.S. 160 (1991).

Under the statute, the Attorney General is to make a determination as to whether the act was accomplished within the scope of employment and may defend the employee and the United States if it is so determined. If the action against the employee was brought in a State court, the Attorney General's determination of scope of employment is conclusive for purposes of removal from the State court to a federal district court. However, that determination has been found not to be conclusive after the case has been removed to the district court, *Nasuti v. Scannell*, 906 F.2d 802 (1st Cir. 1990). If the federal court determines that the certification should not have been made, it has been held that the case is to be remanded to the relevant State court, *Haddon v. United States*, 68 F.3d 1420 (D.C. Cir. 1995). In *Aversa v. United States*, 99 F.3d 1200 (1st Cir. 1996), the court held that while federal law "does determine whether a person is a federal employee and the nature and contours of his or her federal responsibilities[,] . . . state law governs whether the person was acting within the scope of that employment and those responsibilities."

VI. AUTHORITY OF CONTRACTOR PERSONNEL

In contrast to the special rules pertaining to Government representatives, general principles of agency law apply to contractor representatives. There is considerably less litigation in this area.

A. Delegation

Authority may be expressly or impliedly delegated to contractor representatives. When a corporation is involved, the plenary authority to transact all the ordinary business of the corporation within its charter powers is vested in the board of directors. Express delegation of authority to others is normally contained in resolutions of the board of directors, which are often furnished to the Government agencies with which the corporate contractor does business.

Standard Form 129, Solicitation Mailing List Application, provides for the listing of officers, owners, or partners of the prospective contractor and a list of the persons authorized to sign bids, offers, and contracts.

B. Apparent Authority

The major difference between the legal rules applicable to Government versus contractor representatives is that a contractor may be bound by a representative possessing apparent authority. See *American Anchor & Chain Corp. v. United States*, 166 Ct. Cl. 1, 331 F.2d 860 (1964), where the court stated at 4:

> Although the Federal Government still stands on the stricter requirements of actual authority for its own agents (see, e.g., *Federal Crop Ins. Corp. v.*

> *Merrill*, 332 U.S. 380 (1947)), the agents of Government contractors are governed by the usual rules.

See also *Western Box-O-Matic Corp.*, GSBCA 3562, 73-1 BCA ¶ 9968, where it was held that the Government was entitled to rely on the apparent authority of the contractor's plant manager to interpret contract language. In *Menches Tool & Die, Inc.*, ASBCA 21469, 78-1 BCA ¶ 13,167, the board rejected the contractor's arguments that it had never authorized its attorney to make certain statements, finding instead that "[t]he Government has the right to assume an agent has actual or apparent authority to bind its principal."

However, if Government employees know or should know that a contractor representative does not have contracting authority, that representative will not be found to have apparent authority. See, for example, *Tectonics Asia Architects & Eng'rs, Inc.*, ASBCA 17067, 75-2 BCA ¶ 11,456, where the board stated at 54,567:

> It is also clear from the record that Mr. a'Becket was not an officer of the corporation and this fact should have been known to AID contracting personnel since he always signed correspondence and invoices as "contract administrator," acted in that capacity and did not represent himself as a corporate officer. There is nothing in the record to indicate that AID was ever notified that Mr. a'Becket had contracting authority. His participation in negotiations for Amendment No. 1, together with [the contractor's] vice-president Mr. Anderson, did not clothe him with apparent or implied authority on which AID personnel could have been [relying.] The authorities cited in [the Government's] brief (*American Anchor & Chain Corporation v. United States,* 166 Ct. Cl. 1 (1964) and *Video Engineering Company, Inc.*, DOT CAB No. 72-5, 72-1 BCA ¶ 9432) involve distinctly different factual situations and thus do not support the proposition that Mr. a'Becket had apparent authority to act for the corporation and bind it contractually.

See also *Piracci Corp.*, GSBCA 6007, 82-2 BCA ¶ 16,047 (contractor not bound by a settlement negotiated by attorney when Government negotiator had no reason to believe that attorney had authority to settle a claim); *Ray Wilson Co.*, ASBCA 17084, 75-1 BCA ¶ 11,066 (Government was not justified in inferring that a second-tier subcontractor's employees had authority to bind the contractor); Comp. Gen. Dec. B-171802, Mar. 2, 1971, *Unpub.* (contractor not bound by the actions of its employees who had no real, implied, or apparent authority); *Colorado Sec. Agency, Inc.*, GSBCA 5650, 84-1 BCA ¶ 16,940 (contractor not bound because contracting officer knew contractor's employee had no authority); and *Kahaluu Constr. Co.*, ASBCA 33248, 90-2 BCA ¶ 22,663 (proposed settlement agreement approved by an agent of a contractor and an agent of the Government, both without authority, was not an offer to settle).

C. Ratification and Estoppel

Even where the Government deals with an unauthorized representative, the contractor will be bound if the action is ratified by an authorized official. In *Tectonics Asia Architects & Eng'rs, Inc.*, ASBCA 17067, 75-2 BCA ¶ 11,456, the contractor was held bound by an unauthorized amendment when it had continued performance for two and one-half months with full knowledge of the terms of the amendment.

The principles of estoppel are similarly applicable to the contractor. In *Ampex Corp.*, GSBCA 5913, 82-1 BCA ¶ 15,738, *recons. denied*, 82-2 BCA ¶ 15,858, the board held that the contractor was estopped to deny an agreement where a contractor representative had informed the Government that the contractor had agreed to accept the agreement. The board found that the representative did not have authority to make the agreement but did have authority to convey information to the Government, stating at 77,861:

> Granted, [the contractor representative] was not an agent of the company authorized to bind it contractually. We have already indicated that we do not consider that to be the point in dispute. Rather, the issue is whether [the representative] had the authority to tell the Government that [the contractor] had agreed to be bound. If she had that authority, then [the contractor] is bound by her representation:
>
> > "Except as to statements with relation to the agent's authority, in actions brought upon a contract or to rescind a contract, a disclosed or partially disclosed principal is responsible for unauthorized representations made incidental to it, if the contract is otherwise authorized and if true representations as to the same subject matter are within the authority or the apparent authority of the agent, unless the other party thereto has notice that the representations are untrue or unauthorized." *Restatement (Second), Agency* (1958), § 162.

See also *Detroit Diesel Allison Div., Gen. Motors Corp.*, ASBCA 20199, 77-1 BCA ¶ 12,414, where the contractor was estopped to deny applicability of longstanding accounting practice. Compare *CRF v. United States*, 224

Ct. Cl. 312, 624 F.2d 1054 (1980), where the court stated that the contractor was not estopped to deny the validity of a contract awarded in a manner contrary to the regulations. In *Piracci Corp.*, GSBCA 6007, 82-2 BCA ¶ 16,047, the board held that the contractor was not estopped on the basis, among others, that there was no justifiable reliance by the Government.

VII. STANDARDS OF CONDUCT

In order to maintain public confidence in the federal procurement process, Government and contractor employees must follow exemplary standards of conduct. There are numerous statutory and regulatory provisions outlining the standards to be followed and the stringent penalties for noncompliance. This section discusses these standards in three broad categories — those dealing with improper influence on Government decisions, those requiring honesty and disclosure of relevant facts in dealing with the Government, and those barring improperly disclosing or obtaining information. The focus of the material is on proscribed conduct.

A. Sanctions

Each statute prohibiting a certain type of conduct contains its own sanction or penalty. Since most of these sanctions involve straightforward criminal or civil fines or imprisonment, this section does not discuss the precise way that these penalties have been interpreted and enforced. In this regard, a Government contractor or a Government employee is treated the same as any other person guilty of a "white collar" crime. However, Government contractors are also subject to additional sanctions that are considerably broader than the normal criminal and civil sanctions. In many if not most cases, these broader sanctions are a more serious threat to Government contractors than the criminal or civil sanctions contained in the specific statutes covering the prohibited conduct. There are also additional sanctions applicable to Government employees. This section considers those additional sanctions that provide drastic penalties for those engaged in improper conduct in the contracting process.

1. *Forfeiture and Cancellation*

The first of these general sanctions against Government contractors is *forfeiture* of all rights under the contract. The Supreme Court has held that the Government can cancel a contract and need not pay for work done or benefit conferred if it is tainted with illegal conduct, *United States v. Mississippi Valley Generating Co.*, 364 U.S. 520 (1961) (conflict of interest); *Pan Am. Petroleum & Transp. Co. v. United States*, 273 U.S. 456 (1927). The Court of Claims went even further and held that the Government can recover the full amount paid on a *completed contract* that is subsequently found to have been tainted with illegal conduct, *K & R Eng'g Co. v. United States*, 222 Ct. Cl. 340, 616 F.2d 469 (1980) (bribery and conflict of interest). Fraudulent *claims* are also forfeited. Under 28 U.S.C. § 2514, see *O'Brien Gear & Mach. Co. v. United States*, 219 Ct. Cl. 187, 591 F.2d 666 (1979) (forfeiting a renegotiation claim because it was tainted with fraud); and *Supermex, Inc. v. United States*, 35 Fed. Cl. 29 (1996) (forfeiting a contract claim because the contractor had bribed a Government official during contract performance). Contracts containing a contingent fee arrangement are also void and unenforceable, *Quinn v. Gulf & Western Corp.*, 644 F.2d 89 (2d Cir. 1981); *LeJohn Mfg. Co. v. Webb*, 222 F.2d 48 (D.C. Cir. 1955). The fact that Congress may have specifically provided for other statutory or criminal sanctions does not deprive the United States of the right to cancel such contracts "tainted with illegal conduct," *United States v. Acme Process Equip. Co.*, 385 U.S. 138 (1966) (statutory sanction for violation of Anti-Kickback Act, 41 U.S.C. § 51); *Horton J. Brown v. United States*, 207 Ct. Cl. 768, 524 F.2d 693 (1975) (criminal sanction for violation of False Statement Act, 18 U.S.C. § 1001).

The Government may lose its right of forfeiture if it does not exercise this right in a timely manner. For example, it has been held that the Government could not cancel a contract for breach of the covenant against contingent fees where it knew of the arrangement during prolonged negotiations and the arrangement had many indicia of a bona fide covenant, *Companhia Atlantica De Desenvoluimento E Exploracao De Minas v. United States*, 148 Ct. Cl. 71, 180 F. Supp. 342, *cert. denied*, 364 U.S. 862 (1960). See also *Paradyne Corp. v. United States*, 647 F. Supp. 1228 (D.D.C. 1986), prohibiting the Government from exercising a contract option at the same time it was charging the contractor with fraud pertaining to the option.

There is some question as to which officials in the Government are authorized to cancel contracts and the nature of the activity that would entitle the Government to cancel. In *Medico Indus., Inc.*, ASBCA 22141, 80-2 BCA ¶ 14,498, *recons. denied*, 80-2 BCA ¶ 14,665, *mot. to suspend hearings granted*, 81-1 BCA ¶ 14,983, it was held that the contracting officer was not authorized to cancel a contract because of improper conduct by a former Government employee. The board distinguished *Mississippi Valley Generating Company* on the grounds that it involved the more serious violation — action by a "public official having simultaneous conflicting interests." The board also questioned whether improper conduct of a former Government employee was a sufficiently serious violation to allow the Government to cancel. Following the board's suspension of the hearing, the Government sued in U.S. District Court for a declaratory judgment that the contract cancellation was authorized. The district court granted the contractor's motion to dismiss for lack of jurisdiction. In *United States v. Medico Indus., Inc.*, 685 F.2d 230 (7th Cir. 1982), however, the circuit court reversed, holding that the board of contract appeals did not have jurisdiction under the Disputes clause to determine whether 18 U.S.C. § 207(a) was violated and remanding the matter to the district court for disposition. Contrast *Four-Phase Sys., Inc.*, ASBCA 27487, 84-1 BCA ¶ 17,122, suggesting that the Contract Disputes Act gives jurisdiction to the appeals boards over a Government affirmative defense of cancellation for a violation of 18 U.S.C. § 208. Section 218 of 18 U.S.C. provides for cancellation by the President or, under presidentially prescribed regulations, the head of any department or agency if there has been a final conviction for offenses involving bribery, gratuities, and conflicts of interest during and after Government employment. Exec. Order No. 12448, 48 Fed. Reg. 5128 (1983), delegates the authority to exercise this power to heads of executive agencies and provides that implementing regulations should contain specified procedural protections. FAR 3.705 sets forth the procedures for exercising this authority and states that "the agency head or designee may declare void and rescind contracts with respect to which a final conviction has been entered."

2. Debarment

The second broad sanction is debarment of the contractor or its employees, that is, precluding participation in the Government contracts process for a stated period of time. FAR 9.406-2 states:

> (a) The debarring official may debar a contractor for a conviction of or civil judgment for —

> (1) Commission of fraud or a criminal offense in connection with (i) obtaining, (ii) attempting to obtain, or (iii) performing a public contract or subcontract;
>
> (2) Violation of Federal or State antitrust statutes relating to the submission of offers;
>
> (3) Commission of embezzlement, theft, forgery, bribery, falsification or destruction of records, making false statements, or receiving stolen property;
>
> (4) Intentionally affixing a label bearing a "Made in America" inscription (or any inscription having the same meaning) to a product sold in or shipped to the United States, when the product was not made in the United States (see section 202 of the Defense Production Act (Pub. L. 102-558)); or
>
> (5) Commission of any other offense indicating a lack of business integrity or business honesty that seriously and directly affects the present responsibility of a Government contractor or subcontractor.

Debarment precludes contracts with any agency of the Federal Government for a period of up to three years or longer in some cases, FAR 9.406-4. Debarment of a company has been sustained for submitting false claims, *Dowling Group v. Williams*, Civ. Action No. 82-1775 (D.D.C. 1982), and for bribery, *Atlantic Chem. Co.*, GSBCA 5822-D, 80-2 BCA ¶ 14,801. Debarment of an officer of a company was also sustained when the company bribed Government officials, *Taylor v. Marsh*, Civ. Action No. 81-2643 (D.D.C. 1982).

3. Suspension or Dismissal of Government Employees

A third broad sanction is suspension or dismissal of a Government employee who has violated the standards of conduct. Such actions must be taken in accordance with 5 U.S.C. § 7513, which permits appeal by the employee to the Merit System Protection Board. See 5 C.F.R. Part 1200. Dismissal of an employee was upheld in *Womer v. Hampton*, 496 F.2d 99 (5th Cir. 1974), where a Government inspector had taken payments from a contractor and did not give a satisfactory explanation for the payments. Dismissal was also sustained in *Polcover v. Secretary of Treasury*, 477 F.2d

1223 (D.C. Cir. 1973), on the basis that the employee accepted a bribe even though he was later acquitted in a criminal prosecution. The court held that the evidence was sufficient to meet a "preponderance of the evidence" test in the dismissal proceeding despite failing to meet the "beyond a reasonable doubt" test of the criminal action. The Court of Claims repeatedly held that agencies have broad discretion in selecting administrative sanctions for acceptances of bribes and gratuities. In *Jones v. United States*, 223 Ct. Cl. 138, 617 F.2d 233 (1980), the court upheld a decision of the Civil Service Commission Appeals Review Board sustaining the dismissal of a Department of Agriculture meat inspector who had accepted a single bottle of whiskey from a meat packer. In *Parker v. United States*, 224 Ct. Cl. 618, 650 F.2d 287 (1980), the court rejected the contention that dismissal of an employee who had accepted meals and entertainment valued at more than $3,000 from a contractor constituted an abuse of agency discretion. In *Lane v. United States*, 225 Ct. Cl. 209, 633 F.2d 1384 (1980), the court upheld the dismissal of IRS auditors who had accepted a "whole series" of free meals from a firm being audited. See also *Monahan v. United States*, 173 Ct. Cl. 734, 354 F.2d 306 (1965), sustaining the dismissal of a procuring agency employee for permitting a contractor to pay for hotel rooms and accepting loans from three contractors; *Brewer v. United States Postal Serv.*, 227 Ct. Cl. 276, 647 F.2d 1093 (1981), *cert. denied*, 454 U.S. 1144 (1982), upholding the dismissal of an employee with 27 years of service for falsifying time cards; and *Miller v. United States Postal Serv.*, 712 F.2d 1006 (6th Cir. 1983), sustaining the dismissal of an employee for using inside information to benefit a company in which he had an interest.

B. Improper Influence of Government Decisions

One of the most serious threats to the integrity of the procurement process is the possibility of conduct by contractors that will improperly influence the decisions of contracting officers and other Government employees. To protect against this threat, there are a number of very strict criminal statutes.

1. Bribery

18 U.S.C. § 201(b) makes it a criminal offense to *offer* or *give* a bribe to a Government official or for a Government official to *solicit* or *receive* a bribe. The crimes are defined as follows:

(b) Whoever —

(1) directly or indirectly, corruptly gives, offers or promises anything of value to any public official or person who has been selected to be a public official, or offers or promises any public official or any person who has been selected to be a public official to give anything of value to any other person or entity, with intent —

(A) to influence any official act; or

(B) to influence such public official or person who has been selected to be a public official to commit or aid in committing, or collude in, or allow, any fraud, or make opportunity for the commission of any fraud, on the United States; or

(C) to induce such public official or such person who has been selected to be a public official to do or omit to do any act in violation of the lawful duty of such official or person;

(2) being a public official or person selected to be a public official, directly or indirectly, corruptly demands, seeks, receives, accepts, or agrees to receive or accept anything of value personally or for any other person or entity, in return for:

(A) being influenced in the performance of any official act;

(B) being influenced to commit or aid in committing, or to collude in, or allow, any fraud, or make opportunity for the commission of any fraud, on the United States; or

(C) being induced to do or omit to do any act in violation of the official duty of such official or person.

a. Anything of Value

To constitute bribery, the statute requires that something "of value" be given, offered, promised, solicited, or received. Courts have adopted an expansive reading of the value requirement for both bribery and gratuities. Most cases involving bribery under the statute understandably concern cash payments, *United States v. Hollingshead*, 672 F.2d 751 (9th Cir. 1982) (cash payment to employee of Federal Reserve Bank); *United States v. Myers*, 635 F.2d 932 (2d Cir.), *cert. denied*, 449 U.S. 956 (1980) (cash paid by undercover agents to members of Congress); *United States v. Johnson*, 621 F.2d 1073 (10th Cir. 1980) (cash payment offered to FAA procurement official); *United States v. Strand*, 574 F.2d 993 (9th Cir. 1978) (cash payment by undercover agent to summer border guard); *United States v. Arroyo*, 581 F.2d 649 (7th Cir. 1978), *cert. denied*, 439 U.S. 1069 (1979) (cash payments to Small Business Administration loan officers from loan applicant); *United States v. Brasco*, 516 F.2d 816 (2d Cir. 1975), *cert. denied*, 423 U.S. 860 (1975) (cash payments to Post Office officials to obtain contracts); *United States v. Deutsch*, 475 F.2d 55 (5th Cir. 1973) (cash payments to Post Office employees to obtain stolen credit cards); *United States v. Rosner*, 485 F.2d 1213 (2d Cir. 1973), *cert. denied*, 417 U.S. 950 (1974) (cash payments by lawyer to undercover agent to obtain secret grand jury minutes); and *United States v. Jacobs*, 431 F.2d 754 (2d Cir. 1970), *cert. denied*, 402 U.S. 950 (1971) (cash payment to IRS auditor). However, a variety of other benefits have also been considered as "value" by courts in relation to bribery charges, *United States v. Harary*, 457 F.2d 471 (2d Cir. 1972) (prostitutes and cameras); *United States v. Ellenbogen*, 365 F.2d 982 (2d Cir. 1966), *cert. denied*, 386 U.S. 923 (1967) (an automobile). It is not necessary for the Government to establish the exact value of a bribe, since the express language of 18 U.S.C. § 201(b)(1) defines the offense as giving "anything of value" to a public official, *United States v. Rasco*, 853 F.2d 501 (7th Cir.), *post-conviction proceedings*, 697 F. Supp. 343 (N.D. Ill.), *cert. denied*, 488 U.S. 959 (1988).

b. Corrupt Intent

To establish a violation of the provision, a specific "corrupt" intent on the part of the giver or receiver of the bribe must be proved. The requisite intent is proved by showing a quid pro quo — an expectation of a favorable official act in return for the bribe. In *United States v. Strand*, 574 F.2d 993 (9th Cir. 1978), where a U.S. Customs Service official was found to have violated this provision by soliciting and accepting an $800 payment in return for allowing drugs to be smuggled through a border checkpoint, the court discussed the intent required under 18 U.S.C. § 201(c) (now § 201(b)(2)(c)) at 995:

> To be guilty under § 201(c)(3), Strand must have "corruptly" accepted the $800 from the Customs agent for himself or some other person in return for knowingly violating his official duty. The requisite "corrupt" intent has been defined as "incorporating a concept of the bribe being the prime mover

> or producer of the official act." *United States v. Brewster*, 165 U.S. App. D.C. 1, 21, 506 F.2d 62, 82 (D.C. Cir. 1974). It is this element of quid pro quo that distinguishes the heightened criminal intent requisite under the bribery sections of the statute from the simple mens rea required for violation of the gratuity sections.

In proving the exchange or quid pro quo element, the accompanying intent to influence some identifiable public act must be shown. In *United States v. Heffler*, 402 F.2d 924 (3d Cir. 1968), a Government technical employee was convicted for having solicited a bribe in return for an offer to influence an award, even though he was not the awarding officer. The nexus between solicitation and intent was found in the employee's purported ability to indirectly affect award, his offer to do so, and the specificity of the act to be performed. Similarly, in *United States v. Arroyo*, 581 F.2d 649 (7th Cir. 1978), *cert. denied*, 439 U.S. 1069 (1979), an SBA loan officer was convicted of accepting a bribe even though the loan had already been consummated, because the loan officer had told the borrower that the loan had not yet been finalized. In *United States v. Pommerening*, 500 F.2d 92 (10th Cir.), *cert. denied*, 419 U.S. 1088 (1974), loan applicants were convicted of bribery for giving an SBA official a $5,000 automobile in exchange for expediting a $200,000 loan application to finance their car dealership. The number of reported cases involving Government procurement officials and contractors is relatively small. The typical case involves payments made in the hope of influencing contract awards. In *United States v. Johnson*, 621 F.2d 1073 (10th Cir. 1980), the court found the requisite indicia of an expected quid pro quo where the contractor, who had given a $10,000 check to a Government procurement agent, credited it on its books to Government contracts it expected to win. *United States v. Iaconetti*, 540 F.2d 574 (2d Cir.), *cert. denied*, 429 U.S. 1041 (1976), involved a GSA inspector who was assigned to conduct a preaward survey of a contractor and was convicted of soliciting a bribe for offering to ensure the favorable treatment of the contractor by the "upper echelon" of GSA in exchange for one percent of the contract price.

c. *Public Official*

The statute prohibits payments to a "public official," defined at 18 U.S.C. § 201(a), as follows:

> Member of Congress, Delegate, or Resident Commissioner, either before or after such official has qualified, or an officer or employee or person acting

> for or on behalf of the United States, or any department, agency or branch of Government thereof, including the District of Columbia, in any official function under or by authority of any such department, agency, or branch of Government, or a juror.

The class of "public officials" is an expansive one, consisting of federal prison administrators, *United States v. Alessio*, 528 F.2d 1079 (9th Cir.), *cert. denied*, 426 U.S. 948 (1976); IRS agents, *United States v. Johnson*, 647 F.2d 815 (8th Cir. 1981); congressional aides, *United States v. Carson*, 464 F.2d 424 (2d Cir. 1972), *cert. denied*, 409 U.S. 949 (1972); *United States v. Dixon*, 658 F.2d 181 (3d Cir. 1981); a privately employed grain inspector licensed by the Department of Agriculture, *United States v. Kirby*, 587 F.2d 876 (7th Cir. 1978); a COR, *K & R Eng'g Co. v. United States*, 222 Ct. Cl. 340, 616 F.2d 469 (1980); and a private broker for HUD, *United States v. Griffin*, 401 F. Supp. 1222 (S.D. Ind. 1975), *aff'd*, 541 F.2d 284 (7th Cir. 1976). There is some conflict, however, regarding the propriety of classifying persons not directly employed by the Federal Government as "public officials." Compare *United States v. Loschiavo*, 531 F.2d 659 (2d Cir. 1976) (model cities program administrator was not acting on behalf of Federal Government by suggesting leasing arrangement with one who bribed administrator), with *Griffin* (privately employed broker under HUD contract was "public official") and *United States v. Velazquez*, 847 F.2d 140 (4th Cir. 1988) (county jailer was "public official" where jail housed federal as well as state prisoners, county jailers supervised federal inmates, and jail was subject to inspections by federal prison authorities).

2. Gratuities

There is a general gratuity statute in the criminal code and a special statute applicable to the DOD.

a. General Restrictions

18 U.S.C. § 201(c) makes it a crime to offer or give a gratuity to a Government official or for a Government official to solicit or receive a gratuity. The crimes are defined as follows:

(c) Whoever —

(1) otherwise than as provided by law for the proper discharge of official duty —

(A) directly or indirectly gives, offers, or promises anything of value to any public official, former public official, or person selected to be a public official, for or because of any official act performed or to be performed by such public official, former public official, or person selected to be a public official; or

(B) being a public official, former public official, or person selected to be a public official, otherwise than as provided by law for the proper discharge of official duty, directly or indirectly demands, seeks, receives, accepts, or agrees to receive or accept anything of value personally for or because of any official act performed or to be performed by such official or person.

This statute is implemented by Exec. Order No. 12674, 54 Fed. Reg. 15159 (1989), as modified by Exec. Order No. 12731, 55 Fed. Reg. 42547 (1990), and by the regulations at 5 C.F.R. § 2635 Subpart B, which provide a uniform set of rules for all executive branch employees.

(1) ANYTHING OF VALUE

A variety of benefits have been deemed to constitute "value" in relation to gratuities, including cash, meat, liquor, and clothing, *United States v. Romano*, 583 F.2d 1 (1st Cir. 1978); paid vacations, *United States v. Hartley*, 678 F.2d 961 (11th Cir. 1982); and loans and promise of future employment, *United States v. Gorman*, 807 F.2d 1299 (6th Cir. 1986), *cert. denied*, 484 U.S. 815 (1987). In *Gorman*, the court noted that the term "anything of value" should be broadly construed and not limited to gratuities as that word is commonly understood. In determining what constitutes a "thing of value," the court placed the focus on the subjective value the receiver of the gratuity attached to the items received. See *United States v. McDade*, 827 F. Supp. 1153 (E.D. Pa. 1993), *aff'd*, 28 F.3d 283 (3d Cir. 1994), where a United States congressman charged with accepting illegal gratuities argued that many of the gifts allegedly received, such as a golf jacket, a golf bag, and a golf umbrella, had only nominal value and were thus not "things of value" under the gratuities statute. The congressman cited *Gorman* to support the proposition that the term "anything of value" should be construed as meaning "substantial value." The court could find nothing in *Gorman* to support this argument and denied the congressman's motion to dismiss the indictment. The court noted that even the smallest of the items allegedly received was objectively valuable enough under the gratuities statute, and that the items may have also had additional subjective value to the congressman. As an example, the court noted that the golf jacket was a green jacket similar to the one awarded each year to the winner of the Masters Golf Tournament and, thus, presumably covetable by a golf lover.

The federal standards of conduct in 5 C.F.R. § 2635 contain extensive guidance on "gifts" to federal employees. 5 C.F.R. § 2635(b) provides the following definition of the term "gift":

> *Gift* includes any gratuity, favor, discount, entertainment, hospitality, loan, forbearance, or other item having monetary value. It includes services as well as gifts of training, transportation, local travel, lodgings, and meals, whether provided in-kind, by purchase of a ticket, payment in advance, or reimbursement after the expenses has been incurred.

The regulation contains nine exceptions to this definition which are summarized as follows:

> (1) Modest items of food and refreshments offered other than as part of a meal.
>
> (2) Greeting cards and plaques, certificates and trophies of little intrinsic value.
>
> (3) Commercial loans on terms generally available to the public.
>
> (4) Favorable rates and discounts available to the public or all Government employees.
>
> (5) Rewards and prizes unrelated to an employee's duties and open to a broad class of people.
>
> (6) Pension and other benefits resulting from continued participation in an employee welfare and benefits plan maintained by a former employer.

(7) Anything paid for by the Government.

(8) Gifts accepted under specific statutory authority.

(9) Anything paid for at market value.

5 C.F.R. § 2635.204 contains detailed guidance on a number of additional exceptions that pertain to special situations. See, for example, the small value exception in 5 C.F.R. § 2635.204(a), which permits employees to accept unsolicited gifts with a value of $20 or less and an aggregate annual value of $50 per giver. Even though acceptance of a gift may be permitted by one of the described exceptions, the regulations note at 5 C.F.R. § 2635.204 that "it is never inappropriate and frequently prudent for an employee to decline a gift offered by a prohibited source or because of his official position." Additionally, 5 C.F.R. § 2635.202(c) contains the following broad restrictive guidance:

> Notwithstanding any exception provided in this subpart . . . an employee shall not:
>
> (1) Accept a gift in return for being influenced in the performance of an official act:
>
> (2) Solicit or coerce the offering of a gift;
>
> (3) Accept gifts from the same or different sources on a basis so frequent that a reasonable person would be led to believe that the employee is using his public office for private gain;
>
> (4) Accept a gift in violation of any statute . . . ;
>
> (5) Accept vendor promotional training contrary to applicable regulations, policies or guidance relating to the procurement of supplies and services for the Government, except pursuant to § 2635.204(l).

This would appear to make it inappropriate for a Government employee to accept any gift from a contractor if the employee has official duties with regard to the contract. See 5 C.F.R. § 3601.103 for supplemental guidance provided for DOD employees.

(2) PURPOSE OF GRATUITY

The laws relating to gratuities are less rigorous than the laws relating to bribery, *United States v. Brewster*, 165 U.S. App. D.C. 1, 506 F.2d 62 (D.C. Cir. 1974). In *United States v. Campbell*, 684 F.2d 141 (D.C. Cir. 1982), the court concluded that a gift offered or solicited merely to "generally influence" an official is sufficient to satisfy the "for or because of" element of the statute. Contrast the Fourth Circuit's ruling in *United States v. Arthur*, 544 F.2d 730 (4th Cir. 1976), stating that a gift given to create "goodwill" was not a gratuity.

There is also a lesser degree of intent with gratuities as compared to bribes. In *United States v. Niederberger*, 580 F.2d 63 (3d Cir. 1978), where an IRS employee violated the gratuity statute by accepting five golfing trips, the court discussed the different degrees of intent required for establishing violations of the bribery and gratuity sections at 68:

> It is clear, then, that § 201(c)(1) [now § 201(b)(1)] requires as one of its elements a quid pro quo. In fact, we find this to be the primary distinction between subsections (c)(1) and (g) [now § 201(c)]. Support for this view is found in *United States v. Brewster*, 165 U.S. App. D.C. 1, 506 F.2d 62 (1974), where the court, analyzing the differences between subsections (c)(1) and (g), held that "[t]he bribery section [(c)(1)] makes necessary an explicit quid pro quo which need not exist if only an illegal gratuity is involved." *Id.*, at 11, 506 F.2d at 72.
>
> Thus, we find it unnecessary for the Government to allege in an indictment charging a § 201(g) offense that a gratuity received by a public official was, in any way, generated by some specific, identifiable act performed or to be performed by the official. A quid pro quo is simply foreign to the elements of a subsection (g) offense.

In *United States v. Bishton*, 463 F.2d 887 (D.C. Cir. 1972), a supervisor was convicted under this section for soliciting a $400 gift from an employee for whom the supervisor had previously obtained a promotion. In *United States v. Evans*, 572 F.2d 455 (5th Cir. 1978), acceptance of a $500 gratuity by an official who had previously accepted an offer of Government employment but had not commenced work was sufficient to establish a violation of this section.

Since a gratuity need only be paid "for or because of any official act" (18 U.S.C. § 201(c)) and no quid pro quo need be proved, it may be difficult to discern whether the alleged payment was made out of friendship or other disinterested motive. While it is clear that *corrupt* intent need not be shown, the Government must at least demonstrate *some* nexus between the giving or receiving of the thing of value and the employee's official position. In *United States v. Standefer*, 610 F.2d 1076 (3d Cir. 1979), *aff'd*, 447 U.S. 10 (1980), sufficient evidence of intent was found despite a corporate officer's assertion that certain vacation trips to Florida given to an IRS employee were motivated by disinterested friendship, because no evidence was offered that similar gifts were given either prior or subsequent to the recipient's employment in the Government, and a subordinate of the corporate officer characterized the relationship as a "business friendship." However, many of the reported cases actually involve facts reflecting an expectation of a quid pro quo, perhaps reflecting a prosecutorial reluctance to impose bribery sanctions in cases involving small payments. For example, in *United States v. Mosley*, 659 F.2d 812 (7th Cir. 1981), an Illinois state official, whose salary was entirely paid by the Federal Government under the CETA program, was convicted of violating 18 U.S.C. § 201(g) (now § 201(c)(1)(B)) for soliciting $50 payments from applicants for CETA jobs in exchange for favorable referral to CETA hiring agencies. In *United States v. Kirby*, 587 F.2d 876 (7th Cir. 1978), the defendants were convicted of conspiring to violate 18 U.S.C. § 201(f) (now § 201(c)(1)(A)) by making payments to grain inspectors in exchange for false certifications that inspected grain was of a higher quality than it actually was.

b. Department of Defense Statute

10 U.S.C. § 2207, as modified by Section 801 of the Clinger-Cohen Act of 1996, P.L. 104-106, provides as follows:

> (a) Money appropriated to the Department of Defense may not be spent under a contract other than a contract for personal services unless that contract provides —
>
> > (1) the United States may, by written notice to the contractor, terminate the right of the contractor to proceed under the contract if the Secretary concerned or his designee finds, after notice and hearing, that the contractor, or his agent or other representative, offered or gave any gratuity, such as entertainment or a gift, to an officer, official, or employee of the United States to obtain a contract or favorable treatment in the awarding, amending, or making of determinations concerning the performance, of a contract; and

> (2) if a contract is terminated under clause (1), the United States has the same remedies against the contractor that it would have had if the contractor had breached the contract and, in addition to other damages, is entitled to exemplary damages in an amount at least three, but not more than 10, as determined by the Secretary or his designee, times the cost incurred by the contractor in giving gratuities to the officer, official, or employee concerned.
>
> (b) This section does not apply to a contract that is for an amount not greater than the simplified acquisition threshold (as defined in section 4(11) of the Office of Federal Procurement Policy Act (41 U.S.C. § 403(11)).

See *Heinrich Wilhem Koehler v. United States*, 37 Cont. Cas. Fed. (CCH) ¶ 76,241 (D.D.C. 1991), where the court found proper an agency's decision to suspend a foreign contractor on the ground that the contractor offered gratuities to Government personnel in violation of regulations. The court stated that given the fact that all Government contracts involving defense appropriations are to contain a clause indicating the Government's right to terminate a contractor's right under a contract if the contractor offered a gratuity in order to obtain a contract, it was presumed that the contract in question contained the clause and the contractor was thus on notice of the illegality of the gifts.

3. Conduct of Former Employees

The Government has sought to prevent former Government employees and military officers from making unfair use of their prior positions and affiliations. At the same time, the Government recognizes the legitimate interest and rights of former employees to seek employment and to enter into business ventures. Thus, activity that seeks to influence Government action or that would undermine confidence in the fairness of Government activities is prohibited, but former Government employees and military officers retain a great amount of freedom to pursue legally permissible activity.

a. General Restrictions

18 U.S.C. § 207 restricts "officers and employees" in the following circumstances:

(1) A former employee is prohibited for life from representing anyone else before the Government on a particular matter the employee handled personally and substantially while a Government official.

(2) A former employee is prohibited for two years from representing a party on a particular matter that had been under the employee's official responsibility during the last year of the employee's Government service.

(3) A former senior-level employee is prohibited for one year from making any communication or appearance before the employee's former agency regardless of prior involvement in the matter.

(4) A former employee is prohibited for one year from assisting others in trade or treaty negotiations the employee had been engaged in during the employee's final year of Government service.

(5) A former senior-level employee is prohibited for one year from assisting foreign entities before the Government.

Criminal prosecutions under this statute are rare. However, alleged violations of this statute are frequently raised in contesting the validity of contracts. The most egregious conduct falling within this provision is hiring Government employees before the award of a contract when they have worked on the procurement. A contracting officer's disqualification of an offeror for such conduct was sustained in *NKF Eng'g, Inc. v. United States*, 805 F.2d 372 (Fed. Cir. 1986). In that case, a former Navy civilian employee, who had participated substantially in the procurement process on a particular RFP, left federal employment to take a job with one of the offerors before the contract was awarded. That offeror subsequently submitted a price revision that was 33 percent lower than its earlier offer. The court upheld the disqualification of the offeror on the basis of an appearance of impropriety, even though the offeror claimed that it had carefully isolated the former Government employee from its preparation of the final offer. The court agreed that the potential for an unfair competitive advantage so tainted the procurement process that the integrity of the process had been damaged.

(1) Particular Matter

Violations of the first two restrictions require participation in a "particular matter" that was in the agency during the official's employment. Such a matter typically involves a "proceeding affecting legal rights" or transactions "between identifiable parties," 5 C.F.R. § 2637.201(c)(1). Excluded are formulation of general policy, rulemaking, and legislation. For a violation to occur, the subsequent representation must concern the same matter in which the employee participated during employment, 5 C.F.R. § 2637.201(c)(4). In *CACI, Inc.-Fed. v. United States*, 1 Cl. Ct. 352, *rev'd*, 719 F.2d 1567 (Fed. Cir. 1983), the Justice Department issued an RFP for ADPE services for the Information Systems Support Group (ISSG) of the department. Before award was made, an offeror who had provided these services for some time alleged that a conflict existed in that a vice president of a competitor had previously served as chief of the ISSG. In issuing an injunction barring award, the Claims Court found that the employee was involved in the "same particular matter" while working for the Government, a criterion that satisfies either Section 207(a) or Section 207(b). The Federal Circuit reversed, holding that a follow-on service contract did not cover the "same particular matter" as the prior contract because the nature of the services had evolved and were broader than those on the earlier contract. The court appears to have read the statute narrowly in arriving at this conclusion. Contrast the *CACI* decision with *United States v. Medico Indus., Inc.*, 784 F.2d 840 (7th Cir. 1986), holding that a contract amendment adding a large quantity of units to an existing contract was sufficiently related to the original contract to be the same particular matter.

(2) Personal and Substantial Participation

Violation of the first restriction occurs only when there has been a personal and substantial participation in the matter during employment, as stated at 5 C.F.R. § 2637.201(d)(1):

> Basic requirements. The restrictions of section 207(a) apply only to those matters in which a former Government employee had "personal and substantial participation," exercised "through decision, approval, disapproval, recommendation, the rendering of advice, investigation or otherwise." To participate "personally" means directly, and includes the participation of a subordinate when actually directed by the former Government employee in the matter. "Substantially" means that the employee's involvement must be of significance to the matter, or form a basis for a reasonable appearance of

> such significance. It requires more than official responsibility, knowledge, perfunctory involvement, or involvement on an administrative or peripheral issue. A finding of substantiality should be based not only on the effort devoted to a matter, but on the importance of the effort. While a series of peripheral involvements may be insubstantial, the single act of approving or participation in a critical step may be substantial.

Review of a proposed notice of income tax deficiency and recommendation for its issuance constituted personal and substantial participation, *United States v. Nasser*, 476 F.2d 1111 (7th Cir. 1973). Preparing a memorandum and answering a legal question were also held to be such participation. Review of a patent application was held to be sufficient involvement in *Kearney & Trecker Corp. v. Giddings & Lewis, Inc.*, 452 F.2d 579 (7th Cir. 1971), *cert. denied*, 405 U.S. 1066 (1972).

(3) Representation

The basic prohibition in 18 U.S.C. § 207(a)(1) is on representational activities carried out "with the intent to influence." "Representation" may occur in the course of formal or informal appearances and in written or oral communications. In 5 C.F.R. § 2637.201(b), representation is defined as "acting as agent or attorney, or other representative in an appearance, or communication with intent to influence." Furthermore, 5 C.F.R. § 2637.201(b)(3) states:

> An appearance occurs when an individual is physically present before the United States in either a formal or informal setting or conveys material to the United States in connection with a formal proceeding or application. A communication is broader than an appearance and includes, for example, correspondence or telephone calls.

The following example is set forth at 5 C.F.R. § 2637.201(b)(5):

> A Government employee, who participated in writing the specifications of a contract awarded to Q Company for the design of certain education testing programs, joins Q Company and does work under the contract. She is asked to accompany a company vice-president to a meeting to state the results of a series of trial tests, and does so. No violation occurs when she provides the information to her former agency. During the meeting a dispute arises as to some terms of the contract, and she is called upon to support Q Company's position. She may not do so. If she had reason to believe that the

> contractual dispute would be a subject of the meeting, she should not have attended.

See *Robert E. Derecktor of R.I., Inc. v. United States*, 762 F. Supp. 1019 (D.R.I. 1991), where the court, interpreting the predecessor to Section 207(a), held that a former employee's delivery of a bid package to his former agency did not constitute an appearance within the meaning of this restriction and that the employee did not deliver the bid with the intent to influence. See, however, *United States v. Coleman*, 805 F.2d 474 (3d Cir. 1986), where a former employee's presence at a meeting related to tax cases, which had been within the employee's supervisory responsibility before retiring, was found to constitute representation within the meaning of this restriction.

18 U.S.C. § 207(j)(5) permits "communications solely for the purpose of furnishing scientific or technological information" to the agency. See *J. L. Assocs.*, Comp. Gen. Dec. B-201331.2, 82-1 CPD ¶ 99, where this exception was applied by the Air Force to a "briefing" by a retired military officer concerning the same activity that he had commanded. The briefing concerned the contractor's experience on similar work with other agencies and occurred before issuance of an RFP.

Under a predecessor statute, participation in the preparation of a claim for reimbursement was held not to violate the statute since it did not amount to "prosecution" of a claim, *Acme Process Equip. Co. v. United States*, 171 Ct. Cl. 324, 347 F.2d 509 (1965), *rev'd on other grounds*, 385 U.S. 138 (1966).

(4) TYPES OF EMPLOYMENT OR CONTRACTING PERMITTED

Absent a violation of the specific provisions of 18 U.S.C. § 207, there is no general prohibition in this statute against *employment* of a former Government employee by a contractor, as provided at 5 C.F.R. § 2637.101(c)(5):

> The provisions of 18 U.S.C. § 207 do not, however, bar any former Government employee, regardless of rank, from employment with any private or public employer after Government service. Nor do they effectively bar employment even on a particular matter in which the former Government employee had major official involvement except in certain circumstances

> involving persons engaged in professional advocacy. Former Government employees may be fully active in high-level supervisory positions whether or not the work is funded by the United States and includes matter in which the employee was involved while employed by the Government. The statutory provisions are not intended to discourage the movement of skilled professionals in Government, to and from positions in industry, research institutions, law and accounting firms, universities and other major sources of expertise. Such a flow of skills can promote efficiency and communication between the Government and private activities, and it is essential to the success of many Government programs. Instead, only certain acts which are detrimental to public confidence in the Government are prohibited.

For cases not applying this statute to mere employment, see *Bray Studios, Inc.*, Comp. Gen. Dec. B-207723, 82-2 CPD ¶ 373 (former agency employee now president of contractor and working in same area); and *Culp/Wesner/Culp*, Comp. Gen. Dec. B-212318, 84-1 CPD ¶ 17 (former agency employee in charge of preparing solicitation subsequently awarded subcontract).

There is also no general prohibition against entering into contracts with former Government employees, *Sterling Med. Assocs.*, 62 Comp. Gen. 230 (B-209493), 83-1 CPD ¶ 215 (former employee of Veterans Administration awarded contract by the Department of the Navy); *Edward R. Jereb*, 60 Comp. Gen. 298 (B-200092), 81-1 CPD ¶ 178 (restriction prohibiting award of services contract to former agency employees held invalid); *Western Eng'g & Sales Co.*, Comp. Gen. Dec. B-205464, 82-2 CPD ¶ 277 (former employee awarded contract by agency based on proposal submitted after employment terminated). See, however, *Aviation Enters., Inc. v. Orr*, 29 Cont. Cas. Fed. (CCF) ¶ 82,053 (D.D.C. 1981), *vacated*, 716 F.2d 1403 (D.C. Cir. 1983), where a contract award to a company owned by a former military officer was enjoined because of a "conflict of interest," without reference to the statute.

b. Additional Statutory Restrictions

A broader post-employment restriction applicable to specific "former officials" is set forth at 41 U.S.C. § 423(d). This new statute in Section 4304 of the Clinger-Cohen Act of 1996 states:

(1) A former official of a Federal agency may not accept compensation from a contractor as an employee, officer, director, or consultant of the contractor within a period of one year after such former official —

(A) served, at the time of selection of the contractor or the award of a contract to that contractor, as the procuring contracting officer, the source selection authority, a member of the source selection evaluation board, or the chief of a financial or technical evaluation team in a procurement in which that contractor was selected for award of a contract in excess of $10,000,000;

(B) served as the program manager, deputy program manager, or administrative contracting officer for a contract in excess of $10,000,000 awarded to that contractor; or

(C) personally made for the Federal agency —

(i) a decision to award a contract, subcontract, modification of a contract or subcontract, or a task order or delivery order in excess of $10,000,000 to that contractor;

(ii) a decision to establish overhead or other rates applicable to a contract or contracts for that contractor that are valued in excess of $10,000,000;

(iii) a decision to approve issuance of a contract payment or payments in excess of $10,000,000 to that contractor; or

(iv) a decision to pay or settle a claim in excess of $10,000,000 with that contractor.

(2) Nothing in paragraph (1) may be construed to prohibit a former official of a Federal agency from accepting compensation from any division or affiliate of a contractor that does not produce the same or similar products or services as the entity of the contractor that is responsible for the contract referred to in subparagraph (A), (B), or (C) of such paragraph.

FAR 3.104-8 provides guidance on the calculation of the one-year period — stating that the period begins on the date of the last activity of the official. FAR 3.104-7 contains guidance on obtaining advice from agency ethics officials on the application of these rules. 41 U.S.C. § 423(g) also provides that protests may no longer be filed based on an allegation that this statute has been violated.

This restriction replaces prior restrictions in 41 U.S.C. § 423(f) that became applicable when an employee's participation occurred during the conduct of a procurement. In that event, the former procurement official was prohibited for two years from participating with a competing contractor in subsequent negotiations on that contract or from participating in the performance of that contract. Those restrictions also applied to first- and second-tier subcontractors with contracts in excess of $100,000, subcontractors who significantly assisted the prime contractor in negotiations of the prime contract, subcontractors specifically directed to the prime contractor by the procurement official, and subcontractors reviewed or approved by the procurement official. The Comptroller General held that the interpretation and enforcement of the postemployment restrictions found in 41 U.S.C. § 423 are primarily matters for the procuring agency and the Department of Justice — with the result that protests will determine only "whether any action of the former government employee may have resulted in prejudice for, or on behalf of, the awardee," *Central Texas College*, 71 Comp. Gen. 164 (B-245233.4), 92-1 CPD ¶ 121. In *FHC Options, Inc.*, Comp. Gen. Dec. B-246793.3, 92-1 CPD ¶ 366, the Comptroller denied a protest based on the employment of a former Government employee by the awardee's subcontractor because, although the former employee had assisted in the initial development of the performance work statement and the source selection plan for the solicitation, he had left the Government before the RFP was issued, was not involved in the preparation of the awardee's proposal, and would not be involved in performing the contract.

There were also special purpose post-employment restrictions applicable only to defense or procurement personnel, 10 U.S.C. § 2397c. These provisions were repealed by Section 4304(b)(1) of the Clinger-Cohen Act of 1996.

Formerly, a retired military officer was subject to two additional restrictions under 37 U.S.C. § 801 and 18 U.S.C. § 281. The Federal Acquisition Streamlining Act of 1994, P.L. 103-355, repealed 37 U.S.C. § 801. Under the provisions of that statute, a retired regular officer could not be paid from any appropriation for three years after retirement if the former officer was selling for himself or herself or for others or was contracting or negotiating to sell supplies or war materials to the DOD, the Coast Guard, NASA, or the Public Health Service. Section 4304(b)(3) of the Clinger-Cohen Act of 1996 repealed 18 U.S.C. § 281. This statute made it unlawful for a period of two years after retirement for a former military officer to be compensated for representing any person in the sale of goods or services to the military service from which the officer retired.

Section 4304(b)(6) of the Clinger-Cohen Act of 1996 also repealed 42 U.S.C. § 7216, prohibiting the Department of Energy from using employees of "energy concerns" in departmental matters involving that concern for a period of one year after employment. In *TRW Envtl. Safety Sys., Inc. v. United States*, 18 Cl. Ct. 33 (1989), award to an offeror was permanently enjoined when the court found a violation of that statute. In that case, an ex-employee of a competitor had participated in drafting the statement of work and was appointed chairman of the source evaluation board within the one-year period.

4. Conduct of Current Employees

There are numerous statutes and regulations circumscribing the activities of Government employees. See, for example, 18 U.S.C. § 203 (limitation on receiving payment from others for official activity); 18 U.S.C. § 205 (prohibition against prosecuting claims); and 18 U.S.C. § 209 (prohibition against receiving compensation from other than United States for official duties). This section discusses the two major statutes applicable to Government contracting. It also discusses administrative restrictions on contracting with organizations owned or controlled by Government employees.

a. General Restrictions

Officers and employees of the Government with a financial interest in an organization are prohibited from participating personally and substantially in any matter concerning that organization and the Government, 18 U.S.C. § 208. This provision was intended to expand the proscriptions against employee participation with the private sector beyond the prior Section 434, which merely prohibited certain "transactions of business."

The Standards of Ethical Conduct contained in 5 C.F.R. § 2635 Subpart D provide detailed guidance implementing this statutory proscription. The following definition of "financial interest" is found at 5 C.F.R. § 2635.403(c):

(1) Except as provided in paragraph (c)(2) of this section, the term financial interest is limited to financial interests that are owned by the employee or by the employee's spouse or minor children. However, the term is not limited to only those financial interests that would be disqualifying under 18 U.S.C. § 208(a) and § 2635.402. The term includes any current or contingent ownership, equity, or security interest in real or personal property or a business and may include an indebtedness or compensated employment relationship. It thus includes, for example, interests in the nature of stocks, bonds, partnership interests, fee and leasehold interests, mineral and other property rights, deeds of trust, and liens, and extends to any right to purchase or acquire any such interest, such as a stock option or commodity future. It does not include a future interest created by someone other than the employee, his spouse or dependent child or any right as a beneficiary of an estate that has not been settled.

(2) The term financial interest includes service, with or without compensation, as an officer, director, trustee, general partner or employee of any person, including a nonprofit entity, whose financial interests are imputed to the employee under § 2635.402(b)(2)(iii) or (iv).

The Ethics in Government Act of 1978, 5 U.S.C. App. § 201 et seq., further requires the public disclosure of financial information by all political appointees and all civil service employees of GS-16 and above.

A financial interest is present if it is more than insubstantial, remote, or inconsequential. The Office of Government Ethics ruled in 83 OGE 1 (1983), that vested rights in a private corporation's pension plan constituted a financial interest. In another ruling dated August 17, 1979, the Office ruled that leaves of absence or reemployment rights with a former employer were financial interests in that company.

Case law indicates that a statutory violation occurs when the employee has both a financial stake in the outcome of the transaction and a sufficient contact with the transaction. It seems clear that the threshold is quite low for both elements. In *United States v. Mississippi Valley Generating Co.*, 364 U.S. 520 (1961), the Court gave an expansive reading to the term "transacting business" in prior Section 434 and found a violation of the statute where the employee's financial stake consisted of the potential business he had generated for another employer and where his contact with the transaction involved him in preliminary contract negotiations on behalf of both parties. In that case, a temporary employee of the Bureau of the Budget who served at the request of the bureau chief without pay also served as an officer of a bank. An offeror on an RFP for construction of a power plant negotiated the early stages of the contract with the temporary employee and also asked him to inquire into financing with bank officials. The temporary employee was not involved in the final contract negotiations but confidentially suggested revisions to the offeror's second proposal. Regarding the employee's financial stake, the Court held that positive corruption is not a prerequisite for violation of the conflicts statute and stated at 550, "[T]he statute is more concerned with what might have happened than with what actually happened." See also *Smith v. United States*, 305 F.2d 197 (9th Cir. 1962), where the court found a violation of Section 434 even though the "transaction" consisted merely of an employee's failure to circumscribe the activities of subordinates who were involved in a conflict.

Although Section 208 is much broader in scope than was Section 434, the cases decided under this section do not appear to have given it as strict an interpretation as was given to the prior statute. See, for example, *Grassetti v. Weinberger*, 408 F. Supp. 142 (N.D. Cal. 1976), where a grant applicant had been denied a grant by the National Cancer Institute, a division of the National Institutes of Health, whose evaluation team consisted of members also competing for research grants. Though the team had sufficient contact with the transaction, the court stated that although a conflict would arise where team members contributed to a decision as to whether to award themselves a grant, the allegation that a denial of a grant to another applicant would leave more money for the team was too remote to create a conflict. Thus, the cases that have enforced Section 208 have dealt with considerably greater financial interests and contact than that in *Mississippi Valley* or *Smith*. See, for example, *K & R Eng'g Co. v. United States*, 222 Ct. Cl. 340, 616 F.2d 469 (1980) (chief of a branch of the Corps of Engineers took kickbacks and profits from contracts awarded by his office to a particular contractor after giving contractor advance notice of the IFB and of the maximum amount the Corps would pay); *United States v. Conlon*, 628 F.2d 150 (D.C. Cir. 1980) (indictment under Section 208 reinstated where it was shown that the director of the Bureau of Engraving, who was also president of the American Bank Note Development Corp. (ABNC), participated in decisionmaking regarding replacement of a Bureau signature system with one developed by ABNC); *United States v. Irons*, 640 F.2d 872 (7th Cir. 1981) (program officer for HEW recommended to a contracting officer that an IFB be sent to a company he established for the purpose of receiving the IFB); and *United Tel. Co.*, GSBCA 10031-P, 89-3 BCA ¶ 22,108 (offeror disqualified because its subcontractor had used a Government employee participating in the procurement as a consultant during the competition).

Conducting employment negotiations has also been held to be a conflict of interest under 18 U.S.C. § 208. Employment discussions are considered a financial interest by the Standards of Ethical Conduct, 5 C.F.R. § 2635.603. The following definition of "seeking employment" is found at 5 C.F.R. § 2635.603(b):

> An employee is seeking employment once he has begun seeking employment within the meaning of paragraph (b)(1) of this section and until he is no longer seeking employment within the meaning of paragraph (b)(2) of this section.
>
> (1) An employee has begun seeking employment if he has directly or indirectly:
>
> (i) Engaged in negotiations for employment with any person. For these purposes, as for 18 U.S.C. § 208(a), the term negotiations means discussion or communication with another person, or such person's agent or intermediary, mutually conducted with a view toward reaching an agreement regarding possible employment with that person. The term is not limited to discussions of specific terms and conditions of employment in a specific position;
>
> (ii) Made an unsolicited communication to any person, or such person's agent or intermediary, regarding possible employment with that person. However, the employee has not begun seeking employment if that communication was:
>
> (A) For the sole purpose of requesting a job application; or
>
> (B) For the purpose of submitting a resume or other employment proposal to a person affected by the performance or nonperformance of the employee's duties only as part of an industry or other discrete class. The employee will be considered to have begun seeking employment upon receipt of any response indicating an interest in employment discussions; or
>
> (iii) Made a response other than rejection to an unsolicited communication from any person, or such person's agent or intermediary, regarding possible employment with that person.

Once an employment discussion has commenced, it may be terminated by "rejection" of any possibility of employment. However, it is clear that terminating an immediate employment discussion will not result in "rejection" of an offer of employment if the discussion is only deferred. See *Express One Int'l, Inc. v. United States Postal Serv.*, 814 F. Supp. 93 (D.D.C. 1992), where the court enjoined award of a contract because the employee of a consultant of the procuring agency had told the winning offeror "he would not be available for a personal meeting or to discuss a position until after [award of the contract]."

In *AT&T Communications, Inc.*, GSBCA 9252-P, 88-2 BCA ¶ 20,805, an offeror was disqualified after receiving information from a Government employee with whom it had discussed employment. Similarly, in *Four-Phase Sys., Inc.*, ASBCA 26794, 86-2 BCA ¶ 18,924, a violation of Section 208 was found where employment negotiations occurred during the negotiation of a change order. Less stringent enforcement of this rule occurred in *Chemonics Int'l Consulting Div.*, 63 Comp. Gen. 14 (B-210426), 83-2 CPD ¶ 426, where the Comptroller General held that it was improper to withhold award from a firm that had offered employment to a Government employee who had attended subsequent negotiations, and *CACI, Inc.-Fed. v. United States*, 1 Cl. Ct. 352, *rev'd*, 719 F.2d 1567 (Fed. Cir. 1983), where the court found no violation of Section 208 when contract negotiations with a Government employee occurred 16 months after an employment discussion had occurred.

b. Procurement Integrity Restrictions

Additional restrictions on employment contacts or discussions are contained in 41 U.S.C. § 423(c). This statute, as amended by Section 4304(a) of the Clinger-Cohen Act of 1996, provides:

> (1) If an agency official who is participating personally and substantially in a Federal agency procurement for a contract in excess of the simplified acquisition threshold contacts or is contacted by a person who is a bidder or offeror in that Federal agency procurement regarding possible non-Federal employment for that official, the official shall —
>
> > (A) promptly report the contact in writing to the official's supervisor and to the designated agency ethics official (or designee) of the agency in which the official is employed; and

(B) (i) reject the possibility of non-Federal employment; or

(ii) disqualify himself or herself from further personal and substantial participation in that Federal agency procurement until such time as the agency has authorized the official to resume participation in such procurement, in accordance with the requirements of section 208 of title 18, United States Code, and applicable agency regulations on the grounds that —

(I) the person is no longer a bidder or offeror in that Federal agency procurement; or

(II) all discussions with the bidder or offeror regarding possible non-Federal employment have terminated without an agreement or arrangement for employment.

The new Act provides for completely different procedures from those in the former Act. The first step in the new procedures is an immediate reporting requirement when an agency official receives an employment contract. This report must be submitted to the official's supervisor and the agency ethics official. The second step is for the official to either "reject the possibility of non-Federal employment" or disqualify himself or herself from further participation in the procurement. Under the new Act, this disqualification decision seems to be in the sole discretion of the official, while under the former Act recusal was a decision of the agency. However, FAR 3.104-11(c) states that an official who "refuses to terminate employment discussions may be subject to agency administrative actions under 5 C.F.R. § 2635.604(d) if the official's disqualification from participation in a particular procurement interferes substantially with the individual's ability to perform assigned duties." Thus, an agency retains considerable control over this decision under the regulations.

The new Act also narrows the scope of these restrictions. First, the rule only applies to contracts over the simplified acquisition threshold of $100,000. Second, the rule applies only to "Federal agency procurement" — which excludes sole source contracts and contract modifications. Note, however, that entertaining employment discussions or negotiations during such transactions would be a violation of 18 U.S.C. § 208 and 5 C.F.R. § 2635.603(b). A third narrowing is that the new Act restricts only bidders and offerors making contacts to officials regarding future employment while the former Act restricted "any entity that is, or is reasonably likely to become, a competitor for or recipient of a contract or subcontract . . . and includes any other person acting on behalf of such an entity." FAR 3.104-6(a) warns that the disqualification may be required even where contacts are through an agent or intermediary of the bidder or offeror because that contact would be a violation of 18 U.S.C. § 208. See also 5 C.F.R. § 2635.603(c). However, neither the new Act nor the FAR define "proprietary or source selection information" prior to the award of a contract. The new Act, 41 U.S.C. § 423(b), substantially broadens this rule by prohibiting a "person" from knowingly obtaining "contractor bid or proposal information" or "source selection information" before the award of the "Federal agency procurement" to which the information relates. It applies the prohibition to any contractor, other business entity, or individual that obtains information even if that person is not participating in the procurement. It also seems to apply the prohibition without regard to the source of the information, with the result that it could arguably be a violation to obtain the information from a newspaper reporter or some other person not connected with the procurement. The only narrowing of the rule is that it is no longer a violation of the Act to *solicit* information if the information is not obtained.

5. Anti-Kickback Act

Contractors and subcontractors are prohibited from soliciting, accepting, or attempting to accept any kickbacks from their subcontractors by the Anti-Kickback Act of 1986, 41 U.S.C. §§ 51–58. The Act contains a broad definition of the term "kickback," as follows:

> The term "kickback" means any money, fee, commission, credit, gift, gratuity, thing of value, or compensation of any kind which is provided, directly or indirectly, to any prime contractor, prime contractor employee, subcontractor, or subcontractor employee for the purpose of improperly obtaining or rewarding favorable treatment in connection with a prime contract or in connection with a subcontract relating to a prime contract.

The purpose of this statute is to prevent payments that impede the competitive process. The typical kickback is paid to a purchasing agent of a contractor or subcontractor to obtain the award of a subcontract without having to participate in a fair competition. The purchasing agent, in turn, takes some action that distorts the competition. The presumption is that the Government eventually pays the amount of the kickback in higher prices, and the Act permits the procuring agency to reduce the price by the amount of the kickback. The Act also contains criminal and civil sanctions.

The Act is implemented in FAR 3.502 and the Anti-Kickback Procedures clause at FAR 52.203-7. This clause requires the contractor to have internal procedures to detect and prevent kickbacks. It also requires the prompt reporting of kickbacks and cooperation with Government agencies in the investigation of kickbacks. The FASA makes this clause inapplicable to contracts under $100,000 (Section 4104(a)) or to a prime contract for the acquisition of commercial items (Section 8301(c)).

6. Covenant against Contingent Fees

The Government has a longstanding policy against the payment of contingent fees. This policy developed because of the Government's concern that contingent fee arrangements expose Government agencies to corrupting influences. It also reflects the Government's recognition that such agreements could allow for the payment of exorbitant fees by contractors, leading to higher costs for the Government, thereby resulting in an unnecessary waste of public funds. See *Quinn v. Gulf & Western Corp.*, 644 F.2d 89 (2d Cir. 1981). Thus, a clause is required in negotiated contracts by statute, 10 U.S.C. § 2306(b) and 41 U.S.C. § 254(a), and in sealed bid procurements by regulation, FAR 3.404. The FASA removes the requirement for such a clause in contracts at or below the simplified acquisition threshold of $100,000 (Section 4103(c) and Section 4102(b), civilian agencies and armed services, respectively) or in contracts for the acquisition of commercial items (Section 8204(b) and Section 1105(a), civilian agency and armed services, respectively). The clause to be used is contained in FAR 52.203-5:

COVENANT AGAINST CONTINGENT FEES (APR 1984)

(a) The Contractor warrants that no person or agency has been employed or retained to solicit or obtain this contract upon an agreement or understanding for a contingent fee, except a bona fide employee or agency. For breach or violation of this warranty, the Government shall have the right to annul this contract without liability or, in its discretion, to deduct from the contract price or consideration, or otherwise recover, the full amount of the contingent fee.

(b) "Bona fide agency," as used in this clause, means an established commercial or selling agency, maintained by a contractor for the purpose of securing business, that neither exerts nor proposes to exert improper influence to solicit or obtain Government contracts nor holds itself out as being able to obtain any Government contract or contracts through improper influence.

> "Bona fide employee," as used in this clause, means a person, employed by a contractor and subject to the contractor's supervision and control as to time, place, and manner of performance, who neither exerts nor proposes to exert improper influence to solicit or obtain Government contracts nor holds out as being able to obtain any Government contract or contracts though improper influence.
>
> "Contingent fee," as used in this clause, means any commission, percentage, brokerage, or other fee that is contingent upon the success that a person or concern has in securing a Government contract.
>
> "Improper influence," as used in this clause, means any influence that induces or tends to induce a Government employee or officer to give consideration or to act regarding a Government contract on any basis other than the merits of the matter.

The covenant does not prohibit the payment of all contingent fees — only those made for the purpose of obtaining a contract. In *Browne v. R & R Eng'g Co.*, 264 F.2d 219 (3d Cir. 1959), the court held that contingent fee services in connection with a proposed contract that did not involve any dealings with officials responsible for the award of contracts were not prohibited. The Comptroller General has followed this ruling. See *Holmes & Narver Servs., Inc.*, 70 Comp. Gen. 424 (B-242240), 91-1 CPD ¶ 373, where an incumbent contractor offered to sell access to its employees and competitively useful contract information to potential offerors who agreed to purchase inventory and equipment at set prices if they won the contract. The Comptroller General held that this was not a prohibited contingent fee arrangement because the payment would not be made for the purpose of soliciting or obtaining the contract at issue and the arrangement did not involve any dealings with Government officials. See also *Kasler Elec. Co.*, DOTCAB 1425, 84-2 BCA ¶ 17,374, where a payment to a nonemployee estimator was contingent on award of the contract. The board held that the arrangement did not violate the covenant, since the estimator's function was to price out a bid and not to solicit a Government contract. Compare *Howard Johnson Lodge*, Comp. Gen. Dec. B-244302.2, 92-1 CPD ¶ 305, finding a violation of the covenant because the sales agent was directly contacting Government agencies about potential contracts.

In addition, the covenant does not apply to a "bona fide employee" or "bona fide agency." The factors to be considered in determining whether the recipient of a contingent fee falls within these exceptions are set forth at FAR 3.408-2(c), as follows:

> (1) The fee should not be inequitable or exorbitant when compared to the services performed or to customary fees for similar services related to commercial business.
>
> (2) The agency should have adequate knowledge of the contractor's products and business, as well as other qualifications necessary to sell the products or services on their merits.
>
> (3) The contractor and the agency should have a continuing relationship or, in newly established relationships, should contemplate future continuity.
>
> (4) The agency should be an established concern that has existed for a considerable period, or be a newly established going concern likely to continue in the future. The business of the agency should be conducted in the agency name and characterized by the customary indicia of the conduct of regular business.
>
> (5) While an agency that confines its selling activities to Government contracts is not disqualified, the fact that an agency represents the contractor in Government and commercial sales should receive favorable consideration.

In *General Sales Agency*, Comp. Gen. Dec. B-247133.2, 92-1 CPD ¶ 544, a newly established arrangement with a sales organization for a seven and one-half percent contingent fee was held proper because the parties anticipated that the arrangement would be longstanding and no improper influence had been exerted to obtain the contract. Similarly, in *Convention Mktg. Servs.*, Comp. Gen. Dec. B-245660.3, 92-1 CPD ¶ 144, no violation was found where contractors had entered into contingent fee arrangements with sales agents to assist in the acquisition and preparation of contracts, but they had exerted no improper influence to solicit or obtain the contracts. The Comptroller General stated:

> The fact that an agent's fee is contingent upon the contractor receiving the contract award is insufficient to bring a fee arrangement under the contingent fee prohibition; rather, the regulation contemplates a specific demonstration that an agent is retained for the express purpose of contacting Government officials.

See *Wickes Indus., Inc.*, ASBCA 17376, 75-1 BCA ¶ 11,180, for a decision in which the Government was not allowed to cancel a contract where a contingency arrangement was "bona fide" considering the factors set forth in the DAR. See also Comp. Gen. Dec. B-157815, Jan. 21, 1966, *Unpub.*

The bona fide employee exemption focuses on the nature of the arrangement between the agent and the contractor, FAR 3.408-2(b). In *Quinn v. Gulf & Western Corp.*, 644 F.2d 89 (2d Cir. 1981), a contract was held to be unenforceable because the contingent fee arrangement between the turbine blade manufacturer and the owner of the consulting firm, who was also a special Government employee, failed to satisfy the "bona fide employee" criterion.

C. Honesty and Disclosure of Facts

One of the most important requirements of the public contracting process is that contractors and subcontractors be honest in their dealings with governmental agencies and contractors. This section reviews this requirement by first discussing the applicable statutes and then considering the major types of conduct that have been found to violate this requirement.

1. Statutory Requirements

In federal contracting, the requirement for honesty and disclosure of facts is supported by a number of criminal and civil statutes imposing a variety of penalties on contractors and others who do not comply with the minimum standards of disclosure and honesty.

a. False Claims

The fundamental federal statute with the goal of promoting honesty in dealing is the False Claims Act. This Act was originally enacted in 1863 to prevent fraud in Civil War defense contracts and is now divided into a civil provision in 31 U.S.C. § 3729 and a criminal provision in 18 U.S.C. § 287.

(1) CIVIL FRAUD

For many years this provision was set forth in 31 U.S.C. § 231. In 1982, it was codified in 31 U.S.C. § 3729, and then it was amended by the False Claims Amendments Act of 1986 to read as follows:

(a) Liability for certain acts. Any person who —

(1) knowingly presents, or causes to be presented, to an officer or employee of the United States Government or a member of the Armed Forces of the United States a false or fraudulent claim for payment or approval;

(2) knowingly makes, uses, or causes to be made or used, a false record or statement to get a false or fraudulent claim paid or approved by the Government;

(3) conspires to defraud the Government by getting a false or fraudulent claim allowed or paid;

(4) has possession, custody, or control of property or money used, or to be used, by the Government and, intending to defraud the Government or willfully to conceal the property, delivers, or causes to be delivered, less property than the amount for which the person receives a certificate or receipt;

(5) authorized to make or deliver a document certifying receipt of property used, or to be used, by the Government and, intending to defraud the Government, makes or delivers the receipt without completely knowing that the information on the receipt is true;

(6) knowingly buys, or receives as a pledge of an obligation or debt, public property from an officer or employee of the Government, or a member of the Armed Forces, who lawfully may not sell or pledge the property; or

(7) knowingly makes, uses, or causes to be made or used, a false record or statement to conceal, avoid, or decrease an obligation to pay or transmit money or property to the Government,

is liable to the United States Government for a civil penalty of not less than $5,000 and not more than $10,000, plus 3 times the amount of damages which the Government sustains because of the act of that person, except if the court finds that —

(A) the person committing the violation of this subsection furnished officials of the United States responsible for investigating false claims violations with all information known to such person about the violation within 30 days after the date on which the defendant first obtained the information;

(B) such person fully cooperated with any Government investigation of such violation; and

(C) at the time such person furnished the United States with the information about the violation, no criminal prosecution, civil action, or administrative action had commenced under this title with respect to such violation, and the person did not have actual knowledge of the existence of an investigation into such violation;

the court may assess not less than 2 times the amount of damages which the Government sustains because of the act of the person. A person violating this subsection shall also be liable to the United States Government for the costs of a civil action brought to recover any such penalty or damages.

In *Hughes Aircraft Co. v. Schumer*, 117 S. Ct. 1871 (1997), the Court held that the 1986 amendment does not apply to actions that took place prior to its enactment.

(A) INTENT

Under the False Claims Act, as amended in 1986, the Government can establish liability without showing that the contractor had a specific intent to defraud as long as the act is committed "knowingly." Not defined in the original Act, "knowingly" is now defined in 31 U.S.C. § 3729(b) as (1) actual knowledge of the information, (2) deliberate ignorance of the truth or falsity of the information, or (3) reckless disregard of the truth or falsity of the information. Further, the Act specifically states that "no proof of specific intent to defraud is required." See *United States v. TDC Management Corp.*, 24 F.3d 292 (D.C. Cir. 1994), stating at 298:

> To prevail under the False Claims Act, the government must prove either that TDC actually knew it had omitted material information from its monthly progress reports or that it recklessly disregarded or deliberately ignored that possibility. The government need not prove that TDC intended to deceive the government by omitting such information.

See also *First Interstate Bank v. United States*, 27 Fed. Cl. 348 (1992) (mere negligence by bank would not satisfy False Claims Act).

Since what constitutes the offense is not an intent to deceive but a knowing presentation of a claim that is either "fraudulent" or simply "false," the fact that the germane Government officials knew of a claim's falsity is not a defense, *Hagood v. Sonoma Cty. Water Agency*, 92 F.2d 1416 (9th Cir. 1991) (Government officials condoned contractor's inaccurate cost allocation violating federal water supply law). However, the Government's knowledge may be relevant in proving that the defendant did not submit a claim with "deliberate ignorance" or "reckless disregard" of the "truth or falsity of the information." For example, in *Chemray Coatings Corp. v. United States*, 29 Fed. Cl. 278 (1993), the court held that the Government's knowledge of the condition of paint pigment contaminated by fire debris for which the contractor received payment under a termination for convenience settlement was relevant to the determination of liability under the Act, stating at 284:

> GSA's knowledge of the contents of the drums is relevant for purposes of section 3729(a). Intent to deceive need not be proved under the Act. . . . What must be proved is that the contractor knowingly presented a false or fraudulent claim. . . . If GSA officials knew that the drums referred to in the termination for convenience settlement contained debris and [the contractor] did not know that its representation of the contents was false, [the contractor] is not guilty of "knowingly" making a false or fraudulent statement to the Government.

(B) DEFINITION OF CLAIM

A "claim" for purposes of the False Claims Act is any demand upon the Government for the payment of money or the transfer of property, *United States v. Tieger*, 234 F.2d 589 (3d Cir.), *cert. denied*, 352 U.S. 941 (1956). For example, in *Tieger* the court found no claim, although the defendant had fraudulently induced the Government to guarantee loans, because no demand for satisfaction of the guarantee had been made against the Government. Similarly, no claim was found in *United States v. Farina*, 153 F. Supp. 819 (D.N.J. 1957), where a bidder had conspired with a Government employee to submit a lower bid after the bids had been opened. While the court recognized that such conduct subverted the competitive bidding process, it found no claim because no contract had been awarded and, hence, no request for payment was made. But any request for payment will constitute a claim. See *United States ex rel. Marcus v. Hess*, 317 U.S. 537 (1943), where the Court found a claim because the contractor submitted a payment voucher on a contract obtained through collusive bidding. The Court held that the Act covered all claims "grounded in fraud." See also *United States ex rel. Luther v. Consolidated Indus.*, 720 F. Supp. 919 (N.D.

Ala. 1989), finding a claim where the defendant submitted false invoices even though Government discovered fraud and withheld payments.

The demand for payment need not be one based on an existing contractual relationship since the Act encompasses all fraudulent attempts to cause the Government to pay out a sum of money, *United States v. Neifert-White Co.*, 390 U.S. 228 (1968) (false application to Federal Commodity Credit Corp. for loan held to be claim). The Act has been held to apply to endorsement and deposit of Government checks known to have been issued by mistake, *United States v. McLeod*, 721 F.2d 282 (9th Cir. 1983); repeated inclusion of rejected items in shipments, *United States v. Milton Marks Corp.*, 240 F.2d 838 (3d Cir. 1957); fraudulently submitted Medicare health insurance claim forms by health care providers, *United States v. Lorenzo*, 768 F. Supp. 1127 (E.D. Pa. 1991); cashing fraudulently obtained social security checks, *United States v. Fowler*, 282 F. Supp. 1 (E.D.N.Y. 1968); and submission of false payroll reports, *United States v. Greenberg*, 237 F. Supp. 439 (S.D.N.Y. 1965).

In a novel case, *United States v. Eilberg*, 507 F. Supp. 267 (E.D. Pa. 1980), the court found a false claim when a Congressman submitted a false certification that toll telephone calls pertained to Government business in order to prevent the Government from demanding reimbursement of funds previously paid.

(C) QUI TAM

Any person may bring a civil action (termed "qui tam") under the Act "for the person and the United States," and the action is "brought in the name of the United States," 31 U.S.C. § 3730(b). The qui tam plaintiff (termed "the relator") files a civil complaint. The complaint is sealed while the Government decides whether to take over the case. If the Government intervenes, it bears primary responsibility for prosecuting the action, 31 U.S.C. § 2730(c)(1). If the Government elects not to proceed with the action, the person who initiated the action has the right to conduct the action, 31 U.S.C. § 3730(c)(3).

A three-part inquiry determines whether jurisdiction exists for a qui tam action: (1) have allegations made by the plaintiff been publicly disclosed; (2) if so, is the disclosed information the basis of the plaintiff's suit; and

(3) if so, is the plaintiff the original source of that information, 31 U.S.C. § 3730(e).

Public disclosure occurs when the allegations upon which the qui tam suit is based are affirmatively disclosed to the public, *United States ex rel. Ramseyer v. Century Healthcare Corp.*, 90 F.3d 1514 (10th Cir. 1996). In this case, the court held that a relator whose allegations were similar to findings made in a routine state audit report did not base her suit upon publicly disclosed information because the report remained in Government files and was never released to the public. In *United States ex rel. v. MK-Ferguson Co.*, 99 F.3d 1538 (10th Cir. 1996), however, the court held that a qui tam suit filed by a former Government auditor was barred under § 3730(e). The court found that the complaint was substantially identical to a Government audit report that had been sent to a state without any restriction on dissemination. Similarly, in *United States ex rel. Fine v. Advanced Sciences, Inc.*, 99 F.3d 1000 (10th Cir. 1996), the court affirmed a district court's holding that a qui tam suit filed by a former Government auditor was barred under § 3730(e). The court found that the action was substantially identical to a memorandum, which contained allegations and transactions set out in a Government audit, that the relator had given to his representative in an unrelated age discrimination case. The court found that the memorandum was made public when it was disclosed to an American Association of Retired Persons representative. In *United States ex rel. Doe v. John Doe Corp.*, 960 F.2d 318 (2d Cir. 1992), the second circuit held that a public disclosure occurred when federal investigators executing a search warrant informed employees of their investigation into fraudulent overcharging. Information obtained through the Freedom of Information Act (FOIA) prior to filing will be considered publicly disclosed, *United States ex rel. Burns v. A.D. Roe Co., Memorandum Op. & Order*, No. 3:94CV-357-H (W.D.Ky. 1996). But see *United States ex rel. Schumer v. Hughes Aircraft Co.*, 63 F.3d 1512 (9th Cir. 1995), where the court held that information cannot be deemed to be publicly disclosed if it is only theoretically available through the FOIA. Information made available through discovery may also be considered to be publicly disclosed. In *United States ex rel. Stinson v. Prudential Ins. Co.*, 944 F.2d 1149 (3d Cir. 1991), the court held that allegations made available through the discovery process are considered to be publicly disclosed even if the material has not been filed with the court. But see *United States ex rel. Springfield Terminal Ry. Co. v. Quinn*, 14 F.3d 645 (D.C. Cir. 1994), holding that discovery material is considered publicly disclosed only when actually filed and not subject to protective order.

The second prong of the jurisdictional test examines whether the disclosed information is the basis of the plaintiff's suit. In *United States ex rel. v. MK-Ferguson Co.*, 99 F.3d 1538 (10th Cir. 1996), the court examined whether a qui tam complaint was based upon a publicly disclosed audit report. The court held that "based upon" means "supported by" and the inquiry is "whether the relator's complaint is 'substantially identical' to the allegations contained in the public disclosure." The court compared the audit report with the complaint and found substantial identity and, thus, barred the action. Similarly, in *United States ex rel. Fine v. Advanced Sciences, Inc.*, 99 F.3d 1000 (10th Cir. 1996), the court found that the plaintiff's qui tam complaint was "based upon" a memorandum that had been publicly disclosed. The court noted that the plaintiff admitted that the costs specified in the memorandum provided the basis for the allegations in his complaint. The plaintiff also stated that his knowledge about the practices of Advanced Sciences came in part from the work papers of the report. The Second Circuit has held that "based upon" should be defined as "the same as," *United States ex rel. Doe v. John Doe Corp.*, 960 F.2d 318 (2d Cir. 1992). Other circuits interpret the phrase "based upon" to mean "derived from." See *United States ex rel. Siller v. Becton Dickinson & Co.*, 21 F.3d 1339 (4th Cir.), *cert. denied*, 513 U.S. 928 (1994), where the court stated that the "derived from" definition would grant jurisdiction when the relator's suit would not be "based upon" public disclosures of which the relator had no knowledge. In this case, the relator learned of the overcharging through an independent source and thus the court held that the information was not based upon public disclosures.

To be considered an original source a plaintiff must have direct and independent knowledge of the allegations in the qui tam suit, 31 U.S.C. § 3730(e)(4). In *United States ex rel. Devlin, Sidicane, & Kodman v. State of California*, 84 F.3d 358 (9th Cir. 1996), the court held that the relators could not meet the original source test. The court found that the relators, while they were a source for the news article, had learned of the fraud from an employee of the defendant and did not have sufficient firsthand information to satisfy the direct knowledge prong of the original source test. In *United States ex rel. v. MK-Ferguson Co.*, 99 F.3d 1538 (10th Cir. 1996), the court held that the plaintiff did not have direct and independent knowledge because the plaintiff did not discover the alleged fraud but, rather, was the supervisor to whom the auditors reported the fraud. A person who is obligated as part of his or her job to investigate and report fraud will not be considered an original source, *United States ex rel. LeBlanc v. Raytheon Co.*, 913 F.2d 17 (1st Cir. 1990); *United States ex rel. Fine v. Chevron*

U.S.A., Inc., 72 F.3d 740 (9th Cir. 1995). See also *United States ex rel. Pentagen Technologies Int'l Ltd. v. CACI Int'l Inc.*, ___ F. Supp. __ (D.C. S.N.Y. 1997) (federal employee responsible for disclosing defects in software provided by contractors cannot qualify as an original source). The D.C. Circuit adds an additional element to the original source test. According to the D.C. Circuit, to qualify as an original source, a relator must have direct and independent knowledge of the information on which the publicly disclosed allegations are based and must have provided that information to the Government before the public disclosure occurred, *United States ex rel. Findley v. FPC-Boron Employees' Club*, 105 F.3d 675 (D.C. Cir. 1997).

Relators are given a share of the Government's monetary recovery and are granted whistleblower protection. The amount depends on whether the Government elects to proceed with the action. 31 U.S.C. § 3730(d) provides that if the Government proceeds with an action, the relator will receive at least 15 percent but not more than 25 percent of the proceeds, "depending upon the extent to which the person substantially contributed to the prosecution of the action." However, the relator is permitted to receive no more than 10 percent of the recovery if the action is based primarily on disclosures of specific information, allegations, or transactions in a criminal, civil, or administrative hearing; in a congressional, administrative, or Government [General] Accounting Office report, hearing, audit, or investigation; or from the news media. If the Government does not take over the case, the relator receives not less than 25 percent nor more than 30 percent of the proceeds. In either case, the relator receives an amount for reasonable expenses plus reasonable attorneys' fees and costs.

There is a disagreement over whether the Government has the right to challenge a settlement in a case in which it chose not to intervene. In *United States ex rel. Killingsworth v. Northrop Corp.*, 25 F.3d 715 (9th Cir. 1994), the court held that the Government had no right to challenge the settlement agreed to between the relator and the defendant. In *Searcy, Trustee for Bankruptcy Estate of C&P Bus. World Inc. v. Phillips Elecs. North America Corp.*, 117 F.3d 154 (5th Cir. 1997), the court took the opposite position, allowing the Government to enter the case to contest the settlement.

(2) Criminal Fraud

As amended by the False Claims Amendments Act of 1986, 18 U.S.C. § 287, provides:

> Whoever makes or presents to any person or officer in the civil, military, or naval service of the United States, or to any department or agency thereof, any claim upon or against the United States, or any department or agency thereof, knowing such claim to be false, fictitious, or fraudulent, shall be imprisoned not more than five years and shall be subject to a fine in the amount provided in this title.

The same issues have arisen under this provision as those discussed with regard to civil fraud.

(A) SPECIFIC INTENT

The courts have held that proof of specific intent to defraud is not necessary to prove criminal intent. Acting with "knowledge that the claim is false or fictitious" is sufficient, *United States v. Barker*, 942 F.2d 585 (9th Cir. 1991); *United States v. Maher*, 582 F.2d 842 (4th Cir. 1978), *cert. denied*, 439 U.S. 1115 (1979); *United States v. Precision Med. Labs., Inc.*, 593 F.2d 434 (2d Cir. 1978). See also *Giuliano v. Everything Yogurt, Inc.*, 819 F. Supp. 240 (E.D.N.Y. 1993) (dishonesty, recklessness, deceptiveness, and deliberate disregard satisfied the intent requirement for fraud); and *United States v. Irwin*, 654 F.2d 671 (10th Cir. 1981) (comparing the language of the False Statements Act — which includes the term "willfully" — and concluding that the False Claims Act intentionally excludes the question of the "state of mind" of the claimant).

(B) DEFINITION OF CLAIM

The courts have followed the rule used in the civil False Claims Act that a criminal false claim can occur only if there is a request for the payment of money or the transfer of property. However, a "valid" request for payment will be a false claim if it is made under a contract obtained by fraudulent means, *United States v. Winchester*, 407 F. Supp. 261 (D. Del. 1975). Presenting a voucher for payment despite knowing that the goods had not been properly inspected and accepted was also held to be a false claim, *United States v. U.S. Cartridge Co.*, 198 F.2d 456 (8th Cir. 1952), *cert. denied*, 345 U.S. 910 (1953).

The Act encompasses claims submitted indirectly to the Government. For example, a claim submitted to a contractor processing Medicare claims for the Government was held to be a false claim, *United States v. Siddiqi*,

959 F.2d 1167 (2d Cir. 1992). Similarly, in *United States v. Beasley*, 550 F.2d 261 (5th Cir.), *cert. denied*, 434 U.S. 863 (1977), the court held that a claim submitted to the state of Louisiana for housing units never constructed was a claim against the Federal Government since federal funds were to be used for the payments.

b. False Statements

The False Statements Act, 18 U.S.C. § 1001, provides:

> Whoever, in any matter within the jurisdiction of any department or agency of the United States knowingly and willfully falsifies, conceals or covers up by any trick, scheme, or device a material fact, or makes any false, fictitious or fraudulent statements or representations, or makes or uses any false writing or document knowing the same to contain any false, fictitious or fraudulent statement or entry, shall be fined under this title or imprisoned not more than five years, or both.

The key elements of the conduct prohibited by this statute are a false "statement" made "knowingly and willfully."

(1) Definition of Statement

The scope of the False Statements Act is considerably broader than that of the False Claims Act. It has been held that the Act covers all false statements that might support fraudulent claims or that might pervert or corrupt the authorized functions of a Government agency to which the statement was made, *United States v. Bedore*, 455 F.2d 1109 (9th Cir. 1972). The Act covers oral as well as written statements and unsworn as well as sworn statements, *United States v. Poindexter*, 951 F.2d 369 (D.C. Cir. 1991). It also covers the omission of information on a certified statement when the information should have been included, *United States v. Irwin*, 654 F.2d 671 (10th Cir. 1981). In *United States v. Johnson*, 937 F.2d 392 (8th Cir. 1991), the court defined this element of the Act as "concealing material facts from a federal agency by trick, scheme, or device." The transferring of acceptance stamps from goods that had been accepted to goods that had not been inspected was held to be a false statement, *United States v. Steiner Plastics Mfg. Co.*, 231 F.2d 149 (2d Cir. 1956). False statements were also found to be made by an employee of a contractor who included false information on a security questionnaire, *United States v. Dale*,

991 F.2d 819 (D.C. Cir. 1993), and by an applicant for employment with a defense contractor who included false statements on the employment application, *United States v. Giarraputo*, 140 F. Supp. 831 (E.D.N.Y. 1956). False statements have also been found to have been made by Government employees when they included false entries on documents during the transaction of Government business, *United States v. Leviton*, 193 F.2d 848 (2d Cir. 1951), *cert. denied*, 343 U.S. 946 (1952); *United States v. Eisenmann*, 396 F.2d 565 (2d Cir. 1968).

The Act applies to matters that involve a Government agency's activity even though the false statement is not made to the Government, *Ebeling v. United States*, 248 F.2d 429 (8th Cir.), *cert. denied sub nom. Ebeling v. United States*, 355 U.S. 907 (1957) (false invoices submitted by subcontractor to contractor under price redeterminable contract). See also *United States v. Popow*, 821 F.2d 483 (8th Cir. 1987) (false identification presented to custom inspector is a matter concerning INS); and *United States v. Herring*, 916 F.2d 1543 (11th Cir. 1990) (Georgia Department of Labor involves activity of United States Department of Labor).

(2) Knowingly and Willfully

To fall within the scope of the Act, the statement must have been made with the intent to deceive, but the Government need not prove an intent to defraud, *United States v. Lichenstein*, 610 F.2d 1272 (5th Cir. 1980). One court stated that the knowing and willful intent requirement was met when the Government proved that the defendant knew that the false statement was necessary for the fraudulent scheme to succeed, *United States v. Beck*, 615 F.2d 441 (7th Cir. 1980). See also *United States v. Cutaia*, 511 F. Supp. 619 (E.D.N.Y. 1981), where criminal intent was found when the defendant was advised of the Government's requirements and deliberately gave answers to avoid compliance.

An honest misinterpretation of Government forms precludes conviction under the Act, *United States v. Weatherspoon*, 581 F.2d 595 (7th Cir. 1978), but reckless disregard of the truthfulness of the statement will be deemed to be a knowing and willful false statement, *United States v. Puente*, 982 F.2d 156 (5th Cir. 1993). If a contractor has followed a reasonable interpretation of a contract, there can be no conviction under the Act, *United States v. Race*, 632 F.2d 1114 (4th Cir. 1980). In *United States v. Anderson*, 579 F.2d 455 (8th Cir.), *cert. denied*, 439 U.S. 980 (1978), the court stated that in the case of an ambiguity, the Government had the burden to "negate any reasonable interpretation that would make the defendant's statement factually correct"; in *United States v. Johnson*, 937 F.2d 392 (8th Cir. 1991), the court stated that in such a case, the Government "will ordinarily be unable" to carry this burden. This rule has also been followed in time by ambiguous regulations, *United States v. Migliaccio*, 34 F.3d 1517 (10th Cir. 1994). See, however, *United States. v. Rule*, 878 F.2d 535 (1st Cir. 1989), refusing to follow the rule in a case involving the interpretation of the Buy American Act and its regulations. In one case, the Government overcame the rule by showing willful deception. See *United States v. Carrier*, 654 F.2d 559 (9th Cir. 1981), stating that the "true holding" of these cases "is that if there is sufficient evidence to show that the defendant acted knowingly and willfully, the question of honest misinterpretation is precluded, unless the form is so vague on its face as to violate the due process clause as a matter of law." Other cases have accepted the rule but found that the contractor's interpretation was not reasonable, *United States v. Dale*, 991 F.2d 819 (D.C. Cir. 1993); *United States v. White*, 765 F.2d 1469 (11th Cir. 1985). Still others have accepted the rule but found that failure to permit expert testimony on the reasonableness of the rule was a "harmless error," *United States v. Barsanti*, 943 F.2d 428 (4th Cir. 1991).

It has been held that the maker of the false statement can be convicted even if that person does not know that the Federal Government is involved in the transaction, *United States v. Wright*, 988 F.2d 1036 (10th Cir. 1993).

(3) Materiality

Materiality in a false statement is a question of law to be determined by the courts. See *United States v. Arcadipane*, 41 F.3d 1 (1st Cir. 1994) (claim for workers' compensation); *United States v. Meuli*, 8 F.3d 1481 (10th Cir. 1993) (application for loan from federal agency); and *United States v. Gribben*, 984 F.2d 47 (2d Cir. 1993) (police officer's statements to assistant attorney general). The test of materiality is whether a statement has a natural tendency to influence, or is capable of influencing, the actions of a federal agency, *Kungys v. United States*, 485 U.S. 759 (1988); *United States v. Gaudin*, 515 U.S. 506 (1995). There is no need to prove either reliance by the Government, *United States v. Hicks*, 619 F.2d 752 (8th Cir. 1980), or actual pecuniary loss by the Government, *United States v. Lichenstein*, 610 F.2d 1272 (5th Cir. 1980). Thus, a criminal false statement can occur even if the Government employee hearing the statement knows that it is false at the time, *United States v. LeMaster*, 54 F.2d 1224 (6th Cir. 1995). In *United States v. Coastal Contracting & Eng'g Co.*, 174 F. Supp. 474 (D. Md. 1959), a contractor knowingly submitted fictitious statements in connection with a change order proposal. They were not relied upon by the Government negotiator because he thought the prices were entirely out of line. Nevertheless, the contractor violated the Act because the misstatements were material and were calculated to induce reliance and action.

c. Truth in Negotiations

The Truth in Negotiations Act (TINA) was added to the Armed Services Procurement Act in 1962 to improve the Government's ability to negotiate contracts and contract modifications by ensuring that the Government had the same factual data as the contractor at the time of price negotiations. The Act does this by requiring that offerors and contractors submit and certify "cost or pricing data" in circumstances where the Government has no way, other than cost analysis, to determine that a price is reasonable. This Act was modified from time to time to include more detailed provisions on the administration and interpretation of this requirement. The requirement was added to the FPASA in 1984, with significantly less detail. The FASA amends these statutes to contain conforming language in 10 U.S.C. § 2306a and 41 U.S.C. § 254b (previously § 254(d)). These statutes now require the submission of cost or pricing data on all negotiated contracts over $500,000 unless any of five exceptions applies. The application of these statutes is considered in more detail in Chapter 9.

These statutes contain elaborate guidance on the contractual remedies available to the Government if a contractor fails to comply with their requirements. See 10 U.S.C. § 2306a(e) and 41 U.S.C. § 254b(e), as follows:

> Price Reductions for Defective Cost or Pricing Data. (1)(A) A prime contract (or change or modification to a prime contract) under which a certificate under subsection (a)(2) is required shall contain a provision that the price of the contract to the United States, including profit or fee, shall be adjusted to exclude any significant amount by which it may be determined by the head of the agency that such price was increased because the contractor (or any subcontractor required to make available such a certificate) submitted defective cost or pricing data.

(B) For the purposes of this section, defective cost or pricing data are cost or pricing data which, as of the date of agreement on the price of the contract (or another date agreed upon between the parties), were inaccurate, incomplete, or noncurrent. If for the purposes of the preceding sentence the parties agree upon a date other than the date of agreement on the price of the contract, the date agreed upon by the parties shall be as close to the date of agreement on the price of the contract as is practicable.

(2) In determining for purposes of a contract price adjustment under the contract provision required by paragraph (1) whether, and to what extent, a contract price was increased because the contractor (or a subcontractor) submitted defective cost or pricing data, it shall be a defense that the United States did not rely on the defective data submitted by the contractor or subcontractor.

(3) It is not a defense to an adjustment of the price of a contract under a contract provision required by paragraph (1) that —

(A) the price of the contract would not have been modified even if accurate, complete, and current cost or pricing data had been submitted by the contractor or subcontractor because the contractor or subcontractor —

(i) was the sole source of the property or services procured; or

(ii) otherwise was in a superior bargaining position with respect to the property or services procured;

(B) the contracting officer should have known that the cost or pricing data in issue were defective even though the contractor or subcontractor took no affirmative action to bring the character of the data to the attention of the contracting officer;

(C) the contract was based on an agreement between the contractor and the United States about the total cost of the contract and there was no agreement about the cost of each item procured under such contract; or

(D) the prime contractor or subcontractor did not submit a certification of cost or pricing data relating to the contract as required under subsection (a)(2).

The statutory provisions are implemented, with almost no additional guidance, in FAR 15.407-1 and two mandatory contract clauses: Price

Reduction for Defective Cost or Pricing Data in FAR 52.215-10 and Price Reduction for Defective Cost or Pricing Data — Modifications in FAR 52.215-11.

(1) When the Government Is Entitled to a Reduction

Although the statutes provide for price reduction only when the effect of the defective data is to increase the contract price by a "significant amount," the Government has been permitted to recover any amount that the price has been increased by a defect. See, for example, *Conrac Corp. v. United States*, 214 Ct. Cl. 561, 558 F.2d 994 (1977), where the court interpreted the statutory language as relieving agencies from having to pursue trivial claims but permitted claims in any amount that an agency considered to be meaningful. In that case, the claim was for an overpricing of $8,050 on a $548,100 contract. In *American Bosch Arma Corp.*, ASBCA 10305, 65-2 BCA ¶ 5280, the board held that a claim for $20,746 on a contract over $15 million was significant. In *Kaiser Aerospace & Elecs. Corp.*, ASBCA 32098, 90-1 BCA ¶ 22,489, *recons. denied*, 90-2 BCA ¶ 22,695, the board awarded a price reduction of $5,527.82 on orders under a basic ordering agreement of $2,754,581, holding that even if this might "appear to be insignificant," it was bound to award that amount by *Conrac*.

(2) Government Reliance on Defective Data

In order to obtain a price reduction, the Government must demonstrate that the contract price negotiated by the parties was increased because of Government reliance on defective data. The Government is aided in this task by the "natural and probable consequence" rule developed by the Armed Services Board in *Lambert Eng'g Co.*, ASBCA 13338, 69-1 BCA ¶ 7663; *McDonnell Douglas Corp.*, ASBCA 12786, 69-2 BCA ¶ 7897. This rule holds that the natural and probable consequence of the furnishing of defective data is a dollar-for-dollar increase in the negotiated price. This rule has been termed a "rebuttable presumption," *American Mach. & Foundry Co.*, ASBCA 15037, 74-1 BCA ¶ 10,409. However, it has the effect of requiring the contractor, in order to avoid a price reduction, to demonstrate that the price was not impacted by the defective data, *Sylvania Elec. Prods., Inc. v. United States*, 202 Ct. Cl. 16, 479 F.2d 1342 (1973). See *EDO Corp.*, ASBCA 41448, 93-3 BCA ¶ 26,135, where the price was reduced by the full amount of a reduced price that a supplier gave a subcontractor, because the contractor could not furnish evidence to overcome the presumption that the contract price had been impacted by this amount.

The natural and probable consequence rule has led to a number of rulings that the contractor was responsible for a dollar-for-dollar price increase. See *Hughes Aircraft Co.,* ASBCA 46321, 97-1 BCA ¶ 28,972; *Limpiezas Corona S.A.*, ASBCA 45504, 96-1 BCA ¶ 28,137; *P.A.L. Sys. Co.*, GSBCA 10858, 91-3 BCA ¶ 24,259; *Millipore Corp.*, GSBCA 9453, 91-1 BCA ¶ 23,345; *Kaiser Aerospace & Elecs. Corp.*, ASBCA 32098, 90-1 BCA ¶ 22,489, *recons. denied*, 90-2 BCA ¶ 22,695; *Etowah Mfg. Co.*, ASBCA 27267, 88-3 BCA ¶ 21,054; *Boeing Military Airplane Co.*, ASBCA 33168, 87-2 BCA ¶ 19,714; *Sylvania Elec. Prods., Inc.*, ASBCA 13622, 70-2 BCA ¶ 8387, *aff'd*, 202 Ct. Cl. 16, 479 F.2d 1342 (1973); and *Aerojet-General Corp.*, ASBCA 12264, 69-1 BCA ¶ 7664, *modified*, 70 BCA ¶ 8140. This result is now called for in DFARS 215.804-7(b)(2), which states:

> Unless there is clear evidence to the contrary, the contracting officer may presume the defective data were relied on and resulted in a contract price increase equal to the amount of the defect plus related overhead and profit or fee. The contracting officer is not expected to reconstruct the negotiation by speculating as to what would have been the mental attitudes of the negotiating parties if the nondefective data had been known.

However, contractors have been successful in demonstrating lack of reliance in several cases. See, for example, *Texas Instruments, Inc.*, ASBCA 30836, 89-1 BCA ¶ 21,489; and *Hughes Aircraft Co.*, ASBCA 30144, 90-2 BCA ¶ 22,847, where the board found that the Government would not have used current prices of materials because the contract price had been negotiated using average prices of materials based on accumulated costs after the materials went through the manufacturing process. Thus, the board concluded that no price reduction was called for because the Government would not have used the data had it been disclosed. See also *Levinson Steel Co.*, ASBCA 16520, 73-2 BCA ¶ 10,116 (contracting officer testified he would not have used data); *Muncie Gear Works, Inc.*, ASBCA 18184, 75-2 BCA ¶ 11,380 (auditor would not have used data because he rejected similar data as inaccurate); and *Rose, Beaton & Rose*, PSBCA 459, 80-1 BCA ¶ 14,242 (Government would not have reduced its offer because it contained far less overhead than indicated by undisclosed data).

Several defenses demonstrating that the Government did not rely on defective data have been barred by the language in 10 U.S.C. § 2306a(3) and 41 U.S.C. § 254b(3). Thus, it may no longer be possible to argue that there was no reliance because the contractor would not have accepted a lower price. This argument had been used successfully in *Universal Restoration, Inc. v. United States*, 798 F.2d 1400 (Fed. Cir. 1986). See also *Luzon Stevedoring Corp.*, ASBCA 14851, 71-1 BCA ¶ 8745 (contractor made take-it-or-leave-it offer); and *American Mach. & Foundry Co.*, ASBCA 15037, 74-1 BCA ¶ 10,409 (contractor in strong bargaining position). Similarly, in *J.S. Latsis Group of Cos.*, ENGBCA 4276, 86-2 BCA ¶ 18,853, the board denied any price reduction for nondisclosure of detailed information on overhead because the contracting officer had negotiated overhead rates on a gross basis without regard to the contents of the overhead pool.

(3) Computing the Price Reduction

In computing the amount of a price reduction, the court or board must determine (1) the dollar amount that would have been included in the price had the data been disclosed and (2) the dollar amount that was included in the contract price because of the nondisclosure. The determination of the latter amount has led to significant controversy. In *Sperry Corp. Computer Sys.*, ASBCA 29525, 88-3 BCA ¶ 20,975, *aff'd sub nom. Unisys Corp. v. United States*, 888 F.2d 841 (Fed. Cir. 1989), the board used the labor dollars that the Government's documents indicated had been included in the contract price. The board rejected the contractor's argument that a lower amount should be used because the parties had arrived at the price through a "bottom line" settlement. In *Grumman Aerospace Corp.*, ASBCA 35188, 90-2 BCA ¶ 22,842, the board used the labor rates agreed to by the parties in the negotiation of the contract price rather than the labor rate originally proposed by the contractor because "a contractor is not liable for overstated costs that were eliminated during the price negotiation process." In that case, the board rejected the Government's argument that the labor hours in the contract price would have been derived from labor hours on a prior contract projected down a learning curve. The board found that the parties had concluded during the price negotiation that difficulties in performing the work would prevent learning and had therefore used the same number of hours for the new contract as had been incurred on the previous contract. In *Etowah Mfg. Co.*, ASBCA 27267, 88-3 BCA ¶ 21,054, the board used the Government estimate prior to the negotiation rather than the considerably higher amount included in the contract price. The board apparently concluded that the contractor's nondisclosure of relevant data was not the cause of the Government's willingness to include a higher amount in the price and, therefore, that the contractor was not responsible for any amount greater than the difference between the Government estimate and the amount derived from the undisclosed data.

The dollar amount that would have been included in the contract price had the data been disclosed has also created controversy. In *Sperry Corporation Computer System*, the board used the undisclosed labor dollars incurred in manufacturing the product 18 months before the negotiations even though there was evidence that the parties had agreed in the negotiations that a higher figure would be required for the instant contract because of decreases in volume. The precise amount in the undisclosed data was also used in *Etowah Manufacturing*. In earlier cases, the boards had been more willing to base the computation of this figure on the record of the actual negotiations. For example, in *Aerojet-General Corp.*, ASBCA 12873, 69-1 BCA ¶ 7585, the board noted that the parties had arrived at the contract price by splitting the difference in their final negotiation positions. The board therefore assumed that the defective data would have decreased the Government's negotiation position by the amount of the defect and that the parties would have split the difference — resulting in a price reduction of one-half of the amount of the defective data. Similarly, in *Bell & Howell Co.*, ASBCA 11999, 68-1 BCA ¶ 6993, the board concluded that had the data been disclosed, the parties would not have been able to negotiate a firm-fixed-price contract. It therefore assumed that they would have negotiated an incentive contract with a 60/40 share and awarded a price reduction in the amount of 60 percent of the defect. For a later case using the negotiation history, see *Aerojet Ordnance Tenn.*, ASBCA 36089, 95-2 BCA ¶ 27,922, where the board concluded that the parties would not have arrived at a price reduced by the entire amount of the defects in submitting the data. The board reached a compromise reduction based on the figures generated by each party in a precontract technical analysis.

In order to make a full computation of the impact of the price reduction on the contract price, the price must be reconstructed using the pricing structure that the parties used in the original negotiation. Thus, the computation must also include all elements of the contractor's costs that would normally be added to the cost item that is adjusted because of the defective data. See, for example, *Grumman Aerospace Corp.*, ASBCA 35188, 90-2 BCA ¶ 22,842, where the board computed the price reduction for defective data on labor dollars by adding all categories of work that were estimated as percentages of labor dollars (manufacturing engineering, sustaining engineering, program management, and foreign sales) plus all applicable overheads, general and administrative expense, and profit. Similarly, in *Kaiser Aerospace & Elecs. Corp.*, ASBCA 32098, 90-1 BCA ¶ 22,489, *recons. denied*, 90-2 BCA ¶ 22,695, the price reduction for defective data on labor rates was computed by adding overhead, general and administrative expense, warranty, and profit.

(4) OFFSET

Early in the litigation of price reductions for defective cost or pricing data, it was determined that a contractor was entitled, up to the amount of any price reduction, to offset any amount due to underpricing that had occurred because of defective data in the same pricing action, *Cutler-Hammer, Inc. v. United States*, 189 Ct. Cl. 76, 416 F.2d 1306 (1969); *Lockheed Aircraft Corp. v. United States*, 193 Ct. Cl. 86, 432 F.2d 801 (1970). This rule was incorporated in the statutes in 10 U.S.C. § 2306a(e) and 41 U.S.C. § 254b(e), as follows:

> (4)(A) A contractor shall be allowed to offset an amount against the amount of a contract price adjustment under a contract provision required by paragraph (1) if —
>
> > (i) the contractor certifies to the contracting officer (or to a designated representative of the contracting officer) that, to the best of the contractor's knowledge and belief, the contractor is entitled to the offset; and
> >
> > (ii) the contractor proves that the cost or pricing data were available before the date of agreement on the price of the contract (or price of the modification) and that the data were not submitted as specified in subsection (a)(3) before such date.
>
> (B) A contractor shall not be allowed to offset an amount otherwise authorized to be offset under subparagraph (A) if —
>
> > (i) the certification under subsection (a)(2) with respect to the cost or pricing data involved was known to be false when signed; or
> >
> > (ii) the United States proves that, had the cost or pricing data referred to in subparagraph (A)(ii) been submitted to the United States before the date of agreement on the price of the contract (or price of the modi-

> fication), the submission of such cost or pricing data would not have resulted in an increase in that price in the amount to be offset.

Offsets are permitted only when the contractor proves that there was an understatement of "factual pricing data," *J.S. Latsis Group of Cos.*, ENGBCA 4276, 86-2 BCA ¶ 18,853. In that case, the board found that the evidence was very unclear, but if there were any errors to which a low price could be attributed, they were errors of judgment, not errors in cost or pricing data. Compare *Hughes Aircraft Co.*, ASBCA 46321, 97-1 BCA ¶ 28,972, where offsetting mistakes in the same packages of data as the nondisclosed reduced cost were permitted as offsets.

Offsets may not be made between different contracts, *Norris Indus., Inc.*, ASBCA 15442, 74-1 BCA ¶ 10,482; *Minnesota Mining & Mfg. Co.*, ASBCA 20266, 77-2 BCA ¶ 12,823, or between unrelated contract modifications, *Muncie Gear Works, Inc.*, ASBCA 18184, 75-2 BCA ¶ 11,380. Neither can offsets lead to a price increase by the contractor, *Baldwin Elecs., Inc.*, ASBCA 19683, 76-2 BCA ¶ 12,199 (offsets exceeding the claimed price reduction led to sustaining of contractor's appeal), or be used when the omitted costs have been recovered from the Government through inclusion in an overhead account, *Aerojet Ordnance Tenn.*, ASBCA 36089, 95-2 BCA ¶ 27,922. However, offsets are proper even when the contractor has intentionally understated the dollar amounts in the data, *Rogerson Aircraft Controls*, ASBCA 27954, 85-1 BCA ¶ 17,725, *aff'd*, 785 F.2d 296 (Fed. Cir. 1986) (Government knew of understatements and was not "hindered or deceived" by them). A contractor has also been permitted to offset its omitted in-house costs of completing work from an overstated subcontract price for the same work, *TGS Int'l, Inc.*, ASBCA 31120, 87-2 BCA ¶ 19,683, *recons. denied*, 87-3 BCA ¶ 19,989.

(5) Defective Subcontractor Data

If subcontractor cost or pricing data have been submitted to the Government before the negotiation of the contract price of a firm-fixed-price contract, the contractor is liable for defects in that data, *Lockheed Aircraft Corp. v. United States*, 193 Ct. Cl. 86, 432 F.2d 801 (1970). In that case, the court held the contractor liable even though the subcontractor data had been submitted directly to the Government, not to the contractor. The court reasoned that the contractor's liability was dictated by the contract clause requiring price reductions. See also *McDonnell Aircraft Co.*, ASBCA

44504, 97-1 BCA ¶ 28,977 (contractor liable for not furnishing updated subcontractor information when it had furnished original subcontractor data with its proposal). If subcontractor cost or pricing data are not submitted to the contractor until after the negotiation of the price of a firm-fixed-price contract, there is no contractor liability for a price reduction because there could be no Government reliance on that data.

The contractor is expected to include price reduction clauses in all subcontracts under cost-reimbursement or fixed-price-incentive or redeterminable contracts, and price reductions obtained through such clauses are expected to be credited to the costs billed to the Government, FAR 15.407-1(f)(2). This applies even though the subcontractor's cost or pricing data were never submitted to the Government or used as the basis for the original contract price.

(6) Interest and Penalties

The statutes require the addition of interest and penalties in certain cases where the Government has overpaid the contractor as a result of defective cost or pricing data, as stated at 10 U.S.C. § 2306a and 41 U.S.C. § 254b:

> (f) Interest and penalties for certain overpayments. (1) If the United States makes an overpayment to a contractor under a contract with an executive agency subject to this section and the overpayment was due to the submission by the contractor of defective cost or pricing data, the contractor shall be liable to the United States —
>
> (A) for interest on the amount of such overpayment, to be computed —
>
> (i) for the period beginning on the date the overpayment was made to the contractor and ending on the date the contractor repays the amount of such overpayment to the United States; and
>
> (ii) at the current rate prescribed by the Secretary of the Treasury under section 6621 of the Internal Revenue Code of 1986; and
>
> (B) if the submission of such defective data was a knowing submission, for an additional amount equal to the amount of the overpayment.
>
> (2) Any liability under this subsection of a contractor that submits cost or pricing data but refuses to submit the certification required by subsection

(a)(2) with respect to the cost or pricing data shall not be affected by the refusal to submit such certification.

d. Contract Disputes Act of 1978

The Contract Disputes Act of 1978, 41 U.S.C. § 605(c)(1), provides that each claim over $100,000 must be certified with regard to four specific elements:

> For claims of more than $100,000, the contractor shall certify that the claim is made in good faith, that the supporting data are complete and accurate to the best of his knowledge and belief, that the amount requested accurately reflects the contract adjustment for which the contractor believes the government is liable, and that the certifier is duly authorized to certify the claim on behalf of the contractor.

Neither the statutes nor regulations specifically require the submission of supporting data. All that is expressly required is that the contractor certify that "supporting data" are accurate and complete. Although a certification that the data are "complete" could be interpreted as a requirement for submission, there has been disagreement over whether the contractor is *affirmatively* required to submit data. See *Joseph P. Mentor*, GSBCA 6757, 85-1 BCA ¶ 17,887, where the board held that the certification was not intended to force contractors to submit evidence in support of their claims, but was merely an "honesty" requirement designed to discourage inflated claims. See, however, *LaBarge Elecs.*, ASBCA 44401, 93-2 BCA ¶ 25,617, where the board held that supporting data for a claim cannot be limited to data concerning the amount but must also include data in support of entitlement. See Chapter 13 of Cibinic and Nash, *Administration of Government Contracts* (3d ed., 1995) for an in-depth discussion of the certification requirements under the Contract Disputes Act.

The Contract Disputes Act contains additional sanctions for the misrepresentation of facts or fraud when submitting a claim, as provided at 41 U.S.C. § 604:

> If a contractor is unable to support any part of his claim and it is determined that such inability is attributable to misrepresentation of fact or fraud on the part of the contractor, he shall be liable to the Government for an amount equal to such unsupported part of the claim in addition to all costs to the Government attributable to the cost of reviewing said part of his claim. Li-

> ability under this subsection shall be determined within six years of the commission of such misrepresentation of fact or fraud.

The Act contains no definition of fraud. However, 41 U.S.C. § 601(7) defines "misrepresentation of fact" as follows:

> The term "misrepresentation of fact" means a false statement of substantive fact, or any conduct which leads to a belief of a substantive fact material to proper understanding of the matter in hand, made with intent to deceive or mislead.

It is not possible to enforce this section in litigation before the appeals boards under the Contract Disputes Act because of the following language in 41 U.S.C. § 605(a):

> Each claim by a contractor against the government relating to a contract and each claim by the government against a contractor relating to a contract shall be submitted within 6 years after the accrual of the claim. The preceding sentence does not apply to a claim by the government against a contractor that is based on a claim by the contractor involving fraud. . . . The authority of this subsection shall not extend to a claim or dispute for penalties or forfeitures prescribed by statute or regulation which another Federal agency is specifically authorized to administer, settle or determine.

Thus, the boards of contract appeals have refused to rule on a counterclaim for the penalty prescribed in § 604, *Comada Corp.*, ASBCA 26613, 83-2 BCA ¶ 16,681 ("actions to enforce the Government's rights under [Section 604] would be solely the responsibility of the Department of Justice and would be instituted by the United States in a court of competent jurisdiction"); or on a defense that the claim was fraudulent, *Schmalz Constr., Ltd.*, AGBCA 86-207-1, 91-3 BCA ¶ 24,183 ("[I]t is sufficient for the Board to determine whether statements in a claim are correct or incorrect. The Board does not need to determine whether incorrect statements were made knowingly or with an intent to deceive."). Following this view that the appeals boards have no jurisdiction over claims involving Section 604, a board has also refused to hear a contractor's claim that the contracting officer improperly assessed the penalty prescribed in Section 604, *Warren Beaves*, DOTBCA 1324, 83-1 BCA ¶ 16,232. Another board denied jurisdiction over a contractor's claim because the contractor had pled guilty to fraudulently computing the amount of the claim, *P.H. Mechanical Corp. v. General Servs. Admin.*, GSBCA 10567, 94-2 BCA ¶ 26,785.

Counterclaims for the Section 604 penalty can be asserted in the Court of Federal Claims in the same manner that all fraud counterclaims are asserted in that court, *Simko Constr., Inc. v. United States*, 852 F.2d 540 (Fed. Cir. 1988). Such counterclaims are generally asserted along with counterclaims under the False Claims Act and the False Statements Act, *Chemray Coatings Corp. v. United States*, 29 Fed. Cl. 278 (1993); *Tyger Constr. Co. v. United States*, 28 Fed. Cl. 35 (1993). See *JANA, Inc. v. United States*, 34 Fed. Cl. 447 (1995), where the court held that the Government's counterclaim alleging fraud under the CDA was timely because the Act's six-year statute of limitations for fraud could begin to run no earlier than the submission of the contractor's certified claim, regardless of when the conduct rendering the contractor's false claim allegedly occurred.

e. Certification under 10 U.S.C. § 2410

Another statute dealing with certifying supporting data for requests for equitable adjustment and requests for relief under P.L. 85-804 on DOD contracts is 10 U.S.C. § 2410. This statute was amended by the FASA to make it clear that the provision applies only to requests for equitable adjustment or for relief under P.L. 85-804. As amended, 10 U.S.C. § 2410 establishes the following certification requirement:

> (a) Certification Requirement.— A request for equitable adjustment to contract terms or request for relief under Public Law 85-804 (50 U.S.C. 1431 et seq.) that exceeds the simplified acquisition threshold may not be paid unless a person authorized to certify the request on behalf of the contractor certifies, at the time the request is submitted, that —
>
> > (1) the request is made in good faith, and
> >
> > (2) the supporting data are accurate and complete to the best of that person's knowledge and belief.

Note that this statute also does not contain a clear requirement for the submission of data. The FASA also repealed the DOD-unique claim certification requirement contained in 10 U.S.C. § 2410e, thus leaving the Contract Disputes Act claim certification as the single Government-wide standard.

2. Types of Illegal Conduct

In the 1980s and 1990s, Government contractors have been heavily investigated and prosecuted for failure to deal openly and honestly with the Federal Government. The major types of conduct that have led to such accusations of criminality are covered in this section.

a. Product Substitution

Product substitution generally refers to attempts by the contractor to deliver to the Government a product that does not conform to the contract requirements. Such substitution can occur by mismarking products, deviating from specifications, and other types of conduct that may indicate an intention to deceive the Government in the performance of the contract. The Government has clear contractual remedies when such substitution occurs. Thus, it may obtain a price reduction equivalent to the amount of costs saved plus overhead and profit, *Santa Fe Engrs., Inc.*, ASBCA 44906, 93-1 BCA ¶ 25,298 (substitution of less expensive door); *Arnold M. Diamond, Inc.*, ASBCA 38974, 92-2 BCA ¶ 24,869 (use of fewer expansion joints than called for by specifications); *J.S. Alberici Constr. Co.*, GSBCA 10630, 92-1 BCA ¶ 24,392 (substitution of less expensive doors); *Bruce Andersen Co.*, ASBCA 29412, 89-2 BCA ¶ 21,872 (omission of work called for by contract). It may also void final acceptance if the substitution constitutes fraud, *BMY v. United States*, 38 Fed. Cl. 109 (1997); *D & H Constr. Co.*, ASBCA 37482, 89-3 BCA ¶ 22,070 (substitution of refrigerators with counterfeited certification labels), or gross mistake amounting to fraud, *Catalytic Eng'g & Mfg. Corp.*, ASBCA 15257, 72-1 BCA ¶ 9342 (substitution of material in product). There are several reasons for strict enforcement of these contract requirements, including the need to obtain requisite quality levels to ensure that the agency mission is performed, to ensure the safety of personnel using the equipment, and to maintain the integrity of the procurement process. Even if the substitute is equal to that specified in the contract, acceptance may harm the procurement system, which is based on all competitors offering to furnish only the product called for in the contract specifications. Allowing offerors to substitute products according to their own judgment would defeat the concept of bidding on an equal basis. See *Ideal Restaurant Supply Co.*, VACAB 570, 67-1 BCA ¶ 6237, where the board found that the Government was justified in rejecting equivalent supplies that did not meet contract specifications and noted that allowing the contractor to substitute aluminum for nickel alloy and stainless steel in steam kettle parts could have a negative effect on the competitive bidding process. Similarly, in *J.L. Malone & Assocs.*, VABCA 2335, 88-3 BCA ¶ 20,894, *aff'd*, 879 F.2d 841 (Fed. Cir. 1989), the Government rejected a contractor's substitution of a technically equivalent computer in the installation of a fire alarm system. The board stated that the preservation of the integrity of the competitive procurement system was more important than any benefits that could derive from replacing the specified computer with an even more advanced one at no extra cost to the Government.

Product substitution may also subject contractors to criminal or civil sanctions under the False Claims Act, criminal sanctions under the False Statements Act, and sanctions under other criminal statutes. The DOD Inspector General Semiannual Report to Congress, Apr. 1 through Sept. 30, 1993, identified product substitution as a critical issue of concern, stating at page 3-1:

> Since the infusion of inferior, substandard parts and equipment renders the military forces vulnerable to serious safety threats, the DoD will continue to give allegations of product substitution the highest investigative priority.

A few of these cases are prosecuted under the criminal provisions of the False Claims Act, 18 U.S.C. § 287. See *Imperial Meat Co. v. United States*, 316 F.2d 435 (10th Cir.), *cert. denied*, 375 U.S. 820 (1963), where a false claim was found when the contractor substituted an inferior grade of meat on a DOD contract and then submitted an invoice for the contract price. However, most product substitution cases are brought under the civil provisions of the False Claims Act 31 U.S.C. § 3729. In *United States v. National Wholesalers*, 236 F.2d 944 (9th Cir. 1956), *cert. denied*, 353 U.S. 930 (1957), the contractor indicated to the Government that it would supply brand name regulators, but instead manufactured the regulators itself and attached false brand name labels before delivery. The court found the contractor liable for a false claim even though the regulators were in fact equal. In *United States v. Aerodex, Inc.*, 469 F.2d 1003 (5th Cir. 1972), the court found a false claim when the contractor knowingly substituted aircraft bearings that differed from the contract specifications, even though there was no proof that they were inferior. See also *United States v. Advance Tool Co.*, 86 F.3d 1159 (8th Cir. 1996), where the court found a false claim when the contractor did not deliver brand name tools but supplied tools that it had reversed engineered and that had been manufactured by small machine shop operators. Other statutes used to prosecute product substitution include the

False Statements Act, 18 U.S.C. § 1001; the conspiracy statutes, 18 U.S.C. § 286 and § 371; the mail and wire fraud statutes, 18 U.S.C. § 1341 and § 1343; and the Racketeer Influenced and Corrupt Organizations Act, 18 U.S.C. §§ 1961–1968.

The DOD Inspector General Semiannual Report to Congress, Oct. 1, 1993 through Mar. 31, 1994, reflected this emphasis by including four product substitution cases among the summaries of the significant fraud cases resolved during the six-month period. Two of the cases involved contractors entering into settlements for violations of the False Claims Act. In one case, the contractor supplied electrical cable that did not meet contract specifications and was not "lowsmoke," as the contractor claimed. In the second case, the contractor presented reconditioned reel-to-reel computer tapes as new. The tapes had numerous data storage and programming problems and caused lengthy computer downtime. Two other product substitution cases resulted in guilty pleas. In one case, the contractor pleaded guilty to conspiracy to conceal flaws and defects in the assembly of the Maverick missile launcher. Another case involved parts purchased for use in support equipment for the space shuttle, the Hubble space telescope, and the USS Kitty Hawk aircraft carrier. In this case, the contractor pleaded guilty to defrauding customers by selling substandard O-rings and ordinary commercial fasteners and fittings. The contractor used inadequate plating and baking processes on fasteners, falsified certifications, provided O-rings that could not withstand high temperatures, and represented itself as having an elaborate quality control system.

b. Mischarging/Accounting Fraud

Mischarging is the term used to describe a particular type of fraud involving the accounting treatment of costs by contractors. Mischarging is the false description and the improper charging of costs to a Government contract. The contractual remedy for mischarging is the disallowance of the costs including all costs incurred because of the mischarging. See FAR 31.205-15(b), providing:

> Costs incurred in connection with, or related to, the mischarging of costs on Government contracts are unallowable when the costs are caused by, or result from, alteration or destruction of records, or other false or improper charging or recording of costs. Such costs include those incurred to measure or otherwise determine the magnitude of the improper charging, and costs

incurred to remedy or correct the mischarging, such as costs to rescreen and reconstruct records.

Mischarging can arise in several instances, including improper allocation of costs and charging of expressly unallowable costs to a contract. If a contractor includes an "expressly unallowable" cost in a proposal to settle indirect costs, the agency must assess a penalty against the contractor, in addition to disallowance of the cost, in the amount of the cost claimed plus interest on those costs, 10 U.S.C. § 2324(b); 41 U.S.C. § 256(b). These sections also provide that the penalty will be double the amount of the claimed cost if it had been "determined to be unallowable in the case of such contractor before the submission of such proposal."

Mischarging is also subject to criminal and civil sanctions under the False Claims Act as well as other criminal sanctions. In *United States v. McGunnigal*, 151 F.2d 162 (1st Cir.), *cert. denied*, 326 U.S. 776 (1945), a criminal conspiracy was found where welders and counters who manufactured and constructed ships under a cost-reimbursement contract inflated payroll costs. See also *United States v. Maher*, 582 F.2d 842 (4th Cir. 1978), *cert. denied*, 439 U.S. 1115 (1979), where false claims requesting payments under a time-and-materials contract were submitted. The accountant involved was instructed to inflate labor hours on monthly billings, prepare new time sheets that conformed to the changes, trace over employees' signatures on the new time sheets, and destroy the originals. More recently, in *United States v. Sperry Corp.*, Civ. 89-2472 (E.D.N.Y. 1991), contractor employees falsely filled out time cards indicating work on one contract when the work was properly chargeable to other costs. See also *United States v. Richmond*, 700 F.2d 1183 (8th Cir. 1983). For an in-depth analysis of other mischarging cases, see Graham, "Mischarging: A Contract Dispute or a Criminal Fraud?" 15 Pub. Cont. L.J. 208 (1985).

c. Fraudulent Pricing

As discussed previously, the Truth in Negotiations Act provides contractual remedies when certified cost or pricing data are not accurate, complete, and current. However, the failure to submit complete, current, and accurate cost or pricing data has been treated as fraud in only a few cases. There are two types of defective pricing situations that are often treated as instances of fraud — the falsification of cost or pricing data and the submission of bad estimates.

(1) FRAUDULENT DATA

For many years, *United States v. Foster Wheeler Corp.*, 447 F.2d 100 (2d Cir. 1971), which affirmed a district court decision that the contractor had committed civil fraud by submitting defective cost or pricing data, was the only reported decision in this area. More recently, in *United States v. Poarch*, 878 F.2d 1355 (11th Cir. 1989), the circuit court affirmed the conviction of a defense firm's contracts administrator for conspiracy to defraud the United States and for criminal false statements. Fraud was found where an administrator (1) told an employee to charge time to a wrong account in order to build up labor hours and (2) omitted current labor-hour data from the submission of cost or pricing data that had been required by the contracting officer. A number of fraud cases in this area involve the creation and submission of false data by the contractor. See *United States v. Barnette*, 800 F.2d 1558 (11th Cir. 1986), *cert. denied*, 480 U.S. 935 (1987), where the contractor created false payroll records and false invoices from bogus vendors to inflate its proposed contract prices; and *United States v. Busher*, 817 F.2d 1409 (9th Cir. 1987), where the contractor falsified data relating to performance of work by subcontractors. The DOD Inspector General pamphlet IGDPH 4200.50, *Criminal Defective Pricing and the Truth in Negotiations Act* (March 1988), reported four similar cases where the contractors pleaded guilty to fraud. In these cases, the contractors created false labor records and false vendor information to support high estimates of the cost of performance. These fraud cases, involving the *submission* of false data, concern conduct that goes considerably beyond the mere failure to disclose complete cost or pricing data to the Government, and they should be contrasted with normal defective pricing cases where the Government obtains a price adjustment because of the *nonsubmission* of cost or pricing data.

Cases litigating the issue of whether the Government should obtain a price reduction for defective pricing appear to be distinguishable from those involving prosecution for civil or criminal fraud. Price reduction cases largely deal with technical interpretations of the submission requirement. In most instances, the contractor has made major submissions but has omitted some discrete data. The fraud cases generally involve either falsification of data or a scheme to obtain a higher price. Thus, if a contractor makes a serious effort to disclose the cost or pricing data used in preparing its proposal, it is probably not in jeopardy of being charged with fraud. However, a contractor that adopts practices that permit regular nondisclosure of such data is taking an unreasonable business risk. If the Government concludes that higher prices are being obtained through the use of such practices, a charge of fraud is likely.

(2) False Estimate

Contractors have also been held liable for submitting other than their best estimates as certified on the Standard Form 1411 (Rev. 7-87), stating, "This proposal . . . reflects our best estimates and/or actual costs as of this date." See *United States v. Singer Co.*, 889 F.2d 1327 (4th Cir. 1989), accepting the validity of this type of civil fraud. Similarly, in *United States v. Sperry Corp.*, Civ. 89-2472 (E.D.N.Y. 1991), the Government alleged that the contractor submitted a low estimate on the original contract and, after "buying in," submitted high estimates on the follow-on contracts where the contractor was the sole source. In *United States v. Bicoastal Corp.*, Cr. No. 92-CR-261 (N.D.N.Y. 1992), a contractor pleaded guilty to charges arising from the submission of inflated, fraudulent labor estimates on negotiated sole source contracts for flight simulators. The contractor had submitted cost estimates that included amounts allocated for fictitious jobs and personnel that purported to be necessary costs. The contractor certified that each cost estimate was its "best estimate," while it routinely concealed a lower estimate. In response to industry criticism of these cases, Standard Form 1411 (Rev. 10-95) was revised in 1995 to state "This proposal . . . reflects our estimated and/or actual costs as of this date." This removes the issue of whether the estimate submitted was the "best" estimate but does not affect the question of whether the estimate was fraudulently compiled.

Other fraud cases also involve the submission of estimates of a contract's cost of performance when the contractor is aware that it will incur much lower costs. See *United States v. White*, 765 F.2d 1469 (11th Cir. 1985), where the contractor submitted an estimate of the cost of fully performed work under change orders that was far higher than the actual costs that had been incurred and recorded in its accounting data. The court held that the contractor had represented to the Government that its estimate reflected actual costs. See also *United States v. Pimental & Duroyd Mfg. Co.*, 810 F.2d 366 (2d Cir. 1987), where the contractor obtained quotations from eight vendors but submitted only the highest quote to the contracting officer while buying at the low price.

D. Obtaining Information Improperly

There are several sanctions on disclosing or obtaining information related to the procurement process. 18 U.S.C. § 1905 imposes criminal sanctions on any Government employee that discloses trade secrets and other proprietary data obtained from any person or organization. The procurement integrity provisions of the Office of Procurement Policy Act of 1989, 41 U.S.C. § 423, prohibit any person from disclosing "contractor bid or proposal information" or "source selection information" before contract award, 41 U.S.C. § 423(a). There may also be improper conduct involved in obtaining information about a competitor.

1. Disclosure of Confidential Information

18 U.S.C. § 1905 provides:

> Whoever, being an officer or employee of the United States or of any department or agency thereof, any person acting on behalf of the Office of Federal Housing Enterprise Oversight, or agent of the Department of Justice as defined in the Antitrust Civil Process Act (15 U.S.C. 1311–1314), publishes, divulges, discloses, or makes known in any manner or to any extent not authorized by law any information coming to him in the course of his employment or official duties or by reason of any examination or investigation made by, or return, report or record made to or filed with, such department or agency or officer or employee thereof, which information concerns or relates to the trade secrets, processes, operations, style of work, or apparatus, or to the identity, confidential statistical data, amount or source of any income, profits, losses, or expenditures of any person, firm, partnership, corporation, or association; or permits any income return or copy thereof or any book containing any abstract or particulars thereof to be seen or examined by any person except as provided by law; shall be fined not more than $1,000, or imprisoned not more than one year, or both; and shall be removed from office or employment.

The conviction of a Government employee under 18 U.S.C. § 1905 for improper disclosure of information was affirmed in *United States v. Wallington*, 889 F.2d 573 (5th Cir. 1989) (Act not overly broad to constitute a valid criminal statute).

2. Disclosure of Bid or Proposal Information or Source Selection Information

The Clinger-Cohen Act of 1996 amended the Procurement Integrity Act, 41 U.S.C. § 423, to streamline the provisions on disclosure of information. The former Act contained two prohibitions on disclosing information. First, it prohibited "procurement officials" from knowingly disclosing proprietary or source selection information to "persons." Second, it prohibited "persons" with authorized or unauthorized access to proprietary or source selection information from knowingly disclosing that information to "persons." The new Act consolidates this into a single provision, 41 U.S.C. § 423(a), prohibiting a "person" from knowingly disclosing "contractor bid or proposal information" or "source selection information" before award of a contract. The "persons" covered are defined in the Act, 41 U.S.C. § 423(a)(2), as any person who

> (A) is a present or former official of the United States, or a person who is acting or has acted for or on behalf of, or who is advising or has advised the United States with respect to, a Federal agency procurement; and
>
> (B) by virtue of that office, employment, or relationship has or had access to contractor bid or proposal information or source selection information.

The term "official" is defined in 41 U.S.C. § 423(f)(7) as (1) an officer as defined in 5 U.S.C. § 2104, (2) an employee as defined in 5 U.S.C. § 2105, and (3) a member of the uniformed forces as defined in 5 U.S.C. § 2101(3). FAR 3.104-3 adds to this the category of "special Government employees" as defined in 18 U.S.C. § 202.

The new statute thus gives a new test as to what persons are covered by the Act. They are persons who have either "acted" or "advised" regarding a federal agency procurement and have obtained information through that contact with the procurement. Neither the statute nor the implementation of this part of the Act in FAR 3.104-4(a) contain any guidance on the meaning of the terms "acted" or "advised," with the apparent effect that this rule applies to persons who have acted or advised no matter how small their contact with the procurement. This would seem to apply this part of the Act to virtually anyone who obtained information in the course of participating in the procurement, unless he or she was a total bystander that obtained information in the course of observing the procurement.

The Act applies only to "federal agency procurement," and this term is defined in 41 U.S.C. § 423(f)(4) to mean only acquisitions using competitive procedures. This is an important reduction from the coverage of the prior Act because officials who have participated in sole source procurements or contract modifications are not covered by the new Act. This provision is implemented in FAR 3.104-4(a). However, FAR 3.104-5(a) contains a broader statement: "Except as specifically provided for in this subsection, no person or other entity may disclose contractor bid or proposal information or source selection information to any person other than a person authorized, in accordance with applicable agency regulations or procedures, by the head of the agency or designee, or the contracting officer, to receive such information." This paragraph is probably a drafting mistake because it is not limited to "federal agency procurement" but, as it stands, it appears to substantially broaden the scope of the Act. It may have been intended to reflect the fact that 18 U.S.C. § 1905 continues to prohibit disclosure of proprietary information.

The information protected from disclosure is essentially the same as under the prior Act — the only change being one of terminology with "contractor bid or proposal information" replacing "proprietary information." The term "contractor bid or proposal information" is defined in 41 U.S.C. § 423(f)(1) as

> any of the information submitted to a Federal agency as part of or in connection with a bid or proposal to enter into a Federal agency procurement contract, if that information has not been previously made available to the public or disclosed publicly;
>
> > (A) Cost or pricing data (as defined by section 2306a(h) of title 10, United States Code, with respect to procurements subject to that section, and section 304A(h) of the Federal Property and Administrative Services Act of 1949 (41 U.S.C. 254b(h)), with respect to procurements subject to that section).
> >
> > (B) Indirect costs and direct labor rates.
> >
> > (C) Proprietary information about manufacturing processes, operations, or techniques marked by the contractor in accordance with applicable law or regulation.
> >
> > (D) Information marked by the contractor as "contractor bid or proposal information," in accordance with applicable law or regulation.

The term "source selection information" is defined in 41 U.S.C. § 423(f)(2) as

> any of the following information prepared for use by a Federal agency for the purpose of evaluating a bid or proposal to enter into a Federal agency procurement contract, if that information has not been previously made available to the public or disclosed publicly:
>
> (A) Bid prices submitted in response to a Federal agency solicitation for sealed bids, or lists of those bid prices before public bid opening.
>
> (B) Proposed costs or prices submitted in response to a Federal agency solicitation, or lists of those proposed costs or prices.
>
> (C) Source selection plans.
>
> (D) Technical evaluation plans.
>
> (E) Technical evaluations of proposals.
>
> (F) Cost or price evaluations of proposals.
>
> (G) Competitive range determinations that identify proposals that have a reasonable chance of being selected for award of a contract.
>
> (H) Rankings of bids, proposals, or competitors.
>
> (I) The reports and evaluations of source selection panels, boards, or advisory councils.
>
> (J) Other information marked as "source selection information" based on a case-by-case determination by the head of the agency, his designee, or the contracting officer that its disclosure would jeopardize the integrity or successful completion of the Federal agency procurement to which the information relates.

However, Section 4304(h) of the new statute contains a number of "savings provisions," as follows:

(h) Savings Provisions. — This section does not —

(1) restrict the disclosure of information to, or its receipt by, any person or class of persons authorized, in accordance with applicable agency regulations or procedures, to receive that information;

(2) restrict a contractor from disclosing its own bid or proposal information or the recipient from receiving that information;

(3) restrict the disclosure or receipt of information relating to a Federal agency procurement after it has been canceled by the Federal agency before contract award unless the Federal agency plans to resume the procurement;

(4) prohibit individual meetings between a Federal agency official and an offeror or potential offeror for, or a recipient of, a contract or subcontract under a Federal agency procurement, provided that unauthorized disclosure or receipt of contractor bid or proposal information or source selection information does not occur;

(5) authorize the withholding of information from, nor restrict its receipt by, Congress, a committee or subcommittee of Congress, the Comptroller General, a Federal agency, or an inspector general of a Federal agency;

(6) authorize the withholding of information from, nor restrict its receipt by, the Comptroller General of the United States in the course of a protest against the award or proposed award of a Federal agency procurement contract; or

(7) limit the applicability of any requirements, sanctions, contract penalties, and remedies established under any other law or regulation.

These provisions are implemented at FAR 3.104-5(e) and (f). It seems clear that these rules should not prevent open communication between contracting agencies and potential offerors regarding the work to be procured and the procurement strategy before solicitations are issued as long as specific finalized source selection plans and technical evaluation plans are not revealed.

The former Act prohibited a "competitive contractor" from knowingly soliciting or obtaining from an officer or employee of an agency "proprietary or source selection information" prior to the award of a contract. The new Act, 41 U.S.C. § 423(b), substantially broadens this rule by prohibiting a "person" from knowingly obtaining "contractor bid or proposal information" or "source selection information" before the award of the "Federal agency procurement" to which the information relates. It applies the prohibition to any contractor, other business entity, or individual that obtains information even if that person is not participating in the procurement. It also seems to apply the prohibition without regard to the source of the information, with the result that it could arguably be a violation to obtain the information from a newspaper reporter or some other person not connected with the procurement. The only narrowing of the rule is that it is no longer a violation of the Act to *solicit* information if the information is not obtained.

3. Information about Competitors

The techniques for gaining information about competitors are diverse and may or may not be proper. These techniques range from the benign, such as reading a competitor's sales brochure, to the potentially criminal, such as business espionage. In *Compliance Corp. v. United States*, 22 Cl. Ct. 193 (1990), *aff'd*, 960 F.2d 157 (Fed. Cir. 1992), the offeror approached employees of the incumbent contractor, who was competing for a follow-on services contract, to obtain detailed information on how the incumbent contractor was performing the work and to discover the contents of the incumbent's proposal for the follow-on work. Upon learning of this conduct, the contracting officer disqualified the offeror, and the Comptroller General sustained this action, *Compliance Corp.*, Comp. Gen. Dec. B-239252, 90-2 CPD ¶ 126, *recons. denied*, 90-2 CPD ¶ 435. The Claims Court agreed with this decision, stating at 204:

> The court finds actual or attempted "industrial espionage" to be outside the realm of normal business practices, and the contracting officer is entitled to disqualify those who engage in such conduct, not only to protect the integrity of the contracting process, but also to deter others from similar conduct.

Both the Comptroller General and the GSBCA have disqualified companies that have improperly obtained information during the procurement process. In *Litton Sys., Inc.*, 68 Comp. Gen. 422 (B-234060), 89-1 CPD ¶ 450, *recons. denied*, 68 Comp. Gen. 677, 89-2 CPD ¶ 228, the Comptroller disqualified an offeror that had obtained source selection information through a "marketing consultant." See also *AT&T Communications, Inc.*,

GSBCA 9252-P, 88-2 BCA ¶ 20,805, where the board disqualified an offeror that had been given the competitive range prices by a Government employee.

E. Conspiracy

It is a crime for two or more persons to agree to (1) commit any offense against the United States, 18 U.S.C. § 371, or (2) defraud the United States, 18 U.S.C. § 286, if any of the persons performs an act to effect the conspiracy. The unlawful object of a conspiracy could be the violation of any civil or criminal statute, *United States v. Feola*, 420 U.S. 671 (1975). A conspiracy to commit bribery is clearly included, and conspiracies involving gratuities or conflicts of interest also fall within 18 U.S.C. § 371, *United States v. Razete*, 199 F.2d 44 (6th Cir.), *cert. denied*, 344 U.S. 904 (1952). However, it is not necessary for the agreed-upon action to be a violation of statute; an agreement to defraud the United States in any manner would qualify. It is not necessary that the Government lose money or property as a result of the fraud. All that is required is that the Government's "legitimate official action and purpose shall be defeated by misrepresentation, chicane or . . . overreaching," *Hammerschmidt v. United States*, 265 U.S. 182 (1924).

CHAPTER 2

CONTRACT FORMATION PRINCIPLES

Although the Federal Government's purchasing procedures are governed extensively by statutes and regulations, the creation or modification of a contractual relationship between the Government and contractor is, for the most part, determined by common-law legal rules. See *Priebe & Sons, Inc. v. United States*, 332 U.S. 407 (1947). As these rules have been applied to Government contract cases, a body of federal law has developed as the primary source of law in this area. This federal law is generally consistent with the legal rules summarized in the *Restatement of Contracts*. The *Uniform Commercial Code* (U.C.C.), although not binding upon the Federal Government, is also used to determine the rights and liabilities of the contracting parties when not inconsistent with federal law.

An enforceable promise is the essential requirement for a contract. See *Restatement, Second, Contracts* § 1, which defines "contract" as follows:

> a promise or a set of promises for the breach of which the law gives a remedy, or the performance of which the law in some way recognizes as a duty.

This chapter focuses on the legal principles used by courts and boards of contract appeals to determine whether the Government has entered into a relationship involving one or more enforceable promises. It first considers whether the parties have entered into a contractual relationship — whether they have manifested mutual assent. It then deals with whether their agreement is binding. Where applicable, this chapter includes a discussion of contract formation issues involving electronic transactions.

I. MANIFESTATION OF MUTUAL ASSENT

In order to create a contractual relationship, the parties must each assent to the same terms and conditions. This mutual assent occurs when one party manifests an intent to be bound to a set of terms and conditions and the other party timely agrees to that relationship. Most often this process can be analyzed in terms of an offer and an acceptance. The party making the offer, referred to as the "offeror," communicates to the other party an intention to form a contract. To accept the offer forming a contract, the other party must assent in the manner invited or authorized. The manifestation of mutual assent may also occur absent an identifiable offer or acceptance. These concepts are stated in *Restatement, Second, Contracts* § 22, which provides:

> (1) The manifestation of mutual assent to an exchange ordinarily takes the form of an offer or proposal by one party followed by an acceptance by the other party or parties.
>
> (2) A manifestation of mutual assent may be made even though neither offer nor acceptance can be identified and even though the moment of formation cannot be determined.

See also U.C.C. § 2-204.

This section first covers basic requirements, specifically capacity to contract and contractual intent and definiteness. It then analyzes the rules of offer and acceptance as they have been applied to the various types of contractual relationships entered into by the Federal Government. The section concludes with a discussion of the circumstances where the actions of the parties create an implied-in-fact contract.

A. Basic Requirements

There are a number of basic requirements which must be satisfied in order for parties' communications to result in contractual obligations. Both parties must possess the legal capacity to contract, they must have contractual intent, and their agreement must be sufficiently definite to permit enforcement by a court or board of contract appeals.

1. Capacity to Contract

Capacity to contract refers to the common law principle which provides that a person cannot be bound unless that person "has capacity to incur at least voidable contractual duties," *Restatement, Second, Contracts* § 12. This rule is applicable to Government contracts although its application is not common. There are also a number of special Government contracts rules which deal with the same or analogous issues. For example, questions concerning the legal capacity of Government agencies to contract are dealt with in Chapter 1, Section II under the topic "contracting powers." Similarly, those seeking to deal with the Government are subject to rules concerning eligibility, suspension and debarment. See Chapter 4, Section II. In some cases, the term "capacity to contract" has been used, mistakenly, to refer to the question of whether a specific officer, employee or agent has the authority to bind an offeror. See *Video Eng'g Co.*, DOTCAB 72-5, 72-1 BCA ¶ 9432. Questions concerning such authority are dealt with in Chapter 1, Section III under the topic "authority of Government personnel," and Section VI under the topic "authority of contractor personnel."

a. Nature of Capacity to Contract

Determination of a party's capacity to contract depends on whether the party is a natural person, a partnership, a joint venture, or a corporation. For natural persons, *Restatement, Second, Contracts* § 12 states:

> A natural person has the legal capacity to contract unless he or she is:
>
> (a) under guardianship, or
>
> (b) an infant, or
>
> (c) mentally ill or defective, or
>
> (d) intoxicated.

However, this does not mean that such parties cannot enter into contracts. If a contracting party has no knowledge, or reason to know, that the other party is mentally ill or intoxicated, the lack of capacity will not prevent the formation of a contract. Further, a contract will be found if the party fails to disaffirm the transaction within a reasonable time after recovering from the mental illness or intoxication. With respect to infancy, the other party's notice or reason to know of the infancy is not required in order to permit the infant from rescinding the agreement. However, the failure to do so within a reasonable time after reaching the age of majority will permit the other party to enforce the contract, *Lonchyna v. Brown*, 491 F. Supp. 1352 (N.D. Ill. 1980) (armed services enlistment contract). These types of agreements are commonly referred to as "voidable."

Corporations are artificial persons and their contracting capacity is determined by their charters or articles of incorporation. Agreements which are not within the authority of such documents are called "ultra vires" and are considered to be *void ab initio*, meaning that a contract never came into being, *Rose Island Co. v. United States*, 105 Ct. Cl. 192 (1945). There, the court permitted the Government to cancel an agreement for the purchase of stone on the grounds that the corporation it dealt with had no legal capacity to contract. The court found that the corporation's charter authorized it to conduct a public entertainment and amusement park but not to sell stone from a quarry which it owned. The laws of the state of incorporation will determine whether a corporation has the capacity to contract, *BLH, Inc. v. United States*, 2 Cl. Ct. 463 (1983); *Mather Constr. Co.v. United States*, 201 Ct. Cl. 219, 475 F.2d 1152 (1973). Thus, if questions arise concerning capacity to contract, a certificate from the proper agency of the state of incorporation will be used to determine capacity, *Valley Constr. Co.*, Comp. Gen. Dec. B-184391, 75-2 CPD ¶ 393.

Most of the cases challenging corporate capacity involve situations where a corporation's charter has been suspended for failure to pay taxes or failure to file reports. State corporation laws contain elaborate provisions governing the conduct of a corporation whose charter has been suspended for such reasons. See *Easterbrook/Ramco*, ASBCA 42176, 94-2 BCA ¶ 26,658, where the board dismissed an appeal without prejudice because the company had entered into the contract during a period when its charter had been suspended but the applicable California law appeared to permit the company to sue for restitution of any benefits it had conferred on the party to the contract. Compare *Micro Tool Eng'g, Inc.*, ASBCA 31136, 86-1 BCA ¶ 18,680, where the board dismissed an appeal with prejudice because the company had entered into a contract at a time when it had been "involuntarily dissolved" for failure to file annual reports and the time for reinstatement under Florida law had expired. The same result was reached in *West Point Research, Inc.*, ASBCA 27185, 83-2 BCA ¶ 16,845 (applying Connecticut law); and *Services, Inc.*, ASBCA 42929, 93-1 BCA ¶ 25,514 (applying South Carolina law).

Loss of corporate capacity may also preclude a contractor from bringing a suit or appeal concerning a contract that was entered into when the company had capacity. See *Computer Prods., Int'l, Inc. v. United States*, 26 Cl. Ct. 518 (1992), where a suit was dismissed because it was filed during a period when the company's charter had been suspended by the state of California and the Contract Disputes Act statute of limitations had run during the period of suspension. Compare *Ricmar Eng'g, Inc.*, ASBCA 44260, 97-2 BCA ¶ 29,084 (board rejected motion to dismiss because the company had been reinstated by the state of California and the board construed state law to require no prejudicial action to companies that had filed suits during suspension); *Teller Entl. Sys., Inc.*, ASBCA 42092, 93-1 BCA ¶ 25,330 (board rejected motion to dismiss because the appeal had been filed within three years of dissolution, as permitted by Massachusetts law); *Allied Production Management, Inc.*, DOTBCA 2466, 92-1 BCA ¶ 24,585 (board rejected motion to dismiss because California law permitted suits during suspension if company subsequently reinstated).

Questions concerning the contracting capacity of a partnership or a joint venture would be determined by reference to the partnership or joint venture agreement. See GSAR 552.270-6 providing that for leases of real property, "a copy of either the partnership agreement or current Certificate of Limited Partnership" shall be furnished if required by the Government. FAR 4.102(d) provides as follows with respect to joint ventures:

> A contract with joint venturers may involve any combination of individuals, partnerships, or corporations. The contract shall be signed by each participant in the joint venture in the manner prescribed in paragraphs (a) through (c) above for each type of participant. When a corporation is participating, the contracting officer shall verify that the corporation is authorized to participate in the joint venture.

As long as an organization possesses the capacity to contract, it is not necessary to spell out that capacity in the contract, *Pacific Far East Line, Inc.*, ASBCA 7629, 1963 BCA ¶ 3835.

b. Time for Determining Capacity to Contract

A number of cases have involved the question of whether a corporation's capacity to contract is to be determined at time of bidding or time of award. In *West Point Research, Inc.*, ASBCA 27185, 83-2 BCA ¶ 16,845, no valid contract was found where the company had capacity at the time of bid opening but had lost capacity, through revocation of its corporate charter, at the time of award. Conversely, in *Casper Constr. Co.*, Comp. Gen. Dec. B-253887, 93-2 CPD ¶ 247, a corporation had been dissolved at the time of bid opening. It later became reinstated and under the laws of the state of incorporation, and the reinstatement was made retroactive to the time of dissolution. Nevertheless, the Comptroller General held that the bid could not be accepted. The Comptroller General rationalized this position as follows:

> As a general rule, a sealed bid award may not be made to any entity different from that which submitted the bid, and where a bid represents that it was submitted by a corporation, it should be disregarded if no such corporation exists. *General Chem. Servs. Inc.*, B-241595, Jan. 30, 1991, 91-1 CPD ¶ 94. Otherwise, irresponsible parties could undermine sound competitive bidding procedures by submitting bids that could be avoided or backed up by real principals as their interests might dictate. *Id.* We believe Casper's bid was properly rejected. At the time of bid opening, on June 7, the corporation had been dissolved under the laws of Oregon since January 20, and was not reinstated until after award on June 15. Consequently, at the time of bid opening Casper was not a legally sufficient corporation for bidding purposes.

The Comptroller General reached the opposite result in a line of cases holding that bids may be accepted even though submitted in a corporate name prior to the date of incorporation. See *PHE/Master, Inc.*, 70 Comp. Gen. 689 (B-238367.5), 91-2 CPD ¶ 210, stating at 695:

> As PHE/Master pointed out to the Air Force in its letter dated May 22, 1990, there is ample legal authority permitting an entity, formed for the purpose of performing a particular government contract, to submit a proposal in the name of the corporation prior to formally incorporating. *See Telex Communications, Inc., Mil-Tech Sys., Inc.*, B-212385; B-212385.2, *supra* [84-1 CPD ¶ 127, *aff'd*, 84-1 CPD ¶ 440]; *see also Protectors, Inc.*, B-194446, Aug. 17, 1979, 79-2 CPD ¶ 128; *Oscar Holmes & Son, Inc.*; *Blue Ribbon Refuse Removal Inc.*, B-184099, Oct. 24, 1975, 75-2 CPD ¶ 251. At a minimum, these cases provided PHE/Master with a good faith basis for submitting its initial proposal under the corporate name. Accordingly, we find no reasonable basis for the Air Force to conclude that PHE/Master engaged in misrepresentation by submitting its proposal in the name of the corporation that was formally incorporated after proposal submission.

It is difficult to understand this distinction. It would seem that the offeror, by not going forward with the incorporation, would have the same ability to avoid any obligation as would the bidder in *Casper*. In *Tours, Lodging and Conferences, Inc.*, Comp. Gen. Dec. B-270478, 96-1 CPD ¶ 144, the Comptroller General held that an award to a joint venture was proper even though one of the venturers was a corporation which had been dissolved at time of submission of the offer but had been reinstated prior to award. The fact that the other joint venturer possessed the capacity to contract would appear to justify this result.

The Comptroller General has also dealt with the situation where an award was made to an offeror, which at the time of proposal submission and the time of award, had its corporate status automatically terminated for "an apparently inadvertent failure to pay an annual registration fee," *Triad Research, Inc.*, Comp. Gen. Dec. B-225793, 87-2 CPD ¶ 16. The Comptroller General held that the award was proper since the award was made to the "same entity" which submitted the offer. See also *Forbes Aviation, Inc.*, Comp. Gen. Dec. B-248056, 92-2 CPD ¶ 58. In these cases, the Comptroller General relied on state statutes which provided "that the corporation is responsible for any liabilities incurred during the period of termination, including 'contracts, acts, matters and things made, done or performed in its name and on its behalf by its officers and agents prior to its reinstatement, as if its articles of incorporation had remained at all times in full force and effect.' "

2. Contractual Intent and Definiteness

In order for a contract to be formed, the parties must possess contractual intent and their agreement must be sufficiently definite to be enforced, *Modern Sys. Technology Corp. v. United States*, 24 Cl. Ct. 360 (1991), *aff'd*, 979 F.2d 200 (Fed. Cir. 1992). While the absence of definite terms may be evidence that the parties do not intend to enter into a contractual relationship, their existence does not necessarily require a finding that the parties had contractual intent.

a. Contractual Intent

Whether the parties have indicated an intent to enter into a contractual relationship will be determined on a case-by-case basis, taking into consideration all the facts and circumstances surrounding the transaction. See *Mayfair Constr. Co.*, NASABCA 478-6, 80-2 BCA ¶ 14,772 ("entire context" of Government granting of contractor's request for deviation was contractual).

(1) Preliminary Negotiations

One of the problems in determining contractual intent is whether the communications between the parties are merely preliminary negotiations contemplating future contractual agreements or whether they indicate an intent to presently enter into a contract.

Occasionally, the Government announces publicly its desire to receive proposals for specified programs, services, or commodities. They may be included in statutes, regulations, circulars, or other media. Normally, these announcements are treated as preliminary inquiries or requests for offers, *Primary Metal & Mineral Corp. v. United States*, 214 Ct. Cl. 90, 556 F.2d 507 (1977) (Department of Treasury regulation stating that all "requests" for silver bullion in exchange for silver certificates be directed to the fiscal assistant secretary held not to be an offer). If the statement merely reflects a future intent or a desire to begin negotiations, it will not be considered an offer. Such statements are invitations to begin negotiations or to submit offers and cannot be accepted to form a contract for goods and services. See *Elkhorn-Hazard Coal Co. v. Kentucky River Corp.*, 20 F.2d 67 (6th Cir. 1927).

However, they may constitute offers if they are sufficiently definite. In *Radium Mines, Inc. v. United States*, 139 Ct. Cl. 144, 153 F. Supp. 403 (1957), the Atomic Energy Commission issued a circular expressing the Commission's desire to stimulate domestic production of uranium ore. The circular contained information as to the minimum price to be paid for ore, the time period in which the commission would purchase ore, grade specifications, and application instructions. The court held that the circular constituted an offer since it was sufficient to induce performance. Similarly, in *Griffin v. United States*, 215 Ct. Cl. 710 (1978), the service secretary published procedures and guidelines requesting meritorious suggestions relating to Minuteman Missile silos. Since the service secretary adopted suggestions that benefited the service, the court held that a valid contract was created. But see *Hayes v. United States*, 20 Cl. Ct. 150 (1990), which held that although a suggestion of a former Postal Service employee was implemented as part of the Employee Suggestion Program, a contractual relationship was not formed between the former employee and the Government. The court found that the statutory and procedural requirements necessary to elevate such an agreement to the level of a contract had not been met. Compare *Cutler-Hammer, Inc. v. United States*, 194 Ct. Cl. 788, 441 F.2d 1179 (1971), where a Treasury Department regulation regarding the sale of silver at a specific price was held not to be an offer because it was interpreted not to contain a promise by the Government.

(2) NON-CONTRACTUAL AGREEMENTS

The Government enters into several different types of agreements which it specifically indicates are not contracts. FAR 16.702 describes "basic agreements," which are instruments of "understanding" between agencies and contractors on contract clauses that will be used in future contracts between the parties. FAR 16.702(a) states that "[a] basic agreement is not a contract." "Basic ordering agreements," described in FAR 16.703, contain not only contract clauses, but a description of supplies or services to be provided and methods for "pricing, issuing, and delivering future orders" under the agreement. FAR 16.703(a) states that "[a] basic ordering agreement is not a contract." In addition, FAR 16.703(c) states:

> *Limitations.* A basic ordering agreement shall not state or imply any agreement by the Government to place future contracts or orders with the contractor or be used in any manner to restrict competition.

"Blanket purchase agreements," described in FAR 13.303, are agreements that agencies establish with contractors for placing orders within the simplified acquisition threshold. FAR 13.303-3(a)(2) requires that such agreements contain a statement that the Government "is obligated only to the extent of authorized purchases actually made."

Modern Sys. Technology Corp. v. United States, 24 Cl. Ct. 360 (1991), *aff'd*, 979 F.2d 200 (Fed. Cir. 1992), dealt with a basic pricing agreement used by the Postal Service. The court concluded that the "plain language" of the agreement "appears to be contemplative of future contracts." It found "no language indicating any present intent that either party be bound." The court went on to state at 362–63:

> According to the Procurement Manual and its companion publication, the Procurement Handbook, a basic pricing agreement is similar to an ordering agreement, the difference being that "ordering agreements are used for large dollar amounts and basic pricing agreements are used for simplified purchases. The similarity is that they both set up terms and conditions prior to the need for supplies and services so that when the need arises, delivery time can be shortened." United States Postal Service Procurement Handbook 5.1-4 (June 1988). The Procurement Manual states that "[a]n ordering agreement is not itself a contract. It is a written agreement negotiated between a purchasing activity and a contractor that contains terms and conditions applying to future contracts (orders) between the parties." United States Procurement Manual 5-10 (Oct. 1987).

> The view of the BPA is echoed in other federal regulations applicable to basic agreements. The Government commonly uses basic agreements, such as the BPA in this case, to facilitate procurement of various products and services. The Federal Acquisitions Regulations (FAR) System "prescribes policies and procedures for establishing and using basic agreements and basic ordering agreements." 48 C.F.R. § 16.701 (1988). Both "basic agreements" and "basic ordering agreements" contain "contract clauses applying to future contracts between the parties during [the] term [of the contract]." 48 C.F.R. §§ 16.702(a), 16.703(a) (1988). The principal difference between the two is that a basic ordering agreement, in addition to containing the elements of a basic agreement, also describes the goods or services to be furnished, the methods by which prices are determined, and the parties authorized to issue orders to the contractor. Because the BPA in the present case contained these additional elements, it appears to be more representative of a "basic ordering agreement."
>
> The regulations list a number of terms that a basic ordering agreement must contain. The BPA in the present case appears to have been drafted so as to comply with these regulations because all of these terms are included. The applicable regulations go on to state that "[a] basic ordering agreement is not a contract," 48 C.F.R. § 16.703.3(a), and "shall not state or imply any agreement by the Government to place future contracts or orders with the contractor or be used in any manner to restrict competition." 48 C.F.R. § 16.703(c).

Another type of agreement envisioning future transactions is a "trading partner agreement." To engage in electronic commerce (Electronic Data Interchange (EDI) or Electronic Funds Transfer (EFT)), a contractor must become a trading partner, which means that it has agreed to exchange business information electronically. In order to become a trading partner, a contractor must first register with the Government's Central Contractor Registration. It then must execute a trading partner agreement which prescribes the general procedures and policies when using EDI. In addition to a trading partner agreement, some agencies require a trading partner to sign another agreement setting forth the standard contract clauses for electronic solicitations. For example, the Defense Industrial Supply Center (DISC) requires all trading partners to sign a simplified purchase agreement which contains solicitation provisions, certification requirements, and award clauses.

b. Definiteness

The parties' agreement must be sufficiently complete and certain in its terms so that the promises and performances to be rendered can be reasonably determined. However, this does not mean that there be complete agreement on all terms. See *Penn-Ohio Steel Corp. v. United States*, 173 Ct. Cl. 1064, 354 F.2d 254 (1965), where the court found a contract because there had been agreement on "major matters in issue." Similarly, in *Town of North Bonneville, Wash. v. United States*, 5 Cl. Ct. 312 (1984), the court found a binding agreement in spite of the need for future agreements because the parties had indicated a present intent to be bound.

Restatement, Second, Contracts § 33 recognizes these concepts, providing:

> (1) Even though a manifestation of intention is intended to be understood as an offer, it cannot be accepted so as to form a contract unless the terms of the contract are reasonably certain.
>
> (2) The terms of a contract are reasonably certain if they provide a basis for determining the existence of a breach and for giving an appropriate remedy.
>
> (3) The fact that one or more terms of a proposed bargain are left open or uncertain may show that a manifestation of intention is not intended to be understood as an offer or as an acceptance.

See *Western States Constr. Co.*, ASBCA 16003, 72-2 BCA ¶ 9508 (contract found to exist even though price of contract was never agreed upon).

(1) AGREEMENTS TO AGREE

In *Folk Constr. Co.*, ENGBCA 5839, 93-3 BCA ¶ 26,094, the board found that the parties mutually agreed to rescind the contract. The Government argued that the condition that the unit prices would be determined through future negotiations made the bargain unenforceable. The board rejected this defense, stating at 129,726:

> Agreements in which certain terms are reserved for future negotiation ("agreements to agree"), while not favored traditionally, have been gaining approval where the criteria for resolution of the terms to be negotiated are sufficiently definite. The reservation of some terms for future agreement

> does not necessarily preclude a finding that a binding agreement has been made. However, this arrangement impliedly places an obligation on the parties to negotiate in good faith in an effort to resolve the outstanding issues. Courts then will evaluate the *bona fides* of the parties toward negotiation in order to ascertain when a breach has occurred if the remaining issues are not resolved.

See also *Aviation Contractor Employees, Inc. v. United States*, 945 F.2d 1568 (Fed. Cir. 1991), where the court reversed the Armed Services Board's holding that a contract modification containing a requirement for determination of the price in the future was not binding because of lack of certainty. The court found sufficient indications of the basis of the future pricing in the previous negotiations between the parties and held that the Government was bound by the modification. To be binding, a contract generally must be "sufficiently definite to permit determination of breach and remedies," *Modern Sys. Technology Corp. v. United States*, 24 Cl. Ct. 360 (1991), *aff'd*, 979 F.2d 200 (Fed. Cir. 1992). In *Trauma Serv. Group, Ltd. v. United States*, 33 Fed. Cl. 426 (1995), the court held that CHAMPUS Memoranda of Understandings (MOUs) were unenforceable agreements because they did not set forth any remedy for breach, did not demonstrate definitively the Government's intent to be bound, and contained no method for determining a breach. However, in *Total Med. Management, Inc. v. United States*, 104 F.3d 1314 (Fed. Cir. 1997), the Government, relying on *Trauma*, argued CHAMPUS MOUs were unenforceable agreements because they set forth no method for determining breach. The Federal Circuit disagreed, finding that the contractor was to provide discounted medical services while the hospital was to provide free space and support staff and encourage military dependents to use the services. The CHAMPUS regulatory scheme provided payment details. The court held that the determination of damages or specific performance would flow naturally from a breach of these duties. The Federal Circuit decided the appeal from the Court of Federal Claim's decision in *Trauma* on the same day it issued *Total*. See *Trauma Serv. v. United States*, 104 F.3d 1321 (Fed. Cir. 1997). Here, the Federal Circuit stated that an MOU can be an enforceable contract, but found it unnecessary to decide whether the specific MOU in *Trauma* was such a contract because the health care provider had failed to show that the MOU created a duty for the Government to pay the salary of the X-ray technician that the provider furnished.

(2) LETTER CONTRACTS

The terms of a letter contract have been found sufficiently definite to bind the parties even though the parties failed to definitize the contract. In *Saul Bass & Assocs. v. United States*, 205 Ct. Cl. 214, 505 F.2d 1386 (1974), the Government issued a letter of intent incorporating a contractor's design agreement, stating a monetary limitation and proposing the execution of a formal contract. The contractor performed, but no formal contract was agreed upon. The court found contractual agreement on the basis of the letters exchanged between the parties. For another case providing a remedy when the contractor completed performance but the parties failed to definitize the letter contract, see *Sanders Assocs. v. United States*, 191 Ct. Cl. 157, 423 F.2d 291 (1970). See also *Wilco Floor Serv., Inc. v. United States*, 197 Ct. Cl. 902 (1972) (plaintiff entitled to costs from beginning of letter-contract term as opposed to date of definitized contract); *Kavourvas, Inc.*, Comp. Gen. Dec. B-226782, Oct. 20, 1987, *Unpub.* (even though expected definitized contract never came into existence, Comptroller General ordered claimant be paid according to terms of letter contract).

B. Offer and Acceptance

Restatement, Second, Contracts § 24 defines "offer" as follows:

> An offer is the manifestation of willingness to enter into a bargain, so made as to justify another person in understanding that his assent to that bargain is invited and will conclude it.

Restatement, Second, Contracts § 50(1) defines "acceptance" as

> a manifestation of assent to the terms thereof made by the offeree in a manner invited or required by the offer.

The time, manner, form, and any other conditions associated with the method of acceptance are generally within the control of the offeror and may be specified in the offer. When the offeror requests that the acceptance be in the form of a return promise the acceptance creates what is termed a "bilateral contract." The offeror may also request that the acceptance be in the performance of an act or forbearance; this been referred to as a "unilateral contract."

Except for simplified acquisitions, the Government prefers to have the contractor make the offer, thereby obtaining the favored position of offeree. The Government then has full control of when the contract is formed because it will not be bound to that contract until it manifests its acceptance. This is extremely important as it enables the contracting officer to determine which offer is most advantageous to the Government and whether funds are available before deciding to accept. The Government controls the terms of the offer by requiring that offerors agree to submit their offers in accordance with the terms provided in the solicitation.

1. Solicitation and Submission of Offers or Quotations

a. Sealed Bid Procurement

In sealed bid procurement, the Government solicits offers by issuing an Invitation for Bids (IFB) on Standard Form 33 (FAR 53.301-33). See Chapter 5, **Figure 5-1**. The IFB is not an offer by the Government to purchase goods or services. The prospective contractor's bid is intended to be the offer and the Government's award is the acceptance. See 42 Comp. Gen. 490 (B-150798) (1963), which held that a bid submitted in response to a solicitation is an offer that may be accepted if sufficiently responsive.

b. Negotiated Procurement

The process of negotiated procurement is more complex than that of sealed bid procurement. The opportunity to hold oral or written discussions in the procurement process raises the possibility that offerors may be requested to submit sequential offers. See *United States v. John McShain, Inc.*, 258 F.2d 422 (D.C. Cir. 1958), *cert. denied*, 358 U.S. 832 (1958), where the court stated at 424:

> Negotiation is a process of submission and consideration of offers until an acceptable offer is made, and accepted, or until it becomes apparent that no acceptable offer will be made.

The negotiation process is sufficiently flexible so that the Government can also make an offer during the course of negotiations. The various forms of negotiated procurement are discussed below.

(1) REQUEST FOR PROPOSALS OR OFFERS

The major form of solicitation in negotiated procurement is the Request for Proposals (RFP). This type of solicitation is generally accomplished using Optional Form 307 or Standard Form 33. The RFP is not an offer but, like the IFB, requests the proposer to submit an offer, *Space Research Corp. v. United States*, 225 Ct. Cl. 721 (1980). See FAR 15.203(a). In competitive negotiation, if acceptance without discussions is not possible or desirable, the Government conducts oral or written negotiations with all offerors within the competitive range. These offerors are then given the opportunity to submit another offer, which is called a "final proposal revision," FAR 15.307(b). Before FAC 97-02, September 30, 1997, these offers were called "best and final offers" (BAFOs), FAR 15.611(a) (pre-1997 FAR). If the Government is not satisfied with any such offer the process may be repeated and, in rare cases, the Government may be the party making the ultimate offer.

(2) REQUEST FOR QUOTATIONS

When the Government does not intend that offers be submitted in response to the initial solicitation in a negotiated procurement, it uses a Request for Quotations (RFQ) rather than an RFP. This procedure is used most commonly with sole source procurements. RFQs are normally prepared on Standard Form 18 (FAR 53.301-18). See **Figure 2-1**. Unlike bids or proposals following an IFB or RFP, quotations submitted in response to an RFQ are not considered to be offers that can be accepted, FAR 13.004(a). Prior to FAC 97-02, September 30, 1997, the FAR permitted the use of RFQs in negotiated procurement. The FAR is now silent on this issue.

A variety of procedures may be used following the receipt of a quotation. In some cases, a quotation serves as the basis for beginning negotiations. Following the conclusion of these negotiations in major procurements, the Government usually requests the prospective contractor to submit an offer that can be accepted by the Government. This is often accomplished by the Government sending a formal contract document to be signed by the contractor and presented to the Government for acceptance. However, various other procedures may be followed, and in some instances the Government becomes the offeror.

REQUEST FOR QUOTATION
(THIS IS NOT AN ORDER)

THIS RFQ ☐ IS ☐ IS NOT A SMALL BUSINESS SET-ASIDE

PAGE OF PAGES

1. REQUEST NO.
2. DATE ISSUED
3. REQUISITION/PURCHASE REQUEST NO.
4. CERT. FOR NAT. DEF. UNDER BDSA REG. 2 AND/OR DMS REG. 1 ▶ RATING

5a. ISSUED BY

6. DELIVER BY *(Date)*

5b. FOR INFORMATION CALL *(NO COLLECT CALLS)*

NAME | TELEPHONE NUMBER: AREA CODE | NUMBER

7. DELIVERY ☐ FOB DESTINATION ☐ OTHER *(See Schedule)*

8. TO:
a. NAME
b. COMPANY
c. STREET ADDRESS
d. CITY
e. STATE
f. ZIP CODE

9. DESTINATION
a. NAME OF CONSIGNEE
b. STREET ADDRESS
c. CITY
d. STATE
e. ZIP CODE

10. PLEASE FURNISH QUOTATIONS TO THE ISSUING OFFICE IN BLOCK 5A ON OR BEFORE CLOSE OF BUSINESS *(Date)*

IMPORTANT: This is a request for information, and quotations furnished are not offers. If you are unable to quote, please so indicate on this form and return it to the address in Block 5A. This request does not commit the Government to pay any costs incurred in the preparation of the submission of this quotation or to contract for supplies or services. Supplies are of domestic origin unless otherwise indicated by quoter. Any representations and/or certifications attached to this Request for Quotations must be completed by the quoter.

11. SCHEDULE *(Include applicable Federal, State and local taxes)*

ITEM NO. (a)	SUPPLIES/SERVICES (b)	QUANTITY (c)	UNIT (d)	UNIT PRICE (e)	AMOUNT (f)

12. DISCOUNT FOR PROMPT PAYMENT ▶

a. 10 CALENDAR DAYS (%)	b. 20 CALENDAR DAYS (%)	c. 30 CALENDAR DAYS (%)	d. CALENDAR DAYS NUMBER	PERCENTAGE

NOTE: Additional provisions and representations ☐ are ☐ are not attached.

13. NAME AND ADDRESS OF QUOTER
a. NAME OF QUOTER
b. STREET ADDRESS
c. COUNTY
d. CITY
e. STATE
f. ZIP CODE

14. SIGNATURE OF PERSON AUTHORIZED TO SIGN QUOTATION

15. DATE OF QUOTATION

16. SIGNER
a. NAME *(Type or print)*
b. TELEPHONE: AREA CODE | NUMBER
c. TITLE *(Type or print)*

AUTHORIZED FOR LOCAL REPRODUCTION
Previous edition not usable

STANDARD FORM 18 (Rev. 6-95)
Prescribed by GSA - FAR (48 CFR) 53.215-1(a)

Figure 2-1

2. Requests for Information

When the Government needs information on prices, delivery or other terms, it uses a Request for Information (RFI). Responses to RFIs are not offers that can be accepted, FAR 15.201(e).

a. Simplified Acquisition

The standard procedure for simplified acquisitions is for the Government to request quotations and to make offers through the issuance of purchase orders. The quoter is then free to reject or accept the offer. FAR 13.004(a) provides in part:

> Therefore, issuance by the Government of an order in response to a supplier's quotation does not establish a contract. The order is an offer by the Government to the supplier to buy certain supplies or services upon specified terms and conditions. A contract is established when the supplier accepts the offer.

See *Harney County Gypsum Co.*, AGBCA 93-190-1, 94-1 BCA ¶ 26,455, in which the firm's response to a request for price quotes and discussion of the firm's availability did not manifest an offer by the firm that could be accepted by the Government. Once the purchase order has been issued, the supplier may then manifest acceptance through promise or performance, FAR 13.004(b). See *Sunshine Cordage Corp.*, ASBCA 38904, 90-1 BCA ¶ 22,382 (initial request for quotation on price of rope was not an offer, but purchase order by Government in response to quotation by supplier was an offer).

The purchase order, in simplified acquisitions, may be made on Optional Form 347 (FAR 53.302-347) or, for purchases not exceeding $2,500, Standard Form 44 (FAR 53.301-44). See FAR 53.213. Agencies may use their own forms and the military agencies must use DD Form 1155 (DFARS 253.303-1155). See DFARS 213.505-2.

b. Obligation to Consider Responses

Although the issuance of a solicitation may not be an offer by the Government to contract for goods or services, the Government may be obligated to fairly and honestly consider responses conforming to the solicitation. In determining whether such an obligation exists, the courts have used offer-and-acceptance analysis. This analysis has served as the basis for giving the Court of Federal Claims jurisdiction to grant relief for bid protests under 28 U.S.C. § 1491, *United States v. John C. Grimberg Co.*, 702 F.2d 1362 (Fed. Cir. 1983). See also *Y.S.K. Constr. Co., Inc. v. United States*, 30 Fed. Cl. 449 (1994) (court may grant declaratory and injunctive relief in bid protest actions filed before the contract is awarded). In *CACI, Inc.-Fed. v. United States*, 1 Cl. Ct. 352, *rev'd*, 719 F.2d 1567 (Fed. Cir. 1983), the court held that issuance of a solicitation implied an offer to fairly and honestly consider all bids. See also *Aerolease Long Beach & Satsuma Inv. Co. v. United States*, 31 Fed. Cl. 342, *aff'd*, 39 F.3d 1198 (Fed. Cir. 1994) (court had jurisdiction on any contract claim including the implied contract to fairly and honestly consider bids and proposals "pursuant to an invitation for bids or solicitation for offers").

The Government has also been held to have made an offer to give fair and impartial consideration to responses to a procurement notice published in the *Commerce Business Daily* (CBD), *Standard Mfg. Co. v. United States*, 7 Cl. Ct. 54 (1984); *Magnavox Elec. Sys. Co. v. United States*, 26 Cl. Ct. 1373 (1992). But see *Motorola, Inc. v. United States*, 988 F.2d 113 (Fed. Cir. 1993), which criticized the rationale of *Standard Manufacturing* and *Magnovox* and stated at 116:

> Government requests for information and responses from prospective bidders are not the equivalents of offer and acceptance. Such exchanges are not carried on with an expectation to presently affect legal relations. Rather, the parties are dealing . . . with an eye to the future, each being free, . . . to withdraw from the dialogue.

The court then differentiated this situation from the situation that arises when a bid actually has been submitted, finding at 116:

> In that circumstance there is a promise — the contractor's bid — which empowers the Government, upon acceptance, to bind the contractor to the terms of the solicitation. The essence of the contractor's engagement — the manifestation of an intention to be bound — warrants reading into the situation a reciprocal commitment from the Government, i.e, a promise to fairly and honestly consider the contractor's bid.

Similarly, in *El Dorado Springs v. United States*, 28 Fed. Cl. 132 (1993), the court held that a Department of Housing and Urban Development invitation to submit an application for mortgage insurance did not imply a request for offers by the Government. The court was therefore unwilling to find that an implied contract to fairly and honestly consider all offers existed. See also *Garchik v. United States*, 37 Fed. Cl. 52 (1996), where the court held that a CBD notice stating explicitly that it was not a request for offers did not create an implied contract to fairly and honestly consider the response. The court stated that the *Motorola* decision "implicitly" overrules *Standard Manufacturing* and *Magnovox.*

3. Withdrawal or Modification of Offers

According to general contract-law principles, unless an offeror has made an enforceable agreement not to revoke an offer, the offer is freely revocable. See *Restatement, Second, Contracts* § 42:

> An offeree's power of acceptance is terminated when the offeree receives from the offeror a manifestation of an intention not to enter into the proposed contract.

Despite this general rule, there are a number of limitations on revocability. See *Restatement, Second, Contracts* § 87, which provides:

> (1) An offer is binding as an option contract if it
>
> > (a) is in writing and signed by the offeror, recites a purported consideration for the making of the offer, and proposes an exchange on fair terms within a reasonable time; or
> >
> > (b) is made irrevocable by statute.
>
> (2) An offer which the offeror should reasonably expect to induce action or forbearance of a substantial character on the part of the offeree before acceptance and which does induce such action or forbearance is binding as an option contract to the extent necessary to avoid injustice.

These general limitations on revocability have been subsumed, to a degree, in the rules developed for Government contracts. However, the term "option contract" has not been used in Government contracts to describe all irrevocable offers.

In the procurement of goods and services, the revocability of an offer is dependent upon the type of procurement involved and the stage of the procurement. Revocation may occur through either modification or withdrawal of the offer. In sealed bid procurement, offers may be modified or withdrawn prior to the time set for bid opening, FAR 14.303. Another longstanding rule, however, is that bids may not be modified or withdrawn after the exact time for bid opening unless they are based on a mistake, *Refining Assocs. v. United States*, 124 Ct. Cl. 115, 109 F. Supp. 259 (1953).

In negotiated procurement, proposals (offers) may be withdrawn at any time prior to award, FAR 15.208(g). See paragraph (c)(8) of the solicitation provision contained in FAR 52.215-1, which permits such withdrawal: "Proposals may be withdrawn at any time before award. Withdrawals are effective upon receipt of notice by the Contracting Officer." See *United Elec. Motor Co.*, Comp. Gen. Dec. B-191996, 78-2 CPD ¶ 206. Paragraph (c) of this solicitation provision contains the following guidance on modifications and revisions to proposals:

> (6) The Government reserves the right to make multiple awards if, after considering the additional administrative costs, it is in the Government's best interest to do so.
>
> (7) Communications with offerors after receipt of a proposal do not necessarily constitute a rejection or counteroffer by the Government.

Under FAR 15.412, in effect prior to FAC 97-02, September 30, 1997, "modifications" could be considered after the time or receipt of proposals only in response to a request for BAFOs. However, "normal revisions" to offers were permitted "during the conduct of negotiations by offerors selected for discussion." After BAFOs, modifications are generally not considered unless provisions for such modifications were specifically stated in the solicitation, FAR 15.611(b)(4). See *Sunset Realty Sales Assocs.*, Comp. Gen. Dec. B-221390, 86-1 CPD ¶ 303; and *United Tractor Co.*, Comp. Gen. Dec. B-231127, 88-1 CPD ¶ 428. It is questionable whether the Government could ignore an offeror's modification that is favorable to the offeror and instead accept the original offer; it could be argued that such a modification by the offeror is tantamount to a withdrawal of the original proposal. Thus, unless the modification indicates that no withdrawal of the original proposal is intended, it would appear that the Government could not ignore the modification and accept the original proposal.

The solicitation provision at FAR 52.214-7(f) (sealed bids) requires consideration of modifications with terms more favorable to the Government if submitted by the successful offeror. This requirement was applicable to negotiated procurements prior to FAC 97-02, September 30, 1997. The FAR is now silent on this issue.

The rules on modification and withdrawal are inconsistent with the specific provisions in Item 12 of Standard Form 33, which require the offeror to agree to be bound if the "offer is accepted within" a specified number of days "from the date of receipt of offers." In sealed bid procurement, this inconsistency could be resolved by interpreting receipt of offers to mean opening of bids. However, there is no way to resolve the inconsistency in negotiated procurement. Thus, it is likely that the issue will be governed by the more specific provision of the solicitation provision in FAR 52.215-1, which allows withdrawal and modification in certain limited circumstances.

The Government also uses option clauses, giving it the right to order additional goods or services. These offers are irrevocable for the stipulated period, FAR 17.201 and FAR 17.202. See *Contel Page Servs., Inc.*, ASBCA 32100, 87-1 BCA ¶ 19,540 (Government timely exercised its option to extend contract when it sent the contractor written notice as well as an unsigned bilateral modification). Proposed amendments to existing contracts could also constitute irrevocable offers. However, since there is no regulatory guidance on this issue, each occurrence must be analyzed on a case-by-case basis.

The legal theories supporting the irrevocability of Government contract offers have never been fully articulated. There is no Government contract statute similar to U.C.C. § 2-205 making "firm" offers irrevocable. In dealing with sealed bids, the court in *Refining Assocs. v. United States*, 124 Ct. Cl. 115, 109 F. Supp. 259 (1953), enforced the solicitation provision precluding withdrawal on the grounds that otherwise "innumerable frauds could be perpetrated against the United States." Irrevocability might also be supported on the theory that the offeror responding to solicitations receives consideration for agreeing not to revoke the offer in the form of the Government's obligation to fairly and honestly consider all bids and proposals. As FAR 17.201 defines "option" as a "unilateral right" in an already existing contract, the consideration supporting the irrevocability of offers in option clauses is provided by the consideration present in the contract that contains the option clause, *Holly Corp.*, ASBCA 24975, 83-1 BCA ¶ 16,327.

While the theory of detrimental reliance in Paragraph (2) of *Restatement, Second, Contracts* § 87 is potentially available to support the irrevocability of offers to contract with the Government, it would appear to be applicable only to sealed bid contracting and to offers for amendments to existing contracts. In these situations, the Government's expenditure of time and effort in evaluating the offers and preparing for acceptance could well be sufficient to bind offerors that agreed not to revoke. Although significantly more effort is expended by the Government in negotiated procurements, the offeror's broad right of withdrawal makes this theory inapplicable.

Government offers in the form of purchase orders for simplified acquisitions may also be revoked at any time prior to acceptance, FAR 13.004(c). See *Harney County Gypsum Co.*, AGBCA 93-190-1, 94-1 BCA ¶ 26,455 (Government's withdrawal of a purchase order for the rental of an excavator and operator did not constitute a breach of contract when the contractor had not yet accepted the offer in writing nor furnished an excavator and operator). The contracting officer may also modify purchase orders, without the contractor's written acceptance of the modification, FAR 13.302-3. See *University Sys., Inc. v. Department of Commerce*, GSBCA 10896-COM, 92-3 BCA ¶ 25,182 (insertion of a Termination for Default clause by unilateral modification to an already existing contract did not have to be accepted in writing by the contractor).

The procedures for withdrawing offers contain safeguards. Withdrawal is to be accomplished by written or telegraphic notice, facsimile, or in person if the identity of the person withdrawing the bid is established and such person signs a receipt, FAR 14.303. Guidance also may be found in the solicitation provision, FAR 52.214-7. Less detailed guidance for negotiated procurements is found in FAR 15.208(g). See also *John A. Maney*, GSBCA 6550, 83-2 BCA ¶ 16,744 (withdrawal of offers in Government contracts regulated by provisions specific to the field and not necessarily by common law).

4. Acceptance of Bids, Proposals, and Purchase Orders

To be binding, an acceptance must contain a manifestation of present intention to be bound. See *D&S Universal Mining, Inc.*, Comp. Gen. Dec. B-200815, 81-2 CPD ¶ 186, where the Comptroller General stated:

> In order for a binding contract to result, the contracting officer must unequivocally express an intent to accept an offer. Also, the acceptance of a contractor's offer by the Government must be clear and unconditional; it must appear that both parties intended to make a binding agreement at the time of the acceptance of the contractor's offer.

In *DeMatteo Constr. Co. v. United States*, 220 Ct. Cl. 579, 600 F.2d 1384 (1979), mere notification to an offeror that its offer was "selected as the lowest responsive bid" did not constitute an acceptance. Similarly, in *Greenwood Co.*, ASBCA 12232, 67-2 BCA ¶ 6650, the contracting officer asked the bidder to come in and sign contract documents and to bring payment and performance bonds. The bidder complied. Subsequently, the contracting officer determined that it would be to the Government's advantage to split the award as permitted by the IFB. The bidder contended that the entire contract had been awarded, but the board disagreed, finding that there had been no contract made for full performance because the contracting officer's request was not a "clear-cut expression of intention" to accept. The board stated at 30,829:

> Here, no clear-cut expression of intention to accept the bid and award a contract exists. [The bidder] was asked to bring in the payment and performance bonds undated, indicating that a contract date had not been established and the contract not yet awarded. In fact, the bonds were provisional, subject to annulment if a contract was not entered into. Nor did the contracting officer even sign the proposed contract on behalf of the Government, after [the bidder] had signed on its own behalf. In this light, that which transpired on 20 and 21 June 1966 must be considered as preparatory to the homologation of the contract. When the contracting officer failed to sign the proposed instrument signed by [the bidder], he did not, acting on behalf of [the Government], breach a contract, but preserved the STATUS QUO ANTE that no contract had yet come into existence.

See also *City of Klawock v. United States*, 2 Cl. Ct. 580 (1983), *aff'd*, 732 F.2d 168 (Fed. Cir. 1984), and *Edwards v. United States*, 22 Cl. Ct. 411 (1991), which appear to find no present intent to be bound because there were details remaining to be resolved. In both cases, the communications between the parties were susceptible to being read as conditional acceptances. In *Goldberger Foods, Inc. v. United States*, 23 Cl. Ct. 295 (1991), neither telephonic notice to a bidder that it was the lowest bidder nor public release of award information constituted a binding acceptance.

a. Time for Acceptance

Acceptance must occur within the time stated in the offer or a reasonable time if no time is stated. See *Restatement, Second, Contracts* § 41, which provides:

> (1) An offeree's power of acceptance is terminated at the time specified in the offer, or, if no time is specified, at the end of a reasonable time.
>
> (2) What is a reasonable time is a question of fact, depending on all the circumstances existing when the offer and attempted acceptance are made.

In IFBs and RFPs using Standard Form 33, the standard acceptance period is 60 days from opening of bids (in the case of IFBs) or from the date set for receipt of proposals (in the case of RFPs). Note that Item 12 of this form uses the term "date of receipt of offers" to imprecisely describe both situations. This clause also permits offerors to insert a longer or shorter acceptance period. But see *Imperial Maintenance, Inc.*, 71 Comp. Gen. 407 (B-247371), 92-1 CPD ¶ 464, where the Comptroller General held that a 56-day bid guarantee period, made in the form of letters of credit, established the bid acceptance period even though the bidder did not insert that period in the bid form.

The regulations also provide for the use of minimum acceptance periods. In construction IFBs and RFPs using Standard Form 1442 (FAR 53.301-1442), the contracting officer is required to insert a minimum acceptance period in Item 13D, and the offeror is permitted to offer a longer period in Item 17. FAR 52.214-16, applicable to contracts for other than construction, contains a solicitation provision for IFBs that is to be used when the contracting officer determines that a minimum acceptance period is necessary, FAR 14.201-6(j).

If acceptance does not occur during the specified period, no contract is formed. See 46 Comp. Gen. 371 (B-159639) (1966), where the Comptroller General stated at 372:

> [I]t is clear that expiration of the acceptance period operated to deprive the Government of any right to create a contract by acceptance action and to confer upon the bidder a right to refuse to perform any contract awarded to him thereafter.

This rule is applied inflexibly in the case of an attempted exercise of an option, *International Tel. & Tel. v. United States*, 197 Ct. Cl. 11, 453 F.2d 1283 (1972).

Where no time for acceptance is specified by the offer, the Government must accept within a reasonable time, *International Graphics, Div. of Moore Business Forms, Inc. v. United States*, 4 Cl. Ct. 515 (1984) (reasonable period held to be "obviously in excess of 14 days"). See *National Movers Co. v. United States*, 181 Ct. Cl. 419, 386 F.2d 999 (1967), where acceptance at 3:00 p.m. on Friday, two days after bid opening, was held to be within a reasonable time even though work was required to begin on the following Monday morning. See also *One Way Constr., Inc.*, AGBCA 84-301-1, 85-1 BCA ¶ 17,839, holding that 23 days is not "an unduly long period of time from bid opening to award of contract."

The acceptance period may be extended in a number of different ways. The contracting officer may request bidders to extend the period if administrative difficulties prevent award before expiration of the bids, FAR 14.404-1(d), or if a protest prevents awarding the contract before expiration of the offers, FAR 33.103(a)(3). The acceptance period may also be extended on negotiated procurements without reopening discussions with offerors, *Science Info. Servs., Inc.*, Comp. Gen. Dec. B-207149.2, 82-2 CPD ¶ 477. While offerors are not required to extend their offers, such extensions are commonly granted because the offeror wishes to continue to be considered for award. However, it may be disadvantageous for a low bidder to extend in view of FAR 33.103(a)(3), which suggests that the contracting officer should consider award prior to resolution of a protest and expiration of a bid if the bidder refuses to extend the offer.

The acceptance period may also be extended through the submission of a bid protest. The Comptroller General has held that such an extension of the protester's acceptance period is automatic until the date of the decision and may be extended for a reasonable time thereafter, 52 Comp. Gen. 863 (B-177165) (1973). In *International Graphics v. United States*, 4 Cl. Ct. 515 (1984), the court ruled that an acceptance period may be extended through and beyond protest litigation if the "parties, through litigation or otherwise, have actually or constructively expressed their intent to accept the award." In *Uffnor Textile Corp.*, Comp. Gen. Dec. B-205050, 81-2 CPD ¶ 443, the Comptroller General found another type of automatic extension when the bidder withdrew from the protest but agreed to accept the contracting officer's decision. The Comptroller General reasoned that such expression of interest had the effect of extending the acceptance period.

Offerors submitting offers with acceptance periods equal to or greater than those requested by the solicitation have been permitted to revive their offers after the period has expired if doing so will not compromise the integrity of the competitive bidding system, *Strom Contracting Co.*, Comp. Gen. Dec. B-216115, 84-2 CPD ¶ 705; *Rubbermaid, Inc.*, Comp. Gen. Dec. B-238631, 90-1 CPD ¶ 444. See also *Rentfrow, Inc.*, Comp. Gen. Dec. B-243215, 91-2 CPD ¶ 25, holding that where a firm proposed an adequate acceptance period in its original proposal, it could revive the offer once the original acceptance period had passed because doing so would not prejudice other offerors. However, a bidder that offers a bid acceptance period shorter than that requested in an IFB may not extend that period or revive the bid in order to qualify for award because such an extension would be prejudicial to other bidders that offered the requested acceptance period. However, where the contract is awarded to another firm within the shorter acceptance period and the bidder that offered the shorter period protests the award, that bid may be accepted if the protest is sustained even though the acceptance period otherwise would have expired, *Professional Materials Handling Co.*, Comp. Gen. Dec. B-205969, 82-1 CPD ¶ 297.

b. Time When Acceptance Occurs

The time when acceptance occurs depends upon the type of acceptance requested by the offer and the mode of communication used. When the parties are face-to-face or communicating by telephone or teletype, the acceptance occurs as soon as the offeree has given assent to the transaction by statement or signature, *Restatement, Second, Contracts* § 64. There is little opportunity for controversy in such cases. Where the communication is by mail or telegraph, there are two views as to when acceptance occurs. The private common-law view holds that acceptance is effective when dispatched, *Adams v. Lindsell*, 106 Eng. Rep. 250 (K.B. 1818). This is commonly referred to as the "mailbox rule" and requires only that the offeree properly dispatch the notice of acceptance, *Restatement, Second, Contracts* § 63. In Government contracts, a contrary view was adopted by the Court of Claims, which ruled that an acceptance must be received by the offeror before a contract is created, *Rhode Island Tool Co. v. United States*, 130 Ct. Cl. 698, 128 F. Supp. 417 (1955). That decision was premised on postal regulations that permitted reclaiming letters after deposit in the mail and on solicitation language that stated that a binding contract would be formed upon "receipt" of the notice of award. Subsequently, this solicitation language was changed by the Government, and the solicitation provisions in the FAR now provide that a binding contract is formed when a notice of award is "mailed or otherwise furnished" to the offeror, FAR 52.214-10(d) and FAR 52.215-1(f)(9).

Subsequent litigation involving solicitations containing this revised language demonstrate that a potential conflict still remains. A concurring opinion in *G.C. Casebolt Co. v. United States*, 190 Ct. Cl. 783, 421 F.2d 710 (1970), stated that "a valid contract is not formed until the acceptance is received by the offeror." The majority of the court disposed of the case on other grounds. In *Emeco Indus. v. United States*, 202 Ct. Cl. 1006, 485 F.2d 652 (1973), the court endorsed the requirement for an actual "communication" of the acceptance. See also *Romala Corp. v. United States*, 20 Cl. Ct. 435 (1990) (provisions included in letter sent by Government after acceptance of original offer had been communicated were not part of contract). In contrast, the appeals boards have followed the reasoning of the Comptroller General in finding that the acceptance need only be mailed for a valid contract to come into being when specific language to that effect is used in the solicitation. See *Computer Wholesale Corp.*, GSBCA 4217, 76-1 BCA ¶ 11,859, *recons. denied*, 76-2 BCA ¶ 12,163 (board's reasoning was not necessarily inconsistent with the Court of Claims when solicitation specifically provided that once a written acceptance of award was mailed, contract formed); *Cisco Supply Co.*, GSBCA 5678, 81-1 BCA ¶ 15,103 (IFB required removal of purchased property within 15 days after award, and board found that time period began to run when notice of award was mailed as per solicitation language); and *Singleton Contracting Corp.*, IBCA 1770-1-84, 86-2 BCA ¶ 18,800 (relief from bid error was denied because board found mailed notice of award had already completed the contract as designated in solicitation). In cases involving an acceptance not governed by this solicitation language, it has been held that the Court of Claims rule should be followed. In *Titan Atl. Constr. Corp.*, ASBCA 26007, 83-2 BCA ¶ 16,791, the board, noting the absence of controlling language, held that an acceptance of a contract amendment by the contractor was not effective until received by the Government.

The mailbox rule requires that the notice of award be placed in the United States mail, not in the agency mail system, *Albert H. Voight, Inc.*, GSBCA 4433, 76-1 BCA ¶ 11,789. The Government, as offeree, carries the burden of proving timely and proper mailing of the award notice. See *C & L*

Petroleum Co., ASBCA 39844, 91-1 BCA ¶ 23,490, where the Government failed to mail the notice of award by either registered or certified mail and thus could only submit evidence of usual practices to prove timely acceptance. The board found that type of evidence insufficient to carry the burden.

There is unanimity regarding the rule for exercise of options under existing contracts. Unless a contrary agreement is shown, all authorities hold that the acceptance is not effective until *received* by the offeror, *Dynamics Corp. of Am. v. United States*, 182 Ct. Cl. 62, 389 F.2d 424 (1968); and *Restatement, Second, Contracts* § 63(b). FAR 17.207(a) requires that written notice of the exercise of the option be "provided" to the contractor within the time specified in the contract. While the *Restatement* uses the term "option contract" broadly to apply to all irrevocable offers — those in new contracts as well as those in existing contracts — the special acceptance rule for options has generally not been applied to firm offers for new Government contracts. As discussed above, the *Rhode Island Tool* case reached the same conclusion. In *Cessna Aircraft Co.*, ASBCA 43196, 96-1 BCA ¶ 27,966, the board held that an option exercised by facsimile at 6:00 p.m. on a Saturday and received on the contractor's fax machine was effective even though the contractor did not become aware of the fax until the following Monday. The Government had warned the contractor that it intended to exercise the option, which was due to expire at 12:00 midnight on Saturday, as soon as funds became available. It alerted the contractor to "stand by their fax machine."

When acceptance is to be accomplished by performance rather than promise, such as in simplified acquisitions, *Restatement, Second, Contracts* § 45 provides that *the beginning of performance* binds the offeror but not the offeree. FAR 13.004(b) attempts nevertheless to permit later Government withdrawal of its unilateral offer by defining acceptance as occurring when the supplier either furnishes the supplies or services or substantially performs the work; it is doubtful, however, that this definition will be used to permit the Government to withdraw an offer after the supplier has begun performance. The FAR definition does not address, and should not alter, the *Restatement* rule that the offeree is not bound. See *Harney County Gypsum Co.*, AGBCA 93-190-1, 94-1 BCA ¶ 26,455, where the board found no acceptance, citing the substantial performance requirement in the FAR, but finding no significant performance. See also *Federal Acquisition Management Training Serv.*, Comp. Gen. Dec. B-248871, 92-2 CPD ¶ 214 (agency may cancel purchase order prior to beginning of performance); *Sunshine Cordage Corp.*, ASBCA 38904, 90-1 BCA ¶ 22,382 (finding that the supplier/offeror is not bound to perform under a Government offer for a unilateral contract).

c. Conditional Acceptance

Under certain circumstances, the contracting officer wants to accept the offer but is unable or unwilling to obligate the Government at that time. The most common situations occur when the contracting officer's acceptance is contingent upon either the availability of funding for the contract or the approval of higher authority. FAR 32.703-2 permits the contracting officer to initiate a contracting action properly chargeable to funds of the new fiscal year before these funds are available, provided that the solicitation and contract document include the following clause at FAR 52.232-18:

AVAILABILITY OF FUNDS (APR 1984)

> Funds are not presently available for this contract. The Government's obligation under this contract is contingent upon the availability of appropriated funds from which payment for contract purposes can be made. No legal liability on the part of the Government for any payment may arise until funds are made available to the Contracting Officer for this contract and until the Contractor receives notice of such availability, to be confirmed in writing by the Contracting Officer.

The contracting officer may use this procedure for procurements involving operation and maintenance and continuing services necessary for normal operations, and for which Congress previously has consistently appropriated funds, unless statutory authority exists for use in other areas, FAR 32.703-2.

Another type of conditional acceptance is one subject to approval of higher authority. FAR 4.103 requires that the contracting officer use the following clause at FAR 52.204-1 in solicitations and contract documents if required by agency procedures:

APPROVAL OF CONTRACT (DEC 1989)

> This contract is subject to the written approval of ______________ [*identify title of designated agency official here*] and shall not be binding until so approved.

If the condition occurs within a stated or reasonable time without attempted withdrawal by either party, both parties will be bound, *Thomson v. United States*, 174 Ct. Cl. 780, 357 F.2d 683 (1966) (once condition of approval of contract by Attorney General's office was attained, parties to contract were bound); *Delco Elecs. Corp. v. United States*, 12 Cl. Ct. 367 (1987) (failure to issue required formal modification of contract prevented formation of a binding contract). Further, if the condition never occurs, neither party is bound unless one party has undertaken an obligation regarding the occurrence of the condition, *Monroe v. United States*, 184 U.S. 524 (1902) (lack of approval by chief of engineers as specified in contract prevented contract from being enforceable); *Municipal Leasing Corp. v. United States*, 1 Cl. Ct. 771 (1983) (Government's motion for summary judgment denied due to its failure to use "best efforts" to secure the necessary funding that was condition of contract). See also *United States v. Newport News Shipbuilding & Dry Dock Co.*, 571 F.2d 1283 (4th Cir.), *cert. denied*, 439 U.S. 875 (1978) (negotiated settlement not binding on the Government because condition of ultimate approval by Attorney General never received); and *Blackhawk Heating & Plumbing Co.*, VACAB 823, 81-2 BCA ¶ 15,400 (Government not obligated to pay contractor full amount due under a settlement agreement because the agreement made the Government's payment obligation contingent upon the availability of funds and Congress withdrew the appropriation of funds for the agreement before the final payment was due).

There is less certainty as to the degree to which either party is bound during the period prior to the occurrence of the condition or the passage of a reasonable or stated time for its occurrence. Since the offeror has usually invested considerable effort in the procurement, there is normally no desire to withdraw. Thus, most of the cases in this area have involved the Government's refusal to proceed with the contractual action. One view of this legal issue is that either party is free to withdraw during this period. See *3 Williston on Contracts*, § 77A (4th ed., 1992), stating, in part, that an acceptance to take effect in the future is one that

> adopts unequivocally the terms of the offer but states that it will not be effective until a certain contingency happens or fails to happen. . . . There is, so to speak, an acceptance in escrow, which is not to take effect until the future. In the meantime, of course, neither party is bound and either may withdraw. Moreover, if the time at which the acceptance was to become effectual is unreasonably remote, the offer may lapse before the acceptance becomes effective. But if neither party withdraws and the delay is not un-

reasonable, a contract will arise when the contingency happens or stipulated event occurs.

The applicability of this reasoning should depend upon which party has control of the condition. If the condition is under the control of a third party, there would appear to be no sound reason for permitting either party to withdraw from such a conditional acceptance envisioned in the terms of the solicitation. In such an agreement, it could be argued that since neither party has control of the condition, both have agreed to be bound while awaiting its outcome. See, however, *City of Klawock v. United States*, 2 Cl. Ct. 580 (1983), *aff'd*, 732 F.2d 168 (Fed. Cir. 1984), and *American Gen. Leasing, Inc. v. United States*, 218 Ct. Cl. 367, 587 F.2d 54 (1978), both supporting the proposition that if a contract is conditioned upon the action of a third party, no contract comes into existence until such action is completed. A better rule would be that a contract for the goods or services does not come into being but that the parties are contractually bound to await the occurrence of the condition for a reasonable period of time.

The more common conditions included in Government contract solicitations are those within the control of the Government. In such cases, some official above the contracting officer or outside the contracting agency must approve the transaction or provide funding. In *American Gen. Leasing, Inc. v. United States*, 218 Ct. Cl. 367, 587 F.2d 54 (1978), it was held that the approving or funding official is under no obligation to the offeror. Similarly, in *Congress Constr. Corp. v. United States*, 161 Ct. Cl. 50, 314 F.2d 527 (1963), *cert. denied*, 375 U.S. 817 (1963), the court assumed, arguendo, that the Government was legally bound to use its "best efforts" to obtain the higher approval needed to complete negotiations, but that such efforts did not include "unreasonable and improper conduct," such as ignoring the orders of a superior officer. Compare *Municipal Leasing Corp. v. United States*, 1 Cl. Ct. 771 (1983), where the contract provided that the Air Force would "use its best efforts to obtain appropriations." The court found that the Conditional Funding clause was modified by this provision. If the ultimate decisionmaker within the Government has no obligation, the Government also is free of obligation as a practical matter.

If the Government can freely avoid obligation in this manner, basic contract principle would give the offeror the same right unless there is an independent promise to be bound. For example, a conditional acceptance should not override a bidder's agreement not to withdraw a sealed bid. Once the period has expired, the bidder should be free to withdraw unless the

Government has assumed some obligation such as to use good faith in the decisional process. However, in one case, the Comptroller General held that a bidder could not withdraw following a conditional acceptance, 31 Comp. Gen. 477 (B-103842) (1952). There was no discussion of Government obligation and no indication that the required approval was obtained within the bid acceptance period. The decision was supported by the questionable reasoning that a bid bond provided an independent basis for liability.

An offeror should not be bound to conditions not included in solicitations but unilaterally inserted by the offeree at the time of attempted acceptance. Since such an "acceptance" would not conform to the terms of the offer, no contract would be formed, *United States v. Braunstein*, 75 F. Supp. 137 (S.D.N.Y. 1947). This rule has been applied to the attempted exercise of an option where the board held that the contractor was not bound by an acceptance conditioned on the availability of funds; this clause was not present in the original contract which the contractor had satisfactorily performed, *Lear Siegler Inc.*, ASBCA 30224, 86-3 BCA ¶ 19,155.

d. Nonacceptance Responses to Offers

In some cases, offerees' communications are not intended to be acceptances; in others, attempted acceptances do not properly manifest an intent to accept. In such situations, the communication may be held to be a rejection of the offer, a counteroffer, or a request that the offeror alter the terms of the offer. Under traditional contract law, an acceptance must unequivocally conform to the terms of the offer in order to create a binding contractual agreement. See *United States v. Braunstein*, 75 F. Supp. 137 (S.D.N.Y. 1947). *Restatement, Second, Contracts* § 58 provides:

> An acceptance must comply with the requirements of the offer as to the promise to be made or the performance to be rendered.

However, an acceptance is not invalid if it merely requests a change or addition to terms and is not made to depend on assent to the changed or added terms, *Restatement, Second, Contracts* § 61. See *Best Foam Fabricators, Inc. v. United States*, 38 Fed. Cl. 627 (1997), where the Government argued that the contractor never accepted the offer because its letter accompanying the signed contract took exception to the inclusion of MIL-I-45208 and, therefore, constituted a counteroffer. The court disagreed, stating that the contractor's letter unequivocally requested that the contract be modified to remove MIL-I-45208. The court stated that neither this request nor any other portion of the letter even remotely suggested that the contractor's acceptance was dependent on the Government's assent to the deletion. Thus, the court held that the request was not a counteroffer and did not invalidate the contractor's acceptance.

Rejections and counteroffers terminate the offer unless a different intention is manifested. See *Restatement, Second, Contracts* § 38 and § 39:

> § 38. Rejection
>
> (1) An offeree's power of acceptance is terminated by his rejection of the offer, unless the offeror has manifested a contrary intention.
>
> (2) A manifestation of intention not to accept an offer is a rejection unless the offeree manifests an intention to take it under further advisement.
>
> § 39. Counter-offers
>
> (1) A counter-offer is an offer made by an offeree to his offeror relating to the same matter as the original offer and proposing a substituted bargain differing from that proposed by the original offer.
>
> (2) An offeree's power of acceptance is terminated by his making of a counter-offer, unless the offeror has manifested a contrary intention or unless the counter-offer manifests a contrary intention of the offeree.

The *Restatement* further provides that a rejection or counteroffer does not terminate an offer where there is a binding promise by the offeror not to revoke the offer, *Restatement, Second, Contracts* § 37. In Government contracts, this latter rule would prevent termination of offers in option clauses and in irrevocable offers in sealed bid procurements. In contrast, offers in negotiated contracts would be terminated by a rejection or counteroffer in view of the offeror's broad right to revoke the offer.

The most common type of counteroffer in Government contracts occurs where the offeree attempts to conclude the transaction with different terms. Thus, an acceptance by the Government that materially varies from the contractor's offer will be treated as a counteroffer, 26 Comp. Gen. 567 (B-63244) (1947) (Government's insertion of level of permitted price increase in its acceptance made such acceptance a counteroffer); *Northpoint Investors*, Comp. Gen. Dec. B-209816, 83-1 CPD ¶ 523 (Government's acceptance conditioned upon future actions by Government was neither clear nor unconditional and thus constituted a counteroffer); *Aero Corp.*, ASBCA 8178, 1963 BCA ¶ 3665 (purchase order by Government containing terms "not previously set out, referred to or incorporated" turned purchase order into counteroffer); *Ford Aerospace & Communications Corp.*, ASBCA 34994, 91-3 BCA ¶ 24,108 (Government's acceptance of offer only at lower sales rate found to be a counteroffer and not an acceptance). The *Aero Corporation* case holds further that such a counteroffer may then be accepted by the original offeror. See also *Bloch Lumber Co.*, ASBCA 23512, 79-2 BCA ¶ 14,167, where the Government accepted a counteroffer by accepting delivered items without objecting to the new terms. Compare, however, *Ford Aerospace & Communications Corp.*, ASBCA 34994, 91-3 BCA ¶ 24,108, where before and during performance, the contractor maintained that a discrepancy had to be corrected by the Government. The board refused to find acceptance by the contractor through performance because the Government was unclear and ambiguous as to what course of action it would take. In *Dunrite Tool & Die Corp.*, ASBCA 16708, 73-1 BCA ¶ 9940, the board found that there were two counteroffers. The Government was found to have made one counteroffer when it included different terms in its purported acceptance. The second counteroffer was found when the offeror's response incorporated different terms. Since the Government subsequently rejected the offeror's counteroffer, the board concluded that no contract was ever formed. A Government notice of award citing the RFP was held to be a counteroffer to an offer containing specifications different from those in the RFP, *Data Gen. Corp.*, ASBCA 21865, 79-2 BCA ¶ 14,185.

Generally, late acceptances have also been treated as counteroffers. See *Restatement, Second, Contracts* § 70, which states in part:

> A late or otherwise defective acceptance may be effective as an offer to the original offeror.

In order to prevent these types of acceptance communications from terminating the offer, the offeree must manifest an intention to keep the offer open. If such an intention is manifested, the offeree can make inquiries, suggest different terms, or propose a counteroffer while retaining the right to accept the original offer. See *Dudek & Bock Spring Mfg. Co.*, ASBCA 9753, 65-2 BCA ¶ 4931, where a Government telegram requesting that a bidder confirm the unit price, provide an extended price, and confirm that it had received certain data was held not to terminate the Government's power to accept the offer.

C. Implied-in-Fact Contracts

An implied-in-fact contract occurs when the conduct of the parties indicates that they have actually manifested their mutual assent but an express offer or acceptance is absent. See *Restatement, Second, Contracts* § 4 and § 19, stating that promises may be inferred and that mutual assent may be determined from words or acts. Implied-in-fact contracts are also recognized in Government contracts, *Baltimore & Ohio R.R. v. United States*, 261 U.S. 592 (1923). However, as in the case of express contracts, implied-in-fact contracts must be consistent with statutory and regulatory requirements, *Prestex Inc. v. United States*, 162 Ct. Cl. 620, 320 F.2d 367 (1963), and based on the conduct of authorized employees, *Essen Mall Properties v. United States,* 21 Cl. Ct. 430 (1990); *Pacific Gas & Elec. Co. v. United States,* 3 Cl. Ct. 329 (1983), *aff'd*, 738 F.2d 452 (Fed. Cir. 1984); *Woodcraft Corp. v. United States*, 146 Ct. Cl. 101, 173 F. Supp. 613 (1959).

1. Course of Conduct

The implied-in-fact agreement may be established from a course of conduct followed by the parties. In *Algonac Mfg. Co. v. United States*, 192 Ct. Cl. 649, 428 F.2d 1241 (1970), a contract was awarded for the production of armor-plated gun carriage parts. By a contract modification, the Government was to furnish the necessary armor plate and the contractor was to maintain, repair, protect, and preserve it so long as it was in its possession. Following completion of performance, the contractor asked the Government to remove the surplus armor plate from its plant. It was not removed. The contractor stored it for 11 years and later informed the Government that it would assess a storage charge for that time. The court held that the Government was liable for a reasonable charge on the basis of an implied-in-fact contract, as stated at 676:

> In view of the duties, responsibilities, and obligations imposed on the [contractor] by the foregoing provisions to maintain, repair, protect, and preserve the armor plate as long as it was in its possession, it was reasonable for the [contractor] to conclude, after the contract was finished and it had requested the government several times in writing, as outlined above, to take possession of the property and the government failed to do so, that the

> government wished it to continue to care for, preserve, and store such property and that the government would pay it for doing so.

Similarly, in *Bruce-Andersen Co.*, ASBCA 28125, 83-2 BCA ¶ 16,892, a contractor made an agreement with the Government to substitute five-eighth-inch plywood furring for the three-quarter-inch solid furring called for in the contract in order to correct a one-eighth-inch gap resulting from the Government's contract drawings. At the time this agreement was reached, it was clear to both parties that each would benefit from the change. The contractor was silent as to the matter of potential net increased cost of the change. In addition, the contractor knew, or should have known, that the Government agent with whom it dealt did not have the authority to approve changes involving additional costs to the Government. Nevertheless, a year later, the contractor attempted to claim increased costs from the Government for the change. The board held that, under the circumstances, there was an implied-in-fact agreement that the change was to be made on a no-cost basis, stating at 84,060:

> [The contractor] is in error in conceiving that express words that the change would be on a no-cost basis was [sic] the only mode for making an agreement to that effect. It is well settled that an agreement may be effected not only through the exchange of express verbal undertakings by the parties but also through conduct between them that, evaluated in the light of surrounding circumstances, manifests a mutual, albeit tacit, intent to be contractually bound. Such an agreement, implied in fact from such conduct is as actual as one reached verbally.

See also *OAO Corp. v. United States,* 17 Cl. Ct. 91 (1989), where the Government encouraged the contractor to begin performance before the contract was awarded but later canceled the acquisition. The court granted relief for the contractor's costs based on an implied-in-fact contract.

2. *Acceptance of Benefits*

Implied-in-fact contracts may also be created through the acceptance of benefits with the knowledge that the contractor expects to be compensated, *Pacific Maritime Ass'n v. United States*, 123 Ct. Cl. 667, 108 F. Supp. 603 (1952) (labor referral services by the contractor accepted with knowledge that compensation was expected); *Buffalo & Fort Erie Pub. Bridge Auth. v. United States*, 106 Ct. Cl. 731, 65 F. Supp. 476 (1946) (premises used with knowledge that contractor expected compensation); *Equitable Life Assur-*

ance Soc'y, GSBCA 8909, 90-3 BCA ¶ 23,130 (directive to contractor/lessor to replace carpet in leased office space made with knowledge that contractor expected compensation); *Robert J. DiDomenico*, GSBCA 5539, 82-2 BCA ¶ 16,093 (building alterations not called for in the contract ordered with knowledge that contractor expected compensation).

Since implied-in-fact contracts require conduct of the parties manifesting assent, the mere conferring of a benefit on the Government does not create a contractual relationship, *Mega Constr. Co. v. United States*, 29 Fed. Cl. 396 (1993). In private transactions, conferring a benefit may permit recovery under a restitutionary theory.

In Government contracts, however, sovereign immunity from suit has not been waived for restitutionary actions. Such claims have been called "quasi-contract" or "implied-in-law" contract claims, which are not actionable under the Tucker Act, 28 U.S.C. § 1491, or the Contract Disputes Act of 1978, 41 U.S.C. § 601 et seq. These statutes waiving sovereign immunity for suits on express or implied contracts have been held to exclude suits on contracts implied in law. See *Merritt v. United States*, 267 U.S. 338 (1925), stating at 341:

> The Tucker Act does not give a right of action against the United States in those cases where, if the transaction were between private parties, recovery could be had upon a contract implied in law.

In *Russell Corp. v. United States*, 210 Ct. Cl. 596, 537 F.2d 474 (1976), the court recognized this distinction and its inability to grant remedies on quasi- or implied-in-law contracts, stating at 609:

> Implied-in-fact contracts differ from contracts implied in law (quasi-contracts), where a duty is imposed by operation of law without regard to the intent of the parties. Such arrangements are treated as contracts for the purposes of remedy only. This court, of course, has no jurisdiction to render judgment against the United States based upon a contract implied in law.

See also *United States v. Mitchell,* 463 U.S. 206 (1983), confirming that the Tucker Act does not waive sovereign immunity for claims based on contracts implied in law. Therefore, the Claims Court lacks jurisdiction in such cases.

3. Incomplete Contract Formation

Implied-in-fact contracts have also been found to exist where the Government and the contractor have unsuccessfully attempted to form an express contract, *Hughes Transp., Inc. v. United States*, 128 Ct. Cl. 221, 121 F. Supp. 212 (1954). Similarly, such contracts have sometimes been found to exist where the Government and a contractor enter into an incomplete agreement. If the parties have nonetheless exhibited contractual intent, a contract will be found to exist. See *Western States Constr. Co.*, ASBCA 16003, 72-2 BCA ¶ 9508, where the board commented on the failure of the parties to agree to a contract price at 44,302:

> In this case there was no manifestation of mutual assent or "meeting of the minds" as to the contract price. [The contractor] took the firm position that the legal contract price was $1,208,300, and the Government knew it. The Government took the equally firm position that the correct legal contract price was $1,098,300, and [the contractor] knew it. Each party clearly manifested to the other party its position as to the correct contract price, and each party manifested to the other party its disagreement with the other party's position as to the contract price. It does not follow, however, that the failure of the parties to arrive at a meeting of the minds on the contract price resulted in there being no contract. An agreed on contract price is not essential to the existence of a contract when there is agreement on all the other terms of contract and a manifestation of intent to make a contract, such as we have here.

See also *Howard Nettleton*, PSBCA 3454, 94-3 BCA ¶ 27,038, where the absence of an express agreement on price was insufficient to prevent recovery on a contract implied in fact.

An implied-in-fact contract may be found to exist on the basis of an implied acceptance of an express offer. In *Thomson v. United States*, 174 Ct. Cl. 780, 357 F.2d 683 (1966), acceptance of a contractor's offer to perform surveying services was contingent upon approval of higher authority. The contracting office received notice of such approval but did not inform the contractor of that fact, and did not therefore expressly accept the offer. However, the court held that there was an implied acceptance by the actions and communications of the contracting officer that encouraged the contractor to perform. As a result, an implied-in-fact contract was held to have come into existence. In discussing the relationship between an implied acceptance and an implied-in-fact contract, the court stated at 791:

> It is fundamental, however, that acceptance of an offer may be manifested either expressly (as by words) or impliedly by conduct indicating assent to the proposed bargain. *Restatement 2d, Contracts* §§ 5, 21, 21A, 52 (Comment c) (Tent. ed. 1, 1964); I *Williston, Contracts* §§ 90, 91A (3d ed. 1957). The notion that assent to the terms of an agreement (i.e., acceptance) may be evinced by action or conduct underlies the rule, repeatedly recognized by the courts, that contracts may be "implied in fact."

See also *Padbloc Co. v. United States*, 161 Ct. Cl. 369 (1963), where because the contractor stipulated that the Government could use its data only if the data were kept confidential, the Government's use of the data constituted an implied promise of confidentiality.

II. BINDING THE PARTIES

The manifestation of mutual assent is not in itself sufficient to bind a party to perform as promised. The law requires either that something be exchanged for the promise or that the promise be reasonably relied upon. The term given by the law to the former is "consideration," while the latter is called "promissory estoppel."

A. Requirement for Signed Document

In private contract law, state Statutes of Frauds permit a party being charged in a contract suit who has not signed a document evidencing a contract to plead that as a defense. See generally *Restatement, Second, Contracts* § 110 and § 138; and U.C.C. § 2-201. There is no similar statute concerning Government contracts, and it has been held that the absence of a signed written document does not preclude the enforceability of a Government contract, *Escote Mfg. Co. v. United States*, 144 Ct. Cl. 452, 169 F. Supp. 483 (1959) (valid contract existed despite the absence of the contracting officer's signature on the Government's acceptance form because the form was sent with a letter indicating acceptance that was signed by the contracting officer).

1. Writing

Although there is no federal Statute of Frauds, there are a number of statutory and regulatory references to written contract documents. See 10 U.S.C. § 2305(b)(3); 41 U.S.C. § 253b(c) and (d)(4); FAR 14.408-1; and

FAR 15.504, which require written notices of award for sealed bid and competitive negotiated procurement. The FAR 2.101 definition of "contracts" states that the term "includes all types of commitments that obligate the Government . . . and that, except as otherwise authorized, are in writing." The term "writing" is defined in 1 U.S.C. § 1 to include "printing and typing and reproduction of visual symbols by photography, multigraphing, mimeographing, manifolding, or otherwise." The fiscal statutes contain a provision relating to this issue. 31 U.S.C. § 1501(a)(1) states that one of the bases for recording an obligation of the United States is a "binding agreement . . . in writing . . . and executed." The Comptroller General has held that for purposes of the statute, electronic data interchanges constitute writings, *National Inst. of Standards & Technology*, 71 Comp. Gen. 109 (B-245714), 96-2 CPD ¶ 225.

In *United States v. American Renaissance Lines, Inc.*, 494 F.2d 1059 (D.C. Cir.), *cert. denied*, 419 U.S. 1020 (1974), the court construed the appropriations recording statute to be a Statute of Frauds in refusing to hold a contractor to an oral agreement. The court rejected the Government's argument that the statute was merely for purposes of recording obligations to facilitate auditing and that it was not applicable to Government contracts. *Escote Mfg. Co. v. United States*, 144 Ct. Cl. 452, 169 F. Supp. 483 (1959), and *Penn-Ohio Steel Corp. v. United States*, 173 Ct. Cl. 1064, 354 F.2d 254 (1965), earlier Court of Claims cases holding that Government contracts need not be in writing to be binding, were dismissed in a statement that in neither case did a citation to the statute appear. The court's interpretation of the statute is unique and appears to be a misapplication, since the statute's purpose is to provide an effective means of budgetary control as reflected in the Report of the Committee on Appropriations, H. Rep. 2266, 83d Cong., 2d Sess. 49-50 (1954).

The *American Renaissance Lines* holding is inapplicable where the contracts involve the obligation of nonappropriated funds. See *Sam Won Dev. Co.*, ASBCA 16541, 74-2 BCA ¶ 10,730, recognizing a binding oral contract and distinguishing *American Renaissance Lines* on the ground that the statute has no application to agreements where nonappropriated funds are involved. See also *Robert P. Maier, Inc.*, GSBCA 4382, 76-1 BCA ¶ 11,873, and *Robert P. Maier, Inc.*, Comp. Gen. Dec. B-185177, 76-1 CPD ¶ 137, *recons. denied*, 76-2 CPD ¶ 163, holding that *American Renaissance Lines* is not applicable to sales of Government property.

American Renaissance Lines has also been distinguished where the Government's bidding documents specify that acceptance will be oral, *Ross Indus.*, ASBCA 19563, 75-1 BCA ¶ 11,212, and where the parties acted with the mutual understanding that a contract had been formed, *Superior Asphalt & Concrete Co.*, AGBCA 75-142, 76-2 BCA ¶ 12,022, *recons. denied*, 77-2 BCA ¶ 12,851. In the latter case, the board stated at 62,559:

> We are persuaded that the weight of authority to the effect that there is no Federal Statute of Frauds applies in the case before us. Where the terms and conditions are fixed by the writing in the bid package which becomes the offer, oral acceptance with execution of the document intended by both parties in a routine manner results in an enforceable contract even though the parties fail to actually execute the document. The oral acceptance must, of course, be by a duly authorized contracting officer acting within the scope of his authority.

For a similar discussion, see the concurring opinion in *Eastern Salvage Assocs.*, ENGBCA 4046, 80-1 BCA ¶ 14,216. However, the Claims Court opinion in *Prestex Inc. v. United States*, 3 Cl. Ct. 373 (1983), contains dicta in note 5 stating that express oral contracts fail on the ground that they violate the recording statute.

Although the 31 U.S.C. § 1501 requirement for a signed document may preclude recovery on an express oral contract, it may not be enough to preclude recovery on a contract implied in fact. In *Narva Harris Constr. Corp. v. United States*, 216 Ct. Cl. 238, 574 F.2d 508 (1978), the Court of Claims recognized that an implied contract could exist even though some of the indicia of the agreement were oral statements concerning the transaction. In rejecting the Government's claim that 31 U.S.C. § 1501 barred the contractor's recovery, the court stated at 244:

> In almost all such cases, there is some sort of oral representation on the part of some Government agent. Although the party seeking to recover from the Government may not rely on the oral representation, and may rely totally on other, independent facts to establish the presence of an implied in fact contract or to recover in quantum meruit, the Government now seeks to make the mere existence of the oral representation, characterized as an oral express contract not reduced to writing, sufficient to compel this court to close its eyes to all other surrounding facts. Clearly such an expansive interpretation of § 200 [1501] is unacceptable.

The Claims Court has more recently noted that while 31 U.S.C. § 1501 "is rarely, if ever, the sole basis for invalidating an otherwise valid express oral agreement[,] . . . the provision manifests the general view that generally oral agreements provide a very shaky basis for granting relief by way of money judgments," *Edwards v. United States*, 22 Cl. Ct. 411 (1991).

2. Signature

A handwritten signature is probably the most universally accepted evidence of an agreement to be bound by a contract's terms. As early as 1951, the Comptroller General held that a signature does not have to be handwritten and that "any symbol adopted as one's signature when affixed with his knowledge and consent is a binding and legal signature," Comp. Gen. Dec. B-104590, Sept. 12, 1951, *Unpub.* 1 U.S.C. § 1 provides that " 'signature' or 'subscription' includes a mark when the person making the same intended it as such." Under common law, it has been determined that audio tape recordings can be considered to constitute a "signed writing" and are sufficient to create a contract. See *Ellis Canning Co. v. Berstein*, 348 F. Supp. 1212 (D. Colo. 1972).

The Comptroller General has concluded that EDI technology offers evidence of an intent to be bound that has the same attributes as a handwritten signature, *National Inst. of Standards & Technology*, 71 Comp. Gen. 109 (B-245714), 96-2 CPD ¶ 225. In this case, the Comptroller General held that EDI systems using message authentication codes that follow the National Institute of Standards and Technology's (NIST) Computer Data Authentication Standard or digital signatures following NIST's Digital Standard, can produce a form of evidence of a signature.

In an August 22, 1996 audit report (96-214), the DOD's Inspector General found that FACNET lacks the digital signature and encryption capabilities needed to ensure that the transactions are authentic and properly authorized and protected from loss, modification, or unauthorized disclosure. The IG recommended that until FACNET acquires such a digital signature capability, the network's use should be limited to transactions that do not require a signature.

Where facsimile transmission is authorized, a facsimile signature will be sufficient. In *American Eagle Indus, Inc.*, Comp. Gen. Dec. B-256907, 94-2 CPD ¶ 156, the Comptroller General held that a bidder's faxed modification did not render its bid nonresponsive merely because it instructed the agency to replace the original first page of its bid with a faxed page, thereby replacing the authorized agent's original signature with a faxed copy of the same agent's signature. Similarly, in *International Shelter Sys., Inc.*, 71 Comp. Gen. 142 (B-245466), 92-1 CPD ¶ 34, the protester argued that the facsimile and photocopy signatures did not equal an original signature and thus the bid was nonresponsive. The Comptroller General denied the protest and held that a photocopy of a signed bid document is binding as a duplicate of the original signed document because the signature still prevents the bidder from disavowing its obligations under the signed document.

An appeals board has followed the Comptroller General's reasoning that evidence of an intent to be bound has the same attributes as a handwritten signature. In *Regional Trucking, Inc.*, PSBCA 3918, 97-1 BCA ¶ 28,733, the board held that the hand-printed name and title of the contractor's president constituted acceptable evidence of the contractor's intent to be bound by the bid on which it was placed. The president had also hand-signed three other documents that were submitted as part of the bid and referred to the specific solicitation involved and the contractor subsequently completed, signed, and returned the preaward surveys. In reaching its decision, the board stated at 143,404:

> Courts, as well as the General Accounting Office, have long indicated a willingness to accept other than a handwritten signature on executory documents such as bid proposals. *See Ohl & Co. v. Smith Iron Works*, 288 U.S. 170, 176 (1932) (initials); *Benedict v. Lebowitz*, 346 F.2d 120 (2d Cir. 1965) (typed name); *Tabas v. Emergency Fleet Corporation*, 9 F.2d 648, 649 (E.D. Penn., 1926) (typed, printed or stamped signatures); *See also National Institute of Standards and Technology*, 71 Comp. Gen. 109 (1991) (use of electronic data interchange technology to create valid obligations). What is necessary is evidence of an intent to be bound. *Benedict v. Lebowitz, supra*; *see also*, *Peter J. O'Brien*, 96-2 CPD ¶ 91 (Aug. 29, 1996). In this case, Appellant hand printed the title of the corporation on the signature line, and hand printed "M.C. Johnson President" on the line calling for the name and title of the bidder. Mr. Johnson also hand signed three other documents which were submitted as a part of its bid, all of which either referred to the solicitation or highway route number. These actions constitute sufficient evidence of an intent to be bound by the bid documents. Furthermore, the fact that Appellant subsequently completed, signed and returned to Respondent the pre-award surveys, resolve any doubt of Appellant's intent to be bound by the bid it submitted.

3. Standard Form 30

Statutory or regulatory requirements and questions concerning the authority of the Government representatives have been involved in a number of decisions dealing with whether the parties' communications were intended to effect contractual relations. These matters might be grounds for making agreements unenforceable even if the parties had subjectively intended to contract. See Chapter 1. Thus, in some cases it is not clear whether the agreement is held to be unenforceable on the basis of the statute or regulation or because it was concluded that the parties did not intend to be bound until the statutory or regulatory provision has been satisfied. In *SCM Corp. v. United States*, 219 Ct. Cl. 459, 595 F.2d 595 (1979), the court held that the contractor and the contracting officer did not intend to be bound by their oral agreement settling a claim, stating at 464:

> Oral understandings which contemplate the finalization of the legal obligations in a written form are not contracts in themselves. When legal obligations between the parties *will be deferred* until the time when a written document is executed, there will not be a contract until that time. *See Restatement of Contracts* § 26 (1932). *See also Corbin on Contracts* § 30 (1963). Under the regulations, Government funds were not obligated until the execution of standard form 30. The parties were well aware of the fact that only the written contract modification could finalize their agreement. No commitments in the oral understanding to act in any way by either party were to be consummated until execution of the supplemental agreement. Whether the parties had reached a clear understanding of the terms of the settlement makes no difference and we specifically intimate no decision on that issue. We thus conclude that neither party was bound by its negotiations until standard form 30 was executed. This interpretation of the understanding and intent of the parties is supported by the actions of plaintiff in later seeking inclusion in the contract of an additional term for interest. Thus, we conclude that the representations made by telephone on January 6, 1976, did not constitute a contract.
>
> We note that this case does not squarely present the question of the enforceability of oral contracts with the Government. Instead, the case deals with the problem of what effect the parties' clear understanding of the procedures and regulations governing settlements had on their intent to consummate a binding contract. It should be kept in mind that oral understandings must first be contracts before they are enforceable. In this case, we simply hold that the understanding between the parties was not a contract and cannot sustain a breach of contract action in this court.

While the *SCM Corporation* decision was clearly based upon the conclusion that both parties did not intend to have a binding agreement until Standard Form (SF) 30 was signed, later decisions have focused on the need for a signed writing to modify an integrated contract. In *Mil-Spec Contractors, Inc. v. United States*, 835 F.2d 865 (Fed. Cir. 1987), the court cited the regulatory requirement for the use of a signed SF 30 in holding that an oral agreement was not a binding contract amendment. See also *Daly Constr., Inc. v. Garrett*, 5 F.3d 520 (Fed. Cir. 1993), stating at 521:

> To recover on an express agreement with a government agency, the agreement must be in writing and signed by an authorized person. *Mil-Spec Contractors, Inc. v. United States*, 835 F.2d 865 (Fed. Cir. 1987). We need not here discuss whether any circumstances might warrant departure from that standard, for as to this particular contract modification Daly, although poorly used by the pattern of lengthy negotiation, apparent agreement, unwarranted delay, and broken promises, was not deceived. Daly knew the government was not bound in contract until a formal written modification was executed.

The use of SF 30 was held to be a "mere formality" as long as the parties' agreement was in a signed writing, *Robinson Contracting Co. v. United States*, 16 Cl. Ct. 676 (1989), *aff'd*, 895 F.2d 1420 (Fed. Cir. 1989). See also *Adams Constr. Co.*, VABCA 4669, 97-1 BCA ¶ 28,801. While these decisions affect modifications to contracts, they do not deal with the initial formation of a contract.

B. Consideration

Consideration can be described as the price bargained and paid for a promise. It may consist of an act, a forbearance, or a return promise. *Restatement, Second, Contracts* § 71 defines "consideration" as follows:

> (1) To constitute consideration, a performance or a return promise must be bargained for.
>
> (2) A performance or return promise is bargained for if it is sought by the promisor in exchange for his promise and is given by the promisee in exchange for that promise.

(3) The performance may consist of

(a) an act other than a promise, or

(b) a forbearance, or

(c) the creation, modification, or destruction of a legal relation.

(4) The performance or return promise may be given to the promisor or to some other person. It may be given by the promisee or by some other person.

The requirement for consideration flowing to the Government is supported not only by the common-law rules but also by the rule that Government officials generally do not have the authority to give up vested rights of the Government without receiving consideration, *Simpson v. United States*, 172 U.S. 372 (1899). See also *Aviation Contractor Employees, Inc. v. United States*, 945 F.2d 1568 (Fed. Cir. 1991); *Metzger, Shadyac & Schwarz v. United States*, 12 Cl. Ct. 602 (1987); and *Joseph Pickard's Sons Co.*, ASBCA 13585, 73-1 BCA ¶ 10,026. The major exception to this rule is P.L. 85-804, 50 U.S.C. §§ 1431–35, which authorizes executive agencies to make or amend contracts without consideration when to do so would facilitate national defense. See FAR Part 50.

1. Form of Consideration

Generally, consideration in the typical sealed bid or negotiated Government contract is found in the exchange of promises to perform positive duties. A bid or proposal is a promise to furnish supplies or services offered in exchange for the Government's promise to pay for the work. The promise of compensation induces the offeror's promise of performance, and the offeror's promise to perform induces the award of the contract containing the Government's promise to pay upon completion. Each party's promise serves as consideration for the other's. In unilateral contracts, as in some simplified acquisitions, consideration takes the form of an act, i.e., performance, induced by the Government's promise to pay.

Consideration in contract modifications normally takes the form of promises by the contractor to perform work that is different from that originally required in exchange for the Government's promise to pay a different price. In some cases, the consideration may be the agreement to forbear from exercising a right such as asserting a claim.

a. Promises to Perform Duties

Cases in which consideration is not present may arise under different fact situations. In one type of case, the alleged promise or performance confers no benefit on the other party. In Government contracts, this most often occurs when the Government modifies a contract to benefit the contractor but receives no additional or different promise or performance in return. Under *Restatement, Second, Contracts* § 73, such modifications are without consideration because they involve performance of a preexisting duty that is neither doubtful nor the subject of honest dispute. See *Montefiore Hosp. v. United States*, 5 Cl. Ct. 471 (1984) (alleged agreement to modify contractual interest rate unenforceable because Government received no benefit); *AAA Eng'g & Drafting, Inc.*, ASBCA 36176, 91-2 BCA ¶ 23,812 (contract clause that provided for additional compensation as workload increased unenforceable where the Government did not order the minimum amount of work specified in the contract); *States Roofing & Metal Co.*, ASBCA 22091, 78-2 BCA ¶ 13,287 (change order that directed contractor to do work required under original contract for increased compensation not binding); and *A.O. Smith Corp.*, ASBCA 16788, 72-2 BCA ¶ 9688 (modification covering repair costs unenforceable since contractor was already obligated to make repairs). Furthermore, the Comptroller General has stated that a defaulted firm's bid on a reprocurement contract must be rejected if it is higher than the original contract price, on the grounds that acceptance of a higher bid would be tantamount to a contract modification increasing the price without any consideration for the Government, *A.R.E. Mfg. Co.*, Comp. Gen. Dec. B-246161, 92-1 CPD ¶ 210; *Air, Inc.*, Comp. Gen. Dec. B-233501, 88-2 CPD ¶ 505. See, however, *Salsbury Indus. v. United States*, 17 Cl. Ct. 47 (1989), *aff'd*, 905 F.2d 1518 (Fed. Cir. 1990), indicating that the requirement to give notice would be sufficient to enforce the contract.

Another situation where no consideration exists is where one party has a right to avoid any contractual duties. See *Restatement, Second, Contracts* § 77. See also *3 Williston, Contracts* § 7:13 (4th ed., 1992), which states at 271, "An agreement wherein one party reserves the right to cancel at his pleasure cannot create a contract." This issue has been raised concerning the present Termination for the Convenience of the Government clause. An early Government contracts case dealing with the question of lack of consideration and termination clause is *Sylvan Crest Sand & Gravel Co. v. United States*, 150 F.2d 642 (2d Cir. 1945). In that case, the clause stated, "Cancellation by the Procurement Division may be effected at any time." The appellate court held that the contract was not illusory because it contained an implied promise by the Government to give notice of cancellation within a reasonable time if it did not want to accept the goods. In *Torncello v. United States*, 231 Ct. Cl. 20, 681 F.2d 756 (1982), the court extensively discussed the consideration issue and concluded that the scope of termination rights had to be limited to prevent the absence of consideration. The court also indicated that it disagreed with the reasoning in *Sylvan Crest* that the bare requirement to give notice constituted consideration. See also *Salsbury Indus. v. United States*, 17 Cl. Ct. 47 (1989), *aff'd*, 905 F.2d 1518 (Fed. Cir. 1990), where the court in a footnote reiterated that notice of impending termination might not constitute sufficient consideration in a contract with a Termination clause. In *Krygoski Constr. Co. v. United States*, 94 F.3d 1537 (Fed. Cir. 1996), the court interpreted *Torncello* to impose only the limitation of bad faith on such terminations without discussing whether this constituted consideration. See *Judiciary Plaza Limited Partnership v. Securities & Exchange Comm'n*, GSBCA 12920-SEC, 96-2 BCA ¶ 28,596, holding that a lease that granted the landlord broad termination rights was not invalid for lack of consideration. The board stated that upon signing the lease, the parties became subject to the obligations thereunder. The lease expressly described the parties' obligations in the event of a termination.

b. Forbearance

Forbearance is a kind of consideration that does not involve the performance of any additional or modified duties. Perhaps the most common type of forbearance is involved in the settlement of claims. See *Restatement, Second, Contracts* § 74(1), which states:

> Forbearance to assert or the surrender of a claim or defense which proves to be invalid is not consideration unless
>
> (a) the claim or defense is in fact doubtful because of uncertainty as to the facts or the law, or
>
> (b) the forbearing or surrendering party believes that the claim or defense may be fairly determined to be valid.

See *Penn-Ohio Steel Corp. v. United States*, 173 Ct. Cl. 1064, 354 F.2d 254 (1965), where the Government argued that a contractor's agreement to vacate a building was not consideration because a contract clause entitled the Government to revoke the lease in case of a national emergency. The court found consideration because the contractor could have instituted a suit to enjoin the contractor's eviction from the plant under this legally questionable provision. Thus, the forbearance need not be on a claim that is legally correct. In *American Air Filter Co.*, ASBCA 14794, 72-1 BCA ¶ 9219, the Government believed that a high-pressure cutout switch was a required item in a contract to furnish air conditioners. The contractor contended that the item was not required. The board held that the position of the contractor was incorrect, but because the claim was not completely unreasonable or in bad faith, the settlement of the claim by the Government through contract modification was supported by consideration (the agreement by contractor to withdraw the claim). See also *Institutional & Envtl. Management*, ASBCA 32924, 90-3 BCA ¶ 23,118, where a modification lacked consideration because the contractor's relinquished claim had "no color or claim of right." The board's reasoning is consistent with the general principle that consideration exists if one party is relinquishing a legal right or forbearing to exercise it in exchange for something from the other party, *Busby School Bd. of the N. Cheyenne Tribe*, IBCA 3007, 94-1 BCA ¶ 26,327; *ITT Gilfillan, Inc. v. United States*, 200 Ct. Cl. 367, 471 F.2d 1382 (1973).

Another type of consideration through forbearance exists where the parties agree to release each other from a contract that has not been completely performed on either side. In *Savage Arms Corp. v. United States*, 266 U.S. 217 (1924), the Court stated at 220-21:

> A good deal is said by [the contractor] to the effect that this agreement was without consideration; but we need not stop to review the contention. It is enough to say that the parties to a contract may release themselves, in whole or in part, from its obligations so far as they remain executory, by mutual agreement without fresh consideration. The release of one is sufficient consideration for the release of the other. If authority for a rule so elementary be required, see, for example: *Hanson & Parker v. Wittenberg*, 205 Mass. 319, 326; *Collyer & Co. v. Moulton*, 9 R.I. 90, 92; *McCreery v. Day*, 119 N.Y. 1, 7; *Dreifus, Block & Co. v. Salvage Co.*, 194 Pa. St. 475, 486.

One example of such an agreement would be the no-cost termination authorized in FAR 49.402-4(c). In *Folk Constr. Co.*, ENGBCA 5839, 93-3

BCA ¶ 26,094, although not following the reasoning of *Savage Arms*, the board found that the release of claims for additional compensation was valid consideration, stating at 129,728:

> [We] conclude that the release of claims element of the agreement satisfies the requirement for consideration. The claims were neither meritless on their face nor manufactured. Even if a tribunal subsequently determines that released or settled claims would have been resolved on their merits against the party advancing them, it will not *nunc pro tunc* divest the settlement of its consideration value. . . . Furthermore, withdrawal of even specious claims has been recognized as supplying consideration, where the defendant realizes the "nuisance value" of not defending against the allegations. See *Restatement, Second, Contracts* § 74(1).

Similarly, in *Aviation Contractor Employees, Inc. v. United States*, 945 F.2d 1568 (Fed. Cir. 1991), the claims were determined by the court to be meritless but were held to be the subject of an "honest dispute," with the result that their withdrawal was found to constitute consideration for a modification.

2. Adequacy of Consideration

It is a well-established rule that the boards and courts will inquire only into whether there has been a bargained-for exchange and not into the adequacy of the consideration, *Silverman v. United States*, 230 Ct. Cl. 701, 679 F.2d. 865 (1982); *Mills v. United States*, 187 Ct. Cl. 696, 410 F.2d 1255 (1969). There is no requirement that the partys' obligations be relatively equal, *United States v. American Trading Co.*, 138 F. Supp. 536 (N.D. Cal. 1956); *Aywon Wire & Metal Corp.*, ASBCA 4966, 1963 BCA ¶ 3912. The Claims Court has stated that a contract does not lack mutuality merely because a particular promise is not offset by a similar promise or obligation. Rather, "the pertinent question is whether the agreement as a whole is supported by mutual consideration," *Florida Keys Aqueduct Auth. v. United States*, 7 Cl. Ct. 297 (1985). However, if the consideration furnished by a party is so inadequate as to cause the tribunal to determine that the agreement would be unconscionable, it will not be enforced. See *Hume v. United States*, 132 U.S. 406 (1889), stating at 410:

> That an agreement to pay $1200 a ton for shucks, actual worth not more than $35 a ton, is a grossly unconscionable bargain, defined in Bouvier's Law Dictionary to be "a contract which no man in his senses, not under delusion, would make, on the one hand, and which no fair and honest man

> would accept on the other," nobody can doubt. Such a contract, whether founded on fraud, accident, mistake, folly, or ignorance, is void at common law. It is not necessary to invoke the aid of a court of equity to reform it. Courts of law will always refuse to enforce such a bargain, as against the public policy of honesty, fair dealing, and good morals.

Similarly, the Comptroller General has also indicated that he will not inquire into adequacy of the bargain when determining whether consideration exists. See, e.g., 47 Comp. Gen. 170 (B-160886) (1967), where the Comptroller stated at 173:

> However, it is well settled that the legal sufficiency of a promise or benefit is not dependent upon the adequacy of the bargain. In other words, an extravagant promise for an inadequate consideration will still be held to constitute legally sufficient consideration. See *Contracts*, 17 Am. Jur. 2d, sections 85, 92 and 102. Accordingly, we conclude that the portion of the amendment dealing with the culler-stacker is supported by consideration.

The Comptroller General has indicated that the reasoning behind the refusal to address the adequacy of the consideration lies in the belief that it is an issue of contract administration, better left to the individual agencies. See *Stancil-Hoffman Corp.*, Comp. Gen. Dec. B-193001.2, 80-2 CPD ¶ 226, stating:

> The issue as to adequacy of the consideration received by the Air Force for relaxing the delivery schedule of VRC's contract pertains to a matter of contract administration since the reinstatement of the contract has been found to be proper. As such, it is not for resolution within our bid protest function. See *Acadian Airmotive Inc.*, B-196414, 80-1 CPD ¶ 270.

3. Severability of Consideration

Most Government contracts involve a number of obligations of or benefits to each party. In general, such contracts are not divided into individual exchanges. Thus, the total benefit or detriment of one party is normally thought to be consideration for the total obligations of the other. Further, a single obligation or benefit can support a number of promises. However, these rules do not apply when the agreements are severable, for example, when a benefit or promise runs to only one portion of the contract. In *Shipco Gen., Inc.*, ASBCA 29206, 86-2 BCA ¶ 18,973, the Government granted an extension of the contract completion date in consideration of the contractor's release of a valid claim. The contract modification contained a separate provision applying liquidated damages to a more demanding delivery requirement. The board held that the parties did not intend that the time extension relate to the altered provisions regarding the delivery schedule. Therefore, the agreements were severable and the revised delivery schedule failed for lack of consideration by the Government. See also 47 Comp. Gen. 170 (B-160886) (1967), where the Comptroller General divided a contract amendment into three separate agreements for the purpose of consideration and found one to lack sufficient consideration. In *Pennsylvania Exch. Bank v. United States*, 145 Ct. Cl. 216, 170 F. Supp. 629 (1959), the contract called for work in four steps. Steps I, II, and III required the contractor to tool up and get ready to manufacture exchange tees. Step IV required the contractor to stand by and be prepared to manufacture the tees. The contractor claimed it was not bound since the Government was not obligated to order any tees under Step IV. The court first found that the contract was not severable. It then held that consideration existed even though the contractor was reimbursed only for its costs in Steps I, II, and III. The contractor was benefited by obtaining, at Government expense, the capacity to produce the tees. See also *Hemet Valley Flying Serv. Co. v. United States*, 7 Cl. Ct. 512 (1985), where the Forest Service paid the contractor to be available to fly. This payment was an indivisible part of the contract which furnished consideration for the contractor's obligation to satisfy all the Forest Service's flight order needs.

Because a release of a claim must be supported by consideration, severability of consideration has been used to avoid general releases included in change orders. For example, compensation for the increased costs of change orders was held to be inadequate to support a general release of the contractor's subsequent claims arising from the defective Government property that precipitated the change orders, *Dero Indus., Inc.*, ASBCA 16473, 72-1 BCA ¶ 9462. See also *Sam Won Dev. Co.*, ASBCA 16541, 74-2 BCA ¶ 10,730, where the board stated that such a release by the contractor would be gratuitous. Furthermore, when the parties do not intend a time extension to be the sole consideration for a change order, claims for additional compensation arising from the change order are not precluded, *Discon Corp.*, ASBCA 15981, 71-2 BCA ¶ 9069. Where, however, the amount agreed upon by the negotiating parties is not clearly related solely to the change order involved, or there is a good faith dispute concerning either the entitlement to the adjustment or its amount, the inclusion of a broader release or waiver will be supported by the compromise agreement, *Boston Shipyard Corp. v. United States Military Sealift Command*, 886 F.2d 451 (1st Cir. 1989); *Spellman Eng'g Inc.*, NASABCA 367-11, 69-2 BCA

¶ 7891. Of course, a release already called for by the contract upon completion of performance is not lacking consideration even though the contractor receives only amounts otherwise due, *Inland Empire Builders, Inc. v. United States*, 191 Ct. Cl. 742, 424 F.2d 1370 (1970); *Optimum Designs, Inc.*, ASBCA 16986, 74-1 BCA ¶ 10,622. Such releases are based on the consideration contained in the Government's promises in the original contract.

4. Consideration in Variable Quantity Contracts

When the Government wishes to obtain firm contractual commitments from contractors but is unable to forecast its precise needs, an indefinite-quantity contract is often used. There are three basic types of indefinite-quantity contracts. The most commonly used of these contract forms is the requirements contract, wherein the Government agrees to purchase its "needs" or "requirements" from one contractor for a particular period of time. See FAR 16.503(a). Consideration issues arise in this type agreement because the contractor is bound to furnish items but the Government is not bound to make any orders. In response, boards and courts hold that consideration is found in the Government's agreement to purchase its requirements solely from the contractor and in its implied obligation to order and identify those requirements in good faith, *United States v. Purcell Envelope Co.*, 249 U.S. 313 (1919); *Ceredo Mortuary Chapel, Inc. v. United States,* 29 Fed. Cl. 346 (1993); *Vehicle Maintenance Servs. v. General Servs. Admin.*, GSBCA 11663, 94-2 BCA ¶ 26,893. In *Machlett Labs., Inc.*, ASBCA 16194, 73-1 BCA ¶ 9929, the board found an enforceable contract even though the Government never placed a single order. Similarly, in 52 Comp. Gen. 732 (B-176901) (1973), it was held that the use of a clause providing that "no guarantee is given that any quantities will be purchased" did not render a requirements contract unenforceable for lack of consideration. An unusual case where the court enforced a requirements contract is *Torncello v. United States*, 231 Ct. Cl. 20, 681 F.2d 756 (1982). In this case, the contractor was awarded a requirements contract by the Navy for grounds maintenance and refuse removal. The contractor's bid itemization, accepted by the Government, specified a per-call charge of $500 for any call under the pest control item. It turned out, however, that the Navy only needed gopher-control work which was customarily cheaper than $500 per call. Therefore, the Navy did not call the contractor for this work but instead requested such work from a competing bidder on the original solicitation. The contractor claimed that the Navy had breached its contract when it diverted work to a competing bidder.

The court agreed and rejected the Government's argument that the Termination for Convenience clause creates in the Government an implicit right to refrain from giving a contractor work if it is not in the best interests of the Government. The court stated at 42:

> It must be concluded, then, that the government's promise to turn to Soledad for all of its pest control work, if it was also implicit in the termination for convenience clause that the Government could give Soledad none, was no promise at all. The contract would thus fail [for lack of consideration].

A second type of indefinite-quantity contract requires the contractor to furnish all supplies or services ordered by the Government but obligates the Government to order only a stated minimum quantity. See FAR 16.504 and FAR 52.216-22. After the Government has ordered the minimum quantity, it is free to order the remainder of its "needs" or "requirements" from either the same contractor or from any other source. However, the contractor continues to be bound to supply all that is ordered from it even after the minimum amount. Consideration to support this unique obligation of the contractor is found in the Government's agreement to order the minimum quantity. The minimum order, however, must be for more than just a nominal amount in order for consideration to exist, *Mapco Alaska Petroleum, Inc. v. United States,* 27 Fed. Cl. 405 (1992); *Tennessee Soap Co. v. United States*, 130 Ct. Cl. 154, 126 F. Supp. 439 (1954); FAR 16.501(a)(2). In *Tennessee Soap*, the Government agreed to purchase only a $10 minimum amount, which was held to be nominal. See also *Goldwasser v. United States*, 163 Ct. Cl. 450, 325 F.2d 722 (1963). In *C.W. Over & Sons, Inc.*, Comp. Gen. Dec. B-274365, 96-2 CPD ¶ 223, the Comptroller General held that the requirement that the value of an indefinite-quantity contract be more than nominal does not apply to individual task orders under a contract. In this case, the Comptroller General found it sufficient that there was a guarantee minimum value of $800,000 for the base contract period.

Another type of indefinite-quantity contract is one that does not bind the Government either to purchase its requirements or to place a minimum order. Such contracts are often referred to as "wish, want or will" contracts and are unenforceable for lack of consideration where no order is placed, *Modern Sys. Technology Corp.*, 24 Cl. Ct. 360 (1991); *Updike v. United States*, 69 Ct. Cl. 394 (1930). However, if the Government places an order with the contractor, it will be treated as an offer that the contractor may accept to form a binding agreement as to that particular order. See, for example, *Bel Pre Health Care Ctr. v. United States,* 24 Cl. Ct. 495 (1991);

Ann Riley & Assocs., DOTBCA 2418, 93-3 BCA ¶ 25,963. In *Ralph Constr., Inc. v. United States*, 4 Cl. Ct. 727 (1984), the court found lack of consideration in an indefinite-quantity contract that contained no promised minimum quantity and no firm requirements promise because the Government had reserved the right to assign work to its own workforce. However, rather than finding that the entire contract was unenforceable for lack of consideration, the court found that it was valid only to the extent it was performed. On this basis, the court held that the contractor was entitled to the reasonable value of the work completed but was not entitled to additional costs.

If a contract is susceptible to interpretation as either an indefinite-quantity contract without a specified minimum order or a requirements contract, the general rule is that the court should uphold it as a requirements type, *A-Transport Northwest Co. v. United States,* 27 Fed. Cl. 206 (1992).

5. Consideration to Contractor

Although it is clear that the Government must receive consideration for the execution of a contract modification, there is a split of authority on the need for the contractor to receive consideration. The Comptroller General has held that a contractor need not receive consideration to be bound by a contract modification, Comp. Gen. Dec. B-151383, Nov. 3, 1966, *Unpub.* See also *Mid-State Prods. Co. v. Commodity Credit Corp.*, 196 F.2d 416 (7th Cir. 1952); and *Equipment Corp. v. United States*, 98 Ct. Cl. 159 (1942).

However, three boards of contract appeals have held that a contractor must receive consideration. In one case, a $700 credit to the Government for substitution of a conforming brand was held to be without consideration since the Government was obligated to accept a conforming brand under the original contract, *Hunt Bldg. Marts*, DOTCAB 69-6, 69-2 BCA ¶ 8042. The second case involved the Government's reduction of the contract price for a nonconforming item. Having determined that the item was acceptable, the board held that the agreement reducing the price was without consideration and, thus, not binding, *Airco Eng'rs*, AGBCA 245, 72-1 BCA ¶ 9215. In a third case, the Government issued a unilateral contract modification adding a Liquidated Damages clause to the contract. The board held that because the amount of liquidated damages to be assessed in the event of delay is a vital condition affecting the price of a contract, the Government's unilateral modification was not supported by consideration and, therefore, was not binding upon the contractor, *Jacqueline Howell, Ltd.*, ASBCA 27026, 82-2 BCA ¶ 16,086.

In addition, at least one board of contract appeals has adopted the view in *Restatement, Second, of Contracts* § 89 that allows modification of an executory agreement without consideration to the contractor: "(a) if the modification is fair and equitable in view of circumstances not anticipated by the parties when the contract was made; or (b) to the extent provided by statute; or (c) to the extent that justice requires enforcement in view of a material change of position in reliance on the promise." See *Florida East Coast Properties, Inc.*, GSBCA 7538, 86-3 BCA ¶ 19,070; *Universal Bldg. Servs. Inc.*, GSBCA 7396, 85-1 BCA ¶ 17,732; *Zebra Corp.*, GSBCA 4723, 80-2 BCA ¶ 14,484.

C. Promissory Estoppel

Promissory estoppel is a concept developed by the courts to enforce agreements on the basis of fairness and justice when consideration is not present but a person has reasonably relied on a promise. Whereas equitable estoppel is used to bar a party from raising a defense or objection, promissory estoppel is used to create a cause of action, *Knaub v. United States*, 22 Cl. Ct. 268 (1991). The necessary requirements for application of promissory estoppel are stated in *Restatement, Second, Contracts* § 90:

> (1) A promise which the promisor should reasonably expect to induce action or forbearance on the part of the promisee or a third person and which does induce such action or forbearance is binding if injustice can be avoided only by enforcement of the promise. The remedy granted for breach may be limited as justice requires.

Promissory estoppel has been infrequently used in Government contracts, and it would appear that in some of the cases where is has been applied, it has been used unnecessarily. See, for example, *George H. Whike Constr. Co. v. United States*, 135 Ct. Cl. 126, 140 F. Supp. 560 (1956), where the bidder entered into a written contract and performed it upon the assurance that the provision for reimbursement included in its bid would protect it from increased costs resulting from changes in labor regulations. It seems apparent that either the contractor's agreement or its subsequent performance should have been sufficient consideration. There was no need to resort to promissory estoppel since the "acts in reliance" were the very things bargained for by the Government. See also *Lockheed Shipbuilding & Constr. Co.*, ASBCA 18460, 75-1 BCA ¶ 11,246, *recons. denied*, 75-2 BCA ¶ 11,566, and *Mercury Mach. & Mfg. Co.*, ASBCA 20068, 76-1 BCA ¶ 11,809, where all of the elements of consideration were present but the board held for the contractor based on "equitable or promissory estoppel." In *Louisiana Lamps & Shades*, ASBCA 45294, 95-1 BCA ¶ 27,577, the board held that the Government did not establish promissory estoppel because the Government did not prove that the terminating contracting officer relied on the contractor's promise to deliver the work by a certain date when deciding not to terminate the contractor for default.

The Claims Court has stated that it has no jurisdiction to render judgment against the United States on the theory of promissory estoppel since it is "founded on contracts implied-in-law," *Lichtefeld-Massaro, Inc. v. United States*, 17 Cl. Ct. 67 (1989); *Pacific Gas & Elec. Co. v. United States*, 3 Cl. Ct. 329 (1983), *aff'd*, 738 F.2d 452 (Fed. Cir. 1984) (court affirmed decision without a discussion of promissory estoppel).

This rationale does not recognize the distinction between promissory estoppel and implied-in-fact contracts. Although both concepts are based upon considerations of justice and fairness, promissory estoppel requires that the person being charged make an actual promise, express or implied in fact. On the other hand, the "promises" referred to in contracts implied in law (alternatively referred to as "quasi contracts") are legal fictions. They are "implied" by courts to recognize that a person of good faith would want to pay compensation for a benefit that they received from another. They are based upon the legal and equitable rules of restitution, which, according to the Supreme Court, are not covered by the Tucker Act, *Merritt v. United States*, 267 U.S. 338 (1925). Nevertheless, the court continues to hold that it has no jurisdiction of claims based upon promissory estoppel, e.g., *Gregory v. United States*, 37 Fed. Cl. 388 (1997).

The lack of jurisdiction rationale does not seem to have affected claims based on promissory estoppel at the boards of contract appeals. See, for example, *Systems Management American Corp.*, ASBCA 45704, 97-1 BCA ¶ 28,820 (claim reinstated to determine whether contractor's reliance was based on assurances that option would be exercised). The focus of the cases has been whether the requirements of § 90 of the *Restatement* are satisfied. See *State Street Management Corp. v. General Servs. Admin.*, GSBCA 12374, 94-1 BCA ¶ 26,500 (Government statements not specific enough for reliance); and *Louisiana Lamps & Shades*, ASBCA 45294, 95-1 BCA

¶ 27,577 (Government did not prove reliance in its claim based on promissory estoppel).

In *Law Mathematics & Technology, Inc. v. United States*, 779 F.2d 675 (Fed. Cir. 1985), on appeal from a board of contract appeals, the contractor argued that it took certain actions in reliance on the Government's assurances that it would provide additional funds on the contract. The court held that even if the Government had made such assurances and the contractor had relied upon them, the contractor still could not recover. The court held that the contractor's reliance would not have been reasonable, stating at 679:

> Finally, even if LMT had relied to its detriment on any promises or assertions, such reliance could not have been reasonable in this case. Dr. Sponsler is an attorney, with the ability to understand the specific limitations of the contract language. Moreover, Sponsler is also a former Navy employee, and should have been, if he was not, familiar with the uncertainty of relying on additional allocations to Navy research contracts.

In another appeal from a board of contract appeals, the Government argued that promissory estoppel was not available against the Government. In a decision not for precedent, the court did not address this argument, disposing of the appeal on the grounds that the contractor did not offer "any concrete evidence that it relied on a promise to change its position for the worse," *Delfour, Inc. v. Runyon*, 95 F. 3d 1163 (Fed. Cir. 1996).

CHAPTER 3

ACQUISITION PLANNING

"Acquisition planning" is an expansive term that includes actions aimed at stating the Government's needs, identifying potential sources, and determining the techniques to be used to satisfy those needs. It is the first step in the procurement process. FAR 7.101 contains the following broad definition:

> "Acquisition planning" means the process by which the efforts of all personnel responsible for an acquisition are coordinated and integrated through a comprehensive plan for fulfilling the agency need in a timely manner and at a reasonable cost. It includes developing the overall strategy for managing the acquisition.

A well-planned procurement will be structured to comply with the numerous acquisition laws and regulations as well as to obtain, most effectively, the goods or services needed by the agency. A procurement that is not well planned can lead to numerous problems that waste the time and funds of both the procuring agency and the offerors.

This chapter reviews all elements of acquisition planning conducted by a procuring agency. The first section explains the planning process as mandated by law and implemented by regulation. The next two sections cover the requirement for competition and the selection of the contracting technique. The fourth section addresses identifying sources for obtaining goods or services. The fifth section deals with the preparation of the statement of work. The sixth section deals with the consideration of overall cost to the Government in the acquisition planning process. The final section covers public announcements and solicitations.

I. PLANNING PROCESS

The planning process brings all members of the acquisition team together to formulate the strategy that will be used to conduct a procurement.

A. Requirement for Planning

As a result of deficiencies in the planning process, a number of agencies began to focus on the need for more formalized acquisition planning in the 1970s. Congress also identified this need during discussions on the Competition in Contracting Act of 1984 (CICA). As a result, the Armed Services Procurement Act and the Federal Property and Administrative Services Act now require that an executive agency "use advance procurement planning and market research" in preparing for the procurement of property or services, 10 U.S.C. § 2305(a)(1)(A)(ii); 41 U.S.C. § 253a(a)(1)(B). FAR Part 7 implements this requirement.

FAR 7.102(b) states that "[t]he purpose of this planning is to ensure that the Government meets its needs in the most effective, economical, and timely manner." The acquisition planning requirement in FAR 7.102 is pervasive:

> Agencies shall perform acquisition planning and conduct market research (see part 10) for all acquisitions in order to promote and provide for —
>
> (1) Acquisition of commercial items or, to the extent that commercial items suitable to meet the agency's needs are not available, nondevelopmental items, to the maximum extent practicable (10 U.S.C. 2377 and 41 U.S.C. 251, et seq.); and
>
> (2) Full and open competition (see part 6), or, when full and open competition is not required in accordance with part 6, to obtain competition to the maximum extent practicable, with due regard to the nature of the supplies or services to be acquired (10 U.S.C. 2301(a)(5) and 41 U.S.C. 253a(a)(1)).

In some cases, the lack of adequate acquisition planning will place the agency in a position where it will attempt to acquire supplies and services without obtaining full and open competition. See *Freund Precision, Inc.*, 66 Comp. Gen. 90 (B-223613), 86-2 CPD ¶ 543 (failure to plan ahead precluded agency from evaluating protester's alternate product and resulted in sole source procurement); and *TeQcom, Inc.*, Comp. Gen. Dec. B-224664, 86-2 CPD ¶ 700 (failure to plan ahead effectively deprived offerors of any opportunity to qualify their products so that they could compete with the brand name manufacturer). In this regard, lack of advance planning does not justify noncompetitive procurement, as stated in 10 U.S.C. § 2304(f)(5) and 41 U.S.C. § 253(f)(5):

> In no case may the head of an agency —
>
> > (A) enter into a contract for property or services using procedures other than competitive procedures on the basis of the lack of advance planning.

Cases finding a lack of advance planning include *K-Whit Tools, Inc.*, Comp. Gen. Dec. B-247081, 92-1 CPD ¶ 382 (agency took 10 months to determine requirements when it knew that the items were required by a fixed deadline); *Service Contractors*, Comp. Gen. Dec. B-243236, 91-2 CPD ¶ 49 (lack of advance planning found where procurement process for ongoing services commenced six months after expiration of prior contract); and *Pacific Sky Supply, Inc.*, 66 Comp. Gen. 370 (B-225513), 87-1 CPD ¶ 358 (nine-week delay in processing paperwork on qualification requirement deprived protester of a reasonable opportunity to compete).

Advance planning need not be entirely error-free or actually successful, *Sprint Communications Co.*, Comp. Gen. Dec. B-262003.2, 96-1 CPD ¶ 24. However, the planning actions must be reasonable. In *New Breed Leasing Corp.*, Comp. Gen. Dec. B-274201, 96-2 CPD ¶ 202, the Comptroller General sustained a protest, finding that had the agency engaged in reasonable advance planning, it would not have taken more than a year after the solicitations were issued to realize that the solicitations were fundamentally flawed in failing to contain basic information. Similarly, in *Commercial Drapery Contractors, Inc.*, Comp. Gen. Dec. B-271222, 96-1 CPD ¶ 290, an agency sought to justify its issuance of purchase orders to a Multiple Award Federal Supply Schedule contractor at higher prices than offered by other Federal Supply Schedule contractors by arguing that it urgently needed the supplies and only the selected contractor could meet the delivery time frame. The Comptroller General sustained the protest, finding that the urgency resulted from delays caused by the agency's prior improper issuance of purchase orders to the same contractor for the same requirement and the subsequent cancellation of those orders in response to clearly meritorious protests. See, however, *Datacom, Inc.*, Comp. Gen. Dec. B-274175, 96-2 CPD ¶ 199, where the Comptroller General rejected the protester's claim that the urgency necessitating a noncompetitive sole source award and contract modification resulted from the lack of advance planning. In this case, the decision on how to conduct the procurement was the subject of significant congressional action. The Comptroller General would not fault the Air Force for failure to compete its procurement in the face of a congressional report directing the agency to go no further in its effort to hold a competition of any kind.

The fact that a procurement is noncompetitive does not necessarily establish that there was a lack of acquisition planning. See *Honeycomb Co. of Am.*, Comp. Gen. Dec. B-225685, 87-1 CPD ¶ 579, where the agency made a reasonable but unsuccessful effort to obtain competition. The Comptroller General distinguished such a case from those where there was an absence of advance planning. See also *Sprint Communications Co.*, Comp. Gen. Dec. B-262003.2, 96-1 CPD ¶ 24, where the Comptroller General stated that there was no requirement that planning be successful. In *Rex Sys., Inc.*, Comp. Gen. Dec. B-239524, 90-2 CPD ¶ 185, the agency's continued negotiations with a failing contractor placed it in a position of urgency requiring a sole source award. Although the Comptroller General in "hindsight" indicated that he might disagree with how long the negotiations were allowed to continue, he was unable to say that such actions were unreasonable. The Comptroller General found that the efforts sought to establish the failing contractor as an alternate source and were therefore related to procurement planning and fostering competition. The fact that the efforts were unsuccessful did not constitute a lack of planning. In *Federal Data Corp.*, GSBCA 8488-P, 86-3 BCA ¶ 19,068, the agency held up a procurement at the request of a congressman until after a study was completed and awarded a sole source contract to the incumbent contractor on an interim basis so that operations would continue. The board held that the need to award the sole source contract was not due to a lack of advance planning but, rather, was a result of permissible cooperation with Congress.

B. Statement of Need

The acquisition plan should begin with a brief statement of need. The need for the acquisition is identified and documented by the program or technical personnel in the agency who prepare the budget justification. Generally, the need will have been fully justified during the budget process and can merely be restated in the acquisition plan. If the acquisition planning is being done prior to preparing the budget, the agency will have to analyze its needs in a thorough manner as part of the acquisition plan.

The plan should "[s]pecify the required capabilities or performance characteristics of the supplies or services being acquired and state how they are related to the need," FAR 7.105(a)(4). This requirement should assist the agency in identifying restrictive provisions in the statement of work that may preclude potential contractors from participating in the procurement. When such provisions are identified, an agency can address possible ways to eliminate them. The guidance on restrictive specifications is reviewed below in the discussion of specifications.

C. Contents of Plan

The acquisition plan must identify all actions essential to the conduct of a successful procurement and establish milestones for their performance. See FAR 7.105, which provides the following general guidance regarding the elements of the acquisition plan:

> In order to facilitate attainment of the acquisition objectives, the plan must identify those milestones at which decisions should be made (see subparagraph (b)(18) below). The plan shall address all the technical, business, management, and other significant considerations that will control the acquisition. The specific content of plans will vary, depending on the nature, circumstances, and stage of the acquisition.

FAR 7.105(a) contains a brief description of the elements of the acquisition plan under the category "Acquisition Background and Objectives," while FAR 7.105(b) describes additional elements under the category "Plan of Action." The Background and Objectives section considers what the Government is buying, how it will evaluate price and other cost factors, where the work is to be performed, and the risks involved. The Plan of Action section describes the steps necessary to procure the identified articles or services. Although the elements are discussed separately, they are interrelated.

The contents of the acquisition plan also should include a summary of any contractual history. This summary, normally done by the contracting officer, should identify each previous procurement that impacts the current planning. This is a key element in the planning process because it identifies how the current procurement fits in the overall conduct of the agency's business. The contractual history also identifies those cases where the procurement is part of an ongoing program, such as the development of a new product. In such cases, the agency normally will have adopted an acquisition plan for the entire program, and the planning for each step in the program will merely verify that the overall plan is still valid. On the other hand, the contractual history may identify previous procurements that have been unsuccessful — indicating that a new approach is needed. Thus, the contractual history is a key starting point for the preparation of the plan.

The plan should contain a concise statement of the acquisition strategy to be followed. See, for example, DOD Regulation 5000.2-R, Part 3 (Mar. 15, 1996), which contains general guidance on arriving at a sound acquisition strategy within the Department of Defense (DOD). This regulation describes the planning of an acquisition strategy for a new system as an iterative process that becomes increasingly more definitive as the system progresses from the initial stages of advanced research to production. Curiously, the FAR does not require agencies to include a summary of the acquisition strategy in the plan. Nonetheless, planners should strive to draft a clear and explicit statement of the agency's strategy to ensure that all agency personnel understand how the procurement goal is to be achieved.

In formulating the acquisition strategy, the entire planning team should review all acquisition alternatives that could be used to conduct the procurement. Any acquisition strategy that will enhance the procurement should be considered as an alternative, and all members of the team should be encouraged to propose ideas. This element of the plan calls for innovative thinking, especially if the acquisition techniques used in the past have not been fully successful.

The contents of the plan also should include such considerations as the method for obtaining and using priorities, allocations, and allotments; consideration of make-or-buy programs; description of the test and evaluation program of the contractor and Government; description of logistical support; applicable environmental issues associated with the acquisition; how security will be established, maintained, and monitored; what Government property or information will be furnished to the contractor; what management system will be used by the Government to monitor the contractor's effort; as well as any other consideration that might impact the procurement. For a discussion of these elements of the acquisition plan, see Nash and Cibinic, *Competitive Negotiation: The Source Selection Process* (1993).

1. Acquisition Milestones

Each acquisition plan should contain a specific set of milestones for the procurement. The basic milestones are set forth in FAR 7.105(b)(19):

> *Milestones for the acquisition cycle.* Address the following steps and any others appropriate:
>
> Acquisition plan approval.
>
> Statement of work.
>
> Specifications.
>
> Data requirements.
>
> Completion of acquisition-package preparation.
>
> Purchase request.
>
> Justification and approval for other than full and open competition where applicable and/or any required D&F approval.
>
> Issuance of synopsis.
>
> Issuance of solicitation.
>
> Evaluation of proposals, audits, and field reports.
>
> Beginning and completion of negotiations.
>
> Contract preparation, review, and clearance.
>
> Contract award.

Any additional steps that are required to implement the acquisition plan should also be included in the milestone chart.

2. Applicable Conditions

This part of the plan identifies the *constraints* that must be imposed on the end product of the procurement, as set forth in FAR 7.105(a)(2):

> *Applicable conditions.* State all significant conditions affecting the acquisition, such as (i) requirements for compatibility with existing or future systems or programs and (ii) any known cost, schedule, and capability or performance constraints.

Precise identification of significant conditions early in the procurement process enables the agency to explore steps that can be taken to reduce or eliminate constraints that could have a detrimental impact on the procurement being planned. For example, if a product to be procured must be fully compatible with items in the agency's inventory, the agency may have to provide detailed drawings in the procurement package or induce the original manufacturer to license other sources in order to obtain sufficient competition to ensure a reasonable price. In this case, identification of this constraint would lead to the adoption of a strategy that would make detailed drawings available to a number of competitors.

Of course, identification of a constraint does not guarantee that there is a strategy that will completely overcome it. Many constraints must be accepted as an inherent element of the procurement. However, early identification of such constraints is beneficial because it assists all members of the planning team in recognizing the limitations that must be accepted in the conduct of the procurement being planned.

3. Justifications and Approvals

When the acquisition plan proposes a strategy that entails using a procurement that is "other than competitive," 41 U.S.C. § 253(f) and 10 U.S.C. § 2304(f) require the contracting officer to provide written justification for the use of such procedures. These statutes require that the justification contain the following six elements:

> (A) a description of the agency's needs;
>
> (B) an identification of the statutory exception from the requirement to use competitive procedures and a demonstration, based on the proposed contractor's qualifications or the nature of the procurement, of the reasons for using that exception;
>
> (C) a determination that the anticipated cost will be fair and reasonable;
>
> (D) a description of the market survey conducted or a statement of the reasons a market survey was not conducted;

(E) a listing of the sources, if any, that expressed in writing an interest in the procurement; and

(F) a statement of the actions, if any, the agency may take to remove or overcome any barrier to competition before a subsequent procurement for such needs.

See FAR 6.303-2 for additional guidance on the contents of this justification.

This justification must be certified as accurate and complete by the contracting officer responsible for awarding the contract, 41 U.S.C. § 253(f)(1)(A), 10 U.S.C. § 2304(f)(1)(A). It must then be reviewed and approved pursuant to Section 253(f)(1)(B) and Section 2304(f)(1)(B), as amended by § 4102 of the Clinger-Cohen Act of 1996, as follows:

Contract Amount		Approval Authority
Over	Not in excess of	
$500,000	$10,000,000	Competition advocate without delegation
$10,000,000	$50,000,000	Head of Procuring Activity or delegate (Flag Officer or GS-16 rank or above)
$50,000,000	--------	Senior Procurement Executive of Agency without delegation

Justification and Approvals (J&As) should be prepared and approved during the acquisition planning process. However, they may be made subsequently and even after award if circumstances warrant, FAR 6.303-1(e). While late preparation of a J&A may not represent good planning, the lateness will not affect the validity of an otherwise proper J&A, *AUTOFLEX, Inc.*, Comp. Gen. Dec. B-240012, 90-2 CPD ¶ 294 (J&A executed after the closing date for receipt of proposals but prior to award); and *Magnavox Elec. Sys. Co.*, Comp. Gen. Dec. B-258076.2, 94-2 CPD ¶ 266 (J&A not invalidated even though modified and signed by the approving authority after the lower-level officials had signed it and after a protest was filed). Similarly, if additional facts are learned after a J&A has been prepared, an amended J&A will satisfy the detailed requirements for information that must be included, *Minowitz Mfg. Co.*, Comp. Gen. Dec. B-228502, 88-1 CPD ¶ 1.

Procurements will be overturned if the J&A does not contain a reasonable explanation for the avoidance of full and open competition, *NI Indus., Inc.*, Comp. Gen. Dec. B-223941, 86-2 CPD ¶ 674 (elimination of one of two mobilization base contractors was not adequately justified where the J&A contained no statement of the particular facts and circumstances that would justify a sole source award); *Sturm, Ruger & Co.*, Comp. Gen. Dec. B-235938, 89-2 CPD ¶ 375 (documentation not meeting the specific requirements applicable to J&As was insufficient to justify the avoidance of full and open competition).

Class J&As are permitted if approved in writing in accordance with agency procedures, FAR 6.304(c). When class J&As are used, the approval level should probably be determined by the estimated total value of the class. Class J&As will not be sufficient if they do not relate to the particular facts and circumstances of the specific procurement being questioned, *NI Indus., Inc.*, Comp. Gen. Dec. B-223941, 86-2 CPD ¶ 674.

D. Preparation of Plan

An effective plan must be timely prepared and have the participation of all agency personnel whose input can affect its viability. In addition, attention should be given to program requirements as well as individual contracts.

1. Time of Preparation

It is essential that acquisition planning be done early in the process to ensure that all actions necessary to carry out an effective procurement can be performed within the procurement cycle. FAR 7.104(a) provides that "[a]cquisition planning should begin as soon as the agency need is identified, preferably well in advance of the fiscal year in which contract award is necessary." This recognizes that a complex procurement may require up to several years from the time the requirement is identified until a contract is awarded. In such cases, acquisition planning must start at essentially the same time as the budget process and must be executed simultaneously. This, of course, means that if the requirement is ultimately not funded, some planning effort will be wasted. However, to ensure that the ultimate procurement is carried out effectively, such a risk may be unavoidable.

DOD Directive 5000.1, Mar. 15, 1996, identifies that, in the acquisition of a new system, the acquisition process is concurrent with both the budgeting process and the requirements generation process. See **Figure 3-1**. These three key management processes, then, are completely interactive, and acquisition planning must be done very early in the life of a new system.

Other agencies have also sought to ensure that acquisition planning is conducted on a timely basis. For example, NFS 1807.102(b) states that, regardless of the method employed, all acquisitions must be planned to allow sufficient time to complete the competitive procurement process and award a contract by the required date. Similarly, the Department of Health and Human Services requires early acquisition planning to overcome the problem of having an inordinate percentage of contract awards being made in the closing weeks, or even days, of the fiscal year, 48 C.F.R. § 307.7101.

The acquisition plan should be revised and changed whenever necessary. FAR 7.104(a) provides:

> At key dates specified in the plan or whenever significant changes occur, and no less often than annually, the planner shall review the plan and, if appropriate, revise it.

2. *Form of Plan*

The FAR does not deal with the question of whether written or formal acquisition plans should be prepared but, rather, places this responsibility on agency heads, FAR 7.103(c). Some agencies, such as the DOD, require written plans only for large-dollar acquisitions (acquisitions for development when costs are $5 million or more and for production or services when costs are $30 million or more for all years) but permit the use of written plans for smaller procurements, DFARS 207.103(c)(i). The Army delegates the authority for determining thresholds for written plans to each head of contracting activity, AFARS 7.190. The Air Force requires written acquisition plans for all acquisitions of $5 million or more as well as for other "high risk" acquisitions, AFFARS 5307.103(c)(i)(C). The Navy requires written acquisition plans for all acquisitions involving the development, production, or support of weapon systems, subsystems, or equipment that meet or

Feb 23, 91
5000.1 (Part 2)

PART 2

INTEGRATED MANAGEMENT FRAMEWORK

A. OVERVIEW

The policies established in Part 1 forge a closer, more effective interface among the Department's three major decisionmaking support systems affecting acquisition. These are the:

- Requirements Generation System.
- Acquisition Management System.
- Planning, Programming, and Budgeting System.

This part describes the major characteristics of each system and highlights the complex relationships that must be maintained for effective decisionmaking. These characteristics and relationships define the integrated management framework for defense acquisition. This part describes the disciplined integration of the three systems and is not intended to establish policy. Elements of the decisionmaking systems described below are adjusted as necessary to assist the Secretary of Defense in decisionmaking as circumstances change.

THE THREE SYSTEMS

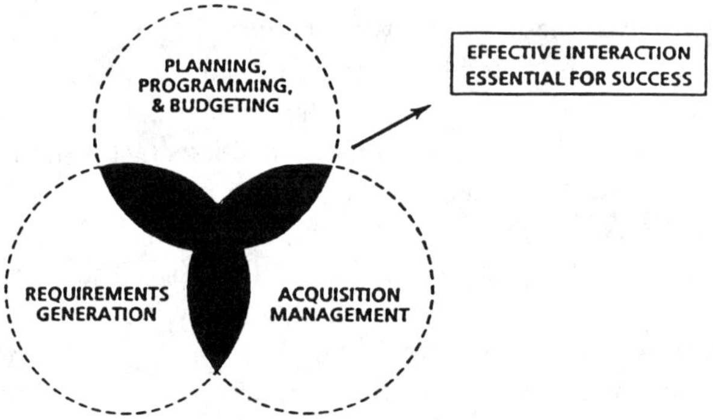

Figure 3-1 (cont'd on next page)

B. REQUIREMENTS GENERATION SYSTEM

1. Overview. The requirements generation system produces information for decisionmakers on projected mission needs.

   a. The needs identified are expressed initially in broad operational terms. They are progressively translated into system-specific performance requirements.

   b. This evolutionary approach enables decisionmakers to make informed cost-performance-schedule trade-offs at critical points in a program's implementation.

REQUIREMENTS EVOLUTION

2. Identifying and Processing Mission Needs. Mission needs are identified as a direct result of continuing assessments of current and projected capabilities in the context of changing military threats and national defense policy.

   a. The assessments are conducted by the Unified and Specified Commands, the Military Departments, the Office of the Secretary of Defense, and the Chairman of the Joint Chiefs of Staff. Their purpose is to identify deficiencies that may result in a need to:

      (1) Change doctrine, tactics, training, or organization;

      (2) Fix shortcomings in existing materiel; or

      (3) Introduce new operational capabilities.

   b. Assessments may also identify opportunities made possible by technological breakthroughs that could reduce ownership costs or improve the effectiveness of current materiel.

   c. Decisionmakers review the results of these assessments to determine what actions, if any, should be taken to meet the needs identified.

      (1) Needs that can be satisfied by changes in doctrine, tactics, training, or organization are sent to the Military Departments for consideration and action.

Figure 3-1 (cont'd from previous page)

exceed the thresholds of DFARS 207.103(c)(i) unless an exemption is applicable, NAPS 5207.103(c)(i).

Civilian agencies tend to require written acquisition plans at lower-dollar thresholds. For example, the General Services Administration (GSA) requires that plans for acquisitions over the simplified acquisition threshold ($100,000) must be in writing unless waived, GSAR 507.102. This regulation also notes that the heads of contracting activities may authorize oral plans for acquisitions not exceeding $100,000, as long as the file contains the name of the individual who approved the plan. NASA requires the preparation of written procurement plans for most procurements in categories of $250,000 or more or $500,000 or more, depending on the center conducting the procurement, NFS 1807.103.

3. *Responsibility for Preparing Plan*

Although FAR 7.102 requires agencies to conduct acquisition planning, it does not require the contracting officer to manage the planning process — it merely permits each procuring agency to designate the person or office responsible for acquisition planning. The DOD provides that the program manager or other official responsible for the program has overall responsibility for acquisition planning, DFARS 207.103(f). The Navy states that the acquisition program manager has overall responsibility for acquisition planning and implementing the acquisition plan, *Department of the Navy Acquisition Planning Guide* (Apr. 1992). The Air Force requires that an acquisition strategy panel be held for all acquisitions requiring a written acquisition plan, AFFARS 5307.104-91. NASA charges contracting officers with the responsibility of preparing a "procurement plan" (which is essentially the same as the normal acquisition plan), NFS 1807.103(a). These procurement plans are submitted to the procurement officer of the agency for approval, NFS 1807.103(b).

FAR 7.104(a) contemplates that acquisition planning be performed by a team:

> In developing the plan, the planner shall form a team consisting of all those who will be responsible for significant aspects of the acquisition, such as contracting, fiscal, legal, and technical personnel. The planner should review previous plans for similar acquisitions and discuss them with the key personnel involved in those acquisitions.

FAR 1.102(c) also states that the team includes the users of the supplies or services being procured. See also FAR 1.102-2(a)(7) stating:

> All members of the Team are required to employ planning as an integral part of the overall process of acquiring products or services. Although advance planning is required, each member of the Team must be flexible in order to accommodate changing or unforeseen mission needs. Planning is a tool for the accomplishment of tasks, and application of its discipline should be commensurate with the size and nature of a given task.

The members of the team should be identified in the acquisition plan, FAR 7.105(b)(10). See also DLAR 90.601 noting that the acquisition planning team normally consists of customer and technical personnel, budget personnel, and a representative from contracting.

The most comprehensive listing of team members is found in the *Department of the Navy Acquisition Planning Guide* (Apr. 1992), which states at paragraph 2.1:

> The APM [Acquisition Program Manager] is responsible for convening acquisition planning meetings with representatives from logistics, technical, fiscal, security, contracting, legal counsel, small business, and other areas, as appropriate, to prepare initial [acquisition plans] or revise [acquisition plans].
>
> All personnel engaged in the management of the acquisition process; including program, contracts, logistics, technical and financial personnel; are essential to the comprehensive acquisition planning and preparations necessary to achieve the acquisition objectives. These personnel must be made cognizant of their responsibilities and actively participate in the development and preparation of the [acquisition plan], if acquisition planning is to be successful. Planning meetings are strongly encouraged in order to coordinate planning efforts, which should significantly reduce [acquisition plan] development time.

Although the FAR does not discuss the role of competition advocates in the planning process, their participation is essential in each executive agency and in each procuring activity within the agency. Appointed pursuant to 41 U.S.C. § 418, competition advocates are responsible for challenging barriers to competition and promoting full and open competition. The agency-level advocate is given the additional duty of providing an annual report to the senior procurement executive on the agency's use of competition in contracting. They have become actively involved in acquisition planning in most procuring agencies. They generally work at a high level in the procuring agency with commensurate influence in determining the strategy that will be used by the agency in the prospective procurement. They also approve or review virtually all justifications for the use of other than competitive procedures. Thus, their agreement with the acquisition plan is essential to ensuring the success of the procurement.

4. Extent of Plan

Acquisition planning has been performed by some agencies in a sporadic and fragmented manner. Requirements have often been identified and justified on a contract-by-contract basis without regard for long-term acquisition needs. There are, after all, relatively few regulations requiring plans to be made on a program basis. The DOD provides that written acquisition plans for large-dollar acquisitions should be prepared on a program basis, while other acquisition plans may be written on either a program or individual-contract basis, DFARS 207.103(d). The Army policy is that, when feasible, acquisition plans will be written on a program/project basis for all procurement actions generally above $30 million, AFARS 7.103(c). The Navy regulations provide examples of program-based acquisition plans (e.g., aircraft, tracked and wheeled vehicles, electronic warfare) but do not state when or if an acquisition plan is required to be developed on a program basis, NAPS 5207.103(d). DLAR 7.103 states that acquisition plans required by DLAR 7.102(91) may be effected on a system basis using a comprehensive plan for a specified period of time. The civilian agencies generally are silent on this point. The GSA provides for the use of "comprehensive acquisition" plans that cover the acquisition process from identification of agency need through contract performance and administration, GSAR 507.101 and GSAR 507.104(a).

II. COMPETITION REQUIREMENT

A major goal of acquisition planning is the use of competition whenever feasible. The Competition in Contract Act of 1984 (CICA) specifically requires "full and open competition" to be attained by executive agencies in the conduct of sealed bid or competitive negotiation except as specifically permitted by statute. The CICA also lists five other "competitive procedures." Full and open competition and other than full and open competition are discussed in this section.

A. Full and Open Competition

The extent of competition required by the procurement statutes has been the subject of extensive debate and a number of statutory changes. Prior to passage of the CICA, the statutes provided that specifications and invitations for bids (IFBs) for formal advertising (now sealed bidding) "permit such free and full competition as is consistent with the procurement of property and services needed by the agency concerned," 10 U.S.C. § 2305(a) (pre-CICA version). See also the prior version of 41 U.S.C. § 253. For negotiated procurement, the Armed Services Procurement Act required that proposals be solicited from "the maximum number of qualified sources consistent with the nature and requirements of the supplies or services to be procured," 10 U.S.C. § 2304(g) (pre-CICA version). In 1984, the CICA required that "full and open competition" be used in sealed bid and competitive proposal procurements except when specifically exempted, 10 U.S.C. § 2304(a)(1)(A) and 41 U.S.C. § 253(a)(1)(A). The CICA defined the term "full and open competition" to mean that "all responsible sources are permitted to submit sealed bids or competitive proposals on the procurement," 41 U.S.C. § 403(6).

Based upon claims that receipt in some cases of inordinately large numbers of proposals placed an undue and unnecessary burden on procurements, attempts were made to narrow the statutory definition. One draft of the Clinger-Cohen Act of 1996 provided for "efficient competition." However, the definition was not changed. Instead, Section 4101 of the Act added a new provision to 10 U.S.C. § 2304(j) and 41 U.S.C. § 253(h), as follows:

> The Federal Acquisition Regulation shall ensure that the requirement to obtain full and open competition is implemented in a manner that is consistent with the need to efficiently fulfill the Government's requirements.

Efficiency in competition was addressed in Section 4103 of the Act, which provides that the contracting officer can limit the number of proposals in the competitive range "to the greatest number that will permit an efficient competition among the offerors rated most highly," 10 U.S.C. § 2305(b)(4)(B) and 41 U.S.C. § 253b(d)(2).

There are a number of procurements where all responsible offerors are not necessarily permitted to submit bids or proposals. Nevertheless, Congress has by statute provided that these procurements, when properly conducted, are included in the definition of full and open competition.

10 U.S.C. § 2302(2) and 41 U.S.C. § 259(b) specify five special procedures that are "competitive procedures" meeting the statutory requirement for full and open competition. See Section III for a listing of these special procedures.

Under the previous statutory provisions, the Comptroller General upheld awards if the Government obtained "adequate competition" and stated that the adequacy of competition did not depend upon whether every prospective bidder was afforded an opportunity to bid. See *Culligan, Inc.*, 56 Comp. Gen. 1011 (B-189307), 77-2 CPD ¶ 242, which involved advertised procurement, and *John Bransby Productions, Ltd.*, Comp. Gen. Dec. B-198360, 80-2 CPD ¶ 419, dealing with negotiated procurement. These decisions were based upon the Government's reasonable efforts to inform offerors generally of the proposed procurements and upon the absence of probative evidence that the Government had a conscious or deliberate intent to impede the participation of the prospective bidders.

The Comptroller General has continued this line of cases and will not require cancellation of a solicitation or an award merely because a prospective offeror was not furnished a copy of the solicitation, absent probative evidence of a conscious or deliberate effort to exclude the offeror. See *International Ass'n of Firefighters*, Comp. Gen. Dec. B-220757, 86-1 CPD ¶ 31, stating:

> Generally, the risk of nonreceipt of a solicitation amendment rests with the offeror. *Maryland Computer Services, Inc.*, B-216990, Feb. 12, 1985, 85-1 CPD ¶ 187. The propriety of a particular procurement is determined on the basis of whether full and open competition was achieved and reasonable prices were obtained, *Metro Medical Downtown*, B-220399, Dec. 5, 1985, 85-2 CPD ¶ 631, and whether the agency made a conscious and deliberate effort to exclude an offeror from competing for the contract. *Reliable Service Technology*, B-217152, Feb. 25, 1985, 85-1 CPD ¶ 234.

See also *Metro Med. Downtown*, Comp. Gen. Dec. B-220399, 85-2 CPD ¶ 631 (full and open competition was present despite failure to solicit firm through apparent oversight since *Commerce Business Daily* (CBD) notice resulted in solicitation of 24 firms, of which four submitted offers); *Denver X-Ray Instruments, Inc.*, Comp. Gen. Dec. B-220963, 85-2 CPD ¶ 562 (no evidence that prospective offeror was deliberately excluded from competition); and *Shemya Constructors*, Comp. Gen. Dec. B-232928.2, 89-1 CPD ¶ 108 (24 firms were solicited and there was no attempt by the agency to exclude the offeror from the competition). However, in *Trans World Maintenance, Inc.*, 65 Comp. Gen. 401 (B-220947), 86-1 CPD ¶ 239, the Comptroller General found that the agency failed to obtain full and open competition when it failed to solicit bids from the incumbent contractor, which had requested a copy of the solicitation at least four times before its issuance. In addition, the CBD notice did not indicate the date of the IFB or of the bid opening. See also *Abel Converting, Inc. v. United States*, 679 F. Supp. 1133 (D.D.C. 1988), where the court held that an agency's failure to solicit an incumbent contractor on a 33-item procurement would not be adequately remedied by the Comptroller General's recommendation that the agency resolicit the 14 items on which it had received only one bid, because the agency had not received full and open competition. The court reasoned at 1141:

> While the GAO concluded that two bids constituted adequate competition on nineteen of the line items, the Court disagrees. When so few bidders participate in a solicitation, the absence of even one responsible bidder significantly diminishes the level of competition. This is particularly so when the absent bidder is the incumbent contractor since that contractor previously submitted the lowest bids. Because GSA's actions "prevented a responsible source from competing[,] . . . the CICA mandate for full and open competition was not met."

In *Republic Floors, Inc.*, Comp. Gen. Dec. B-242962, 91-1 CPD ¶ 579, the agency failed to send the protester two material solicitation amendments, in violation of applicable regulatory requirements governing the dissemination of solicitation materials. The Comptroller General found that as a result of the agency's actions, of the four bids received, only two were responsive. The Comptroller General held that where so few firms participate in a competition, the absence of even one responsive firm due to the agency's regulatory violation so diminished the level of competition and undermined the CICA mandate for full and open competition that it constituted a compelling reason to resolicit the requirement. See also *Custom Envtl. Serv., Inc.*, 70 Comp. Gen. 563 (B-242900), 91-1 CPD ¶ 578, where competition was found to be inadequate where only one responsive bid was received and at least three other prospective bidders were eliminated from the bidding as a result of using an obsolete mailing list.

B. Other Than Full and Open Competition

"Other than competitive procedures" are not statutorily defined; the statutes merely list seven specific procurement situations where full and open competition is not required. Depending upon the circumstances, such procurements may be made on either a sole source basis or with limited competition. These exceptions, set forth in 41 U.S.C. § 253(c) and 10 U.S.C. § 2304(c), state that other than competitive procedures may be used *only* in the following situations:

> (1) the property or services needed by the executive agency are available from only one responsible source or only from a limited number of responsible sources and no other type of property or services will satisfy the needs of the executive agency;
>
> (2) the agency's need for the property or services is of such an unusual and compelling urgency that the United States would be seriously injured unless the agency is permitted to limit the number of sources from which it solicits bids or proposals;
>
> (3) it is necessary to award the contract to a particular source or sources in order (A) to maintain a facility, producer, manufacturer, or other supplier available for furnishing property or services in case of a national emergency or to achieve industrial mobilization, (B) to establish or maintain an essential engineering, research, or development capability to be provided by an educational or other nonprofit institution or a federally funded research and development center, or (C) to procure the services of an expert for use, in any litigation or dispute (including any reasonably foreseeable litigation or dispute) involving the Federal Government, in any trial, hearing, or proceeding before any court, administrative tribunal, or agency, or to procure the services of an expert or neutral for use in any part of an alternative dispute resolution process, whether or not the expert is expected to testify;
>
> (4) the terms of an international agreement or a treaty between the United States and a foreign government or international organization, or the written directions of a foreign government reimbursing the agency for the cost of the procurement of the property or services for such government, have the effect of requiring the use of procedures other than competitive procedures;
>
> (5) subject to subsection (j), a statute expressly authorizes or requires that the procurement be made through another executive agency or from a specified source, or the agency's need is for a brand-name commercial item for authorized resale;

> (6) the disclosure of the agency's needs would compromise the national security unless the agency is permitted to limit the number of sources from which it solicits bids or proposals; or
>
> (7) the head of the agency —
>
> > (A) determines that it is necessary in the public interest to use procedures other than competitive procedures in the particular procurement concerned, and
> >
> > (B) notifies the Congress in writing of such determination not less than 30 days before the award of the contract.

Justification for the use of other than competitive procedures on the basis of any exception other than (c)(1) does not necessarily permit the use of sole source contracting. Competition is required from as many potential sources as is practicable. See 41 U.S.C. § 253(e) and 10 U.S.C. § 2304(e), which state:

> The head of an agency using procedures other than competitive procedures to procure property or services by reason of the application of subsection (c)(2) or (c)(6) shall request offers from as many potential sources as is practicable under the circumstances.

The FAR requirement to solicit offers from as many sources as is practicable is not limited to (c)(2) and (c)(6) only. FAR 6.301(d) is applicable to (c)(3), (c)(4), (c)(5), and (c)(7) as well:

> When not providing for full and open competition, the contracting officer shall solicit offers from as many potential sources as is practicable under the circumstances.

Thus, procurements under all subsections except (c)(1) should be conducted with some degree of competition when circumstances permit. Protests in this area have primarily been under Subsection (c)(2). For instance, the Comptroller General has held that even though urgency permitted a procurement without full and open competition, the agency violated the statute by awarding a sole source contract, *Data Based Decisions, Inc.*, Comp. Gen. Dec. B-232663, 89-1 CPD ¶ 87; *TMS Bldg. Maintenance*, 65 Comp. Gen. 222 (B-220588), 86-1 CPD ¶ 68. The Comptroller General has also held that an agency violated the statute where it had conducted the procurement so inefficiently that a competitor did not have time to compete for the entire quantity, *Arrow Gear Co.*, 68 Comp. Gen. 612 (B-235081), 89-2 CPD ¶ 135. Other such protests have been sustained in *Kahn Indus., Inc.*, Comp. Gen. Dec. B-251777, 93-1 CPD ¶ 356 (agency failed to contact one of the potential sources because the firm's phone number was missing from the file and the agency opined that three quotes would be "good enough" in a situation of urgency); *Ferranti Int'l Defense Sys., Inc.*, Comp. Gen. Dec. B-237760, 90-1 CPD ¶ 317 (agency could have negotiated with a third source that had expressed interest and had prior experience, without significantly delaying the ongoing procurement); *Charles Snyder*, 68 Comp. Gen. 659 (B-235409), 89-2 CPD ¶ 208 (agency could have solicited nonlocal company that had previously expressed interest in procurement); and *AT&T Info. Servs., Inc.*, 66 Comp. Gen. 58 (B-223914), 86-2 CPD ¶ 447 (agency could have conducted fast negotiations with another known source of the work). In *Earth Property Servs., Inc.*, Comp. Gen. Dec. B-237742, 90-1 CPD ¶ 273, the agency was prohibited from soliciting only one source in an urgent procurement where a second offeror, which had previously done similar work for the agency, was available to perform on short notice. Similarly, in *Olmpic Marine Servs., Inc.*, Comp. Gen. Dec. B-246143, 92-1 CPD ¶ 205, the Comptroller General sustained a protest where an agency failed to solicit a firm that had previously done similar work and had specifically requested to be solicited by the agency in the future. See also *Bay Cities Servs., Inc.*, Comp. Gen. Dec. B-239880, 90-2 CPD ¶ 271, where the Comptroller General held that the incumbent contractor's refusal to provide cost data did not justify failing to solicit a proposal for an urgent procurement of additional effort for four months (two other proposals had been solicited).

1. Only One Source Available

The first exception is the broadest and possibly most utilized exception to the requirement for full and open competition. It is intended to permit a sole source procurement "only when truly warranted," Competition in Contracting Act: Report of Government Affairs Committee to Accompany S. 338, S. Rep. No. 8-50, 98th Cong., 1st Sess. 21 (1983). This section discusses the decisions contesting sole source procurements under both the prior statutes and the current statute to determine the meaning of this exception.

a. Agency Discretion

An agency determination that a proposed contractor is the only source capable of meeting the technical needs of the agency is subject to close scrutiny but will not be overturned if the agency has properly justified its needs and there is a reasonable basis for its determination, *Mine Safety Appliances Co.*, Comp. Gen. Dec. B-233052, 89-1 CPD ¶ 127; *WSI Corp.*, Comp. Gen. Dec. B-220025, 85-2 CPD ¶ 626. However, when a responsible source has expressed interest in the procurement, the agency must make reasonable efforts to permit the source to compete, *Neil R. Gross & Co.*, 69 Comp. Gen. 292 (B-237434), 90-1 CPD ¶ 212. If such efforts fail, however, the Comptroller General is reluctant to question agency decisions. See, for example, *Automated Prod. Equip. Corp.*, Comp. Gen. Dec. B-210476, 84-1 CPD ¶ 269, where, despite observing that the agency's technical personnel were impressed with the protester's equipment demonstration, the Comptroller General did not disturb the agency's determination that the protester did not supply sufficient data from which the agency could evaluate the functional equivalence of the protester's equipment. Similarly, in *Technology for Communications Int'l*, Comp. Gen. Dec. B-236922, 89-2 CPD ¶ 603, the Comptroller General did not question an agency's determination that the protester, in response to a CBD notice seeking sources, did not submit sufficient technical data to justify permitting the protester to compete on the basis of developing a new product if it won the competition.

The Comptroller General has held that the availability of only one source has to be demonstrated "convincingly," *Daniel H. Wagner Assocs.*, 65 Comp. Gen. 305 (B-220633), 86-1 CPD ¶ 166. In most protests of sole source awards, agencies have been able to meet this test. For example, in *Amray, Inc.*, Comp. Gen. Dec. B-209186, 83-2 CPD ¶ 45, the protester complained of a sole source procurement for a scanning microscope on the grounds that it, too, could meet the agency's needs. In rejecting the protest, the Comptroller General noted that the agency's technical personnel reviewed the literature published by various manufacturers, spoke to their representatives, including Amray's, and reasonably determined the microscope to be unique. See also *Mnemonics, Inc.*, Comp. Gen. Dec. B-261476.3, 96-1 CPD ¶ 7 (agency reasonably determined that only one source could supply critically required items under an expedited delivery schedule); *Navistar Marine Instrument Corp.*, Comp. Gen. Dec. B-262221, 95-2 CPD ¶ 232 (sole source procurement proper where no other barometer had the ability to fit into a preexisting opening on the instrument control panel of the engine); *Nomura Enter., Inc.,* Comp. Gen. Dec. B-260977.2, 95-2 CPD ¶ 206 (sole source contract for engineering support services related to howitzer proper because agency reasonably concluded that unacceptable delays would occur if award was made to another source); *Pilkington Aerospace, Inc.*, Comp. Gen. Dec. B-259173, 95-1 CPD ¶ 180 (agency reasonably awarded sole source contract for advanced design windshields for the F-15 aircraft); *Midwest Dynamometer & Eng'g Co.*, Comp. Gen. Dec. B-257323, 94-2 CPD ¶ 91 (agency reasonably determined that only one source could furnish a dynamometer system meeting its requirement for a system capable of running on existing software); *Litton Computer Servs.*, Comp. Gen. Dec. B-256225, 94-2 CPD ¶ 36 (agency reasonably determined that only the developer of the original system had the necessary extensive system knowledge and experience to accomplish task); *Essex Electro Eng'rs, Inc.*, Comp. Gen. Dec. B-250437, 93-1 CPD ¶ 74 (procurement from only immediately available source justified to obtain backup electric power plants, which were in short supply because of Operation Desert Storm — even though units would be placed on standby status); *AGEMA Infrared Sys.*, Comp. Gen. Dec. B-240961, 91-1 CPD ¶ 4 (protester's equipment did not contain essential technical features needed by agency); *EG&G Astrophysics Research Corp.*, Comp. Gen. Dec. B-241171, 90-2 CPD ¶ 525 (agency had thoroughly reviewed protester's equipment and had reasonably determined it did not meet agency's needs); *Elbit Computers, Ltd.*, Comp. Gen. Dec. B-239038, 90-2 CPD ¶ 26 (agency's determination that no other contractor could supply the equipment reasonable); *C & S Antennas, Inc.*, Comp. Gen. Dec. B-224549, 87-1 CPD ¶ 161 (agency determination that only one product was compatible with its needs reasonable even though protester was meeting similar needs of another agency); and *Abbott Labs.*, Comp. Gen. Dec. B-230220, 88-1 CPD ¶ 468 (reasonable determination of agency requirement and no other source).

Protest of sole source determinations have, however, been sustained if the facts indicate that other sources could satisfactorily meet the Government's needs. In *Sidereal Corp.*, Comp. Gen. Dec. B-210969, 83-2 CPD ¶ 92, the Comptroller General sustained a protest to a sole source award for automatic data processing equipment. The protester had recently won contracts for equipment similar to that which was procured, thus demonstrating that meaningful competition was possible. See also *Design Pak, Inc.*, Comp. Gen. Dec. B-212579, 83-2 CPD ¶ 336, where the Comptroller General sustained a protest to a noncompetitive award because the agency confused its requirements with the characteristics of the sole source contractor's product, and *Data Based Decisions, Inc.*, Comp. Gen. Dec.

B-232663, 89-1 CPD ¶ 87, where a protest was sustained because the incumbent contractor was not solicited although able to compete for the work. In making a determination that only one contractor is capable of meeting an agency's needs, it is improper for an agency to rely on the putative sole source contractor for technical advice and expertise. The agency should independently evaluate technical data and draw its own conclusions, *Aero Corp. v. Department of the Navy*, 558 F. Supp. 404 (D.D.C. 1983).

b. Privately Developed Items

The determination to procure on a sole source basis may be justified under certain circumstances if the items being procured were developed at private expense. The following material discusses the circumstances that preclude or permit sole source procurement of privately developed items.

(1) Patented Items

The mere fact that an item is patented will *not* justify a sole source procurement. The statutory basis for this rule is 28 U.S.C. § 1498(a), which gives patent owners the right to reasonable compensation if an invention is used "by or for the United States without license," but does not permit patent owners to enjoin the use of patents in such cases. In 38 Comp. Gen. 276 (B-136916) (1958), the Comptroller General ruled that this statute requires the use of competitive procurement techniques when purchasing patented items. The Comptroller General reasoned at 278:

> It is our view, however, that section 1498 appears clearly to constitute a modification of the patent law by limiting the rights of patentees insofar as procurement of supplies by the Government may be concerned, and by vesting in the Government a right to the use of any patents granted by it upon payment of reasonable compensation for such use. We believe that the statute is not consistent with any duty on the part of a contracting agency of the Government to protect the interests of patentees or licensees with respect to articles which it proposes to purchase, since the statute itself defines and provides an exclusive remedy for enforcement of the patentee's rights as to the Government. Any other interpretation would appear to us to impose an impossible burden upon Government procurement officials to determine the applicability and validity of any patents affecting any articles desired.

See also 53 Comp. Gen. 270 (B-177835) (1973), indicating that competitive negotiation could be used to obtain patented items if the circumstances for negotiation are present. It is proper to use a Patent Indemnity clause (transferring the risk of patent infringement to the contractor) in such cases, *Barrier-Wear*, Comp. Gen. Dec. B-240563, 90-2 CPD ¶ 421; FAR 27.203-1(b)(2).

(2) Copyrighted Items

Although 28 U.S.C. § 1498(b) contains substantially the same language relating to copyrights as 28 U.S.C. § 1498(a), the presence of a copyright has been held to be a valid reason for sole source procurement. See *ALK Assocs.*, Comp. Gen. Dec. B-237019, 90-1 CPD ¶ 113, where the Comptroller General upheld a sole source procurement of copyrighted software because the agency needed the identical software to meet its needs. The Comptroller General apparently reasoned that competitors could not recreate such software and/or that the agency or its contractors could not take the software through eminent domain procedures (as can occur with patents). The same logic probably explains the copyright provisions in Paragraph (c)(2) of the Rights in Data — General clause in FAR 52.227-14 and Paragraph (d) of the Rights in Technical Data — Noncommercial Items clause in DFARS 252.227-7013, stating that a contractor may not use copyrighted material in the performance of the contract without the consent of the contracting officer.

(3) Items Described by Proprietary Data

Since there is no statute comparable to 28 U.S.C. § 1498 covering proprietary data, it is the policy of the Government to honor proprietary rights in technical data, FAR 27.402(b). This policy, now incorporated in 41 U.S.C. § 418a(a) and 10 U.S.C. § 2320(a)(1), states that procurement regulations may not impair "any other right in technical data otherwise established by law." However, 10 U.S.C. § 2320(c)(1) does permit the use of contract clauses calling for expiration of a contractor's proprietary rights to the technical data after no more than seven years, a policy that is implemented at DFARS 227.403-70(c)(3). The Government's policy of honoring proprietary rights in technical data does not prevent the Government from meeting its needs with an independent development project.

In some cases, the Comptroller General has held that agencies should prepare data packages or use performance specifications to facilitate competitive procurement. The fact that the agency would incur substantial cost in drafting a specification that could be used for competitive procurement was not adequate justification for sole source procurement in *Techniarts*, Comp. Gen. Dec. B-193263, 79-1 CPD ¶ 246. But see *Compressor Eng'g Corp.*, Comp. Gen. Dec. B-213032, 84-1 CPD ¶ 180, where the Comptroller General stated that it would be unreasonable for the agency to bear the cost of testing parts that would facilitate a competitive procurement. In *Command, Control & Communications Corp.*, Comp. Gen. Dec. B-210100, 83-2 CPD ¶ 448, the Comptroller General rejected the agency's arguments that the urgency of its needs and the lack of proprietary data precluded a competitive award. While the Comptroller General recognized that the agency might have to satisfy its immediate needs on a sole source basis, urgency could not justify acquisition of computer systems over a five-year period where the systems were not complex technologically and the agency acknowledged that other vendors could duplicate the system "if given enough time."

Agencies frequently create nonproprietary technical data packages by reverse engineering proprietary products. Reverse engineering is the process of developing design specifications by inspection and analysis of a product. Although DFARS 217.503(d) provides that reverse engineering by the Government is the least desirable means of obtaining competition in the face of proprietary data, this practice has been found to be legal, *Westech Gear Corp. v. Department of the Navy*, 907 F.2d 1225 (D.C. Cir. 1990); *American Hoist & Derrick, Inc. v. United States*, 3 Cl. Ct. 198 (1983). Sometimes nonproprietary technical data packages are created by awarding a contract to perform the reverse engineering, *EG&G Sealol*, Comp. Gen. Dec. B-232265, 88-2 CPD ¶ 558. When reverse engineering is too expensive to justify the effort to obtain competition, an agency can reasonably decide to continue the sole source procurement, *Gel Sys., Inc.*, Comp. Gen. Dec. B-231680, 88-2 CPD ¶ 316. See also *AAI ACL Technologies, Inc.*, Comp. Gen. Dec. 258679.4, 95-2 CPD ¶ 243, finding a sole source award proper given the risk and cost associated with reverse engineering.

The most prevalent form of reverse engineering is for the Government to suggest that companies reverse engineer a product in order to compete for a quantity of items to be procured. The major way that an agency initiates this type of reverse engineering is by providing proprietary items to competitors. With regard to spare parts, this procedure is encouraged by 10 U.S.C. § 2320(d), which states:

> The Secretary of Defense shall by regulation establish programs which provide domestic business concerns an opportunity to purchase or borrow replenishment parts from the United States for the purpose of design replication or modification, to be used by such concerns in the submission of subsequent offers to sell the same or like parts to the United States.

This technique is sometimes called "competitive copying."

Agencies also attempt to obtain competition in the face of proprietary data by having the contractor with the proprietary data license other contractors. In *Leigh Instruments, Ltd.*, Comp. Gen. Dec. B-233642, 89-1 CPD ¶ 149, the licensee complained that the contractor had failed to honor the license with the result that the licensee could not successfully compete on a procurement. The Comptroller General did not entertain the protest, characterizing such situations as disputes between two private parties.

The Comptroller General has sustained sole source procurements where the product being procured could only be described by proprietary data, *Aerospace Eng'g & Support, Inc.*, Comp. Gen. Dec. B-258546, 95-1 CPD ¶ 18; *TSI Microelectronics Corp.*, Comp. Gen. Dec. B-243889, 91-2 CPD ¶ 172; *Hydra Rig Cryogenics, Inc.*, Comp. Gen. Dec. B-234029, 89-1 CPD ¶ 442; *Turbo Mechanical, Inc.*, Comp. Gen. Dec. B-231807, 88-2 CPD ¶ 299; *Quality Diesel Engines, Inc.*, Comp. Gen. Dec. B-210215, 83-2 CPD ¶ 1. In such cases, the Comptroller General generally will not question an agency's legal determination that the sole source contractor has proprietary rights, *Fil-Coil Co.*, Comp. Gen. Dec. B-198105, 80-2 CPD ¶ 304.

Sole source procurements have also been justified where, "as a practical matter," it was not feasible to create a nonproprietary data package. See *Kessler Int'l Corp.*, Comp. Gen. Dec. B-230662, 88-2 CPD ¶ 27, where it was held that the agency reasonably determined that only one source could timely supply the needed part because it was a critical application part necessary for performing safety, mission, and readiness requirements. The Government had no technical data package because the item had been developed at private expense under a nondevelopmental item. In *Rack Eng'g Co.*, Comp. Gen. Dec. B-194470, 79-2 CPD ¶ 385, the Comptroller General upheld the Navy's sole source procurement for interchangeable spare parts cabinets because the supplier had already supplied 87 percent of the Atlantic Fleet Carrier Force's needs. The Comptroller General reasoned that the cost of redesigning and retooling to meet the interchangeability requirement would necessarily preclude any other offerors from competing. Thus, the most economically sound alternative to ensure interchangeability was to procure sole source from the existing supplier. In *Worldwide Marine, Inc.*, Comp. Gen. Dec. B-212640, 84-1 CPD ¶ 152, the Comptroller General acknowledged there may have been some degree of agency negligence in failing to draft specifications, but nevertheless held that, faced with an urgent need for the purchase in question, the agency was justified in making a sole source award to the only company that possessed adequate data to produce the item. See also *Piezo Crystal Co.*, 69 Comp. Gen. 97 (B-236160), 89-2 CPD ¶ 477, and *Rotek, Inc.*, Comp. Gen. Dec. B-240252, 90-2 CPD ¶ 341, where the Comptroller General upheld sole source procurements justified by the agency's lack of a data package and an urgent need for initial deliveries of the product. In *Masbe Corp.*, Comp. Gen. Dec. B-260253.2, 95-1 CPD ¶ 253, the Comptroller General upheld a sole source procurement for a critical military aircraft engine part. The Air Force stated that it did not have adequate data to establish qualification requirements for the part because this data was possessed by the original designer of the engine. The Air Force asserted that without the technical data it could not tell what variation in the configuration and manufacturing process led to acceptable performance. The Comptroller General found this rationale to be reasonable.

The Small Business and Federal Procurement Competition Enhancement Act of 1984, P.L. 98-577, and the Defense Reform Act of 1984, P.L. 98-525, both contain provisions requiring agencies to consider requiring offerors for production contracts for major systems to propose methods for obtaining competition. See 41 U.S.C. § 253b(j)(2) and 10 U.S.C. § 2305(d)(2), which describe such proposals as follows:

> (B) Proposals referred to in the first sentence of subparagraph (A) are proposals identifying opportunities to ensure that the United States will be able to obtain on a competitive basis items procured in connection with the system that are likely to be reprocured in substantial quantities during the service life of the system. Proposals submitted in response to such requirement may include the following:
>
> > (i) Proposals to provide to the United States the right to use technical data to be provided under the contract for competitive reprocurement of the item, together with the cost to the United States, if any, of acquiring such technical data and the right to use such data.
> >
> > (ii) Proposals for the qualification or development of multiple sources of supply for the item.

c. *Unsolicited Proposals*

Unsolicited proposals can provide the basis for a determination that the property or services are available from only one source. See 41 U.S.C. § 253(d)(1)(A), which states:

> [I]n the case of a contract for property or services to be awarded on the basis of acceptance of an unsolicited research proposal, the property or services shall be considered to be available from only one source if the source has submitted an unsolicited research proposal that demonstrates a unique and innovative concept the substance of which is not otherwise available to the United States and does not resemble the substance of a pending competitive procurement.

10 U.S.C. § 2304(d)(1)(A) is substantively the same.

FAR Subpart 15.6 goes beyond these statutes and provides guidance on the handling of all unsolicited proposals for research work and other types of work. FAR 15.606-2(a) requires that each proposal be comprehensively evaluated, considering, at a minimum, the following factors:

> (1) Unique, innovative and meritorious methods, approaches, or concepts demonstrated by the proposal;
>
> (2) Overall scientific, technical, or socioeconomic merits of the proposal;
>
> (3) Potential contribution of the effort to the agency's specific mission;
>
> (4) The offeror's capabilities, related experience, facilities, techniques, or unique combinations of these that are integral factors for achieving the proposal objectives;
>
> (5) The qualifications, capabilities, and experience of the proposed principal investigator, team leader, or key personnel who are critical in achieving the proposal objectives; and
>
> (6) The realism of the proposed cost.

FAR 15.607 contains limitations on award of contracts based on unsolicited proposals:

> (a) A favorable comprehensive evaluation of an unsolicited proposal does not, in itself, justify awarding a contract without providing for full and open

competition. Agency contact points shall return an unsolicited proposal to the offeror, citing reasons, when its substance —

> (1) Is available to the Government without restriction from another source;
>
> (2) Closely resembles a pending competitive acquisition requirement;
>
> (3) Does not relate to the activity's missions; or
>
> (4) Does not demonstrate an innovative and unique method, approach, or concept, or is otherwise not deemed a meritorious proposal.

FAR 15.607(b) goes on to state that if the unsolicited proposal has received a favorable comprehensive evaluation and is not subject to the above impediments, the agency can procure the work covered by the proposal. If it is for research work, such procurement can be on a sole source basis in accordance with FAR 6.302-1(a)(2)(i):

> Supplies or services may be considered to be available from only one source if the source has submitted an unsolicited research proposal that [meets the statutory requirements].

If the proposal is for other than research work, FAR 15.607(b) requires full and open competition unless one of the statutory exceptions is justified.

The Comptroller General has held that these provisions *do not* require award of a contract to a submitter of an unsolicited proposal — they merely *permit* award if the proposal is unique and innovative. Even when the proposal is unique and innovative, agencies have the discretion not to award a sole source contract, *S. T. Research Corp.*, Comp. Gen. Dec. B-231752, 88-2 CPD ¶ 152; *University of Dayton Research Inst.*, Comp. Gen. Dec. B-220589, 86-1 CPD ¶ 108. Further, the Comptroller General "does not consider it appropriate to review a protest that an agency should procure from a particular firm on a sole-source basis," *Arctic Energies Ltd.*, Comp. Gen. Dec. B-224672, 86-2 CPD ¶ 571. Thus, it is very difficult to challenge an agency decision to reject an unsolicited proposal.

It is appropriate not to issue a sole source contract based on an unsolicited proposal where the data necessary for a competitive procurement are otherwise available to the Government, *Saratoga Indus.*, Comp. Gen. Dec. B-219341, 85-2 CPD ¶ 247 (information in the unsolicited proposal was available from previous specifications or from publicly available information); *Georgetown Air & Hydro Sys.*, Comp. Gen. Dec. B-210806, 84-1 CPD ¶ 186 (unsolicited proposal incorporated information related to a forthcoming solicitation). In *LW Planning Group*, Comp. Gen. Dec. B-215539, 84-2 CPD ¶ 531, the Government was found to have properly decided that the work in the unsolicited proposal required the work of an architect-engineer contractor and thus the work could not be done by the submitter.

It appears that a proposal could be "unique and innovative" even though it does not include proprietary information. FAR 15.609 permits unsolicited proposals to contain a legend prohibiting the disclosure, outside the Government, of all information in the proposal or the use of such information for any purpose other than evaluation of the proposal. This regulation also establishes a procedure for Government protection of the information even if the legends are not placed on the proposal. It has been held that the Government does not violate a protectable trade secret by competitively soliciting for the item using data that were independently developed by the Government, *Zodiac of North Am., Inc.*, Comp. Gen. Dec. B-220012, 85-2 CPD ¶ 595; *Sellers, Connor & Cuneo*, 53 Comp. Gen. 161 (B-177436), *recons. denied*, 74-1 CPD ¶ 126.

Many agencies now screen unsolicited research proposals to determine if they can be reviewed and considered under the broad agency announcement in effect at the time of receipt of the proposal. In most cases, the proposal will fall within one of the categories of research covered by this announcement and can be treated as a research proposal.

d. Follow-On Contracts

Follow-on contracts are awards made to the contractor that has previously been awarded a design or manufacturing contract for the same item or that has previously performed the services being procured. The CICA enacted two different provisions on this issue. Sole source contracting for follow-on contracts is permitted by 41 U.S.C. § 253(d)(1)(B) in the following circumstances:

> [I]n the case of a follow-on contract for the continued development or production of a major system or highly specialized equipment when it is likely that award to a source other than the original source would result in (i) substantial duplication of cost to the Government which is not expected to be

> recovered through competition, or (ii) unacceptable delays in fulfilling the executive agency's needs, such property may be deemed to be available only from the original source and may be procured through procedures other than competitive procedures.

The same provision is contained in 10 U.S.C. § 2304(d)(1)(B) with additional language making it applicable to follow-on contracts for "highly specialized services." The Act requires the agency to determine and document that the cost of the initial capital investment made by the developer of new items cannot be offset by savings that would result from openly competing the item.

There have been no decisions on the scope of these statutes. However, the Comptroller General has considered the issue of follow-on contracts in a variety of cases. In *International Harvester Co.*, 61 Comp. Gen. 388 (B-205073), 82-1 CPD ¶ 459, involving a sole source award to the company that developed and hand-built four prototypes, the Comptroller General urged the Army to limit its first production run to the minimum number needed to validate a data package and to consider whether competing the remainder of its requirements would result in savings despite the initial tooling cost incurred by the incumbent contractor. In *Sprint Communications Co.*, Comp. Gen. Dec. B-262003.2, 96-1 CPD ¶ 24, the agency justified a 15-month "bridge" contract on a sole source basis to the original contractor to permit the award of several contracts designated to achieve significant economies of scale. See also *Univox Cal., Inc.*, Comp. Gen. Dec. B-225449.2, 87-2 CPD ¶ 569, where the Comptroller General permitted the limitation of competition to the two contractors that had developed competitive prototypes, but recommended that the agency quickly obtain technical data packages so that quantities in future years could be fully competed. Compare *Berkey Mktg. Cos.*, Comp. Gen. Dec. B-224481, 86-2 CPD ¶ 596, where the agency was permitted to continue buying "the only commercially available item within an acceptable price range that would meet the [agency's] minimum requirements," and *SEAVAC Int'l, Inc.*, Comp. Gen. Dec. B-231016, 88-2 CPD ¶ 134, where urgency justified the agency's continuing to buy services from the incumbent contractor. See also *Magnavox Elec. Sys. Co.*, Comp. Gen. Dec. B-258076.2, 94-2 CPD ¶ 266, where the Comptroller found that a sole source award on a follow-on contract was permissible because award to any other source would cause unacceptable delays. The Comptroller General noted that another basis for awarding sole source to a follow-on contractor would be if the award to any other source would result in substantial duplication of cost that would not be expected to be recovered through competition. Since the decision was based on unreasonable delay, the Comptroller did not address the question of duplication of costs.

Mere prior experience of a contractor has been found to be insufficient grounds to support a sole source procurement. In *Electronic Sys., U.S.A., Inc.*, Comp. Gen. Dec. B-200947, 81-1 CPD ¶ 309, the Comptroller General stated:

> A company's prior experience with the procuring agency which may facilitate the company's performance of the required services and enable it to better anticipate problems in the implementation of the system is not a legally adequate justification to support a sole-source procurement. Furthermore, the fact that a particular contractor may be able to perform the services with greater ease than any other contractor does not justify a noncompetitive procurement to the exclusion of others.

In another decision, a sole source procurement of repairs to an oil distribution system was improper when justified on the basis that the selected contractor had installed the original system and had previously made repairs to it, *Titan Atl. Constr. Corp.*, Comp. Gen. Dec. B-200986, 81-2 CPD ¶ 12. See also *Metropolitan Radiology Assocs.*, Comp. Gen. Dec. B-195559, 80-1 CPD ¶ 265, where the Comptroller General ruled that a sole source procurement was not justified on the basis of a past, long-standing relationship with a single contractor.

Justifications for award of sole source procurements to the prior contractor have been most successfully challenged by the submission of proof that the competitor is equally capable of performing the work. For example, in *Techniarts*, Comp. Gen. Dec. B-193263, 79-1 CPD ¶ 246, the Comptroller General determined that the protester was capable of producing the desired product, and the sole source procurement was therefore improper. Similarly, sole source procurement was found improper in *Federal Data Corp.*, Comp. Gen. Dec. B-196221, 80-1 CPD ¶ 167, where, after the agency's publication of intent to procure on a sole source basis, the agency received alternative responses indicating the likelihood that other concerns could meet the Government's needs. In *Aerospace Research Assocs.*, Comp. Gen. Dec. B-201953, 81-2 CPD ¶ 36, a sole source procurement for armored helicopter seats was improper since the agency was aware of two other contractors that could possibly "satisfy the Government's minimum needs without undue technical risk . . . within the required time," yet failed to contact them about the solicitation. See also *Consolidated Elevator Co.*, 56 Comp. Gen. 434 (B-187624), 77-1 CPD ¶ 210, where sole source awards for elevator maintenance to the manufacturers of the respective elevators were found to be improper because evidence showed that companies other than the manufacturers could meet the Government's maintenance needs. Similarly, in *Berkshire Computer Prods.*, Comp. Gen. Dec. B-240327, 91-1 CPD ¶ 464, sole source awards to the original computer system contractor were found improper because the protester sold compatible equipment and software.

2. Unusual and Compelling Urgency

The second exception in the statute permits a procurement without full and open competition based on "unusual and compelling" urgency. This exception is narrowly construed because the acquisition planning process is intended to overcome all but the most compelling urgency situations. Urgency has generally been found in circumstances where the agency has made reasonable efforts to obtain competition but has been unable to accomplish this goal because of insufficient time to fulfill critical agency requirements. For example, the need to continue weapon tests vital to the national security has met the urgency requirement, *Support Sys. Assocs.*, Comp. Gen. Dec. B-232473, 89-1 CPD ¶ 11. Urgency was also found to exist in *Greenbrier Indus., Inc.*, Comp. Gen. Dec. B-241304, 91-1 CPD ¶ 92, where the Marine Corps reasonably determined that only one company was capable of immediately supplying chemical protective suits for use in Operation Desert Shield; and *E. Huttenbauer & Son, Inc.,* Comp. Gen. Dec. B-252320.2, 93-1 CPD ¶ 499, where the agency reasonably determined that only one known firm was capable of meeting urgent supply requirement caused by Operation Restore Hope in Somalia. In *Alektronics, Inc.*, Comp. Gen. Dec. B-261431, 95-2 CPD ¶ 146, the Comptroller General found reasonable a sole source award of a critical military item where there was an inventory shortage and the awardee was the only approved source. Similarly, in *Gentex Corp.*, Comp. Gen. Dec. B-233119, 89-1 CPD ¶ 144, the Comptroller General agreed that the agency was justified in refusing to consider an untested competitive product in a weapons program, and in *Forster Enters., Inc.*, Comp. Gen. Dec. B-237910, 90-1 CPD ¶ 363, the Comptroller General permitted a sole source contract to the only company with a qualified product for an unforeseen quantity of essential military items needed during the period the protester was qualifying its product under a new contract. See also the following decisions finding that urgency justified other than full and open competition: *BlueStar Battery Sys. Corp.*, Comp. Gen. Dec. B-270111.2, 96-1 CPD ¶ 67 (procurement restricted to two manufacturers that had supplied batteries to the Army under previous contracts); *All Points Int'l, Inc.*, Comp. Gen. Dec. B-260134, 95-1 CPD ¶ 252 (only one contractor was capable of meeting requirement relating to the growing Cuban and Haitian refugee population at the U.S. Naval Facility); *Purdy Corp.*, Comp. Gen. Dec. B-257432, 94-2 CPD ¶ 127 (no other source possessed or could reasonably access test stand that was needed quickly for examining discovered gearbox problem); *Logics, Inc.*, Comp. Gen. Dec. B-256171, 94-1 CPD ¶ 314 (agency solicited only known sources that had successfully manufactured filter assemblies because the agency encountered a critical supply shortage); *Sargent & Greenleaf, Inc.*, Comp. Gen. Dec. B-255604.3, 94-1 CPD ¶ 208 (sole source award to only qualified firm for limited quantities of security containers because existing mechanical locks placed classified information at risk); *Braswell Servs. Group, Inc.*, Comp. Gen. Dec. B-245507, 92-1 CPD ¶ 72 (ship repair was urgent and critical to ship operations and the ship's limited availability did not permit resolicitation on either a competitive basis or the basis of a limited competition); *Rotair Indus.*, Comp. Gen. Dec. B-239503, 90-2 CPD ¶ 154 (competition limited to two sources with qualified products when the protester had not completed the qualification of its product and the agency could wait no longer); and *Racal Corp.*, Comp. Gen. Dec. B-235441, 89-2 CPD ¶ 213 (contract awarded to the only contractor that could proceed without first article testing and the agency had concluded that the risk of failure by another contractor was too great).

Unusual and compelling circumstances have also been found when there was insufficient time to test a nondevelopmental item, *Astron*, Comp. Gen. Dec. B-236922.2, 90-1 CPD ¶ 441. A finding of urgency has also been justified where the contractor currently performing the work provided an additional quantity while competition was being conducted for future requirements, *Elbit Computers, Ltd.*, Comp. Gen. Dec. B-239038, 90-2 CPD ¶ 26; *Abbott Prods., Inc.*, Comp. Gen. Dec. B-231131, 88-2 CPD ¶ 119, and while an award protest was being decided, *Unified Indus., Inc.*, 70 Comp. Gen. 142 (B-241010), 91-1 CPD ¶ 11. However, unusual and compelling circumstances will not be found if the agency is slow in conducting the procurement. For example, in *Honeycomb Co. of Am.*, Comp. Gen. Dec. B-227070, 87-2 CPD ¶ 209, the Comptroller General held that no urgency could be justified when the agency took eight months to award a contract for products to be delivered from 16 months to four years after award. Unusual and compelling circumstances also will not be found when there is a lack of advance planning, *New Breed Leasing Corp.*, Comp. Gen. Dec. B-274201, 96-2 CPD ¶ 202; *TLC Servs., Inc.*, Comp. Gen. Dec. B-252614, 93-1 CPD ¶ 481.

Although urgency does not necessarily justify sole source procurement, an agency conducting a procurement under the urgency exception may limit competition to the only firm it reasonably believes can perform the work promptly and properly, *Arthur Young & Co.*, Comp. Gen. Dec. B-221879, 86-1 CPD ¶ 536; *Gentex Corp.*, Comp. Gen. Dec. B-221340, 86-1 CPD ¶ 195. See also *IMR Sys. Corp.*, Comp. Gen. Dec. B-222465, 86-2 CPD ¶ 36, where urgency justified a sole source procurement even though the protester had notified the agency that it could take over the work on three to five days' notice. Compare *Earth Property Serv., Inc.*, Comp. Gen. Dec. B-237742, 90-1 CPD ¶ 273, where the Comptroller General sustained a protest of a sole source procurement based on urgency because the protester showed that it could begin performance "on short notice."

Although the statute does not indicate what type of "serious injury" must result to justify limiting competition, the Comptroller General has included possible financial injury within the scope of the term, *Arthur Young Co.*, Comp. Gen. Dec. B-221879, 86-1 CPD ¶ 536. In that case, the Navy was permitted to make a sole source award because it claimed that the incumbent was the only firm that could perform a management study in time and that the study was necessary to achieve an estimated $1.5 billion savings. Serious injury was also found in a potential failure of the agency's telephone system, *AT&T Info. Servs., Inc.*, 66 Comp. Gen. 58 (B-223914), 86-2 CPD ¶ 447, and potential poor operation of the agency's computer facility, *Data Transformation Corp.*, Comp. Gen. Dec. B-220581, 86-1 CPD ¶ 55.

Potential expiration of funds is not a justification under the urgency exception. See *Computer Lines*, GSBCA 8206-P, 86-1 BCA ¶ 18,653, where the board stated at 93,805:

> We can first quickly dispel the notion that [the agency's] actions in this acquisition are somehow made legitimate by its concern that the period of availability for obligation of its funds was shortly to expire. *See* 31 U.S.C. § 1552(a)(2) (1982) (the unobligated balance of funds available for obligation for a definite period is withdrawn at the end of the period of availability for obligation, and it reverts to the Treasury). The procurement provisions of the CICA have put an end to the idea that the statutory duty to ob-

> tain maximum practicable competition is somehow suspended at the end of each fiscal year. The legislative history of the CICA clearly depicts Congressional disgust with unconscionable year-end spending abuses. *See*, H.R. Rep. No. 98-861, 98th Cong., 2d Sess. 1428 (1984), *reprinted in* 1984 U.S. Code Cong. & Ad. News 2116. We do not suggest that this acquisition was the sort of abusive spending that Congress had in mind when it prohibited agencies from entering into noncompetitive contracts "on the basis of the lack of advance planning or concerns related to the amount of funds available to the agency for procurement functions." [10 U.S.C. § 2304(f)(5)(A)] Nonetheless, we have previously held that concerns as to expiring funds have no place in protest proceedings before this Board, *Wordplex Corp.*, GSBCA No. 8193-P, 86-1 BCA ¶ 18,655 (Dec. 3, 1985), and we see no reason to depart from that holding here.

Frequently, the threat of appropriations expiring occurs because of a protest against the award. See, for example, *Federal Technology Corp.*, GSBCA 10188-P, 89-3 BCA ¶ 22,134, where the board refused to permit award pending the outcome of a protest that could have resulted in a decision on the last day of the fiscal year. This problem has been ameliorated with regard to protests before the agency, the General Accounting Office, or the courts by the provisions of 31 U.S.C. § 1558, which keep appropriations from expiring for 100 calendar days after the date of the final ruling on the protest.

3. Industrial Mobilization and Maintaining Critical Capability

The third exception permits a procurement under less than competitive procedures in order to achieve industrial mobilization or to establish or maintain critical engineering, research, or development capability provided by an educational or other nonprofit organization or federally funded research and development center. An agency's decision under this exception will not be questioned as long as it can demonstrate that its determinations are related to its industrial mobilization needs, *Minowitz Mfg. Co.*, Comp. Gen. Dec. B-228502, 88-1 CPD ¶ 1. See also *Right Away Foods/Shelf Stable Foods*, Comp. Gen. Dec. B-259859.3, 95-2 CPD ¶ 34 (award to third mobilization base producer proper where agency reasonably determined that the failure of either of the current producers would be catastrophic in the event of a military emergency); *Kilgore Corp.*, Comp. Gen. Dec. B-253672, 93-2 CPD ¶ 220 (sole source award to operate and maintain an ammunition plant based on mobilization need); *Lance Ordnance Co.*, Comp. Gen. Dec.

B-246849, 92-2 CPD ¶ 29 (sole source award made to one of two mobilization base producers for smoke and illumination signals); *Greebrier Indus., Inc.*, Comp. Gen. Dec. B-248177, 92-2 CPD ¶ 74 (agency divided its requirements for chemical suits among four active mobilization base producers to provide a continuation of each firm's minimum sustaining rate of production); and *Propper Int'l, Inc.*, Comp. Gen. Dec. B-229888, 88-1 CPD ¶ 296 (Navy hat considered an essential part of the enlisted person's uniform and designated industrial mobilization item).

4. Terms of International Agreement or Treaty

This exception may be used when the terms of an international agreement or treaty have the effect of requiring the use of other than competitive procedures. There is no requirement that the foreign government initiate a sole source designation. Thus, in the absence of bad faith or an intention to circumvent competition, it is immaterial whether a United States agency recommends specific items or advises a foreign government as to what items might satisfy its needs. See *Julie Research Labs. Inc.*, GSBCA 8070-P, 85-3 BCA ¶ 18,375; and *Kahn Indus., Inc.*, Comp. Gen. Dec. B-225491, 87-1 CPD ¶ 343.

5. Authorized by Another Statute

The use of other than competitive procedures is permitted when a statute expressly authorizes or requires that a procurement be made through another agency or from a specified source. Sole source awards under the 8(a) set-aside are usually justified under this exception. See *Bosco Contracting Inc.*, Comp. Gen. Dec. B-236989, 89-2 CPD ¶ 346, where the Comptroller General held that the CICA's mandate for full and open competition does not apply to a procurement being conducted as an 8(a) set-aside under 15 U.S.C. § 637(a). 10 U.S.C. § 2304(c)(5) also authorizes the use of other than competitive procedures when "the agency's need is for a brand-name commercial item for authorized resale." See *Defense Commissary — Request for Advance Decision*, Comp. Gen. Dec. B-262047, 96-1 CPD ¶ 115, holding that under the CICA, the Defense Commissary Agency could noncompetitively procure items bearing the USO Always Home brand name for resale in military stores.

6. National Security

This exception permits an agency to limit the number of sources from which it offers if the disclosure of the agency's needs would compromise the national security. There are no protests on the use of this exception.

7. Public Interest

This exception enables the head of the agency to make a determination that it is necessary in the public interest to use other than competitive procedures in a particular procurement. See *Zublin Del., Inc.*, Comp. Gen. Dec. B-227003.2, 87-2 CPD ¶ 149, where the Comptroller General denied a protest that the Navy, after submission of initial offers, unreasonably restricted competition to United States firms for construction of Navy housing in the Philippines. The Comptroller General held that the Secretary of the Navy, under 10 U.S.C. § 2304(c)(7), made the required determination that such a restriction was in the public interest because hiring foreign firms could jeopardize United States bases in the Philippines.

8. Competition Excluding Particular Sources

41 U.S.C. § 253(b)(1) and 10 U.S.C. § 2304(b)(1) provide that executive agencies are permitted to exclude particular sources in order to establish or maintain alternate sources if the agency head determines that to do so:

> (A) would increase or maintain competition and would likely result in reduced overall costs for such procurement, or for any anticipated procurement, of property or services;
>
> (B) would be in the interest of national defense in having a facility (or a producer, manufacturer, or other supplier) available for furnishing the property or service in a case of a national emergency or industrial mobilization;
>
> (C) would be in the interest of national defense in establishing or maintaining an essential engineering, research, or development capability to be provided by an educational or other nonprofit institution or a federally funded research and development center.

The second and third of these reasons are similar to the former 10 U.S.C. § 2304(a)(16), which permitted the use of negotiated procurement for mobilization purposes. The first reason gives statutory authority for developing a competitive second source by precluding an existing sole source contractor from participating in the second source competition or maintaining an alternate source by precluding the primary source from being awarded all of an agency's requirements. FAR 6.202(a) states the following justifications that may be used for the action:

> Agencies may exclude a particular source from a contract action in order to establish or maintain an alternate source or sources for the supplies or services being acquired if the agency head determines that to do so would —
>
> (1) Increase or maintain competition and likely result in reduced overall costs for the acquisition, or for any anticipated acquisition;
>
> (2) Be in the interest of national defense in having a facility (or a producer, manufacturer, or other supplier) available for furnishing the supplies or services in case of a national emergency or industrial mobilization;
>
> (3) Be in the interest of national defense in establishing or maintaining an essential engineering, research, or development capability to be provided by an educational or other nonprofit institution or a federally funded research and development center;
>
> (4) Ensure the continuous availability of a reliable source of supplies or services;
>
> (5) Satisfy projected needs based on a history of high demand; or
>
> (6) Satisfy a critical need for medical, safety, or emergency supplies.

FAR 6.202(b) provides that a determination and findings (D&F) by an agency head or designee must support the decision to exclude particular sources. Class D&Fs are not permitted; thus, a D&F must be made for each individual procurement action. After exclusion of particular sources, an agency is required to establish full and open competition using one of the competitive procedures, FAR 6.201.

9. Reprocurement after Default Termination

FAR 49.402-6 provides that after a default termination, reprocurements of no more than the amount of work remaining to be performed are not subject to the statutory competition requirements, while reprocurements over the remaining quantity of work are to be treated as "new acquisitions." The FAR requires in the former case that the agency obtain competition "to the maximum extent practicable." The Comptroller General has held that in the case of a reprocurement after default, the statutes and regulations governing regular federal procurements are not strictly applicable, *Aerosonic Corp.*, 68 Comp. Gen. 179 (B-232730), 89-1 CPD ¶ 45. See *AT&T Corp.*, Comp. Gen. Dec. B-270344, 96-1 CPD ¶ 117, denying a protest against the sole source award of a contract for a telecommunications circuit following the protester's default termination. But see *Master Sec., Inc.*, Comp. Gen. Dec. B-235711, 89-2 CPD ¶ 303, where the Comptroller General ruled that the inclusion of two one-year options in a sole source reprocurement of a defaulted service contract was unreasonable. In reaching this conclusion, the Comptroller General used the same reasoning applied under the statutory requirements — because there was adequate time to obtain competition for this optional work, not obtaining such competition was improper. Contracting officers are invested with wide latitude to determine how needed supplies or services are to be reprocured after a default and may automatically exclude a defaulted contractor from the competition for the reprocurement, *Montage Inc.*, Comp. Gen. Dec. B-277923.2, 97-2 CPD ¶ ___.

C. Ordering Work under Existing Contracts

Merely because work is added to an existing contract by modification or change order does not justify the use of "other than competitive" procedures if the work is in reality a new procurement action. Thus, it is necessary to determine whether the work can properly be ordered on a noncompetitive basis under existing contracts.

1. Change Orders

Change orders issued under the various Changes clauses may be made on a sole source basis if they are within the general scope of the contract. Although the Comptroller General does not review contract administration matters, the Comptroller will review an allegation that the Government action should have been the subject of a new procurement, *LDDS World-Com*, Comp. Gen. Dec. B-266257, 96-1 CPD ¶ 50; *Arjay Elecs. Corp.*, Comp. Gen. Dec. B-243080, 91-2 CPD ¶ 3; *Memorex Corp.*, 61 Comp. Gen.

42 (B-200722), 81-2 CPD ¶ 334; *Webcraft Packaging*, Comp. Gen. Dec. B-194087, 79-2 CPD ¶ 120.

A "scope of the competition" test is employed to determine whether work has been improperly added to a contract. See *American Air Filter Co.*, 57 Comp. Gen. 567 (B-188408), 78-1 CPD ¶ 443, stating at 573:

> The impact of any modification is in our view to be determined by examining whether the alteration is within the scope of the competition which was initially conducted. Ordinarily, a modification falls within the scope of the procurement provided that it is of a nature which potential offerors would have reasonably anticipated under the changes clause.
>
> To determine what potential offerors would have reasonably expected, consideration should be given, in our view, to the procurement format used, the history of the present and related past procurements, and the nature of the supplies or services sought. A variety of factors may be pertinent, including: whether the requirement was appropriate initially for an advertised or negotiated procurement; whether a standard off-the-shelf or similar item is sought; or whether, *e.g.*, the contract is one for research and development, suggesting that broad changes might be expected because the Government's requirements are at best only indefinite.

The Comptroller General held that a change substituting diesel for gasoline engines in heating units was beyond the scope of an advertised manufacturing contract because it required significant development work, doubled the performance time, and increased the price by 29 percent. In *W.H. Mullins*, Comp. Gen. Dec. B-207200, 83-1 CPD ¶ 158, a modification of an existing requirements contract was also found to be beyond the scope of competition for the original contract because the parties could not have reasonably anticipated such a major change. See also *MCI Telecommunications Corp.*, Comp. Gen. Dec. B-276659.2, 97-2 CPD ¶ 90, where the Comptroller General found that a modification of the FTS 2000 contract under which AT&T Communications, Inc. supplies 60 percent of the Federal Government's inter-city telecommunications services exceeded the scope of the original contract and therefore must be purchased on a competitive basis. The Comptroller General distinguished the network design and management services purchased under NSAP II from the services purchased under earlier modifications, thereby distinguishing the case from *AT&T Communications, Inc. v. Wiltel, Inc.*, 1 F.3d 1201 (Fed. Cir. 1993). See, however, *LDDS WorldCom*, Comp. Gen. Dec. B-266257, 96-1 CPD ¶ 50, finding the modification to be within the scope of the original contract because the added services could have been anticipated from the face of the contract and the added services were not materially different than the services currently produced under the contract.

A slightly different test was used in *Cray Research v. Department of the Navy*, 556 F. Supp. 201 (D.D.C. 1982), where the court stated at 203:

> The "cardinal change" doctrine prevents government agencies from circumventing the competitive process by adopting drastic modifications beyond the original scope of a contract. The basic standard is whether the modified contract calls for essentially the same performance as that required by the contract when originally awarded so that the modification does not materially change the field of competition.

Utilizing this analysis, the court examined the claim that installation by an incumbent contractor of more advanced computer equipment following a performance test failure of the specified equipment was a "cardinal change." The court held that where new equipment is provided at no additional cost and the original contract specifications remain unchanged, the field of competition is not changed sufficiently to constitute a cardinal change.

The General Services Board of Contract Appeals followed essentially the same analysis as that used by the Comptroller General. See *MCI Telecommunications Corp. v. General Servs. Admin.*, GSBCA 11963-P, 93-1 BCA ¶ 25,541. In *Wiltel, Inc. v. General Servs. Admin.*, 93-1 BCA ¶ 25,314, *rev'd*, 1 F.3d 1201 (Fed. Cir. 1993), the board held that a modification to a telecommunications contract to add a new service that had become available commercially after contract award was outside the scope of the services for which the contract had been awarded. However, the Federal Circuit reversed, stating that the services added by the modification would have been anticipated by the original competitors because the solicitation called for services that were commercially available and the contract contained a "Service Improvements" clause, *AT&T Communications, Inc. v. Wiltel, Inc.*, 1 F.3d 1201 (Fed. Cir. 1993). The court noted that "a broad original competition may validate a broader range of later modifications."

Contract actions held to be outside the scope of the procurement include a change order issued almost immediately after contract award substituting a mail delivery system of electric cars on fixed tracks in lieu of the specialized system of stationary trays on moving belts, *Lamson Div. of Diebold, Inc.*,

Comp. Gen. Dec. B-196029.2, 80-1 CPD ¶ 447; a modification substituting a newer model disk drive and changing an "option to purchase" or a "lease-to-ownership" plan envisioning a five-year lease period, *Memorex Corp.*, 61 Comp. Gen. 42 (B-200722), 81-2 CPD ¶ 334; an extension of a requirements contract for word processing equipment, *CPT Corp.*, Comp. Gen. Dec. B-211464, 84-1 CPD ¶ 606; a modification to the performance specifications in the purchase description for aircraft generator test stands, *Avtron Mfg., Inc.*, 67 Comp. Gen. 404 (B-229972), 88-1 CPD ¶ 458; and a modification adding quantities to an indefinite-quantity contract when the added quantities were beyond the quantity evaluated in the initial award, *Valix Fed. Partnership I v. National Transp. Safety Bd.*, GSBCA 12109-P, 93-2 BCA ¶ 25,587.

2. Extensions and Options

Contract extensions, exercise of contract options, and lease renewals can also constitute de facto sole source procurements. Extensions adding only time to permit the contractor to complete performance of the original work are almost always within the scope of the procurement. However, if the original contract is seen as a procurement of services for a specified period of time, extensions calling for additional time will frequently be held to be de facto sole source procurements. The Comptroller General has stated that "competition should be sought whenever it appears likely that the Government's position can be improved whether in terms of cost or performance," 51 Comp. Gen. 57 (B-165218) (1971). In *Washington Nat'l Arena Ltd. Partnership*, 65 Comp. Gen. 25 (B-219136), 85-2 CPD ¶ 435, the Government issued an amendment retroactively extending a contract that had expired four months earlier. The Comptroller General held that this action constituted a cardinal change and an improper de facto sole source award. See also *Intermem Corp.*, Comp. Gen. Dec. B-187607, 77-1 CPD ¶ 263, where a mandatory requirements contract was modified twice to extend its expiration date. The agency issued a D&F (a written approval by an authorized official, clearly justifying the specific determination made), concluding that the extensions were in the best interests of the Government because a lapse would disrupt a Government-wide mandatory source of equipment and services, and user agencies would lose accumulated purchase credits. The Comptroller General found that the extensions became necessary only because the agency failed to timely solicit a follow-on contract, and the extensions were therefore not justified. In *Varian Assocs.*, Comp. Gen. Dec. B-208281, 83-1 CPD ¶ 160, the exercise of a contract option by the contracting agency constituted an unjustifiable sole source procurement even though the contracting officer sought and obtained a reduction in the price called for in the original contract. In *Federal Data Corp.*, Comp. Gen. Dec. B-196221, 80-1 CPD ¶ 167, a short renewal of an ADPE lease pending replacement with Government-owned equipment constituted an unjustified sole source procurement where responses to a CBD notice evidenced competitive interests in a solicitation. See also *Techno-Sciences, Inc.*, Comp. Gen. Dec. B-257686, 94-2 CPD ¶ 164, where the Comptroller General found that the agency had improperly extended a contract on a sole source basis, stating that other responsible sources could have competed for the requirement had the agency engaged in adequate advance procurement planning to allow a phase-in period for a new contractor.

Before an agency can exercise an option, in order to satisfy the requirement for full and open competition, "the option must have been evaluated as part of the initial competition," FAR 17.207(f). See also FAR 6.001, which contains the following statement of applicability of the competition requirements:

> This part applies to all acquisitions except —
>
> * * *
>
> (c) Contract modifications, including the exercise of priced options that were evaluated as part of the initial competition (see 17.207(f)), that are within the scope and under the terms of an existing contract.

If an option is not evaluated under the initial competition, FAR 17.207(f) prevents its exercise absent an appropriate justification and authorization that full and open competition is not required, *Kollsman Instrument Co.*, Comp. Gen. Dec. B-233759, 89-1 CPD ¶ 243. See *Stoehner Sec. Servs., Inc.*, Comp. Gen. Dec. B-248077.3, 92-2 CPD ¶ 285.

Even if it has been determined that Government action in modifying a contract has gone beyond the scope of the procurement, and therefore constitutes a de facto sole source procurement, the Comptroller General will deny the protest if a new sole source procurement could have been justified. See *Tilden-Coil Constructors, Inc.*, Comp. Gen. Dec. B-211189.3, 83-2 CPD ¶ 236, where the Army modified an ongoing contract, for the construction of eight buildings and a central energy plant, to authorize the incumbent to construct two additional buildings. The Comptroller General accepted the Army's explanation that additional costs and delayed completion dates would result from the overcrowding of the congested work site occasioned by the presence of another contractor. Similarly, in *Die Mesh Corp.*, Comp. Gen. Dec. B-190421, 78-2 CPD ¶ 36, modifications incorporating Phase II research into Phase I contracts, although outside of the scope of the procurement, were allowed. The procuring agency had claimed that Phase II was treated as a new (noncompetitive) procurement and that the contracts were modified "purely for administrative convenience." The Comptroller General found sufficient sole source justification to support the amendment because award to a new source would have precluded meeting statutory deadlines for the program. See also *Mediax Assocs.*, Comp. Gen. Dec. B-211350, 84-1 CPD ¶ 71, where the Comptroller General declined to determine whether a modification exceeded the scope of a procurement after first concluding that a sole source award was justified. Similarly, in *Hercules Aerospace Co.*, Comp. Gen. Dec. B-254677, 94-1 CPD ¶ 7, the protester asserted that a contract modification for additional rocket motors and engineering services amounted to a de facto sole source procurement. Without deciding this issue, the Comptroller General held that the agency's decision to modify the contract of the only qualified contractor due to unusual and compelling circumstances was reasonable. Compare *Kent Watkins & Assocs.*, Comp. Gen. Dec. B-191078, 78-1 CPD ¶ 377, where the Government apparently added another year's work by modification and later wrote a sole source justification for a new procurement after the protest had been lodged. The supporting reasons cited included that the incumbent contractor submitted the only response to the solicitation, the incumbent had gained special experience, and additional costs would be incurred in changing contractors. However, because the agency was aware of other companies interested in the solicitation, the Comptroller found the sole source award improper. In 41 Comp. Gen. 484 (B-145598) (1962), a Navy decision to renovate a portion of Bancroft Hall at the Naval Academy by giving a change order to a contractor that was performing other work at the Academy was held to be improper. The Comptroller General found no justification for the Navy's contention that it would have been impracticable to obtain competitive proposals. The Navy's primary reason for failing to procure competitively was a desire to ensure that the incumbent contractor performed the work.

3. *Task and Delivery Orders*

Task (services) and delivery (supplies) order contracts are contracts that do not specify a "firm quantity," 10 U.S.C. § 2304d(1) and (2) and 41 U.S.C. § 253k(1) and (2). FAR 16.5 provides that task or delivery order contracts may take the form of requirements contracts or indefinite-quantity contracts. In addition, the FAR does not preclude the use of unique arrangements as long as contractor receives consideration. See Chapter 8 for a complete discussion of this type of contracting.

Procurement notices and competition are not required for the issuance of task or delivery orders under either single award or multiple award contracts, 10 U.S.C. § 2304c(a) and 41 U.S.C. § 253j(a). However, 10 U.S.C. § 2304c(b) and 41 U.S.C. § 253j(b) require that each contractor receiving an award be "provided a fair opportunity to be considered" for each order unless:

> (1) the [executive] agency's need for the services or property ordered is of such unusual urgency that providing such opportunity to all such contractors would result in unacceptable delays in fulfilling that need;
>
> (2) only one such contractor is capable of providing the services or property required at the level of quality required because the services or property ordered are unique or highly specialized;
>
> (3) the task or delivery order should be issued on a sole-source basis in the interest of economy and efficiency because it is a logical follow-on to a task or delivery order already issued on a competitive basis; or
>
> (4) it is necessary to place the order with a particular contractor in order to satisfy a minimum guarantee.

The statutory exemption of task and delivery orders from competition is implemented in FAR 6.001(d) – (f).

A task or delivery order may not "increase the scope, period or maximum value" of the contract. Such increases may only be accomplished "by modification of the contract," 10 U.S.C. § 2304a(e) and 41 U.S.C. § 253h(e). Although not specifically stated in these sections, procurement notices and competition would be required for such actions unless a noncompetitive award could be justified since the exemption from competition is only applicable to task orders. By contrast, the FASA's coverage of task orders for advisory and assistance services specifically provides that contract modifications are subject to competition requirements, 10 U.S.C. § 2304b(f)(2) and 41 U.S.C. § 253i(f)(2). Under limited circumstances, a one-time extension not exceeding six months may be made on a "sole source basis," 10 U.S.C. § 2304b(g) and 41 U.S.C. § 253i(g).

The FASA permits the award of task and delivery order contracts using "[a] statement of work, specifications, or other description that reasonably describes the general scope, nature, complexity, and purposes of the services or property to be procured under the contract," 10 U.S.C. § 2304a(b)(3) and 41 U.S.C. § 253h(b)(3). Thus, task orders can potentially cover a broad spectrum, depending upon the nature of the work statement. Although no cases on this issue have been decided under the new FASA rules, a number of cases decided under the prior rules have dealt with the question of what can be ordered noncompetitively under indefinite-quantity and requirements contracts.

In *Bulova Technologies, Inc.*, Comp. Gen. Dec. B-252660, 93-2 CPD ¶ 23, the Comptroller General suggested that the criterion for determining whether an order or modification is outside the scope is whether potential offerors would have considered that such a modification might be made:

> Preservation of the integrity of the competitive procurement system requires that contracting parties not make changes to contracts which have the effect of circumventing the competitive procurement statutes; this principle is violated when a modification so substantially changes the purpose or nature of a contract that the contract for which the competition was held and the contract which is to be performed are essentially different. Ordinarily, a modification falls within the scope of the contract originally competed where potential offerors could reasonably have anticipated that such a modification might be made under the changes or other contract clauses.

See also *AT&T Communications, Inc. v. Wiltel, Inc.*, 1 F.3d 1201 (Fed. Cir. 1993), where the court noted that the length of the contract and the need to meet changing Government needs placed the competitors on notice that "a broad range of modifications would fall within the scope," stating at 1205:

> In determining whether a modification falls within CICA's competition requirement, this court examines whether the contract as modified materially departs from the scope of the original procurement. [citations omitted] The analysis thus focuses on the scope of the entire original procurement in comparison to the scope of the contract as modified. Thus a broad original

> competition may validate a broader range of later modifications without further bid procedures.

See also *Astronautics Corp. of Am.*, 70 Comp. Gen. 554 (B-242782), 91-1 CPD ¶ 531, where the Comptroller General stated that protesters were precluded from contesting the issuance of a delivery order on the ground that the statement of work in the contract was too broad, reasoning at 557:

> Since the delivery order falls within the scope of the existing engineering services contract, there is no basis to require a separately-competed procurement as urged by the protester. *See Stanford Telecommunications, Inc.*, B-241449, Dec. 10, 1990, 90-2 CPD ¶ 475.
>
> Here, the basic contract appears to encompass an extremely broad spectrum of items and services, which prompted the protester to hypothesize that DOD could use the contract routinely to obtain a wide range of electronic items without meaningful competition. While on the limited record presented in this case we could not resolve the question, we recognize that where an agency conducts a procurement for a total package or for broadly aggregated needs without a legitimate basis for bundling its requirements rather than breaking them out, competition is inhibited in derogation of the mandate for "full and open competition" under the Competition in Contracting Act of 1984, 10 U.S.C. § 2304(a)(1)(A)(1988). *See LaBarge Products, Inc.*, B-232201, Nov. 23, 1988, 88-2 CPD ¶ 510; *Pacific Sky Supply, Inc.*, B-228049, Nov. 23, 1987, 87-2 CPD ¶ 504; *Systems, Terminals & Communications Corp.*, B-218170, May 21, 1985, 85-1 CPD ¶ 578. However, as the protester also acknowledges, the [*Commerce Business Daily*] synopsis indicated the broad range of services which could be acquired. [The protester] did not timely protest the scope of the procurement in 1988. To the extent that [the protester] is now protesting the scope of the requirements under the basic contract, the protest is untimely.

Task orders were also found to be within the scope of the contract in *Information Ventures, Inc.*, Comp. Gen. Dec. B-240458, 90-2 CPD ¶ 414 (tasks "logically related to the overall purpose" of the agreement); *Liebert Corp.*, Comp. Gen. Dec. B-232234.5, 91-1 CPD ¶ 413 (work within the general scope but quantity beyond maximum stated in contract outside scope); and *Lockheed Martin Fairchild Sys.*, Comp. Gen. Dec. B-275034, 97-1 CPD ¶ 28 (modernization of computer-based training within scope of contract for automatic data processing systems integration and support services).

The background and circumstances surrounding the award of a contract may indicate that an order under an otherwise broad work statement is not within the scope of the contract. In *Octel Communications Corp. v. General Servs. Admin.*, GSBCA 12975-P, 95-1 BCA ¶ 27,315, the board found that the ordering of voice mail under a telecommunications contract was outside the scope because, when the solicitation for the contract was issued, the Government knew that it had a requirement for voice mail but excluded it from the solicitation "to avoid protests from voice mail providers who desired to separately compete to satisfy such requirements." The board found that based on these circumstances, the original competitors would not have expected voice mail to be ordered under the contract. See also *Dynamac Corp.*, Comp. Gen. Dec. B-252800, 93-2 CPD ¶ 37, where the Comptroller General determined that an order for support of a computerized information system was outside the scope of a contract that was intended to provide engineering support for an agency's information resources management systems because the original solicitation for the contract did not adequately advise offerors of the potential for this type of order. Similar reasoning was used in *Data Transformation Corp.*, Comp. Gen. Dec. B-274629, 97-1 CPD ¶ 10, where operation of a nationwide debt collection system was held to be outside of the scope of a litigation support contract. The Comptroller General stated that one factor supporting the decision was that the agency had "historically procured [the work] under a separate contract." In *Comdisco, Inc.*, Comp. Gen. Dec. B-277340, 97-2 CPD ¶ 105, the Comptroller General sustained a protest where an agency exceeded the scope of its task orders for computer equipment and related services by permitting computer hardware/software to constitute more than its allotted share of a contract. See also *Marvin J. Perry & Assocs.*, Comp. Gen. Dec. B-277684, 97-2 CPD ¶ ___, where the Comptroller General found that the Navy's modification of Federal Supply Schedule delivery orders to permit substitution of lower-grade, less expensive furniture materially altered the nature of the orders from those originally issued and thereby prejudiced the protester.

III. SELECTION OF CONTRACTING TECHNIQUE

One of the major changes to procurement policy in the CICA was the elimination of the absolute preference for formal advertising (renamed "sealed bidding") over negotiation. Instead, the CICA substituted the following rule in 10 U.S.C. § 2304(a)(2) and 41 U.S.C. § 253(a)(2):

> In determining the competitive procedures appropriate under the circumstance, an executive agency —
>
> (A) shall solicit sealed bids if —
>
> (i) time permits the solicitation, submission, and evaluation of sealed bids;
>
> (ii) the award will be made on the basis of price and other price-related factors;
>
> (iii) it is not necessary to conduct discussions with the responding sources about their bids; and
>
> (iv) there is a reasonable expectation of receiving more than one sealed bid;

10 U.S.C. § 2304(a)(1)(B) and 41 U.S.C. § 253(a)(1)(B) provide that in conducting a procurement, an agency

> shall use the competitive procedure or combination of competitive procedures that is best suited under the circumstances of the procurement.

These provisions are implemented by FAR 6.401, which states:

> Sealed bidding and competitive proposals, as described in Parts 14 and 15 are both acceptable procedures for use under Subparts 6.1, 6.2 and, when appropriate, under Subpart 6.3. Contracting Officers shall exercise good judgment in selecting the method of contracting that best meets the needs of the Government. If the choice is to use competitive proposals rather than sealed bidding, the contracting officer shall briefly explain, in writing, which of the four conditions [in the above mentioned statute] has not been met. No additional documentation or justification is required.

A. Sealed Bidding

Contracting officers must use sealed bidding if none of the four exceptions set forth in 10 U.S.C. § 2304(a)(2) and 41 U.S.C. § 253(a)(2) can be demonstrated. The Comptroller General enunciated this rule in *Defense Logistics Agency*, 67 Comp. Gen. 16 (B-227055.2), 87-2 CPD ¶ 365 at 17:

> It is true . . . that CICA eliminates the specific preference for formally advertised procurements ("sealed bids") and directs an agency to use the

> competitive procedures, or combination of procedures, that is best suited under the circumstances of the procurement. However, CICA . . . does provide, in determining which competitive procedure is appropriate under the circumstances, that an agency "shall solicit sealed bids if": (1) time permits, (2) award will be based on price, (3) discussions are not necessary, and (4) more than one bid is expected to be submitted. As is evident, the plain language of the CICA provision is mandatory in nature. When the enumerated statutory conditions are present, the solicitation of sealed bids is, therefore, required, leaving no room for the exercise of discretion by the contracting officer in determining which competitive procedure to use.

In reaching this conclusion, the Comptroller General relied on the legislative history of the CICA, stating:

> The legislative history of CICA also indicates the mandatory nature of the requirement to use sealed bidding when the statutory conditions are present. Senate Report No. 98-50, 98th Cong., 2nd Sess., *reprinted in* 1984 U.S. Code Cong. & Admin. News 2191, states, in pertinent part:
>
>> While competitive negotiation is recognized in S.338 as a bona fide competitive procedure, the Committee emphasizes that traditional formal advertising procedures are by no means cast aside. In fact, agencies are *required* . . . to solicit sealed bids [when the enumerated conditions are present]. . . .
>
> House Conference Report No. 98-861, 98th Cong., 2nd Sess., *reprinted in* 1984 U.S. Code Cong. & Admin. News 2110, states:
>
>> In effect, the substitute, like the Senate amendment, removes the restriction from — and written justification required for — competitive proposal procedures and places them on a par with sealed bid procedures. *The substitute maintains minimum criteria for sealed bid procedures to ensure their use when appropriate.*

Where all the elements enumerated in the CICA for the use of sealed bidding procedures are present, agencies are required to use these procedures and do not have the discretion to use negotiated procedures, *Knoll N. Am., Inc.*, Comp. Gen. Dec. B-250234, 93-1 CPD ¶ 26. In *Racal Corp.*, 70 Comp. Gen. 127 (B-240579), 90-2 CPD ¶ 453, the Comptroller General ruled that negotiation could not be used in a price only procurement to ensure that offerors had a complete understanding of the specifications and to permit changes to the agency's requirements after submission of offerors. See also *Northeast Constr. Co.*, 68 Comp. Gen. 406 (B-234323), 89-1 CPD

¶ 402, where the Comptroller General held that negotiation was not appropriate because the procurement was based on price alone and the RFP did not call for technical proposals.

An agency's decision to use sealed bidding procedures instead of competitive negotiation will be upheld unless it is clearly unreasonable. In *Eagle Fire Inc.*, Comp. Gen. Dec. B-257951, 94-2 CPD ¶ 214, the protester argued that technical proposals were needed and discussions required; thus, the procurement should have been conducted using competitive procedures rather than sealed bidding procedures. The Comptroller General found no basis to object to the Navy's choice of using sealed bidding because there was no ambiguity in the specification requirements and the Navy could conduct a preaward survey to determine whether the low bidder was qualified and capable of performing the contract. See also *Tennessee Apparel Corp.*, Comp. Gen. Dec. B-253178.3, 94-1 CPD ¶ 104, where the protester contended that negotiation procedures were required. The Comptroller General found that the specifications identified in the IFB made price and price-related factors the only relevant evaluation criteria and made discussions unnecessary. Further, the Comptroller General stated that the matters identified by the protester as necessary for discussions concerned a bidder's capacity to perform, which could be resolved through the conduct of a preaward survey. In *Machinewerks, Inc.*, Comp. Gen. Dec. B-258123, 94-2 CPD ¶ 238, the Comptroller General found sealed bidding with bid samples an appropriate technique to ensure that the proposed product met the agency's needs. The protester had argued that a negotiated procurement requiring first articles was less burdensome on the competitors. Similarly, in *Virginia Blood Servs.*, B-259717, 95-1 CPD ¶ 185, the Comptroller General upheld the agency's decision to use sealing bidding procedures, stating that the agency reasonably concluded that there was no reason to conduct discussions or to consider factors other than price in selecting the contractor.

B. Competitive Negotiation

It is frequently determined in the planning process that one of the statutory conditions for the use of sealed bidding is absent. In such cases, competitive negotiation is the proper procurement technique.

1. *No Time nor Expectation of Receiving More Than One Bid*

Conditions (i) and (iv) of 10 U.S.C. § 2304(a)(2) and 41 U.S.C. § 253(a)(2) do not frequently arise in protests of the use of competitive negotiation. When these conditions are called into question, the Comptroller General gives contracting officers a large amount of discretion. In *Milbar Corp.*, Comp. Gen. Dec. B-232158, 88-2 CPD ¶ 509, the contracting officer used competitive negotiation because only one offer was anticipated on a number of the items being procured. The Comptroller General denied the protest even though the contracting officer's logic was questionable. Although five firms participated in the previous procurement, only two firms were expected to bid on the current procurement. The contracting officer expected to receive only one offer on nine of the 32 items and expected the other firm to be financially capable of supplying only three of the items. The contracting officer therefore determined that the agency could not reasonably expect more than one bid on the vast majority of items.

2. *Non-Price-Related Factors*

The most common reason for using competitive proposals (negotiation) will probably be the need to make award on the basis of non-price-related factors. There appears to be little controversy as to the discretion of agencies to use negotiation procedures in these circumstances. See Comp. Gen. Dec. B-219998.2, Feb. 18, 1986, *Unpub.*, where the Comptroller General dismissed the protest against the use of competitive proposals without requesting a separate report from the agency because the solicitation indicated award would not be based solely on price and price-related factors. In both *A.J. Fowler Corp.*, Comp. Gen. Dec. B-233326, 89-1 CPD ¶ 166, and *KIME Plus, Inc.*, Comp. Gen. Dec. B-231906, 88-2 CPD ¶ 237, the Comptroller General sustained the decision to use competitive negotiation in order to award on the basis of technical/management factors as well as price, although the work was relatively routine and had been previously obtained through sealed bidding. In *Premiere Vending*, Comp. Gen. Dec. B-256437, 94-1 CPD ¶ 380, the solicitation was initially issued as an IFB, but the contracting officer subsequently decided that the procurement should be conducted using competitive proposals. The Comptroller General upheld the agency's decision to use negotiated procedures, stating that award would be based on non-price-related factors and that discussions might be required. Similarly, in *Specialized Contract Servs., Inc.*, Comp. Gen. Dec. B-257321,

94-2 CPD ¶ 90, the Comptroller General upheld an agency's decision to use negotiated procedures because the agency reasonably determined that, based on its experience, it was desirable to evaluate technical factors in addition to price. In *Vantex Serv. Corp.*, Comp. Gen. Dec. B-266199, 96-1 CPD ¶ 29, the Comptroller General found that the agency properly determined to use competitive negotiation. The RFP listed three technical evaluation factors that the agency stated would be evaluated on a go/no-go basis. Thus, the Comptroller General stated that award would be based on technical acceptability and price — not just price, as the protester contended. In addition, based on prior performance problems, the Comptroller found that the agency reasonably determined that discussions would be necessary to ensure that offerors understood the requirements. See also *Comfort Inn South*, Comp. Gen. Dec. B-270819.2, 96-1 CPD ¶ 225, finding that the use of negotiated procedures was justified because the agency reasonably determined that it was necessary to evaluate offeror past performance.

3. Need to Conduct Discussions

When the agency intends to make award on the basis of only price and price-related factors, the use of negotiation procedures is subject to much greater scrutiny. See *ARO Corp.*, Comp. Gen. Dec. B-227055, 87-2 CPD ¶ 165, *recons. denied*, 67 Comp. Gen. 16 (B-227055.2), 87-2 CPD ¶ 365, finding that the use of negotiation procedures in order to conduct price negotiations violated the statute because discussions were not necessary and all of the other conditions for sealed bidding had been met.

One case found that in order to justify negotiation on the basis of discussions, the agency is required to solicit technical proposals, *Saxon Corp.*, Comp. Gen. Dec. B-221054, 86-1 CPD ¶ 225. However, there have been subsequent cases where negotiation has been permitted without obtaining technical proposals. See *Carter Chevrolet Agency, Inc.*, Comp. Gen. Dec. B-228151, 87-2 CPD ¶ 584, where negotiation was permitted because prior sealed bid procurements had demonstrated that offerors had many exceptions to the solicitation and that only one bid had been submitted on a number of bid items. Similarly, in *Claude E. Atkins Enters., Inc.*, Comp. Gen. Dec. B-241047, 91-1 CPD ¶ 42, the Comptroller General permitted negotiation of a construction contract where the specifications were complex and prior sealed bid procurements had indicated that the agency could expect numerous queries as to the proper interpretation of the specifications. The distinguishing feature in these cases is the prior experience of the agency on similar procurements, indicating that discussions may be needed to effect a successful procurement. In *Saxon Corp.*, Comp. Gen. Dec. B-216148, 85-1 CPD ¶ 87, negotiation was held appropriate for a base vehicle operations and maintenance services contract requiring a high level of technical and managerial competence that could not be defined adequately in the specifications. The Comptroller General reasoned that prebid conferences and preaward surveys would not be adequate substitutes for discussions. See also *JT Constr. Co.*, Comp. Gen. Dec. B-244404.2, 92-1 CPD ¶ 1 (use of competitive negotiation procedures was appropriate where contracting officer determined that discussions were necessary to gauge offeror understanding of complex specifications); and *Essex Electro Eng'rs, Inc.*, 65 Comp. Gen. 242 (B-221114), 86-1 CPD ¶ 92 (refusing to question the judgment of the agency that technical data regarding a new engine were sufficiently important to warrant discussions).

4. Fixed-Price Contract Not Appropriate

Another reason for not using sealed bidding is that the agency determines that a firm-fixed-price or fixed-price with economic price adjustment type contract cannot be used for the procurement. If this choice is correctly made, it will rule out sealed bidding and require the use of one of the other competitive procedures — in most cases the solicitation of competitive proposals. For example, in *United Food Servs., Inc.*, Comp. Gen. Dec. B-220367, 86-1 CPD ¶ 177, the Comptroller General found that the Army's decision to use a cost-plus-award-fee contract for food service was justified by a number of factors, including the uncertainty in the quantities of meals to be served. The Comptroller General had found in an earlier decision, *United Food Servs., Inc.*, 64 Comp. Gen. 880 (B-217211), 85-2 CPD ¶ 326, that variation in quantity alone was not a sufficient justification for the use of a cost-type contract requiring negotiation. In *United Food Servs., Inc. — Recons.*, 65 Comp. Gen. 643 (B-218165.2), 86-1 CPD ¶ 538, the Comptroller General modified the 64 Comp. Gen. 880 decision to recommend that the Army assess the overall risks and uncertainties to determine whether use of a cost-type contract would be warranted.

C. Other Competitive Procedures

10 U.S.C. § 2302(2) and 41 U.S.C. § 259(b) specify five special procedures that are "competitive procedures" meeting the statutory requirement for full and open competition:

(A) procurement of architectural or engineering services conducted in accordance with title IX of the Federal Property and Administrative Services Act of 1949 (40 U.S.C. 541 et seq.);

(B) the competitive selection for award of basic research proposals resulting from a general solicitation and the peer review or scientific review (as appropriate) of such proposals;

(C) the procedures established by the Administrator of General Services for the multiple award schedule program of the General Services Administration if —

(i) participation in the program has been open to all responsible sources; and

(ii) orders and contracts under such program result in the lowest overall cost alternative to meet the needs of the United States;

(D) procurements conducted in furtherance of section 15 of the Small Business Act (15 U.S.C. 644) as long as all responsible business concerns that are entitled to submit offers for such procurements are permitted to compete; and

(E) a competitive selection of research proposals resulting from a general solicitation and peer review or scientific review (as appropriate) solicited pursuant to section 9 of the Small Business Act (15 U.S.C. 638).

These procedures are generally used in preference to sealed bidding or competitive negotiation when the special circumstances set forth in the statutes apply. See Chapter 7 for a detailed discussion of these procedures.

D. Commercial Supplies and Services

CBD doesn't have to be out for 15 da

The FASA added 10 U.S.C. § 2377 and 41 U.S.C. § 264b stating a preference for acquisition of commercial items. Agencies are required to "define requirements in terms that enable and encourage offerors to supply commercial items," FAR 11.002(a)(2)(ii). In addition, offerors of commercial items are to be provided an opportunity to compete in any procurement, FAR 11.002(a)(2)(iii). When commercial items are procured, certain statutes and clauses applicable to other procurements do not apply and special price analysis does apply. FAR 12.203 provides that contracting officers are required to use the policies unique to the acquisition of commercial items in conjunction with the policies and procedures for solicitation, evaluation and award prescribed in FAR Part 13, FAR Part 14, or FAR Part 15, as appropriate for the particular acquisition. The contracting officer may use the streamlined procedure for soliciting offers for commercial items prescribed in FAR 12.603. For acquisitions exceeding the simplified acquisition threshold but not exceeding $5,000,000, contracting activities must use the simplified procedures authorized by Subpart 13.5 to the maximum extent practicable. A detailed discussion of commercial item procedures in contained in Chapter 7.

E. Simplified Acquisition

In order to promote efficiency and economy in contracting, Congress enacted a provision under the FASA for special simplified procedures for contracts for acquisition of property and services at amounts not greater than the simplified acquisition threshold. FAR 2.101 provides the following definition:

> "Simplified acquisition procedures" means the methods prescribed in part 13 for making purchases of supplies or services.

FAR 13.003(h) provides broad guidance on the procedures that may be used:

> (1) The simplified acquisition threshold for other than commercial items, use any appropriate combination of the procedures in parts 13, 14, 15, 35, or 36, including the use of Standard Form 1442, Solicitation, Offer, and Award (Construction, Alteration, or Repair), for construction contracts (see 36.701(b));
>
> (2) $5 million for commercial items, use any appropriate combination of the procedures in parts 12, 13, 14, and 15 (see paragraph (d) of this section).

In choosing among these techniques, contracting officers are required to use the "simplified manner that is most suitable, efficient, and economical in the circumstances of each acquisition," FAR 13.003(h).

The simplified acquisition threshold stated in 41 U.S.C. § 403(11) is for purchases not exceeding $100,000. FAR 13.003 provides, in part:

> (a) Agencies shall use simplified acquisition procedures to the maximum extent practicable for all purchases of supplies or services not exceeding the

simplified acquisition threshold (including purchases at or below the micro-purchase threshold).

* * *

(d) The contracting officer shall not use simplified acquisition procedures to acquire supplies and services if the anticipated award will exceed the simplified acquisition threshold (or $5,000,000), including options, for acquisitions of commercial items using Subpart 13.5). Do not break down requirements aggregating more than the simplified acquisition threshold (or for commercial items, the threshold in Subpart 13.5) or the micro-purchase threshold into several purchases that are less than the applicable threshold merely to —

(1) Permit use of simplified acquisition procedures; or

(2) Avoid any requirement that applies to purchases exceeding the micro-purchase threshold.

Thus, the use of simplified acquisition procedures requires that the procurement be within the threshold at two stages in the procurement action — the solicitation stage and the award stage. First, the Government's estimate of the dollar value of the procurement determines whether the procurement can be solicited using simplified acquisition procedures. Next, the quoted or offered prices determine whether a simplified acquisition award can be made. For example, if the Government's estimate of the procurement is $98,500, a simplified acquisition solicitation can be issued. However, if the lowest price received exceeds $100,000, a simplified acquisition award cannot be made unless a price reduction is obtained that brings the amount within the threshold. Thus, in this example, if the lowest quotation received is $102,500, the contracting officer can seek to obtain price reductions to come within the $100,000 threshold. If that fails, the procurement must be resolicited using sealed bid or competitive proposal procedures. A detailed discussion of simplified acquisition procedures is contained in Chapter 7.

IV. IDENTIFYING SOURCES

In planning a procurement, it is necessary to determine what sources, if any, exist to meet the Government's needs. The number and nature of the sources will, in large part, determine the technique that can be used in the procurement. Other determinations that must be made in the planning stages deal with whether to satisfy the agency's needs from private or Government sources. It is also essential to determine whether there are any mandatory sources.

The prospective sources of supplies and/or services that can meet the need must be stated in the acquisition plan, FAR 7.105(b)(1). In determining what sources can be used to fulfill their needs, the agencies may not be free to make a choice. Statutes, regulations, and existing contractual obligations often dictate what sources may or may not be used. One example is when purchases are required to be set aside for performance solely by small business concerns, 15 U.S.C. § 644(j). Another example is when products or services fall under the Buy American Act, 41 U.S.C. §§ 10a–d. See Chapter 10 for an in-depth discussion of collateral policies that play a role in determining what sources are available to meet the Government's procurement needs.

In most cases, the agency technical and program personnel and the contracting officer will know of potential sources that should be solicited. In addition, the contracting officer may find it necessary to publicize the requirement with a solicitation of sources. The contracting officer will also determine whether the procurement must be directed to a mandatory source or set aside for small or disadvantaged businesses.

A. Market Research

Market research is defined in FAR 2.101:

> "Market Research" means collecting and analyzing information about capabilities within the market to satisfy agency needs.

In *Coulter Corp.; Nova Biomedical; Ciba Corning Diagnostics Corp.*, Comp. Gen. Dec. B-258713, 95-1 CPD ¶ 70, the Comptroller General stated the purpose of market research:

> A market survey is an attempt to ascertain whether other qualified sources capable of satisfying the government's requirements exist and may be informal, i.e., phone calls to federal or non-federal experts, or formal, i.e., sources-sought announcements in the CBD or solicitations for information or planning purposes.

An increased emphasis on market research began in the early 1980s. In hearings before the Senate Armed Services Committee, the General Accounting Office stated that the failure to perform market research was a "major processing deficiency." Many witnesses testified that the failure to perform market research was one of the key factors responsible for the absence of competition in Government procurement, Competition in Contracting Act of 1983: Hearings on S. 338 Before the Committee on Armed Services, United States Senate, 98th Cong., 1st Sess. (1983). The Senate Report on the CICA stated that "[c]ompetition in contracting depends on the procuring agency's understanding of the marketplace . . . [M]arket research is essential to developing this understanding," S. Rep. No. 50, 98th Cong., 2d Sess. (1984).

As a result, CICA included a general requirement for market research in 10 U.S.C. § 2305(a)(1)(A) and 41 U.S.C. § 253a(a)(1). The Federal Acquisition Streamlining Act of 1994 (FASA) added new, more specific provisions at 10 U.S.C. § 2377(c) and 41 U.S.C. § 264b(c), requiring that market research be conducted "appropriate to the circumstances":

> (A) before developing new specifications for a procurement by that agency; and
>
> (B) before soliciting bids or proposals for a contract in excess of the simplified acquisition threshold.

These statutes impose a unique requirement that market research be conducted *before* new specifications are prepared. This is to ensure that such specifications are drafted to maximize the use of commercial items.

These statutes are implemented in new FAR Part 10. FAR 10.002(a) provides that the Government's need should be stated in sufficient terms to allow market research to be conducted. Once the acquisition need is sufficiently stated, market research is conducted to determine if commercial items or nondevelopmental items are available to meet the Government's needs or could be modified to meet the Government's needs, FAR 10.002(b). Market research can also be used to determine the availability of additional or more competent sources to perform Government work. The extent of market research conducted varies depending on the circumstances and complexity of the procurement, FAR 10.002(b)(1).

When other than full and open competition procedures are used, FAR 6.303-2(a)(8) requires that justifications describe the market research conducted or the reasons why it was not conducted. The Comptroller

General has held that an agency's reason for not conducting a market survey was adequate where it had supported the fact that a directed source was designated pursuant to an international agreement, *PacOrd*, Comp. Gen. Dec. B-238366, 90-1 CPD ¶ 466. The Comptroller General also upheld an agency's decision not to conduct a market survey where the agency stated that it had recently determined that there was only one domestic source for a product, *Lister Bolt & Chain, Ltd.*, Comp. Gen. Dec. B-224473, 86-2 CPD ¶ 305. The technique used for the market survey is in the discretion of the contracting officer, *AAA Eng'g & Drafting, Inc.*, Comp. Gen. Dec. B-236034.3, 93-1 CPD ¶ 295.

1. Inadequate Market Research

Inadequate market research can be a fatal defect in the procurement process if there are sources available to meet the agency's needs that were not discovered. In *K-Whit Tools, Inc.*, Comp. Gen. Dec. B-247081, 92-1 CPD ¶ 382, the Comptroller General held that the failure to conduct a market survey indicated that the need to contract sole source was due to a lack of advance planning and was unauthorized. See also *TMS Bldg. Maintenance*, 65 Comp. Gen. 222 (B-220588), 86-1 CPD ¶ 68 (failure to contact other potential sources or to conduct a market survey evidenced a lack of advance planning and rendered the sole source award improper); *BFI Medical Waste Sys. of Arizona, Inc.*, Comp. Gen. Dec. B-270881, 96-1 CPD ¶ 239 (failure to conduct market survey led to improper small business set aside); *Rocky Mountain Trading Co.*, GSBCA 9569-P, 89-1 BCA ¶ 21,216 (inadequate market research led to unclear specification which invalidated procurement); *Jervis B. Webb Co.*, Comp. Gen. Dec. B-211724, 85-1 CPD ¶ 35 (lack of even a limited market survey led, in part, to a finding that the Defense Logistics Agency's sole source justification was inadequate). In contrast, the results of a market survey may justify a sole source award, *Interscience Sys., Inc.*, Comp. Gen. Dec B-201943, 82-2 CPD ¶ 187 (upholding determination to award contract on a sole source basis as a result of two market surveys). The results of a market survey have also been used to support the reasonableness of a bid price, *Eclipse Sys., Inc.*, Comp. Gen. Dec. B-216002, 85-1 CPD ¶ 267.

2. Solicitations for Planning Purposes

One technique for conducting market research is the use of solicitations for information or planning purposes. FAR 15.201(e) permits requests for information (RFIs) to be used in this manner as follows:

> RFIs may be used when the Government does not presently intend to award a contract, but wants to obtain price, delivery, other market information, or capabilities for planning purposes. Responses to these notices are not offers and cannot be accepted by the Government to form a binding contract. There is no required format for RFIs.

FAR 14.405-1 permits the use of solicitations for information or planning purposes for sealed bid procurements.

NASA's guidance on the use of solicitations for information or planning purposes is set forth in NFS 1815.405-70, which provides:

> (a) Except for acquisitions described in 18-15.602(b), contracting officers shall issue draft requests for proposals (DRFPs) for all competitive negotiated acquisitions expected to exceed $1,000,000 (including all options or later phases of the same project). DRFPs shall invite comments from potential offerors on all aspects of the draft solicitation, including the requirements, schedules, proposal instructions, and evaluation approaches. Potential offerors should be specifically requested to identify unnecessary or inefficient requirements. When considered appropriate, the statement of work or the specifications may be issued in advance of other solicitation sections.
>
> (b) Contracting officers shall plan the acquisition schedule to include adequate time for issuance of the DRFP, potential offeror review and comment, and NASA evaluation and disposition of the comments.
>
> (c) When issuing DRFPs, potential offerors should be advised that the DRFP is not a solicitation and NASA is not requesting proposals.
>
> (d) Whenever feasible, contracting officers should include a summary of the disposition of significant DRFP comments with the final RFP.
>
> (e) The procurement officer may waive the requirement for a DRFP upon written determination that the expected benefits will not be realized given the nature of the supply or service being acquired. The DRFP shall not be waived because of poor or inadequate planning.

When solicitations are used in this manner, they must contain a clear statement that the agency does not intend to award a contract and will not pay for the information submitted.

Some agencies require that solicitations for information or planning purposes may be used only when approved at a level above the contracting officer. See, for example, GSAR 515.405-1 (the chief of the contracting office) and DEAR 915-405-1 (the head of contracting activity).

3. Sources-Sought Synopsis

Another technique for identifying potential sources is the issuance of a sources-sought synopsis in the CBD. FAR 5.205 states that contracting officers may publish in the CBD advance notices of their interest in potential research and development programs when existing solicitation mailing lists do not include a sufficient number of concerns to obtain adequate competition. Under the FAR, such advance notices are called "Research and Development Sources Sought." Although the FAR appears to limit this technique for identifying potential sources to research and development contracts, it has been used for all types of procurement. The GSA provides a better definition of the term "sources-sought synopsis" in GSAR 505.204-70(a):

> The term "sources-sought synopsis" means the type of *Commerce Business Daily* (CBD) notice designed to identify potential sources for procurements. The sources-sought synopsis provides an opportunity for the marketplace to indicate its interest in submitting offers for future acquisitions. It is normally used to discover if more than one firm is interested and qualified to provide a particular product or service, although a solicitation is not yet available. This type of synopsis has particular application when one contractor is thought to be uniquely capable of meeting the Government's minimum requirements and verification of this opinion is needed.

If an agency uses a sources-sought synopsis, it must make its essential requirements clear to potential offerors and allow them an opportunity to demonstrate their ability to comply before rejecting them as potential sources. In *Masstor Sys. Corp.*, 64 Comp. Gen. 118 (B-215046), 84-2 CPD ¶ 598, the Comptroller General sustained a protest where the agency rejected a potential source for failing to demonstrate compliance with a requirement that was neither set forth in the sources-sought synopsis nor otherwise made known to the vendor. The Government should not, however, include proprietary information in the sources-sought synopsis. In *Research, Analysis & Dev., Inc. v. United States*, 8 Cl. Ct. 54 (1985), the plaintiff submitted an unsolicited proposal pertaining to a novel concept in state-of-the-art aircraft-sensor technology. The proposal included the proper restrictive proprietary legend. After having agreed to maintain the confidentiality of the information, the agency issued a sources-sought synopsis requesting responses regarding the feasibility of a sensor system concept identical to that proposed by the plaintiff. The court held that the disclosure in the CBD of the proprietary information associated with the unsolicited proposal violated the Government's implied-in-fact contractual obligation to protect the data and entitled the company to damages.

The results of a sources-sought synopsis may bear on the Comptroller General's review of an agency's reasonableness in choosing specifications. In *Motorola, Inc.*, Comp. Gen. Dec. B-247913.2, 92-2 CPD ¶ 240, the protester challenged the agency's choice of procuring on a nondevelopmental item (NDI) basis. In concluding that the agency had a reasonable basis for its selection of NDI-only specifications, the Comptroller General stated that through a sources-sought synopsis, the agency learned that there were offerors who would have an NDI available either by making minor modifications to existing items or by developing an item that would meet the agency's specifications and that such items would be available by the time the agency would award the contract. Thus, the Comptroller General found that the agency had a sufficient basis to conclude that an NDI procurement was feasible.

Similarly, the results of a sources-sought synopsis may support the Comptroller General's finding that an agency reasonably awarded on a sole source basis. In *Polaris, Inc.*, Comp. Gen. Dec. B-218008, 85-1 CPD ¶ 401, the protester alleged that the agency improperly awarded a sole source contract. The Comptroller General stated that the agency had made a significant effort to determine whether other firms could meet the agency's needs. The agency had issued a sources-sought synopsis and received responses from six potential offerors. The agency, however, determined that none of the six potential offerors could meet all of its requirements. In denying the protest, the Comptroller General stated that it was incumbent upon the protester in responding to the CBD announcement to do more than restate the agency's needs. Thus, the Comptroller General found the agency's decision to award on a sole source basis to be reasonable.

The Comptroller General will not consider a protest against a procuring agency issuing a potential sources-sought announcement in the CBD. The Comptroller General only considers protests against solicitations already issued by agencies and awards made or proposed to be made under those solicitations, *Pancor Corp.*, Comp. Gen. Dec. B-234168, 89-1 CPD ¶ 328.

B. Contractor versus Government Performance

Once a need has been identified by a Government agency, there are usually a number of sources available to satisfy those needs. These sources may either be private commercial sources or Government agencies, including the procuring agency itself.

This section first examines the executive branch policy of reliance on private sources contained in Office of Management and Budget (OMB) Circular No. A-76, *Policies for Acquiring Commercial or Industrial Services Needed by the Government* (A-76). It then considers mandatory sources and procurements through other Government agencies.

1. Reliance on Private Sources

As a result of concerns that Government competition with the private sector is detrimental to the free enterprise system, the executive branch policy is that, to the extent practicable, the Government should rely on the private sector for commercially available goods and services. This policy was first enunciated in Bureau of the Budget Bulletin No. 55-4, Jan. 15, 1955. Today, detailed guidance for determining whether commercial activities should be performed under contract with commercial sources or in-house using Government facilities and personnel is contained in A-76. Legislative agencies, however, are not subject to A-76's requirements, *International Graphics v. United States*, 4 Cl. Ct. 186 (1983).

This policy is implemented by FAR Subpart 7.3. FAR 7.301 contains the following summary of A-76's policy:

> The Circular provides that it is the policy of the Government to (a) rely generally on private commercial sources for supplies and services, if certain criteria are met, while recognizing that some functions are inherently Governmental and must be performed by Government personnel, and (b) give appropriate consideration to relative cost in deciding between Government performance and performance under contract. In comparing the costs of

Government and contractor performance, the Circular provides that agencies shall base the contractor's cost of performance on firm offers.

A-76 requires that each agency designate an official at the assistant secretary or equivalent level to be responsible for implementing its policies and to create an office that will be a contact point for information regarding inventories, reviews, and results of cost comparison studies.

Each agency contracting office is required to maintain an inventory list of all its functions that are eligible for A-76 review. The inventory is updated annually and is available upon request to other agencies and to the public. To compile this inventory, the agency must first evaluate its activities and functions and then determine which are Governmental and which are commercial. All the commercial activities are listed on an inventory that includes known expansions and new requirements. Activities involving 10 full-time equivalent (FTE) personnel or fewer are listed separately from those with more than 10 FTEs. The inventory must, at a minimum, describe the number of FTEs involved, the nature and location of the activity, and the dates of last and next reviews.

FAR 7.302 provides that agencies must:

(1) Prepare an estimate of the cost of Government performance based on the same work statement and level of performance as apply to offerors; and

(2) Compare the total cost of Government performance to the total cost of contracting with the potentially successful offeror.

In-house commercial activities involving 11 or more FTEs may be converted to private-sector contracts without cost comparison if (1) fair and reasonable prices can be obtained from qualified sources and (2) all directly affected federal employees can be reassigned to comparable federal positions for which they are qualified. In-house commercial activities of 10 FTEs or less may be contracted out without cost comparison, if fair and reasonable prices can be obtained from qualified commercial sources. The requirement for reassignment of employees to comparable federal positions does not apply where 10 or fewer FTEs are involved. Note, however, that commercial activities involving 11 or more FTEs may not be modified, reorganized, or divided for the purpose of avoiding any of the foregoing procedures.

Other waivers of the cost comparison requirements for activities exceeding 10 FTEs may be authorized by an agency official at the assistant secretary level. The waiver request must include a written report explaining why (1) the waiver will be in the best interests of the Government, (2) effective price competition is not readily available, or (3) the in-house operation has no reasonable expectation of winning the competition.

Where waivers are not warranted, a cost comparison is required prior to authorizing in-house performance if an agency anticipates an in-house expansion in any given budget cycle — including the modernization, replacement, upgrading, or enlargement of a Government activity — involving a 30 percent increase in the operating cost of the activity, a 30 percent increase in the total capital investment to perform the activity, or a 10 percent FTE staffing increase. Cost comparisons should be completed within 18 months for a single activity or 36 months for multiple activities from the comparison start date (i.e., public announcement and designation of the study team). Agencies must provide an annual report to the OMB identifying all cost comparisons that exceed these time frames.

The Supplemental Handbook, which was substantially revised in 1996, requires that a new private-sector contract be competitively awarded. If there is reason to believe that the private-sector contract service quality or prices will be unreasonable, a cost comparison must be conducted to justify conversion to in-house performance. Paragraph 7.c.(8) states that A-76 "shall not be construed to create any substantive or procedural basis for anyone to challenge any agency action or inaction."

The cost of contracting out must be based on a firm bid or proposal, FAR 7.301(b) and FAR 7.304(c)(2). Thus, the first step in the cost comparison process is the preparation of a statement of work. Once the statement of work is completed, bids or proposals are solicited. Concurrently, an in-house estimate is prepared for submission to the contracting officer not later than the time established for receipt of proposals or bid opening, FAR 7.304. The evaluation procedure to be followed after the contracting officer receives the cost estimate for Government performance and the responses to the solicitation differs from conventional contracting procedures. Under sealed bidding, the contracting officer opens the sealed cost comparison from the Government estimate, enters the cost comparison from the price of the lowest bidder, and announces the result. No final determination for performance by the Government or under contract is made until after a public review period, which is a minimum of 15 and a maximum of 30 working days, FAR

7.306(a). After the review period, the responsible agency official will make the final determination for performance by the Government or under contract and provide written notification to the contracting officer, who then either awards a contract or cancels the solicitation as required, FAR 7.306(a)(3). Under competitive negotiation, the contracting officer will receive proposals, evaluate them, conduct negotiations, and select the most advantageous proposal in accordance with normal contracting procedures, FAR 7.306(b). The contracting officer then, prior to public announcement, opens the sealed cost estimate for Government performance and enters the amount of the most advantageous proposal on the cost comparison form. If the result of the cost comparison favors performance under contract and the responsible agency official approves, the contracting officer will award the contract and publicly notify interested parties of the result of the cost comparison, FAR 7.306(b)(1). If, on the other hand, the result of the cost comparison favors Government performance, the contracting officer must notify interested parties of the result of the comparison, announce the price of the offer most advantageous to the Government, and conduct a public review period. The remaining part of the process is the same as under sealed bidding.

If serious problems with the cost comparison are revealed during the review process, A-76 allows an attempt at correction. Where an error lies with the in-house estimate that cannot be timely corrected, A-76 states that the in-house estimate should be rejected and a contract awarded. But see *International Graphics v. United States*, 5 Cl. Ct. 100 (1984), where the court allowed the Government to reestimate its cost after the submission of bids for cost comparison. However, if the cost comparison concerns a review of an existing Government-operated commercial or industrial activity, A-76 provides that the solicitation may be canceled and the review rescheduled.

The Comptroller General will review whether an offeror was unfairly treated because the agency failed to conduct a cost comparison in accordance with applicable procedures, *Dyneteria, Inc.*, Comp. Gen. Dec. B-222581.3, 87-1 CPD ¶ 30. See, for example, *Tecom, Inc.*, Comp. Gen. Dec. B-253740.3, July 7, 1994, *Unpub.*, where the Comptroller General found that the agency had followed applicable procedures and that the protester failed to show that the methodology used in its cost comparison was unreasonable or inconsistent with A-76. Compare *DynCorp*, Comp. Gen. Dec. B-233727.2, 89-1 CPD ¶ 543, where the Comptroller General sustained a protest, stating that the agency failed to include all costs required for in-house performance and otherwise miscalculated costs in conducting a cost comparison. The Comptroller General will not review the validity of an agency cost comparison until the protester has exhausted the administrative appeals procedure provided by the agency, *RAI, Inc.*, Comp. Gen. Dec. B-244725, 91-2 CPD ¶ 48.

Existing contracts are not required by A-76 to be kept on the inventory list. However, most agencies maintain an inventory of commercial contracting activities. A-76 requires that the contracted activities be continually monitored. If the Government believes that quality or prices may be unreasonable, or if competitive prices are not available, a cost comparison is conducted to determine whether the contract should be converted to in-house performance.

The Comptroller General takes the position that the decision of whether to contract out is a matter of executive branch policy and is not reviewable, *Schonstedt Instrument Co.*, Comp. Gen. Dec., B-215531, 84-2 CPD ¶ 141; *Research, Analysis & Management Corp.*, Comp. Gen. Dec., B-215712.2, 85-1 CPD ¶ 54. Likewise, the courts have held that agency decisions under A-76 are internal managerial decisions that are not subject to judicial review, *International Graphics v. United States*, 4 Cl. Ct. 186 (1983).

2. Exceptions

Paragraph 7.c. of A-76 contains the following limitations on the contracting-out policy:

> This Circular and its Supplement shall not:
>
> (1) Be applicable when contrary to law, Executive Orders, or any treaty or international agreement;
>
> (2) Apply to Governmental functions as defined in paragraph 6.e.;
>
> (3) Apply to the Department of Defense in times of a declared war or military mobilization;
>
> (4) Provide authority to enter into contracts;
>
> (5) Authorize contracts which establish an employer-employee relationship between the Government and contractor employees. An employer-employee relationship involves close, continual supervision of individual contractor

employees by Government employees, as distinguished from general oversight of contractor operations. However, limited and necessary interaction between Government employees and contractor employees, particularly during the transition period of conversion to contract, does not establish an employer-employee relationship. Additional guidance on this subject is provided in the Federal Personnel Manual issued by the Office of Personnel Management;

(6) Be used to justify conversion to contract solely to avoid personnel ceilings or salary limitations;

(7) Apply to the conduct of research and development. However, severable in-house commercial activities in support of research and development, such as those listed in Attachment A, are normally subject to this Circular and its Supplement.

a. Statutory Limitations on Contracting Out

Congress has placed a number of statutory limitations on the procurement of services by contract.

(1) DOD Authorization Acts

Chapter 146 of Title 10 of the U.S. Code regulates the DOD's contracting-out process. The statute provides that the Secretary of Defense must procure supplies or services necessary for DOD functions from a private-sector source if such a source can provide the supplies or services at a lower cost level than the comparable in-house cost, 10 U.S.C. § 2462. Such a cost comparison must include consideration of all relevant costs that are fair and reasonable. Note, however, that Section 2461 prohibits conversion to private-contractor performance of an in-house function unless extensive notice to Congress has occurred.

This statute imposes restrictions on the DOD's ability to contract out. In particular, 10 U.S.C. § 2464 places limitations on the contracting out of "core logistics functions." The section applies to those DOD activities that are necessary "to ensure a ready and controlled source of technical competence and resources" if there is a situation that involves the national security. The statute provides that the Secretary of Defense will identify activities that are to be exempt from contacting out under A-76. Once an activity has been identified as a core logistics function, it may only be contracted out if the Secretary waives the requirements of the section.

Another restriction is in 10 U.S.C. § 2466, whereby defense agencies and military departments are prevented from contracting out more than 50 percent of their respective depot maintenance workloads. Any funds that are not used for such a contract must be used for the performance of depot-level maintenance and repair workload by employees of the DOD.

(2) NATIONAL PARK SERVICE

The Volunteers in the Parks Act of 1969, Amendments, P.L. 98-540, 98 Stat. 2718 (1984), 43 U.S.C. § 1457a note, states that A-76 will not apply to activities conducted by the National Park Service, United States Fish and Wildlife Service, and the Bureau of Land Management if those activities involve 10 FTEs or fewer.

After the enactment of this amendment, three cases before the Department of the Interior Board of Contract Appeals (IBCA) were dismissed as moot because this statute deprived the contracting officer of authority to contract despite challenges to the cost comparisons conducted by the National Park Service. See *Applicators, Inc.*, IBCA 1797-(A-76), 85-1 BCA ¶ 17,797; *Crimson Enters., Inc.*, IBCA 1876(A-76), 85-1 BCA ¶ 17,798; and *B & W Serv. Indus., Inc.*, IBCA 1859(A-76), 85-1 BCA ¶ 17,799. In another case, the same board affirmed a prior dismissal for lack of jurisdiction over an appeal of a decision not to renew a contract. The board did not rely on P.L. 98-540 as it did in the above cases, but chose rather to rely on A-76. The board stated that A-76 did not provide for an appeal "for a decision to terminate a contracted service resulting from a cost comparison study," despite an Office of Federal Procurement Policy (OFPP) letter to the appellant that an appeal should be heard, *Ontario Flight Serv., Inc.*, IBCA 1812(A-76), 84-3 BCA ¶ 17,630, *recons. denied*, 85-1 BCA ¶ 17,775.

(3) VETERANS' HOSPITALS

In enacting the Veterans' Compensation, Education and Employment Act of 1982, P.L. 97-306, Congress decided that cost savings alone would not justify a conversion of patient-care-related services from in-house performance to contractor performance. See S. Rep. No. 7-550, 97th Cong., 2d Sess. 100 (1982). The Act amended 38 U.S.C. § 5010 (now § 8110(c)(1)) to provide that activities directly related to patient care or any activities incident to patient care should not be contracted out. The amendment also states that if an activity is deemed by the chief medical director to be neither of the above, that activity may be contracted out by the secretary of the

Department of Veterans' Affairs only after two determinations are made: first, "that the cost to the Government of the performance of such activity under such a contract over the first five years of such performance (including the cost to the Government of conducting the study) would be lower by 15 percent or more than the cost of performance of such an activity by Federal Employees;" and second, that the quality of patient care would be enhanced or at least maintained by contracting out. These two provisos establish clear congressional intent that activities relating to veterans' patient care should be performed by federal employees. They are also stricter than the guidelines set out in the Supplemental Handbook.

(4) EDGAR AMENDMENT

The jobs of General Services Administration (GSA) guards, elevator operators, messengers, and custodians are protected by P.L. 97-377, 96 Stat. 1830, 1913 (1983), which prohibits the use of funds available under the Act to the GSA from being expended for these services. As a result, the Comptroller General dismissed a protest to the cancellation of a solicitation for custodial services as "academic" because the GSA was prohibited by the Act from awarding such a contract, *Consolidated Maintenance Co.*, Comp. Gen. Dec. B-209766, 83-1 CPD ¶ 225.

b. Inherently Governmental Functions Excepted

Certain governmental functions may not be contracted out to private firms. FAR 7.501 defines the term "inherently Governmental function" as follows:

> [A]s a matter of policy, a function that is so intimately related to the public interest as to mandate performance by Government employees. This definition is a policy determination, not a legal determination. An inherently governmental function includes activities that require either the exercise of discretion in applying Government authority, or the making of value judgments in making decisions for the Government. Governmental functions normally fall into two categories: the act of governing, i.e., the discretionary exercise of Government authority, and monetary transactions and entitlements.

Paragraph 6.e. of A-76 defines "Governmental function" as follows:

> A *Governmental function* is a function which is so intimately related to the public interest as to mandate performance by Government employees.

> These functions include those activities which require either the exercise of discretion in applying Government authority or the use of value judgment in making decisions for the Government. Services or products in support of Governmental functions, such as those listed in Attachment A, are commercial activities and are normally subject to this Circular. Governmental functions normally fall into two categories:
>
> > (1) *The act of governing*; i.e., the discretionary exercise of Government authority. Examples include criminal investigations, prosecutions and other judicial functions; management of Government programs requiring value judgments, as in direction of the national defense; management and direction of the Armed Services; activities performed exclusively by military personnel who are subject to deployment in a combat, combat support or combat service support role; conduct of foreign relations; selection of program priorities; direction of Federal employees; regulation of the use of space, oceans, navigable rivers and other natural resources; direction of intelligence and counter- intelligence operations; and regulation of industry and commerce, including food and drugs.
> >
> > (2) *Monetary transactions and entitlements*, such as tax collection and revenue disbursements; control of the treasury accounts and money supply; and the administration of public trusts.

The executive branch policy relating to inherently governmental functions is further articulated in OFPP Policy Letter 92-1. The policy letter states that whether a function is inherently governmental depends upon the facts of the case and involves a consideration of a number of factors such as the degree to which official discretion would be limited, the finality of any contractor's action affecting individual claimants, or the contractor's ability to take action that will significantly affect the public. The policy letter provides illustrative lists of both functions considered to be inherently governmental and functions that are not considered as such. In *Nuclear Regulatory Comm'n Licensing Examiners*, 70 Comp. Gen. 682 (B-242942) (1991), the Comptroller General found that the Nuclear Regulatory Commission's (NRC) use of contract employees to perform testing procedures involved in licensing operators for nuclear facilities did not involve the performance of inherently governmental functions. Although the contract examiners prepared, administered, and graded examinations, the NRC's internal guidelines provided such extensive detail and guidance that the contract examiners could not exercise discretion and make value judgments to decide who would passed the examination and be licensed. However, in *Socolar*,

Comp. Gen. Dec. B-237356, Dec. 29, 1989, *Unpub.*, the Comptroller General found that determining eligibility for a DOE security clearance was an inherently governmental function. In this case, the hearing officers had to consider and rule on disputed matters, make specific findings as to the truth of the information provided, and preliminarily determine whether the access should be granted, denied, or invoked.

FAR 7.501(b) states that inherently governmental functions do not normally include

> gathering information for or providing advice, opinions, recommendations, or ideas to Government officials. They also do not include functions that are primarily ministerial and internal in nature, such as building security, mail operations, operation of cafeterias, housekeeping, facilities operations and maintenance, warehouse operations, motor vehicle fleet management operations, or other routine electrical or mechanical services. The list of commercial activities included in the attachment to Office of Management and Budget (OMB) Circular No. A-76 is an authoritative, nonexclusive list of functions which are not inherently governmental functions.

Examples of both types are contained in FAR 7.503.

c. Circular Exceptions

Paragraph 8 of A-76 authorizes Government performance of a commercial activity in four specific cases.

(1) No Satisfactory Commercial Source Available

Paragraph 8.a. permits in-house performance if "[e]ither no commercial source is capable of providing the needed product or service, or use of such a source would cause unacceptable delay or disruption of an essential program." Before an agency can claim that no commercial source is capable, there must be at least three notices describing the requirement published in the CBD over a 90-day period. The specifications and requirements cannot be unduly restrictive nor exceed the in-house requirements. In cases of bona fide urgency, the requirement may be two notices published in a 30-day period.

The finding that a commercial source would cause unacceptable delay must be accompanied by a written explanation from the assistant secretary, detailing the specific impact on the agency in terms of cost and performance. In-house performance is not justified on the basis of urgency alone, nor on the basis of the temporary disruption associated with conversion to contract. Further, the possibility of strikes by contract employees is not sufficient to support this claim. Finally, this exception does not justify in-house performance solely on the basis that the activity involves or supports a classified program. Documentation for the finding that no commercial source is capable is available to the public upon request.

(2) National Defense

Paragraph 8.b. of A-76 provides a national defense exception that allows the Government to operate a "commercial or industrial" activity where necessary to maintain military preparedness. This exception authorizes military personnel to perform commercial or industrial activities if the activity is subject to deployment in a direct combat support role, provides essential training in military skills, or is needed to provide appropriate overseas rotation. Certain maintenance activities are also allowed if necessary to maintain technical competence for meeting military contingencies, but these must be justified by detailed explanations of why commercial sources or contract operation of Government-owned facilities would not be sufficient.

(3) Patient Care

Paragraph 8.c. of A-76 states that commercial activities performed by Government employees shall be retained in-house if it would be in the best interests of the patients. This is determined by the agency head in consultation with the agency's chief medical officer.

(4) Lower Cost

Paragraph 8.d. provides that in-house performance of a commercial or industrial activity can be justified by an agency on the basis of a cost comparison conducted in accordance with the Supplemental Handbook. A-76 sets forth basic policies governing the cost comparison process, while the Supplemental Handbook contains detailed guidelines for performing the comparison. If on the basis of a cost comparison it is determined that the estimated cost of Government (in-house) performance is lower than that offered by commercial sources, Government performance of the activity is authorized by A-76. However, the fact that Government performance may be cheaper does not require an agency to perform the work in-house. Note that applicable federal statutes override any duty the Government may have had under A-76 to conduct cost comparisons or to rely on commercial production. See *Techniarts Eng'g v. United States*, 51 F.3d 301 (1995), where the court stated that the production of television newscasts in-house without first comparing the costs of private and agency production did not violate A-76 because the TV Marti Act overrode any duty that the Government might have had under A-76 to conduct cost comparisons. This Act instructed the Government to establish newscasts to Cuba and authorized the Government to move production in-house and to enter into service contracts. In its reasoning, the court stated at 304:

> [T]o the extent that the Economy Act and the OMB Circular require use of commercial resources when cheaper, they are at odds with the TV Marti Act's mandate to "make maximum feasible utilization" of USIA resources and, as laws of general application, must give way to that specific mandate.

3. Mandatory Sources

Various statutes and regulations require agencies to attempt to satisfy their needs for goods and services from specific sources prior to contracting with commercial sources. FAR Part 8 contains detailed guidance on mandatory sources. See also DFARS Part 208 for guidance on mandatory sources for defense procurement.

FAR 8.001 ranks mandatory sources in order of priority. Existing agency inventory is the first source considered. If the needed supply is not available from existing inventory, FAR 8.001 directs the agency to consider other sources in the following order: other agencies (excess supplies), Federal Prison Industries, the Committee for Purchase from People Who Are Blind or Severely Disabled, Government wholesale supply sources, federal supply schedules, and commercial sources. If the agency's requirement is for services, sources are considered in the following sequence: the Committee for Purchase from People Who Are Blind or Severely Disabled, federal supply schedules, Federal Prison Industries, and commercial sources, FAR 8.001. The following discussion examines these other sources of supply.

a. *Excess Personal Property*

The administrator of the GSA is authorized to prescribe policies and methods to promote utilization of excess personal property by the federal agencies pursuant to 40 U.S.C. § 483. This statute requires agencies to utilize excess personal property of other agencies to the fullest extent possible. The statute also charges agencies with the duty of monitoring excess property and either transferring or disposing of it as promptly as possible. The GSA maintains catalogs of available excess property, issues bulletins, and provides other assistance to facilitate acquisition of excess personal property. FAR 8.102 requires procurement personnel to make "positive efforts" to utilize excess personal property before taking other procurement action.

b. *Government Printing Office*

Virtually all printing, binding, and blank-book work for Congress, the Executive Office of the President, the judiciary (except the Supreme Court), and every executive department, independent office, and establishment of the Government must be done by or through the Government Printing Office (GPO). Exceptions include those classes of work the Congressional Joint Committee on Printing considers sufficiently urgent or necessary to be done elsewhere, as well as work printed in field printing plants operated by an executive department, 44 U.S.C. § 501. FAR 8.802 mandates compliance with the regulations of the Congressional Joint Committee on Printing and vests responsibility for obtaining waivers and dealing with the Joint Committee in certain officials.

Section 207 of the Legislative Branch Appropriations Act of 1993, P.L. 102-392, prohibits, with limited exceptions, the use of appropriated funds by the executive branch agencies for the procurement of printing other than by or through the GPO. Section 207 was amended by the Legislative Branch Appropriations Act of 1995, P.L. 103-283, and added "duplicating" to the definition of "printing." Congress specifically deleted language from the proposed amendment that would have added to the definition of "printing" those processes involving "production of an image on paper or other substrate." The conference report accompanying the amendment stated that the deletion was made so that the revised definition would not encompass "ADP output, CD-ROMs, video discs, and other material that fall within the Brooks Act or other statutes," H.R. Conf. Rep. 567, 103 Cong. 2d

Sess. 13 (1994). See Comp. Gen. Dec. B-251481.4, Sept. 30, 1994, *Unpub.*, holding that printing includes duplicating processes using high-speed duplicating equipment. But see Comp. Gen. Dec. B-251481.3, Feb. 15, 1994, *Unpub.*, stating that a contract modification requiring a design system to have the capability of developing "reproducible masters" from the technical manual source data did not fall within the definition of printing.

Individual printing orders costing not more than $1,000 are, under certain conditions, not required to be printed by the GPO, P.L. 102-392, Title II § 207(a), codified at 44 U.S.C. § 501 note.

c. General Services Administration Stores Stock

The administrator of the GSA is authorized to operate supply centers and procure and supply personal property for executive agencies, 40 U.S.C. § 481. Pursuant to this authority, the GSA operates supply distribution facilities and maintains an inventory of stock items that constitute a mandatory source for executive agencies located within the United States. See 41 C.F.R. § 101-26.301. The GSA publishes a supply catalog that lists all items available from GSA stock. The GSA also has an electronic catalog, "GSA Advantage!," which is an on-line ordering system that allows agencies to search through all GSA sources of supply and select the item that best meets their requirements.

d. General Services Administration Motorpools

The Federal Property and Administrative Services Act of 1949 authorizes the General Services administrator to "consolidate, take over, acquire, or arrange for the operation by any executive agency of" motor vehicles, 40 U.S.C. § 491. The Act authorizes the GSA to enter into rental or other arrangements and to utilize Government-owned vehicles. The Act provides that requisitioning agencies should be charged for services rendered at prices calculated to recover all elements of cost.

e. Federal Prison Industries

Federal Prison Industries (FPI) is a wholly owned Government corporation created by Congress in 1934 to administer industrial operations in federal penal and correctional institutions. FPI is authorized to produce commodities for consumption in penal institutions or for sale to the Government, but is prohibited from selling to the public, 18 U.S.C. § 4122. All

Government agencies are required to purchase available quantities that meet their needs from FPI, 18 U.S.C. § 4124. Such commodities are listed on the Schedule of Products made in federal penal and correctional institutions and may be purchased either directly from FPI or from GSA store depots, depending on the quantities involved and which sources are most convenient, FAR 8.604. If a supply not listed in the Schedule is of a type normally produced by federal penal and correctional institutions, agencies are encouraged to suggest that FPI consider adding it to the Schedule, FAR 8.602(c).

f. Surplus Strategic and Critical Materials

The General Services administrator has the authority to purchase strategic and critical materials for Government stockpiles and for use or resale to stimulate exploration, development, and mining of these materials under Exec. Order No. 10480, 18 Fed. Reg. 4939 (1953), which delegates presidential authority as contained in 50 U.S.C. App. § 2093. Pursuant to this authority, the GSA issues a bulletin entitled *Transfer of Excess Strategic and Critical Materials from GSA Inventories*. This bulletin lists excess stockpile materials that are available for transfer to agencies. FAR 8.002 directs the procuring activity to use this source prior to procurement of such materials. The agency is required to screen the list to determine whether its requirements can be met through transfer from the GSA, with consideration given to quantity, quality, location of materials, and timeliness of availability, 41 C.F.R. § 101-14.2.

g. The Committee for Purchase from People Who Are Blind or Severely Disabled

Federal agencies are required to procure goods and services from a nonprofit agency serving people who are blind or a nonprofit agency serving people with other severe disabilities if those agencies can provide the needed commodities or services, 41 U.S.C. § 48. This committee, appointed by the President, compiles a list of services and commodities that qualified agencies may provide. Agencies must purchase these supplies or services if they are available within the period required, FAR 8.704. Copies of the list are obtained by submission of GSA Form 457, in accordance with the instructions in FAR 8.703.

h. Jewel Bearings and Related Items

Public Law 90-469 provided for the operation, by contract or otherwise, of the William Langer Jewel Bearing Plant to produce jewel bearings and related items for Government use or for sale at prices to be determined by the GSA to be sufficient to cover the estimated or actual costs of production, including depreciation, without fiscal year limitation. In 1995, § 2852 of P.L. 104-201 conveyed the land that the plant is on (including the improvements and all associated personal property) to the Job Development Authority of the city of Rolla, North Dakota, subject to the condition that the land and property be used "for economic development relating to the jewel bearing plant." Section 4301 of the Clinger-Cohen Act of 1996 provided for the elimination of certain regulatory certification requirements for contractors and offerors that are not specifically imposed by statute. As a result of this Act, FAR Subpart 8.2, requiring the acquisition of jewel bearings from the William Langer Plant, was removed by FAC 90-45, January 2, 1997.

4. Procurement through Another Government Agency

In some cases, the most efficient procurement can be achieved by obtaining the goods and services through another agency. This permits agencies to pool their requirements to achieve higher volume procurements or to reduce the administrative expenses of multiple procurement actions.

a. Economy Act

The Economy Act, 31 U.S.C. § 1535, authorizes contract off-loading — the use by one procurement office of the contracts of another office to fulfill its requirements. Used in conjunction with task and delivery order contracts, contract off-loading can be beneficial to both the ordering and servicing offices. The ordering office is saved the time and expense of awarding and administering a separate contract. The servicing office can benefit because the ordering agency will pay the servicing office's share of the costs, and the servicing office's orders can be used, if necessary, to fulfill obligations under indefinite-quantity contracts.

Contract off-loading can also enhance efficiency through centralizing the contracting function or where a requiring agency lacks essential technical capability to evaluate contractor proposals. See *Dictaphone Corp.*,

Comp. Gen. Dec. B-244691.2, 92-2 CPD ¶ 380 (user agency reasonably determined that it could purchase dictaphones at a lower cost through another agency than through the Federal Supply Schedule); and *Liebert Corp.*, 70 Comp. Gen. 448 (B-232234.5), 91-1 CPD ¶ 413 (agency concluded that at the time of the original competition, the awardee's prices were less than half of the prices submitted by its competitors; thus, it determined that this contract was likely to be cheaper and more convenient than a separate agreement). The CICA prohibits an agency from procuring goods or services from another agency unless that agency complies with the requirements of the Act, 10 U.S.C. § 2304(f)(5)(B); 41 U.S.C. § 253(f)(5)(B).

The practice of contract off-loading increased dramatically in the late 1980s and the early 1990s. This led to criticism of the practice, several Department of Defense Inspector General (DODIG) audits, and, in July 1993, congressional hearings. The DODIG expressed concern that many DOD procurement offices were taking advantage of the procurement process by awarding contracts through agencies in order to avoid putting contracts out for competitive bids. The Office of the Inspector General issued an audit report on allegations of improprieties involving DOD acquisition services through the Department of Energy (DOE), Rep. No. 93-042 (Jan. 21, 1993). In the report, the DODIG determined that DOD program officials had circumvented normal procurement channels via placing Economy Act orders with DOE facilities. The DODIG recommended that additional guidance be given on the format and content of interagency agreements, on who should perform the determinations that the interagency acquisition is in the best interests of the Government, and what should be included in the determinations. Subsequently, Section 1074 of the FASA required that the FAR be amended to include a number of limitations on the practice. A discussion of these and subsequent events is contained in an October 1995 Letter Report of the Comptroller General titled *Interagency Contracting: Controls Over Economy Act Orders Being Strengthened* (GAO/NSAID-96-10).

The authority for the use of both intra- and interagency ordering is contained in 31 U.S.C. § 1535, as amended by the FASA, as follows:

> (a) The head of an agency or major organizational unit within an agency may place an order with a major organizational unit within the same agency or another agency for goods or services if —

(1) amounts are available;

(2) the head of the ordering agency or unit decides the order is in the best interest of the United States Government;

(3) the agency or unit to fill the order is able to provide or get by contract the ordered goods or services; and

(4) the head of the agency decides ordered goods or services cannot be provided by contract as conveniently or cheaply by a commercial enterprise.

In addition, Congress directed that regulations be adopted to place controls on the use of contract off-loading. These directions were added as notes to 31 U.S.C. § 1535. The first of these directions, applicable only to the DOD, was adopted in 1993 in Section 844 of the National Defense Authorization Act for Fiscal Year 1994, P.L. 103-160. In essentially the same language, this requirement was extended to all agencies by FASA § 1074.

FASA § 1074 required the Administrator of the OFPP to ensure that "systems for collecting and evaluating procurement data are capable of collecting and evaluating appropriate data" on Economy Act procurements. Note that while the Economy Act applies to both intra- and interagency transactions, these limitations apply only to orders placed with another agency.

The FAR implementation of FASA § 1074 is set forth in FAR Subpart 17.5. FAR 17.503 requires that these limitations be addressed in a D&F as follows:

(a) Each Economy Act order shall be supported by a Determination and Finding (D&F). The D&F shall state that —

(1) Use of an interagency acquisition is in the best interest of the Government; and

(2) The supplies or services cannot be obtained as conveniently or economically by contracting directly with a private source.

(b) If the Economy Act order requires contracting action by the servicing agency, the D&F shall also include a statement that at least one of the following circumstances is applicable —

(1) The acquisition will appropriately be made under an existing contract of the servicing agency, entered into before placement of the order, to meet the requirements of the servicing agency for the same or similar supplies or services;

(2) The servicing agency has capabilities or expertise to enter into a contract for such supplies or services which is not available within the requesting agency; or

(3) The servicing agency is specifically authorized by law or regulation to purchase such supplies or services on behalf of other agencies.

(c) The D&F shall be approved by a contracting officer of the requesting agency with authority to contract for the supplies or services to be ordered, or by another official designated by the agency head, except that, if the servicing agency is not covered by the Federal Acquisition Regulation, approval of the D&F may not be delegated below the senior procurement executive of the requesting agency.

Procedures for issuing orders are contained in FAR 17.504:

(a) Before placing an Economy Act order for supplies or services with another Government agency, the requesting agency shall make the D&F required in 17.503. The servicing agency may require a copy of the D&F to be furnished with the order.

(b) The order may be placed on any form or document that is acceptable to both agencies. The order should include —

(1) A description of the supplies or services required;

(2) Delivery requirements;

(3) A funds citation;

(4) A payment provision (see 17.505); and

(5) Acquisition authority as may be appropriate (see 17.504(d)).

(c) The requesting and servicing agencies should agree to procedures for the resolution of disagreements that may arise under interagency acquisitions, including, in appropriate circumstances, the use of a third-party forum. If a third party is proposed, consent of the third party should be obtained in writing.

(d) When an interagency acquisition requires the servicing agency to award a contract, the following procedures also apply:

(1) If a justification and approval or a D&F (other than the requesting agency's D&F required in 17.503) is required by law or regulation, the servicing agency shall execute and issue the justification and approval or D&F. The requesting agency shall furnish the servicing agency any information needed to make the justification and approval or D&F.

(2) The requesting agency shall also be responsible for furnishing other assistance that may be necessary, such as providing information or special contract terms needed to comply with any condition or limitation applicable to the funds of the requesting agency.

(3) The servicing agency is responsible for compliance with all other legal or regulatory requirements applicable to the contract, including

(i) Having adequate statutory authority for the contractual action, and

(ii) Complying fully with the competition requirements of part 6 (see 6.002). However, if the servicing agency is not subject to the Federal Acquisition Regulation, the requesting agency shall verify that contracts utilized to meet its requirements contain provisions protecting the Government from inappropriate charges (for example, provisions mandated for FAR agencies by part 31), and that adequate contract administration will be provided.

* * *

While recognizing that the Economy Act applies to both intra- and interagency procurements, the FAR, like the FASA, places the limitations only on interagency transactions.

More restrictive limitations were applied to the DOD in Section 844 of the 1994 Defense Authorization Act. A DOD ordering agency must find that the use of the Economy Act is *both* more convenient and more economical than contracting by the ordering agency itself. Compare FAR 17.503(a)(2), which permits ordering through another agency if it is *either* more convenient or more economical. In addition, for acquisitions where the DOD uses contracts of other agencies, the D&F must be approved by a high-level official, as opposed to FAR 17.503(c), which merely requires approval by the contracting officer. These more restrictive provisions were adopted by a memorandum and are not contained in the DFARS. However, the Air Force had adopted them in AFFARS 5317.5.

b. Federal Supply Schedules

Administered by the GSA, the Federal Supply Schedule (FSS) program provides agencies with a simple process for acquiring commonly used supplies and services in varying quantities at volume discounts, FAR 38.101. The FSS program includes single and multiple award schedules, and contracts under the schedules are indefinite-delivery, indefinite-quantity contracts for the sale of products and services to any agency at stated prices for a certain period of time. Because these schedules are competitively awarded, FAR 6.102(d)(3), ordering agencies do not issue solicitations or conduct competitions.

FSS are lists of standard commercial products (often with related services) stating the discounted commercial prices, obtained by the GSA, that contractors will charge Government agencies. Single award schedules list only one contractor on the schedule against which the agency can place its order. Multiple award schedules are used when multiple suppliers are able to furnish similar products, thereby permitting agencies with the variety and the flexibility necessary to select the best value item that meets their needs at the lowest overall cost.

For a detailed discussion of the procedures for ordering from multiple award schedules, see Chapter 7.

V. DESCRIBING THE WORK

The selection of the specification is a key element of the acquisition planning process because it is inherently related to the extent of competition and the procurement technique that can be used. Another critical decision is the amount of work that will be included in each solicitation. As discussed earlier, "new specifications" may not be prepared until market research has been conducted, 10 U.S.C. § 2377(c) and 41 U.S.C. § 264b(c).

A. Specifications

The term "specifications" is used in this material to refer to work descriptions generally, including statements of work, drawings, and documents bearing the title "specifications."

With respect to specifications to be used in the procurement process, 41 U.S.C. § 253a(a)(2) and 10 U.S.C. § 2305(a)(1)(B) provides:

> Each solicitation under this title shall include specifications which —
>
> (A) consistent with the provisions of this title, permit full and open competition;
>
> (B) include restrictive provisions or conditions only to the extent necessary to satisfy the needs of the executive agency or as authorized by law.

To meet the requirement for seeking "full and open competition," agencies should draft specifications "in terms that enable and encourage offerors to supply items" to the maximum extent possible. This requires that specifications be drafted only after there is full knowledge of what goods and services are commercially available. See FAR 11.002(a)(2)(ii).

1. Generic Nature of Specifications

Once the market situation is known, agencies can choose among a number of types of specifications or combine types of specifications to identify its needs. 41 U.S.C. § 253a(a)(3) and 10 U.S.C. § 2305(a)(1)(C), as modified by the FASA, provides:

> [T]he type of specification included in a solicitation shall depend on the nature of the needs of the executive agency and the market available to satisfy such needs. Subject to such needs, specifications may be stated in terms of —
>
> (A) function, so that a variety of products or services may qualify;
>
> (B) performance, including specifications of the range of acceptable characteristics or of the minimum acceptable standards; or
>
> (C) design requirements.

FAR 11.002(a)(2)(i) includes the same types in slightly different language:

> State requirements with respect to an acquisition of supplies or services in terms of —
>
> (A) Functions to be performed;
>
> (B) Performance required; or
>
> (C) Essential physical characteristics;

These provisions state no preference regarding the type of specification to be used, giving the agency full discretion to prepare the type of specification best suited to satisfy its needs, *Motorola Computer Sys., Inc.*, GSBCA 8596-P, 86-3 BCA ¶ 19,309. See, however, FAR 11.101(a) stating a preference for "performance-oriented" specifications over "design-oriented" specifications. Regardless of the type of specification used, it must contain only those provisions necessary to meet the agency's needs.

Note that few specifications are composed solely of one type. The Government must often combine specification types in order to describe its needs adequately and ensure full and open competition. See *Blake Constr. Co. v. United States*, 987 F.2d 743 (Fed. Cir. 1993), stating at 746:

> [T]he distinction between design and performance specifications is not absolute, and does not dictate the resolution of this case. Contracts may have both design and performance characteristics. *See, e.g., Utility Contractors, Inc. v. United States*, 8 Cl. Ct. 42, 50 n.7 (1985) ("Certainly one can find numerous government contracts exhibiting both performance and design specifications."), *aff'd mem.*, 790 F.2d 90 (Fed. Cir. 1986); *Aleutain Constructors v. United States*, 24 Cl. Ct. 372, 379 (1991) ("Government contracts not uncommonly contain both design and performance specifications." It is not only possible, but likely that a contractor will be granted at least limited discretion to find the best way to achieve goals within the design parameters set by a contract. *See, e.g., Penguin Indus., Inc. v. United States*, 209 Ct. Cl. 121, 530 F.2d 934, 937 (Ct. Cl. 1976). "On occasion the labels 'design specification' and 'performance specification' have been used to connote the degree to which the government has prescribed certain details of performance on which the contractor could rely. However, those labels do not independently create, limit, or remove a contractor's obligations." *Zinger Constr. Co. v. United States*, 807 F.2d 979, 981 (Fed. Cir. 1986) (citations omitted). These labels merely help the court discuss the

> discretionary elements of a contract. It is the obligations imposed by the specification which determine the extent to which it is "performance" or "design," not the other way around.

See also *Purification Envtl.*, Comp. Gen. Dec. B-270762, 96-1 CPD ¶ 203, where the performance specification included a requirement that only a specified type of water treatment system be used. In such a case, the Comptroller General noted that

> where the government does specify a certain design, it has long been established that the risk that the design is unsuited for the intended purpose is allocated to the government, based on a theory of implied warranty.

a. Design Specifications

In *Blake Constr. Co. v. United States*, 987 F.2d 743 (Fed. Cir. 1993), the court described design specifications at 744:

> Design specifications . . . describe in precise detail the materials to be employed and the manner in which the work is to be performed. The contractor has no discretion to deviate from the specifications, but is "required to follow them as one would a road map." "Detailed design specifications contain an implied warranty that if they are followed, an acceptable result will be produced." *Stuyvesant Dredging Co. v. United States*, 834 F.2d 1576, 1582 (Fed. Cir. 1987) (citing *United States v. Spearin*, 248 U.S. 132 (1918)).

When the Government uses a design specification, it impliedly warrants that the specifications are suitable for their intended purposes. See Chapter 3 of *Administration of Government Contracts* (3d. ed 1995). The Government undertakes the same obligation when it includes design requirements in a performance specification, e.g., *Purification Envtl.*, Comp. Gen. Dec. B-270762, 96-1 CPD ¶ 203.

b. Performance Specifications

In *Blake Constr. Co. v. United States*, 987 F.2d 743 (Fed. Cir. 1993), the court discussed performance specifications at 744:

> Performance specifications "set forth an objective or standard to be achieved, and the successful bidder is expected to exercise his ingenuity in achieving that objective or standard of performance, selecting the means

and assuming a corresponding responsibility for that selection." *J.L. Simmons Co. v. United States*, 188 Cl. Ct. 684, 412 F.2d 1360, 1362 (Ct. Cl. 1969).

In general, performance type specifications describe the Government's requirements in terms of the agency's needs rather than in terms of a precise description of the work to be done. In many cases, they promote more competition by giving contractors more flexibility. The Comptroller General denied a protest that the use of such specifications placed too much risk on the contractor by requiring substantial design effort, *McDermott Shipyards*, Comp. Gen. Dec. B-237049, 90-1 CPD ¶ 121. The Comptroller General cited *Pitney Bowes*, 68 Comp. Gen. 249 (B-233100), 89-1 CPD ¶ 157, for the view that such specifications are favored under the CICA.

Performance specifications are much less likely than design specifications to be found to be unduly restrictive unless they contain a restrictive design feature. See, for example, *Sun Refining & Mktg. Co.*, Comp. Gen. Dec. B-239973, 90-2 CPD ¶ 305 (requirement for delivery of oil products by pipeline rather than by truck). Performance requirements, however, can be unduly restrictive in some instances, *Prime-Mover Co.*, Comp. Gen. Dec. B-201970, 81-2 CPD ¶ 325 (unnecessary speed and mechanical requirements for forklift vehicles); *Globe Air, Inc.*, Comp. Gen. Dec. B-180969.2, 75-1 CPD ¶ 57 (requirement that rotor blades on helicopter be no more than 37 feet in diameter). Compare *Glock, Inc.*, Comp. Gen. Dec. B-236614, 89-2 CPD ¶ 593 (requirement that handguns be double-action first shot, single-action subsequent shots reasonable for safety purposes); *Fluid Eng'g Assocs.*, 68 Comp. Gen. 447 (B-234540), 89-1 CPD ¶ 520 (requirement for independent roughing/backing pump system reasonable based on analysis of agency needs); and *Hallmark Packaging Prods., Inc.*, Comp. Gen. Dec. B-232218, 88-2 CPD ¶ 390 (requirement that trash bags pass tear-resistance test reasonable because it is a standard commercial test).

c. Functional Specifications

A functional specification describes the work to be performed in terms of end purpose or the Government's ultimate objective, rather than how the work is to be performed. Functional specifications may be regarded as a particular type of performance specification — ones that describe the Government's ultimate need or objective without specifying any particular approach or type of product that should be used to achieve the objectives. This should be contrasted with a so-called "product-oriented" performance type specification, which indicates the ultimate performance objectives of the Government but also specifies a particular type of product or approach that must be used and the performance standards that must be met. Functional specifications have the advantage of permitting the widest possible competition. However, before functional specifications are introduced, the commercial market should be examined to guarantee that the needs of the Government can and will be met through use of such specifications.

It has been very difficult to distinguish functional specifications from performance specifications when drafting a specification for procurement of equipment. See, for example, Federal Property Management Regulation Temporary Regulation E-69, 45 Fed. Reg. 9269, Feb. 12, 1980, which implemented a policy favoring purchase of commercially available products through so-called commercial item descriptions (CIDs) by providing the following definition of "functional specifications" at Section 7(i):

> *Functional specification.* A description of a product in terms of its performance characteristics and intended use. It may include a statement of the qualitative nature of the product and, when necessary, will contain those minimum essential characteristics to which the product must conform in order to satisfy its intended use.

Section 11(b) emphasized the use of functional specifications in both CIDs and any new or revised federal specifications:

> Stressing functional or performance requirements. Functional or performance requirements will be specified instead of design requirements. Design will be specified only to the extent that controls are necessary to achieve commonality and interchangeability or when it is clearly more efficient and effective to do so and is reflective of general industry practice. Design requirements such as dimensions, materials, composition, and formulation may be included only to the extent that these requirements are essential to the end use . . . and when the requirements are common practice.

Thus, functional specifications used on contracts for equipment are only slightly broader than performance specifications.

Functional specifications must be carefully prepared to ensure that competitors are not misled by overly general statements of the agency's requirements. In *CompuServe*, Comp. Gen. Dec. B-188990, 77-2 CPD ¶ 182, the Comptroller General discussed the benefits and disadvantages of functional specifications:

> To use the approach advocated by the protester — functional specifications — in a procurement such as the present one can increase competition, which is desirable. However, using functional specifications is not free from complex, and potentially costly, difficulties. Initially, the Government must expend considerable effort in drafting the specifications. Offerors must then translate the specifications into their own individual equipment and software approaches. This can involve a considerable amount of detail, may result in a variety of solutions to the Government's requirements and may be quite costly. A substantial effort on the part of the Government is then required to evaluate the proposals. Whether an agency conducting a procurement like the present one should be required to take a functional approach, as opposed to specifying a DBMS package, is a question which cannot be answered in the abstract.

In *Project Software & Dev., Inc.*, GSBCA 8471-P, 86-3 BCA ¶ 19,082, the board held that the agency's failure to use a completely functional specification was not improper since major portions of the specification were stated in functional terms.

2. Sources of Specifications

For many years, Government specifications were required to be used when available. However, the FAR was revised in 1995 to drop this requirement and substitute the following broad guidance in FAR 11.101(a):

> Agencies may select from existing requirements documents, modify or combine existing requirements documents, or create new requirements documents to meet agency needs, consistent with the following order of precedence:
>
> (1) Documents mandated for use by law.
>
> (2) Performance-oriented documents.
>
> (3) Detailed design-oriented documents.
>
> (4) Standards, specifications and related publications issued by the Government outside the Defense or Federal series for the non-repetitive acquisition of items.

a. Government Specifications

Federal and military specifications are generally detailed and include specific requirements on the characteristics of a product and the standards that it must meet. They provide for a clearly stated, mandatory level of quality that any contractor subject to them will be required to meet.

(1) MILITARY SPECIFICATIONS

Traditionally, DOD had used thousands of military specifications and standards in its procurements. However, it became increasingly difficult to keep these specifications and standards attuned to normal commercial practices. In 1994, Defense Secretary William Perry issued a DOD policy mandating greater use of performance and commercial specifications in lieu of military specifications. The Memorandum for Secretaries of the Military Departments (June 29, 1994), states:

> Military Specifications and Standards: Performance specifications shall be used when purchasing new systems, major modifications, upgrades to current systems, and nondevelopmental and commercial items, for programs in any acquisition category. If it is not practicable to use a performance specification, a non-government standard shall be used. Since there will be cases when military specifications are needed to define an exact design solution because there is no acceptable non-government standard or because the use of a performance specification or non-government standard is not cost effective, the use of military specifications and standards is authorized as a last resort, with an appropriate waiver.

The intent of the policy is not to eliminate military specifications altogether, but to curtail the automatic development and imposition of unique military specifications as the cultural norm at DOD. When DOD was the leader in advanced technology, military specifications served a logical purpose. In recent years, however, industry has taken the lead in technological developments, and military specifications in lieu of industry standards are no longer cost-effective for either the Government or the contractor. Thus, a DOD solicitation must describe the agency's needs with performance specifications or non-Government standards. According to Secretary Perry, military specifications are to be used only as a "last resort," and only after obtaining the proper waiver.

Although industry seems pleased with the cancellation of overly burdensome "how to" military specifications, there is concern from the Aerospace Industry Association (AIA) regarding the effect of canceling specifications that define parts and materials used in aircraft manufacture worldwide. As DOD is canceling documents that constitute state of the art in actual commercial practices, the burden falls on industry to prepare new documents to replace those that are canceled. The AIA argues that where a military specification has in fact become a de facto commercial specification or international standard, its cancellation may not result in cost savings to the Government or the contractors.

In addition, the shift from military specifications to commercial specifications may require successful offerors to assume substantially greater levels of performance risk when the commercial specification is performance-oriented. In such cases, contractors encountering performance problems can no longer routinely assert that the contract requirements were met by showing that military specifications were precisely followed. The use of performance specifications also threatens the availability of the traditional Government contractor defense to tort liability.

(A) PERFORMANCE SPECIFICATIONS

DOD Policy Memo 95-2A, "Processing Performance Specifications," issued on March 10, 1995, by the Defense Standards Improvement Council, defines "performance specification" as "a specification that states requirements in terms of the required results with criteria for verifying compliance, but without stating the methods for achieving the required results." It defines the functional requirements for the item, the environment in which it must operate, and interface and interchangeability characteristics.

There are four types of performance-based specifications: commercial item descriptions (CIDs), guide specifications, standard performance specifications, and program-peculiar performance specifications. CIDs are only to describe requirements in terms of function, performance, and essential form and fit requirements. The guidance for CIDs is in the GSA Federal Standardization Manual and the Defense Standardization Manual, DOD 4120.3-M. Numerous military specifications are CID candidates.

Guide specifications standardize the function or performance requirements of common procurements like systems, subsystems, equipments, and assemblies. The guidance for guide specifications is also in the Defense Standardization Manual, DOD 4120.3-M.

Approved performance specifications are listed in the DOD Index of Specifications and Standards (DODISS). A special section lists standard performance specifications that are used in multiple applications. The guidance for program-peculiar performance specifications is still being developed.

(B) WAIVERS

DOD Policy Memo 95-1, "Waivers for Use of Specifications and Standards," issued on December 22, 1994, by the Defense Standards Improvement Council, outlines the policies and procedures for obtaining waivers for military specifications in DOD solicitations. When citing requirements in solicitations, the following types of documents require waivers: military specifications and standards; program-unique detail specifications and standards that define exact design solutions; and federal specifications and standards.

There are, however, six exemptions for these three types of documents. They can be used in a solicitation without a waiver if the solicitation is for reprocurement of an item not requiring major modification or upgrade, the offeror proposes the use of a specification or standard in response to a solicitation, the solicitation is for specifications and standards under Federal Supply Group 11 for Nuclear Ordnance and Federal Supply Class 4470 for Nuclear Reactors, a non-DOD customer requires the use of a specification or standard, the solicitation is a combined or joint acquisition program where another federal agency or another country has the lead in the design or acquisition of an item, or the specification or standard is cited for guidance only.

If the military specification is cited for guidance only, it must be clearly stated in the solicitation what performance criteria will be used in evaluating proposals, and that the specification represents only one possible acceptable solution. Policy Memo 95-1 strongly discourages the excessive listing of specifications for guidance only.

According to Policy Memo 95-1, only the component acquisition executive or the milestone decision authority can approve a waiver. A waiver should be approved only if an exact design solution is required and an acceptable non-Government solution does not exist or if a performance specification or non-Government standard would not meet user needs, not be cost-effective, or not be practicable.

(2) FEDERAL SPECIFICATIONS

There are four basic categories of federal standardization documents that control the content of solicitations from the various federal agencies. First, federal specifications describe essential and technical requirements for items, materials, or services bought by the Federal Government. Federal specifications are coordinated with interested Government agencies and industry during their development and are mandatory for use in procurement by Government agencies.

Second, federal standards provide standard data for reference in federal specifications. There are two major categories of standards: federal test method standards, which are developed by the Federal Government when appropriate industry standards are not available; and packaging, marking, and material identification standards.

Third, Commercial Item Descriptions are simplified specifications intended to be used in the acquisition of products available in the commercial marketplace. Finally, Qualified Products Lists are lists of products, by plant, that have been tested for conformance with the appropriate specification requirements. A complete list of all federal standardization documents can be found in the Index of Federal Specifications available from the GSA.

b. Non-Government Standards

Non-Government standards are authored and published privately, usually with the help of and in conjunction with professional and technical societies or associations, such as the American Defense Preparedness Association. Two common sources of non-Government standards are the American Society for Testing and Materials and the American National Standards Institute.

3. Improper Specifications

Specifications that unnecessarily require certain features or preclude certain products or services from being offered, and specifications that are unclear or ambiguous are improper.

a. *Unduly Restrictive Specifications*

The use of unduly restrictive specifications is prohibited by 41 U.S.C. § 253a(a)(2) and 10 U.S.C. § 2305(a)(1)(B). An unduly restrictive specification is one that limits competition by including a requirement that exceeds the needs of the Government, *Kohler Co.*, Comp. Gen. Dec. B-257162, 94-2 CPD ¶ 88. The procuring agency has considerable discretion in determining its needs, and the Comptroller General will not disturb the agency's determination unless a protester shows that the restrictive provision is unreasonable, *AT&T Corp.*, Comp. Gen. Dec. B-270841, 96-1 CPD ¶ 237. In *AT&T Corp.*, the Comptroller General stated:

> The governing statutes and regulations allow contracting agencies broad discretion in determining their minimum needs and the appropriate method for accommodating them. See 10 U.S.C. § 2305(a)(1)(A) (1994); Federal Acquisition Regulation §§ 6.101(b) and 7.103(c). Government procurement officials who are familiar with the conditions under which supplies, equipment, or services have been used in the past, and how they are to be used in the future, are generally in the best position to know the government's actual needs, and therefore, are best able to draft appropriate specifications. *Gel Sys., Inc.*, B-234283, May 8, 1989, 89-1 CPD ¶ 433. Although an agency is required to specify its needs in a manner designed to achieve full and open competition, and is required to include restrictive provisions or conditions only to the extent necessary to satisfy its needs, without a showing that competition is restricted, agencies are permitted to determine how best to accommodate their needs, *Mine Safety Appliances Co.*, B-242379.2; B-242379.3, Nov. 27, 1991, 91-2 CPD ¶ 506, and we will not substitute our judgment for that of the agency. *Simula, Inc.*, B-251749, Feb. 1, 1993, 93-1 CPD ¶ 86; *Purification Envtl.*, B-259280, Mar. 14, 1995, 95-1 CPD ¶ 142.

The Comptroller General has also stated that an agency's basis for using a restrictive specification will be held to be reasonable if it can "withstand logical scrutiny," *Glock, Inc.*, Comp. Gen. Dec. B-236614, 89-2 CPD ¶ 593. The General Services Board of Contract Appeals stated the test in slightly different language. See *Motorola Computer Sys., Inc.*, GSBCA 8596-P, 86-3 BCA ¶ 19,309, stating at 97,641:

> In making [this] determination we will not take issue with an agency's narrowing of competition in pursuit of legitimate agency requirements, but we can and will overturn those expression of requirements which improperly limit competition. We will grant deference to the agency's technical judg-

> ment, but will not slavishly follow it where the result is lacking in justification.

However, a stricter rule is applicable when the provision limits the competition to a single source, *Daniel H. Wagner, Assocs.*, 65 Comp. Gen. 305 (B-220633), 86-1 CPD ¶ 166.

The Comptroller General will not rule on protests that the specification was less restrictive than proper to meet the needs of an agency, *Purification Envtl.*, Comp. Gen. Dec. B-259280, 95-1 CPD ¶ 142; *Technology Scientific Servs., Inc.*, Comp. Gen. Dec. B-245039, 91-2 CPD ¶ 233; *Terex Corp.*, 64 Comp. Gen. 691 (B-217053), 85-2 CPD ¶ 76. The same rule was applied by the GSBCA, *Teradata Corp. v. Department of the Air Force*, GSBCA 11642-P, 92-2 BCA ¶ 24,895.

Of the various kinds of specifications, design specifications are the most likely to be unduly restrictive. They are likely to contain specific requirements that are not necessary to meet the agency's needs but that preclude some contractors from competing. See, for example, *Kohler Co.*, Comp. Gen. Dec. B-257162, 94-2 CPD ¶ 88 (requirement that diesel engines in power generators be four-cycle); *Bardex Corp.*, Comp. Gen. Dec. B-252208, 93-1 CPD ¶ 461 (requirement for electromechanical shiplift rather than hydraulic lifting devices); *Data-Team, Inc.*, 68 Comp. Gen. 368 (B-233676), 89-1 CPD ¶ 355 (requirement that copying machines use dry toner); *North Am. Reporting, Inc.*, 60 Comp. Gen. 64 (B-198448), 80-2 CPD ¶ 364 (exclusion of electronic stenographic equipment); *Lanier Business Prods., Inc.*, Comp. Gen. Dec. B-193693, 79-1 CPD ¶ 232 (overly intricate features on text editing equipment); and *Constantine N. Polites & Co.*, Comp. Gen. Dec. B-189214, 78-2 CPD ¶ 437 (exclusion of metric threaded parts).

Specifications written around a certain product are particularly susceptible to being found unduly restrictive. See, for example, *Racal Corp.*, Comp. Gen. Dec. B-233240, 89-1 CPD ¶ 169 (make and model specification); *Julie Research Labs., Inc.*, GSBCA 9474-P, 88-3 BCA ¶ 20,966 (make and model specification); *Southern Technologies, Inc.*, 66 Comp. Gen. 208 (B-224328), 87-1 CPD ¶ 42 (specific product required); *Jarrell-Ash Div. of the Fisher Scientific Co.*, Comp. Gen. Dec. B-185582, 77-1 CPD ¶ 19 (specified feature found in only one product); and 48 Comp. Gen. 345 (B-164993) (1968) ("commercial" specification describing, in great part, the desk of one manufacturer). See, however, *Stavely Instruments, Inc.*, Comp.

Gen. Dec. B-259548.3, 95-1 CPD ¶ 256, where the Comptroller General held that the specifications for X-ray units were not unduly restrictive even though only one company manufactured the product and the specifications were written around that product; Stavely did not challenge the technical specifications or otherwise assert that the specifications overstated or otherwise exceeded the Air Force's actual needs.

A specification will not be held to be unduly restrictive if the agency can show that it has a legitimate need for the specified restrictive feature. See, for example, *Purification Envtl.*, Comp. Gen. Dec. B-270762, 96-1 CPD ¶ 203 (requirement to use one particular design approach (oxidation process rather than new accelerated chemical treatment process) was not unduly restrictive because agency reasonably determined that it was the only way to remove the contaminant without creating a hazardous waste); *Building Sys. Contractors, Inc.*, Comp. Gen. Dec. B-266180, 96-1 CPD ¶ 18 (specifications for a brand name computerized energy management control system not unduly restrictive because the system had to be compatible with the other 23 facilities at the base); *T&S Products, Inc.*, Comp. Gen. Dec. B-261852, 95-2 CPD ¶ 161 (requirement for pressure-sensitive adhesive shipping tape with a specified length not unduly restrictive where agency reasonably demonstrated that tape quality was necessary to secure fiber-board shipping boxes); *Fisons Instruments, Inc.*, Comp. Gen. Dec. B-261371, 95-2 CPD ¶ 31 (specifications for a mass spectrometry system not unduly restrictive); *Electronic Office Env'ts*, Comp. Gen. Dec. B-254571, 93-2 CPD ¶ 342 (detailed design specifications for file cabinets not unduly restrictive because necessary to maintain aesthetic appearance); *Lenderking Metal Prods.*, Comp. Gen. Dec. B-252035, 93-1 CPD ¶ 393 (suspension system incorporating features of brand name product not unduly restrictive because agency experience indicated that features necessary to meet agency's needs); *Absecon Mills, Inc.*, Comp. Gen. Dec. B-251685, 93-1 CPD ¶ 332 (upholstery fabrics to be used by Federal Prison Industries not unduly restrictive because necessary for aesthetics); *Trilectron Indus., Inc.*, Comp. Gen. Dec. B-248475, 92-2 CPD ¶ 130 (requiring air conditioners to use new coolant that reduces ozone release not unduly restrictive even though EPA regulations do not require its use); *Electro-Methods, Inc.*, 70 Comp. Gen. 53 (B-239141.2), 90-2 CPD ¶ 363 (buying entire modification kits rather than individual parts not unduly restrictive); *Pulse Elecs., Inc.*, Comp. Gen. Dec. B-240105, 90-2 CPD ¶ 309 (MIL-Q-9858A quality assurance requirement not unduly restrictive for complex item); *Allen Organ Co.*, Comp. Gen. Dec. B-231473.2, 88-2 CPD ¶ 196 (requirement for wind-blown pipe organ to harmonize with historic building not unduly restrictive even though it excluded electronic organs); *Milcare, Inc.*, Comp. Gen. Dec. B-230876, 88-2 CPD ¶ 29 (inward-opening doors on storage cabinets not unduly restrictive when agency had space shortage); and *Honeywell Inc.*, Comp. Gen. Dec. B-230224, 88-1 CPD ¶ 568 (detailed salient characteristics describing features of brand name product not unduly restrictive when agency demonstrated its need for specified features).

b. Unclear or Ambiguous Specifications

If specifications are vague or ambiguous, they will not communicate the exact needs of the agency to the offerors. This will generally result in proposals that do not fully meet the agency's needs or do not give rise to the most satisfactory product or service that the offeror can provide. It may even result in some potential offerors deciding not to submit proposals because they assume the agency is not seeking their product or service. The outcome of such specifications is, thus, either reduced competition or the need for considerably greater clarification or discussion after the proposals have been submitted. Most protests of ambiguous or vague specifications have occurred in sealed bid procurements where specification problems cannot be cleared up easily after bid opening. While there is more flexibility in negotiated procurements, agencies are still required to provide clear and unambiguous specifications. The Comptroller General stated the following rule in *Alpha Q, Inc.*, Comp. Gen. Dec. B-248706, 92-2 CPD ¶ 189:

> The government has a general obligation when seeking bids or proposals to draft solicitations in a way that identifies the agency's needs with sufficient detail and clarity so that all vendors have a common understanding of what is required under the contract in order that they can compete on an equal basis. *Dynalectron Corp.*, B-198679, Aug. 11, 1981, 81-2 CPD ¶ 115; *Worldwide Marine, Inc.*, B-212640, Feb. 7, 1984, 84-1 CPD ¶ 152. This means that a contracting agency normally must provide or at least reference the applicable specifications and drawings which are to govern the contractor's performance. Federal Acquisition Regulation (FAR) 10.008(d). Solicitations are not required to be so detailed as to eliminate all uncertainties, *AAA Eng'g & Drafting, Inc.*, B-236034, Oct. 31, 1989, 89-2 CPD ¶ 404, and in some cases the government cannot provide drawings or other data because they are either not available or not releasable. See *Oktel*, B-244956, B-244956.2, Dec. 4, 1991, 91-2 CPD 512; *American Diesel Engineering Co., Inc.*, B-245534, Jan. 16, 1992, 92-1 CPD ¶ 79. However, where relevant information is available for inclusion in a solicitation and would give offerors seeking to meet government requirements a clearer un-

> derstanding of those requirements than they would otherwise have, the information should be provided.

The following discussion includes decisions on both sealed bid and competitively negotiated procurements where guidance is provided to ensure fair competition and obtain the best product or service to meet the agency's needs.

(1) REQUIREMENT FOR CLARITY

Specifications and solicitations that are susceptible to more than one reasonable interpretation of what kind of performance is contemplated are ambiguous. Such requirements are objectionable since they impede full and open competition by failing to ensure that offerors are competing on a "common" or "equal" basis. This rule is strictly enforced in sealed bid procurements and would appear to be equally applicable to competitively negotiated procurements using design specifications. See *North Am. Reporting, Inc.*, 60 Comp. Gen. 64 (B-198448), 80-2 CPD ¶ 364, where the Comptroller General stated at 69:

> We agree with the protester that the term "other service" as used in the amended IFB is ambiguous. . . . [T]he term "other service" may be *any* other delivery service each bidder cares to offer as long as the FERC is so advised. Thus, the bidders are, in effect, defining the term and, as they do so differently, their bids are not comparable because they are not bidding on the same delivery bases. *See* 39 Comp. Gen. 570, 572 (1960). Therefore, we believe that this portion of the IFB accelerated delivery specification is not sufficiently definite to permit the preparation and evaluation of bids on a common basis.

In *M.J. Rudolph Corp.*, Comp. Gen. Dec. B-196159, 80-1 CPD ¶ 84, the Comptroller General recommended resolicitation of a contract to lease cranes for loading ships where the specifications were susceptible to more than one reasonable interpretation as to the necessary performance characteristics of the cranes. See also *MLC Fed., Inc.*, Comp. Gen. Dec. B-254696, 94-1 CPD ¶ 8 (RFP's system architecture requirement that equipment proposed be of the latest line could have referred only to the conceptual structure and functional behavior of the machine as distinct from the physical design); *Consolidated Devices, Inc. — Recons.*, Comp. Gen. Dec. B-225602.2, 87-1 CPD ¶ 437 (RFP did not adequately define the torque/force tension ranges within which the calibrators were to operate); *University Research Corp.*, 64 Comp. Gen. 273 (B-216461), 85-1 CPD

¶ 210 (RFP contained vague description of training courses with result that incumbent contractor had unfair advantage); *Maron Constr. Co.*, Comp. Gen. Dec. B-193106, 79-1 CPD ¶ 169 (specifications were ambiguous as to the quantity of doors and frames required); *Kemp Indus., Inc.*, Comp. Gen. Dec. B-192301, 78-2 CPD ¶ 248 (specifications were ambiguous regarding a requirement that a specific motor assembly be used in the power pack supplying howitzers); *Orthopedic Equip. Co.*, Comp. Gen. Dec. B-189971, 78-1 CPD ¶ 391 (specifications were unclear as to whether or not leaded steel could be used in the production of mountain pilon snap links); *Flo Tek, Inc.*, 56 Comp. Gen. 378 (B-187571), 77-1 CPD ¶ 129 (specifications were ambiguous as to the type of stainless steel required under the contract); *Learning Resources Mfg. Co.*, Comp. Gen. Dec. B-180642, 74-1 CPD ¶ 308 (specifications did not indicate whether modular counter units were to be constructed of particle board or plywood and particle board); 51 Comp. Gen. 635 (B-174813) (1972) (specifications did not indicate whether photocomposition, Linotron 1010 system, or master typography program was to be furnished); 51 Comp. Gen. 518 (B-173244) (1972); Comp. Gen. Dec. B-173452, Sept. 27, 1971, *Unpub.* (inconsistent provisions in solicitation); 49 Comp. Gen. 713 (B-169368) (1970) (solicitation failed to specify delivery time); 52 Comp. Gen. 87 (B-175254) (1972) (unclear whether solicitation referred to gear box components formerly or currently used by manufacturer); 52 Comp. Gen. 842 (B-177879) (1973) (solicitation incorporated two inconsistent bid acceptance provisions causing 10 of 13 bidders to submit nonresponsive bids); *Air Plastics, Inc.*, 53 Comp. Gen. 622 (B-179836), 74-1 CPD ¶ 100 (specifications did not detail descriptive data required); *Jacobs Transfer, Inc.*, 53 Comp. Gen. 797 (B-180195), 74-1 CPD ¶ 213 (specifications failed to estimate the number of work units required); *Allied Contractors, Inc.*, Comp. Gen. Dec. B-186114, 76-2 CPD ¶ 55 (specification ambiguous as to whether prefabricated metal building was needed in sewage treatment plant).

Specifications are not ambiguous when they contain clear performance requirements. Thus, an agency can properly elect to state its needs in terms of performance or functional requirements in order to encourage greater competition. See *Memorex Corp.*, Comp. Gen. Dec. B-212660, 84-1 CPD ¶ 153, where the Comptroller General found that it was proper to define the requirement in terms of the "required capability and characteristics of the requested equipment" in order to invite innovative and independent approaches to meeting the agency's needs. The Comptroller General relied to some extent on the fact that five proposals had been submitted in response to the RFP. See also *Jackson Jordan, Inc.*, Comp. Gen. Dec. B-198072, 80-2

CPD ¶ 104, where, on a sealed bid procurement, the Comptroller General held that a specification requiring "tamping 100% of the switch" was not ambiguous, although performance was impossible, because it provided the "best method presently available" to describe the performance characteristic. It is also proper to define the work in terms of sample tasks, *International Sec. Technology, Inc.*, Comp. Gen. Dec. B-215029, 85-1 CPD ¶ 6.

An agency can also impose risks on competitors when it does not have necessary information. See *ANV Enters., Inc.*, Comp. Gen. Dec. B-270013, 96-1 CPD ¶ 40 (specification to test soil for the proper fertilizer requirements and to furnish and apply fertilizer did not impose undue risk where agency provided information on the types and quantities of fertilizer used historically); *Cobra Technologies, Inc.*, Comp. Gen. Dec. B-254890, 94-1 CPD ¶ 35 (failure to include an estimate of the hours required to assist tenant moves not undue risk because there was no historical data to use and the IFB described what was to be required); *Newport News Shipbuilding & Dry Dock Co.*, Comp. Gen. Dec. B-221888, 86-2 CPD ¶ 23 (statement that offerors should assume the work was similar to prior overhauls and that, if not, price would be adjusted provided sufficient clarity); *Korean Maintenance Co.*, 66 Comp. Gen. 12 (B-223780), 86-2 CPD ¶ 379 (requirement that offeror bear risk of utility costs for three-year performance period not undue risk where past usage data were included in RFP); *Dynalectron Corp.*, 65 Comp. Gen. 290 (B-220518), 86-1 CPD ¶ 151 (requirement that offeror bear risk of amount of materials needed to perform work not undue risk where neither agency nor offerors could make a good estimate because the past usage data were not segregated); *Analytics Inc.*, Comp. Gen. Dec. B-215092, 85-1 CPD ¶ 3 (requirement that equipment function with other unspecified equipment to be procured in the future not overly vague); and *Klein-Sieb Advertising & Pub. Relations, Inc.*, Comp. Gen. Dec. B-200399, 81-2 CPD ¶ 251, *recons. denied*, 82-1 CPD ¶ 101 (statement that agency could not compute amount of services required not overly vague where seven proposals received).

The apparent confusion of bidders evidenced by their varied responses to the solicitation can be indicative of ambiguity in the specification. One solicitation was canceled because six of nine bidders took exception to the specifications, Comp. Gen. Dec. B-177660, Apr. 24, 1973, *Unpub*. See also *Ferguson-Williams, Inc.*, Comp. Gen. Dec. B-258460, 95-1 CPD ¶ 39 (agency canceled solicitation where refuse collection and disposal requirements did not identify the agency's actual requirements and the three low bidders were misled). However, in *Bentley, Inc.*, Comp. Gen. Dec.

B-200561, 81-1 CPD ¶ 156, the Comptroller General overturned the agency's decision to cancel a solicitation for alleged ambiguity, relying in part upon the fact that none of the several bidders had complained that the solicitation was ambiguous. The mere fact that there is a great variation in bid prices is not sufficient evidence of inadequate specifications to require cancellation, *Broken Lance Enters., Inc.*, Comp. Gen. Dec. B-193066, 78-2 CPD ¶ 328 (submission of low bids does not indicate ambiguity and is not a basis to challenge an award); *Arvol D. Hays Constr. Co.*, Comp. Gen. Dec. B-187526, 76-2 CPD ¶ 378 (wide disparity in bid prices does not automatically indicate defective IFB); *J.C.L. Servs., Inc.*, Comp. Gen. Dec. B-181009, 74-1 CPD ¶ 198 (that a wide range of bids was received does not necessarily indicate defect in the specifications).

(2) Errors or Omissions in Specifications

Specifications may be improper due to errors or omissions even though they are definite and unambiguous, *Day & Zimmerman, Inc.*, Comp. Gen. Dec. B-212017, 84-1 CPD ¶ 377 (current operating data needed for competition for services); 50 Comp. Gen. 50 (B-169977) (1970) (erroneous provision expressed fixed level of man hours required as opposed to estimated level); 51 Comp Gen. 426 (B-174010) (1972) (solicitation omitted data requirements); Comp. Gen. Dec. B-173740.1, Nov. 17, 1971, *Unpub.* (specifications omitted test capability and one specific item); Comp. Gen. Dec. B-178482, July 10, 1973, *Unpub.* (explosive was erroneously classified in specifications as class "C" rather than class "B"); *Kleen-Rite Janitorial Servs., Inc.*, Comp. Gen. Dec. B-180345, 74-1 CPD ¶ 210 (bid sheet omitted blank space for an itemized price).

Government construction contracts often attempt to overcome this problem by including an Omissions and Misdescriptions clause that requires a contractor to perform omitted or misdescribed details of the work that are necessary to carry out the intent of the drawings or specifications. However, this clause applies only to details, not to new sections of unspecified work. For example, in *Strauss Constr. Co.*, ASBCA 22791, 79-1 BCA ¶ 13,578, a contractor was not required to provide a particular fire extinguishing system whose description was omitted from the specifications because the particular system was not a "detail" under the clause.

Furthermore, the Government may include contract clauses that require the contractor to assume the risk of specification or drawing errors or omissions. In 48 Comp. Gen. 750 (B-165953) (1968), the Comptroller General approved the use of such a clause, stating at 754:

> [W]e are not aware of any situations where [the] doctrine of implied warranty or representation as to the adequacy of Government specifications has been extended to cases where the Government discloses the inadequacies of such specifications and permits or requires the contractor to make necessary corrections.

See also *Varo, Inc.*, Comp. Gen. Dec. B-193789, 80-2 CPD ¶ 44.

(3) Open or Indefinite Specifications

Provisions permitting offerors to select the applicable specification, like ambiguous specifications, may preclude competition on a common basis. In *Alpha Q, Inc.*, Comp. Gen. Dec. B-248706, 92-2 CPD ¶ 189, the Comptroller General ruled that a specification was improper because it required offerors to deliver parts for General Electric engines meeting "the latest revision of the General Electric drawing." The Comptroller General reasoned that FAR 10.008(b) required that the Government furnish such information. That provision, now in FAR 11.201, states:

> Do not use general identification references, such as "the issue in effect on the date of the solicitation."

See also *Pulse Elecs., Inc.*, Comp. Gen. Dec. B-244764, 91-2 CPD ¶ 468, where the Comptroller General found a specification improper because it required offerors to comply with military specifications and standards "in effect as of the date set for receipt of proposals."

B. Bundling

One of the major decisions that must be made in the acquisition planning process is how much work to bundle or package in a single procurement. The bundling (also known as "packaging) decision is usually a tradeoff between the type of competition that is obtained and the achievement of efficiencies in procuring the work. When different types of work are bundled into a single procurement, there will inevitably be some companies that cannot compete because they are only capable of performing a segment of the work. On the other hand, other companies with broader capabilities will be attracted to the job and may be more vigorous competitors than if the work were fragmented into a number of procurements. Thus, the type of competition shifts when bundling occurs. In addition, efficiencies are achieved through bundling. One efficiency is a reduction of the administrative costs of awarding contracts by reducing the number of procurements that must be processed. Another efficiency is frequently achieved by having only one contractor responsible for coordinating the work. This ensures that the work is performed in a more coherent manner than if it were performed by multiple contractors. An additional efficiency is the reduction in the amount of contract administration that the procuring agency must perform. These efficiencies make bundling an attractive alternative when planning procurements.

Agencies have considerable discretion in determining what work will be bundled in a single procurement. See *LaBarge Prods., Inc.*, Comp. Gen. Dec. B-232201, 88-2 CPD ¶ 510, stating:

> We recognize that procurements on a total package or consolidated basis can restrict competition. *See The Caption Center*, B-220659, Feb. 19, 1986, 86-1 CPD ¶ 174. However, we have upheld use of a total package approach where the agency has reasonably concluded that such an approach was necessary to meet the agency's minimum needs. *See MASTOR Systems Corp.*, B-211240, Dec. 27, 1984, 84-1 CPD ¶ 23. For instance, we have rejected challenges to a total package approach where a single contractor was required to ensure the effective coordination and integration of interrelated tasks, or where procurement by means of separate acquisitions involved undue technical risk or would defeat a requirement for interchangeability and compatibility. *Id.*; *Batch-Air, Inc.*, B-204574, Dec. 29, 1981, 81-2 CPD ¶ 509. Additionally, recognizing that an agency's minimum needs include the need to procure services and supplies on the most cost-effective basis, we have found that the possibility of obtaining economies of scale or avoiding the unnecessary duplication of costs may also justify a total package approach. *See Eastman Kodak Co.*, [68 Comp. Gen. 57] B-231952 et al., Nov. 8, 1988, 88-2 CPD ¶ 455; *The Caption Center*, B-220659, *supra*. Ultimately, the decision whether to procure by means of a total package approach or to break out divisible portions of the total requirement for separate procurement is a matter generally within the discretion of the contracting agency, which we will not disturb absent a clear showing that the agency's determination lacks a reasonable basis. *IVAC Corp.*, B-231174, July 20, 1988, 67 Comp. Gen. 531, 88-2 CPD ¶ 75; *Ampex Corp.*, B-191132, June 16, 1978, 78-1 CPD ¶ 439 (total package approach justified for procurement of a complex computer system where agency required compatibility among the components).

Thus, it is permissible to include design and manufacture of a product in a single contract and limit competition to firms capable of performing both types of work, *Argus Research Corp.*, Comp. Gen. Dec. B-249055, 92-2 CPD ¶ 260. The Comptroller General accepted the agency's reasoning that this type of packaging would result in the most efficient completion of the work. See *Express Signs Int'l.*, Comp. Gen. Dec. B-227144, 87-2 CPD ¶ 243, where similar reasoning was used to justify packaging design and installation services in a single procurement. Compare *Southern Technologies, Inc.*, Comp. Gen. Dec. B-239431, 90-2 CPD ¶ 191, where a requirement that the product be designed, manufactured, and delivered by a single contractor was found to be improper.

The Comptroller General has denied protests against packaging of work in numerous situations where the agency has been able to describe a satisfactory benefit to be derived from the packaging. See, for example, *Space Vector Corp.*, 73 Comp. Gen. 24 (B-253295.2), 93-2 CPD ¶ 273, where the Comptroller General found it proper to bundle the procurement of three launch vehicles into a single procurement based on the agency's explanation that the use of different vehicles for the series of launches contemplated would have had technical repercussions. The Comptroller accepted bundling based on a "legitimate technical need." Similarly, in *Sequoia Group, Inc.*, Comp. Gen. Dec. B-252016, 93-1 CPD ¶ 405, the Comptroller General found bundling of building maintenance services in two cities proper because the agency had incurred staffing cuts that made it difficult to administer separate contracts and there had been inadequate competition on the prior separate contracts. In *Aalco Forwarding, Inc.*, Comp. Gen. Dec. B-277241.12, 97-2 CPD ¶ ___, the Comptroller General found that a solicitation implementing a pilot program to reengineer the personal property of military service members and civilian employees did not constitute improper bundling. The Comptroller General stated that the requirements reasonably reflected the agency's needs and were necessary to implement the pilot program's goals of reducing administrative burdens on the agency and improving the reliability and quality of the service. See also *Phoenix Technical Servs.*, Comp. Gen. Dec. B-274694.2, 97-2 CPD ¶ ___ (Air Force's decision to consolidate engineering support services for C-130 and C-141 aircraft systems for purposes of systems integration upheld); *Advanced Elevator Servs., Inc.*, Comp. Gen. Dec. B-272340, 96-2 CPD ¶ 125 (use of five regional task order contracts instead of 103 local contracts for elevator maintenance necessary because of agency downsizing and budget reductions); *Building Sys. Contractors, Inc.*, Comp. Gen. Dec. B-266180, 96-1 CPD ¶ 18 (requirement for heating ventilation and air conditioning installation bundled with the acquisition of a computerized energy management control system); *Border Maintenance Serv., Inc.*, Comp. Gen. Dec. B-260954, 95-1 CPD ¶ 287 (putting building maintenance services at separate facilities in four cities into a total-package commercial facilities management procurement); *Iowa-Illinois Cleaning Co.*, Comp. Gen. Dec. B-260463, 95-1 CPD ¶ 272 (custodial and mechanical maintenance services for single building in one procurement); *Magnavox Elec. Sys. Co.*, Comp. Gen. Dec. B-258037.2, 94-2 CPD ¶ 227 (bundling of guidance system and the missile it serves into one procurement); *Tucson Mobilephone, Inc.*, Comp. Gen. Dec. B-256802, 94-2 CPD ¶ 45 (single contract to provide, install, and warrant equipment for emergency communications system); *Titan Dynamics Simulations, Inc.*, Comp. Gen. Dec. B-257559, 94-2 CPD ¶ 139 (bundling requirements for weapon simulators); *Resource Consultants, Inc.*, Comp. Gen. Dec. B-255053, 94-1 CPD ¶ 59 (combining several tasks to support a modification to a weapon training system); *Ryder Aviall, Inc.*, Comp. Gen. Dec. B-249920, 92-2 CPD ¶ 438 (both parts and labor for engine overhaul); *Delta Oaktree Prods.*, Comp. Gen. Dec. B-248903, 92-2 CPD ¶ 230 (various types of graphic arts services); *LaQue Center for Corrosion Technology, Inc.*, Comp. Gen. Dec. B-245296, 91-2 CPD ¶ 577 (corrosion control services for life of product); *Institutional Communications Co.*, Comp. Gen. Dec. B-233058.5, 91-1 CPD ¶ 292 (design, build, and service entire telecommunications system); *Electro-Methods, Inc.*, 70 Comp. Gen. 53 (B-239141.2), 90-2 CPD ¶ 363 (modification kits and engineering services for many modifications to an aircraft engine); *Massa Prods. Corp.*, Comp. Gen. Dec. B-236892, 90-1 CPD ¶ 38 (manufacturing of a number of similar transducers); *Great Lakes Towing Co.*, Comp. Gen. Dec. B-235023, 89-1 CPD ¶ 570 (maintenance and repair of vessel); *Eastman Kodak Co.*, 68 Comp. Gen. 57 (B-231952), 88-2 CPD ¶ 455 (photocopiers and related services); *Southwestern Bell Tel. Co.*, Comp. Gen. Dec. B-231822, 88-2 CPD ¶ 300 (entire telecommunications system); *IVAC Corp.*, 67 Comp. Gen. 531 (B-231174), 88-2 CPD ¶ 75 (six commonly used IV solutions and IV sets); *Korean Maintenance Co.*, 66 Comp. Gen. 12 (B-223780), 86-2 CPD ¶ 379 (custodial services for several buildings); and *Southwest Marine, Inc.*, Comp. Gen. Dec. B-204136, 82-2 CPD ¶ 60 (overhaul of two ships).

When bundling a large amount of work restricts competition without providing a commensurate benefit to the Government, the technique will be overturned. See, for example, *Allfast Fastening Sys., Inc.*, Comp. Gen. Dec. B-251315, 93-1 CPD ¶ 266, where the agency had packaged a three-year indefinite-quantity procurement of 97 types of rivets into four lots. Each of these lots contained at least one rivet type that the protester was barred from supplying for a one-year period under an administrative debarment-type agreement with the procuring agency. The Comptroller General found that although these lots were rationally structured, the effect was to preclude one of three competitors from participating in the procurement. Thus, the Comptroller General sustained the protest, stating that restructuring the procurement would "significantly increase competition and will probably achieve even greater savings than the current structure." Similarly, in *National Customer Eng'g*, Comp. Gen. Dec. B-251135, 93-1 CPD ¶ 225, the Comptroller General found that bundling computer hardware and software maintenance restricted competition because it clearly excluded companies that performed only one of these types of maintenance. See also *Better Serv.*, Comp. Gen. Dec. B-265751.2, 96-1 CPD ¶ 90, finding the bundling of copier machine service for Government-owned machines with sales of copiers under a federal supply schedule to be improper because it unduly restricted competition; and *Airport Markings of Am., Inc.*, 69 Comp. Gen. 511 (B-238490), 90-1 CPD ¶ 543, where the Comptroller General permitted inclusion of airfield removal and restriping services in a single procurement but rejected the bundling of 84 airfields in four regional procurements as unduly restricting competition.

Bundling is most frequently rejected when there is no strong relationship among the items that are included in the package. For example, in *Technology Servs., Inc.*, GSBCA 8178-P, 86-1 BCA ¶ 18,656, the board permitted packaging of 47 automatic data processing systems, including maintenance and training, but held that it was improper to package assorted equipment that did not constitute systems. Similarly, in *Richard M. Milburn High School*, Comp. Gen. Dec. B-244933, 91-2 CPD ¶ 496, the Comptroller General rejected the packaging of five different types of training programs where only one required college accreditation. See also *Systems, Terminals & Communications Corp.*, Comp. Gen. Dec. B-218170, 85-1 CPD ¶ 578, where it was held to be improper to package a number of peripherals for a Wang computer system where the items being bought were add-ons rather than a system. In *Pacific Sky Supply, Inc.*, Comp. Gen. Dec. B-228049, 87-2 CPD ¶ 504, it was held to be improper to package all replacement parts for an aircraft engine in a five-year requirements contract. The agency had included a contract clause permitting breakout of any part that became competitive, but the Comptroller General held that even with this clause, award of the contract on a sole source basis would be inherently restrictive of competition. Similarly, in *DSI, Inc.*, GSBCA 8568-P, 87-1 BCA

¶ 19,407, it was found improper to require that a single vendor provide both computer hardware and maintenance services.

Small business associations lobbied Congress to place some restrictions on bundling. This resulted in the inclusion of Sections 411–417 in the Small Business Reauthorization Act of 1997, P.L. 105-135. Under the Act, agencies must "avoid unnecessary and unjustified bundling of contract requirements that precludes small business participation in procurements as prime contractors." In addition, the Act defines what constitutes a bundled contract, requires agencies to conduct market research to determine whether consolidation of the requirements is necessary and justified, and permits the SBA to challenge an agency's decision to consolidate two or more small contracts into a large contract.

C. Draft Solicitations and Specifications

Several agencies use draft solicitations or draft specifications as a means of improving their clarity when the procurement is complex or of a high dollar amount, AFARS 15.405-90; NFS 1815.405-70 (draft RFPs mandatory for all competitive negotiated procurements over $1 million). See *Formal Source Selection for Major Acquisitions*, AFFARS Appendix AA, stating at paragraph AA-104:

> (e) Early industry involvement including the use of draft RFPs is recommended to obtain industry comments. The contracting officer may request industry feedback on contract type, performance, schedule, Contract Data Requirements Lists (CDRLs), specifications, statements of work, and other requirements that impact costs or restrict technical solutions. Equal access for all potential offerors must be afforded and a cutoff date will be established for receipt of comments to permit government evaluation and incorporation of accepted changes into the formal solicitation. The Program Office shall evaluate recommendations, make appropriate changes and provide industry feedback on disposition of the recommendations.

See also *NAVSEA Source Selection Guide* § 5.1 (Mar. 1989), which encourages the use of draft RFPs to obtain feedback from prospective offerors and states:

> A draft RFP is a solicitation which includes all the requirements (statement of work, specifications, data requirements, and general and specific provisions), but which is sent to prospective offerors to request information. An

offeror's response to a draft RFP is not an offer and cannot be accepted by the Government to create a binding contract.

NAVSEA also notes that to be useful, a draft solicitation must be as complete as possible, and sufficient time should be allowed to permit prospective offerors to respond meaningfully. See also *The Source Selection Process*, AMC-P 715-3 Vol. 1 § 5-16, where the Army encourages the use of draft RFPs, noting that draft RFPs "can be used to identify cost driver and problem areas and request alternative approaches from industry." This allows industry to start work on the problems and point out areas where additional acquisition streamlining steps can be taken. The Army points out that the draft RFP should reflect as closely as possible the RFP that will be formally issued at a later date and therefore requires draft RFPs to contain as much information as is feasible.

When draft solicitations or specifications are circulated for comment, they should be sent to all prospective offerors, and a CBD announcement of their availability should be published. FAR 5.205(c) provides guidance on the preparation of such CBD announcements. Sufficient time should be given to potential bidders or offerors to submit meaningful comments, and the agency should take steps to assure all submitters that their comments have been given full consideration. The use of a draft RFP led the Comptroller General to reject a protest that a procuring agency had given insufficient performance time in a subsequent procurement, *International Technology Corp.*, Comp. Gen. Dec. B-233742.2, 89-1 CPD ¶ 497.

VI. OVERALL COST TO THE GOVERNMENT

One of the major considerations in acquisition planning is the overall cost to the Government. Acquisition techniques should be chosen to induce contractors to provide products and services at the lowest possible cost commensurate with high quality and timely performance. The costs considered should be both the initial acquisition cost of the product or service and the operating or usage costs because amount to be paid to a contractor may not be the only, or even the major, expenditure by the Government in using the work obtained. Thus, it is important for the Government to consider more than the contract price in determining what award is most advantageous to the Government. FAR 7.105(a)(3) states:

> *Cost.* Set forth the established cost goals for the acquisition and the rationale supporting them, and discuss related cost concepts to be employed, including, as appropriate, the following items:
>
> (i) *Life-cycle cost.* Discuss how life-cycle cost will be considered. If it is not used, explain why. If appropriate, discuss the cost model used to develop life-cycle-cost estimates.
>
> (ii) *Design-to-cost.* Describe the design-to-cost objective(s) and underlying assumptions, including the rationale for quantity, learning-curve, and economic adjustment factors. Describe how objectives are to be applied, tracked, and enforced. Indicate specific related solicitation and contractual requirements to be imposed.
>
> (iii) *Application of should-cost.* Describe the application of should-cost analysis to the acquisition (see 15.810).

This part of the plan contains the agency's best analysis of the expected cost of the procurement and some of the techniques that will be used to ensure that this cost is reasonable and attainable.

A. Acquisition Cost

The plan must contain the agency's estimate of the amount of funds that will be needed to support the contract effort. Prior to FAC 97-01, September 30, 1997, FAR 15.803(b) contained the following requirement:

> Before issuing a solicitation, the contracting officer shall (when it is feasible to do so) develop an estimate of the proper price level or value of the supplies or services to be purchased. Estimates can range from simple budgetary estimates to complex estimates based on inspection of the product itself and review of such items as drawings, specifications, and prior data.

Although this requirement was deleted from the FAR, it is still good practice to develop an estimate of the cost of the procurement. Ideally, this estimate of the acquisition cost will be made in conjunction with the budget process so that sufficient funds can be obtained to carry out the procurement. The cost estimate can be made using parametric data on the class of products or services being procured, data from past procurements of the same or similar products or services, or any other data that are relevant to arriving at the estimate. The higher the degree of accuracy of this cost estimate, the more smoothly the procurement will proceed because funds will be available as necessary to execute it. Thus, good acquisition planning demands that the agency devote sufficient effort to arriving at a valid cost estimate to ensure a satisfactory degree of accuracy.

The plan should also address measures that will be taken to ensure reasonable acquisition costs. When price competition is anticipated, it is generally assumed that the Government will be able to contract at a reasonable price. Where price competition is not anticipated, the acquisition plan must address the efforts that will be made to ensure that reasonable prices can be negotiated. See Chapter 9 for a full discussion of this issue. In this situation, the acquisition plan should also address the type of contract that will be used to share the risks and motivate the contractor to control the costs of performance. Chapter 8 sets forth the guidance on selecting the contract type.

B. Life-Cycle Cost

The plan must contain a discussion of how life-cycle cost logic will be used in the procurement. FAR 7.101 defines life-cycle cost to mean "the total cost to the Government of acquiring, operating, supporting, and (if applicable) disposing of the items being acquired," but contains no guidance on the application of this technique. See also DFARS 207.103(h)(ii), which requires that life-cycle costs be considered in all acquisitions of systems and equipment within the DOD. Essentially, the technique attempts to acquire products that impose the lowest costs on the agency over the total period that the product will be used. It requires factoring costs of using a product into the original source selection decision (which is frequently made only on the basis of the initial acquisition costs). The best guidance available on the use of this technique is found in the *Department of Defense Life Cycle Costing Procurement Guide (Interim)* (July 1970), which states at Paragraph 1-1:

> *Life Cycle Costing (LCC).* LCC is an acquisition or procurement technique which considers operating, maintenance, and other costs of ownership as well as acquisition price, in the award of contracts for hardware and related support. The objective of this technique is to insure that the hardware procured will result in the lowest overall ownership cost to the Government during the life of the hardware.

For a broader definition of LCC, see Paragraph 1.1(a) of *Life Cycle Costing Guide For System Acquisitions (Interim)*, DOD, LCC-3 (Jan. 1973), noting that the life-cycle cost of a system is the total cost to the Government of acquisition and ownership of that system over its lifetime, including cost of development, acquisition, operation, support, and disposal.

In instances where the cost of operating and maintaining the acquired product will be much greater than the initial acquisition cost, conducting a procurement without factoring in life-cycle costs can greatly increase the ultimate costs to the Government. For example, it may be more expensive to purchase equipment with a low initial price that requires significantly more personnel or energy to operate than higher priced equipment. Similarly, low-priced equipment that will be expensive to maintain may not be the best buy for the agency. Generally, these life-cycle costs are included in a procurement in one of two ways: (1) by including specific contract provisions establishing design goals or stating mandatory contract requirements for such factors as operating costs, maintainability, and reliability; or (2) by making life-cycle costs a part of the evaluation process in competitive source selections when the agency has a methodology to evaluate such costs during source selection.

Factoring life-cycle costs into a procurement by using clauses containing mandatory contract requirements forces the contractor to consider the cost in computing the contract price. Thus, a warranty clause calling for the equipment to function over a specified period of time would induce the contractor to include in its price either the cost of repair of equipment that did not meet the warranty or the cost of designing and manufacturing equipment that had the required life. Similarly, a clause requiring the contractor to reimburse the Government for all energy costs over a certain required amount would motivate the contractor to include such costs in the price if its equipment did not meet the requirement. Such clauses are the most direct way of factoring life-cycle costs into the procurement process because they ensure that the offered prices include each offeror's evaluation of the cost impact of the requirement. It is difficult, however, for agencies to formulate a complete set of contract clauses covering all life-cycle costs anticipated in the use of a product.

Another way to deal with life-cycle costs is to include contract clauses establishing goals, such as maintenance man-hours per aircraft flight hour or fuel consumption of vehicles. In order to ensure that such goals are effective, agencies frequently specify contractual penalties for missing the goal or incentives for making the goal. Alternatively, these goals can be taken into account in subjective award-fee determinations. Such clauses generally have a less direct impact on the contractor than a clause requiring full reimbursement of the Government for failure to meet the life-cycle cost requirement.

The use of evaluation factors in the source selection process is the other way of addressing life-cycle costs. If sufficient information is available, the agency can make a reasonable estimate of the life-cycle cost of each competitor and add that to the offered prices to determine whose price is lowest, *Columbia Inv. Group*, Comp. Gen. Dec. B-214324, 84-2 CPD ¶ 632, or the estimate can be used to assist the source selection official in making a best value determination, *Storage Technology Corp.*, Comp. Gen. Dec. B-215336, 84-2 CPD ¶ 190. See also *Lockheed Missiles & Space Co. v. Department of the Treasury; AT&T Fed. Sys., Intervenor*, GSBCA 11776-P, 93-1 BCA ¶ 25,401, where the board found proper the agency's cost/technical tradeoff that resulted in an award to the highest technical, highest price offeror. The agency compared the differences in the value of technical features with the difference in overall cost to the Government. Overall cost to the Government included the offeror's prices for equipment, software, maintenance, support and any other solicited items while the differences in value included the "productivity" of the proposed computer systems. Another possible technique is to make a subjective evaluation of life-cycle costs in the evaluation of the technical competence of the offeror. Such evaluation techniques will be far more accurate if the agency has valid information on the prospective life-cycle costs of the offered equipment — such as its energy usage or maintenance costs.

C. Design-to-Cost

When the acquisition is for the designated development of a new product, the plan must also contain a discussion of the use of design-to-cost techniques. FAR 7.101 defines "design-to-cost" as

> a concept that establishes cost elements as management goals to achieve the best balance between life-cycle cost, acceptable performance, and schedule. Under this concept, cost is a design constraint during the design and development phases and a management discipline throughout the acquisition and operation of the system or equipment.

The purpose of this technique is to focus the contractor on the need to design an item that can be procured in the future at an affordable cost. The FAR contains no further guidance on how to use design-to-cost techniques in the procurement process. See also DFARS 207.103(h)(i).

In order to enhance the ability of contractors to meet cost goals in the design of a new product, DOD has adopted the practice of treating cost as an independent variable. Paragraph 3.3.3.1 of DOD 5000.2-R, Mandatory Procedures for Major Defense Acquisition Programs and Major Automated Information System Acquisition Programs, March 15, 1996, calls for continual cost/performance tradeoffs during system design and contemplated lowering performance requirements in order to achieve life-cycle goals.

D. Cost As an Independent Variable

Another technique for controlling program costs is "cost as an independent variable." The Office of the Secretary of Defense guidance describes this concept as follows:

> This strategy entails setting aggressive, realistic cost objectives for acquiring defense systems, and managing risks to obtain those objectives. Cost objectives must balance mission needs with projected out-year resources, taking into account existing technology as well as high-confidence maturation of new technologies. This concept has become known as "cost as an independent variable," meaning that, once the system performance and objective cost are decided (on the basis of cost-performance tradeoffs), the system acquisition process will make cost more of a constraint, and less of a variable, while nonetheless obtaining the needed military capability of the system.

This description sounds as if cost of a weapon system may be a variable in the initial planning stages but becomes a fixed number once development is under way. Thus, the term "independent variable" apparently means "fixed constraint." In addition, the policy guidance seems to emphasize that this fixed cost number should be an "aggressive" number — apparently meaning a low number. The guidance also emphasizes that the cost number is not only the acquisition cost but includes the cost of operating and maintaining the system throughout its life. Thus, "cost as an independent variable" process appears to involve "sticking to" the cost goals throughout the life of the program by varying performance and schedule requirements as necessary.

VII. PROCUREMENT NOTICES

Procurement notices are aimed at soliciting proposals or increasing meaningful competition by explaining the Government's requirements.

There are several ways to disseminate information concerning the Government's needs, the primary method being the CBD. There are also different techniques used to publicize solicitations, i.e., mailing lists and public posting of solicitations. This section covers the various notice requirements and concludes with a discussion on the use of publicizing procurements electronically through the use of the Federal Acquisition Computer Network (FACNET), the Internet, and e-mail.

A. Presolicitation Notices and Conferences

Some procurement notices are designed primarily to give notice of present and planned procurements. The primary vehicle used is a synopsis of the proposed procurement in the CBD. The agency may also use presolicitation notices and conferences or other techniques to develop competition well in advance of the prospective procurement.

1. CBD Notice Requirements

The Small Business Act, 15 U.S.C. § 637(e), and the Office of Procurement Policy Act, 41 U.S.C. § 416(a), establish *minimum standards* for the development of competition by requiring that contracting officers transmit a notice (synopsis) to the CBD for each proposed procurement in excess of $25,000 and for proposed orders under basic agreements, basic ordering agreements, or similar agreements exceeding $25,000. The format and content of synopses are specified in FAR 5.207. The purposes served by this policy of publicizing proposed contract actions is stated as follows in FAR 5.002:

> Contracting officers shall publicize contract actions in order to —
>
> (a) Increase competition;
>
> (b) Broaden industry participation in meeting Government requirements; and
>
> (c) Assist small business concerns, small disadvantaged business concerns, and women-owned small business concerns in obtaining contracts and subcontracts.

This publicizing policy gives potential competitors a short period to determine if they are capable of performing the proposed work. It provides that solicitations may not be issued earlier than 15 days after publication of the notice, and the closing date for the receipt of proposals may not be earlier than 30 days after issuance of the solicitation, FAR 5.203. FAR 5.203(d) calls for a "response time" of not less than 30 days from issuance of the notice for architect-engineer services and orders under basic ordering agreements. For research and development procurements, the required waiting period for the closing date for receipt of proposals is 45 days, FAR 5.203(e). For commercial items, FAR 12.603 permits the use of a combined synopsis/solicitation with a response time of not less than 15 days. These requirements set forth minimum periods only; many procuring agencies have found that extending the periods increases competition.

FAR 5.203(g) provides that contracting officers may, unless they have evidence to the contrary, presume that the notices are published 10 days after transmittal to the CBD (six days for electronic transmittal), but this presumption does not negate the statutory waiting periods. See *AUL Instruments, Inc.*, 64 Comp. Gen. 871 (B-216543), 85-2 CPD ¶ 324, reaching this same conclusion. Thus, the FAR requires contracting officers, upon learning that the notice was not published within the 10-day period, to determine whether the date for receipt of proposals should be extended or the notice requirement waived under FAR 5.202(a)(2). In *Shiloh Forestry, Inc.*, Comp. Gen. Dec. B-235449, 89-2 CPD ¶ 229, the Comptroller General upheld a decision to waive the requirement based on the urgency of the procurement even though the notice was never published. See also *Electro-Methods, Inc.*, Comp. Gen. Dec. B-250931, 93-1 CPD ¶ 181, where the Air Force reasonably decided it had an "urgent need" for airplane engine duct supports and was therefore not required to synopsize the proposed acquisition. Similarly, in *JRW Management Co.*, Comp. Gen. Dec. B-260396.2, 95-1 CPD ¶ 276, the Comptroller General held that the agency's need for shuttle bus services had been classified as urgent, and the procurement was consequently exempt from the FAR's general synopsis and time period requirements.

According to 15 U.S.C. § 637(f) and 41 U.S.C. § 416(b), the following information must be contained in CBD notices:

> (1) [An] accurate description of the property or services to be contracted for, which description (A) shall not be unnecessarily restrictive of competition, and (B) shall include, as appropriate, the agency nomenclature, National Stock Number or other part number, and a brief description of the item's form, fit, or function, physical dimensions, predominant material of

manufacture, or similar information that will assist a prospective contractor to make an informed business judgment as to whether a copy of the solicitation should be requested;

(2) provisions that —

(A) state whether the technical data required to respond to the solicitation will not be furnished as part of such solicitation, and identify the source in the Government, if any, from which the technical data may be obtained; and

(B) state whether an offeror, its product, or service must meet a qualification requirement in order to be eligible for award, and, if so, identify the office from which the qualification requirement may be obtained;

(3) the name, business address, and telephone number of the contracting officer;

(4) a statement that all responsible sources may submit a bid, proposal, or quotation (as appropriate) which shall be considered by the agency;

(5) in the case of a procurement using procedures other than competitive procedures, a statement of the reason justifying the use of such procedures and the identity of the intended source; and

(6) in the case of a contract in an amount estimated to be greater than $25,000 but not greater than the simplified acquisition threshold, or a contract for the procurement of commercial items using simplified procedures—

(A) a description of the procedures to be used in awarding the contract; and

(B) a statement specifying the periods for prospective offerors and the contracting officer to take the necessary preaward and award actions.

A number of exemptions from the requirement for CBD notices are contained in 15 U.S.C. § 637(g) and 41 U.S.C. § 416(c). These are summarized as follows in FAR 5.202:

The contracting officer need not submit the notice required by 5.201 when —

(a) The contracting officer determines that —

(1) The synopsis cannot be worded to preclude disclosure of an agency's needs and such disclosure would compromise the national security (e.g., would result in disclosure of classified information). The fact that a proposed solicitation or contract action contains classified information, or that access to classified matter may be necessary to submit a proposal or perform the contract does not, in itself, justify use of this exception to synopsis;

(2) The contract action is made under the conditions described in 6.302-2 (or, for purchases conducted using simplified acquisition procedures, if unusual and compelling urgency precludes competition to the maximum extent practicable) and the Government would be seriously injured if the agency complies with the time periods specified in 5.203;

(3) The contract action is one for which either the written direction of a foreign government reimbursing the agency for the cost of the acquisition of the supplies or services for such government, or the terms of an international agreement or treaty between the United States and a foreign government or international organizations, has the effect of requiring that the acquisition shall be from specified sources;

(4) The contract action is expressly authorized or required by a statute to be made through another Government agency, including acquisitions from the Small Business Administration (SBA) using the authority of section 8(a) of the Small Business Act (but see 5.205(f)), or from a specified source such as a workshop for the blind under the rules of the Committee for the Purchase from the Blind and Other Severely Handicapped;

(5) The contract action is for utility services other than telecommunications services and only one source is available;

(6) The contract action is an order placed under Subpart 16.5;

(7) The contract action results from acceptance of a proposal under the Small Business Innovation Development Act of 1982 (P.L. 97-219);

(8) The contract action results from the acceptance of an unsolicited research proposal that demonstrates a unique and innovative concept (see 6.003) and publication of any notice complying with 5.207 would improperly disclose the originality of thought or innovativeness of the

proposed research, or would disclose proprietary information associated with the proposal. This exception does not apply if the contract action results from an unsolicited research proposal and acceptance is based solely upon the unique capability of the source to perform the particular research services proposed (see 6.302-1(a)(2)(i));

(9) The contract action is made for perishable subsistence supplies, and advance notice is not appropriate or reasonable;

(10) The contract action is made under conditions described in 6.302-3, or 6.302-5 with regard to brand name commercial items for authorized resale, or 6.302-7, and advance notice is not appropriate or reasonable;

(11) The contract action is made under the terms of an existing contract that was previously synopsized in sufficient detail to comply with the requirements of 5.207 with respect to the current contract action;

(12) The contract action is by a Defense agency and the contract action will be made and performed outside the United States, its possessions, or Puerto Rico, and only local sources will be solicited. This exception does not apply to contract actions subject to the Trade Agreements Act (see Subpart 25.4). This exception also does not apply to North American Free Trade Agreement contract actions, which will be synopsized in accordance with agency regulations;

(13) The contract action is for an amount expected to exceed $25,000 but not expected to exceed the simplified acquisition threshold and is made by a contracting activity that has been certified as having implemented a system with interim (until December 31, 1999) or full (after December 31, 1999) FACNET and the contract action will be made through FACNET;

(14) The contract action is for an amount at or below $250,000 and is made through FACNET after Governmentwide FACNET has been certified pursuant to 4.505-3; or

(15) The contract action is made under conditions described in 6.302-3 with respect to the services of an expert to support the Federal Government in any current or anticipated litigation or dispute.

(b) The head of the agency determines in writing after consultation with the Administrator for Federal Procurement Policy and the Administrator of the Small Business Administration, that advance notice is not appropriate or reasonable.

It has also been held that the synopsis requirement is not directly applicable to reprocurements against defaulted contracts, *United States Pollution Control, Inc.*, Comp. Gen. Dec. B-225372, 87-1 CPD ¶ 96.

The Government's failure to properly publish the required notice may invalidate a procurement. See *Gourmet Distributors*, Comp. Gen. Dec. B-259083, 95-1 CPD ¶ 130, where the Comptroller General held that an agency did not use reasonable methods to obtain full and open competition when it improperly classified the announcement of a beverage vending services procurement under the classification category for leasing or renting equipment. In *RII*, Comp. Gen. Dec. B-251436, 93-1 CPD ¶ 223, the Comptroller General found cancellation and resolicitation of the procurement to be proper where the agency had misclassified a listing in the CBD as "research and development" instead of "professional, administrative, and management support services." The Comptroller General stated that this error did not allow all potential offerors to compete and did not meet the requirement of full and open competition. In *Frank Thatcher Assocs.*, 67 Comp. Gen. 77 (B-228744), 87-2 CPD ¶ 480, the Comptroller General ruled that misclassification of the notice was a statutory violation requiring the award of protest costs (the contract had been performed). See also *Pacific Sky Supply, Inc.*, Comp. Gen. Dec. B-225420, 87-1 CPD ¶ 206, holding that a notice not listing all of the items to be procured from a single source was defective; and *United States Marshals Serv.*, Comp. Gen. Dec. B-224277.3, 87-1 CPD ¶ 430, holding that the agency had improperly failed to synopsize a procurement based on national security when it failed to include a full explanation of its use of this exception in the internal agency justification. Compare *Morris Guralnick Assocs.*, Comp. Gen. Dec. B-214751.2, 84-2 CPD ¶ 597, where the CBD notice appeared in the section for communications equipment rather than in the section on services where it properly belonged. The Comptroller General refused to cancel the contract because the statute contains no expression of congressional intent to require agencies to cancel otherwise proper awards where the exact letter of the statute was not followed. The Comptroller General noted that the Navy complied with the spirit of the statute because notice was actually published and two firms were aware of the procurement. In *Pilkington Aerospace, Inc.*, Comp. Gen. Dec. B-259173, 95-1 CPD ¶ 180, the Air Force failed to publish an amended CBD synopsis increasing the quantity of goods from 35 to 325. The Comptroller General agreed with the protester that the Air Force erred but denied the protest because the protester was not capable of meeting the increased needs. See also *Gott Corp.*, Comp. Gen. Dec. B-222586, 86-2 CPD ¶ 154, where the Comptroller General refused to cancel the award for improper notice because the protester actually knew of the procurement in time to compete. Similarly, in *Space Vector Corp.*, Comp. Gen. Dec. B-253295.2, 93-2 CPD ¶ 273, the Comptroller General held that although the "GPS receiver integration" was a critical factor in the agency's sole source determination that should have been disclosed in the CBD synopsis, the protester was informed of this requirement during qualification discussions and was given the opportunity to demonstrate its capability.

One of the major functions of CBD notices is to alert potential competitors that an agency intends to conduct a procurement using other than competitive procedures. Thus, notices of procurements involving other than competitive procedures must contain a statement of the reason justifying such procedures and must identify the intended source, 41 U.S.C. § 416(b)(5); FAR 5.207(c)(2)(xiv). The failure to comply with this publication requirement was held not to require termination of the resulting sole source award in *AUL Instruments, Inc.*, 64 Comp. Gen. 871 (B-216543), 85-2 CPD ¶ 324, because the Comptroller General found no prejudice to the protester who did not appear able to meet the urgent requirements. However, the publication of this notice is mandatory; and when a potential contractor responds to such a notice, the agency must consider the response, 10 U.S.C. § 2304(f)(1)(C); 41 U.S.C. § 253(f)(1)(C). See *Masstor Sys. Corp.*, 64 Comp. Gen. 118 (B-215046), 84-2 CPD ¶ 598, where the Comptroller General held that a sole source award was unreasonable because the agency rejected the responding offer for reasons not stated in the notice or otherwise made known to the offeror. See also *Standard Mfg. Co. v. United States*, 7 Cl. Ct. 54 (1984), where the court held that the protester's reply to a CBD notice stating that it was capable of performing the proposed work bound the Government to an implied promise to fairly and honestly consider the response. Similarly, in *Magnavox Elec. Sys. Co. v. United States*, 26 Cl. Ct. 1373 (1992), the court held that the Government's CBD market survey notice and prospective bidder's response resulted in an implied contract to give fair and impartial consideration to a bid. But see *Motorola, Inc. v. United States*, 988 F.2d 113 (Fed. Cir. 1993), where the court stated that it is only the contractor's submission of a formal bid manifesting its intent to be bound by the solicitation's provision that justifies implying a reciprocal Government commitment to fairly and honestly consider the bid. *Motorola* impliedly overrules *Standard* and *Magnavox* to the extent that those cases held that anything less than a formal, responsive bid can create an implied contract of fair and honest dealing. See also *Garchik v. United States*, 37 Fed. Cl. 52 (1996), where the Securities and Exchange Commission (SEC) published a notice in the CBD indicating its intent to enter into a sole source lease with its current landlord. The CBD notice invited property owners throughout the Washington, D.C. area to submit proposals, but stated that the SEC was only interested in leasing property located within a narrowly-defined geographic area. The CBD notice also made clear that the request for proposals was "not a request for competitive proposals" and the information received "will normally be considered solely for the purpose of determining whether to conduct a competitive procurement." The plaintiffs submitted a proposal that was rejected by the SEC because it offered property outside the geographic area described in the CBD notice. The court held that it had no jurisdiction over the case because the plaintiffs did not submit a formal, responsive bid.

Mere inclusion in the notice of the identity of the intended source and the reason justifying the lack of competition may be insufficient. However, in *Berkshire Computer Prods.*, Comp. Gen. Dec. B-240327, 91-1 CPD ¶ 464, the Comptroller General indicated that the notice should contain sufficient information to permit prospective offerors to respond in a meaningful way with alternative approaches. In *Racal-Milgo*, 66 Comp. Gen. 430 (B-225681), 87-1 CPD ¶ 472, the Comptroller General held that this did not require the inclusion of the agency's evaluation factors in the notice.

If a potential competitor fails to submit a timely expression of interest in response to a CBD notice that other than competitive procedures will be used, it will be precluded from contesting the agency decision before the Comptroller General. Thus, when the agency specified in the CBD notice that there was a 45-day period for the submission of expressions of interest in competing on a procurement, the Comptroller General refused to rule on a protest from a firm that had not responded within that time, *Fraser-Volpe Corp.*, Comp. Gen. Dec. B-240499, 90-2 CPD ¶ 397. See also *Allerion, Inc.*, Comp. Gen. Dec. B-256986, 94-1 CPD ¶ 281 (protester must respond to CBD notices with a timely expression of interest in fulfilling the potential sole source requirement and must receive a negative agency response as a prerequisite to filing a protest challenging the agency's sole source decision). When a potential competitor submits a timely expression of interest that is subsequently rejected, a protest will be untimely if it is not filed within 10 days of the rejection, *Keco Indus., Inc.*, Comp. Gen. Dec. B-238301, 90-1 CPD ¶ 490.

2. Presolicitation Exchanges with Industry

FAR 15.201 encourages early exchanges with industry when competitive negotiations are employed. It states:

> (a) Exchanges of information among all interested parties, from the earliest identification of a requirement through receipt of proposals, are encouraged. Any exchange of information must be consistent with procurement integrity requirements (see 3.104). Interested parties include potential offerors, end users, Government acquisition and supporting personnel, and others involved in the conduct or outcome of the acquisition.
>
> (b) The purpose of exchanging information is to improve the understanding of Government requirements and industry capabilities, thereby allowing potential offerors to judge whether or how they can satisfy the Government's requirements, and enhancing the Government's ability to obtain quality supplies and services, including construction, at reasonable prices, and increase efficiency in proposal preparation, proposal evaluation, negotiation, and contract award.
>
> (c) Agencies are encouraged to promote early exchanges of information about future acquisitions. An early exchange of information among industry and the program manager, contracting officer, and other participants in the acquisition process can identify and resolve concerns regarding the acquisition strategy, including proposed contract type, terms and conditions, and acquisition planning schedules; the feasibility of the requirement, including performance requirements, statements of work, and data requirements; the suitability of the proposal instructions and evaluation criteria, including the approach for assessing past performance information; the availability of reference documents; and any other industry concerns or questions. * * *

The techniques used to promote early exchanges of information are set forth in FAR 15.201(c), as follows:

> (1) Industry or small business conferences;
>
> (2) Public hearings;
>
> (3) Market research, as described in part 10;
>
> (4) One-on-one meetings with potential offerors (any that are substantially involved with potential contract terms and conditions should include the

> contracting officer; also see paragraph (f) of this section regarding restrictions on disclosure of information);
>
> (5) Presolicitation notices;
>
> (6) Draft RFPs;
>
> (7) RFIs;
>
> (8) Presolicitation or preproposal conferences; and
>
> (9) Site visits.

In all these presolicitation techniques it is important that any information be consistent with the Procurement Integrity Act. FAR 15.201 provides:

> (a) . . . Any exchange of information must be consistent with procurement integrity requirements (see 3.104). . . .
>
> * * *
>
> (f) General information about agency mission needs and future requirements may be disclosed at any time. After release of the solicitation, the contracting officer shall be the focal point of any exchange with potential offerors. When specific information about a proposed acquisition that would be necessary for the preparation of proposals is disclosed to one or more potential offerors, that information shall be made available to the public as soon as practicable, but no later than the next general release of information, in order to avoid creating an unfair competitive advantage. Information provided to a particular offeror in response to that offeror's request shall not be disclosed if doing so would reveal the potential offeror's confidential business strategy. When a presolicitation or preposposal conference is conducted, materials distributed at the conference should be made available to all potential offerors, upon request.

Note that one-on-one exchanges with potential offerors meets the procurement integrity requirements, FAR 15.201(c)(4).

After a presolicitation conference has been held, attendees must be diligent in following up with the agency to ensure that they receive an RFP. See *Ktech Corp.*, Comp. Gen. Dec. B-240578, 90-2 CPD ¶ 447, where a protest was denied when the protester inadvertently did not receive a copy of the RFP. The Comptroller General held that no recourse was available because the protester made only one inquiry to the agency in the two months between the presolicitation conference and the mailing of the RFP.

B. Traditional Solicitation Techniques

The Government has traditionally used a number of different techniques to publicize solicitations, the most common being solicitation mailing lists and publicly posted solicitations.

1. Mailing Solicitations

Agencies have attempted to mail solicitations to all qualified firms that are known to the agency. This subsection discusses the creation and maintenance of mailing lists, omission of firms from the solicitation, and rules precluding the sending of solicitations to firms.

a. Mailing Lists

Agencies maintain mailing lists of firms that have expressed interest in their procurements. FAR 14.205 states that the contracting agencies shall establish mailing lists to assure access to adequate sources of supplies and services. Agencies are expected to keep their mailing lists up to date and to include new firms on the list when the agency determines they are qualified to furnish the product or service covered by the list. Thus, a firm that responds to a CBD notice, in either the presolicitation or solicitation stage, should be placed on the list as soon as the qualification decision is made.

FAR 14.205-1(a) states that mailing lists need not be used when (1) the requirements of the agency can be obtained through use of simplified acquisition procedures, (2) the requirements are nonrecurring, or (3) electronic commerce methods are used which transmit solicitations or presolicitation notices to all interested sources participating in electronic contracting with the purchasing activity. FAR 14.205-1(b) provides that a prospective contractor may be included in the list in two ways: (1) the prospective contractor submits a Bidders' Mailing List Application (SF 129) to the procuring activity, or (2) the procuring activity places an apparently capable source on the list. In *Trans World Maintenance, Inc.*, 65 Comp. Gen. 401 (B-220947), 86-1 CPD ¶ 239, the Comptroller General held that a firm's failure to submit a SF 129 should not preclude it from being furnished a copy of a solicitation if it requests a copy.

The procedure for removal of names from mailing lists is outlined in FAR 14.205-2(a):

> The name of each concern failing to either (1) submit a bid, (2) respond to a presolicitation notice (see 14.205-4(c)), or (3) otherwise respond to an invitation for bids may be removed from the solicitation mailing list without notice to the concern. However, the removal shall be limited to the items involved in the invitation or notice. When a concern fails to respond to two consecutive invitations or presolicitation notices, its name shall be removed from the list to the extent indicated in this paragraph. However, in individual cases, concerns failing to respond may be retained on a list if retention is in the best interest of the Government. Both actual bids and written requests for retention on the lists shall be deemed to be "responses" to invitations for bids or presolicitation notices. If this procedure results in limited solicitation mailing lists, the contracting officer should request an explanation from the concerns that did not respond.

FAR 14.205-2(b) also states that debarred or otherwise ineligible concerns shall be removed from the mailing lists to the extent required by the debarment or ineligibility.

FAR 14.205-3 provides for reinstatement on mailing lists, as follows:

> Concerns that have been removed from solicitation mailing lists may be reinstated (a) upon written request, (b) by filing a new application on Standard Form 129, or (c) by the submission of a bid. Debarred or suspended firms shall not be reinstated during the period of a debarment or suspension.

If practicable, all firms on the list will receive a copy of the solicitation. However, FAR 14.205-4 recognizes circumstances where providing all contractors on the list with the solicitation would be impracticable:

> (a) *General.* Solicitation mailing lists should be used to promote competition commensurate with the dollar value of the proposed contract. As much of the solicitation mailing list shall be used as is compatible with efficiency and economy in securing competition. Where the number of bidders on a mailing list is excessive in relation to a specific acquisition, the list may be reduced consistent with this paragraph and paragraphs (b) and (c) below. Nonetheless, solicitations should be furnished to others upon request, in accordance with 5.102. Also, bids shall not be disregarded merely because the bidder was not formally invited to bid.

> (b) *Rotation of lists.* By using different portions of a list for separate acquisitions, solicitation mailing lists may be rotated. However, considerable judgment must be exercised in determining whether the size of the acquisition justifies the rotation. The use of a presolicitation notice (see paragraph (c) below), time permitting, also should be considered. In rotating a list, the interests of small, small disadvantaged and women-owned small businesses (see 19.202-4) shall be considered. Whenever a list is rotated, bids shall be solicited from (1) the previously successful bidder, (2) prospective suppliers who have been added to the solicitation mailing list since the last solicitation, and (3) concerns on the segment of the list selected for use in a particular acquisition. However, the rule does not apply when such action would be precluded by use of a total set-aside (see Part 19).

The regulations also provide that procuring agencies may send presolicitation notices to concerns on the mailing list and forward complete bid sets to those who respond to the presolicitation notice, FAR 14.205-4(c).

The procuring activity need not make enough copies of the solicitation to satisfy all requests. The number made is determined by the size and significance of the procurement. Fifty-two IFB sets were adequate on a procurement of less than $15,000 where 19 names were on the bidders' mailing list, *Welmetco, Ltd.*, Comp. Gen. Dec. B-186403, 76-2 CPD ¶ 111. Twenty copies were considered adequate where 14 were sent to bidders on the rotated portion of the bidders' mailing list, *Lake States Constr., Inc.*, Comp. Gen. Dec. B-187151, 76-2 CPD ¶ 435. In *Metropolitan Int'l Resources, Inc.*, Comp. Gen. Dec. B-258011, 94-2 CPD ¶ 196, the protester objected to the agency's failure to furnish it with copies of the solicitation. The Comptroller General denied the protest, finding that the agency had mailed copies of a presolicitation notice to over 500 sources and copies of the solicitation to the sources that responded. In these cases, refusal to mail additional copies after the supply was exhausted did not adversely affect the validity of the procurement since adequate competition and a reasonable price were obtained and there was no indication of an intent to deliberately exclude a party from the competition. Although agencies are not explicitly required to issue solicitation packages to all contractors, it was not Congress's intent to deny packages arbitrarily. Thus, 41 U.S.C. § 416(d) provides:

> An executive agency shall make available to any business concern, or the authorized representative of such concern, the complete solicitation package for any on-going procurement announced pursuant to a notice of solicitation under subsection (a). An executive agency may require the payment of a

fee, not exceeding the actual cost of duplication, for a copy of such package.

b. Omission of Firms

There are numerous instances where firms are not sent solicitations, either through mistake or because the agency has determined that they are not qualified to meet the agency's needs.

(1) INADVERTENT OMISSION

Before the passage of the CICA, the Comptroller General upheld awards if the Government obtained "adequate competition" and held that the adequacy of competition did not depend upon whether every prospective offeror was afforded an opportunity to submit a proposal, *John Bransby Prods., Ltd.*, 60 Comp. Gen. 104 (B-198360), 80-2 CPD ¶ 419. This decision was based upon the Government's reasonable efforts to inform offerors generally of the proposed procurement and upon the absence of probative evidence that the Government had a conscious or deliberate intent to impede the participation of the prospective bidders.

In view of the language of the CICA that all responsible sources be "permitted" to submit bids or proposals, it appears that the Comptroller General will continue to follow this line of cases and not require cancellation of a solicitation or an award merely because a prospective offeror was not furnished a copy of the solicitation, absent clear evidence of Government fault. See *Price Waterhouse*, Comp. Gen. Dec. B-239525, 90-2 CPD ¶ 192, stating:

> A firm bears the risk of not receiving solicitation materials unless it is shown that the contracting agency made a deliberate effort to prevent the firm from competing, or that, even if not deliberate, the agency failed to provide the solicitation materials after the firm availed itself of every reasonable opportunity to obtain it. *Crown Management Servs., Inc.*, B-232431.4, Apr. 20, 1989, 89-1 CPD ¶ 393; *Uniform Rental Serv.*, B-228293, Dec. 9, 1987, 87-2 CPD ¶ 571.

See also *Sentinel Security & Patrol Servs.*, Comp. Gen. Dec. B-261018, 95-2 CPD ¶ 67 (inadvertent failure to provide solicitation amendment that set the revised bid opening date); *Lewis Jamison Inc. & Assocs.*, Comp. Gen. Dec. B-252198, 93-1 CPD ¶ 433 (inadvertent mailing of solicitation to wrong address); *International Ass'n of Fire Fighters*, Comp. Gen. Dec. B-220757, 86-1 CPD ¶ 31 (inadvertent failure to mail solicitation amendment); *Viktoria F.I.T., GmbH*, Comp. Gen. Dec. B-233125, 89-1 CPD ¶ 70 (inadvertent mailing of solicitation amendments to wrong address). In *Eagle Creek Archaeological Servs, Inc.*, Comp. Gen. Dec. B-258480, 95-1 CPD ¶ 43, the Comptroller General found a series of errors by the agency to be inadvertent. Here, the protester had informed the agency of a change of address and had subsequently received a solicitation amendment at its new address. However, the contracting officer failed to update the mailing list with the result that a second amendment was mailed to the protester's former address and subsequently returned by mail to the agency rather than forwarded to the new address. Further, a personnel shortage resulted in the agency's failure to promptly forward the amendment to the protester. The protest was denied because these inadvertent errors did not show any deliberate attempt by the agency to exclude the protester. Compare *EMSA Ltd. Partnership*, Comp. Gen. Dec. B-237846, 90-1 CPD ¶ 326, in which the Comptroller General found agency fault when the offeror had requested that the RFP and its amendments be sent by Federal Express and the agency did not send them until the day before the proposal was due. The Comptroller General found sufficient diligence by the offeror, which apparently believed that the procurement had been delayed.

(2) Incumbent Contractors

Although it might be expected that agencies would be required to exercise special care to ensure that incumbent contractors are solicited in order to ensure full and open competition, there does not appear to be any special rule with regard to such offerors. See *Rut's Moving & Delivery Serv., Inc.*, 67 Comp. Gen. 240 (B-228406), 88-1 CPD ¶ 139, where the Comptroller General found that the requirement for full and open competition had been met even though the agency inadvertently failed to solicit the incumbent contractor. The agency had publicized the procurement in the CBD and had received three proposals. See also *Cutter Lumber Prods.*, Comp. Gen. Dec. B-262223.2, 96-1 CPD ¶ 57, finding that the agency's inadvertent failure to solicit the incumbent contractor did not warrant sustaining the protest where the RFP had been issued to 62 prospective small business contractors and the agency received 12 offers. In contrast, the General Services Board of Contract Appeals found a lack of full and open competition where only one offeror submitted a proposal and the agency failed to solicit the incumbent contractor, *Thorson Co.*, GSBCA 8185-P, 85-3 BCA ¶ 18,516, *recons. denied*, 86-1 BCA ¶ 18,594. In that case, a solicitation was mailed to 13 companies on a mailing list and notice of the proposed procurement was published in the CBD. However, the incumbent contractor contended that it did not receive the solicitation or amendments that the Government alleged it had sent. Agreeing with the protester, the board stated at 92,990:

> Given the peculiar facts of this case, we conclude that full and open competition did not occur. We would not reach this conclusion if, without further facts, a potential contractor had submitted a late proposal and said its participation would result in savings to the Government. By statute, solicitations for competitive proposals "shall at a minimum include . . . the time and place for submission of proposals." CICA, § 1191, 98 Stat. 1175, 1179 (1984) (to be codified at 10 U.S.C. § 2305). Here, excusable circumstances for a late submission of a proffered price occurred, award has not been made, and respondent is on notice that it may be able to enlarge the number of participants in the procurement process beyond a single potential contractor whose price has not been revealed. Resolicitation should help to assure that respondent achieves full and open competition to obtain any of its necessary maintenance services.
>
> Our decision finds further support in the legislative history of CICA, where, regarding full and open competition, the House Committee on Government Operations has noted:
>
> > Full and open competition is accomplished only when (1) all qualified vendors are allowed and encouraged to submit offers on Federal procurements, and (2) a sufficient number of offers is received to ensure that the government's requirements are filled at the lowest possible cost. H.R. Rep. No. 98-1157, 98th Cong., 2d Sess. 17 (1984).

For other cases finding a lack of full and open competition, see *Qualimetrics, Inc.*, Comp. Gen. Dec. B-262057, 95-2 CPD ¶ 228 (agency mailed solicitation to wrong address after having been advised that the contractor had executed a novation agreement approved by another agency and of the correct address of the successor contractor); *Professional Ambulance Inc.*, Comp. Gen. Dec. B-248474, 92-2 CPD ¶ 145 (agency failed to mail a solicitation to the incumbent contractor and received only three offers); *Kimber Guard & Patrol, Inc.*, Comp. Gen. Dec. B-248920, 92-2 CPD ¶ 220 (agency failed to mail a solicitation to the incumbent contractor and received only one bid); and *Pratt & Lambert, Inc.*, Comp. Gen. Dec. B-245537, 92-1 CPD ¶ 48 (agency failed to mail a solicitation to the incumbent contractor and received only one offer).

2. Posting Notices of Solicitations

41 U.S.C. § 416, as amended by FASA § 4202, requires the posting of notices of solicitations, as follows:

> (B) an executive agency intending to solicit bids or proposals for a contract for property or services for a price expected to exceed $10,000, but not to exceed $25,000, shall post, for a period of not less than ten days, in a public place at the contracting office issuing the solicitation a notice of solicitation described in subsection (b);

FAR 5.101(a) calls for displaying a notice of or a copy of these solicitations on bulletin boards in the contracting office and/or at additional public places if required by agency regulations.

FAR 5.101(b) suggests other methods of publicizing solicitations:

> In addition, one or more of the following methods may be used:
>
> (1) Preparing periodic handouts listing proposed contracts, and displaying them as in 5.101(a)(2).
>
> (2) Assisting local trade associations in disseminating information to their members.
>
> (3) Making brief announcements of proposed contracts to newspapers, trade journals, magazines, or other mass communication media for publication without cost to the Government.
>
> (4) Placing paid advertisements in newspapers or other communications media, subject to [restrictions].

See *Minotaur Eng'g*, Comp. Gen. Dec. B-258367, 95-1 CPD ¶ 137, concerning a protest against the issuance of a purchase order under small purchase procedures. The Comptroller General sustained the protest because the agency did not publicly display notice of the procurement or solicit quotations from a reasonable number of sources as required by the regulations.

3. Central Contractor Registration

Central Contractor Registration (CCR) is envisioned as a method for the Government to have one list of all entities wishing to contract with any agency of the Government. Although operated by DOD, CCR is meant to serve the entire Government. Essentially, it would replace the solicitation mailing lists maintained by individual agencies. The Federal Electronic Commerce Acquisition Registration Instructions (FECAI) state that "[w]e are creating a single, master registration database of all contractors that want to do business with any Federal government agency," the "primary purpose" of which is to "avoid registrations with each procurement office." The only reference to CCR in the FAR is contained in FAR 4.503(a), as follows:

> In order for a contractor to conduct electronic commerce with the Federal Government, the contractor must provide registration information to the Central Contractor Registration (CCR). Phone (800) EDI-3414 for information regarding FACNET.

There are three methods of registration: (1) obtaining a registration kit by calling the Electronic Commerce Information Center and mailing in the registration; (2) using the electronic bulletin board; or (3) registering on the Internet at <http://ccr.edi.disa.mil/>. There are two options on registration. A contractor can register as an Electronic Commerce Trading Partner. This means that the contractor wishes to contract with the Government electronically (no paper and probably using FACNET). The other option is to register as a Non-Electronic Commerce Contractor, meaning that the contractor wishes to contract using other means (such as paper, faxes, telephone). The former will require the contractor to furnish considerably more information and agree to the terms contained in the FECAI.

C. Electronic Solicitations

It is becoming more common for agencies to publicize procurements electronically through the use of electronic bulletin boards and other means. FAR 5.101(a)(2)(iv) states:

> Electronic posting of requirements in a place accessible by the general public at the Government installation may be used to satisfy the public display requirement. Contracting offices utilizing electronic systems for public posting shall periodically publicize the methods for accessing such information.

This provision permits electronic dissemination for procurements of $25,000 or less. However, electronic solicitations are being used more widely in some agencies. See FAR 15.203(c), which states:

> Electronic commerce may be used to issue RFPs and to receive proposals, modifications, and revisions. In this case, the RFP shall specify the electronic commerce method(s) that offerors may use (see subpart 4.5).

In *NuWestern USA Constructors, Inc.*, Comp. Gen. Dec. B-275514, 97-1 CPD ¶ 90, the Comptroller General held that an agency's issuance of a solicitation only in electronic format (CD-ROM) was not unduly restrictive of competition or otherwise inconsistent with applicable law and regulation). The Comptroller General stated:

> Federal agencies have traditionally issued their solicitations on paper and furnished paper copies to interested vendors, who then responded with paper proposals. With advances in the information technology field, however, agencies have found that the use of an electronic format, in place of a paper format, can be more efficient and economical. For example, submission of quotation prices on a floppy disk was required in *Latins American, Inc.*, 71 Comp. Gen. 436 (1992), 92-1 CPD ¶ 519, cost spreadsheets were required on disk in *D.O.N. Protective Servs., Inc.*, B-249066, Oct. 23, 1992, 92-2 CPD ¶ 277, and complete cost proposals on a disk were required in *W.B. Jolley*, 68 Comp. Gen. 443 (1989), 89-1 CPD ¶ 512. Further, in both *Continental Airlines, Inc.*, B-258271, B-258271.4, July 31, 1995, 95-1 CPD [¶ 5], and *Spectronics Corp.*, B-260924, July 27, 1995, 95-2 CPD ¶ 47, the agency furnished offerors with certain solicitation-related information on a computer disk, while in *Arcy Mfg. Co., Inc.*, et al., B-261538 et al., Aug. 14, 1995, 95-2 CPD ¶ 283, the agency conducted entire procurements electronically, posting solicitations on its electronic bulletin board and requiring electronic responses only. Moreover, with the enactment of the Federal Acquisition Streamlining Act of 1994, which called for the development and utilization of a federal acquisition computer network, 41 U.S.C. § 426 (1994), Congress clearly signaled its desire that agencies use electronic acquisition methods.

The solicitation was sent to 63 firms. The Comptroller General found nothing in the procurement statutes or the Small Business Act that requires agencies to provide paper copies of solicitation documents upon request. Requiring firms to have access to computerized CD-ROM printing equipment or incur a charge to have another company do the printing is not unduly burdensome to prospective contractors.

1. Federal Acquisition Computer Network

In an effort to streamline procurement through the use of electronic commerce, the FASA required the administrator of the OFPP to establish a program for the development and implementation of a Federal Acquisition Computer Network (FACNET). FACNET is a universal electronic capability that will permit potential contractors to, at a minimum, obtain information on proposed procurements, submit responses, query the system, and receive awards on a Government-wide basis. FAR Subpart 4.5 provides policy and procedures for the establishment and use of FACNET. Section 850 of the National Defense Authorization Act for Fiscal Year 1998, P.L. 105-85 repealed the requirement to use FACNET as a single-face-approach in conducting electronic commerce. This amendment allows federal agencies greater flexibility in implementing uniformly the electronic commerce capability requirements of FASA. Under Section 850, agencies are required to give due consideration to the use or partial use of existing electronic commerce systems, such as FACNET, before developing new systems using this authority. In addition, the Administrator of OFPP is required to submit annual reports to the Congress detailing progress made in implementing this section.

FAR 4.502(b) states that:

> Before using FACNET, or any other method of electronic data interchange, the agency head shall ensure that the electronic data interchange system is capable of ensuring authentication and confidentiality commensurate with the risk and magnitude of the harm from loss, misuse, or unauthorized access to or modification of the information.

The FACNET functions are described in FAR 4.504 as follows:

> (a) For agencies —
>
> > (1) Provide widespread public notice of contracting opportunities, and issue solicitations;
> >
> > (2) Receive responses to solicitations and associated requests for information;
> >
> > (3) Provide widespread public notice of contract awards and issuance of orders (including price);

(4) Receive questions regarding solicitations, if practicable;

(5) Issue contracts and orders, if practicable;

(6) Initiate payments to contractors, if practicable; and

(7) Archive data relating to each procurement action.

(b) For the private sector —

(1) Access notices of solicitation;

(2) Access and review solicitations;

(3) Respond to solicitations;

(4) Receive contracts and orders, if practicable;

(5) Access information on contract awards and issuance of orders; and

(6) Receive payment by purchase card, electronic funds transfer, or other automated means, if practicable.

2. Internet

Section 5062 of the FASA provides NASA with a statutory waiver from the CBD synopsis requirement for mid-range procurements valued up to $500,000. The statute states that NASA "may conduct a test of alternative notice and publication requirements for procurements." NASA established the NASA Acquisition Internet Service (NAIS) (http://procurement.nasa.gov/) to serve as the only source for mid-range procurements valued between $25,000 and $500,000. See NFS 1871.302, which states that "[s]ynopses are not to be sent to or published in the *Commerce Business Daily* except where the basic award is expected to exceed $500,000." For presolicitation notices, NASA requires that such procurements must be published on the NAIS, NFS 1871.302(b). For procurements above and below the statutory waiver, NASA uses a dual-track method for procurements: synopses are posted in the CBD as well as on the Internet.

The GSA provides that proposed acquisitions must be publicized in local newspapers and may also be posted on on-line information systems, GSAR 505.101 (http://www.gsa.gov/). The administrator of the GSA has determined that advertising in local newspapers as well as optional posting on on-line information systems are more appropriate than synopsizing in the CBD for proposed acquisition of leasehold interests in real property and real property appraisal services, GSAR 505.202(c).

NASA, the FAA, and the OFPP have created a "single face" for federal acquisitions on the Internet by creating the Federal Acquisition Jumpstation (http://procure.msfc.nasa.gov/fedproc/home.htm/). This site links industry to servers of federal procurement information on the Internet. It is a pilot project designed to provide the business community with a central starting point to quickly access federal procurement documents. Although all known federal procurement sites are linked to the Jumpstation, each agency page has varying capabilities. Some agency pages only offer regulatory, policy, and procedural information, while others, such as NASA's, offer solicitation notices, draft RFPs, RFPs, amendments, and award notices.

3. Electronic Mail

NASA is piloting an e-mail on-line register where a contractor can register its name, address, and specific types of contracts it is interested in. It is called the NAIS List Serve Subscription Form and is, in effect, an on-line mailing list. The register is used to give automatic notification of upcoming acquisitions. A contractor can receive all NASA solicitations or can choose from among the 11 NASA Centers and the 99 categories of Federal Supply Codes to customize its geographic and industrial needs. When a NASA solicitation is placed on the Internet that matches a contractor's choices, the solicitation is sent to the contractor's e-mail address.

E-mail also provides a convenient method for contractors to communicate with contracting officials. The Internet sites of the various agencies provide contractors the opportunity to write directly to procurement officials with general or specific questions about a solicitation.

4. Bulletin Boards

Bids and proposals may also be solicited by an electronic bulletin board. In *Arcy Mfg. Co.*, Comp. Gen. Dec. B-261538, 95-2 CPD ¶ 283, the Comptroller General found proper an agency's requirement that requests for quotations be transmitted directly to an electronic bulletin board. The Comptroller General found that the agency's determination to require that quotes be electronically submitted was reasonably based and was not overly burdensome to prospective vendors.

5. *Facsimile*

FAR 15.203(d) permits the solicitation and receipt of proposals by facsimile, as follows:

> Contracting officers may issue RFPs and/or authorize receipt of proposals modifications, or revisions by facsimile.
>
> (1) In deciding whether or not to use facsimiles, the contracting officer should consider factors such as —
>
> (i) Anticipated proposal size and volume;
>
> (ii) Urgency of the requirement;
>
> (iii) Availability and suitability of electronic commerce methods; and
>
> (iv) Adequacy of administrative procedures and controls for receiving, identifying, recording, and safeguarding facsimile proposals, and ensuring their timely delivery to the designated proposal delivery location.
>
> (2) If facsimile proposals are authorized, contracting officers may request offeror(s) to provide the complete, original signed proposal at a later date.

Although the FAR is silent as to the use of facsimile for sealed bid procurements, this would appear to be permissible.

D. Oral Solicitations

Oral solicitations may be used for any procurement falling within the simplified acquisition threshold. In addition, FAR 15.203(f) permits the use of oral solicitations for negotiated procurements as follows:

> Oral RFPs are authorized when processing a written solicitation would delay the acquisition of supplies or services to the detriment of the Govern-

ment and a notice is not required under 5.202 (*e.g.*, perishable items and support of contingency operations or other emergency situations).

(1) The contract files supporting oral solicitations should include —

(i) A description of the requirement;

(ii) Rationale for use of an oral solicitation;

(iii) Sources solicited, including the date, time, name of individuals contacted, and prices offered; and

(iv) The solicitation number provided to the prospective offerors.

(2) The information furnished to potential offerors under oral solicitations should include appropriate items from paragraph (e) of this section.

CHAPTER 4

CONTRACTOR QUALIFICATION

An essential step in every procurement involves a determination that the potential contractor is qualified to serve as a Government contractor. This is based on the well-established policy that awards will be made only to "responsible" contractors. It has long been recognized that the Government has broad discretion in determining those firms with which it will enter into contractual agreements. The basic rule was stated in *Perkins v. Lukens Steel Co.*, 310 U.S. 113 (1940), at 127:

> Like private individuals and businesses, the Government enjoys the unrestricted power to produce its own supplies, to determine those with whom it will deal, and fix the terms and conditions upon which it will make needed purchases.

While this rule has been modified in recent years, it still retains its basic vitality.

Determination of contractor qualification requires consideration of whether the firm: (1) can be expected to complete the contract work on time and in a satisfactory manner; (2) is organized in such a way that doing business with it will promote various social and economic goals; and (3) satisfies other special standards of eligibility imposed by statutes and regulations.

The Government uses two separate techniques to avoid awarding contracts to unqualified firms: (1) nonresponsibility determinations, and (2) debarment and suspension actions. The most critical difference between these two types of disqualification techniques is that a nonresponsibility determination is made by a contracting officer and results in disqualification from a specific contract, while a debarment or suspension action is taken by an agency official or agency board and results in disqualification on an extended (or even permanent) basis. This chapter analyzes the important substantive and procedural aspects of each of these disqualification techniques.

I. RESPONSIBILITY

While Government agencies had long followed the practice of refraining from awarding contracts to firms lacking qualifications to perform the specified work, 7 Comp. Gen. 547 (A-21012) (1928); *O'Brien v. Carney*, 6 F. Supp. 761 (D.C. Mass. 1934), the concept of responsibility was not formalized as part of the procurement process until 1948. At that time, the Armed Services Procurement Act (ASPA) adopted the following language relevant to advertised procurement at 10 U.S.C. § 2305(c):

> Awards shall be made with reasonable promptness by giving written notice to the responsible bidder whose bid conforms to the invitation and will be the most advantageous to the United States, price and other factors considered.

Similar language was included in the Federal Property and Administrative Services Act of 1949, 41 U.S.C. § 253(b). In 1962, when 10 U.S.C. § 2304(g) was added to the ASPA to provide negotiation procedures, the concept of responsibility was specifically recognized as applying to negotiation as well as to contracting by formal advertising (now sealed bidding). The Competition in Contracting Act of 1984 (CICA), P.L. 98-369, which amended 10 U.S.C. § 2305 and 41 U.S.C. § 253, provides fresh emphasis on the imperative of contractor responsibility. That Act reiterates earlier policy on providing for award in negotiated procurements only to a "responsible source," 10 U.S.C. § 2305(b)(4)(C); 41 U.S.C. § 253b(d)(2), and for award in sealed bid procurements only to a "responsible bidder," 10 U.S.C. § 2305(b)(3); 41 U.S.C. § 253b(4).

The regulations promulgated pursuant to these statutes have expressly required an *affirmative responsibility determination* as a prerequisite to award of a Government contract. This requirement, as well as an expression of the policy on which it is based, is contained in FAR 9.103:

> (a) Purchases shall be made from, and contracts shall be awarded to, responsible prospective contractors only.
>
> (b) No purchase or award shall be made unless the contracting officer makes an affirmative determination of responsibility. In the absence of information clearly indicating that the prospective contractor is responsible, the contracting officer shall make a determination of nonresponsibility. If the prospective contractor is a small business concern, the contracting officer shall comply with Subpart 19.6, Certificates of Competency and Deter-

> minations of Eligibility. (If Section 8(a) of the Small Business Act (15 U.S.C. 637) applies, see Subpart 19.8.)
>
> (c) The award of a contract to a supplier based on lowest evaluated price alone can be false economy if there is subsequent default, late deliveries, or other unsatisfactory performance resulting in additional contractual or administrative costs. While it is important that Government purchases be made at the lowest price, this does not require an award to a supplier solely because that supplier submits the lowest offer. A prospective contractor must affirmatively demonstrate its responsibility, including, when necessary, the responsibility of its proposed subcontractors.

As noted in paragraph (b) of this regulation, when the offeror is a small business, the Small Business Administration (SBA) can override a contracting officer's determination of nonresponsibility by issuing a Certificate of Competency (COC). See Chapter 10 for a complete discussion of this procedure.

Unlike the issue of "responsiveness," the responsibility of a prospective contractor is judged as of the time of award and not as of the time of submission of the offer, *CardioMetrix*, Comp. Gen. Dec. B-255748.2, 94-1 CPD ¶ 364; *Vulcan Eng'g Co.*, Comp. Gen. Dec. B-214595, 84-2 CPD ¶ 403; *Heli-Jet Corp. v. United States*, 2 Cl. Ct. 613 (1983). Thus, a firm that appears unqualified at the time of bid opening may nevertheless gain eligibility for award of the contract so long as it takes the steps necessary to become responsible by the time of award. In addition, information pertaining to how performance requirements will be met (rather than to the requirements themselves) relates to bidder responsibility and not to bid responsiveness; such information may be provided at any time prior to award, *LORS Med. Corp.*, Comp. Gen. Dec. B-259829.2, 95-1 CPD ¶ 222. The distinction between matters of responsiveness and responsibility is reviewed in detail in Chapter 5.

In most situations, this timing issue does not become a source of controversy because the prospective contractor's status will not be expected to vary significantly between the time of evaluation and the time of award. However, when there is a marked change of status, the rule can affect the outcome. For example, when a low bidder obtained adequate financing by forming a joint venture after bid opening, the Comptroller General held that the responsibility determination should be based on the resources of the joint venture, *International Business Investments*, Comp. Gen. Dec. B-206474, 82-1 CPD ¶ 500; *Masoneilan Regulator Co.*, Comp. Gen. Dec. B-189908,

77-2 CPD ¶ 343. Similarly, it has been held that a bidder is responsible if it obtains required licenses and permits after bid opening but before award, even though the invitation required the inclusion of the permits with the bids, *International Business Investments*, Comp. Gen. Dec. B-206474, 82-1 CPD ¶ 500; 47 Comp. Gen. 539 (B-163156) (1968). This principle is also reflected in the timing of the submission of the FAR 52.222-25 certification of affirmative action program requirements that need not be submitted until immediately prior to award, *McCarthy Mfg. Co.*, 56 Comp. Gen. 369 (B-186550), 77-1 CPD ¶ 116; *Royal Indus.*, Comp. Gen. Dec. B-185571, 76-1 CPD ¶ 139. Administrative convenience does not justify making a responsibility determination at the time of negotiations rather than at the time of award, *Mercury Consolidated, Inc.*, Comp. Gen. Dec. B-212077.2, 84-2 CPD ¶ 186, *recons. denied*, *CFE Servs., Inc.*, Comp. Gen. Dec. B-212077.3, 84-2 CPD ¶ 459.

A. Standards of Responsibility

There are two basic issues addressed in making responsibility determinations. The first is whether the prospective contractor will perform the contract. The second is whether the prospective contractor meets the eligibility requirements imposed by statute or regulation for the type of procurement. In the following material, the term "responsibility" is broadly used to encompass all matters relating to determination of contractor eligibility made on a contract-by-contract basis. However, statutes and regulations setting forth collateral social and economic standards of eligibility frequently do not use the term "responsibility."

1. Performance-Related Standards of Responsibility

Ability and Will to perform

Performance-related standards are of two basic types: (1) general standards, which are mandated by the procurement regulations for application to all prospective contractors regardless of whether there is any mention of responsibility in the solicitation; and (2) special standards, or "definitive criteria," which are imposed in the solicitation at the discretion of the contracting officer. Special standards may be desirable when it is evident that unusual expertise or special facilities are needed for adequate contract performance, FAR 9.104-2.

a. General Standards

General standards of responsibility address two distinct issues relating to whether the prospective contractor will perform in accordance with the contract terms. First, they deal with the question of whether the contractor possesses *the ability to render satisfactory performance*, that is, whether it can perform the work. Second, they relate to whether the contractor has *the determination to use this ability* to complete the contract work in a satisfactory manner and whether the contractor has sufficient *integrity* to justify reliance on its agreement to perform.

(1) Ability to Perform

In determining whether a firm possesses the capability to satisfactorily perform the work, the contracting officer is required to consider several distinct aspects of the prospective contractor's business structure.

(A) FINANCIAL RESOURCES

A prospective contractor must, according to FAR 9.104-1(a),

> "[h]ave adequate financial resources to perform the contract, or the ability to obtain them (see 9.104-3(b))."

Although the FAR does not contain specific guidance on techniques for determining financial responsibility, the criteria in practice are those traditionally used to gauge the financial health of any business organization. They include the ratio of assets to liabilities, working capital, cash flow projections, and credit ratings. Other factors, such as the firm's profitability and the liquidity of assets, are also frequently considered.

The contracting officer has broad discretion to use any current facts indicating financial weakness in making responsibility determinations. In 39 Comp. Gen. 895 (B-143208) (1960), the Comptroller General upheld a determination of nonresponsibility of a bidder on a $4.7 million contract to charter aircraft to the Military Transportation Service. The procuring agency based its determinations on the facts that the bidder's net worth amounted to only $66,000 and that it had incurred an operating loss of $22,000 thus far that year. Even with the bidder's promised bank loan of $300,000, the cash flow position was still deemed unsatisfactory because it appeared that the contractor would suffer a loss on the contract. Although not necessarily endorsing such action, the Comptroller General found that the procuring agency did not abuse its discretion by not informing the bidder of the amount of working capital that it believed sufficient to permit a finding of financial responsibility. In *Costec Assocs.*, Comp. Gen. Dec. B-215827, 84-2 CPD ¶ 626, the Comptroller General concluded that a new business with unproven profitability was properly held nonresponsible based upon a financial responsibility report finding that the protester's working capital of $32,500 was insufficient to maintain a $230,000 contract. Similarly, in *Tomko, Inc.*, 63 Comp. Gen. 218 (B-210023.2), 84-1 CPD ¶ 202, an offeror was found nonresponsible because it acquired only merchants' lines of credit rather than a bank line of credit. The Comptroller General ruled that the contracting officer and the SBA properly determined that a bank line of credit was necessary to assure performance. See also *West State, Inc.*, Comp. Gen. Dec. B-255693, 94-1 CPD ¶ 211, where the contracting officer reasonably determined that the receipt of a judgment and the obtaining of a loan did not cure the negative net worth and negative working capital situation that had led to the prior SBA denial of a COC. Conversely, in *Schwendener/Riteway (J.V.)*, Comp. Gen. Dec. B-250865.2, 93-1 CPD ¶ 203, the Comptroller General reversed a finding of nonresponsibility when it concluded that the contracting officer had misinterpreted information concerning the protester's bonding capacity and schedule of values, and had also failed to seek relevant information regarding the true status of its current performance, thereby deciding unreasonably that the protester was financially and otherwise nonresponsible.

An offeror whose financial resources are questionable may obtain necessary assistance through association with another firm. The form of association may vary. However, if the entity submitting the bid or proposal ceases to exist as a legal entity, award may not be made to the firm that has succeeded to the interests of the offeror. Another limitation is that the transaction may not appear to be the mere transfer of a bid to a nonbidding entity. Arrangements that have been found to be appropriate include the establishment of a joint venture after bid opening, *Harper Enters.*, 53 Comp. Gen. 496 (B-179026), 74-1 CPD ¶ 131; the sale of all the offeror's stock to an organization with the necessary financial resources, *Telex Communications, Inc.*, Comp. Gen. Dec. B-212385, 84-1 CPD ¶ 127; and the sale of all the offeror's assets to an organization that has agreed to "assume" all open contracts and has guaranteed the performance of the transaction in question, *Gull Airborne Instruments, Inc.*, 57 Comp. Gen. 67 (B-188743), 77-2 CPD ¶ 344. In *Gull Airborne*, the transaction was approved on the grounds that the offeror did not cease to exist as a legal entity. The Comptroller General appears to have ignored the prohibition against transferring a bid to a nonbidding party. This prohibition will preclude any arrangement involving the acquisition of an offeror with insubstantial assets, *Mil-Tech Sys., Inc. v. United States*, 6 Cl. Ct. 26 (1984).

A bidder may demonstrate financial capability by offering a performance bond, 33 Comp. Gen. 549 (B-119030) (1954). See also *G & C Enters., Inc.*, Comp. Gen. Dec. B-186748, 77-1 CPD ¶ 155, stating that additional resources may be obtained through a subcontractual or guaranteeship arrangement.

The fact that a contractor has filed a petition of bankruptcy does not, per se, require a finding of nonresponsibility, *Hunter Outdoor Prods., Inc.*, 54 Comp. Gen. 276 (B-179922), 74-2 CPD ¶ 207; *Domar Indus. Co.*, Comp. Gen. Dec. B-202735, 81-2 CPD ¶ 199, but may be considered as a factor in such determination, *Wallace & Wallace, Inc.*, Comp. Gen. Dec. B-209859.2, 83-2 CPD ¶ 142. The appropriate question is whether the contractor has the necessary financial capability in spite of the bankruptcy.

(B) ABILITY TO COMPLY WITH DELIVERY SCHEDULE

According to FAR 9.104-1(b), a prospective contractor must

> [b]e able to comply with the required or proposed delivery or performance schedule, taking into consideration all existing commercial and governmental business commitments.

A variety of factors may indicate inability to meet the schedule. In *50 State Security Serv., Inc.*, Comp. Gen. Dec. B-272114, 96-2 CPD ¶ 123, the Comptroller General upheld a contracting officer's determination that the protester did not have the ability to have a sufficient number of guards in place when performance of the contract was to begin. The contracting officer considered the critical nature of the services, as well as the fact that there were only 18 days remaining prior to commencement of contract performance and the protester had not provided the contracting officer with a list of names of prospective employees. In *X-Tyal Int'l Corp.*, Comp. Gen. Dec. B-190101, 78-1 CPD ¶ 248, the Comptroller General upheld a contracting officer's determination that X-Tyal would not be able to comply with the required delivery schedule where it had recently moved to a new facility, had undergone a labor strike, and had delivery problems with a majority of its other Government contracts. In *System Dev. Corp.*, Comp. Gen. Dec. B-212624, 83-2 CPD ¶ 644, SDC's failure to present written confirmation of suppliers' and subcontractors' commitments to deliver items and equipment with long lead times led to a negative responsibility determination. In *Sermor, Inc.*, Comp. Gen. Dec. B-210872, 83-2 CPD ¶ 87, the procuring agency found the protester nonresponsible because eight of its 10 current contracts were delinquent under original performance schedules and six continued to be delinquent under revised schedules. In *Johnson Graphic Indus. Inc.*, Comp. Gen. Dec. B-205070, 82-1 CPD ¶ 409, a nonresponsibility determination was reasonably based on the firm's record of late deliveries under two of six contracts during the preceding four-month period. See *Victor Graphics, Inc.*, Comp. Gen. Dec. B-249297, 92-2 CPD ¶ 252, where the protester's late deliveries under a number of recent contracts were found to provide a reasonable basis for a nonresponsibility determination in view of the solicitation's short (27-workday) delivery schedule. See also *Computer Support Sys., Inc.*, Comp. Gen. Dec. B-261166, 95-2 CPD ¶ 30, where a protester was properly found nonresponsible when the contracting officer observed and obtained information during a preaward survey that it lacked the resources and ability to comply with the IFB's short delivery schedule.

(C) FACILITIES AND EQUIPMENT

A prospective contractor must, according to FAR 9.104-1(f),

> [h]ave the necessary production, construction, and technical equipment and facilities, or the ability to obtain them (see 9.104-3(b)).

See *S.A.F.E. Export Corp.*, Comp. Gen. Dec. B-208744, 83-1 CPD ¶ 437, *recons. denied*, 83-2 CPD ¶ 90, where the Comptroller General upheld the contracting officer's determination of nonresponsibility based in part on the fact that S.A.F.E. apparently had no plant in either the United States or Europe, although the prospective contract required work in both places.

Contractors that do not have the necessary equipment and facilities at the time of evaluation for award can demonstrate responsibility by submitting "acceptable evidence" of ability to obtain the required resources, as stated at FAR 9.104-3(b):

> Acceptable evidence normally consists of a commitment or explicit arrangement, that will be in existence at the time of contract award, to rent,

purchase, or otherwise acquire the needed facilities, equipment, other resources, or personnel.

See also *McLaughlin Research Corp.*, Comp. Gen. Dec. B-247118, 92-1 CPD ¶ 422, where the agency reasonably relied upon an "intent to leave" agreement as demonstrating the awardee's ability to use certain warehouse facilities during its performance; and *Norfolk Shipbuilding & Drydock Corp.*, Comp. Gen. Dec. B-248549.2, 92-2 CPD ¶ 127, where a certification of drydocking availability was deemed to relate to a contractor's ability to perform and therefore was a matter of responsibility (not responsiveness) that need only be met prior to award. The Comptroller General stated that the solicitation cannot convert a matter of responsibility into one of responsiveness.

The Comptroller General upheld a contracting officer's nonresponsibility determination based on the offeror's lack of a "written commitment" for the purchase of essential equipment, but did comment that the offeror should have been given the chance to prove that it could have acquired the equipment by the time needed for performance, 52 Comp. Gen. 240 (B-176227) (1972).

Plant and equipment are evaluated for safety as well as capacity to meet contract requirements, and the failure to correct prior safety deficiencies may be a basis for a finding of nonresponsibility, Comp. Gen. Dec. B-175545, Aug. 17, 1972, *Unpub.*

(D) MANAGEMENT AND TECHNICAL CAPABILITY

According to FAR 9.104-1(e), a prospective contractor must

> [h]ave the necessary organization, experience, accounting and operational controls, and technical skills, or the ability to obtain them (including, as appropriate, such elements as production control procedures, property control systems, quality assurance measures, and safety programs applicable to materials to be produced or services to be performed by the prospective contractor and subcontractors) (see 9.104-3(b)).

The best means of ascertaining whether the offeror has these capabilities is to appraise the offeror's present organization. See, for example, *Certified Testing Corp.*, Comp. Gen. Dec. B-212242, 83-2 CPD ¶ 542, where the Comptroller General affirmed the finding that the low bidder was not responsible in part because its quality control manager was unfamiliar with the quality assurance provisions of the solicitation. The preaward survey report showed that the company's quality control manager lacked knowledge of quality control procedures and test equipment. See also *Omneco, Inc.*, Comp. Gen. Dec. B-218343, 85-1 CPD ¶ 660 (protester's inability to implement an adequate quality assurance program plan in time to meet the performance schedule constituted a reasonable basis for a determination of nonresponsibility); and *Products Research & Chem. Corp.*, Comp. Gen. Dec. B-214293, 84-2 CPD ¶ 122 (poor quality control system, production capacity, and purchasing ability).

The determination of capability is often approached by investigating the prior experience of the prospective contractor. Determinations as to types and degree of experience and the method of proving experience are solely within the discretion of the procuring agency, but any such requirements must be necessary to meet the agency's needs, 39 Comp. Gen. 173 (B-140481) (1959). Nonresponsibility can be based on either unsatisfactory experience, *Columbus Jack Corp.*, Comp. Gen. Dec. B-211829, 83-2 CPD ¶ 348 (poor quality assurance history), or lack of experience, Comp. Gen. Dec. B-169160, May 4, 1970, *Unpub.* (firm had no experience in type of work being procured). A responsibility finding was properly based on the individual experience of a firm's principal officers in *D.H. Kim Enters., Inc.*, Comp. Gen. Dec. B-255124, 94-1 CPD ¶ 86.

The past performance of a contractor can be used to determine that it does not have the capability to perform the current contract. For example, in *Pittman Mechanical Contractors, Inc.*, Comp. Gen. Dec. B-242499, 91-1 CPD ¶ 439, the Comptroller General affirmed determinations of nonresponsibility based on a thorough evaluation of the performance records from eight prior contracts. The contracting officers had concluded that this performance record indicated that the contractor had problems with the quality of the work, the timeliness of performance, the effectiveness of management, and compliance with labor and safety standards. See also *North American Constr. Corp.*, Comp. Gen. Dec. B-270085, 96-1 CPD ¶ 44. Similarly, in *Shepard Printing*, Comp. Gen. Dec. B-260362, 95-2 CPD ¶ 119, the Comptroller General agreed with a determination of nonresponsibility based on the contractor's performance record on several recent contracts for the same type of work.

The performance of a predecessor firm may be considered in determining the bidder's technical and management capability. For example, in *Sun Elec. Corp.*, Comp. Gen. Dec. B-202325, 81-2 CPD ¶ 112, although the prospective contractor was not established until 1980, it was the successor in interest to a prior corporation that had manufactured a similar product. The contracting officer properly considered this information in concluding that the prospective awardee had the requisite experience. Similarly, in *Oklahoma County Newspapers, Inc.*, Comp. Gen. Dec. B-270849, 96-1 CPD ¶ 213, the experience of the predecessor firm was relevant because the new firm had retained all of the key employees of the predecessor firm. The Comptroller General stated that the "key consideration is whether the experience evaluated reasonably can be considered predictive of the offeror's performance under the contract." It is also proper to evaluate the experience of key employees who have worked for another firm, *J.D. Miles & Sons, Inc.*, Comp. Gen. Dec. B-251533, 93-1 CPD ¶ 300; *Hawco Mfg. Co.*, Comp. Gen. Dec. B-265795, 95-2 CPD ¶ 191.

A contracting agency may also consider the experience of an offeror's parent firm in evaluating a proposal where the offeror has represented that all of the parent's resources would be committed to the project, *Tri-Star Indus., Inc.*, Comp. Gen. Dec. B-254767.2, 94-1 CPD ¶ 20; *Hardie-Tynes Mfg. Co.*, 69 Comp. Gen. 359 (B-237938), 90-1 CPD ¶ 347. Compare *Pope, Evans & Robbins, Inc.*, Comp. Gen. Dec. B-200265, 81-2 CPD ¶ 29, which affirmed a contracting officer's determination that a bidder was nonresponsible even though the parent corporation stated it would "stand behind" its subsidiary. See *Medical Servs. Consultants, Inc.*, Comp. Gen. Dec. B-203998, 82-1 CPD ¶ 493, where the Comptroller General stated that in evaluating the experience of a newly formed subsidiary, an agency could use, but was not obligated to consider, the experience of a parent company.

In evaluating the management and technical capability of a corporation, it is proper to consider the experience of one or more of its principal officers, 36 Comp. Gen. 673 (B-130910) (1957). In *Hydromatics Int'l Corp.*, Comp. Gen. Dec. B-180669, 74-2 CPD ¶ 66, a newly formed company was declared nonresponsible for reasons of inadequate management because the firm's president and general manager had been instrumental in managing contracts awarded to other firms on which there was an unsatisfactory record of performance. Similarly, in *Data Flow Corp.*, 62 Comp. Gen. 506 (B-209499), 83-2 CPD ¶ 57, the Comptroller General specifically held that in evaluating a new business, an agency could consider the experience of supervisory personnel.

Contracting officers frequently include provisions in the solicitation specifying precise minimum-experience requirements. These so called "definitive criteria" of responsibility are discussed in the section on special standards of responsibility.

(E) LICENSES AND PERMITS

FAR 9.104-1(g) provides generally that a prospective contractor must be "otherwise qualified" to receive an award under applicable laws and regulations. The major application of this provision is with regard to licenses and permits. The decisions, which have been somewhat confusing, have focused on whether the licenses and permits are federal, state, or local and whether they are specifically required by the solicitation. However, two rules appear to have clearly emerged regardless of these considerations. First, an affirmative determination of responsibility may be made if the offeror can obtain the license or permit prior to the time of performance even though it has not been obtained prior to award, 46 Comp. Gen. 326 (B-160085) (1966) (Atomic Energy Commission license and California license); *New Haven Ambulance Serv., Inc.*, 57 Comp. Gen. 361 (B-190223), 78-1 CPD ¶ 225 (license from the state office of Emergency Medical Services); *Carolina Waste Sys., Inc.*, Comp. Gen. Dec. B-215689.3, 85-1 CPD ¶ 22 (state certification of waste disposal sites); *Impact Instrumentation, Inc.*, Comp. Gen. Dec. B-250968.2, 93-1 CPD ¶ 241 (premarketing approval by Food & Drug Administration); *Olson & Assocs. Eng'g, Inc.*, Comp. Gen. Dec. B-215742, 84-2 CPD ¶ 129 (state surveyor's license). Second, a determination of nonresponsibility will be upheld if the contracting officer reasonably concludes that a required or necessary license or permit will, if not obtained, impair performance, *What-Mac Contractors, Inc.*, 58 Comp. Gen. 767 (B-192188), 79-2 CPD ¶ 179 (state license, not required by solicitation, which state intended to enforce); *U.S. Jet Aviation*, Comp. Gen. Dec. B-214093, 84-1 CPD ¶ 575 (FAA certificate required by solicitation).

There is a great deal of discussion in the cases concerning the degree of specificity of the solicitation requirement for licenses or permits. This discussion is primarily related to the question of whether the contracting officer must consider the lack of a license or permit in making a responsibility determination. Where the solicitation merely includes a statement requiring offerors to "obtain any necessary licenses," as in the Permits and Responsibilities clause for construction contracts in FAR 52.236-7, the contracting officer is not required to consider state or local licenses or permits. The contracting officer can leave the matter of such licenses or permits to be resolved between the contractor and the state or local authorities, *Mercury Business Servs., Inc.*, Comp. Gen. Dec. B-237220, 89-2 CPD ¶ 443; *James C. Bateman Petroleum Servs., Inc.*, 67 Comp. Gen. 591 (B-232325), 88-2 CPD ¶ 170; *North Park Village Homes, Inc.*, Comp. Gen. Dec. B-216862, 85-1 CPD ¶ 129; *John Baker Janitorial, Inc.*, Comp. Gen. Dec. B-206292, 82-1 CPD ¶ 157; *E.I.L. Instruments, Inc.*, 54 Comp. Gen. 480 (B-182004), 74-2 CPD ¶ 339. However, where the contracting officer reasonably determines that enforcement attempts by state or local officials are likely and that there is a reasonable possibility that such enforcement attempts could interrupt and delay performance if award is made to the unlicensed contractor, the contracting officer may consider lack of such license as bearing on responsibility, *Recyc Sys., Inc.*, Comp. Gen. Dec. B-216772, 85-2 CPD ¶ 216; *What-Mac Contractors, Inc.*, 58 Comp. Gen. 767 (B-192188), 79-2 CPD ¶ 179. If the contracting officer does not have reasonable grounds for determining that enforcement attempts by the state will impair performance, the absence of a license or permit cannot properly be considered, *Career Consultants, Inc.*, Comp. Gen. Dec. B-195913, 80-1 CPD ¶ 215. These same rules have been held to be applicable to federal licenses and permits, *Chipman Van & Storage, Inc.*, Comp. Gen. Dec. B-188917, 77-2 CPD ¶ 299. See, however, *What-Mac Contractors, Inc.*, 58 Comp. Gen. 767 (B-192188), 79-2 CPD ¶ 179, which indicates that the contracting officer must make a determination regarding federal licenses or permits in this situation. See also *Israel Aircraft Indus. Ltd.*, Comp. Gen. Dec. B-242552, 91-1 CPD ¶ 454, where denial of an Israeli import license was deemed sufficient to render an offeror nonresponsible.

A contracting officer may include a specific requirement for a state or local license or permit in the solicitation if it is reasonably determined that it is necessary to have a licensed contractor, 53 Comp. Gen. 51 (B-174634) (1973). Federal licensing requirements are not subject to such limitations but may be freely incorporated in solicitations. When such mandatory requirements for licenses or permits are placed in solicitations, the contracting officer must consider whether the offeror has, or will be able to obtain, the license or permit in making the responsibility determination. Thus, the Comptroller General has treated such requirements as definitive responsibility criteria, *Coastal Elecs., Inc.*, Comp. Gen. Dec. B-250718, 93-1 CPD ¶ 144; *Aero Sys., Inc.*, Comp. Gen. Dec. B-215892, 84-2 CPD ¶ 374; *Fry Communications, Inc.*, 62 Comp. Gen. 164 (B-207605), 83-1 CPD ¶ 109; *Sillco, Inc.*, Comp. Gen. Dec. B-188026, 77-1 CPD ¶ 296. The language of the solicitation relative to licenses and permits will be read very closely to determine whether the requirement is general or specific. See, for example, *Washington Patrol Serv., Inc.*, Comp. Gen. Dec. B-195900, 80-2 CPD ¶ 132 (requirement to meet state laws regarding security services not specific requirement to obtain state handgun permits); *Mark Danning Indus., Inc.*, Comp. Gen. Dec. B-258373, 94-2 CPD ¶ 226 (contract line item requiring a bid price for a refuse disposal fee not a specific requirement for a dumping franchise agreement with a local government); and *Honolulu Marine, Inc.*, Comp. Gen. Dec. B-248380, 92-2 CPD ¶ 87 (solicitation statement "directing" offerors to state hazardous waste materials requirement not a specific requirement).

(2) WILL TO PERFORM

Offerors having the requisite ability to perform may, nevertheless, be declared nonresponsible if there is evidence indicating that they lack the will to complete the work in a satisfactory way. Determining whether an offeror possesses the necessary will to perform generally involves the evaluation of two factors: (1) tenacity and perseverance and (2) integrity.

(A) TENACITY AND PERSEVERANCE

A prospective contractor's performance record must be satisfactory to demonstrate responsibility, FAR 9.104-1(c). This qualification standard is essentially related to the issue of whether a prospective contractor has the will to perform, and is treated as an independent basis of responsibility by FAR 9.104-3(b), which states:

> *Satisfactory performance record.* A prospective contractor that is or recently has been seriously deficient in contract performance shall be presumed to be nonresponsible, unless the contracting officer determines that the circumstances were properly beyond the contractor's control, or that the contractor has taken appropriate corrective action. Past failure to apply sufficient tenacity and perseverance to perform acceptably is strong evidence of nonresponsibility. Failure to meet the quality requirements of the contract is a significant factor to consider in determining satisfactory performance. The contracting officer shall consider the number of contracts involved and the extent of deficient performance in each contract when making this determination. If the pending contract requires a subcontracting plan pursuant to Subpart 19.7, Subcontracting with Small, Small Disadvantaged Business and Women-Owned Small Business Concerns, the contracting officer shall also consider the prospective contractor's compliance with subcontracting plans under recent contracts.

This provision creates a strong presumption that a poor performance record indicates a lack of tenacity and perseverance. See *Information Resources Inc.*, Comp. Gen. Dec. B-271767, 96-2 CPD ¶ 38, where the Comptroller General upheld the agency's finding that the protester was nonresponsible based on poor past performance while awarding contracts to other firms with poor records where the performance records of the other firms were substantially better than the protester's, who recently had experienced serious performance deficiencies on similar contracts with the same agency. See also *Mine Safety Appliances Co.*, Comp. Gen. Dec. B-266025, 96-1 CPD ¶ 86, where the Comptroller General upheld the contracting officer's determination of nonresponsibility based on a history of serious deficient contract performance. This presumption may be applied to the poor performance history of a subcontractor that is proposed for a major portion of the work, *L & M Mercadeo Int'l, S.A.*, Comp. Gen. Dec. B-250637, 93-1 CPD ¶ 124.

The issue in judging tenacity and perseverance is whether a firm that possesses adequate capability will apply it in sufficient measure to ensure satisfactory completion of the contract, *United Power & Control Sys., Inc.*, Comp. Gen. Dec. B-184662, 78-2 CPD ¶ 436; *Eastern Tank, Inc.*, Comp. Gen. Dec. B-188559, 77-2 CPD ¶ 76; *Boiler Servs.*, Comp. Gen. Dec. B-187080, 77-1 CPD ¶ 372.

Tenacity and perseverance, by their nature, must be determined from past performance, *Ford Motor Co.*, Comp. Gen. Dec. B-207179, 83-1 CPD ¶ 72; *Particle Data, Inc.*, Comp. Gen. Dec. B-179144, 74-2 CPD ¶ 30. This may include performance on both private and Government contracts, and such determination must be based on substantial evidence, 51 Comp. Gen. 288 (B-171729) (1971). The fact of poor performance or of a default on one or several prior contracts is not per se a sufficient reason for a determination that the contractor lacks the requisite tenacity and perseverance — inquiry must be made into the nature and causes of the poor performance, *Marine Eng'rs Beneficial Ass'n*, Comp. Gen. Dec. B-181265, 74-2 CPD ¶ 298; 39 Comp. Gen. 705 (B-142055) (1960). If the offeror was delinquent in performance of numerous contracts while possessing the necessary equipment and production personnel, a finding of lack of tenacity and perseverance is justified, 49 Comp. Gen. 139 (B-166969) (1969); *Pittman Mechanical Contractors, Inc.*, Comp. Gen. Dec. B-242499, 91-1 CPD ¶ 439. In *United Power & Control Sys., Inc.*, Comp. Gen. Dec. B-184662, 78-2 CPD ¶ 436, the Comptroller General affirmed the Navy's nonresponsibility determination where the bidder delivered nonconforming items under current Government contracts that were similar to those called for in the procurement at hand even though it had the ability to perform. Similarly, in Comp. Gen. Dec. B-170224, Oct. 8, 1970, *Unpub.*, performance deficiencies were properly attributed to lack of tenacity and perseverance where previous contract administrators had tried to work with the contractor to improve its performance but the contractor was unresponsive to their suggestions. See, however, 49 Comp. Gen. 600 (B-168917) (1970) and 39 Comp. Gen. 868 (B-142939) (1960) for cases in which the Comptroller General has stated that he will not affirm a nonresponsibility determination based on a bidder's lack of tenacity and perseverance where the evidence fails to (1) relate to those nonresponsibility factors or (2) adequately establish a reasonable basis for the determination.

A contractor may be found nonresponsible for lack of tenacity and perseverance based on prior failures to adhere to contract specifications, *Kennedy Van & Storage Co.*, Comp. Gen. Dec. B-180973, 74-1 CPD ¶ 334, even where the alleged deficiencies are still the subject of dispute between the contractor and the agency, *Halo Optical Products, Inc.*, Comp. Gen. Dec. B-178573, 74-1 CPD ¶ 263; *Howard Elec. Co.*, 58 Comp. Gen. 303 (B-193899), 79-1 CPD ¶ 137; *Ford Motor Co.*, Comp. Gen. Dec. B-207179, 83-1 CPD ¶ 72. A lack of tenacity or perseverance has been found based on late deliveries caused by factors within the contractor's control, such as poor business practices, *Transport Tire Co.*, Comp. Gen. Dec. B-179098, 74-1 CPD ¶ 27; poor management and technical judgment, *Campbell Indus.*, Comp. Gen. Dec. B-238871, 90-2 CPD ¶ 5; a failure to diligently or aggressively take action to correct production problems, *Marine Eng'rs Beneficial Ass'n*, Comp. Gen. Dec. B-181265, 74-2 CPD ¶ 298; a failure to perform safely on a prior contract, *Air Unlimited*, Comp. Gen. Dec. B-189428, 77-2 CPD ¶ 294; and inadequate surveillance and supervision of subcontractors, *Bill Ward Painting & Decorating*, Comp. Gen. Dec. B-184612, 76-1 CPD ¶ 57. Even though a contractor has substantially performed its prior contracts on time, meeting minimum contract requirements, it may still be found to lack tenacity and perseverance based on the cumulative effect of a number of relatively minor deficiencies that, individually, would not warrant termination for default or finding unsatisfactory performance, 43 Comp. Gen. 257 (B-151121) (1963) (numerous minor deficiencies in performance of 11 of last 12 contracts); 49 Comp. Gen. 139 (B-166969) (1969) (almost 60 percent of recent contracts not completed on schedule); *Leslie & Elliott Co.*, Comp. Gen. Dec. B-237190, 90-1 CPD ¶ 100 (numerous deficiencies in five previous contracts). But see *Pulse Companies, Inc.*, Comp. Gen. Dec. B-184463, 76-1 CPD ¶ 376, where the

Comptroller General objected to a nonresponsibility determination after the contractor had taken steps necessary to prevent recurrence of deficiencies.

The contracting officer has considerable discretion in determining what information will be used in appraising past performance. In *Flameco Div. of Barnes Group, Inc.*, Comp. Gen. Dec. B-243872, 91-2 CPD ¶ 123, a finding of nonresponsibility was properly reached after consultation with the administrative contracting officer and consideration of inadequate performance under prior contracts for manufacture of the same part. See also *S.A.F.E. Export Corp.*, Comp. Gen. Dec. B-208744, 83-1 CPD ¶ 437, where a determination of nonresponsibility was found proper because it was based on default terminations of four previous contracts plus performance difficulties on two others. Even if there have been no default terminations, nonresponsibility can be properly determined based on delinquencies in performance, *NJCT Corp.*, 64 Comp. Gen. 883 (B-219434), 85-2 CPD ¶ 342 (delinquencies on numerous contracts); *C.W. Girard, C.M.*, 64 Comp. Gen. 175 (B-216004), 84-2 CPD ¶ 704 (a number of delinquencies on one contract); *Pittman Mechanical Contractors, Inc.*, Comp. Gen. Dec. B-242243.2, 91-1 CPD ¶ 525 (recent contract performance on similar work inadequate); *Marathon Watch Co., Ltd.*, Comp. Gen. Dec. B-247043, 92-1 CPD ¶ 384 (serious performance problems on four recent contracts). Conversely, the contracting officer may make an affirmative determination of responsibility despite unfavorable information concerning past performance, *REDM Corp.*, Comp. Gen. Dec. B-211197, 83-1 CPD ¶ 428. Both the FAR and the Comptroller General decisions in this area indicate that circumstances surrounding nonperformance must be weighed to ascertain the seriousness of the delinquency in performance. See *Girard*, stating at 178:

> [T]he mere fact of unsatisfactory performance under one prior contract does not necessarily establish a lack of responsibility. Nevertheless, the circumstances of the contractor's failure to perform properly and in a timely manner under the contract are for consideration, and may provide a reasonable basis for a nonresponsibility determination. 39 Comp. Gen. 705 (1960).

Thus, the Comptroller General will not normally review protests of favorable determinations of responsibility even if the successful offeror has had a previous contract terminated for default, *Pacific Fabrication*, Comp. Gen. Dec. B-219837.2, 85-2 CPD ¶ 263, or has not met obligations on prior contracts, *Norfolk Shipbuilding & Drydock Corp.*, Comp. Gen. Dec. B-218618, 85-1 CPD ¶ 604.

Responsibility generally is measured from information of record at the time of award. A determination of nonresponsibility based on past unsatisfactory performance must, under the terms of FAR 9.104-3(c), be related to serious deficiencies in current or recent contracts. In *United Office Machs.*, 56 Comp. Gen. 411 (B-187193), 77-1 CPD ¶ 195, the Comptroller General held that the contracting officer's determination of nonresponsibility for lack of tenacity and perseverance may not be based on events that occurred more than three years prior to the determination when there is an adequate record of more recent experience. See *Universal Am. Enters., Inc.*, Comp. Gen. Dec. B-185430, 76-2 CPD ¶ 373, and *Consolidated Airborne Sys., Inc.*, 55 Comp. Gen. 571 (B-183293), 75-2 CPD ¶ 395, indicating that contracts completed within one year of the responsibility determination are "recent" contracts. Compare *Maywood Cab Co.*, Comp. Gen. Dec. B-187550, 77-1 CPD ¶ 288, finding improper a determination of nonresponsibility based on termination for default of similar contracts nine months earlier, where no preaward survey had been conducted in the interim and the deficiencies were readily correctable.

(B) INTEGRITY

FAR 9.104-1(d) states that a prospective contractor must have "a satisfactory record of integrity and business ethics," but it does not define the term "integrity." However, the term has been given its generally accepted connotation of probity, honesty, and uprightness, 48 Comp. Gen. 769 (B-165915) (1969). As in most cases involving nonresponsibility determinations based on lack of integrity, the finding in that case was based on criminal violations — the indictment of an officer and the conviction of an employee of the company for criminal offenses, income tax evasion, and fraud. See also *Traffic Moving Sys., Inc.*, Comp. Gen. Dec. B-248572, 92-2 CPD ¶ 152, affirming a nonresponsibility determination based upon a prior criminal conviction of the protester's president.

The Comptroller General has held that the causes for suspension, now enumerated in FAR 9.407-2, may be used to determine a bidder's integrity, *Drexel Indus., Inc.*, Comp. Gen. Dec. B-189344, 77-2 CPD ¶ 433. These causes also primarily deal with the violation of criminal statutes. Findings of lack of integrity have been upheld based on an allegedly false certification submitted under requirements of prior Government contracts, *Mayfair Constr. Co.*, Comp. Gen. Dec. B-192023, 78-2 CPD ¶ 187; repeated violations of state environmental laws, *Standard Tank Cleaning Corp.*, Comp. Gen. Dec. B-245364, 92-1 CPD ¶ 3; an indictment that had been dismissed because of procedural deficiencies, *P.T. & L. Constr. Co.*, 55 Comp. Gen. 343 (B-183966), 75-2 CPD ¶ 208; a pending debarment for violations of the Service Contract Act, *Greenwoods's Transfer & Storage Co.*, Comp. Gen. Dec. B-186438, 76-2 CPD ¶ 167; and a plea of nolo contendere in an antitrust case, *Colonial Baking Co.*, Comp. Gen. Dec. B-185305, 76-2 CPD ¶ 59. See, however, *Pulse Companies, Inc.*, Comp. Gen. Dec. B-184463, 76-1 CPD ¶ 376, where the Comptroller General found insufficient proof to sustain a finding of lack of integrity where the offeror had corrected isolated violations of the Service Contract Act on prior contracts; *Universal Technologies Inc.*, Comp. Gen. Dec. B-248808.2, 92-2 CPD ¶ 212, where failure to identify criminal convictions did not influence an affirmative responsibility determination because it was not made in bad faith; and *Tutor-Saliba Corp.*, Comp. Gen. Dec. B-255756, 94-1 CPD ¶ 223, where allegations of involvement in Brazilian government scandals were found to be insubstantial.

See also *Garten-und Landschaftsbau GmbH Frank Mohr*, Comp. Gen. Dec. B-237276, 90-1 CPD ¶ 186, and *Frank Cain & Sons, Inc.*, Comp. Gen. Dec. B-236893, 90-1 CPD ¶ 44, where the agency reasonably determined that the protester was nonresponsible based upon a criminal investigation report that called into question the protester's integrity under recent procurements; *Becker & Schwindenhammer, GmbH*, Comp. Gen. Dec. B-225396, 87-1 CPD ¶ 235, where the contracting officer properly relied on an Army CID report of improper substitution of materials to support a nonresponsibility determination; *Americana de Comestibles S.A.*, Comp. Gen. Dec. B-210390, 84-1 CPD ¶ 289, where the Comptroller General upheld a nonresponsibility determination based on confidential information contained in a discontinued Army CID investigative file; and *Drexel Indus., Inc.*, Comp. Gen. Dec. B-189344, 77-2 CPD ¶ 433, where the Comptroller General overturned a nonresponsibility determination for lack of integrity because the evidence in the contract file indicated that the contractor's prior performance problems were apparently due to financial circumstances and not lack of integrity.

Determinations of nonresponsibility may be based on the lack of integrity of those having close relationships with the offeror. In *Speco Corp.*, Comp. Gen. Dec. B-211353, 83-1 CPD ¶ 458, the Comptroller General held that the lack of integrity of a bidder's key employee may properly constitute grounds for finding that bidder nonresponsible when it appears that significant influence might be exercised by the key employee in performance of the contract. See also *Americana de Comestibles S.A.*, Comp. Gen. Dec.

B-210390, 84-1 CPD ¶ 289, where the unsatisfactory record of integrity of the company's president was deemed sufficient in itself to justify the contracting officer's finding that the firm was not responsible.

Similarly, the integrity of a predecessor firm may be considered in determining the responsibility of a bidder. In *R.H. Ritchey*, Comp. Gen. Dec. B-205602, 82-2 CPD ¶ 28, the Comptroller General based its nonresponsibility determination on the fact that the managing partner of the predecessor firm had been convicted of false pretenses in connection with a previous contract. A low bidder's relationship with another contractor that, it was conceded, lacked integrity, may also support a finding of nonresponsibility, *John Carlo, Inc.*, Comp. Gen. Dec. B-204928, 82-1 CPD ¶ 184. In that case, although the protester argued there was no substantial relationship between it and the disreputable contractor, the Comptroller General found that there were both past and present dealings between the two contractors in which the protester allowed the other to both bid and perform work in the protester's name.

Determinations of nonresponsibility based upon lack of integrity involve special considerations because of the rule requiring "due process" if such a determination "stigmatizes" the offeror, *Old Dominion Dairy Prods., Inc. v. Secretary of Defense*, 631 F.2d 953 (D.C. Cir. 1980); *Related Indus., Inc. v. United States*, 2 Cl. Ct. 517 (1983). See *Omneco, Inc.*, Comp. Gen. Dec. B-218343, 85-1 CPD ¶ 660, stating that this rule does not apply to an initial determination of nonresponsibility. The elements of such "due process" are discussed below.

b. Special Standards

Contracting officers are permitted to define the responsibility criteria more specifically by including special standards of responsibility, sometimes called "definitive performance criteria," in the solicitation. FAR 9.104-2(a) states:

> When it is necessary for a particular acquisition or class of acquisitions, the contracting officer shall develop, with the assistance of appropriate specialists, special standards of responsibility. Special standards may be particularly desirable when experience has demonstrated that unusual expertise or specialized facilities are needed for adequate contract performance. The special standards shall be set forth in the solicitation (and so identified) and shall apply to all offerors.

Since imposition of special standards has the effect of limiting competition, they must be thoughtfully drawn. However, when they are based on essential Government needs, they effectively narrow the field of eligible firms by warning unqualified firms not to expend needless effort in preparing offers.

Contracting officers may not waive special standards of responsibility, *Mary Kathleen Collins Trust*, Comp. Gen. Dec. B-261019.2, 96-1 CPD ¶ 164. Thus, an affirmative determination of responsibility will be overruled if the contracting officer does not have a reasonable basis to conclude that the low responsible bidder satisfies a special responsibility standard, *George Hyman Constr. Co.*, Comp. Gen. Dec. B-265798, 95-2 CPD ¶ 173 (there was a "reasonable possibility of prejudice" in the waiver of a "very restrictive" key personnel experience requirement). The GSBCA followed this rationale in *C3, Inc.*, GSBCA 10647-P, 90-3 BCA ¶ 23,180.

The contracting officer is, however, granted some discretion in determining whether the offeror has the equivalent experience to meet such special standards of responsibility, *Haughton Elevator Div., Reliance Elec. Co.*, 55 Comp. Gen. 1051 (B-184865), 76-1 CPD ¶ 294 (employee's experience used to satisfy corporate experience requirement); *Evans, Inc.*, Comp. Gen. Dec. B-216260.2, 85-1 CPD ¶ 535 (regular dealer permitted to certify as manufacturer). See also *Aero Sys., Inc.*, Comp. Gen. Dec. B-215892, 84-2 CPD ¶ 374, where the Comptroller General determined that despite the offeror's failure to meet the precise definitive criteria, it could still be found responsible because it had clearly demonstrated that it had equivalent capability (possession of Canadian license instead of FAR 13.5 certificate), and *Stocker & Yale, Inc.*, Comp. Gen. Dec. B-238251, 90-1 CPD ¶ 475, where the agency's right to determine if an awardee's licenses were the equivalent of the IFB requirements was acknowledged. This discretion is not granted, however, if the definitive criteria are stated with specificity, *Power Sys.*, Comp. Gen. Dec. B-210032, 83-2 CPD ¶ 232. In that case, the solicitation required experience on the same product offered in the bid, and the Comptroller General ruled that experience on no other product would suffice.

The definitive criteria must be necessary to assure satisfaction of the Government's needs. See *Software City*, Comp. Gen. Dec. B-217542, 85-1 CPD ¶ 475, concurring with an agency requirement that offerors present a letter from the source of the goods guaranteeing the supply of the product because the agency needed a continuous supply. Compare *Keeson, Inc.*,

Comp. Gen. Dec. B-245625, 92-1 CPD ¶ 108, where the Comptroller General found the following requirement unduly restrictive:

> The [contractor] has an established asbestos abatement business for 5 years; has conducted within the last 3 years 5 asbestos abatement projects 3 of which are of comparable complexity and dollar value with this project; has not defaulted on any project within the last five years; has not been cited or has not been a defending party of any legal action for violation of asbestos regulations during the last five years; [and] . . . has an adequate number of qualified personnel available for this project.

The Comptroller General found the provisions on regulatory violations and prior defaults unreasonably broad and the provision requiring that the organization have five years' experience unduly restrictive in that it did not recognize experience of the personnel working for the organization. See also *Haughton Elevator Div., Reliance Elec. Co.*, 55 Comp. Gen. 1051 (B-184865), 76-1 CPD ¶ 294, where the Comptroller General found that an experience requirement was unduly restrictive because the awardee, while not meeting the requirement, was successfully performing the contract. In *International Computaprint Corp.*, 55 Comp. Gen. 1043 (B-185403), 76-1 CPD ¶ 289, and *Topley Realty Co.*, 65 Comp. Gen. 510 (B-221459), 86-1 CPD ¶ 398, the Comptroller General found definitive responsibility criteria unduly restrictive because the agency had ignored the requirement in making the award. To the extent that a special standard requires the offeror to complete a "testing or other quality assurance demonstration" before award, it must be justified in writing pursuant to 10 U.S.C. § 2319 or 41 U.S.C. § 253c. See FAR Subpart 9.2. In *Altex Enters., Inc.*, 67 Comp. Gen. 184 (B-228200), 88-1 CPD ¶ 7, a blanket requirement that all individual sureties provide a first deed of trust on the unencumbered value of real estate was found not reasonably related to the needs of the agency because there were no unusual circumstances justifying its presence.

To qualify as definitive responsibility criteria, solicitation provisions must be specific, objective, and mandatory, *Weldtest, Inc.*, Comp. Gen. Dec. B-216747.2, 84-2 CPD ¶ 612. In that case, a requirement that "offerors may be required to prove that they have experience in comparable work" was held to be neither "specific and objective" nor "mandatory." In *AT&T Corp.*, Comp. Gen. Dec. B-260447.4, 96-1 CPD ¶ 200, the Comptroller General found a lack of specificity when the solicitation stated that the "facilities and services under the contract shall be in accordance with all applicable tariffs, rates, charges, rules, regulations or requirements of the FCC." Similarly, a provision "reserving the right" to consider performance in the last two years was held not to meet these requirements, *Old Dominion Sec.*, Comp. Gen. Dec. B-216534, 85-1 CPD ¶ 78, and a requirement for "corporate experience" was held not to be sufficiently specific or objective, *Alliance Properties Inc.*, Comp. Gen. Dec. B-214769, 84-2 CPD ¶ 14. Compare *J. Baranello & Sons*, 58 Comp. Gen. 509 (B-192221), 79-1 CPD ¶ 322, where the standards were met by a solicitation requiring three years' experience and installation of comparable equipment on two prior projects.

Definitive responsibility criteria must also be distinguished from specification requirements. See *Power Testing Inc.*, Comp. Gen. Dec. B-197190, 80-2 CPD ¶ 72, where a statement in the solicitation requiring the contractor to use a foreperson with at least five years' experience was treated as a statement of how the work was to be performed rather than an aspect of responsibility that had to be satisfied at the time of award. Specification statements rather than definitive responsibility criteria were also found in *Markhurd Aerial Surveys, Inc.*, Comp. Gen. Dec. B-210108, 83-1 CPD ¶ 51, where a solicitation requirement stated that the contractor was required to use personnel with minimum crew experience; *Data Gen. Corp.*, Comp. Gen. Dec. B-252239, 93-1 CPD ¶ 457, where the solicitation stated that "all personnel performing under the resulting contract must have a minimum of one year experience" in similar work; and *Satellite Servs., Inc.*, Comp. Gen. Dec. B-219679, 85-2 CPD ¶ 224, where the solicitation stated that all personnel must be fully qualified to perform.

In order to properly find that an awardee meets the criteria, an agency must base its determination upon adequate and objective evidence, *T. Warehouse Corp.*, Comp. Gen. Dec. B-248951, 92-2 CPD ¶ 235. In that case, the Comptroller General reviewed the facts and determined that they did not support the agency's determination that the criteria had been met. Similarly, in *Prime Mortgage Corp.*, 69 Comp. Gen. 618 (B-238680.2), 90-2 CPD ¶ 48, the Comptroller General reversed a finding of responsibility when the contracting officer had no objective evidence that the offeror had $100,000 working capital as required by the solicitation. Compare *Coastal Elecs., Inc.*, Comp. Gen. Dec. B-250718, 93-1 CPD ¶ 144, where the Comptroller General reviewed certificates of training and determined that they met the criteria.

A contract requirement that a commercial product be furnished is not a definitive responsibility criterion, *PTR-Precision Technologies, Inc.*, Comp. Gen. Dec. B-243439, 91-2 CPD ¶ 110; *Blue Tee Corp.*, Comp. Gen. Dec

B-246623, 92-1 CPD ¶ 289. See also *Symtron Sys., Inc.*, Comp. Gen. Dec. B-242244, 91-1 CPD ¶ 282, holding that a commercial product requirement involves an affirmative determination of responsibility and generally is not reviewable. At one time, the Comptroller General ruled that requirements that commercial products be furnished were definitive responsibility criteria, *Data Test, Inc.*, 54 Comp. Gen. 499 (B-181199), 74-2 CPD ¶ 365, *recons. denied*, 54 Comp. Gen. 715, 75-1 CPD ¶ 138. In *Clausing Mach. Tools*, Comp. Gen. Dec. B-216113, 85-1 CPD ¶ 533, the Comptroller General stated that this rule had been changed. See, however, *Presto Lock, Inc.*, Comp. Gen. Dec. B-218766, 85-2 CPD ¶ 183, following the *Data Test* rule and not citing *Clausing*. See also *Evans, Inc.*, Comp. Gen. Dec. B-216260.2, 85-1 CPD ¶ 535, holding that a required manufacturer's certification that spare parts be available for 10 years was a definitive criterion.

One of the most common types of special standards deals with experience requirements. The Comptroller General has recognized the propriety of limiting contract awards to those bidders that have had a minimum amount of experience doing work comparable to that required by the contract, 35 Comp. Gen. 161 (B-124614) (1955) (service contract); *American Sterilizer Co.*, Comp. Gen. Dec. B-207518, 82-2 CPD ¶ 453 (supply contract for biohazardous use); *Karl Doll GmbH*, Comp. Gen. Dec. B-213556, 84-1 CPD ¶ 604 (boiler firing services); *Urban Masonry Corp.*, Comp. Gen. Dec. B-213196, 84-1 CPD ¶ 48 (erection of precast concrete); *R.R. Mongeau Eng'rs, Inc.*, Comp. Gen. Dec. B-213330, 84-1 CPD ¶ 333 (installation of cathodic protection equipment). The Comptroller General has accepted the use of such provisions where the interests of the Government would thereby be served, provided that the special standards are included in the invitation, 37 Comp. Gen. 196 (B-133707) (1957); 45 Comp. Gen. 4 (B-156520) (1965).

Requirements for special facilities have also been expressed as definitive responsibility criteria, *Aero Corp.*, Comp. Gen. Dec. B-201581, 81-1 CPD ¶ 338. See *Auto Discount Rent-N-Drive Sys., Inc.*, Comp. Gen. Dec. B-197236, 80-2 CPD ¶ 73, finding that a requirement that the awardee demonstrate that its dispatching facility is located in a certain geographical area was a definitive criterion. Business reference requirements have been treated as definitive responsibility criteria, *Ampex Corp.*, Comp. Gen. Dec. B-212356, 83-2 CPD ¶ 565. Accreditation requirements have also been treated as definitive responsibility criteria, *United States Crane Certification Bureau, Inc.*, Comp. Gen. Dec. B-197433, 80-1 CPD ¶ 247; *School for Educ. Enrichment*, Comp. Gen. Dec. B-199003, 80-2 CPD ¶ 286. See *E.J.*

Nachtwey, Comp. Gen. Dec. B-209562, 83-1 CPD ¶ 104, where a music degree from a special music school was held to be a definitive responsibility criterion, and *Townsco Contracting Co.*, Comp. Gen. Dec. B-240289, 90-2 CPD ¶ 313, where a requirement for bidders that have been regularly engaged "in airfield paving for the three years immediately preceding" was found to be a definitive responsibility criteria.

Definitive responsibility criteria can be demonstrated by showing that affiliates or subcontractors meet the criteria, *Tutor-Saliba Corp.*, Comp. Gen. Dec. B-255756, 94-1 CPD ¶ 223. In that case, the Comptroller General stated the following:

> As a general rule, the experience of a technically qualified subcontractor or third party — such as an affiliate or consultant — may be used to satisfy definitive responsibility criteria relating to experience for a prospective prime contractor. *Gelco Servs., In.*, B-253376, Sept. 14, 1993, 93-2 CPD ¶ 163, *recon. denied*, B-253376.2, Oct. 27, 1993, 93-2 CPD ¶ 261; *Tama Kensetsu Co., Ltd, and Nippon Hodo*, B-233118, Feb. 8, 1989, 89-1 CPD ¶ 128. However, where a solicitation contains a criterion which by its express language prohibits satisfying a particular experience requirement through the experience of a prospective subcontractor, such a provision limits the prime contractor from relying on a subcontractor to comply with the experience criterion. See *Allen-Sherman-Hoff Co.*, B-231552, Aug. 4, 1988, 88-2 CPD ¶ 116.

The Comptroller General has also held that a joint venture meets a definitive criteria requirement if only one of the venturers satisfies the requirement, *Hellenic Technodomiki, S.A.*, Comp. Gen. Dec. B-265931, 96-1 CPD ¶ 91. Experience of employees working for other companies can also be used to demonstrate that the offeror meets an experience requirement, *Tuscon Mobilephone, Inc.*, Comp. Gen. Dec. B-258408.3, 95-1 CPD ¶ 267.

For a number of years, the Comptroller General held that these special standards or "definitive criteria" of responsibility could be waived if the agency determined that the contractor was responsible even though it did not meet the standards, 39 Comp. Gen. 881 (B-143073) (1960). In one case, the Comptroller General held that the contracting officer could not declare an offeror nonresponsible for failure to meet the "literal requirements" of such provisions, 45 Comp. Gen. 4 (B-156520) (1965). This line of decisions was expressly reversed in *Haughton Elevator Div., Reliance Elec. Co.*, 55 Comp. Gen. 1051 (B-184865), 76-1 CPD ¶ 294, because of the potential prejudicial effect of waiving definitive responsibility criteria, and further clarified in

Lesko Assocs., Comp. Gen. Dec. B-209703, 83-1 CPD ¶ 443, where the Comptroller General stated that a waiver is misleading and prejudicial both to offerors that met the requirement and to any prospective offerors that did not participate in the competition because of the stated requirement.

In granting a COC, the SBA must consider, but is not bound by, the definitive responsibility criteria in the solicitation, *Baxter & Sons Elevator Co.*, 60 Comp. Gen. 97 (B-197595), 80-2 CPD ¶ 414; *E-Systems, Inc.*, 60 Comp. Gen. 283 (B-199550.5), 81-1 CPD ¶ 137. Thus, the Comptroller General will not review the proper application of a definitive responsibility criterion unless the SBA has not been informed of its application to the procurement under protest, *Eastern Marine, Inc.*, 63 Comp. Gen. 551 (B-212444.2), 84-2 CPD ¶ 232.

2. Collateral Requirements

Offerors that do not meet specific requirements imposed by statute or regulation may be excluded from contracting even though they appear otherwise fully able and willing to perform the work specified in the solicitation. These requirements are termed "collateral" because they are not involved with the performance of the work called for by the contract. In some cases, they are closely related to the responsibility issue, while in others they are separate eligibility considerations. See, however, FAR 9.104-1(g), apparently making all such issues matters of responsibility.

a. Equal Employment Opportunity

The equal employment opportunity policies of the Federal Government are covered in Chapter 10. A major element of these policies is the development of affirmative action plans and programs. FAR 22.802(b) prohibits award of a contract to a person "who has been found ineligible" by the Office of Federal Contract Compliance Programs (OFCCP) of the Department of Labor. In addition, 41 C.F.R. § 60-2.2(b) requires a nonresponsibility determination if a contracting officer finds that a contractor does not have an affirmative action program that complies with the Government's standards. See 51 Comp. Gen. 551 (B-174816) (1972), where the Comptroller General, citing 41 C.F.R. § 60-2.2, stated that the contracting officer was correct in finding the prospective contractor nonresponsible because the contractor was not in compliance with the equal employment opportunity requirements at one of its establishments.

For awards of contracts of $1 million or more, excluding construction, the contracting officer must request a determination from the OFCCP that the contract is "awardable," FAR 22.805(a).

b. Small Business Subcontracting

In 1978, P.L. 95-507 amended 15 U.S.C. § 637 to require that solicitations for certain contracts that offer subcontracting possibilities contain a clause requiring any bidder who is selected for award to submit a detailed small business subcontracting plan to the procuring agency. 15 U.S.C. § 637(d)(5)(B) indicates that failure to comply with these requirements will result in a nonresponsibility determination:

> If, within the time limit prescribed in regulations of the Federal agency concerned, the bidder selected to be awarded the contract fails to submit the subcontracting plan required by this paragraph, such bidder shall become ineligible to be awarded the contract. Prior compliance of the bidder with other subcontracting plans shall be considered by the Federal agency in determining the responsibility of such bidder for the award of the contract. The subcontracting plan of the bidder awarded the contract shall be included in and made a material part of the contract.

See *Devcon Sys. Corp.*, Comp. Gen. Dec. B-197935, 80-2 CPD ¶ 46, affirming the contracting officer's holding that submission of a small business subcontracting plan is a matter of responsibility rather than responsiveness, and permitting the firm, until the time of award, to submit an acceptable plan. Accord *A.B. Dick Co.*, Comp. Gen. Dec. B-233142, 89-1 CPD ¶ 106. See also *Columbia Research Corp.*, 61 Comp. Gen. 194 (B-202762), 82-1 CPD ¶ 8, finding a 16-page plan adequate although the offeror proposed no small business subcontracts for the procurement under consideration.

c. Government Employees

FAR 3.601(a) provides explicit policy guidance on contracting with employees of the Federal Government:

> Except as specified in 3.602, a contracting officer shall not knowingly award a contract to a Government employee or to a business concern or other organization owned or substantially owned or controlled by one or more Government employees. This policy is intended to avoid any conflict of interest that might arise between the employees' interests and their Gov-

ernment duties, and to avoid the appearance of favoritism or preferential treatment by the Government toward its employees.

Valiant Sec. Agency, Comp. Gen. Dec. B-205087, 81-2 CPD ¶ 367, *recons. denied*, 81-2 CPD ¶ 501, explains this policy as follows:

> Contracts between the Government and its employees are not expressly prohibited by statute except where the employee acts for both the Government and the contractor in a particular transaction or where the service to be rendered is such as could be required of the contractor in his capacity as a Government employee. 18 U.S.C. § 208 (1976); *Hugh Maher*, B-187841, March 31, 1977, 77-1 CPD ¶ 204. However, it has long been recognized that such contracts are undesirable because among other reasons they invite criticism as to alleged favoritism and possible fraud and that they should be authorized only in exceptional cases where the Government cannot reasonably be otherwise supplied. 27 Comp. Gen. 735 (1948); *Capital Aero, Inc.*, B-183833, September 30, 1975, 75-2 CPD ¶ 201; *Burgos & Associates, Inc.*, 59 Comp. Gen. 273 (1980), 80-1 CPD ¶ 155. The fact that a service would be more expensive if not obtained from an employee of the Government does not by itself provide support for a determination that the service cannot reasonably be obtained from other sources. 55 Comp. Gen. 681 [B-184716] (1976).

The sole exception to the prohibition in FAR 3.602 requires a determination by a high-level official that there is a "most compelling reason to [enter into a contract], such as when the Government's needs cannot reasonably be otherwise met." The contracting officer has discretion in determining whether this exemption applies. Compare the *Valiant* case with *International Alliance of Sports Officials*, Comp. Gen. Dec. B-210172, 83-2 CPD ¶ 328. In the latter case, the Comptroller General sustained a contracting officer's decision to award a contract to an employee-owned company at approximately $223,000 in contrast to the next low offer of $275,000.

Substantial ownership or control is determined by the facts of each individual case. Mere employment by a Government contractor is not prohibited by this restriction. See *National Serv. Corp.*, Comp. Gen. Dec. B-205629, 82-2 CPD ¶ 76 (no substantial ownership or control when Government employee gave up partnership and became part-time bookkeeper); *HH & K Builders, Inc.*, Comp. Gen. Dec. B-238095, 90-1 CPD ¶ 219 (sole owner's husband was Government employee, but sufficient separation of ownership). Compare *Electronics West, Inc.*, Comp. Gen. Dec. B-209720, 83-2 CPD ¶ 127 (change in title from president to treasurer did not prevent disqualification). An agency does not have to establish with certainty that an employee has a substantially controlling interest but rather need only have "a reason to believe" that the Government employee has such control, *Gurley's, Inc.*, Comp. Gen. Dec. B-253852, 93-2 CPD ¶ 123. See *Elogene Thurman*, Comp. Gen. Dec. B-206325, 82-1 CPD ¶ 487 (award to wife of Government employee improper when husband in fact ran the business); *Applied Resources Corp.*, Comp. Gen. Dec. B-249258, 92-2 CPD ¶ 272 (disqualification proper where spouse of firm's president was the contracting officer's supervisor and relationship was not disclosed on financial disclosure form); *American Truss & Mfg. Corp.*, Comp. Gen. Dec. B-205962, 82-1 CPD ¶ 477 (award improper where Government employee owned 50 percent of stock and wife owned balance); *Marc Indus.*, Comp. Gen. Dec. B-246528, 92-1 CPD ¶ 273 (substantial control found where Government employee represented the firm in prework conferences under prior contracts with the agency, served as the contact for any complaints about contract performance, and, based on his involvement with the firm, was disciplined for violating his agency's conflict of interest regulations); and *KSR, Inc.*, Comp. Gen. Dec. B-250160, 93-1 CPD ¶ 37 (substantial control found where Government employee was president and was one of five owners).

Some agencies have restrictions on dealing with close relatives of employees. See *Joann Flora*, Comp. Gen. Dec. B-212776, 83-2 CPD ¶ 520 (regulation prohibiting contract with "immediate member of the household" of agency employee barred contract with unmarried party living as spouse); and *Heidi Holley*, Comp. Gen. Dec. B-211746, 83-2 CPD ¶ 241 (regulations stating that contracts should generally not be awarded to members of an agency employee's family and requiring close scrutiny barred award to spouse of agency employee required to supervise contract). However, see *J. Allen Grafton*, Comp. Gen. Dec. B-212986, 84-1 CPD ¶ 263, in which the Comptroller General found that an agency unreasonably rejected a quotation from the son of an agency employee, when there was no showing that the employee had responsibility for the resulting contract and no indication that the father had disclosed any confidential agency information or otherwise influenced the procurement.

If the contracting officer inadvertently makes an award to a company owned or controlled by a Government employee, the Comptroller General will not disturb the award absent an indication of favoritism or other impropriety, *Sterling Medical Assocs.*, Comp. Gen. Dec. B-209493, 83-1 CPD ¶ 215; *Biosystems Analysis, Inc.*, Comp. Gen. Dec. B-198846, 80-2

CPD ¶ 149. In both cases, the employee worked for an agency other than the one awarding the contract.

d. Guard and Security Service

The Anti-Pinkerton Act of 1893, as revised in 5 U.S.C. § 3108, states:

> An individual employed by the Pinkerton Detective Agency, or similar organization, may not be employed by the Government of the United States or the government of the District of Columbia.

FAR 37.109 narrowly defines this statute to cover "quasi-military armed forces" by stating:

> Contracts with "Pinkerton Detective Agencies or similar organizations" are prohibited by 5 U.S.C. § 3108. This prohibition applies only to contracts with organizations that offer quasi-military armed forces for hire, or with their employees, regardless of the contract's character. An organization providing guard or protective services does not thereby become a "quasi-military armed force," even though the guards are armed or the organization provides general investigative or detective services.

This guidance limiting the application of the Act to "quasi-military" forces is derived from *United States ex rel. Weinberger v. Equifax, Inc.*, 557 F.2d 456 (5th Cir. 1977), *cert. denied*, 434 U.S. 1035 (1978). It was adopted by the Comptroller General in 57 Comp. Gen. 524 (B-139965) (1978). In *Old Dominion Sec.*, Comp. Gen. Dec. B-216534, 85-1 CPD ¶ 78, it was held that the low bidder was not precluded by the Anti-Pinkerton Act from receiving a contract for security guard services since all personnel assigned to the project were licensed and employed solely as uniformed security guards. Whether a prospective contractor must be precluded from Government contracting due to the Anti-Pinkerton Act is a matter for contracting officer determination subject to the Comptroller General review, *Inter-Con Sec. Sys., Inc.*, Comp. Gen. Dec. B-192188, 79-1 CPD ¶ 86.

e. Organizational Conflicts of Interest

It is the policy of the Government to avoid awarding contracts where the contractor would have either an actual or potential bias in making judgments required by contract performance or have an unfair competitive advantage in competing for future contracts, FAR 9.505. In implementing this policy, the contracting officer must decide whether to disqualify an offeror or to include a contract provision imposing restraints designed to "avoid, neutralize, or mitigate" the bias or competitive advantage, FAR 9.504(a)(2). The particular action the contracting officer should take depends on the nature of the conflict and the point in the procurement process at which it is identified.

The possibility of bias exists when a contractor's judgment in advising the Government might be influenced because of potential future gain or past involvement in the area. Unfair competitive advantage may result from access to Government information not available to others or information from competitors obtained in the performance of a Government contract. In some cases, both bias and unfair competitive advantage can be involved. This could occur, for instance, if a contractor were permitted to draft specifications favoring its own product or services. See FAR 9.509 and DEAR 209.570-14 for examples of these situations. Identification of a potential organizational conflict of interest often involves complex facts that require careful analysis. FAR 9.505 states:

> The exercise of common sense, good judgment, and sound discretion is required in both the decision on whether a significant potential conflict exists and, if it does, the development of an appropriate means for resolving it.

The Comptroller General has recognized the judgmental nature of decisions in this area and has stated that the responsibility for determining whether award to a particular firm would result in an organizational conflict of interest lies with the procuring agency. Such determinations are subject to objection only if they are directly contrary to statute or regulation or are shown to be clearly unreasonable, *Abt Assocs.*, Comp. Gen. Dec. B-253220.2, 93-2 CPD ¶ 269; *NAHB Research Found., Inc.*, Comp. Gen. Dec. B-219344, 85-2 CPD ¶ 248; *John J. McMullen Assocs.*, Comp. Gen. Dec. B-188703, 77-2 CPD ¶ 270.

FAR 9.505 describes three types of situations in which an organizational conflict of interest is most likely to arise. The first situation is procurement of systems engineering and technical direction. FAR 9.505-1(b) defines these terms as follows:

> Systems engineering includes a combination of substantially all of the following activities: determining specifications, identifying and resolving interface problems, developing test requirements, evaluating test data, and supervising design. Technical direction includes a combination of substantially all of the following activities: developing work statements, determin-

> ing parameters, directing other contractors' operations, and resolving technical controversies.

It has been held that "sustaining engineering" by a contractor on an aircraft program did not bar that contractor from performance of overhaul and maintenance contracts on the same aircraft because sustaining engineering was not the same as technical direction or systems engineering, *Hayes Int'l Corp. v. McLucas*, 509 F.2d 247 (5th Cir.), *cert. denied*, 423 U.S. 864 (1975). The Comptroller General has stated that mere employment of a former Government employee, who is familiar with the type of work required but not privy to the contents of proposals or any other "inside" information, does not confer any unfair competitive advantage, *Central Texas College*, 71 Comp. Gen. 164 (B-245233.4) (1992). Compare *MAR, Inc.*, Comp. Gen. Dec. B-215798, 85-1 CPD ¶ 121, where a contract for "scientific, engineering, analytical, technical and prototype-fabrication services" was held to involve a potential conflict of interest.

The second situation is a contract for the preparation of specifications or statements of work for nondevelopmental items, FAR 9.505-2. This situation may occur where the specifications contain substantial detail, *Nelson Erection Co.*, Comp. Gen. Dec. B-217556, 85-1 CPD ¶ 482 (specifications for repair of hangar door outlining specific repairs needed), as well as where the specifications are very general, *LW Planning Group*, Comp. Gen. Dec. B-215539, 84-2 CPD ¶ 531 (broad work statement for contract to revise a facility's master plan). See also *Ressler Assocs., Inc.*, Comp. Gen. Dec. B-244110, 91-2 CPD ¶ 230 (organizational conflict where protester had earlier prepared portions of the statement of work without contracting officer's knowledge), and *Network Solutions, Inc. v. Department of the Air Force*, GSBCA 11498-P, 92-3 BCA ¶ 25,083 (improper competitive advantage found where offeror, under an RFP for engineering of LANs, had previously installed the network on which a sample task set out in the RFP was based). Since most services, including construction, will be construed to involve nondevelopmental work, contractors drafting specifications for such work will generally be excluded under this rule, e.g., *Danish Arctic Contractors*, Comp. Gen. Dec. B-212957, 84-1 CPD ¶ 131; *Ressler Assocs.*, Comp. Gen. Dec. B-244110, 91-2 CPD ¶ 230.

FAR 9.505-2(a) defines two situations where no conflict of interest will be found:

(i) Contractors that furnish at Government request specifications or data regarding a product they provide, even though the specifications or data may have been paid for separately or in the price of the product; or

(ii) Situations in which contractors, acting as industry representatives, help Government agencies prepare, refine, or coordinate specifications, regardless of source, provided this assistance is supervised and controlled by Government representatives.

The first rule is amplified in FAR 9.505-2(b)(1). See *Analytic Sciences Corp.*, Comp. Gen. Dec. B-218074, 85-1 CPD ¶ 464, where the Comptroller General questioned the exclusion of a company that had prepared a broad work statement, because it was not clear whether the work statement involved existing software or software to be developed.

The third conflict situation involves contracts for technical evaluation or consulting services concerning the products or activities of the contractor or its competitors, FAR 9.505-3. In *Acumenics Research & Technology, Inc.*, Comp. Gen. Dec. B-211575, 83-2 CPD ¶ 94, the contractor properly was eliminated from competition on a contract that would require the firm to evaluate the usefulness of its work under an earlier contract. Similarly, in *Engineered Air Sys., Inc.*, Comp. Gen. Dec. B-230878, 88-2 CPD ¶ 77, it was proper to exclude the protester from a competition that would have required it to test and evaluate its own product. In *ICF Inc.*, Comp. Gen. Dec. B-241372, 91-1 CPD ¶ 124, a protester was excluded from a competition that would have involved its evaluation of the efficiency of sister corporations that had "response action" contracts with the Environmental Protection Agency (EPA). In *KPMG Peat Marwick*, Comp. Gen. Dec. B-255224, 94-1 CPD ¶ 111, a conflict was found where the protester would have been reviewing its own audits performed for the agency's predecessor. See also *Women's Energy, Inc.*, Comp. Gen. Dec. 258785, 95-1 CPD ¶ 86. Compare *Tymshare, Inc.*, Comp. Gen. Dec. B-198020, 80-2 CPD ¶ 267, where the Comptroller General held that there was no conflict of interest under a solicitation that called for the contractor to provide "technical assistance" to the Government in evaluating the reliability of the data system being procured. In *N.D. Lea & Assocs.*, Comp. Gen. Dec. B-208445, 83-2 CPD ¶ 21, the Comptroller General held that serving as a subcontractor on one prior contract was not sufficient involvement in the rail standardization program to justify barring the awardee from reviewing new awards in that program. Similarly, in *Battelle Memorial Inst.*, Comp. Gen. Dec. B-218538, 85-1 CPD ¶ 726, a contract to prepare "general methodologies" to solve a technical problem including the summarization of technical data from past contract performance was properly awarded to a contractor that was performing one of the prior contracts. The Comptroller General reasoned that the contract did not require the assessment of the adequacy of its performance under the prior contract. See also *CH2M Hill, Ltd.*, Comp. Gen. Dec. B-259511, 95-1 CPD ¶ 203, where the Comptroller General found no conflict of interest when the president of a subcontractor chaired a community commission that was the "focal point" for relocation efforts caused by Government downsizing. The Comptroller concluded that the commission had no control over the agency's efforts that would be facilitated by the contract.

When the contracting officer identifies a potential organizational conflict of interest, the offeror must be disqualified unless a restraint can be included in the contract to neutralize or mitigate the conflict. If the conflict results from past actions of the contractor, disqualification may be the only logical course of action. Most often this occurs when a prior contract has included a clause restraining participation in the present procurement. However, the absence of a clause does not preclude disqualification, *LW Planning Group*, Comp. Gen. Dec. B-215539, 84-2 CPD ¶ 531; *Acumenics Research & Technology, Inc.*, Comp. Gen. Dec. B-211575, 83-2 CPD ¶ 94. The *LW Planning* case involved a contractor that had participated in the drafting of specifications or work statements. The *Acumenics* case, discussed above, involved a situation where bias could result under a contract that required the firm to evaluate the usefulness of its own work under an earlier contract. Similarly, in *Cardiocare*, 59 Comp. Gen. 355 (B-195827), 80-1 CPD ¶ 237, the Comptroller General upheld the Veterans Administration's finding of potential bias where the offeror was determined ineligible to do the follow-up service work on pacemakers because approximately 50 percent of them were produced by the offeror's parent company.

Disqualification under a current procurement can be avoided through the imposition of restraints. In such cases, the solicitation and the contract must contain appropriate provisions, FAR 9.508. However, the FAR contains no clauses for this purpose. See DEAR 952.209-72 and NFS 1852.209-71 for agency clauses. The most common restraint is a bar to participation in future procurements. For example, this type of clause has been used to eliminate bias in drafting specifications, *Analytic Sciences Corp.*, Comp. Gen. Dec. B-218074, 85-1 CPD ¶ 464. Similarly, a clause may only warn a contractor that disqualification in future contracts could result from biased drafting of specifications, *Iris Int'l, Inc.*, Comp. Gen.

Dec. B-216084.2, 85-1 CPD ¶ 524. Other types of restraints have been used to eliminate bias. For example, in *Columbia Research Corp.*, 61 Comp. Gen. 194 (B-202762), 82-1 CPD ¶ 8, the agency included a clause requiring the contractor to give notice of any organizational conflicts during a study and providing for default termination if the notice was not given. See also *Calspan Corp.*, Comp. Gen. Dec. 258441, 95-1 CPD ¶ 28, where preparation of an acceptable conflict of interest plan was sufficient to allay any conflicts. In *PRI, Inc.*, Comp. Gen. Dec. B-210714, 84-1 CPD ¶ 345, the Comptroller General denied a protest of bias concerning the overlapping roles of the awardee in separate contracts with the agency. It was held that potential bias could be avoided by having the agency monitor the placing of task orders to avoid such conflict. See *Gold Appraisal Co.*, Comp. Gen. Dec. B-259201, 95-1 CPD ¶ 144 , where the Comptroller General found that a conflict could be mitigated by monitoring the work under a clause in the contract. Unfair advantage through use of competitor's proprietary data can be eliminated by a clause requiring the contractor to agree with other companies to protect the data and refrain from using them for other purposes, FAR 9.505-4. See *MAR, Inc.*, Comp. Gen. Dec. B-215798, 85-1 CPD ¶ 121, where the Comptroller General agreed with the use of such a clause even though a protester contended that no competitors would disclose the data under such conditions.

It can be argued that the contracting officer is required to attempt to negotiate restraints, when appropriate, before disqualifying an offeror because of an organizational conflict, FAR 9.505. See *Orkand Corp.*, Comp. Gen. Dec. B-209662.2, 83-1 CPD ¶ 349, where the Comptroller General agreed with an agency determination that a contracting officer should have attempted to negotiate an appropriate contract clause. With respect to unfair advantage resulting from obtaining proprietary data of competitors, FAR 9.505-4 indicates that a restraint is the only proper course of action. But see *Aetna Gov. Health Plans, Inc.*, Comp. Gen. Dec. B-254397.15, 95-2 CPD ¶ 129, where severance of communications between two affiliates and the absence of direct financial interests by employees were insufficient to mitigate a conflict situation.

B. Subcontractor Responsibility

In many Government contracts, much of the work is done by subcontractors. In these circumstances, it may be important for the contracting officer to evaluate the capabilities and character of an offeror's proposed subcontractors in order to make an accurate assessment of the prospects for successful completion of work through award to that offeror. See *Linde Constr.*, Comp. Gen. Dec. B-206442, 83-1 CPD ¶ 271. FAR 9.104-4 addresses the matter as follows:

> (a) Generally, prospective prime contractors are responsible for determining the responsibility of their prospective subcontractors (but see 9.405 and 9.405-2 regarding debarred, ineligible, or suspended firms). Determinations of prospective subcontractor responsibility may affect the Government's determination of the prospective prime contractor's responsibility. A prospective contractor may be required to provide written evidence of a proposed subcontractor's responsibility.
>
> (b) When it is in the Government's interest to do so, the contracting officer may directly determine a prospective subcontractor's responsibility (e.g., when the prospective contract involves medical supplies, urgent requirements, or substantial subcontracting). In this case, the same standards used to determine a prime contractor's responsibility shall be used by the Government to determine subcontractor responsibility.

This regulation provides that the qualifications of a proposed subcontractor may form the basis for the determination of the contractor's responsibility. See *Omneco, Inc.*, Comp. Gen. Dec. B-218343, 85-1 CPD ¶ 660, holding a contractor nonresponsible when a preaward survey of a major subcontractor's facilities revealed the absence of a quality assurance plan; *Linde Constr.*, Comp. Gen. Dec. B-206442, 83-1 CPD ¶ 271, where the two lowest bidders in the procurement failed to demonstrate adequately the ability of proposed subcontractors to meet hiring goals for women and minorities and were thus deemed nonresponsible; and *L & M Mercadeo Int'l, S.A.*, Comp. Gen. Dec. B-250637, 93-1 CPD ¶ 124, concluding that the major subcontractor's failure to perform under an earlier contract was sufficient support for a nonresponsibility finding. Conversely, a proposed subcontractor's qualifications may sometimes overcome deficiencies of the contractor. In *Contra Costa Elec., Inc.*, Comp. Gen. Dec. B-200660, 81-1 CPD ¶ 196, the Comptroller General held that a subcontractor's experience could properly be considered in determining whether a definitive experience requirement in the solicitation was satisfied even though the solicitation did not mention that subcontractor experience would be considered. See also *Dineen Mechanical Contractors, Inc.*, Comp. Gen. Dec. B-204420, 82-1 CPD ¶ 516, where the bidder was able to satisfy the definitive experience requirement through the satisfactory completion of past projects using subcontractors, even though it did not itself possess the expertise to do the job. In such cases, there would be no need to demonstrate experience by a prospective subcontractor. Similarly, in 39 Comp. Gen. 173 (B-140481) (1959), the Comptroller General required compliance with a solicitation specifically limiting award to offerors with three years' experience "either with their own organizations or through the Subcontractor they will use on this project."

The contracting officer is not required to independently investigate the responsibility of each proposed subcontractor. The Comptroller General has stated that if the contracting officer is satisfied that the prospective contractor is responsible, it may be presumed, with nothing further, that the contractor has ascertained the responsibility of subcontractors to perform properly, *FHC Options, Inc.*, Comp. Gen. Dec. B-246793.3, 92-1 CPD ¶ 366; *R.G. Robbins Co.*, Comp. Gen. Dec. B-187365, 77-2 CPD ¶ 33.

C. Responsibility Determination Procedure

The contracting officer is charged with the duty to make an affirmative responsibility determination before awarding a contract. In discharging this duty, the contracting officer must obtain relevant information and exercise discretion in assessing this data. If an affirmative determination cannot be made, the contracting officer must make a determination of nonresponsibility. See, however, FAR 9.103(b) requiring referral of nonresponsibility determinations to the Small Business Administration if the prospective contractor is a small business. Generally, responsibility determinations are made only with regard to offerors in line for award, FAR 9.105-1(b). This section considers the process of obtaining information, the rules governing the exercise of discretion, and special procedures including the role of the SBA in responsibility matters.

1. Obtaining Information

The contracting officer must obtain sufficient information to be satisfied that the offeror meets all applicable responsibility standards, FAR 9.105-1(a). FAR 9.105-1(c) provides the following guidance on sources of information:

> In making the determination of responsibility (see 9.104-1(c)), the contracting officer shall consider relevant past performance information (see 48 CFR part 42, subpart 42.15). In addition, the contracting officer should use the following sources of information to support such determinations:

(1) The Lists of Parties Excluded from Federal Procurement and Non-procurement Programs maintained in accordance with subpart 9.4.

(2) Records and experience data, including verifiable knowledge of personnel within the contracting office, audit offices, contract administration offices, and other contracting offices.

(3) The prospective contractor — including bid or proposal information, questionnaire replies, financial data, information on production equipment, and personnel information.

(4) Preaward survey reports (see 9.106).

(5) Other sources such as publications; suppliers, subcontractors, and customers of the prospective contractor; financial institutions; Government agencies; and business and trade associations.

The contracting officer may be able to make a determination based only on data in the agency's possession, such as the first three categories listed above. If this information is not sufficient, the agency may conduct its own investigation through a preaward survey or may seek information from outside sources such as that described in the fifth category listed above. In *A. & M. Gregos, Inc. v. Hoffman*, 18 G.C. 227 (D.N.J. 1976), the court upheld a nonresponsibility determination based on performance information compiled by another contracting officer. Similarly, the Comptroller General has sustained a nonresponsibility determination based partially on unfavorable evaluations of the offeror by other procuring activities, *Propserv Inc.*, Comp. Gen. Dec. B-184698, 75-2 CPD ¶ 405.

FAR 9.106-1(a) provides that preaward surveys should not be conducted for procurements at or below the simplified acquisition threshold or for procurements involving the acquisition of commercial items. Further, there is no requirement for the contracting officer to call for such a survey if adequate evidence is already available, *Beacon Winch Co.*, Comp. Gen. Dec. B-206513.3, 82-2 CPD ¶ 304; *Klein-Sieb Advertising & Public Relations, Inc.*, Comp. Gen. Dec. B-194553.2, 81-1 CPD ¶ 214. The contracting officer has the discretion not to conduct a preaward survey, and unless a protester shows possible fraud or bad faith on the part of the contracting officer or the failure to apply definitive criteria, as in *Saratoga Indus.*, Comp. Gen. Dec. B-219341, 85-2 CPD ¶ 247, the Comptroller General will not review that decision, *Carolina Waste Sys., Inc.*, Comp. Gen. Dec. B-215689.3, 85-1 CPD ¶ 22; *Xtek, Inc.*, Comp. Gen. Dec.

B-213166, 84-1 CPD ¶ 264; *Metalcastello, s.r.l.*, Comp. Gen. Dec. B-244510, 91-2 CPD ¶ 350. In *Oliver Prods. Co.*, Comp. Gen. Dec. B-245762.2, 92-1 CPD ¶ 501, the Comptroller General held that the agency's failure to investigate the results of several related audits of the awardee's performance did not rise to the level of bad faith.

A preaward survey is the process of obtaining information from a contract administration office or other Government organization, FAR 9.101. The contracting officer initiates the survey by forwarding Standard Form 1403, identifying the factors to be investigated. The surveying authority then conducts an investigation at a level commensurate with the size and complexity of the procurement and the information currently available, FAR 9.106-4(d). In many cases, Government teams visit the offeror's place of business to obtain firsthand information concerning plant, equipment, and personnel. Making a preaward survey does not commit the Government to award a contract, nor may an offeror recover for costs of a preaward survey if the procurement is later properly canceled, Comp. Gen. Dec. B-174225, Nov. 22, 1971, *Unpub.* Information obtained from a preaward survey can be highly useful in making a responsibility determination. In *Computer Support Sys., Inc.*, Comp. Gen. Dec. B-261166, 95-2 CPD ¶ 30, findings made through a preaward survey were deemed sufficient to support such a determination.

Much of the responsibility information is furnished by the contractor at the request of the Government. Frequently, such requirements are included in the solicitation. Additional information may be requested by the contracting officer or the surveying activity. Offerors may also voluntarily furnish information in order to satisfy the requirement that they "must affirmatively demonstrate . . . responsibility," FAR 9.103(c). It was held that an offeror had no obligation to voluntarily furnish the information that the president of the offeror's parent corporation had been recently convicted for conspiring to defraud the Government, *Trilon Educ. Corp. v. United States*, 217 Ct. Cl. 266, 578 F.2d 1356, *aff'd*, 217 Ct. Cl. 284 (1978). It is likely that this conclusion would not apply to all instances where information is consciously withheld, since this could constitute a violation of the False Statements Act, 18 U.S.C. § 1001. Further, failure of the firm to provide access to relevant information specifically requested by the contracting officer or by a preaward survey team may become a basis for a nonresponsibility determination, *Donald L. Markley*, PSBCA 831, Nov. 7, 1980, *Unpub.* See *Security Assistance Forces & Equip. Int'l, Inc.*, Comp. Gen. Dec. B-194876, 80-2 CPD ¶ 68, upholding a nonresponsibility determination based upon the contractor's refusal to cooperate with the preaward survey team. Accord *Collins Mach. Corp.*, Comp. Gen. Dec. B-184428, 75-2 CPD ¶ 277. In both cases, the contracting officers relied upon the language in DAR 1-902 requiring prospective contractors to "affirmatively demonstrate" their responsibility and requiring a nonresponsibility determination if the information obtained does not "indicate clearly" that the firm is responsible. The language in DAR 1-902 has been replaced by similar language in FAR 9.103. In *Wallace & Wallace, Inc.*, Comp. Gen. Dec. B-209859.2, 83-2 CPD ¶ 142, the Comptroller General held that the contracting officer's determination that a bidder is not financially responsible may include consideration of the bidder's inability or unwillingness to fully disclose information relating to performance, particularly its corporate organization and contractual relationships.

2. Exercise of Discretion

The fundamental rule is that an offeror must be determined nonresponsible in "the absence of information clearly indicating that the prospective contractor is responsible," FAR 9.103(b). The application of this rule involves the exercise of discretion by the contracting officer. See 43 Comp. Gen. 228 (B-151834) (1963), stating at 230:

> Deciding a prospective contractor's probable ability to perform a contract to be awarded involves a forecast which must of necessity be a matter of judgment. Such judgment should of course be based on fact and reached in good faith; however, it is only proper that it be left largely to sound administrative discretion of the contracting officers involved who should be in the best position to assess responsibility, who must bear the major brunt of any difficulties experienced in obtaining required performance, and who must maintain day to day relations with the contractor on the Government's behalf. 39 Comp. Gen. 705, 711.

The Comptroller General has justified this view because reasonable persons can easily disagree on these issues, 37 Comp. Gen. 430 (B-132604) (1957); 49 Comp. Gen. 553 (B-168518) (1970); *Riocar*, Comp. Gen. Dec. B-180361, 74-1 CPD ¶ 282; *Triad Mechanical, Inc.*, Comp. Gen. Dec. B-258129, 94-2 CPD ¶ 224. The discretion of the contracting officer was illustrated in *S.A.F.E. Export*, Comp. Gen. Dec. B-208744, 83-1 CPD ¶ 437, where the fact that the protester was recently found responsible by other contracting officers did not show that the present contracting officer acted unreasonably in making a nonresponsibility determination. See also *MCI*

Constructors, Inc., Comp. Gen. Dec. B-240655, 90-2 CPD ¶ 431, stating that the fact that others could have reached different conclusions does not demonstrate the unreasonableness of a nonresponsibility determination. Similarly, an affirmative determination of responsibility in the face of unfavorable information concerning past performance may be a proper reflection of the business judgment of the contracting officer, *REDM Corp.*, Comp. Gen. Dec. B-211197, 83-1 CPD ¶ 428.

Since the criteria for determining responsibility are not readily susceptible to reasoned review and because they essentially involve business judgment, affirmative determinations of responsibility generally are not overturned absent fraud or bad faith. See *Hayes Int'l Corp. v. United States*, 7 Cl. Ct. 681 (1985); *Seaton Van Lines, Inc.*, Comp. Gen. Dec. B-217298, 85-1 CPD ¶ 26; *Clark Int'l Sec., Inc.*, Comp. Gen. Dec. B-216320, 84-2 CPD ¶ 369; and *Brandhurst Inc.*, Comp. Gen. Dec. B-214829, 84-1 CPD ¶ 669. In *Robert E. Dereckter of R.I., Inc. v. Goldschmidt*, 516 F. Supp. 1085 (D.R.I. 1981), the court held that to prove arbitrary and capricious conduct sufficient to permit a court to overturn an affirmative responsibility decision, the aggrieved bidder must demonstrate the lack of a reasonable or rational basis for the agency decision. The court further stated that either subjective bad faith on the part of the contracting officer or a clear and prejudicial violation of relevant statutes and regulations would be tantamount to finding a lack of a reasonable basis.

The standard for review of nonresponsibility determinations is similarly narrow. In *Keco Indus., Inc. v. United States*, 203 Ct. Cl. 566, 492 F.2d 1200 (1974), the court stated at 576:

> A party submitting a responsive and low bid may still be adjudged not "responsible," and thus denied the award. ASPR § 2.404-2(g); FPR § 1-2.404-2(e). Ordinarily, the contracting officer will have very wide discretion in making this determination (standards are set forth at ASPR § 1.900 et seq. and FPR § 1-1.1203), and thus a complaining bidder would normally have to demonstrate bad faith or lack of any reasonable basis in order to prevail.

A determination of nonresponsibility will not be disturbed unless the protester can demonstrate agency bad faith, or unless the record fails to provide a reasonable basis for the nonresponsibility determination, *System Dev. Corp.*, Comp. Gen. Dec. B-212624, 83-2 CPD ¶ 644; *Decision Sciences Corp.*, Comp. Gen. Dec. B-188454, 77-2 CPD ¶ 485; *United Office*

Machs., 56 Comp. Gen. 411, 77-1 CPD ¶ 195. In *Automated Datatron, Inc.*, 68 Comp. Gen. 89 (B-232048), 88-2 CPD ¶ 481, the Comptroller General held that in order to show bad faith, a protester must submit virtually irrefutable proof that procurement officials had a specific and malicious intent to harm. See *Trilon Educ. Corp. v. United States*, 217 Ct. Cl. 266, 578 F.2d 1356, *aff'd*, 217 Ct. Cl. 284 (1978), where the court held that the contracting officer improperly canceled a contract based upon information, obtained after award, that would have supported a determination of nonresponsibility. See also *Samuel A. Moore*, PSBCA 1063, 83-1 BCA ¶ 16,376. Compare *Aviation Enters., Inc. v. Orr*, 29 Cont. Cas. Fed. (CCF) ¶ 82,053 (D.D.C. 1981), *vacated,* 716 F.2d 1403 (D.C. Cir. 1983), where the court limited the contracting officer's broad discretion under circumstances it determined would impair the integrity of the competitive bidding process.

a. Adequacy and Timeliness of Information

Inherent in the exercise of discretion is that the decision be based upon adequate information, *Automated Datatron, Inc.*, 68 Comp. Gen. 89 (B-232048), 88-2 CPD ¶ 481. An affirmative determination of responsibility is improper if it is not based upon sufficient information, FAR 9.105-1(a). The amount of information needed may vary depending upon whether conflicting conclusions can be drawn. See 52 Comp. Gen. 977 (B-172061) (1973), where the Comptroller General stated at 981:

> Where, as here, conflicting information on the responsibility of a prospective contractor is a matter of record, a contracting officer has an information-gathering duty that cannot be avoided, and this duty has a direct relationship to the existence of reasonable doubts as to capacity. See 50 Comp. Gen. 281, 289 (1970).

Similarly, in *L.A. Anderson Constr. Co.*, GSBCA 6235, 82-1 BCA ¶ 15,507, the board found that the contracting officer's determination of nonresponsibility was "arbitrary, capricious or both" because, among other reasons, of his failure to seek information from third parties.

Infrequently, a contracting officer's determination has been found to be improper because it was not supported by the record. In *John F. Small & Co.*, Comp. Gen. Dec. B-207681.2, 82-2 CPD ¶ 505, the Comptroller General found a determination of nonresponsibility to be arbitrary. The contracting officer's findings of lack of integrity and poor performance were improperly based upon a technical conflict of interest that had occurred a year earlier and upon allegations of poor performance not supported by the record. A similar decision is *Mesa Constructors, P.S. Protest 83-39*, Sept. 20, 1983, *Unpub.*, where the contracting officer's finding that a bidder lacked tenacity and perseverance was not supported by substantial evidence. The contracting officer focused on the delay in the bidder's performance of one project but failed to consider evidence that it had satisfactorily performed another project.

All determinations dealing with responsibility must also be based on the most current information available, FAR 9.105-1(b)(1). In *Hayes Int'l Corp. v. United States*, 7 Cl. Ct. 681 (1985), the court held that reevaluation of responsibility in light of changed conditions is required, since responsibility determinations are to be based on the most recent information. Thus, in 51 Comp. Gen. 588 (B-174455) (1972), the Comptroller General held a nonresponsibility determination improper when based on a five-week-old preaward survey and when the bidder had submitted to the agency a statement specifying the action taken to correct a particular apparent deficiency. However, where a bidder submitted to the agency "only a vague statement that more complete and updated information" was available, the Comptroller General upheld a nonresponsibility determination based on a seven-week-old preaward survey, *Camel Mfg. Co.*, Comp. Gen. Dec. B-218473.3, 85-2 CPD ¶ 40. See *Orlotronics Corp.*, Comp. Gen. Dec. B-180467, 74-1 CPD ¶ 245, where a six-week-old preaward survey was found to be sufficient to support a determination of nonresponsibility, and *Firm Otto Einhaupl*, Comp. Gen. Dec. B-241553, 91-1 CPD ¶ 192, where unfavorable performance ratings all issued within eight months of the nonresponsibility determination were deemed sufficiently timely. See also *Construcciones Electromecanicas*, S.A., Comp. Gen. Dec. B-242656, 91-1 CPD ¶ 448 (agency's failure to consider a more current financial statement was determined not to affect the reasonableness of its nonresponsibility finding), and *Oliver Prods. Co.*, Comp. Gen. Dec. B-245762.2, 92-1 CPD ¶ 501 (affirmative responsibility finding was based upon recent preaward surveys and other current documents). In *Maywood Cab Co.*, Comp. Gen. Dec. B-187550, 77-1 CPD ¶ 288, the Comptroller General stated that a contracting officer's determination of nonresponsibility based on a termination for default of a similar contract nine months earlier was improper where no preaward survey had been conducted and the earlier deficiencies were easily correctable. In *Roarda, Inc.*, Comp. Gen. Dec. B-204524.5, 82-1 CPD ¶ 438, the Comptroller General held that while a determination of responsibility should not be made on the basis of "stale" information, a procuring agency is not required to delay award indefinitely while a bidder attempts to cure the causes for its being found nonresponsible. See also *Noble Pine Prods. Co.*, Comp. Gen. Dec. B-189420, 78-2 CPD ¶ 65, where award to another offeror was found proper after the agency waited and worked six months with the low bidder to see if it could meet the responsibility standards.

b. Recommendations to the Contracting Officer

The duty to consider information does not bind the contracting officer to follow recommendations included in the information, because it is the contracting officer's discretion that must be exercised. Thus, the contracting officer is not bound to follow the recommendation made by the preaward survey team but may arrive at the opposite conclusion based upon other evidence. See *Carl Weissman & Sons, Inc.*, Comp. Gen. Dec. B-190304, 78-1 CPD ¶ 140, upholding a nonresponsibility determination made prior to the contracting officer's receipt of a preaward survey recommending award, where the contracting officer had independently learned of performance and integrity problems. See also Comp. Gen. Dec. B-165562, Jan. 6, 1969, *Unpub.*; and *X-Tyal Int'l Corp.*, Comp. Gen. Dec. B-190101, 78-1 CPD ¶ 248. However, in 45 Comp. Gen. 4 (B-156520) (1965), the Comptroller General found that a determination of nonresponsibility was arbitrary where the preaward survey contained a recommendation that the firm be found responsible and there was no contrary evidence available.

The contracting officer must consider evidence both favorable and unfavorable to the prospective contractor in making a responsibility determination. In 52 Comp. Gen. 977 (B-172061) (1973), the Comptroller General objected to a nonresponsibility determination based "exclusively" on unfavorable data and a recommendation in a second preaward survey, where the contracting officer made no attempt to "rationalize" this conclusion with a favorable recommendation on responsibility contained in the initial preaward survey. See also *Decision Sciences Corp.*, Comp. Gen. Dec. B-188454, 77-2 CPD ¶ 485, where the Comptroller General held that when conflicting information relative to the responsibility of a prospective contractor is a matter of record, the contracting officer has the duty to resolve inconsistencies before making a reasoned judgment of responsibility. Compare *Hydromatics Int'l Corp.*, Comp. Gen. Dec. B-180669, 74-2 CPD ¶ 66, upholding a nonresponsibility determination based on an unfavorable recommendation on a second preaward survey despite a favorable recommendation on the initial survey, because the first survey did not include a review of the contractor's record of performance.

3. Contesting Nonresponsibility Determinations

The FAR and its predecessor regulations have had no requirement that offerors be notified before award of a determination of nonresponsibility. As a result, nonresponsible offerors in most instances have no opportunity to contest such a determination with the contracting officer.

There are, however, several situations where offerors are given an opportunity to contest a determination of nonresponsibility. The most important of these is a contracting officer's decision that a small business is nonresponsible. In such cases, the offeror must be notified of the decision and must be given the opportunity to apply to the SBA for a COC. This procedure is discussed in detail in Chapter 10.

GSAR 509.105-3 contains another exception to the general rule. This regulation requires the contracting officer to send written notice of nonresponsibility to all offerors that the agency has found to be nonresponsible. The notice must be sufficient to "provide the offeror with the opportunity, where applicable, to cure the factors that lead to the nonresponsibility determination." This requirement is unique among the present supplements to the FAR. However, contracting officers may voluntarily notify offerors of unfavorable responsibility information and provide an opportunity to submit additional information. See FAR 9.105-3(b) permitting discussion of preaward survey information with the prospective contractor. When there is any question as to the reliability, accuracy, or currency of the information, contracting officers are well advised to provide such an opportunity.

The courts have also ruled in several cases that an offeror is entitled to notice of a nonresponsibility determination and an opportunity to be heard. While these decisions have not been implemented in the procurement regulations, they would appear to be binding on contracting officers. They apply specifically to those instances where an offeror is found to be nonresponsible because of a lack of integrity. In these cases, the courts have reasoned that an offeror is entitled to protection of a constitutional "liberty interest." In the first case of this type, *Old Dominion Dairy Prods., Inc. v. Secretary of Defense*, 631 F.2d 953 (D.C. Cir. 1980), the plaintiff had been performing several contracts to provide dairy products at Government installations around the world, and this activity constituted nearly 100 percent of its business. Based upon an audit report that raised questions about Old Dominion's billing practices under these contracts, Old Dominion was found to be nonresponsible due to lack of integrity when it submitted the low bid on a milk supply contract (Okinawa contract). Shortly thereafter, Old Dominion was found to be nonresponsible in another procurement (Yokohama contract), based solely upon the audit report and the prior finding of nonresponsibility. It was not notified of the basis for the nonresponsibility determinations or given a chance to respond to the charges of improper bidding practices. Old Dominion argued that the communications between Government officials about the firm's lack of integrity had the effect of "stigmatizing" the firm and had such a negative impact upon the firm's business that it constituted a deprivation of a "liberty interest" without due process of law. The court agreed, noting that the nonresponsibility determination on the Yokohama contract had been based solely upon communications "through official Government channels" about the audit report and, further, that the nonresponsibility determination on the Okinawa contract established that Old Dominion had in effect been barred from receiving further Government contracts. The court stated at 964:

> [I]t cannot be disputed that the Government action in this case effectively foreclosed Old Dominion's freedom to take advantage of other Government employment opportunities, and barred ODDPI from all public employment. As illustrated by the Yokohama contract, the determination that Old Dominion lacked integrity would follow ODDPI in any attempt to procure Government work. This is particularly true in light of the Government's admission at oral argument that the case would be no different if eight contracts had been denied. As noted above, the Government action in this case had the effect of putting Old Dominion out of business. These actions were taken without any amount of due process. Despite the fact that numerous conversations were conducted between ODDPI and the Government, between the time the determination was made and the time the contracts were denied, at no point was it even mentioned that the integrity of Old Dominion was in issue. Old Dominion never received any notice of the charges against it. Needless to say, ODDPI was never afforded the slightest opportunity to respond to those charges.

Finding that a liberty interest had been invaded without due process, the court went on to discuss what kind of due process protection was necessary, stating at 968 that due process included the right to be notified

> of the specific charges concerning the contractor's alleged lack of integrity, so as to afford the contractor the opportunity to respond to and attempt to persuade the contracting officer, in whatever time is available, that the allegations are without merit. This requirement to give notice will impose ab-

> solutely no burden on the Government. Since a determination that a contractor lacks integrity may not be made without reference to specific charges or allegations, it will impose no burden on the Government to notify the contractor as to those charges. In so doing, the contractor will at least have the opportunity to explain its actions before adverse action is taken. In this way, a simple misunderstanding or mistake may be clarified before significant injury is done to both the Government and the contractor.
>
> We do not suggest that the Government was required to afford the contractor any type of a formal hearing. Government scheduling need not be delayed while the contractor puts on evidence. We simply hold that when a determination is made that a contractor lacks integrity and the Government has not acted to invoke formal suspension or debarment procedures, notice of the charges must be given to the contractor as soon as possible so that the contractor may utilize whatever opportunities are available to present its side of the story before adverse action is taken. This minimal requirement will not burden the Government and, indeed, is in the interest of both parties.

See also *Conset Corp. v. Community Servs. Admin.*, 655 F.2d 1291 (D.C. Cir. 1981), indicating that circulation of a memorandum alleging a "conflict of interest" and the subsequent refusal to approve a firm for a contract under a federal grant based upon this memo could constitute a deprivation of a liberty interest calling for due process safeguards, and *Related Indus., Inc. v. United States*, 2 Cl. Ct. 517 (1983), where the contracting officer stated that under no circumstances would he award any contract to the prospective contractor. The court held at 526:

> [T]he due process clauses of the fifth and fourteenth amendments require that a determination by governmental authority stigmatizing a person as so lacking in integrity that he is to be deprived of property or the liberty to enjoy rights which he would otherwise enjoy must be preceded by written notice of the facts upon which the charge is based and a reasonable opportunity to submit facts in response.

The issue of due process in nonresponsibility determinations has also been addressed by the Comptroller General. See 43 Comp. Gen. 140 (B-151269) (1963), where the Comptroller General stated at 141:

> There can be no doubt that your Administration, as a contracting agency, may base an initial determination of nonresponsibility upon the evidence of record without advising the bidder of the nature of the evidence and without affording the bidder an opportunity to explain or otherwise defend against

> such evidence. Although, as we stated in B-150791, B-150861, April 25, 1963, we believe it preferable that such opportunity be given. It is apparent that the continued refusal to award contracts to a particular company on the basis of nonresponsibility subsequent to the initial determination of nonresponsibility could operate to deny the bidder of the right to defend himself against the charge of nonresponsibility and to indefinitely deprive him of procurement awards from your administration.

The Comptroller General has pointed out that the *Old Dominion* rule does not apply to single determinations based on factors other than integrity, *Omneco, Inc.*, Comp. Gen. Dec. B-218343, 85-1 CPD ¶ 660 (lack of capability); *Lithographic Publications, Inc.*, Comp. Gen. Dec. B-217263, 85-1 CPD ¶ 357 (unsatisfactory past performance); *System Dev. Corp.*, Comp. Gen. Dec. B-212624, 83-2 CPD ¶ 644 (inability to meet delivery schedule); *United Aircraft & Turbine Corp.*, Comp. Gen. Dec. B-210710, 83-2 CPD ¶ 267 (lack of capacity and facilities). The Comptroller has also held that the *Old Dominion* rule does not apply to a single nonresponsibility determination based on lack of integrity, *Frank Cain & Sons, Inc.*, Comp. Gen. Dec. B-236893.2, 90-1 CPD ¶ 516.

A contracting officer's failure to seek SBA review of a nonresponsibility determination was not fatal where the SBA had refused to issue COCs under three similar procurements. The Comptroller General ruled that the SBA, in effect, ratified the determinations, *W.H. Smith Hardware Co.*, Comp. Gen. Dec. B-219654, 85-2 CPD ¶ 536. See also *Small Business Admin.*, Comp. Gen. Dec. B-219654.3, 86-1 CPD ¶ 420. It is not clear what position the Comptroller General will take on multiple, non-integrity-related determinations. When multiple determinations are involved, the matter may be considered a constructive debarment, which is discussed in the next section.

4. Prequalification

Prior to 1984, prequalification of offerors — the limiting of competitors to those firms that had been determined to be responsible prior to the solicitation — had been held by the Comptroller General to be a restriction on competition. See 53 Comp. Gen. 209 (B-178624) (1973), stating at 211:

> It is the cornerstone of the competitive system that bids and/or proposals be solicited in such a manner as to permit the maximum amount of competition consistent with the nature and extent of the services or items being pro-

> cured. Any establishment of presolicitation procedures for determining a prospective bidder's/offeror's responsibility whether relating to the manner of manufacture or capability to manufacture, is a restriction of full and free competition [the pre-CICA standard]. The question to be answered concerning the validity of the procedure is not whether it restricts competition per se, but whether it unduly restricts competition.
>
> * * *
>
> While determinations concerning a contractor's responsibility must be made before contract award, we have not ordinarily sanctioned such determinations prior to bid opening since to do so might foreclose the receipt of proposals from responsible contractors of whom the procurement agency is not aware. Thus, in the usual case, such prebid opening determinations have been considered as unduly restricting competition within the meaning of the statutes governing competition.

Following this reasoning, the Comptroller General ruled that prequalification procedures were improper in contracts for restoration of historic buildings, 52 Comp. Gen. 569 (B-176940) (1973); supply of aircraft parts, *D. Moody & Co.*, 55 Comp. Gen. 1 (B-180732), 75-2 CPD ¶ 1; and operation of a sonobuoy test program, *VAST, Inc.*, Comp. Gen. Dec. B-182844, 75-1 CPD ¶ 71. None of these cases directly addressed the issue of whether there was a compelling agency need for prequalification. In *Department of Agriculture's Use of Master Agreement*, 54 Comp. Gen. 606 (B-182337), 75-1 CPD ¶ 50, the Comptroller General ruled that mere administrative convenience was not a valid reason for the use of prequalification procedures. In that case, the agency had used a system of prequalifying the 10 "most qualified" companies for each type of consulting services being procured. The Comptroller General noted that this was considerably more restrictive than a system that prequalified *all qualified firms*. In *Department of Agriculture's Use of Master Agreements*, 56 Comp. Gen. 78 (B-182337), 76-2 CPD ¶ 390, the Comptroller General approved modified prequalification procedures, awarding a master agreement to *all qualified firms,* on the grounds that this would enhance competition by permitting more firms to compete than the alternative of awarding a single requirements contract for the consulting services.

In spite of the general view that prequalification was restrictive, a number of prequalification systems were approved as not being *unduly* restrictive. For example, prequalification of film and videotape producers was approved to permit more meaningful evaluation of offerors, *John Bransby*

Productions, Ltd., Comp. Gen. Dec. B-198360, 80-2 CPD ¶ 419, and prequalification of production lines for microcircuitry by the National Aeronautics and Space Administration was also approved on the basis that such prequalification was necessary to assure a continuous supply of these items under stringent quality requirements, 50 Comp. Gen. 542 (B-171597) (1971). The Comptroller General also permits the Navy to require contractors to have or be eligible for a Master Ship Repair Contract (MSRC), which is a certification of responsibility, in order to receive an award, *Carolina Drydocks, Inc.*, Comp. Gen. Dec. B-218186.2, 85-1 CPD ¶ 629; *Fairburn Marine Aviation*, Comp. Gen. Dec. B-187062, 76-2 CPD ¶ 523. The Comptroller General in *Carolina Drydocks* upheld a determination that the protester would not qualify for an MSRC. The determination was based on a survey revealing inadequate facilities and organization. Prequalification was also approved for use in the cut-make-and-trim industry where the agency demonstrated that reputable firms would not submit bids under normal sealed bidding conditions, Comp. Gen. Dec. B-135504, May 2, 1958, *Unpub.* See Lieblich, "Bidder Prequalifications: Theory in Search of Practice," 5 Pub. Cont. L.J. 32 (1972). The Comptroller General summarized this reasoning in *Rotair Indus.*, 58 Comp. Gen. 149 (B-190392), 78-2 CPD ¶ 410, as follows at 152-53:

> The general rule is that prequalification of offerors is an undue restriction on competition. . . . We have, however, tentatively approved special agency procedures which limit competition to offerors which have previously entered into certain types of agreements with the procuring activity. . . . The validity of any procedure which limits the extent of the competition depends upon whether the restriction serves a bona fide need of the Government. Such restrictions include those essential to assure procurement of a satisfactory end product, . . . or to determine the high level of quality and reliability assurance necessitated by the criticality of the product. . . . Use of restrictive procedures will not be sanctioned merely because obtaining maximum competition is administratively burdensome; rather, a showing that the exigencies of the procurement in question are such that the Government's interests would be adversely affected by the delay necessary to obtain maximum competition is required. . . . Basic characteristics of approved, albeit restrictive, procedures are that they function so that 1) no firm which is able to provide a satisfactory product is necessarily precluded from competing on procurements of that item, and 2) a firm may become eligible to compete at any time it demonstrates under applicable procedures that it is able to furnish an acceptable item which meets the Government's needs. . . . We have, therefore, found improper the use of restrictive procedures under which an offeror's disqualification would not be based on a

> finding that it could not provide a satisfactory product. . . . Moreover, even a prequalification system for which there may be valid reasons would be rendered invalid by a lack of regulation and procedures for its use.

The lack of fair prequalification procedures was the basis for sustaining a protest in *Algonquin Parts, Inc.*, 60 Comp. Gen. 361 (B-198464), 365, 81-1 CPD ¶ 270.

Prequalification was formally recognized by Congress in 1984, shortly after the passage of the CICA, with the enactment of 41 U.S.C. § 253c and 10 U.S.C. § 2319. These statutes provide that before enforcing any prequalification requirement with regard to a firm or a product, the head of the contracting agency must (1) demonstrate in writing a need for establishing the requirement; (2) specify all requirements that must be satisfied to become qualified in the least restrictive manner possible in the circumstances; (3) specify an estimate of the costs of testing and evaluation likely to be incurred by a potential offeror in order to become qualified; (4) ensure that prospective contractors are given a prompt opportunity to demonstrate their ability to meet the requirement; and (5) ensure that a potential offeror seeking qualification is promptly informed as to whether qualification is attained and, if not attained, is promptly furnished specific information explaining the outcome. These requirements are implemented in FAR Subpart 9.2. Neither the regulation nor the statutes contain any guidance as to the situations that can justify the necessity for qualification requirements.

These statutes may authorize greater use of prequalification procedures if the statutory procedures are strictly followed. See *Vac-Hyd Corp.*, 64 Comp. Gen. 658 (B-216840), 85-2 CPD ¶ 2, commenting that although the applicable prequalification statute was not yet applicable to the procurement being protested, it "establishes a framework for future procurements." In *Vac-Hyd*, the Comptroller General stated that the protested prequalification process for jet engine repair contracts was proper because it

> serves a bona fide need of the government — that is, it ensures a high level of maintenance on a critical aircraft part — yet it also allows nonapproved sources to submit proposals and become qualified.

However, the Comptroller General criticized the way the agency had implemented the prequalification procedure because it had not given the protester sufficient time to become qualified. Prequalification procedures have been approved for repair and alteration of nuclear ships, *Southwest*

Marine, Inc., Comp. Gen. Dec. B-225559, 87-1 CPD ¶ 431; production of films and videos, *Video Educ. Television*, Comp. Gen. Dec. B-248596, May 19, 1992, *Unpub.*; and ship dismantling under master ship repair contracts, *Stevens Technical Servs., Inc.*, Comp. Gen. Dec. B-250515.2, 93-1 CPD ¶ 385. In *Stevens*, however, the Comptroller General ruled that the protester was entitled to have the agency's determination that it was not a qualified contractor referred to the SBA in order to obtain a COC. The Comptroller General reached this conclusion because the factors evaluated by the agency were the normal responsibility factors and did not include any of the exceptions in FAR 9.202(d) such as special testing requirements or quality assurance demonstrations. See also *Digicomp Research Corp.*, Comp. Gen. Dec. B-262139, 95-2 CPD ¶ 246, holding that the prequalification statutes, including all of their procedural requirements, are applicable to procurements where the agency has justified limited competition rather than full and open competition.

II. DEBARMENT AND SUSPENSION

Debarment and suspension are drastic sanctions, precluding a company or individual from contracting with executive agencies. Debarments "exclude a contractor from Government contracting and Government-approved subcontracting for a reasonable, specified period," FAR 9.403, following notice and an opportunity to submit evidence, FAR 9.406-3. Suspensions are temporary exclusions "pending the completion of investigation or legal proceedings, when it has been determined that immediate action is necessary to protect the Government's interest," FAR 9.407-1(b)(1). Contractors "proposed for debarment" are also excluded temporarily, FAR 9.404(a). While this exclusion appears to relate only to contractors proposed for debarment for procurement violations, it has also been permitted in the case of a contractor proposed for debarment under the Davis-Bacon Act, *Salazar Constr. Co.*, 67 Comp. Gen. 115 (B-228071), 87-2 CPD ¶ 542.

There are two types of debarments: *procurement* and *inducement*. Procurement debarments and suspensions are carried out following the procedures in FAR Subpart 9.4, with the purpose of avoiding certain business risks associated with engaging in a contractual relationship with a firm. These risks relate directly to the procurement involved and include delivery of unacceptable products or services, waste of public funds, and contractor fraud. Thus, procurement debarment and suspension are the "appropriate means to effectuate" an express regulatory policy of ensuring "the Government's protection" by allowing contracting "with responsible contractors only," FAR 9.402(a)–(b). This basis for debarment and suspension involves behavior "of so serious or compelling a nature that it affects the present responsibility" of the contractor, FAR 9.406-2(c) and FAR 9.407-2(c). This type of sanction, referred to as "procurement," "nonresponsibility," or "administrative" debarment or suspension, is used by procuring agency officials as an integral part of the procurement process.

Inducement debarments have a different purpose — to induce contractors to perform Government contracts in ways that will further fundamental social and economic goals, such as equal employment opportunity, the payment of prescribed minimum wages, and environmental protection. Debarments based upon a contractor's failure to participate effectively in furtherance of these goals have been referred to as "inducement" or "statutory" debarments because they are generally based upon statutory provisions. The grounds and procedures for these debarments are set forth in a variety of regulations issued by agencies outside of the procurement process such as the DOL and the EPA. While the statutes, executive orders, and regulations creating and implementing these debarments are often imprecise in their terminology (using either "listing" or "ineligible," for example, apparently to mean the same thing) all sanctions that preclude contract awards for a specific period of time are encompassed in the discussion of debarment in this section (suspension is not used to induce contractors to carry out these goals). FAR 9.400(b) describes inducement debarments as "declarations of ineligibility" and states that it does not prescribe the policies or procedures applicable to them. However, they have the same effect as debarments issued by the procuring agencies.

All contractors that are "debarred, suspended, proposed for debarment or declared ineligible" are included on the List of Parties Excluded from Procurement Programs and Nonprocurement Programs, FAR 9.404(a). The list also includes all entities excluded from nonprocurement transactions, Exec. Order No. 12549, 51 Fed. Reg. 6370 (1986). This list is compiled by the General Services Administration (GSA) and is published monthly. An electronic version of the list is updated daily, FAR 9.404(d). This list is used by contracting officers in carrying out the policies regarding debarred and suspended contractors.

Procurement debarment or suspension decisions are made by agency heads or designees rather than contracting officers. FAR 9.403 defines these designees as the "debarring official" and the "suspending official." Debarment or suspension actions preclude contracting officers awarding contracts to debarred or suspended contractors, FAR 9.405(a). Thus, debarment and suspension override the responsibility determination process including the SBA COC procedure.

Procurement and inducement debarments are treated differently when contracts are awarded to debarred firms through Government inadvertence. Contracts awarded to firms debarred under statutes are void ab initio, *Paisner v. United States*, 138 Ct. Cl. 420, 150 F. Supp. 835 (1957), *cert. denied*, 355 U.S. 941 (1958), while contracts awarded to firms debarred pursuant to agency regulation are voidable at the option of the Government, *P.E.C. Corp.*, ASBCA 14241, 69-2 BCA ¶ 8056.

This section discusses the bases for debarment and suspension, the impact of these actions, and the procedures used to impose these sanctions.

A. *Exercise of Discretion*

Even though the purposes of procurement and inducement debarments are different, both require the exercise of discretion in making the debarment or suspension decision. Thus, even though a cause for debarment has been clearly demonstrated, the debarring official must consider such factors as the seriousness of the improper conduct, mitigating circumstances, and remedial actions that have been taken.

1. *Procurement Debarments or Suspensions*

Procurement debarments or suspensions are generally considered actions to be taken to protect the Government from future misconduct, as FAR 9.402(b) states:

> The serious nature of debarment and suspension requires that these sanctions be imposed only in the public interest for the Government's protection and not for purposes of punishment. Agencies shall impose debarment or suspension to protect the Government's interest and only for the causes and in accordance with the procedures set forth in this subpart.

Under this policy, the primary consideration in imposing these sanctions should be the offeror's "present and likely future responsibility" rather than the mere fact that a past offense has been committed, *Roemer v. Hoffman*,

419 F. Supp. 130 (D.D.C. 1976). While most circuit courts have rejected the contention that debarment is punitive, *Bae v. Shalala*, 44 F.3d 489 (7th. Cir. 1995); *United States v. Bizzell*, 921 F.2d 263 (10th Cir. 1990), one has stated that every debarment "is a form of punishment," *Fischer v. RTC*, 59 F.3d 1344 (D.C. Cir. 1995).

Conduct constituting grounds for debarment is sufficient to raise doubts concerning present responsibility. However, debarment officials must consider the seriousness of the contractor's conduct and any mitigating circumstances in deciding whether to impose debarment. FAR 9.406-1(a) provides:

> The existence of a cause for debarment, however, does not necessarily require that the contractor be debarred; the seriousness of the contractor's acts or omissions and any remedial measures or mitigating factors should be considered in making any debarment decision.

This regulatory policy establishes two key points. First, debarment is not to be an automatic consequence of a cause for debarment; rather, the debarment official is to exercise discretion. Second, it is appropriate not to debar in circumstances where the contractor's acts or omissions are not serious or where mitigating factors are strong. For example, the Housing and Urban Development (HUD) Board of Contract Appeals did not impose debarment where the contractor had rectified the misdeeds (making false statements to HUD) and produced letters indicating its present responsibility, *Lawrence C. Shank*, HUDBCA 82-724-D43, 83-1 BCA ¶ 16,439. In *Roemer*, the court remanded the debarment of a contractor based upon a conviction for accepting monies from a manufacturer's representative because the agency had not given a "hard look" to factors affecting the question of the firm's "present responsibility." The court discussed the kind of mitigating factors it considered relevant at 132:

> [T]he plaintiff has suggested a number of factors which appear to diminish the force of that conviction as an indication of Roemer's present responsibility. These factors touch on Roemer's character before the offense occurred, the circumstances surrounding the offense, the deterrent effect of the prior 29-month suspension, of the conviction, and of the payment to the government of $3,600 in restitution, the length of time which has passed since the offense and since the conviction, and Roemer's character since the offense and conviction.

In *Silverman v. Defense Logistics Agency*, 817 F. Supp. 846 (D.S.D. Cal. 1993), the court terminated a debarment based on a plea of guilty to a misdemeanor (with a fine of $250), because the debarring official had failed to consider the mitigating circumstance that the plea had been made to avoid an indictment for an offense of which the plaintiff did not believe he was guilty. The court also doubted if the agency was correct in finding the plaintiff not presently responsible when it had continued to contract with his company for six years after the alleged offense. In *C. & J. Harmon*, AGBCA 77-198, 79-1 BCA ¶ 13,705, the Agriculture board overturned a debarment based upon a firm's failure to satisfy contract requirements where the agency "mechanically" applied the debarment sanction without giving consideration to "surrounding" circumstances. Compare *Puma Co.*, GSBCA 6934-D, 83-1 BCA ¶ 16,349, and *Atlantic Chem. Co.*, GSBCA 5822-D, 80-2 BCA ¶ 14,801, where the board agreed that mitigating factors should be considered but deferred to the discretionary decision of the debarring official. See *David K. Alberta*, AGBCA 93-189-7, 94-2 BCA ¶ 26,923, where the board reduced the length of a contractor's debarment because its conviction for previous illegal activities did not demonstrate that it lacked present responsibility justifying continuation of the debarment. In *United States Testing Co.*, EPADEBAR 89-0021-00, Apr. 23, 1991, *Unpub.*, the board analogized the standard of "adequate evidence" in support of suspension to that of "probable cause" in support of a warrant. It noted that an adequate evidence showing need not rise to the level of that necessary for a successful criminal prosecution or a formal debarment.

The Department of Defense (DOD) has placed certain limitations on the debarring official's discretion when proposed debarments are based on felony convictions. The apparent purpose of these limitations is to ensure that in most cases debarments based on such crimes will be for a period of more than one year. DFARS 209.406-1(d) requires that any decision not to debar or to debar for a period of one year or less be made only where mitigating factors "demonstrate clearly to the debarring official's complete satisfaction" that the contractor has eliminated circumstances contributing to the improper act and has implemented effective remedial measures. DFARS 209.406-4(a) requires approval of higher authority in such cases.

2. Inducement Debarments

Statutes and other regulations providing for inducement debarments do not contain the clear statement of purpose included in FAR 9.402(b), but similar principles have been applied. Thus, under the Service Contract Act of 1965, 41 U.S.C. §§ 351–358, the Secretary of Labor is given discretion to refrain from debarring violators upon a finding of "unusual circumstances." See *White Glove Bldg. Maintenance, Inc. v. Hodgson*, 459 F.2d 175 (9th Cir. 1972), affirming the discretion of the Secretary not to debar violators under the pre-1972 version of the Act, which simply stated that contracts should not be awarded to violators "unless the Secretary otherwise recommends." In *Washington Moving & Storage Co.*, SCA-168, Mar. 12, 1974, the Secretary of Labor identified the factors to be considered in deciding whether "unusual circumstances" are present:

> Whether "unusual circumstances" are present in a case within the meaning of the Act must be determined on the basis of the facts and circumstances of the particular case. Some of the principal factors which must be considered in making this determination are whether there is a history of repeated violations of the Act; the nature, extent, and seriousness of past or present violations; whether the violations were willful, or the circumstances show there was culpable neglect to ascertain whether certain practices were in compliance, or culpable disregard of whether they were or not, or other culpable conduct (such as deliberate falsification of records); whether the respondent's liability turned on bona fide legal issues of doubtful certainty; whether the respondent has demonstrated good faith, cooperation in the resolution of issues, and a desire and intention to comply with the requirements of the Act; and the promptness with which employees were paid the sums determined to be due them. It is clear that the mere payment of sums found due employees after an administrative proceeding, coupled with an assurance of future compliance, is not in itself sufficient to constitute "unusual circumstances" warranting relief from the ineligible list sanction. It is also clear that a history of recurrent violations of identical nature, such as repeated violations of identical minimum wage or recordkeeping provisions, does not permit a finding of "unusual circumstances."

See also *Federal Food Serv., Inc. v. Donovan*, 658 F.2d 830 (D.C. Cir. 1981), where the D.C. Circuit reversed a decision of the Secretary of Labor debarring a contractor for "de minimis" underpayments under the Service Contract Act, concluding that the Secretary's failure to consider whether the facts warranted a finding of "unusual circumstances" constituted an "arbitrary" act. The court held that "use of debarment against innocent and petty violations was not intended."

The Davis-Bacon Act, 40 U.S.C. § 276a, authorizes the Comptroller General to debar firms that have "disregarded their obligations" under the

Act. The Comptroller General acts on recommendations of the Secretary of Labor and has held that he will exercise limited discretion — debarring firms for "substantial violations" but not for "technical violations," *Bryant Paint Contracting, Inc.*, 64 Comp. Gen. 549 (B-217337) (1985). Thus, in *Rams-Head Constr., Inc.*, Comp. Gen. Dec. B-222063, Aug. 13, 1986, *Unpub.*, the Comptroller General refused to follow the debarment recommendation of the Secretary of Labor because there was insufficient evidence of "willful" violation of the Act; the contractor's not paying workers was based on either inadvertence or a justified concern that they had improperly reported hours worked. Compare *Phoenix Paint Co.*, Comp. Gen. Dec. B-242728, Jan. 2, 1992, *Unpub.*, debarring a contractor that had falsified payroll records even though it claimed that the violation was inadvertent (based on bad advice), had cooperated in the investigation, and had made restitution to the workers. See also *Mashburn Elec. Co.*, Comp. Gen. Dec. B-189471, 78-1 CPD ¶ 277, holding that such mitigating circumstances will not preclude debarment when there have been substantial violations of the Act. The Secretary of Labor also exercises discretion in determining whether to recommend debarment of a firm to the Comptroller General.

Executive Order No. 11246, as amended, gives the Secretary of Labor the power to refrain from debarring firms not in compliance with contractual equal employment obligations, because Section 209 of the executive order states that the Secretary "may" provide for debarment of noncomplying firms. See also the implementing regulations, at 41 C.F.R. § 60-1.24(c)(2), indicating that the director of the OFCCP should seek to resolve instances of violations through "informal means," such as conciliation agreements, before invoking sanctions.

Clean Air Act and Federal Water Pollution Control Act regulations provide for the debarment of companies that violate the Acts, 40 C.F.R. § 32.110(d). However, an agency or the EPA may grant an exception to the regulations and permit a contractor to be eligible for a contract, 40 C.F.R. § 32.215.

B. Causes for Debarment

Statutes and regulations list a number of causes that, in the absence of mitigating or other circumstances, will support debarment.

1. Procurement Debarments

FAR 9.406-2 contains a list of acts that are sufficiently serious to warrant debarment proceedings — *conviction* of or *civil judgment* for offenses showing lack of business integrity, *serious* violation of contract terms, and other causes showing a lack of present responsibility.

a. Lack of Business Integrity

FAR 9.406-2(a) lists types of conduct that indicate a lack of business integrity:

> (1) Commission of fraud or a criminal offense in connection with (i) obtaining, (ii) attempting to obtain, or (iii) performing a public contract or subcontract;
>
> (2) Violation of Federal or State antitrust statutes relating to the submission of offers;
>
> (3) Commission of embezzlement, theft, forgery, bribery, falsification or destruction of records, making false statements, or receiving stolen property;
>
> (4) Intentionally affixing a label bearing a "Made in America" inscription (or any inscription having the same meaning) to a product sold in or shipped to the United States, when the product was not made in the United States; or
>
> (5) Commission of any other offense indicating a lack of business integrity or business honesty that seriously and directly affects the present responsibility of a Government contractor or subcontractor.

Most business integrity debarments have been based upon conviction of criminal offenses in dealing with the Federal Government. Included are such acts as bid rigging and mail fraud in violation of 18 U.S.C. § 1341, *John F. Azzarelli*, HUDBCA 82-671-D12, 82-1 BCA ¶ 15,677; bribing public officials in violation of 18 U.S.C. § 201, *Thomas P. Prickett,* GSBCA 6311-D, 82-1 BCA ¶ 15,736; perjury before a grand jury in connection with investigation of another Government contractor, *William A. Fuhrman*, HUDBCA 79-431-D46, Oct. 14, 1980, *Unpub.*; presenting fraudulent claims in violation of 18 U.S.C. § 287, *Ira F. Gassman*, GSBCA D-3, 79-1 BCA ¶ 13,771; submitting false income tax information in violation of 18 U.S.C.

§ 1001, *Clarence L. White*, HUDBCA 79-382-D32, July 12, 1979, *Unpub.* (later reinstated); failing to file a federal income tax return in violation of 26 U.S.C. § 7203, *Nathan A. Hicks*, HUDBCA 79-438-D51, Jan. 7, 1980, *Unpub.*; taking kickbacks in violation of 18 U.S.C. § 874, *Thomas M. Zakucia*, HUDBCA 79-348-D7, Dec. 3, 1979, *Unpub.*; failing to immediately notify the appropriate agency of an unlawful release of a hazardous substance as required by 42 U.S.C. § 9603(b), *John R. Fields*, EPADEBAR 93-0289-00, Nov. 13, 1995, *Unpub.*; and knowingly failing to dispose of asbestos contaminated material in accordance with the Clean Air Act, 42 U.S.C. § 7412, *Ellis "Ray" Kiser*, EPADEBAR 93-0253-01, Nov. 2, 1995, *Unpub.*

Occasionally, a debarment will be based upon convictions of criminal acts in connection with other governmental dealings. See, for example, *Lundin Constr. Co.*, DOT Fin. Asst. Pgm. Dkt. No. 2, Mar. 11, 1985, 43 Fed. Cont. Rep. 657 (bid rigging conviction in state court). The FAR gives no guidance as to what other offenses might indicate a lack of business integrity or honesty. It is not clear, for example, whether conviction for commission of a crime of violence might fall within this category.

FAR 9.403 contains the following broad definition of "conviction":

> "Conviction" means a judgment or conviction of a criminal offense by any court of competent jurisdiction, whether entered upon a verdict or a plea, and includes a conviction entered upon a plea of nolo contendere.

Generally, convictions establish the facts necessary to support a debarment without the submission of additional evidence to the debarring official. However, there is some disagreement on this rule in the case of a conviction based on a plea of nolo contendere. Despite the clearly stated intention of the Government in the above definition, the HUD Board of Contract Appeals has held that independent evidence must be introduced in a debarment proceeding to prove the alleged criminal acts when a conviction is based upon a plea of nolo contendere, *Milton H. Girard*, HUDBCA 82-730-D47, 83-1 BCA ¶ 16,544; *Willie J. Hope*, HUDBCA 80-521-D52, 81-1 BCA ¶ 15,045. See also *Sam Ligon*, HUDBCA 83-798-D29, Jan. 4, 1984, *Unpub.*, where independent evidence of the facts was used to prove the commission of the criminal act in lieu of the plea of nolo contendere. The EPA board has reached a similar conclusion. In *Mark P. Young*, EPADEBAR 93-00-25-03, Jan. 6, 1994, *Unpub.*, the board stated that "fundamental fairness requires that the respondents be provided an opportunity to complete their submission of information and arguments."

b. Serious Violation of Contract Terms

FAR 9.406-2 contains the following description of this category:

> (b)(1) The debarring official may debar a contractor, based upon a preponderance of the evidence, for —
>
> > (i) Violation of the terms of a Government contract or subcontract so serious as to justify debarment, such as —
> >
> > > (a) Willful failure to perform in accordance with the terms of one or more contracts; or
> > >
> > > (b) A history of failure to perform, or of unsatisfactory performance of, one or more contracts.

This provision appears to give considerable discretion to debarring officials — both as to the conduct that will justify debarment and the amount of evidence necessary to prove the conduct. Thus, failure to perform repairs within the time specified in the contract and failure to obtain a timely extension of the period of performance provided grounds for debarment in *Wilbert T. Alexander & Alexander Realty Co.*, HUDBCA 81-648-D47, 82-1 BCA ¶ 15,649. See also *Andrew Calhoun*, HUDBCA 82-676-D14, 82-2 BCA ¶ 15,921, where a contractor was debarred for unexcused failure to perform 17 contracts for purchase and repair of rental property. In *Mayer Co.*, HUDBCA 81-544-D1, 82-1 BCA ¶ 15,473, serious inadequacies in supervision and control by corporate managers of a property management firm, including the failure to make mortgage payments and obtain liability insurance, led to a one-year debarment from HUD programs. See also *Donald Schutte*, AGBCA 77-189, 79-2 BCA ¶ 13,902 (three-year debarment for installing a well within a building foundation in violation of state requirements the contractor knew or should have known); *Howard Bigelow*, HUDBCA 80-467-D15, 82-2 BCA ¶ 15,798 (three-year debarment for persistent failure to supervise employees and poor business practices leading to noncompliance with HUD regulations). However, in *Rudy Barnes & Rudy Barnes Co.*, HUDBCA 81-588-D15, 82-2 BCA ¶ 16,001, the contractor's failure to complete two HUD contracts was held insufficient where the contractor's difficulties arose in part from an excessive agency delay in awarding one of the contracts, and a history of failure on a large number of contracts was not involved.

FAR 9.406-2(b) also permits debarment, based on a preponderance of the evidence, for violations of the Drug-Free Workplace Act, intentionally mislabeling a product "Made in America," or commission of an unfair practice relating to foreign trade.

c. *Other Causes Showing Lack of Present Responsibility*

FAR 9.406-2(c) contains the following omnibus category of causes for debarment:

> Any other cause of so serious or compelling a nature that it affects the present responsibility of a Government contractor or subcontractor.

This provision, which gives extremely broad discretion to the debarring official, can relate either to performance or integrity issues. See, for example, *Robert Walker, Mark Walker, Alto Leasing Corp.*, GSBCA 7585-D, Mar. 11, 1985, *Unpub.*, where the board found that the contractor's misrepresentation to third parties of its contractual relationship with the GSA demonstrated absence of integrity and lack of present responsibility, and *Kiesel Co.*, EPADEBAR 94-0091-00, Aug. 28, 1995, *Unpub.*, where the charge was improper storage of one drum of hazardous waste (PCB) without required markings. In *Robinson v. Cheney*, 876 F.2d 152 (D.C. Cir. 1989), the court affirmed the debarment of a military clothing supplier that had been indicted for bribing a Government official and collusive bidding. The court found no abuse of discretion in finding that the contractor did not have present responsibility based on uncontroverted evidence supplied by one witness that had been granted immunity from criminal prosecution.

2. *Inducement Debarments*

Causes for inducement debarments are specifically enunciated in each statute or regulation covering the public policy at issue.

a. *Equal Employment Opportunity*

Section 209(a)(6) of Exec. Order No. 11246 empowers the Secretary of Labor to debar any firm that fails to comply with the terms of the Equal

Employment clause. FAR 22.809(c) incorporates this policy, specifically authorizing "[d]ebarment from future Government contracts" as a possible sanction for violation of these requirements.

This debarment sanction has been invoked against firms failing to submit acceptable affirmative action plans, *Ingersoll Milling Mfg. Co.*, 42 Fed. Reg. 41330 (1977); *Loffland Bros. Co.*, 44 Fed. Reg. 22835 (1979). In the latter debarment action, the director of OFCCP rejected the contractor's contention that its failure to submit an acceptable affirmative action plan should not be grounds for debarment since it had successfully completed performance of the specified contract work. Failure to meet the minority utilization goals in an affirmative action plan has also been used as the basis for debarment, *Anastasia Bros. Corp.*, 42 Fed. Reg. 42932 (1977). See also *Painting Corp. of Detroit, Inc.*, 43 Fed. Reg. 30919 (1978), where a debarment action was based in part upon a contractor's failure to make a good faith effort to meet minority utilization goals.

The debarment authority under Exec. Order No. 11246 has also been invoked for certain procedural violations. In *Uniroyal, Inc. v. Marshall*, 482 F. Supp. 364 (D.D.C. 1979), the court upheld an OFCCP debarment order based upon the contractor's failure to comply with regulations giving the Government access to employment records needed to conduct a discrimination investigation. In *First Ala. Bank of Montgomery v. Donovan*, 692 F.2d 714 (11th Cir. 1982), the court upheld a debarment based upon a refusal to cooperate in a compliance review under Exec. Order No. 11246. See also *OFCCP v. Prudential Ins. Co.*, 23 F.E.P. Cases 492 (DOL 1980), where debarment resulted from a contractor's failure to give OFCCP computer tapes containing detailed personnel, salary, and organizational material, and *Painting Corp. of Detroit, Inc.*, 43 Fed. Reg. 22836 (1978), where a debarment order was based in part upon a firm's refusal to supply workforce data.

b. Labor Statutes

While only the Davis-Bacon Act, 40 U.S.C. § 276a-2(a), the Walsh-Healey Act, 41 U.S.C. § 37, and the Service Contract Act, 41 U.S.C. § 354, specifically provide for debarment, the Secretary of Labor has adopted a rule authorizing debarment for violations of labor-related statutes that do not, in themselves, specifically authorize debarment, 29 C.F.R. § 5.1. The Contract Work Hours and Safety Standards Act, 40 U.S.C. § 328, is perhaps the most important among these. See *Copper Plumbing & Heating Co. v. Campbell*,

290 F.2d 368 (D.C. Cir. 1961), and *Janik Paving & Constr., Inc. v. Brock*, 828 F.2d 84 (2d Cir. 1987), sustaining the right of the Secretary of Labor to debar in the absence of statutory provisions. The standard for debarment under the Davis-Bacon Act is a showing of disregard of obligations to employees and subcontractors. The standard in the other labor statutes is aggravated or willful violation of the statutory requirements, 29 C.F.R. § 5.6(b)(1).

The DOL has also adopted the debarment sanction for violations of the Vietnam-Era Veterans Readjustment Assistance Act of 1974, 41 C.F.R. § 60-250.28(e), and the Rehabilitation Act of 1973, 41 C.F.R. § 60-741.28(e). See *Commonwealth Aluminum Corp.*, 59 Fed. Reg. 22178 (1994); *Blaine Constr. Co.*, 59 Fed. Reg. 17120 (1994); and *Layton Constr. Co.*, 58 Fed. Reg. 61922 (1993).

c. Buy American

41 U.S.C. § 10b(b) authorizes the head of a contracting agency to debar a contractor from receiving future construction contracts for violations of the Buy American Act in performing construction contracts. See FAR 25.204 implementing this statute.

Although Buy American Act requirements also apply to supply contracts, neither the statute nor the FAR explicitly provides for debarment for violations. However, it would appear that debarment in this area could be accomplished as a serious violation of contract terms under FAR 9.406-2(b).

d. Environmental Statutes

The EPA is directed to notify procuring agencies of facilities that are in violation of the Federal Water Pollution Control Act, 33 U.S.C. § 1368, and the Clean Air Act, 42 U.S.C. § 7606. These statutes prohibit agencies from awarding contracts to be performed at such facilities. These statutes are implemented by Exec. Order No. 11738, 38 Fed. Reg. 25161 (1973), and regulations set forth at 40 C.F.R. Part 32, which charge an EPA listing official with responsibility for "listing" those facilities found to be in violation of clean air and clean water standards, 40 C.F.R. § 32.110(d). The EPA regulation at 40 C.F.R. § 32.305 provides five causes other than conviction as grounds for listing of a facility: (i) civil adjudications for noncompliance, (ii) violation of a public agreement, (iii) knowingly doing business with a debarred, suspended, ineligible, or voluntarily excluded person, (iv) failure to pay a single substantial debt or multiple outstanding debts owed to an agency, excluding the IRS, and (v) any cause so serious or compelling a nature that affects the present responsibility of a person. The authority of the EPA to adopt these broader grounds for listing has been upheld in *United States v. Del Monte de Puerto Rico, Inc.*, 9 E.R.C. 1495 (D.P.R. 1976); *United States v. Interlake, Inc.*, 432 F. Supp. 987 (N.D. Ill. 1977); and *United States v. United States Steel*, 10 E.R.C. 1751 (N.D. Ill. 1977). In *ITT Rayonier Inc. v. United States*, 651 F.2d 343 (5th Cir. 1981), the plaintiff contended that these opinions did not examine the legislative history of the Federal Water Pollution Control Act, which would show that EPA was denied this authority. The court deemed the issue moot and did not rule on it.

These provisions are implemented in FAR Subpart 23.104, which gives the head of a procuring agency authority to exempt any contract for one year when it is "in the paramount interest of the United States."

C. *Causes for Suspension*

The causes for suspension are somewhat narrower than those for debarment. There are no inducement-type causes, and the procurement causes are limited to integrity issues and "serious and compelling" causes that affect the present responsibility of the contractor.

FAR 9.407-2 specifies the following causes for suspension:

> (a) The suspending official may suspend a contractor suspected, upon adequate evidence, of —
>
> > (1) Commission of fraud or a criminal offense in connection with (i) obtaining, (ii) attempting to obtain, or (iii) performing a public contract or subcontract;
> >
> > (2) Violation of Federal or State antitrust statutes relating to the submission of offers;
> >
> > (3) Commission of embezzlement, theft, forgery, bribery, falsification or destruction of records, making false statements, tax evasion, or receiving stolen property; or
> >
> > (4) Violations of the Drug-Free Workplace Act of 1988 (Public Law 100-690), as indicated by —

(i) Failure to comply with the requirements of the clause at 52.223-6, Drug-Free Workplace; or

(ii) Such a number of contractor employees convicted of violations of criminal drug statutes occurring in the workplace as to indicate that the contractor has failed to make a good faith effort to provide a drug-free workplace (see 23.504);

(5) Intentionally affixing a label bearing a "Made in America" inscription (or any inscription having the same meaning) to a product sold in or shipped to the United States, when the product was not made in the United States (see section 202 of the Defense Production Act (Pub L. 102-558));

(6) Commission of an unfair trade practice as defined in 9.403 (see section 201 of the Defense Production Act (Pub L. 102-558)); or

(7) Commission of any other offense indicating a lack of business integrity or business honesty that seriously and directly affects the present responsibility of a Government contractor or subcontractor.

(b) Indictment for any of the causes in paragraph (a) above constitutes adequate evidence for suspension.

(c) The suspending official may upon adequate evidence also suspend a contractor for any other cause of so serious or compelling a nature that it affects the present responsibility of a Government contractor or subcontractor.

Because suspensions may be ordered before conviction or judgment, the FAR requires that a suspension action be based upon "adequate evidence." FAR 9.407-1(b)(1) provides:

> In assessing the adequacy of the evidence, agencies should consider how much information is available, how credible it is given the circumstances, whether or not important allegations are corroborated, and what inferences can reasonably be drawn as a result. This assessment should include an examination of basic documents such as contracts, inspection reports, and correspondence.

FAR 9.407-2(b) indicates that an outstanding indictment for criminal conduct of the type identified in the regulations as grounds for debarment by itself constitutes "adequate evidence" of criminal conduct upon which a suspension may be based. See *James A. Merritt & Sons v. Marsh*, 791 F.2d 328 (4th Cir. 1986), and *Alexander & Alexander, Ltd.*, HUDBCA 82-727-D46, 83-1 BCA ¶ 16,229. However, the Department of Transportation has held an indictment to be a rebuttable presumption of adequate evidence, thereby shifting the burden of rebutting the adequacy of the evidence to the contractor, *Mainelli, DOT Fin. Asst. Prog.*, Dkt. No. 12, July 22, 1985. Adequate evidence has been likened to the probable cause necessary for an arrest, a search warrant, or a preliminary hearing, *Horne Bros., Inc. v. Laird*, 463 F.2d 1268 (D.C. Cir. 1972); *McCoy's Super Tread, Inc.*, GSBCA 7039-S, 83-2 BCA ¶ 16,751. In *Bio-Tech Research Labs., Inc.*, HUDBCA 94-C-154-D21, Sept. 28, 1995, *Unpub.*, the HUD board defined the "adequate evidence" needed to support a suspension as a "minimal standard of proof" and as "information sufficient to support the reasonable belief that a particular act or omission has occurred." See also *United States Testing Co.*, EPADEBAR 89-0021-00, Apr. 23, 1991, *Unpub.*

In *TS Generalbau GmbH*, Comp. Gen. Dec. B-246034, 92-1 CPD ¶ 189, the Comptroller General approved a suspension that was based upon "an ongoing investigation of the alleged bribery of Government employees." In *SDA Inc.*, Comp. Gen. Dec. B-253355, 93-2 CPD ¶ 132, approval was given to a suspension based upon "unrebutted, detailed allegations" of misconduct involving fraudulent real estate transactions and substantial sums of money that were contained in a civil complaint filed by the Resolution Trust Corporation (a Government entity). See also *BASIX, Inc.*, Comp. Gen. Dec. B-255613, 94-1 CPD ¶ 194, where the Comptroller General approved exclusion of a company from a competition because of its suspension based upon an indictment alleging conspiracy to commit securities fraud, bank fraud, and mail fraud.

D. *Scope and Duration*

Because debarments and suspensions are for the protection of the Government, debarring officials have considerable discretion in tailoring their scope and duration. In certain areas, however, the regulations limit this discretion but provide for waivers or exemptions. This section discusses the Government agencies that must respect debarment or suspension orders, the entities to which such orders apply, the duration of such orders, their effect during the procurement process, and the permissible activities of debarred or suspended entities.

1. Agencies Affected

FAR 9.406-1(c) and FAR 9.407-1(d) provide that debarments and suspensions are "effective throughout the executive branch" unless waived by the procuring agency. It is clear that these provisions make debarments and suspensions by any executive branch agency binding on all other executive branch agencies. FAR 9.404 requires the GSA to issue a current consolidated List of Parties Excluded from Federal Procurement and Nonprocurement Programs containing the names of all contractors that are debarred, suspended, proposed for debarment, or ineligible for contracts as well as all entities excluded from participation in nonprocurement transactions under the "Nonprocurement Common Rule." FAR 9.403 gives examples of these nonprocurement transactions as "grants, cooperative agreements, scholarships, fellowships, contracts of assistance, loans, loan guarantees, subsidies, insurance, payments for specified use and donation agreements." Since FAR 9.405 precludes contracting officers from awarding contracts to any entity on this list, this "common rule" bars contracting with a broad spectrum of entities that have been excluded from participation in federal programs.

It is clear from the statutes that most inducement-type debarments are binding throughout the Federal Government. Debarments ordered by the Secretary of Labor under the Walsh-Healey Act, 41 U.S.C. § 37, the Service Contract Act, 41 U.S.C. § 354, and debarments ordered by the Comptroller General for violations of the Davis-Bacon Act, 40 U.S.C. § 276a-2(a), are mandatory for all Government agencies. Listing of a facility by the EPA for violations of the Clean Air Act and the Federal Water Pollution Control Act generally precludes all Government agencies from making award of any contract to be performed at the listed facility. See 40 C.F.R. § 32.110(d). The construction provisions of the Buy American Act, 41 U.S.C. § 10b(b), also apply to all agencies of the Government. In contrast, equal employment debarments under Exec. Order No. 11246 apply only to executive branch agencies. All of these inducement debarments are included on the GSA consolidated list.

Procuring agencies generally are permitted to contract with debarred or suspended firms or individuals. FAR 9.406-1(c) and FAR 9.407-1(d) provide that such waivers may be made by the agency head or the agency head's designee and must be based on "compelling reasons." While these provisions appear to permit contracting in the face of all debarments, the only statutory provisions that explicitly grant such discretion to procuring activities are the Clean Air Act and the Federal Water Pollution Control Act. DFARS 209.405 contains the following guidance:

> Examples of compelling reasons are —
>
> (1) Only a listed contractor can provide the supplies or services;
>
> (2) Urgency requires contracting with a listed contractor;
>
> (3) The contractor and a department or agency have an agreement covering the same events which resulted in the listing and the agreement includes the department/agency decision not to debar or suspend the contractor; or
>
> (4) The national defense requires continued business dealings with the listed contractor.

2. *Entities Covered*

Debarment and suspension orders may apply to those entities sufficiently connected with the misconduct to make dealing with them detrimental to the interest of the Government. Under FAR 9.406-1(a) and FAR 9.407-1(a), "contractors" are debarred or suspended. FAR 9.403 contains the following definition:

> "Contractor," as used in this Subpart, means any individual or other legal entity that—
>
> (a) Directly or indirectly (*e.g.*, through an affiliate), submits offers for or is awarded, or reasonably may be expected to submit offers for or be awarded, a Government contract, including a contract for carriage under Government or commercial bills of lading, or a subcontract under a Government contract; or
>
> (b) Conducts business, or reasonably may be expected to conduct business, with the Government as an agent or representative of another contractor.

This definition includes affiliates of a company as well as its officers and employees. It also reaches companies for which tainted officers or employees perform work. The following discussion treats business entities separately from officers and employees.

a. Business Entities

The Government deals with four types of business entities: corporations, partnerships, sole proprietorships, and joint ventures. An entity may be debarred or suspended based on the acts of its own employees or based upon its association with entities or individuals that have committed improper acts. An entity may also escape debarment or suspension if it purges itself by severing its relationship with offending individuals or entities.

FAR 9.406-1(b) deals with the breadth of the debarment with respect to business entities and permits the debarring official to include "affiliates" within the scope of the debarment:

> Debarment constitutes debarment of all divisions or other organizational elements of the contractor, unless the debarment decision is limited by its terms to specific divisions, organizational elements, or commodities. The debarring official may extend the debarment decision to include any affiliates of the contractor if they are (1) specifically named and (2) given written notice of the proposed debarment and an opportunity to respond (see 9.406-3(c)).

FAR 9.403 contains the following definition of "affiliates":

> Business concerns, organizations, or individuals are affiliates of each other if, directly or indirectly, (a) either one controls or has the power to control the other, or (b) a third party controls or has the power to control both.

One of the issues raised by these provisions is whether an entire entity should be debarred or suspended. Although FAR 9.406-1 gives broad discretion, it has been very rare for a debarment or suspension to cover less than the entire business entity. However, debarments under the Clean Air Act or the Federal Water Pollution Control Act apply only to particular noncomplying "facilities." For a case narrowing the scope of a procurement debarment, see *Peter Kiewit & Sons' Co. v. U.S. Army Corps of Eng'rs*, 534 F. Supp. 1139 (D.D.C. 1982), *rev'd on other grounds*, 714 F.2d 163 (D.C. Cir. 1983), where the district court held that the contractor "should not be prevented from doing business with the United States." The court reasoned that criminal acts that had been committed by two small subsidiaries and one small division were not sufficient to exclude the balance of the organization from being awarded contracts for different types of work, given that the contractor had discharged the employees responsible for the illegal acts. The circuit did not rule on this issue but reversed on the grounds that the district court should not have taken the case until the administrative process had been completed. Compare *Dowling Group v. Williams*, Civ. Action No. 82-1775 (D.D.C. 1982), permitting debarment of all entities of a small company and agreeing with the debarring official's distinction of the *Kiewit* case on the ground that *Kiewit* was "a large corporation with over 11,000 employees."

FAR 9.406-1(b) also gives broad discretion to include affiliates in a debarment order if notice is given. Debarment of affiliates is proper to prevent circumvention of the sanctions by operating through separate entities. Normally, however, an affiliate would not be debarred if it was not connected in any way to the entity that committed the improper act. See 51 Comp. Gen. 65 (B-173016) (1971), affirming an agency decision not to debar an affiliate because there could have been valid reasons for the creation of the affiliate other than avoidance of the debarment. See also *Roy C. Markey*, HUDBCA 82-712-D33, 83-2 BCA ¶ 16,688, affirming the decision to debar two companies as long as they were controlled by an individual who had committed improper acts in his capacity as a sole proprietor. Even though there was no proof that they had participated in the improper acts, it was clear that these affiliates could be used to circumvent the debarment were they not included within the scope of it.

Affiliation depends on control, and control is a question of fact to be determined by the debarment official. For example, in *Alexandria Printing & Photo Servs.*, EBCA 285-3-83(D), 83-2 BCA ¶ 16,570, the appellant company argued that it was not an affiliate because it was a sole proprietorship under the control of Mary P., who was legally separated from Earl P. and who had filed for divorce. However, in looking at all the facts, including the facts that the wife was employed as a full-time cashier at another store, was not an experienced printer, and was subsidized in her business operations by the husband, the board found a factual basis for debarment of the appellant company on the ground of affiliation. See also *Michael C. Kantrow*, HUDBCA 95-A-109-D7, Aug. 2, 1995, *Unpub.*, finding affiliation where an individual who pleaded guilty to causing submission of a false change order was part owner of and exercised management authority over the affiliated company; *Detek, Inc.*, Comp. Gen. Dec. B-261678, 95-2 CPD ¶ 177, where a finding of affiliation was reached where one entity was purchased by a key employer of the other, both shared several key management employees, and they planned to engage in a prime/subcontractor relationship; and *ABL Indus., Inc.*, Comp. Gen. Dec. B-207335, 82-2 CPD ¶ 119, where affiliation was found when the owner of a suspended firm transferred ownership of another firm to his wife, and that second firm used the key employees and facilities of the suspended firm. Compare *Provident Maintenance Servs., Inc.*, GSBCA 7640-D, Apr. 23, 1985, *Unpub.*, where no affiliation was found even though there was friendship, joint use of office space, and previous business relationships. The Comptroller General has also upheld an agency determination that a debarred company's wholly owned subsidiary was ineligible for award where the debarred company created the affiliate after the agency debarred the parent company, *Solid Waste Servs., Inc.*, Comp. Gen. Dec. B-218445, 85-1 CPD ¶ 703.

FAR 9.406-5(c) provides that entities participating in a joint venture may be debarred for acts of the venture:

> The fraudulent, criminal, or other seriously improper conduct of one contractor participating in a joint venture or similar arrangement may be imputed to other participating contractors if the conduct occurred for or on behalf of the joint venture or similar arrangement, or with the knowledge, approval, or acquiescence of these contractors. Acceptance of the benefits derived from the conduct shall be evidence of such knowledge, approval, or acquiescence.

Generally, misconduct of an officer or employee of a business entity may result in the debarment or suspension of the entity. FAR 9.406-5(a) recognizes this fact but implicitly recognizes that there may be circumstances when such acts should not be imputed to the business entity:

> The fraudulent, criminal, or other seriously improper conduct of any officer, director, shareholder, partner, employee or other individual associated with a contractor may be imputed to the contractor when the conduct occurred in connection with the individual's performance of duties for or on behalf of the contractor, or with the contractor's knowledge, approval, or acquiescence. The contractor's acceptance of the benefits derived from the conduct shall be evidence of such knowledge, approval, or acquiescence.

Thus, a debarment would be improper if an employee's misconduct was totally outside the knowledge or control of the business entity.

Where the employee is an officer of the entity or exercises significant control over the entity, the acts are generally imputed to the entity. See, for example, *Robinson v. Cheney*, 876 F.2d 152 (D.C. Cir. 1989), where a company was debarred for acts of its president even though the other employees knew nothing of the acts. See also *Mikulec v. Department of the Air Force*, Civ. Action No. 84-2248 (D.D.C. 1985) (president at time of misconduct and "corporate official" at time of suspension); *Park Poly Bag Corp.*, GSBCA 5744-S, 80-2 BCA ¶ 14,600 (president, vice president, and sole shareholders); *Arun Gaind, & Gaind Assocs., Inc.*, EPADEBAR 92-0007-01, Mar. 3, 1995, *Unpub.* (president at all times); and *Hy-Tex Marketing, Inc.*, EPADEBAR 93-0217-04, Nov. 22, 1994, *Unpub.* (president, principal stockholder, and sole managerial employee). In *Joseph E. Berrigan & Berrigan, Daniel, Litchfield & Olsen*, HUDBCA 84-894-D46, July 12, 1985, *Unpub.*, a lawyer was debarred but his law firm was not because there was no evidence that the law firm was aware of the lawyer's culpable conduct or that the lawyer controlled the firm. Business entities have also been debarred because they have associated with persons who were debarred or guilty of prior misconduct. In such cases, the entity is described as an affiliate and control is required. See, for example, *Thomas P. Prickett,* GSBCA 6311-D, 82-1 BCA ¶ 15,736, where a company was debarred based on the previous debarment of its sole shareholder. In *Jerry A. Costacos*, GSBCA 7547-D, Apr. 9, 1985, *Unpub.*, a company escaped debarment by showing that its debarred vice president for operations did not "control" the company because he was "walled off" from involvement in Government contracts. Compare *Robinson*, where the court sustained debarment of a company where the president and sole stockholder placed the company in trust after being indicted for alleged criminal conduct. The court agreed that, in such a situation, there was not a sufficient divesting of interest.

b. Individuals

The FAR does not directly discuss the debarment of individuals, but FAR 9.403 includes within the definition of "contractor" "any individual" who "[c]onducts business, or reasonably may be expected to conduct business, with the Government as an agent or representative of another contractor." In addition, FAR 9.406-5(b) permits imputation of acts of a contractor to any employee connected to the misconduct:

> The fraudulent, criminal, or other seriously improper conduct of a contractor may be imputed to any officer, director, shareholder, partner, employee, or other individual associated with the contractor who participated in, knew of, or had reason to know of the contractor's conduct.

Thus, not being a contractor employee does not shield an individual from being debarred from future Government contracts.

The debarment of an individual operating as a sole proprietorship was accomplished under the FPR pursuant to regulations that permitted debarment of individuals. See *Dimitrious A. Mavrophilipos*, GSBCA D-5, 80-1 BCA ¶ 14,446. Under HUD regulations, individuals operating as a sole proprietorship were debarred as contractors, *Robert C. Gennaro*, HUDBCA 81-632-D37, 83-1 BCA ¶ 16,141. This result also could be proper under the current FAR. The confusion of terminology in this area is illustrated in *Charles Kirkland*, HUDBCA 80-541-D60, 82-1 BCA ¶ 15,743, where an individual was debarred for improper conduct, and a sole proprietorship and a company through which he dealt were also debarred as affiliates. See also *Edward M. Alba*, HUDBCA 83-820-D39, 84-2 BCA ¶ 17,242. In *Harold Estes*, HUDBCA 83-793-D24, 84-2 BCA ¶ 17,241, an individual was debarred for illegal acts as a subcontractor and his sole proprietorship was debarred as an affiliate.

When an individual has not been operating as a sole proprietorship but is an employee of a business entity, debarment has been based on several different theories. Under the HUD regulations, 24 C.F.R. § 24.105, employees have been debarred under a broad definition of "contractor." See *Marvin B. Awaya*, HUDBCA 84-834-D6, 84-2 BCA ¶ 17,320, where a housing program analyst came within the definition of contractor because he administered funds; *Nathaniel H. Armstrong, John A. Breland & Bo-rite Co.*, HUDBCA 82-687-D20, 84-3 BCA ¶ 17,634, where officers, directors, and part owners of a subcontractor came within the definition of contractor because they were indirect recipients of HUD funds; and *John F. Azzarelli*, HUDBCA 82-671-D12, 82-1 BCA ¶ 15,677, where a vice president of a company was debarred for illegal acts because he was a "contractor." See also *Facchiano Constr. Co. v. Department of Labor*, 987 F.2d 206 (3d Cir. 1993), where the court concluded that the DOL had the authority to debar "responsible officers" of a contractor but not officers who did not know of the conduct; *Janik Paving & Constr., Inc. v. Brock*, 828 F.2d 84 (2d Cir. 1987), where the court affirmed the debarment of a company's president without discussing his connection to the misconduct; and *TS Generalbau GmbH*, Comp. Gen. Dec. B-246034, 92-1 CPD ¶ 189, where the Comptroller General approved a DOD suspension of "an individual authorized to sign contracts" by imputing the contractor's misconduct (bribery) to the individual. Compare *John R. Morris*, HUDBCA 84-836-D8, 84-2 BCA ¶ 17,245, where the Government did not prove that a maintenance man was a contractor. Under the FPR, which provided for debarment of individuals, the corporation's president and vice president who participated in the illegal conduct were suspended, *Park Poly Bag Corp.*, GSBCA 5744-S, 80-2 BCA ¶ 14,600.

Under the FAR standard, individuals can be debarred if they "participated in, knew of or had reason to know" of the contractor's misconduct. See *Novicki v. Cook*, 946 F.2d 938 (D.C. Cir. 1991), where the court vacated the debarment of the president and CEO of a contractor because there was inadequate proof of "reason to know" of the misconduct, and the agency may have erroneously applied a strict liability or "should have known" standard to the individual's conduct. See also *Caiola v. Carroll*, 851 F.2d 395 (D.C. Cir. 1988), where the court overturned a debarment of two company officers that was based on the "reason to know" standard when the agency could not explain why it had terminated debarment proceedings against a third officer, seemingly in similar circumstances. Compare *Kisser v. Cisneros*, 14 F.3d 615 (D.C. Cir. 1994), where the court sustained the debarment of an executive vice president who had participated in the alleged misconduct. The court rejected the argument that the debarring agency was required to explain why all officers and employees who participated in the conduct were not similarly debarred. See also *Taylor v. Marsh*, Civ. Action No. 81-2643 (D.D.C. 1982), where an officer and 50 percent shareholder was debarred under the DAR based upon her own negligence, and *Mikulec v. Department of the Air Force*, Civ. Action No. 84-2248 (D.D.C. 1985), where the president of a company was suspended following an indictment.

3. *Duration of Orders*

Debarment orders are normally for a specified fixed period of time while suspension orders are for an indefinite but limited period.

a. Debarment Orders

FAR 9.406-4(a) contains the following provision concerning the duration of procurement debarment:

> (1) Debarment shall be for a period commensurate with the seriousness of the cause(s). Generally, debarment should not exceed 3 years, except that —

> (i) Debarment for violation of the provisions of the Drug-Free Workplace Act of 1988 (see 23.506) may be for a period not to exceed 5 years; and
>
> (ii) If suspension precedes a debarment, the suspension period shall be considered in determining the debarment period.

FAR 9.406-1(a) requires the debarring official to consider "the seriousness of the contractor's acts or omissions and any remedial measures or mitigating factors" in making the debarment decision. These issues are also considered in determining the period of a debarment. See *Thomas M. Zakucia*, HUDBCA 79-348-D7, Dec. 3, 1979, *Unpub.*, where a proposed debarment of five years for taking illegal kickbacks was reduced to 30 months where there was no evidence that the individual had acted improperly in the intervening six years since the conviction, and he was remorseful for his criminal activities. Similarly, in *Normal D. Wilhelm*, HUDBCA 82-679-D15, 82-2 BCA ¶ 16,002, the board reduced a debarment period based on a corporate president's conviction for bid rigging because it was convinced he had partially reformed. A "nominal period of debarment" was still necessary, however, because the president did not seem to understand why collusive bidding was illegal, because he did not sufficiently alter the operations of the firm, and because he retained individuals formerly involved in the crime. In *Bruce E. Betterton*, EPADEBAR 93-0217-02, Apr. 25, 1995, *Unpub.*, mitigating circumstances, including lesser culpability for the offenses and cooperation with investigating officials, persuaded the board to reduce the debarment to a two-year period including the suspension period. In *Ellis "Ray" Kiser*, EPADEBAR 93-0253-01, Nov. 2, 1995, *Unpub.*, a three-year debarment of the CEO and owner of a contractor that had improperly disposed of asbestos was reduced to two years after considering the owner's one-year preliminary exclusion under the FAR, the seriousness of the misconduct, the fact that the present facility contained no asbestos, and information presented as mitigating factors and remedial measures. See also *James J. Wannamacher*, HUDBCA 81-585-D14, 82-1 BCA ¶ 15,474, where the board stated that the contractor's conviction for submission of a false certification, based on a plea of nolo contendere, along with extensive evidence showing the violation to be of a continuing pattern and practice, would normally warrant the imposition of a substantial period of debarment. However, only a one-year debarment was imposed because the term was all the agency had sought. In *Shane Meat Co. v. Department of Defense*, 800 F.2d 334 (3d Cir. 1986), the court affirmed a three-year debarment based on the failure of the contractor to ensure that delivery of defective products would not be repeated by changing its senior officers. The court held that the debarring official was reasonable in reaching this conclusion even though the contractor had a record of satisfactory performance for the five years subsequent to the illegal conduct. In *Sidney Spiegal*, HUDBCA 91-5908, 93-1 BCA ¶ 25,294, the board held that the fact that bid rigging was a regular practice in public real estate auctions in the District of Columbia did not excuse or mitigate the practice and should not be used to reduce an individual's three-year debarment.

Debarments for periods longer than three years have been affirmed when the causes for the actions have been egregious. See *Coccia v. Defense Logistics Agency*, Civ. Action No. 89-6544 (D.E.D. Pa. 1992), where the court affirmed the DLA's debarment of an individual for 15 years because, acting as a procurement official, he had seriously corrupted the procurement system by taking bribes in exchange for procurement information. The court agreed with the judgment of the debarring official that the evidence did not demonstrate that the individual could deal honestly with the Government within the 15-year period. It appears, however, that long debarments will be carefully scrutinized. See, for example, *Lake Doctors, Inc.*, EPADEBAR 93-0133-00, Aug. 8, 1995, *Unpub.*, where a five-year debarment for using pesticides in a manner inconsistent with its labeling was reduced to a four-year period with full credit for the period of suspension, due to the presence of mitigating and remedial measures. See also *William R. Absalom*, HUDBCA 82-746-D45, 83-1 BCA ¶ 16,390, where, even though the appellant's mitigating factors were unpersuasive, the board reduced the period of debarment from five to three years because the Government's evidence did not support the longer period for the contractor's false statements made to HUD.

The FAR does not specifically address the permissibility of debarments for indefinite periods. However, under HUD regulations, a few such debarments have been ordered in exceptional cases. In *Don L. Blankenship*, HUDBCA 81-547-D3, Mar. 27, 1981, *Unpub.*, the board imposed debarment for an indefinite period of time because the firm willfully violated the terms of a prior debarment settlement agreement; in 1993, the board declined to reinstate Blankenship because his conduct "remains unexplained, uncorrected and unrepented," *Don Louis Blankenship*, HUDBCA 93-C-D15, June 29, 1993, *Unpub.* In *Charles Kirkland*, HUDBCA 80-541-D60, 82-1 BCA ¶ 15,743, an individual who procured two false certifications, breached his fiduciary obligations as a broker to the parties in a HUD-assisted transaction, and willfully violated HUD regulations and procedures displayed a course of conduct "so fraught with improprieties" that debarment "for an indefinite period of not less than five years" was imposed. Some years later, in *Charles Kirkland*, HUDBCA 90-5285-D57, Jan. 14, 1991, *Unpub.*, the HUD board, after comparing Kirkland's sanctions to those imposed for similar violations, granted his request for reinstatement and ordered the debarment terminated immediately. See also *Charles Howell*, HUDBCA 85-933-D17, Sept. 13, 1985, *Unpub.*, where the board reversed an indefinite debarment imposed five-and-one-half years earlier, on the basis of newly discovered material evidence that the conduct that gave rise to the debarment was neither egregious nor willful. In *Joseph A. Strauss, The Phoenix Assocs., Ltd.*, HUDBCA 95-G-113-D11, May 19, 1995, *Unpub.*, the board considered an imposing list of mitigating factors and changed an indefinite debarment to a five-year debarment with credit given for the period of suspension; in *Philip D. Winn*, HUDBCA 95-G-108-D6, June 9, 1995, *Unpub.*, an indefinite debarment was changed to a four-year debarment.

FAR 9.406-4(a)(2) provides that debarring officials shall give consideration to a preceding period of suspension in determining the period of debarment. Under prior regulations, the board, in *Park Poly Bag Corp.*, GSBCA 5826-D, Mar. 9, 1981, *Unpub.*, held that setting a debarment period without considering a preceding period of suspension was arbitrary and capricious. See *Thomas P. Prickett*, GSBCA 6311-D, 82-1 BCA ¶ 15,736, remanding a case to the debarring official to consider adjusting the debarment period. Although the HUD regulations do not contain such a provision, the HUD Board of Contract Appeals has followed this practice, *Curtis Jerome Kennedy*, HUDBCA 78-319-D49, 79-2 BCA ¶ 13,896; *Thomas M. Zakucia*, HUDBCA 79-348-D7, Dec. 3, 1979, *Unpub.* See also *Bradley Shane Hartman*, HUDBCA 93-0133-10, Oct. 11, 1995, *Unpub.*, where the board, after considering the record, agreed to a two-and-one-half-year debarment "with full credit for the period of suspension." Compare, however, *Andrew Nuccitelli*, HUDBCA 78-321-D51, July 17, 1979, *Unpub.*, where the board refused to reduce the debarment period by the period of suspension because of the particularly egregious nature of the contractor's activities and the absence of mitigating factors. In *Arun Gaind, & Gaind Assocs., Inc.*, EPADEBAR 92-0007-01, Mar. 3, 1995, *Unpub.*, the board, after considering limited mitigating factors and finding that the original violations were egregious, sustained the refusal to "give credit" for Gaind's 33-month suspension in imposing a three-year debarment.

The duration of inducement debarments is controlled primarily by the statute or regulations establishing the debarment. For example, the Davis-Bacon Act specifies a three-year period of debarment for firms found to be in violation of the statute, 40 U.S.C. § 276a-2(a). While the Walsh-Healey Act, 41 U.S.C. § 37, and the Service Contract Act of 1965, 41 U.S.C. § 354, also specify a three-year debarment period, the Secretary of Labor has discretion to impose a shorter-term or no debarment. The Buy American Act, 41 U.S.C. 10b(6), also specifies a three-year period. In *J.B. Kies Constr. Co.*, Comp. Gen. Dec. B-250797, 93-1 CPD ¶ 127, the company was debarred for five and one-half years because the debarment was effective for three years after date of publication of the list of ineligible firms, and the company's name was not included on the list until two and one-half years after it was debarred.

In contrast, facilities listed for noncompliance with the Federal Water Pollution Control Act and the Clear Air Act will remain on the list until compliance is demonstrated. EPA regulations at 40 C.F.R. § 32.321 state that a written petition to reinstate the eligibility of a facility may be submitted to the EPA debarring official. The petitioner bears the burden of providing sufficient information and documentation to establish, by a preponderance of the evidence, that the condition giving rise to the ineligibility finding has been corrected.

Section 209(a)(6) of Exec. Order No. 11246 also provides that the Secretary of Labor may debar a firm "until such contractor has satisfied the Secretary of Labor that such contractor has established and will carry out personnel and employment policies in compliance with the provisions of this order." Implementing regulations under the order provide that a firm declared ineligible may be entitled to reinstatement upon submitting proof that "it has established and will carry out employment practices in compliance with the equal opportunity clause," 41 C.F.R. § 60-1.31.

FAR 9.406-4(b) and (c) offer guidance on reduction or extension of procurement debarments after the order has been issued. Under these regulations, extension of debarments must be based on new evidence and not "solely on the basis of the facts and circumstances upon which the initial debarment action was based." In *S.A.F.E. Export Corp.*, 65 Comp. Gen. 530 (B-222308), 86-1 CPD ¶ 413, the Comptroller General permitted the extension of an earlier debarment based on continued lack of integrity by the company in subsequent business dealings. Reduction of the duration of a debarment at the request of a contractor may be based on new information or a change in circumstances.

Debarring officials may not have as much discretion to reduce the duration of all inducement debarments. See *Mashburn Elec. Co.*, Comp. Gen. Dec. B-189471, 78-1 CPD ¶ 277, where the Comptroller General stated that while the duration of debarments under the Walsh-Healey Act and Service Contract Act could be reduced, there was no similar authority to reduce the duration of a debarment under the Davis-Bacon Act. See 29 C.F.R. § 5.12(c), stating that firms shall be removed from the ineligible bidders list upon demonstrating current responsibility to comply with the labor standards of the applicable statutes.

b. Suspension Orders

FAR 9.407-4 gives specific guidance on the duration of suspension orders:

> (a) Suspension shall be for a temporary period pending the completion of investigation and any ensuing legal proceedings, unless sooner terminated by the suspending official or as provided in this subsection.
>
> (b) If legal proceedings are not initiated within 12 months after the date of the suspension notice, the suspension shall be terminated unless an Assistant Attorney General requests an extension, in which case it may be extended for an additional 6 months. In no event may a suspension extend beyond 18 months, unless legal proceedings have been initiated within that period.
>
> (c) The suspending official shall notify the Department of Justice of the proposed termination of the suspension, at least 30 days before the 12-month period expires, to give that Department an opportunity to request an extension.

The regulation was promulgated in response to *Horne Bros., Inc. v. Laird*, 463 F.2d 1268 (D.C. Cir. 1972), where the court criticized an indefinite suspension. The regulation, however, provides for suspension as long as a criminal proceeding is actively being conducted without regard to the total length of the suspension. For instance, in *BASIX, Inc.*, Comp. Gen. Dec. B-255613, 94-1 CPD ¶ 194, the suspension remained in effect "pending resolution of the indictment" of the contractor's CEO. Similarly, in *MetaTRACE, Inc.*, EPADEBAR 90-0001-00, Aug 30, 1990, *Unpub.*, the suspension remained in effect "pending completion of investigation or ensuing proceedings, including debarment action." There is some question as to whether this complies with the spirit of the *Horne Brothers* decision. In *U.S. Testing Co.*, EPADEBAR 89-0021-00, Apr. 23, 1991, *Unpub.*, the board, after concluding that additional information evidenced "an altered corporate culture as well as organizational and procedural changes," ordered the company's suspension terminated.

4. Effect of Listing

FAR 9.405(a) precludes the award of contracts or the solicitation of offers from contractors that are debarred, suspended, or proposed for debarment. FAR 9.405(b) refers contracting officers to the List of Parties Excluded from Procurement Programs and Nonprocurement Programs, issued by the GSA, to determine which contractors are subject to this requirement. However, it is possible for a debarred contractor to submit a bid or proposal, even if it is listed. Thus, FAR 9.405(d) contains the following procedures to ensure that the Government does not deal with listed contractors:

> (1) After the opening of bids or receipt of proposals, the contracting officer shall review the List of Parties Excluded from Procurement Programs.
>
> (2) Bids received from any listed contractor in response to an invitation for bids shall be entered on the abstract of bids, and rejected unless the agency head or a designee determines in writing that there is a compelling reason to consider the bid.
>
> (3) Proposals, quotations, or offers received from any listed contractor shall not be evaluated for award or included in the competitive range, nor shall discussions be conducted with a listed offeror during a period of ineligibility, unless the agency head or a designee determines, in writing, that there is a compelling reason to do so. If the period of ineligibility expires or is terminated prior to award, the contracting officer may, but is not required to, consider such proposals, quotations, or offers.
>
> (4) Immediately prior to award, the contracting officer shall again review the List to ensure that no award is made to a listed contractor.

Under prior similar regulations, it was held that a contracting officer could properly refuse to award a contract to a bidder that had been proposed for debarment at the time of bid opening but had settled the issues (ending the debarment proceedings) at the time of award, *Instruments by Precision*

Ltd., Comp. Gen. Dec. B-235339, 89-2 CPD ¶ 138. Compare *Tracor Applied Sciences, Inc.*, Comp. Gen. Dec. B-221230.2, 86-1 CPD ¶ 189, holding that a contracting officer had discretion to award to a firm that was suspended or debarred at the time the offer was submitted, so long as it was not ineligible at the time of award, or to deny award even if the suspension or debarment was being reconsidered at the time of evaluation. The current FAR gives the contracting officer discretion to award to such a contractor when there is a "compelling reason," but it appears that agencies may be reluctant to find such compelling reasons. See *J.B. Kies Constr. Co.*, Comp. Gen. Dec. B-250797, 93-1 CPD ¶ 127, affirming a finding of no compelling reason where the bids were opened two days before the debarment ended and the debarment had been delayed for over two years because of "administrative oversight." In *TS Generalbau GmbH*, Comp. Gen. Dec. B-246034, 92-1 CPD ¶ 189, the Comptroller General rejected the argument that the contractor had been arbitrarily suspended "just days before the bid opening and contract award," and in *Baxter Healthcare Corp.*, Comp. Gen. Dec. B-253455.3, 94-1 CPD ¶ 301, the protester was found ineligible for award where its suspension was not lifted until the afternoon after award and the contracting officer did not know that the suspension was about to end.

Contracting officers must be diligent in determining the status of offerors. See *R.J. Crowley, Inc.*, Comp. Gen. Dec. B-253783, 93-2 CPD ¶ 257, where the Comptroller General sustained a protest when the contracting officer had checked the latest monthly list but had not reviewed the electronic update, and the "monthly" list was several months out of date.

5. Permissible Activities

While debarment and suspension are Government-wide, they do not bar entities from all activities related to Government contracting. Some inducement debarments are limited to a certain type of activity. Further, debarments and suspensions do not necessarily affect existing contracts or subcontracting activities.

a. Limited Debarments

Some inducement debarments are limited in nature. For example, a Buy American Act debarment under 41 U.S.C. § 10b extends to contracts for construction, alterations, or repairs of public buildings or public works. The statute is silent as to other types of work. In debarments under the Clean Air

Act and the Federal Water Pollution Control Act, debarments apply only to a "facility." 40 C.F.R. § 32.110(a) includes an exemption for any procurement contract for goods or services that does not exceed the simplified acquisition threshold. This exemption does not apply when the facility is listed because of a conviction under either Section 113(c)(1) of the Air Act or Section 309(c) of the Water Act.

b. Existing Contracts

FAR 9.405-1 provides guidance on whether current contracts are to be continued:

> (a) Notwithstanding the debarment, suspension, or proposed debarment of a contractor, agencies may continue contracts or subcontracts in existence at the time the contractor was debarred, suspended, or proposed for debarment unless the agency head or a designee directs otherwise. A decision as to the type of termination action, if any, to be taken should be made only after review by agency contracting and technical personnel and by counsel to ensure the propriety of the proposed action.
>
> (b) Ordering activities may continue to place orders against existing contracts, including indefinite delivery contracts, in the absence of a termination.
>
> (c) Agencies shall not renew or otherwise extend the duration of current contracts, or consent to subcontracts, with contractors debarred, suspended, or proposed for debarment, unless the agency head or a designee authorized representative states, in writing, the compelling reasons for renewal or extension.

Within the GSA, the regulation provides that termination for default is appropriate if the circumstances giving rise to the debarment or suspension also constitute a default in performance under the contract. If the debarment is based on reasons unrelated to performance, default termination is inappropriate. However, termination for convenience or cancellation is authorized "if the contractor presents a significant risk to the Government in completing a current contract," GSAR 509.405-1(2). See *Integrated Sys. Group, Inc. v. Department of the Army*, GSBCA 12613-P, 94-2 BCA ¶ 26,618, where the board approved the convenience termination of a contractor that had been proposed for debarment. NFS 1809.405-1 provides simply that "the contracting officer may terminate a contract under FAR 9.405-1(a) if it is in the best interest of the Government." There is no special DOD regulatory provision on the effect of debarment on current contracts.

c. Subcontracts

FAR 9.405-2(a) states that only subcontracts "subject to consent" are precluded by debarment or suspension:

> When a contractor debarred, suspended, or proposed for debarment is proposed as a subcontractor for any subcontract subject to Government consent (see Subpart 44.2), contracting officers shall not consent to subcontracts with such contractors unless the agency head or a designee states in writing the compelling reasons for this approval action.

The FAR is silent as to the eligibility of debarred firms for subcontracts where the contract does not require approval of the subcontractor selected by the contractor. See, however, 51 Comp. Gen. 65 (B-173016) (1971), where the Comptroller General stated that debarment does not preclude the sale of products to the Government through a distributor. See also Comp. Gen. Dec. B-149781, Oct. 29, 1962, *Unpub.*, where the Comptroller General precluded the nonresponsibility determination of a contractor planning to use a debarred subcontractor. In spite of this decision and the lack of guidance in the regulations on this issue, a contractor runs the risk of being declared nonresponsible if significant purchases are to be made from debarred or suspended subcontractors. Thus, the proposed use of a debarred subcontractor has been considered partially relevant to the determination of responsibility of a contractor in *Medical Devices of Fall River, Inc.*, Comp. Gen. Dec. B-232336, 88-2 CPD ¶ 247, and *Nuclear Supply & Serv. Co.*, Comp. Gen. Dec. B-151543, Jan. 17, 1964, *Unpub.*

Some inducement debarments cover subcontractors. It appears that firms listed for violation of the equal employment requirements under Exec. Order No. 11246 are ineligible for subcontracts whether or not Government approval is required. See 41 C.F.R. § 60-1.31. Likewise, it seems clear under EPA regulations that agencies may not award contracts where part of the performance would take place in a subcontractor facility that has been listed for violation of the Clean Air Act or the Federal Water Pollution Control Act. See 40 C.F.R. § 32.225.

E. Debarment and Suspension Procedures

This section considers the debarment and suspension procedures employed by the various contracting agencies and discusses the procedural due process requirements in debarment and suspension actions. Because suspension and debarment of a firm is quite serious and may even be fatal, the courts have recognized that certain due process protections must be afforded before these measures are invoked. See FAR 9.406-3(b) and FAR 9.407-3(b), stating that agencies shall establish procedures governing the debarment and suspension decision-making process that are "as informal as is practicable, consistent with principles of fundamental fairness." Exec. Order No. 12549 created a set of procedural "Common Rules" that retained the due process structure outlined in FAR 9.406-3(b) and FAR 9.407-3(b). The final guidelines were accepted, with certain modifications, by 28 administrative agencies, including the EPA, HUD, and the DOE, 53 Fed. Reg. 19161 (1988).

1. Notice

An agency is not required to provide notice that it is contemplating the suspension of a contractor. Usually, once a contractor receives notice that it has been proposed for debarment or suspension, it is already included on the GSA's List of Parties Excluded from Federal Procurement and Nonprocurement Programs.

a. Referral and Investigation

FAR 9.406-3(a) and Common Rule .311 require agencies to establish "procedures for the prompt reporting, investigation, and referral to the debarring official of matters appropriate for that official's consideration." Usually, suspension and debarment actions are initiated upon receipt by the agency of information of an indictment or conviction. Suspension and debarring officials receive indictment and conviction notice from U.S. Attorneys' offices, Inspector General offices, and other Government investigative organizations, as well as such sources as newspaper articles, competitors, and qui tam relators.

b. No Presuspension Notice

No notice of contemplated proceedings is required. Although there have been initiatives to require such notice, agencies have resisted. While there may be valid arguments that lack of advance notice of suspension violates due process, the courts have not yet reached this conclusion. In *Shermco Indus. v. Secretary of the Air Force*, 584 F. Supp. 76 (N.D. Tex. 1984), the court observed at 88:

> Whether notice given a suspended contractor is sufficient depends on several considerations. The first is whether timing of the notice allowed meaningful opportunity to rebut the charges. Two recent Court of Appeals decisions seem to impose different due process requirements for the timing of notice of a suspension. In *Transco*, above, at 320, 323, the contractor received no notice until after the suspension. Although the Sixth Circuit discussed whether the notice there involved was constitutionally infirm due to vagueness and the inconsistent explanations given by the agency for its decision to suspend, the court gave no indication that notice, to be constitutionally sufficient, had to be given before suspension.
>
> On the other hand, in *Old Dominion Dairy Products, Inc. v. Secretary of Defense*, 631 F.2d 953 (D.C. Cir. 1980), the D.C. Circuit held that a contractor was denied due process when it was not told, before two non-responsibility determinations, that it was under investigation and, after the determinations, was told only that they were based on the lack of a "satisfactory record of integrity."
>
> * * *
>
> Under the circumstances of this case, the constructive notice provided to Shermco, by way of a draft of the proposed indictment against it, was constitutionally sufficient. This draft indictment was delivered to Shermco several months before suspension proceedings were instituted; it sufficiently informed Shermco of the existence of an investigation and the substance of the charges against it.

This same issue arises with the listing of contractors that are proposed for debarment — the notice is received after they are included on the list.

Some agencies have adopted the practice of sending an informal notice, commonly known as a "shock and alarm" letter. This letter informs the recipient that suspension is contemplated but that the respondent is being afforded a presuspension opportunity to submit information in opposition to the proposed suspension.

While agencies reject any notion that presuspension notice is required, they generally will allow a contractor the opportunity to present matters of present responsibility prior to suspension if the contractor so requests and if a timely meeting can be scheduled. Thus, a contractor that knows an indictment or suspension is imminent is well advised to request an opportunity to present information and argument before any action by the agency is taken.

The procedures for such preventive communication vary with each agency. For example, the DOD has incorporated a particular avenue of communication into its acquisition regulations, stating at DFARS 209.402, App. H-103:

> A contractor who becomes aware of a pending indictment or allegations of wrongdoing that the contractor believes may lead to a suspension or debarment action may contact that debarring and suspending official or designee to provide information as to the contractor's present responsibility.

This communication may take the form of appealing to the agency's pragmatism. For instance, the contractor may argue to the agency that it would be against its interest to begin debarment procedures because debarment or listing will disrupt the flow of a product that is indispensable to the Government or will affect future procurements that have few competitors.

If the contractor is successful in proving its responsibility to the agency's satisfaction, the result is usually described in a settlement or compliance agreement. This document sets forth the findings of the informal communications between the parties and the terms upon which the finding of responsibility has been conditioned. In the event that this communication does not prevent a debarment, early recognition of the problem will accelerate the fact-finding and hearing process and result in the removal of the contractor's name from the proposed debarment list with as little damage as possible (assuming, of course, that the proposed debarment is unsuccessful).

c. *Notice of Suspension or Notice of Proposed Debarment*

Contractors must be given notice of the grounds upon which suspension and debarment actions are based. However, as stated above, once a contractor receives notice that it has been proposed for debarment or suspension, it is already included on the GSA's List of Parties Excluded from Federal Procurement and Nonprocurement Programs, FAR 9.404. In *Horne Bros., Inc. v. Laird*, 463 F.2d 1268 (D.C. Cir. 1972), the court concluded that a contractor could not be subjected to a "protracted suspension" without being given "some specific notice" of the charges upon which the suspension was based. In *Transco Sec., Inc. v. Freeman*, 639 F.2d 318 (6th Cir. 1981), the court overturned the suspension of a contractor suspected of fraud in obtaining a Government contract since the agency had failed to give adequate notice of the charges, stating at 323:

> The general notice which appellants received did not permit adequate preparation for participation in a meaningful way in any forthcoming hearing or equivalent proceeding. Appellants were suspended for, among other things, "billing irregularities." At the time this information was received, appellants had performed a number of contracts for the GSA over several years at various locations. Appellants were not told to which of these contracts the "billing irregularities" referred. Without further identifying information of at least the contract involved, and approximate date of misbillings, it would be at best onerous and at worst virtually impossible to effectively gather and present relevant information refuting this general charge.

See also *ATL, Inc. v. United States*, 736 F.2d 677 (Fed. Cir. 1984), requiring notice "sufficiently specific to permit the suspended contractor to collect and present relevant evidence refuting the charges," and *Electro-Methods, Inc. v. United States*, 728 F.2d 1471 (Fed. Cir. 1984), finding adequate notice where the contractor had been provided and in fact rebutted all the evidence considered by the suspension authority. In *SDA Inc.*, Comp. Gen. Dec. B-253355, 93-2 CPD ¶ 132, the Comptroller General found sufficient notice where a contractor had been suspended on the basis of detailed, unrebutted allegations of misconduct contained in a civil complaint filed by the Federal Government. See also *Reeve Aleutian Airways, Inc. v. United States*, 982 F.2d 594 (D.C. Cir. 1993), where the court found sufficient notice in a letter referring to an adverse report on the contractor's performance.

FAR 9.406-3(c) requires that contractors and "specifically named affiliates" be given advance notification of proposed debarment actions as well as at least a general statement of the reasons for the proposed debarment. See *S.A.F.E. Export Corp.*, Comp. Gen. Dec. B-222308.2, 86-2 CPD ¶ 44, where the Comptroller General found adequate notice to an unnamed affiliate because the principal officer of the affiliate and the principal company received actual notice. With respect to suspension actions, the regulations provide for notice *immediately after* the suspension has been invoked, FAR 9.407-3(c).

d. Designation of Lead Agency

Because contractors often do business with various Government agencies, more than one agency may have an interest in suspension or debarment of an entity. FAR 9.402(c) and Common Rule .115(c) provide for the designation of a lead agency as follows:

> When more than one agency has an interest in the debarment or suspension of a [person or contractor], consideration shall be given to designating one agency as the lead agency for making the decision. Agencies are encouraged to establish methods and procedures for coordinating their debarment or suspension actions.

The procedures for designating the lead agency are informal. Where a contractor is known to have involvement with more than one agency, the agencies consult with one another to determine which agency will handle the matter. Often, the agency with which the contractor does the most business (based on dollar value of contracts and subcontracts) is designated the lead agency. However, there may be extenuating circumstances where there is an overriding interest in another agency being the lead agency. For example, the EPA may take the lead for cases involving violations of the environmental laws.

2. Presentation of Matters in Opposition

Basic fairness in debarment proceedings requires that a party be given an "opportunity to present evidence," *Gonzales v. Freeman*, 118 U.S. App. D.C. 180, 334 F.2d 570 (D.C. Cir. 1964). Moreover, after a reasonable period of time following imposition of a suspension, the firm may be entitled to a "hearing" involving at least an opportunity to refute the basis for the suspension, unless a hearing would be inappropriate for reasons of national security or would prejudice a pending or imminent criminal prosecution of the firm, *Horne Bros., Inc. v. Laird*, 463 F.2d 1268 (D.C. Cir. 1972).

a. *Opportunity to Be Heard in Opposition*

FAR 9.406-3(b)(1) and FAR 9.407-3(b)(1) contain the minimal guidance that debarment and suspension proceedings "shall afford the contractor (and any specifically named affiliates) an opportunity to submit, in person, in writing, or through a representative, information and argument in opposition to the proposed" action. FAR 9.406-3(b)(2) and FAR 9.407-3(b)(2) then state that in debarment actions not based on conviction or civil judgment and in suspension actions not based on an indictment, if it is found that the contractor's submission *raises a genuine dispute over facts material to the proposed action*, the agency must:

> (i) Afford the contractor an opportunity to appear with counsel, submit documentary evidence, present witnesses, and confront any person the agency presents; and
>
> (ii) Make a transcribed record of the proceedings and make it available at cost to the contractor upon request, unless the contractor and the agency, by mutual agreement, waive the requirement for a transcript.

Agencies have been granted considerable discretion in following this two-step procedure in deciding whether there is a genuine dispute of fact to justify such an actual hearing. See *Robinson v. Cheney*, 876 F.2d 152 (D.C. Cir. 1989), affirming the agency's denial of a hearing on the grounds that the alleged factual disputes were minor in nature and did not go to the central issues in the case. See also *IMCO, Inc. v. United States*, 33 Fed. Cl. 312 (1995), affirming the debarring official's denial of a hearing on the basis that there were no seriously contested facts. This limited-hearing approach was also upheld in *Transco*, where the court stated at 322-23:

> Under the present regulations, promulgated following *Horne Brothers*, suspended contractors denied a hearing are provided the opportunity to present information or argument, in person, in writing, or through representation in opposition to the suspension. Thus under the current regulations, suspended contractors will not "dangle in suspension for a period of one year or more" before being given an opportunity to rebut charges. 463 F.2d at 1271. Under most circumstances, this opportunity coupled with proper notice will timely

cure such errors as suspending the wrong contractor or suspending a contractor based on mere suspicion, unfounded allegation, or error.

Thus, when an agency follows this two-step procedure, a contractor that is proposed for debarment or is suspended must, in order to obtain a hearing, demonstrate in its initial written submission that there are significant factual disputes. On the other hand, there is nothing in the FAR precluding an agency from granting hearings in less restrictive circumstances.

FAR 9.406-3(d) and FAR 9.407-3(d)(2) call for written findings of fact when an actual hearing is conducted. They also permit the debarring official to delegate the conduct of such a hearing by stating that "matters involving disputed material facts" may be referred to another official. Some agencies have established a separate hearing officer as a matter of course. For example, GSA provides that if there is a genuine dispute of material fact, the suspending official must refer the matter to the fact-finding official, GSAR 509.407-3(b)(6).

Obtaining a hearing does not necessarily give the contractor the same due process rights it would have in civil litigation. For example, in *Electro-Methods, Inc. v. United States*, 728 F.2d 1471 (Fed. Cir. 1984), the Federal Circuit, commenting on a suspension, held that the "concept of due process cannot be extended so far, in the circumstances of this case, as to mandate that a 'meaningful' hearing include permitting the contractor to subpoena and examine FBI agents involved in an on-going criminal investigation, as well as other government and industry officials, to prove its case." However, some minimal evidentiary standards may apply. See *James J. Burnett*, HUDBCA 80-501-D42, 82-1 BCA ¶ 15,716, where the board held that hearsay evidence alone would not normally be sufficient to support a debarment.

b. Right of Confrontation

Although the court in *Horne Bros., Inc. v. Laird*, 463 F.2d 1268 (D.C. Cir. 1972) suggested that there may be a right to confront adverse witnesses if a suspension is protracted, FAR 9.406-3(b)(2)(i) and FAR 9.407-3(b)(2)(i) provide for an opportunity to confront agency witnesses *only* when there is a dispute as to material facts. *Robinson v. Cheney*, 876 F.2d 152 (D.C. Cir. 1989) significantly limits this right by analogizing the situation to that of courts deciding motions for summary judgment without a hearing. See also *Reeve Aleutian Airways, Inc. v. United States*, 982 F.2d 594 (D.C. Cir.

1993), commenting that hearing where no Government witnesses were present was sufficient because the contractor could have called them.

The agencies that use appeals boards to hear these cases generally provide for an opportunity to cross-examine adverse witnesses prior to imposition of a debarment. HUD regulations mimic the FAR by providing an opportunity to "confront any witness the agency presents" when there is a factual dispute, 24 C.F.R. § 24.313. The GSA likewise provides an "opportunity for the affected contractor to . . . cross-examine any witness GSA presents," GSAR 509.406-3(b). However, confrontation and cross-examination of adverse witnesses have not been required where material facts are not in dispute, *Titan Constr. Co. v. Weinberger*, Civ. Action No. 85-5533 (D.N.J. 1986); *Taylor v. Marsh*, Civ. Action No. 81-2643 (D.D.C. 1982); *Commonwealth Labs., Inc.*, AGBCA 94-0059-01, Apr. 17, 1995, *Unpub.*

3. Timing Requirements

FAR 9.406-3(c) and Common Rule .313(a) provide that within 30 days of receipt of notice of proposed debarment or suspension, the respondent may present information or argument in opposition. In actions based upon "a conviction or judgment, or in which there is no genuine dispute over material facts," the debarring official will make a decision based upon the administrative record. No time is specified for this decision. If no suspension is in effect, the decision must be made within 30 working days after receipt of "any information and argument submitted by the contractor, unless the debarring official extends this period for good cause," FAR 9.406-3(d).

4. Procedures of Particular Agencies

The agencies have implemented the general prescriptions of the FAR and the Common Rule in varying ways.

a. Department of Defense

The DOD has 10 designated suspending and debarring officials, identified in DFARS 209.403 as follows:

Army — Commander, U.S. Army Legal Services Agency

Navy — The General Counsel of the Department of the Navy

Air Force — Deputy General Counsel (Contractor Responsibility)

Advanced Research Projects Agency — The Director

Defense Information Systems Agency — The General Counsel

Defense Logistics Agency — The Special Assistant for Contracting Integrity

Defense Mapping Agency — The General Counsel

Defense Special Weapons Agency — The Director

National Security Agency — The Director

Ballistic Missile Defense Organization — The General Counsel

Appendix H of the DFARS sets forth the debarment and suspension procedures. Contractors are notified of the proposed debarment or suspension in accordance with FAR 9.406-3 or FAR 9.407-3. DFARS Appendix H-101 provides that a copy of the record that formed the basis for the decision by the debarring and suspending official will be made available to the contractor.

There are two distinct proceedings that may be involved in the suspension or debarment process. The first is the presentation of matters in opposition to the suspension or debarment. Matters in opposition may be presented "in person, in writing, or through a representative," DFARS Appendix H-103. If, however, a contractor desires to present matters in person or through a representative, any written matters should be delivered at least five working days prior to the presentation.

The second proceeding is fact-finding, which only occurs in cases where the contractor's presentation of matters raises a genuine dispute over one or more material facts. The debarring official determines whether the contractor's presentation has raised a genuine dispute of material fact. Fact-finding is normally held within 45 working days of the contractor's presentation of matters, DFARS Appendix H-104(b). Both the Government and the contractor have an opportunity to present evidence. The fact-finder determines the disputed facts by a preponderance of the evidence. A copy of the findings are provided to the debarring and suspending official, the Government, and the contractor. The debarring and suspending official then determine whether to continue the suspension or to debar the contractor based on the entire administrative record, including the findings of fact.

b. Environmental Protection Agency

The EPA, unlike most other agencies, has two mechanisms for rendering contractors ineligible to receive federal agency contracts and subcontracts. First, the EPA pursues suspension and debarment actions pursuant to FAR Subpart 9.4 and the Common Rule. The EPA's suspension and debarment program is administered by the Office of Administration and Resources Management (OARM). Second, the Federal Water Pollution Control Act and the Clean Air Act provide an additional means for statutory ineligibility (known as "listing") for criminal convictions of certain offenses. The Contractor Listing Program is also administered by OARM.

Generally, suspension and debarment actions are initiated by or through a Suspension and Debarment Division (SDD) attorney. The SDD attorney prepares an Action Request Memorandum (ARM) and submits it to the EPA's suspending/debarring official. The ARM sets forth the information, the evidence supporting the request, applicable rules, and rationale for requesting the action. The suspending/debarring official reviews the ARM and, if in agreement, issues a Notice of Action to the respondent. Subsequent to receipt of Notice, respondent's counsel and the agency's counsel meet to discuss the evidence that led to the agency's action. In some cases, the matter is resolved prior to formal proceedings by a settlement or compliance agreement that addresses action to be taken to correct the problem. If the matter cannot be resolved informally, it is docketed for a hearing. The hearing officer then permits both parties to "present evidence, witnesses or any other information," *B.E.S. Envtl. Specialists, Inc. and Richard Baranowski*, EPA Debarment Case Nos. 88-044-00 and 88-0044-01 (June 12, 1989). The hearing official serves as a fact-finder and makes recommendations to the suspending/debarring official. Note that the functions related to investigations, suspension or debarment requests, and oversight are separate from the functions related to suspension or debarment decision making. The EPA's suspending/debarring official is the director of the Office of Grants Debarment (OGD). The director of the OGD reports to the OARM deputy assistant administrator for finance and acquisition and has several hearing officers to assist in carrying out suspension and debarment duties. The functions related to investigation are often referred to the SDD by the Office of the Inspector General or Office of Enforcement.

c. Department of Housing and Urban Development

HUD's debarment regulation is set forth in 24 C.F.R. Part 24. HUD does not have a single debarring official. Every assistant secretary, the HUD Inspector General, and the president of Ginnie Mae (GNMA) all have the authority to suspend and to propose debarment, 24 C.F.R. § 24.105.

Under HUD's procedures, the authorized HUD official sends a letter notifying a party of suspension or proposed debarment. If no hearing is requested, a proposed debarment becomes final. Often, HUD proposes debarments in excess of three years, which is allowed by regulation, 24 C.F.R. § 24.320(a)(1). If a hearing is requested, the hearing is conducted by a judicial hearing officer who is either an administrative judge of HUD's Board of Contract Appeals or a HUD administrative law judge. Assignments of debarment and suspension cases are made by rotation. After the filing of a complaint and answer, the parties may engage in discovery and oral argument. Prehearing conferences and prehearing orders are also available. The judicial hearing officer then issues a written decision with findings of fact and conclusions of law. This decision is final unless either party requests Secretarial review within 15 days of receipt of decision. The Secretary must decide to accept review within 40 days.

d. Department of Agriculture

The regulations governing debarment and suspension for the Department of Agriculture are set forth in 48 C.F.R. Subpart 409.4. The regulations provide that the director of the Office of Operations serves as the debarment official, except for contracts awarded under the School Lunch and Surplus Removal Program, where debarring authority is delegated to the Agricultural Marketing Service, 48 C.F.R. § 409.403. Any contracting officer may refer a case through the head of contracting activity (HCA) to the debarring official upon detecting information that is sufficient cause for debarment, 48 C.F.R. § 409.406-3.

The Department's procedures for debarment are set out in 48 C.F.R. § 409.406-3 and for suspension in 48 C.F.R. § 409.407-3. Despite the separate regulations, procedures for both suspension and debarment are essentially the same. A contracting officer referring a case through the HCA to the debarring official must also provide a complete statement of the facts and a recommendation for action. The HCA must then consult with the

Office of the Inspector General to determine whether further investigation is necessary before the case is referred to the debarring official.

The debarring official reviews the recommendations and consults with the Office of the Inspector General and the Office of the General Counsel, as appropriate. If the debarring official determines that debarment is justified, the official proceeds in accordance with FAR 9.406-3(c). The debarring official then informs the HCA whether the proposed debarment was initiated.

Where the action is listed under FAR 9.406-3(b)(2)(i), the contractor is given the opportunity to appear at an informal hearing. The hearing is to be held at a convenient time and location for all parties, if possible. Parties may be represented by counsel or any duly authorized representative. Each party may call witnesses and each has the opportunity to present all pertinent information in an expeditious manner. The contractor is provided a transcript of the proceedings under the conditions established in FAR 9.406-3(b)(2)(ii).

e. General Services Administration

The debarring official designated by the GSA is the associate administrator for acquisition policy or a designee, 48 C.F.R. § 509.403. The GSA regulations also designate the chairman of the Debarment and Suspension Board within the GSA Board of Contract Appeals as the fact-finding official, 48 C.F.R. § 509.403. Any element of the GSA acting as a contracting activity has the authority to refer a matter to the debarring official for review, 48 C.F.R. § 509.406-3(a). Where criminal or fraudulent activities are involved, the matter must first be reported to the Office of the Inspector General, which determines whether to then refer it to the debarring official.

Referrals for consideration of debarment action must include:

(i) The recommendation and rationale for the referral;

(ii) A statement of facts;

(iii) Copies of documentary evidence and a list of all witnesses, including addresses and telephone numbers, together with a statement concerning their availability to appear at a fact-finding proceeding and the subject matter of their testimony;

(iv) A list of parties including the contractor, principals, and affiliates (including last known home and business addresses, zip codes, and DUNS Number);

(v) GSA's acquisition history with the contractor, including recent experience under contracts and copies of the pertinent contracts;

(vi) A list of any known active or potential criminal investigations, criminal or civil proceedings, or administrative claims before the Board of Contract Appeals; and

(vii) A statement regarding the impact of the debarment action on GSA programs. This statement is not required for referrals by the Inspector General.

If the debarring official requires further information, the referral is returned to the originator.

The debarring official coordinates with assigned legal counsel to determine whether to initiate debarment action. Notice of the debarring official's decision is provided to the originating agency. Upon receipt of notice of a proposed debarment, the contracting activity has 30 calendar days to respond before the debarment becomes final. If such response is made, the party may make an oral presentation of information and arguments before the debarring official within 20 calendar days. Written supplements will be accepted. The affected party may also request a copy of the administrative record that led to the decision to propose debarment. The party is informed if any portion of the record is withheld. If a genuine issue of material fact remains, the party may request a fact-finding hearing. The debarring official must determine whether such issue exists and, if so, must refer the matter to the fact-finding official. A hearing is scheduled within 20 calendar days of receipt of the debarring official's referral.

GSA regulations provide several goals of fact-finding hearings:

(i) Afford the affected party the opportunity to dispute material facts relating to the proposed debarment through the submission of oral and written evidence;

(ii) Resolve facts in dispute and provide the debarring official with written findings of fact based on a preponderance of evidence; and

(iii) Provide the debarring official with a determination as to whether a cause for debarment exists, based on facts as found.

The hearings must be conducted in accordance with rules consistent with FAR 9.406-3(b)(2) as promulgated by the fact-finding official. The fact-finding official submits a written report to the debarring official within 20 days of the close of the hearings.

F. De Facto Debarment and Suspension

There have been a number of decisions finding actions of the Government that exclude contractors from the opportunity to receive award to be de facto debarments. The reasoning in such cases is that since the effect of the action was the same as a suspension or debarment, it was improper, because the agency did not observe due process requirements. The FAR contains no guidance on the type of actions that constitute de facto debarments. The decisions giving such guidance are covered in this section.

1. Multiple Nonresponsibility Determinations

Multiple determinations of nonresponsibility may be tantamount to a debarment. See 43 Comp. Gen. 140 (B-151269) (1963), holding it improper to make successive nonresponsibility determinations for the same criminal offense without initiating debarment proceedings. See also Comp. Gen. Dec. B-175845, Mar. 9, 1973, *Unpub.*, where the Comptroller General upheld a nonresponsibility determination for alleged labor violations without the agency having undertaken formal debarment proceedings, but stated that "continued refusal to award contracts . . . as a result of a nonresponsibility determination based upon the same alleged labor violations as involved here without invoking and following the applicable debarment procedures would be of doubtful validity." In *Myers & Myers, Inc. v. United States Postal Serv.*, 527 F.2d 1252 (2d Cir. 1975), the court found de facto debarment where the Postal Service refused to renew six delivery contracts because of suspected criminal conduct. See *Dynamic Aviation v. Department of the Interior*, 898 F. Supp. 11 (D.D.C. 1995), where the court recognized a possibility of a de facto debarment in the Government's one-year revocation of a contractor's pilot's credentials coupled with a refusal to test and inspect until a federal bureau specifically requested the contractor's services, which would not occur until a card has been issued; and *Leslie & Elliott Co. v. Garrett*, 732 F. Supp. 191 (D.D.C. 1990), where a de facto debarment was found because the Navy attacked the contractor's integrity and developed a policy to declare the contractor nonresponsible on all contracts. In *Shermco Indus. v. Secretary of the Air Force*, 584 F. Supp. 76 (N.D. Tex. 1984), involving integrity issues, the court said "a procuring agency cannot make successive determinations of nonresponsibility on the same basis; rather it must initiate suspension or debarment procedures at the earliest practicable date following the first determination of nonresponsibility."

The Comptroller General has refused to find de facto debarments when the finding of nonresponsibility can be referred to the SBA for the granting of a COC, *Sermor, Inc.*, Comp. Gen. Dec. B-219132.2, 85-2 CPD ¶ 444 (five consecutive nonresponsibility determinations based on financial capability); *Pittman Mechanical Contractors, Inc.*, Comp. Gen. Dec. B-242499, 91-1 CPD ¶ 439 (four contemporaneous nonresponsibility determinations). The Comptroller General has also refused to find de facto debarments when a number of nonresponsibility determinations have been made contemporaneously, *Mexican Intermodal Equip., S.A. de C.V.*, Comp. Gen. Dec. B-270144, 96-1 CPD ¶ 31, (two nonresponsibility determinations did "not demonstrate that they were part of a long-term disqualification attempt . . . [but were] . . . merely a reflection of the fact that the determinations were based on the same current information"); *Shepard Printing*, Comp. Gen. Dec. B-260362, 95-2 CPD ¶ 119 (seven nonresponsibility determinations within three-month period based on same information as to deficient quality); *Government Contract Advisory Servs., Inc.*, Comp. Gen. Dec. B-255918, 94-1 CPD ¶ 181 (three concurrent nonresponsibility determinations by different contracting officers based on same information); *Garten-und Landschaftsbau GmbH Frank Mohr*, Comp. Gen. Dec. B-237276, 90-1 CPD ¶ 186 (two nonresponsibility determinations based on integrity issues).

2. Blacklists, Holdups, and Passovers

No longer allowed

Actions or communications indicating a refusal to deal with a contractor in the future have been held to be de facto debarments or suspension. In *Airco, Inc. v. Cecil D. Andrus*, 26 Cont. Cas. Fed. (CCF) ¶ 83,636 (D.D.C. 1979), the contractor was threatened with placement of an "informal blacklist" by the Department of the Interior (DOI). Specifically, the agency threatened to notify its customers and contractors that Airco was in violation of an agency regulation that would prevent such customers from doing business with Airco. The court found that while the DOI had not canceled or terminated any contract with Airco and had not put Airco on an "ineligible" list, the effect on Airco was the same as a formal debarment but without the protective procedures to which Airco would have been entitled by a formal debarment action. Similarly, in *Peter Kiewit & Sons' Co. v. U.S. Army Corps of Eng'rs*, 534 F. Supp. 1139 (D.D.C. 1982), *rev'd on other grounds*, 714 F.2d 163 (D.C. Cir. 1983), the court found a de facto debarment by the Army when it held Kiewit in abeyance under a "temporary declaration of ineligibility" and denied it a contract award without providing notice and an opportunity to be heard. See also *Art-Metal USA, Inc. v. Solomon*, 473 F. Supp. 1 (D.D.C. 1978), where the court found de facto debarment where the GSA terminated for convenience a contract to furnish vertical file cabinets and then held in abeyance four other contract awards pending the completion of a GSA investigation into possible contract abuses by Art-Metal.

Informal statements of the contracting officer may be sufficient to indicate an intention not to award future contracts. For example, in *Related Indus., Inc. v. United States*, 2 Cl. Ct. 517 (1983), the court found de facto debarment where the contracting officer proposed to find Related nonresponsible on one award but also declared that he would not award any future contract to plaintiff or to any company with which plaintiff was associated. Compare *Community Economic Dev. Corp. v. United States*, 577 F. Supp. 425 (D.D.C. 1983), where there was a justifiable basis for a single nonresponsibility determination. Although the contractor contended that the contracting officer told him he was debarred, the subsequent deposition of the contracting officer stating that the contractor was welcome to bid on future procurements and regularly would be sent future solicitations led the court to conclude that the alleged statement, if true, was made in the heat of the moment. In *Bannum, Inc.*, Comp. Gen. Dec. B-249758, 92-2 CPD ¶ 373, while an agency official's remark that she and her supervisors "were tired of Bannum's rhetoric," a remark made over two years earlier, may have reflected a lack of judgment, the facts did not support the contractor's contention that it had been de facto debarred.

It has also been held that the "passover" procedure under Exec. Order No. 11246, where contractors are found not in compliance with equal employment obligations, constitutes a de facto debarment, *Pan Am. World Airways, Inc. v. Marshall*, 439 F. Supp. 487 (S.D.N.Y. 1977); *Sundstrand Corp. v. Marshall*, 17 FEP Cases 432 (N.D. Ill. 1978).

Although not decided under the de facto debarment rubric, two cases have found that stigmatizing communications that inhibit the award of future contracts constitute a deprivation of a contractor's "liberty interest," *Old Dominion Dairy Prods., Inc. v. Secretary of Defense*, 631 F.2d 953 (D.C. Cir. 1980); *Conset Corp. v. Community Servs. Admin.*, 655 F.2d 1291 (D.C. Cir. 1981). In both cases, the stigmatizing communications related to the integrity of the contractor, and there is some question as to whether this logic would apply to other grounds of nonresponsibility. See *John Carlo, Inc. v. Corps of Eng'rs of the U.S. Army*, 539 F. Supp. 1075 (N.D. Tex. 1982), listing four factors to consider when deciding if a finding of nonresponsibility amounts to a de facto debarment:

> (1) were other persons or government agencies apprised of the contracting officer's finding of nonresponsibility; (2) was the information circulated for the purpose of preventing [contractor] from securing future contracts with the government; (3) did circulation of the information in fact stigmatize [contractor]; and (4) has [contractor] suffered any losses in government business attributable to the contracting officer's determination of nonresponsibility.

In *Frank Cain & Sons, Inc.*, Comp. Gen. Dec. B-236893, 90-1 CPD ¶ 44, the Comptroller General found proper the contracting agency's determination that the bidder was nonresponsible based on information in a criminal investigation report that called into question the bidder's integrity.

CHAPTER 5

SEALED BIDDING

Sealed bidding, previously known as formal advertising, has long been used by the Federal Government to select contractors on the basis of price competition with publicly opened bids. Congress passed the first statute dealing with advertising in 1809, requiring that "all purchases and contracts for supplies or services . . . shall be made either by open purchase, or by previously advertising for proposals," 2 Stat. 536. The Attorney General stated that the purpose of this statute was to prevent favoritism, 2 Ops. Att'y Gen. 257 (1829), and to prevent the notorious mischief of making contracts privately, 6 Ops. Att'y Gen. 99 (1853). From time to time, additional formalities were adopted. See, e.g., 5 Stat. 522, 526 (1842), 5 Stat. 614, 617 (1843), 5 Stat. 790, 795 (1845). In 1861, the statutory requirements for advertising were reaffirmed, 12 Stat. 220. This statute was subsequently incorporated into Revised Statute 3709, the forerunner of 41 U.S.C. § 5. In the years that followed, numerous Comptroller of the Treasury, Comptroller General, and court decisions implemented the statute by further defining the procedures to be followed in formal advertising. Following World War II, these procedures were adopted by Congress in the Armed Services Procurement Act of 1947, 10 U.S.C. § 2301 et seq., and the Federal Property and Administrative Services Act, 41 U.S.C. § 252 et seq. These statutes were further modified by the Competition in Contracting Act of 1984 (CICA), 98 Stat. 1175.

Sealed bidding was the predominant technique used in Government contracting until World War II. During the war its use was suspended in order to efficiently award contracts to obtain necessary war materials. After the war the statutes reinstated it as the preferred technique, but negotiation was permitted under specified statutory exceptions. Thereafter, sealed bidding was used for the majority of the procurement actions, but the more significant dollar expenditures were made using negotiation procedures. As discussed in Chapter 3, the CICA ended the practice of "favoring" the use of sealed bidding when it made sealed bidding and competitive negotiation parallel procedures for meeting the statutory competition requirements. At the present time, less than 10 percent of federal procurement dollars are spent in sealed bid procurements.

The statutory procedures for sealed bidding are now contained in 10 U.S.C. § 2305 and 41 U.S.C. § 253a and b. The key provisions describing the unique features of sealed bidding are in 10 U.S.C. § 2305(b)(3) and 41 U.S.C. § 253b(c):

> Sealed bids shall be opened publicly at the time and place stated in the solicitation. The head of the agency shall evaluate the bids in accordance with paragraph (1) without discussions with the bidders and, except as provided in paragraph (2), shall award a contract with reasonable promptness to the responsible bidder whose bid conforms to the solicitation and is most advantageous to the United States, considering only price and the other price-related factors included in the solicitation. The award of a contract shall be made by transmitting, in writing or by electronic means, notice of the award to the successful bidder. Within three days after the date of contract award, the head of the agency shall notify, in writing or by electronic means, each bidder not awarded the contract that the contract has been awarded.

The statutory requirements for sealed bidding are implemented in FAR Part 14.

This chapter first considers the procedures applicable to the submission and public opening of sealed bids. It then deals with the concept of responsiveness — whether the bid conforms in all material respects to the invitation. The evaluation of bids and the award of the contract is next discussed. The last two sections cover mistakes in bids and two-step sealed bidding. The other key aspect of sealed bidding — determining whether the prospective contractor is responsible — is covered in Chapter 4.

I. BIDDING AND OPENING PROCEDURE

The fundamental concept of sealed bidding is that the public interest is best served when the Government describes its needs with precision, conducts an open competition to obtain the best price, opens the bids publicly, and awards to the responsible bidder that submits the lowest price and agrees without qualification to meet all the material contract requirements. In this system, discretion of Government employees is reduced to a minimum, and public opening ensures that the award decision is subject to public scrutiny. Thus, it has been stated that sealed bidding is aimed at securing the most advantageous contract for the Government by maximizing free and open competition; preventing favoritism, collusion, or fraud; and giving all interested parties an opportunity to compete, *United States v.*

Brookridge Farm, Inc., 111 F.2d 461 (10th Cir. 1940). Bidders must prepare their bids independently without the knowledge of whether other bidders are competing for award or of the contents of other bids. Public opening assures all parties that the award is being made in conformance with the IFB. Bids are "firm" for a specified period of time — with the result that withdrawal or modification of a bid after opening is permitted only in the limited circumstances of mistake.

Sealed bidding does not afford the Government the option of evaluating the merits of technical proposals and paying somewhat more to obtain a higher quality product or service. It *requires* that if award is made, it must be made to the responsive bidder with the lowest price even if the product or service offered is only minimally acceptable. Thus, its successful use is almost completely dependent on the Government's ability to describe its needs in a way that ensures that the winning contractor will be *contractually bound* to perform satisfactory work.

A. Solicitation of Bids

The solicitation of sealed bids is accomplished through a written document called an Invitation for Bids (IFB). The Government mails or otherwise furnishes copies of IFBs to prospective bidders and may give further notice of the solicitation through advertising or posting notices of the solicitation in public places. See Chapter 3, Section IV for a discussion of public announcements and solicitations.

1. Invitation for Bids

In order to ensure that all bidders compete on an equal basis, IFBs must contain all of the essential terms of the contract so that bidders may submit offers by merely filling in the price and schedule, if required, completing the necessary certifications, and signing the offer, FAR 14.101(a). Solicitations are issued on multipurpose standard forms used for both sealed bid and negotiated procurements. The contracting officer may use Standard Form 33 (Solicitation, Offer and Award) (see **Figure 5-1**) or Standard Form 1447 (Solicitation/Contract) or may issue the solicitation on a special form, FAR 14.201-2(a); FAR 53.214. Standard Form 1442 (Solicitation, Offer, and Award) is prescribed for use on construction contracts, FAR 36.701(b); FAR 53.236-1(e). One of these standard forms is used in most cases

PART 53—FORMS 53.301-33

OMB Approved No. 9000-0002

SOLICITATION, OFFER AND AWARD

1. THIS CONTRACT IS A RATED ORDER UNDER DPAS (15 CFR 350) ▶ RATING | PAGE OF PAGES

2. CONTRACT NO.	3. SOLICITATION NO.	4. TYPE OF SOLICITATION ☐ SEALED BID (IFB) ☐ NEGOTIATED (RFP)	5. DATE ISSUED	6. REQUISITION/PURCHASE NO.

7. ISSUED BY CODE

8. ADDRESS OFFER TO *(If other than Item 7)*

NOTE: In sealed bid solicitations "offer" and "offeror" mean "bid" and "bidder".

SOLICITATION

9. Sealed offers in original and ________ copies for furnishing the supplies or services in the Schedule will be received at the place specified in Item 8, or if handcarried, in the depository located in ________________ until ______ local time ________
(Hour) *(Date)*

CAUTION – LATE Submissions, Modifications, and Withdrawals: See Section L, Provision No. 52.214-7 or 52.215-10. All offers are subject to all terms and conditions contained in this solicitation.

10. FOR INFORMATION CALL: ▶ A. NAME | B. TELEPHONE NO. *(Include area code) (NO COLLECT CALLS)*

11. TABLE OF CONTENTS

(✓)	SEC.	DESCRIPTION	PAGE(S)	(✓)	SEC.	DESCRIPTION	PAGE(S)
		PART I – THE SCHEDULE				PART II – CONTRACT CLAUSES	
	A	SOLICITATION/CONTRACT FORM			I	CONTRACT CLAUSES	
	B	SUPPLIES OR SERVICES AND PRICES/COSTS				PART III – LIST OF DOCUMENTS, EXHIBITS AND OTHER ATTACH.	
	C	DESCRIPTION/SPECS./WORK STATEMENT			J	LIST OF ATTACHMENTS	
	D	PACKAGING AND MARKING				PART IV – REPRESENTATIONS AND INSTRUCTIONS	
	E	INSPECTION AND ACCEPTANCE			K	REPRESENTATIONS, CERTIFICATIONS AND OTHER STATEMENTS OF OFFERORS	
	F	DELIVERIES OR PERFORMANCE					
	G	CONTRACT ADMINISTRATION DATA			L	INSTRS., CONDS., AND NOTICES TO OFFERORS	
	H	SPECIAL CONTRACT REQUIREMENTS			M	EVALUATION FACTORS FOR AWARD	

OFFER *(Must be fully completed by offeror)*

NOTE: Item 12 does not apply if the solicitation includes the provisions at 52.214-16, Minimum Bid Acceptance Period.

12. In compliance with the above, the undersigned agrees, if this offer is accepted within ____________ calendar days *(60 calendar days unless a different period is inserted by the offeror)* from the date for receipt of offers specified above, to furnish any or all items upon which prices are offered at the price set opposite each item, delivered at the designated point(s), within the time specified in the schedule.

13. DISCOUNT FOR PROMPT PAYMENT *(See Section I, Clause No. 52-232-8)* ▶	10 CALENDAR DAYS %	20 CALENDAR DAYS %	30 CALENDAR DAYS %	CALENDAR DAYS %

14. ACKNOWLEDGMENT OF AMENDMENTS *(The offeror acknowledges receipt of amendments to the SOLICITATION for offerors and related documents numbered and dated:*	AMENDMENT NO.	DATE	AMENDMENT NO.	DATE

15A. NAME AND ADDRESS OF OFFEROR — CODE — FACILITY

16. NAME AND TITLE OF PERSON AUTHORIZED TO SIGN OFFER *(Type or print)*

15B. TELEPHONE NO. *(Include area code)*

15C. CHECK IF REMITTANCE ADDRESS IS DIFFERENT FROM ABOVE - ENTER SUCH ADDRESS IN SCHEDULE. ☐

17. SIGNATURE

18. OFFER DATE

AWARD *(To be completed by Government)*

19. ACCEPTED AS TO ITEMS NUMBERED

20. AMOUNT

21. ACCOUNTING AND APPROPRIATION

22. AUTHORITY FOR USING OTHER THAN FULL AND OPEN COMPETITION:

☐ 10 U.S.C. 2304(c)(☐ 41 U.S.C. 253(c)(

23. SUBMIT INVOICES TO ADDRESS SHOWN IN *(4 copies unless otherwise specified)* ▶ ITEM

24. ADMINISTERED BY *(If other than Item 7)* CODE

25. PAYMENT WILL BE MADE BY CODE

26. NAME OF CONTRACTING OFFICER *(Type or print)*

27. UNITED STATES OF AMERICA

(Signature of Contracting Officer)

28. AWARD DATE

IMPORTANT – Award will be made on this Form, or on Standard Form 26, or by other authorized official written notice.

NSN 7540–01–152–8064
PREVIOUS EDITION NOT USABLE

33-134

STANDARD FORM 33 (REV. 4-85)
Prescribed by GSA
FAR (48 CFR) 53.214(c)

53-25

Figure 5-1

because they contain blanks with the essential information that must be filled in by both the contracting officer and the bidder. This entire package is designed so that all bidders can make legally sufficient and comparable offers under the same terms and conditions by furnishing the required information and inserting their price and delivery schedule.

FAR 14.201-1 requires, with certain exceptions such as construction contracts, that solicitations and resulting contracts be prepared using the Uniform Contract Format "to the maximum practicable extent." Standard Form 33 is the most commonly used standard form because it is structured to use this format. However, the contracting officer is permitted to use a "simplified contract format," FAR 14.201-9, and should use Standard Form 1447 when this format is used, FAR 53.214(d).

The Uniform Contract Format consists of the following Parts and Subparts:

Uniform Contract Format	
Part I—The Schedule	
Section	Title
A	Solicitation/contract form
B	Supplies or services and prices
C	Description/specifications
D	Packaging and marking
E	Inspection and acceptance
F	Deliveries or performance
G	Contract administration data
H	Special contract requirements
Part II—Contract Clauses	
I	Contract clauses
Part III—List of Documents, Exhibits, and Other Attachments	
J	List of attachments

Uniform Contract Format	
Part IV—Representations and Instructions	
K	Representations, certifications, and other statements of offerors or quoters
L	Instructions, conditions, and notices to offerors or quoters
M	Evaluation factors for award

This format is structured so that Parts I, II, and III become the contract, when awarded, while Part IV is retained in the contract file, FAR 14.201-1(c). Part I of the format contains the unique provisions pertaining to the procurement, including, as Section A, Standard Form 33, FAR 14.201-2. Part II, Section I, contains the clauses for the proposed contract, FAR 14.201-3, including standard contract clauses contained in FAR Part 52 and special clauses used by the agency and not included in Part I. FAR 52.3 contains a matrix giving guidance on the required and optional clauses to be incorporated into the various types of contracts. FAR 52.102-1 encourages incorporation of clauses by reference, "to the maximum extent practicable," if permitted by FAR 52.3 or they are contained in agency-wide procurement regulations such as the Department of Defense Federal Acquisition Regulation Supplement (DFARS).

Part III, Section J, contains a list of all attachments to the contract providing the title, date, and number of pages for each document, FAR 14.201-4. Part IV, Section K, contains all representations and certifications as well as any other provision that must be filled in by the bidders, FAR 14.201-5(a). This section, by clustering all of these requirements in a single section, reduces the possibility of bidders failing to fill out a necessary form. Section L contains all of the instructions to bidders on procedures that will be followed in evaluating bids and selecting the bidders — commonly known as "solicitation provisions." See FAR 52.101, which defines a solicitation provision as "a term or condition used only in solicitations and applying only before contract award." FAR 14.201-6 contains a long list of the standard solicitation provisions used in sealed bid procurements. Section M contains all of the "price-related factors" other than bid price that will be evaluated in selecting the low bidder, FAR 14.201-5(c).

Once a solicitation is issued, communication between the procuring agency and prospective bidders is discouraged except through the procurement official named in the solicitation for that purpose. Routine questions that do not require an amendment to the solicitation or do not involve the clarification of ambiguous provisions may be answered orally or by letter. If the procurement is complex or numerous questions have been raised, the procuring agency may convene a prebid conference for all interested parties.

The solicitation therefore serves a number of functions in the procurement process. It must: (1) lay out the ground rules of the competition, including the information to be supplied by bidders and the bid opening time; (2) contain the specifications or incorporate them by reference when permitted; and (3) contain all the terms and conditions of the proposed contract. Both the substantive requirements of the solicitation and the procedures by which it is publicized can influence the degree of competition that is obtained.

2. *Amendment of IFBs*

A contracting officer may — because of revised needs, or errors or deficiencies in the solicitation — find it necessary to change the solicitation by issuing an amendment. FAR 14.208 outlines the procedures for the issuance of amendments to IFBs:

> (a) If it becomes necessary to make changes in quantity, specifications, delivery schedules, opening dates, etc., or to correct a defective or ambiguous invitation, such changes shall be accomplished by amendment of the invitation for bids using Standard Form 30, Amendment of Solicitation/Modification of Contract. The fact that a change was mentioned at a pre-bid conference does not relieve the necessity for issuing an amendment. Amendments shall be sent, before the time for bid opening, to everyone to whom invitations have been furnished and shall be displayed in the bid room.
>
> (b) Before amending an invitation for bids, the period of time remaining until bid opening and the need to extend this period shall be considered. When only a short time remains before the time set for bid opening, consideration should be given to notifying bidders of an extension of time by telegrams or telephone. Such extension must be confirmed in the amendment.
>
> (c) Any information given to a prospective bidder concerning an invitation for bids shall be furnished promptly to all other prospective bidders as an amendment to the invitation (1) if such information is necessary for bidders to submit bids or (2) if the lack of such information would be prejudicial to

> uninformed bidders. The information shall be furnished even though a pre-bid conference is held. No award shall be made on the invitation unless such amendment has been issued in sufficient time to permit all prospective bidders to consider such information in submitting or modifying their bids.

Even though the regulations provide that amendment shall be sent to each concern to whom the invitation for bids has been furnished, the Comptroller General has consistently held that the bidder bears the risk of not receiving an amendment, assuming that such failure is not the result of a conscious and deliberate effort by the agency to exclude the bidder from participating in the competition, *Monterey Advanced Imaging Ctr.*, Comp. Gen. Dec. B-253152, 93-2 CPD ¶ 118; *Southwestern Enters., Inc.*, Comp. Gen. Dec. B-245491.2, 92-1 CPD ¶ 88; *GSX Gov. Servs., Inc.*, Comp. Gen. Dec. B-239549.2, 91-1 CPD ¶ 12; *Crown Management Servs., Inc.*, Comp. Gen. Dec. B-232431.4, 89-1 CPD ¶ 393; *C-Way Constr. Co.*, Comp. Gen. Dec. B-198885, 80-2 CPD ¶ 41.

The underlying theory is that the agency discharges its legal responsibility when it issues and dispatches an amendment in sufficient time to permit all bidders to consider the amendment in formulating their bids, *Southern Technologies, Inc.*, 67 Comp. Gen. 204 (B-228516), 88-1 CPD ¶ 57; *Maintenance Pace Setters, Inc.*, Comp. Gen. Dec. B-212757, 84-1 CPD ¶ 98; *Eugene Ricciardelli, Inc.*, Comp. Gen. Dec. B-212871, 83-2 CPD ¶ 640. Hence, in *Electro-Mechanical Indus., Inc.*, 52 Comp. Gen. 281 (B-176839) (1972), an amendment issued to the bidder, but addressed incorrectly, provided no basis for cancellation. The Comptroller General stated that "the propriety of a particular procurement must be determined from the Government's point of view upon the basis of whether adequate competition and reasonable prices were obtained, not upon whether every possible prospective bidder was afforded an opportunity to bid." Thus, late receipt of an amendment will require cancellation and resolicitation if adequate competition is not received as a result of the transmission defect. For example, in *Andero Constr., Inc.*, 61 Comp. Gen. 253 (B-203898), 82-1 CPD ¶ 133, the Comptroller General ignored the general rule that the bidder bears the risk of nondelivery of an amendment to the solicitation, because the agency failed to affirmatively establish that it complied with DAR 2-208 (similar to FAR 14.208), and three of four bidders appeared not to have received the amendment in the mail. The agency never affirmatively stated that the amendments were mailed, and thus the Comptroller General recommended that the agency cancel the IFB and resolicit its requirements. See also *Gadsden Moving & Storage Co.*, Comp. Gen. Dec. B-250658, 93-1

CPD ¶ 134, where the Comptroller General found that the agency had deprived the protester of the opportunity to compete by not providing the protester with a copy of the amendment in a timely manner. The Comptroller General stated that the agency conceded that it used an incorrect mailing address, the protester took reasonable steps to obtain the amendment, and the agency had received only one bid. In *Phillip Sitz Constr.*, Comp. Gen. Dec. B-245941, 92-1 CPD ¶ 101, the Comptroller General found that because the agency had sent the IFB to the protester, it was required to place the protester on the mailing list and to send it any solicitation amendments. The agency conceded that the protester was not included on the mailing list and that it did not send the amendment. Further, the Comptroller General stated that as a result of the agency's actions, only one responsive bid was received, thereby undermining the CICA mandate for full and open competition.

3. Time for Submission of Bids

Bidders must be given sufficient time to submit bids. See FAR 14.202-1, which states:

> (a) *Policy.* A reasonable time for prospective bidders to prepare and submit bids shall be allowed in all invitations, consistent with the needs of the Government. (For construction contracts, see 36.303(a).) A bidding time (i.e., the time between issuance of the solicitation and opening of bids) of at least 30 calendar days shall be provided when synopsis is required by Subpart 5.2.
>
> (b) *Factors to be considered.* Because of unduly limited bidding time, some potential sources may be precluded from bidding and others may be forced to include amounts for contingencies that, with additional time, could be eliminated. To avoid unduly restricting competition or paying higher-than-necessary prices, consideration shall be given to such factors as the following in establishing a reasonable bidding time: (1) degree of urgency; (2) complexity of requirement; (3) anticipated extent of subcontracting; (4) whether use was made of preinvitation notices; (5) geographic distribution of bidders; and (6) normal transmittal time for both initiations and bids.

Contracting officers may extend (or postpone) the bidding time in order to increase competition, *Ling Dynamic Sys., Inc.*, Comp. Gen. Dec. B-252091, 93-1 CPD ¶ 407; *Combustion Equip. Co.*, Comp. Gen. Dec. B-228291, 87-2 CPD ¶ 627.

FAR 14.208(b) provides that no award should be made on an invitation unless an amendment has been issued in sufficient time to permit all prospective bidders to consider such information in submitting or modifying their bids. However, the amount of time necessary will be determined by the complexity of the amendment. In *Pacific Contractors, Inc.*, Comp. Gen. Dec. B-190568, 78-2 CPD ¶ 297, the Comptroller General found that the contracting officer acted reasonably in affording four of five bidders less than one day and a fifth bidder less than one hour to consider the effect of an amendment, where the amendment was simple in nature and none of the bidders (including the protester) objected prior to bid opening. In *Tom Walsh & Assocs.*, Comp. Gen. Dec. B-212750, 84-1 CPD ¶ 78, the Comptroller General again determined that the protester had been given sufficient time (six days) to consider the amendment. Conversely, 45 Comp. Gen. 651 (B-158766) (1966) held that no award should be made where amendments to the IFB were furnished to prospective bidders only two days before bid opening. The Comptroller General rejected the Government's argument that since six bidders were able to respond, sufficient time was available; the six bidders were all located nearer to the bidding site than the protester.

It is within the contracting officer's discretion to extend the bidding time when it appears that there was insufficient time to consider an amendment to a solicitation. See *Tolina Constr. Co.*, Comp. Gen. Dec. B-213028, 84-1 CPD ¶ 244, where it was determined that the contracting officer had not abused his discretion when he extended bid opening by one week in order to allow potential bidders additional time to consider a material amendment to the IFB. The contracting officer made this decision on the day prior to bid opening because no bids had been received, and he feared that competition had been restricted by the issuance of the amendment.

B. Submission of Bids

Bids that are submitted in accordance with the IFB bind the bidder once they are opened. However, the regulations permit their withdrawal before bid opening.

1. Method of Submission

As discussed in Chapter 2, bids are *offers* submitted in the precise form specified by the Government in the IFB. The method of submission of sealed bids is covered by a standard solicitation provision set forth in FAR 52.214-5:

SUBMISSION OF BIDS (FEB 1997)

(a) Bids and bid modifications shall be submitted in sealed envelopes or packages (unless submitted by electronic means) (1) addressed to the office specified in the solicitation, and (2) showing the time and date specified for receipt, the solicitation number, and the name and address of the bidder.

(b) Bidders using commercial carrier services shall ensure that the bid is addressed and marked on the outermost envelope or wrapper as prescribed in subparagraphs (a)(1) and (2) of this provision when delivered to the office specified in the solicitation.

(c) Telegraphic bids will not be considered unless authorized by the solicitation; however, bids may be modified or withdrawn by written or telegraphic notice.

(d) Facsimile bids, modifications, or withdrawals, will not be considered unless authorized by the solicitation.

(e) Bids submitted by electronic commerce shall be considered only if the electronic commerce method was specifically stipulated or permitted by the solicitation.

Bids may be submitted through the United States Postal Service, any other delivery service, or may be hand delivered. Bids may also be submitted by facsimile, if authorized by the solicitation, FAR 14.202-7. Bids transmitted by facsimile must be received in the office designated for the receipt of bids before the time set for bid opening, *Butt Constr. Co.*, Comp. Gen. Dec. B-258507, 95-1 CPD ¶ 45. The controlling time is the time the *last page* of the bid is received by the agency (not when the transmission begins), *Radar Devices, Inc.*, Comp. Gen. Dec. B-249118, 92-2 CPD ¶ 287. However, if the bid is late due to mishandling on the part of the Government, the bid will be considered timely.

Bids (other than those sent by facsimile) should be submitted in a sealed envelope or package on the forms provided in the IFB. However, such submission is not required if the bidder is careful to comply fully with the IFB. Failure to seal a bid envelope is a minor informality that will not prevent the consideration of the bid, Comp. Gen. Dec. B-153288, Mar. 19,

1964, *Unpub.*; *Rhoads Constr. Co.,* Comp. Gen. Dec. B-242992, 91-1 CPD ¶ 561. Upon receipt of an unsealed bid the Government should place the bid in a sealed envelope.

Bids must be submitted prior to bid opening. Paragraph (d) of the Late Submissions, Modifications, and Withdrawals of Bids solicitation provision in FAR 52.214-7 states that "[t]he only acceptable evidence to establish the time of receipt at the Government installation is the time/date stamp of that installation on the bid wrapper or other documentary evidence of receipt maintained by the installation." This provision has been strictly enforced, *Pershield, Inc.*, Comp. Gen. Dec. B-256827, 94-2 CPD ¶ 46; *Isometrics, Inc.*, Comp. Gen. Dec. B-245095, 91-2 CPD ¶ 477; *Monitor Northwest Co.*, Comp. Gen. Dec. B-193357, 79-1 CPD ¶ 437.

a. *Bids Sent by Other Than U.S. Mail*

Extreme care must be exercised in sending bids by means other than United States mail. The Submission of Bids solicitation provision allows the use of telegraphic bids or facsimile bids only when they are permitted by the IFB. This limitation has been strictly enforced, *Marbex, Inc.*, Comp. Gen. Dec. B-221995, 86-1 CPD ¶ 212; *Electro-Mechanical Indus., Inc.*, 52 Comp. Gen. 281 (B-176839) (1972) (telegraphic bids may not be considered unless they are explicitly authorized by the solicitation). Similarly, a facsimile bid modification will be rejected if the solicitation does not authorize the submission by facsimile, *H. Bendzulla Contracting*, Comp. Gen. Dec. B-246112, 91-2 CPD ¶ 441. See also *Recreonics Corp.*, Comp. Gen. Dec. B-246339, 92-1 CPD ¶ 249 (bid nonresponsive where bidder acknowledged a material amendment by facsimile transmission, which was not permitted by the solicitation). A bidder was not permitted to rely on a contracting officer's oral authorization that a facsimile transmission was permissible because it was not explicitly authorized in the solicitation. In *Michelin Aircraft Tire Corp.*, Comp. Gen. Dec. B-248498, 92-2 CPD ¶ 142, the Comptroller General agreed that an agency had properly rejected a bid modification sent by facsimile when the bidder had been orally advised by an agency contract specialist that the modification should be sent in that manner because the agency's telegraphic equipment had become inoperative. The Comptroller General reasoned that oral modification of these rules prejudiced other offerors.

The standard Submission of Bids solicitation provision permits submission of bid modifications telegraphically. However, if the IFB does not contain a current telex number, the bidder assumes the risk in using a prior number in sending a modification to the agency's telex machine, *Kings Point Indus., Inc.*, Comp. Gen. Dec. B-244398, 91-2 CPD ¶ 331. In that case, the Comptroller General ruled that the contracting officer had properly rejected proof that a modification had been received by the agency's telex machine when the agency had discontinued its direct receipt of such communications. On the other hand, if the solicitation contains telex numbers, it is improper to disconnect the machine without informing bidders, *Kings Point Mfg. Co.*, Comp. Gen. Dec. B-199992, 81-1 CPD ¶ 293; *Singleton Contracting Co.*, Comp. Gen. Dec. B-215186, 84-2 CPD ¶ 471; to allow the telex machine to run out of paper, *Hydro Fitting Corp.*, 54 Comp. Gen. 999 (B-183438), 75-1 CPD ¶ 331; or to lose the service because of failure to pay the service fee, *Standard Prods. Co.*, Comp. Gen. Dec. B-215832, 85-1 CPD ¶ 86.

If the IFB contains either the Telegraphic Bids solicitation provision in FAR 52.214-13 or the Facsimile Bids solicitation provision in FAR 52.214-31, the bidder may submit the bid in the form permitted, but care must be exercised to ensure that the bid precisely complies with the technical requirements of the applicable provision. For example, both clauses require that all required representations and information be submitted just as if the bid had been mailed, *Triple D Orchards, Inc.*, Comp. Gen. Dec. B-219648, 85-2 CPD ¶ 525. The Telegraphic Bids provision also requires the submission of a signed confirming copy of the bid. The Facsimile Bids provision requires that a proper signature be included and makes the offeror responsible for all defects in the bid due to faulty transmission or reception. This provision has been strictly enforced against the offeror even in cases where the offeror had proof of transmission of the facsimile, *Southern CAD/CAM*, 71 Comp. Gen. 78 (B-244745), 91-2 CPD ¶ 453; *S.W. Elecs. & Mfg. Corp.*, Comp. Gen. Dec. B-249308, 92-2 CPD ¶ 320; *Microscope Co.*, Comp. Gen. Dec. B-257015, 94-2 CPD ¶ 157.

If the IFB permits the submission of bids or modifications by telegraph or facsimile, the Late Submissions, Modifications, and Withdrawals of Bids solicitation provision subjects them to the same stringent rules applied to late submission of mailed bids. See *Singleton Contracting Corp.*, 68 Comp. Gen. 149 (B-232760), 88-2 CPD ¶ 592, where the Comptroller General held that since the only acceptable evidence of time of receipt is the agency time/date stamp, the late bid modification was properly rejected even though there was evidence from Western Union that the modification was timely delivered.

Bidders must be certain to correctly and carefully instruct telegraph company employees on such matters as the exact date, time, and place of delivery. In *Western Alaska Contractors, J.V.*, Comp. Gen. Dec. B-241839, 91-1 CPD ¶ 248, the telegraph company attempted to send telephone notice of a bid modification to the agency, but stated to the agency employee that it had a "bid wire." The agency employee reasonably assumed that this was an attempted telephone bid, which was not permitted by the IFB. The agency employee so informed the telegraph company and hung up the telephone. The Comptroller General sustained the agency's decision to reject the protester's subsequent written modification, which was received after bid opening.

b. Notice of Nonsubmission of Bid

The following standard solicitation provision at FAR 52.214-9 calls for notification if a firm does not intend to submit a bid:

FAILURE TO SUBMIT BID (JUL 1995)

> Recipients of this solicitation not responding with a bid should not return this solicitation, unless it specifies otherwise. Instead, they should advise the issuing office by letter, postcard, or established electronic commerce methods, whether they want to receive future solicitations for similar requirements. If a recipient does not submit a bid and does not notify the issuing office that future solicitations are desired, the recipient's name may be removed from the applicable mailing list.

A firm should comply with the requirements of this provision because it is not uncommon for an agency to remove a company's name from the mailing list if it fails to respond to a number of solicitations.

2. Firm Bid Rule

As discussed in Chapter 2, sealed bids are subject to the "firm bid rule," which prohibits modification or withdrawal of bids after bid opening. The rationale for this rule is that it would be detrimental to the competitive bidding system if bidders were allowed to change their bids after they have had an opportunity to discover what other bidders have offered. The only major exception to the firm bid rule is for mistakes in bid. This is discussed fully in Section IV of this chapter.

The firm bid rule is incorporated in both Standard Form 33 and Standard Form 1447. Block 12 of Standard Form 33 provides:

> [T]he undersigned agrees, if this offer is accepted within ____ calendar days (60 calendar days unless a different period is inserted by the offeror) from the date for receipt of offers specified above, to furnish any or all items upon which prices are offered at the price set opposite each item, delivered at the designated point(s), within the time specified in the schedule.

Block 11 of Standard Form 1447 provides:

> If offer is accepted by the government within ____ calendar days (60 calendar days unless offeror inserts a different period) from the date set forth in blk 9 above, the contractor agrees to hold its offered prices firm for the items solicited herein and to accept any resulting contract subject to the terms and conditions stated herein.

In *W.A. Scott v. United States*, 44 Ct. Cl. 524 (1909), the Court of Claims recognized the distinction between private and Government contracts and would not allow the withdrawal of a bid deposit, stating at 527:

> The agents of the Government stand upon a different footing from private individuals in the matter of advertising for the letting of contracts in behalf of the United States. They have no discretion. They must accept the lowest or the highest responsible bid, or reject all and readvertise. Private individuals are not required thus to act. Hence it is apparent that Government agents should be allowed a reasonable time after the opening of bids before they are allowed to be withdrawn so they can be afforded opportunities to ascertain whether collusion or fraud had been perpetrated against the United States by the parties engaged in the bidding. It is also apparent that if the rule of allowing immediate withdrawals after the results of the bidding are made known, frauds innumerable could be perpetrated against the United States and thus public justice would be greatly hampered.

In *Refining Assocs. v. United States*, 124 Ct. Cl. 115, 109 F. Supp. 259 (1953), the court reiterated that bids were irrevocable for the time stated in the invitation. In that case, the invitation for bids stipulated that after the opening of bids no bid could be withdrawn. In holding the bid to be irrevocable, the court stated at 122:

> [The bidder] submitted its bid subject to these provisions, and agreed that [the Government] should have 15 days from the date of opening to consider the bids. In so doing, [the bidder] was accorded the right of having its bid

> considered on the merits, and this right was conditioned on the premise that the bid would remain open during the time specified.

See *Nation-Wide Reporting & Convention Coverage*, GSBCA 8309, 88-2 BCA ¶ 20,521, where the IFB specifically required that the bidder keep its offer open for 90 days from the opening of bids. The board held that the bidder could not revoke its bid during this period and that, once the bids were opened, the Government's "acceptance after an attempted withdrawal . . . create[d] a valid contract" and failure to perform after this acceptance justified default termination. See also *Western Adhesives*, GSBCA 7449, 85-2 BCA ¶ 17,961 (acceptance of bid during an extended acceptance period created a valid contract even though bidder attempted to withdraw bid); and 19 Comp. Gen. 761 (B-8531) (1940) (agreement to perform contract if awarded within 20 days of bid opening is held the same as an agreement not to revoke offer in that period).

3. Modification or Withdrawal of Bids Prior to Bid Opening

Bids may be freely modified or withdrawn as long as this is accomplished no later than *the exact time set for bid opening*. Such modification or withdrawal is effective if it is in accordance with the procedures set forth in the Late Submissions, Modifications, and Withdrawal of Bids solicitation provision in FAR 52.214-7. These procedures are summarized in FAR 14.303 as follows:

> (a) Bids may be modified or withdrawn by any method authorized by the solicitation, if notice is received in the office designated in the solicitation not later than the exact time set for opening of bids. Unless proscribed by agency regulations, a telegraphic modification or withdrawal of a bid received in such office by telephone from the receiving telegraph office shall be considered. However, the message shall be confirmed by the telegraph company by sending a copy of the written telegram that formed the basis for the telephone call. If the solicitation authorizes facsimile bids, bids may be modified or withdrawn via facsimile received at any time before the exact time set for receipt of bids, subject to the conditions specified in the provision prescribed in 14.201-6(w). Modifications received by telephone (including a record of those telephoned by the telegraph company) or facsimile shall be sealed in an envelope by a proper official. The official shall write on the envelope (1) the date and time of receipt and by whom, and (2) the number of the invitation for bids, and shall sign the envelope. No in-

formation contained in the envelope shall be disclosed before the time set for bid opening.

(b) A bid may be withdrawn in person by a bidder or its authorized representative if, before the exact time set for opening of bids, the identity of the persons requesting withdrawal is established and that person signs a receipt for the bid.

(c) Upon withdrawal of an electronically transmitted bid, the data received shall not be viewed and shall be purged from primary and backup data storage systems.

These procedures have been held to preclude a bidder from withdrawing a bid by telephone, *Ruggiero v. United States*, 190 Ct. Cl. 327, 420 F.2d 709 (1970); *John A. Maney*, GSBCA 6550, 83-2 BCA ¶ 16,744. See *Satellite Servs.*, Comp. Gen. Dec. B-207631.2, 83-1 CPD ¶ 357, where a bidder telephonically requested that the agency return its bid. When the agency failed in its attempt to comply with the request, the bidder continued to participate in the procurement and was eventually awarded the contract. The Comptroller General denied a protest of a competitor, holding that a telephone request for withdrawal from other than a telegraph company will not be honored. It appears that a valid withdrawal would have occurred if the agency had returned the bid. Withdrawal in person is permitted, but failure to return the bid has been considered sufficient evidence that such withdrawal did not occur, *Tomahawk Constr. Co.*, Comp. Gen. Dec. B-243582, 91-2 CPD ¶ 137.

Bid modifications must be submitted in sufficient time so that they will be delivered to the bid opening room prior to opening. When they are sent telegraphically, time must be allowed for the receiving employee to take the telegram (or telephone message from the telegraph company) to the bid opening. See *Roy McGinnis & Co.*, Comp. Gen. Dec. B-275988, 97-1 CPD ¶ 156 (bid modification received five seconds before deadline was insufficient); and *Sanchez Painting & Constr. Co.*, Comp. Gen. Dec. B-232287, 88-2 CPD ¶ 554, (bid received one minute before deadline was insufficient). See also *Monitor Northwest Co.*, Comp. Gen. Dec. B-193357, 79-1 CPD ¶ 437, where the Comptroller General stated that it is unrealistic to assume that a document not marked as a bid or bid modification received five minutes before bid opening would reach the designated office on time. When the telegraph company attempts to notify the agency by telephone that a modification has been sent, the bidder bears the risk that the agency will reject the call, *Western Alaska Contractors, J.V.*, Comp. Gen. Dec. B-241839, 91-1 CPD ¶ 248. In case of an IFB for multiple items, a telegraphic modification may include prices on items that were not in the original bid, 39 Comp. Gen. 163 (B-140552) (1959).

C. Public Opening

Public opening of bids is one of the key elements of sealed bidding. The importance of public opening was recognized by the Comptroller General in *Computer Network Corp.*, 55 Comp. Gen. 445 (B-183639), 75-2 CPD ¶ 297, as stated at 451:

> The public advertising statute, 41 U.S. Code § 253(b) (1970), requires that: "All bids shall be publicly opened at the time and place stated in the advertisement." We have interpreted this requirement for a public opening to mean that the bid must publicly disclose the essential nature and type of the products offered and those elements of the bid which relate to price, quantity and delivery terms. 53 Comp. Gen. 24 (1973). The purpose of public opening of bids for public contracts is to protect both the public interest and bidders against any form of fraud, favoritism or partiality and such openings should be conducted to leave no room for any suspicion of irregularity. *Page Airways, Inc., et al.*, 54 Comp. Gen. 120 (1974), 74-2 CPD ¶ 99; 48 Comp. Gen. 413 (1968).

Bids must be closely guarded prior to opening to ensure that no bidder has access to the bids of competitors. FAR 14.401 provides the following guidance on the safeguarding of bids received prior to the time for bid opening:

> (a) All bids (including modifications) received before the time set for the opening of bids shall be kept secure. Except as provided in paragraph (b) of this section, the bids shall not be opened or viewed, and shall remain in a locked bid box, a safe, or in a secured, restricted-access electronic bid box. If an invitation for bids is cancelled, bids shall be returned to the bidders. Necessary precautions shall be taken to ensure the security of the bid box or safe. Before bid opening, information concerning the identity and number of bids received shall be made available only to Government employees. Such disclosure shall be only on a "need to know" basis. When bid samples are submitted, they shall be handled with sufficient care to prevent disclosure of characteristics before bid opening.
>
> (b) Envelopes marked as bids but not identifying the bidder or the solicitation may be opened solely for the purpose of identification, and then only

> by an official designated for this purpose. If a sealed bid is opened by mistake (e.g., because it is not marked as being a bid), the envelope shall be signed by the opener, whose position shall also be written thereon, and delivered to the designated official. This official shall immediately write on the envelope (1) an explanation of the opening, (2) the date and time opened, and (3) the invitation for bids number, and shall sign the envelope. The official shall then immediately reseal the envelope.

If a bid is returned unopened to the bidder, it may not be considered even if the basis for return was improper, *Leggett & Platt, Inc.*, Comp. Gen. Dec. B-246733, 92-1 CPD ¶ 314 (Federal Express envelope contained two bids, and agency returned envelope to bidder unopened because of action taken with respect to the other procurement); *Dima Contracting Corp.*, Comp. Gen. Dec. B-186487, 76-2 CPD ¶ 208 (bid was returned unopened because of reference on envelope to another IFB).

The procedures for public opening of unclassified bids are contained in FAR 14.402-1:

> (a) The bid opening officer shall decide when the time set for opening bids has arrived and shall inform those present of that decision. The officer shall then (1) personally and publicly open all bids received before that time, (2) if practical, read the bids aloud to the persons present, and (3) have the bids recorded. The original of each bid shall be carefully safeguarded, particularly until the abstract of bids required by 14.403 has been made and its accuracy verified.
>
> (b) Performance of the procedure in paragraph (a) above may be delegated to an assistant, but the bid opening officer remains fully responsible for the actions of the assistant.
>
> (c) Examination of bids by interested persons shall be permitted if it does not interfere unduly with the conduct of Government business. Original bids shall not be allowed to pass out of the hands of a Government official unless a duplicate bid is not available for public inspection. The original bid may be examined by the public only under the immediate supervision of a Government official and under conditions that preclude possibility of a substitution, addition, deletion, or alteration in the bid.

A different bid opening procedure must be used for classified bids. See FAR 14.402-2 stating:

> The opening of classified bids shall not be accessible to the general public. Openings may be witnessed and the results recorded by those bidder representatives (a) who have been previously cleared from a security standpoint and (b) who represent bidders who were invited to bid. Bids shall be made available to those persons authorized to attend the opening of bids. No public record shall be made of bids or bid prices received in response to classified invitations for bids.

Public opening is required even if only one bid is received and the contracting officer knows before reading the bid that it will be rejected, *Wessel Co.*, Comp. Gen. Dec. B-189629, 77-2 CPD ¶ 152.

Inherent in the public opening procedure is the availability of the bid and its accompanying documents for public inspection. Thus, it is improper not to read an unclassified bid publicly and not to make it available for public inspection, Comp. Gen. Dec. B-170049, Aug. 2, 1970, *Unpub.* However, the failure to publicly read a bid is a deviation of form, not substance, which does not affect the validity of an otherwise proper award. If the bidders have an opportunity to examine the awardee's bid, there is no prejudice in failing to publicly read it, *A. A. Beiro Constr. Co.*, Comp. Gen. Dec. B-192664, 78-2 CPD ¶ 425. See also *George C. Martin, Inc.*, 55 Comp. Gen. 110 (B-182175), 75-2 CPD ¶ 55; and *Moir Ranch & Constr. Co.*, Comp. Gen. Dec. B-191616, 78-1 CPD ¶ 423. However, bids that may not be publicly read because they contain information that the bidder considers "proprietary" must be rejected even if the bidder authorizes disclosure after bids are opened, *Sperry-Univac*, Comp. Gen. Dec. B-200378, 81-1 CPD ¶ 38; *Computer Network Corp.*, 55 Comp. Gen. 445 (B-183639), 75-2 CPD ¶ 297. See also *Industrial Acoustics Co.*, Comp. Gen. Dec. B-255123.2, 94-1 CPD ¶ 220 (prohibition against disclosing required test data); *Prestex, Inc.*, Comp. Gen. Dec. B-195251.2, 79-2 CPD ¶ 411 (prohibition against revealing place of performance in a small business set-aside); *Warner Labs., Inc.*, Comp. Gen. Dec. B-189502, 77-2 CPD ¶ 314 (prohibition against disclosure of unit prices); and 53 Comp. Gen. 24 (B-178140) (1973) (prohibition against disclosure of descriptive data relating to responsiveness of bid). However, a prohibition on disclosure of information that deals only with a bidder's responsibility will not require rejection, *Ace-Federal Reporters, Inc.*, 54 Comp. Gen. 340 (B-181451), 74-2 CPD ¶ 239.

The premature opening of bids raises a serious question regarding the propriety of the procurement. Ordinarily such a circumstance requires that all bids be rejected and the matter resolicited unless later bidders did not obtain an unfair advantage, 34 Comp. Gen. 395 (B-122707) (1955). In *Chemical Compounding Corp.*, Comp. Gen. Dec. B-210317, 83-1 CPD ¶ 499, the Comptroller General held that it was not unreasonable to cancel a solicitation where the premature opening coincided with inadequate and ambiguous specifications. In determining whether the solicitation should be canceled when bids are prematurely opened through error or inadvertence, the Comptroller General considers the impact on both the bidders who submitted the prematurely opened bids and the other bidders. An alternate remedy is to give the bidder whose bid has been prematurely opened sufficient time to revise its bid, even if that requires extending the period for bidding, *Bartomeli Co.*, 71 Comp. Gen. 237 (B-246060), 92-1 CPD ¶ 170. See *Leach Corp.*, Comp. Gen. Dec. B-212534, 83-2 CPD ¶ 623, and *Boyd Lumber Co.*, Comp. Gen. Dec. B-189641, 77-2 CPD ¶ 315, holding that giving the bidders of the prematurely opened bids the opportunity to confirm, modify, or withdraw the bids was sufficient protection. It is not clear how the opportunity to modify a bid assists the bidder whose bid has been prematurely opened when there is evidence that other bidders have learned of the amount of the bid. However, there is no adequate means of correcting this error once it has been made, and to restrict the procurement to the bidders whose bids have been opened prematurely would be prejudicial to other bidders, *Air, Inc.*, 69 Comp. Gen. 504 (B-238468), 90-1 CPD ¶ 533.

D. Bid Opening Time

To be considered for award, bids must be "submitted so that they will be received in the office designated in the Invitation for Bids . . . not later than the exact time set for opening of bids," FAR 14.302(a). The regulations provide that the contracting officer should announce to those present when the time for bid opening has arrived, FAR 14.402-1(a). A bid may be submitted up to, or simultaneously with, the time the bid opening officer announces that the time for bid opening has arrived, *Carothers Constr., Inc. v. United States*, 18 Cl. Ct. 745 (1989); *Amfel Constr., Inc.*, Comp. Gen. Dec. B-233493.2, 89-1 CPD ¶ 477.

The determination of the bid opening officer of when the opening time has arrived is binding unless it is clearly unreasonable. See *W.W. Asphalt*, Comp. Gen. Dec. B-235560, 89-2 CPD ¶ 106, upholding a determination that a bid was untimely when late by the opening officer's clock even though it was one minute early by the Federal Express courier's hand-held computer. See also *Swinerton & Walberg Co.*, Comp. Gen. Dec. B-242077.3, 91-1 CPD ¶ 318, and *Chattanooga Office Supply Co.*, Comp. Gen. Dec. B-228062, 87-2 CPD ¶ 221 (bid untimely when late by bid opening office clock even though timely by telephonic report); *Lambert Constr. Co.*, Comp. Gen. Dec. B-181794, 74-2 CPD ¶ 131 (bid modification found to be late based on agency time stamp even though modification was timely according to Western Union); and 51 Comp. Gen. 173 (B-173392) (1971) (bid found to be late based on the time shown on the clock in the bid opening room even though bid was timely according to the clock in the hall). See also *General Eng'g Corp.*, Comp. Gen. Dec. B-245476, 92-1 CPD ¶ 45, upholding a determination that a bid was late based on the bid opening room clock even though the watch of an Army civil engineering technician, who was in the bid room when the protester first appeared with its bid, stated that the time was 10:59 and 45 seconds a.m., and the bid opening room clock was shown, after bid opening, to be about three minutes fast.

Occasionally, a bid opening officer's declaration of bid opening time has been shown to be unreasonable. See *William F. Wilke, Inc. v. Department of the Army*, 485 F.2d 180 (4th Cir. 1973), where a bid that was hand delivered four minutes after the scheduled bid opening could not be considered even though no other bids had been opened, and the bid opening officer announced after receipt of the late bid: "It is now 3:00 p.m." Similarly, contracting officers cannot arbitrarily use the time on their own watch as evidence of the bid opening time when the clock in the bid opening room shows another time, 41 Comp. Gen. 807 (B-148972) (1962). However, opening officers may reasonably rely on the time shown by their watch if the bid opening room is not equipped with a clock, and only "persuasive independent evidence" will rebut the reasonableness of this reliance, *Tate Architectural Prods., Inc.*, Comp. Gen. Dec. B-191361, 78-1 CPD ¶ 389. This rule is based on the Comptroller General's view that the bid opening officer's declaration is prima facie evidence of the time for bid opening. Unless there is a clear record to contradict this evidence, the authorized declaration serves as the criterion of lateness, *MACETO, Inc.*, Comp. Gen. Dec. B-207878, 82-2 CPD ¶ 300; *Peter Kiewit & Sons' Co.*, Comp. Gen. Dec. B-189022, 77-2 CPD ¶ 41; *Hyster Co.*, 55 Comp. Gen. 267 (B-182995), 75-2 CPD ¶ 176.

If the Government admits that its time determination was incorrect, it may accept a bid that was determined to be late but was actually submitted on time. In *Washington Mechanical Contractors, Inc. v. United States*, 612

F. Supp. 1243 (N.D. Cal. 1984), bids were due by 2:30 p.m., and the bidder's agent had been standing at a wall phone until 2:29 p.m. waiting for a final figure. The agent had previously synchronized his watch with the phone company's time service. The agent received the final figure and inserted it into the bid forms, walked to the bid opening room (which took less than 30 seconds), and tried to submit its bid. The bid opening officer said the bid was late and would not stamp it. An assistant who was present in the room said that the bid opening officer should at least stamp the envelope as received. By this time 30 seconds had passed, and the stamp read 2:31 p.m. Subsequent testing by the Government indicated that the clock was one to three minutes fast and the bid was held to have been properly accepted.

The relevant time for determining whether a bid is timely received by the Government is that time when the bidder relinquishes possession of its bid. If a bidder does not relinquish control of a bid prior to the bid opening officer's announcement of bid opening, it will be considered late even if the bid is time/date stamped before bid opening. In *J. C. Kimberly Co.*, Comp. Gen. Dec. B-255018.2, 94-1 CPD ¶ 79, although the bid was time/date stamped 2:29 p.m., the bid was late because it was not tendered to the bid opening officer until after the 2:30 p.m. announcement that the time for receipt of bids has passed. Similarly, in *Reliable Builders, Inc.*, Comp. Gen. Dec. B-249908.2, 93-1 CPD ¶ 116, a bid that was time/date stamped at 2:01 p.m. was not considered late because the record showed that the bidder relinquished control of the bid by 2:00 p.m., the exact time called for in the solicitation, and prior to the bid opening officer's declaration of the time for bid opening. A bid handed to and returned by the agency receptionist outside the designated bid opening room does not constitute submission of the bid, *J.C.N. Constr. Co.*, Comp. Gen. Dec. B-250815, 93-1 CPD ¶ 166. Even if the bidder is in the bid opening room, a bid received an instant late must be rejected. In *Lucero*, Comp. Gen. Dec. B-228425, 87-2 CPD ¶ 566, the Comptroller General rejected a bid as late under the following circumstances:

> Bids were due by 2:00 p.m. September 25, 1987 in the conference room of the District Ranger's Office. At approximately 1:50 or 1:55 p.m. of that day, Lucero entered the conference room after returning from an unsuccessful attempt to locate and inspect the timber sale area. When Lucero arrived, the bid receiving agent introduced himself, inquired as to whether Lucero had an updated form, advised him to complete the appropriate forms "right away," and answered Lucero's questions. Another Forest Service agent

> then assisted Lucero in completing the forms and at 1:59 p.m. advised him that he had one minute remaining in which to submit the bid. At 1:59 p.m. and 55 seconds, Lucero placed the unsealed envelope in front of him, but did not submit it. At 2:00 the bid receiving agent announced that the time for receiving sealed bids had expired. Lucero attempted then to submit his bid but was advised that it could not be accepted since it was after 2:00 p.m.

A bid that is relinquished simultaneously with the announcement of closing will be considered timely. In *Carothers Constr., Inc. v. United States*, 18 Cl. Ct. 745 (1989), the court upheld the Comptroller General's decision that the bid was submitted on time. In holding that the Comptroller General's decision had a rational basis, the court stated at 750:

> The GAO's finding that Townsend relinquished control of Barron's bid (including all bid documents) simultaneously with Quinton's announcement that the time for receipt of bids had passed had ample support in the record. The GAO based its finding on the unsworn declarations of Quinton, Brignole and Thoele. The Comptroller General focused on the following: Quinton declared that she was watching the clock, and "when the second hand reached the 12 she began to announce that the time for receipt of bids had passed. At that time . . . [Townsend] threw the other copies of the bid (and other bid documents) on the table in front of her." Supporting this was the statement of Brignole that Townsend placed the other bid documents simultaneously with Quinton's announcement. Finally, the Comptroller General noted Thoele's declaration that he picked up the documents on the table. Based on these unsworn declarations, the court finds that a rational basis existed for the GAO's decision.

The timeliness requirement is not satisfied merely because the bid is in the Government's possession. The bid must be delivered to the exact location specified in the solicitation or it will be considered late, unless the failure to arrive on time is a result of Government mishandling, *Alpha Technical Servs., Inc.*, Comp. Gen. Dec. B-243715, 91-2 CPD ¶ 56 (bid delivered to Government installation approximately two hours before bid opening but not received in bid opening room until next day was late); *Larry J. Robinson & Co.*, Comp. Gen. Dec. B-234991, 89-1 CPD ¶ 559 (delivery to central switchboard area insufficient); *Four Thirteen, Inc.*, ASBCA, 84-1 BCA ¶ 17,155 (telegram delivered to guard in lobby approximately three hours before opening insufficient).

FAR 14.402-3 permits bid opening officers to postpone the time scheduled for bid opening. Generally this occurs when the contracting officer has reason to believe that an "important segment" of bidders have been delayed for causes beyond their control and without their fault or negligence (i.e., flood, fire, weather conditions), or when an emergency or unanticipated event interrupts the normal Government process, making the scheduled bid opening impractical. See *B.L.I. Constr. Co.*, Comp. Gen. Dec. B-239246.2, 90-2 CPD ¶ 85, in which an extension was permitted so that bidders could get to the designated room on time. Note, however, that postponing the date set for bid opening is strictly within the contracting officer's discretion, *Educational Planning & Advice, Inc.*, Comp. Gen. Dec. B-274513, 96-2 CPD ¶ 173 (determination to proceed with bid opening despite hurricane not an abuse of discretion). When a postponement occurs due to an interruption in the normal Government process and urgent Government requirements prevent amendment of the solicitation under FAR 14.208, bid opening is extended to "the first work day on which normal Government processes resume," at the same time of day as originally specified in the solicitation.

E. Late Bids

The Government has adopted very strict requirements precluding the consideration of late bids unless precisely defined exceptions are met. See FAR 14.304-1 stating:

> (a) A late bid, modification of bid, or withdrawal of bid shall not be considered unless received before contract award, and —
>
> > (1) It was sent to a contracting office in the United States or Canada by registered or certified mail not later than 5 calendar days before the bid receipt date specified;
> >
> > (2) It was sent by mail (or telegram or facsimile, if authorized) or hand-carried (including delivery by a commercial carrier) if it is determined by the Government that the late receipt was due solely to mishandling after receipt at the Government installation;
> >
> > (3) It was sent to a contracting office in the United States or Canada by U.S. Postal Service Express Mail Next Day Service—Post Office to Addressee not later than 5:00 p.m. at the place of mailing 2 working days prior to the date specified for receipt of bids. The term "working days" excludes weekends and Federal holidays; or
> >
> > (4) It was transmitted through an electronic commerce method authorized by the solicitation and was received at the initial point of entry to

> the Government infrastructure not later than 5:00 p.m. one working day prior to the date specified for receipt of bids.

> (b) The only acceptable evidence to establish the date of mailing of a late bid, modification, or withdrawal sent to a contracting office in the United States or Canada either by registered or certified mail is a U.S. or Canadian Postal Service postmark both on the envelope or wrapper and on the original receipt from the U.S. or Canadian Postal Service. Both postmarks must show a legible date, or the bid, modification, or withdrawal shall be deemed to have been mailed late. (The term "postmark" means a printed, stamped, or otherwise placed impression (exclusive of a postage meter machine impression) that is readily identifiable without further action as having been supplied and affixed on the date of mailing by employees of the U.S. or Canadian Postal Service. Therefore, bidders should request the postal clerk to place a legible hand cancellation bull's-eye postmark on both the receipt and the envelope or wrapper.)

> (c) Acceptable evidence to establish the time of receipt at the Government installation includes the time/date stamp of such installation on the bid wrapper, other documentary evidence of receipt maintained by the installation, or oral testimony or statements of Government personnel.

> (d) The only acceptable evidence to establish the date of mailing of a late bid, modification, or withdrawal sent by U.S. Postal Service Express Mail Next Day Service—Post Office to Addressee is the date entered by the post office receiving clerk on the "Express Mail Next Day Service—Post Office to Addressee" label and the postmark on the envelope or wrapper and on the original receipt from the U.S. Postal Service. "Postmark" has the same meaning as defined in paragraph (b) of this subsection, excluding postmarks of the Canadian Postal Service. Therefore, bidders should request the postal clerks to place a legible hand cancellation bull's-eye postmark on both the receipt and the envelope or wrapper.

> (e) Notwithstanding the above, a late modification of an otherwise successful bid which makes its terms more favorable to the Government will be considered at any time it is received and may be accepted.

Bids that cannot meet the exceptions in the regulations are considered late even though received immediately after the bid opening time. See *James L. Ferry & Sons, Inc.*, Comp. Gen. Dec. B-181612, 74-2 CPD ¶ 245 (hand-delivered bid not considered even though only three minutes late); *National Blower & Sheet Metal Co.*, Comp. Gen. Dec. B-194895, 79-2 CPD ¶ 240 (bid not accepted though only two minutes late and no bids had yet been opened); and *Parmatic Filter Corp.*, Comp. Gen. Dec. B-209296, 83-1 CPD ¶ 234 (telegraphic bid recorded as being received two minutes late was rejected where protester was unable to prove record was inaccurate).

1. Government Mishandling

A late bid may be considered for award if Government mishandling after timely receipt at the agency is the sole or paramount cause for its late receipt, FAR 14.304-1. In *Watson Agency, Inc.*, Comp. Gen. Dec. B-241072, 90-2 CPD ¶ 506, the Comptroller General found Government mishandling where a guard placed the bid in the wrong safe, and the agency subsequently failed to remove the bid from the guardhouse and deliver it to the Center's Classified Mails and Files Branch for distribution, in accordance with agency procedures. Government mishandling also was found in *John J. Kirlin, Inc.*, Comp. Gen. Dec. B-250244, 92-2 CPD ¶ 419, where a contractor representative delivered a hand-carried bid to the wrong bid opening officer, relying upon a sign on the entrance door to the building that the bid opening room for an IFB for "Compilation of 13 Construction Jobs" had been changed. The representative interpreted the sign to mean that the IFB for his construction project had been combined with other solicitations and that the room had been changed. Compounding the confusion, the bid opening officer for the combined construction jobs accepted the bid and clocked it at 1:46 p.m. without noticing that the envelope listed a different solicitation number. For other cases finding Government mishandling, see *AABLE Tank Servs., Inc.*, Comp. Gen. Dec. B-273010, 96-2 CPD ¶ 180 (contract specialist identified in the solicitation as contact person for further information misdirected bid); *Gair's Med. Transcription Servs.*, Comp. Gen. Dec. B-257426, 94-2 CPD ¶ 115 (contracting officer failed to remove bid from safe prior to bid opening); *Victoria Inn Ltd.*, Comp. Gen. Dec. B-256724, 94-2 CPD ¶ 37 (bid package misfiled in bid cabinet); and *Data Gen. Corp.*, Comp. Gen. Dec. B-252239, 93-1 CPD ¶ 457 (installation postal authorities received bid two days prior to bid opening but did not deliver bid to contracting office due to the absence of a driver with a security clearance).

Despite the apparent simplicity of the current late bid regulations, there are frequent controversies concerning what constitutes "mishandling by the Government." In *Butt Constr. Co.*, Comp. Gen. Dec. B-258507, 95-1 CPD ¶ 45, the Comptroller General found that Government mishandling was the paramount cause of the late receipt of the modification, noting that:

> When facsimile transmission is authorized, however, it is not unreasonable for bidders to expect that they can take advantage of that technology shortly before the bid opening — the transmission normally consumes very little time (here less than a minute), and agencies, before authorizing facsimile bids, are expected to have in place adequate procedures for ensuring timely delivery of such bids upon receipt.

In this case the Comptroller General stated that the facsimile bid modification was received at least seven minutes prior to bid opening time; the facsimile machine was only a short distance from the room designated in the solicitation for receipt of bids and the bid opening room; the bid modification was properly identified as directed by the solicitation; and the record established that mail room clerks unreasonably delayed prompt delivery. In *Hydro Fitting Mfg. Corp.*, 54 Comp. Gen. 999 (B-183438), 75-1 CPD ¶ 331, a telegraphic bid received late due to the malfunction of a Government telex machine was considered Government mishandling. Similarly, in *Brazos Roofing, Inc.*, Comp. Gen. Dec. B-275113, 97-1 CPD ¶ 43, the Comptroller General held that where the agency amended a solicitation so close to the deadline for submitting bids that submission by facsimile was the only practicable alternative to bidders, a bid received late due to an inoperable facsimile machine was considered Government mishandling. However, in *Stack-On Prods. Co.*, Comp. Gen. Dec. B-181862, 74-2 CPD ¶ 220, a late bid modification could not be considered even though it was received on the telex machine on time but was not transcribed for 50 minutes because the operator was busy. The Comptroller General found that this was an example of ordinary delay and not Government mishandling. See also *PDP Analytical Servs.*, Comp. Gen. Dec. B-251776.2, 93-1 CPD ¶ 294, in which the Comptroller General found no Government mishandling where, due to accumulation of mail over the Christmas holidays, the mail took longer to sort and was not distributed until after bid opening. In *Environmental Control Technologies*, Comp. Gen. Dec. B-250859, 93-1 CPD ¶ 172, the Comptroller General found no Government mishandling where the bid was received at the installation post office 40 minutes prior to bid opening but, as a result of the installation's normal mail delivery, did not arrive at the place for receipt of bids until after bid opening. See, however, *Frequency Eng'g Labs.*, Comp. Gen. Dec. B-186390, 76-2 CPD ¶ 166, where a mailed bid sat for one hour because only two of four mail handlers were on duty, and the Comptroller General found Government mishandling. In an unusual case, *Scherr Constr. Co. v. United States*, 5 Cl. Ct. 249 (1984), the failure of the Government to inform a bidder of the flex-time schedule during which the Government officer operated was found to be the primary cause of the nonreceipt of the contractor's telegraphic modification on the day before bid opening. The late bid rule, however, remained intact since the court ultimately determined that Western Union's lack of diligence in delivering the modification the following day when the Government office was open was the primary cause for nonreceipt.

The Comptroller General will not consider the Government mishandling exception to the late bid rule until the bidder establishes, with documented evidence, that the bid was actually received at the Government facility prior to bid opening, *Power Connector, Inc.*, Comp. Gen. Dec. B-256362, 94-1 CPD ¶ 369. The record of a commercial carrier is not sufficient evidence to support the contention that the bid was timely delivered, *J.C.N. Constr. Co.*, Comp. Gen. Dec. B-270068, 96-1 CPD ¶ 42; *Qualimetrics, Inc.*, Comp. Gen. Dec. B-213162, 84-1 CPD ¶ 332. However, commercial carrier records may be considered if the record contains corroborating relevant evidence, including statements by Government personnel, *Santa Cruz Constr., Inc.*, Comp. Gen. Dec. B-226773, 87-2 CPD ¶ 7. In *Eliscu & Co.*, Comp. Gen. Dec. B-211617, 84-1 CPD ¶ 75, the Comptroller General would not consider the issue of Government mishandling because the only proof available for bid receipt was the Government stamp that recorded the delivery as being late.

Though the regulations refer to Government mishandling only at the Government installation after receipt, the Comptroller General has avoided strict application of the rule where Government mishandling in the process of receipt caused the lateness. See, for example, *Kings Point Mfg. Co.*, Comp. Gen. Dec. B-199992, 81-1 CPD ¶ 293 (Government cancellation of authorized Western Union terminal without notice constituted Government mishandling); *I & E Constr. Co.*, 55 Comp. Gen. 1340 (B-186766), 76-2 CPD ¶ 139 (locking the building designated for receipt of bids constituted Government mishandling under the "intent and the spirit" of the late bid regulations); *Sun Int'l*, Comp. Gen. Dec. B-208146, 83-1 CPD ¶ 78 (Government failure to follow established procedures for receiving express mail on the weekends was the paramount cause of the bid's late receipt; the bid was therefore acceptable despite never being in the Government's possession); *Howard Management Group*, Comp. Gen. Dec. B-221889, 86-2 CPD ¶ 28 (mishandling found when agency misinformed bidder that it had a telex machine); and *Standard Prods. Co.*, Comp. Gen. Dec. B-215832, 85-1 CPD ¶ 86 (mishandling found when agency failed to pay for telex service). In *Microflect*, 66 Comp. Gen. 269 (B-225118), 87-1 CPD ¶ 173, the agency provided that mailed offers be sent to a post office call number.

The Comptroller General found mishandling when a bid mailed by express mail was delivered to the post office four and one-half hours before bid opening but was not picked up by the agency in time for bid opening. The Comptroller General ruled that an agency must pick up items from the post office when it designates that as a proper place for submission.

If the bidder significantly contributes to late receipt of a bid, any subsequent Government mishandling is not the paramount reason for the bid's late receipt. In *Bill Strong Enters., Inc.*, Comp. Gen. Dec. B-260721, 95-2 CPD ¶ 10, the Comptroller General found that Bill Strong and its agent, Federal Express, contributed significantly to the late receipt of the bid by not including the correct label on the bid. Thus, the bid was held to be late even though it was delivered to the mail room prior to noon but was not delivered to the bid opening room in time for the 2:00 p.m. bid opening. The Comptroller General found no mishandling because the mail clerk had no way of ascertaining that it was a bid to be opened that day.

2. Hand-Carried Bids

The regulations do not provide exceptions for late bids that are hand carried. See *Nueva Constr. Co.*, Comp. Gen. Dec. B-270009, 96-1 CPD ¶ 84 (hand-carried bid delivered seconds after bid opening officer declared that the time for bid opening stated in the solicitation had arrived was late); *J. C. Kimberly Co.*, Comp. Gen. Dec. B-255018.2, 94-1 CPD ¶ 79 (hand-carried bid received after bid opening officer declared that the time for bid opening had arrived was late); and *GS Edwards*, Comp. Gen. Dec. B-255202, 94-1 CPD ¶ 54 (hand-carried bid delivered three minutes late could not be considered). See also *Boulder Constr., Inc.*, Comp. Gen. Dec. B-250671, 93-1 CPD ¶ 122; *Wyoming Sawmills, Inc.*, Comp. Gen. Dec. B-248331, 92-2 CPD ¶ 45; and *General Eng'g Corp.*, Comp. Gen. Dec. B-245476, Jan. 9, 1992, *Unpub.*

A bid that is delivered by commercial carrier is considered to be "hand carried" and is considered late if it does not arrive timely at the location designated in the solicitation, *Barnes Elec. Co.*, Comp. Gen. Dec. B-241391.2, 91-1 CPD ¶ 10; *Hans Olsen Egg Co.*, Comp. Gen. Dec. B-235085, 89-2 CPD ¶ 75.

The Comptroller General permits the consideration of late hand-carried bids where the Government is responsible for the lateness. In *Kelton Contracting, Inc.*, Comp. Gen. Dec. B-262255, 95-2 CPD ¶ 254, the

Comptroller General found that the agency properly accepted a late hand-carried bid because the Government's mishandling was the paramount cause of the lateness. Here, the agency clerk placed the bid package in the wrong mail slot, which was the reason for the bid arriving late. See also *Palomar Grading & Paving, Inc.*, Comp. Gen. Dec. B-274885, 97-1 CPD ¶ 16 (incorrect address specified in the solicitation for the delivery of bids); *Ed Kocharian & Co.*, Comp. Gen. Dec. B-271186, 96-1 CPD ¶ 170 (office designated for bid opening was locked); *Power Connector, Inc.*, Comp. Gen. Dec. B-256362, 94-1 CPD ¶ 369 (agency personnel misdirected delivery of bid package to the wrong floor); *Pearl Properties*, Comp. Gen. Dec. B-249519, 92-2 CPD ¶ 333 (bid received three and one half hours prior to bid opening but placed in the bottom of a mail tote); *Ranco Constr., Inc.*, Comp. Gen. Dec. B-246345, 92-1 CPD ¶ 234 (employee failed to expedite delivery of package as instructed and instead placed bid in normal delivery); *Baeten Constr., Co.*, Comp. Gen. Dec. B-210681, 83-2 CPD ¶ 203 (Government official misdirected the delivery person); *Dale Woods*, Comp. Gen. Dec. B-209459, 83-1 CPD ¶ 396 (Government changed the room for bid delivery without informing all bidders); *Empire Mechanical Contractors, Inc.*, Comp. Gen. Dec. B-202141, 81-1 CPD ¶ 471 (commercial carrier delivered the bid before opening, but the bid was delivered late to the opening official due to mishandling); *Scot, Inc.*, Comp. Gen. Dec. B-189345, 77-2 CPD ¶ 425 (commercial carrier delivered the bid late due to Government misdirection); *LeChase Constr. Corp.*, Comp. Gen. Dec. B-183609, 75-2 CPD ¶ 5 (delay was caused by a change in the room designated for bid opening); and *Fredericks Rubber Co.*, 51 Comp. Gen. 69 (B-172974) (1971) (bid was placed in the wrong box due to the Government's failure to mark the correct bid box clearly). See also *Richards Painting Co.*, Comp. Gen. Dec. B-232678, 89-1 CPD ¶ 76, where mishandling was found where a hand-carried bid was delivered three minutes after bid opening because the front door of the Government building was locked, and the bid opening room was different from the unstaffed room designated for the receipt of hand-carried bids. But see *L.V. Anderson & Sons, Inc.*, Comp. Gen. Dec. B-189835, 77-2 CPD ¶ 249, where mishandling did not "save" a returned bid that may have been altered subsequent to opening.

If the Government is not the cause of the lateness of the hand-carried bid, no other excuse will assist the bidder in having its bid considered. See *Great Plains Asbestos Control, Inc.*, Comp. Gen. Dec. B-271841, 96-2 CPD ¶ 19 (commercial carrier leaving bid at military installation's freight terminal no excuse); *Ironhorse, Ltd.*, Comp. Gen. Dec. B-256582, 94-1 CPD ¶ 176, and *B.E.C. Med. Products*, Comp. Gen. Dec. B-256483, 94-1 CPD

¶ 159 (severe weather no excuse); *Braceland Bros., Inc.*, Comp. Gen. Dec. B-248234, 92-2 CPD ¶ 69 (messenger delivering bids to wrong address no excuse); *John Holtman & Sons, Inc.*, Comp. Gen. Dec. B-246062, 92-1 CPD ¶ 187 (bid delivered to warehouse rather than the office specified in the solicitation was late); *High Vacuum Equip. Corp.*, Comp. Gen. Dec. B-224511, 86-2 CPD ¶ 189 (flight delays no excuse); *National Minority Research Dev. Corp.*, Comp. Gen. Dec. B-220057, 85-2 CPD ¶ 303 (automobile accident no excuse); *Key Airlines*, Comp. Gen. Dec. B-214122, 84-1 CPD ¶ 242 (late bid properly rejected despite bidder never receiving an official copy of the IFB); *Northwest Instrument*, Comp. Gen. Dec. B-200873, 80-2 CPD ¶ 373 (traffic delays and business necessity do not excuse late bid); and *Unitron Eng'g Co.*, 58 Comp. Gen. 748 (B-194707), 79-2 CPD ¶ 155 (closing of a common carrier's offices due to the Three Mile Island nuclear emergency did not serve as an excuse for late delivery of hand-carried bid).

The general rules regarding Government mishandling apply to hand-carried bids. If the bidder significantly contributes to a hand-carried bid being received late, any subsequent Government mishandling will not be considered the cause of the lateness, *Scherr Constr. Co. v. United States*, 5 Cl. Ct. 249 (1984) (Western Union had final opportunity to deliver a bid modification on time and did not). Similarly, a bidder's failure to follow solicitation procedures will generally be considered the primary reason for the late delivery rather than improper Government action, *Sencland CDC Enters.*, Comp. Gen. Dec. B-252796, 93-2 CPD ¶ 36 (bid rejected as late where commercial carrier delivered bids to the mail room rather than to the bid depository for hand-carried bids in accordance with the solicitation instructions). In *Gould Metal Specialists Inc.*, Comp. Gen. Dec. B-246686, 92-1 CPD ¶ 311, the protester's bid was delivered to the mailing address rather than the address for hand-carried bids. The Comptroller General held that when a bidder "dispatches its agent — a common carrier — to an address other than that designated for hand-carried bids, it bears the risk of untimely receipt, if the time spent by the agency rerouting the bid package is reasonable." Although the bid arrived at 10:00 a.m., it did not get rerouted in time for the 3:00 p.m. bid opening. The Comptroller General stated that the bidder's error in sending the bid to the wrong location did not obligate the Government to send a special messenger to get it to bid opening on time. *George W. Kane, Inc.*, Comp. Gen. Dec. B-245382.2, 92-1 CPD ¶ 143, is a particularly harsh decision. Here, the protester arrived at 10:53 a.m. to deliver its bid. Not seeing a receptionist or signs posted by the agency with information regarding the bid opening, the protester walked down a corridor and asked a secretary, "Is this where the bid goes in for the Holly Point bid?" Supposedly the secretary answered, "Yes sir. Go right in," although this was not confirmed by the agency. The protester proceeded to the bid opening room. This, however, was not the room designated as the bid depository location. Meanwhile, the bid opening officer waited in the bid depository room, where the date/time stamp machine was located, until at least 11:00 a.m. and then proceeded to the bid opening room. The protester's bid was sitting on the desk when the bid opening officer entered the room, and the bid opening officer said that it was late. The protester argued that "I've been here for six minutes I know and no one told me any different about where to turn the bid in." The Comptroller General held that the bidder is responsible for delivering its bid to the proper place at the proper time. See also *Federal Contracting Corp.*, 54 Comp. Gen. 304 (B-181286), 74-2 CPD ¶ 229; and *Greer Hydraulics, Inc.*, Comp. Gen. Dec. B-182826, 75-1 CPD ¶ 249. This line of cases was distinguished in *Scot, Inc.*, 57 Comp. Gen. 119 (B-189345), 77-2 CPD ¶ 425, where the commercial carrier attempted to deliver a bid to the office designated for hand-delivered bids rather than the office designated for mailed bids, but was directed elsewhere by Government personnel. The Comptroller General found the bid late due to Government mishandling and advised the protester to seek bid preparation costs. See also *Cost Bros., Inc.*, Comp. Gen. Dec. B-213257.2, 84-1 CPD ¶ 469. The same result was reached in *Visar Co.*, Comp. Gen. Dec. B-208701, 83-1 CPD ¶ 100, where the commercial carrier gave the bid package to a Government official not affiliated with the contracting process, and that official did not properly deliver the bid.

II. RESPONSIVENESS

A key element of the sealed bidding system is that nonresponsive bids may not be considered by contracting officers and must be rejected. This *responsiveness* requirement is derived from the statutory provision providing that award be made to the bidder "whose bid conforms to the solicitation," 10 U.S.C. § 2305(b)(3); 41 U.S.C. § 253b(c). The purpose of this requirement is to promote fairness and objectivity, and to encourage wide competition by requiring all bidders to bid on exactly the same work and to the same terms and conditions — permitting the selection of the winning bidder solely on the basis of price. Thus, the responsiveness requirement ensures that a bidder will not receive an award by offering to perform the work perhaps less expensively but in a manner that represents a material deviation from the terms of the IFB. This promotes the integrity of the procurement process by protecting other bidders that might also have proposed such a method had they known that the Government was willing to accept it.

The mandatory rejection rule also prevents bidders with ambiguous bids from having "two bites at the apple" by contending, after seeing the competing bids, that their bids conformed to the solicitation (or did not conform), depending on the interpretation that is most beneficial to them.

The requirement for mandatory rejection has made responsiveness a focal point for award controversies. If the low bidder can be disqualified as nonresponsive, the next bidder in line becomes eligible to receive the award at a higher price. Thus, both the Government and the bidder could be "losers" if a bid is found to be nonresponsive. This section first examines the criteria used in determining whether a nonconformity is sufficient to require the bid being classified as nonresponsive. It next considers the disposition of nonconforming bids and the limited circumstances under which an award may be made on the basis of a nonresponsive bid. The section concludes with an analysis of the types of nonconforming bids and the factors that determine whether such bids are nonresponsive.

A. Criteria for Determining Responsiveness

A bid is nonconforming if it fails to comply exactly with the literal requirements of the IFB. However, not all nonconforming bids are nonresponsive. In determining whether a nonconforming bid is nonresponsive, the focus may be either on the nature of the nonconformity or on the effect of the nonconformity on the competition. This section first considers whether the nonconformity is *sufficiently material* to warrant rejection of the bid or is merely an *immaterial deviation* that may be waived. The next section examines the extent to which *prejudice to other bidders* resulting from a nonconformity determines responsiveness. The section concludes with a discussion of the distinction between responsiveness of bids and responsibility of bidders.

1. Materiality of Nonconformity

The FAR defines responsiveness in terms of materiality of the nonconformity. See FAR 14.301(a), which states:

> To be considered for award, a bid must comply in all material respects with the invitation for bids. Such compliance enables bidders to stand on an equal footing and maintain the integrity of the sealed bidding system.

Thus, a bid that contains an immaterial nonconformity is not considered to be a nonresponsive bid. Such nonconformities are called *minor informalities.* FAR 14.405 defines a "minor informality":

> A minor informality or irregularity is one that is merely a matter of form and not of substance. It also pertains to some immaterial defect in a bid or variation of a bid from the exact requirements of the invitation that can be corrected or waived without being prejudicial to other bidders. The defect or variation is immaterial when the effect on price, quantity, quality, or delivery is negligible when contrasted with the total cost or scope of the supplies or services being acquired. The contracting officer either shall give the bidder an opportunity to cure any deficiency resulting from a minor informality or irregularity in a bid or waive the deficiency, whichever is to the advantage of the Government. Examples of minor informalities or irregularities include failure of a bidder to —
>
> (a) Return the number of copies of signed bids required by the invitation;
>
> (b) Furnish required information concerning the number of its employees;
>
> (c) Sign its bid, but only if —
>
> (1) The unsigned bid is accompanied by other material indicating the bidder's intention to be bound by the unsigned bid (such as the submission of a bid guarantee or a letter signed by the bidder, with the bid, referring to and clearly identifying the bid itself); or
>
> (2) The firm submitting a bid has formally adopted or authorized, before the date set for opening of bids, the execution of documents by typewritten, printed, or stamped signature and submits evidence of such authorization and the bid carries such a signature;
>
> (d) Acknowledge receipt of an amendment to an invitation for bids, but only if —
>
> (1) The bid received clearly indicates that the bidder received the amendment, such as where the amendment added another item to the invitation and the bidder submitted a bid on the item; or

(2) The amendment involves only a matter of form or has either no effect or merely a negligible effect on price, quantity, quality, or delivery of the item bid upon;

(e) Furnish affidavits concerning parent company and affiliates, if required pursuant to the clause at 52.214-8, Parent Company and Identifying Data, and 52.214-17, Affiliated Bidders; and

(f) Execute the representations with respect to Equal Opportunity and Affirmative Action Programs, as set forth in the clauses at 52.222-22, Previous Contracts and Compliance Reports, and 52.222-25, Affirmative Action Compliance.

The clearest example of a minor informality is the failure to meet IFB requirements that deal with the form rather than the substance of the bid. For example, minor informalities have been found when a bidder failed to initial an erasure correction on the bid form as required by the IFB, *Werres Corp.*, Comp. Gen. Dec. B-211870, 83-2 CPD ¶ 243, and when a bidder failed to initial changes to a bid as required by the IFB, *Stone Forest Indus., Inc.*, Comp. Gen. Dec. B-246123, 92-1 CPD ¶ 161. In *E-Systems, Inc.*, Comp. Gen. Dec. B-190693, 78-1 CPD ¶ 236, the Comptroller General upheld the contracting officer's determination that the bidder's use of "n/c" instead of "n" to indicate items for which the Government would not be charged was a minor informality. See also *Image Contracting*, Comp. Gen. Dec. B-253038, 93-2 CPD ¶ 95 (failure to indicate to which of two locations bidder intended to deliver the items); *Storage Technology Corp. v. Department of the Army*, GSBCA 12626-P, 94-1 BCA ¶ 26,548 (use of dashes instead of "none" in procurement integrity certificate); *Boardsen Assocs.*, Comp. Gen. Dec. B-245876, 92-1 CPD ¶ 115 (failure to insert "none" in procurement integrity certificate to indicate no previous violations); *Grumman Aerospace Corp.*, 64 Comp. Gen. 553 (B-216068), 85-1 CPD ¶ 596 (failure to include positive dollar amount for separate line item contrary to procuring agency's requirements); and *Dyneteria, Inc.*, 54 Comp. Gen. 345 (B-181470) (1975) (dashes inserted in lieu of price).

Nonconformities that have a trivial or de minimis effect on price will also be considered immaterial. What constitutes "de minimis" will be determined on a case-by-case basis. For example, in *Brutoco Eng'g & Constr., Inc.*, 62 Comp. Gen. 111 (B-209098), 83-1 CPD ¶ 9, the Comptroller General waived as a minor informality a bidder's failure to acknowledge a wage rate amendment that increased bid price by only 0.8 percent of the $95,213 difference between the low bidder and the second low bidder. The Comptroller General concluded at 112:

> [I]nsofar as the effect on the competitive bid system is concerned, Brutoco's failure to acknowledge the amendment cannot reasonably be construed to affect the competition such that the competitive bid system will be adversely affected if the firm is permitted now to cure the defect by acknowledging the amendment.

See also *Marine Power & Equip. Co.*, 62 Comp. Gen. 75 (B-208393), 82-2 CPD ¶ 514 ($100 deficiency in required bid deposit of 20 percent of $75,522 properly waived as minor deviation); and *Roan Corp.*, Comp. Gen. Dec. B-211228, 84-1 CPD ¶ 116, *recons. denied*, 84-1 CPD ¶ 211 (heavily front-loaded bid with option periods presented waivable minor informality because of project's high startup costs). For an example of an amendment whose provisions could not be waived, despite the de minimis effect of the amendment on bid price, see *Grade-Way Constr. v. United States*, 7 Cl. Ct. 263 (1985), where it was held that the Government could not waive an amendment modifying wage rate schedules because failure to acknowledge the amendment would give the bidder the opportunity to become ineligible for award by not curing the defect. The Comptroller General has followed this logic, holding that failure to acknowledge a wage rate amendment can only be waived if the bidder can demonstrate that it was already obligated to pay the wages in the amendment; *ABC Project Management, Inc.*, Comp. Gen. Dec. B-274796.2, 97-1 CPD ¶ 74. See *Tri-Tech Int'l, Inc.*, Comp. Gen. Dec. B-246701, 92-1 CPD ¶ 304, where failure to acknowledge an amendment increasing wage rates made the bid nonresponsive even though the fringe benefit rate decreased more than the wages increased.

Failure to submit mandatory information has been held to be an immaterial deviation when the agency does not intend to use the information to determine which bid is in line for award. Thus, a bid not furnishing required price lists was held to be responsive because the agency did not intend to use the lists to determine the bid prices, *American Spare Parts, Inc.*, Comp. Gen. Dec. B-224745, 87-1 CPD ¶ 4. See also *W.M. Schlosser Co.*, Comp. Gen. Dec. B-258284, 94-2 CPD ¶ 234, where a bid was found responsive, in spite of the fact that it did not contain required descriptive literature, because the agency had no intention of using the literature to determine if the proposed work complied with the contract requirements.

The minor informality rule has also been applied to technically nonresponsive bids where the bid otherwise leaves no doubt as to the intention of the bidder to offer an acceptable bid. In *AABCO, Inc. v. United States*, 3 Cl. Ct. 109 (1983), the failure of a bidder to code each of the prices on a magnetic tape exactly as required by the solicitation was properly waived as a minor informality. The Claims Court held that there was no doubt whatsoever as to the intended bids, stating at 119:

> A mere glance at the printout that accompanied the submitted tape would confirm the exact dollars and cents that the [contractor] intended to bid.

See also *Sere Constr. Corp.*, Comp. Gen. Dec. B-205098, 82-1 CPD ¶ 453 (failure to provide unit prices waivable because single unit price provided sufficient bidding pattern to allow accurate pricing of any contract modification); *MKB Constructors (J.V.)*, Comp. Gen. Dec. B-250413, 93-1 CPD ¶ 50 (failure to submit a price for 1 of 60 line items was a minor informality where the intended price of the missing line item could be determined from the bid itself); *Mike Johnson, Inc.*, Comp. Gen. Dec. B-271943, 96-2 CPD ¶ 66 (failure to break the contract work into three line items of work per revised bid schedule was a minor informality because the revised schedule did not add any additional work beyond that encompassed in the original bid schedule). However, when the bid fails to provide sufficient information to allow the contracting officer to determine the details of the intended bid, it must be rejected. See *Childrey Contract Servs., Inc.*, Comp. Gen. Dec. B-258653, 95-1 CPD ¶ 60 (insufficient information in bid to determine what prices bidder intended to bid for option years without prices); and *Norris Paint & Varnish Co.*, Comp. Gen. Dec. B-206079, 82-1 CPD ¶ 425 (no information in bid to determine whether bidder had a valid Qualified Products List test number as required by IFB).

Statements in invitations as to the automatic effect of noncompliance with certain provisions on responsiveness are not controlling where noncompliance involves a minor deviation, *Mid-South Metals, Inc.*, Comp. Gen. Dec. B-257056, 94-2 CPD ¶ 78 (submission of multiple credit card accounts as bid guarantee was responsive, even though solicitation prohibited the use of multiple credit card accounts); *Isometrics, Inc.*, Comp. Gen. Dec. B-212434, 83-2 CPD ¶ 618 (failure to supply shipping information as required by the IFB does not render bid nonresponsive when agency was able to derive the information from other bids). In *D.N. Owens Co.*, 57 Comp. Gen. 231 (B-190749), 78-1 CPD ¶ 66, even though the solicitation required rejection of bids for nonresponsiveness if bidders failed to submit bid samples, the Comptroller General held that the failure to submit the sample was a minor irregularity since the extent of detail in the specifications made the sample unnecessary.

The decision as to whether a particular nonconformity constitutes a minor deviation has sometimes been characterized as a discretionary one for the contracting officer, Comp. Gen. Dec. B-172227, May 13, 1971, *Unpub.* Cases where proper waiver was found include *Consolidated Contracting Eng'g*, Comp. Gen. Dec. B-274319, 96-2 CPD ¶ 174 (failure to acknowledge amendment properly waived where the amendment results in less stringent obligations on the bidder); *Elliott Co.*, Comp. Gen. Dec. B-212897, 84-1 CPD ¶ 130 (failure to include Qualified Price List information was properly waived when the information could be obtained from other facts within the bid); *Massee Builders, Inc.*, 61 Comp. Gen. 227 (B-204450), 82-1 CPD ¶ 72 (failure to utilize additive method in bid construction as stated in IFB properly waived); *Gillette Indus., Inc.*, B-194552, 79-2 CPD ¶ 59 (failure to acknowledge "trivial amendment" properly waived).

The Comptroller General has required waiver in several cases and has suggested award to the protester, even though the contracting officer "in his discretion" had previously refused to waive the nonconformity, *Schuster Eng'g, Inc.*, Comp. Gen. Dec. B-275044, 97-1 CPD ¶ 29 (failure to acknowledge amendment should have been waived because the amendment only relaxed performance requirements); *Legare Constr. Co.*, Comp. Gen. Dec. B-257735, 94-2 CPD ¶ 173 (failure to meet price limitation should have been waived); *Shipco Gen., Inc.*, Comp. Gen. Dec. B-204259, 81-2 CPD ¶ 161 (failure to complete size status certifications should have been waived); *MB Assocs.*, Comp. Gen. Dec. B-197566, 80-1 CPD ¶ 383 (failure to acknowledge amendment that decreases performance costs should have been waived by the contracting officer). See also *National Radio Co.*, Comp. Gen. Dec. B-198240, 80-2 CPD ¶ 67, *recons. denied*, 80-2 CPD ¶ 165 (failure to list separate price for first article testing should have been waived, regardless of IFB warnings, because the bid indicated that such cost was included in the price of the basic item). In an unusual case, *Champion Road Mach. Int'l Corp.*, Comp. Gen. Dec. B-200678, 81-2 CPD ¶ 27, the Comptroller General reversed the contracting officer by ruling that a two horsepower difference between the item offered and the performance required constituted a minor deviation. Another example of a liberal interpretation of the minor deviation rule is *Albano Cleaners, Inc. v. United States*, 197 Ct. Cl. 450, 455 F.2d 556 (1972), where the contractor had qualified the bid by refusing delivery services for orders of less than $50.

The court held that the contracting officer should have waived the deviation because the qualification was not a substantial deviation from the solicitation.

2. *Prejudice to Other Bidders*

In a number of cases the Comptroller General has focused on the prejudice to other bidders rather than on the degree of nonconformity in determining whether a bid is nonresponsive. Thus, a material nonconformity that gives the bidder no advantage or that operates only to the disadvantage of the bidder will not require rejection. See *Gibraltar Indus., Inc.*, Comp. Gen. Dec. B-218537.3, 85-2 CPD ¶ 24 (failure to acknowledge amendment that reduced quantity of items required under the contract properly waived); and *Action Mfg. Co.*, Comp. Gen. Dec. B-208205.2, 82-2 CPD ¶ 526 (failure to indicate which of two equally acceptable designs would be used, as required by the IFB, was waived and the bid properly accepted). In *Davidson-Kelson, Inc.*, Comp. Gen. Dec. B-212551, 83-2 CPD ¶ 589, where an amendment reduced the cost of performance, and no competitive advantage accrued to the bidder as a result of its failure to acknowledge, the error was waived. The Comptroller General stated:

> [T]he bidder's failure to acknowledge an amendment containing a lessened requirement could only be prejudicial to the bidder's own competitive position and even possibly beneficial to the position of the other bidders.

See also *Conrad Indus., Inc.*, Comp. Gen. Dec. B-213974.2, 84-2 CPD ¶ 156 (failure to acknowledge amendment changing delivery terms from "f.o.b. destination" to "f.o.b. origin" properly waived); and *Patterson Enters. Ltd.*, Comp. Gen. Dec. B-207105, 82-2 CPD ¶ 133 (failure to acknowledge amendment extending completion deadline for construction project properly waived). However, a different result is obtained when, in addition to reducing performance cost, the amendment imposes additional work, *Hutto Appliance & Refrigeration Serv.*, Comp. Gen. Dec. B-201585, 81-1 CPD ¶ 495. See also *Childrey Contract Servs., Inc.*, Comp. Gen. Dec. B-258653, 95-1 CPD ¶ 60 (failure to clearly demonstrate that bid price includes work added by amendment renders bid nonresponsive).

For other cases involving application of the "no prejudice" rule, see *Keco Indus., Inc.*, 64 Comp. Gen. 48 (B-216396.2), 84-2 CPD ¶ 491 (second low bidder could not conceivably become low even if permitted the same nonconformity); *Leslie & Elliott Co.*, 64 Comp. Gen. 279 (B-216676), 85-1

CPD ¶ 212 (failure to provide a price for a bid item waived); and *Energy Maintenance Corp.*, 64 Comp. Gen. 425 (B-215281.3), 85-1 CPD ¶ 341 (ambiguity as to low bidder's price waived where bid would be low by a significant margin under least favorable interpretation). Thus, the Comptroller General has, under limited circumstances, required waiver of an otherwise significant deviation where no competitive advantage would result.

3. Responsiveness versus Responsibility

It is critical to determine whether a nonconformity deals with the responsiveness of a bid or the responsibility of the bidder. Responsiveness, an area in which the contracting officer has limited discretion, deals with the question of whether the contractor *has promised to do exactly what the Government has requested.* Responsibility, however, involves the question of whether the contractor *can or will perform as it has promised*, and the contracting officer is accorded a great deal of discretion. Questions of responsiveness are determined only on the basis of information submitted with the bid and on the facts available at the time of bid opening. Conversely, responsibility determinations are made on the basis of all information that may be submitted or available up to the time of award. These concepts are often confused, particularly when the IFB contains specific requirements concerning bidders' responsibility characteristics — such as the requirement for submission of information relating to responsibility. As a general rule, matters that deal with bidder responsibility cannot be converted into matters of responsiveness merely by inserting a provision into the IFB requiring rejection of bids that do not comply, *LORS Med. Corp.*, Comp. Gen. Dec. B-259829, 95-1 CPD ¶ 222 (requirement for submission of information regarding company's policies and procedures relates to responsibility even though IFB required information to be submitted with bid); *Employers Sec. Co.*, GSBCA 6917, 85-1 BCA ¶ 17,885 (requirement that bidder possess an operating license properly relates to responsibility, notwithstanding solicitation language stating that it affects responsiveness); *Lithographic Pubs. Inc.*, Comp. Gen. Dec. B-217263, 85-1 CPD ¶ 357 (solicitation provision stating that bids would be considered nonresponsive if the bidder had defaulted on prior Government contract could not convert a matter of responsibility into one of responsiveness); *Marine Power & Equip. Co.*, Comp. Gen. Dec. B-208393, 82-2 CPD ¶ 514 (specific solicitation provisions could not convert the issue of an agent's authority into a matter of bid responsiveness). However, some matters, such as those discussed below, although dealing with the likelihood of obtaining promised performance, have been permitted to be treated as matters of responsiveness.

a. Quantity in Use Provisions

The requirement that a product have a "quantity in use" for a stated period of time may be considered to deal with responsiveness, even though the requirement deals more with a bidder's ability to satisfy the Government's needs than with the bidder's agreement to do so. See Comp. Gen. Dec. B-175493.1, Apr. 20, 1972, *Unpub.*, where the Comptroller General discusses quantity in use requirements in a responsiveness context. In *Sunsav, Inc.*, Comp. Gen. Dec. B-205004.2, 82-2 CPD ¶ 476, the Comptroller General held that if the requirement relates to the performance history and reliability of the contract *product* and the solicitation requires that the information be furnished, the requirement relates to bid responsiveness and evidence of compliance must be submitted prior to bid opening. The same result was reached by the General Services Administration Board of Contract Appeals in *Micro Star Co.*, GSBCA 8717-P, 87-1 BCA ¶ 19,474.

The key is whether the solicitation clearly establishes that the agency is seeking to assure itself of the reliability of the equipment rather than the capability of the offeror, *National Energy Resources, Inc.*, Comp. Gen. Dec. B-206275, 83-1 CPD ¶ 108 (requirement of coal analysis reports related to the suitability of the product and not to the producer's qualifications). However, the distinction between quantity in use requirements and "experience" requirements is often obscure. For example, in *Cubic Western Data, Inc.*, 57 Comp. Gen. 17 (B-189578), 77-2 CPD ¶ 279, the Comptroller General found the statement that "each bidder, in order to demonstrate his qualifications . . . shall . . . show that he has successfully executed a contract for the design . . . of equipment of the complexity of this contract within . . . two years" related to the bidder's responsibility. Thus, if a quantity in use requirement does not pertain exclusively to the item procured, but includes generally similar equipment previously produced by the offeror, the quantity in use requirement is a matter of responsibility, *Carco Elecs.*, Comp. Gen. Dec. B-186747, 77-1 CPD ¶ 172; *United Power & Control Sys., Inc.*, Comp. Gen. Dec. B-184662, 76-1 CPD ¶ 340; 52 Comp. Gen. 647 (B-175254.2) (1973). Similarly, if information regarding use of the product is requested, but the agency has established no standards for measuring the level of successful use, it will be a matter of responsibility and not responsiveness, *W.M. Schlosser Co.*, Comp. Gen. Dec. B-258284, 94-2 CPD ¶ 234.

b. Bid Guarantees

Another area where the concepts of responsiveness and responsibility are confused is that of bid guarantees. Such bid guarantees, commonly in the form of bid bonds, are necessary when a performance bond is required from the winning bidder, FAR 28.101-1(a). Despite the fact that the bid guarantee relates to whether the contractor will perform (responsibility), it is considered such a material requirement that it has been made a matter of bid responsiveness. Thus, Paragraph (a) of the Bid Guarantee solicitation provision in FAR 52.228-1 states that failure to furnish a required bid guarantee by the time of bid opening "may be cause for rejection of the bid." FAR 28.101-4(a) *requires* rejection of bids not including required bid guarantees, but FAR 28.101-4(c) gives the contracting officer discretion to waive noncompliance as follows:

> Noncompliance with a solicitation requirement for a bid guarantee shall be waived in the following circumstances unless the contracting officer determines in writing that acceptance of the bid would be detrimental to the Government's interest when —
>
> (1) Only one offer is received. In this case, the contracting officer may require the furnishing of the bid guarantee before award;
>
> (2) The amount of the bid guarantee submitted is less than required, but is equal to or greater than the difference between the offer price and the next higher acceptable offer;
>
> (3) The amount of the bid guarantee submitted, although less than that required by the solicitation for the maximum quantity offered, is sufficient for a quantity for which the offeror is otherwise eligible for award. Any award to the offeror shall not exceed the quantity covered by the bid guarantee;
>
> (4) The bid guarantee is received late, and late receipt is waived under 14.304;
>
> (5) A bid guarantee becomes inadequate as a result of the correction of a mistake under 14.407 (but only if the bidder will increase the bid guarantee to the level required for the corrected bid);
>
> (6) A telegraphic offer modification is received without corresponding modification of the bid guarantee, if the modification expressly refers

to the previous offer and the offeror corrects any deficiency in bid guarantee;

(7) An otherwise acceptable bid bond was submitted with a signed offer, but the bid bond was not signed by the offeror;

(8) An otherwise acceptable bid bond is erroneously dated or bears no date at all; or

(9) A bid bond does not list the United States as obligee, but correctly identifies the offeror, the solicitation number, and the name and location of the project involved, so long as it is acceptable in all other respects.

The Comptroller General acceded to this policy in 38 Comp. Gen. 532 (B-137319) (1958) on the grounds that permitting bidders to submit bid bonds after bids had been opened gave them "two bites at the apple." This damaged the integrity of the procurement process by providing the low bidder that had not furnished a bond with the option of winning the competition by furnishing the bond or dropping out by not furnishing it. Since that time, rejection of bids as nonresponsive because of the lack of a proper bid guarantee has been sustained, *Morrison Constr. Servs.*, Comp. Gen. Dec. B-266233, 96-1 CPD ¶ 26; *Johnston Eng'g, Inc.*, Comp. Gen. Dec. B-258180, 94-2 CPD ¶ 246; *Secur-Data Sys., Inc.*, Comp. Gen. Dec. B-255090, 94-1 CPD ¶ 68; *Hugo Key & Son, Inc.*, Comp. Gen. Dec. B-251053.4, 93-2 CPD ¶ 21; *Minority Enters., Inc.*, Comp. Gen. Dec. B-216667, 85-1 CPD ¶ 57. For a circuit court case agreeing with this reasoning, see *Professional Bldg. Concepts, Inc. v. City of Central Falls*, 974 F.2d 1 (1st Cir. 1992). The Comptroller General has also sustained contracting officers' decisions to waive the requirement that bid security be submitted with the bid when one of the FAR situations applies or where there is another valid reason for waiver, *R.P. Richards Constr. Co.*, Comp. Gen. Dec. B-260965, 95-2 CPD ¶ 128 (bid bond with incorrect solicitation number but with other indicia tying it to the IFB); *Centex-Great Southwest Corp.*, Comp. Gen. Dec. B-258578, 95-1 CPD ¶ 19 (bid bond less than 20 percent of bid price but greater than difference between low and next low bid); *S.J. Amoroso Constr. Co.*, Comp. Gen. Dec. B-240687, 90-2 CPD ¶ 432 (bid bond not listing United States as obligee but containing other indicia that it was for the bid). In a few cases, the Comptroller General has also sustained protests that the contracting officer failed to waive this requirement, *Castle Floor Covering*, 70 Comp. Gen. 530 (B-242718), 91-1 CPD ¶ 510 (cashier's check made out to "Farmers Home Bureau, U.S.

Government" in lieu of "Farmers Home Administration" is minor error); *Haag Elec. & Constr., Inc.*, 70 Comp. Gen. 180 (B-240974), 91-1 CPD ¶ 29 (bid bond for less than amount required but more than difference between bid and next low bid).

c. Ability to Perform

The Comptroller General usually rejects arguments that a bidder's inability to perform should be taken to mean that it does not intend to perform and that the bid is therefore nonresponsive, *Peterson Accounting*, Comp. Gen. Dec. B-257411, Sept. 24, 1994, *Unpub.* (agency allegation that bidder failed to submit information to demonstrate ability to perform work); *Luhr Bros., Inc.*, Comp. Gen. Dec. B-248423, 92-2 CPD ¶ 88 (allegation that "bidder-generated production rate" used to determine low bidder on IFB calling for payment based on bid unit prices "is so much a part of the price structure that it has been elevated to a matter of responsiveness"); *American KAL Enters., Inc.*, Comp. Gen. Dec. B-211938, 84-1 CPD ¶ 66 (protest that bidder was unable to meet domestic products requirement); *Grace Indus., Inc.*, Comp. Gen. Dec. B-212263.3, 84-1 CPD ¶ 212 (allegation that bidder was unable to comply with IFB requirement); *Gillette Indus., Inc.*, Comp. Gen. Dec. B-203157, 81-1 CPD ¶ 389 (allegation that low bidders could not perform contract at their bid prices); *Data Test Corp.*, 54 Comp. Gen. 499 (B-181199), 74-2 CPD ¶ 365 (allegation that the bidder did not have an "off the shelf" item as required by the IFB, however, protest sustained on the basis of nonresponsibility).

For a unique case where a bid valid on its face was held nonresponsive, see Comp. Gen. Dec. B-159560, Oct. 7, 1966, *Unpub.*, where it was found that the bidder did not intend to comply with the IFB although the bid conformed to the IFB. The Comptroller General found that contacts between the bidder and Government personnel prior to bidding indicated that the bidder was unable and did not intend to perform in accordance with the IFB. Compare *Radio TV Reports, Inc.*, Comp. Gen. Dec. B-192958, 79-2 CPD ¶ 27, where the Comptroller General, holding that an allegation that the bidder did not intend to perform was a matter of responsibility, distinguished Comp. Gen. Dec. B-159560, Oct. 7, 1996, *Unpub.*, stating:

> In its bid, Birmingham promised to perform all the work required and further indicated that it intended to use its owned and operated facilities in the four metropolitan areas for contract performance. However, prior to award, the Army learned that Birmingham did not own monitoring, recording, and

transcribing facilities in Chicago and New York. When questioned about this, Birmingham provided the Army's preaward survey team addresses in the two cities, and explained it had representatives at those locations who could easily obtain the requisite tapes and transcripts from the broadcasting stations.

* * *

Radio TV contends, however, that the contract should be terminated because the Army awarded the contract knowing that Birmingham had no facilities in either Chicago or New York. In support of its position, the protester submits that the facts in this case are sufficiently similar to those in B-159560, October 7, 1966, where we recommended a contract be canceled, to warrant a similar result. In that case, the Navy awarded a contract following advertisement for trash removal services to a company knowing that the contractor planned to use a trash collection method which deviated from the specifications. We determined that although the contractor's bid appeared valid on its face, contracting officials, by making the award, in effect improperly agreed to waive the specifications requirements for the benefit of one bidder.

We do not believe the present case is sufficiently analogous to B-159560, *supra*, to warrant a similar result, because in our view, there was no Government waiver of a substantive contract provision for the benefit of Birmingham. For example, the IFB provision quoted above which the protester relies upon for the most part as his basis for protest does not *require* the contractor to perform the desired services either through the use of its own personnel *or* by subcontract. If, as Birminham alleges, the materials can be obtained directly from the broadcasters who presumably make the recordings for their own purposes, we believe no subcontracts are involved and the clause requiring evidence of a "commitment or specific arrangement" is not called into play.

d. Certification Requirements

Bidders are frequently required to submit certifications and representations with their bids. This practice often led to confusion on the part of the bidders when these requirements were scattered throughout the IFB, Comp. Gen. Dec. B-176148, Aug. 14, 1973, *Unpub.* However, under the Uniform Contract Format required by FAR 14.201-1, all certifications and representations must be included in Section K of the IFB. Nonetheless, certifications and representations are often omitted or are furnished with signatures or other information missing. This raises a question of whether a bid submitted with an incomplete, missing, or defective certification or representation must be rejected, as being nonresponsive. As a general rule, if the information in the certification deals with the bidder's responsibility, the bid should not be rejected and the missing information may properly be submitted after bid opening, *J. Morris & Assocs.*, Comp. Gen. Dec. B-259767, 95-1 CPD ¶ 213 (certification that bidder is or is not a small, disadvantaged business is not a matter of responsiveness); *Norfolk Shipbuilding & Drydock Corp.*, Comp. Gen. Dec. B-248549, 92-2 CPD ¶ 127 (although a solicitation required certification of drydocking availability to be submitted with bid, certification concerns bidder's capability to perform and is a matter of responsibility); *PacifiCorp Capital, Inc.*, GSBCA 10884-P, 91-1 BCA ¶ 23,598 (requirement that reconditioned equipment be "certified as new" not a matter of responsiveness); *Grifco*, Comp. Gen. Dec. B-240549, 90-2 CPD ¶ 143 (certificate disclosing whether any facilities are on the EPA list of facilities violating the Clean Air Act or the Clean Water Act is a matter of bidder responsibility); *Intermountain Elec., Inc.*, Comp. Gen. Dec. B-236953.2, 90-1 CPD ¶ 143 (certificate regarding status as debarred or suspended bidder a matter of responsibility); *Jersey Maid Distributors, Inc.*, Comp. Gen. Dec. B-217307, 85-1 CPD ¶ 307 (bid certifications were not necessary to determine whether the bid meets specifications requirements since they relate to responsibility); *Deterline Corp.*, Comp. Gen. Dec. B-208986, 83-1 CPD ¶ 427 (certification that bidder is a regular dealer or manufacturer of product may be submitted up to time of award); *C.R. Hipp, Inc.*, Comp. Gen. Dec. B-212093, 83-2 CPD ¶ 418 (failure to complete Standard Form 19-B, "Representations and Certifications," relates to bidder's responsibility); *Fisher Berkeley Corp.*, Comp. Gen. Dec. B-196432, 80-1 CPD ¶ 26 (failure to include testing certification may be waived if bid indicates equipment has been tested and meets the specifications); *Jets, Inc.*, Comp. Gen. Dec. B-194017, 79-1 CPD ¶ 269 (failure to accurately complete affidavit regarding surety net worth is a matter of responsibility).

However, if a missing or defective certificate raises doubt over whether the bidder has agreed to perform in accordance with the IFB or whether the product offered meets the contract requirements, the bid must be rejected, *New Zealand Fence Sys.*, Comp. Gen. Dec. B-257460, 94-2 CPD ¶ 101 (failure to certify that bidder under a total small business set-aside for supply items would provide end items manufactured or produced by small business concerns); *Camar Corp.*, Comp. Gen. Dec. B-248485, 92-2 CPD ¶ 140 (failure to submit certified test report that product had been tested under specified conditions); *Koch Corp.*, Comp. Gen. Dec. B-212304.4, 84-2 CPD ¶ 132 (failure to certify product's performance history relates to product quality); *Phaostron Instrument & Elec. Co.*, Comp. Gen. Dec. B-214169, 84-1 CPD ¶ 474 (failure to certify that bidder would supply previously approved, identified components); *B.K. Instrument Inc.*, Comp. Gen. Dec. B-212162.2, 84-1 CPD ¶ 189 (failure to meet source control certification requirements); *Fraser-Volpe Corp.*, Comp. Gen. Dec. B-213910, 84-1 CPD ¶ 35 (failure to certify that component parts would be purchased from a designated group).

On occasion, the Government has treated certifications that serve an important public policy as matters of responsiveness even though they relate more directly to issues of responsibility. See *Northeast Constr. Co. v. Romney*, 485 F.2d 752 (D.C. Cir. 1973); *Rossetti Contracting Co. v. Brennan*, 508 F.2d 1039 (7th Cir. 1974); and *Astro Pak Corp.*, Comp. Gen. Dec. B-183556, 75-2 CPD ¶ 97, which deal with affirmative action plans for equal employment opportunity that were required to be submitted along with the bids. In *Northeast Construction*, the bidder failed to fill in its affirmative action goals in the space provided but did sign the document agreeing to comply with the plan included in the IFB, which specified the minimum acceptable goals. Nevertheless, the bid was considered nonresponsive because the omissions created doubts regarding enforceability of the bidder's commitment because its bid was inconsistent with the instructions of the plan. These decisions have been mooted with respect to EEO certificates because of changes in the procedures making the certificate a matter of responsibility, FAR 14.405(f).

The Government had identified proper completion of the Certificate of Procurement Integrity as a matter of responsiveness for procurements that exceeded $100,000. This requirement was upheld even though the Procurement Integrity Act, 41 U.S.C. § 423(e), merely called for obtaining the certificate before award, *S.J. Amoroso Constr. Co. v. United States*, 981 F.2d 1073 (9th Cir. 1992); *McMaster Constr., Inc. v. United States*, 23 Cl. Ct. 679 (1991); *P & R Roofing & Sheet Metal, Inc.*, Comp. Gen. Dec. B-258388, 94-2 CPD ¶ 254; *Stamatis Lykos*, Comp. Gen. Dec. B-257843, 94-2 CPD ¶ 186. Submission of an unsigned certificate was also held to make the bid nonresponsive, *Holly's, Inc.*, Comp. Gen. Dec. B-246444, 92-1 CPD ¶ 261. However, submission of a photocopy of a properly executed certificate met the responsiveness requirement, *C.B.S. Enters., Inc.*, Comp. Gen. Dec. B-252484, 93-1 CPD ¶ 495. Similarly, an undated certificate met the requirement, *General Elec. Ocean & Radar Sys. Div.*, Comp. Gen. Dec. B-250418, 93-1 CPD ¶ 30. This certification requirement has been repealed by Section 4301 of the Clinger-Cohen Act of 1996, P.L. 104-106.

In *Worcester Elec. Assocs.*, Comp. Gen. Dec. B-193064, 79-1 CPD ¶ 236, a specification requirement that bidders submit Underwriter Laboratories (UL) listing cards was held to be a matter of responsiveness, because the purpose of the cards was to provide evidence that the equipment being offered conformed to certain standards of safety and performance. But see *Fisher Berkeley Corp.*, Comp. Gen. Dec. B-196432, 80-1 CPD ¶ 26, where the UL certification itself was considered a matter of responsibility as long as the bidder promised that its product would be and was UL certified.

4. Information or Data to Be Submitted

When data or information is required to be submitted with the bid, the Comptroller General will consider the purpose for which the data or information is to be used when determining whether it is a matter of responsiveness or responsibility. Thus, if descriptive data are to be used to determine a bidder's *ability or capacity to perform*, the matter will be one of *responsibility*, and failure to submit the information with the bid will not cause its rejection, *Savin Business Machs. Corp.*, Comp. Gen. Dec. B-191163, 78-1 CPD ¶ 447 (failure to furnish preventive maintenance plan, key operator instruction plan, and samples of paper to be used with photocopying equipment did not render bid nonresponsive); *Science Applications, Inc.*, Comp. Gen. Dec. B-193479, 79-1 CPD ¶ 167 (failure to submit personnel résumés did not render bid nonresponsive); *Career Consultants, Inc.*, Comp. Gen. Dec. B-198727, 80-2 CPD ¶ 285 (IFB requirement for statement of licensing status was not a matter of responsiveness); *Seacoast Trucking & Moving Co.*, Comp. Gen. Dec. B-200315, 80-2 CPD ¶ 235 (failure to submit description of equipment to be used in performing refuse services did not render bid nonresponsive because equipment was matter of capability to perform); *Career Consultants, Inc.*, Comp. Gen. Dec. B-200506.2, 81-1 CPD ¶ 414 (requirement for security clearances is a matter of responsibility); *Skyline Credit Corp.*, Comp. Gen. Dec. B-209193, 83-1 CPD ¶ 257 (failure to include written performance procedures did not render bid nonresponsive); *Commercial Window & Door Co.*, Comp. Gen. Dec. B-211280, 83-2 CPD ¶ 582 (bid that failed to include test results concerning product performance held responsive because IFB failed to warn bidders that submission requirement involved responsiveness and the information was not necessary to determine conformance with specifications); *Siska Constr. Co.*, 64 Comp. Gen. 384 (B-218208.2), 85-1 CPD ¶ 331 (affiliation and parent company data as well as certificate of independent pricing concern bidder responsibility and may be submitted after bid opening); *Master Power, Inc.*, Comp. Gen. Dec. B-238468.2, 90-2 CPD ¶ 434 (furnishing incorrect qualification test number for qualified product a matter of responsibility); *RKR, Inc.*, Comp. Gen. Dec. B-247619.2, 92-2 CPD ¶ 289 (failure to submit adequate evidence of compliance with zoning laws a matter of responsibility); *CardioMetrix*, Comp. Gen. Dec. B-255748.2, 94-1 CPD ¶ 364 (failure to designate place of performance is matter of responsibility).

On the other hand, information or data may be required to be submitted with the bid for purposes of more precisely determining *the nature of the work that the bidder is agreeing to accomplish.* Such data can be considered to go to the *responsiveness* of the bid. Requiring the submission of such data can protect the Government from bids that are responsive on their face, because they take no exception to the IFB but are based on performing in a manner that does not conform to the solicitation. The two major techniques used by the Government for this purpose are requirements for *descriptive literature* and *bid samples.*

Neither of these techniques should be used indiscriminately because they may unduly increase the cost of bidding. FAR 14.202-4(c) gives the following guidance regarding the use of bid samples:

> The use of bid samples would be appropriate for products that must be suitable from the standpoint of balance, facility of use, general "feel," color, pattern, or other characteristics that cannot be described adequately in the specification. However, when more than a minor portion of the characteristics of the product cannot be adequately described in the specification, products should be acquired by two-step sealed bidding or negotiation, as appropriate.

FAR 14.202-5(b) provides the following guidance with respect to descriptive literature:

> Bidders shall not be required to furnish descriptive literature unless the contracting office needs it to determine before award whether the products offered meet the specification and to establish exactly what the bidder proposes to furnish.

Where the purpose of the data is to enable the procuring agency to determine precisely what the bidder intends to supply, the matter will be considered to deal with responsiveness. This is the only purpose for which bid samples may be submitted, FAR 14.202-4(b)(2). For example, in

Western Waterproofing Co., Comp. Gen. Dec. B-183155, 75-1 CPD ¶ 306, the bidder was required to furnish data demonstrating that the stone proposed for use met the IFB criteria. The Comptroller General reasoned that this provision did not deal with the bidder's ability to perform but was aimed at describing the articles to be supplied. See also *FFR-Bauelemente + Bausanierung GmbH*, Comp. Gen. Dec. B-274828 97-1 CPD ¶ 7 (failure to include descriptive literature to ascertain whether item met salient characteristics of brand name product made bid nonresponsive); *National Energy Resources, Inc.*, Comp. Gen. Dec. B-206275, 83-1 CPD ¶ 108 (failure to include data regarding the suitability of the coal to be provided was a matter of responsiveness); *Thermal Reduction Co.*, Comp. Gen. Dec. B-211405, 83-2 CPD ¶ 180 (failure to include descriptive literature assuring conformance with specifications makes bid nonresponsive); and *RMTC Sys., Inc. v. Department of the Army*, GSBCA 12637-P, 94-2 BCA ¶ 26,614 (failure to submit descriptive literature to demonstrate that product was "equal" to the specified brand name makes bid nonresponsive).

B. Consequences of Nonconforming Bids

The consequences of submitting a nonconforming bid depend on the nature of the nonconformity and the time it is discovered.

1. Minor Informalities

Once a defect is found to be minor, award must be made if at all, to the low bidder who is otherwise responsible. The contracting officer has the choice of either giving the bidder an opportunity to cure the deficiency or waiving it, whichever is in the best interest of the Government, FAR 14.405; *Champion Road Mach. Int'l Corp.*, Comp. Gen. Dec. B-200678, 81-2 CPD ¶ 27; *Astrophysics Research Corp.*, 66 Comp. Gen. 211 (B-224532), 87-1 CPD ¶ 65. If the bidder refuses to cure the deficiency, then award may be made on the basis of the bid as submitted.

If a sealed bid procurement is canceled because the agency determines that the only bid at a reasonable price is nonresponsive, and the agency subsequently determines that the defect in the bid was a minor informality, the agency may reinstate the IFB and award to that bidder, *Bilt-Rite Contractors, Inc.*, Comp. Gen. Dec. B-259106.2, 95-1 CPD ¶ 220.

2. Material Nonconformities

This section discusses the requirement for rejection of nonresponsive bids, the legal effect of an award on the basis of a nonresponsive bid, and the limited cases in which such awards are sanctioned by the Comptroller General.

a. Rejection Required

FAR 14.404-2(a) states that "any bid that fails to conform to the essential requirements of the solicitation shall be rejected." In commenting on the rationale for this rule, the court, in *Toyo Menka Kaisha, Ltd. v. United States*, 220 Ct. Cl. 210, 597 F.2d 1371 (1979), stated at 219-20:

> These principles rest upon and effectuate important public policies. "Rejection of irresponsive bids is necessary if the purposes of formal advertising are to be attained, that is, to give everyone an equal right to compete for Government business, to secure fair prices, and to prevent fraud." *Prestex Inc. v. United States, supra*, 162 Ct. Cl. at 626, 320 F.2d at 372 (footnote omitted). The requirement that a bid be responsive is designed to avoid unfairness to other contractors who submitted a sealed bid on the understanding that they must comply with all of the specifications and conditions in the invitation for bids, and who could have made a better proposal if they imposed conditions upon or variances from the contractual terms the government had specified. The rule also avoids placing the contracting officer in the difficult position of having to balance the more favorable offer of the deviating bidder against the disadvantages to the government from the qualifications and conditions the bidder has added. In short, the requirement of responsiveness is designed to avoid a method of awarding government contracts that would be similar to negotiating agreements but which would lack the safeguards present in either that system or in true competitive bidding. See R. Nash & J. Cibinic, *Federal Procurement Law*, 260 (3d ed. 1977).
>
> Responsiveness is determined by reference to the bids when they are opened and not by reference to subsequent changes in a bid. *Id.* at 261. Allowing a bidder to modify a nonresponsive bid when, upon opening the bids, it appears that the variations will preclude an award, would permit the very kind of bid manipulation and negotiation that the rule is designed to prevent. Otherwise bidders would be encouraged to submit nonresponsive bids on terms favorable to the government but subject to certain conditions, in the hope that if their bids were the top ones, they could then negotiate about and retain some of their proposed changes. In this way they could

> obtain a contract that they could not have received had they complied with the specification in the invitation for bids.

It is immaterial whether the nonconformity is deliberate or occurs by mistake, or whether the bidder is willing to correct or modify the bid to conform to the terms of the invitation, *Legeay, Inc.*, Comp. Gen. Dec. B-218307, 85-1 CPD ¶ 338 (fact that bidder alleged mistake and offered to correct an insufficient acceptance period held irrelevant); *AVS Inc.*, Comp. Gen. Dec. B-218205, 85-1 CPD ¶ 328 (irrelevant that bid guarantee deficiency may have resulted from innocent error on the part of the surety); *Public Entity Underwriters, Ltd.*, Comp. Gen. Dec. B-213745, 84-2 CPD ¶ 326 (clerical error may not be corrected after opening to make bid responsive). In *Amendola Constr. Co.*, Comp. Gen. Dec. B-214258, 84-1 CPD ¶ 255, the Comptroller General stated:

> The fact that [the protester] has subsequently explained that the 15-day period it offered was a mistake and that it is willing to waive its restriction is irrelevant. A bid which is nonresponsive on its face may not be changed, corrected or explained by the bidder after bid opening since to permit this would give the firm the option of accepting or rejecting a contract after bids are exposed.

See also *Parco, A Div. of Blue Mountain Products, Inc.*, Comp. Gen. Dec. B-211016, 83-1 CPD ¶ 318, where the Comptroller General refused to allow a nonresponsive bid to be considered for correction after bid opening because to permit a change after bid opening would be tantamount to permitting the submission of a new bid after the competitors' bids have been revealed.

b. *Validity of Award*

Award to a bidder whose bid contains a material nonconformity has been held to be void ab initio, *Prestex Inc. v. United States*, 162 Ct. Cl. 620, 320 F.2d 367 (1963). See also *Albano Cleaners, Inc. v. United States*, 197 Ct. Cl. 450, 455 F.2d 556 (1972), where the court stated at 455:

> [The Government] may disclaim a contract on the ground of voidness *ab initio* because of the nonresponsiveness of the bid. Where a public contract is to be let pursuant to formal advertising, the strictures upon [the Government's] contracting agent are such "that the contract awarded must be the contract advertised and *** if it is not, the Government is not bound, since [the Government's] contracting agent could not bind the Government be-

> yond his actual authority." *Prestex Inc. v. United States*, 162 Ct. Cl. 620, 625, 320 F.2d 367, 371 (1963).

Thus, a bidder who receives such an award runs a great risk if the Government decides to cancel the award. If the contract is declared void ab initio, the contractor will generally be entitled to payment for benefits conferred on the Government, *United States v. Amdahl Corp.*, 786 F.2d 387 (Fed. Cir. 1986). However, to the extent that any expenditures made in performance do not confer a benefit upon the Government, they may not be recovered, *Toyo Menka Kaisha, Ltd. v. United States*, 220 Ct. Cl. 210, 597 F.2d 1371 (1979). See 40 U.S.C. § 759(f)(6)(B), providing the following guidance on the compensation to be paid when the General Services Board revoked the procurement authority of an agency:

> If the board revokes, suspends, or revises the procurement authority of the Administrator or the Administrator's delegation of procurement authority after the contract award, the affected contract shall be presumed valid as to all goods or services delivered and accepted under the contract before the suspension, revocation, or revision of such procurement authority or delegation.

This statute was repealed by the Clinger-Cohen Act of 1996, P.L. 104-106.

In recent years, the Comptroller General has recommended termination for convenience rather than cancellation when there has been an award to a nonresponsive bidder, *Fischer-White-Rankin Contractors, Inc.*, Comp. Gen. Dec. B-213401, 84-1 CPD ¶ 471, *withdrawn because much work done*, 84-1 CPD ¶ 640; *Harris Constr. Co.*, 64 Comp. Gen. 628 (B-218387), 85-1 CPD ¶ 710. This result follows the reasoning that cancellation is only proper when the illegality of the contract is "plain," *John Reiner & Co. v. United States*, 163 Ct. Cl. 381, 325 F.2d 438 (1963), *cert. denied*, 377 U.S. 931 (1964), or "palpable," *Warren Bros. Roads Co. v. United States*, 173 Ct. Cl. 714, 355 F.2d 612 (1965). This reasoning was also followed by the General Services Board of Contract Appeals, *International Bus. Machs. Corp.*, GSBCA 9703-P, 89-1 BCA ¶ 21,389, *rev'd on other grounds*, 892 F.2d 1006 (Fed. Cir. 1989).

c. *Award*

On a number of occasions the Comptroller General has sanctioned awards on the basis of nonresponsive bids. This is generally done only if all the bids submitted are nonresponsive, the bid in question satisfies the Government's requirements, and no competing bidder would be prejudiced as a result of the award. In *K. B. Constr.*, Comp. Gen. Dec. B-214192, 84-1 CPD ¶ 223, the failure of all bidders to submit required test manufacturer's data permitted award to the low bidder.

A crucial element in the decisions sanctioning award to a nonresponsive bidder is the Comptroller General's finding that, under the circumstances, acceptance of the nonresponsive bid would not prejudice other bidders, *Singleton Contracting Corp.*, Comp. Gen. Dec. B-211259, 83-2 CPD ¶ 270 (award proper where both bids were nonresponsive for same material nonconformity, and acceptance resulted in a contract that satisfied Government needs). In *E.F. Matelich Constr. Co.*, Comp. Gen. Dec. B-207600, 82-2 CPD ¶ 291, the Comptroller General stated that "[t]he test of prejudice . . . is whether it is reasonably clear that another bidder, given the benefit of a similarly relaxed requirement . . . would have bid in such a manner that it would have been in line for award." See *Esko & Young, Inc.*, 61 Comp. Gen. 192 (B-204053), 82-1 CPD ¶ 5, where the failure of the sole bidder to include a conforming bid acceptance period did not require rejection since "no bidding advantage accrues to the single bidder . . . because there were no competitors who . . . subjected themselves to the risks of maintaining their bid process for the longer period." See also *Fluid Sys, Inc.*, Comp. Gen. Dec. B-225880, 87-1 CPD ¶ 20, where an award was upheld where the IFB required a two-inch-diameter drain for feed pump lube oil modification kits, but the low bidder could supply only a one-and-three-quarter-inch-diameter model because it was the only model available. The Comptroller General reasoned that the substituted product met the Government's needs and no other bidders were prejudiced.

In a number of these cases, award is sanctioned because cancellation of the procurement after bids have been exposed is seen as a greater evil. In *Big State Enters.*, 64 Comp. Gen. 482 (B-218055), 85-1 CPD ¶ 459, the Comptroller General stated at 484:

> [W]e believe that in spite of the specification deficiency, the determination to make an award was reasonable and less of a compromise to the competitive bidding system than resolicitation after exposure of all prices would have been. *See GAF Corp. et al.*, 53 Comp. Gen. 586 (1974), 74-1 CPD ¶ 68.

These Comptroller General decisions sanctioning award on the basis of the most advantageous nonresponsive bid are based on pragmatism. The standard alternatives would be for the contracting officer to reject all bids and resolicit sealed bids, *Gulf & Western Healthcare, Inc.*, Comp. Gen. Dec. B-209684, 83-2 CPD ¶ 248, competitive proposals, or two-step sealed bids, 34 Comp. Gen. 364 (B-121831) (1965). In case of urgency, it might also be possible to negotiate with all bidders if less than full and open competition could be justified. See *Bus Indus. of Am., Inc.*, Comp. Gen. Dec. B-208366, 83-1 CPD ¶ 222, approving this technique in a case that arose prior to the Competition in Contracting Act. Since these alternatives would all involve the expenditure of additional time and effort, it is clearly more expedient to make the award to the bidder submitting the most advantageous, albeit nonresponsive, bid.

This pragmatism, however, may be shortsighted. It ignores the possibility that the requirement that was not met may have deterred other potential bidders from entering the competition at all. These decisions also ignore decisions such as *Prestex Inc. v. United States*, 162 Ct. Cl. 620, 320 F.2d 367 (1963), holding that award to a nonresponsive bidder constitutes a prohibited waiver of responsiveness criteria and does not obligate the Government. The courts focus more on the prejudice to potential bidders, while the Comptroller General addresses the issue of prejudice only in terms of actual bidders.

For a questionable case in which the Comptroller General held that the Government could accept a nonresponsive bid even though the second low bid was responsive, see *Dunlin Corp.*, Comp. Gen. Dec. B-207964, 83-1 CPD ¶ 7. The protester, who believed that it was the only bidder with a supply of the window sealant required by the IFB, submitted a bid price of $24.80 per unit. The awardee, offering an alternative sealant that rendered its bid nonresponsive, submitted a bid price of $18.10 per unit. Claiming that the alternative sealant would meet its needs and that the specifications had overstated the needs, the Government made the award to the low bidder. Even though the Comptroller General held that this action was proper, more effective competition could have been promoted by a cancellation and resolicitation in which both those submitting bids and those refraining from bidding could compete to the revised specifications.

C. Types of Nonconforming Bids

The determination of whether a nonconformity is material depends upon the facts of the case and the nature of the nonconformity. This section examines some of the common types of nonconforming bids.

1. Differing Products or Services

Any bid that fails to conform to the essential requirements or applicable specifications of an invitation must be rejected. FAR 14.404-2(b) states that bids offering materially differing products or services from those solicited must be rejected as nonresponsive. See, for example, *Kincaid Equip. Mfg.*, Comp. Gen. Dec. B-246079, 92-1 CPD ¶ 140 (bid offering a belt-driven threshing cylinder rejected as nonresponsive where IFB required a hydrostatically driven threshing cylinder); *Mobile Drilling Co.*, Comp. Gen. Dec. B-216989, 85-1 CPD ¶ 199 (an offer to furnish a drill with a torque capacity of 6,000 ft.-lbs. at 27 R.P.M. instead of the required capacity of 5,800 ft.-lbs. at 50 R.P.M. was properly rejected); *Jensen Corp.*, Comp. Gen. Dec. B-213677, 84-1 CPD ¶ 544 (a bid offering a two-roll flatwork commercial ironer when the IFB called for a four-roll ironer held nonresponsive); and *Sheffield Bldg. Co.*, Comp. Gen. Dec. B-181242, 74-2 CPD ¶ 108 (bidder's failure to include spud engines when the specifications called for derrick-boats equipped with spud engines resulted in bid rejection).

When the Government solicits products on a "brand name or equal" basis, a bidder offering an "equal" product must establish that it conforms to all the salient characteristics of the brand name product listed in the IFB. A failure to do so will result in bid rejection, *RCP Shelters, Inc.*, Comp. Gen. Dec. B-256258, 94-1 CPD ¶ 336 (descriptive literature submitted with bid failed to show compliance with the salient characteristics listed in the IFB); *Alternate Power & Energy Corp.*, Comp. Gen. Dec. B-228746, 87-2 CPD ¶ 440 (although offered product possessed required features, bid rejected where literature submitted with bid did not clearly show conformance with IFB requirements). Any information used to show conformance to the salient characteristics must have been commercially available prior to bid opening and must not have been developed afterward, *Elastomeric Roofing Assocs.*, 68 Comp. Gen. 426, (B-234125), 89-1 CPD ¶ 451. To allow bidders to submit other than preexisting, commercially available material would give the bidder control over the responsiveness of its bid, *Monitronics*, Comp. Gen. Dec. B-228219, 87-2 CPD ¶ 527. However, bidders have been permitted to submit such information after bid opening. See *Lappen Auto Supply Co.*, Comp. Gen. Dec. B-261475, 95-2 CPD ¶ 68.

Bids that fail to meet salient characteristics of the solicitation must be rejected as nonresponsive even if the offered items function as well as the brand name units and satisfy the intent of the specifications, *Advanced Med. Sys., Inc.*, Comp. Gen. Dec. B-258945, 95-1 CPD ¶ 67 (bid rejected as nonresponsive where proposed "equal" product could digitally display one fetal heart rate, but IFB for fetal heart monitor required digital display of two fetal heart rates); *T & T Prods., Inc.*, Comp. Gen. Dec. B-243898, 91-2 CPD ¶ 139 (bid stating "equal" product had cable diameter of "0.75 inches nominal" rejected as nonresponsive where IFB required a cable diameter between 0.8 and 0.875 inches); *United Mach.*, Comp. Gen. Dec. B-227923, 87-2 CPD ¶ 54 (bid rejected as nonresponsive where, although the offered "equal" washer extractor may have functioned as well as the brand name, the protester conceded that the offered product did not meet all the specifications of the IFB); *Paul F. Pugh & Associated Professional Eng'rs*, Comp. Gen. Dec. B-199920, 80-2 CPD ¶ 358 (although aluminum conductors offered may function as well as brand-name units, bid was properly rejected as nonresponsive because IFB for power cables listed copper as a salient characteristic). Even a brand-name product listed in the IFB may not be accepted as responsive if it fails to meet listed salient characteristics and, in effect, constitutes a "differing" product, *Vista Scientific Corp.*, Comp. Gen. Dec. B-185170, 76-1 CPD ¶ 212. But see *Central Power Eng'g Corp.*, Comp. Gen. Dec. B-215658.2, 85-1 CPD ¶ 85, where the bid listed a brand-name model number that represented an upgraded version of the brand-name model solicited. The Comptroller General upheld the agency's determination that although designated somewhat differently, the model offered met all the salient characteristics of the solicitation and was in essence the same brand-name item called for in the IFB. See also *GAF Corp.*, 53 Comp. Gen. 586, (B-179744), 74-1 CPD ¶ 68, where the Comptroller General reinstated a canceled IFB and permitted award to a brand name product that did not conform to all listed salient characteristics.

Nonconformities of bids that are merely a matter of form and not substance or that are immaterial or inconsequential variations from the exact requirements of an IFB may not properly be rejected as nonresponsive. FAR 14.405 requires minor informalities or irregularities to be corrected or waived if no prejudice will result to other bidders, or where the deviation has only a negligible effect on price, quality, quantity, or delivery when compared with the total cost or scope of supplies or work to be furnished.

See, for example, *W.M. Schlosser Co.,* Comp. Gen. Dec. B-258284, 94-2 CPD ¶ 234 (bidder's failure to submit requested equipment history with bid that would not be used to evaluate bid waived as an immaterial deviation); *Universal Applicators, Inc.*, Comp. Gen. Dec. B-232670, 88-2 CPD ¶ 591 (failure to certify that bid price was not based on "spray painting" when IFB required a liquid roof sealant held to be an immaterial deviation); *Astrophysics Research Corp.*, 66 Comp. Gen. 211 (B-224532), 87-1 CPD ¶ 65 (10-pound discrepancy between 410-pound X-ray screening machine bid and 400-pound machine specified in IFB. IFB requirement waived as a minor informality where item met Government needs and there was no prejudice to other bidders); *Evans, Inc.*, Comp. Gen. Dec. B-216260.2, 85-1 CPD ¶ 535 (118.5-inch dryer minor deviation from 120-inch specification requirement); *Magnaflux Corp.*, Comp. Gen. Dec. B-211914, 84-1 CPD ¶ 4 (29.5-inch bath tank minor deviation to specification requiring 30-inch tank); *Champion Road Mach. Int'l Corp.*, Comp. Gen. Dec. B-200678, 81-2 CPD ¶ 27 (bid offering 168-horsepower road grader where solicitation specified 170 horsepower held responsive where deviation had no effect on price, quality, quantity, or delivery); and Comp. Gen. Dec. B-172227, May 13, 1971, *Unpub.* (bid offering uniform with five buttons and a scalloped pocket rather than the required four buttons and plain pocket held responsive since deviations were minor and did not affect quality, utility, or the cost of producing the uniform).

There are a few seemingly inconsistent decisions. See *Yale Materials Handling Corp.*, Comp. Gen. Dec. B-250208, 92-2 CPD ¶ 360 (bid offering forklift exceeding specified dimensions in the IFB by about one-half inch was a material deviation affecting the quality of the forklift and was rejected as nonresponsive); *Taylor-Forge Engineered Sys., Inc.*, 69 Comp. Gen. 54 (B-236408), 89-2 CPD ¶ 421 (bid offering delivery f.o.b. origin where IFB required f.o.b. destination constituted a material deviation); and 43 Comp. Gen. 209 (B-151968) (1963) (award of contract canceled where bid offered paper cutter that materially deviated from the IFB specifications by affecting price and quality, even though the product would better serve the agency's needs).

2. Failure to Agree to IFB Delivery Schedule

An IFB's delivery schedule is a material requirement of the solicitation, and any bid that fails to conform to the delivery schedule is nonresponsive and must be rejected, FAR 14.404-2(c). Thus, a bid offering a delivery period greater than the maximum delivery period permitted under the terms of the solicitation will be rejected as nonresponsive, *Chrysler Corp.*, Comp. Gen. Dec. B-249492, 92-2 CPD ¶ 253 (bid offering "shipments" within 90 days rejected as nonresponsive where IFB required "delivery" within 90 days); *Rhimco Indus., Inc.*, Comp. Gen. Dec. B-247600, 92-1 CPD ¶ 499 (IFB required delivery of all items within 120 days after award, but protester's bid offered delivery of one half of the requirements); *Delta Scientific Corp.*, Comp. Gen. Dec. B-233485, 88-2 CPD ¶ 516 (bid's delivery schedule of 120 days was rejected where IFB stated bidders could offer delivery schedule longer than the desired 60 days but within the required 90 days); *Meyer Tool & Mfg.*, Comp. Gen. Dec. B-222595, 86-1 CPD ¶ 537 (bid rejected as nonresponsive where numbers in proposed delivery period were transposed, due to a clerical error, from 120 days to 210 days, which exceeded the 180 days required by the IFB); *Mar-Mac Precision Corp.*, Comp. Gen. Dec. B-214604, 84-2 CPD ¶ 164 (failure to acknowledge an amendment that doubled the delivery requirements for the first 180 days of the contract rendered bid nonresponsive). Even a bid footnote objecting to and qualifying a required delivery schedule has rendered a bid nonresponsive, *Sunoptic, Inc.*, Comp. Gen. Dec. B-194722, 79-1 CPD ¶ 351. But see *TEREX Corp.*, Comp. Gen. Dec. B-212441, 84-1 CPD ¶ 330, where a bid that failed to offer delivery within 30 days was improperly rejected as nonresponsive because the IFB merely called for a "desired" delivery date of 30 days, and the offered delivery date was "reasonable."

The bid must indicate that the bidder is agreeing to meet the required date. In Comp. Gen. Dec. B-170287, Aug. 18, 1970, *Unpub.*, *recons. denied*, 50 Comp. Gen. 379 (1970), the invitation required delivery in 150 days and had a desired delivery date of 120 days. The bidder offered delivery in "approximately 120 days (as requested)." This deviation was found to be material and rendered the bid nonresponsive since no firm date was bid. But see Comp. Gen. Dec. B-175342, Mar. 27, 1972, *Unpub.*, where an approximate delivery date of 30 days did not render a bid nonresponsive when the required date was 90 days. The Comptroller General distinguished the earlier case by noting that the "approximate period of offered delivery is significantly greater in the instant case than in the earlier case both in terms of the absolute number of days between the approximate date and the deadline and the relative period involved."

When the IFB requires delivery within a certain time from date of contract award, bidders may specify delivery times starting from receipt of contract award documents. In such cases, FAR 11.403(e) requires that five calendar days (normal mail delivery time) be added to the bidder's date, and if this date is later than the IFB required date, the bid is considered nonresponsive. See, for example, *AMP Inc.*, Comp. Gen. Dec. B-230120, 88-1 CPD ¶ 163 (bid offering a delivery schedule of 150 days after receipt of an order rejected as nonresponsive because it effectively added five days to the IFB required schedule as an allowance for delivery through ordinary mails); and *Discount Mach. & Equip.*, Comp. Gen. Dec. B-223048.2, 86-2 CPD ¶ 5 (bid offering a delivery period of 90 days after receipt of contract, where IFB required 90 days from contract award, in effect added five days for delivery of award documents through the mail and was rejected as nonresponsive).

3. Conditions Altering the Invitation

Bids that impose conditions altering the requirements of the invitation or limiting the rights of the Government must be rejected. FAR 14.404-2(d) states:

> A bid shall be rejected when the bidder imposes conditions that would modify requirements of the invitation or limit the bidder's liability to the Government, since to allow the bidder to impose such conditions would be prejudicial to other bidders. For example, bids shall be rejected in which the bidder —
>
> (1) Protects against future changes in conditions, such as increased costs, if total possible costs to the Government cannot be determined;
>
> (2) Fails to state a price and indicates that price shall be "price in effect at time of delivery";
>
> (3) States a price but qualifies it as being subject to "price in effect at time of delivery";
>
> (4) When not authorized by the invitation, conditions or qualifies a bid by stipulating that it is to be considered only if, before date of award, the bidder receives (or does not receive) award under a separate solicitation;
>
> (5) Requires that the Government is to determine that the bidder's product meets applicable Government specifications; or
>
> (6) Limits rights of the Government under any contract clause.

a. Modifying Material Requirements of the IFB

Any bid that imposes conditions that would modify the material requirements of the solicitation will be rejected as nonresponsive, *Antennas for Communications*, Comp. Gen. Dec. B-253950, 93-2 CPD ¶ 48 (bid nonresponsive when it stated that Government damages for delay "shall be billed at a rate of $1,000 per day"); *NR Vessel Corp.*, Comp. Gen. Dec. B-250925, 93-1 CPD ¶ 128 (bid conditioned on the Government disposing of hazardous waste was rejected as nonresponsive where the IFB placed responsibility for disposal on the contractor); *Lathan Constr. Corp.*, Comp. Gen. Dec. B-250487, 93-1 CPD ¶ 107 (bid nonresponsive where document captioned "Contractor's Qualifications and Exclusions" excluded permit and engineering fees required by the IFB); *General Elec. Co.*, Comp. Gen. Dec. B-228191, 87-2 CPD ¶ 585 (bid rejected for taking exception to two parts of the IFB's warranty provision). See also *Garney Companies, Inc.*, Comp. Gen. Dec. 196075.2, 81-1 CPD ¶ 62 (bidder reserved right to use unacceptable pipe installation technique); *State Mut. Book & Periodical Serv., Ltd.*, Comp. Gen. Dec. B-191008.2, 78-1 CPD ¶ 264 (exception to specified delivery method); *National Ambulance Co.*, 55 Comp. Gen. 597 (B-184439), 75-2 CPD ¶ 413 (bid conditioned on receipt of local license); *Joy Mfg. Co.*, 54 Comp. Gen. 237 (B-181136), 74-2 CPD ¶ 183 (bid reserved the right to change prices if costs increase even though the IFB required a firm-fixed-price); and 43 Comp. Gen. 382 (B-152470) (1963) (bid stated that alignment of turbine and generator shafts would be accomplished at contractor's plant in Japan rather than in the United States as specified in the IFB).

If there is no prohibition in the IFB against conditions limiting the size of the award, the imposition of such a condition will not render the bid nonresponsive. In *Orvedahl Constr., Inc.*, 63 Comp. Gen. 288 (B-213408), 84-1 CPD ¶ 405, bids were entered on two line items at $781,000 and $622,000 respectively, along with a condition stipulating that no award over $1,000,000 would be accepted. The rejection of Orvedahl's bid was held improper because the bidder's obligation to perform according to the terms and conditions of the IFB was not affected in any way. See also FAR 14.404-5, which allows bidders to condition acceptance upon award of all or a specified group of items, unless the IFB expressly prohibits "all or none" or similarly restricted bids. See *Mansfield Assocs.*, Comp. Gen. Dec. B-242270, 91-1 CPD ¶ 284 (agency's failure to incorporate a provision expressly permitting "all or none" bids did not constitute an express prohibition of such bidding); and *Phillips Cartner & Co.*, 69 Comp. Gen. 105 (B-236416.2), 89-2 CPD ¶ 492 ("all or none" qualification did not render bid nonresponsive since the IFB did not expressly prohibit such bid qualifications).

A bid may be responsive in spite of a qualifying legend contained in the bid literature where it is reasonably clear from the bid that a "subject to change" legend is not intended to reserve the right to the bidder to change the offered product or to deviate from the material requirements of the invitation, *Syntrex Inc.*, 63 Comp. Gen. 360, (B-212781.2), 84-1 CPD ¶ 522. See also *Yale Materials Handling Corp.*, Comp. Gen. Dec. B-228974.2, 87-2 CPD ¶ 550, where, although the bid was held nonresponsive on other grounds, the Comptroller General stated that a handwritten statement, which immediately followed the "subject to change" clause, that all requirements will be met, effectively deleted the conditional language. Similarly, where a bid statement merely clarifies the bidder's understanding of the IFB without limiting any material provisions, the bid is responsive, *Westinghouse Elec. Corp.*, Comp. Gen. Dec. B-187487, 76-2 CPD ¶ 455.

b. Limiting Rights of the Government

If a bid attempts to limit the rights of the Government under any contract clause, the bid will be rejected as nonresponsive, *New Dimension Masonry, Inc.*, Comp. Gen. Dec. B-258876, 95-1 CPD ¶ 102 (bid rejected as nonresponsive where cover letter conditioned bid upon the use of a Government storage area); *Municipal Leasing Sys., Inc.*, Comp. Gen. Dec. B-242648.2, 91-1 CPD ¶ 495 (bid language "after 12 months" limited the agency's right to exercise a purchase option within the first 12 months of the contract); *F.J. Dahill Co.*, Comp. Gen. Dec. B-235272, 89-2 CPD ¶ 103 (bid nonresponsive because it contained statement that bidder would not work on hazardous substances and would leave site if any were found); *Gelco Payment Sys., Inc.*, Comp. Gen. Dec. B-234957, 89-2 CPD ¶ 27 (bid stating that either party may cancel upon 30 days' notice attempted to limit the Government's rights under the "termination for convenience" clause and was rejected as nonresponsive); *Integrated Research & Info. Sys.*, Comp. Gen. Dec. B-196456, 80-1 CPD ¶ 130 (bid specified that procuring agency rather than the bidder would pay shipping costs); *Kari-Vac, Inc.*, Comp. Gen. Dec. B-194202, 79-2 CPD ¶ 4 (bid conditioned upon payment by the Government of 1½ percent interest charge for payments made after 30 days). But see 48 Comp. Gen. 306 (B-164639) (1968), where the Comptroller General held that a statement on one competitor's own bid form that "no withholding will be allowed without the prior written consent of the seller" did not affect the responsiveness of the bid, even though that it appeared to limit the Government's rights. The Comptroller General stated at 310-11:

> In this instance we do not believe that the acceptance of the MSA bid, including the wording "no withholding will be allowed without the prior written consent of the seller," resulted in any diminution of the rights which the Government would have without that language. If the Government does withhold any or all of the contract price by reason of a claim against the contractor, we are not aware of any remedy available to the contractor except an action for the amount withheld, and in the event of such an action it is our opinion the Government could assert its claim either as a cross-claim or as a separate action.

c. Limiting Liability to the Government

A bid that attempts to limit the bidder's liability to the Government as proposed in the invitation will be rejected as nonresponsive, *AAA Roofing Co.*, Comp. Gen. Dec. B-240852, 90-2 CPD ¶ 485 (form submitted with bid rendered bid nonresponsive since it imposed limitations on bidder's future liability to the Government); *Contech Constr. Co.*, Comp. Gen. Dec. B-241185, 90-2 CPD ¶ 264 (bid nonresponsive when it included notation "impossible" next to two interim schedule requirements; argument that these were only estimator's notes rejected); *Roche Biomedical Labs., Inc.*, Comp. Gen. Dec. B-233123, 88-2 CPD ¶ 368 (bid claiming the right and privilege of terminating contract upon certain conditions limited bidder's liability to the Government); *Southwest Marine of San Francisco, Inc.*, 66 Comp. Gen. 22 (B-224508), 86-2 CPD ¶ 388 (bid stating contractor "shall take every precaution to contain contaminate" from abrasive ship blasting rendered bid nonresponsive since statement attempted to limit its liability to the Government for any environmental violations); *Dr. Beurt R. Servaas*, HUDBCA 83-780-B1, 83-2 BCA ¶ 16,690 (bid request for waiver of first 12 months' interest and principal payment found to be a material deviation from invitation thus requiring rejection); *Dubie-Clark Co.*, Comp. Gen. Dec. B-186918, 76-2 CPD ¶ 194 (exception to liquidated damages); 39 Comp. Gen. 259 (B-140236) (1959) (bid limiting contractor's liability for excess costs for failure or delay in making delivery rendered bid nonresponsive).

d. Barring Public Disclosure

Bids containing restrictions that prevent public disclosure are nonresponsive if they effectively keep competing bidders from knowing the essential nature and type of products offered or those elements of the bid that relate to quantity, price, and delivery terms, *Industrial Acoustics Co.*, Comp. Gen. Dec. B-255123.2, 94-1 CPD ¶ 220 (bid properly rejected as nonresponsive where bid restricted disclosure of required test data necessary to determine responsiveness of bid); *VACAR Battery Mfg. Co.*, B-223244.2, 86-2 CPD ¶ 21 (bid restricting public disclosure rejected as nonresponsive despite disclosure of the restricted bid price at bid opening); *Sperry-Univac*, Comp. Gen. Dec. B-200378, 81-1 CPD ¶ 38 (bid stamped "proprietary" properly rejected as nonresponsive because disclosure of price at bid opening was limited). But where the limitations on disclosure of a company's information relate solely to its ability to perform and not to price, quantity, or delivery, rejection is not required, *Tennessee Apparel Corp.*, Comp. Gen. Dec. B-253178.4, 94-1 CPD ¶ 104.

4. Indefinite, Uncertain, or Ambiguous Bids

Bids that are indefinite, uncertain, or ambiguous are normally rejected as nonresponsive. The test is whether "the face of the bid indicates the bidder's intent to be bound" by the Government's acceptance of the bid, *Orvedahl Constr., Inc.*, 63 Comp. Gen. 288 (B-213408), 84-1 CPD ¶ 405. See *Entwistle Co.*, Comp. Gen. Dec. B-192990, 79-1 CPD ¶ 112, stating:

> When determining the responsiveness of a bid, the controlling factor is not whether the bidder intends to be bound, but whether this intention is apparent from the bid as submitted. 42 Comp. Gen. 502 (1963). Thus, if [the low bidder's] bid is ambiguous, as Entwistle seems to contend, then the intent to be bound is not apparent from the bid submitted and [the low bidder's] bid must be found nonresponsive. See *James W. Boyer Company*, B-187539, November 17, 1976, 76-2 CPD ¶ 433. In 48 Comp. Gen. 757 at 760 (1969), we stated:
>
> > The mere allegation that something is ambiguous does not make it so. Similarly, some factor in a written instrument may be somewhat confusing and puzzling without constituting an ambiguity, provided that an application of reason would serve to remove the doubt. In other words, an ambiguity exists only if two or more *reasonable* interpretations are possible.

Thus, where a bid is subject to two reasonable interpretations, one of which would make it responsive and the other nonresponsive, the bid must be rejected as ambiguous, *Reid & Gary Strickland Co.*, Comp. Gen. Dec. B-239700, 90-2 CPD ¶ 222 (notation on bid schedule stating that bidder had "allowed" $500,000 for doors ambiguous because it could be interpreted as indicating an intent to offer something other than a firm-fixed-price contract); *Banks Ship Rigging Corp.*, Comp. Gen. Dec. B-239853, 90-2 CPD ¶ 181 (two reasonable interpretations concerning bidder's proposed delivery date); *Wasteco Container Servs., Inc.*, Comp. Gen. Dec. B-240309, 90-2 CPD ¶ 372 (bid notation that "prices are based on dumping fees of $26 per ton" created an ambiguity as to intended price under an IFB for a firm-fixed-price contract). The consideration of ambiguous bids for award would give the bidder an unfair competitive advantage by giving it the opportunity to withdraw or affirm the bid after seeing the bids of competitors. In this regard the Comptroller General, in *Fire & Technical Equip. Corp.*, Comp. Gen. Dec. B-192408, 78-2 CPD ¶ 91, stated:

> Only material available at bid opening may be considered by the contracting officer when determining the responsiveness of the bid. To permit explanations after bid opening to render responsive a bid which is nonresponsive on its face would be tantamount to granting an opportunity to submit a new bid. 52 Comp. Gen. 602 (1973). Thus, a nonresponsive bid may not be corrected and it does not matter whether the failure to comply with the requirements of the IFB was due to inadvertence, mistake or otherwise. 45 Comp. Gen. 433 (1966).

In *Don's Wheelchair & Ambulance Serv., Inc.*, Comp. Gen. Dec. B-216790, 85-1 CPD ¶ 82, a bid was found to be nonresponsive because it permitted the bidder to elect one of two prices, only one of which would result in award to the bidder. However, in *Hughes & Hughes*, 68 Comp. Gen. 194 (B-233624), 89-1 CPD ¶ 61, the Comptroller General found no ambiguity where the bidder submitted two conflicting bid sheets, reasoning that it was clear that the bid sheet with the later notations was the one that would be binding on the bidder.

a. *Conditioning the Offer*

Bids that are ambiguous regarding whether they represent an unconditional offer to comply with the specifications are nonresponsive, *B&C Indus., Inc.*, Comp. Gen. Dec. B-244471.4, 91-2 CPD ¶ 314 (shipping information included with bid created an ambiguity as to whether bid would conform to the IFB's packaging requirement); *G.S. Link & Assocs.*, Comp. Gen. Dec. B-238600, 90-1 CPD ¶ 479 (statement that bid would comply with EPA guidelines rendered bid ambiguous with respect to whether the offered paper products would comply with the required waste paper content); *John C. Grimberg, Inc.*, Comp. Gen. Dec. B-218231, 85-1 CPD ¶ 305 (bidder's failure to unconditionally acknowledge referenced sketch created uncertainty concerning whether the bid was an unequivocal offer to meet material requirements of the solicitation). Bids also have been rejected when required descriptive literature submitted with them stated that specifications were "subject to change," *Air & Hydraulic Equip., Inc.*, Comp. Gen. Dec. B-250332, 93-1 CPD ¶ 54. However, if other language negates the "subject to change" provision, the bid has been held to be responsive. See *Yale Materials Handling Corp.*, Comp. Gen. Dec. B-228974.2, 87-2 CPD ¶ 550 (bid need not be rejected as nonresponsive where handwritten statement that all required specifications will be met immediately following the "subject to change" provision effectively deleted such language from bid); and *Waukesha Motor Co.*, Comp. Gen. Dec. B-178494, 74-1 CPD ¶ 329 (cover letter, stating that all equipment would meet specifications, negated the "subject to change" clause and did not render the bid nonresponsive).

If required bid literature — submitted to establish conformance to the specifications — does not clearly indicate such conformance, the bid is considered ambiguous and rejection will result, *AMSCO Scientific*, Comp. Gen. Dec. B-255313, 94-1 CPD ¶ 112. Similarly, where a bidder submits unsolicited bid literature that either takes exception to the specifications or renders the bid ambiguous as to whether or not the item offered will comply with the specifications, the bid will be rejected, *Nu-Lite Elec. Wholesalers, Inc.*, Comp. Gen. Dec. B-248383, 92-2 CPD ¶ 104.

The insertion of unsolicited part or model numbers in a bid, even where included only for a bidder's internal control purposes, creates an ambiguity regarding whether the bidder is offering to comply completely with the specifications, *IFR, Sys., Inc.*, Comp. Gen. Dec. B-222533, 86-2 CPD ¶ 224, *recons. denied*, 86-2 CPD ¶ 601. Thus, a bid containing unsolicited part numbers must be rejected as nonresponsive unless either the bid contains an express statement that the designated parts conform to the specifications or the contracting officer determines, from data available before bid opening, that the parts conform, *Infab Corp.*, Comp. Gen. Dec. B-238423, 90-1 CPD ¶ 506. In *Buckingham Mfg. Co.*, Comp. Gen. Dec. B-239999, 90-2 CPD ¶ 224, a bid ambiguity created by the unsolicited insertion of a part number resulted in rejection because the ambiguity could not be resolved by reference to the bid itself, commercial literature, or other data available at the time of bid opening. See also *Wright Tool Co.*, Comp. Gen. Dec. B-212343, 83-2 CPD ¶ 457; *Abbott Labs.*, Comp. Gen. Dec. B-183799, 75-2 CPD ¶ 171; *Lift Power, Inc.*, Comp. Gen. Dec. B-182604, 75-1 CPD ¶ 13; and 50 Comp. Gen. 8 (B-169813) (1970). However, ambiguities created by unsolicited insertions of model numbers can be resolved by an express bid statement that the designated model numbers comply with the IFB specification, *Millipore Corp.*, Comp. Gen. Dec. B-234979, 89-2 CPD ¶ 31; *Carco Elecs.*, Comp. Gen. Dec. B-186747, 77-1 CPD ¶ 172; *Huey Paper & Material, Stacor Corp.*, Comp. Gen. Dec. B-185762, 76-1 CPD ¶ 382.

Although reference to commercially available literature or to documents that are submitted with the bid may clarify an otherwise ambiguous bid, this literature is to be used only to "fill in the gaps" and may not negate what is in the bid itself, *IFR, Inc.*, Comp. Gen. Dec. B-203391.4, 82-1 CPD ¶ 292. Note, also, that where the contracting agency obtained literature that detracted from the second low bidder's bid, the agency's refusal to consider contemporaneously available literature that showed the bid was in compliance, was irrational, *Essex Electro Eng'rs, Inc. v. United States*, 3 Cl. Ct. 277 (1983).

b. Requests That Vary from the IFB

Bidders can also create uncertainty regarding their bids when they "request" additions to or variations from the IFB, because it is then not clear how such a request should be interpreted. In *National Oil & Supply Co.*, Comp. Gen. Dec. B-198321, 80-1 CPD ¶ 437, one bidder included the following provision:

> Please be advised that National Oil would like to be relieved against freight increases. Due to the unsteady trend of increasing freight rates by the common carriers, we are unable to predict an adequate freight rate. . . . We would wish to escalate our freight rates with verification along with those imposed upon us by carriers.

The Comptroller General upheld the agency's determination of nonresponsiveness, explaining:

> With regard to National's contention that the wording in its cover letter was merely precatory in nature, i.e., the expression of a request rather than tak-

> ing exception to the terms of the invitation, the meaning of those words must be determined within the context of existing circumstances. Here, we do not find it unreasonable to view National's "request" as something more than a mere wish or desire, for if National's bid were accepted it could be argued that DLA would be legally bound, contrary to the IFB's cited clauses, to absorb unanticipated increases in freight costs above and beyond those which might be included in increases in posted prices.
>
> * * *
>
> At best, National's bid, including its cover letter, is subject to two possible interpretations, under one of which it would be responsive and under the other nonresponsive. We have consistently held that the rejection of such a bid is required and that it would be prejudicial to other bidders to permit the bidder creating the ambiguity to select, after bid opening, the interpretation to be adopted.

See also *A & Z Eng'g Co.*, Comp. Gen. Dec. B-222806, 86-1 CPD ¶ 388 (bid containing a request to use a different type of alloy than required in the IFB was properly rejected as nonresponsive since the request indicated that without the deviation the bidder could not manufacture the item as specified in the invitation).

The Comptroller General has allowed bidders to "confirm" bids to a contracting officer who finds them ambiguous. The Comptroller General has stated that in such situations, the low bidder is not given any advantage in being permitted to confirm its intended bid price because the confirmation is not inconsistent with the only reasonable interpretation of the bid, *Wismer & Becker Contracting Eng'rs*, Comp. Gen. Dec. B-198674, 80-2 CPD ¶ 170. See also 39 Comp. Gen. 653 (B-141591) (1960).

FAR 52.232-15 prescribes a standard solicitation clause for use when no progress payments are intended:

> PROGRESS PAYMENTS NOT INCLUDED (APR 1984)
>
> A progress payments clause is not included in this solicitation, and will not be added to the resulting contract at the time of award. Bids conditioned upon inclusion of a progress payment clause in the resulting contract will be rejected as nonresponsive.

In contrast, FAR 32.405(b) does not prohibit the request for advance payments:

> Bidders may request advance payments before or after award, even if the invitation for bids does not contain an advance payment provision. However, the contracting officer shall reject any bid requiring that advance payments be provided as a basis for acceptance.

Prior to the Comptroller General decision in *Canadian Commercial Corp.*, 62 Comp. Gen. 113 (B-207777), 83-1 CPD ¶ 16, *recons. denied*, 83-1 CPD ¶ 275, bids containing requests for advance payments were held responsive while bids requesting progress payments were held as conditions that rendered the bid nonresponsive. Compare *Potomac Iron Works, Inc.*, Comp. Gen. Dec. B-200075, 81-1 CPD ¶ 15 (bid "requesting" advance payments was not a condition or qualification, and rejection was improper) with 45 Comp. Gen. 809 (B-158915) (1966) (bid stating "Progress Payments are Requested" under an IFB that did not provide for progress payments renders bid nonresponsive, even though the word "request" is, in the ordinary sense, precatory in nature).

In *Canadian Commercial Corp.*, the distinction between progress payments and advance payments was held irrelevant. The Comptroller General stated that the issue is not whether a bidder requests advance or progress payments, but whether the request is a condition or a mere wish or desire. Whether a "request" is a condition or a mere wish or desire must be determined from the meaning of the words under the circumstances. The Comptroller General, relying primarily on the reasoning in *Potomac Iron Works, Inc.*, Comp. Gen. Dec. B-200075, 81-1 CPD ¶ 15, determined that the statement, "Progress payments, in accordance with governing U.S. procurement regulations, are requested" was a precatory request that did not affect the responsiveness of the bid. See also *GMI, Inc.*, 69 Comp. Gen. 557 (B-239064), 90-2 CPD ¶ 8, where a request for progress payments did not render a bid nonresponsive in the absence of circumstances showing that the request was more than a mere wish or desire.

c. *Uncertainties As to Price*

If a total bid price is uncertain, the bid is not responsive, *Associated Mechanical, Inc.*, Comp. Gen. Dec. B-243892, 91-2 CPD ¶ 192 (telegram submitted prior to bid opening created uncertainty as to whether bidder proposed to deduct $311.00 from bid or $311,000 because it was unclear whether a comma or period preceded the zeros); *Harris Constr. Co.*, 64 Comp. Gen. 702 (B-218387.2), 85-2 CPD ¶ 92 (garbled telegraphic modification increasing bid price to an uncertain amount received prior to bid opening required rejection of bid). Similarly, a bid is nonresponsive if its intended price cannot be determined from all the bid documents submitted at the time of bid opening, *United States Coast Guard — Advance Decision*, Comp. Gen. Dec. B-252396, 93-1 CPD ¶ 286 (cover letter submitted with bid requesting additional charge of $1,000 per hour for Government preacceptance tests rendered bid nonresponsive; the IFB provided no means of estimating the amount of testing and, thus, the bid price could not be calculated with any certainty). Note, however, that an ambiguity as to a low bidder's intended price does not render a bid nonresponsive if the bid would be low by a significant margin under all possible interpretations, *The Ryan Co.*, Comp. Gen. Dec. B-238932, 90-1 CPD ¶ 557. The Comptroller General holds that these ambiguities can be resolved without prejudice to other bidders, *Energy Maintenance Corp.*, 64 Comp. Gen. 425 (B-215281.3), 85-1 CPD ¶ 341. Similarly, the Comptroller General has stated that when it is clear from the bid itself what price was intended, or where on the basis of logic and experience it can be determined that only one price makes sense, correction of a bid and displacement of another bidder is allowed, *J&J Maintenance, Inc.*, Comp. Gen. Dec. B-251355, 93-1 CPD ¶ 187. See also *R.R. Gregory Corp.*, Comp. Gen. Dec. B-217251, 85-1 CPD ¶ 449, where the Comptroller General held that award to the bidder was proper even though the bid contained a price discrepancy because only one price could reasonably be regarded as the intended bid.

d. Offers to Comply

Bidders often attempt to resolve ambiguities in their bids by including statements to the effect that they are offering to comply with all terms of the invitation. Overall offers to comply will cure bid discrepancies only if they are specific, resolve all doubts as to the bidder's intention, and remove any option to deviate from the invitation, Comp. Gen. Dec. B-179024, Oct. 30, 1973, *Unpub.* Successful offers to comply were present in *Millipore Corp.*, Comp. Gen. Dec. B-234979, 89-2 CPD ¶ 31 (insertion of a model number did not render bid ambiguous since the bid contained an express statement that the product identified conformed to the technical requirements of the IFB); *Syntrex Inc.*, Comp. Gen. Dec. B-212781.2, 84-1 CPD ¶ 522 (bidder's cover letter offering to comply with all material specifications overcame "subject to change" clause contained in bid literature); *Calma Co.*, Comp.

Gen. Dec. B-209260.2, 83-2 CPD ¶ 31 (statement in bidder's descriptive literature indicating that it intends to supply processors with the 500,000 bytes of memory required by the IFB clarifies preprinted literature indicating that the processors have only 440,000 bytes of memory).

However, a "blanket" promise of compliance with the specifications of an IFB is not sufficient to establish the responsiveness of a bid that does not demonstrate compliance apart from that promise, *Electrophysics Corp.*, Comp. Gen. Dec. B-258674, 95-1 CPD ¶ 63 (bid rejected as nonresponsive where descriptive literature submitted with bid failed to demonstrate that the offered product would satisfy a salient characteristic in the IFB, despite a blanket statement of compliance); *Amjay Chemicals*, Comp. Gen. Dec. B-252502, 93-1 CPD ¶ 426 (blanket offer in bid cover letter to comply with all IFB specifications was properly rejected as nonresponsive where unsolicited descriptive literature established noncompliance); *IRT Corp.*, Comp. Gen. Dec. B-233134, 89-1 CPD ¶ 216 (blanket statement in cover letter that bidder will meet specification requirements did not cure bid's failure to provide required descriptive literature); *JoaQuin Mfg. Corp.*, Comp. Gen. Dec. B-228515, 88-1 CPD ¶ 15 (bid rejected as nonresponsive where required descriptive literature demonstrated nonconformance with IFB requirement, despite blanket statement of compliance); *Eclipse Sys., Inc.*, Comp. Gen. Dec. B-216002, 85-1 CPD ¶ 267 (bidder's general reference to supplying item in accordance with military specification did not overcome ambiguity raised in cover letter). See also *Zero Mfg., Co.*, Comp. Gen. Dec. B-210123.2, 83-1 CPD ¶ 416 (bid that did not conform was not cured by statement that item would be equal to or better than that specified).

5. Failure to Furnish Required Items or Information

Failure to furnish items or information required to be submitted with the bid can render a bid nonresponsive. However, if sufficient information is otherwise contained in the bid documents to determine the missing information, the bid will be responsive, *Inland Assocs.*, Comp. Gen. Dec. B-213579, 84-1 CPD ¶ 398 (registration status of modem is matter of FCC public record); *Abbot Power Corp.*, Comp. Gen. Dec. B-192792, 79-1 CPD ¶ 295 (failure to submit dimensions on drawing was a minor deviation since the information could be obtained from other information in the bid).

a. Descriptive Literature and Bid Samples

When descriptive literature or bid samples are necessary to determine if the items being offered meet the specifications, standard solicitation provisions are used to alert the bidders to this requirement. See the Bid Samples provision in FAR 52.214-20 and the Descriptive Literature provision in FAR 52.214-21. These provisions state that failure to furnish the literature or samples will require rejection of the bid. They are operative only when the IFB specifies the precise descriptive literature or bid samples that are required. Alternate provisions are to be used if there is a possibility that the requirement will be waived for some of the bidders. FAR 14.202-5(e) provides that an agency may waive the descriptive literature requirements for specific bidders. It states that:

> (1) The requirement for furnishing descriptive literature may be waived if—
>
> > (i) The bidder states in the bid that the product being offered is the same as a product previously or currently being furnished to the contracting activity; and
> >
> > (ii) The contracting officer determines that the product offered by the bidder complies with the specification requirements of the current invitation for bids. When the requirement may be waived, see 14.201-6(p)(2).
>
> (2) When descriptive literature is not considered necessary and a waiver of literature requirements of a Federal, Military, or other formal specification has been authorized, a statement shall be included in the invitation that, notwithstanding the requirements of the specifications, descriptive literature will not be required.
>
> (3) If the solicitation provides for a waiver, a bidder may submit a bid on the basis of either the descriptive literature to be furnished or a previously furnished product. If the bid is submitted on one basis, the bidder is precluded from having it considered on the other basis after bids are opened.

FAR 14.202-4(f) contains a similar provision permitting the waiver of the requirement for bid samples. See *Entwistle Co.*, Comp. Gen. Dec. B-192990, 79-1 CPD ¶ 112, permitting waiver of a descriptive literature requirement where the bidder instead provided the contract number of a contract where it had supplied equipment that met the contract specifications. The Comptroller General affirmed the contracting officer's determination that this was an expression of intent to supply that equipment on the current contract.

Failure to furnish the descriptive literature called for by the IFB will result in a bid's rejection as nonresponsive, *TIMCO Elec. Power & Controls, Inc.*, Comp. Gen. Dec. B-248308, 92-2 CPD ¶ 84 (bid nonresponsive because it did not contain specific descriptive literature required by IFB); *BSC Indus., Inc.*, Comp. Gen. Dec. B-237299, 90-1 CPD ¶ 152 (bid nonresponsive because agency received only partial descriptive literature; bidder contention that far more literature had been provided with bid was unproven); *AMSCO Scientific*, Comp. Gen. Dec. B-255313, 94-1 CPD ¶ 112 (bid nonresponsive because descriptive literature was ambiguous). Even where the descriptive literature requirement is imprecise, a bid may be rejected for failure to include any of the required literature or if what was furnished evidences nonconformance with the specifications, *Baker Co.*, Comp. Gen. Dec. B-216220, 85-1 CPD ¶ 254; *Clackamas Communications, Inc.*, Comp. Gen. Dec. B-209387, 83-1 CPD ¶ 549.

Imprecise requirements for descriptive data will be less likely to lead to a determination that a noncompliant submission is nonresponsive. For example, failure to furnish "drawings . . . showing overall dimensions of reactors" as required by the IFB did not render a bid nonresponsive in *Abbot Power Corp.*, Comp. Gen. Dec. B-192792, 79-1 CPD ¶ 295. In that case, the Comptroller General found that the agency reasonably determined that the purpose of the clause was "substantially met" by the material furnished, though the bidder did not state that the offered product was a previously furnished one. See also *Tri-Servs., Inc.*, Comp. Gen. Dec. B-245698, 92-1 CPD ¶ 75, where the Comptroller General stated that a bidder's failure to include required information regarding overhead and costs did not render the bid nonresponsive since the information was not material to bid evaluation or the bidder's obligation to perform.

Failure to provide bid samples as required by an invitation will also render a bid nonresponsive, *EEV, Inc.*, Comp. Gen. Dec. B-253061, 93-2 CPD ¶ 52; *Canon U.S.A., Inc.*, Comp. Gen. Dec. B-249521, 92-2 CPD ¶ 388, *recons. denied*, 93-1 CPD ¶ 219. Where an invitation requires that bid samples strictly comply with listed specifications, a sample that fails to demonstrate conformance renders a bid nonresponsive, *Aqua-Trol Corp.*, Comp. Gen. Dec. B-246473.2, 92-1 CPD ¶ 420; *ATD-American Co.*, Comp. Gen. Dec. B-227134, 87-2 CPD ¶ 58. Note, however, that bid samples need not meet every specification requirement that the items to be furnished under the contract must meet, but rather may be evaluated solely for the characteristics specified in the solicitation's bid sample provision, *LSL Indus., Inc.*, Comp. Gen. Dec. B-239486, Sept. 10, 1990, *Unpub.*; *Sherwood Med. Co.*, Comp. Gen. Dec. B-231184, 88-2 CPD ¶ 171; FAR 14.202 4(b)(3) and (e)(ii). In addition, a bid is not necessarily nonresponsive for failing to include a bid sample "as part of the bid" as long as the sample is submitted to the agency in a responsive manner that identifies it with the procurement before bid opening, *Alan Scott Indus.*, Comp. Gen. Dec. B-200391.2, 81-1 CPD ¶ 525; *Unique Packaging, Inc.*, 54 Comp. Gen. 157 (B-181940), 74-2 CPD ¶ 125.

Submission of bid samples or descriptive literature not required by the IFB will generally not be considered as qualifying the bid and will be disregarded, FAR 14.202-4(g) and FAR 14.202-5(f). However, if the literature or sample indicates that the bidder is conditioning its bid, it will be rejected as nonresponsive, *Products for Indus.*, Comp. Gen. Dec. B-257463, 94-2 CPD ¶ 128.

b. Bid Guarantees

FAR 14.404-2(j) states that when a bid bond or guarantee is required and a bidder fails to furnish it in accordance with the IFB, the bid shall be rejected as nonresponsive unless one of the stated exceptions in FAR 28.101-4, as discussed in A.3.b. of this section, is otherwise applicable, *Secur-Data Sys., Inc.*, Comp. Gen. Dec. B-255090, 94-1 CPD ¶ 68 (bid that did not include required bid guarantee was properly rejected despite the bidder's assertion that the guarantee was included in its bid package).

Submission of a defective bid bond or bid guarantee is as fatal to a bid as the total failure to submit a bid bond or guarantee. The determinative question as to the acceptability of bonds and guarantees containing defects is whether the bid documents submitted with the bid establish that the bond or guarantee is enforceable by the Government should the bidder fail to meet its obligations, *A.W. & Assocs.*, 69 Comp. Gen. 737 (B-239740), 90-2 CPD ¶ 254; *F&F Pizano*, 64 Comp. Gen. 805 (B-219591.2), 85-2 CPD ¶ 234. For example, in *Darla Envtl., Inc.*, Comp. Gen. Dec. B-234560, 89-1 CPD ¶ 454, a bid bond that contained signatures of individual sureties that were photocopied on the bid form prior to its completion rendered the bid nonresponsive. The Comptroller General stated that the reproduction created serious doubts about the bonds enforceability, because after bid opening, the sureties could argue that the bonding documents were executed without their knowledge. See also *Hydro-Dredge Corp.*, Comp. Gen. Dec. B-214408, 84-1 CPD ¶ 400 (although penal amount listed on the bid bond was sufficient, the attorney-in-fact who signed the bond had the authority to bind the surety for only a fraction of the amount required by the IFB); *H.W. Houston Constr. Co.*, Comp. Gen. Dec. B-258581, 95-1 CPD ¶ 47 (bid properly rejected where the solicitation number on the bid bond was "whited out" and retyped without evidence of the surety's consent, and there was another ongoing procurement to which the altered number could refer); and *Pioneer Constr. Co.*, Comp. Gen. Dec. B-227948, 87-2 CPD ¶ 279 (bid properly rejected where the penal amount was typed over "white out," and there was no evidence that the surety had consented to an alteration). Compare *Castle Floor Covering*, 70 Comp. Gen. 530 (B-242718), 91-1 CPD ¶ 510, where waiver of the defect was required because a cashier's check made out to "Farmers Home Bureau, U.S. Government" would be binding even though the procurement was by the "Farmers Home Administration."

Failure to include a penal sum on a bond also results in a nonresponsive bid, *Allen County Builders Supply*, 64 Comp. Gen. 505 (B-216647), 85-1 CPD ¶ 507. Failure to provide a bid bond or guarantee that is effective for the entire bid acceptance period also renders a bid nonresponsive, *J.C. & N. Maintenance, Inc.*, Comp. Gen. Dec. B-229556, 87-2 CPD ¶ 567; *McNamara — Lunz Warehouses, Inc.*, Comp. Gen. Dec. B-188100, 77-1 CPD ¶ 448, *recons. denied*, 77-2 CPD ¶ 149. However, where the Government extends the bid acceptance period but fails to require extension of the bid bond, expiration of the bid bond prior to award does not render a bid nonresponsive, *Holk Dev., Inc.*, Comp. Gen. Dec. B-230830.2, 88-2 CPD ¶ 543; *Engle Acoustic & Tile, Inc.*, Comp. Gen. Dec. B-190467, 78-1 CPD ¶ 72.

FAR 28.101-2(b) requires bid guarantees to be for a minimum of 20 percent of the bid price but not to exceed $3 million. However, FAR 28.101-4(c)(2) requires waiver of the deficiency in the amount of the bid guarantee if the guarantee amount submitted is "equal to or greater than the difference between the offer price and the next higher acceptable offer." Such waiver has been accepted by the Comptroller General, *Centex-Great Southwest Corp.*, Comp. Gen. Dec. B-258578, 95-1 CPD ¶ 19, and waiver was required in one case, *Haag Elec. & Constr., Inc.*, 70 Comp. Gen. 180 (B-240974), 91-1 CPD ¶ 29. However, the Comptroller General has affirmed the exercise of discretion by a contracting officer that determined that the bid guarantee was not sufficient to equal the difference in bids in an indefinite-delivery, indefinite-quantity contract where the bids were stated in terms of multipliers, not dollar amounts, *Apex Servs., Inc.*, Comp. Gen. Dec. B-255118, 94-1 CPD ¶ 95. See also *P.B. Eng'g Co.*, Comp. Gen. Dec. B-244640, 91-2 CPD ¶ 80 (bid nonresponsive when bid guarantee 24 percent lower than required amount); and *Drill Constr. Co.*, Comp. Gen. Dec. B-239783, 90-1 CPD ¶ 538 (submission of bid bond for half the required penal amount rendered bid nonresponsive).

FAR 28.202 provides guidance on the use of corporate sureties for bid bonds and requires that only sureties listed in Department of Treasury Circular 570 will be acceptable. Thus, bids submitting bonds by other corporate sureties are nonresponsive, *Envirotox Technologies, Inc.*, Comp. Gen. Dec. B-250091, 92-2 CPD ¶ 186 (bid bond executed by corporate surety not listed in Treasury Circular 570 rendered bid nonresponsive); *Siska Constr. Co.*, Comp. Gen. Dec. B-218428, 85-1 CPD ¶ 669, *recons. denied*, 85-2 CPD ¶ 102 (lack of notice in solicitation that unlisted surety was unacceptable is not an excuse for using unlisted surety, because the requirement for listed surety is in regulations and instructions to bond form).

Bid bonds may be furnished by individual sureties if the surety pledges assets equal to the amount of the bond, FAR 28.203. See *C. E. Wylie Constr. Co.*, Comp. Gen. Dec. B-234225, 89-1 CPD ¶ 427 (bid responsive where individual sureties demonstrated sufficient net worth to cover the penal amounts of the bonds); and *O.V. Campbell & Sons Indus., Inc.*, Comp. Gen. Dec. B-229555, 88-1 CPD ¶ 259 (completed SF 24 is proper "on its face" when executed by two individual sureties whose affidavits indicate that, subject to further investigation, they both have a net worth at least equal to the penal amount of the bond). A bid containing bid bonds furnished by individual sureties is responsive even if the sureties fail to file a pledge of assets, *Burtch Constr.*, Comp. Gen. Dec. B-240695, 90-2 CPD ¶ 423; *R.C. Benson & Sons, Inc.*, Comp. Gen. Dec. B-240251.2, 90-2 CPD ¶ 92. This is because a pledge of assets assists the contracting officer in determining the financial acceptability of individual sureties, which is a matter of responsibility, not responsiveness.

Where the bidder named on the bid form differs from the principal name on the bid bond, the bid must be rejected unless it can be established that the bidder is "the same legal entity as the principal," *Gem Eng'g Co.*, Comp. Gen. Dec. B-251644, 93-1 CPD ¶ 303; *Scotsman Group, Inc.*, Comp. Gen. Dec. B-245634, 92-1 CPD ¶ 57 (bid properly rejected where publicly available information submitted after bid opening did not demonstrate that the principal named on the bid bond and the named bidder were the same legal entity); *New Solid, Ltd.*, Comp. Gen. Dec. B-246357, 92-1 CPD ¶ 163 (bid properly rejected where bid bond identified "Eugene E. and Ingride Harmon" as principals, and the bidder identified in the bid form was "Eugene E. Harmon, owner"). See also *Tower Elevator Corp.*, Comp. Gen. Dec. B-192064, 78-2 CPD ¶ 188, where the Comptroller General stated that wholly owned subsidiaries and parent corporations are not "identical legal entities."

The form of the bid guarantee may vary so long as the requisite monetary obligation by the surety is certain, *Niles Janitor Serv. & Supply, Inc.*, Comp. Gen. Dec. B-246575.3, 92-1 CPD ¶ 256 (bid properly rejected as nonresponsive where irrevocable letter of credit incorporated a force majeure provision of the Uniform Customs and Practices for Documentary Credits Act, which created uncertainty as to the liability of the issuing bank); *Central Mechanical, Inc.*, 61 Comp. Gen. 566 (B-206555), 82-2 CPD ¶ 150 (bidder's offer to assign funds allegedly due the bidder from the Government was rejected because the amount actually owed was undetermined); *Colorado Elevator Serv., Inc.*, Comp. Gen. Dec. B-206950.2, 82-1 CPD ¶ 434 (letter of credit from a bank stating that it is subject to the bank's standard review process is not a firm commitment and renders bid nonresponsive). Where a bid guarantee does not list the United States as the obligee, an agency may waive the noncompliance since the guarantee correctly identified the offeror, the solicitation number, and the name of the location of the project involved, *S.J. Amoroso Constr. Co.*, Comp. Gen. Dec. B-240687, 90-2 CPD ¶ 432; *Nationwide Roofing & Sheet Metal, Inc.*, 64 Comp. Gen. 474 (B-216845), 85-1 CPD ¶ 454 (use of United States Postal Service bond form for a GSA procurement did not render bid nonresponsive where the intent of the surety and the principal to be bound to the Government was clearly shown).

c. List of Subcontractors

Generally, a requirement to list subcontractors or suppliers in bids involves a matter of responsibility, because an agency utilizes these lists to evaluate subcontractor qualifications or the bidder's ability to meet equal employment opportunity requirements, *CDM Fed. Programs Corp.*, Comp. Gen. Dec. B-249022, Jun. 23, 1992, *Unpub.*; *Norfolk Dredging Co.*, Comp. Gen. Dec. B-229572.2, 88-1 CPD ¶ 62; *A. Metz, Inc.*, Comp. Gen. Dec. B-213518, 84-1 CPD ¶ 386. However, if the requirement for bidders to list their proposed subcontractors is intended to prevent "bid shopping," the failure to furnish required subcontractor lists requires rejection of a bid as nonresponsive, *Industrial Structures, Inc.*, 64 Comp. Gen. 768 (B-219500), 85-2 CPD ¶ 165; *Lazos Constr. Co.*, Comp. Gen. Dec. B-211966, 83-2 CPD ¶ 201; *McCrory Constr. Co.*, Comp. Gen. Dec. B-192913, 79-1 CPD ¶ 64. A contractor who plans to do categories of work with its own employees must so indicate if required by the IFB, or the bid will be found nonresponsive for failure to list subcontractors, *Brisk Waterproofing Co. v. GSA*, Civ. Action No. 77-0659 (D.D.C. 1977). The listing of alternate subcontractors also renders a bid nonresponsive, *Burn Constr. Co.*, Comp. Gen. Dec. B-192196, 78-2 CPD ¶ 139. See also *Dawson Constr. Co.*, Comp. Gen. Dec. B-208547, 82-2 CPD ¶ 551, where the Comptroller General found the rejection of a bid for failing to list all subcontractors improper because the IFB called only for a listing of those doing on-site work.

6. Accurate Completion of Bids and Documents

Bids and accompanying documents must be accurately completed if they are to be considered responsive. FAR 14.301(d) states:

> Bids should be filled out, executed, and submitted in accordance with the instructions in the invitation. If a bidder uses its own bid form or a letter to submit a bid, the bid may be considered only if (1) the bidder accepts all the terms and conditions of the invitation and (2) award on the bid would result in a binding contract with terms and conditions that do not vary from the terms and conditions of the invitation.

This rule was applied in *J.C. Adams, Inc.*, Comp. Gen. Dec. B-252132, 93-1 CPD ¶ 394, where a bid was held nonresponsive because the bidder submitted a bid schedule that it had prepared itself, which varied from the material requirements of the solicitation's bid schedule. Similarly, in *Weber Constr.*, Comp. Gen. Dec. B-233848, 89-1 CPD ¶ 309, a bidder's omission of SF 1442, which contained material provisions of the solicitation, rendered the bid nonresponsive, because it was unclear whether the bidder would be unequivocally committed to all the material requirements of the invitation. See also *Dillingham Ship Repair*, Comp. Gen. Dec. B-218653, 85-2 CPD ¶ 167, where a bid was held nonresponsive for failure to include unit prices as required by the solicitation, even though the bid contained a lump sum for the total amount. In addition, a bid that contains uncertainties as to the identity of the bidder must be rejected as nonresponsive because, upon award, the bidder could avoid its obligations under the contract, *Sunrise Int'l Group, Inc.*, Comp. Gen. Dec. B-252735.2, 93-2 CPD ¶ 58 (award was improper where contracting officer concluded that the bid was submitted by T.B.F. Enterprises using Budget Inns of America (BIA) as a trade name without contemporaneous, publicly available evidence demonstrating that "BIA" was in fact "T.B.F. Enterprises"); *Martin Co.*, Comp. Gen. Dec. B-178540, 74-1 CPD ¶ 234 (bid in the name of "Martin Co., Inc." was properly rejected as nonresponsive because the company bidding was in fact "Martin Co.," a sole proprietorship, and award to anyone other than the bidder named in the bid would be an improper substitution of entities).

Bids may be accepted despite a failure to complete the bid accurately if the deficiency is not material and the obligations of the parties are not altered, *J & K Plumbing & Heating Co.*, 71 Comp. Gen. 241 (B-246000), 92-1 CPD ¶ 174 (bidder's failure to return bid schedule was waived as a minor informality where bidder signed and submitted SF 1442, which incorporated the specifications of the IFB and therefore obligated the bidder to perform in accordance with the material requirements of the IFB); *Walker Constr.*, Comp. Gen. Dec. B-246759, 92-1 CPD ¶ 319 (failure to submit a bid for an alternate item does not render a bid nonresponsive where the alternate item was not awarded); *S.J. Amoroso Constr. Co.*, Comp. Gen. Dec. B-240687, 90-2 CPD ¶ 432 (bid guarantee that did not list the United States as the obligee was waived as a minor defect because the guarantee correctly identified the bidder, the solicitation number, and the name of the location of the project involved); *Hild Floor Mach. Co.*, Comp. Gen. Dec. B-217213, 85-1 CPD ¶ 456 (failure to furnish spare parts price list is waivable because bidders were not required to commit to specific prices).

Unsigned bids are generally nonresponsive, *FCC Constr., Inc.*, Comp. Gen. Dec. B-250304, 93-1 CPD ¶ 28; *Stafford Grading & Paving Co.*, Comp. Gen. Dec. B-245907, 92-1 CPD ¶ 66; *Loop to Loop Messenger Serv.*, Comp. Gen. Dec. B-241068, 90-2 CPD ¶ 519. Unsigned bids, even though accompanied by bid samples must be considered nonresponsive, *Jonard Indus. Corp.*, Comp. Gen. Dec. B-192979, 79-1 CPD ¶ 65. See also Comp. Gen. Dec. B-148235, Mar. 23, 1962, *Unpub.*, where the Comptroller General stated that the presence of a bidder's representative at bid opening was not sufficient to overcome the lack of a signature on the bid or to indicate an intention to be bound to the material requirements of the solicitation.

If it can independently be established that the bidder submitting an unauthorized bid intended to be bound, the bid should be accepted. See

FAR 14.405(c), which allows a bidder's failure to sign a bid to be waived as a minor informality only if:

> (1) The unsigned bid is accompanied by other material indicating the bidder's intention to be bound by the unsigned bid (such as the submission of a bid guarantee or a letter signed by the bidder, with the bid, referring to and clearly identifying the bid itself); or
>
> (2) The firm submitting a bid has formally adopted or authorized, before the date set for opening of bids, the execution of documents by typewritten, printed, or stamped signature and submits evidence of such authorization and the bid carries such a signature[.]

See *Micon Corp.*, Comp. Gen. Dec. B-249231, 92-2 CPD ¶ 293 (bidder's failure to sign SF 1442 waived where bid bond accompanying the bid was properly signed and referenced the solicitation); *Tomahawk Constr. Co.*, Comp. Gen. Dec. B-243582, 91-2 CPD ¶ 137 (failure to submit an originally signed bid held a minor informality because accompanying amendments, bid bond, and letter contained original signature of bidder); and *Wilton Corp.*, 64 Comp. Gen. 233 (B-218064), 85-1 CPD ¶ 128 (bidder's failure to sign bid waived as a minor informality where bid was accompanied by a signed amendment acknowledgment). However, an irrevocable letter of credit does not negate a bidder's failure to sign its bid in the same fashion as a properly executed bid bond, because it does not require the bidder's signature as a party to the instrument, *Cable Consultants, Inc.*, Comp. Gen. Dec. B-215138, 84-2 CPD ¶ 127.

The evidence of intent to be bound must be submitted prior to bid opening. To permit submission of this evidence after bid opening would give the bidder an improper advantage, *A & E Indus., Inc.*, Comp. Gen. Dec. B-239846, 90-1 CPD ¶ 527 (bid signed with a rubber stamp signature was properly rejected because there was no evidence that prior to bid opening, the use of a rubber stamp signature had been authorized); *Power Master Elec. Co.*, Comp. Gen. Dec. B-223995, 86-2 CPD ¶ 615 (bid that included typewritten signature does not evidence intent to be bound when typewritten signature was not authorized). In this regard, the Comptroller General stated in Comp. Gen. Dec. B-160856, Mar. 16, 1967, *Unpub.*:

> The reasoning behind this rule is that when a bid lacks a proper signature, and there is no other clear indication in the bid submission that the purported bidder intended to submit the bid, the contracting officer has no assurance that the bid was submitted by someone with authority to bind the

> bidder. For that reason, acceptance of such a bid would not have automatically obligated the named bidder to perform the contract advertised. The test in cases where bids are not manually signed is whether the bid as submitted will result in a binding contract upon acceptance of the bid by the Government without confirmation of the bidder's intention.

Bids must also be signed by authorized employees of the bidder. The Comptroller General has held that the level of evidence required to establish the authority of a particular person to sign and thus bind a corporation is for the contracting officer to determine, and that the burden of proof rests with the bidder, *Alpha Q, Inc.*, Comp. Gen. Dec. B-234403.2, 89-2 CPD ¶ 401; *Central Mechanical Constr., Inc.*, Comp. Gen. Dec. B-220594, 85-2 CPD ¶ 730; *Dragon Servs., Inc.*, Comp. Gen. Dec. B-208081, 82-2 CPD ¶ 86. The evidence required to establish the authority of the signer to bind a corporation may be presented at any time prior to award. Failure to furnish such information at bid opening will not render a bid nonresponsive, *Southwest Maintenance Serv.*, Comp. Gen. Dec. B-258178, 94-2 CPD ¶ 243; *Goss Fire Protection, Inc.*, Comp. Gen. Dec. B-253036, 93-2 CPD ¶ 97.

For other irregularities in the completion of the bid form that may be waived as minor informalities, see *Corbin Superior Composites, Inc.*, Comp. Gen. Dec. B-236777.2, 90-1 CPD ¶ 2 (bidder's failure to complete "contingent fee representation" clause); *Alpha Q, Inc.*, Comp. Gen. Dec. B-234403.2, 89-2 CPD ¶ 401 (failure to return SF 33, the cover sheet used in most Government procurements, with signature); *O.V. Campbell & Sons Indus., Inc.*, Comp. Gen. Dec. B-229555, 88-1 CPD ¶ 259 (failure of surety to properly complete bid bonds); *All Star Maintenance, Inc.*, Comp. Gen. Dec. B-231618, 88-2 CPD ¶ 181 (bidder's failure to submit the required certifications and representations with bid at bid opening); *TCI, Ltd.*, 65 Comp. Gen. 23 (B-220578), 85-2 CPD ¶ 433 (failure to return the number of copies required by the invitation); *Bond Transfer & Storage Co.*, Comp. Gen. Dec. B-210251, 83-1 CPD ¶ 87 (failure to mark the solicitation number, date, and time of opening on the bid envelope); *Patterson Pump Co.*, Comp. Gen. Dec. B-200165, 80-2 CPD ¶ 453 (failure to return all specification pages where SF 33 was properly executed); *Johnson Auto Parts*, Comp. Gen. Dec. B-182102, 74-2 CPD ¶ 157 (submission of the bid on the addendum rather than on the IFB forms). See also *Excavation Constr., Inc. v. United States*, 204 Ct. Cl. 299, 494 F.2d 1289 (1974), which held that reference to an incorrect date for an addendum and the use of a superseded job number in the bid were waivable informalities.

7. *Accompanying Letter, Literature, and Other Material*

Letters, preprinted forms, descriptive literature, or other material submitted with a bid are considered part of the bid and can affect its responsiveness. Thus, if they condition the bid, they may render it nonresponsive. For example, bids accompanied by cover letters that conditioned the bid were found nonresponsive in *Air Prep Technology, Inc.*, Comp. Gen. Dec. B-252833, 93-1 CPD ¶ 459 (cover letter stating bidder's proposed conveyor system will be powered by a hydraulic motor rendered bid nonresponsive where IFB required a compressed air motor); *Perkin-Elmer Corp.*, 63 Comp. Gen. 27 (B-236175.2), 89-2 CPD ¶ 352 (bid was properly rejected as nonresponsive where cover letter offered a shorter bid acceptance period than required by the IFB); *Taylor-Forge Engineered Sys., Inc.*, 69 Comp. Gen. 54 (B-236408), 89-2 CPD ¶ 421 (bid was properly rejected because the cover letter and bid form contained conflicting delivery terms, thus rendering the bid ambiguous); *Northwest Ground Covers & Nursery*, Comp. Gen. Dec. B-201609, 81-1 CPD ¶ 81 (cover letter requested that bidder be allowed to withdraw bid if it was a successful bidder on another Government contract).

FAR 14.202-5(f) provides that unsolicited descriptive literature will be treated under the same procedures set forth in FAR 14.202-4(g) for unsolicited bid samples:

> Bid samples furnished with a bid that are not required by the invitation generally will not be considered as qualifying the bid and will be disregarded. However, the bid sample will not be disregarded if it is clear from the bid or accompanying papers that the bidder's intention was to qualify the bid. (See 14.404-2(d) if the qualification does not conform to the solicitation.)

Thus, unsolicited descriptive literature will not be considered as qualifying a bid unless it is clear from the bid as a whole that it is intended as a qualification. In *Balantine's South Bay Caterers, Inc.*, Comp. Gen. Dec. B-250223, 93-1 CPD ¶ 39, the Comptroller General stated that unsolicited descriptive literature, which reasonably raised a question regarding whether the offered services complied with the material requirements of the IFB, could not be disregarded, because the cover letter referenced the solicitation number and described the literature as "pertinent information." See also *Delta Chem. Corp.*, Comp. Gen. Dec. B-255543, 94-1 CPD ¶ 175 (bid was properly rejected where unsolicited literature rendered uncertain the bidder's obligation to furnish the exact product called for under the IFB). However, unsolicited descriptive literature that takes exception to the IFB requirements to an immaterial extent only, will not render the bid nonresponsive, *Brown Boveri Elec., Inc.*, Comp. Gen. Dec. B-209338, 83-1 CPD ¶ 342.

When descriptive literature is required for bid evaluation, any statements reserving the right to alter or change the specifications generally will render the bid nonresponsive, *Air & Hydraulic Equip., Inc.*, Comp. Gen. Dec. B-250332, 93-1 CPD ¶ 54; *Erincraft, Inc.*, Comp. Gen. Dec. B-235829, 89-2 CPD ¶ 332 (uncontradicted legend on descriptive literature submitted with bid stating that "all specifications are subject to change"); *Galaxy Distrib., Inc.*, Comp. Gen. Dec. B-220535, 85-2 CPD ¶ 441 ("subject to change" legend in required descriptive literature rendered bid nonresponsive because nothing else in the bid indicated that the legend was not intended to reserve the right to change or deviate from the material requirements of the IFB). However, when a bid contains sufficient assurances that the bidder intends to meet all contract requirements, despite the subject to change disclaimer, it may properly be held responsive, *Yale Materials Handling Corp.*, Comp. Gen. Dec. B-228974.2, 87-2 CPD ¶ 550; *Tektronix, Inc.*, 66 Comp. Gen. 704 (B-227800.2), 87-2 CPD ¶ 315 ("subject to change" legend included in unsolicited descriptive literature does not render bid nonresponsive where the bid otherwise indicates the bidder's intent to conform to the specifications); *Syntrex Inc.*, 63 Comp. Gen. 360 (B-212781.2), 84-1 CPD ¶ 522 (bid was properly viewed as responsive where there was sufficient indication in the bid that the bidder intended to meet all the contract requirements despite "subject to change" legend contained in the required descriptive literature); *Waukesha Motor Co.*, Comp. Gen. Dec. B-178494, 74-1 CPD ¶ 329 ("subject to change" legend in preprinted descriptive literature was effectively negated because cover letter stated that "all equipment and tests will be completed to specifications").

Other materials have resulted in findings of nonresponsiveness, even though the bid forms conformed exactly to the IFB. See *Star Brite Constr. Co.*, Comp. Gen. Dec. B-255206, 94-1 CPD ¶ 89 (notation in bid bond that stated bond was null and void if the "contract includes the removal of asbestos" rendered the bid nonresponsive); *Northwestern Motor Co.*, Comp. Gen. Dec. B-244334, 91-2 CPD ¶ 249 (bid properly rejected as nonresponsive where handwritten note on bid created an ambiguity regarding a material requirement of the IFB); and *Contech Constr. Co.*, Comp. Gen. Dec. B-241185, 90-2 CPD ¶ 264 (bid was properly rejected where notations in bid that the required performance schedule was "impossible" created uncertainty as to whether bidder agreed to the required performance terms).

8. Failure to Acknowledge Amendments

The failure of a bidder to acknowledge receipt of an amendment containing a material requirement prior to bid opening renders a bid nonresponsive, *Hackney Group*, Comp. Gen. Dec. B-261241, 95-2 CPD ¶ 100 (amendment eliminated inconsistency in amount of work to be performed); *Farrar Aerospace*, Comp. Gen. Dec. B-259364, 95-1 CPD ¶ 165 (amendment required the manufacturing of parts stated in the specifications); *G.R. Spanaugle & Sons, Inc.*, Comp. Gen. Dec. B-257784, 94-2 CPD ¶ 178 (amendment limited the hours after regular work hours during which certain construction work could be performed); *Mike Vanebo*, 64 Comp. Gen. 780 (B-219019), 85-2 CPD ¶ 184 (amendment required upward wage rate revision). This is because, absent acknowledgment of a material amendment, a bidder would not be obligated to the terms of the IFB as amended, *Jenness Woodkuts*, Comp. Gen. Dec. B-257345, 94-2 CPD ¶ 112. Even if the amendment was not acknowledged because it was never received, a bid must be rejected as nonresponsive unless the failure was the result of a deliberate and conscious effort to exclude the bidder from competing for the contract, *Southeastern Enters., Inc.*, Comp. Gen. Dec. B-245491.2, 92-1 CPD ¶ 88; *Shemya Constructors*, 68 Comp. Gen. 213 (B-232928.2), 89-1 CPD ¶ 108; or unless the record indicates that the agency did not make a reasonable effort to mail the amendment in accordance with regulatory requirements, *Andero Constr., Inc.*, 63 Comp. Gen. 253 (B-203898), 82-1 CPD ¶ 133 (agency compliance with a regulation is not established where three of four bidders appear not to have received the amendment in the mail).

FAR 14.405(d)(1) allows a bidder's failure to return an amendment to be waived as a minor informality if the bid demonstrates that the bidder received the amendment. Therefore, a bidder's failure to explicitly acknowledge receipt of an amendment may be waived if there is an implicit or constructive acknowledgment through submission of a bid reflecting some change made by the amendment. For examples of constructive acknowledgment of amendments, see *Bonded Maintenance Co.*, Comp. Gen. Dec. B-235207, 89-2 CPD ¶ 51 (bid included a new pricing schedule established by an amendment); and *Professional Aviation Maintenance & Management Servs., Inc.*, Comp. Gen. Dec. B-232078, 88-2 CPD ¶ 350 (bidder's cover letter included statements that it would perform in accordance with two unacknowledged amendments). But see *C Constr. Co.*, 67 Comp. Gen. 107 (B-228038), 87-2 CPD ¶ 534, where the Comptroller General stated that award to the bidder was improper because submission of the bid on the amended bid opening date is not sufficient to show that the bidder constructively acknowledged an amendment extending the bid opening date.

FAR 14.405(d)(2) also permits a bidder's failure to acknowledge an amendment to be waived if the amendment is trivial in nature. Thus, in *Pro Alarm Co.*, 69 Comp. Gen. 727 (B-240137), 90-2 CPD ¶ 242, the Comptroller General stated that a bidder's failure to acknowledge an amendment could be waived since the amendment had no effect or a negligible effect on quantity, quality, delivery, or price. See also *Wirco, Inc.*, 65 Comp. Gen. 255 (B-220327), 86-1 CPD ¶ 103 (failure to acknowledge amendment that added two containers to the previously scheduled deliveries waived as a minor informality because the bidder was obligated to provide the correct number of containers, and the effect on price, if any, was negligible).

In determining whether an amendment has a trivial impact, the increase in the cost of performance and the relative difference between the bid prices will be considered, *Marino Constr. Co.*, 61 Comp. Gen. 269 (B-204970), 82-1 CPD ¶ 167. Thus, a minimal cost increase will not be considered trivial if it represents a material difference between the two lowest bidders, *Gulf Elec. Constr. Co.*, 68 Comp. Gen. 719 (B-235635), 89-2 CPD ¶ 272 (failure to acknowledge amendment with an estimated cost impact of $650 rendered bid nonresponsive because that increase in price was double the difference between the low and second low bid, and 30 percent of the difference between the lowest bid and the protester's third lowest responsive bid); *Power Sys. Diesel Inc.*, Comp. Gen. Dec. B-224635, 86-2 CPD ¶ 599 (bidder's failure to acknowledge amendment rendered bid nonresponsive because the estimated increase in costs was 9.5 percent of the difference between the two lowest bids); *M. C. Hodom Constr. Co.*, Comp. Gen. Dec. B-209241, 83-1 CPD ¶ 440 (bidder's failure to acknowledge amendment that increased bid price only 0.25 percent rendered bid nonresponsive because that increase constituted 11.25 percent of the difference between the two low bidders); *Navaho Corp.*, Comp. Gen. Dec. B-192620, 79-1 CPD ¶ 24 (bid rejected as nonresponsive because bidder failed to acknowledge amendment that increased bid price by only 0.25 percent of low bid but was 13.34 percent of the difference between two lowest bidders).

However, in *K Servs.*, Comp. Gen. Dec. B-238744, 90-1 CPD ¶ 556, the procuring agency properly waived the failure to acknowledge an amendment with an estimated cost impact of $502.50, which was only 0.1 percent of the bidder's bid and 6.6 percent of the difference between the low and second low bid. Similarly in *G.C. Smith Constr. Co.*, Comp. Gen. Dec. B-213525, 84-2 CPD ¶ 100, the low bidder's failure to acknowledge an amendment with an estimated increase in contractor costs of $2,390 should not have been rejected, because this was 0.262 percent of the bidder's bid and 4.92 percent of the difference between the two low bids. See also *Universal Contracting & Brick Pointing Co.*, Comp. Gen. Dec. B-188394, 77-1 CPD ¶ 347 (low bidder's failure to acknowledge an amendment with an estimated value of $820 was properly waived where the next lowest bid was $59,903 higher in price). The determination regarding the price impact of an amendment to an IFB may not be based on the value placed on it by the bidder seeking a waiver, but rather on the Government's estimate, *Ira Gelber Food Servs., Inc.*, 55 Comp. Gen. 599, (B-184308) 75-2 CPD ¶ 415; 53 Comp. Gen. 64 (B-178640) (1973).

Generally, a bidder's failure to acknowledge an amendment that merely restates or clarifies the original solicitation and does not change the legal obligations it imposed, may be waived as a minor informality, *Futura Sys. Inc.*, 70 Comp. Gen. 365 (B-242060), 91-1 CPD ¶ 327 (rejection was improper where amendment made no substantial changes to the original warranty provision, and, by signing its bid, the bidder was bound to the original IFB); *Adak Communications Sys., Inc.*, 67 Comp. Gen. 208 (B-228341), 88-1 CPD ¶ 74 (although bidder failed to acknowledge an amendment that changed line items for costs and required the use of manufacturer-approved parts and equipment, rejection of the bid was improper because the amendment merely clarified the bidder's obligations to provide parts for maintenance and repair work under the IFB).

However, amendments that have more than a negligible effect on price, quantity, quality, or delivery are material, and the failure to acknowledge them may not be waived, *Specialty Contractors, Inc.*, Comp. Gen. Dec. B-258451, 95-1 CPD ¶ 38 (bidder's failure to acknowledge amendment that changed required color of roofing panels from "dark bronze" to "medium bronze" rendered bid nonresponsive under circumstances indicating that color was a material requirement); *MIBO Constr. Co.*, Comp. Gen. Dec. B-224744, 86-2 CPD ¶ 678 (failure to acknowledge amendment deleting the optional use of asbestos roofing materials significantly affected the quality of performance and rendered the bid nonresponsive); *Belfort Instrument Co.*,

Comp. Gen. Dec. B-218561, 85-2 CPD ¶ 135 (bid properly rejected as nonresponsive where bidder failed to acknowledge amendment issued to correct defective and ambiguous technical specifications which affected the quality of the services solicited).

Because amendments revising wage rates implement statutory requirements, the failure to acknowledge such amendments may not be waived, *Promethean Constr., Co.*, Comp. Gen. Dec. B-255222, 94-1 CPD ¶ 78, unless the bidder is already obligated to pay wages not less than those prescribed by the revised wage determination, *Tri-Tech Int'l, Inc.*, Comp. Gen. Dec. B-246701, 92-1 CPD ¶ 304. Thus, if the bidder's employees are already covered by a collective bargaining agreement calling for wages as high as those in the revised wage determination, the failure to acknowledge an amendment containing that determination may be waived, *ABC Paving Co.*, 66 Comp. Gen. 47 (B-224408), 86-2 CPD ¶ 436; *Brutoco Eng'g & Constr., Inc.*, 62 Comp. Gen. 111 (B-209098), 83-1 CPD ¶ 9.

Oral rather than written acknowledgment of a material amendment is unacceptable and renders a bid nonresponsive, *Alcon, Inc.*, Comp. Gen. Dec. B-228409, 88-1 CPD ¶ 114; *Protex Sys., Inc.*, Comp. Gen. Dec. B-201146, 84-1 CPD ¶ 265. In *MET Elec. Testing, Inc.*, 60 Comp. Gen. 321 (B-201146), 81-1 CPD ¶ 202, the Comptroller General stated at 322-23:

> Permitting oral acknowledgment of a material amendment is detrimental to the competitive bidding process in two ways. First, it allows a bidder "two bites at the apple," by giving it the sole discretion to accept or reject the contract after bid opening, by affirming or denying that it intended to be bound by the amendment and, hence, the agreement. See *National Investigation Bureau, Inc.*, B-191759, July 18, 1978, 78-2 CPD ¶ 44. Second, because of the bidder's failure to timely acknowledge the amendment in writing, the terms of the resulting contract are not clear since the written bid acknowledges the terms of the solicitation, but not relevant amendments.

In *Construction Catering, Inc.*, Comp. Gen. Dec. B-207987, 82-2 CPD ¶ 49, the Comptroller General stated, referring to 33 Comp. Gen. 508 (B-119732) (1954), that oral acknowledgment of an immaterial amendment is permissible.

III. EVALUATION AND AWARD

The CICA amended 10 U.S.C. § 2305(b)(3) and 41 U.S.C. § 253b(c) with respect to evaluation and award of sealed bids as follows:

> Sealed bids shall be opened publicly at the time and place stated in the solicitation. The head of the agency shall evaluate the bids . . . without discussions with the bidders and, except as provided in paragraph (2), shall award a contract with reasonable promptness to the responsible bidder whose bid conforms to the solicitation and is most advantageous to the United States, considering only price and the other price-related factors included in the solicitation. The award of a contract shall be made by transmitting, in writing or by electronic means, notice of the award to the successful bidder. Within three days after the date of contract award, the head of the agency shall notify, in writing or by electronic means, each bidder not awarded the contract that the contract has been awarded.

This language is substantially the same as was included in the prior statutes except that the term "the other price-related factors included in the solicitation" has been used in place of the term "other factors." This change continues the fundamental goal of sealed bid procurement — to base the award solely on objectively determined cost to the Government, 47 Comp. Gen. 658 (B-163890) (1968).

The evaluation process necessary to determine which bidder is offering the lowest cost to the Government can vary from the simple to the complex, depending on the circumstances of the procurement. For procurements involving the purchase of multiple items, indefinite quantities, or for an extended performance period, the evaluation process becomes more complicated, and evaluation criteria must be stated in the IFB. Price adjustment provisions such as discounts or economic price adjustment clauses can also become part of the evaluation process. The greatest complexity sometimes occurs when "other price-related factors" are introduced into the evaluation formula. All of these issues are addressed in this section.

The section also considers the procedures followed in awarding sealed bid contracts. Difficulties can arise when multiple awards are contemplated or when the contracting agency cannot make the award decision by the time the bids expire. Award based upon bids at below cost (so called "buy-ins") are also considered.

The section concludes with a discussion of cancellation of the procurement after bid opening. 10 U.S.C. § 2305(b)(2) and 41 U.S.C. § 253b(b) give broad discretion in the area, stating:

> All sealed bids or competitive proposals received in response to a solicitation may be rejected if the head of the agency determines that such action is in the public interest.

However, cancellation is a serious matter because of the time and expense involved in preparing a bid and because bidders can be prejudiced if the competition is reopened after bids have been exposed. Thus, cogent and compelling reasons are usually required to support this course of action.

A. Evaluation Process

The Comptroller General has consistently emphasized that the bid evaluation process must be performed on the basis of the factors set forth in the IFB so that bidders are able to compete on a fair and equal basis, 36 Comp. Gen. 380 (B-127801) (1956).

1. Evaluation of Bid Prices

The solicitation must set forth the price evaluation method that will be used and the contracting officer must adhere to it. See *Jacobs Transfer, Inc.*, 53 Comp. Gen. 797 (B-180195), 74-1 CPD ¶ 213, where the invitation stated the evaluation would be on the basis of prices under Schedule A and B combined. However, just before bid opening the contracting officer orally stated that only the price of Schedule A would be evaluated. This was held improper because the contracting officer did not adhere to the price evaluation criteria set forth in the invitation. In *Southeastern Servs., Inc.*, 56 Comp. Gen. 668 (B-187872), 77-1 CPD ¶ 390, the Comptroller General stated the basic principle at 670:

> Revised evaluation criteria may not be used after bid opening to justify award, because bidders have not competed on that basis.

However, if the protester cannot show harm from the alteration of the price evaluation scheme, the Comptroller General will not require cancellation of the IFB. See *Williams Elevator Co.*, Comp. Gen. Dec. B-210049, 83-2 CPD ¶ 327, where the solicitation called for the evaluation of contract prices for a one-year period, but the contracting officer changed the evaluation method by tripling the prices to reflect the total cost to the Government for the full three-year contract. The alteration was upheld because the disappointed bidder failed to show that its price would have been low had the IFB evaluation scheme been followed. Thus, it was not prejudiced by the different evaluation method.

a. Accurate Reflection of Lowest Cost

The IFB evaluation criteria must reflect the lowest cost to the Government based on the total work to be performed. If the evaluation scheme does not assure that award will be made to the bidder offering the lowest overall cost to the Government during actual performance, cancellation of the IFB is required, *Maintenance Inc.*, Comp. Gen. Dec. B-208036, 83-1 CPD ¶ 631.

Agencies sometimes use evaluation criteria that preclude them from determining which bidder offers the lowest cost to the Government. The most common error is overestimating the agency's needs. In *Southeastern Servs., Inc.*, 56 Comp. Gen. 668 (B-187872), 77-1 CPD ¶ 390, *recons. denied*, *Dyneteria, Inc.*, Comp. Gen. Dec. B-187872, 77-2 CPD ¶ 134, the solicitation for a food service contract calling for the evaluation of meal prices outside the contract range was held improper because it bore no relation to the agency's actual requirements. The Comptroller General stated at 670:

> Our office has held that the lowest bidder must be measured by the total and actual work to be awarded. Any measure which incorporates more or less than the work to be contracted in selecting the lowest bidder does not obtain the benefits of full and free competition required by the procurement statutes.

In this case the IFB evaluation method was based on more meals than the Air Force needed; it did not assure, therefore, that award would be made to the bidder offering the most favorable cost to the Government. See also *Heritage Reporting Corp.*, Comp. Gen. Dec. B-248860.2, 92-2 CPD ¶ 276 (IFB for the base period of an option contract grossly overestimated quantities of transcripts needed by the Government, and using those estimates would not assure award to the lowest bidder); and *W.H. Smith Hardware Co.*, Comp. Gen. Dec. B-228127, 87-2 CPD ¶ 556 (IFB listed a unit as four casters instead of one, which was an overstatement of the agency's needs; thus, there was a possibility of an award that would not result in the lowest cost to the Government).

Sometimes the Government's estimated quantities for evaluation purposes is unclear, thereby making it difficult to ascertain the lowest bidder. See *Duramed Homecare, Inc.*, Comp. Gen. Dec. B-260047, 95-1 CPD ¶ 257 (IFB failed to provide estimated quantities for some of the items); *Ferguson-Williams, Inc.*, Comp. Gen. Dec. B-258460, 95-1 CPD ¶ 39 (after bid opening, the agency determined that the three lowest bidders had misunderstood the estimated quantities); *MTL Sys., Inc.*, Comp. Gen. Dec. B-245363, 91-2 CPD ¶ 569 (IFB failed to include a price adjustment for accelerated delivery or the number of items that required the accelerated delivery); and *Robinson Mills & Williams*, Comp. Gen. Dec. B-236956.3, 90-1 CPD ¶ 156 (IFB failed to provide estimates for any of the specific services to be performed).

In some cases, the lowest bidder cannot be ascertained because the line items in the IFB do not include all factors that need to be considered in the evaluation equation. See, for example, *Bayfone of Tampa*, Comp. Gen. Dec. B-242925, 91-1 CPD ¶ 535 (the line item for telephone usage did not account for the number of telephones that would be using each type of service); and *Temps & Co.*, 65 Comp. Gen. 640 (B-221846), 86-1 CPD ¶ 535 (IFB calling for an assortment of personnel, but hourly wages excluded the amount of time that each temporary employee would work). In *Exclusive Temporaries of Ga.*, Comp. Gen. Dec. B-220331.2, 86-1 CPD ¶ 232, the line items included both full- and part-time work. It was unclear whether one or both line items should be filled out and what would be used to evaluate the bids. Thus, the IFB resulted in bids that "could not be evaluated on an equal basis" and would not necessarily render the lowest cost. In *S.W. Monroe Constr. Co.*, Comp. Gen. Dec. B-256382, 94-1 CPD ¶ 362, the IFB failed to include a complete line item for a service that the Government wanted performed and the quantity required on a different line item. Although some of the bidders did include the omitted item, the IFB did not elicit full and open competition, because it was unclear to the agency whether or not the other bids included the price for that item. Also, there was no common basis for comparison on the omitted quantity, since "the relative standing of bidders could change depending on the number . . . and economies of scale used by each bidder."

In some instances the Comptroller General has found that the Government used a mathematical method in the evaluation scheme that did not result in arriving at the actual lowest bid. In *Chemical Technology, Inc.*, Comp. Gen. Dec. B-187940, 77-1 CPD ¶ 126, the price evaluation entailed the averaging of five prices for varying quantities of monthly meals.

However, historical data revealed that 50 percent of the time the meal service fell under only two of the five meal quantities. Since the method of evaluation gave no assurance that award would be made to the bidder offering the lowest cost to the Government, the Comptroller General decided that the evaluation scheme was faulty. For another case where averaging was found not to render the lowest bidder, see *Temps & Co.*, 65 Comp. Gen. 640 (B-221846), 86-1 CPD ¶ 535, where the IFB requested an assortment of personnel at different wage prices, and the agency attempted to average the wages to come up with a low bidder. This evaluation scheme was found defective, since it failed to provide any assurance that an award would, in fact, result in the most favorable cost to the Government.

A defect in the evaluation scheme caused by a mistake by the agency may also make the lowest bidder difficult to determine. In *Earthworks of Sumter, Inc.*, Comp. Gen. Dec. B-232067.2, 89-1 CPD ¶ 9, bids were to be evaluated on a base period of four months. However, the Air Force mistakenly sent Earthworks a seven-month schedule, on which it consequently bid. The contracting officer tried to rectify the mistake by calculating a four-month bid out of Earthworks' estimate, but after protest, this method was deemed faulty. See also *Balva Financial Corp.*, Comp. Gen. Dec. B-235872, 89-2 CPD ¶ 263 (IFB called for evaluation of the price of one item two times, and therefore the lowest overall price to the Government could not be calculated); and *R.P. Densen Contractors, Inc.*, 66 Comp. Gen. 31 (B-222627), 86-2 CPD ¶ 401 (evaluation clause used an algebraic sum of all adjustments applied to the base bid, which the Comptroller General found to be faulty for measuring the cost to the Government).

As noted earlier, a defective evaluation scheme, such as those mentioned above, does not alone preclude award. Where award of the contract to the current lowest bidder under the defective IFB would serve the best interests of the Government and the other bidders would not be prejudiced, the Comptroller General may permit award to the lowest bidder. In *Square Deal Trucking Co.*, Comp. Gen. Dec. B-183695, 75-2 CPD ¶ 206, *recons. denied*, 75-2 CPD ¶ 303, the invitation specified evaluation based on unit prices. One bidder's prices were low for monthly unit charges, but the price for the entire year of the contract was not low. The Comptroller General recommended award of the contract on the basis of the lowest overall price rather than on the basis of unit prices.

In cases where the award was unavoidably delayed for administrative reasons or due to protests, resulting in a shortened contract period, the

Comptroller General has permitted award to a bidder who was evaluated as low under the IFB performance period, even though that bidder's price was not low for the actual, shorter performance period, *Maintenance Pace Setters, Inc.*, Comp. Gen. Dec. B-208768.3, 83-2 CPD ¶ 514; *International Technical Servs. Corp.*, Comp. Gen. Dec. B-198314, 81-1 CPD ¶ 18. Even though the evaluation of bid prices did not reflect the actual work to be performed, award was sanctioned because bid prices had been exposed, and to resolicit would cost the Government as much or more than it would cost to make the award to the current low bidder.

b. Unbalanced Bids

There are two aspects to unbalanced bidding — "mathematical" unbalancing and "material" unbalancing. A bid is not subject to rejection because of unbalancing unless it is found to be *both* mathematically and materially unbalanced. The first involves a mathematical evaluation to determine whether a bid is based upon understated prices for some work and inflated prices for other work. In this regard, it is necessary to show that a bid contains *both* understated and overstated prices in order to conclude that it is mathematically unbalanced. The second aspect — material unbalancing — involves an assessment of the cost impact of a mathematically unbalanced bid. A bid is materially unbalanced if there is a reasonable doubt that the acceptance of a mathematically unbalanced bid will result in the lowest ultimate cost to the Government, *Continental Collection & Disposal, Inc.*, Comp. Gen. Dec. B-238842.2, 90-1 CPD ¶ 591. Unbalanced bidding is used for several reasons: (a) it may help a bidder to conceal its pricing strategy from its competitors; (b) it may permit a bidder to recover larger sums for earlier performed work, giving it both a monetary advance as well as shifting some of the risk of the contract to the Government; (c) it may enable a bidder to become the lowest evaluated bidder through speculation on the accuracy of the Government's quantity estimates in the invitation for bids; and (d) it may be used by bidders as a hedge against losses in cases where a program does not run to completion.

Reliable Trash Serv., Comp. Gen. Dec. B-194760, 79-2 CPD ¶ 107, first established the two-pronged test to determine whether award may be made to an unbalanced bidder. Award may be made to a mathematically unbalanced bid, but not if the bid is also materially unbalanced. If a bid is both mathematically and materially unbalanced, then the Government should reject it, FAR 14.404-2(g). In *Reliable*, the Comptroller General defined "materially unbalanced," stating:

> A bid is not materially unbalanced unless there is a reasonable doubt that award to the bidder submitting a mathematically unbalanced bid will not result in the lowest ultimate cost to the Government. Consequently, only a bid found to be materially unbalanced may not be accepted.

This test is set forth in the Contract Award — Sealed Bidding solicitation clause in FAR 52.214-10(e), which provides:

> The Government may reject a bid as nonresponsive if the prices bid are materially unbalanced between line items or subline items. A bid is materially unbalanced when it is based on prices significantly less than cost for some work and prices which are significantly overstated in relation to cost for other work, and if there is a reasonable doubt that the bid will result in the lowest overall cost to the Government even though it may be the low evaluated bid, or if it is so unbalanced as to be tantamount to allowing an advanced payment.

Another provision at FAR 9.306(j) requires contracting officers to warn offerors not to submit unbalanced offers for contracts that involve separately priced first articles. See also FAR 14.404-2. A bid can be found to be materially unbalanced if it creates a reasonable doubt as to whether award will be made to the lowest cost bid. The Comptroller General's view of what constitutes "reasonable doubt" has evolved over the years. In *Lear Siegler, Inc.*, Comp. Gen. Dec. B-205594.2, 82-1 CPD ¶ 632, the Comptroller General recognized that when a bid is front-loaded, so that it only becomes low "late" in the contracting period, and the program does not run to completion, the Government will not be able to take advantage of the low prices, and therefore will pay more than would be the case if prices had been balanced over the total contracting period. In *Lear Siegler*, the IFB called for the operation of a transportation motor pool with one base period and three option periods. The contracting officer awarded the contract to SAE, and Lear Siegler protested, claiming that the bid was mathematically and materially unbalanced. The Comptroller General found that, "in view of SAE's front-loaded bid structure and the fact that it is not until well after the exercise of the third and final option year that SAE's total cost becomes low, there is reasonable doubt that award to SAE will result in the lowest ultimate cost to the Government."

The Comptroller General has sometimes determined that an agency's intent to exercise all options suffices to overcome an unbalancing situation. See *Rust Int'l Corp.*, Comp. Gen. Dec. B-256886.2, 94-2 CPD ¶ 84, where the Comptroller General found that there was no doubt that the agency intended to have construction work completed over the option period of two years. However, other cases have made contractor reliance upon this logic dangerous. See, e.g., *Residential Refuse Removal, Inc.*, Comp. Gen. Dec. B-247198.6, 92-2 CPD ¶ 444, where the Comptroller General observed that despite "a contracting agency's intent to exercise all options, there is sufficient reason to doubt the low ultimate cost anticipated from a mathematically unbalanced bid where it does not become low until very late in a contract term." The effect of this rationale is to force contractors to allocate front-end costs across the option years of a long-term contract, with the commensurate risk to them that they will not recover their costs if the Government does not fully exercise the options. This is discussed further below.

Another theory advanced by the Comptroller General for rejecting a materially unbalanced bid is that a grossly front-loaded bid is "tantamount to an advance payment," which is prohibited by 31 U.S.C. § 3324, except when otherwise expressly authorized by law, *Riverport Indus., Inc.*, 64 Comp. Gen. 441 (B-216707), 85-1 CPD ¶ 364. The rationale for rejection on this basis is that such an advance payment is analogous to an interest-free loan, thereby giving the bidder a competitive advantage, *F & E Erection Co.*, Comp. Gen. Dec. B-234927, 89-1 CPD ¶ 573 (bid should be rejected as materially unbalanced when the bidder would receive payment for inflated line items early in the contract); *Barnard-Slurry Walls*, Comp. Gen. Dec. B-274973, 97-1 CPD ¶ 23 (lump sum price for preparatory work line item was many multiples higher than the reasonable value of the work). See also *ACC Constr. Co.*, Comp. Gen. Dec. B-250688, 93-1 CPD ¶ 142, where the Comptroller General rejected a low bid because the protester could receive progress payments on inflated prices for work performed early in the contract period — tantamount to an advance payment.

At the same time, the "tantamount to an advance payment" logic has been limited in application. See *Integrated Protection Sys., Inc.*, Comp. Gen. Dec. B-254457.2, 94-1 CPD ¶ 24, where the Comptroller General stated the rule as follows:

> Even where a mathematically unbalanced bid represents the lowest overall cost to the government, there are certain limited situations where it should not be accepted because it grossly front-loaded and its acceptance would be tantamount to allowing an advance payment. See FAR 52.214-10(e); *Riverport Indus., Inc.*, 64 Comp. Gen. 441 (1985), 85-1 CPD ¶ 364, *aff'd*, B-218626.2, July 31, 1985, 85-2 CPD ¶ 108 (first article unit prices were

> $185,000 and the production unit prices were $250); *ACC Constr. Co. Inc.*, B-250688, Feb. 16, 1993, 93-1 CPD ¶ 142 (line item bid price of $2.2 million to $3.2 million higher than the government's estimate and other bids); *Islip Transformer & Metal Co.*, B-225257, Mar. 23, 1987, 87-1 CPD ¶ 327 (first article unit prices were $15,000 and the production unit prices were $408.90); *Nebraska Aluminum Castings*, B-222476, June 24, 1986, 86-1 CPD ¶ 582, *aff'd*, B-222476.2, Sept. 23, 1986, 86-2 CPD ¶ 335, *reaff'd*, B-222476.3, Nov. 4, 1986, 86-2 CPD ¶ 515 (first article unit prices were $22,510 and the production unit prices were $19.17); *Edgewater Mach. & Fabricators, Inc.*, B-219828, Dec. 5, 1985, 85-2 CPD ¶ 630 (first article unit prices were $125,000 and the production unit prices were $301).
>
> Front-loaded bids that are not grossly front-loaded may be accepted, however. See *Aydin Corp.*, B-245461, Jan. 13, 1992, 92-1 CPD ¶ 51 (first article units priced approximately twice the production unit price); *Dodge Romig Tex Corp.*, B-241810, Mar. 5, 1991, 91-1 CPD ¶ 246 (first article priced two to three times production unit price).
>
> Here, [the awardee's] installation price is less than three times the government estimate and is not even two times greater than the protester's next low bid. We see no basis for finding gross front-loading in these circumstances.

Thus, only *gross* front-loading is tantamount to an advance payment. See *Rust Int'l Corp.*, Comp. Gen. Dec. B-256886.2, 94-2 CPD ¶ 84, where the Comptroller General granted a protest where the agency had rejected a bid as being grossly front-loaded, but the Comptroller General found, on the basis of an analysis of the offeror's projected costs, that is was not. See also *Grumley Schlosser*, Comp. Gen. Dec. B-274012, 96-2 CPD ¶ 158, where the Comptroller General held that a base bid that was less than two times greater than the Government estimate or the protester's next low bid was not so grossly front-loaded as to be tantamount to an improper advance payment.

(1) Front-Loaded Construction Contracts

Front-loading of a construction contract follows the same general pattern found in all unbalancing situations, that is, a bidder will usually structure its bid to recover progress payments for early work in amounts significantly in excess of the cost of that work. For an example of a front-loaded construction bid, see *Dement Constr. Co.*, Comp. Gen. Dec. B-192794, 78-2 CPD ¶ 399, where the two low bidders for the construction job submitted the following figures for the first two items of work to be performed:

Item	Universal	Dement	Government's Estimated Cost
1. Mobilization	$2,749,318	$30,000	$22,600
2. Clearing & Grubbing	$120,505	$1,192,000	$202,860

Based on the Government's estimated cost, the Comptroller General held that the bids must be rejected since "both bidders unbalanced their bids for these early items of work in an effort to recover the sums that must be expended for mobilization and preparation prior to actual commencement of construction."

As mentioned above, the Comptroller General has deemed grossly front-loaded bids as tantamount to advance payments, *Rust Int'l Corp.*, Comp. Gen. Dec. B-256886.2, 94-2 CPD ¶ 84; *Riverport Indus., Inc.*, 64 Comp. Gen. 441 (B-216707), 85-1 CPD ¶ 364. Front-loading is undesirable from the Government's point of view for a variety of reasons, including instances where contractors may have a reduced incentive to complete the work properly after receiving payment, *ACC Constr. Co.*, Comp. Gen. Dec. B-250688, 93-1 CPD ¶ 142.

To justify a front-loaded bid, the bidder will sometimes state that it included start-up costs in the progress payment schedule, *Jasper Painting Serv., Inc.*, Comp. Gen. Dec. B-251092, 93-1 CPD ¶ 204. In that case, the Comptroller General stated:

> Because start-up costs properly may be factored into an offer, a relatively front-loaded price does not automatically establish that an offer is unbalanced. However, the start-up costs may not carry a disproportionate share of the total contract price.

When start-up costs have been factored into the front end of a bid, the Comptroller General generally will not allow award to that bid, *ACC Constr. Co.*, Comp. Gen. Dec. B-250688, 93-1 CPD ¶ 142, unless the front-loading is so minor that it represents no more than a proportionate share of the contract work, *Cottrell Eng'g Corp.*, Comp. Gen. Dec. B-252891, 93-2 CPD ¶ 66 (bidder had unique mobilization costs because it was located far away, and prices were not deemed to be inflated). Another situation where some unbalancing has been found unobjectionable is in cases where a bidder intends to acquire unique equipment for which it will have no other use. See *Roan Corp.*, Comp. Gen. Dec. B-211228, 84-1 CPD ¶ 116. There have been no recent cases utilizing this concept.

(2) Quantity Estimates

Unbalancing can also occur in multiple item requirements and indefinite-quantity contracts. In these contracts, bids are evaluated on the basis of estimated quantities, and unbalancing can occur when a bidder believes that the actual quantities ordered by the Government will vary from the estimates. In such cases, the bidder submits an unbalanced bid, with higher prices on items believed to have underestimated quantities and lower prices on items believed to have been overestimated.

For an example of such unbalanced bidding, see *Michael O'Connor, Inc.*, Comp. Gen. Dec. B-183381, 76-2 CPD ¶ 8, involving the installation of partitions in certain Government buildings where the bidder submitted the following bids:

IFB Item	IFB Estimated Quantities	Actual Prior Year Requirements	Bid
5	16,000	0	0 (N/C)
31	10	426	$249 per unit

The Government based its estimates on an average of the previous years' requirements. The bidder based its bid on only the prior year's actual requirements. For Item 5, the IFB estimate significantly overstated the quantity, and the bidder took advantage of this by bidding "no charge." For Item 31, the bidder increased its unit bid price because the Government had underestimated its needs. As a result, the bidder was evaluated low but would not have represented the actual lowest cost to the Government. See also *Alice Roofing & Sheet Metal Works, Inc.*, Comp. Gen. Dec. B-275477, 97-1 CPD ¶ 86; and *Copy Graphics*, Comp. Gen. Dec. B-273028, 96-2 CPD ¶ 185.

The Comptroller General stated in *Robertson & Penn, Inc.*, Comp. Gen. Dec. B-234082, 89-1 CPD ¶ 365, that "a low bid for a requirements type contract is not materially unbalanced unless it can be shown that the Government's estimates are so unreliable that award to the low bidder will not result in the lowest cost to the Government." See *Belton Roofing & Remodeling Co.*, Comp. Gen. Dec. B-277651, 97-2 CPD ¶ __; and *Ostrom Painting & Sandblasting, Inc.*, Comp. Gen. Dec. B-250827.2, 93-1 CPD ¶ 390, where the Comptroller General recommended that the IFB be canceled due to inaccurate Government estimates. Thus, to determine that a mathematically unbalanced bid is not materially unbalanced, the Government estimate must be sufficiently accurate to ensure that the mathematically unbalanced bid does not create a reasonable doubt that the Government will be awarding to the lowest bidder. See *Adam II, Ltd.*, Comp. Gen. Dec. B-209194, 83-2 CPD ¶ 102, where Air Force estimates based on historical experience were sufficiently accurate. If the estimates in the IFB are not sufficiently accurate, the bids will be found unbalanced and the IFB will be canceled, *Edward B. Friel, Inc.*, 55 Comp. Gen. 231 (B-183381), 75-2 CPD ¶ 164. However, there is no requirement that the Government's estimates be absolutely correct; they need only come from the best information available, thereby providing a reasonably accurate representation of the agency's needs, *Custom Envtl. Serv., Inc.*, 70 Comp. Gen. 184 (B-241052), 91-1 CPD ¶ 38.

(3) Option Contracts

Unbalanced bidding occurs in option contracts when prices submitted for the base period are higher than the option year prices. As in other types of contracts, a two-step analysis is followed. First, it must be determined if a bid is mathematically unbalanced. If so, it must then be determined if the bid is materially unbalanced.

The Comptroller General has altered the analysis of mathematical unbalancing of option contracts in recent years. Originally, a bid with high base-year prices was found to be balanced if the base year contained only those costs chargeable to that year through normal accounting practices. Thus, a bid would be found to be mathematically balanced if it allocated all start-up costs to the base year or included a high base-year price because it used generally accepted accelerated techniques for allocating equipment costs. See *M & M Servs., Inc.*, Comp. Gen. Dec. B-228717, 87-2 CPD ¶ 382 (start-up and equipment costs make up high base-period cost); and *Professional Reprographic Servs.*, Comp. Gen. Dec. B-210608, 83-1 CPD ¶ 653 (high start-up costs accounted for the price differential). See *Fidelity Moving & Storage Co.*, Comp. Gen. Dec. B-222109.2, 86-1 CPD ¶ 476, where the Comptroller General stated that:

> [A]ssessment [of mathematical unbalancing] must go beyond the mere percentage differentials between base and option period prices to determine whether those prices are accurate reflections of the actual costs that will be borne by the bidder in performing each year of the contemplated contract. *See Integrity Management International, Inc.*, B-217016, Dec. 11, 1984, 84-2 CPD ¶ 654.
>
> While this Office has previously recognized that a 25 to 50 percent differential between base and option period prices does not necessarily constitute mathematical unbalancing . . . these cases do not establish conclusively in this particular instance that Fidelity's bid, with 10 to 25 percent base/option period differentials, contains neither overstated nor understated prices. Rather, the determinative question is whether Fidelity's bid pricing structure is reasonably related to the actual costs to be incurred in each year.

However, in making this analysis the Comptroller General stated that a large pricing differential between the base year and option years, or between option years, would be prima facie evidence that the bid was mathematically unbalanced, *Howell Constr., Inc.*, 66 Comp. Gen. 413 (B-225766), 87-1 CPD ¶ 455. This placed the burden on the contractor to prove that the costs were allocated using generally accepted established accounting practices. When a contractor met this burden, award to the apparently unbalanced bid was sustained because it had been demonstrated that, in fact, the bid was not mathematically unbalanced, *Roan Corp.*, Comp. Gen. Dec. B-211228, 84-1 CPD ¶ 116; *Applicators, Inc.*, Comp. Gen. Dec. B-215035, 84-1 CPD ¶ 656.

In recent years the Comptroller General has rejected this reasoning and has held that a bid will be found to be mathematically unbalanced if the Government pays more than "reasonable value" for the work even though the "high" prices are based upon the contractor's projected costs, *Eastex Maritime, Inc.*, Comp. Gen. Dec. B-256164, 94-1 CPD ¶ 340 (bid found unbalanced when it allocated all start-up costs to base bid). This rule has been applied to both start-up costs and equipment depreciation costs. See *Residential Refuse Removal*, Comp. Gen. Dec. B-247198, 92-2 CPD ¶ 444, stating:

> An individual bidder's business decisions for front-loading costs, e.g., the bidder's use of a particular depreciation method, are not generally material

> to the issue of mathematical unbalancing. *Mitco Water Labs., Inc.*, B-249269, Nov. 2, 1992, 92-2 CPD ¶ 301 (reasons for front-loading bid to cover equipment renovation costs are irrelevant); *Government Leasing Corp.*, [B-245939, Jan. 27, 1992, 92-1 CPD ¶ 117] (accelerated depreciation method not considered for determination of mathematical unbalancing); *Westbrook Indus., Inc.*, [71 Comp. Gen. 139 (1991), 92-1 CPD ¶ 30] (reason for front-loading of equipment costs not considered for determination of mathematical unbalancing); *Professional Waste Sys., Inc.*; *Tri-State Servs. of Tex.*, 67 Comp. Gen. 68 (1987), 87-2 CPD ¶ 477] (method of financing a bidder's equipment costs not considered for determination of mathematical unbalancing). It is only where, because of the unique nature of the contract or of the equipment required to perform the contract, the equipment will have little or no value to the ordinary bidder in the event of early contract termination that we will consider a bidder's reasons for front-loading. See, e.g., *Roan Corp.*, B-211228, Jan. 25, 1984, 84-1 CPD ¶ 116 (front-loading costs in the base year of a bid for a contract to lease a fleet of law enforcement vehicles did not mathematically unbalance the bid where, in the event of early termination, there was no market for leasing fleets of used law enforcement vehicles.)

See also *Government Leasing Corp.*, Comp. Gen. Dec. B-245939, 92-1 CPD ¶ 117 (an admission that the bid was structured by factoring in depreciation and following other generally accepted accounting principles, which allowed the bidder to recover the greatest portion of its acquisition costs in the base year, is an admission that a front-loaded bid was submitted and that each price was not reflective of the value of the work it represented); *Inventory Accounting Serv.*, Comp. Gen. Dec. B-245906, 92-1 CPD ¶ 116 (even though business reasons existed for front-loading, the fact that it would result in advance payment and possibly a windfall to the bidder made bid mathematically unbalanced); *DGS Contract Servs., Inc.*, Comp. Gen. Dec. B-245400, 92-1 CPD ¶ 16 (offeror expected to "apportion" cost of generic equipment over entire contract period to avoid mathematical unbalancing); and *Omega One Co.*, Comp. Gen. Dec. B-251316.2, 93-1 CPD ¶ 254 (mathematically unbalanced when base was 31 to 46 percent higher than option prices, and work required no "unique or specialized" equipment). The rule has also been applied to unique performance techniques where an offeror justifies the high front-end costs by the cost of initiating "sophisticated" techniques, *McConico Investment Management Corp.*, Comp. Gen. Dec. B-251895, 93-1 CPD ¶ 346. These decisions demonstrate that in order to escape the onus of mathematically unbalancing, option prices must be essentially the same as base year prices. This has been characterized as "value-based analysis" — meaning that the Comptroller

General is insisting that the analysis be based upon "value" to the Government not the costs to be incurred by the contractor.

As already noted, the determination of whether a mathematically unbalanced bid containing options is materially unbalanced has also changed. In early cases, if the Government expected to exercise an option and there was a reasonable expectation that funds would be available, the Comptroller General held that a mathematically unbalanced bid was not materially unbalanced, *K.P. Food Servs., Inc.*, 60 Comp. Gen. 1 (B-198427.2), 82-1 CPD ¶ 289. However, in *Lear Siegler, Inc.*, Comp. Gen. Dec. B-205594.2, 82-1 CPD ¶ 632, and subsequent cases, the Comptroller General found that even if the Government agency expected to exercise the options and funds were available, a bid would be found to be materially unbalanced if the Government would not actually realize the cost advantage associated with the mathematically unbalanced bid until late in the contract term. The Comptroller General reasoned that there was a risk that the Government would not realize such cost advantage if intervening events occurred, such as termination by default or failure to exercise an option, and the contractor would experience a windfall. See, for example, *Williams Elec. Co.*, Comp. Gen. Dec. B-275019, 97-1 CPD ¶ 25 (bid was materially unbalanced because the agency was unsure if it would exercise any of the options, and the protester's bid was low only if all three options were exercised); *Crown Laundry & Dry Cleaners, Inc.*, Comp. Gen. Dec. B-208795.2, 83-1 CPD ¶ 438 (bid was not low until fourth month of second option period, so despite the agency's intent to exercise all options, intervening events could cause a windfall); and *Westbrook Indus., Inc.*, 71 Comp. Gen. 139 (B-245019.2) (1992) (when bid is not low until the thirty-fifth month, there is reason to believe intervening events could occur). The Comptroller General has held that a bid that does not become low until the final contract year is materially unbalanced on its face, *Fidelity Moving & Storage Co.*, Comp. Gen. Dec. B-222109.2, 86-1 CPD ¶ 476; *Inventory Accounting Serv.*, Comp. Gen. Dec. B-245906, 92-1 CPD ¶ 116. In other situations, the Comptroller General has determined that when the agency intends to use all of the option periods and there is no evidence to the contrary, there is no reasonable doubt, *MCI Constructors, Inc.*, Comp. Gen. Dec. B-274347, 96-2 CPD ¶ 210. This is more apt to occur when the bid will become low relatively early in the contract, *Grunley Schlosser*, Comp. Gen. Dec. B-274012, 96-2 CPD ¶ 158 (bid became low with the exercise of the first option); *Tri-Ark Indus.*, Comp. Gen. Dec. B-270756, 96-1 CPD ¶ 194 (bid became low in the second month of the first option period); *Integrated Protection Sys., Inc.*, Comp. Gen. Dec. B-254457.2, 94-1 CPD ¶ 24 (bid became low in first six months of first option year); *Omega One Co.*, Comp. Gen. Dec. B-251316.2, 93-1 CPD ¶ 254 (bid became low in second month of second option year, so no reasonable doubt existed); *Aquasis Servs., Inc.*, Comp. Gen. Dec. B-228044, 87-2 CPD ¶ 426 (bid became low in eighth month of first option year, so no reasonable doubt existed). But see *Storage Technology Corp.*, GSBCA 9345-P, 88-2 BCA ¶ 20,667, where, although the bid did not become low until its fourth option year, the board held that because the contract was for maintenance, the Army would reasonably exercise all options since it intended to keep the equipment.

(4) FIRST ARTICLE CONTRACTS

Unbalanced bidding may also occur in contracts requiring the delivery of first articles. In this situation, a contractor charges a large amount for the first article and lower amounts for production articles. The Comptroller General has followed the same reasoning as that used in contracts containing options, holding that, even if special equipment and tooling are needed for those first articles, it is improper not to amortize these costs over all of the articles when that tooling will be needed throughout the period of the contract, *Nebraska Aluminum Castings, Inc.*, Comp. Gen. Dec. B-222476, 86-1 CPD ¶ 582, *recons. denied*, 86-2 CPD ¶ 335, *recons. denied*, 86-2 CPD ¶ 515. Thus, if costs other than the unique costs of manufacturing and testing first articles are allocated to the first article, a mathematically unbalanced bid is likely to be found, *Star Dynamic Corp.*, Comp. Gen. Dec. B-248919.3, 93-1 CPD ¶ 63; *LBCO, Inc.*, Comp. Gen. Dec. B-254995, 94-1 CPD ¶ 57.

(5) ALTERNATIVE TO CANCELLATION

The Comptroller General has suggested a number of alternatives to cancelling the invitation in the case of unbalanced bids. In *TWI Inc.*, 61 Comp. Gen. 99 (B-202966), 81-2 CPD ¶ 424, the Comptroller General ruled that the Navy's estimate was not sufficiently accurate to assure that a mathematically unbalanced bid would represent the actual lowest cost to the Government. It therefore recommended award to the next lowest mathematically balanced bid. In *Dement Constr. Co.*, Comp. Gen. Dec. B-192794, 78-2 CPD ¶ 399, the Comptroller General condoned negotiation with an unbalanced bidder to reduce the effect of the unbalancing. The Army originally canceled the IFB because award on the basis of the front-loaded bid would result in an advance payment of funds for work not yet performed. However, after "an understanding" was reached that payment for the item would be "over the life of the contract," the IFB was reinstated.

c. *Time Value of Money*

In order to determine which bid represents the actual lowest cost to the Government, the time value of money should be considered. See, for an explanation of this basic concept, *Linolex Sys., Inc.*, 53 Comp. Gen. 895 (B-179047), 74-1 CPD ¶ 296, stating at 901:

> A dollar received today is worth more than a dollar received next year, and conversely, to postpone spending a dollar until next year gives one the opportunity to earn interest on that dollar or otherwise productively use it for the 1-year period.

For procurements involving a considerable length of time, such as option contracts where base and several option years must be evaluated, good procurement practice would consider the time value of money to ensure that award is made to the bidder representing the "actual" lowest cost to the Government. In order for the contracting agency to be able to consider the time value of money in the evaluation of bids, it must be itemized in the IFB as an evaluation factor, *General Tel. Co.*, 57 Comp. Gen. 89 (B-187793), 77-2 CPD ¶ 376 (not appropriate to consider present value in deciding whether to purchase or lease equipment in absence of IFB provision). Conversely, absent such a provision in the IFB, consideration of the time value of money is prohibited. Yet, neither the FAR nor most agency implementing regulations contain provisions for such consideration.

The Government has included IFB provisions for the present value of money in the evaluation process in some procurements. See *Linolex Sys., Inc.*, 53 Comp. Gen. 895 (B-179047), 74-1 CPD ¶ 296, where the following paragraph was used in an ADPE procurement:

> A present value method will be used in calculation of all costs. The discount rate will be applied annually. The rate used will be current average market yield, rounded to the nearest one-eighth of one percent, on outstanding treasury marketable obligations with approximately five years remaining to maturity at the time proposals are received. As an example, if the rate were six percent, the factors would be:

Year from Contract Award	Discount Factor
1	.943
2	.890
3	.840
4	.792
5	.747

This evaluation method could be used in the evaluation process for procurements where front-loading is expected to occur. However, it does not preclude other types of unbalancing. In future solicitations, the Government might consider using the rate of interest established by the Secretary of the Treasury. For another example of a bid that took present value into consideration, see *Centurial Prods.*, 64 Comp. Gen. 858 (B-216517), 85-2 CPD ¶ 305 (guidelines established by the Water Resources Council required that agencies determine the present value of future expenditures before converting them to an annual equivalent cost).

Factoring in the time value of money in an evaluation removes much of the advantage that bidders attempt to gain through unbalanced bids, and it is proper to structure an IFB calling for such an evaluation, *Solon Automated Servs., Inc.,* Comp. Gen. Dec. B-206449.2, 82-2 CPD ¶ 548. However, absent a clause requiring consideration of the cost of money, the Comptroller General will not consider the additional cost to the Government in interest expense that would result from award to a bidder that front-loaded its prices for earlier items, *Farrell Constr. Co.*, 57 Comp. Gen. 597 (B-191786), 78-2 CPD ¶ 45.

One means of quantifying the time value of money was the prompt payment discount. However, FAR 14.408-3 prohibits the consideration of prompt payment discounts for evaluation purposes. See *Alco Envtl. Servs., Inc.*, Comp. Gen. Dec. B-251053.6, 93-2 CPD ¶ 192; *IFR Sys., Inc.*, Comp. Gen. Dec. B-222533, 86-2 CPD ¶ 224; *Hayes Int'l Assocs.*, Comp. Gen. Dec. B-220471, 86-1 CPD ¶ 8; and *O.K. Tool & Die Co.*, Comp. Gen. Dec. B-219806, 85-2 CPD ¶ 398.

As a legislative agency, the Government Printing Office (GPO) is not subject to FAR 14.408-3, and the GPO may therefore consider prompt payment discounts in the evaluation of its bids, *Capitol Hill Blueprint Co.*, Comp. Gen. Dec. B-220354, 85-2 CPD ¶ 550. The IFB must provide that the discount will be used in evaluation, *Advanced Design Fabrication Corp.*, Comp. Gen. Dec. B-246341, 92-1 CPD ¶ 250; *Western Pub. Co.*, Comp. Gen. Dec. B-224376, 86-2 CPD ¶ 249.

d. Bids Including Price Adjustments

Since only contracts with fixed prices or fixed prices subject to economic adjustment can be used in sealed bid procurements, a bid stating that a price adjustment could be made if the cost of petroleum increased was required to be rejected as nonresponsive, *Re Con Paving, Inc.*, Comp. Gen. Dec. B-198294, 80-1 CPD ¶ 297. See also *Margaret Greenidge*, Comp. Gen. Dec. B-265979, 96-1 CPD ¶ 80, where the Comptroller General found that an agency properly rejected a bid as nonresponsive when the protester included a handwritten notation on the bid schedule stating that "yearly increases is based on 3% or COLA, whichever is greater." Bids containing ceilings on such adjustments have been permitted but such bids must be evaluated at the ceiling. In the absence of a stated ceiling, practical considerations may permit consideration of the bid. See *Copes-Vulcan Div., Blaw-Knox Co.*, 36 Comp. Gen. 259 (B-127372) (1956), where the low bidder stated that if more than three X-rays per valve were required, the price would be increased by $2.50 per X-ray. The invitation had stated that bids were to include the cost of all X-rays required but did not specify the number of X-rays. The Comptroller held that rejection of the low bid was improper since 35 extra X-rays per unit would be necessary before the low bidder's price would be greater than the next low bid. There was no real possibility that such a large number would be required.

Bids based on economic price adjustment (EPA) provisions may be considered for award. FAR 14.408-4 gives the following guidance on the evaluation of EPA provisions:

> (a) *Bidder proposes economic price adjustment.*
>
> (1) When a solicitation does not contain an economic price adjustment clause but a bidder proposes one with a ceiling that the price will not exceed, the bid shall be evaluated on the basis of the maximum possible economic price adjustment of the quoted base price.

(2) If the bid is eligible for award, the contracting officer shall request the bidder to agree to the inclusion in the award of an approved economic price adjustment clause (see 16.203) that is subject to the same ceiling. If the bidder will not agree to an approved clause, the award may be made on the basis of the bid as originally submitted.

(3) Bids that contain economic price adjustments with no ceiling shall be rejected unless a clear basis for evaluation exists.

(b) *Government proposes economic price adjustment.*

(1) When an invitation contains an economic price adjustment clause and no bidder takes exception to the provisions, bids shall be evaluated on the basis of the quoted prices without the allowable economic price adjustment being added.

(2) When a bidder increases the maximum percentage of economic price adjustment stipulated in the invitation or limits the downward economic price adjustment provisions of the invitation, the bid shall be rejected as nonresponsive.

(3) When a bid indicates deletion of the economic price adjustment clause, the bid shall be rejected as nonresponsive since the downward economic price adjustment provisions are thereby limited.

(4) When a bidder decreases the maximum percentage of economic price adjustment stipulated in the invitation, the bid shall be evaluated at the base price on an equal basis with bids that do not reduce the stipulated ceiling. However, after evaluation, if the bidder offering the lower ceiling is in a position to receive the award, the award shall reflect the lower ceiling.

This evaluation procedure gives a bid including an EPA clause no advantage, because the bid must be evaluated at the ceiling price. Most EPA clauses contain the required price ceiling since such ceilings are included in the standard clauses in FAR 52.216. For an example of a solicitation that contained a 15 percent ceiling on option-year prices, see *Echelon Serv. Co.*, 62 Comp. Gen. 542 (B-208720.2), 83-2 CPD ¶ 86. In *Phipps Products Corp.*, Comp. Gen. Dec. B-194840, 79-2 CPD ¶ 200, the solicitation included a 20 percent ceiling, but the bidder inserted an escalation clause without a price ceiling. The Comptroller General held that where a price ceiling cannot be determined with certainty, the bid must be rejected as nonresponsive.

To allow for fair evaluation of bids, EPA clauses must reflect some objective standard, other than the bidder's own prices upon which price adjustments will be made, *Roarda, Inc.*, Comp. Gen. Dec. B-204524.5, 82-1 CPD ¶ 438 (IFB defective because it allowed the contractor to adjust prices for petroleum products based on its own price changes). Similarly, in *Hampton Metropolitan Oil Co.*, Comp. Gen. Dec. B-186509, 76-2 CPD ¶ 471, the solicitation for petroleum products allowed bidders to use their own posted prices in conjunction with the EPA provision. The Comptroller General concluded that the IFB was properly canceled because it was impossible to ensure that bidders would not indiscriminately raise their posted prices after contract award. It was therefore impossible for the Government to determine which bids ultimately would result in the lowest cost to the Government. For an example of the type of objective factor that can be used to determine price adjustments, see *American Transparents Plastics Corp.*, Comp. Gen. Dec. B-210898, 83-2 CPD ¶ 539 (Department of Labor's Producer Price Index for the market price of resin used to make plastic bags was upheld as a valid method for price adjustment).

The analysis used for EPA clauses also extends to other types of price adjustments. In *H. Edward Chozick*, 50 Comp. Gen. 733 (B-171938) (1971), the bid provided for 1½ percent interest per month on past due invoices, and the Comptroller General stated at 735:

> So far as concerns your position that the inclusion of the demand for interest on past due invoices should be treated as a reverse prompt payment, in addition to the fact that its consideration would be contrary to 5 Comp. Gen. 649, the solicitation form has no provision for reverse prompt payment discounts and to consider such discounts could well add a substantial conjectural factor to the evaluation process to the detriment of the competitive bid system's integrity.

The Comptroller General would not allow this clause in a bid because it obligated the Government to pay interest on unpaid invoices, and the contracting officer did not have the authority — at that time — to obligate the Government for such payments.

2. Evaluation of "Other Price-Related Factors"

For many years the procurement statutes specified that award was to be made on the basis of "price and other factors." This was held to permit the use of any factor that could be assessed in terms of *cost to the Government*,

37 Comp. Gen. 550 (B-132596) (1958). It was subsequently held that such "other factors" had to be directly related to the procurement. See 45 Comp. Gen. 59 (B-155725) (1965), where the Comptroller General stated at 68:

> Our Office has generally taken the position that a proper determination of the lowest responsible bidder under advertised procurements may properly include consideration of costs, over and above the bid price, which the Government would incur in the event of an award to each bidder, if the amount of such costs can be ascertained with reasonable certainty. . . . The economic impact or "ripple" effect of a particular procurement are not pertinent factors to be considered in making an award under competitive procedures especially where bidders are not requested to prepare their bids in the light of possible adverse effects their bids might have on a segment of the economy.

The CICA has clarified this issue by requiring award on the basis of "price and other price-related factors."

While the contracting officer has considerable discretion in selecting which price-related factors will be evaluated, any factors chosen must be identified in the solicitation so that all bidders may prepare their bids on an equal and well-informed basis, *Respiratory & Convalescent Specialties Inc.*, Comp. Gen. Dec. B-255176, 94-1 CPD ¶ 101 (IFB failed to include oxygen rental charges as a price-related factor, failed to advise bidders how these rental charges would be evaluated, and gave no quantity estimate); *E & T Elecs., Inc.*, Comp. Gen. Dec. B-238099.2, 90-2 CPD ¶ 24 (evaluation factors including cost to Government of shipping equipment, cost savings from using a local contractor, and a discount offered for certain repairs could not be utilized because they were not specified in the IFB); *Fairchild Weston Sys., Inc.*, Comp. Gen. Dec. B-211650, 83-2 CPD ¶ 347 (contracting officer was correct in not considering development risks and the cost of future modifications because these "other factors" were not stated in the IFB). See also *Old Dominion Sec.*, Comp. Gen. Dec. B-216534, 85-1 CPD ¶ 78, where the incumbent contractor argued that its bid ($52,560) was lower than a competing bid ($52,122) if the agency considered the cost of changing contractors. Such costs could not be considered because the IFB did not include transition costs as a factor in evaluating bids.

The evaluation method for price-related factors must permit objective determination of the cost to the Government, as well as being described in the IFB with sufficient clarity that it can be understood by the bidders. In

36 Comp. Gen. 380 (B-127801) (1956), the Comptroller General stated at 385:

> The "basis" of evaluation which must be made known in advance to the bidders should be as clear, precise and exact as possible. Ideally, it should be capable of being stated as a mathematical equation. In many cases, however, that is not possible. At the minimum, the "basis" must be stated with sufficient clarity and exactness to inform each bidder prior to bid opening, no matter how varied the acceptable responses, of objectively determinable factors from which the bidder may estimate within reasonable limits the effect of the application of such evaluation factor on his bid in relation to other possible bids. By the term "objectively determinable factors" we mean factors which are made known to or which can be ascertained by the bidder at the time his bid is being prepared.

See *Envirotronics, Inc.*, Comp. Gen. B-215622, 84-2 CPD ¶ 18, where the protester contended that a competitor's past experience, its limited plant capacity and personnel, and its late deliveries on other Government contracts were "other factors" that, when considered, should preclude award. In holding that all these factors relate to responsibility, not "other factors," the Comptroller General stated:

> The term "other factors" in the context of a formally advertised procurement concerns only objectively determinable elements of cost, such as shipping costs, that are identified in the IFB as factors to be evaluated in the selection of a contractor.

See also *Emerson Elec. Co.*, Comp. Gen. Dec. B-209272, 82-2 CPD ¶ 409 (usage of recovered materials held not to be an "objectively determinable" element of bid pricing and therefore should not have been included as an evaluation factor); and *Balimoy Mfg. Co.*, Comp. Gen. Dec. B-253287.2, 93-2 CPD ¶ 207 (even though solicitation was denoted as an IFB, it should have been clear to the bidders that it was not a sealed bid procurement because it stated that the agency would take non-price-related factors into consideration, such as mobilization base consideration, contractor capacity, and premium cost).

FAR 14.201-8 lists some of the "other factors" that may be considered in bid evaluation:

> (a) Foreseeable costs or delays to the Government resulting from such factors as differences in inspection, locations of supplies, and transportation. If

> bids are on a f.o.b. origin basis (see 47.303 and 47.305), transportation costs to the designated points shall be considered in determining the lowest cost to the Government.
>
> (b) Changes made, or requested by the bidder, in any of the provisions of the invitation for bids, if the change does not constitute a ground for rejection under 14.404.
>
> (c) Advantages or disadvantages to the Government that might result from making more than one award (see 14.201-6(q)). The contracting officer shall assume, for the purpose of making multiple awards, that $500 would be the administrative cost to the Government for issuing and administering each contract awarded under a solicitation. Individual awards shall be for the items or combinations of items that result in the lowest aggregate cost to the Government, including the assumed administrative costs.
>
> (d) Federal, State, and local taxes (see Part 29).
>
> (e) Origin of supplies, and, if foreign, the application of the Buy American Act or any other prohibition on foreign purchases (see Part 25).

FAR 14.201-8 is not an inclusive list of price-related factors. In *Tek-Lite, Inc.*, Comp. Gen. Dec. B-230298, 88-1 CPD ¶ 241, the Comptroller General found an evaluation factor set forth in the solicitation for a value engineering royalty to be a proper evaluation factor even though it is not listed in FAR 14.201-8, stating:

> [T]he cited language nowhere suggests that the listed factors were meant to be exclusive. . . . [S]ince the royalty fee evaluation factor allows consideration for what the actual cost to the Government would be if a bid based on the VECP alternate were accepted, we think the use of such an evaluation factor is appropriate.

a. Transportation

The most common of the "other factors" is the cost of transportation. If the IFB provides that bids are to be made on an f.o.b. destination basis, the costs of transportation are included in the bid price and separate evaluation is not required. When bids are on an f.o.b. origin basis, FAR 14.201-8(a) requires consideration of transportation costs to the designated place of delivery. See, e.g., *Marlen C. Robb & Son*, B-256516, 94-1 CPD ¶ 392 (a reasonable estimate of the cost per mile was included in evaluating the bids to ensure that the Government would obtain the lowest actual cost). If the exact destination is unknown at the time of the solicitation and the procuring agency is unable to predict even the general destination, transportation costs cannot be a factor in bid evaluation, *Wachtel, Wiener & Ross*, 52 Comp. Gen. 679 (B-177763) (1973). FAR 47.305-3 provides guidance on f.o.b. origin solicitations and requires the use of the Evaluation — F.O.B. Origin solicitation clause in FAR 52.247-50 to inform bidders that costs of transportation will be evaluated. If the exact destination is unknown at the time of solicitation but the general geographic locations can be reasonably established, the solicitation should include a tentative destination for the purposes of evaluation only, FAR 47.305-5(b). See *Entron, Inc.*, Comp. Gen. Dec. B-189362, 77-2 CPD ¶ 414, where the Comptroller General upheld the contracting agency's use of hypothetical delivery points for evaluation purposes since the actual destinations were unknown at the time of solicitation.

In order to evaluate transportation costs accurately, the procuring agency must require bidders to provide certain information with their bids such as minimum size of shipments, guaranteed shipping weights, and information regarding packing and crating, FAR 47.305-1. Part 52 of the FAR contains a number of standard solicitation provisions used to obtain this information. The most commonly used provision of this type is the Guaranteed Shipping Characteristics solicitation provision in FAR 52.247-60. This clause provides that if the specified information is not included in a particular bid, the Government may include either the highest bidder's information or a Government estimate to evaluate the bid. In *F&H Mfg. Corp.*, Comp. Gen. Dec. B-212254, 83-2 CPD ¶ 676, the Comptroller General affirmed the validity of using Government estimates to evaluate bids where the bidders did not submit guaranteed maximum shipping weights and dimensions for shipments of Army vehicle parts. The clause also provides for a price adjustment as follows:

> If the item shipping costs, based on the actual shipping characteristics, exceed the item shipping costs used for evaluation purposes, the Contractor agrees that the contract price shall be reduced by an amount equal to the difference between the transportation costs actually incurred, and the costs which would have been incurred if the evaluated shipping characteristics had been accurate.

In *Kalyn Inc.*, Comp. Gen. Dec. B-237909, 90-1 CPD ¶ 331, the Comptroller General denied a protest contending that this solicitation provision permitted bidders to provide false information that reduced their evaluated transportation costs, thereby giving them an unfair competitive advantage. The Comptroller General reasoned that the provision compensated for this problem by providing for a downward adjustment in price if the actual shipping costs were higher than those estimated because the bid's shipping weights or dimensions were exceeded. Similarly, in *Capital Indus., Inc.*, Comp. Gen. Dec. B-190818, 78-2 CPD ¶ 17, the Comptroller General recognized the practice of bidders' intentionally understating shipping dimensions as an alternative to reducing the bid price. The only limit on this practice appears to be that bidders may not understate the guaranteed weight or dimensions in a manner that creates doubt as to their intent to comply with the solicitation's specifications, *Survival Products, Inc.*, Comp. Gen. Dec. B-235431.3, 89-2 CPD ¶ 464, *modified*, 90-1 CPD ¶ 118 (Comptroller recommended cancellation of the procurement because of shipping information indicating bidder's intent not to comply with one possible interpretation of ambiguous specification). See, for example, *Canadian Commercial Corp.*, Comp. Gen. Dec. B-236850, 90-1 CPD ¶ 3 (dimensions in bid that exceeded the IFB's dimensions did not render the bid nonresponsive); *Trojan Indus. Inc.*, Comp. Gen. Dec. B-220620, 86-1 CPD ¶ 143 (assertion that the transportation costs of the machine were based on incorrect dimensions had no bearing because a bidder may understate the guaranteed dimensions to effectuate a price reduction); and *Drexel Contract Furniture*, Comp. Gen. Dec. B-180598, 74-1 CPD ¶ 324 (in procurement of household furniture for use abroad, bidders were allowed to guarantee less weight than actual in order to meet competition).

Once the agency has the information from the bids, it is required to evaluate transportation costs on the basis of the most economical means of transportation available at bid opening. Thus, lower rates secured by the bidder after bid opening cannot be considered, *Williams & Jensen*, 52 Comp. Gen. 614 (B-176346) (1973). The Comptroller General has held that an evaluation of bids that was not based upon freight rates available to the Government at bid opening was improper because permitting bidders to shop for attractive shipping rates after opening is inconsistent with the sealed bidding system, *Isometrics, Inc.*, Comp. Gen. Dec. B-219057.3, 86-1 CPD ¶ 2. The method of shipment used for evaluation must not vary from that required in the IFB. See *Ellinor Corp.*, 54 Comp. Gen. 901 (B-182384), 75-1 CPD ¶ 254, where the Comptroller General recommended cancellation of an award to the low evaluated bidder because transportation costs had been evaluated on the basis of uneconomical, albeit realistic, partial truck loads rather than full truck loads as required by the invitation. The Government need not use commercial methods of transportation in its evaluation of its potential costs; it can transport the products itself if this would be most economical, since the Government is not limited to commercial methods of transportation, *Capital Indus., Inc.*, Comp. Gen. Dec. B-190818, 78-2 CPD ¶ 17.

b. Life-Cycle Costs (How long will it last)

The procuring agency can provide for evaluation of life-cycle costs such as the cost of operation, maintenance, and other costs of ownership when the basis for determining these costs is identified in the IFB. See *Mor-Flo Indus., Inc.*, Comp. Gen. Dec. B-192687, 79-1 CPD ¶ 390, where life-cycle cost estimates for gas and electric water heaters were used in bid evaluation. See also *Swintec Corp.*, Comp. Gen. Dec. B-225657, 87-1 CPD ¶ 378, where life-cycle costs such as the cost of downtime, repairs, parts, supplies, etc., were evaluated in the procurement of electric typewriters.

To evaluate life-cycle costs, the IFB need not spell out the evaluation methodology with mathematical precision. It is sufficient if the bidders can arrive at a reasonable estimate of the costs that will be used by the Government to make the evaluation. For example, in 36 Comp. Gen. 380 (B-127801) (1956), the IFB for the construction of a radio communications system provided for evaluation of maintenance costs over 15 years of service. After bid opening the contracting officer fixed these costs at $3,000 per repeater station. The Comptroller General held that the evaluation factors were stated with sufficient clarity in the invitation to enable a bidder, on the basis of available data and past expenses, to make an estimate of the effect of the evaluation factor on its bid; and an award under the IFB was, therefore, proper.

While FAR 7-105(a)(3)(i) requires the consideration of life-cycle costs in acquisition planning decisions, and there are obvious benefits from including such factors in the evaluation of bids, there has been relatively little use of such factors. The Comptroller General has recommended that the procuring agencies make greater use of life-cycle costing, Comp. Gen. Dec. B-178214, May 21, 1973, *Unpub.* See also Office of Management and Budget Memorandum for Agency Senior Procurement Executives, Sept. 9, 1991, where the Administrator noted that the application of life-cycle costing has been inadequate and needs to be expanded, and OFPP Policy Letter 92-4, which requested that agencies implement life-cycle costing whenever feasible and appropriate in order for the Government to save money in the long run.

c. Miscellaneous

As discussed in Chapter 10, the Buy American Act prescribes evaluation factors for foreign products or materials. See *Gardner Zemke Co.*, Comp. Gen. Dec. B-234857, 89-2 CPD ¶ 66, and *Dictaphone Corp.*, 58 Comp. Gen. 234 (B-192318), 79-1 CPD ¶ 49, where, for evaluation purposes, a 6 percent Buy American factor was added to the price bid to furnish a foreign product. The Comptroller General has also stated that an agency may not consider the Buy American Act differential if it is not included in the IFB.

Other evaluation factors that may be used if mentioned in the IFB include storage and time-related costs, *Borg Warner Corp.*, 57 Comp. Gen. 103 (B-189275), 77-2 CPD ¶ 420; the cost of potential delays and changes in the course of contract performance, *ACS Constr. Co.*, B-250372.2, 93-1 CPD ¶ 106; the cost of first article testing to the extent that such cost can be realistically estimated, FAR 9.306(i); and the cost that results from varying locations of performance, *Cascade Gen., Inc.*, Comp. Gen. Dec. B-272271, 96-2 CPD ¶ 52. See *Homexx Int'l Corp.*, Comp. Gen. Dec. B-192034, 78-2 CPD ¶ 219, where $70,000, the estimated cost of first article testing, was added to the bid price of any bidder that had not previously produced the procurement items. See also *Flexfab, Inc.*, Comp. Gen. Dec. B-221186, 86-1 CPD ¶ 188, where the Comptroller General determined that the agency properly considered the protester's price for first article testing when the IFB specifically required that bidders include a price for it, which would be evaluated. Government inspection costs may also be added to the bids for evaluation purposes, but in 52 Comp. Gen. 997 (B-177887) (1973), the Comptroller General stated that it was inappropriate to add such costs for evaluation purposes when there was already an inspector in residence in the contractor's plant. The reasoning is that "no actual cost to the Government is incurred nor can it be said at the time of evaluation of bids that any costs would, in fact, be incurred if the award were made to a prospective contractor with an inspector already in residence." In determining whether multiple awards would be less costly to the Government than an aggregate award, FAR 14.201-8(c) requires that $500 be considered for evaluation purposes as the administrative cost to the Government of issuing and administering each contract awarded. See *Weather Experts, Inc.*, Comp. Gen. Dec. B-255103, 94-1 CPD ¶ 93 (agency accepted the low aggregate bid, but should have accepted multiple bids, because even with the $500 administrative costs, the multiple bid option was lower); and *Patrick Loman*,

B-254527, 93-2 CPD ¶ 340 (protest against aggregate award provision denied where IFB provided a reasonable method of assuring the lowest cost to the Government).

3. Evaluation of Equal Low Bids

FAR 14.408-6 outlines the procedures that must be followed when two or more equal low bids are received:

> (a) Contracts shall be awarded in the following order of priority when two or more low bids are equal in all respects:
>
> (1) Small business concerns that are also labor surplus area concerns.
>
> (2) Other small business concerns.
>
> (3) Other business concerns. (large businesses)
>
> (b) If two or more bidders still remain equally eligible after application of paragraph (a) above, award shall be made by a drawing by lot limited to those bidders. If time permits, the bidders involved shall be given an opportunity to attend the drawing. The drawing shall be witnessed by at least three persons, and the contract file shall contain the names and addresses of the witnesses and the person supervising the drawing.
>
> (c) When an award is to be made by using the priorities under this 14.408-6, the contracting officer shall include a written agreement in the contract that the contractor will perform, or cause to be performed, the contract in accordance with the circumstances justifying the priority used to break the tie or select bids for a drawing by lot.

In *Randy Int'l, Ltd.*, 53 Comp. Gen. 466 (B-179880), 74-1 CPD ¶ 11, the Comptroller General stated that once a tie has occurred between two low evaluated bids, no other evaluation factors should be considered if not delineated in the IFB. Thus, additional factors such as past performance record, experience of a bidder's personnel, and shipment security may not be considered. Similarly, in *Richard A. Schwartz Assocs.*, Comp. Gen. Dec. B-214979, 84-1 CPD ¶ 695, the protester's greater technical competence was held an extraneous factor that could not be used to break the tie. Thus, lots must be drawn to determine the winner when there are tie bids, *Van Ben Indus., Inc.*, Comp. Gen. Dec. B-234875, 89-2 CPD ¶ 52; *Berklay Air Servs. Corp.*, Comp. Gen. Dec. B-179880, 74-1 CPD ¶ 115.

The tied bidders should be given the opportunity to attend the drawing to avoid raising doubts concerning its fairness. See *Alderson Reporting Co.*, Comp. Gen. Dec. B-205552.2, 82-1 CPD ¶ 128, where the Comptroller General criticized the procuring agencies for performing the drawing by lot without inviting the tied bidders. Note that since equal low bids may indicate price fixing, identical bids may be reported to the Department of Justice for investigation of possible collusive bidding practices. FAR 3.303(d) states:

> Identical bids shall be reported under this section if the agency has some reason to believe that the bids resulted from collusion.

B. Award

The following guidance on the award of contracts is provided in 10 U.S.C. § 2305(b)(3) and 41 U.S.C.§ 253b(c):

> The head of the agency . . . shall award a contract with reasonable promptness to the responsible bidder whose bid conforms to the solicitation and is most advantageous to the United States, considering only price and the other price-related factors included in the solicitation. The award of a contract shall be made by transmitting, in writing or by electronic means, notice of the award to the successful bidder. Within three days after the date of contract award, the head of the agency shall notify, in writing or by electronic means, each bidder not awarded the contract that the contract has been awarded.

The major issues involved in awarding a sealed bid contract are the procedures to be followed, the determination of whether to make a single award or multiple awards, and the treatment of below-cost bids (also referred to as "buy-ins").

1. Procedures

FAR 14.408-1 outlines the award procedures in sealed bid procurements as follows:

> (a) The contracting officer shall make a contract award (1) by written or electronic notice, (2) within the time for acceptance specified in the bid or an extension (see 14.404-1(d)), and (3) to that responsible bidder whose bid, conforming to the invitation, will be most advantageous to the Government, considering only price and the price-related factors (see 14.201-8) included in the invitation. Award shall not be made until all required ap-

provals have been obtained and the award otherwise conforms with 14.103-2.

* * *

(c)(1) Award shall be made by mailing or otherwise furnishing a properly executed award document to the successful bidder.

(2) When a notice of award is issued, it shall be followed as soon as possible by the formal award.

(3) When more than one award results from any single invitation for bids, separate award documents shall be suitably numbered and executed.

(4) When an award is made to a bidder for less than all of the items that may be awarded to that bidder and additional items are being withheld for subsequent award, the award shall state that the Government may make subsequent awards on those additional items within the bid acceptance period.

(5) All provisions of the invitation for bids, including any acceptable additions or changes made by a bidder in the bid, shall be clearly and accurately set forth (either expressly or by reference) in the award document. The award is an acceptance of the bid, and the bid and the award constitute the contract.

a. Notice of Award

Award can be made by using the award portion of Standard Form 33, Solicitation, Offer and Award. FAR 14.408-1(d) provides that if "an offer leads to further changes," the resulting contract shall be prepared as a bilateral document on SF 26, Award/Contract. This regulation further provides that use of the award portion of SF 33 or SF 26 does not preclude the additional use of informal documents, including telegrams and notices of awards.

Notice of award must be in writing. Oral notice is not sufficient since the Government's acceptance of an offer must be clear and unconditional, *James M. Smith, Inc.*, Comp. Gen. Dec. B-233877, 89-1 CPD ¶ 390 (low bidder sought and received assurances that it would be awarded the contract, but Comptroller General held that retraction of the oral award was proper); *Phillip C. Clarke Elec. Constr. Inc.*, Comp. Gen. Dec. B-226594, 87-1 CPD

¶ 629 (low bidder was notified by telephone, but IFB was subsequently canceled and Comptroller General held the oral notice ineffective). See also *R.J. Crowley, Inc.*, ASBCA 28730, 86-1 BCA ¶ 18,739, where oral notification without a follow-up ratification was held insufficient to establish award.

The award must be made on the basis of the IFB and the responsive bid. The contracting officer may not unilaterally impose different terms on the low bidder, *CRF v. United States*, 224 Ct. Cl. 312, 624 F.2d 1054 (1980). See Chapter 2 for further discussion of Government acceptance issues.

b. Determining the Acceptance Period

As discussed earlier, bidders are subject to the firm bid rule if they include a promise in their bids to hold them open for a specified period of time. The standard cover sheets for sealed bid procurements, Standard Forms 33 and 1447, call for an acceptance period of 60 days but permit the bidder to insert a different period of time. In instances where neither of these forms is used, FAR 14.201-6(i) provides a Period for Acceptance of Bids solicitation provision (FAR 52.214-15) containing the same provisions. These provisions permit sealed bid procurements that will result in no minimum acceptance period if a bidder inserts "0 days" in the blank. See *Perkin-Elmer Corp.*, 69 Comp. Gen. 27 (B-236175.2), 89-2 CPD ¶ 352, where the Comptroller General held that, even though the bidder had filled in "30 days" in another part of the bid, the bid's inclusion of the FAR 52.214-15 clause superseded that number because the bidder did not include its own 30-day period in the clause.

When the contracting officer determines that a minimum acceptance period "must be specified," FAR 14.201-6(j) provides a Minimum Bid Acceptance Period solicitation provision (FAR 52.214-16) to be used in all contracts except those for construction. The use of this provision is at the sole discretion of the contracting officer because the FAR contains no guidance as to its use. The provision allows the agency to designate a number of calendar days as the minimum acceptance period and permits bidders to enter a longer acceptance period, but warns that a bid with a shorter period will be rejected. See *Paragon Investment Corp.* Comp. Gen. Dec. B-241715, 91-1 CPD ¶ 95, where a provision required a minimum acceptance period of 90 days, but the bidder entered 30 days. Although Paragon claimed that the insertion of "30 days" was a clerical error because it meant 30 days longer than the specified 60 days in Block 12 of SF 33, the

Comptroller General held that the "error" was not a minor informality and the bid was nonresponsive. See also *Winsar Corp.*, Comp. Gen. Dec. B-226507, 87-1 CPD ¶ 585, where the bidder sent with the bid a standard letter containing a shorter acceptance period, and the Comptroller General held the bid nonresponsive. Similarly, in *Sundt Corp.*, Comp. Gen. Dec. B-274203, 96-2 CPD ¶ 171, the Comptroller General found a bid nonresponsive where the bidder acknowledged the solicitation amendment changing the minimum acceptance period from 90 to 120 calendar days, but inserted 90 in the bid form blank for proposing an acceptance period. In *Kim's Gen. Maintenance, Inc.*, Comp. Gen. Dec. B-275823, 97-1 CPD ¶ 128, the Comptroller General reasoned that because the protester failed to include SF 1447 with its bid, there was no way for the agency to verify whether the protester took exception to the 120-day minimum acceptance period and thus found the bid to be nonresponsive.

The FAR 52.214-16 provision provides that it supersedes any other provisions in the IFB dealing with the minimum acceptance period. However, care must be taken not to insert acceptance periods in these other provisions. See, for example, *Siems Rental & Sales Co.*, Comp. Gen. Dec. B-257773, 95-1 CPD ¶ 51, where the FAR 52.214-16 provision required an acceptance period of 60 days, but the bidder inserted "30 days" in Block 12 of SF 33. The bidder asserted that its insertion of "30 days" was of no consequence because SF 33 contained a note stating: "Item 12 does not apply if the solicitation includes the provisions at 52.214-16, Minimum Bid Acceptance Period." The Comptroller General rejected this argument holding that, at best, the bid was ambiguous and therefore nonresponsive. See also *Perkin-Elmer Corp.*, 69 Comp. Gen. 27 (B-236175.2), 89-2 CPD ¶ 352, where the IFB incorrectly contained both the FAR 52.214-15 and the FAR 52.214-16 provisions, calling for a 60-day bid acceptance period. The Comptroller General held that the insertion of "30 days" in the FAR 52.214-15 clause rendered the bid ambiguous and therefore nonresponsive.

c. *Extensions from Bidders*

The contracting officer frequently finds that award cannot be made within the time that the bids are firm. When this occurs, bidders are usually requested to extend the time for acceptance. FAR 14.404-1(d) provides:

> Should administrative difficulties be encountered after bid opening that may delay award beyond bidders' acceptance periods, the several lowest bidders whose bids have not expired (irrespective of the acceptance period specified

> in the bid) should be requested, before expiration of their bids, to extend in writing the bid acceptance period (with consent of sureties, if any) in order to avoid the need for resoliciting.

This practice gives bidders the opportunity to choose to remain in the competition or to withdraw. Since the low bidders make this decision with knowledge of how their bids compare to the other bids, they can assess the likely profitability of the contract and make a decision based on this assessment.

To remain in the competition, a bidder's extension must be unqualified and unconditional. In *Klein Constr. Co.*, Comp. Gen. Dec. B-201599, 81-1 CPD ¶ 158, an extension was rejected when the bidder also reserved the right to request additional time or money, even though that qualification was subsequently withdrawn. See *S.J. Groves & Sons Co.*, Comp. Gen. Dec. B-207172, 82-2 CPD ¶ 423, where, when the bidder conditioned an extension on an increase in its bid price, the Comptroller General interpreted this as a refusal to extend the bid "as originally submitted." See also *Dawson Constr. Co.*, Comp. Gen. Dec. B-244204, 91-1 CPD ¶ 523; and *GTA Containers, Inc.*, Comp. Gen. Dec. B-234395.3, 89-2 CPD ¶ 37 (bidder conditioned extension of bid acceptance period upon an increase in price and thus was ineligible for award).

Although the regulations only permit extension of bids before they expire, the Comptroller General has held that the Government may accept *an expired bid* that has subsequently been revived through a bidder's actual or constructive waiver, provided that such waiver is not done with the intention of taking advantage of the other bidders. See *Mission Van & Storage Co.*, 53 Comp. Gen. 775 (B-180112), 74-1 CPD ¶ 195, where the Comptroller General stated at 778–79:

> In 46 Comp. Gen. 371 (1966), the low bidder extended its bid acceptance period when requested to do so 3 days after the original 60 day period had lapsed. We held that the bid properly could be accepted because the integrity of the competitive bidding system would not be compromised thereby and because there would be no prejudice to another bidder whose 60 day acceptance period had also expired. We distinguished that situation from the one in 42 Comp. Gen. 604, *supra*, in which the low bidder offered an acceptance period of only 20 days while the second low bidder offered the more customary 60 days. There we held that the low bid, which was not extended until more than 2 weeks after expiration of the original 20 day period, should not be accepted because the low bidder "sought and gained an

> advantage after bid opening in the nature of an option not sought by other bidders, of renewing its bid in short increments or allowing it to lapse as dictated by market conditions," and that "the integrity of the competitive bidding system would best be served by making an award to the second low bidder." 46 Comp. Gen. 371, 373.
>
> * * *
>
> We do not think that acceptance of DeWitt's bid would compromise the competitive bidding system. Unlike the bidders in 42 Comp. Gen. 604 and 48 *id.* 19, DeWitt did not seek any advantage over other bidders. It offered the standard 60 day acceptance period rather than an unusually short one. Furthermore, it is reasonably clear that DeWitt intended and considered its bid to be viable at least during the pendency of this protest. We have taken the position that a protest to this Office during a bidder's acceptance period could be viewed as tolling the bid acceptance period pending resolution of the protest, 50 Comp. Gen. 357 (1970). . . . Accordingly, we would not object to an award to DeWitt.

For cases involving prejudice to other bidders, see *MKB Mfg. Corp.*, Comp. Gen. Dec. B-208451, 83-1 CPD ¶ 204, where, when other bidders extended their bids before expiration of their 60-day acceptance period, it was held improper to allow MKB to revive its bid more than 15 days after expiration of its 60-day acceptance period because it would give MKB an unfair advantage over the other bidders; and *Esprit Int'l Corp.*, Comp. Gen. Dec. B-276294, 97-1 CPD ¶ 106, where the Comptroller General found that to allow the protester to revive its bid after the expiration of its 14-day acceptance period would afford the protester an unfair advantage since its initial exposure to the risk of the marketplace was for a shorter period.

A waiver will be deemed to have occurred if, following expiration of the acceptance period, the bidder is still willing to accept award on the basis of the bid as submitted, *Cecile Indus., Inc.*, Comp. Gen. Dec. B-207277.3, 82-2 CPD ¶ 299. For an unusual case, see *Input Data, Inc.*, GSBCA 4937-R, 80-2 BCA ¶ 14,711, where the board found that the contractor was bound to perform a contract awarded after bid expiration, even though it had failed to execute a bid extension mailed to the contracting officer. Its failure to disavow a notice of award and the request for a modification delaying performance were "consistent with ratification of his bid and acceptance of the signed contract." The board distinguished *A.C. Ball Co.*, ASBCA 19375, 75-1 BCA ¶ 11,298, where a contractor fulfilled only the minimum quantity on an indefinite-quantity contract awarded after bid expiration. The board found that the contractor had accepted only a "counter-offer," the terms of which were limited to performance of the minimum quantity order, reasoning that the transaction lacked the strong evidence of communications and meetings between the parties which were consistent only with contract recognition.

The Comptroller General has also held that participation in a protest tolls the acceptance period, *Phillips Cartner & Co.*, 69 Comp. Gen. 105 (B-236416.2), 89-2 CPD ¶ 492. Thus, where the award is made to another firm within the protester's shorter acceptance period, the protester's bid may be accepted if the protest is sustained, even though the acceptance period otherwise would have expired, *Professional Materials Handling Co.*, Comp. Gen. Dec. B-205969, 82-1 CPD ¶ 297. Similarly, award to a bidder that actively participated in a bid protest filed by another bidder may be proper, if award was made within the intended awardee's offered acceptance period, as tolled by the protest, *Native Resource Dev., Inc.*, Comp. Gen. Dec. B-246597.2, 92-2 CPD ¶ 15; *Werres Corp.*, Comp. Gen. Dec. B-211870, 83-2 CPD ¶ 243. In *International Graphics v. United States*, 4 Cl. Ct. 515 (1984), the court extended the tolling concept by holding that "the bid acceptance period should remain open as long as the parties, through litigation or otherwise, have actually or constructively expressed their intent to accept the award."

Bids that have expired due to cancellation of a solicitation may generally be revived upon reinstatement of the solicitation, unless the bids have been returned and reinstatement would compromise the integrity of the competitive bidding system, *Baker Mfg. Co.*, 59 Comp. Gen. 573 (B-197016), 80-2 CPD ¶ 1. Even though the Government has requested multiple extensions, it is not required to make an award, *Maceto Inc.*, Comp. Gen. Dec. B-216166, 84-2 CPD ¶ 277 (although Navy requested four extensions of the original bid acceptance period, Maceto had no legal right to require the Navy to award the contract).

2. Multiple versus Aggregate Awards

Considerable confusion has surrounded the award of contracts for multiple items. Part of the problem stems from the number of alternatives available to both the Government and bidders when dealing with multiple items. The Contract Award — Sealed Bidding solicitation provision in

FAR 52.214-10, used for all procurements except construction contracts, states:

> (c) The Government may accept any item or group of items of a bid, unless the bidder qualifies the bid by specific limitations. *Unless otherwise provided in the Schedule, bids may be submitted for quantities less than those specified. The Government reserves the right to make an award on any item for a quantity less than the quantity offered, at the unit prices offered, unless the bidder specifies otherwise in the bid.*

The Contract Award — Sealed Bidding — Construction solicitation provision in FAR 52.214-19 contains a slightly different provision:

> (c) The Government may accept any item or combination of items, unless doing so is precluded by a restrictive limitation in the solicitation or the bid.

Under these provisions awards may be made to one or more bidders for one or more items or to one bidder for all items, whichever is in the best interests of the Government, Comp. Gen. Dec. B-149085, Aug. 28, 1962, *Unpub.*; 47 Comp. Gen. 233 (B-162092) (1967).

Absent solicitation language requiring an aggregate award, the Government must make multiple awards if different bidders offer the low evaluated price on each item to be awarded, *Action Mobile Transportation, Inc.*, Comp. Gen. Dec. B-275427.2, 97-1 CPD ¶ 132; *TAAS Israel Military Indus. Ltd.*, Comp. Gen. Dec. B-258039.3, 95-1 CPD ¶ 32; *Weather Experts, Inc.*, Comp. Gen. Dec. B-255103, 94-1 CPD ¶ 93; *HFS Inc.*, Comp. Gen. Dec. B-246018, 92-1 CPD ¶ 160. In this respect, the Comptroller General has required that in order to make an aggregate award, it must result in the lowest cost to the Government, *S.J. Groves & Sons Co.*, 55 Comp. Gen. 936 (B-184260), 76-1 CPD ¶ 205; 47 Comp. Gen. 233 (B-162092) (1967) (aggregate award improper when based on considerations of centralized management and administration, when multiple awards would have resulted in a lower cost to the Government). But if a bidder offers a low aggregate bid that is less than the sum of its bids on individual items, award should be made to the low aggregate bid. See 47 Comp. Gen. 658 (B-163890) (1968), where the Comptroller General upheld the agency's consideration of a combination bid for tractors and loaders that resulted in a lower overall cost to the Government than on an item-by-item basis. In *Moir Ranch & Constr. Co.*, Comp. Gen. Dec. B-191616, 78-1 CPD ¶ 423, a bidder, offering an additional 10 percent discount if all eight of its bid items were accepted, was properly awarded the contract even though other bidders offered lower prices on individual items and without the discount, the total cost would have been lower under multiple awards.

If the solicitation notifies bidders that award will be made to the low aggregate bidder, then an aggregate award must be made even though such an award may be more costly to the Government, *Northeast Constr. Co.*, 61 Comp. Gen. 317 (B-205246), 82-1 CPD ¶ 293. In *Northeast*, the Comptroller General sustained a protest because the agency split the base bid requirement between two bidders instead of making one aggregate award to the low bidder. However, it is proper to make a partial award if funds to make an aggregate award are not available. In *FBF Indus., Inc.*, Comp. Gen. Dec. B-252574, 93-1 CPD ¶ 477, the protester asserted that the agency should have evaluated bids on an item-by-item basis and made partial award. The Comptroller General denied the protest, stating that the solicitation provided that bids would be evaluated on an "all or none" basis for all items and did not contain a multiple awards clause. If the solicitation requires an aggregate award but multiple awards would serve the Government's needs and there is no reasonable basis for an aggregate award, the solicitation must be canceled and the work reprocured, *Hawthorne Uniform Mfg. Co.*, Comp. Gen. Dec. B-200363, 81-1 CPD ¶ 68 (resolicitation recommended since there was no reason for the aggregate award restriction in the solicitation, and the contracting officer could have made multiple awards at a lower total cost to the Government); *Roy's Rabbitry*, Comp. Gen. Dec. B-193628, 79-1 CPD ¶ 305 (resolicitation recommended because aggregate award restricted the competition unnecessarily to large producers, and multiple awards could meet the Government's needs). See also *Com-Tran of Michigan, Inc.*, Comp. Gen. Dec. B-200845, 80-2 CPD ¶ 407. But see *Alcon Div. of Boyles Bros. Drilling Co.*, Comp. Gen. Dec. B-241058, 91-1 CPD ¶ 46, where a partial award was sustained where the only bidder submitting an aggregate bid within the agency funding limitation had bid some of the items at amounts exceeding the statutory funding limitations. The Comptroller General held that the aggregate award language did not preclude the agency from making an award to that bidder for all of the items that were within the statutory limitation.

In construction contracts, the agency frequently obtains bids on additive and deductive elements of the work and reserves the right to award to the lowest aggregate bidder on the combination of items that fall within the agency's funding limitation. See DFARS 236.303-70 for guidance on the use of this technique.

The Additive or Deductive Items solicitation provision in DFARS 252.236-7007 states:

> (a) The low offeror and the items to be awarded shall be determined as follows —
>
> (1) Prior to the opening of bids, the Government will determine the amount of funds available for the project.
>
> (2) The low offeror shall be the Offeror that —
>
> (i) Is otherwise eligible for award; and
>
> (ii) Offers the lowest aggregate amount for the first or base bid item, plus or minus (in the order stated in the list of priorities in the bid schedule) those additive or deductive items that provide the most features within the funds determined available.
>
> (3) The Contracting Officer shall evaluate all bids on the basis of the same additive or deductive items.
>
> (i) If adding another item from the bid schedule list of priorities would make the award exceed the available funds for all offerors, the Contracting Officer will skip that item and go to the next item from the bid schedule of priorities; and
>
> (ii) Add that next item if an award may be made that includes that item and is within the available funds.
>
> (b) The Contracting Officer will use the list of priorities in the bid schedule only to determine the low offeror. After determining the low offeror, an award may be made on any combination of items if —
>
> (1) It is in the best interest of the Government;
>
> (2) Funds are available at the time of award; and
>
> (3) The low offeror's price for the combination to be awarded is less than the price offered by any other responsive, responsible offeror.

Under this clause the low bidder is determined by the low bid for the best combination of items within the funding limitation applicable *at the time of bid opening*, even if this amount varies from the funding limitation set forth in the solicitation, *Rodriguez & Del Valle, Inc.*, Comp. Gen. Dec. B-239224, 90-2 CPD ¶ 29 (award to bidder not low on base bid but low on base bid plus all additives was sustained because agency budget officer certified prior to bid opening that sufficient funds were available); *Martz Constr. Corp.*, Comp. Gen. Dec. B-213320, 84-1 CPD ¶ 29 (award to bidder not low on base bid and all additives but low on base bid plus two additives sustained because that was all that could be awarded within the funding limitation); *Applicators, Inc.*, Comp. Gen. Dec. B-270162, 96-1 CPD ¶ 32 (award to bidder not low on base bid and additives but low on base bid sustained because that was all that could be awarded within the funding limitation); *Atherton Constr., Inc.*, Comp. Gen. Dec. B-266345, 96-1 CPD ¶ 51 (award made to low base bidder, without including additives, because funds available prior to bid opening were insufficient to cover even the lowest base bid). Once this low bidder has been determined, award can be made for more items if more funds become available thereafter — even if such award would not be to the low bidder for those items, *Sammy Garrison Constr. Co.*, Comp. Gen. Dec. B-215453, 84-2 CPD ¶ 545. In this case, the award was sustained even though the protester had submitted the low bid on the items included in the award — because the awardee was the low bidder on the items that could be included within the funding limitation. In one unusual case, there were no funds available at the time of bid opening, but the Comptroller General ruled that it was proper to award subsequently to the low bidder on the base bid minus all deductive items when funds became available for that amount of work, *Gartrell Constr., Inc.*, Comp. Gen. Dec. B-237032, 90-1 CPD ¶ 46. The Comptroller General rejected the protester's contention that it should have received the award because it was the low bidder on the base bid. An earlier solicitation provision gave the agency the flexibility to select the additive or deductive items after bid opening, but the funds available at the time of bid opening still controlled the determination of the low bidder, *Delta Industrial Contractors, Inc.*, Comp. Gen. Dec. B-226949, 87-1 CPD ¶ 569 (award to bidder not low on base bid but low on base bid plus additives sustained where such items were within the funding limitation); *Huntington Constr., Inc.*, 67 Comp. Gen. 499 (B-230604), 88-1 CPD ¶ 619 (protest sustained when agency determined low bidder based on lower figure than the funding limitation at the time of bid opening). It has been held improper to treat options the same as additive items when the solicitation does not call for the evaluation of options, *N-K Constr. Co.*, Comp. Gen. Dec. B-224534, 87-1 CPD ¶ 188.

Prices may generally be submitted for individual items, for combinations of items, or on an "all or none" basis. An "all or none" bid precludes award to that bidder for less than the total number of items. FAR 14.404-5 provides:

> Unless the solicitation provides otherwise, a bid may be responsive notwithstanding that the bidder specifies that award will be accepted only on all, or a specified group, of the items. Bidders shall not be permitted to withdraw or modify "all or none" qualifications after bid opening since such qualifications are substantive and affect the rights of other bidders.

See *Steel King Indus., Inc.*, Comp. Gen. Dec. B-209239, 83-1 CPD ¶ 473, where the Comptroller General recommended award to an all or none bidder who submitted the lowest overall price for the items bid. In *Canova Moving & Storage Co.*, Comp. Gen. Dec. B-207168, 83-1 CPD ¶ 59, the Comptroller General stated that an "all or none" bidder does not have the option to decide after bid opening whether it will accept an award on less than the total number of items.

The Contract Award — Sealed Bidding solicitation provision in FAR 52.214-10 gives the Government the right to make an award for less than the quantity advertised unless the bidder has restricted the Government's right to do so by an "all or none" bid or by a provision limiting award for less than a stated quantity of any item. Awards for a lesser quantity of an item than that advertised could have a serious impact on the bidder's pricing. Thus, the Government is only permitted to make such awards when the contracting officer learns of a reduced need after bid opening or has accepted a lower bid on a portion of the quantity, Comp. Gen. Dec. B-173666, Oct. 1, 1971, *Unpub.* If the contracting officer learns of a reduced need before award, FAR 14.208(a) requires an amendment to the IFB reflecting the reduction. Failure to follow this procedure would make it unconscionable to hold the bidder to the bid price, Comp. Gen. Dec. B-170808, May 14, 1971, *Unpub.* The Government is not required to award for lesser quantities and may award the total quantity of an item or the entire group of items advertised even though a partial award would result in a lower cost to the Government for the items awarded, *General Fire Extinguisher Corp.*, 54 Comp. Gen. 416 (B-181796), 74-2 CPD ¶ 278. There the Comptroller General stated that "an all or none bid, lower in the aggregate than any combination of individual bids available, may be accepted by the Government even though a partial award could be made at a lower unit cost." See also *George C. Martin, Inc.*, 55 Comp. Gen. 100 (B-182175), 75-2 CPD ¶ 55, where the IFB called for separate bid prices for two facilities on Schedule A and B, respectively. X submitted the low total bid for both schedules and bid on an "all or none" basis, which was not precluded by the IFB. Y bid low on Schedule B. Had the Government desired to award only on Schedule B (a partial award), it would have awarded that item to Y. However, since both schedules were being awarded, it was proper to make the award to X.

3. Award to Below-Cost Bidders

Receipt of a below-cost bid requires the contracting officer to exercise special care in the evaluation and award process. Such bids cannot be summarily rejected, because they offer the Government a low price for obtaining the work. Yet they may pose the risk of default or poor contract performance such as deviating from the specifications to reduce costs. The actions the Government should take depend on the circumstances underlying the bid.

There are several reasons a bidder may submit a below-cost bid: (1) by mistake, *Darwin Constr. Co.*, Comp. Gen. Dec. B-213314, 84-1 CPD ¶ 154; (2) through incompetence; (3) to eliminate competitors, *National Reporting Co.*, Comp. Gen. Dec. B-199497, 80-2 CPD ¶ 142; (4) to retain a team of employees within its organization; (5) to break into a new Government market, *Flexible Metal Hose Mfg. Co. v. United States*, 4 Cl. Ct. 522 (1984); (6) to cover a portion of its fixed costs in a period of slow sales; or (7) to obtain work with the intention of recouping losses through future changes or contracts (known as "buying-in"); *Diemaster Tool, Inc.*, Comp. Gen. Dec. B-238877, 90-1 CPD ¶ 375.

The FAR does not contain comprehensive guidance on dealing with below-cost bids. However, the FAR coverage of improper business practices does address "buying-in," which FAR 3.501-1 defines as

> submitting an offer below anticipated costs, expecting to —
>
> (a) Increase the contract amount after award (e.g., through unnecessary or excessively priced change orders); or
>
> (b) Receive follow-on contracts at artificially high prices to recover losses incurred on the buy-in contract.

The regulations do not require that contracting officers reject such bids. FAR 3.501-2 cautions the contracting officer to be certain that possible losses are not recouped during performance or on follow on contracts. The regulation states:

> (a) Buying-in may decrease competition or result in poor contract performance. The contracting officer must take appropriate action to ensure buying-in losses are not recovered by the contractor through the pricing of (1) change orders or (2) follow-on contracts subject to cost analysis.
>
> (b) The Government should minimize the opportunity for buying-in by seeking a price commitment covering as much of the entire program concerned as is practical by using —
>
> > (1) Multiyear contracting, with a requirement in the solicitation that a price be submitted only for the total multiyear quantity; or
> >
> > (2) Price options for additional quantities that, together with the firm contract quantity, equal the program requirements (see Subpart 17.2).
>
> (c) Other safeguards are available to the contracting officer to preclude recovery of buying-in losses e.g., amortization of nonrecurring costs (see 15.804-6(f) and treatment of unreasonable price quotations (see 15.803(d)).

Although not likely, if the below-cost bid violates antitrust laws, such as predatory pricing, the procuring agency must report this practice to the Department of Justice, 41 U.S.C. § 253(b)(e); 10 U.S.C. § 2305(b)(5); and FAR 3.303(a).

The other major issues raised by below-cost bids are mistakes and non-responsibility, which are more fully discussed in Section IV of this chapter and Chapter 4. An unusually low bid must be verified to assure that no mistake has been made, but upon such verification, award is proper, *Associated Contractors & Renovators, Inc.*, HUDBCA 83-809-B4, 83-2 BCA ¶ 16,755. The board stated at 83,308:

> There is no requirement that a contractor must submit a bid that provides for any profit, let alone a substantial profit. In fact, a bidder can even submit a negative profit "buy-in" so long as that bid is submitted with full knowledge of its cost implications and is not based on a mistake.

The contracting officer must also assure that the prospective contractor is responsible. See *TECOM Inc.*, Comp. Gen. Dec. B-215291, 84-1 CPD ¶ 644, stating:

> The submission of a below-cost bid is not illegal and provides no basis for challenging the award of a government contract to a responsible prospective contractor. Whether the low bidder can perform the contract at the price bid is a matter of responsibility. Our office does not review protests concerning affirmative determinations of responsibility absent a showing that the contracting officer acted fraudulently or in bad faith or that definitive responsibility criteria in the solicitation have not been met.

See also *Seaton Van Lines, Inc.*, Comp. Gen. Dec. B-217298, 85-1 CPD ¶ 26.

C. Cancellation after Bid Opening

Cancellation of a procurement after bid opening is a serious matter because it can give bidders an unfair advantage if they are later permitted to recompete with knowledge of the prior bids. FAR 14.404-1(a) permits such cancellation only for compelling reasons:

> (1) Preservation of the integrity of the competitive bid system dictates that, after bids have been opened, award must be made to that responsible bidder who submitted the lowest responsive bid, unless there is a compelling reason to reject all bids and cancel the invitation.

The Comptroller General has stated that the determination of whether a sufficiently compelling reason exists for bid cancellation is "primarily within the discretion of the administrative agency and will not be disturbed absent proof that the decision was clearly arbitrary, capricious, or not supported by substantial evidence," *Ace-Federal Reporters, Inc.*, Comp. Gen. Dec. B-237414, 90-1 CPD ¶ 144. In some cases the Comptroller General has sustained a cancellation because there was no showing of bad faith or fraud on the part of the agency, *J. Morris & Assocs.*, Comp. Gen. Dec. B-256840, 94-2 CPD ¶ 47 (cancellation was proper where the agency determined that prices were unreasonable and there was no showing of bad faith or fraud); *Moore's Cafeteria Servs., Inc.*, Comp. Gen. Dec. B-234063.4, 89-2 CPD ¶ 11 (cancellation of an IFB in order to initiate a solicitation under Section 8(a) of the Small Business Administration Act was upheld because there was no showing of bad faith or fraud on the part of the agency). In cases where the agency erroneously cancels the solicitation after bid opening, reinstatement of the IFB may be proper if it would not prejudice other bidders and if the award under the original solicitation would serve the actual needs of the Government, *Bilt-Rite Contractors, Inc.*, Comp. Gen. Dec. B-259106.2, 95-1 CPD ¶ 220.

When an agency cancels a solicitation after opening, all facts and circumstances will be considered in determining whether appropriate grounds for cancellation existed, *International Graphics, Div. of Moore Business Forms, Inc. v. United States*, 5 Cl. Ct. 100 (1984) (A-76 cost comparison was conducted after cancellation of a solicitation and was used to prove that the Government had a compelling reason to cancel the solicitation); *McGhee Constr., Inc.*, Comp. Gen. Dec. B-250073.3, 93-1 CPD ¶ 379 (all relevant information was considered to determine that cancellation was appropriate); *I.T.S. Corp.*, Comp. Gen. Dec. B-242725, 91-1 CPD ¶ 518 (when agency's initial reason was inadequate, other information justified cancellation).

In most cases where an IFB is defective, the Comptroller General will recommend cancellation of the entire IFB. However, there may be certain situations where only partial cancellation of the solicitation is appropriate. In such a case, the Government may cancel the defective portion of the IFB and award a contract for the remainder of the solicitation items to the bidder submitting the lowest bid for those items, *Adrian Supply Co.*, Comp. Gen. Dec. B-240871, 90-2 CPD ¶ 515.

The FAR offers guidance to determine when cancellation is proper. FAR 14.404-1(b) requires cancellation in only one circumstance — when the agency finds that it has not properly disclosed the identity or availability of the necessary specifications. In all other situations, cancellation is discretionary provided that there is a compelling reason. FAR 14.404-1(c) lists some compelling reasons:

> Invitations may be canceled and all bids rejected before award but after opening when . . . the agency head determines in writing that —
>
> (1) Inadequate or ambiguous specifications were cited in the invitation;
>
> (2) Specifications have been revised;
>
> (3) The supplies or services being contracted for are no longer required;
>
> (4) The invitation did not provide for consideration of all factors of cost to the Government, such as cost of transporting Government-furnished property to bidders' plants;

(5) Bids received indicate that the needs of the Government can be satisfied by a less expensive article differing from that for which the bids were invited;

(6) All otherwise acceptable bids received are at unreasonable prices, or only one bid received and the contracting officer cannot determine the reasonableness of the bid price;

(7) The bids were not independently arrived at in open competition, were collusive, or were submitted in bad faith . . . ;

(8) No responsive bid has been received from a responsible bidder;

(9) A cost comparison as prescribed in the OMB Circular A-76 and Subpart 7.3 shows that performance by the Government is more economical; or

(10) For other reasons, cancellation is clearly in the public's interest.

1. Compelling Reasons for Cancellation

Cancellation is only proper if the interests of the Government in canceling outweigh the expense and time of resolicitation and the impact on the competitive system resulting from disclosure of bidders and bid prices. This section discusses the major compelling reasons.

a. Solicitation Defects

Failure to state proper evaluation criteria in the solicitation is a compelling reason to cancel, *Armco, Inc.*, Comp. Gen. Dec. B-210018, 83-1 CPD ¶ 553 (evaluation criteria inconsistent with other provisions of the solicitation). Where there is no assurance that compliance with a bid evaluation formula would result in the lowest cost to the Government, the solicitation is materially defective, and cancellation is proper, *Earthworks of Sumter, Inc.*, Comp. Gen. Dec. B-232067.2, 89-1 CPD ¶ 9 (no basis for determining low bidder because IFB ambiguities permitted bids on different bases); *S.W. Monroe Constr. Co.*, Comp. Gen. Dec. B-256382, 94-1 CPD ¶ 362 (evaluation scheme did not set forth a common basis for evaluating offers); *Bayfone of Tampa*, Comp. Gen. Dec. B-242925, 91-1 CPD ¶ 535 (line item prices were based on defective criteria); *Reliable Reproductions, Inc.*, Comp. Gen. Dec. B-201137, 81-1 CPD ¶ 100 (defective evaluation method permitted bidders to submit materially unbalanced bids).

Solicitations have been properly canceled when it was apparent that a majority of bidders were misled by the solicitation, *Neals Janitorial Serv.*, Comp. Gen. Dec. B-276625, 97-2 CPD ¶ 6 (cancellation proper where information in solicitation and ascertainable from site visit were inadequate for bidders to establish the actual work load requirements); *Ferguson-Williams, Inc.*, Comp. Gen. Dec. B-258460, 95-1 CPD ¶ 39 (cancellation proper where three lowest bidders misunderstood the estimated quantities in the IFB); *P.J. Dick, Inc.*, Comp. Gen. Dec. B-259166, 95-1 CPD ¶ 131 (bidders were misled where conflicting terms in IFB caused some bidders to include sales taxes in price while others did not); *Hughes & Smith, Inc.*, Comp. Gen. Dec. B-245969, 91-2 CPD ¶ 530 (cancellation proper where bidders were misled because Certification of Procurement Integrity in IFB contained no signature line); *A&P Surgical Co.*, 62 Comp. Gen. 256 (B-206111.2), 83-1 CPD ¶ 263 (IFB misled five out of six bidders to offer foreign melted specialty metals when the Government required specialty metals melted in the United States); *Kleen-Rite Janitorial Servs., Inc.*, Comp. Gen. Dec. B-180345, 74-1 CPD ¶ 210 (bidding instructions were ambiguous causing the failure of three bidders (including two lowest bidders) to insert separate bid prices for a certain item).

Estimated quantities that are found to differ significantly from actual anticipated quantities provide a proper basis for cancellation, *Ferguson-Williams, Inc.*, Comp. Gen. Dec. B-258460, 95-1 CPD ¶ 39. See *Heritage Reporting Corp.*, Comp. Gen. Dec. B-248860.2, 92-2 CPD ¶ 276 (estimates for base period were exaggerated by 68 percent). In *Heuer, Inc.*, Comp. Gen. Dec. B-202017.2, 81-2 CPD ¶ 460, the Comptroller General held that cancellation was proper stating:

> Where there is a substantial variation between the IFB estimates and the actual estimated requirements, there is substantial doubt that award to any bidder will result in the lowest cost to the Government.

See also *Downtown Copy Ctr.*, 62 Comp. Gen. 65 (B-206999.6), 82-2 CPD ¶ 503, where the agency concluded that volume estimates were inaccurate and could have given an unfair advantage to the incumbent contractor. Cancellation is also proper where award is based on estimated quantities, but the solicitation failed to include estimated quantities for all items, *MTL Sys., Inc.*, Comp. Gen. Dec. B-245363, 91-2 CPD ¶ 569.

b. Specification Defects

FAR 14.404-1(c)(1) states that "inadequate or ambiguous specifications" can be compelling reasons for cancellation. Use of specifications that do not adequately describe the Government's actual needs generally provide a compelling reason for cancellation, *Cycad Corp.*, Comp. Gen. Dec. B-255870, 94-1 CPD ¶ 253 (IFB did not reflect the agency's needs where a requirement for commercial, off-the-shelf products was omitted); *Renic Gov't Sys.*, Comp. Gen. Dec. B-249484, Nov. 9, 1992, *Unpub.* (IFB failed to include the agency's requirement that work be done by a lawyer licensed in Texas); *United States Elevator Corp.*, Comp. Gen. Dec. B-225625, 87-1 CPD ¶ 401 (agency did not include specifications for major repairs and replacement parts); *Intercomp Co.*, Comp. Gen. Dec. B-213059, 84-1 CPD ¶ 540 (without revised weight and testing requirements for aircraft scales, specifications did not reflect the Navy's needs); *Heart of Am. Police Supply*, Comp. Gen. Dec. B-210911, 84-1 CPD ¶ 423 (specification failed to describe all required features of a brand-name product adequately which resulted in unacceptable bids); *Kings Point Mfg. Co.*, Comp. Gen. Dec. B-210757, 83-2 CPD ¶ 342 (design deficiencies in harness specifications resulted in harnesses that did not meet Government's needs).

Vague and ambiguous specifications are another compelling reason for cancellation, *Meds Mktg., Inc.*, Comp. Gen. Dec. B-213352, 84-1 CPD ¶ 318 (specification was so vague that it was not clear what Meds' legal obligation would be if awarded the contract); *Commercial Envelope Mfg. Co.*, Comp. Gen. Dec. B-213272, 84-1 CPD ¶ 206 (specification was not specific enough to procure center-seam envelopes needed by the IRS). Preservation of the integrity of the competitive bidding system requires that an agency not award a contract if it intends to negotiate specifications after award. In *W.M. Grace, Inc.*, Comp. Gen. Dec. B-202842, 81-2 CPD ¶ 121, the Comptroller General stated:

> An attempt by the contracting officer to negotiate changes with the low bidder which amount to a substantial deviation from the original specifications would be prejudicial to the other bidders because the contract after negotiation would not be the same as that offered the other bidders under the invitation.

See also *Source AV, Inc.*, Comp. Gen. Dec. B-238017, 90-1 CPD ¶ 336, where the Comptroller General upheld cancellation of an IFB and denied the protester's argument that modification after award was appropriate, because an agency cannot award a contract with the intention of significantly modifying the terms of the solicitation.

A compelling reason for cancellation exists when an agency concludes that the Government's needs can be satisfied by a less expensive design differing from that called for by the IFB, *Jarrett S. Blankenship Co.*, Comp. Gen. Dec. B-211582, 83-2 CPD ¶ 516 (specification of air-conditioning units with copper coils and fins properly canceled where aluminum coils could meet agency needs at a lesser cost); *Sunrise Int'l Group*, Comp. Gen. Dec. B-256912, 94-2 CPD ¶ 31 (cancellation of IFB for short-order meals was reasonable when full-course meals would meet Government's needs at lesser cost); *Uffner Textile Corp.*, Comp. Gen. Dec. B-204358, 82-1 CPD ¶ 106 (specifications overstated minimum needs when smaller zipper and less restrictive batting specifications would be more cost effective and satisfy the needs of the Government).

Cancellation is also appropriate if the agency determines that its specification is unduly restrictive, *Siemens Power Corp.*, Comp. Gen. Dec. B-257167, 94-2 CPD ¶ 160 (specifications overstated type of equipment needed); *Washex Mach. Corp.*, Comp. Gen. Dec. B-191224, 78-2 CPD ¶ 54 (specifications limited competition to one type of washing machine).

c. *Alternate Performance by Government*

When the services covered by the invitation could be performed by in-house personnel at a cost savings to the Government, cancellation is proper, *Currents Constr., Inc.*, Comp. Gen. Dec. B-236735.2, 90-1 CPD ¶ 236. See also *Ameriko Maintenance Co.*, Comp. Gen. Dec. B-243728, 91-2 CPD ¶ 191 (GSA determined that it could save nearly $3 million by maintaining in-house performance of the services required by the solicitation). In *Powertronic Sys., Inc.*, Comp. Gen. Dec. B-210283, 83-2 CPD ¶ 346, the Comptroller General stated that when the Government can build an urgently needed item faster in-house than by contracting out, cancellation of an IFB that would not meet the urgency of the need is proper. See also *Bush-Herrick, Inc.*, Comp. Gen. Dec. B-209683, 83-1 CPD ¶ 669. Cancellation is also appropriate where a solicited item is available within the Government at a lower cost, and the available item meets the agency's needs, *Nedlog Co.*, Comp. Gen. Dec. B-212665, 84-1 CPD ¶ 215 (Army's needs met by substituting in-house dry mix beverages for the solicited liquid beverages). See also *Essex Electro Eng'rs, Inc.*, Comp. Gen. Dec. B-206012.3, 82-2 CPD ¶ 307, where solicitation for generator sets was canceled because adequate decommissioned generator sets were available within the Government.

d. Lack of Fair Competition

Cancellation is appropriate when competition on an equal basis has been thwarted, *Honeywell, Inc.*, Comp. Gen. Dec. B-210000, 83-1 CPD ¶ 445 (because Air Force did not make historical data or estimates of number of required service calls available, nonincumbent contractors lacked necessary information for intelligent bid preparation). See also *GS Elektro-Schewe GmbH*, Comp. Gen. Dec. B-259103.2, 95-1 CPD ¶ 196 (because agency sent a document to at least one bidder which required a specification that was not included in the IFB, competition on an equal basis was not assured); *HDL Research Lab, Inc.*, Comp. Gen. Dec. B-254863.3, 94-1 CPD ¶ 298 (specifications were biased in favor of the awardee and may have restricted competition when only three of the 66 bidders who were solicited submitted a bid); *Werres Corp.*, Comp. Gen. Dec. B-255379, 94-1 CPD ¶ 153 (solicitation was ambiguous and misled bidders because of an inconsistency between the pricing schedule and the specifications); *Air Inc.*, 69 Comp. Gen. 504 (B-238468), 90-1 CPD ¶ 533 (potential bidders had an unfair advantage where four bids were opened prematurely); *Jackson Marine Cos.*, Comp. Gen. Dec. B-212882, 84-1 CPD ¶ 402 (payment provision put undue economic risk on contractor and discouraged potential bidders from participating in the procurement); and *Downtown Copy Ctr.*, 62 Comp. Gen. 65 (B-206999.6), 82-2 CPD ¶ 503 (inaccurate estimated quantities gave incumbent contractor an unfair advantage). In *Mott Haven Truck Parts, Inc.*, Comp. Gen. Dec. B-210775, 83-2 CPD ¶ 189, untimely dispatch of a material IFB amendment (one day prior to bid opening) was a compelling reason for cancellation due to lack of adequate competition.

e. Insufficient Funds

The procurement agency's determination that funds are not available for the contract is a compelling reason for cancellation, *Michelle F. Evans*, Comp. Gen. Dec. B-259165, 95-1 CPD ¶ 139; *Armed Forces Sports Officials, Inc.*, Comp. Gen. Dec. B-251409, 93-1 CPD ¶ 261. In *Kato/Intermountain Elec. (J.V.)*, Comp. Gen. Dec. B-245807, 92-1 CPD ¶ 129, the Army Corps of Engineers canceled the solicitation when the bid price of the lowest eligible bid was greater than the funds available for the contract. See also *Metric Constructors, Inc.*, Comp. Gen. Dec. B-229947,

88-1 CPD ¶ 311. Where Congress passes legislation that prohibits obligating funds, cancellation is proper, *Consolidated Maintenance Co.*, Comp. Gen. Dec. B-209766, 83-1 CPD ¶ 225 (Joint Continuing Resolution of Dec. 21, 1982, prohibited the agency from obligating funds for the custodial services involved in the solicitation). See also *Satellite Servs., Inc.*, Comp. Gen. Dec. B-225624, 87-1 CPD ¶ 314, where the Comptroller General found that cancellation was proper where a congressional appropriations restriction created uncertainties concerning funding.

f. Inaccurate Statement of Government Needs

FAR 14.404-1(c)(2) states that cancellation may be appropriate where specifications require revision. A compelling reason for cancellation exists where the other parts of the original IFB are inaccurate and must be revised to reflect the needs of the Government, *Days Inn Marina*, Comp. Gen. Dec. B-254913, 94-1 CPD ¶ 23 (preaward surveys showed that the stated geographic restriction was insufficient to satisfy Government's requirements); *McGhee Constr., Inc.*, Comp. Gen. Dec. B-250073.3, 93-1 CPD ¶ 379 (solicitation failed to reflect agency's need where additional construction services were required); *I.T.S Corp.*, Comp. Gen. Dec. B-242725, 91-1 CPD ¶ 518 (IFB for mail and message services omitting material duties and functions did not reflect agency's requirements); *News Printing, Inc.*, Comp. Gen. Dec. B-274773.2, 97-1 CPD ¶ 68 (significant decrease in estimated quantity provided compelling reason to cancel the IFB).

Changing the specifications of a procurement after bid opening to express the Government's new needs constitutes sufficient reason for cancellation, *I.T.S. Corp.*, Comp. Gen. Dec. B-243223, 91-2 CPD ¶ 55 (deployment of troops to hostile area created a need for additional counseling services); *Holk Dev., Inc.*, Comp. Gen. Dec. B-236765.2, 90-1 CPD ¶ 65 (additional work required when asbestos was discovered); *Dyneteria, Inc.*, Comp. Gen. Dec. B-211525.2, 84-2 CPD ¶ 484 (Air Guard conversion from F-4 to F-16 fighters and C-130 to C-5A transports would significantly change manning requirements, aircraft servicing, and fuel consumption); *Tecom, Inc.*, Comp. Gen. Dec. B-213815.2, 84-2 CPD ¶ 152 (material workload changes caused IFB to fail to represent the Government's needs); *Electric Maintenance & Installation Co.*, Comp. Gen. Dec. B-213005, 84-1 CPD ¶ 292 (Army Corps of Engineers advised that change in river water level would require use of two motors involved in IFB earlier than the expected delivery time).

FAR 14.404-1(c)(3) states that cancellation is proper where supplies or services are no longer required. See *Orange Personnel Servs., Inc. — Recons.*, Comp. Gen. Dec. B-256164.2, 95-1 CPD ¶ 26 (cancellation of solicitation of layberthing services for two Ready Reserve Force ships proper where the ships were being repositioned and services were no longer needed); *International Typewriter Exch.*, Comp. Gen. Dec. B-205989.3, 82-2 CPD ¶ 279 (cancellation of solicitation for manual typewriters was proper where conversion to electric typewriters negated the requirement for solicited item).

g. Unreasonable Prices

Solicitations may properly be canceled if bid prices are unreasonable. FAR 14.404-1(c)(6) permits cancellation if the contracting officer determines in writing that "[a]ll otherwise acceptable bids received are at unreasonable prices." A determination of price unreasonableness may be based upon a comparison of bid prices with such factors as Government estimates, past procurement history, current market conditions, or any other relevant factors, *Bay Cities Refuse Serv., Inc.*, Comp. Gen. Dec. B-250807, 93-1 CPD ¶ 151 (solicitation was canceled because all bids were unreasonably high compared with the independent Government estimate); *Omega Container, Inc.*, Comp. Gen. Dec. B-206858.2, 82-2 CPD ¶ 475 (agency properly compared Omega's small business bid prices with Government estimates, the bid prices of an ineligible bidder, and past procurement prices of the item). Similarly, in *Logistics Int'l, Inc.*, Comp. Gen. Dec. B-254810, 94-1 CPD ¶ 28, a contracting officer properly compared an incumbent large business contractor's price for similar contracts with small business bids and found that the small business bids were unreasonable.

Cancellation is a proper exercise of agency discretion where bids exceed Government estimates, even where the low responsible bid was as little as 7.2 percent greater than the Government estimate, *Building Maintenance Specialists, Inc.*, Comp. Gen. Dec. B-186441, 76-2 CPD ¶ 233. See *Kinetic Structures Corp. v. United States*, 6 Cl. Ct. 387 (1984) (court affirmed a cancellation where the sole bidder's price was 27 percent above the Government estimate); *J. Morris & Assocs.*, Comp. Gen. Dec. B-256840, 94-2 CPD ¶ 47 (cancellation proper where low bid exceeded the Government estimate by 23 percent). See also *Photo Data, Inc.*, Comp. Gen. Dec. B-208272, 83-1 CPD ¶ 281, where cancellation was found proper when Photo's bid was more than two times the Government estimate for in-house performance, three times the bid prices received on the original solicitation, and well in excess of unit prices obtained for other comparable work.

A bid submitted by a commercial concern may be unreasonably high if the marketplace, which includes nonprofit associations, can satisfy the Government's needs for substantially less, *International Alliance of Sports Officials*, 63 Comp. Gen. 162 (B-210491), 84-1 CPD ¶ 63 (where nonprofit organization could perform for 30 percent less). The Comptroller General stated at 165:

> We agree with the Army that whether a bid is unreasonable does not depend on whether that bidder can account for every element in its bid price and can demonstrate that its price does not include exorbitant markups. In other words, a bidder's price may accurately reflect the costs unique to it plus a moderate profit and yet not be reasonable if the Government can obtain the same supplies or services from the marketplace for substantially less. Here, it is clear that officiating services are available from several sources other than IASO at prices substantially less than what IASO bid. In determining what it reasonably should expect to pay in the Savannah area for sports officiating services, we do not see how the Army could ignore the existence of local organizations offering to perform the same services at IASO for approximately 30 percent less.

A determination of unreasonable price will be sustained barring bad faith or fraud, *California Shorthand Reporting*, Comp. Gen. Dec. B-250302.2, 93-1 CPD ¶ 202. In *Stewart-Thomas Indus., Inc.*, Comp. Gen. Dec. B-196295, 80-1 CPD ¶ 175, the contracting officer asked a prior supplier to explain its failure to bid. The supplier responded by offering a price 40 percent lower than the lowest bidder. In discussing the propriety of the contracting officer's cancellation of the invitation, the Comptroller stated:

> Stewart-Thomas [low bidder] believes that any award to other than itself at its bid price would be improper because the actions of the contracting activity constituted an impermissible auction. After bids were opened and prices disclosed, the activity, in essence, allegedly attempted to find firms which could offer better prices, notwithstanding the fact that 80 firms had already been solicited on the original solicitation and only seven cared to bid. *Stewart-Thomas*, citing *Interscience Systems, Inc.*, 59 Comp. Gen. 68 (B-194497), 79-2 CPD ¶ 306, states the activity not only improperly permitted a potential bidder to possibly adjust its price knowing the prices offered by other parties, but it also gave a bidder who had not bothered to bid originally a second bite at the procurement.

* * *

> The contracting activity's purpose in contacting the prior contractor was not to require a bid from it, but only to ascertain the validity of the former prices in the current market. In the circumstances, we consider the action proper. Although any cancellation for unreasonable prices may result in nonbidders having another chance to bid (and with the knowledge of the prior bid prices), the competition the second time also provides those bidders who bid unreasonable prices the first time another opportunity to bid as well and this time at reasonable prices.

In some instances, rejected bids are used as the standard of reasonableness. See *Sigma West Corp.*, Comp. Gen. Dec. B-247916, 92-2 CPD ¶ 31 (agency reasonably found the low responsive bid unreasonably high when nonresponsive bid was 12.5 percent lower and the defect of the nonresponsive bid had a negligible impact on price); *Dutra/AmClyde (J.V.)*, Comp. Gen. Dec. B-249364.2, 92-2 CPD ¶ 453 (Government estimate and nonresponsive bid were used to determine that bid prices were unreasonable); *Colonial Ford Truck Sales, Inc.*, Comp. Gen. Dec. B-179926, 74-1 CPD ¶ 80 (determination that the low responsive bid was unreasonably high was supported by a 13 percent lower nonresponsive bid even though the Government had paid higher prices in three of five previous procurements); and *Hercules Demolition Corp.*, Comp. Gen. Dec. B-186411, 76-2 CPD ¶ 173 (even though the only responsive bid was within the Government estimate, cancellation was permitted because the bid was 36 percent higher than an "unacceptable" bid).

h. Miscellaneous

Compelling reasons to cancel the IFB have been found where the agency discovered after bid opening that a similar item was on the Federal Supply Schedule from which the agency was required to make its purchases, *Raymond Corp.*, Comp. Gen. Dec. B-246410, 92-1 CPD ¶ 252; *Security Management Assocs.*, Comp. Gen. Dec. B-214186, 84-2 CPD ¶ 83; where the agency failed to include required wage determination provision in the solicitation, *Dismantlement & Envtl. Management Co.*, Comp. Gen. Dec. B-257632, 94-2 CPD ¶ 151 (Service Contract Act); *Sunspot Garden Ctr. & Country Craft Gift Shop*, Comp. Gen. Dec. B-237065.2, 90-1 CPD ¶ 224 (Davis-Bacon); *Logistical Support, Inc.*, Comp. Gen. Dec. B-212689.3, 84-1 CPD ¶ 191 (Service Contract Act); where the solicitation violates a statute, *Pavel Enters., Inc.*, Comp. Gen. Dec. B-249332, 92-2 CPD ¶ 330; where improper set-aside provisions were included in the IFB, *Midland Transp., Co.*, Comp. Gen. Dec. B-201319, 81-2 CPD ¶ 89; where the agency, although required to do so, did not set the procurement aside, *Baker Support Servs., Inc.*, Comp. Gen. Dec. B-256192.3, 95-1 CPD ¶ 75; *Ryon, Inc.*, Comp. Gen. Dec. B-256752.2, 94-2 CPD ¶ 163; where the completion of another construction project would allow the Air Force to continue its missions without disruption, *S. Sys. Corp.*, Comp. Gen. Dec. B-259827, 95-1 CPD ¶ 221; where delays in completing another construction project made installation of fire sprinkler system impractical, *Gaffny Plumbing & Heating Corp.*, Comp. Gen. Dec. B-209815, 83-1 CPD ¶ 648; where, because of delay in award, the work could not be completed within the Government preferred time, 53 Comp. Gen. 92 (B-178106) (1973); where the Government was unable to timely furnish required Government-furnished material and equipment, *Aul Instruments, Inc.*, Comp. Gen. Dec. B-195887, 80-1 CPD ¶ 98; *Monarch Enters., Inc.*, Comp. Gen. Dec. B-201688, 81-1 CPD ¶ 483; where an "or equal" component of a "brand name or equal" clause was inadvertently omitted, *Seaward Int'l, Inc.*, Comp. Gen. Dec. B-199040, 81-1 CPD ¶ 23; and where inconsistent provisions rendered performance impossible, *Champion Structure Co.*, Comp. Gen. Dec. B-198863, 80-2 CPD ¶ 291.

Occasionally bidders protest an agency's decision to go forward with the solicitation. If the Comptroller General agrees that a compelling reason exists and disagrees with the agency's decision not to cancel, the Comptroller General will recommend cancellation, *Gourmet Distribs.*, Comp. Gen. Dec. B-259083, 95-1 CPD ¶ 130 (agency misclassified the invitation in the *Commerce Business Daily* (CBD)); *Respiratory & Convalescent Specialties, Inc.*, Comp. Gen. Dec. B-255176, 94-1 CPD ¶ 101 (IFB failed to identify an evaluation factor and failed to provide estimates for an item); *Duramed Homecare*, 71 Comp. Gen. 193 (B-245766) 92-1 CPD ¶ 126 (requirements in the IFB were 12 times the amount of the agency's actual past use); *Bartomeli Co.*, 71 Comp. Gen. 237 (B-246060), 92-1 CPD ¶ 170 (protester's bid was prematurely opened and disclosed); *Elrich Constr. Co.*, Comp. Gen. Dec. B-187726, 77-1 CPD ¶ 105 (no quantity estimates were specified in a requirement-type IFB).

2. Reasons for Cancellation — Not Compelling

Even though competition is somewhat flawed, the defects may not be sufficiently compelling to call for cancellation.

a. No Prejudice and Low Bidder Meets Agency's Needs

Cancellation after bid opening is generally inappropriate where an IFB or specification defect did not cause any competitive prejudice and an award under the solicitation would serve the actual needs of the Government, *Canadian Commercial Corp.*, Comp. Gen. Dec. B-255642, 94-1 CPD ¶ 202 (no bidder prejudiced where an allegedly ambiguous provision only had one reasonable interpretation); *Sierra Forest Prods.*, Comp. Gen. Dec. B-245393, 92-1 CPD ¶ 4 (failure to send required form to prospective bidders did not prejudice bidders when they were on notice of the requirement and could have obtained a copy of the missing form); *Richard Hoffman Corp.*, Comp. Gen. Dec. B-212775.2, 83-2 CPD ¶ 656 (solicitation was ambiguous regarding pricing of informational items but no bidder was misled); *American Mut. Protective Bureau*, 62 Comp. Gen. 354 (B-209192), 83-1 CPD ¶ 469 (IFB ambiguous but no prejudice where all six bidders correctly computed their bids); *Tennessee Valley Serv. Co. — Recons.*, Comp. Gen. Dec. B-188771, 77-2 CPD ¶ 241 (no bidder prejudiced by having the contracting officer multiply the unit prices by the applicable estimated quantities to determine the low bidder). See also *Twehous Excavating Co.*, Comp. Gen. Dec. B-208189, 83-1 CPD ¶ 42, where the solicitation did not fully describe the mathematical calculations for one of 32 items but the simple calculation was obvious. The Comptroller General stated:

> The fact that some terms of an invitation are in some way deficient does not, of itself, constitute a compelling reason to cancel. Our Office generally regards cancellation after opening as inappropriate when other bidders would not be prejudiced by an award under the ostensibly deficient solicitation.

In *Immigration & Naturalization Serv.*, Comp. Gen. Dec. B-182949, 75-1 CPD ¶ 165, the Comptroller General indicated that cancellation for ambiguous specifications would not be appropriate

> if no prejudice would result from an award to an otherwise responsive bidder whose bid would meet the Government's actual needs, i.e., (1) where there was no reason to believe that additional firms would bid on revised specifications included in a resolicitation or that the original bidders would have offered any different equipment on a resolicitation . . . and (2) that there was in any event only one responsive bidder.

A solicitation was improperly canceled on the grounds of a purported ambiguity where evidence available from the offeror's cost proposals that tended to disprove the ambiguity was ignored, *Apex Int'l Management Servs., Inc.*, 60 Comp. Gen. 172 (B-200008), 81-1 CPD ¶ 24.

b. Potential Competitor Not Solicited

Failure to solicit a potential competitor is not a compelling reason for cancellation if competition is otherwise adequate, prices are reasonable, the agency does not deliberately exclude a bidder, and it complies with all regulations governing the distribution and advertisement of a solicitation, *Eagle Creek Archaeological Servs., Inc.*, Comp. Gen. Dec. B-258480, 95-1 CPD ¶ 43 (no compelling reason for cancellation when agency did not deliberately exclude bidder, and the record showed there was adequate competition and reasonable prices); *Energy Management Sys.*, Comp. Gen. Dec. B-258391, 94-2 CPD ¶ 208 (no showing that agency deliberately excluded a bidder from competition where bidder failed to review the CBD and to apply for inclusion on the mailing list); *Cinema Color Group*, Comp. Gen. Dec. B-210666, 83-2 CPD ¶ 257 (advertising procurement under heading of "photographic equipment" not shown to be a deliberate attempt to preclude protester from bidding). In 52 Comp. Gen. 281 (B-176839) (1972), a potential supplier was precluded from bidding because the IFB amendment, which advanced the bid opening 10 days, was sent to San Benito, California, rather than San Benito, Texas. The Comptroller General stated at 283:

> We have also held that the propriety of a particular procurement must be determined from the Government's point of view upon the basis of whether adequate competition and reasonable prices were obtained, not upon whether every possible prospective bidder was afforded an opportunity to bid. . . . While it is unfortunate that your address was not correctly recorded on the bidders list, we do not find anything in the record to indicate that the error was other than an inadvertent mistake, or that it was occasioned by any deliberate attempt on the part of the procuring personnel to exclude you from participating in the procurement. In such circumstances, although we recognize the resulting hardship which may be experienced by your firm, it has been our consistent position that the nonreceipt or delay in receiving bidding documents by a prospective bidder does not require cancellation or amendment of the invitation.

However, where an agency fails to comply with the statutory and regulatory requirements regarding distribution of solicitations, cancellation is appropriate, *Kertzman Contracting, Inc.*, Comp. Gen. Dec. B-259461.2, 95-1 CPD ¶ 226 (agency failed to send amendment to a bidder on the mailing list); *Telos Field Eng'g*, Comp. Gen. Dec. B-257747, 94-2 CPD ¶ 172 (agency failed to obtain "full and open" competition when it only provided copies of the solicitation to four firms considered to be industry leaders). In addition, an agency's failure to solicit an incumbent contractor may not satisfy "full and open" competition as required by the Competition in Contracting Act, *Pratt & Lambert, Inc.*, Comp. Gen. Dec. B-245537, 92-1 CPD ¶ 48; *Kimber Guard & Patrol, Inc.*, Comp. Gen. Dec. B-248920, 92-2 CPD ¶ 220.

c. *Increases in Quantity Only*

Where the Government determines that additional quantities of the same item are needed after bid opening, cancellation is not generally deemed compelling. FAR 14.404-1(a)(3) provides:

> As a general rule, after the opening of bids, an invitation should not be canceled and resolicited due solely to increased requirements for the items being acquired. Award should be made on the initial invitation for bids and the additional quantity should be treated as a new acquisition.

FAR 14.404-1(a)(3) only applies in cases where an agency is procuring products and not where the agency is procuring services, *Bangar Contractors Corp.*, Comp. Gen. Dec. B-240071, 90-2 CPD ¶ 295; *Bill McCann*, Comp. Gen. Dec. B-234199.2, 89-1 CPD ¶ 554. The Comptroller General has discussed this regulation on several occasions but has not decided any case where increases in quantity alone were at issue, *Dyneteria, Inc.*, Comp. Gen. Dec. B-211525.2, 84-2 CPD ¶ 484 (closely interrelated aspects of fuel management operations made the above provision inapplicable). See *Genco Tool & Eng'g Co.*, 61 Comp. Gen. 281 (B-204582), 82-1 CPD ¶ 175 (insufficient funds were also at issue); and *ABC Demolition Corp.*, Comp. Gen. Dec. B-192111, 78-2 CPD ¶ 339 (change in agency needs involved additional performance of a different nature than that required under the solicitation).

3. *Partial Cancellation*

There are situations after bid opening where partial cancellation of the solicitation is justified. In *Hampton Metropolitan Oil Co.*, Comp. Gen. Dec. B-186030, 76-2 CPD ¶ 471, the Comptroller General stated:

> [W]e believe the provisions of ASPR 2-404.1(b) [now FAR 14.404-1(b)], which merely refer to cancellation of an IFB, must be read as permitting cancellation of either all or a portion of the IFB, as may be required by the circumstances, and not as requiring cancellation of the IFB *in toto* or not at all.

Where the solicitation includes, but is not limited to, work for an item that the agency does not need, or where there is a solicitation defect that directly affects only a portion of the invitation's bid items, and the Government has the right under the solicitation to accept any item or groups of items, the contracting officer should cancel only the affected portion of the IFB, *Telemarc, Inc.*, Comp. Gen. Dec. B-242339, 91-1 CPD ¶ 375 (ambiguous specification for a line item of the solicitation justified cancellation of that one item); *Hartridge Equip. Corp.*, Comp. Gen. Dec. B-230039, 88-1 CPD ¶ 284 (cancellation proper for line item where specification for line item was defective); *Kan-Du Tool & Instrument Corp.*, Comp. Gen. Dec. B-210819, 83-2 CPD ¶ 12 (proper for Army to cancel 8,699 items and award 1,549 items to responsive bidders). See also *Adrian Supply Co.*, Comp. Gen. Dec. B-240871, 90-2 CPD ¶ 515 (partial cancellation appropriate where bid prices for line item exceeded Government estimate by more than 100 percent); *Duracell, Inc.*, Comp. Gen. Dec. B-229538, 88-1 CPD ¶ 145 (partial cancellation proper where agency could not legally award 40 percent of the solicitation to bidder); and *McGregor Printing Corp.*, Comp. Gen. Dec. B-207084, 82-2 CPD ¶ 240 (proper for GSA to cancel portions of two solicitations because of decreased demand and amount of space available in certain depots).

4. Reinstatement of the Solicitation

Although the FAR does not directly address reinstatement of a procurement after cancellation, FAR 14.404-1 does contain the following guidance on "completion of the acquisition after cancellation":

> (e) Under some circumstances, completion of the acquisition after cancellation of the invitation for bids may be appropriate.
>
> > (1) If the invitation for bids has been canceled for the reasons specified in subparagraphs (c) (6), (7), or (8) of this subsection, and the agency head has authorized, in the determination in paragraph (c) of this subsection, the completion of the acquisition through negotiation, the contracting officer shall proceed in accordance with 15.103.

> (2) If the invitation for bids has been canceled for the reasons specified in subparagraphs (c) (1), (2), (4), (5), or (10) of this subsection, or for the reasons in subparagraphs (c) (6), (7), or (8) of this subsection and completion through negotiation is not authorized under subparagraph (e)(1) of this subsection, the contracting officer shall proceed with a new acquisition.

The Comptroller General has stated that this provision only prohibits reinstatement of a procurement that was properly canceled. See *KAL Maintenance, Inc.*, Comp. Gen. Dec. B-225429, 87-1 CPD ¶ 207, stating:

> Although, as the protester points out, the FAR, 48 C.F.R. § 14.404-1(e)(2), does not expressly state that it applies only to IFB's which have been canceled properly, we think it logical to apply it only in that context, because the provision's purpose is to prescribe a second competition where the results of the first have been invalidated by some defect. It permits the government to set things right — through revising the specifications, for example — and obtain competition based upon an accurate statement of the government's needs. Here, the original IFB in fact was not defective (although for some time after bid opening the Air Force erroneously thought that it was) and it did result in competition from 17 bidders, including the protester. Since an award under the original IFB would serve the government's needs, a second competition would only prejudice those bidders whose prices have been exposed and afford the protester, the eighth low bidder, an opportunity to improve its competitive position. *See ADAK* [*Communications Sys., Inc.*, B-222546, July 24, 1986, 86-2 CPD ¶ 103]; *Woodson Construction Co. — Reconsideration*, B-221530.2, May 23, 1986, 86-1 CPD ¶ 483; *Suburban Industrial Maintenance Co.*, B-188179, June 28, 1977, 77-1 CPD ¶ 459. Reinstatement therefore is necessary to protect the integrity of the competitive procurement system by avoiding an unfair bidding situation after the bids were made public. *See ADAK, supra*; *Lanier Business Products, Inc.*, B-203977, Feb. 23, 1982, 82-1 CPD ¶ 159.

Thus, reinstatement is appropriate as a means of promoting the integrity of the bidding system when the cancellation was improper, *Bilt-Rite Contractors, Inc.*, Comp. Gen. Dec. B-259106.2, 95-1 CPD ¶ 220 (reinstatement was proper where IFB was erroneously canceled because agency incorrectly believed that low bid was nonresponsive); *U.S. Rentals*, 69 Comp. Gen. 395 (B-238090), 90-1 CPD ¶ 367 (IFB reinstated where apparent inconsistency in solicitation did not prejudice any bidder). However, where the agency's actual needs have changed since the issuance of the original solicitation, the Comptroller General will recommend resolicitation, rather than reinstatement, see *TWI Inc.*, Comp. Gen. Dec. B-202966.4, 82-2 CPD ¶ 487.

Upon reinstatement of the solicitation, bids may generally be revived, *U.S. Rentals*, 69 Comp. Gen. 395 (B-238090), 90-1 CPD ¶ 367; *Sac & Fox Indus., Ltd.*, Comp. Gen. Dec. B-231873, 88-2 CPD ¶ 250. This is appropriate even where bids have been returned to all offerors, if a record of the contents of the bids has been made. In *Baker Mfg. Co.*, 59 Comp. Gen. 573 (B-197016), 80-2 CPD ¶ 1, an abstract of bids provided suitable evidence of original bid prices and responsiveness. However, bids could not be revived in *L.V. Anderson & Sons, Inc.*, Comp. Gen. Dec. B-189835, 77-2 CPD ¶ 249, where no record of the contents of the bids was made prior to their return.

IV. MISTAKES

Mistakes are a major exception to the firm bid rule used in sealed bidding, *Refining Assocs. v. United States*, 124 Ct. Cl. 115, 109 F. Supp. 259 (1953). The process of bid preparation and submission is frequently hectic. Specifications and drawings must be analyzed, subcontractors' and vendors' bids coordinated, and costs estimated — usually in a short period of time. In such an environment, mistakes are common. It has long been recognized that it would not be fair for the Government to take advantage of a bid containing a mistake when the Government knew or should have known of the mistake, *Chernick v. United States*, 178 Ct. Cl. 498, 372 F.2d 492 (1967). See also *Pavco, Inc.*, ASBCA 23783, 80-1 BCA ¶ 14,407; *Black Diamond Energies, Inc.*, Comp. Gen. Dec. B-241370, 91-1 CPD ¶ 119.

This exception has been exceedingly difficult to administer. Once bids are opened and announced, low bidders may be tempted to assert that mistakes have been made in order to increase their price or to avoid award. Bidders that are not low may identify mistakes that, if corrected, would make them low. In all such cases, the integrity of the bidding process may be threatened if correction of mistakes is too liberally permitted. Hence, a sophisticated set of rules has evolved to deal with mistakes in bids.

The first section analyzes the types of mistakes that are covered by these rules. The second section discusses the responsibility of the contracting officer when mistakes are suspected. Finally, the third section reviews the actions that can be taken after it has been ascertained that a mistake in bid has occurred.

A. Defining Mistake

Relief is only provided for certain types of mistakes. Although the FAR is silent on this issue, the courts, boards, and Comptroller General make a distinction between *ministerial errors* and *judgmental errors* in granting relief for mistakes in bids. In *Ruggiero v. United States*, 190 Ct. Cl. 327, 420 F.2d 709 (1970), the court stated at 335:

> The mistake . . . must be . . . a clear cut clerical or arithmetical error, or misreading of specifications, and the authorities cited do not extend to mistakes of judgment.

The court also ruled that negligence by the bidder was not a bar to relief since in most cases where relief had been granted the bidders had been "guilty of egregious blunders." See *BCM Corp. v. United States*, 2 Cl. Ct. 602 (1983), pointing out that "the reasonableness of the mistake is not relevant" to the rules relating to mistakes in bid.

1. Business Judgment

Bidders make numerous business judgments in the process of submitting bids. They must assess the complexity of the task, determine the amount of effort required to perform the work, and decide whether to perform the work with their own forces or by subcontract. If their judgments in these areas prove to be in error, relief will not be granted. Thus, when a bidder makes a business judgment, it assumes the responsibility that the judgment may be faulty and is "taking a conscious gamble with known risks," *Liebherr Crane Corp. v. United States*, 810 F.2d 1153 (Fed. Cir. 1987). See also *Aydin Corp. v. United States*, 229 Ct. Cl. 309, 669 F.2d 681 (1982) (errors concerning the nature and costs of materials necessary to perform the work were mere "errors in judgment"); *American Ship Bldg. Co. v. United States*, 228 Ct. Cl. 220, 654 F.2d 75 (1981) (bidder did not fully assess the difficulty of the work); *National Line Co. v. United States*, 221 Ct. Cl. 673, 607 F.2d 978 (1979) (determinations of the adequacy of plant, equipment, personnel, and the attainable rate of production were mistakes of business judgment); *Wyodak Enters., Inc.*, VABCA 3678, 95-1 BCA ¶ 27,493 (underestimation of effort required to comply with contract requirements); *Franklin Pavkov Constr. Co.*, HUDBCA 93-C-C13, 94-3 BCA ¶ 27,078 (underestimation of square footage due to bidder's lack of site inspection); *Fan, Inc.*, GSBCA 7836, 91-1 BCA ¶ 23,364 (bidder used past experience to estimate the number of ventilation units needing adjustment); *EDC/MTI*

(J.V.), ENGBCA 5631, 90-2 BCA ¶ 22,669 (bidder made inaccurate assessments of the availability and cost of insurance); *Overhead Elec. Co.*, ASBCA 25656, 85-2 BCA ¶ 18,026 (bidder neglected to obtain prices from a supplier); *SCM Corp.*, ASBCA 26544, 85-1 BCA ¶ 17,783 (bidder knowingly used a low overhead rate); and *Superior Servs.*, ASBCA 28300, 84-3 BCA ¶ 17,547 (bidder failed to consider the costs of providing supplies and equipment).

2. *Clerical or Arithmetical Errors*

Clerical or arithmetical errors are the most common types of mistakes for which relief is granted. See, for example, *Paragon Energy Corp. v. United States*, 227 Ct. Cl. 176, 645 F.2d 966 (1981), *recons. denied*, 230 Ct. Cl. 884 (1982) (omission of one element of cost estimates); *McCarty Corp. v. United States*, 204 Ct. Cl. 768, 499 F.2d 633 (1974) (numbers transposed on bid document); *Government Micro Resources, Inc. v. Department of the Treasury*, GSBCA 12364-TD, 94-2 BCA ¶ 26,680 (reversal of discount and cost rates in offer preparation); *Allen L. Bender, Inc.*, LBCA 80-BCA-103, 81-2 BCA ¶ 15,435 (cost of several items omitted from recap sheets); *Michaels Constr. Co.*, Comp. Gen. Dec. B-257764, 94-2 CPD ¶ 176 (using incorrect number of square feet to calculate the unit price); *Pipeline Constr., Inc.*, Comp. Gen. Dec. B-256799, 94-2 CPD ¶ 21 (omitting a zero when transcribing from worksheet to final bid); *C Constr. Co.*, Comp. Gen. Dec. B-253198.2, 93-2 CPD ¶ 198 (mistaken use of macro computer command resulted in a misleading screen); *Columbia Pac. Constr. Co.*, Comp. Gen. Dec. B-207313, 82-1 CPD ¶ 436 (bidder divided rather than multiplied in making metric conversion); and *PK Contractors, Inc.*, Comp. Gen. Dec. B-205482, 82-1 CPD ¶ 368 (error in pagination resulted in failure to include estimated costs on one page of estimating sheets).

Relief has also been given for clerical or arithmetical errors made by suppliers and subcontractors. See *R.P. Richards Constr. Co.* Comp. Gen. Dec. B-258923, 95-1 CPD ¶ 103, where the Comptroller General granted relief for a subcontractor's typographical error, stating that the error "precludes the bidder from making a knowing judgment about its actual intended bid." See also *Chemtronics, Inc.*, ASBCA 30883, 88-2 BCA ¶ 20,534, where the board granted relief when the bidder relied on erroneous quotation from the only supplier of a particular commodity. But see *Triax Pac., Inc.*, ASBCA 41891, 94-1 BCA ¶ 26,380, where relief was denied because the subcontractor's price misquotation was obviously lower than any other quote received. The board reasoned that the bidder "assumed the risk of [the subcontractor's] mistaken . . . quote because it failed to investigate thoroughly the 'dramatically higher' . . . quote it received."

In some cases determining whether there is a clerical or arithmetical error or a mistake in judgment is very difficult. See, for example, *Ruggiero v. United States*, 190 Ct. Cl. 327, 420 F.2d 709 (1970), where the court concluded that failure to include an "all or none" stipulation in a multiple item contract was a clerical mistake because the price of one item made no commercial sense without the other items; and *JAL Constr., Inc.*, AGBCA 80-117-3, 81-1 BCA ¶ 14,850, where an omission of work in a subcontractor's estimate due to a misunderstanding between the bidder and the subcontractor was held to be a clerical error. In *Rockwell Int'l Corp.*, ASBCA 41095, 95-1 BCA ¶ 27,459, the board found it unnecessary to determine whether the selection of the wrong algorithm was a clear cut clerical or mathematical error or an error in judgment. Rather, it denied relief on the grounds that the "error" occurred in the use of a complex algorithm which was not "clear cut" and, therefore, did not meet the test for an arithmetical mistake.

3. Misreading Specifications

Misreading of specifications is not considered to be an error in business judgment when it involves the quantity or nature of the work rather than the effort required to perform the work. See *Walter Straga*, ASBCA 26134, 83-2 BCA ¶ 16,611, where the contractor's estimate was based upon an unreasonable but mistaken interpretation of the specifications. The board granted relief, finding the misreading of the specifications as to the quantity of items covered was not an error in business judgment. See also *Faulkner Corp.*, VABCA 2998, 90-1 BCA ¶ 22,507, where relief was granted when the contractor misread ambiguous plan headings and mistakenly substituted one for the other; and *BDF Tesa Corp.*, GSBCA 8307, 89-3 BCA ¶ 21,925, where relief was granted when the contractor mistakenly believed its masking tape would meet the military's strict specifications. Similarly, in *BCM Corp. v. United States*, 2 Cl. Ct. 602 (1983), a contractor who unreasonably misinterpreted the contract specification obtained relief because a mistake in judgment had not occurred. When determining its bid price the bidder failed to include a particular, identifiable portion of work and had not underestimated the work it thought was included. See *Derek & Dana Contracting, Inc. v. United States*, 7 Cl. Ct. 627 (1985) (bidder mistakenly believed that one part of the specified work would be included only when an addendum was issued); *WICO, Inc.*, EBCA 125-6-80, 80-2 BCA ¶ 14,790 (bidder based bid on obsolete drawings); and *Ralph Larsen & Son, Inc. v. United States*, 17 Cl. Ct. 39 (1989) ("unilateral mistake" when subcontractors misinterpreted specifications). For a case finding no mistake when the contractor's subcontractor misinterpreted the specifications, see *H. Fair Assocs.*, ASBCA 26950, 82-2 BCA ¶ 16,112. There the board concluded that the contractor had made a judgmental error in relying on the subcontractor and the subcontractor had made a judgmental error in "not examining all of the specifications and drawings" — apparently reasoning that they were so clear that the subcontractor would not have arrived at its interpretation if it had conducted a thorough examination.

No misreading of the specifications is found where the contractor makes a judgment as to the amount of effort or the cost that is required to perform the work. See *Northern NEF, Inc.*, ASBCA 44996, 94-3 BCA ¶ 27,094 (decision to use an employee at a lower wage than permitted by Service Contract Act wage determination); *Boeing Computer Servs.*, ASBCA 42674, 94-3 BCA ¶ 27,114 (decision to use fewer employees than required to perform work); *Klinger Constructors, Inc.*, ASBCA 41006, 91-3 BCA ¶ 24,218 (failure to include state tax in price); *Dick & Kirkman, Inc.*, VABCA 1545, 84-3 BCA ¶ 17,662 (assumption, on advice of a supplier, that a portion of the specifications could be ignored); *Technology Chem., Inc.*, ASBCA 26304, 82-2 BCA ¶ 15,927 (deliberate choice to use a cheaper, nonconforming material).

Failure to read and consider the contract specifications does not constitute a "misreading," *Liebherr Crane Corp. v. United States*, 810 F.2d 1153 (Fed. Cir. 1987) (failure to read 94 of 98 specifications was a "conscious gamble with known risks" and treated as an error in business judgment). See also *Minority Enters., Inc.*, ASBCA 45549, 95-1 BCA ¶ 27,461 (relief denied when contractor correctly read three golf course drawings but did not read fourth); *Electrical Sys. Eng'g Co.*, ASBCA 37147, 90-2 BCA ¶ 22,715 (relief denied when reprocurement contractor used bill of materials of terminated contractor but did not read contract specifications); and *Universal Constr. Co.*, NASABCA 83-1092, 93-3 BCA ¶ 26,173 (relief denied where contractor failed to read drawings along with specifications as contract stipulated). But see *Minnesota Well Drillers*, ASBCA 26097, 82-1 BCA ¶ 15,539, where the board found a mistake where the contractor failed to read revised specifications describing harder material to be drilled than that called out in the original IFB. The board stated at 77,045:

> [The contractor's] stupidity in bidding without reading the revised specifications does not forfeit relief because such foolishness or a variation thereof is common to most bidders who err in bidding and such conduct is of diminished importance in deciding whether to reform a contract. *Chris Berg v. United States*, 192 Ct. Cl. 176, 426 F.2d 314 (1970).

The board reached this decision partially on the theory that there had not been a mistake in business judgment because most contractors in this area did not read specification revisions.

B. Knowledge of Error and Verification

Although some mistakes are identified by the bidder, most of the controversy over mistakes revolves around the question of whether the Government should have identified the mistake. The rationale underlying relief in this situation is that it would be unfair for the Government to hold a bidder to a bargain when the Government knew of or should have discerned the mistake and called it to the attention of the bidder. If the Government appropriately notifies the bidder of a possible mistake or the bidder alleges a mistake, the bidder can request withdrawal or modification of the bid or can elect to stand by the bid as originally submitted.

If the Government fails to notify the bidder of a suspected mistake, it may subsequently be subject to claims for price adjustment, or the contractor may use a claimed mistake as a basis for avoiding performance obligations. To eliminate these problems the regulations impose verification requirements on the contracting officer. FAR 14.407-1 provides the following guidance:

> After the opening of bids, contracting officers shall examine all bids for mistakes. In cases of apparent mistakes and in cases where the contracting officer has reason to believe that a mistake may have been made, the contracting officer shall request from the bidder a verification of the bid, calling attention to the suspected mistake. If the bidder alleges a mistake, the matter shall be processed in accordance with this section 14.407. Such actions shall be taken before award.

The verification process must be followed precisely in order to assure the bidder fair treatment. This section first discusses the circumstances under which the Government obtains actual knowledge of a mistake or is held to have reason to know of it. It then deals with the adequacy of the verification process.

1. Knowledge or Reason to Know

There are relatively few litigated cases where the Government actually knows of an error and awards without adequate verification. One example is *Walter Straga*, ASBCA 26134, 83-2 BCA ¶ 16,611, where the Government project manager's actual knowledge of the contractor's error was imputed to the contracting officer. See also *Derek & Dana Contracting, Inc. v. United States*, 7 Cl. Ct. 627 (1985), where the bidder orally advised the bid opening official that certain costs were not included in the bid.

In determining whether the Government *should have known* of the mistake, the general test is whether a reasonable person, knowing all the facts and circumstances, would have suspected a mistake. See *Chernick v. United States*, 178 Ct. Cl. 498, 372 F.2d 492 (1967), where the court stated at 504:

> The test of what an official in charge of accepting bids "should" have known must be that of reasonableness, *i.e.*, whether under the facts and circumstances of the case there were any factors which reasonably should have raised the presumption of error in the mind of the contracting officer; among such factors are obvious wide range of bids, and gross disparity between the price bid and the value of the article which was the subject of the bid.

The circumstances that can put the contracting officer on notice are more specifically detailed in *BCM Corp. v. United States*, 2 Cl. Ct. 602 (1983), at 610:

> An oft-cited article, Doke, *Mistakes in Government Contracts — Error Detection Duty of Contracting Officer*, 18 S.W.L.J. 1 (1964) ("Doke"), delineates these general categories: (1) facially apparent errors, such as multiplication errors made when computing unit prices into total price; (2) disparity in prices among the bids; (3) disparity between the bid and the private government estimate; (4) disparity between the bid and the cost of prior procurements of the same item; (5) disparity between the bid price and, if the contracting officer knows it, the market value for the goods.

These rules are not applied mechanically, and no single rule is either necessary or sufficient to impute knowledge of error. Thus, the Government will properly be charged with knowledge only after a full consideration of all the circumstances, *Darwin Constr. Co.*, GSBCA 6590, 84-1 BCA ¶ 17,230, *recons. denied*, 84-2 BCA ¶ 17,356. See *Troise v. United States*, 21 Cl. Ct. 48 (1990), where the contractor purposely deviated from the contract specifications to arrive at its bid as it had done in a previous contract. The court held that since the bid was not out of line with the Government estimate and the other bids, the contracting officer did not have to "speculate as to the basis of the contractor's bid" because to hold thus "would make the United States an insurer of its contractor's mistakes."

The most common situation putting the contracting officer on constructive notice of a possible error is a disparity between a favorable bid and the other bids or the Government's estimate. In *Government Micro Resources, Inc. v. Department of the Treasury*, GSBCA 12364-TD, 94-2 BCA ¶ 26,680, constructive notice was imputed when the bidder's price of $864,482 was 62 percent less than the Government's lowest estimate, 31 percent less than the supplier's schedule price, and 33 percent less than the other vendor's comparison quote. The board rejected the Government argument that, based upon an audit report on a proposed contract of $130 million, it could expect large discounts on the supplier's list price. Constructive notice was also imputed in *L & D Indus., Inc.*, ASBCA 38239, 91-2 BCA ¶ 23,718, where there was an "obvious and substantial" disparity among the bidder's bid of $50.45, bids of $132.00 and $145.70 by the other low vendors, and a previous solicitation price of $157.40 received for the same item; *George A. Harris Enters., Inc.*, GSBCA 9888, 90-1 BCA ¶ 22,405, where the bid was over 24 percent lower than the next lowest bid and "the contract was not large or particularly complex" so should not have produced the disparity that it did; *Figgie Int'l, Inc.*, ASBCA 27541, 83-1 BCA ¶ 16,421, where the bidder's failure to include costs for packaging should have been noted by the contracting officer because all other responsive bids were from 43 percent to 82 percent higher than the bid, and the bidder had not significantly increased its price from that of a prior contract with significantly less costly packaging requirements. The Comptroller General has found constructive notice when there was a disparity between the mistaken bid, the only other bid, and the prior year's contract price, *Ace Window Cleaning Co.*, Comp. Gen. Dec. B-183380, 75-1 CPD ¶ 379; a significant variation from the average of all other bids (127 percent higher) and from the next low bidder (59 percent higher), *American Food Serv. Equip., Inc.*, Comp. Gen. Dec. B-181878, 74-2 CPD ¶ 83; a variation from the bidder's general pattern of prior bids and the market prices for that item, *Calumet Y Farm Store*, Comp. Gen. Dec. B-181284, 74-2 CPD ¶ 11; and when the only bid received varied 21 percent over the Government estimate, *Murphy Elevator Co.*, Comp. Gen. Dec. B-180607, 74-1 CPD ¶ 164.

Other factors in the bid may also place the contracting officer on notice that a mistake may have been made. See *Franklin Pavkov Constr. Co.*, HUDBCA 93-C-C13, 94-3 BCA ¶ 27,078 (constructive notice imputed where the bidder's estimate was based on 200 square feet of work and the contracting officer knew the need far exceeded that figure and the only other bid estimated 2,000 square feet); and *Carter Chevrolet Agency*, GSBCA 10142, 90-2 BCA ¶ 22,804 (constructive notice imputed where the bidder inconsistently priced vehicles with extra options the same or less than vehicles without options). Another example can be seen in *Connelly Containers, Inc. v. United States*, 7 Cl. Ct. 423 (1985), where, while a bid was only 5 percent lower than the other lowest bid, the disparity of individual bid prices should have alerted the contracting officer to the possibility of mistake. In that instance, the prices for shipping identical containers were higher for shorter distances than for longer distances.

Constructive knowledge will not be found if the disparity is insufficiently wide and there are no other indications that a mistake has been made. Insufficient disparity has been found where the bid is far below the Government estimate but is close to other bids, *R.J. Sanders, Inc. v. United States*, 24 Cl. Ct. 288 (1991) (no notice found where bid is 32 percent less than Navy's estimate but only 18 percent less than next low bid); *Electrical Sys. Eng'g Co.*, ASBCA 37147, 90-2 BCA ¶ 22,715 (no notice found where bid is 18.4 percent lower than Government estimate and 6.7 percent away from next low bid). Insufficient disparity has also been found where the bid is far below all other bids but is close to the Government estimate, *T.R. Orr, Inc.*, IBCA 3143, 94-2 BCA ¶ 26,865 (no notice found where bid of $37,750 was much less than only other bid of $59,711, when the Government estimate was $41,100); *AQA Sys., Inc.*, ASBCA 45051, 93-3 BCA ¶ 25,996 (no notice found where bid of $154,000 is close to Government estimate of $167,450 even though the only other two bids are much higher at $274,700 and $600,000). See also *Triax Pac., Inc.*, ASBCA 41891, 94-1 BCA ¶ 26,380 (no notice where bid was 1.63 percent higher than Government estimate, 13.78 percent lower than second low bid, and 14.94 percent lower than third low bid); *Edsall Constr. Co.*, IBCA 2450, 89-3 BCA ¶ 22,177 (no constructive notice found due to disparity of $1,540,000, $1,678,010, and $1,712,000 in bids); *Boeing Computer Servs.*, ASBCA 42674, 94-3 BCA ¶ 27,114 (no notice found where bidder underestimated manpower needed, because bid price of $12.8 million was substantially more than the Government estimate of $6.9 million); and *C.E. Wylie Constr. Co.*, ASBCA 25587, 81-2 BCA ¶ 15,427 (no constructive notice of a $10,000 error on a $6 million procurement).

Even in instances where the disparity may be sufficiently wide, if the Government can successfully explain the reasoning that led to a decision not to request verification, constructive notice will not be found. In *Hankins Constr. Co. v. United States*, 838 F.2d 1194 (Fed. Cir. 1988), a cluster of higher bids was explained with the theory of "high balling" from offerors that were not interested in receiving the job unless they would make a large profit. See also *Packard Constr. Corp.*, ASBCA 45996, 94-1 BCA ¶ 26,512 (bid was 13 percent less than Government estimate but contracting officer knew that in a similar previous situation the same bidder had bid below the Government estimate, had made no complaint of error, and had performed the contract); *Triax Pac., Inc.*, ASBCA 41891, 94-1 BCA ¶ 26,380 (Government explained that it believed the bidder had bid low to "buy in" or because it did not make a site visit); *Wheeled Coach Indus. v. General Servs. Admin.*, GSBCA 10314, 93-1 BCA ¶ 25,245 (Government's two-part price analysis search for errors was accepted even though a line item search would have discerned error); *Folgore Mobile Welding, Inc.*, ASBCA 33250, 88-3 BCA ¶ 21,172 (low bid partially explained because contracting officer knew the bidder was experienced, with excellent references, and that there had been a business slump in the oil industry); and *Singleton Contracting Co.*, ASBCA 26862, 82-2 BCA ¶ 15,994, *aff'd*, 723 F.2d 68 (Fed. Cir. 1983) (allegedly mistaken bid, only other bid, and Government estimate were $123,460, $247,000, and $98,000, respectively, but variations did not place the contracting officer on notice of a mistake because (a) the contracting officer reasonably believed the high bid contained errors, (b) the bidder "enjoyed a reputation of skill, integrity and competency in bidding and contracting," and (c) there was reason to believe that the Government estimate was adequate, although low, while the bidder's bid was "exactly on target.") But see *James R. Sloss*, Comp. Gen. Dec. B-180402, 74-1 CPD ¶ 53, where the Comptroller General was concerned that some explanations had the appearance of being created after the fact to win the protest. In refusing to accept a farfetched Government explanation, the Comptroller General stated:

> To rule otherwise would permit Government estimates to be rationalized away at any time a contractor made a substantial error, especially in a sole bidder situation, merely by evolving a possible hypothesis which might explain a lower bid. 48 Comp. Gen. 672, 676 (1969).

2. Adequacy of Verification Request

A contracting officer on notice of a possible mistake must not only request verification of the bid, but also disclose the particular reasons that led to the suspicion, FAR 14.407-3(g)(1). In *Klinger Constructors, Inc.*, ASBCA 41006, 91-3 BCA ¶ 24,218, the board summarized this concept, stating at 121,125:

> [T]he bid verification request should aim at informing the bidder of all the pertinent factors that indicate to the contracting officer that an error might have been made. The adequacy of verification will turn on an assessment of the reasonableness of the contracting officer's disclosure.

Absent such a disclosure, the request is inadequate, *United States v. Metro Novelty Mfg. Co.*, 125 F. Supp. 713 (S.D.N.Y. 1954). See *United States v. Hamilton Enters., Inc.*, 711 F.2d 1038 (Fed. Cir. 1983) (bidder not informed of large variation in manhours between its bid and Government estimate, 1,941 versus 6,402 hours, respectively); *BCM Corp. v. United States*, 2 Cl. Ct. 602 (1983) (the third low bidder was told neither of the 18 percent variation between its bid price and the Government estimate nor that the contracting officer was on notice of a possible misinterpretation of the solicitation); *BDF Tesa Corp.*, GSBCA 8307, 89-3 BCA ¶ 21,925 (verification request only stated that bid was too low without disclosing 70.7 to 79.3 percent disparity with other bids and a 10.3 to 36.3 percent disparity between bid and previous purchase prices for similar item); *Chemtronics, Inc.*, ASBCA 30883, 88-2 BCA ¶ 20,534 (form letter not adequate verification request where letter did not inform contractor of the gross disparity between its offer and that of the next lowest bidder or the Government's funding estimate); *Ardmore Constr. Co.*, VABCA 2026, 85-1 BCA ¶ 17,743 (request for cost breakdown without advising bidder of suspected error not adequate); *Manistique Tool & Mfg. Co.*, ASBCA 29164, 84-3 BCA ¶ 17,599 (verification request did not state a mistake was suspected and did not disclose wide difference in bid prices); and *Walter Straga*, ASBCA 26134, 83-2 BCA ¶ 16,611 (verification request identifying price disparity was inadequate where Government knew exact nature of error).

A verification request was found to be adequate in *Solar Foam Insulation*, ASBCA 46921, 94-2 BCA ¶ 26,901, where the contracting officer alerted the bidder to a disparity between its bid, the next two low bids, and the Government estimate. The board found the verification request adequate even though the contracting officer failed to note that the error was found in a particular column of the bid and mistakenly said that the difference between the bid and the next lowest was $32,699, where it was really $113,669. See also *Fields Roof Serv., Inc.*, VABCA 3147, 90-3 BCA ¶ 23,232 (bidder told of difference between its bid of $417,545 and next lowest bid of $460,000); *Tri-States Serv. Co.*, ASBCA 31139, 90-3 BCA ¶ 23,059 (bidder told that its bid of $694,000 was less than the Government's estimate of $779,983 for direct labor, and much less than the Government's total estimate of $911,187); *W.B. & A., Inc.*, ASBCA 32524, 89-2 BCA ¶ 21,736 (Government informed bidder that its overall bid was low and called attention to five specific areas: edging, storm drainage, grass cutting, trash pickup, and tree removal); and *Central Mechanical, Inc.*, ASBCA 26543, 85-1 BCA ¶ 17,711 (bidder advised of disparity between its bid and the Government estimate and that the bid was 10.2 percent under second low bid).

If verification is obtained but the contracting officer still has reason to believe a mistake has been made, a second verification request is required if the Government has not revealed all of the information to the bidder, *United States v. Hamilton Enters., Inc.*, 711 F.2d 1038 (Fed. Cir. 1983). In *Hamilton*, the verification request pointed out a disparity with the other bids and asked for a manning chart. After verification, a contract was awarded. The court held that a second verification request was required because the Government had not revealed that the bidder's estimate of manhours was significantly lower than the Government's estimate.

C. Action after Mistake Identification

When a mistake in bid has been identified, the bidder must determine what course of action to follow. The easiest course is to request withdrawal of the bid. However, in many cases the bidder may attempt to persuade the agency to correct the mistake. If correction will maintain the status of a low bidder at a higher bid price, this is generally the bidder's most desirable course of action. However, it raises questions as to the integrity of the competitive bidding process. If correction results in the bid no longer being low, it is tantamount to withdrawal. In some cases, a low bidder may request correction but also be willing to accept award at the mistaken price if correction is denied. Finally, bidders that are not low may attempt to correct mistakes in order to become low. This course of action is the most controversial in terms of its effect on the integrity of the competitive bidding process. All of these courses of action are discussed below.

1. Withdrawal of Bid

The power to allow a bidder to withdraw its bid is vested in "an official above the contracting officer," FAR 14.407-3(c). For many years, the regulations permitted withdrawal of a bid after bid opening if the bidder could prove the existence of a mistake by "clear and convincing" evidence, FPR 1-2.406-3(a)(3); DAR 2-406.3(a)(1). However, the Comptroller General followed a considerably more lenient policy concerning withdrawal after bid opening, generally permitting withdrawal even though there had been little more than a bare allegation of error by the bidder. For example, in 52 Comp. Gen. 258 (B-176111) (1972), the Comptroller General allowed withdrawal of the bid where the only evidence to support a mistake consisted of admittedly self-serving employee affidavits and unverified worksheets. This lenient withdrawal policy was apparently based on the rule that acceptance of a bid with knowledge of error does not consummate a valid and binding contract, *Alta Elec. & Mechanical Co. v. United States*, 90 Ct. Cl. 466 (1940). See also 36 Comp. Gen. 441 (B-129736) (1956), where the Comptroller General stated at 444:

> In undertaking to bind a bidder by acceptance of a bid after notice of a claim of error by the bidder, the Government virtually undertakes the burden of proving either that there was no error or that the bidder's claim was not made in good faith.

In *Texas Turbo Jet, Inc.*, Comp. Gen. Dec. B-195303, 79-2 CPD ¶ 117, the Comptroller General stated that withdrawal would be permitted if the bidder is able to make a "prima facie" case in support of the alleged mistake. See also *Murphy Bros., Inc.*, 58 Comp. Gen. 185 (B-189756), 78-2 CPD ¶ 440.

FAR 14.407-3(c)(2) moved toward the Comptroller General's practice by permitting withdrawal of bids even if the evidence of mistake is less than clear and convincing but still "reasonably supports the existence of a mistake."

Recent Comptroller General decisions have continued to follow this lenient withdrawal policy. See *H.A. Lewis, Inc.*, Comp. Gen. Dec. B-249368, 92-2 CPD ¶ 351 (withdrawal permitted where agency finds calculations used to allege mistake "make no sense under the circumstances"); *Weather Data Servs., Inc.*, Comp. Gen. Dec. B-241621, 91-1 CPD ¶ 185 (withdrawal allowed where bidder alleges mistake without any documentation showing how mistake was made); *McGeary Co.*, Comp.

Gen. Dec. B-230713, 88-1 CPD ¶ 586, (withdrawal permitted even though Navy's allegation that "mistaken" price was a conscious choice to bid low is found reasonable); *Southwest Marine, Inc.*, Comp. Gen. Dec. B-225686, 87-1 CPD ¶ 510 (withdrawal granted even where the credibility of worksheet used to establish mistake is in doubt and the only testimony was from interested parties); and *C.T. Lighting, Inc.*, Comp. Gen. Dec. B-214462, 84-2 CPD ¶ 102 (withdrawal permitted despite contracting officer's contention that evidence of mistake was fabricated).

FAR 14.407-3(c)(1) also permits withdrawal of a bid if the evidence of the existence of a mistake is clear and convincing but the evidence of the intended bid is not. This is the typical case when withdrawal is the only possible course of action other than contract award. See, for example, *American Block Co.*, Comp. Gen. Dec. B-235053, 89-2 CPD ¶ 90, where evidence of a mistake was clear and convincing because the bidder clearly based its bid price on the wrong type of item, but a discrepancy in a worksheet prevented the establishment of the intended bid. See also *Northwest Builders*, 67 Comp. Gen. 278 (B-228555), 88-1 CPD ¶ 200, where discrepancies in computer-generated estimates and printouts established a mistake, but because of wide range of possibilities, the intended bid could not be established.

2. Rejection of Bid

Although the FAR does not deal directly with rejection of mistaken bids, where it is clear that a mistake in bid has been made, rejection of the bid is proper unless it is apparent that the bid both as submitted and intended will remain low. FAR 14.407-3(g)(5) indirectly recognizes the possibility of rejection of bids containing serious mistakes in providing the following guidance regarding when to evaluate a bid as submitted:

> Where the bidder fails or refuses to furnish evidence in support of a suspected or alleged mistake, the contracting officer shall consider the bid as submitted unless (i) the amount of the bid is so far out of line with the amounts of other bids received, or with the amount estimated by the agency or determined by the contracting officer to be reasonable, or (ii) there are other indications of error so clear, as to reasonably justify the conclusion that acceptance of the bid would be unfair to the bidder or to other bona fide bidders. Attempts made to obtain the information required and the action taken with respect to the bid shall be fully documented.

The Comptroller General has recognized that this provision provides authority for the rejection of bids containing mistakes. See *Orbas & Assocs.*, Comp. Gen. Dec. B-255276, 94-1 CPD ¶ 139, stating:

> A contracting officer's decision to reject an apparently mistaken bid under the authority of FAR 14.406-3(g)(5) is subject to question only where it is shown to be unreasonable. *See Pamfilis Painting, Inc.*, B-237968, Apr. 3, 1990, 90-1 CPD ¶ 355; *TLC Fin. Group*, [Comp. Gen. Dec;. B-237384, 90-1 CPD ¶ 116]. Where it is clear that a mistake has been made, the bid cannot be accepted, even if the bidder verifies the bid price, denies the existence of a mistake, or seeks to waive an admitted mistake, unless it is clear that the bid, both as submitted and intended, would remain low. *Trataros Constr., Inc.*, B-254600, Jan. 4, 1994, 94-1 CPD ¶ [1]; *Atlantic Serv., Inc.*, B-245763, Jan. 30, 1992, 92-1 CPD ¶ 125. Acceptance of such clearly erroneous bids would be unfair to other bidders. *See* 51 Comp. Gen. 498 (1972); *Atlantic Serv., Inc., supra*; *Panoramic Studios*, B-200664, Aug. 17, 1981, 81-2 CPD ¶ 144; FAR § 14.406-3(g)(5). Clearly erroneous bids requirements. *See, e.g., Atlantic Servs., Inc., supra*; *Innovative Refrigeration Concepts*, B-242515, Mar. 27, 1991, 91-1 CPD ¶ 332; *Martin Contracting*, B-241229.2, Feb. 6, 1991, 91-1 CPD ¶ 121.

Thus, rejection of mistaken low bids is proper even if the bidder verifies the bid price. See *Trataros Constr., Inc.*, Comp. Gen. Dec. B-254600, 94-1 CPD ¶ 1 (bid verified where bid price on item would not even cover the cost to produce that item); *Suffield Serv. Co.*, Comp. Gen. Dec. B-245579, 92-1 CPD ¶ 54 (bid verified where a group of percentage markups were obviously miscalculated); and *Prince Constr. Co.*, Comp. Gen. Dec. B-213496, 84-1 CPD ¶ 159 (bidder orally stated that an error had been made but refused to furnish evidence and later verified bid).

Rejection is also proper when the bidder denies the existence of a mistake. See *DGS Contract Servs., Inc.*, Comp. Gen. Dec. B-237157.2, 90-1 CPD ¶ 162 (bidder first claimed mistake based on subcontractor error and then claimed that there was no mistake); and *MTR, Inc.*, Comp. Gen. Dec. B-216685, 84-2 CPD ¶ 457, *recons. denied*, 84-2 CPD ¶ 624 (bidder refused to acknowledge mistake but contracting officer concluded, on convincing evidence, that bid was grossly low).

Rejection is proper even when the bidder seeks to waive an admitted mistake. See *Atlantic Servs. Inc.*, Comp. Gen. Dec. B-245763, 92-1 CPD ¶ 125, where the erroneous bid was rejected even though the bidder tried to "stand by" the bid and accept award. This decision was reached because award would be prejudicial to the other bidders if the bidder's mistaken bid would not have remained low after correction. See also *H. Martin Constr. Co.*, Comp. Gen. Dec. B-201352, 81-1 CPD ¶ 268, where the Comptroller General stated that the contracting officer "must reject" a clearly mistaken bid even though there had been no allegation of mistake.

The last basis for rejection would permit the contracting officer to reject the bid in those cases where award might result in an unfair contract. See *Southern Cal. Eng'g Co.*, Comp. Gen. Dec. B-255945, 94-1 CPD ¶ 271 (bid rejected because it was much lower than all other bids and did not conform to specifications); and *Zeta Constr. Co.*, Comp. Gen. Dec. B-244672, 91-2 CPD ¶ 428 (bid rejected because of major misinterpretation of the specifications).

An unstated reason for rejection of bids containing serious mistakes, even where there has been a proper verification, is to avoid the risk of a subsequent claim for reformation based on unconscionability. See, for example, *White Abstract Co.*, Comp. Gen. Dec. B-183643, 75-2 CPD ¶ 98 (would have cost $5,500 to perform item priced at $100); *Yankee Eng'g Co.*, Comp. Gen. Dec. B-180573, 74-1 CPD ¶ 333 ($106,000 mistake on $199,669 contract not discovered through verification); and 53 Comp. Gen. 187 (B-178795) (1973) (bid 74 percent below next low bid and only 1/12 of next low bid for first article unit).

3. Correction of Mistake

The most frequent request of a contractor after discovery of a mistake is that the mistake be corrected. The precise facts of the procurement determine the rules that apply to such requests. Unless the mistake is an apparent clerical error (discussed below), the power to allow a bidder to correct a mistake in its bid is vested in the agency head, FAR 14.407-3(a), and is subject to the following guidelines.

a. Correction of Low Bid Upward

Where the low bidder seeks to correct the bid upward — but the corrected bid remains the low bid — both the existence of the mistake and the bid actually intended must be established by "clear and convincing evidence," FAR 14.407-3(a). The clear and convincing standard has been strictly adhered to in the case of correction. See 53 Comp. Gen. 232

(B-179084) (1973), where the Comptroller General stated that correction will be permitted if the bidder establishes by clear and convincing evidence:

1. That an error has occurred;

2. The manner in which the error occurred; and

3. The amount of the intended bid price.

This three-part standard has been used regularly by the Comptroller General. See, for example, *Pipeline Constr. Inc.*, Comp. Gen. Dec. B-256799, 94-2 CPD ¶ 21; *J. Schouten Constr., Inc.*, Comp. Gen. Dec. B-256710, 94-1 CPD ¶ 353; and *L.F. Leiker Constr. Co.*, Comp. Gen. Dec. B-238496, 90-1 CPD ¶ 453. FAR 14.407-3(g)(2) provides the following similar guidance:

> The request [of the contractor] must be supported by statements (sworn statements, if possible) and shall include all pertinent evidence such as the bidder's file copy of the bid, the original worksheets and other data used in preparing the bid, subcontractors' quotations, if any, published price lists, and any other evidence that establishes the existence of the error, the manner in which it occurred, and the bid actually intended.

Despite the skepticism evidenced by some contracting officers as to the accuracy of worksheets offered by bidders to prove the amount of a mistake, an agency cannot refuse a bidder an opportunity to demonstrate the amount of the intended bid by clear and convincing evidence, *Chris Berg, Inc. v. United States*, 192 Ct. Cl. 176, 426 F.2d 314 (1970); Comp. Gen. Dec. B-163284, Apr. 1, 1968, *Unpub.*

(1) Types of Evidence

Since the bidder must prove the amount of the intended bid price as well as the mistake, documentary evidence of the details of the original estimate must almost always be submitted. Such evidence is usually in the form of worksheets and other materials used during bid preparation. The Comptroller General has been quite liberal in accepting the validity of such materials. For example, a bidder was allowed to correct its bid despite erasures on the worksheets where the worksheet figures were corroborated by subcontractor bids and internal estimates for work intended to be done in-house, 51 Comp. Gen. 503 (B-174608) (1972). See also *H.A. Sack Co.*, Comp. Gen. Dec. B-278359, 98-1 CPD ¶ ___ (computer diskette containing a spreadsheet file dated on the date of bid opening and a statement that these were the original documents used in preparing bid were sufficient evidence to support mistake claim); *Black Diamond Energies, Inc.*, Comp. Gen. Dec. B-241370, 91-1 CPD ¶ 119 (worksheet confirmed the costs of omitted installation work and total corrected price for item (delivered and installed) was still less than Government estimate and in line with other bids); *BAL/BOA Servs., Inc.*, Comp. Gen. Dec. B-233157, 89-1 CPD ¶ 138 (correction allowed where the entry of one subcontractor quote for landscaping was erased and substituted by another lower quote when this price was omitted from final bid and it was very unlikely that this cost was included in any other cost); and *Vrooman Constructors, Inc.*, Comp. Gen. Dec. B-226965.2, 87-1 CPD ¶ 606 (numerous crossouts on the worksheet were allowed because they were corrections of obvious arithmetic errors or erroneously repeated figures, and the worksheet was otherwise in good order).

When the prebid materials do not contain erasures or other evidence of modification, correction has been even more readily allowed. See *Huber, Hunt & Nichols, Inc.*, Comp. Gen. Dec. B-271112, 96-1 CPD ¶ 246 (worksheets and affidavits established clear and convincing evidence of the mistake and the intended bid); *Severino Trucking Co.*, Comp. Gen. Dec. B-259080.2, 95-1 CPD ¶ 160 (comparison between three worksheets revealed that two were calculated by adding a 25 percent profit/overhead factor but the third omitted this factor); *R.P. Richards Constr. Co.*, Comp. Gen. Dec. B-258923, 95-1 CPD ¶ 103 (bidder offered $48,200 instead of $148,200 because the worksheet was not made to accommodate six digit numbers); *ACS Constr. Co.*, Comp. Gen. Dec. B-257775, 94-2 CPD ¶ 179 (worksheets and subcontractor quotes showed that bidder failed to include in final bid the price for steel hooks that were essential to contract requirements); *Southern Technologies Inc.*, Comp. Gen. Dec. B-256190, 94-1 CPD ¶ 321 (subcontractor facsimile demonstrated that bidder omitted costs for certain equipment by overlooking the relevant number on the facsimile); *Shoemaker & Alexander, Inc.*, Comp. Gen. Dec. B-241066, 91-1 CPD ¶ 41 (examination of worksheet and adding machine tape showed the bidder dropped a zero when transferring electrical work price from worksheet to final bid and bid $200,000 rather than $2,000,000); *Continental Heller Corp.*, Comp. Gen. Dec. B-230559, 88-1 CPD ¶ 571 (worksheets, project fee analysis, and adding machine tapes established transcription error of $450,000); *Riverport Indus., Inc.*, 64 Comp. Gen. 441 (B-216707), 85-1 CPD ¶ 364, *recons. denied*, 85-2 CPD ¶ 108 (worksheet showed that material costs had been calculated but not added to the bid price); and

Hughes & Smith, Inc., Comp. Gen. Dec. B-181140, 74-2 CPD ¶ 68 (presence of a mathematical error was plain on the worksheets).

In *Schoutten Constr. Co.*, Comp. Gen. Dec. B-215663, 84-2 CPD ¶ 318, a protester questioned the validity of worksheets supporting the correction of a mistake placing the low bid within 1.9 percent of the second low bidder. In finding that the criminal statutes partially protected the competitive bidding system from fraudulent evidence, the Comptroller General stated:

> Finally, Schoutten has, in essence, questioned the bona fides of the worksheets and has pointed out in this regard that they are not accompanied by a sworn statement as required under FAR 14.406.3(g)(2), 48 Fed. Reg. 42181 (1983). This section of the FAR provides that correction requests "must be supported by statements (sworn statements if possible) and shall include all pertinent evidence such as . . . original worksheets." First, we point out that we have found that the penalties prescribed by 18 U.S.C. § 1001 (1982) could apply to false statements or representations by a bidder. *D.L. Draper Associates*, B-213177, Dec. 9, 1983, 83-2 CPD ¶ 662. In part because of this statutory protection, we have sanctioned the use of handwritten and computer printout worksheets which are readily susceptible to tampering. *D.L. Draper*, B-213177, *supra.* Moreover, we have explicitly accepted the agency consideration of handwritten worksheets which contained numerous erasures. 51 Comp. Gen. 503, 505 (1972). Schoutten's misgivings about the bona fide nature of the alleged mistake and the worksheets were not shared by the contracting officer. Nor do we find that they are supported by the record which appears to reflect only a rather elementary error in mathematics. Accordingly, we find that the protestor has failed to meet its burden of affirmatively proving its case in this respect. *Grandville Electric, Inc.*, B-213406, Feb. 22, 1984, 84-1 CPD ¶ 222.

See also *Ogden Allied E. States Maintenance*, Comp. Gen. Dec. B-239550, 90-2 CPD ¶ 166, where the bidder did not use affidavits to prove mistake. The Comptroller General accepted this partially because the criminal code provided statutory protection against false statements or representations made by a bidder. But see *American Block Co.*, Comp. Gen. Dec. B-235053, 89-2 CPD ¶ 90, where correction was denied because the credibility of the bidder's evidence was in doubt. In that case, the bidder claimed the subcontractor gave a quote for the wrong item, the subcontractor claimed the bidder solicited quotes for the wrong item, and there were unexplained discrepancies between the original and corrected worksheets.

Even if the credibility of the evidence submitted is not directly questioned, if the documents are found insufficient, correction will still not be permitted. See *CRK-JVC/Shockley*, Comp. Gen. Dec. B-265937, 96-1 CPD ¶ 85, where the bidder offered varying explanations for the mistake and based its claim on two different base bid worksheets, neither of which reflected the actual base bid; *Special Sys. Servs., Inc.*, Comp. Gen. Dec. B-259865.2, 95-1 CPD ¶ 241, where the bidder did not explain how the bid was prepared or how the mistake occurred and the worksheets were not "in good order;" *U.S. Gen., Inc.*, Comp. Gen. Dec. B-245452, 92-1 CPD ¶ 8, where correction was denied because the only evidence provided was an undated worksheet containing a series of previously unsubmitted line item prices and where there were no backup documents to support the source of the numbers; *Imprints From the Past*, Comp. Gen. Dec. B-240447, 90-2 CPD ¶ 413, where correction was denied because of uncertainty between two conflicting groups of worksheets; *Gunco, Inc.*, Comp. Gen. Dec. B-238910, 90-2 CPD ¶ 46, where correction was denied because there were "unexplained inconsistencies" between two worksheets that confirmed the bid price and a third worksheet that seemed to establish a $100,000 larger bid under the vague heading "Additional Costs"; and *Edmonds Elec. Co.*, Comp. Gen. Dec. B-214063, 84-1 CPD ¶ 615, where the Comptroller General refused correction based on a "worksheet" prepared after bid opening to show the mistake that had been made.

The Comptroller General has treated computer evidence in the same manner as worksheets. In *Applied Constr. Technology, Inc.*, Comp. Gen. Dec. B-258426, 95-1 CPD ¶ 22, correction was allowed when the mistake was due to a computer spreadsheet program that had not been updated to account for an IFB amendment. See *PLC Constructors Canada, Inc.*, Comp. Gen. Dec. B-274697, 96-2 CPD ¶ 239 (correction allowed where computer spreadsheet showed how bidder made a mistake when it attempted to substitute one subcontractor's quote for its own estimate); *Interstate Constr., Inc.*, Comp. Gen. Dec. B-248355, 92-2 CPD ¶ 86 (correction allowed where computer spreadsheet showed bid of $600 for electrical work instead of an intended $600,000); and *Price/CIRI Constr.*, Comp. Gen. Dec. B-230603, 88-1 CPD ¶ 500 (correction allowed where computer spreadsheet, including handwritten notations, demonstrated how bidder broke down the cost for 13 items and then failed to submit a price for one of them). See also *D.L. Draper Assocs.*, Comp. Gen. Dec. B-213177, 83-2 CPD ¶ 662, where the Comptroller General following the same logic as in *Schoutten* found that the criminal statutes were applicable to computer-generated information and adequately protected the Government from deception.

The most common failure in meeting the clear and convincing evidence standard occurs in proving the intended amount of the bid. For example, a bidder was not allowed to correct a bid where it could not substantiate the additional overhead and profit claimed as a result of having omitted several subcontract prices from the bid price, Comp. Gen. Dec. B-176357, Aug. 29, 1972, *Unpub.* The bidder omitted $488,065 in subcontract items from the bid and substantiated that figure. It then added $20,000 for additional overhead and $30,000 for additional profit on the omitted figures. The bidder, however, did not normally use a fixed percentage rate in bidding overhead and profit, but rather derived those figures "after considering all of the other variable factors." Accordingly, the figures for overhead and profit were held to be arbitrary and not substantiated by the bidder's worksheets or records. A bid that indicated the bidder mistakenly bid on a quantity 24 times greater than that called for in the IFB could not be corrected by taking 1/24 of it because the bidder might well have included price reductions in its bid for the larger quantities, 49 Comp. Gen. 48 (B-165852) (1969). In *Three O Constr., S.E.*, Comp. Gen. Dec. B-255749, 94-1 CPD ¶ 216, correction was denied because the bidder gave inconsistent explanations of its intended bid price without supplying conclusive evidence to show which explanation was accurate. First, the bidder claimed a mistaken portion of the bid had to be increased by 40 percent for payroll tax; then the bidder claimed that the payroll tax had been accounted for, but that the mistaken portion needed to be marked up by 15 percent for workers' compensation. See also *4-S Constr., Inc.*, Comp. Gen. Dec. B-248090, 92-1 CPD ¶ 523 (worksheet indicates the price for mechanical work was omitted but presence of subcontractor quote for that item is not enough to establish intended bid because the bidder used different subcontractors for the job and might have done so again); and *L.F. Leiker Constr. Co.*, Comp. Gen. Dec. B-238496, 90-1 CPD ¶ 453 (blank line on worksheet for concrete work is evidence of mistake, but bidder's use of one cost analysis for concrete work at one site does not mean that the bidder would use same analysis to compute omitted price).

If there is a factor that prevents the intended bid from being established conclusively, but the bid would remain low even if that factor were included, the bid can be corrected. Where a bidder requests only the addition of direct labor and materials and does not request the addition of overhead and profit, the bid may be so corrected, provided that the bid would have been low even if overhead and profit had been included, 49 Comp. Gen. 480 (B-167068) (1970); 51 Comp. Gen. 503 (B-174608) (1972). If the addition of overhead or profit might make the bid as corrected no longer low, then such correction (without overhead and profit) will not be allowed, *Camp Lewis Tent & Awning Co.*, Comp. Gen. Dec. B-182047, 74-2 CPD ¶ 174. In *Western Alaska Contractors*, Comp. Gen. Dec. B-220067, 86-1 CPD ¶ 66, correction was allowed to include a missing subcontractor quote because work papers showed that it was on the spreadsheet but not carried over to the final bid. However, markup on this omitted quote was not allowed because a formula for calculating this percentage was not on the worksheet and a pattern for calculating this percentage could not be derived from examining other subcontractor quotes. See also *Severino Trucking Co.*, Comp. Gen. Dec. B-259080.2, 95-1 CPD ¶ 160 (correction allowed where bidder rounded up final number in original bid, but did not attempt to do so in corrected bid when even rounded bid remained low); and *Avanti Constr. Corp.*, Comp. Gen. Dec. B-229839, 88-1 CPD ¶ 262 (correction allowed for error in transcription between worksheets, but overhead and profits were not allowed to be added because the bidder originally used an estimate rather than the final bid to calculate these numbers).

The clear and convincing test does not require absolute precision in ascertaining the amount the bidder could have bid. In *Chris Berg, Inc. v. United States*, 192 Ct. Cl. 176, 426 F.2d 314 (1970), the court stated that an "uncertainty within a relatively narrow range is not inconsistent with 'clear and convincing evidence' of what the bid would have been." In that case, the low bidder sought correction, but the Government would not agree because the "rounding off" of numbers in the worksheets made it impossible to precisely ascertain the intended bid. The Court of Claims stated that the bidder had successfully established the intended bid price and that the "rounding off" was de minimis. The Comptroller General expanded this reasoning in *P.K. Painting Co.*, Comp. Gen. Dec. B-247357, 92-1 CPD ¶ 424, where the bidder was required to round down its corrected bid because it had done so with all numbers before correction. The Comptroller General stated, "In [these] circumstances, correction is limited to increasing the contracting price only to the bottom end of the range of uncertainty." See *Hampton Rds. Mechanical Contractors, Inc.*, Comp. Gen. Dec. B-257908, 94-2 CPD ¶ 201 (range of $35 in $350,000 procurement is inconsequential); *Precon Constr. Co.*, Comp. Gen. Dec. B-255294.1, 94-1 CPD ¶ 239 (despite several discrepancies between the worksheet and bid price and despite an admitted mistake that bidder does not attempt to correct, correction was allowed because highest in range is still $80,000 low in $1 million procurement); and *Red Samm Constr., Inc.*, Comp. Gen. Dec. B-250891.2, 93-1 CPD ¶ 178 (rounding up and down in bid calculation prevented determination of exact number of intended bid, but correction was allowed when bid would remain low even if always rounded up). See also *Bromley Contracting Co. v. United States*, 219 Ct. Cl. 517, 596 F.2d 488 (1979), where a mistake of failing to add overhead and profit to a bid was remedied by assuming that these factors would have been computed at the same rates used on previous bids.

(2) When Corrected Bid Comes Very Close to Next Bid

Sometimes the corrected bid price is extremely close to the next low bid. In this situation, there is a balancing required between the clarity of the evidence and the closeness of the bids. The closer the correction brings the bid to the next low bid, the greater the need for clear evidence, and the stricter the examination of that evidence, *Vrooman Constructors, Inc.*, Comp. Gen. Dec. B-226965.2, 87-1 CPD ¶ 606. This policy serves as a safeguard against bidders knowingly bidding low, declaring mistake, and fraudulently increasing their bid to an amount just under the second low bid by showing how the "error" was made, *R.H. Whelan Co.*, Comp. Gen. Dec. B-203248, 81-2 CPD ¶ 123. There is no specific percentage or dollar amount at which bids automatically become too close to be corrected, *International Serv. Corp.*, Comp. Gen. Dec. B-246159, 92-1 CPD ¶ 191.

If the evidence presented is sufficient, correction will be allowed even to the smallest of margins. In *J. Schouten Constr., Inc.*, Comp. Gen. Dec. B-256710, 94-1 CPD ¶ 353, correction was permitted to bring the bid within $700 of the next low bid in a $338,000 procurement because there was an obvious addition error on a worksheet, there was an affidavit from the worksheet compiler, and the worksheet was provided within 24 hours of the opening of bids. See also *Pacific Components, Inc.*, Comp. Gen. Dec. B-252585, 93-1 CPD ¶ 478 (correction was allowed to within 1 percent when mistake is obvious from review of erroneous quote from only subcontractor); *International Serv. Corp.*, Comp. Gen. Dec. B-246159, 92-1 CPD ¶ 191 (correction allowed to within 0.0235 percent when the worksheets showed that the bidder neglected to multiply unit price by quantity); *Vrooman Constructors, Inc.*, Comp. Gen. Dec. B-226965.2, 87-1 CPD ¶ 606 (correction allowed to 0.6 percent where 15 of 16 divisions were carried from a worksheet to the final bid, but one was not); and *Guardian Constr.*, Comp. Gen. Dec. B-220982, 86-1 CPD ¶ 224 (correction permitted to bring bid within 1 percent where misplaced decimal is obvious from adding machine tape); and *George C. Martin, Inc.*, Comp. Gen. Dec. B-187638, 77-1 CPD ¶ 39 (permitting correction of a bid to within $68,000 of the next lower bid in a $4.8 million procurement because the contractor's entire bid file of estimate sheets, subcontractor quotes, and personal testimony established the intended bid).

Even though correction would place the bid very close to the next bid, correction will almost always be permitted if the mistake is apparent on the face of the bid. See *Ogden Allied E. States Maintenance*, Comp. Gen. Dec. B-239550, 90-2 CPD ¶ 166, where correction was allowed to within 1 percent where transcription error was apparent on the face of the bid. But see 48 Comp. Gen. 748 (B-166748) (1969), where the Comptroller General denied relief where correction would be within $613 in a $272,000 procurement. The Comptroller General stated at 750:

> The correction of mistakes in bid has always been a vexing problem. It has been argued that bid correction after bid opening and disclosure of prices quoted compromises the integrity of the competitive bidding system, and, to some extent at least, this is true. For this reason, it has been advocated that the Government should adopt a policy which would permit contractors to withdraw, but not to correct, erroneous bids. We do not agree completely with this position since we believe there are cases in which bid correction should be permitted. We do agree that, regardless of the good faith of the party or parties involved, correction should be denied in any case in which there exists any reasonable basis for argument that public confidence in the integrity of the competitive bidding system would be adversely affected thereby. The present case, it seems to us, falls in this category.

When correction would bring the bid close to the next low bid and the evidence of the mistake and the intended bid is not clear, correction will be denied. In *RJS Constructors*, Comp. Gen. Dec. B-257457, 94-2 CPD ¶ 130, correction was denied to within 0.13 percent of the next low bid even though the worksheet showed that if it had been added correctly the bid total should have been $375,960 rather than $276,379. Correction was denied because the credibility of the worksheet was in question, it did not contain entries for overhead and profit, and there were many inconsistencies between subcontractor quotes and the bid submitted. See also *Metric Constr. Co.*, Comp. Gen. Dec. B-259573, 95-1 CPD ¶ 197 (numerous discrepancies in addition and percentage calculation prevent correction to within 0.28 percent); *Northwest Builders*, 67 Comp. Gen. 278 (B-228555), 88-1 CPD ¶ 200 (correction to within 1 percent not allowed because changes were undocumented and unexplained); and *Conner Bros. Constr. Co.*, Comp. Gen. Dec. B-228232.2, 88-1 CPD ¶ 103 (no correction to within 1 percent where worksheets and affidavits do not explain why certain costs were added and deducted from one subcontractor total, but not from two others). Similarly, correction was denied when the evidence was not clear in *Sam Gonzales, Inc.*, Comp. Gen. Dec. B-216728, 85-1 CPD ¶ 125 (amount of overhead not clear); and *D.L. Draper Assocs.*, Comp. Gen. Dec. B-213177, 83-2 CPD ¶ 662 (computer printout and unsworn statement not sufficiently strong evidence).

b. Displacement of Otherwise Low Bid

Stricter

A stricter standard than the clear and convincing evidence standard applies if correction would reduce the bid price and displace the otherwise low bid. FAR 14.407-3(a) provides that mistakes cannot be corrected in such circumstances unless both the mistake and the bid actually intended are ascertainable substantially from the invitation and the bid itself. This requirement makes it very difficult to displace a low bidder through bid correction. See *Armstrong & Armstrong, Inc. v. United States*, 356 F. Supp. 514 (E.D. Wash. 1973), *aff'd*, 514 F.2d 402 (9th Cir. 1975), where a discrepancy between the sum of unit prices and the total bid price was found to be insufficient evidence to support a downward correction of the final price displacing the low bidder.

For cases were the Comptroller General denied correction, see *Nabholz Building & Management Corp.*, Comp. Gen. Dec. B-274930, 96-2 CPD ¶ 196 (bidder claimed an ambiguity that let it to mistakenly include its bond costs under both a base bid line item and a bond costs line item); *Mallory Elec. Co.*, Comp. Gen. Dec. B-244699, 91-2 CPD ¶ 394 (clerical error apparent on the face of the bid was subject to two interpretations as to the intended bid, only one of which made the bid low); *Bullrun Mountain Honey Co.*, Comp. Gen. Dec. B-243325, 91-1 CPD ¶ 344 (bidder claimed a waiver of a 10 percent small business preference was an obvious mistake on the face of the bid); *R.C. Constr. Co.*, Comp. Gen. Dec. B-241176.2, 91-1 CPD ¶ 118 (bidder obviously overbid for an item, but it could not be determined whether the unit should be one square foot or 100 square feet); *Christos Painting & Contracting Corp.*, Comp. Gen. Dec. B-225647, 87-1 CPD ¶ 361 (bidder claimed line item entered in units of 100 as "19(19)" should be read as zero instead of $1,900); *Crystal Contracting Corp.*, Comp. Gen. Dec. B-223531, 86-2 CPD ¶ 433 (bid not corrected because "error" occurred in a schedule of deductions not appearing on the bid itself); and *Mayrant Constructors, Inc.*, Comp. Gen. Dec. B-215274, 84-1 CPD ¶ 617 (bidder claimed it was obvious that an entry of "449,668" was intended to be 49,668). The Comptroller General has used the same reasoning to refuse correction to break a tie bid, *W.G. James, Inc.*, 64 Comp. Gen. 561 (B-218230), 85-1 CPD ¶ 623.

The Comptroller General has permitted the use of rationales based upon past experience and other information in applying this high evidentiary standard. For example, in *Frontier Contracting Co.*, Comp. Gen. Dec. B-214260.2, 84-2 CPD ¶ 40, the bidder submitted an amendment to a bid as follows:

Base Bid			
Item 1	Add	Deduct	$133,752
Item 2	Add	Deduct	$60,000
Total Base Bid			
	Add	Deduct	$193,752
Additive			
Item 3	Add	Deduct	$84,000
Total			
	Add	Deduct	$277,752

The Comptroller General permitted the deduction of the figures, reasoning that the contracting officer had correctly concluded, based on the other bids and past experience with this contractor, that the only logical interpretation was that the figures were to be deducted rather than added. In *Allied Signal Avionics Inc.*, Comp. Gen. Dec. B-258457, 95-1 CPD ¶ 192, the Comptroller General permitted a line item for a two-year warranty to be changed from $50,268 to "no charge." This was allowed because the bidder had inserted "no charge" in 4 of 5 line items for the same warranty, had inserted "no charge" in 5 of 5 line items for the same warranty on an alternate bid, and the amount bid for that line item was the same as an item directly above on the bid sheet. See also *Concorde Battery Corp.*, 68 Comp. Gen. 523 (B-235119), 89-2 CPD ¶ 17 (correction allowed where bidder put total for line items 1 through 3 in line item 4 when line item 4 should have been an "inconsequential expense," and five out of seven bidders made this mistake); *George E. Failing Co.*, Comp. Gen. Dec. B-233207, 89-1 CPD ¶ 203 (bidder's entire bid package used to determine that bidder bid twice for three line items); and *Technical Support Servs., Inc.*, Comp. Gen. Dec. B-232488,

88-2 CPD ¶ 464 (correction allowed where bidder included a line item that was not supposed to be added to the total when five other bidders made this same error). But see *Electronic Space Sys. Corp.*, Comp. Gen. Dec. B-236006, 89-2 CPD ¶ 381, where correction was denied when the bidder offered two different prices on a basic and optional requirements schedule for the same item. Through prior dealings with contracts of this nature, the contracting officer determined that the higher price for the basic schedule was an often used bidding strategy.

In the case of errors in transmission by the telegraph company, the Comptroller General has relaxed the rule that the bid intended must be ascertainable substantially from the IFB and bid (where low bidders are displaced), 41 Comp. Gen. 165 (B-146295) (1960). However, the proof of the intended bid must come from the telegraph company's (not the bidder's) records, Comp. Gen. Dec. B-162627, Nov. 1, 1967, *Unpub.*; Comp. Gen. Dec. B-162740, Jan. 17, 1968, *Unpub.*

The most difficult application of this rule is in cases of a mistake in the extension of unit prices or the addition of subtotals. In most of these cases, it is not clear from the face of the bid whether the mistake is in the total price or in the subtotal or unit price. In *OTKM Constr., Inc.*, 64 Comp. Gen. 830 (B-219619), 85-2 CPD ¶ 273, *recons. denied*, 65 Comp. Gen. 202, 86-1 CPD ¶ 53, the Comptroller General permitted correction based on the internal consistency of the elements of the bid price, but stated the following general principles at 833-34:

> We have previously considered whether a bid may be corrected so as to displace an otherwise low bidder where there is a discrepancy between the correct mathematical total of lump sum and extended price items and the stated total of such items. In *DeRalco, Inc.*, B-205120, May 6, 1982, 82-1 CPD ¶ 430, we sustained a protest against the agency's determination to correct such a discrepancy as an apparent clerical error where neither the nature of the alleged mistake nor the bid actually intended could be determined without benefit of advice from the bidder. We noted that there was no one obvious or apparent explanation for the discrepancy. The difference did not suggest where the mistake might have been made and the stated total was not so grossly out of line with the other bid or with the government's estimate as to be patently erroneous. We found that the discrepancy could reasonably be attributed either to a mistake in totaling the items or to an incorrectly stated item.

See *Patterson Pump Co.*, Comp. Gen. Dec. B-200165, 80-2 CPD ¶ 453, permitting correction in such circumstances. Compare *Wilkinson & Jenkins Constr. Co.*, Comp. Gen. Dec. B-182687, 75-1 CPD ¶ 77, where the protesting bidder inadvertently entered a bid on the original bidding schedule rather than the amended bidding schedule, which had reduced the estimated quantity for one item. The bidder entered a unit price for the item and an extended price based on the larger estimated quantity. The IFB contained a statement that when there was a conflict between the unit price and the extension, the unit price would be considered to be the bid. Nevertheless, the Comptroller General did not permit correction of the extended price to reflect the smaller quantity of work because to do so would displace the low bidder. The Comptroller General reasoned that the intended bid was not ascertainable from the bid documents since it was not clear that the bidder would not have bid a higher unit price for the lower quantity. See also *Argee Corp.*, 67 Comp. Gen. 421 (B-230165.3), 88-1 CPD ¶ 482, where correction was not allowed when a discrepancy existed between the unit prices and the extended prices because neither the unit prices nor the extended total was out of line with the other bids or the Government estimate and there was no indication as to where the mistake occurred. Accord *Roy McGinnis & Co.*, Comp. Gen. Dec. B-239710, 90-2 CPD ¶ 251; and *Virginia Beach Air Conditioning Corp.*, 69 Comp. Gen. 132 (B-237172), 90-1 CPD ¶ 78. But see *J&J Maintenance, Inc.*, Comp. Gen. Dec. B-251355, 93-1 CPD ¶ 187, where correction of a unit price to reflect an extended price was allowed because the unit price total was clearly out of line with the Government estimate and all other bids and the extended price was not. Further, dropping a zero from the unit price and multiplying by the stipulated 12-month period would result in the extended price; and *Marann Inventories, Inc.*, Comp. Gen. Dec. B-237467, 90-1 CPD ¶ 89, where correction was allowed where the uncorrected unit price, if extended, would result in a figure of $1.6 million above the next highest bid.

c. Correction of Nonresponsive Bids

FAR 14.407-3 precludes the use of mistake correction techniques to make nonresponsive bids responsive. However, the Comptroller General has permitted limited correction of nonresponsive bids if the same standards used to correct bids which displace low bids are satisfied, *United Food Servs.*, 65 Comp. Gen. 167 (B-218228.3), 85-2 CPD ¶ 727; and *Fujitsu Imaging Sys. of Am., Inc.*, Comp. Gen. Dec. B-241733.2, 91-1 CPD ¶ 243.

Most cases involving successful correction of nonresponsive bids have involved invitations containing a number of bid items where bidders have incorrectly entered or omitted prices for one or more of the items. In *Slater Elec. Co.*, Comp. Gen. Dec. B-183654, 75-2 CPD ¶ 126, the Comptroller General dealt with this kind of situation, stating:

> Basically, even though a bidder fails to submit a price for an item in a bid, that omission can be corrected if the bid, as submitted, indicates not only the probability of error but also the exact nature of the error and the amount intended. B-151332, June 27, 1963. The rationale for this exception is that where the consistency of the pricing pattern in the bidding documents establishes both the existence of the error and the bid actually intended, to hold that the bid is nonresponsive would be to convert what appears to be an obvious clerical error of omission to a matter of nonresponsiveness. B-157429, August 19, 1965.

See also *MKB Constructors, (J.V.)*, Comp. Gen. Dec. B-250413, 93-1 CPD ¶ 50; *Werres Corp.*, Comp. Gen. Dec. B-211870, 83-2 CPD ¶ 243; and *Lyon Shipyard, Inc.*, Comp. Gen. Dec. B-208978, 82-2 CPD ¶ 287, where a bid was considered to be responsive and the omitted item treated as a mistake when it was shown that the cost of the omitted bid item had been included in the contractor's total bid price. Compare *Automated Marketing Sys., Inc.*, Comp. Gen. Dec. B-230014, 88-1 CPD ¶ 289, where the Comptroller General denied a protest that contended that the contracting officer should have permitted correction when the protester included no bid prices in its bid.

In *Wellco Enters., Inc.*, Comp. Gen. Dec. B-237512, 90-1 CPD ¶ 196, the low bidder neglected to include option prices for two of its block bidding quantities. Correction was permitted because the bid included consistent percentage increases from base to option prices. Correction was allowed in *Burnside-Ott Aviation Training Ctr., Inc.*, Comp. Gen. Dec. B-228937, 87-2 CPD ¶ 461, even though the low bidder had not bid the same price for the omitted device everywhere on the bid. This was allowed because the bidder had bid "NC" (no charge) for all other subitems under which this device was grouped and for all work to be done in the transitional period when this work was to be done. Correction was also permitted on similar facts in *Slater Elec. Co.*, Comp. Gen. Dec. B-183654, 75-2 CPD ¶ 126, even though the bidder had not bid exactly the same price for the item everywhere in the bid. The price of the item wherever found in the bid had only varied by $.02, and the Comptroller General reasoned this was a de minimis variation. This case may be an unwarranted extension of the exception permitting correction of nonresponsive bids. As long as the exception is limited to situations where the mistake and the bid intended are plain on the face of the bid, the opportunities for abuse are small. Once the exception is enlarged to include situations where the intended bid is plainly within a de minimis range, abuses could increase. Bidders would be given the opportunity to press for correction of the bid if award would be advantageous or plead nonresponsiveness if they did not want the award.

d. Clerical Errors

Clerical errors not apparent on the face of the bid are correctable to the same extent as other errors as examined in this section. However, for many years, the regulations have treated apparent clerical errors as a separate class of mistake that can be corrected with less formal procedures than other types of mistakes. Apparent clerical errors are the only type of mistake that the contracting officer can correct without deferring to the agency head or any other higher officer. FAR 14.407-2 provides the following guidance:

> (a) Any clerical mistake, apparent on its face in the bid, may be corrected by the contracting officer before award. The contracting officer first shall obtain from the bidder a verification of the bid intended. Examples of apparent mistakes are —
>
> (1) Obvious misplacement of a decimal point;
>
> (2) Obviously incorrect discounts (for example, 1 percent 10 days, 2 percent 20 days, 5 percent 30 days);
>
> (3) Obvious reversal of the price f.o.b. destination and price f.o.b. origin; and
>
> (4) Obvious mistake in designation of unit.

The difficulty with this guidance is that what is an obvious error to some may not be obvious to everyone. *McCarty Corp. v. United States*, 204 Ct. Cl. 768, 499 F.2d 633 (1974), illustrates the problem. The IFB called for itemized bids on three separate items of work and for a total bid. Bidders were instructed that they must bid on all three items. McCarty's president instructed his subordinate to bid $140,000 for item 1, $434,000 for item 2, $100,000 for item 3, and $674,000 for the total bid. However, the subordinate transposed two numbers on item 2 recording $443,000 rather than

$434,000. All other figures, including the total, were recorded as instructed. Morris, another bidder, included $155,000 for item 1, $389,000 for item 2, $137,000 for item 3, and $690,000 for the total bid. The actual total of the bid prices for items 1, 2, and 3 was $681,000 rather than the $690,000 listed. In reviewing the bids, the Government officials discovered the discrepancies in the bid totals and, without verifying the intended bid, treated these as apparent clerical errors, correcting the totals to reflect the sum of the individual items. This made the other bid total $681,000 and McCarty's bid $683,000. McCarty requested permission to correct its bid to show $434,000 as the amount quoted for item 2 and to leave the total at $674,000. This was denied, and the contract was awarded to Morris. McCarty protested to the Comptroller General and sought damages in the Court of Claims. The Court of Claims held that it was wrong to treat the mistakes in the McCarty and Morris bids as clerical mistakes apparent on the face of the bid. Instead, the mistakes involved a difference between the arithmetical sum of the amounts quoted on the three items comprising the bid and the amount listed as the total bid. It was impossible to tell from the face of the bid whether the bidder had made a mistake in entering one of the three item prices or in calculating the total. Correction of the Morris bid was not appropriate since the correction would have resulted in displacing the low bidder, and the "existence of the mistake and the bid actually intended" were not "ascertainable substantially from the invitation and the bid itself." On the other hand, the McCarty bid could have been corrected since the correction would not change its total price nor result in the displacement of the low bidder since the other bid would not be low without correction. See also *Armstrong & Armstrong, Inc. v. United States*, 356 F. Supp. 514 (E.D. Wash. 1973), *aff'd*, 514 F.2d 402 (9th Cir. 1975), reaching a similar result.

Even though the Court of Claims in the McCarty case stated that the mistake in that case was not an "apparent clerical error," the Comptroller General has continued to so label similar errors. See, for example, *Ace-Federal Reporters, Inc.*, 54 Comp. Gen. 340 (B-181451), 74-2 CPD ¶ 239, where one item of the bid was supposed to equal the difference between two other items but did not. The procuring agency and the Comptroller General treated this as an apparent clerical error and stated as a proposition that when one item is a function of arithmetic between two other items, the initial entries will be considered correct and the error will be in the arithmetic. This decision is inconsistent with both the letter and the spirit of the *McCarty* case. But see *North Landing Line Constr. Co.*, Comp. Gen. Dec. B-239662, 90-2 CPD ¶ 60, where correction in this situation was allowed to conform to the total price of two items. The intended bid for the mistaken item was ascertained by subtracting the price of the other item from the total price bid.

In *DeRalco, Inc.*, Comp. Gen. Dec. B-205120, 82-1 CPD ¶ 430, the Comptroller General sustained a protest against correction by a contracting officer and provided the following guidance:

> Prior decisions of our Office have stressed that, before the authority to correct a mistake under DAR § 2-406.2 may be invoked, the contracting officer must be able to ascertain the intended bid without the benefit of advice from the bidder. *See, e.g.*, 46 Comp. Gen. 77, 82 (1966) (only logical conclusion was that bidder had stated prices in reverse); 45 Comp. Gen. 682 (1966) (written words indicating a price 1,000 times the cost reflected in other bids and in prior contracts were patently in error; bid could be corrected based upon bidder's written figures); *Engle Acoustic & Tile, Inc.*, B-190467, January 27, 1978, 78-1 CPD 72 (obvious misplaced decimal point); *Edward E. Davis, Contracting, Inc.*, B-187132, November 17, 1976, 76-2 CPD 429 (obvious error in designation of unit). By contrast, we have held that, where the intended bid could not be determined from the bid alone, a mistake was not correctable as a clerical error under DAR § 2-406.2. *See, e.g.*, *Western Equipment of Oregon*, B-204125, December 8, 1981, 81-2 CPD 447 (intended bid could not be determined from the bid alone where neither the unit price nor the extended price was grossly out of line; *Sundance Construction, Inc.*, B-182485, February 28, 1975, 75-1 CPD 123 (intended bid could not be determined by multiplying the quoted unit prices by the correct unit).

A good example of a true apparent clerical error is found in 52 Comp. Gen. 604 (B-177368) (1973), where the IFB required bidders to enter prices for an initial quantity of oscilloscopes and four follow-on order quantities, and bidders were required to enter prices for each quantity. The low bidder entered one price for the initial quantity and three of the four follow-on order quantities. However, the bidder failed to enter a price for follow-on order No. 3. Since the bidder had followed a consistent price pattern, bidding the same price for smaller as well as larger numbers of oscilloscopes, it was held that the mistake could be treated as an apparent clerical error and corrected. See *Action Serv. Corp.*, Comp. Gen. Dec. B-254861, 94-1 CPD ¶ 33, where an entry of "$5,0005" was allowed to be corrected to "$5,005" when $5,005 multiplied by 12 months equaled the submitted extended total; the extended total of $60,060, when added with the other extended totals, equaled the total bid; and $5,005 was in line with other bids for this item and $50,005 was not. See also *Northwest Piping, Inc.*, Comp.

Gen. Dec. B-233796, 89-1 CPD ¶ 333 (correction of discrepancy between unit and extended prices is allowed where only the unit price was logical in light of the Government estimate and the other bids); *Technical Support Servs., Inc.* (correction allowed where bidder erroneously added $190,000 to bid for repair parts, and four other bidders made same mistake); *Military Waste Management, Inc.*, Comp. Gen. Dec. B-228862, 87-2 CPD ¶ 424 (correction permitted where bidder inserted its unit price on a per-housing-unit basis instead of the proper per-month basis); and *S.C. Jones Servs., Inc.*, Comp. Gen. Dec. B-226972, 87-1 CPD ¶ 583 (bidder failed to add a certain portion of the work into the final bid).

The Preparation of Bids solicitation clause in FAR 52.214-12 contains the following curious statement in paragraph (c):

> In case of discrepancy between a unit price and an extended price, the unit price will be presumed to be correct, subject, however, to correction to the same extent and in the same manner as any other mistake.

No protest has been found where a contracting officer relied on this statement in determining that a clerical error should be corrected. However, this provision would not appear to give any stronger weight to the unit prices than would be obtained by a thorough analysis of the bid documents.

4. Award after Unsuccessful Request for Correction

One of the parties may desire award at the original bid price after a mistake has been alleged or suspected. The Government may want to take advantage of the low bid, or the bidder may want to take the risk of performing the work at the original bid price.

a. Award Required

The FAR is not clear on whether award is required on the basis of the bids as submitted when evidence does not establish that a mistake has been made. FAR 14.407-3(d) states that the agency head "*may* make a determination that the bid be neither withdrawn nor corrected" when the evidence does not establish the existence of a mistake or an intended bid. On the other hand, FAR 14.407-3(g)(2) states that the contracting officer "*shall* consider the bid as originally submitted" if the bidder verifies that there is no mistake. Similarly, FAR 14.407-3(g)(5) states that the "contracting officer *shall* consider the bid as submitted" if the bidder fails or refuses to submit evidence of the mistake. Gross errors are excepted from this requirement. While it is common practice to award the contract on the original bid after the bidder has verified the bid, it is much less common for the contracting officer to award the contract if the contractor requests withdrawal of the bid. Award in such cases conflicts with the liberal withdrawal policy of the Comptroller General. The Comptroller has stated, however, that when the low responsible bidder submitting a responsive bid alleges error and seeks to withdraw its bid but is unable to make at least a prima facie showing of the existence of error, the firm bid rule prohibits the bidder from revoking the original bid, *Texas Turbo Jet, Inc.*, Comp. Gen. Dec. B-195303, 79-2 CPD ¶ 117. See also *Duro Paper Bag Mfg. Co.*, 65 Comp. Gen. 186 (B-217227), 86-1 CPD ¶ 6.

b. Award Permitted

In some cases, bidders desire to obtain the award even though a mistake has been established. The first section discusses the situation where the bidder seeks award of the contract at the original bid price if correction of an alleged mistake is denied. The second section discusses those cases where the bidder seeks award at the original bid price but reserves the right to assert a claim for reformation of the contract after award.

(1) Waiver

If a bidder seeks correction but is unable to prove the intended bid, it is ordinarily not permitted to then waive the mistake and be awarded the contract at the actual bid price. The rationale for this policy is that it would give such a bidder a competitive advantage if it could decide whether to accept the award after opening had exposed the other bids, 37 Comp. Gen. 579 (B-135272) (1958); 52 Comp. Gen. 706 (B-177482) (1973). Nevertheless, limited exceptions to the rule have developed. In early decisions, the Comptroller General ruled that if the bidder agreed to accept the award at the bid price notwithstanding that a mistake was established by clear and convincing evidence, the contract could be awarded at the bid price provided that the bid would remain low even if the correction were allowed, Comp. Gen. Dec. B-168673, Apr. 7, 1970, *Unpub.* However, the bidder had to request award at its original bid price if correction was not granted and the bid had to be clearly low before and after correction, 52 Comp. Gen. 706 (B-177482) (1973); *Teledyne McCormick Selph*, Comp. Gen. Dec. B-182026, 75-1 CPD ¶ 136. The Comptroller General reasoned in such cases that award of the contract to the bidder at the mistaken bid price would not result in prejudice to another bidder, *Arkay Products Corp.*, Comp. Gen. Dec. B-181596, 74-2 CPD ¶ 219. These cases did not make clear when the contractor was required to indicate its willingness to accept award at the original bid price if correction of the mistake was denied. However, it was clear that the contracting officer had no obligation to offer award at the original price if the bidder had remained silent on the issue. In a subsequent decision, the Comptroller General clarified this area by stating that when the bidder does not include with the request for correction a statement of willingness to accept the award at the original bid price, the contracting officer may either make award to another bidder or request the protesting bidder to accept award at the original bid price, *Guy F. Atkinson Co.*, 55 Comp. Gen. 546 (B-183842), 75-2 CPD ¶ 378. This policy permits the bidder to wait to see if the bid is corrected before deciding whether or not to accept the award at the bid price if it is willing to take the risk that the contracting officer will not offer award at the original price. See *Edmonds Elec. Co.*, Comp. Gen. Dec. B-214063, 84-1 CPD ¶ 615.

Clear evidence that the bid would remain low was found in *National Heat & Power Corp.*, Comp. Gen. Dec. B-212923, 84-1 CPD ¶ 125, where the requested correction, while not sufficiently clear to support correction, would have had to be tripled for the bid to cease being low. Compare *William G. Tadlock Constr.*, Comp. Gen. Dec. B-251996, 93-1 CPD ¶ 382, where waiver of a mistake was denied because the bidder's worksheets did not demonstrate the intended bid price and comparison of the allegedly mistaken item with the Government estimate indicated that the bid as corrected might not have remained the low bid; *C Constr. Co.*, Comp. Gen. Dec. B-242717, 91-1 CPD ¶ 540, where waiver was denied because the requested correction would have brought the bid within 1.2 percent of the next low bidder; *LABCO Constr., Inc.*, Comp. Gen. Dec. B-219437, 85-2 CPD ¶ 240, where waiver was denied because the correction requested did not contain all potential costs of alleged mistake and inclusion of such costs would have raised bid against next low bidder; *DSG Corp.*, Comp. Gen. Dec. B-210818.3, 84-1 CPD ¶ 476, where waiver was held improper because two conflicting sets of worksheets made it very unclear that the bid would have remained low; and *Hanauer Mach. Works*, Comp. Gen. Dec. B-196369, 80-1 CPD ¶ 178, where waiver was held improper because the addition of all potential costs of the alleged mistake brought the bidder very close to or even over the next low bid.

(2) Accepting Award with a Reservation of Right

Award without correction following an allegation of mistake may be permitted where the contractor agrees to accept award at the original price while reserving a right to seek reformation of the resulting contract. In *JAL Constr., Inc.*, AGBCA 80-117-3, 81-1 BCA ¶ 14,850, the board took jurisdiction of a contractor's claim for reformation under a contract that had been awarded at the original bid price with an understanding that the awardee would be permitted to present evidence in support of a claim for an increase in contract price attributable to an alleged mistake in bid. The board denied the claim for reformation, however, holding that the contractor had failed to establish the intended bid by clear and convincing evidence. See also *Fortec Constructors*, Comp. Gen. Dec. B-179204, 74-1 CPD ¶ 285, where the Comptroller General agreed that this was a proper procedure.

V. TWO-STEP SEALED BIDDING

Two-step sealed bidding is a procurement method that combines elements of sealed bidding and negotiation. The first step is flexible and resembles negotiation. In this step, the Government agency initiates the purchase procedure by publishing a Request for Technical Proposals (RFTP), which outlines the Government's requirements. Bidders then submit one or more unpriced technical proposals to satisfy these requirements, and discussions may be held with the offerors. Only those offerors who have submitted acceptable technical proposals are invited to submit step-two sealed bids on price. Offerors bid only on their own proposals, under rules similar to sealed bidding. Award is made to the low responsible bidder submitting a responsive bid.

Two-step formal advertising was suggested in 1957 during the course of the investigation of the Armed Services Procurement Act of 1947 by the House Armed Services Subcommittee for Special Investigations. The subcommittee recommended that the Air Force attempt a two-step procurement procedure in an effort to obtain more competition in military procurements. The Air Force agreed to test the procedure, and in 1959 the procedure was officially adopted by the Armed Services. In a series of decisions published in 1960, the Comptroller General concurred with the Armed Services Procurement Regulation (ASPR) on two-step formal advertising, 40 Comp. Gen. 35 (B-143277) (1960) and 40 Comp. Gen. 40 (B-143277)

(1960). In 1963, similar provisions were incorporated in the Federal Procurement Regulations (FPR).

This procedure was adopted at a time when sealed bidding was the statutorily preferred method of procurement but negotiated procurement was more commonly used for major procurements, and there was some Congressional dissatisfaction with this situation. Thus, two-step sealed bidding was seen as a means of satisfying the need for flexibility obtained through the use of negotiation while still selecting the winner through sealed bid procedures. The Competition in Contracting Act did away with much of the need for two-step sealed bidding by elevating negotiated procurement to the same status as sealed bidding procurement. However, the CICA still authorized the use of two-step sealed bidding by providing that the agencies "shall use the competitive procedure or combination of competitive procedures that is best suited under the circumstances of the procurement," 10 U.S.C. § 2304(a)(1)(B) and 41 U.S.C. § 253(a)(1)(B). The current regulations concerning two-step sealed bidding are set forth at FAR Subpart 14.5.

Two-step sealed bidding procedures offer certain advantages. First, it encourages competition for Government contracts. Contractors that might not have competed under the more structured sealed bidding process may participate in the first step of this process because alternative approaches in the design specifications are encouraged. Second, the price competition of step two makes the award decision public and easily defendable because the decision is based on price alone. Third, the FAR provisions for two-step sealed bidding are the only regulations that explicitly authorize a procedure for the submission of multiple bids by an offeror, FAR 14.503-1(a)(10). Fourth, step one allows the Government to take full advantage of industry's expertise and experience without the costly use of development or research contracts. In addition, the Government hopes to develop adequate technical data packages through the two-step procedure to allow subsequent acquisitions to be made by conventional sealed bidding, FAR 14.501.

Two-step sealed bidding also has disadvantages. The process is generally time-consuming and costly for the Government and for bidders who must draw up detailed technical proposals to meet the Government's specifications. The two-step procedure also may result in the procurement of a product that is not the best or most cost-effective overall because, in contrast to competitive negotiation, there are no tradeoffs between technical performance and cost in either step. Thus, in step one the Government might deem a less desirable proposal unacceptable because it is unable to evaluate how a cost savings would counterbalance the proposal's comparatively diminished performance or quality. Similarly, in step two an offeror will generally quote on its least costly design in order to maximize the chance of success even though a better value would be obtained if the Government obtained the more expensive design. Since the Government must accept the least costly proposal in step two, it may be compelled to turn down proposals that, though slightly higher priced, are markedly superior technically to the lowest cost proposal. Finally, the system allows a bidder to forbid competitors from examining its technical proposal by including a restrictive legend on the proposal. This raises serious questions concerning the public nature of the procurement. Despite the disadvantages, two-step sealed bidding can be an effective procurement technique.

A. Decision to Use Two-Step Sealed Bidding

The factors to be considered by an agency in selecting two-step sealed bidding are treated in FAR 14.502, which provides:

> (a) Unless other factors require the use of sealed bidding, two-step sealed bidding may be used in preference to negotiation when all of the following conditions are present:
>
> > (1) Available specifications or purchase descriptions are not definite or complete or may be too restrictive without technical evaluation, and any necessary discussion, of the technical aspects of the requirement to ensure mutual understanding between each source and the Government.
> >
> > (2) Definite criteria exist for evaluating technical proposals.
> >
> > (3) More than one technically qualified source is expected to be available.
> >
> > (4) Sufficient time will be available for use of the two-step method.
> >
> > (5) A firm-fixed-price contract or a fixed-price contract with economic price adjustment will be used.

(b) None of the following precludes the use of two-step sealed bidding:

(1) Multi-year contracting.

(2) Government-owned facilities or special tooling to be made available to the successful bidder.

(3) A total small business set-aside (see 19.502-2).

(4) A first or subsequent production quantity is being acquired under a performance specification.

1. *Sufficient Technical Data and Appropriate Specifications*

The regulations, written before the passage of the CICA, provide that the nature of the available specifications is a major factor in determining whether to use two-step sealed bidding. The regulations permit its use when performance specifications ("criteria . . . for evaluating technical proposals") are available, FAR 14.502(a)(2), but the agency does not have detailed specifications or only has detailed specifications that are "too restrictive," FAR 14.502(a)(1). Thus, two-step procurement was devised for the situation where an agency sees a need for evaluating the detailed specifications before awarding a contract and wants to induce contractors to develop detailed specifications.

There are no objective guidelines for deciding whether the available specifications are too indefinite, incomplete, or restrictive to permit two-step procurement. Thus, the fulfillment of the prerequisite that detailed specifications are lacking has been granted wide agency discretion. See 52 Comp. Gen. 854 (B-177206) (1973) (two-step sealed bidding appropriate where the Air Force had detailed specifications for all aspects of a procurement of management services, except with respect to data processing and software operations); Comp. Gen. Dec. B-170135, Feb. 5, 1971, *Unpub.* (Navy's statement accepted that the required antenna coupler groups lacked detailed specifications although similar items were already used by Navy); 40 Comp. Gen. 514 (B-144432) (1961) (contracting officers found to be best qualified to review and evaluate the sufficiency of available technical data for procurement of diesel engine generators). Compare *ALS Elecs. Corp.*, Comp. Gen. Dec. B-181731, 74-2 CPD ¶ 214 (lack of experience of an agency in procuring a technical item was not a sufficient justification for using two-step procurement if the specification was sufficiently detailed to permit sealed bidding).

Although lack of detailed specifications may require the use of two-step sealed bidding, the contracting officer must have definite performance specifications providing criteria for the evaluation of the technical proposals, FAR 14.502(a)(2). Again, there are no objective guidelines for determining the adequacy of the available performance specifications, and fulfillment of the prerequisite of definite performance specifications has also been granted wide agency discretion, 50 Comp. Gen. 346 (B-170268) (1970) (determination of how to best satisfy Navy's requirement of ship hull blast cleaner is left to the discretion of contracting officer).

2. *Availability of Competition*

The availability of competition is the other major factor to be considered in deciding whether to use two-step sealed bidding, FAR 14.502(a)(3). If there is likely not to be any competition for the contract, the Comptroller General recommends using negotiation rather than two-step procurement, *Allen Osborne Assocs.*, Comp. Gen. Dec. B-235568.2, 89-2 CPD ¶ 279. The competition requirement is met if there is more than one technically qualified source at the end of the step-one competition, even if only one responsive bid is submitted in step two, *Exide Power Sys. Div. of ESB, Inc.*, Comp. Gen. Dec. B-186793, 76-2 CPD ¶ 140. However, if there is only one qualified source at the end of step one, two-step sealed bidding should be discontinued, and negotiated procurement should be used, *Exide Power Sys. Div., ESB, Inc.*, 57 Comp. Gen. 653 (B-191159), 78-2 CPD ¶ 106. It is proper to cancel a negotiated procurement and use two-step sealed bidding when the agency learns of the availability of competition through the submission of an unsolicited proposal, Comp. Gen. Dec. B-154070, June 24, 1964, *Unpub.* See also *Radionics, Inc.*, ASBCA 22727, 81-1 BCA ¶ 15,011, where two-step sealed bidding was used to develop a second source for an item that had been previously procured through sole source negotiation.

3. *Agency Discretion*

To date, the Comptroller General has not overturned any agency decision to use two-step procurement — holding that the agencies have broad discretion in deciding whether to use this technique, 50 Comp. Gen. 346 (B-170268) (1970); 40 Comp. Gen. 514 (B-144432) (1961). The few cases concerning the selection of two-step sealed bidding that have found their way to the courts have been resolved in favor of the procuring agency. For example, in *Wheelabrator Corp. v. Chafee*, 455 F.2d 1306 (D.C. Cir. 1971), the court stated that the decision to use two-step formal advertising rather than negotiation was "an exercise of discretion which Congress committed solely to the discretion of the head of the agency, and which is not reviewable in court."

B. Step One

FAR 14.501(a) contains the following description of step one:

> Step one consists of the request for, submission, evaluation, and (if necessary) discussion of a technical proposal. No pricing is involved. The objective is to determine the acceptability of the supplies or services offered. As used in this context, the word "technical" has a broad connotation and includes, among other things, the engineering approach, special manufacturing processes, and special testing techniques. It is the proper step for clarification of questions relating to technical requirements. Conformity to the technical requirements is resolved in this step, but not responsibility as defined in 9.1.

The focus in this step is on the preparation of the RFTPs, the evaluation of proposals, and discussions with offerors.

1. Request for Technical Proposals

FAR 14.503-1(a) requires that the RFTP contain the following information:

> (1) A description of the supplies or services required.
>
> (2) A statement of intent to use the two step method.
>
> (3) The requirements of the technical proposal.
>
> (4) The evaluation criteria, to include all factors and any significant subfactors.
>
> (5) A statement that the technical proposals shall not include prices or pricing information.

(6) The date, or date and hour, by which the proposal must be received (see 14.201-6(r)).

(7) A statement that (i) in the second step, only bids based upon technical proposals determined to be acceptable, either initially or as a result of discussions, will be considered for awards and (ii) each bid in the second step must be based on the bidder's own technical proposals.

(8) A statement that (i) offerors should submit proposals that are acceptable without additional explanation or information, (ii) the Government may make a final determination regarding a proposal's acceptability solely on the basis of the proposal as submitted, and (iii) the Government may proceed with the second step without requesting further information from any offeror; however, the Government may request additional information from offerors of proposals that it considers reasonably susceptible of being made acceptable, and may discuss proposals with their offerors.

(9) A statement that a notice of unacceptability will be forwarded to the offeror upon completion of the proposal evaluation and final determination of unacceptability.

(10) A statement either that only one technical proposal may be submitted by each offeror or that multiple technical proposals may be submitted. When specifications permit different technical approaches, it is generally in the Government's interest to authorize multiple proposals. If multiple proposals are authorized, see 14.201-6(s).

The RFTP may include delivery or "performance requirements," but these requirements are not considered evaluation factors under step one and are not binding on the Government, FAR 14.503-1(b). In this context, the term "performance requirements" should be construed as factors unrelated to the technical competency of a proposal. For example, in *Diversified Contract Servs., Inc.*, Comp. Gen. Dec. B-234660, 89-1 CPD ¶ 590, the Comptroller General held that the Government was not required to announce a bonding requirement in its RFTP because the bond was a performance requirement that did not affect the technical focus of step one. Additionally, quantities specified in the RFTP are not binding on the Government, Comp. Gen. Dec. B-163050, Mar. 27, 1968, *Unpub.*

However, performance requirements (also known as "performance specifications") are considered evaluation factors under step one when the performance requirements state the needs of the Government that must be met by the step one proposal. For example, in *Aerostat Servs. Partnership*,

Comp. Gen. Dec. B-244939.2, 92-1 CPD ¶ 71, the Comptroller General upheld the Air Force's rejection of a technical proposal because the manning levels for the operation of a radar system did not fulfill the Air Force's performance requirements. See also *Halter Marine, Inc.*, Comp. Gen. Dec. B-239119, 90-2 CPD ¶ 95 (performance requirement of a patrol boat's speed is a technical evaluation factor); and *HSQ Technology*, Comp. Gen. Dec. B-227054, 87-2 CPD ¶ 77 (performance requirement of computer communications rate at 9600 baud is a technical evaluation factor). While performance specifications in the RFTP should be relatively flexible in order to encourage varying proposals, the requirements must be sufficiently definite to state the Government's needs accurately and to provide offerors with equal opportunities for submitting proposals. When the step-one evaluation is based upon requirements not set forth in the RFTP or ambiguously set forth, the Comptroller General has generally found that an unequal basis for competition has arisen. See *Federal Computer Corp.*, 66 Comp. Gen. 139 (B-223932), 86-2 CPD ¶ 665 (improper rejection of step one proposal for failure to meet Navy's unstated requirements for automatic data processing system); *Tenavision, Inc.*, Comp. Gen. Dec. B-216274, 85-1 CPD ¶ 427 (rejection improper when based on GSA contract number listing requirement that was ambiguously set forth in RFTP); *Masstor Sys. Corp.*, Comp. Gen. Dec. B-206091, 82-2 CPD ¶ 262 (where solicitation provision has two reasonable interpretations and the ambiguity is not so obvious as to impose a duty on the offeror to seek clarification, it is improper for the agency to reject the offeror's proposal for failure to comply with the agency's interpretation); and *RCA Corp.*, 57 Comp. Gen. 809 (B-190247), 78-2 CPD ¶ 213 (camera sample not required by RFTP could not be used as evaluation factor).

The Comptroller General may also find an unequal basis for competition if the Government significantly changes its requirements from the RFTP specifications, but does not issue an amendment to all bidders. For example, in 53 Comp. Gen. 47 (B-178192) (1973), the Government was obligated to amend its RFTP before accepting a technical proposal with a ladder incorporated in the antenna rather than separate from the antenna as originally contemplated in the RFTP. See also *Helmets Ltd.*, 71 Comp. Gen. 281 (B-246301), 92-1 CPD ¶ 241 (proposal that represents a basic change in RFTP helmet design can only be accepted if Navy gives other offerors an opportunity to submit revised proposals); and *Irvin Indus. Can., Ltd. v. Department of the Air Force*, 924 F.2d 1068 (D.C. Cir. 1990) (when no acceptable technical proposals were submitted, agency was not allowed to disregard material changes of its RFTP for only one offeror, but must negotiate with all offerors).

The determinative question regarding the adequacy of the specifications is whether the bidders are competing on a common basis, *Simulaser Corp.*, Comp. Gen. Dec. B-233850, 89-1 CPD ¶ 236, *recons. denied*, 89-2 CPD ¶ 65. However, absent a showing of prejudice to the protesting offeror, the mere existence of an improper evaluation of technical requirements does not provide a compelling reason to cancel or redo step one of the procurement.

Early Comptroller General decisions treated late technical proposals with some leniency, 45 Comp. Gen. 24 (B-156466) (1965); Comp. Gen. Dec. B-160324, Feb. 16, 1967, *Unpub.* However, in 1973, the General Accounting Office advised the General Services Administration "that in our view late proposals under step one should be treated in strict accordance with the terms of the solicitations" and heralded a shift toward more rigid adherence to deadlines, 52 Comp. Gen. 726 (B-177284) (1973). Currently, FAR 14.201-6(r) requires that the RFTP include the solicitation provision set forth at FAR 52.214-23. This provision provides that late technical proposals shall not be considered unless (1) they are received before issuance of the step two IFB, and (2) any of the five following conditions is present:

> (1) Was sent by registered or certified mail not later than the fifth calendar day before the date specified for receipt of technical proposals (e.g., a technical proposal submitted in response to a solicitation requiring receipt of technical proposals by the 20th of the month must have been mailed by the 15th);
>
> (2) Was sent by mail (or telegram or facsimile, if authorized) or hand-carried (including delivery by a commercial carrier) if it is determined by the Government that the late receipt was due primarily to Government mishandling after receipt at the Government installation;
>
> (3) Was sent by U.S. Postal Service Express Mail Next Day Service—Post Office To Addressee, not later than 5:00 p.m. at the place of mailing two working days prior to the date specified for receipt of technical proposals. The term "working days" excludes weekends and U.S. Federal holidays.
>
> (4) Was transmitted through an electronic commerce method authorized by the solicitation and was received at the initial point of entry to the Govern-

ment infrastructure not later than 5:00 p.m. one working day prior to the date specified for receipt of technical proposals; or

(5) Is the only technical proposal received.

Accordingly, late technical proposals submitted under two-step procurement will be rejected unless they fall within one of the exceptions defined in the late proposal clause, *Baron & Assocs.*, Comp. Gen. Dec. B-213898, 84-1 CPD ¶ 80. However, once a timely proposal is submitted that is acceptable or reasonably susceptible to being made acceptable, late responses to amendments of the RFTP or to agency requests for revisions may be accepted if further negotiations under step one are to be conducted. See *Control Central Corp.*, Comp. Gen. Dec. B-214466.2, 84-2 CPD ¶ 28 (failure to submit a timely revised proposal did not exclude bidder from further competition when negotiations are reopened by subsequent amendment); and *Angstrom, Inc.*, 59 Comp. Gen. 588 (B-193261), 80-2 CPD ¶ 20 (late response to amendment of RFTP allowed because subsequent amendments continued negotiations under step one). Additionally, there is no regulatory requirement for a common cutoff date for receipt of revised proposals after discussions, *J&J Maintenance, Inc.*, Comp. Gen. Dec. B-240802, 90-2 CPD ¶ 504, *recons. denied*, 91-1 CPD ¶ 396.

2. Evaluation of First-Step Proposals

FAR 14.503-1(e)(1) states that after proposals have been received, they are to be categorized as acceptable, unacceptable, or reasonably susceptible to being made acceptable. Offerors who submit unacceptable proposals are to be notified of that determination promptly and are to be advised that revisions will not be considered, FAR 14.503-1(g). However, failure to give prompt notice is a mere procedural irregularity and, therefore, does not invalidate the procurement, *Shughart & Assocs.*, Comp. Gen. Dec. B-226970, 87-2 CPD ¶ 56; 48 Comp. Gen. 349 (B-165050) (1968).

Contracting officers are given wide latitude in the evaluation of technical proposals, *Hughes Missile Sys. Co.*, Comp. Gen. Dec. B-257627.2, 94-2 CPD ¶ 256. This discretion on the part of the contracting officer provides broad grounds for disputes between the offeror and the Government regarding whether a proposal was properly evaluated and leads to many protests which delay two-step sealed bidding procurement. For example, in *Angstrom, Inc.*, 59 Comp. Gen. 588 (B-193261), 80-2 CPD ¶ 20, bidding disputes extended the procurement time of a commercial, off-the-shelf item to 33 months.

a. *Acceptable Proposals*

To be acceptable, a technical proposal must conform to the basic or essential requirements of the specifications, FAR 14.503-1(e)(2). However, variations from less significant details of the specifications are permissible in an acceptable proposal. See *Angstrom, Inc.*, 59 Comp. Gen. 588 (B-193261), 80-2 CPD ¶ 20, holding that a proposal need comply only with basic or essential requirements, not all details of specifications. The difficulty is that it is not always readily ascertainable which of the RFTP requirements are "basic" and, therefore, must be complied with and which are minor details that may be waived. Because there are few objective standards by which basic requirements of specifications may be differentiated from specification details, the contracting officer is given wide discretion in making this determination. See *Hughes Missile Sys. Co.*, Comp. Gen. Dec. B-257627.2, 94-2 CPD ¶ 256, where the Comptroller denied a protest of an agency's evaluation of a proposal as acceptable, even though one agency evaluator disagreed with the decision.

Once a proposal is classified as acceptable, it is permitted to compete in step two. There are no degrees of qualification within the acceptable category. Thus, superior and more costly proposals may compete with those that are minimally adequate and less costly, Comp. Gen. Dec. B-159469, Mar. 22, 1967, *Unpub.*

b. *Proposals That Are Reasonably Susceptible to Being Made Acceptable*

FAR 14.503-1(f) provides the following guidance on dealing with proposals that are reasonably susceptible to being made acceptable:

> (1) The contracting officer may proceed directly with step two if there are sufficient acceptable proposals to ensure adequate price competition under step two, and if further time, effort and delay to make additional proposals acceptable and thereby increase competition would not be in the Government's interest. If this is not the case, the contracting officer shall request bidders whose proposals may be made acceptable to submit additional clarifying or supplementing information. The contracting officer shall identify the nature of the deficiencies in the proposal or the nature of the additional

> information required. The contracting officer may also arrange discussions for this purpose. No proposal shall be discussed with any offeror other than the submitter.

Despite this guidance, the Comptroller General has stated that the first step of two-step sealed bidding contemplates the qualification of as many proposals as possible, *Hughes Missile Sys. Co.*, Comp. Gen. Dec. B-257627.2, 94-2 CPD ¶ 256. However, this goal of maximization of competition does not mean that an agency is required to classify a proposal as reasonably susceptible of being made acceptable if it fails to meet the basic requirements of the RFTP or can only be made acceptable through extensive revisions. See *Technology Research Int'l*, Comp. Gen. Dec. B-245174, 91-2 CPD ¶ 470 (agency is not required to afford an offeror an opportunity to revise its proposal if major rewrite is necessary); and *Infotec Dev., Inc.*, Comp. Gen. B-235568, 89-2 CPD ¶ 215 (although only one acceptable proposal was left after step one, agency was not required to consider other proposals that required major revisions). Although the Comptroller General will commonly defer to the Government's decision to reject a proposal where substantial revision is necessary, *Network Sys. Solutions, Inc.*, Comp. Gen. Dec. B-249733, 92-2 CPD ¶ 410, the Comptroller General may overturn the decision if there is evidence that the Government's evaluation was unreasonable and the proposal was susceptible to being made acceptable. See *Coastal Gov't Servs., Inc.*, Comp. Gen. Dec. B-250820, 93-1 CPD ¶ 167 (agency unreasonably determined that proposal was technically unacceptable based on minor informational deficiencies and proposal ambiguities); and *A.R.E. Mfg. Co.*, Comp. Gen. Dec. B-224086, 86-2 CPD ¶ 395 (decision unreasonable where Navy cannot explain how or why conclusion of unacceptability was reached).

The amount of discussion or clarification that is appropriate and which proposals are reasonably susceptible to being made acceptable are matters of agency discretion, *Ronnoc, Inc.*, Comp. Gen. Dec. 243729, 91-2 CPD ¶ 163. Although the step-one process is stated to be similar to negotiated procurement, when the Government decides that a step one proposal is reasonably susceptible to being made acceptable, there is no requirement that the Government hold "meaningful discussions" with the offeror, *Datron Sys., Inc.*, Comp. Gen. Dec. B-220423.2, 86-1 CPD ¶ 264. It is sufficient if the offeror is notified of deficiencies and afforded the opportunity to address them, *Lockheed Cal. Co.*, Comp. Gen. Dec. B-218143, 85-1 CPD ¶ 676. See also FAR 14.503-1(f)(1).

Discussions resulting in revised proposals that are classified as acceptable are regularly upheld as proper, Comp. Gen. Dec. B-179587, Sept. 27, 1973, *Unpub.* (modification effected in step one discussions substituted hydraulic actuators for mechanical ones); and *Guardian Elec. Mfg. Co.*, Comp. Gen. Dec. B-191871, 79-1 CPD ¶ 321 (extensive discussions needed to qualify proposal upheld). Additionally, protests alleging that a deficiency in discussions resulted in a proposal's rejection are generally denied. See *Applied Research Technology*, Comp. Gen. Dec. B-240230, 90-2 CPD ¶ 358 (agency not required to conduct successive rounds of discussions and revisions of proposals); and *Anchor Conveyors, Inc.*, Comp. Gen. Dec. B-215624, 84-2 CPD ¶ 451 (FAA's effort to qualify proposal upheld as reasonable where agency identified deficient areas and afforded bidder an opportunity to correct those deficiencies in revised proposal).

The Comptroller General may find step-one discussions improper if there is evidence that technical transfusion or technical leveling occurred. Technical transfusion is prohibited by federal statutes, 18 U.S.C. § 1905 and 41 U.S.C. § 423(b), as amended by Section 4304 of the Clinger-Cohen Act of 1996, and this prohibition is reflected in FAR 14.503-1(f)(1). For examples of cases involving technical transfusion in two-step procurement, see *Aerial Image Corp.*, Comp. Gen. Dec. B-219174, 85-2 CPD ¶ 319, where the Comptroller General upheld an agency's decision not to hold discussions because of the danger of disclosing another offeror's innovative approach to an audio-video slide show, and *General Elec. Can., Inc.*, Comp. Gen. Dec. B-230584, 88-1 CPD ¶ 512, where the Comptroller General denied a protest alleging technical transfusion as being based on mere speculation by the protester.

The FAR does not explicitly ban technical leveling during step-one discussions. However, the Comptroller General has applied the general prohibition on technical leveling during discussions found in FAR 15.610(d) (pre FAC 97-02, September 30, 1997 version). In *Applied Research Technology*, Comp. Gen. Dec. B-240230, 90-2 CPD ¶ 358, the Comptroller stated that successive rounds of discussion during step one are precluded because of the FAR 15.610(d) ban on technical leveling. See also *Essex Electro Eng'rs, Inc.*, Comp. Gen. Dec. B-210366, 83-1 CPD ¶ 650, where the Comptroller General held that an agency is not required to engage in technical leveling to bring a proposal up to the level of other proposals. It is difficult to determine when step one discussions are permissible dialogues about a proposal's deficiencies rather than technical leveling's prohibited coaching. Thus, if a protest is comprised of allegations of both technical leveling and technical transfusion, the Comptroller General may address the technical transfusion claim, which is easier to establish, and ignore the difficult technical leveling claim. See *J&J Maintenance, Inc.*, Comp. Gen. Dec. B-240802, 90-2 CPD ¶ 504, where the Comptroller General approved acceptance of revised proposal following discussions after finding no evidence of technical transfusion, but disregarded claims of technical leveling.

The amount of time to be allotted to discussion is also a discretionary matter. For example, in Comp. Gen. Dec. B-178071, May 22, 1973, *Unpub.*, the Comptroller General upheld the contracting officer's decision to allow 60 additional days to make a proposal acceptable after the date on which two other proposals qualified as acceptable.

c. Unacceptable Proposals

FAR 14.503-1(e)(2) states:

> Any proposal which modifies, or fails to conform to the essential requirements or specifications of, the request for technical proposals shall be considered nonresponsive and categorized as unacceptable.

A proposal may also be unacceptable because it contains insufficient information to permit a determination that the offeror possesses sufficient technical understanding of the work, *Radiation Sys., Inc.*, Comp. Gen. Dec. B-211732, 83-2 CPD ¶ 434. The cases uniformly follow the principle established in FAR 14.503-1(g) that the Government does not have a duty to initiate or continue discussions with the offeror in order to clarify a clearly unacceptable proposal, that would require considerable time and effort to be made acceptable, *Network Sys. Solutions, Inc.,* Comp. Gen. Dec. B-249733, 92-2 CPD ¶ 410 (offeror should not have assumed that it would be afforded opportunity to make further clarifications); *Gichner Iron Works, Inc.*, Comp. Gen. B-230009, 88-1 CPD ¶ 459 (upholding rejection of proposal that would require substantial revisions); and *Colbar, Inc.*, Comp. Gen. Dec. B-227555.4, 88-1 CPD ¶ 168 (upholding evaluation team consensus upheld that proposal for food service would require total rewrite).

d. Erroneous Evaluations

In reviewing protests of allegedly improper evaluations, the Comptroller General will not substitute his judgment for that of the agency that retains wide discretion, but will examine the record to determine whether the evaluation was reasonable and in accord with listed criteria, and whether there were any violations of procurement statutes or regulations, *Anchor Conveyors, Inc.*, Comp. Gen. Dec. B-215624.2, 84-2 CPD ¶ 451. The Comptroller General lacks technical expertise to oversee the judgments of the procuring agencies and, therefore, is reluctant to review the step one evaluation process. Thus, the technical judgment of the agency is accepted unless it is shown to be erroneous, arbitrary, or not in good faith, *Kay & Assocs.*, Comp. Gen. Dec. B-234509, 89-1 CPD ¶ 567.

In contrast, the Comptroller General exercises judgment in matters considered to be legal in nature. See, e.g., Comp. Gen. Dec. B-170825.2, Mar. 12, 1971, *Unpub.*, where the meaning and effect of a specification as opposed to whether a product met the specification was declared to be a matter of law within the province of the Comptroller General's office to decide. See also *Federal Computer Corp.*, 66 Comp. Gen. 139 (B-223932), 86-2 CPD ¶ 665 (protest that evaluation factor was not set forth in RFTP); and *E.C. Campbell, Inc.*, Comp. Gen. Dec. B-205533, 82-2 CPD ¶ 34 (award overturned because agency improperly failed to consider awardee's noncompliance with material specification requirement).

Offerors that can demonstrate that a determination of unacceptability is improper are not foreclosed from further participation in the procurement. In 43 Comp. Gen. 255 (B-152261) (1963), a contractor revised a proposal and submitted a second-step bid based on the revised proposal within three days of learning that the proposal had been rejected. The Comptroller General permitted the contractor to participate in the second step, stating that the speed with which the proposal was made acceptable showed it had been erroneously rejected as unacceptable in the first instance. See also *Tenavision, Inc.*, Comp. Gen. Dec. B-218794, 85-2 CPD ¶ 62, where the Comptroller General awarded a protester bid preparation costs incurred in step one of a two-step sealed bid procurement because the offeror's proposal was improperly rejected in step one. However, if the unacceptable proposal is not corrected prior to the submission of the step-two bids, it may not be considered for award. Such proposals are still nonresponsive, and the strict rules of formal advertising applicable to the second step do not permit correction of the proposal at that stage. See 45 Comp. Gen. 487 (B-157084) (1966), where the Comptroller General held improper the revision of a proposal during step two. Compare Comp. Gen. Dec. B-160324, Apr. 5, 1967, *Unpub.*, where the Comptroller General allowed a step-two bid on a proposal initially deemed unacceptable but made competitive before step two.

C. Step Two

Generally, the second step of two-step sealed bidding is conducted in accordance with the procedures applicable to sealed bidding. See FAR 14.501(b), which states:

> Step two involves the submission of sealed priced bids by those who submitted acceptable technical proposals in step one. Bids submitted in step two are evaluated and the awards made in accordance with Subparts 14.3 and 14.4.

However, there are a number of unique aspects of the sealed bidding procedures used in step two.

Upon completion of step one, invitations for bids are issued to offerors whose technical proposals have been determined acceptable under step one. Limiting competition in step two to acceptable proposals is an exception to the normal sealed bid procedures but is an essential element of two-step sealed bidding. This limitation has been strictly enforced. See Comp. Gen. Dec. B-170175, Apr. 21, 1971, *Unpub.*, where a successful participant in the first step, unable to obtain the required bond, was prohibited from bidding in the second step under the name of a different company that could be bonded. But see *G&C Enters., Inc.*, Comp. Gen. Dec. B-186748, 76-2 CPD ¶ 367, *recons. denied*, 77-1 CPD ¶ 155, where an acceptable step one proposer was permitted to bid in a joint venture with an outside party in step two.

While participants in step two are limited to those submitting acceptable proposals in step one, step-one participants are not legally bound to participate in step two. The application of this rule could lead to the situation where only one bid is submitted in step two. However, this should not cause cancellation of the procurement unless the bidder was aware that the other successful step-one offerors did not intend to bid.

The regulations provide that the step-two invitation for bids shall "prominently state that the bidder shall comply with the specifications and the bidder's technical proposal," FAR 14.503-2(a)(3). This requirement has been strictly enforced. Products that vary from the RFTP and the accepted technical proposals in step one cannot be accepted in step two, *Qualimetrics,*

Inc., Comp. Gen. Dec. B-227044.3, 87-2 CPD ¶ 100. However, when the bidder deviates from the solicitation in the technical proposal, but would still be the lowest bidder, absent such deviation, the award is proper, *Lusardi Constr. Co.*, Comp. Gen. Dec. B-210276, 83-2 CPD ¶ 297 (price benefit of deviations from specifications did not affect relative standing of bidders); *Essex Electro Eng'rs, Inc.*, Comp. Gen. Dec. B-213892, 84-1 CPD ¶ 434 (relaxation of requirements found not to result in price advantage).

FAR 14.503-2(a)(4) states that it is unnecessary to publish and synopsize second-step IFBs. However, "names of firms which have submitted acceptable proposals in step one are required to be listed in the *Commerce Business Daily* for the benefit of prospective subcontractors," FAR 14.503-2(b). Negligent failure to list the names of acceptable proposals before the second step has not been fatal to the procurement, *Bailey Controls Co.*, Comp. Gen. Dec. B-256189, 94-1 CPD ¶ 320. However, a failure to publish that is done in bad faith could require readvertisement if the Government's interest in full competition has been affected or if the omitted bidder can establish prejudice, Comp. Gen. Dec. B-166315, Aug. 15, 1969, *Unpub.*

1. Responsiveness

There are two unique aspects of responsiveness in two-step sealed bidding. First, the bid must conform to all of the significant procurement documents. Second, the Comptroller General has sometimes stated that there is a presumption of responsiveness.

a. Nonconforming Bids

In order to be eligible for award in two-step sealed bidding, bids must conform to the RFTP, to the technical proposal as approved by the procuring agency in step one, and to any additional requirements in the step two invitation for bids. However, it is not necessary for the bidder to physically incorporate the technical proposal in the second-step bid. The bid is considered responsive if it summarizes the technical proposal, as long as the summary is consistent with the acceptable technical proposal. Incorporation by reference or acknowledgment that the bid is in accordance with the accepted proposal is also sufficient, 52 Comp. Gen. 821 (B-177423) (1973).

An invitation to submit a second-step bid does not eliminate the possibility that the offeror will be found nonresponsive after receipt of second-step bids based on a nonconformity included in the step-one proposal. In *International Med. Indus., Inc.*, 62 Comp. Gen. 31 (B-208235), 82-2 CPD ¶ 386, an offeror was invited to submit a bid in step two after the step-one proposal was found technically acceptable. The offeror's step-one proposal included a 30-day bid acceptance period rather than the 45-day period included in the RFTP. Based upon this nonconformity the company was found nonresponsive in step two. See also *American Tel. & Tel. Co.*, Comp. Gen. Dec. B-193454, 79-1 CPD ¶ 365 and 52 Comp. Gen. 783 (B-177220) (1973). When the Comptroller General states that such a bid is nonresponsive, it is tantamount to a finding that the procuring agency has made an erroneous determination of acceptability in step one.

Bidders can also be found nonresponsive by failing to comply with the requirements of the IFB. These requirements may include price schedules, delivery requirements and bid bond requirements. See *Parsons Precision Prods., Inc.*, Comp. Gen. Dec. B-249940, 92-2 CPD ¶ 431 (cover letter to bid changing payment terms makes bid nonresponsive); *American Monorail, Inc.*, Comp. Gen. Dec. B-181226, 74-2 CPD ¶ 69 (bid with exception to required delivery schedule nonresponsive); and 52 Comp. Gen. 223 (B-176138) (1972). See generally *Metric Sys. Corp.*, Comp. Gen. Dec. B-256343, 94-1 CPD ¶ 360 (exception to indemnification clause); and *KW Control Sys., Inc.*, Comp. Gen. Dec. B-246963, 91-2 CPD ¶ 543 (total payment obligation inconsistent with IFB requirements).

However, if a price for a certain item is not necessary for the agency's determination of the low bidder, failure to include the price in the step-two bid does not make the bidder nonresponsive, *Educational Computer Corp.*, Comp. Gen. Dec. B-227078, 87-2 CPD ¶ 156.

b. Presumption of Responsiveness

The Comptroller General has sometimes stated that bidders in the second step are entitled to a presumption of responsiveness. See *Spectrolab, Inc.*, Comp. Gen. Dec. B-180008, 74-1 CPD ¶ 321 (bid was ambiguous but Comptroller presumed offeror meant to be responsive); *Federal Aviation Admin.*, Comp. Gen. Dec. B-193238, 79-1 CPD ¶ 136 (offeror specifically addressed in step one an item that was omitted in step two). The rationale for this rule is that the time, effort, and money a bidder expends in participating in two-step sealed bidding would make it unlikely that the bidder would disqualify the bid by varying from the accepted proposal or the requirements of the specifications, 45 Comp. Gen. 221 (B-157454) (1965). Using this presumption of responsiveness, the Comptroller General has approved awards to firms despite deviations that would lead to determinations of nonresponsiveness in a regular sealed bid procurement. For example, in 45 Comp. Gen. 221 (B-157454), the bidder placed "N/A," indicating "not applicable," in the amount column of the item covering the furnishing of certain data related to the end item of the procurement. This created an ambiguity as to whether the bidder was refusing to provide the item or was offering to provide it at no cost. In similar situations in standard sealed bid procurements, such bids are routinely found nonresponsive. However, in this case the Comptroller General held that the bidder was responsive based on the asserted presumption of responsiveness. Similarly, in 50 Comp. Gen. 337 (B-169874) (1970), the bidder submitted descriptive literature with the bid that was not consistent with the Government's requirements. The Comptroller General found the bid responsive. See also *Spectrolab, Inc.*, Comp. Gen. Dec. B-180008, 74-1 CPD ¶ 321; and Comp. Gen. Dec. B-178764, June 27, 1973, *Unpub.*

The presumption of responsiveness is not applicable when the step-two bid takes specific exception to a material requirement that has a significant effect on price, *Universal Comm. Sys., Inc.*, Comp. Gen. Dec., B-205032, 82-2 CPD ¶ 236. See also *Parsons Precision Prod., Inc.*, Comp. Gen. Dec. B-249940 92-2 CPD ¶ 431 (conflict in payment terms); *Southwestern Bell Corp.*, GSBCA 10321-P, 90-1 BCA ¶ 22,545 (omission of cost of growth requirement); and *Abar Ipsen Indus.*, Comp. Gen. Dec. B-219499.2, 86-1 CPD ¶ 7 (delivery schedule and price terms in conflict).

2. Data Protection

The two-step regulations require the contracting officer to safeguard step-one proposals against disclosure to unauthorized persons. See FAR 14.503-1, which states:

> (c) Upon receipt, the contracting officer shall —
>
> (1) Safeguard proposals against disclosure to unauthorized persons;
>
> (2) Accept and handle data marked in accordance with 15.413 as provided in that section.

Thus, competitors have no way of determining whether the step-one proposal, as accepted by the Government, varies from the RFTP. This conflicts with the public opening concept of sealed bidding. See FAR 14.404-4, which states that if a bidder restricts the disclosure of sufficient information to permit competing bidders to know the essential nature of the offer, the bid is nonresponsive. This special procedure has been accepted by the Comptroller General as a necessary part of two-step sealed bidding, 46 Comp. Gen. 34 (B-158865) (1966); Comp. Gen. Dec. B-164106, Nov. 8, 1968, *Unpub.* See also *Powers Regulator Co.*, Comp. Gen. Dec. B-181251, 74-2 CPD ¶ 98, where the Comptroller General rejected a protester's contention that only a competitor's review of step-one proposals could protect the integrity of the competitive bidding system. The Comptroller General indicated that review by the GAO was sufficient.

This rule does not apply to elements of the bid that are not included in the step-one proposal. Thus, the prices bid in step two must be disclosed. Therefore, a bid that restricts release of a price in a two-step sealed bid procurement must be found nonresponsive and be rejected, *Northern Telecom, Inc.*, Comp. Gen. Dec. B-209412, 83-1 CPD ¶ 382. Additionally, an agency may disclose prices for a similar prior contract so that potential bidders on the current contract have the same opportunity to bid competitively, *B.C. Cleaning & Maintenance Corp.*, Comp. Gen. Dec. B-225909, 87-1 CPD ¶ 56.

3. Discontinuing Step Two

FAR 14.404-1 lists the circumstances under which cancellation of two-step sealed bid procurement is permitted after the step-two bids are opened. Cancellation at this stage most often results because the Government has not obtained sufficient price competition, evidenced by the fact that the bid prices are too high. See *Aero Innovations, Ltd.*, Comp. Gen. Dec. B-227677, 87-2 CPD ¶ 332, where the Comptroller General upheld cancellation and resolicitation when restrictive specifications resulted in limited competition. The contracting officer has substantial discretion in concluding that lack of price competition justifies cancellation and may use the bid of a nonresponsive bidder in this determination of price unreasonableness, *McCarthy Mfg. Co.*, 56 Comp. Gen. 369 (B-186550), 77-1 CPD ¶ 116; Comp. Gen. Dec. B-168972, Apr. 14, 1970, *Unpub.* The procurement may also be canceled because the specifications failed to state or overstated the needs of the Government. However, the presence of ambiguous specifications is a justification for cancellation only if there is a compelling reason, for instance, where an award would not meet the Government's needs or a bidder would be prejudiced. See *Diversified Energy Sys.*, Comp. Gen. Dec. B-245593.3, 92-1 CPD ¶ 293, where cancellation was held to be appropriate because ambiguous specifications led to an overstatement of the agency's needs. Compare *Hydro Power Equip. Co.*, Comp. Gen. Dec. B-205263, 82-1 CPD ¶ 466, finding no compelling reason to cancel despite ambiguous specifications. Additionally, the procurement may be canceled if the agency determines from a cost comparison that it would be more advantageous to perform the services with agency personnel, *United Media Corp.*, Comp. Gen. Dec. B-259425.2, 95-1 CPD ¶ 289.

If the procurement is canceled in step two, the contracting agency may readvertise step two, initiate a new sealed bid procurement, or negotiate the contract. If negotiation is selected as the best means of obtaining the work, the competition may not be limited to the companies that submitted acceptable technical proposals, 46 Comp. Gen. 360 (B-159665) (1966). In one interesting case, the Comptroller General ruled that it was proper for an agency to obtain the item by negotiating a lease/purchase arrangement after cancellation of the two-step sealed bid procurement because the bids exceeded the funds available to the agency, 48 Comp. Gen. 471 (B-165013) (1968). Although the Comptroller General suggests cancellation of step two and initiation of negotiations when step one results in only one acceptable proposal, the contracting officer has the discretion to proceed to step two, *Allen Osborne Assocs.*, Comp. Gen. Dec. B-235568.2, 89-2 CPD ¶ 279.

CHAPTER 6

BASIC NEGOTIATION PROCEDURES

The term "negotiation" has been broadly used to refer to any procurement technique other than sealed bidding (previously known as formal advertising). In use since World War II, it was initially introduced into the procurement statutes by the Armed Services Procurement Act in 1948 as an "exception" to procurement by formal advertising. Its use was authorized only if formal advertising was determined not to be "feasible and practicable" and one of a number of enumerated "exceptions" was present. This statute did not specify any procedures to be used in negotiating contracts. However, subsequent statutes have incorporated various requirements aimed at insuring fair treatment of competitors. Rather than specifying any single technique, the present statutes provide a framework within which procuring agencies have flexibility to devise varying strategies.

Following complaints that noncompetitive practices were used by the Department of Defense (DOD) in negotiating contracts, the statute was amended by P.L. 87-653, 76 Stat. 528 (1962) to require "oral or written discussions" with all offerors submitting proposals within a "competitive range." Award without discussions was permitted only if the reasonableness of price could be determined through adequate competition or prior cost experience. These requirements were subsequently imposed on civilian agencies by the Federal Procurement Regulations. The Competition in Contracting Act (CICA) of 1984 restated and supplemented these requirements and made them statutorily applicable to civilian agency contracts. In addition, it introduced the term "competitive proposals" for negotiated contracts. Subsequent statutory changes, including the Federal Acquisition Streamlining Act of 1994 (FASA), P.L. 104-355, and the Clinger-Cohen Act of 1996, P.L. 104-106, required increased detail in stating evaluation factors and subfactors, removed restrictions on making awards without discussions, permitted limitation of the competitive range for purposes of efficiency, and required extensive debriefing of offerors.

The purpose of negotiation is to permit agencies to use flexible procedures not permitted in the sealed bidding process. As a result, proposals are not available for public inspection prior to award. The concept of responsiveness does not apply and proposals which vary from the RFP are not required to be rejected. Discussions and bargaining are permitted which can result in modifications of proposals by offerors to correct deficiencies or to enhance their offers. Contracting by negotiation also enables the Government to use techniques which allow it to make tradeoffs between cost or price and other factors when selecting a proposal for award. The flexibility of negotiation is reflected in FAR 15.306(d), stating:

> Negotiation are exchanges . . . between the Government and offerors, that are undertaken with the intent of allowing the offeror to revise its proposal. These negotiations may include bargaining. Bargaining includes persuasion, alteration of assumptions and positions, give-and-take, and may apply to price, schedule, technical requirements, type of contract, or other terms of a proposed contract.

The negotiation process gives contracting officials the option to seek proposal modifications but they are not required to do so if acceptance of the most favorable initial proposals is in the best interests of the Government. The options available are shown in **Figure 6-1**.

Through the years much of the flexibility available in negotiated procurements became lost due to overly complex solicitations including unnecessarily large numbers of evaluation factors and subfactors. In an attempt to reverse this trend, FAR 15.002 establishes a policy aimed at minimizing the complexity of negotiated procurements as follows:

> (a) *Sole-source acquisitions.* When contracting in a sole source environment, the request for proposals (RFP) should be tailored to remove unnecessary information and requirements; e.g., evaluation criteria and voluminous proposal preparation instructions.
>
> (b) *Competitive acquisitions.* When contracting in a competitive environment, the procedures of this part are intended to minimize the complexity of the solicitation, the evaluation, and the source selection decision, while maintaining a process designed to foster an impartial and comprehensive evaluation of offerors' proposals, leading to selection of the proposal representing the best value to the Government (see 2.101).

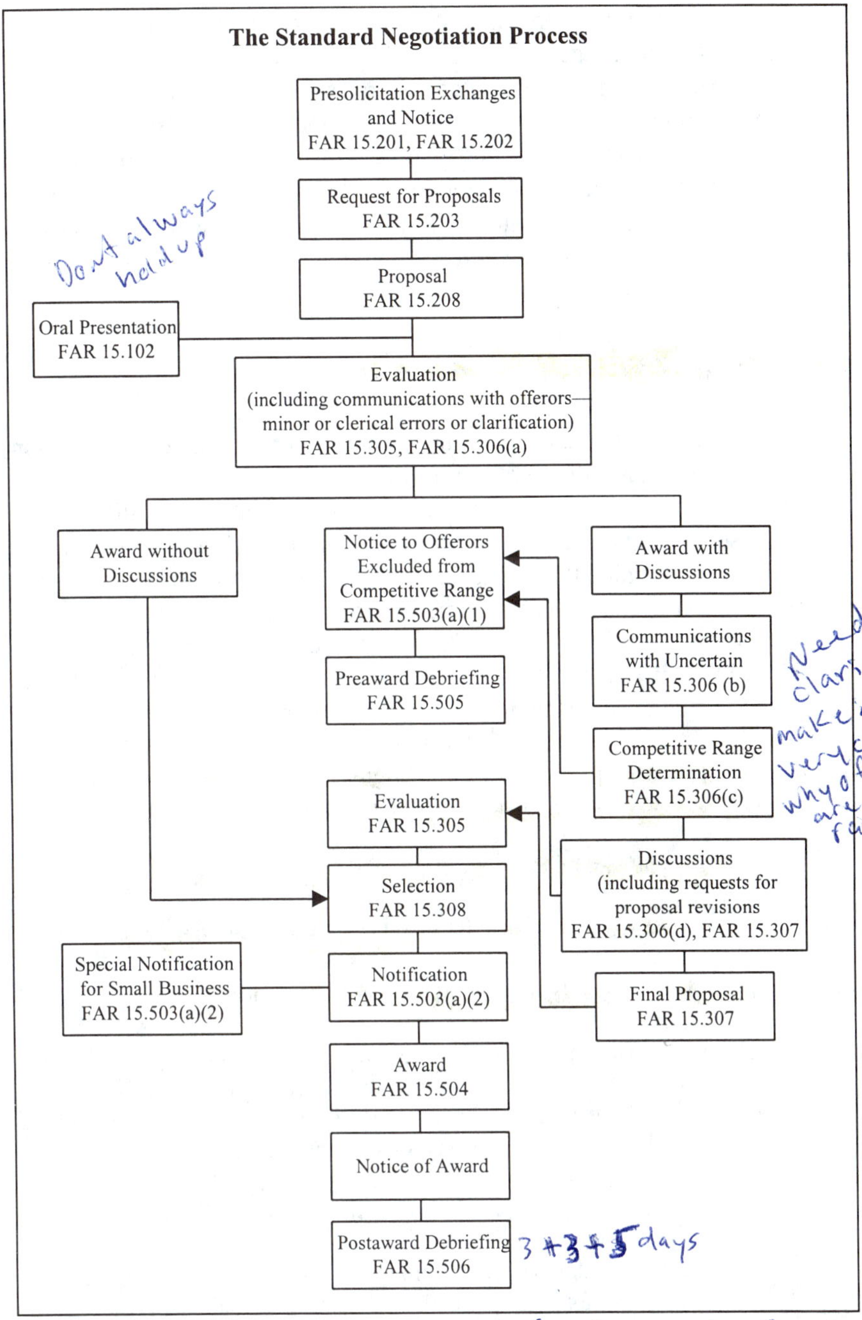

The Standard Negotiation Process

Figure 6-1

It's recommended for face-to face discussions get a Court Reporter versus videotape or tape recorder.

3 Days for post award debriefing. provide answers to relevant questions.

This Chapter covers the basic negotiation procedures covered by FAR Part 15. First, the procedures applicable to competitive negotiation are discussed. Although most negotiated contracts result from solicitations for competitive proposals, negotiation also encompasses sole source procurements. The abbreviated procedures involved in such noncompetitive awards are then discussed. Special negotiation procedures involved in specific types of procurements are dealt with in Chapter 7. The pricing of all types of negotiated contracts, both competitive and noncompetitive, is covered in Chapter 9.

I. PROCUREMENT STATEGIES

The procurement statutes give the agencies a great degree of discretion in devising strategies designed to fulfill the Government's needs. This permits the source selection decision to be made by balancing other factors against costs to the Government. Thus, a starting point in the process is for the agency to determine the fundamental basis that will be used to make the source selection decision. The statement of this basis has been described as the "decisional rule." 41 U.S.C. § 253a(c)(1)(C) and 10 U.S.C. § 2305(a)(3)(A)(iii) contain the following minimal requirements to be observed in stating the decisional rule for a procurement:

> [The solicitation] shall disclose to offerors whether all evaluation factors other than cost or price, when combined, are —
>
> (i) significantly more important than cost or price;
>
> (ii) approximately equal in importance to cost or price; or
>
> (iii) significantly less important than cost or price.
>
> (B) The regulations implementing clause (iii) of subparagraph (A) may not define the terms "significantly more important" and "significantly less important" as specific numeric weights that would be applied uniformly to all solicitations or a class of solicitations.
>
> (4) Nothing in this subsection prohibits an agency from —
>
> (A) providing additional information in a solicitation, including numeric weights for all evaluation factors and subfactors on a case-by-case basis; or

> (B) stating in a solicitation that award will be made to the offeror that meets the solicitation's mandatory requirements at the lowest cost or price.

Although previous versions of FAR Part 15 did not use the term, procurements in which the selection was based on a tradeoff between price and other factors came to be known as "best value" procurements. However, the "Rewrite" of FAR Part 15, contained in FAC 97-02, 62 Fed. Reg. 51224, September 30, 1997, uses the term "best value" more broadly. It encompasses all the strategies, whether or not based on tradeoffs. FAR 15.302 states: "The objective of source selection is to select the proposal that represents the best value." The term is now defined in FAR 2.101 as follows:

> Best value means the expected outcome of an acquisition that, in the Government's estimation, provides the greatest overall benefit in response to the requirement.

FAR 15.101, entitled "Best value continuum," elaborates on this concept as follows:

> An agency can obtain best value in negotiated acquisitions by using any one or a combination of source selection approaches. In different types of acquisitions, the relative importance of cost or price may vary. For example, in acquisitions where the requirement is clearly definable and the risk of unsuccessful contract performance is minimal, cost or price may play a dominant role in source selection. The less definitive the requirement, the more development work required, or the greater the performance risk, the more technical or past performance considerations may play a dominant role in source selection.

Under this concept, procurement officials determine, in advance of soliciting proposals, what type of selection process will be best for the Government. Where differences in non-cost factors will not materially impact the agency's needs, award on the basis of the lowest evaluated price would be appropriate. Where differences in non-cost factors will be material, a tradeoff process would be called for. The following material discusses these two processes. It also considers a strategy which consists of a combination of the two processes.

A. Tradeoff Process

As previously indicated, this strategy had previously been known as the best value technique. The hallmark of the system is that it permits the determination of best value to be made after the receipt of proposals. It is described in FAR 15.101-1 as follows:

> (a) A tradeoff process is appropriate when it may be in the best interest of the Government to consider award to other than the lowest priced offeror or other than the highest technically rated offeror.
>
> (b) When using the tradeoff process, the following apply:
>
> > (1) All evaluation factors and significant subfactors that will affect contract award and their relative importance shall be clearly stated in the solicitation; and
> >
> > (2) The solicitation shall state whether all evaluation factors other than cost or price, when combined, are significantly more important than, approximately equal to, or significantly less important than cost or price.
>
> (c) This process permits tradeoffs among cost or price and non-cost factors and allows the Government to accept other than the lowest priced proposal. The perceived benefits of the higher-priced proposal shall merit the additional cost, and the rationale for tradeoffs must be documented in the file in accordance with 15.406.

This process gives the source selection official very broad discretion because the ultimate decision is made on a *subjective* basis. In other terms, the official is permitted to make a business judgment on whether the higher price is worth the added value of non-price factors. See *TRW, Inc., v. Widnall*, 98 F.3d 1325 (Fed. Cir. 1996); *Environmental Chemical Corp.*, Comp. Gen. Dec. B-275819, 97-1 CPD ¶ 154. It is clear that this judgment as to the value of the non-cost factors need not be quantified, FAR 15.308. See *Widnall v. B3H Corp.*, 75 F.3d 1577 (Fed. Cir. 1996), stating that these tradeoff decisions must be based on a "reasoned explanation" of the decision but need not be based on quantification of the non-cost factors. The same result was reached by the Comptroller General in *Kay & Assoc., Inc.*, Comp. Gen. Dec. B-258243.7, 96-1 CPD ¶ 266, and *EG&G Team*, Comp. Gen. Dec. B-259917.3, 95-2 CPD ¶ 175. If the agency does quantify some of the non-cost evaluation factors, the Comptroller General will not scrutinize the quantification for accuracy but will focus on the overall rationality of the best value decision, *DDD Co.*, Comp. Gen. Dec. B-276708, 97-2 CPD ¶ 44.

In the past, some agencies have attempted to devise numerical formulas to make this tradeoff appear to be *objective*. Some of these formulas have used a total point system by assigning points to the price, others have assigned dollar values to the non-price factors and a third has divided the price by the points assigned to non-price factors to come up with a dollars per point figure. Such techniques have been accepted as tools to be used in evaluating the relative merits of proposals. However, the Comptroller General has indicated that these are only evaluation techniques and that the source selection official should still exercise judgment in determining whether the merits of the highest scored proposal are worth paying a higher price. See, e.g., *Harrison Sys., Ltd.*, 63 Comp. Gen. 244 (B-212675), 84-1 CPD ¶ 572 (recommending that a total point system not be used in combination with a statement that award will be made to the offeror receiving the highest number of points); *Storage Technology Corp.,* Comp. Gen. Dec. B-215336, 84-2 CPD ¶ 190 (dollar values assigned to non-price factors only to be used as a *guide* to the selection official); and *Moran Assocs.*, Comp. Gen. Dec. B-240564.2, 91-2 CPD ¶ 495 (cost/technical ratio formula only one tool to assure that the Government was getting the best buy). In addition, a number of agencies have prohibited or strongly discouraged the use of such formulas.

B. Lowest Price Technically Acceptable Source Selection Process

This strategy has been used for many years. The FAR now describes it as a "best value" procedure but the best value determination is made by the agency at the time the strategy is chosen, before receipt or analysis of proposals. FAR 15.101-2 describes this process as follows:

> (a) The lowest price technically acceptable source selection process is appropriate when best value is expected to result from selection of the technically acceptable proposal with the lowest evaluated price.
>
> (b) When using the lowest price technically acceptable process, the following apply:

> (1) The evaluation factors and significant subfactors that establish the requirements of acceptability shall be set forth in the solicitation. Solicitations shall specify that award will be made on the basis of the lowest evaluated price of proposals meeting or exceeding the acceptability standards for non-cost factors. If the contracting officer documents the file pursuant to 15.304(c)(3)(iii), past performance need not be an evaluation factor in lowest price technically acceptable source selections. If the contracting officer elects to consider past performance as an evaluation factor, it shall be evaluated in accordance with 15.305. However, the comparative assessment in 15.305(a)(2)(i) does not apply. If the contracting officer determines that a small business' past performance is not acceptable, the matter shall be referred to the Small Business Administration for a Certificate of Competency determination, in accordance with the procedures contained in subpart 19.6 and 15 U.S.C. § 637(b)(7).
>
> (2) Tradeoffs are not permitted.
>
> (3) Proposals are evaluated for acceptability but not ranked using the non-cost/price factors.
>
> (4) Exchanges may occur (see 15.306).

It is important to note that when using this technique, the non-cost evaluation factors are all of equal importance. Thus, the failure of a proposal to meet any *one* of the factors will preclude award to the offeror submitting the proposal. However, the offeror may be given an opportunity to cure the noncompliance through oral or written discussions if award on initial proposals will not be made and the proposal would otherwise be in the competitive range.

The term "technically acceptable proposals" as used in the FAR refers to all non-cost factors. Thus, it includes factors dealing with the capability of the offerors as well as the technical details of the performance which is offered in the proposal. While FAR 15.101-2(b) refers only to "past performance" as requiring reference to Small Business Administration (SBA), the same rule would apply to other "capability" factors. See, e.g., *Vantex Serv. Corp.*, Comp. Gen. Dec. B-266199, 96-1 CPD ¶ 29, holding that when "traditional" responsibility factors such as "experience" are evaluated on a "go/no-go" basis, the matter must be referred to the SBA if the proposal is determined unacceptable because of such factors. See also *Dynamic*

Aviation — Helicopters, Comp. Gen. Dec. B-274122, 96-2 CPD ¶ 166; and *Environsol, Inc.*, Comp. Gen. Dec. B-254223, 93-2 CPD ¶ 295.

This technique has been used extensively in the past. See, for example, *Weinschel Eng'g Co.*, 64 Comp. Gen. 524 (B-217202), 85-1 CPD ¶ 574, where the Comptroller General agreed with a source selection when the Navy awarded a fixed-price contract to the lowest priced offeror meeting the RFP's technical specifications. In *Saxon Corp.*, Comp. Gen. Dec. B-216148, 85-1 CPD ¶ 87, the RFP provided for award to the offeror with the lowest overall price among those offers found acceptable in the technical and management areas. Technical and management factors were thus scored on a go, no-go basis. In *Computer Sciences Corp.*, Comp. Gen. Dec. B-213287, 84-2 CPD ¶ 151, the RFP for a data base management system called for award to the vendor with the lowest evaluated price offering a system judged to have a "user-friendly, English-like syntax." Award may also be made to the technically acceptable proposal with the lowest total discounted life cycle cost, *Hawaiian Tel. Co.*, Comp. Gen. Dec. B-187871, 77-1 CPD ¶ 298; *University Sys.*, GSBCA 10600-P, 90-3 BCA ¶ 23,085.

The use of this method has on several occasions led to protests that sealed bidding was required for the procurement. In *Saxon Corp.*, Comp. Gen. Dec. B-216148, 85-1 CPD ¶ 87, the Comptroller General upheld the use of negotiation, finding that it was impossible to draft sufficiently precise specifications for a sealed bid procurement where a high level of technical and management competence was needed. Similarly, in *Essex Electro Eng'rs, Inc.*, 65 Comp. Gen. 242 (B-221114), 86-1 CPD ¶ 92, the use of negotiation was upheld because of the agency's need to conduct discussions with offerors. The protester's argument that the agency could have obtained the necessary information through a preaward survey was rejected, as the discussion process can be used to negotiate contractual terms as well as to obtain responsibility related information. See also *Vantex Serv. Corp.*, Comp. Gen. Dec. B-266199, 96-1 CPD ¶ 29, where the RFP listed three technical evaluation factors which the agency stated would be evaluated on a go/no-go basis to determine the acceptability of an offeror's proposal. Once technical acceptability was established based on the evaluation factors, price would become the determinative factor for award. The Comptroller General found proper the use of competitive negotiation because the agency reasonably determined that discussions were necessary.

C. Combination of Tradeoff and Low Price Acceptable Processes

Although FAR Part 15 does not directly address the combination of these two processes, FAR 15.101 indicates that a "combination of source selection approaches" may be used. Thus an agency could subject some of the evaluation factors to a "go, no-go" test, while providing that others can be evaluated on the relative merits provided. This technique would enable tradeoffs to be made for those factors subject to evaluation on their relative merits while requiring rejection of the proposals not meeting the minimum requirements for those subject to the "go, no-go" test. Another strategy might be to subject all factors to a "go, no-go" test for the proposal to receive further consideration and then to evaluate the relative merits of those determined to be acceptable. These types of strategies were discussed in Chapter 2 of the GSA Handbook, Source Selection Procedures, APD P 2800.2, July 21, 1987, which provided the following guidance:

> [A] go, no-go approach can be applied to some or all of the major evaluation factors or subfactors identified in the solicitation. When all factors are go, no-go the process is equivalent to the lowest-priced acceptable proposal approach discussed above. When the "greatest value concept" is used, some evaluation factors may be used as discriminators and be evaluated on a go, no-go basis. An evaluation factor such as "management" may be used as a discriminator for evaluation on a go, no-go basis. If the "management" factor is scored adequate, it may, or may not, have further relevance in the evaluation process. . . . The evaluation process may be structured so that the factor has no further relevance . . . if it is scored adequate. On the other hand, the evaluation process may be structured so that the factor is scored and the merits of the proposal considered in the ultimate award decision. An adequate score in such an area is therefore a minimum requirement for selection. . . . This approach is frequently used in situations in which the product is subject to testing to establish whether it meets certain requirements outlined in the solicitation.

This method has been used in a number of situations and has been approved by the Comptroller General. See *ECI Telecom, Inc.*, 64 Comp. Gen. 688 (B-218533), 85-2 CPD ¶ 73, where the Comptroller General upheld a selection based on a go, no-go evaluation of all technical subfactors. See also *FMB Laundry, Inc.*, Comp. Gen. Dec. B-261837.2, 95-2 CPD ¶ 274, where the protester argued that the RFP was deficient because it failed to specify what weight would be accorded to the technical factors in relation to price. The Comptroller General stated that the fact that relative weight of acceptability verses price was not spelled out was irrelevant because the solicitation did not contemplate gradations in acceptability rankings as it was essentially a go/no-go determination. This procedure has been upheld in a procurement containing a "5000 round service life" requirement, *Smith & Wesson Div., Bangor Punta Corp. v. United States*, 782 F.2d 1074 (1st Cir. 1986), *reh'g and reh'g en banc denied, Unpub.* (1986), where a product was excluded from further consideration based on tests of samples which cracked before firing 5000 rounds. The Comptroller General has approved similar procedures where offerors had an opportunity to correct deficiencies found in initial testing, *Centennial Computer Prods., Inc.*, Comp. Gen. Dec. B-212979, 84-2 CPD ¶ 295.

Very important

II. EVALUATION FACTORS AND SUBFACTORS

Evaluation factors and subfactors describe the matters which are to be considered in determining which proposal will be most advantageous to the Government. See FAR 15.304:

> (b) Evaluation factors and significant subfactors must —
>
> (1) Represent the key areas of importance and emphasis to be considered in the source selection decision; and
>
> (2) Support meaningful comparison and discrimination between and among competing proposals.

While the statutes and regulations use the term "evaluation factors," they are also often called "criteria."

The specific number and types of evaluation factors and subfactors depend upon the nature of the procurement and the needs of the Government. Procuring officials have broad discretion in selecting the factors and in determining their relative importance. See *Augmentation, Inc.*, Comp. Gen. Dec. B-186614, 76-2 CPD ¶ 235, where the Comptroller General stated:

> [I]t is well settled that a determination of an agency's minimum needs and the selection and weights of evaluation criteria to be used to measure how well offerors will meet those needs are within the broad discretion entrusted to agency procurement officials.

Should be based on 100 points its easier

Within this broad authority, Congress has required that, as a minimum, the evaluation factors must deal with cost to the Government and quality of the products or services and all significant factors and subfactors and their relative importance must be disclosed in the solicitation, 10 U.S.C. § 2305(a)(3) and 41 U.S.C. § 253a(c). FAR 15.304 implements these requirements.

The evaluation factors specified in a solicitation not only notify the offerors of what will be evaluated, they also serve as the basis for determining what is to be submitted by offerors. Some of the submissions will be used only for evaluation while others will also be incorporated into the contract. They include price or estimated cost and fee and the other features that will become part of the offeror's contractual undertaking. These other features might be the precise product or service to be furnished, the offered delivery schedule, a specific warranty, or any other promise made by the offeror that will become part of the contract. This classification of factors has been referred to as "offer factors" as opposed to "capability factors," which deal with an offeror's ability to perform. Some "capability factors" can become "offer factors" if the agency decides to incorporate the information submitted by the offeror into the contract. As far as evaluation and source selection is concerned, the classification is not relevant, but the solicitation should inform the offerors which factors will be made contractual promises and which will be used solely for evaluation purposes. This matter will be discussed in Section III, below. This section deals with the types of evaluation factors and subfactors which might be used by an agency, the requirements for their disclosure and the indication of their relative importance.

A. Categories of Evaluation Factors

Neither the statutes nor the FAR deal coherently with the classification of evaluation factors. Both statutes combine non-cost factors dealing with the capability of the offeror with those describing offers solicited by the RFP under the broad category "quality." See 10 U.S.C. § 2305(a)(3)(A)(i) and 41 U.S.C. § 253a(c)(1)(A) specifying evaluation of the "quality of the product or services to be provided (including technical capability, management capability, prior experience, and past performance of the offeror)." FAR 15.304(c)(2) contains this same classification, expanding upon it as follows:

> The quality of the product or service shall be addressed in every source selection through consideration of one or more non-cost evaluation factors

> such as past performance, compliance with solicitation requirements, technical excellence, management capability, personnel qualifications, and prior experience.

Rather than combining non-cost factors under this general heading of quality, the following material distinguishes between factors dealing with the capability of the offeror and those which relate to offers solicited by the RFP.

1. Offer Factors

Offer factors are those factors that will result in contractual promises made by the contractor to the Government. Such promises are solicited by the Request for Proposals and incorporated into the resulting contract, either by reference or, preferably, by specific contract terms that are agreed to by both parties.

a. Cost to the Government

The one offer evaluation factor that is present in every negotiated procurement is cost to the Government. Offerors submit this offer by filling out Section B of the Uniform Contract Format when they submit their proposals. This discussion of cost to the Government includes the amount to be paid to the contractor and other costs which the Government might incur in procuring and using articles or services.

(1) Amount to Be Paid to the Contractor

The amount to be paid to the Government depends on the pricing arrangement to be used in the contract. When a firm-fixed-price contract is involved, the offeror's proposed price, not a mere estimate of the "realistic" cost, is the criterion which must be used in evaluating the proposal, *Planning Research Corp.*, Comp. Gen. Dec. B-237201, 90-1 CPD ¶ 131, *recons. denied*, 90-1 CPD ¶ 362; *Litton Sys., Inc.*, 63 Comp. Gen. 585 (B-215106), 84-2 CPD ¶ 317. This rule is followed because the contractor bears the risk of costs exceeding the price of a firm-fixed-price contract. If the agency doubts the offeror's ability to perform at the offered price, the problem should be treated in the evaluation of non-price factors or as a matter of responsibility, *Triple P Servs., Inc.*, Comp. Gen. Dec. B-271629.3, 96-2

CPD ¶ 30. Similarly, if the agency believes that the offeror's price indicates a lack of understanding of the work to be performed, this should be taken into consideration in the evaluation of capability or determination of responsibility. See *Systems Processes & Eng'g Corp.*, Comp. Gen. Dec. B-234142, 89-1 CPD ¶ 441, *recons. denied*, 89-2 CPD ¶ 191; and *Sarasota Measurements & Controls, Inc.*, Comp. Gen. Dec. B-252406.3, July 15, 1994, *Unpub*. In this regard, FAR 15.305(a)(1) provides that cost realism analyses may be used "in exceptional cases, on other competitive fixed-price-type contracts (see 15.404-1(d)(3))."

There has been considerable confusion over the evaluation of fixed-price incentive contracts and the FAR does not address this issue. In the past, the Comptroller General stated that target cost should be used to evaluate the proposed prices, *Televiso Elecs.*, 46 Comp. Gen. 631 (B-159922) (1967). In *Serv-Air, Inc.*, 58 Comp. Gen. 362, 79-1 CPD ¶ 212, the Comptroller General held that the target price of one offeror could be contrasted with the ceiling price of another offeror in a "best case/worst case" comparison. In *Motorola, Inc.*, Comp. Gen. Dec. B-236294, 89-2 CPD ¶ 484, the Comptroller General condoned the use of the ceiling price to evaluate cost to the Government. The use of target prices alone might be logical if all offerors are proposing to use the same fixed-price incentive formula with the same ceiling. However, if the RFP permits the use of different formulas, it is better practice to use the ceiling price as the evaluation factor because this is the only element of the formula that is common to all offerors. With respect to realism of target cost proposals, FAR 15.305(a)(1) states that "Cost realism analyses may also be used on fixed-price incentive contracts" — apparently permitting use of probable target cost as an evaluation factor. However, the Comptroller General has held that it is improper to adjust the ceiling price upward in connection with increasing the target cost based on a cost realism analysis, *Raytheon Co.*, Comp. Gen. Dec. B-242484.2, 91-2 CPD ¶ 131.

In cost-reimbursement contracts, both the realistic expected cost of performance and the proposed fee should be used as evaluation factors. FAR 15.305(a)(1) requires that a cost realism analysis be conducted "to determine what the Government should realistically expect to pay for the proposed effort," and FAR 15.404-1(d)(2)(i) states that the probable cost "shall be used for purposes of evaluation to determine the best value." This is consistent with Comptroller General decisions, 50 Comp. Gen. 739 (B-171663) (1971); *DOT Sys., Inc.*, Comp. Gen. Dec. B-185558, 76-2 CPD ¶ 186; *Boeing Sikorsky Aircraft Support*, Comp. Gen. Dec. B-277263.2,

97-2 CPD ¶ 91. The Comptroller General has held that where the RFP is amended to call for a cost-reimbursement rather than fixed-price contract, the agency should also amend the RFP to explicitly include cost realism as an evaluation factor and notify offerors that proposed costs may be adjusted accordingly, *Varian Assocs., Inc.*, Comp. Gen. Dec. B-209658, 83-1 CPD ¶ 658. In this case, the initial RFP had listed "Lowest Evaluated Cost to the Government" as a factor, but although the protest was denied the Comptroller General stated that the better practice was to amend the solicitation.

The evaluation of fee depends on what type of cost-reimbursement contract is used. In a cost-plus-fixed-fee contract, the proposed fixed-fee should be used as the evaluation factor, rather than a "realistic" estimate of the fee, since the former reflects a more reliable judgment, *Booz, Allen & Hamilton*, 63 Comp. Gen. 599 (B-213665), 84-2 CPD ¶ 329. In a cost-plus-award-fee contract, it is proper to use the offeror's proposed fee structure as the evaluation factor, *Management Servs., Inc.*, Comp. Gen. Dec. B-206364, 82-2 CPD ¶ 164.

(2) Other Costs to the Government

Products or services purchased by the Government, on either a fixed-price or cost-reimbursement basis, may result in the Government incurring costs of acquisition or ownership which are not included in the contract price or cost. There is little clear guidance on the consideration of such costs as evaluation factors. The procurement statutes might be interpreted to require that other costs to the Government be specified as evaluation factors. They state that solicitations "shall at a minimum include" evaluation factors, "including cost or price, cost-related or price-related factors and subfactors," 10 U.S.C. § 2305(a)(2)(A)(i) and 41 U.S.C. § 253a(b)(1)(A). However, the FAR does not repeat this language, with FAR 15.304(c)(1) merely stating that "[p]rice or cost to the Government shall be evaluated in every source selection." The Comptroller General has not interpreted the statutes or the regulations as requiring the consideration of such costs in evaluating proposals, *Kastle Sys., Inc.*, Comp. Gen. Dec. B-231990, 88-2 CPD ¶ 415. See also *Sensis Corp.*, Comp. Gen. Dec. B-265790.2, 96-1 CPD ¶ 77 (life cycle costs are not required to be evaluated as part of the cost/price evaluation). However, the failure to consider other costs to the Government could lead to poor procurement decisions. As a matter of practice, other costs to the Government are frequently used as evaluation factors or subfactors whether objectively quantified or subjectively determined.

The most common cost of acquisition used as an evaluation criterion is transportation costs. This is one of the few areas in which evaluation of costs incurred by the Government is mandated. FAR 47.305-2 provides that a solicitation for supplies will specify that offers may be f.o.b. origin, f.o.b. destination, or both, and that they will be evaluated on the basis of the lowest overall cost to the Government. In such cases, the solicitation must require the offeror to furnish the Government with applicable data necessary to compute transportation costs.

Costs incurred as a result of owning an item are known as "life cycle" costs, and should be considered during acquisition planning, FAR 7.105(a)(3)(i). Such costs include the cost to the Government of installation, operation, maintenance, security, and disposal. The magnitude of these costs can greatly exceed the item's purchase price or production cost. See, for example, *Lockheed Missiles & Space Co. v. Department of the Treasury; AT&T Fed. Sys., Intervenor*, GSBCA 11776-P, 93-1 BCA ¶ 25,401, in which such costs resulted in awarding the contract to an offeror whose price totaled $1.4 billion over others whose prices were $900 and $700 million. Extensive agency analysis, quantified in dollar figures, illustrated the differences between the technical proposals and justified paying the price premium. See also *Ingalls Shipbuilding, Inc.*, B-275830, 97-1 CPD ¶ 180 (price premium justified because awardee's proposed life cycle cost reduction approach provided the greatest probability of achieving the greatest life cycle cost savings); *Sundstrand Corp.*, Comp. Gen. Dec. B-227038, 87-2 CPD ¶ 83 (approving award to offeror with substantially higher unit price on turbine engines due to superior life cycle cost savings); and *American Airlines Training Corp.*, Comp. Gen. Dec. B-217421, 85-2 CPD ¶ 365 (finding that future flight training costs more than made up for the large price differential).

DFARS 207.103(h)(ii) states that evaluators should "consider life cycle costs in all acquisitions of systems and equipment." However, this apparently does not require the use of life cycle costs as evaluation factors, as identical language was contained in DAR 1-335 and that regulation was not interpreted as imposing such a requirement, *Big Bud Tractors, Inc. v. United States*, 2 Cl. Ct. 188, *aff'd*, 727 F.2d 1118 (Fed. Cir. 1983); *Big Bud Tractors, Inc.*, Comp. Gen. Dec. B-209858, 83-1 CPD ¶ 127. The Comptroller General found that although the regulation "requires" that life cycle costs be considered as a factor during the procurement cycle, "we do not read the regulation as requiring that [life cycle costs] be an evaluation factor for each award." Whether to use life cycle costs as evaluation factors in defense procurements is thus left to the discretion of the contracting officer. The agency's decision not to include the cost of Government self-insurance as an evaluation factor was upheld, as this cost was considered too "indefinite" and "speculative." See also *Hawaiian Tel. Co.*, Comp. Gen. Dec. B-187871, 77-1 CPD ¶ 298, approving an agency's decision not to take into account possible termination costs since they would be too speculative. Similarly, there is no requirement that the life cycle cost of limited rights in technical data be included in the evaluation of proposals, *General Elec. Aerospace Sys.*, Comp. Gen. Dec. B-250514, 93-1 CPD ¶ 101.

When life cycle costs are an evaluation factor, it is unclear whether a general statement in the solicitation informing offerors that such costs are to be evaluated is adequate, or whether it is necessary to specify the particular costs to be evaluated. In *Lanier Bus. Prods., Inc.*, 60 Comp. Gen. 306 (B-223555), 81-1 CPD ¶ 188, *recons. denied ex rel., Dictaphone Corp.*, Comp. Gen. Dec. B-200695.2, 81-2 CPD ¶ 511, resolicitation was recommended where the RFQ merely stated that life cycle costing would be employed and did not adequately inform offerors of the specific evaluation factors to be used. See also *Systemhouse Fed. Sys., Inc.*, GSBCA 9313-P, 88-2 BCA ¶ 20,603, granting a protest because the agency did not disclose the manner in which life cycle cost analysis would be used (where it had a major impact on the evaluation). However, in *Southwestern Bell Tel. Co.*, Comp. Gen. Dec. B-200523.3, 82-1 CPD ¶ 203, the Comptroller General stated:

> Where an agency makes it clear that its evaluation will be based on an analysis of expected system life-cycle costs without qualification, offerors may reasonably expect that all determinable elements of cost will be taken into account.

These cases illustrate the difficulties created by vague language describing the life cycle costs that will be evaluated. The offerors clearly had difficulty ascertaining what costs would be evaluated, with the result that the ground rules of the competition were not clearly disclosed in the RFP. See also *AM Int'l*, Comp. Gen. Dec. B-200200, 81-1 CPD ¶ 258, stating that "[w]hen life-cycle costs are to be evaluated, we believe that the solicitation should not only indicate the fact, but also the useful life period that will be utilized in the evaluation."

However, the agency is given broad discretion when the solicitation language clearly describes what life cycle costs will be evaluated. In *ViON*

Corp., Comp. Gen. Dec. B-256363, 94-1 CPD ¶ 373, the solicitation clearly set forth what factors would be considered in determining life cycle costs. The protester argued that the solicitation's model for evaluating life cycle cost was incomplete and unreasonable because it did not consider environmental costs, such as cooling, electricity, and space. The Comptroller General denied the protest, stating that the agency properly decided not to consider environmental factors as part of life cycle costs because the agency's prior experience indicated that this was not a useful discriminator between technical solutions.

b. Non-Cost Factors

Where the contractor is merely required to comply with specifications furnished by the Government and the terms and conditions in the RFP, there will be no non-cost offer evaluation factors and no need for technical or management proposals, *International Data Prods., Inc.*, Comp. Gen. Dec. B-275480.2, 97-1 CPD ¶ 179 (offeror "global certification" that its product met all of the requirements of the solicitation was an adequate substitute for a detailed technical proposal explaining how each requirement was met). However, in many procurements the Government solicits or permits offerors to propose alterations to the specifications or terms and conditions and treats these offers as evaluation factors. When such alterations are used as evaluation factors, the agency is indicating to offerors that they are of value to the agency and that the agency will therefore consider paying a higher price to obtain that value. When this is done, the general practice is to subsequently amend the specifications and terms and conditions so that the awarded contract makes these offers contractually binding.

The use of non-cost offer factors greatly complicates the task of offerors because they must attempt to anticipate the value that the agency will give to different amounts of enhanced performance or alteration of terms and conditions. To ease this problem, the best practice is for agencies to use such factors only when they can not specify their precise requirements in the RFP.

(1) Enhancements

Probably the most common type of non-cost offer factor is enhancements to the work or results called for by the specifications. In such cases the specification generally will call for a minimum level of performance and the RFP will indicate that the agency will evaluate greater performance. In such cases, the best practice is for the agency to clearly delineate the range of enhancements it is willing to consider so that offerors do not propose enhancements that are of no benefit to the agency. It is also good practice to obtain price proposals for different levels of enhancements to enable the agency to compare proposals at each level of performance. However, the use of general language stating that enhancements will be evaluated has been approved even when the offerors had to speculate as to the value of specific enhancements, *Telos Sys. Integration v. Administrative Office of the Courts*, GSBCA 13315-P, 96-1 BCA ¶ 27,990. See also *Lexis-Nexis*, Comp. Gen. Dec. B-260023, 95-1 CPD ¶ 14, where the Comptroller General held that the RFP was sufficiently specific as to enhancements when it listed the areas where enhancements would be evaluated and gave some examples of features that were of value to the agency.

Enhancement factors are frequently used in procurements of products such as computer systems. See, for example, *Engineering & Professional Servs., Inc.*, Comp. Gen. Dec. B-262179, 95-2 CPD ¶ 266, where the Comptroller General denied a protest arguing that the RFP had not clearly stated that such enhancements would be evaluated.

(2) Specific Products or Services

In some cases, an agency will use a performance specification and evaluate specific products or services that will meet that specification. This technique is most practicable when there are a variety of products or services in the marketplace that will meet the agency's performance requirements and the agency will benefit by obtaining competitive prices for each product or service in order to identify the best value at the time of contract award. See, for example, *Integrated Sys. Group*, Comp. Gen. Dec. B-272336, 96-2 CPD ¶ 144, where the agency used this technique to procure central processing units. This technique is more difficult to use when the offered product or service has not been sold or provided because, in such cases, the agency may have little ability to evaluate whether the offeror can actually deliver the product or perform the service and whether the product or service will actually meet the contract requirement. In such cases, the best practice is to perform a risk analysis in an attempt to ensure that the best value decision is based not only on the quality of the offered product or service but also on the risk that the offeror may not be able to perform as promised. See, for example, *Alliant Techsystems, Inc.*, Comp. Gen. Dec.

B-276162, 97-1 CPD ¶ 141, where the Comptroller General denied a protest challenging the risk assessment of the technical feasibility of manufacturing the proposed product at the offered price. See also *Martin Marietta Corp.*, Comp. Gen. Dec. B-259823.4, 96-1 CPD ¶ 265, where the Comptroller General denied a protest that the agency had found that the protester's technical approach to meeting the specification was "unsatisfactory," and had awarded the contract to an offeror whose approach was rated "good."

(3) Process or Techniques to be Used

Another non-cost offer factor is the process or technique that the offeror intends to use to meet the Government's performance requirements. This factor can be used in two ways. If it is used to evaluate the offeror's understanding of the work or capability to perform the work, it is a capability factor. However, if the agency intends to incorporate the technique or process into the contract, making it contractually binding, it will be an offer factor. In most instances, the best practice is to treat this as a capability factor — giving the contractor the freedom to meet the performance requirements using some other technique or process — but there are some instances where an agency has determined that the specific technique or process has an identified value that will not be achieved by the use of any other technique or process. In such cases, this should be treated as an offer factor.

When a proposed process or technique is used as an evaluation factor, it is good practice to evaluate the comparative risk of using different techniques. See, for example, *Robbins-Gioia, Inc.*, Comp. Gen. Dec. B-274318, 96-2 CPD ¶ 222, where the Comptroller General denied a protest that the agency had evaluated a proposal for the use of "state-of-the-art software architecture" as having moderate risk as compared to a proposal to use off-the-shelf software. In such cases, the agency is conducting a form of design competition requiring the evaluation of the potential effectiveness of the offered designs. See, for example, *AT&T Corp.*, Comp. Gen. Dec. B-261154.4, 96-1 CPD ¶ 232, where the Comptroller General agreed that the agency's evaluation of competing designs was performed effectively.

(4) Terms and Conditions

A fourth type of non-cost offer factor is the enhanced or specific term or condition. Enhanced terms and conditions should be treated in the same manner as other enhancements — the agency should state a minimum acceptable level and the range of enhanced performance which it considers to be of potential value. Specific terms and conditions that the agency requires to be filled out with explicit information should be clearly stated so that the offerors clearly understand the information that will be incorporated in the contract.

Perhaps the most common enhanced term or condition is the warranty clause where the agency solicits better warranty coverage than the minimum specified in the RFP. See *Integrated Sys. Group*, Comp. Gen. Dec. B-272336, 96-2 CPD ¶ 144, where offers were obtained for "extended warranties" of one and two years.

A common example of a specific term or condition is the Key Personnel clause that is used in many service procurements. As discussed below, key personnel is a frequently used capability factor but when the names of the key personnel are incorporated into a Key Personnel clause, this factor becomes an offer factor because the contractor promises to use the specified personnel unless they become unavailable. While the evaluation of key personnel can be a strong predictor of performance, it is only completely valid if the personnel proposed by the offer actually work on the contract. Yet, that is not the effect of a Key Personnel clause. Almost all of the clauses in use call for the use of key personnel listed in the clause or equally qualified personnel approved by the contracting officer. This is, of course, a necessary part of the process because the contractor cannot guarantee that employees will stay with the company or be willing to work on the contract.

The Comptroller General has given contractors a substantial amount of freedom to operate under these clauses. See, for example, *Laser Power Technologies, Inc.*, Comp. Gen. Dec. B-233369, 89-1 CPD ¶ 267, where the protester argued that a competing offeror had to propose "permanent" employees to meet the key personnel requirements in the solicitation. The Comptroller General denied the protest, stating:

> Laser power essentially contends the RFP requires that proposed key personnel must be for permanent positions. However, the RFP, which contains the "key personnel" clause referenced above, does not require designated key personnel to be permanent, nor even that the contractor commence performance with the personnel listed in its proposal, so long as the contractor provides personnel as qualified as those listed in the proposal and obtains the Air Force's approval for all substituted key personnel. *A.B. Dick Co.*,

> B-233142, Jan. 31, 1989, 89-1 CPD ¶ [106]. Indeed, there is nothing unusual or inherently improper for an awardee to recruit and hire personnel employed by the incumbent contractor. *A.B. Dick Co.*, 233142, *supra*, at 5; *Applications Research Co.*, B-230097, May 25, 1988, 88-1 CPD ¶ 499.

On the other hand, the Comptroller General will intervene if there is a substitution of lesser qualified personnel. See *KPMG Peat Marwick, LLP*, Comp. Gen. Dec. B-259479.2, 95-2 CPD ¶ 13, *recons. denied*, 95-2 CPD ¶ 26, where the Comptroller General sustained a protest where the agency had ordered the winning contractor to substitute less qualified personnel. The Comptroller General stated the following rule:

> The agency asserts that under the RFP's "Key Personnel" clause, a standard provision which allows the contracting officer to authorize substitutions of personnel so long as the replacement personnel qualifications "are equal to or better [than] the qualifications of the personnel being replaced," it had unfettered authority to change [the contractor's] proposed personnel. Contrary to [the agency's] position, the RFP's key personnel clause cannot be used by the agency if the effect of the substitution is to significantly modify the contract awarded; such an interpretation would render meaningless the competition on the original solicitation requirements. See *Planning Research Corp. v. United States*, 971 F.2d 736 (Fed. Cir. 1992). Rather, the key personnel clause is simply intended to permit the natural turnover of personnel that tends to occur during the performance of a contract.

Thus, the Comptroller General will find that the competition has not been fairly conducted if the Key Personnel clause is not enforced as written and will require that the procurement be recompeted. The same result was reached by the General Services Administration Board of Contract Appeals in *PSI Int'l, Inc. v. Department of Energy*, GSBCA 11521-P, 92-2 BCA ¶ 24,775, where it was held that it was improper to award a contract to an offeror that had not named its key personnel but had reserved the right to staff the contract with competent personnel.

The most difficult problem is the enforceability of the clause when the contractor requests the contracting officer's approval of substitution of personnel. While there appears to be no litigated case on the subject, cases regarding clauses requiring contracting officer approval to substitute subcontractors are a sufficiently close analogy to be usable in this area. These cases find it to be an abuse of discretion for the contracting officer to deny approval when the substitute subcontractor is equally competent to the subcontractor listed in the contract, *Hoel-Steffen Constr. Co. v. United*

States, 684 F.2d 843 (Ct. Cl. 1982); *Liles Constr. Co. v. United States*, 455 F.2d 527 (Ct. Cl. 1972); *Richard Constr., Inc. v. General Servs. Admin.*, GSBCA 11161, 93-1 BCA ¶ 25,239. It could also be a constructive change to the contract if the contracting officer demands that the contractor use more qualified personnel than those listed in the clause, *Watson, Rice & Co.*, HUDBCA 89-4468-C6, 90-1 BCA ¶ 22,499. In that case, however, the Department of Housing and Urban Development Board of Contract Appeals found that the contracting officer's "suggestions" that different, more qualified subcontractor personnel be used did not rise to the level of an "order" for purposes of finding a constructive change.

(5) DELIVERY OF COMPLETION SCHEDULE

In some instances, the agency will use the delivery or completion schedule as an offer factor. In such cases, the RFP will state the time of performance that the agency must have and will permit offerors to propose shorter times of performance. This technique should never be used unless the agency has determined that it will benefit from faster performance, and, in such cases, the RFP should clearly state the amount of faster performance that will be of value. Like other enhancements, it is also good practice to obtain price proposals on a step ladder basis so that offers can be rationally compared.

2. Capability

"Capability factors" are those factors that will be used to evaluate the relative ability of the competing offerors to perform the contract.

a. Responsibility Determinations Distinguished

Since these factors deal with the same matters that are considered in making responsibility determinations, it is important to distinguish between them. Agencies commonly evaluate factors and subfactors related to responsibility, notwithstanding the fact that a formal responsibility determination must ultimately be made before award of the contract. Such factors and subfactors frequently include experience, staffing, and past performance. This process does not officially constitute a responsibility determination as long as these factors are evaluated on a variable basis. Therefore, it does not conflict with the Small Business Administration's (SBA) authority to resolve questions concerning the responsibility of small businesses. In *Electrospace Sys., Inc.*, 58 Comp. Gen. 415 (B-192574), 79-1 CPD ¶ 264, the Comptroller General stated at 425:

> Since neither 10 U.S.C. § 2304(g) nor applicable regulations in any way restrict the "other factors" that may be used by agencies in selecting the proposal having the greatest value to the Government, we have not prohibited procuring agencies from using responsibility-related factors in making *relative* assessments of the merits of competing proposals. There is no indication on the face of Public Law 95-89 or in the legislative history of the law that Congress intended to eliminate this long-standing practice as far as the evaluation of small business proposals are concerned. Thus, neither the cited precedent (40 Comp. Gen., *supra*) of advertised procurements nor the 1977 Public Law prevents the relative-assessment evaluation of responsibility-related information contained in small business proposals.

See also *Southwest Maine, Inc.*, Comp. Gen. Dec. B-198701, 80-2 CPD ¶ 123. In *T. Head & Co.*, Comp. Gen. Dec. B-275783, 97-1 CPD ¶ 169, the Comptroller General held that an evaluation of capability factors that resulted in the conclusion that the offeror's proposal was "unacceptable" was not a determination of nonresponsibility because the evaluation had been arrived at in the course of a best value procurement where past performance was being evaluated on a variable basis. Thus, factors and subfactors relating to responsibility are often used when evaluating technical and management criteria.

It is improper to use responsibility-related factors or subfactors if the evaluation is merely to determine acceptability of a proposal, *Sanford & Sons Co.*, 67 Comp. Gen. 612 (B-231607), 88-2 CPD ¶ 266; *Angelo Warehouses Co.*, Comp. Gen. Dec. B-196780, 80-1 CPD ¶ 228. In *Sanford*, the agency determined that the offeror's past performance did not meet the minimum acceptable standard of performance. The Comptroller General ruled that since this was tantamount to a determination that the protester was not responsible, Sanford, who was a small business, was entitled to request a Certificate of Competency from the Small Business Administration. See also *Federal Support Corp.*, 71 Comp. Gen. 152 (B-245573), 92-1 CPD ¶ 81, and *Clegg Indus., Inc.*, 70 Comp. Gen. 679 (B-242204.3), 91-2 CPD ¶ 145, where the Comptroller General found that an agency had improperly used responsibility factors to determine technical acceptability and pointed out that responsibility factors should be used only to make a comparative evaluation of the proposals. These cases could be read as precluding the use of responsibility factors or subfactors in any procurement where the award was to be made to the offeror that submitted the lowest priced technically acceptable proposal since any negative evaluation of responsibility could only be used to disqualify the offeror. However, there are other decisions of the Comptroller General permitting rejection of proposals submitted by large businesses as being technically unacceptable based on responsibility-type factors related to the experience of the offeror, *Oak Ridge Associated Univ.*, Comp. Gen. Dec. B-245694, 92-1 CPD ¶ 86 (lack of experience required by RFP); *Aerostat Servs. Partnership*, Comp. Gen. Dec. B-244939.2, 92-1 CPD ¶ 71 (failure to propose manning adequate to meet specifications); *Color Ad Signs & Displays*, Comp. Gen. Dec. B-241544, 91-1 CPD ¶ 154 (lack of required experience); *Sach Sinha & Assocs., Inc.*, 69 Comp. Gen. 108 (B-236911), 90-1 CPD ¶ 50 (personnel did not meet education and experience requirement of RFP). These decisions appear to indicate that responsibility-type factors may be used to determine lack of acceptability of proposals from large businesses, but not from small ones.

The critical question then is whether the agency can make a valid assessment of capability from these two factors alone or whether additional capability factors should be used. The answer depends on the specific procurement. For example, in some manufacturing contracts, the agency may believe that it is essential to evaluate the facilities of each offeror. In service contracts, some agencies believe it is crucial to evaluate key personnel. In either type of contract, the agency may find it advantageous to evaluate major subcontractors. It is important to select an array of factors that provide a balanced assessment of the capability of each offeror to perform the work called for by the contract.

b. Past Performance

FASA amended 10 U.S.C. § 2305(a)(3)(A) and 41 U.S.C. § 253a(c) to add past performance as one of the potential evaluation factors in source selection, and amended 41 U.S.C. § 401 to require the adoption of procedures "that encourage the consideration of the offerors' past performance in the selection of contractors." FAR 15.304(c)(3) makes past performance a mandatory factor as follows:

> (i) Except as set forth in paragraph (c)(3)(iii) of this section, past performance shall be evaluated in all source selections for negotiated competitive acquisitions expected to exceed $1,000,000.

> (ii) Except as set forth in paragraph (c)(3)(iii) of this section, past performance shall be evaluated in all source selections for negotiated competitive acquisitions issued on or after January 1, 1999, for acquisitions expected to exceed $100,000. Agencies should develop phase-in schedules that meet or exceed this schedule.

See also OFPP Policy Letter 92-5 and *A Guide to Best Practices for Past Performance.*

The evaluation of past performance reduces the emphasis on merely writing good proposals in favor of focusing on actual performance on prior contracts. Past performance can be evaluated as a separate evaluation factor or as a subfactor. There is no question that this is a proper factor in the evaluation process, *Ferranti Int'l Defense Sys., Inc.*, Comp. Gen. Dec. B-237555, 90-1 CPD ¶ 239, even though it may give the incumbent contractor with a good performance record an advantage in the competition, *Bendix Field Eng'g Corp.*, Comp. Gen. Dec. B-241156, 91-1 CPD ¶ 44; *Engineering & Computation, Inc.*, Comp. Gen. Dec. B-275180.2, 97-1 CPD ¶ 47. It has also been held proper to evaluate past performance even if poor performance is attributable, to some extent, to subcontractors, *Neal R. Gross & Co.*, Comp. Gen. Dec. B-275066, 97-1 CPD ¶ 30 (noting that the prime contractor always bears responsibility for the work of subcontractors). See also *Federal Envtl. Servs., Inc.*, Comp. Gen. Dec. B-260289, 95-1 CPD ¶ 261; and *CORVAC, Inc.*, Comp. Gen. Dec. B-244766, 91-2 CPD ¶ 454. An offeror may also be given a good past performance rating based on the consideration of a proposed subcontractor's prior contracts under the past performance factor, *GZA Remediation, Inc.*, Comp. Gen. Dec. B-272386, 96-2 CPD ¶ 155.

FAR 15.305(a)(2) contains the following detailed requirements when past performance is used as an evaluation factor:

> (i) Past performance information is one indicator of an offeror's ability to perform the contract successfully. The currency and relevance of the information, source of the information, context of the data, and general trends in contractor's performance shall be considered (41 U.S.C. 401). This comparative assessment of past performance information is separate from the responsibility determination required under subpart 9.1.
>
> (ii) The solicitation shall describe the approach for evaluating past performance, including evaluating offerors with no relevant performance history, and shall provide offerors an opportunity to identify past or current

(including Federal, State, and local government and private) for efforts similar to the Government requirement. The solicitation shall also authorize offerors to provide information on problems encountered on the identified contracts and the offeror corrective actions. The Government shall consider this information, as well as information obtained from any other sources, when evaluating the offeror past performance. The source selection authority shall determine the relevance of similar past performance information.

(iii) The evaluation should take into account past performance information regarding predecessor companies, key personnel who have relevant experience, or subcontractors that will perform major or critical aspects of the requirement when such information is relevant to the instant acquisition.

This guidance is somewhat more detailed than in prior regulations, and appears to require a more through description in the RFP of the methodology that will be used to evaluate past performance. The RFP should also contain a clear statement of the precise information that each offeror is required to furnish to facilitate the evaluation of past performance.

The Air Force Materiel Command (AFMC) uses past performance as a specific risk assessment factor which is given to the source selection official to be used with the technical/management color codes and a technical proposal risk factor, AFMCFARS Appendix BB, May 15, 1996. Performance risk is defined according to one of the following categories:

(1) High — Significant doubt exists, based on the offeror's performance record, that the offeror can perform the proposed effort.

(2) Moderate — Some doubt exists, based on the offeror's performance record, that the offeror can perform the proposed effort.

(3) Low — Little doubt exists, based on the offeror's performance record, that the offeror can perform the proposed effort.

(4) Not Applicable — No significant performance record is identified.

See *Universal Technologies, Inc.*, Comp. Gen. Dec. B-241157, 91-1 CPD ¶ 63, *recons. denied*, Comp. Gen. Dec. B-241157.2, 91-1 CPD ¶ 505, fully displaying and affirming the use of these factors. In *Instrument Control Serv., Inc.*, Comp. Gen. Dec. B-247286, 92-1 CPD ¶ 407, the Comptroller General found proper a past performance risk assessment based upon information obtained from another agency regarding a default termination of the offeror. See also *Dragon Servs., Inc.*, Comp. Gen. Dec. B-255354, 94-1 CPD ¶ 151, an Army procurement, where the Comptroller General found proper a past performance risk assessment of "moderate" based upon unfavorable information received concerning the protester's performance under a similar contract at another agency.

While past performance can be used as either a factor or a subfactor, it is good practice to avoid using it in both situations simultaneously. For example, in *Center for Educ. & Manpower Resources*, Comp. Gen. Dec. B-191453, 78-2 CPD ¶ 21, it was held impermissible to evaluate past performance as a factor and also use past performance in the evaluation of technical and management factors. The Comptroller General reasoned that this gave a higher weight to past performance than was indicated in the RFP. A similar result was reached in *Metric Sys. Corp.*, Comp. Gen. Dec. B-210218.2, 83-2 CPD ¶ 394. Compare *Global Assoc., Ltd.*, Comp. Gen. Dec. B-275534, 97-1 CPD ¶ 129, where the Comptroller General rejected a protest that undue weight had been given to past performance. See also *Halter Marine, Inc.*, B-255429, 94-1 CPD ¶ 161, where the Comptroller General found the evaluation to be unreasonable because the agency gave overwhelming emphasis to past performance by repeated consideration of that factor in both the technical merit and quality control capability factors. In *United Ammunition Container, Inc.*, Comp. Gen. Dec. B-275213, 97-1 CPD ¶ 58, the solicitation identified technical approach, management, and past performance as separate and independent evaluation factors. The protester asserted that the agency's evaluation of the awardee's proposal was flawed because the agency only considered the awardee's past performance record under the past performance factor and should have considered the awardee's past performance record under the other evaluation factors as well. The Comptroller General denied the protest stating that this would have resulted in an exaggeration of the importance of the past performance factor.

c. Experience

In most procurements, the best practice is to assess the capability of the offerors be evaluating experience as well as past performance. This is so because the cases are conflicting on the issue of whether experience is included within the assessment of past performance. See, for example, *Telcom Sys. Servs., Inc. v. Department of Justice*, GSBCA 13272-P, 95-2 BCA ¶ 27,849, where the board stated that experience must be considered when evaluating past performance. In that case, the board stated that "[i]t is unreasonable to suggest that past performance does not encompass experience." In contrast, in *Hughes Georgia, Inc.*, Comp. Gen. Dec. B-272526, 96-2 CPD ¶ 151, the Comptroller General indicated that experience was not included in the evaluation of past performance. Other cases appear to indicate that there is a good deal of confusion on this issue. For example, in *Ameriko, Inc.*, Comp. Gen. Dec. B-272989, 96-2 CPD ¶ 167, the Comptroller General did not object to the consideration of past performance when the evaluation factor in the RFP was "experience," while in *Myers Investigative & Security Servs., Inc.*, Comp. Gen. Dec. B-272947.2, 96-2 CPD ¶ 114, the Comptroller General agreed that experience could be evaluated as part of the past performance evaluation factor when the RFP stated that the agency would assess "relevant corporate experience and past performance."

These cases make it essential that past performance and experience be evaluated separately. See *Executive Court Reporters, Inc.*, Comp. Gen. Dec. B-272981, 96-2 CPD ¶ 227, stating that past performance and experience should be separate factors and evaluated separately. See also *PW Constr., Inc.*, Comp. Gen. Dec. B-272248, 96-2 CPD ¶ 130, where the Comptroller General concluded that the evaluation of both experience and past performance was properly performed. The fact that they are two components of a contractor's capability that involve inquires into the past have led some to believe that they are the same thing. However, their evaluation requires asking entirely different questions. To determine a contractor's experience the questions are: What have you done? and How many times or for how long have you done it? The question for past performance is: How well have you done it?

Once it has been determined that experience is to be evaluated, the types of experience relevant to the procurement must be determined. Often, RFPs merely indicate that experience on "similar" projects will be considered. There are many factors to be considered in determining similarity, including dollar value, complexity, and nature of the work. Some RFPs go into great detail specifying the types of experience considered important and, in some cases, their relative importance, *Telestar Corp.*, Comp. Gen. Dec. B-275855, 97-1 CPD ¶ 150 (experience required on projects "of similar size and scope related to this effort"); *Sigmatech, Inc.*, Comp. Gen. Dec. B-271821, 96-2 CPD ¶ 101 (corporate experience plus "sufficient personnel with ample qualifications"), and agencies have been permitted to specify very limited types of relevant experience, *Systems Application & Technologies, Inc.*, Comp. Gen. Dec. B-270672, 96-1 CPD ¶ 182 (experience with contracting agency); *CAN Indus. Eng'g, Inc.*, Comp. Gen. Dec. B-271034, 96-1 CPD ¶ 279 (experience with the agency's system that was to be tested under the contract). See *Computer Sys. Dev. Co.*, Comp. Gen. Dec. B-275356, 97-1 CPD ¶ 91, where the Comptroller General noted the following description contained in the solicitation:

> Under the corporate experience factor, the RFP provided that consideration would be given to the breadth (i.e., variety or number of contracts) and significance (i.e., size, complexity, participation) of corporate experience (including subcontractors and consultants of this proposal) in accomplishing efforts relevant to those described in the [statement of work]. The RFP also provided that [w]hen cited contracts cover a variety of size and complexity, greater weight goes to relevant contracts of a size and complexity equal to or greater than this solicitation, and that [p]articular emphasis shall be placed on contracts that provide [AIS] services in a dynamic environment . . . [such as] . . . [o]pen architecture or systems migration experience.

Even where solicitations use terms such as "similar" or "relevant" in describing the nature of the experience, the cases have been quite liberal in permitting the Government to use specific discriminators that are not stated in the solicitation. See *EastCo Building Servs., Inc.*, Comp. Gen. Dec. B-275334.2, 97-1 CPD ¶ 83, where the Comptroller General held that the totality of the RFP will be considered in determining whether offerors were given appropriate notice of the factors to be considered. The Comptroller General stated:

> EastCo argues that the agency improperly applied — and downgraded its proposal under the past performance/experience on similar projects factor based on — two undisclosed criteria: whether previously performed contracts were of at least a 3-year duration, and whether the areas of the buildings maintained under prior contracts had been at least 500,000 square feet.
>
> This argument is without merit. The RFP required offerors to list prior contracts, which would be evaluated for past performance/experience, and to indicate for each contract (among other things) the type of facility, gross square footage, services performed, and duration. EastCo and the other offerors were on notice from these requirements that, in judging whether a prior contract would be deemed a "similar project," the agency would consider the similarity of the contracts to the RFP requirement in these areas, and reading these requirements together with the rest of the RFP should have put EastCo on notice of the agency's intent to consider these specific elements of its listed contracts. *See ORI Servs. Corp.*, B-261225, July 28, 1995, 95-2 CPD ¶ 55.

See also *Aviate L.L.C.*, Comp. Gen. Dec. B-275058.6, 97-1 CPD ¶ 162, where a factor used in selecting the source was the awardee's experience on "performance based contracting" although the RFP did not specifically call for that type of experience.

When an evaluator has personal knowledge of an offeror's experience, it is improper to disregard such experience in the evaluation, *Safeguard Maintenance Corp.*, Comp. Gen. Dec. B-260983.3, 96-2 CPD ¶ 116.

In some instances, the agency is willing to accept experience not specifically of the type being contracted for but does not explicitly state so. In *HSG-Holzmann Technischer Servs GmbH*, Comp. Gen. Dec. B-274992.2, 97-1 CPD ¶ 87, the agency awarded a contract for operation and maintenance of a fully operational hospital to a firm that had experience only in base maintenance and operating and maintaining a "contingency hospital." The Comptroller General upheld the award based on the agency's determination that the skills and tasks involved in that work were sufficiently similar to those required for the contract being awarded.

d. Key Personnel

One of the most commonly used evaluation factors in best value procurements is the key personnel that the offeror intends to use to perform the contract. It is an especially useful means of assessing the capability of offerors in research and development and service contracts where the quality of the people will likely be a major determinant of the quality of the performance. However, this is only so if the contractor that wins the competition actually uses the key personnel that have been proposed. Many agencies use key personnel clauses in solicitations in an attempt to ensure that this occurs. This raises a question about the effectiveness of these clauses.

There is no doubt that key personnel is a useful evaluation factor. There are numerous protests regarding agency evaluations of the personnel proposed to be used to perform the work — all of which recognize the validity of this means of assessing the offerors' capability. The issues raised are the validity of the scoring and the sufficiency of discussions when there are perceived inadequacies. See, for example, *A.T. Kearney, Inc.*, Comp. Gen. Dec. B-237731, 90-1 CPD ¶ 305, where the agency downgraded an offeror because it believed that the personnel offered might not actually work on the contract. When the issue was raised in discussions, the agency continued to evaluate the factor as only "adequate" because the offeror did not provide a "strong statement" that the offered personnel really would work on the contract. The Comptroller General denied a protest of this procedure, finding that it was reasonable. Compare *Development Alternatives, Inc.*, Comp. Gen. Dec. B-217010, 85-1 CPD ¶ 188, where the Comptroller General affirmed a strong agency evaluation of key personnel even though the contractor did not provide the personnel after award. The Comptroller General stated:

> An agency's evaluation of an offer's key personnel, even though some are changed after award, is not objectionable when the names are submitted in good faith by the offeror with the consent of the respective individuals. *Kirschner Associates, Inc.*, B-187625, June 15, 1977, 77-1 CPD ¶ 426. Here, it appears that [the offeror] submitted the names of key personnel in good faith and with their consent. According to [the offeror], two of the four individuals originally proposed are working on the contract. A third individual informed [the offeror] just after the contract was signed that she had decided to stay at her current job and would be unavailable to serve on the project. A fourth individual introduced new conditions for his employment as project director after the contract was signed, which conditions [the offeror] determined were inappropriate for the project director's role and inconsistent with [the offeror's] administrative policies for full-time administrators. In view of these facts and [the agency's] report that [the offeror] did not propose personnel which it had no intention of providing, we [deny the protest].

Thus, agencies have significant latitude in evaluating this factor.

Included in this latitude is the authority to disqualify an offeror if it offers key personnel that are not committed to work on the contract. See *Planning Research Corp. v. United States*, 971 F.2d 736 (Fed. Cir. 1992), where an offeror was disqualified for submitting 101 resumes of personnel to be employed on the contract with no intention of using them. The Comptroller General has followed this reasoning in *Informatics, Inc.*, 57 Comp. Gen. 217 (B-188566), 78-1 CPD ¶ 53, where the offeror misstated the availability of key personnel, and *Ultra Technology Corp.*, Comp. Gen. Dec. B-230309.6, 89-1 CPD ¶ 42, where the offeror proposed a key person without obtaining that person's permission to use his name in the proposal. See also *Biospherics, Inc.*, Comp. Gen. Dec. B-253891.2, 93-2 CPD ¶ 333, where the Comptroller General agreed that an offeror should be disqualified when it did not disclose that a number of the personnel proposed for the contract had also been proposed for another contract being competed at the same time.

e. Facility

Another evaluation factor that may be used in best value procurements is the evaluation of an offeror's facility. See *Conrex, Inc.*, Comp. Gen. Dec. B-266060.2, 96-1 CPD ¶ 46 (proposal reasonably downgraded because offeror failed to adequately describe its facility); and *Bannum, Inc.*, Comp. Gen. Dec. B-270640, 96-1 CPD ¶ 167 (agency reasonably excluded protester from competitive range because the facility that the protester proposed would require major renovations which could not be completed within the 60-day commencement time frame). An offeror's facility may also be evaluated as a subfactor. See *Schleicher Community Corrections, Inc.*, Comp. Gen. Dec. B-270499.3, 97-1 CPD ¶ 33.

f. Technical and Management Plans

Although there is some question whether technical and management plans are a meaningful measure of an offeror's capability, they have been used for this purpose on numerous occasions. Under this evaluation factor, technical and management plans may be downgraded if they are generic. See *Intown Properties, Inc.*, Comp. Gen. Dec. B-272524, 96-2 CPD ¶ 149, where the Comptroller General found reasonable an agency's exclusion of the protester's proposal from the competitive range. Under the management plan evaluation factor, the evaluators commented that the protester's proposal repeated the solicitation without giving specifics and that the proposal did not accurately reflect the solicitation requirements. Similarly, in *Quality Elevator Co.*, Comp. Gen. Dec. B-271899, 96-2 CPD ¶ 89, the Comptroller General found reasonable an agency's evaluation where the evaluators downgraded the protester's management plan factor because the plan lacked sufficient detail. Compare *Tidewater Homes Realty, Inc.*, Comp. Gen. Dec. B-274689, 96-2 CPD ¶ 241, where the Comptroller General granted a protest where the agency had given the protester low scores for lack of detail but had given the winning offeror high scores when its proposal contained a similar level of detail.

The Comptroller General has accorded agencies considerable latitude in their evaluation of technical and management plans. See, for example, *GTE Hawaiian Tel. Co.*, Comp. Gen. Dec. B-276487.2, 97-2 CPD ¶ 21, where the agency had required each offeror to address compliance with more than 1300 technical requirements but had imposed an 800 page limitation on technical proposals. The Comptroller General denied a protest that the winning offeror had not addressed all of the requirements. See also *JW Assocs., Inc.*, Comp. Gen. Dec. B-275209, 97-1 CPD ¶ 57, where the Comptroller General initially granted a protest, in part because the agency had not documented its evaluation of a technical plan, but subsequently denied the protest when the agency reevaluated the technical plan of the winning offeror and determined that it was adequate even though it contained far less detail than the plan of the protester. Similarly, in *Matrix Int'l Logistics, Inc.*, Comp. Gen. Dec. B-272388.2, 97-2 CPD ¶ 89, the agency had evaluated one proposal as excellent and "clearly superior" to another in the initial procurement but had evaluated the same proposal as "good" and the other proposal as "excellent" in a resolicitation following a sustained protest. The Comptroller General did not comment on the disparity in evaluations in denying the protest on the resolution. Compare *DynaLantic Corp.*, Comp. Gen. Dec. B-274944.2, 97-1 CPD ¶ 101, where the Comptroller General made a detailed review of the agency's evaluation of the protester's technical and management proposal and determined that the identified deficiencies were easily correctable and thus that the protester should not have been dropped from the competitive range.

It is proper to make a risk assessment of the probability that a proposed management or technical plan will create performance problems. See, for example, *Trend Western Technical Corp.*, Comp. Gen. Dec. B-275395.2, 97-1 CPD ¶ 201, where the Comptroller General denied a protest that the agency had assessed a plan as having "moderate risk" because the staffing level was low. See also *Sensis Corp.*, Comp. Gen. Dec. B-265790.2, 96-1 CPD ¶ 77, where the agency properly found moderate risk because the protester did not have a mature software development process, and *Hydro Eng'g, Inc. v. United States*, 37 Fed. Cl. 448 (1997), where the agency properly found specific elements of a technical and management proposal created a risk of timely performance and technical compliance.

g. *Financial Capability*

Not a evaluation factor

There has been considerable controversy over whether the financial ability of offerors should be used as an evaluation factor or subfactor. In *Delta Data Sys. Corp. v. Webster*, 240 U.S. App. D.C. 182, 744 F.2d 197 (D.C. Cir. 1984), the court followed the general rule that factors related to responsibility could be used for comparative purposes and applied this rule to permit the comparative evaluation of the financial condition of the offerors in a long-term contract. In arriving at this result, the court reversed a contrary conclusion of the Comptroller General on the same case, *Delta Data Sys. Corp.*, Comp. Gen. Dec. B-213396, 84-1 CPD ¶ 430. The Comptroller General continues to adhere to the premise that financial condition should be used as an evaluation factor only when there is some special justification for doing so. See *Flight Int'l Group, Inc.*, 69 Comp. Gen. 741 (B-238953.4), 90-2 CPD ¶ 257, where the Comptroller General ruled that downgrading an offeror' management capabilities on the basis of financial weakness was actually a finding of nonresponsibility. However, there are cases where the Comptroller General has permitted the use of financial condition as a specific evaluation factor, *Greyback Concession*, Comp. Gen. Dec. B-239913, 90-2 CPD ¶ 278 (no discussion of special justification used to justify evaluation of financial condition); *E.H. White & Co.*, Comp. Gen. Dec. B-227122.3, 88-2 CPD ¶ 41 (competition between small businesses). In the normal procurement situation, there is little justification for making a comparative evaluation of financial condition and this should be left to the responsibility determination.

B. Unlisted Factors or Subfactors

The best practice is to list in the RFP all evaluation factors and subfactors that the agency intends to evaluate. However, failure of the agency to specifically identify an evaluation factor will be excused if the solicitation fairly advises offerors that the factor will be considered. For example, in *Canadian Commercial Corp.*, Comp. Gen. Dec. B-276945, 97-2 CPD ¶ 48, the solicitation requested proposals for a commercial off-the shelf boat with proven marine performance. The fact that the agency considered the failure of the protester to provide performance data or that protester had not previously built the ship did not constitute the evaluation of unstated factors. These factors were held to be reasonably understood as related to and relevant to the agency's assessment of risk of whether the protester would successfully deliver a product conforming to the solicitation requirements. See also *Israel Aircraft Indus.*, Comp. Gen. Dec. B-274389, 97-2 CPD ¶ 41 (enhanced safety intrinsic to stated evaluation factors and is not an unstated evaluation factor); *Myers Investigative & Security Servs., Inc.*, Comp. Gen. Dec. B-272947.2, 96-2 CPD ¶ 114 (solicitation clearly put offerors on notice that relevant experience would be evaluated under the past performance factor); and *Science & Technology, Inc.*, Comp. Gen. Dec. B-272748, 97-1

CPD ¶ 121 (offerors could not reasonably ignore factor left off the list of subfactors in section M but which was discussed in section L).

The requirement to list "significant subfactors" has been liberally interpreted to permit the nondisclosure of subfactors which are logically and reasonably related to the stated evaluation factors, *Buffalo Organization for Social & Technological Innovation, Inc.*, Comp. Gen. Dec. B-196279, 80-1 CPD ¶ 107. See *Thomas G. Gebhard, Jr., P.E., Ph.D.*, Comp. Gen. Dec. B-196454, 80-1 CPD ¶ 115, where the Comptroller General stated:

> We have held that each evaluation subcriterion need not be disclosed in the solicitation so long as offerors are advised of the basic criteria. *Genasys Corporation*, 56 Comp. Gen. 835 (1977), 77-2 CPD ¶ 60. Additional factors may be used in an evaluation where there is sufficient correlation between an additional subcriterion and the generalized criteria in the RFP so that offerors are on reasonable notice of the evaluation criteria to be applied to their proposals. *Littleton Research and Engineering Corp.*, B-191245, June 30, 1978, 78-1 CPD ¶ 466.

See *Hydro Eng'g, Inc. v. United States*, 37 Fed. Cl. 448 (1997).

Of course, a subfactor that is not logically related to the stated factor may not be used. See, for example, *US Sprint Communications Co. v. Department of Defense*, GSBCA 11769-P, 93-1 BCA ¶ 25,255, where a preference for commercially available equipment was held not related to the factor "characteristics of equipment to be located on Government premises (size, power requirements, noise, etc.)." The board held further that the term "etc." could not be reasonably read to include such a preference.

There have been numerous protests where unlisted subfactors have been held to be logically related to a factor. For example, the requirement that the project director be available at the outset of the procurement was held to be logically related to the "Personnel Qualifications" evaluation factor, *Health Management Sys.*, Comp. Gen. Dec. B-200775, 81-1 CPD ¶ 255. Similarly, the subfactors "Compliance with Stated Minimum Requirements," "Additional Experience/Qualifications of Key Personnel," and "Experience in the Topical Area" were found to be sufficiently related to the "Personnel Qualifications" factor, *Management Sys. Designers, Inc.*, Comp. Gen. Dec. B-244383.4, 91-2 CPD ¶ 518. In *Telos Field Eng'g*, Comp. Gen. Dec. B-258805.2, 95-1 CPD ¶ 186, the protester contended that its proposal was improperly downgraded under the spare parts factor for proposing an inventory of older spare parts and on the ground that its current inventory did not consist of the optimal mix of equipment and was not organized in kits. The spare parts factor provided:

> "[D]oes the contractor have the ability to supply spare parts when needed? Does the contractor have an adequate reserve of parts and the means to quickly deliver them to the site? Could the contractor replace a complete piece of equipment if need be to incur maximum equipment uptime?"

In finding the evaluation reasonable, the Comptroller General stated:

> [T]he type of inventory and the mix of parts reasonably could be expected to affect the ability to furnish parts for certain equipment, as well as the speed with which the contractor can furnish a part for a newer piece of equipment. Similarly, making parts available in kits, rather than individually, reasonably relates to the speed with which parts necessary for a certain repair can be ordered.

In other cases, cost management was held to be clearly related to past performance even though the RFP only listed "technical performance" and "schedule performance" as subfactors, *Bendix Field Eng'g Corp.*, Comp. Gen. Dec. B-241156, 91-1 CPD ¶ 44, and specific experience was held to be reasonably related to general experience, *Technical Servs. Corp.*, 64 Comp. Gen. 245 (B-214634), 85-1 CPD ¶ 152. In *JoaQuin Mfg. Corp.*, Comp. Gen. Dec. B-275185, 97-1 CPD ¶ 48, the Comptroller General found that weight, number of footings, and visibility properly related to the suitability of design evaluation factor. In a very questionable decision, the Comptroller General held that performance of work by segments of the company rather than by subcontractors was clearly related to the factor "Offeror's Ability to Provide Additional Effort," *Specialized Technical Servs., Inc.*, Comp. Gen. Dec. B-247489.2, 92-1 CPD ¶ 510.

Subfactors need not be included on a separate list if they are described in a narrative form in the description of the factor, *Moran Assocs.*, Comp. Gen. Dec. B-240564.2, 91-2 CPD ¶ 495. In that case, the Comptroller General apparently believed that a diligent offeror would identify the subfactors from the narrative description. See also *ITT Electron Technology Div.*, Comp. Gen. Dec. B-242289, 91-1 CPD ¶ 383, where the Comptroller General held that there was no need to disclose an evaluation "checklist" when the items on the list were reasonably related to the evaluation factors. In *Stone Webster Eng'g Corp.*, Comp. Gen. Dec. B-255286.2, 94-2 CPD ¶ 306, the protester contended that the evaluation was improper because the agency evaluated proposals on a basis of an evaluation factor, "general strategy," that was not listed as an evaluation factor in the RFP. The agency stated that general strategy was not a separate evaluation criterion but was, however, considered as part of the evaluation of several factors that were set forth in the RFP. The Comptroller General agreed, finding that the RFP did state that strategy formulation and selection of appropriate tactics would be a significant subfactor under the understanding the anticipated work evaluation factor.

If a subfactor will have an inordinate impact on the evaluation of a factor, it will be found to be a "significant" subfactor which must be identified in the RFP as having such impact, *Systemhouse Fed. Sys., Inc.*, GSBCA 9313-P, 88-2 BCA ¶ 20,603. See *Compuware Corp.*, GSBCA 8869-P, 87-2 BCA ¶ 19,781, where the agency was required to identify a subfactor which altered the focus of the evaluation scheme. See also *Devres, Inc.*, 66 Comp. Gen. 121 (B-224017), 86-2 CPD ¶ 652, where the Comptroller General required listing of a subfactor for specific experience even though it was related to the "general experience" that had been listed. The specific experience subfactor was 60 percent of the general experience factor and 25 percent of the total scoring (it was larger than any other factor).

Listed subfactors must include only elements that bear a relationship to the subfactor. Thus, the Comptroller General has held that the financial condition of an offeror was not properly included in the subfactor "ability to meet the published schedule requirements of the Government at an acceptable level of risk," *Flight Int'l Group, Inc.*, 69 Comp. Gen. 741 (B-238953.4), 90-2 CPD ¶ 257.

C. Relative Importance

There are two aspects of the statutory requirement to provide a statement of relative importance in the RFP. At the highest level, there must be a statement of the procurement strategy described in Section I, above. This is the relationship of cost/price to the non-price factors required by 10 U.S.C. § 2305(a)(3)(iii) and 41 U.S.C. § 253a(c)(1)(C). Below that level, there must be some indication of the relative importance of the factors and subfactors within the non-cost or price areas, 10 U.S.C. § 2305(a)(2)(A)(ii) and 41 U.S.C. § 253a(b)(1)(B).

1. Relationship of Cost/Price to Other Factors

At a minimum, the RFP must indicate the decisional logic that the agency intends to use to make the selection decision. See *Signatron, Inc.*, 54 Comp. Gen. 530 (B-181782), 74-2 CPD ¶ 386, where the Comptroller General stated at 535:

> We believe that each offeror has a right to know whether the procurement is intended to achieve a minimum standard at the lowest cost or whether cost is secondary to quality. Competition is not served if offerors are not given any idea of the relative values of technical excellence and price.

Thus, the solicitation must describe the procurement strategy that will be used to make the award.

If an agency has decided to use the lowest price, acceptable proposal decisional rule, the RFP should include a statement to that effect, FAR 15.101-2(b)(1). If the agency has decided to use a tradeoff decisional rule, it has a variety of ways to state that rule in the RFP. The following is provided, by way of illustration, as language that may be included in an RFP to convey essential information to the offerors:

> Award will be made to that offeror whose proposal contains the combination of those criteria offering the best overall value to the Government. This will be determined by comparing differences in the value of technical and management features with differences in cost to the Government. In making this comparison . . . (select the applicable alternative)
>
> No. 1 (Technical/management most important) — the Government is more concerned with obtaining superior technical or management features than with making an award at the lowest overall cost to the Government. However, the Government will not make an award at a significantly higher overall cost to the Government to achieve slightly superior technical or management features.
>
> No. 2 (Technical/management and cost to the Government of equal importance) — the Government is concerned with striking the most advantageous balance between technical and management features and cost to the Government.
>
> No. 3 (Cost to the Government most important) — the Government is more concerned with making an award at the lowest overall cost to the Government than with obtaining superior technical or management

> features. However, the Government will not make an award based on a proposal with significantly inferior technical or management features in order to achieve a small savings in cost to the Government.

This language attempts to tell offerors that the best value decision would ultimately be made on the basis of marginal differences between the competitors and that the agency would pay more for marginal differences in technical and management features but not a lot more for a little. This, of course, describes the essence of a tradeoff selection.

The shorter version of this rule in 10 U.S.C. § 2305(a)(3)(A)(iii) and 41 U.S.C. § 254a(c)(1)(C), quoted earlier, is implemented in FAR 15.304(e) as follows:

> The solicitation shall also state, at a minimum, whether all evaluation factors other than cost or price, when combined, are —
>
> (1) Significantly more important than cost or price;
>
> (2) Approximately equal to cost or price; or
>
> (3) Significantly less important than cost or price.

It is proper to state in the RFP that past performance is more important than price (rather than "significantly more important" than price) when that is a correct statement, *Braswell Servs., Group. Inc.*, Comp. Gen. Dec. B-276694, 97-2 CPD ¶ 18.

When the relationship among the evaluation criteria is variable rather than fixed, the agency may meet the statutory requirement by including a statement in the RFP describing the relationship that will be used. Usually the variable relationship is that the cost to the Government will vary in importance to the other factors. There may also be variable relationships among other factors. Generally, the actual intent of the agency is to make a tradeoff analysis of the proposals and select that one offering the best overall value to the Government. In such cases, the source selection process can be best described in narrative form. For example, in *DLM&A, Inc. v. United States*, 6 Cl. Ct. 329 (1984), the RFP stated at 330:

> [C]ost is not expected to be the controlling factor in the selection of a Contractor for this solicitation. The degree of importance of cost as a factor could become greater depending upon the equality of the proposals for

> other factors evaluated; where competing proposals are determined to be substantially equal, total cost and other cost factors would become the controlling factor.

Another example can be found in *EG&G Ortec*, Comp. Gen. Dec. B-213347, 84-1 CPD ¶ 182, *recons. denied*, 84-1 CPD ¶ 372, where the RFP contained the full point scoring system plus the following statement:

> You are advised that paramount consideration shall be given to the evaluation of technical proposals rather than cost or price. It is pointed out, however, that should technical competence between offerors be considered approximately the same, then cost or price could become paramount.

In many cases a procuring agency will determine that fixed weights should not control the source selection in all situations. The most common situation where this occurs is where the agency assigns a high weight to technical and management factors and a low weight to cost. In such cases, a competitor earning a higher score on technical and management might have a much higher predicted cost of performance, yet could still earn the highest total score. The agency may want to reserve the right to reevaluate to determine if the difference in cost is worth the difference in technical quality and management. Not surprisingly, the decision is sometimes made that it is more advantageous not to pay the price premium. See, for example, *Systems Integrated*, Comp. Gen. Dec. B-225055, 87-1 CPD ¶ 114 (upholding an agency's exclusion of protester from competitive range who offered a 30 percent higher cost to perform but no significant technical advantage over other offeror). Even if the RFP describes a precise evaluation formula, the source selection official retains the discretion to examine scores between offerors to determine whether point differentials represent tangible differences in the technical merits of the proposals, and where they do not, to award to the lowest-cost offeror, *Crowley Maritime Salvage*, Comp. Gen. Dec. B-234555, 89-1 CPD ¶ 555; *Harrison Sys., Ltd.*, 63 Comp. Gen. 379, (B-212675), 84-1 CPD ¶ 572.

There has been some confusion over the terms "relative weight" and "relative importance." In *CardioMetrix*, Comp. Gen. Dec. B-258108, 94-2 CPD ¶ 191, the agency used language similar to the above quote. The Comptroller General mixed up "relative weight" with "relative importance," stating:

> Here, by stating only that the government is more concerned with obtaining superior technical features than with making an award at the lowest overall price, the RFP was, in effect, silent with regard to the relative weight to be given to price versus technical factors. Where, a solicitation indicates that price will be considered, without explicitly indicating the relative weight to be given to price versus technical factors, price and technical considerations will be accorded approximately equal weight and importance in the evaluation.

See also *ENCORP Int'l, Inc.*, Comp. Gen. Dec. B-258829, 95-1 CPD ¶ 100, where the agency had explicitly refrained from stating the relative weights of the "more important" technical factors listed in the RFP. Instead, the RFP stated:

> When making tradeoff decisions during proposal preparation, offerors should remember that the Government prefers to obtain better offeror experience, past performance, and better savings. However, the *relative influence* that any of these factors will have on the source selection decision will ultimately depend on the marginal differences among the competing offerors, which will not be known until the proposals have been analyzed and compared to one another. Therefore, the Government has not assigned *weights* to these factors. (emphasis added)

In a footnote the Comptroller General stated that this scheme failed to comply with the Competition in Contracting Act, which required, at a minimum, all evaluation factors and significant subfactors and their relative importance. In *Ogden Support Servs., Inc.*, Comp. Gen. Dec. B-270354, 96-1 CPD ¶ 175, the RFP only stated that "cost would become more important as the difference in technical evaluation scores decreases and that cost 'may become' determinative when proposals are technically equal." The Comptroller General stated that this scheme failed to state the relative importance of the cost factor. The Comptroller General further stated that where a solicitation fails to explicitly state the relative weight of cost in the evaluation scheme, it must be presumed that cost and technical considerations will be accorded equal weight and importance in the evaluation.

When the agency has decided that either technical/management or cost are of predominant importance, that should be clearly stated in the RFP. It is proper in such cases to include a statement that the predominant factor will not control when there is a large disparity between proposals. See, for example, *CPT Corp.*, GSBCA 8134-P-R, 86-1 BCA ¶ 18,727, *recons. denied*, 86-2 BCA ¶ 18,818, where the RFP stated at 94,211:

> The technical proposal is of substantially greater importance than the cost proposal. However, if, after evaluation of the Technical and Price Proposals, two or more competing overall proposals are within the competitive range, evaluated probable cost to the Government may be the deciding factor for selection, depending on whether the most acceptable overall proposal (excluding cost consideration) is determined to be worth the cost differential, if any. The Business Management Proposal is of significantly lesser importance than the Technical and Cost Proposals. However, a particular situation regarding one or more business management aspects could strongly influence selection, or in an extreme case, make a proposal unacceptable.

2. Relative Importance of Other Factors

There are a number of different methods of specifying the relative importance factors other than cost or price.

a. Listing Criteria

A questionable technique for disclosing the relative importance of factors is merely to list the factors that will be evaluated in the RFP with no statement of relative importance. In such cases the offerors are expected to assume that all evaluation criteria are of approximately equal importance. See, for example, *Carol Solomon & Assocs.*, Comp. Gen. Dec. B-271713, 96-2 CPD ¶ 28; *Computing & Software, Inc.*, 52 Comp. Gen. 686 (B-176763) (1973); *Dikewood Servs. Co.*, 56 Comp. Gen. 188 (B-186001), 76-2 CPD ¶ 520, where the Comptroller General applied the presumption of equality in the absence of a contrary indication of relative importance in the RFP.

b. Descending Order of Importance

Another inferior method of indicating relative order of importance is to list the factors and state that they are listed in descending order of importance. The Comptroller General has upheld use of this method where the evaluation scheme "reflects a reasonable downward progression of evaluation weights," *Optimum Technology, Inc.*, Comp. Gen. Dec. B-266339.2, 96-1 CPD ¶ 188. See also *A&W Maintenance Servs., Inc.*, Comp. Gen. Dec. B-255711.2, 95-1 CPD ¶ 24; and *North-East Imaging, Inc.*, Comp. Gen. Dec. B-256281, 94-1 CPD ¶ 332. Thus, a mere statement that the evaluation factors are listed in the order of their relative importance, without specifically assigning a weight to each, is satisfactory so long as the difference between the importance assigned to any one factor and that assigned to the factor either immediately preceding or immediately following it is small. See *Sperry Rand Corp.*, Comp. Gen. Dec. B-179875, 74-2 CPD ¶ 158, where the Comptroller General stated that where one factor is to have predominant consideration over the other factors, this should be disclosed. In *BDM Servs. Co.*, Comp. Gen. Dec. B-180245, 74-1 CPD ¶ 237, the Comptroller General stated that a predominant factor should have been identified in the RFP and added:

> Moreover, we believe the general relationship of the remaining factors to each other could have been described in narrative without violating the prohibition against disclosure of precise numerical weights in ASPR 3-501(D)(i). As a matter of sound procurement policy, the fullest possible disclosure of all of the evaluation factors and their relative importance is to be preferred to reliance on the reasonableness of the offeror's judgment as to the relative significance of the various evaluation factors.

Where a solicitation lists evaluation factors and subfactors in descending order of importance, such an evaluation scheme does not indicate that the subfactors of lower-weighted factors are necessarily of less individual weight than subfactors of higher-weighted factors, *Brown & Root, Inc.*, Comp. Gen. Dec. B-270505.2, 96-2 CPD ¶ 143.

c. *Adjectival Descriptions of Importance*

Another technique for disclosing relative importance of the factors is to provide an adjectival description of the importance of each evaluation factor. Prior to the statutory requirement for a statement of the relationship between cost/price factor and the other factors, this was permitted with regard to the entire evaluation. See *Bayshore Sys. Corp.*, Comp. Gen. Dec. B-184446, 76-1 CPD ¶ 146, where the Comptroller General found a mere statement that technical factors were more important than price was proper where the undisclosed technical-to-price ratio was 3:1. See also *Kirk-Mayer, Inc.*, Comp. Gen. Dec. B-208582, 83-2 CPD ¶ 288, where the Comptroller General found satisfactory a statement that the weights attached to the four factors did not differ significantly, where the weights used in the evaluation were 25, 25, 20 and 30 points; and *Technical Servs. Corp.*, 64 Comp. Gen. 245 (B-214634), 85-1 CPD ¶ 152, where the Comptroller concurred with a statement that cost was "secondary" but "important" in a situation where cost was given a 20 percent weight and technical an 80 percent weight. However, the Comptroller General has agreed that an award should be cancelled and the RFP amended where the adjectival description is misleading as to the relative importance of a factor, *Unisys Corp.*, 67 Comp. Gen. 512 (B-230019.2), 88-2 CPD ¶ 35.

d. Numerical Systems

The relative importance of factors and subfactors may also be indicated by disclosing the numerical point score or percentage for each evaluation criterion in the RFP. An agency's RFP disclosures of its numerical systems must be sufficient to inform prospective offerors of how the rating system will apply to their proposals. In *National Capital Med. Found. Inc.*, Comp. Gen. Dec. B-215303.5, 85-1 CPD ¶ 637, the RFP failed to inform offerors that proposals would receive zero points out of a possible 110 allocated to "admission objectives" and 200 allocated to "quality objectives" if any one of the subcriteria under these objectives was rated less than acceptable regardless of the merits of the others. The Comptroller General found that application of such an undisclosed scoring scheme was arbitrary and inconsistent with the RFP requirements.

e. Subcriteria

As with primary areas of the evaluation, an offeror may assume that all subcriteria are of substantially equal importance in the absence of advice to the contrary, *North Am. Tel. Assoc.*, Comp. Gen. Dec. B-187239, 76-2 CPD ¶ 495; *Tracor, Inc.*, 56 Comp. Gen. 62 (B-186315), 76-2 CPD ¶ 386. However, if a subfactor is to play an important role in the source selection decision, that must be stated in the RFP. See, for example, *H. J. Group Ventures, Inc.*, Comp. Gen. Dec. B-246139, 92-1 CPD ¶ 203, where the Comptroller General found improper heavy reliance on past performance when that criterion had been listed as a "general consideration" but not included in the list of other criteria which were stated in relative order of importance. See also *J.A. Jones Management Servs., Inc.*, Comp. Gen. Dec. B-254941.2, 94-1 CPD ¶ 244, where the agency improperly had greatly exaggerated the weight the RFP assigned to the key personnel evaluation factor; *University of Michigan*, 66 Comp. Gen. 538 (B-225756), 87-1 CPD ¶ 643, where it was improper to place heavy reliance on one criterion when the RFP appeared to indicate that four technical criteria were of relatively equal weight; and *Genasys Corp.*, GSBCA 8734-P, 87-1 BCA ¶ 19,556, where the RFP stated that one to three points would be given for technical enhancements to a proposed computer system but gave no indication which enhancements were of greater importance to the agency.

3. Minimum Requirements

If an RFP provides that offerors must meet specified minimum requirements, award may not be made to an offeror that fails to meet the minimum requirements. Conversely, the Government may not reject proposals which do not meet minimum requirements if the RFP does not clearly state those requirements. To impose a minimum requirement not specified in the RFP would be improper, *RJO Enters., Inc.*, Comp. Gen. Dec. B-260126.2, 95-2 CPD ¶ 93. In *ACS Sys. & Eng'g, Inc.*, Comp. Gen. Dec. B-275439.3, 97-1 CPD ¶ 126, the Comptroller General upheld an agency's corrective action allowing resubmission of BAFOs after its requirements had changed, stating that "[i]t is fundamental that offerors must be advised of a procuring agency's actual minimum requirements." See also *Lobar, Inc.*, Comp. Gen. Dec. B-247843.3, 92-2 CPD ¶ 139, where the Comptroller General required the agency to reopen the procurement and amend the RFP to state the minimum requirements that the agency was actually using in the evaluation of proposals. In *CNA Indus. Eng'g, Inc.*, Comp. Gen. Dec. B-271034, 96-1 CPD ¶ 279, the agency awarded a contract to an offeror who had similar experience with a similar software system. The Comptroller General held that the award was based on an improper relaxation of the agency's minimum requirement that offerors demonstrate expertise and experience with the agency's own software system. However, there is no need for an agency to formulate minimum requirements for each evaluation factor in order to satisfy minimum requirements disclosures, if objective measures are not relevant to the source selection, *W.B. Jolley*, 68 Comp. Gen. 443 (B-234490), 89-1 CPD ¶ 512.

Similarly, minimum requirements need not be stated if the agency is open to consideration of varying levels of performance, *Carson & Assocs., Inc.*, GSBCA 9411-P, 88-2 BCA ¶ 20,778 (no need to state minimum staffing levels when agency considered staffing levels variable depending on proposed method of performing the work). Thus, an agency must only disclose in the RFP any minimum requirements that it intends to actually use in the evaluation. See also *Doss Aviation, Inc.*, Comp. Gen. Dec. B-275419, 97-1 CPD ¶ 117, where the protester asserted that the agency improperly awarded additional evaluation credit based on aspects of the awardee's proposal that exceeded the solicitation's minimum requirements. The Comptroller General denied the protest, stating that where detailed technical proposals are sought and technical evaluation criteria are used to enable the agency to make comparative judgments about the relative merits of competing proposals, offerors are on notice that qualitative distinctions among the technical proposals will be made under the various evaluation factors.

III. REQUEST FOR PROPOSALS

Once specifications have been adopted, a procurement strategy has been selected and evaluation factors and subfactors and their relative weights have been determined, the Government must provide this information to potential offerors. In addition, offerors must be advised of the type of contract that will be used and the terms and conditions which it will contain. Finally, offerors must be given instructions on what must be submitted. The Request for Proposals (RFP) is the means by which these matters are communicated. See FAR 15.203(a):

> Requests for proposals (RFPs) are used in negotiated acquisitions to communicate Government requirements to prospective contractors and to solicit proposals. RFPs for competitive acquisitions shall, at a minimum, describe the —
>
> (1) Government's requirement;
>
> (2) Anticipated terms and conditions that will apply to the contract:
>
> (i) The solicitation may authorize offerors to propose alternative terms and conditions, including the contract line item number (CLIN) structure; and
>
> (ii) When alternative CLIN structures are permitted, the evaluation approach should consider the potential impact on other terms and conditions or the requirement (e.g., place of performance or payment and funding requirements) (see 15.206);
>
> (3) Information required to be in the offeror's proposal; and
>
> (4) Factors and significant subfactors that will be used to evaluate the proposal and their relative importance.

Thus, it can be seen that the RFP serves a number of functions and that a well-organized and well-drafted RFP is essential to achieving an effective and efficient procurement.

A. Organization of the RFP

FAR 15.204 requires that RFPs be prepared using the Uniform Contract Format. The Uniform Contract is specified in FAR 15.204-1 (b) as follows:

Uniform Contract Format	
Part I—The Schedule	
Section	Title
A	Solicitation/contract form
B	Supplies or services and prices/costs
C	Description/specifications/statement of work
D	Packaging and marking
E	Inspection and acceptance
F	Deliveries or performance
G	Contract administration data
H	Special contract requirements
Part II—Contract Clauses	
I	Contract clauses required for every contract
Part III—List of Documents, Exhibits, and Other Attachments	
J	List of attachments
Part IV—Representations and Instructions	
K	Representations, certifications, and other statements of offerors or respondents
L	Instructions, conditions, and notices to offerors or respondents
M	Evaluation factors for award

Sections B, C, L, & M are most important to the offerors on a solicitation

Parts I, II and III become part of the contract and Section K is to be incorporated into the contract by reference.

FAR 15.204 provides that the Uniform Contract Format "need not be used" for:

(a) Construction and architect-engineer contracts (see part 36).

(b) Subsistence contracts.

(c) Supplies or services contracts requiring special contract formats prescribed elsewhere in this part that are inconsistent with the uniform format.

(d) Letter requests for proposals (see 15.203(e)).

(e) Contracts exempted by the agency head or designee.

B. Contract Provisions

The contract provisions in Parts I, II, and III of the Uniform Contract Format constitute a complete contract except for the prices or costs and fee in Part B, which the offeror must fill out when the proposal is submitted. Thus, as in the case of sealed bidding, the Government normally writes an entire contract in the course of preparing the RFP. However, in negotiated procurement, the RFP may solicit additive or alternate offers which will vary the terms of the RFP and require rewriting of the contract after negotiation has occurred.

FAR 15.204-2(a) provides that Standard Form 33 (Solicitation, Offer and Award), FAR 53.301-33; or Optional Form 308 (Solicitation and Offer — Negotiated Acquisition) may be used as the cover sheet for the RFP and will constitute Section A of the contract. These forms contain a significant amount of key information, as well as blocks for the signatures of the prospective contractor. In addition, the SF 33 contains a block for the signature of the contracting officer, which permits it to be used as an award form. The most important information is the time by which the proposal must be submitted and the requirement for signature of the proposal by an authorized representative of the contractor. The information contained on these forms must be included in the RFP if these forms are not used. See FAR 15.203(e).

FAR 15.204-2(b) contains the following guidance on the information to be included in Section B of the RFP:

> Include a brief description of the supplies or services; e.g., item number, national stock number/part number if applicable, nouns, nomenclature, and quantities. (This includes incidental deliverables such as manuals and reports.)

The purpose of this section is to give offerors a summary description of the contract requirements and provide a place for offerors to submit their proposed prices. Thus, the descriptions of the work in this section are very brief — with details left to Section C.

The number of line items is discretionary with the procuring agency. However, it is normal practice to include a separate line item whenever a different source of funds is used for the supplies or services being procured. This can result in fragmentation of the same work (such as a single product) into a number of line items in instances where the agency is buying that work for a number of different users or in different years.

Section C contains the detailed description of the work to be performed under the contract. The contract specification is usually a detailed document that has evolved in an agency over a number of procurements or a new document written specifically for the procurement. In either case, the RFP must provide specific information to prospective offerors on the applicable specifications. However, the RFP need not actually contain the specifications except in certain situations. See FAR Subpart 11.2.

FAR 15.204-2(d) provides that Section D should contain packaging, packing, preservation, and marking provisions. Detailed guidance on this issue is left to agency regulations.

Section E should contain the special clauses that the agency will use in inspecting and accepting the work. In most cases, the procuring agency will include the appropriate standard inspection clause from FAR 52.246. FAR Subpart 46.2 contains detailed guidance on the selection of standard inspection clauses or other inspection clauses to minimize the costs to the Government and utilize the contractor's inspection capabilities to the maximum extent consistent with obtaining the necessary quality of work.

Section F contains guidance on the time and place of contract performance in accordance with FAR Subpart 11.4. FAR 52.211-9 contains a number of alternate clauses to be used in specifying the time of delivery as either a firm contract requirement or a desired time. When the time is specified as a firm contract requirement, an offer may be rejected if it fails to comply with the requirement. Note, however, that offerors whose initial proposals do not comply with the required delivery schedules should still be considered for the competitive range. Unlike sealed bid procurements, negotiated procurements permit giving offerors the opportunity to satisfy Government requirements through discussions. Therefore, an offeror in negotiated procurements that fails to comply with delivery times in its proposal should not be automatically labeled nonresponsive and rejected since this error could easily be corrected during discussions. See *Hollingsead Int'l*, Comp. Gen. Dec. B-227853, 87-2 CPD ¶ 372; *Xtek, Inc.*, Comp. Gen. Dec. B-213166, 84-1 CPD ¶ 264; *DPF Inc.*, Comp. Gen. Dec. B-180292, 74-1 CPD ¶ 303. These cases seem to contradict paragraph (b) of the Time of Delivery clause in FAR 52.211-8, which states that if the proposed delivery date is "later than the required delivery date, the offer will be considered nonresponsive and rejected." This language only applies to sealed bid procurements and should be deleted from the clause when it is used in negotiated procurements. Alternates I and II of the Time of Delivery clause in FAR 52.211-9 do not need to be altered in this way because they contain a paragraph (b) which omits such language.

In some cases, agencies use special time of performance clauses which make the time of performance, within a range, an evaluation factor. The Comptroller General has sanctioned the use of time of performance as an evaluation factor, especially when the procurement is urgent. See *Shirley Constr. Corp.*, 70 Comp. Gen. 62 (B-240357), 90-2 CPD ¶ 380 (total time of performance one of four evaluation criteria); and *Hydroscience*, Comp. Gen. Dec. B-227989, 87-2 CPD ¶ 501 (offeror's proposal properly devalued due to uncertainty as to time of performance when swift performance was crucial).

FAR 15.204-2(g) requires that Section G include accounting and appropriation data as well as contract administration information or instructions other than those pertaining to the solicitation. DFARS 204.7107 requires contracting offices to use accounting classification reference numbers (ACRNs) in order to process certain contract data through the Military Standard Contract Administration Procedures (MILSCAP). MILSCAP utilizes the ACRNs to relate contract administration records to the long-line accounting classification used to obligate funds on the contract. NAPS 5232.792 repeats these requirements and adds that "accounting data shall also be shown on any change order or contract amendment to a contract that revises the accounting data for any item or increases or decreases the total amount of a contract."

FAR 15.204-2(h) provides that Section H may contain any special contract requirements that are not contained in Section I. While this gives procuring agencies almost total discretion on how to use this Section, many agencies include clauses which are specially written for the procurement.

Section I contains most of the standard clauses for the proposed contract. Standard contract clauses are contained in FAR Part 52. The matrix in FAR Subpart 52.3 gives guidance on the clauses to be incorporated into the various types of contracts. Clauses are either (1) required, (2) required when applicable, or (3) optional. FAR 52.102-1 and -2 require incorporation of clauses by reference to the "maximum practical extent" if they are used verbatim from the FAR or are contained in agency-wide procurement regulations such as the DFARS. FAR 52.103 provides that when clauses are incorporated by reference they are to be identified by FAR number, date and title or agency regulation number, date and title.

When an agency deviates from a standard clause, FAR 52.107(f) requires it to alert offerors to such deviation by including the following clause from FAR 52.252-6 in the RFP:

> (a) The use in this solicitation or contract of any Federal Acquisition Regulation (48 CFR Chapter 1) clause with an authorized deviation is indicated by the addition of (DEVIATION) after the date of the clause.
>
> (b) The use in this solicitation or contract of any [insert regulation name] (48 CFR ___) clause with an authorized deviation is indicated by the addition of (DEVIATION) after the name of the regulation.

Deviations are only effective if they are approved by an official with the authority to take such actions. See Chapter 1.

Section J contains all attachments and exhibits to the contract. FAR 15.204-4 requires that the title, date, and number of pages be listed for each of these documents. There is no provision dealing with the incorporation of these items by reference.

The numerous requirements for certifications or representations by the offeror are contained in Section K. FAR 52.102-2 states that such provisions must be incorporated in full text in the RFP. The Government uses these provisions to determine the status of the offeror and to ensure that the offeror will be in compliance with the socioeconomic requirements of the procurement. Thus, these provisions create a self-monitoring mechanism permitting offerors to establish their compliance by certification rather than by proving that certain requirements are met.

C. Solicitation Provisions

The solicitation provisions specify the ground rules under which proposals are to be submitted and evaluated and award is to be made. FAR 52.101 contains the following definition:

> "Solicitation provision" or "provision" means a term or condition used only in solicitations and applying only before contract award.

These provisions will consist of standard terms or conditions dealing with the submission of proposals, specialized instructions relating to the specific procurement and a statement of the evaluation factors and subfactors and their relative weights. The RFP may be transmitted by electronic commerce or facsimile and may authorize the submission of proposals using electronic commerce or facsimiles, FAR 15.203(c) and (d).

1. Standard Provisions

FAR 15.209 requires the inclusion of a number of standard provisions in the RFP. FAR 15.209(a) requires that the FAR 52.215-1, Instructions to Offerors — Competitive Acquisition be included in all competitive solicitations where the Government intends to award a contract without discussions. This provision does not prohibit conducting discussions if award without discussions is not feasible. Alternate I is to be added if the Government has determined, in advance, that it will conduct discussions. When Alternate I is included, award without discussions is not permitted. This provision incorporates definitions and rules involving a number of matters, including modification and withdrawal of proposals, consideration of late proposals, acceptable restrictions on disclosure of information, and award. These matters were previously contained in twelve separate clauses. FAR 15.209(a)(2) also calls for the use of Alternate II to this solicitation provision when the Government would be willing to accept alternate proposals. The use of this alternate allows the Government to award a contract to an offeror submitting an alternate proposal without having to amend the RFP and provide all offerors the opportunity to compete on that alternate, *Litton Sys., Inc. v. Department of Transportation*, GSBCA 12911-P, 94-3 BCA ¶ 27,263. However, Alternate II "reserves the right" of the Government to amend the RFP if the agency chooses to obtain competition on the alternate requirements.

FAR 15.209 also provides guidance on a number of additional provisions that are commonly used in RFPs. FAR 15.209(b) requires the use of the FAR 52.215-2, Audit and Records — Negotiation provision or one of its alternate provisions in all negotiated procurements except for simplified acquisitions, acquisition of utility services at established rates or acquisition of commercial items. FAR 15.209(d) requires the use of the FAR 52.215-4, Type of Business Organization provision in all RFPs. FAR 15.209(e) requires the use of the FAR 52.215-5, Facsimile Proposals provision in all RFPs permitting the use of such proposals. FAR 15.209(f) requires use of the FAR 52.215-6, Place of Performance provision in all RFPs where the place of performance is not specified by the Government. FAR 15.209(g) requires the use of the FAR 52.215-7, Annual Representations and Certifications — Negotiation provision in all RFPs providing for such representations and certifications. FAR 15.209(h) requires the use of the FAR 52.215-8, Order of Precedence — Uniform Contract Format provision in all RFPs using the uniform contract format.

2. Specific Instructions — Section L

These instructions are the key to obtaining quality proposals. In the past, the failure to give clear and well organized guidance in Section L has been one of the most common defects in the competitive negotiation process. FAR 15.204-5(b) contains only the following brief discussion of this area, stating:

> Insert in this section solicitation provisions and other information and instructions not required elsewhere to guide offerors or respondents in preparing proposals or responses to requests for information. Prospective offerors or respondents may be instructed to submit proposals or information in a specific format or severable parts to facilitate evaluation. The instructions may specify further organization of proposal or response parts, such as —

(1) Administrative;

(2) Management;

(3) Technical;

(4) Past performance; and

(5) Cost or pricing data (see Table 15-2 of 15.408) or information other than cost or pricing data.

This generalized coverage gives little advice to contracting officers as to the purpose of these specific instructions and the nature of the information which is to be furnished by offerors. It also does not deal with identification of the strategy which the agency has decided to use.

a. Procurement Strategy

The instructions should identify the procurement strategy that will be used in making the award. This entails the inclusion of a clear statement of whether the agency is using the tradeoff process, the lowest price, technically acceptable proposal process or some combination of these two. See Section I, above.

The instructions should also describe the type of contract that is to be used and the objectives that the agency has in the procurement. It is also helpful to include a description of the time that the agency intends to take to evaluate proposals and the intended date of award of the contract. Guidance of this nature is very beneficial to offerors in assisting them to allocate resources to the procurement.

It is also very helpful to offerors if the instructions include specific information on the evaluation process that will be followed. In particular, evaluation standards should be disclosed. See *RJO Enters., Inc.*, Comp. Gen. Dec. B-260126.2, 95-2 CPD ¶ 93, and *Sarasota Measurements & Controls, Inc.*, Comp. Gen. Dec. B-252406, 93-1 CPD ¶ 494, requiring the inclusion of evaluation standards in RFPs when they constituted Government requirements. While the Comptroller General has not required the disclosure of evaluation standards that merely give guidance to evaluators in assessing the relative value of factors or subfactors, *Lexis-Nexis*, Comp. Gen. Dec. B-260023, 95-2 CPD ¶ 14, the inclusion of such standards in the RFP is good practice because it provides fuller information on the agency's acquisition strategy.

b. Required Submissions

In the past, offerors have been requested to submit much information pertaining to their capability to perform in detailed technical and management "proposals." As discussed in Section II, above, much of this type of information comes under the category of "capability factors" to be used solely for evaluation purposes as opposed to "offer factors" to be incorporated into the contract. The RFP should make a clear distinction between these matters and should specify what information is to be furnished. "Technical proposals" should only be required where offerors are permitted to offer differing supplies or services than those specified in the RFP or where the Government is requesting offerors to provide solutions to its needs.

Offerors should be provided detailed guidance on the information to be furnished for evaluation purposes. A well written RFP will contain a precise correlation between the information to be furnished and the evaluation factors and subfactors identified in Section M. Where different evaluation factors are to be evaluated by different personnel, the agency may wish to have the relevant information packaged in separate sections. The RFP should also specifically identify the cost or pricing information needed by the contracting officer to evaluate the cost/price proposal of the offeror. Since there are no standard solicitation provisions in the FAR for requesting such information, the contracting officer must draft a provision for each procurement detailing the information required. See Chapter 9 for a discussion of the types of information that should be requested.

c. Oral Presentations

In recent years agencies have used oral presentations in lieu of written proposals to evaluate whether offerors fully understand the work that will be required to successfully perform the prospective contract. Such presentations have proved to be a superior means of assessing offerors' understanding because they permit the agency to communicate directly with the offeror's personnel that will perform the work rather than reading technical proposals that may have been written by professional proposal writers. FAR 15.102 provides the following guidance on the use of oral presentations:

(a) Oral presentations by offerors as requested by the Government may substitute for, or augment, written information. Use of oral presentations as a substitute for portions of a proposal can be effective in streamlining the source selection process. Oral presentations may occur at any time in the acquisition process, and are subject to the same restrictions as written information, regarding timing (see 15.208) and content (see 15.306). Oral presentations provide an opportunity for dialogue among the parties. Prerecorded videotaped presentations that lack real-time interactive dialogue are not considered oral presentations for the purposes of this section, although they may be included in offeror submissions, when appropriate.

(b) The solicitation may require each offeror to submit part of its proposal through oral presentations. However, certifications, representations, and a signed offer sheet (including any exceptions to the Government's terms and conditions) shall be submitted in writing.

Although FAR 15.102(b) provides that offerors may be required to submit "part of its proposal" through oral presentations, FAR 15.102(f) precludes incorporation of oral statements in the contract by reference and provides that any information from an oral presentation that is to be incorporated in the contract must be put in writing.

FAR 15.102(c) indicates that such presentations are suitable for obtaining information, as follows:

Information pertaining to areas such as an offeror's capability, past performance, work plans or approaches, staffing resources, transition plans, or sample tasks (or other types of tests) may be suitable for oral presentations. In deciding what information to obtain through an oral presentation, consider the following:

(1) The Government's ability to adequately evaluate the information;

(2) The need to incorporate any information into the resultant contract;

(3) The impact on the efficiency of the acquisition; and

(4) The impact (including cost) on small businesses. In considering the costs of oral presentations, contracting officers should also consider alternatives to on-site oral presentations (e.g., teleconferencing, video teleconferencing).

FAR 15.102(d) requires that RFPs provide offerors with sufficient information to understand what is sought in the oral presentation. It suggests a description of the following issues:

> (1) The types of information to be presented orally and the associated evaluation factors that will be used;
>
> (2) The qualifications for personnel that will be required to provide the oral presentation(s);
>
> (3) The requirements for, and any limitations and/or prohibitions on, the use of written material or other media to supplement the oral presentations;
>
> (4) The location, date, and time for the oral presentations;
>
> (5) The restrictions governing the time permitted for each oral presentation; and
>
> (6) The scope and content of exchanges that may occur between the Government's participants and the offeror's representatives as part of the oral presentations, including whether or not discussions (see 15.306(d)) will be permitted during oral presentations.

3. Evaluation Factors and Subfactors — Section M

The evaluation factors and subfactors to be used must be identified in Section M. FAR 15.204-5(c) provides minimal guidance, merely directing that the agency:

> Identify all significant factors and any significant subfactors that will be considered in awarding the contract and their relative importance (see 15.304(d)).

This provision also requires that the contracting officer insert one of the statements of relative importance in FAR 15.304(e) in the RFP (stating that non-price factors are "significantly more important," "approximately equal to," or "significantly less important" than the price factors). However, the Comptroller General has ruled that this requirement was met when the RFP contained an accurate statement that the non-price factor was "more important" than price, rather than "significantly more important," *Braswell Servs., Group*, Comp. Gen. Dec. B-276694, 97-2 CPD ¶ 18. The relative importance of the non-price evaluation factors and subfactors should also be stated in this section.

D. Amendment and Cancellation of the RFP

When needs or circumstances change or when new information or defects in the RFP are discovered, the agency may be required to amend or cancel the RFP. Cancellations resulting from the Government no longer having a need for the procurement or from lack of funds are not at issue. However, where the Government still intends to proceed with the procurement, the RFP must be amended. See FAR 15.206(a), which states:

> When, either before or after receipt of proposals, the Government changes its requirements or terms and conditions, the contracting officer shall amend the solicitation.

Whether the amendment requires or permits cancellation and resolicitation or is such that the procurement is allowed to proceed depends upon the nature and timing of the changes. While both a cancellation followed by a resolicitation with an amended RFP and an amendment without cancellation involve amended RFPs, the latter action permits the Government to continue on with the procurement. Thus, it may be more attractive to procurement officials since it saves both time and administrative effort. Conversely, resolicitation may expand the field of competition and result in a more advantageous deal for the Government.

1. Cancellation and Resolicitation

The only FAR provision dealing with cancellation and resolicitation is FAR 15.206(e), which states:

> If, in the judgment of the contracting officer, based on market research or otherwise, an amendment proposed for issuance after offers have been received is so substantial as to exceed what prospective offerors reasonably could have anticipated, so that additional sources likely would have submitted offers had the substance of the amendment been known to them, the contracting officer shall cancel the original solicitation and issue a new one, regardless of the stage of the acquisition.

The pre-FAR 15 Rewrite version of this regulation had an additional provision which directed that the new solicitation be furnished to all firms originally solicited and any added to the original list. While the normal rules of "full and open competition" would take into consideration those firms added to the list, it would seem appropriate for the Government to resolicit those originally solicited.

a. Required Cancellation

In *Loral Fairchild Corp.*, Comp. Gen. Dec. B-242957.2, 91-2 CPD ¶ 218, the Comptroller General stated that the changes would have to "significantly alter the purpose or nature of the contract" or change the "field of competition" in order to require a cancellation. See *Denwood Properties Corp.*, B-251347.2, 93-1 CPD ¶ 380, where the changes involved a reduction in the amount of space to be leased and the agency's desire to open the competition to consider build-to-suit facilities. The Comptroller General stated that "it would not have been proper" to simply amend the specifications because the changes were substantial and would likely increase the field of competition.

Whether the field of competition would be increased by competition depends upon the facts and circumstances of each individual case. Thus, a number of cases have held that cancellation and resolicitation was not required even though significant changes were made. For example, in *Atkins*, a change from a 690-day, eight-phase construction schedule to one of 630 days with two phases was found not to be an appreciable change. See also *Defense Group, Inc.*, Comp. Gen. Dec. B-253795, 94-1 CPD ¶ 196, where a 12.3 percent increase in overall contract effort was not considered a substantial change to the basic nature of the contemplated contract. For other cases finding that cancellation of a solicitation was not required because the change was not substantial, see *SMS Data Prods. Group v. Austin*, 940 F.2d 1514 (Fed. Cir. 1991) (changing the solicitation by advancing the commercial availability date of laptop computers); *Corporate Jets, Inc.*, GSBCA 11049-P, 91-2 BCA ¶ 23,998, *recons. denied*, 91-2 BCA ¶ 23,999 (adding option with a potential to increase the number of helicopters from 26 to 75); *Cape Fear Paging Co.*, Comp. Gen. Dec. B-252160.2, 93-1 CPD ¶ 347 (elimination of separate line item and combining prices into remaining item); *Di Frances Co.*, Comp. Gen. Dec. B-245492, 91-2 CPD ¶ 323 (5.9 percent decrease in the requirements); *Goodway Graphics of Virginia, Inc.*, Comp. Gen. Dec. B-236386, 89-2 CPD ¶ 491 (change affecting only five of

71 items); *Chromatics, Inc.*, Comp. Gen. Dec. B-224515, 87-1 CPD ¶ 171 (deletion of design requirements from specification); and *Hughes Aircraft Co.*, Comp. Gen. Dec. B-222152, 86-1 CPD ¶ 564 (elimination of one of two alternative technical approaches).

b. Discretionary Cancellation and Resolicitation

Although cancellation and resolicitation after the receipt of proposals subjects the competitors that responded to the solicitation to added cost and effort, because of the possibility of increased competition procurement officials have considerable discretion in making this decision. In this regard, the FAR 14.404-1(a) "compelling reason" basis for cancellation of an IFB after bid opening is not applicable. In *CFM Equip. Co.*, Comp. Gen. Dec. B-251344, 93-1 CPD ¶ 280, the Comptroller General held that an agency needs only a "reasonable basis" to cancel an RFP. In discussing the difference between the standards for canceling an RFP or IFB, the Comptroller General stated:

> Under FAR 15.608(b)(4), a procuring agency may reject all proposals received in response to an RFP if cancellation is clearly in the government's interest. Thus, as a general rule, in a negotiated procurement the contracting agency need only demonstrate a reasonable basis to cancel a solicitation after receipt of proposals, as opposed to the "cogent and compelling" reason required to cancel an IFB where sealed bids have been opened. *Xactex Corp.*, B-241739, May 5, 1992, 92-1 CPD ¶ 423. The standards differ because in procurements using sealed bids, competitive positions are exposed as a result of the public opening of bids, while in negotiated procurements there is no public opening. *ACR Elecs., Inc.*, B-232130.2; B-232130.3, Dec. 9, 1988, 88-2 CPD ¶ 577. The question presented by this protest is whether the agency's second thoughts about its procurement strategy have a reasonable basis.

Cases finding an agency's decision to cancel and resolicit reasonable include, *Robertson Leasing Corp.*, Comp. Gen. Dec. B-275152, 97-1 CPD ¶ 49 (agency canceled solicitation so as to recompete under relaxed specifications in order to increase competition and reduce costs to the Government); *Nidek, Inc.*, Comp. Gen. Dec. B-272255, 96-2 CPD ¶ 112 (agency canceled solicitation until such time as the medical staff developed an accurate statement of its needs, upon which all firms could submit an offer); *Chant Eng'g Co.*, Comp. Gen. Dec. B-270149.2, 96-1 CPD ¶ 96 (agency canceled solicitation because the minimum needs were overstated and the agency determined that enhanced competition would result from a relaxation of the requirements); *JRW Management Co.*, Comp. Gen. Dec. B-260396.2, 95-1 CPD ¶ 276 (agency canceled solicitation because it received only one response and recognized that it could meet its minimum needs with an alternate approach which presented an opportunity for increased competition); and *Best Foam Fabricators, Inc.*, Comp. Gen. Dec. B-259905.3, 95-1 CPD ¶ 275 (agency canceled solicitation so as to obtain the items from the organization designated by the Committee for Purchase from the Blind and Other Severely Handicapped rather than another offeror under the solicitation).

2. Amendment Without Cancellation

Even if the agency decides not to cancel the RFP, an amendment is required if changes would have a significant impact on competition, *Joint Action in Community Serv., Inc.*, Comp. Gen. Dec. B-214564, 84-2 CPD ¶ 228; *Computek, Inc.*, 54 Comp. Gen. 1080 (B-182576), 75-1 CPD ¶ 384. A significant impact on competition occurs when (1) mandatory specifications or terms and conditions are changed, and (2) offerors not receiving notice of the changes would be prejudiced. In *Management Sys. Designers, Inc.*, Comp. Gen. Dec. B-244383.8, 92-1 CPD ¶ 496, prejudice was found where an offeror showed that it might have revised its proposal.

FAR 15.206(d) requires an amendment to take advantage of an offer that deviates from the RFP as follows:

> If a proposal of interest to the Government involves a departure from the stated requirements, the contracting officer shall amend the solicitation, provided this can be done without revealing to the other offerors the alternate solution proposed or any other information that is entitled to protection (see 15.207(b) and 15.306(e)).

See *Loral Terracom*, 66 Comp. Gen. 272 (B-224908), 87-1 CPD ¶ 182 (different technical approach suggested by an offeror).

An amendment is also called for where the relative importance of the evaluation factors is altered, *Unisys Corp.*, 67 Comp. Gen. 512 (B-230019.2), 88-2 CPD ¶ 35 (clarifying the importance of cost), or the overall evaluation scheme is changed, *Galler Assocs., Inc.*, Comp. Gen. Dec. B-210204, 83-1 CPD ¶ 515 (changing from low cost acceptable offer scheme to best value scheme).

Amendments are not required if the claimed deviation is from a provision that is not mandatory, *Howard Cooper Corp. v. United States*, 763 F. Supp. 829 (1991). In *AEL Defense Corp.*, Comp. Gen. Dec. B-251376, 93-1 CPD ¶ 256, the protester alleged that the agency improperly awarded the contract to a firm whose proposal did not conform to a design referenced in a RFP document. The protester asserted that the design was mandatory and, therefore, the RFP should have been amended. The Comptroller General denied the protest stating that the design was not mandatory under the hierarchy established in the specification. Similarly, a contracting officer was not required to issue an amendment to an RFP after changing specified computer systems where the Government provided all equipment necessary for performance of the contract and the change brought about no cost savings to offerors, *Optimum Says., Inc.*, Comp. Gen. Dec. B-194984, 80-2 CPD ¶ 32. See also *Litton Sys., Inc. v. Department of Transportation*, GSBCA 12911-P, 94-3 BCA ¶ 27,263.

a. Issuance of Amendments

FAR 15.210(b) provides that Standard Form 30, Amendment of Solicitation/Modification of Contract or Optional Form 309, Amendment of Solicitation "may be used to amend solicitations." Prior to the FAR 15 Rewrite, the use of Standard Form 30 was mandatory. Whether issued on these forms or otherwise in writing or electronically, the amendment must provide offerors sufficient information to determine the changed requirements. FAR 15.206(g) states that, "At a minimum, the following information should be included in each amendment:"

(1) Name and address of issuing activity.

(2) Solicitation number and date.

(3) Amendment number and date.

(4) Number of pages.

(5) Description of the change being made.

(6) Government point of contact and phone number (and electronic or facsimile address, if appropriate).

(7) Revision to solicitation closing date, if applicable.

FAR 15.206(f) permits oral notice of the amendment when "time is of the essence." It states that, in such a case, "The contracting officer shall document the contract file and formalize the notice with an amendment." The importance of formalizing the notice in writing is illustrated in cases where the protester contends that it did not receive the notice that the agency claimed had been issued orally. In *Lockheed, IMS*, Comp. Gen. Dec. B-248686, 92-2 CPD ¶ 180, the offeror denied that it received oral notice of the amendment. The Government did not follow up with an RFP amendment or other written confirmation. As a result, the protest was successful. See also *CoMont, Inc.*, 65 Comp. Gen. 66 (B-219730), 85-2 CPD ¶ 555 (stressing that amendments must be made in writing); and *I.E. Levick & Assocs.*, Comp. Gen. Dec. B-214648, 84-2 CPD ¶ 695 (failure to issue a written amendment is a procedural defect whenever an offeror effectively denies having been advised orally). However, in *Family Stress Clinics of Am.*, Comp. Gen. Dec. B-270993, 96-1 CPD ¶ 223, an oral amendment extending the closing date for submission of proposals indefinitely was given full effect even though it was not confirmed in writing. The Comptroller General stated that the amendment was issued under exigent circumstances accompanying the shutdown of the contracting agency and the terms of the oral amendment were not in dispute.

In *Labat-Anderson Inc.*, 71 Comp. Gen. 252 (B-246071), 92-1 CPD ¶ 193, the Comptroller General suggested that notification of changes might be accomplished by either raising the issue in discussions with all offerors within the competitive range or issuing an amendment to the RFP. It would appear that the discussion method would only be appropriate for relatively simple changes.

b. Actual Notice or No Prejudice

The failure to issue an amendment has been excused where the protesting offeror had actual notice of the change. See *General Offshore Corp.*, Comp. Gen. Dec. B-249601, 92-2 CPD ¶ 391, where the Comptroller General held that the protester had received adequate notice of changed requirements through negotiations; and *Collins & Aikman Corp.*, Comp. Gen. Dec. B-247961, 92-2 CPD ¶ 41, where the Comptroller General stated in a footnote that an amendment was not required since the protester had knowledge of the change.

Failure to amend an RFP has also been excused where the protester was unable to demonstrate that it was prejudiced by the lack of notice. In *Saratoga Dev. Corp. v. United States*, 777 F. Supp. 29 (D.D.C. 1991), the court held that the test for prejudice is whether the protester would have altered its proposal to its competitive advantage, and further that the protester has the burden of showing how it would have responded to notice of the change. No prejudice was found in *Environmental Tectonics Corp.*, Comp. Gen. Dec. B-209423, 83-1 CPD ¶ 81, because the protester admitted that it could not have bettered its own proposed delivery time. Similarly, in *Canberra Indus.*, Comp. Gen. Dec. B-271016, 96-1 CPD ¶ 269, no prejudice was found for failing to amend a solicitation based on relaxed specifications because the protester did not present any evidence that it would have altered its proposal to its competitive advantage had it been given the opportunity to respond to the altered requirements. The Comptroller General will not overturn an award in which the agency has changed the evaluation criteria without notifying the offerors if the losers are not prejudiced by the change, *Akal Security, Inc.*, Comp. Gen. Dec. B-261996, 95-2 CPD ¶ 216; *Delta Dental Plan*, Comp. Gen. Dec. B-260461, 95-1 CPD ¶ 293; *FKW Inc. Says.*, Comp. Gen. Dec. B-235989, 89-2 CPD ¶ 370.

c. *Firms to Be Notified*

FAR 15.206 specifies that amendments would be furnished as follows:

> (b) Amendments issued before the established time and date for receipt of proposals shall be issued to all parties receiving the solicitation.
>
> (c) Amendments issued after the established time and date for receipt of proposals shall be issued to all offerors that have not been eliminated from the competition.

While an amendment may not be made after submission of proposals so as to intentionally preclude further competition, agencies may amend the solicitation after submission of proposals to take advantage of terms being offered by a particular offeror if other offerors are given the opportunity to respond to the change, *Cel-U-Dex Corp.*, Comp. Gen. Dec. B-195012, 80-1 CPD ¶ 102; *Sub-Sea Says, Inc.*, Comp. Gen. Dec. B-195741, 80-1 CPD ¶ 123. See *Zublin Delaware, Inc.*, Comp. Gen. Dec. B-227003.2, 87-2 CPD ¶ 149, in which an amendment containing new Government needs was permitted even though it excluded some offerors since it was done in the public interest. Similarly, an agency may amend an RFP after the closing date to set aside the procurement exclusively for small business if such action has a reasonable basis, *Gill Mktg. Co.*, Comp. Gen. Dec. B-194414.3, 80-1 CPD ¶ 213. It has also been held that an agency need not issue an amendment after qualifying additional parties to a qualified products list (QPL), even though the RFP lists only one source on the QPL.

Once a competitive range has been established, agencies are not required to issue amendments to offerors outside the competitive range so long as the amendment is not directly related to the reason for the excluded offeror's rejection, *Amperif Corp.*, Comp. Gen. Dec. B-211992, 84-1 CPD ¶ 409. This is the case even where the change is significant, *Labat-Anderson Inc.*, B-246071, 92-1 CPD ¶ 193. For instance, no amendment is required where a contract is amended from a cost-type to a fixed-price contract, *Westinghouse Elec. Corp.*, Comp. Gen. Dec. B-197768, 80-1 CPD ¶ 378. See also *Loral Terracom, Marconi Italiana*, Comp. Gen. Dec. B-224908, 87-1 CPD ¶ 182, where an amendment recognizing alternative methods of satisfying the agency's requirements was properly limited to offerors within the competitive range. Compare *Information Ventures, Inc.*, Comp. Gen. Dec. B-232094, 88-2 CPD ¶ 443, where an amendment relaxing the specifications was required to be sent to an excluded offeror because it directly related to the reasons for exclusion. See also *Hamilton Tool Co.*, Comp. Gen. Dec. B-218260.1, 85-1 CPD ¶ 566, where resolicitation of all offerors was required when different requirements were arrived at with the only offeror in the competitive range. In *Lobar Inc.*, Comp. Gen. Dec. B-247843.3, 92-2 CPD ¶ 139, the Comptroller General found that the agency had acted properly when, after determining that the specifications exceeded the Government's minimum needs, it amended the RFP and reopened with all offerors, both those within and outside the competitive range.

Even though the regulations provide that the amendment shall be sent to each prospective offeror, the Comptroller General has consistently held that the offeror bears the risk of not receiving an amendment, assuming that full and open competition has been found and it has not been shown that there was a conscious and deliberate effort by the agency to exclude the offeror from participating in the competition, *CardioMetrix*, Comp. Gen. Dec. B-270701, 96-1 CPD ¶ 149; *CDA Inc.*, Comp. Gen. Dec. B-224971, 87-1 CPD ¶ 163; *Maryland Computer Servs., Inc.*, Comp. Gen. Dec. B-216990, 85-1 CPD ¶ 187. The underlying theory is that the agency discharges its legal responsibility when it issues and dispatches an amendment in sufficient time to permit all offerors to consider the amendment in formulating their offers. In *CompuServe*, Comp. Gen. Dec. B-192905, 79-1 CPD ¶ 63, an amendment issued to the offeror, but addressed incorrectly, provided no basis for extending the closing date for initial proposals even though the offeror's late acknowledgment was prompted by late receipt of the amendment. However, in *Andero Constr., Inc.*, 61 Comp. Gen. 253 (B-203898), 82-1 CPD ¶ 133, the Comptroller General ignored the general rule that the offeror bears the risk of non-delivery of an amendment to the solicitation because the agency failed to affirmatively establish that it complied with DAR 2-208 (similar to FAR 14.208) where three of four offerors appeared not to have received the amendment in the mail. The agency never affirmatively stated that the amendments were mailed and thus the Comptroller General recommended that the agency cancel the solicitation and resolicit its requirements.

IV. PREPARATION AND SUBMISSION OF PROPOSALS

In the past, the term proposal has been used broadly to refer to an offeror's entire submission in response to an RFP, consisting of both an offer which can be accepted by the Government and information to be considered by the Government in evaluating proposals. The term has also been used to describe separate parts of the submission. Thus, RFPs often requested offerors to organize submissions into separate portions called "Technical Proposals," "Management Proposals," and "Cost Proposals." Although the distinction between the offer and information was recognized in a number of provisions in drafts of FAR Part 15, the final Rewrite eliminated most of these distinctions. Thus, it is necessary to determine whether the final Rewrite's use of the term "proposal" in a particular provision is intended to refer to the offer or information. Some contracting officers have recognized the distinction between these two portions of the submission and have drafted their RFPs so that the offer and information in the offeror's submission can be readily distinguished. The following discussion uses the term "proposal" to refer to the total submission in response to an RFP and the terms "offer" and "information" to distinguish between the two components of the submission.

A. The Offer

The offer describes what the contractor is willing to agree to and its terms becomes part of the contract when accepted by the Government. See FAR 2.101 which contains the following definition of the term "offer":

> "Offer" means a response to a solicitation that, if accepted, would bind the offeror to perform the resultant contract.

In the typical negotiated contract, the offer consists of the terms specified in the RFP (specifications, clauses, etc. contained in Parts I, II and III of the Uniform Contract Format) and the price specified by the offeror. FAR 15.204-2 (a)(1) provides for the use of Optional Form (OF) 308, Solicitation and Offer — Negotiated Acquisition, or Standard Form (SF) 33, Solicitation, Offer and Award to prepare RFPs. These forms reference the various sections of the RFP which will become part of the contract, refer to the prices "which are offered," and provide spaces for a signature and for the "offer date." FAR 15.204-2(a)(2)(ix) requires that the solicitation include the "offer expiration date" when the forms are not used.

1. *Intention to Be Bound*

To be considered for award, the offer must evidence an intent to be bound to the terms and conditions in the RFP and any amendments. This is evidenced by the signature on SF 33 and OF 308, which bind the offeror to the terms and conditions of the RFP. In addition, the offeror must acknowledge receipt of the amendments.

a. Signature

Paragraph (c) of the Instructions to Offerors — Competitive Acquisition solicitation provision in FAR 52.215-1 contains the following guidance making signature of the proposal mandatory:

> (2) The first page of the proposal must show —
>
> * * *
>
> (v) Name, title, and signature of person authorized to sign the proposal. Proposals signed by an agent shall be accompanied by evidence of that

agent's authority, unless that evidence has been previously furnished to the issuing office.

The Comptroller General has held that it is proper to reject a proposal which does not contain a signature if the RFP contemplates award on the basis of initial proposals, *SWR, Inc.*, Comp. Gen. Dec. B-278415, 97-2 CPD ¶ 166; *Valencia Technical Servs., Inc.*, Comp. Gen. Dec. B-223288, 86-2 CPD ¶ 40. In these cases, the Comptroller General relied on cases dealing with unsigned sealed bids and found that it would be unfair to other offerors if a contracting officer permitted an offeror to sign its offer after the time proposals were opened. The Comptroller General also rejected the argument that lack of a signature was a minor informality. In effect, this is an application of the responsiveness requirement to competitive proposals even though this rule is generally not applicable in negotiated procurement. Neither decision contains any recognition of the significant differences between sealed bidding and competitive negotiation. It would appear that unsigned offers could be considered if the RFP included Alternate I to the Instructions to Offerors — Competitive Acquisition provision in FAR 52.215-1, precluding the agency from making an award on the basis of the initial proposals.

The Comptroller General has also followed sealed bidding cases when competitive proposals are signed by agents. Thus, evidence of an agent's authority may be submitted after opening of proposals but proof that an offeror submitting a proposal in its own name was acting as an agent may not be submitted after opening. See *Hay-Holland Co.*, Comp. Gen. Dec. B-233002, 89-1 CPD ¶ 102, where the agency properly rejected an offer which was signed and subscribed by an agent without mention of the agent-principal relationship. The Comptroller General rejected the protester's contention that the incorrect signature was a clerical error which should have been corrected through discussions. In *WorldWide Parts, Inc.*, Comp. Gen. Dec. B-244793, 91-2 CPD ¶ 156, the Comptroller General held that an agent who submits a proposal listing itself as the offeror may not submit evidence after the closing date for receipt of proposals to show the agent-principal relationship because to do so would constitute an improper transfer of a proposal. See also *American Material Handling, Inc.*, Comp. Gen. Dec. B-253818, 93-2 CPD ¶ 246 (award to an entity other than that named in original offer is improper).

A proposal which is properly signed by one offeror may be transferred or assigned to another firm only if such a transfer is affected by operation of law, which is interpreted to include a merger, a corporate reorganization, a sale of an entire business or that portion of a business embraced by a proposal, or other means not barred by anti-assignment statutes, *Numax Elecs., Inc.*, 54 Comp. Gen. 580 (B-181670), 75-1 CPD ¶ 21.

b. Acknowledge Receipt of Amendments

Offerors are required to acknowledge the receipt of amendments to the solicitation either upon receipt or on the cover sheet of the proposal. The Instructions to Offerors — Competitive Acquisition solicitation provision in FAR 52.215-1(b) provides:

> If this solicitation is amended, all terms and conditions that are not amended remain unchanged. Offerors shall acknowledge receipt of any amendment to this solicitation by the date and time specified in the amendment(s).

The failure to acknowledge receipt of a material amendment precludes award to that offeror on the basis of the initial proposal but the contracting officer may establish a competitive range and permit the offeror to acknowledge the amendment in negotiations, *International Filter Mfg. Corp.*, Comp. Gen. Dec. B-235049, 89-1 CPD ¶ 586. See *Nomura Enter., Inc.*, Comp. Gen. Dec. B-277768, 97-2 CPD ¶ 148, where the Comptroller General did not object to an agency's failure to evaluate an offer where the offeror had failed to acknowledge a material amendment and the agency chose to award on the basis of initial proposals; and *Galaxy Aircraft Instruments Co.*, Comp. Gen. Dec. B-194356, 80-1 CPD ¶ 364, where the agency properly included the offer in the competition and, through oral or written discussions, permitted it to acknowledge the amendment. The choice of which alternative to follow will depend upon the degree of competition and the value of the offer in relation to the other offers. The failure to acknowledge an amendment does not preclude award, however, where "the offeror is otherwise obligated to perform in accordance with the terms of the solicitation," *E. Frye Enters., Inc.*, Comp. Gen. Dec. B-258699.2, 95-1 CPD ¶ 64, or where the amendment does not contain material provisions, *International Data Sys., Inc.*, Comp. Gen. Dec. B-277385, 97-2 CPD ¶ 96 (failure to acknowledge amendment waived as minor informality).

The mere fact that an offeror does not receive an amendment is no excuse for failure to acknowledge the amendment where full and open competition and reasonable prices are obtained and the agency did not deliberately exclude the offeror from competition, *CDA, Inc.*, Comp. Gen. Dec. B-224971, 87-1 CPD ¶ 163, and *O.J. Best Servs., Inc.*, Comp. Gen. Dec. B-276954, 97-1 CPD ¶ 231 (of 21 offers received, 19 acknowledged receipt of the amendments).

2. Offer Strategy

There are a number of strategies which may be available to an offeror. These include deciding on the pricing and other aspects of the offer, whether to make an offer on all the items covered by the RFP, and whether to submit alternate or multiple offers.

a. Best Terms

One of the most difficult decisions to make is whether to submit an offer containing the best possible offer the firm can make or one reserving some improvements for the later stages of the process. The problem is that, in a competitive environment, the offeror may not get an opportunity to make concessions and improve the offer. In this regard, paragraph (f)(4) of the FAR 52.215-1 Instructions to Offerors — Competitive Acquisition provision warns offerors that:

> The Government intends to evaluate proposals and award a contract without discussions with offerors (except clarifications described in FAR 15.306(a)). *Therefore, the offeror's initial proposal should contain the offeror's best terms from a cost or price and technical standpoint.* [Emphasis supplied.]

Even where the solicitation indicates that the Government plans to undertake discussions with offerors within the competitive range, an offer at less than the best possible terms runs the risk of being found to be outside the competitive range.

b. Items Offered

Where the RFP calls for a number of severable items and the solicitation does not specifically require that offers be made on all the items, the offeror must decide whether to submit an offer on all the items or only some of them. The only FAR provision dealing with this issue is contained in paragraph (c)(4) of the FAR 52.215-1 Instructions to Offerors — Competitive Acquisition solicitation provision, stating, "Unless otherwise specified in the solicitation, the offeror may propose to provide any item or combination of items." If it decided to submit an offer covering all the items, the offeror should also consider whether to condition its offer on award of all the items. This condition, termed an "all or none" offer, would insure that the offeror would not receive partial awards. In such a case, the all or none prices will be compared with the price combinations for all the items offered by other offerors without an "all or none" condition, *Banknote Corp. of Am., Inc.*, Comp. Gen. Dec. B-245528.2, 92-1 CPD ¶ 53. If no such condition is contained in the offer, paragraphs (f)(5) and (f)(6) of the FAR 52.215-1 Instructions to Offerors — Competitive Acquisition solicitation provision permit the Government to award multiple contracts for all or a part of any contract line items. See Chapter 5, Section III for a further discussion of the rules for evaluating multiple item solicitations.

c. Alternate or Multiple Offers

Offerors may want to consider submitting more than one offer. This may be particularly desirable when the specifications permit the offeror to determine the way that the work will be performed such as in a performance or functional specification. See also FAR 11.002(e) permitting agencies to identify performance levels as targets rather than as fixed or minimum requirements. In other cases, an offeror may conclude that a non-specification offer will have sufficient advantages for the Government to consider amending the specifications to permit its consideration. The term "alternate proposal" has sometimes been used to refer to these two different situations. It has been used to describe the case where an offeror submits two or more offers each meeting the RFP requirements. It has also been used to describe the case where the offeror submits one offer meeting the requirements and another which does not, or merely submits one offer which does not conform to the RFP. The FAR does not provide comprehensive directions as to the treatment to be given the offers when an offeror elects to follow one of these strategies, but it would appear that agencies have substantial discretion in evaluating such offers and conducting the procurement to obtain the best value for the Government.

(1) NONCONFORMING OFFERS

If an offeror submits an alternate offer that deviates from the requirements of the RFP, the Government may not award to that offeror but must revise the RFP to permit other offerors to propose to the deviation, FAR 15.206(d). See *Labat-Anderson, Inc.,* 71 Comp. Gen. 252 (B-246071.5), 92-1 CPD ¶ 193, holding that it was improper to accept an offer which deviated from a staffing level required by the RFP. The proper course was followed in *Simmonds Precision Prods., Inc.*, Comp. Gen. Dec. B-244559.3, 93-1 CPD ¶ 483, where, upon receipt of a deviating offer containing terms that were more attractive than those required by the RFP, other offerors were given the opportunity to submit revised offers.

An offer is not nonconforming, however, if the RFP states that the agency reserves the right to award to a proposal that does not meet all of the mandatory requirements of the solicitation, *Litton Sys., Inc. v. Department of Transportation*, GSBCA 12911-P, 94-3 BCA ¶ 27,263. In that case, the board held that the agency was not required to amend the RFP to permit award to an alternate offer that did not conform to the mandatory requirements because all of the offerors had been informed that the agency might follow that procedure.

The only provision dealing with this issue is FAR 15.209(a)(2), which directs that language similar to the following Alternate II to the FAR 52.215-1 Instructions to Offerors — Competitive Acquisition provision be incorporated into the RFP if the Government would be willing to accept "alternate proposals:"

> (9) Offerors may submit proposals that depart from stated requirements. Such proposals shall clearly identify why the acceptance of the proposal would be advantageous to the Government. Any deviations from the terms and conditions of the solicitation, as well as the comparative advantage to the Government, shall be clearly identified and explicitly defined. The Government reserves the right to amend the solicitation to allow all offerors an opportunity to submit revised proposals based on the revised requirements.

While the presence of this provision appears to indicate that nonconforming offers will be considered, such offers can only be accepted if the solicitation is amended to give other competitors the opportunity to make offers to the revised specifications.

The absence of the Alternate II language does not necessarily mean that offers which deviate from the RFP must be rejected. The sealed bid concept of "responsiveness," does not apply to negotiated procurements, *Gardiner, Kamya & Assocs., P.C.*, Comp. Gen. Dec. B-258400, 95-1 CPD ¶ 191. Thus, the contracting officer has the discretion to include such an offer in the competitive range and seek to have a nonconformity cured through discussions or to amend the solicitation as required by FAR 15.206(g). However, the offeror takes the risk that the offer will be rejected and the offeror excluded from the competitive range. See *Bencor-Petrifond*, Comp. Gen. Dec. B-254205, 93-2 CPD ¶ 208 (proposal departed from RFP's construction schedule); and *Discount Mach. & Equip., Inc.*, Comp. Gen. Dec. B-241444, 90-2 CPD ¶ 474 (offeror unable to meet technical provisions). Which course of action will be taken by the contracting officer will depend upon the number and nature of conforming offers received and the benefits offered by the nonconforming offer. However, an offer that is totally out of compliance with the RFP may not be considered, *Best W. Quantico Inn/Conference Ctr.*, Comp. Gen. Dec. B-209500, 83-1 CPD ¶ 164. In that case, the offeror responded to an RFP with only a "contract pricing proposal" when the RFP required a "technical proposal."

(2) Multiple Conforming Offers

The present FAR, like its predecessor, does not deal with the submission of multiple conforming offers. Nevertheless, the Comptroller General has held that there is no need for the solicitation to contain a provision authorizing multiple offers for them to be considered, *Educational Media, Inc.*, B-225457.2, May 12, 1987, 87-1 CPD ¶ 498, and *Federal Computer Corp.*, 66 Comp. Gen. 139 (B-223932), 81-2 CPD ¶ 665. See also 33 Comp. Gen. 499 (B-119646) (1954); and 39 Comp. Gen. 892 (B-142957) (1960), holding that the submission of multiple offers are appropriate competitive techniques.

While the receipt of multiple offers can be of value to the Government, they do require additional evaluation. This could be unduly burdensome in cases where substantial evaluation effort is required such as where a large number of different approaches are proposed or there are a large number of multiple proposals. See, for example, *Banknote Corp. of Am., Inc.*, Comp. Gen. Dec. B-245528.2, 92-1 CPD ¶ 53, where the evaluation was complicated and delayed by the fact that one offeror submitted four separate price offers and another submitted ten. Thus, agencies may seek to preclude multiple offers by including a provision in the solicitation prohibiting more than one offer, e.g., *Dale Stevens Constr.*, Comp. Gen. Dec. B-24234, 91-1 CPD ¶ 354. However, such a provision will not necessarily prevent separate offers from being submitted by separate, but affiliated, firms. In *Robbins-Gioia, Inc.*, Comp. Gen. Dec. B-274318, 96-2 CPD ¶ 222, the RFP stated that (1) "an offeror may submit a maximum of one fully compliant proposal," (2) "no alternate proposals will be accepted," and (3) "if an offeror submits more than one proposal, all proposals will be returned without evaluation." The Comptroller General denied the protest against consideration of both offers, holding that the general rule is that contracting agencies may accept bids and offers from affiliated firms unless doing so would prejudice the Government's interests or give the affiliated offerors an unfair advantage over other offerors.

d. Unbalanced Offers

Where the solicitation contains multiple items, offerors may seek to obtain a competitive advantage by unbalancing the prices. Paragraph (f)(8) of the FAR 52.215-1 Instructions to Offerors — Competitive Acquisition provision warns offerors that their offers may be rejected if the prices are materially unbalanced, stating:

> The Government may determine that a proposal is unacceptable if the prices proposed are materially unbalanced between line items or subline items. Unbalanced pricing exists when, despite an acceptable total evaluated price, the price of one or more contract line items is significantly overstated or understated as indicated by the application of cost or price analysis techniques. A proposal may be rejected if the Contracting Officer determines that the lack of balance poses an unacceptable risk to the Government.

Though the majority of protests alleging unbalanced pricing occur in sealed bidding cases, the concept of unbalanced pricing has also been applied to negotiated procurements, *Litton Sys., Inc.*, Comp. Gen. Dec. B-239123.3, 90-2 CPD ¶ 276. The Comptroller General has held that a proposed price may not be accepted by a contracting agency if the proposed price in the offer is found to be materially unbalanced, *International Transport, S.A.*, Comp. Gen. Dec. B-244853, 91-2 CPD ¶ 489. The contracting officer may reject such a proposal without discussions, *Ocean Habitability, Inc.*, Comp. Gen. Dec. B-227304, 87-2 CPD ¶ 265, or may seek to remedy the unbalanced price through discussions, *Dynamic Science, Inc.*, Comp. Gen. Dec. B-270448.3, 96-1 CPD ¶ 236.

Prior to the FAR Part 15 Rewrite, unbalanced pricing in competitive proposals was treated in the same manner as in sealed bidding, requiring that to reject an offer it had to be both mathematically unbalanced and materially unbalanced. See Chapter 5, Section III. See *Astrosystems, Inc.*, Comp. Gen. Dec. B-260399.2, 95-2 CPD ¶ 18 (protester failed to show reasonable doubt for material unbalancing); *Laidlaw Envtl. Servs., Inc.*, Comp. Gen. Dec. B-261603, 95-2 CPD ¶ 171 (no evidence of enhanced prices); *Allstate Van & Storage, Inc.*, Comp. Gen. Dec. B-270744, 96-1 CPD ¶ 191 (no basis in record to conclude mathematical unbalancing). However, the current FAR replaces this rule with a discretionary rule stating that an unbalanced proposal may be rejected if the contracting officer determines that the lack of balance "poses an unacceptable risk to the Government," FAR 15.404-1(g)(3).

3. Modification, Revision and Withdrawal

The RFP forms specify the time within which the Government may accept offers. Block 12 of SF 33 provides that the offeror agrees to perform the work "if this offer is accepted within *60 calendar days unless a different date is inserted by the offeror*." Block 4 of OF 308, in turn, states, "Offers valid for 60 days unless a different period is entered here." Neither of these provisions prohibit the offeror from modifying, revising or withdrawing the offer prior to its acceptance. While the relevant FAR sections cited below speak in terms of modification, revision and withdrawal of "proposals," it is evident from the context that they are referring to "offers" and not "information." See, for example, FAR 15.208 which is titled, "Submission, modification, revision, and withdrawal of *proposal*" but which states in paragraph (a), "Offerors are responsible for submitting *offers*, and any revisions and modifications to them."

a. Modification

FAR 15.001 defines a modification as follows:

> Proposal modification is a change made to a proposal before the solicitation closing date and time, or made in response to an amendment, or made to correct a mistake at any time before award.

The correction of a mistake is the only type of modification where there is a question as to the extent to which an offeror can change the offer. This issue will be discussed in the following section dealing with Exchanges and Communications. FAR 15.508 provides that mistakes discovered after award are to be processed substantially in accordance with the mistake in bid procedures set forth in FAR 14.407-4.

b. Revision

FAR 15.001 defines a revision as follows:

> Proposal revision is a change to a proposal made after the solicitation closing date, at the request of or as allowed by a contracting officer, as the result of negotiations.

This definition permits offers to be "revised" only as a result of negotiations and negotiations will take place only after a competitive range has been established. See FAR 15.307. The subject of offer revisions will be covered in the discussion of competitive range below.

c. Withdrawal

Offers may be withdrawn by an offeror at any time prior to acceptance. See paragraph (c) of the Instructions to Offerors — Competitive Acquisition solicitation provision at FAR 52.215-1, which states that "Proposals may be withdrawn at any time before award. Withdrawals are effective upon receipt of notice by the Contracting Officer." This same statement is made in FAR 15.208(g), which also contains the procedures for withdrawal:

> Proposals may be withdrawn at any time before award. Written proposals are withdrawn upon receipt by the contracting officer of a written notice of withdrawal. Oral proposals in response to oral solicitations may be withdrawn orally. The contracting officer shall document the contract file when such oral withdrawals are made. One copy of withdrawn proposals should be retained in the contract file (see 4.803(a)(10)). Extra copies of the withdrawn proposals may be destroyed or returned to the offeror at the offeror's request. Extremely bulky proposals shall only be returned at the offeror's request and expense.

FAR 15.208(h) requires the purging of withdrawn electronic offers as follows:

> Upon withdrawal of an electronically transmitted proposal, the data received shall not be viewed and shall be purged from primary and backup data storage systems.

No explanation is given for the inconsistent treatment between withdrawn hard copy of facsimile offers (one copy retained for the contract file) and withdrawn electronic offers (purged).

The broad right of withdrawal before award in the present FAR is consistent with previous FAR provisions and the Comptroller General has consistently accepted the FAR provision as governing and has held that a signed offer is revocable before acceptance and, therefore, is not a firm offer, *Pedestrian Bus Stop Shelters, Ltd.*, 63 Comp. Gen. 265 (B-212570), 84-1 CPD ¶ 331. The Armed Services Board of Contract Appeals has described an offeror's right to withdraw its offer prior to award as a "fundamental protection," *Toyad Corp.*, ASBCA 26785, 85-3 BCA ¶ 18,354. The procedure for withdrawal is specified in FAR 15.208(g).

4. Timely Submission Required

Although earlier drafts had proposed liberalizing the rule concerning late proposals, the final FAR Part 15 Rewrite reestablished the "late is late" rule. Thus, offerors must use great care to ensure the timely submission of offers, modifications or revisions. This strict rule, with very limited exceptions, is contained in FAR 15.208:

> (a) Offerors are responsible for submitting offers, and any revisions and modifications to them, so as to reach the Government office designated in the solicitation on time. If an emergency or unanticipated event interrupts normal Government processes so that proposals cannot be received at the office designated for receipt of proposals by the exact time specified in the solicitation, and urgent Government requirements preclude amendment of the solicitation closing date, the time specified for receipt of proposals will be deemed to be extended to the same time of day specified in the solicitation on the first work day on which normal Government processes resume. If no time is specified in the solicitation, the time for receipt is 4:30 p.m., local time, for the designated Government office on the date that proposals are due.
>
> (b) Proposals, and modifications to them, that are received in the designated Government office after the exact time specified are "late" and shall be considered only if —

(1) They are received before award is made; and

(2) The circumstances meet the specific requirements of 52.215-1(c)(3)(i).

The late rule does not apply if the late offer is the only offer received. See paragraph (c)(3)(i)(F) of the Instructions to Offerors — Competitive Acquisition provision in FAR 52.215-1. In addition, paragraph (c)(3)(vi) provides a "late modification or revision of an otherwise successful proposal that makes its terms more favorable to the Government will be considered at any time it is received and may be accepted." Other circumstances detailed in this provision which permit consideration of late offers will be discussed below.

The Government's determination of the time of receipt is binding unless it is clearly unreasonable. Thus, a contracting official's reliance on the time/date clock will generally be found to be reasonable, *Pat Mathis Constr. Co.*, Comp. Gen. Dec. B-248979, 92-2 CPD ¶ 236 (contracting official's reliance on a time/date clock which showed offer's proposal to be one minute late rather than relying on clock in conference room which adjoined the proposal delivery point was reasonable). If the agency does not record the time of receipt of proposals, a Federal Express receipt signed by an agency employee may be used to establish that a proposal was timely received, *M.J.S., Inc.*, Comp. Gen. Dec. B-244410, 91-2 CPD ¶ 344.

The late rule has been enforced strictly and the offer must be received by the Government exactly on time and at the place specified in the RFP. See, for example, *Logistics Management Inst.*, Comp. Gen. Dec. B-276143, 97-1 CPD ¶ 186 (7 minutes late). See also *Med-National, Inc.*, Comp. Gen. Dec. B-277430, 97-2 CPD ¶ 67 (offeror could not show by a preponderance of evidence that its hand-carried proposal was "in the proper place by the proper time"); *Koba Assocs., Inc.*, Comp. Gen. Dec. B-265854, 95-2 CPD ¶ 212 (hand-carried proposal delivered to the depository office three minutes after time specified for receipt of proposals late); *Hallcrest Sys., Inc.*, Comp. Gen. Dec. B-215328, 84-2 CPD ¶ 334 (hand-carried proposal received one minute late rejected) and *Priest & Fine, Inc.*, Comp. Gen. Dec. B-213603, 84-1 CPD ¶ 358 (hand-delivered proposal received two minutes late not considered).

The same rules are applied when submission of offers by facsimile is authorized. Receipt by the Government's fax machine is not sufficient. Even if the fax is transmitted before opening, it must get to the place designated in the solicitation on time, *Instrument Assocs.*, Comp. Gen. Dec. B-256814, 94-2 CPD ¶ 52 (bid was rejected where both sender's and agency's fax activity reports showed fax was transmitted on time but did not get to opening on time); *Microscope Co.*, Comp. Gen. Dec. B-257015, 94-2 CPD ¶ 157 (proposal was rejected even though offeror's telephone records showed timely transmission where agency provided sworn statement by contract specialist responsible for checking fax machine that proposal was not received on time); and *R.C. Constr. Co.*, Comp. Gen. Dec. B-250037.2 (Feb. 24, 1993) (bid modification received by fax three minutes before closing in room connected to bid opening room was rejected when received in opening room four minutes after opening). Further, the entire message must be received before the time for submission, *Cyber Digital, Inc.*, Comp. Gen. Dec. B-270107, 96-1 CPD ¶ 20; *Radar Devices, Inc.*, Comp. Gen. Dec. B-249118, 92-2 CPD ¶ 287 (where transmission began before closing but completed after closing, contracting officer could only consider pre-closing transmission). However, the date/time notation on a facsimile has been used as evidence that a BAFO was timely received when the agency did not apply its own date/time stamp upon actual receipt, *Essex Electro Eng'rs, Inc.*, Comp. Gen. Dec. B-238207, 90-1 CPD ¶ 438. The fact that the Government's fax machine is out of order, out of paper, or busy will not excuse the failure to meet the required time, *Brookfield Dev., Inc.*, Comp. Gen. Dec. B-255944, 94-1 CPD ¶ 273 (BAFO due at 4 p.m. rejected where transmission began at 3:50 but was not completed until 4:16 because the Government's fax machine was busy).

5. Circumstances Permitting Acceptance of Late Offers

The FAR 52.215-1 Instructions to Offerors — Competitive Acquisition solicitation provision outlines a number of circumstances which would permit the consideration of late offers, modifications and revisions. These rules vary depending upon the method in which the offer, modification or revision was submitted.

a. Registered or Certified Mail (U.S. or Canadian Postal Service)

A submission which is received before award will be considered if sent by registered or certified mail in accordance with the timing specified in paragraph (c)(3)(i)(A) of the FAR 52.215-1 provision:

> It was sent by registered or certified mail not later than the fifth calendar day before the date specified for receipt of offers (e.g., an offer submitted in response to a solicitation requiring receipt of offers by the 20th of the month must have been mailed by the 15th).

Paragraph (c)(3)(iii) provides that the only evidence of the date of mailing "is the U.S. or Canadian Postal Service postmark both on the envelope or wrapper and on the original receipt from the U.S. or Canadian Postal Service." Postage meter impressions are not acceptable and offerors are cautioned to "request the postal clerk to place a legible hand cancellation bull's eye postmark on both the receipt and the envelope or wrapper."

b. U.S. Postal Service Next Day Delivery

Paragraph (c)(3)(i)(C) of the FAR 52.215-1 provision permits consideration of a submission received before award if:

> It was sent by U.S. Postal Service Express Mail Next Day Service-Post Office to Addressee, not later than 5:00 p.m. at the place of mailing two working days prior to the date specified for receipt of proposals. The term "working days" excludes weekends and U.S. Federal holidays.

Paragraph (c)(3)(v) provides that the only evidence of mailing "is the date entered by the post office receiving clerk on the Express Mail Next Day Service-Post Office to Addressee" label and the postmark on "both the envelope or wrapper and on the original receipt from the U.S. Postal Service." Offerors are cautioned to obtain a "legible hand cancelled bull's eye" to establish these dates.

c. *Government Mishandling of Offers Submitted By Other Means*

Lateness caused by weather or acts of God or other such factors is not excused, *Glyn Group, Inc.*, Comp. Gen. Dec. B-213917, 84-1 CPD ¶ 50 (hand-delivered proposal properly rejected as late even though delay was caused by unusually severe weather); *University of Kansas*, Comp. Gen. Dec. B-222329, 86-1 CPD ¶ 369 (hand-carried proposal late when due to congested air traffic); and *White Horse Assocs.*, Comp. Gen. Dec. B-218872, 85-1 CPD ¶ 581 (proposal late when offeror delayed submission awaiting oral advice of agency).

The only excuse is provided in paragraph (c)(3)(B) of the FAR 52.215-1 provision, which indicates that offers submitted by regular mail, facsimile or hand-carried may be considered only if the lateness was due primarily to Government mishandling. It permits consideration if :

> It was sent by mail (or telegram or facsimile, if authorized) or hand-carried (including delivery by a commercial carrier) if it is determined by the Government that the late receipt was due primarily to the Government mishandling after receipt at the Government installation.

The mishandling must be by the procurement agency. Thus, mishandling by U.S. Postal Service does not constitute "Government mishandling," *California State Univ., Fullerton*, Comp. Gen. Dec. B-243020.2, 91-1 CPD ¶ 452.

It has been extremely difficult for offerors to establish that the lateness was due to improper Government action. In *Vikonics, Inc.*, Comp. Gen. Dec. B-222423, 86-1 CPD ¶ 419, a protester alleged that its hand-carried proposal was late because it was delayed in getting a base pass and the receptionist gave incorrect directions. The Comptroller General denied the protest stating that delays in gaining access to Government buildings are not unusual and should be expected. See also *Einhorn Yaffee Prescott*, Comp. Gen. Dec. B-259552, 95-1 CPD ¶ 153, where the protester's BAFO was logged in at 1:05, five minutes after the time set for receipt. In denying the protester's claim of improper Government action, the Comptroller General stated:

> We cannot conclude that improper government action caused the late delivery here. To begin with, the offeror's messenger's action in attempting to make the delivery only 5 minutes before the time deadline was the paramount cause of the lateness. Further, it is undisputed that an agency mail-

room employee was on the loading dock at 1 p.m. That mailroom employee did not receive Einhorn's BAFO because Einhorn's messenger had gone outside to call the mailroom a second time. If the messenger had remained on the loading dock until 1 p.m., Einhorn's BAFO would have been timely received.

Social Eng'g Technology, Comp. Gen. Dec. B-187194, 77-1 CPD ¶ 234, is a particularly harsh decision. The protester's offer had been delivered to the HUD mailroom. This was the office that would have received the proposal if it had been mailed, but not the office designated for hand-delivered proposals. The Comptroller General found that the proposal was late and could not be considered for award. See also *CSLA, Inc.*, Comp. Gen. Dec. B-255177, 94-1 CPD ¶ 63.

Government mishandling was found in *Wand Elec.*, Comp. Gen. Dec. B-250576, 93-1 CPD ¶ 59 (bid depository was not checked within a reasonable time before offers were due); and *Timber-Mart Southwest, Inc.*, Comp. Gen. Dec. B-274677, 97-1 CPD ¶ 38 (failure to check mailbox until after time for receipt); *Space Ordinance Sys.*, 63 Comp. Gen. 482 (B-214079), 84-2 CPD ¶ 61 (telegraphic proposal modification received two and one-half hours prior to closing, but not delivered to the proper office until two days later).

The previous version of this exception required that the late receipt be due "solely" to the Government's mishandling. Whether the change from "solely" to "primarily" will have any effect on the decisions remains to be seen. Under the prior regulation the Comptroller General has dealt with cases involving joint responsibility for lateness by using a "paramount" cause rationale. See *Bergen Expo Sys., Inc.*, Comp. Gen. Dec. B-236970, 89-2 CPD ¶ 540 (Government at fault for restricting access to bid depository but paramount cause was Federal Express courier's failure to wait or to return on time); *Gulls, Inc.*, Comp. Gen. Dec. 13-232599, 89-1 CPD ¶ 74 (bid delivered two minutes late could not be considered even though front door of Government installation was locked and blocked by construction since bidder's failure to allow sufficient time to deliver bid was the paramount cause); *Bullard & Danbury Auto Processing*, Comp. Gen. Dec. B-226841, 87-2 CPD ¶ 8 (Government officials' failure to redirect misdelivered bid was incidental, rather than paramount, cause of lateness); *Scherr Constr. Co. v. United States*, 5 Cl. Ct. 249 (1984) (Government failure to answer telephone during normal business hours due to flex time was not paramount cause since subsequent action by bidder's delivery agent could have resulted in timely delivery). These cases should be compared with *Rocky Mountain Trading Co.*, GSBCA 8671-P 87-1 BCA ¶ 19,406, where a properly addressed submission was found to be timely even though a United Parcel Service (UPS) courier took it to the shipping and receiving facility instead of the specified room. There, the Government agency unbeknown to bidders, had an arrangement with UPS to deliver all packages to the shipping and receiving facility.

The regulations and solicitations refer to Government actions "after receipt at the installation." Nevertheless, the Government mishandling rationale has been extended to Government actions prior to the receipt of the bid or proposal. In *Richards Painting Co.*, Comp. Gen. Dec. B-232678, 89-1 CPD ¶ 76, the bid opening room was different from the room designated for the receipt of hand-carried bids and the latter room was not staffed when the bidder attempted to deliver the bid prior to the time for opening. In addition, the front door was locked and blocked by construction and the bidder had to go around to the rear of the building. The Comptroller General held that the bid, which arrived in the bid opening room three minutes late, should be considered. See also *I&C Constr. Co.*, Comp. Gen. Dec. B-186766, 76-2 CPD ¶ 139, where the designated building for delivery was locked while all Government employees were attending a retirement luncheon; and *United Teleplex*, Comp. Gen. Dec. B-237160.2, 90-1 CPD ¶ 146, where the Comptroller General found that the solicitation failed to accurately indicate the place of delivery and agency personnel misdirected the offeror upon arrival.

Mishandling will generally not be found if the proposal does not contain the time and date specified for receipt and the solicitation number, as required by paragraph (c)(1) of the FAR 52.215-1 provision. Thus, no mishandling was found in *Human Resources Consulting Serv.*, Comp. Gen. Dec. B-232338, 88-2 CPD ¶ 340, where a proposal not containing the solicitation number or time for receipt was delivered over eight hours before submission time but was misrouted by the agency. The Comptroller General concluded the primary cause of the lateness was the contractor's lack of diligence. In *Alpha Technical Servs., Inc.*, Comp. Gen. Dec. B-243322, 91-2 CPD ¶ 56, proposals were delivered via U.S. mail's express mail delivery service two hours before time set for receipt of proposals. However, the proposals were not routed to the contracting officer until after closing time. The Comptroller General held that lack of identification markings rather than agency mishandling caused the late deliveries. See also *Secure Applications, Inc.*, Comp. Gen. Dec. B-261885, 95-2 CPD ¶ 190, where the

Comptroller General found that late receipt of the protester's proposal was not due to Government mishandling. The offeror had failed to identify its submission as a proposal or otherwise mark the submission with an identifying solicitation number or closing date deadline and time; and had allowed only one day for delivery.

The Comptroller General will not consider the Government mishandling exception to the late proposal rule until the offeror establishes, with documented evidence, that the proposal was actually received by the Government prior to the closing date *Southeastern CAD/CAM*, 71 Comp. Gen. 78 (B-244745), 91-2 CPD ¶ 453 (drawings were allegedly transmitted by facsimile but no proof of receipt); *Microscope Co.*, Comp. Gen. Dec. B-257015, 94-2 CPD ¶ 157 (revised proposal was allegedly transmitted by facsimile but no proof of receipt).

B. Information

The typical RFP will require the offeror to furnish a considerable amount of information. Much of the information will deal with the offeror's capability to perform, including such subjects as past performance, experience, facilities and equipment, financial capacity and key personnel. Requests for information dealing with how the offeror intends to perform the work and what techniques it will use in managing the work often call for the offeror to include this information in what have been called "technical proposals" and "management proposals." Such requests for information have been criticized as creating "essay contests" and many agencies have stopped requiring them. They should be distinguished from RFP provisions which require the offeror to include in the offer details of the work or explanations of the offer which may or may not be incorporated into the contract. When such technical information is to be incorporated into the contract, it should be accomplished through negotiations and included in a revised offer or in the final contract document.

1. Technical Information

Offerors may be required to furnish technical information which will be used in assessing the offeror's "know how" or the degree of risk involved in the way the offeror intends to perform. When such information is required, offerors should devote full attention to ensuring that their information describes sound technical solutions and contains thorough documentation. Weak proposals are excluded as a matter of course, *University Sys., Inc.*, GSBCA 10924-P, 91-1 BCA ¶ 23,617; *Integrated Microcomputer Sys., Inc.*, Comp. Gen. Dec. B-239126.4, 90-2 CPD ¶ 195; and submissions that are not supported with sufficient technical information may be excluded from the competitive range, *Millar Elevator Indus., Inc.*, Comp. Gen. Dec. B-250992.2, 93-1 CPD ¶ 212; *KCI, Inc.*, Comp. Gen. Dec. B-244690, 91-2 CPD ¶ 395; *Wyle Lab.*, Comp. Gen. Dec. B-239671, 90-2 CPD ¶ 231. If the RFP calls for a specific description of how the work will be performed, the offeror can be downgraded for not supplying such information, *Northwestern Travel Agency, Inc.*, Comp. Gen. Dec. B-244592, 91-2 CPD ¶ 363. Merely repeating portions of the RFP (termed "parroting" the RFP) is a poor strategy, *Paragon Dynamics, Inc.*, Comp. Gen. Dec. B-251280, 93-1 CPD ¶ 248. See *Supreme Automation Corp.*, Comp. Gen. Dec. B-224158, 87-1 CPD ¶ 83, where an offeror was eliminated from the competitive range because it repeated back portions of the specification without affirmatively demonstrating the merits of its technical approach. Similarly, merely promising to meet the requirements in the RFP will almost invariably lead to a poor evaluation, *Bannum, Inc.*, Comp. Gen. Dec. B-271075, 96-1 CPD ¶ 248 (exclusion from competitive range proper where the protester merely paraphrased the statement of work requirements); *Eastern Technical Enters., Inc.*, Comp. Gen. Dec. B-259844, 95-1 CPD ¶ 232 (blanket offers of compliance are not adequate substitutes for detailed technical information); *Inter-Con Sec. Sys., Inc.*, Comp. Gen. Dec. B-235248, 89-2 CPD ¶ 148 (exclusion from competitive range proper when proposal merely made a "blanket promise" to comply with RFP). Compare *Moxon, Inc.*, Comp. Gen. Dec. B-179160, 74-1 CPD ¶ 134, where the Comptroller General held that discussions should have been held to determine what the protester was offering. See *Corporate Jets, Inc.*, GSBCA 11049-P, 91-2 BCA ¶ 23,998, *recons. denied*, 91-2 BCA ¶ 23,999, where it was held proper to eliminate an incumbent contractor from the competitive range because it failed to submit detailed technical information and merely stated that it would continue to perform as it had been performing on the current contract. For similar reliance on past performance and subsequent rejection from the competitive range, see *InterAmerica Research Assocs., Inc.*, Comp. Gen. Dec. B-253698.2, 93-2 CPD ¶ 288.

2. Management Information

The offeror may be called upon to explain how it plans to manage the work to attain the promised technical solution. While technical information focuses on how the work will be performed, management information focuses on whether the offeror's organization will manage its resources to achieve those results. The offeror will be required to show the Government what personnel and material resources it will use and how it will organize and control those resources to bring the contract work to a successful conclusion. As is the case with technical proposals, lack of detail in management proposals will generally result in lower scores and general statements will not suffice, *Science & Technology, Inc.*, Comp. Gen. Dec. B-272748, 97-1 CPD ¶ 121 (lower grade justified when management proposal contains statements such as "our managers who are incumbent personnel understand Fort Huachuca's mission").

3. Capability Information

Most RFPs call for the submission of information showing the offeror's capabilities as part of the technical or management proposal or as separate information. As a general rule, submission of specific information is far more effective than the mere inclusion of general statements on the abilities of the organization, *Honolulu Marine, Inc.*, Comp. Gen. Dec. B-245329, 91-2 CPD ¶ 586; *EAP Consultants*, Comp. Gen. Dec. B-238103, 90-1 CPD ¶ 358. Two of the most important types of capability information deal with experience and past performance and the personnel who will perform the contract.

a. Experience and Past Performance

Information concerning an offeror's experience and past performance record will be required to be furnished in almost all procurements. Experience deals with the types of work which the offeror or its employees have performed and past performance deals with how well the work has been performed. While the request may not clearly distinguish between the two, information on both types of background will be important. See *Telcom Sys. Servs., Inc. v. Department of Justice*, GSBCA 13272-P, 95-2 BCA ¶ 27,849 ("unreasonable to suggest that past performance does not encompass experience").

In addition to complying with the RFP's specific requests for past performance information, the offeror should offer additional information which would explain or supplement the information furnished. Thus, the offeror should provide a thorough analysis of its past performance on contracts that are similar to the procurement in question and should demonstrate that those contracts are relevant to the evaluation of its performance for the current effort. Where there have been instances of poor or unsuccessful past performance the offeror should provide any factual information which would establish extenuating circumstances. In addition, factual information on steps taken to correct or avoid such occurrences should be included.

When information on experience is requested, a detailed description of past efforts should be provided, *Sunbelt Properties, Inc.*, Comp. Gen. Dec. B-245729.3, 92-1 CPD ¶ 278. In some cases, the RFP may require information on the experience of both the offeror and its personnel, *General Physics Fed. Sys., Inc.*, Comp. Gen. Dec. B-275934, 97-1 CPD ¶ 171 (personnel experience and corporate experience); and *Global Assocs., Ltd.*, Comp. Gen. Dec. B-275534, 97-1 CPD ¶ 129 (corporate experience and personnel qualifications and experience). Where an offeror has not had the specific experience required, the lack of corporate experience may be overcome by the experience of employees, *Consultants on Family Addiction*, Comp. Gen. Dec. B-274924.2, 97-1 CPD ¶ 80 (nothing improper in evaluating an offeror's capacity to perform services based on the experience of those who will perform those services); and *EBA Eng'g, Inc.*, Comp. Gen. Dec. B-275818, 97-1 CPD ¶ 127 (a competitor for a service contract was entitled to use the experience of the incumbent employees).

b. Key Personnel

If you ask for resumes they better be there.

The personnel that the offeror intends to use in performing the contract are of prime importance. Thus, resumes of key personnel are frequently required and probably should be submitted even when they have not been requested. The importance of complying with resume requirements is demonstrated by *Inter-Con Sec. Sys., Inc.*, Comp. Gen. Dec. B-235248, 89-2 CPD ¶ 148, where an incumbent contractor was properly omitted from the competitive range of the follow-on procurement because it failed to provide resumes of key personnel and other requested information. For a similar result, see *Pyramid Servs., Inc.*, Comp. Gen. Dec. B-257085.2, 94-2 CPD ¶ 79.

Offerors have also been disqualified from the competition because of inaccuracies in listing key personnel, *Electronic Data Sys. Fed. Corp.*, GSBCA 9869-P, 89-2 BCA ¶ 21,655, *recons. denied*, 89-2 BCA ¶ 21,778, *aff'd in part, vacated in part sub. nom. Planning Research Corp. v. United States*, 971 F.2d 736 (Fed. Cir. 1992) (submission of 101 resumes with no intention to use the personnel); *Ultra Technology Corp.*, Comp. Gen. Dec. B-230309.6, 89-1 CPD ¶ 42 (proposing person as "lead technician" without obtaining his permission); *ManTech Advanced Sys. Int'l., Inc.*, Comp. Gen. Dec. B-255719.2, 94-1 CPD 326 (misrepresenting availability of incumbent personnel). In *CBIS Fed., Inc.*, 71 Comp. Gen. 319 (B-245844.2), 92-1 CPD ¶ 308, the Comptroller General stated that when an offeror finds that proposed personnel are no longer available the offeror should withdraw the names and propose substitutes in the best and final offer.

In many cases, the offeror will be required to furnish evidence that the listed key personnel will be available for performance if the offeror receives the award. In such cases, the Comptroller General has ruled that award would be improper if the offeror does not supply information ensuring that key personnel would be available to perform the contract, *ManTech Field Eng'g Corp.*, Comp. Gen. Dec. B-245886.4, 92-1 CPD ¶ 309. Thus, failure to do so will result in the submission being held to be unacceptable or downgraded, *Xeta Int'l Corp.*, Comp. Gen. Dec. B-255182, 94-1 CPD ¶ 109 (failure to provide required letters of commitment for proposed key personnel). In *Scientific Management Assocs., Inc.*, Comp. Gen. Dec. B-238913, 90-2 CPD ¶ 27, the RFP stated that proposed personnel with nonbinding hiring agreements would not be evaluated as highly. The Comptroller General held that the protester was properly excluded from the competitive range because of conditional hiring agreements for several key personnel. Similarly, in *IMR Servs. Corp.*, Comp. Gen. Dec. B-230586, 88-1 CPD ¶ 548, the proposed program manager was also committed to work as a site manager at another location. The Comptroller General held that it was not unreasonable for the agency to downgrade a proposal in which a proposed manager would be stationed at a location different from the center of contract activity.

C. Rules Governing Submission

The RFP will specify the method of submitting offers and information and the format that must be observed. The failure to follow these instructions may result in the submission being rejected. See *Environmental*

Control Div., Inc., Comp. Gen. Dec. B-255181, 94-1 CPD ¶ 115, where the Comptroller General found that the agency properly rejected a protester's BAFO which was transmitted by facsimile in response to the agency's facsimile transmitted request for BAFOs because the solicitation did not allow for offers or modifications to be transmitted by facsimile.

1. *Method of Submission*

The basic method of submission of offers and information is in paper media in a sealed envelope. However, there are a growing number of procurements where facsimile or electronic submission is permitted or required. In addition, part or all of the required information may be submitted in an oral presentation.

a. *Paper Media*

Paragraph (c) of the Instructions to Offerors — Competitive Acquisition solicitation provision in FAR 52.215-1 provides guidance on the basic procedure to be followed in submitting offers and information:

> (1) Unless other methods (e.g., electronic commerce or facsimile) are permitted in the solicitation, proposals and modifications to proposals shall be submitted in paper media in sealed envelopes or packages (i) addressed to the office specified in the solicitation, and (ii) showing the time and date specified for receipt, the solicitation number, and the name and address of the offeror. Offerors using commercial carriers should ensure that the proposal is marked on the outermost wrapper with the information in paragraphs (c)(1)(i) and (c)(1)(ii) of this provision.
>
> (2) The first page of the proposal must show —
>
>> (i) The solicitation number;
>>
>> (ii) The name, address, and telephone and facsimile numbers of the offeror (and electronic address if available);
>>
>> (iii) A statement specifying the extent of agreement with all terms, conditions, and provisions included in the solicitation and agreement to furnish any or all items upon which prices are offered at the price set opposite each item;

(iv) Names, titles, and telephone and facsimile numbers (and electronic addresses if available) of persons authorized to negotiate on the offeror's behalf with the Government in connection with this solicitation; and

(v) Name, title, and signature of person authorized to sign the proposal. Proposals signed by an agent shall be accompanied by evidence of that agent's authority, unless that evidence has been previously furnished to the issuing office.

b. Facsimile or Electronic Submission

FAR 15.203(c) provides that when electronic commerce is an authorized means of submission, the RFP must "specify the electronic commerce method(s) that offerors may use (see Subpart 4.5)." FAR 15.209(e) requires the contracting officer to include the following FAR 52.215-5 Facsimile Proposals provision in an RFP when submission by facsimiles is authorized:

(a) Definition. Facsimile proposal, as used in this provision, means a proposal, revision or modification of a proposal, or withdrawal of a proposal that is transmitted to and received by the Government via facsimile machine.

(b) Offerors may submit facsimile proposals as responses to this solicitation. Facsimile proposals are subject to the same rules as paper proposals.

(c) The telephone number of receiving facsimile equipment is: [insert telephone number].

(d) If any portion of a facsimile proposal received by the Contracting Officer is unreadable to the degree that conformance to the essential requirements of the solicitation cannot be ascertained from the document —

(1) The Contracting Officer immediately shall notify the offeror and permit the offeror to resubmit the proposal;

(2) The method and time for resubmission shall be prescribed by the Contracting Officer after consultation with the offeror; and

(3) The resubmission shall be considered as if it were received at the date and time of the original unreadable submission for the purpose of determining timeliness, provided the offeror complies with the time

and format requirements for resubmission prescribed by the Contracting Officer.

(e) The Government reserves the right to make award solely on the facsimile proposal. However, if requested to do so by the Contracting Officer, the apparently successful offeror promptly shall submit the complete original signed proposal.

The instructions for handling unreadable portions of facsimile or electronic submissions contained in this provision are also set forth in FAR 15.207(c).

Offerors assume the risk of having their facsimile or electronic transmissions considered, *S.W. Electronics & Mfg. Corp.*, Comp. Gen. Dec. B-249308, 92-2 CPD ¶ 320. For electronic transmission, delivery to the offeror's Government approved Value Added Network (VAN) would not appear to be sufficient, *Comspace Corp.*, Comp. Gen. Dec. B-274037, 96-2 CPD ¶ 186 (involving a request for quotations).

c. *Oral Presentations*

Oral presentations, as discussed earlier, have been used for some time to enable procurement officials to obtain information leading to additional understanding of the offerors' capability and features of their offers. However, it was not until the FAR Part 15 Rewrite that comprehensive coverage was adopted for these procedures. FAR 15.102 provides detailed guidance on obtaining information, but not offers, through this process. This regulatory provision for obtaining information through the presentation process is consistent with prior practice. See *Intermagnetics Gen. Corp.*, Comp. Gen. Dec. B-255741.2, 94-1 CPD ¶ 302, holding that while an agency may limit its evaluation to information contained in written submissions, it also may decide to use other information, including that obtained in oral presentations:

> An agency may properly limit its evaluation to information contained in the four corners of a proposal, and [the protester] cites decisions in which we have denied protests alleging that the contracting agency should have used information from other sources, such as a pre-award survey, as a substitute for information that the solicitation directed offerors to include in their proposal. *See, e.g., Numax Elecs. Inc.*, B-210266, May 3, 1983, 83-1 CPD ¶ 470. [The protester] is also correct in noting that we have denied protests where the protester complained that the agency erred in not considering

> orally discussed changes to the protester's proposal, where the protester did not confirm the changes by incorporating them in its BAFO. *See, e.g., Recon Optical, Inc.*, B-232125, Dec 1, 1988, 88-2 CPD ¶ 544.
>
> These decisions are not inconsistent with our denial of [the protester's] protest; they stand for the proposition that offerors act at their peril when they fail to include within the four corners of their proposals information required by the solicitation or requested by the agency during discussions, and that such proposals may properly be rejected. *See Abacus Enters.*, B-248969, Oct. 13, 1992, 92-2 CPD ¶ 242. However, we have also consistently held that, in evaluating proposals, contracting agencies may consider any evidence, even if that evidence is entirely outside the proposal (and, indeed, even if it contradicts statements in the proposal), so long as the use of the extrinsic evidence is consistent with established procurement practice. *See, e.g., Western Medical Personnel, Inc.*, 66 Comp. Gen. 699 (1987), 87-2 CPD ¶ 310; *AAA Eng'g & Drafting, Inc.*, B-250323, Jan. 26, 1993, 93-1 CPD ¶ 287.

See also *NW Ayer, Inc.*, Comp. Gen. Dec. B-248654, 92-2 CPD ¶ 154; and *Palmer Brown Cos.*, 70 Comp. Gen. 667 (B-243544), 91-2 CPD ¶ 134. In *Labat-Anderson, Inc.*, 71 Comp. Gen. 252 (B-246071), 92-1 CPD ¶ 193, the oral presentation resulted in a determination that the offeror lacked capability as it also did in *ARTEL, Inc.*, Comp. Gen. Dec. B-248478, 92-2 CPD ¶ 120, where the agency concluded from an oral presentation that there were serious doubts as to the quality and availability of the offeror's key personnel.

The present regulations make it clear that agency officials may ask questions and seek further detail. This is consistent with prior decisions, *NAHB Research Found., Inc.*, Comp. Gen. Dec. B-219344, 85-2 CPD ¶ 248 (aggressive questioning permissible). Agencies may also adopt reasonable rules governing the nature of the presentations, including limitations on the length and nature of the presentations, *American Sys. Corp.*, 68 Comp. Gen. 475 (B-234449), 89-1 CPD ¶ 537. They may also require that offerors meet mandatory requirements in an RFP before being eligible to make an oral presentation, *Inte-Great Corp.*, Comp. Gen. Dec. B-272780, 96-2 CPD ¶ 159.

Agencies may either preclude or permit discussions during the oral presentation, FAR 15.102(d)(6). However, if discussions occur, the agency must comply with the rules governing negotiations with all offerors in the competitive range, FAR 15.102(g). The Comptroller General has not yet ruled that discussions occurred during an oral presentation. See *General Physics Federal Sys., Inc.*, Comp. Gen. Dec. B-275934, 97-1 CPD ¶ 171, where no ruling on this issue was made because there was no prejudice to the protester when the agency sought information on the commitment of proposed key personnel from all of the offerors during the oral presentations. See also *Telestar Corp.*, Comp. Gen. Dec. B-275855, 97-1 CPD ¶ 150, where the Comptroller General found that no discussions had occurred during an oral presentation.

2. Format and Style

The format and style of a submission are intangible considerations in winning competitions. A good submission is organized and written so that it can be read by Government evaluators of many different functional and technical disciplines such as management, contracting, engineering, legal, accounting, and others. Some features the offeror will want to consider in developing its are:

> Inclusion of an *executive summary* to highlight the salient aspects. A good summary may be read by the source selection official and other agency officials too busy to read the entire document.
>
> An *index* which cross-references the statement of work to the information and the offer. This can be valuable in showing the Government exactly how the offer matches the evaluation factors expressed in the RFP.
>
> The *organization* of the submission should indicate that the offeror is orderly, thorough, and effective. It should be made easy to break out into component parts for evaluation by technical, business, and pricing personnel.

The way in which a submission is presented can have a significant effect on its evaluation. See *Professional Software Eng'g, Inc.*, Comp. Gen. Dec. B-272820, 96-2 CPD ¶ 193 (proposal downgraded for typographical errors); *Engineering & Envt., Inc.*, Comp. Gen. Dec. B-271868.3, 96-2 CPD ¶ 182 ("many typographical errors and misspelling" and "inattention to detail"); and *Pannesma Co.*, Comp. Gen. Dec. B-251688, 93-1 CPD ¶ 333 ("sloppy proposal" reflecting a "casual approach").

It is the offeror's responsibility to ensure its submission is, in all respects, a complete document, *Westvold & Assocs.*, Comp. Gen. Dec. B-201032, 81-1 CPD ¶ 354. It should also be a coherent document — both within each section and among sections. One of the most common failings is the inclusion of conflicting data and information in the technical, management, and cost sections. See, for example, *Earle Palmer Brown Cos.*, 70 Comp. Gen. 667 (B-243544) 91-2 CPD ¶ 134, where the agency properly adjusted the contractor's price upward upon determining that the contractor could not pay the salary of required personnel for the cost offered in its proposal; and *AmerInd, Inc.*, Comp. Gen. Dec. B-248324, 92-2 CPD ¶ 85, where the agency properly determined that the costs offered by the protester bore no relation to the cost of personnel for whom the protester submitted resumes.

Whenever data can be summarized in graphic form, it is wise to include such charts and graphs. They are particularly important when page limitations make it necessary to present information in the most concise form. However, such charts and graphs should be simple and direct. Although the FAR Part 15 Rewrite eliminated the Unnecessarily Elaborate Proposals or Quotations solicitation provision, it is still sound advise not to submit unnecessarily elaborate brochures or other presentations beyond those sufficient to present a complete and effective response to a solicitation. In *Professional Data Servs., Inc.*, Comp. Gen. Dec. B-220002, 33 Cont. Cases Fed. (CCF) ¶ 74,331, *Unpub.*, Dec. 13, 1985, the agency rejected the protester's offer because it was overly elaborate and the Comptroller General upheld that decision, stating:

> [O]ne reason that [the protester] did not receive higher scores for Technical Understanding and Approach was because [the protester] submitted an unnecessarily elaborate proposal that in part was confusing regarding what was being offered. An offeror has the burden of submitting an adequately written proposal permitting the agency to make an intelligent evaluation, and failure to do so justifies lowering the proposal's score.

Conversely, when a proposal has been rejected because it lacks detail or specifics, the Comptroller General has routinely rejected the argument that the proposal could not be more detailed without violating the unnecessarily elaborate proposal prohibition. In *TLC Sys.*, Comp. Gen. Dec. B-243220, 91-2 CPD ¶ 37, the Comptroller General stated that none of the unnecessarily elaborate provisions "can be read to obviate the clearly expressed requirements to submit specified information with the proposal." See also

Global Valuation Serv., Comp. Gen. Dec. B-230753, 88-1 CPD ¶ 604, where the Comptroller General rejected the protester's assertion that its "rather limited proposal" was justified by the RFP's caution against submitting overly elaborate proposals. Thus, offerors must strike a balance between clear and coherent explanation of their proposed method of performance and unduly elaborate detailing.

Another formal requirement in many solicitations is a page limitation for some or all of the sections of the proposal. Page limitations are strictly enforced, *Management & Indus. Technologies Assocs.*, Comp. Gen. Dec. B-257656, 94-2 CPD ¶ 134 (agency properly rejected pages in excess of limitation); *U.S. Envtl. & Indus., Inc.*, Comp. Gen. Dec. B-257349, 94-2 CPD ¶ 51 (smaller typeface created excess pages and improper competitive advantage); *All Star Maintenance, Inc.*, Comp. Gen. Dec. B-244143, 91-2 CPD ¶ 294 (single space, instead of double space created excess pages and improper competitive advantage). However, the Comptroller General has ruled that it is proper to exclude the cover sheet and table of contents from the page limitation requirement, *Trident Sys., Inc.*, Comp. Gen. Dec. B-243101, 91-1 CPD ¶ 604. The Comptroller General has also ruled that it is not proper to evaluate a long appendix to a proposal which exceeded the page limitation in the RFP, *ITT Electron Technology Div.*, Comp. Gen. Dec. B-242289, 91-1 CPD ¶ 383. The General Services Board has held that it was proper to exclude a Contract Start-Up Handbook and a Task Leader Handbook from the page limitation on technical proposals, *TRW, Inc.*, GSBCA 11309-P, 92-1 BCA ¶ 24,389. The board stated that this exclusion was reasonable because the handbooks were not used in scoring the proposal — although they were used to "ameliorate . . . concerns about [the offeror's] ability to effect a smooth transition in the event [the offeror] was awarded the contract." In *Macfadden & Assocs., Inc.*, Comp. Gen. Dec. B-275502, 97-1 CPD ¶ 88, the Comptroller General reasoned that whether an agency can automatically reject an entire proposal that exceeds a page limit rather than evaluate only the proposal pages within the limit depends upon the language of the solicitation. The Comptroller General stated:

> If the solicitation provides that a proposal exceeding a specified page limit will be rejected and an offeror, without protesting that provision, chooses to compete in accordance with the RFP's terms but nevertheless submits a proposal that exceeds the limit, rejection of the proposal, at least in general, would seem to be unobjectionable. Where, however, the solicitation states that a proposal exceeding a page limit may be excluded from consideration, we think offerors are reasonably put on notice that rejection for exceeding

> the page limit will not be automatic but instead will occur only if there is a reasonable basis for such action.

In *HSQ Technology*, Comp. Gen. Dec. B-277048, 97-2 CPD ¶ 57, the RFP stated that noncompliance with the stated page limitation "could result in elimination of the offer from the proposal process." The Comptroller General followed the logic in *Macfadden* stating that "could" meant that such a proposal could not automatically be rejected but rather may properly be rejected only if there was a reasonable basis for the rejection. The Comptroller General found that the agency reasonably concluded that the proposal without the excess pages was unacceptable since it lacked material sections of the technical proposal and the entire price proposal.

Paragraph (c)(iv) of the Instructions to Offerors — Competitive Acquisition solicitation provision in FAR 52.215-1 contains a further formal requirement — that offerors must provide the names, titles, and telephone and facsimile numbers of persons authorized to negotiate on the offeror's behalf. While there is no indication that a proposal can be rejected for failure to comply with this requirement, the information should be furnished as a matter of course in each proposal.

3. Proprietary Data

FAR 15.207(b) provides that proposals must be "safeguarded from unauthorized disclosure throughout the source selection process." This provision merely instructs the contracting officer on the protections that are required to be used in handling the data. Offerors are permitted to place proprietary markings on their proposals to ensure that such protection is given. The following paragraph (e) in FAR 52.215-1 implements this regulation:

> Offerors that include in their proposals data that they do not want disclosed to the public for any purpose, or used by the Government except for evaluation purposes, shall —
>
> (1) Mark the title page with the following legend:
>
> This includes data that shall not be disclosed outside the Government and shall not be duplicated, used, or disclosed — in whole or in part — for any purpose other than to evaluate this proposal. If, however, a contract is awarded to this offeror as a result of — or in connection

> with — the submission of this data, the Government shall have the right to duplicate, use, or disclose the data to the extent provided in the resulting contract. This restriction does not limit the Government's right to use information contained in this data if it is obtained from another source without restriction. The data subject to this restriction are contained in sheets [insert numbers or other identification of sheets]; and
>
> (2) Mark each sheet of data it wishes to restrict with the following legend:
>
> Use or disclosure of data contained on this sheet is subject to the restriction on the title page of this proposal.

This provision permits offerors to mark all data in the proposal — whether technical, management, or financial data — with the prescribed legend, and requires Government agencies to protect such data during the source selection process, and thereafter for the losing offerors. However, if the contract is awarded, this provision states that the Government's obligation to protect the data of the winning offeror ceases, and, thereafter, the Government's right to disclose the information is governed by the clauses of the contract. With regard to properly marked technical data submitted to civilian agencies, protection would be granted by the Rights in Data — General clause in FAR 52.227-14 when it is included in the resulting contract. If this clause is not included in the contract, there may well be no Government promise to protect proprietary technical data. Even if the clause is included in the contract, it contains no Government promise to protect management and financial data. Thus, offerors dealing with civilian agencies desiring to protect such data should request that a clause be included in the contract for that purpose. With regard to proposal data submitted to the Department of Defense, 10 U.S.C. § 2305(g) prohibits disclosure of this data unless it is incorporated in the contract by reference. This statute would appear to override the language in the solicitation provision stating that there is no protection for the winning contractor after award of the contract. To the extent that the data was incorporated in the contract, the only protection would be that granted to properly marked technical data under the Rights in Technical Data — Noncommercial Items clause in DFARS 252.227-7013 when it is included in contracts of the Department of Defense.

FAR 15.309 provides additional instructions concerning the protection of data in unsolicited proposals. This procedure tells contracting officers to protect data in proposals even though legends are omitted and directing contracting officers to attempt to persuade offerors to delete legends that are different from the prescribed legend. This procedure also authorizes contracting officers to reject proposals with deviating legends. FAR 15.609(e) notes that the provisions of the Freedom of Information Act override this Government promise to protect information — as was established in *Petkas v. Staats*, 501 F.2d 887, 163 U.S. App. D.C. 327 (D.C. Cir. 1974).

V. COMMUNICATIONS TO FACILITATE EVALUATION

Following the submission of offers, there are many occasions when communications between the Government and one or more of the offerors would facilitate the evaluation process. After the receipt of initial offers, such communications can assist the Government in determining whether to make an award on initial proposals or in deciding which offerors should be included in the competitive range. Communications can also be helpful if questions arise after the submission of final revised offers. In these situations, communications may also be necessary when mistakes are suspected or alleged. However, if these communications become discussions, the Government loses the right to award without conducting discussions with all offerors in the competitive range. The statutes, regulations and decisions in this area have not been very helpful in assisting contracting officials in deciding what communications with one or more offerors would preclude award without discussions or would require discussion with all other offerors within the competitive range.

While the propriety of preaward communications is one of the major characteristics distinguishing competitive proposals from sealed bidding, a continuing concern by some is that such communications can result in unfair treatment of unfavored offerors. This concern was addressed in the FAR Part 15 Rewrite comments at 62 Fed. Reg. 51226 (1997):

> Some respondents expressed concerns that the increased exchanges between the Government and industry throughout the acquisition process increased the risk of unfair practices. The final rule encourages earlier and more meaningful exchanges of information between the Government and potential contractors to achieve a better understanding of the Government's requirements and the offerors' proposals. This rule contains limits on exchanges that preclude favoring one offeror over another, revealing offerors' technical solutions, revealing prices without the offerors' permission, and knowingly furnishing source selection information.

The concept of equal treatment and fairness was discussed in *General Physics Federal Sys., Inc.*, Comp. Gen. Dec. B-275934, 97-1 CPD ¶ 171:

> Our decisions sustaining protests that an agency held discussions with only one offeror — a scenario found in a minority of our meaningful discussions cases, which usually present distinctions between clarifications and discussions or challenges to the adequacy of discussions the agency intended to hold — have generally focused on the inherent unfairness of agency actions that fail to provide unsuccessful offerors the same opportunity as the awardee to improve their relative standing in a negotiated competition. *Raytheon Co.*, B-261959.3, Jan. 23, 1996, 96-1 CPD ¶ 37, at 11-12; *Paramax Sys. Corp.*; *CAE-Link Corp.*, B-253098.4; B-253098.5, Oct. 27, 1993, 93-2 CPD ¶ 282, at 6. In such cases, we generally conclude that if the protester had been given the opportunity to address evaluator concerns during discussions it would have submitted a materially revised proposal, and the outcome of the competition might have been changed. *Raytheon Co., supra*, at 12, n. 11.

Thus, it appears that in close questions as to the classification of communications, the decision will be based upon considerations of whether an offeror has been treated unfairly or whether another offeror has been given favorable unequal treatment.

A. Development of Statutory and Regulatory Language

At the center of the confusion over the effect of communications are the statutory terms "discussions" and "clarification," neither of which are defined in the statutes. The term "discussions" was originally incorporated into 10 U.S.C. § 2304 by P.L.87-653 on September 10, 1962, providing for oral or written discussions with all offerors within the competitive range and award on initial proposals without discussions. The Comptroller General interpreted these provisions as requiring "discussions" with all offerors in the competitive range "if negotiations (i.e., discussions) be conducted with one of the offerors," 46 Comp. Gen. 191 (B-158686), 1966 CPD ¶ 76. The regulations did not attempt to define "discussions" until the FAR was published in April 1984. At that time the term "clarification" was also defined as communications distinct from "discussions." Shortly thereafter, the Competition in Contracting Act, P.L. 98-369, provided that "discussions conducted for the purpose of minor clarification" would not prohibit award without discussions. The same terminology is now contained in 10 U.S.C.§ 2305(b)(4)(A), as follows:

> The head of an agency shall evaluate competitive proposals in accordance with paragraph (1) and may award a contract —
>
> (i) after discussions with the offerors, provided that written or oral discussions have been conducted with all responsible offerors who submit proposals within the competitive range; or
>
> (ii) based on the proposals received, without discussions with the offerors (other than discussions conducted for the purpose of minor clarification) provided that the solicitation included a statement that proposals are intended to be evaluated, and award made, without discussions, unless discussions are determined to be necessary.

Essentially the same language is contained in 41 U.S.C. § 253b(d)(1).

The following definitions of "clarifications" and "discussions" remained in FAR 15.601 until they were removed by the FAR Part 15 Rewrite:

> "Clarification," as used in this subpart, means communication with an offeror for the sole purpose of eliminating minor irregularities, informalities, or apparent clerical mistakes in the proposal. It is achieved by explanation or substantiation, either in response to Government inquiry or as initiated by the offeror. Unlike discussion (see definition below), clarification does not give the offeror an opportunity to revise or modify its proposal, except to the extent that correction of apparent clerical mistakes results in a revision.
>
> "Discussion," as used in this subpart, means any oral or written communication between the Government and an offeror (other than communications conducted for the purpose of minor clarification), whether or not initiated by the Government, that (a) involves information essential for determining the acceptability of a proposal, or (b) provides the offeror an opportunity to revise or modify its proposal.

In addition, FAR 15.607 contained detailed provisions dealing with mistakes disclosed before award. That entire section was also removed in the Rewrite.

Post-submission communications are now addressed under FAR 15.306 titled, "Exchanges with offerors after receipt of proposals." Three types of exchanges are covered: (1) communications and award without discussion,

(2) communications prior to establishing the competitive range, and (3) negotiations with offerors within the competitive range. The following material discusses the first two types of communications. It also discusses the treatment of mistakes alleged before award. Negotiations with offerors within the competitive range will be discussed in a following section.

B. Communications and Award Without Discussions

FAR 15.306(a) contains the following coverage of communications (termed clarifications) prior to award without discussions:

> (a) *Clarifications and award without discussions.* (1) Clarifications are limited exchanges, between the Government and offerors, that may occur when award without discussions is contemplated.
>
>> (2) If award will be made without conducting discussions, offerors may be given the opportunity to clarify certain aspects of proposals (e.g., the relevance of an offeror's past performance information and adverse past performance information to which the offeror has not previously had an opportunity to respond) or to resolve minor or clerical errors.

The comments accompanying its publication indicate that the deletion of the previous definitions and the adoption of the above language was intended to permit increased exchanges of information while still complying with the statutory requirements for award without discussions. See 62 Fed. Reg. 51228–29 (1997), stating:

> (1) Clarifications. We drafted the rule to allow as much free exchange of information between offerors and the Government as possible, while still permitting award without discussions and complying with applicable statutes. The proposed rule did not differentiate between exchanges of information when award without discussions was contemplated versus when a competitive range would be established. Public comment pointed out that the proposed rule language may allow exchanges beyond what is permitted by applicable statute when making award without discussions. In drafting the second proposed rule, we limited these exchanges. The resulting language still permits more exchange of information between offerors and the Government than the current FAR. This policy is expected to help offerors, especially small entities that may not be familiar with proposal preparation, by permitting easy clarification of limited aspects of their proposals.

An earlier draft would have enabled the Government to obtain "relevant information (in addition to that submitted in the offeror's proposal) needed to understand and evaluate the offeror's proposal." It further provided that, "The nature and extent of communications between the Government and offerors is a matter of contracting officer judgment."

The terms "minor clarification" and "limited exchanges" are not in themselves meaningful. Relatively small bits of information can result in an offer being revised. Thus, in determining the extent to which the final Rewrite "permits more exchange of information" than the prior FAR rules, it is necessary to consider the purpose of the exchange. If the exchange is intended to obtain a revision in the offer, oral or written discussions and final revised offers will be required. Conversely, information exchanges which are conducted with all offerors that are similarly situated and do not vary the terms of their offers should not preclude award without discussions.

1. Communications Concerning Offer Revisions

A major problem with the statutory and regulatory coverage of discussions and clarifications has been the overly broad use of the term "proposal" sometimes referring to the entire submission and other times referring to the offer. While any changes or additions to information will result in a revision to the entire submission, such changes or additions should be distinguished from offer revisions. Revisions are defined in FAR 15.001, as follows:

> "Proposal revision" is a change to a proposal made after the solicitation closing date, at the request of or as allowed by a contracting officer, as the result of negotiations.

While the term "proposal" is used in this definition, a reasonable interpretation is that it refers to offers as opposed to information. It indicates that revisions result from negotiations and it is not likely that the contracting officer would negotiate over information. Negotiations are conducted over the terms of the offer, which will be incorporated into the contract. Such revisions would result from changes in the price, time for performance, description of the work or other terms of the contract.

2. *Communications Concerning Information*

While it is clear that communications concerning revisions to offers are not permitted, information exchanges which do not concern changes to offers may be appropriate. However, it is useful to distinguish between information concerning the capability of the offeror and information relating to the features of the offer. While the former should clearly fall under the FAR 15.206(a) "minor clarification" category, past decisions dealing with information relating to the offer make inclusion of this type of communication more problematic.

a. Capability Information

Capability information deals with the offeror's ability to perform as promised, as opposed to what has been promised. FAR 15.306(a)(2) recognizes that this is an appropriate area of communication, identifying past performance information as an example of the class of information which should be subject to "clarification." This distinction was also recognized under prior regulations. In *Hercules, Inc.*, Comp. Gen. Dec. B-167643, Jan. 20, 1970, *Unpub.*, the Comptroller General stated:

> [W]e conclude that an offeror's responsibility or ability to perform may be discussed without foreclosing the right of the contracting officer to invoke the exception to the requirement for conducting written or oral discussions. Any other conclusion would either deprive the government of the right to make award on the basis of initial proposals or allow such an award only at the peril of dealing with nonresponsible contractors.

See also *Edgewater Machine & Fabricators, Inc.*, Comp. Gen. Dec. B-219828, 85-2 CPD ¶ 630, stating:

> Although we recognize that a successful negotiated procurement requires both an acceptable proposal and a capable contractor, we find no substance to Edgewater's argument that the determination of the acceptability of the proposal and the capability of the prospective contractor are inextricably intertwined. The FAR, at 48 C.F.R. Secs. 15.610 and 15.611, clearly relates to the discussions necessary to determine the acceptability of a proposal and the best and final offers that must follow such discussions. FAR, 48 C.F.R. Sec. 9.100, clearly indicates that the purpose of a preaward survey is to evaluate the capability of the prospective contractor to perform the contract. See *Saxon Corp.*, B-216148, Jan. 23, 1985, 85-1 CPD ¶ 87. Thus, the de-

> terminations as to the acceptability of a proposal and the capability of an offeror involve distinct functions for different purposes usually performed at different times by different people. Moreover, the record here demonstrates that the survey team did not step outside the bounds of its responsibility evaluation. This is illustrated by Edgewater's statement that the survey included:
>
>> ". . . a physical survey of the manufacturing facilities, its equipment, the quality control program, what subcontracting programs were envisaged, inquiries as to quotations from seller of long lead items and all of the other matter which go into a sound manufacturing operation. Before and after the actual day of this visit of the pre-award survey team, [Edgewater] had been supplying financial data to DCAAS in Orlando as a part of the pre-award survey."
>
> These are all appropriate matters on which to base a responsibility determination and are consistent with the requirements of FAR, 48 C.F.R. Sec. 9.104, that set forth the general and special standards to be applied by the survey team in its evaluations.

Accord, *Kitco, Inc.*, Comp. Gen. Dec. B-221386, 86-1 CPD ¶ 321 (requesting and furnishing information regarding background and capability of proposed subcontractor did not preclude award without discussions); *Dynamic Resources, Inc.*, Comp. Gen. Dec. B-277213, 97-2 CPD ¶ 100 (preaward survey not improper discussions); and *Unicco Gov't Servs., Inc.*, Comp. Gen. Dec. B-277658, 97-2 CPD ¶ ___ (site visit to offeror's facility and inspection of equipment did not constitute discussions).

b. Offer Information

Early decisions dealing with offer information made a distinction between obtaining information explaining the features of an offer and revisions to the offer which would preclude award without discussions. See *Amram Nowak Assocs., Inc.*, Comp. Gen. Dec. B-187253, 76-2 CPD ¶ 454, stating:

> The question of what constitutes discussions depends on whether an offeror has been given a chance to revise or modify its proposal. 51 Comp. Gen. 479, 481, *supra*. Thus, we have held that a requested "clarification" which resulted in a price reduction constituted discussions. 48 Comp. Gen. 663 (1969). However, an explanation by an offeror of the basis of its price reduction without an opportunity to change its proposal was held not to constitute discussions. B-170989, B-170990, November 17, 1971.

See also *Keco Indus., Inc.*, Comp. Gen. Dec. B-170990, Nov. 17, 1971, *Unpub.*, where the Comptroller General stated:

> In B-167643, November 14, 1969, we stated that the discussions contemplated by the statute relate to proposals within the competitive range but not to discussions relating to an offeror's responsibility or the ability to perform. In B-170751, September 23, 1970, 50 Comp. Gen. [202], cited by Keco's counsel, one of the offerors failed to acknowledge an addendum which changed the specifications and thereby affected the price. This offeror orally acknowledged the amendment subsequent to the closing time for receipt of proposals. In the written confirmation of the oral acknowledgment requested by the procuring activity, the offeror confirmed that the price offered was based on the specifications as changed by the amendment. It was held that this exchange constituted negotiations and that award could no longer be made on the basis of the initial proposals.
>
> The meeting with Trane on August 21, 1970, was intended only as an opportunity for Trane to explain its price reductions and was in fact so limited. Presumably there was no opportunity for Trane to make any change in its proposal or for the government representatives to effect any change in the solicitation provisions. Therefore, we do not believe that the meeting constitutes a basis for invalidating the award.

However, following the adoption of the definition of "discussion" in the former FAR 15.601, communications were found to be discussion even though the terms of the offer were not changed. Those holdings were based on the language in the definition stating that discussion "involves information essential for determining the acceptability of a proposal." See *Integration Technology Group*, Comp. Gen. Dec. B-274288, 97-1 CPD ¶ 214 (identification of components to be furnished); *Strategic Analysis, Inc.*, Comp. Gen. Dec. B-270075.4, 96-1 CPD ¶ 41 (inquiry of employment status of designated key employee where RFP required letters of intent for proposed key personnel not current employees). Compare *Robotic Sys. Technology*, Comp. Gen. Dec. B-278195.2, 98-1 CPD ¶ ___, where the Comptroller General found that no discussion had been held where the offeror explained its cost proposal but did not add any information that was not included in the original proposal. With the deletion of the FAR 15.601 definition and the language relied on in these decisions, it is arguable that they should no longer be followed and that the principles of the earlier decisions should govern. This would be consistent with the Rewrite's purpose of increasing communications during the evaluation of proposals.

C. Communications Prior to Establishing the Competitive Range

The previous FAR did not deal with the subject of communications with parties prior to the establishment of the competitive range. The following detailed provisions were incorporated into FAR 15.306(b) by the FAR Part 15 Rewrite:

> (b) *Communications with offerors before establishment of the competitive range.* Communications are exchanges, between the Government and offerors, after receipt of proposals, leading to establishment of the competitive range. If a competitive range is to be established, these communications —
>
> (1) Shall be limited to the offerors described in paragraphs (b)(1)(i) and (b)(1)(ii) of this section and —
>
> (i) Shall be held with offerors whose past performance information is the determining factor preventing them from being placed within the competitive range. Such communications shall address adverse past performance information to which an offeror has not had a prior opportunity to respond; and
>
> (ii) May only be held with those offerors (other than offerors under paragraph (b)(1)(i) of this section) whose exclusion from, or inclusion in, the competitive range is uncertain;
>
> (2) May be conducted to enhance Government understanding of proposals; allow reasonable interpretation of the proposal; or facilitate the Government's evaluation process. Such communications shall not be used to cure proposal deficiencies or material omissions, materially alter the technical or cost elements of the proposal, and/or otherwise revise the proposal. Such communications may be considered in rating proposals for the purpose of establishing the competitive range;
>
> (3) Are for the purpose of addressing issues that must be explored to determine whether a proposal should be placed in the competitive range. Such communications shall not provide an opportunity for the offeror to revise its proposal, but may address —
>
> (i) Ambiguities in the proposal or other concerns (e.g., perceived deficiencies, weaknesses, errors, omissions, or mistakes (see 14.407)); and

(ii) Information relating to relevant past performance; and

(4) Shall address adverse past performance information to which the offeror has not previously had an opportunity to comment.

The promulgation comments indicate that these provisions were adopted to assuage the concerns of small business commenters. See 62 Fed. Reg. 51229 (1997):

> Public comments indicated that the second proposed rule did not establish a "bright line" distinction between when communications conducted in order to establish a competitive range end, and when discussions begin. Small businesses were concerned that the Government may conduct inappropriate communications with selected offerors prior to the establishment of the competitive range to the detriment of small businesses. We revised the final rule to accommodate this concern by clearly defining when discussions begin. We adopted this alternative to preclude the occurrence of the inappropriate communications that concerned small businesses.

While these provisions seem unnecessary, they appear to give the contracting officer considerable discretion in seeking both offer and capability information on offers when their inclusion in the competitive range is uncertain. Seeking such information permits the agency to make the competitive range determination based on a full understanding of the proposal — furthering the goal of establishing a competitive range consisting of only those offerors that are most highly rated. The only limitation on such communications is that the offers may not be revised, FAR 15.306(b)(3).

Where the evaluation indicates, with certainty, that an offer is outside the competitive range, communication is required for past performance information which the offeror has not had an opportunity to address, FAR 15.306(b)(1)(i). With respect to offers that are clearly within the competitive range, there is no need for communications prior to the conduct of negotiations.

D. Oral Presentations

As discussed earlier, oral presentations were incorporated into FAR 15.102 by the Rewrite. FAR 15.102(a) states that oral presentations can occur at any time during the acquisition process. Presentations that occur during the discussion process following the establishment of the competitive range will be controlled by the negotiation rules in FAR 15.306(d), which will be discussed in a later section. This section is concerned with communications during presentations prior to award without discussions and prior to the establishment of the competitive range.

The new regulations appear to indicate that oral presentations conducted prior to award without discussions can encompass both capability information and information explaining offers but may not be used to permit an offeror to alter its offer. It is clear that these regulations authorize broadened exchange of information when oral presentations are conducted. FAR 15.102 does not use the term "clarification" and the FAR 15.102(c) suggested subjects for presentations consist of both capability and offer information. FAR 15.102(a) now indicates that such presentations may "substitute for, or augment, written information," and that they are "subject to the same restrictions as written information." Thus, is appears that oral presentations should be subject to the same rules as written information. See also FAR 15.102(g) stating:

> If, during an oral presentation, the Government conducts discussions (see 15.306(d)), the Government must comply with 15.306 and 15.307.

This provision, by its reference to FAR 15.306(d), indicates that award on initial offers would be precluded only where the communications are the negotiations described in FAR 15.306(d).

The very nature of oral presentations involves the exchange of information. Thus, it might be expected that a broader range of communications would be permitted where the presentations involve all offerors submitting acceptable offers. The Government made this argument in *General Physics Federal Sys., Inc.*, Comp. Gen. Dec. B-275934, 97-1 CPD ¶ 171. There, award was made after oral presentations, including a question and answer session, without a call for best and final offers. The protester provided information which was used by the Government in downgrading its ranking. It argued that the oral presentations process constituted discussions and that it should have been given an opportunity to submit a best and final offer. The Comptroller General found that the protester was not prejudiced because the presentation process conducted by the Government did not result in unfair treatment and resolved the protest on those grounds. However, it declined to rule on the issue of whether the oral presentation process should be treated differently from other communications, stating:

> Given our conclusion — discussed in detail below — that General Physics was not prejudiced by the Navy's actions, we conclude that this is not the appropriate case for a substantive ruling on whether the question and answer session constituted discussions. Until such time as this matter is raised by a party with a stake in the outcome, we will hold in abeyance our views on whether this approach is consistent with current statutory and regulatory requirements.

If any agency has decided to establish a competitive range, it does not appear likely that oral presentations would occur until after the range had been established. Then oral presentations would be conducted only with those offerors in the competitive range. If oral presentations were conducted in order to determine which offerors should be placed in the competitive range, the rules in FAR 15.306(b) would apply, but there would appear to be little or no harm if discussions occurred at this time since the offerors would be requested to submit final proposal revisions after the conclusion of discussions. See, e.g., *Dynamic Resources, Inc.*, Comp. Gen. Dec. B-277213.2, 97-2 CPD ¶ 100.

FAR 15.102 contains the following additional guidance on the procedures to be followed when oral presentations are required:

> (e) The contracting officer shall maintain a record of oral presentations to document what the Government relied upon in making the source selection decision. The method and level of detail of the record (e.g., videotaping, audio tape recording, written record, Government notes, copies of offeror briefing slides or presentation notes) shall be at the discretion of the source selection authority. A copy of the record placed in the file may be provided to the offeror.
>
> (f) When an oral presentation includes information that the parties intend to include in the contract as material terms or conditions, the information shall be put in writing. Incorporation by reference of oral statements is not permitted.

E. Mistakes

The statutes do not deal with the subject of mistakes discovered or alleged prior to award. Prior to the Rewrite, FAR 15.607 contained detailed procedures directing contracting officers to examine proposals of mistakes. Where communications were considered to prejudice "the interest of other offerors" or where correction of a mistake would require reference "to documents, worksheets, or other data outside the solicitation and proposal," the mistake could be corrected only through oral or written discussions with all offerors within the competitive range. These provisions were removed in the final Rewrite and the FAR now specifies only fragmentary procedures for correction of mistakes.

Under the FAR Rewrite as was the case under the prior regulations, allegations of error and requests for *verification* and subsequent verifications that mistakes have not been made do not require discussions with all offerors within the competitive range, e.g., *R&B Rubber & Eng'g, Inc.*, Comp. Gen. Dec. B-214299, 84-1 CPD ¶ 595. Similarly, since a proposal may be *withdrawn* freely, communications resulting in withdrawal do not require discussions with all offerors.

The deletion of the pre-Rewrite FAR 15.607 and its requirements for *correction* of mistakes through the discussion process raises the question of what types of mistakes may be corrected without requiring discussions with all offerors. FAR 15.001 indicates that a "Proposal modification" is a change made to a proposal "to correct a mistake at any time before award." The final Rewrite makes limited references to mistakes or errors alleged or discovered prior to award. FAR 15.306(a) includes communications to "resolve minor or clerical errors" under the description of "clarifications." In addition, FAR 15.306(b)(3)(i) includes "errors, omissions, or mistakes (see 14.407)" as items which might be addressed prior to the establishment of the competitive range. In view of this absence of treatment, it would appear that, at the least, the rules for dealing with mistakes applicable to sealed bidding ought to be applicable to competitive proposals. See FAR 14.407 and the discussion in Chapter 5, Section IV. Application of these rules would require that the contracting officer request verification of an offer whenever a mistake was suspected and would permit correction of a mistake at any time that it met the requirements of the regulation. This would permit the contracting officer to deal with mistakes as they were identified or disclosed without losing the right to award the contract without discussions.

VI. EVALUATION OF PROPOSALS

Evaluation is an ongoing process that starts upon the receipt of proposals, continues during communications and negotiations, and concludes with the evaluation of final proposal revisions. The purpose of evaluation is to assess the quality of each offer and to determine the capability of each offeror. However, this may be done only by evaluating proposals in terms of the evaluation factors set forth in the RFP. The results of proposal evaluation are explained in narrative comments of the evaluators and are generally summarized in some type of scoring system. FAR 15.305(a) states the basic rules for proposal evaluation as follows:

> Proposal evaluation is an assessment of the proposal and the offeror's ability to perform the prospective contract successfully. An agency shall evaluate competitive proposals and then assess their relative qualities solely on the factors and subfactors specified in the solicitation. Evaluations may be conducted using any rating method or combination of methods, including color or adjectival ratings, numerical weights, and ordinary rankings. The relative strengths, deficiencies, significant weaknesses, and risks supporting proposal evaluation shall be documented in the contract file.

A. The Evaluation Process

Since there is no guidance in the FAR on the methodology used by agencies to evaluate proposals, they are free to perform the evaluation in any manner that ensures fairness and objectivity. See FAR 1.102-2(c)(3) stating that "[a]ll . . . prospective contractors shall be treated fairly and impartially but need not be treated the same." This requires that, after receipt, all proposals must be evaluated, FAR 15.306(c)(1), and such evaluation should be done with the same degree of care. Thereafter, agencies may drop excessively deficient proposals from the evaluation process. See *W&D Ships Deck Works, Inc. v. United States*, __ Fed. Cl. ___ (1997) ("grossly deficient" proposal may be dropped from consideration); *Inte-Great Corp.*, Comp. Gen. Dec. B—272780, 96-2 CPD ¶ 159 (proposal not furnishing information demonstrating compliance with mandatory requirements may be denied opportunity to make oral presentation); *Dimensions Int'l/QSOFT, Inc.*, Comp. Gen. Dec. B-270966, 96-1 CPD ¶ 257 (proposal with inadequate response to sample task may be removed from further consideration).

When an agency intends to separate the cost and technical evaluations, this procedure is usually facilitated by requiring the offerors to submit their cost and technical proposals in separate packages. In this situation, it has been common practice to withhold the cost information from technical personnel with the result that the technical package describes the work to be done but may not include a description of the resources (labor hours and amount of subcontracted effort) needed to perform the various tasks on the contract. Without such resource information, the technical evaluation will be imprecise at best. The FAR Part 15 Rewrite addresses this problem by providing in FAR 15.305(a)(4) that "[c]ost information may be provided to members of the technical evaluation team." A well-written RFP requires that such information be included in the technical package. If the RFP does not contain this data, the agency should extract the information from the cost proposal and provide it to the technical evaluators. This will permit them to arrive at an accurate assessment of the offerors' technical understanding of the requirements as well as their ability to perform the work described in the RFP. See *AmerInd, Inc.*, Comp. Gen. Dec. B-248324, 92-2 CPD ¶ 85, where the Comptroller General affirmed the contracting officer's adjustment of an offeror's cost proposal to reflect the salaries of personnel discussed in the technical proposal.

Objectivity is generally sought by having the same evaluators review each proposal or portion of a proposal. However, if it is impractical to do so, proposals can be evaluated by different personnel. See *Design Concepts, Inc.*, Comp. Gen. Dec. B-186125, 76-2 CPD ¶ 365 (30 proposals divided among the evaluators); *T.V. Travel, Inc.*, 65 Comp. Gen. 109 (B-218198), 85-2 CPD ¶ 640 (37 proposals evaluated in six groups); *Innovative Logistics Techniques, Inc.*, Comp. Gen. Dec. B-275786.2, 97-1 CPD ¶ 144 (one evaluator reviewed both proposals and two evaluators each reviewed one proposal). Oral presentations can also be evaluated by different personnel, *Quality Elevator Co.*, Comp. Gen. Dec. B-276750, 97-2 CPD ¶ 28. The key question is whether the evaluation fairly reflects the strengths and weaknesses of each proposal.

Agencies may change evaluators during the course of a procurement. For example, initial proposals may be evaluated by one set of evaluators, and BAFOs by another, *Data Flow Corp.*, 62 Comp. Gen. 506 (B-209499), 83-2 CPD ¶ 57. Similarly, an agency may re-evaluate proposals using a more experienced group of evaluators, *Pro-Mark, Inc.*, Comp. Gen. B-247248, 92-2 CPD ¶ 124. New evaluations may also be used after the agency has lost a protest, *PRC, Inc.*, Comp. Gen. Dec. B-233561.8, 92-2 CPD ¶ 215. However, most agencies attempt to use the same evaluation personnel throughout the procurement.

Frequently, the same factors are evaluated by a number of evaluators who arrive at a different assessment of the merits of the proposals and different scores. The Comptroller General has stated "[s]ince evaluating proposals involves subjective as well as objective judgments, it is not unusual for individual evaluators to reach disparate conclusions," *Mounts*

Eng'g, 65 Comp. Gen. 476, 482 (B-218489.4), 86-1 CPD ¶ 358. In *EBA Ernest Bland Assocs.*, Comp. Gen. Dec. B-270496, 96-1 CPD ¶ 148, the Comptroller General found nothing unusual or improper in the fact that two individual agency evaluators gave widely divergent scores to the same proposal. Therefore, disparities in evaluator scores alone do not suffice to show improper or irrational evaluation schemes, even if the final scores are averaged. See *Arthur Anderson & Co.*, 71 Comp. Gen. 233 (B-245903), 92-1 CPD ¶ 168 (consensus score of 27 after initial scores of 25, 25, and 30); *Syscon Servs.*, 68 Comp. Gen. 698 (B-235647), 89-2 CPD ¶ 258 (evaluations ranged from unacceptable to acceptable to better than acceptable); *Monarch Enters., Inc.*, Comp. Gen. Dec. B-233303, 89-1 CPD ¶ 222 (scores from different evaluation panels varied significantly). On the other hand, if factor scores are averaged or added, the agency must make sure that offers are not unreasonably downgraded for notations which are meant to be neutral. See *Inlingua Sch. of Language*, Comp. Gen. Dec. B-229784, 88-1 CPD ¶ 340, finding unfairness in a point adding system which scored questions answered as "not applicable" with zeros, thereby penalizing the protester for meaningless data.

Whenever possible, the agency should attempt to reconcile disparate scores to ensure that the evaluators have not made obvious mistakes in their evaluation. See *Resource Applications, Inc.*, Comp. Gen. Dec. B-274943.3, 97-1 CPD ¶ 137, where the Comptroller General described the flexibility given consensus procedures to achieve this result:

> There is nothing inherently objectionable in an agency's decision to develop a consensus rating. *Appalachian Council, Inc.,* B-256179, May 20, 1994, 94-1 CPD ¶ 319. The fact that the evaluators individually rated TechLaw's proposal for [certain] subfactors less favorably than they did on a consensus basis for those subfactors, and individually rated RAI's proposal for [certain] subfactors more favorably than they did on a consensus basis for those subfactors does not, by itself, warrant questioning the final evaluation results. See *Syscon Servs., Inc.*, 68 Comp. Gen. 698 (1989), 89-2 CPD ¶ 258; *Dragon Servs., Inc.*, B-255354, Feb. 25, 1994, 94-1 CPD ¶ 151. Agency evaluators may discuss the relative strengths and weaknesses of proposals in order to reach a consensus rating, which often differs from the ratings given by individual evaluators, since such discussions generally operate to correct mistakes or misperceptions that may have occurred in the initial evaluation. *Schweizerr Aircraft Corp.*, B-248640.2; B-248640.3, Sept. 14, 1992, 92-2 CPD ¶ 200; *The Cadmus Group, Inc.*, B-241372.3, Sept. 25, 1991, 91-2 CPD ¶ 271. Thus, a consensus score need not be the score of the majority the evaluators initially awarded — the score may

properly be determined after discussions among the evaluators. *GZA Remediation, Inc.*, B-272386, Oct. 3, 1996, 96-2 CPD ¶ 155 (note 3). In short, the overriding concern in the evaluation process is that the final score assigned accurately reflect the actual merits of the proposals, not that it be mechanically traceable back to the scores initially given by the individual evaluators. *Id.*; *Dragon Servs., Inc., supra.*

B. Agency Discretion

Just as the procuring agency has great discretion in selecting evaluation factors, its evaluation will not be disturbed unless it is arbitrary or in violation of procurement statutes or regulations, *Pacific Consultants*, Comp. Gen. Dec. B-198706, 80-2 CPD ¶ 129. See *Buffalo Organization for Social & Technological Innovation, Inc.*, Comp. Gen. Dec. B-196279, 80-1 CPD ¶ 107, where the Comptroller General enunciated his traditional position in this area:

> The determination of the relative merits of proposals is the responsibility of the procuring agency since it must bear the burden of any difficulties incurred by reason of a defective evaluation. In light of this, we have held that procuring officials enjoy a reasonable degree of discretion in the evaluation of proposals and such discretion must not be disturbed unless shown to be arbitrary or in violation of the procurement statutes and regulations.

In more recent decisions, the Comptroller General has summarized this position as follows:

> In reviewing an agency's evaluation of proposals and source selection decision, our review is confined to a determination of whether the agency acted reasonably and consistent with the stated evaluation factors.

See *Matrix Int'l Logistics, Inc.*, Comp. Gen. Dec. B-272388.2, 97-2 CPD ¶ 89; *PRC, Inc.*, Comp. Gen. Dec. B-274698.2, 97-1 CPD ¶ 115; *Main Bldg. Maintenance, Inc.*, Comp. Gen. Dec. B-260945, 95-2 CPD ¶ 214.

Thus, agencies have broad discretion in the evaluation process. In spite of this broad discretion, however, evaluations must be able to withstand scrutiny as to their reasonableness and must be made in accordance with the evaluation scheme described in the RFP. Thus, agency evaluations have been overturned if they are irrational, not in compliance with the RFP, arbitrary, or not based on evidence in the record.

1. Irrational Evaluations

Irrational evaluations involve evaluation decisions which are inherently erroneous and could not be used even if specifically outlined in the RFP. For example, in *Dynalantic v. United States*, 945 F.2d 416 (Fed. Cir. 1991), the offeror's significantly less expensive bid was rejected based on an unreasonable assumption that Dynalantic was ignorant of industry standards. Expert testimony illustrated that the Air Force itself lacked such knowledge. In *Programmatics, Inc.*, Comp. Gen. Dec. B-228916.2, 88-1 CPD ¶ 35, the Comptroller General deemed an evaluation irrational where two of five evaluators significantly reduced the protester's technical scores during a second evaluation without having any reason for doing so. See also *Int'l Business Sys., Inc.*, Comp. Gen. Dec. B-275554, 97-1 CPD ¶ 114, where the Comptroller General found it irrational to ignore the past performance of the incumbent contractor because the agency technical person had not filled out the past performance questionnaire; *PMT Servs., Inc.*, Comp. Gen. Dec. B-270538.2, 96-2 CPD ¶ 98, where the Comptroller General found it irrational to evaluate only the size of prior projects when the evaluation factor called for a review of projects with "similar complexity" to the subject procurement; *Safeguard Maintenance Corp.*, Comp. Gen. Dec. B-260983.3, 96-2 CPD ¶ 116, where the Comptroller General found it irrational to give a low score to a proposal for not furnishing required information when the evaluators had personal knowledge of the information; and *DynCorp*, Comp. Gen. Dec. B-232999, 89-1 CPD ¶ 152, where the Comptroller General overruled the contracting officer's finding that two proposals were technically equal, noting that the awardee's proposal contained many obvious weaknesses not apparent in the protester's offer. Similarly, in *Inlingua Schools of Languages*, Comp. Gen. B-229784, 88-1 CPD ¶ 340, questions answered by an offeror's reference as "not applicable" were irrationally scored as zeros, and in *SDA, Inc.*, Comp. Gen. Dec. B-248528.2, 93-1 CPD ¶ 320, rating past experience by the percentage of past projects that were similar in size to the contract work was inherently irrational. In the latter case, the Comptroller General commented that the rating scheme gave the highest rating to the offeror that listed the fewest irrelevant past projects. Such a system was seen to be inherently illogical and the protest was sustained. *In CBIS Fed., Inc. v. Department of the Interior*, GSBCA 12092-P, 93-2 BCA ¶ 25,643, the board criticized evaluations which gave maximum scores to proposals which met the minimum requirements where the procurement was clearly a best value procurement.

2. Evaluations Not in Compliance with the RFP

Evaluations will be found to be improper if the evaluators do not comply with the evaluation scheme set forth in the RFP. While an agency is free to choose from many possible evaluation schemes, once the scheme is finalized, it must be followed. Thus, in *SIMCO, Inc.*, Comp. Gen. Dec. B-229964, 88-1 CPD ¶ 383, a cost evaluation was overturned for using an "all or nothing" point system not specified in the RFP and for failing to weigh price as 20 percent of the total score as promised. Similarly, a technical evaluation scheme giving no credit for partially unsatisfactory proposals was held noncompliant in *National Capital Medical Found., Inc.*, Comp. Gen. Dec. B-215303.5, 85-1 CPD ¶ 637, because such a grading system was not outlined in the RFP. Compare *Home & Family Servs., Inc.*, Comp. Gen. Dec. B-182290, 74-2 CPD ¶ 366, allowing such a scoring system since it was described in the RFP.

Another noncomplying evaluation was found in *T.V. Travel, Inc.*, 65 Comp. Gen. 323 (B-221526.2), 86-1 CPD ¶ 172, where a protest succeeded after it was determined that the agency failed to deduct points for certain deficiencies in awardee's proposal as set forth in the RFP. *See HG Properties A, L.P.*, Comp. Gen. Dec. B-277572, 97-2 CPD ¶ 123, where an improper evaluation was found where the agency gave the awardee 225 points of the 250 points available for efficient layout even though the awardee's layout was inconsistent with the stated requirement, *Technology Servs. Int'l, Inc.*, Comp. Gen. Dec. B-276506, 97-2 CPD ¶ 113, where an improper evaluation was found where the agency gave the highest rating under a significant quality control technical subfactor even though the awardee's proposal did not submit a detailed work scheduling scheme as contemplated by this subfactor, *Ogden Support Servs., Inc.*, Comp. Gen. Dec. B-270012.2, 96-1 CPD ¶ 177, Comp. Gen. Dec. B-270012.4, 96-2 CPD ¶ 137, where a noncompliant evaluation was found where the agency evaluated past performance on dissimilar work although the RFP called for "successful performance on similar efforts," *RJO Enters., Inc.*, Comp. Gen. Dec. B-260126.2, 95-2 CPD ¶ 93, where an improper evaluation was found when the agency downgraded a proposal for not furnishing sufficient resumes but the resumes were not called for in the RFP, and *Centel Fed. Sys., Inc. v. Department of the Navy*, GSBCA 12011-P, 93-2 BCA ¶ 25,648, where an erroneous evaluation was found when the agency gave unequal weight to subfactors that the RFP said would be "equal." See *also University of Michigan*, 66 Comp. Gen. 538 (B-225756), 87-1 CPD ¶ 643 (agency gave almost total weight to one of four criteria listed in the RFP); *H. J. Group Ventures, Inc.*, Comp. Gen. Dec. B-246139, 92-1 CPD ¶ 203 (agency gave heavy weight to a criterion which was listed as a "general consideration" but not included in the list of relative order of importance of criteria). One protest was sustained where the agency's cost evaluation was done on a 12-month systems-life basis instead of the 60-month basis specified in the RFP, *AM Int'l, Inc.*, Comp. Gen. Dec. B-200200, 81-1 CPD ¶ 258. Compare *Tracor, Inc.*, 56 Comp. Gen. 62 (B-186315), 76-2 CPD ¶ 386, where failure by the agency to follow stated evaluation criteria was not a basis for upsetting the award since proper evaluation would not have significantly modified the assigned scores.

Evaluations have been found not to comply with the RFP even when the agency had no knowledge of the noncompliance. See, for example, *CBIS Fed., Inc.*, 71 Comp. Gen. 319 (B-245844.2), 92-1 CPD ¶ 308, where the agency gave high scores to proposed personnel to perform the work and later found that the contractor had no "letters of commitment" with two of the key personnel. The Comptroller General granted the protest because the evaluation was not in accord with the RFP requirement that each offeror furnish the names of key personnel that would actually be used to perform the contract.

In some instances, a detailed analysis of the RFP is required to determine whether the agency has followed the evaluation scheme. For example, in *University of New Orleans*, 55 Comp. Gen. 1281 (B-184194), 76-1 CPD ¶ 22, the RFP stated that primary emphasis in the evaluation of proposals would be placed on the analysis of "the effects of a particular pollutant on various environmental media," but the actual evaluation rated proposals in terms of whether they treated each of the environmental media equally. The evaluation was held to be improper. In *Safeguard Maintenance Corp.*, Comp. Gen. Dec. B-260983.3, 96-2 CPD ¶ 116, the Comptroller General reviewed the entire scoring of the protester's proposal and found that the evaluation was improper because a number of the low scores were based on noncompliance with agency requirements that were not stated in the RFP. See also *Lithos Restoration, Ltd.*, 71 Comp. Gen. 367 (B-247003.2), 92-1 CPD ¶ 379, where the RFP stated that technical factors were more important than price, technical subfactors were listed in descending order of importance, and the first of four technical subfactors listed would be evaluated on a "go, no-go" basis. The Comptroller General held that failing to score the first evaluation subfactor in these circumstances was a violation of the RFP evaluation scheme because the evaluation procedure could only be reasonably interpreted as requiring point scoring of the most important technical subfactor in making the price/technical tradeoff.

3. Arbitrary Evaluations

Evaluations are occasionally overturned because they are purely arbitrary. For example, the General Services Board rejected a technical evaluation which reduced the score of one offeror simply because the contracting officer did not know the proposed project manager, *Compuware Corp.*, GSBCA 9533-P, 88-3 BCA ¶ 21,109. The board commented that the person in question had excellent credentials and that it was unfair to penalize an offeror for such arbitrary reasons.

Evaluations are also likely to be found to be arbitrary when offerors are not treated equally in the evaluation process. Such situations develop when decisions to award or deduct points are made without rational justification. *J.M. Cashman, Inc.*, Comp. Gen. Dec. B-233733, 89-1 CPD ¶ 380, is a good example of such arbitrary decision making. In that case, the Comptroller General found that downgrading one offeror's score due to a lack of experience without doing the same for a similar offeror was unjustified. Likewise, in *United Int'l Eng'g, Inc.*, 71 Comp. Gen. 177 (B-245448.3), 92-1 CPD ¶ 122, an evaluation was found to be arbitrary for treating offerors differently. There, the contracting officer raised one offeror's labor cost estimate without doing the same for a competitor with a similar estimate. See also *New Breed Leasing Corp.*, Comp. Gen. Dec. B-259328, 96-2 CPD ¶ 84, where the evaluation comments indicated that the protester had addressed all of the agency's concerns in its BAFO and had "enhanced" its proposal but the protester's scores were not raised, *Main Bldg. Maintenance, Inc.*, Comp. Gen. Dec. B-260945.4, 95-2 CPD ¶ 214, where one offeror was evaluated as having none of the six "strengths" of the winning offeror when the Comptroller General found that, in fact, the protester had four of the six strengths, *Deployable Hosp. Sys., Inc.*, Comp. Gen. Dec. B-260778, 95-2 CPD ¶ 65, where two technical proposals were rated as equal because both offerors had the same experience but the Comptroller General found that the protester had significantly more experience than the winning offeror, and *Arco Management of Washington, D.C., Inc.*, Comp. Gen. Dec. B-248653, 92-2 CPD ¶ 173, where the winning offeror's BAFO scores were increased based on very "conclusionary" information while the protester's BAFO scores were not increased after the submission of substantive responses to issues raised in discussions.

An extreme form of arbitrary evaluation is evident in situations where the procuring agency purposely favors one offeror over another. For example, in *Xerox Corp. v. United States*, 21 Cl. Ct. 278 (1990), the agency displayed an unethical and even criminal bias toward the awardee. It changed the RFP to omit a requirement that the awardee could not satisfy. It also met secretly with the awardee to allow it to improve its evaluation by correcting a mistake in its proposal, after BAFOs had been submitted, without allowing other offerors to change their proposals. The entire procurement was eventually voided and Xerox obtained reimbursement for all costs.

4. *Evaluation Not Based on Evidence*

Evaluation decisions must be based on tangible evidence to support an agency's decision. In *Amtec Corp.*, Comp. Gen. Dec. B-240647, 91-2 CPD ¶ 211, *recons. denied*, 91-2 CPD ¶ 473, the Comptroller General overturned a "marginal" technical evaluation because the agency record contained no evidence supporting such a grading. Similarly, in *Compuware Corp.*, GSBCA 9533-P, 88-3 BCA ¶ 21,109, the board rejected a cost realism evaluation in which the contracting officer refused to accept auditor conclusions, deeming them "ludicrous." The board commented that the contracting officer's decision was not supported by any evidence. See also *Matrix Int'l Logistics, Inc.*, Comp. Gen. Dec. B-272388.2, 97-2 CPD ¶ 89 (no evidence to support changing of winning contractor's scores from "good" to "excellent" in evaluating BAFO); *JW Assoc., Inc.*, Comp. Gen. Dec. B-275209, 97-1 CPD ¶ 57 (no evidence to support evaluation of technical proposals); *TRESP Assoc.*, Comp. Gen. Dec. B-258322.5, 96-1 CPD ¶ 8 (contracting officer relied on three supposed discriminators, none of which accurately reflected terms of protester's proposal); *Eng'g Computation, Inc.*, Comp. Gen. Dec. B-261658, 95-2 CPD ¶ 176 (no evidence to support evaluation that protester's proposal posed performance risks); *Telos Field Eng'g*, Comp. Gen. Dec. B-253492.6, 94-2 CPD ¶ 240 (no evidence to support higher scores for winning offeror's BAFO); *TRW, Inc.*, Comp. Gen. Dec. B-254045.2, 94-1 CPD ¶ 18 (high evaluation of selected offeror not supported when questions raised by lower-level evaluators regarding the selected firm's technical proposal and substantial "unquantified" concerns about that firm's evaluated cost were not resolved); *HSI-CCEC*, Comp. Gen. Dec. B-240610, 90-2 CPD ¶ 465 (low evaluation of skills of subcontractors not supported by information submitted by the offeror; low evaluation of minority subcontracting unjustified when offeror stated intention to use minority firms that were part of its joint venture); *Asbestos Management, Inc.*, Comp. Gen. Dec. B-237841, 90-1 CPD ¶ 325 (evaluation of key consultant improper when agency had lost qualification statement submitted with proposal); and *Coastal Science & Eng'g, Inc.*, 69 Comp. Gen. 66 (B-236041), 89-2 CPD ¶ 436 (evaluation not substantiated by the record when two competitors received relatively equal technical scores even though one was found to be "sufficiently technically superior to warrant payment of [a significant] cost premium").

Evaluations will also be overturned when it becomes apparent that the evaluators do not understand the data available to them. For example, in *Computer Sys. & Resources, Inc.*, GSBCA 9176-P, 88-1 BCA ¶ 20,331, an evaluation was overturned when, among other things, the chief evaluator admitted validating a critical portion of a proposal without understanding it. The board questioned how she could approve an offer without knowing if it satisfied the necessary requirements. Another evaluation was overturned when the evaluators "extrapolated" successful performance after the offeror had failed the required tests, *Mine Safety Appliance Co.*, 69 Comp. Gen. 562 (B-238597.2), 90-2 CPD ¶ 11. The Comptroller General concluded that the agency should not have proceeded with the procurement without determining why the item did not perform properly.

C. Using Factors Contained in the RFP

The FAR follows the language in 10 U.S.C. § 2305(b)(1) and 41 U.S.C. § 253(b), stating that evaluation shall be based solely on the factors specified in the RFP. Thus, the Comptroller General has stated that it is generally improper to add or substitute evaluation criteria after proposals have been submitted and reviewed by Government evaluators. See *Grey Advertising, Inc.*, 55 Comp. Gen. 1111 (B-184825), 76-1 CPD ¶ 325, stating that "once offerors are informed of the criteria against which proposals will be evaluated, it is incumbent upon the procuring activity to adhere to those criteria." Thus, unless the solicitation has been amended, the entire evaluation must be based on the stated factors throughout the competitive negotiation process.

1. Scope of Evaluation

Notwithstanding the requirement that only stated factors may be evaluated, the evaluation of a factor may consider all matters that offerors would reasonably have believed to be within the scope of the factor. See *Bank Street College of Educ.*, 63 Comp. Gen. 393 (B-213209), 84-1 CPD ¶ 607, where the Comptroller General stated at 400:

> As far as consistency with the evaluation criteria is concerned, while the source selection official may not judge the merits of the proposals based on criteria that offerors were not advised would be considered, the official may properly take into account specific, albeit not expressly identified, matters that are logically encompassed by or related to the stated criteria.

Thus, agency evaluation personnel are given considerable discretion in determining which considerations are within the scope of an evaluation factor. For example, in *Homequity, Inc.*, Comp. Gen. Dec. B-223997, 86-2 CPD ¶ 685, it was held proper for evaluators to consider the cumulative experience of the offerors' key personnel in evaluating the "organization and experience" factor. Similarly, in *Cygnus Corp.*, Comp. Gen. Dec. B-275957, 97-1 CPD ¶ 202, evaluation of the experience of key personnel was proper when the evaluation factor was "corporate experience;" in *EastCo Bldg. Servs., Inc.*, Comp. Gen. Dec. B-275334, 97-1 CPD ¶ 83, evaluation of past performance of only contracts of a similar size was considered proper even though the RFP did not mention this limitation; in *American Dev. Corp.*, Comp. Gen. Dec. B-251876.4, 93-2 CPD ¶ 49, consideration of the relevance of prior contracts was proper when the evaluation factor was past performance, in *S.C. Jones Servs., Inc.*, Comp. Gen. Dec. B-223155, 86-2 CPD ¶ 158, the experience of a predecessor firm with the same key personnel was properly used to evaluate the factor of "organizational experience and past performance," and in *AWD Technologies, Inc.*, Comp. Gen. Dec. B-250081.2, 93-1 CPD ¶ 83, experience in the specific work called for by the contract was properly given heavy weight when the evaluation factor was denominated "past project experience." See also *Courseware, Inc.*, Comp. Gen. Dec. B-200731, 81-1 CPD ¶ 133, where a proper evaluation was found when the agency gave a considerably higher score to offerors proposing the use of two experts rather than one when the evaluation factor called for evaluation of expertise in a subject area; and *Quantum Research, Inc.*, Comp. Gen. Dec. B-242020, 91-1 CPD ¶ 310, where it was held proper to downgrade a proposal calling for extended work weeks when the evaluation factors called for evaluation of the quality of personnel and their ability to provide services. Similarly, in *Western Medical Personnel, Inc.*, 66 Comp. Gen. 699 (B-227991), 87-2 CPD ¶ 310, it was held that offerors were on notice of the agency's intention to evaluate past performance when the RFP contained an evaluation factor entitled "references;" and in *Omega World Travel, Inc.*, Comp. Gen. Dec. B-271262.2, 96-2 CPD ¶ 44, evaluators were permitted to use their personal knowledge regarding negative aspects of an offeror's past performance to downgrade that offeror's proposal even though this was not mentioned in the RFP. In *International Bus. Machs. Corp. v. Department of the Treasury*, GSBCA 11777-P, 92-3 BCA ¶ 25,401, the board held that the agency properly evaluated the productivity of the proposed computer systems in the technical and cost evaluation even though productivity was not mentioned in the list of factors. The board stated that the protesters should not have been surprised that the agency would be concerned about productivity because it was inherent in the evaluation of computer systems for use by Government agencies. Similarly, in *Israel Aircraft Indus., Ltd.*, Comp. Gen. Dec. B-274389, 97-1 CPD ¶ 41, enhanced aircraft safety was properly evaluated even though it was not stated as an evaluation factor. The Comptroller General reasoned:

> We agree with the Army that enhanced aircraft safety is intrinsic to the stated evaluation factors and is not an unstated factor. Not only was improving the safe operation of the aircraft the underlying basis for the auxiliary fuel monitoring system, but all of the technical elements and most of the subelements stated in the RFP require compliance with the performance specifications, wherein it is stated that the monitoring system:
>
>> "shall afford the crew with a quick, unambiguous indication of fuel status and provide the crew with control capability to easily and directly manage the fuel system [and] shall monitor external auxiliary fuel for imbalance conditions that result in aircraft lateral center-of-gravity changes."
>
> Additionally, the stated subelements under human factors, a stated element under the technical area, include visibility and readability, and operation. Thus, it is obvious that enhanced aircraft safety pervaced this entire procurement and advantages in this regard could properly be considered by the SSA in making her award decision.

Also inherent in the evaluation of technical and management factors is the *risk* involved in successfully carrying out the proposed management or technical approach to be performed under the prospective contract. Thus, the scoring can account for such risks even though the RFP does not describe this aspect of the evaluation process. See, for example, *S-Tron*, Comp. Gen. Dec. B-244767.2, 92-1 CPD ¶ 409 (possibility that protester could not meet expedited delivery schedule was a proper reason to deduct points from the proposal); *Honeywell, Inc.*, Comp. Gen. Dec. B-238184, 90-1 CPD ¶ 435 (proposed reverse engineering of software created the risk of a failure to meet required schedules and costs); *AT&T Technologies, Inc.*, Comp. Gen. Dec. B-237069, 90-1 CPD ¶ 114 (inability to test computerized system until in actual use created great technical and scheduling risks); *Raytheon Support Servs. Co.*, 68 Comp. Gen. 566 (B-234920), 89-2 CPD ¶ 84 (insufficient staff and organization needed to meet program requirements created risk of failure to meet contract requirements); *Kaiser Elecs.*, 68 Comp. Gen. 48 (B-232175), 88-2 CPD ¶ 448 (new design approach created technical risk of malfunction); *Computer Sciences Corp.*, GSBCA 11497-P, 92-1 BCA ¶ 24,703 (schedule risk that offeror would not have its system evaluated by the target date).

In spite of the breadth of the rules permitting significant leeway in interpreting the scope of the listed evaluation factors, an agency may not evaluate an issue that has no relationship to the factors contained in the RFP. See *J.M. Cashman, Inc.*, Comp. Gen. Dec. B-233733, 89-1 CPD ¶ 380 (improper to downgrade an offeror for proposing to subcontract work when there was no mention of the issue in the evaluation factors); *NITCO*, Comp. Gen. Dec. B-246185, 92-1 CPD ¶ 212 (improper to evaluate past experience in manufacturing a product when there was no indication in the RFP that this would be a consideration); *Flight Int'l Group, Inc.*, 69 Comp. Gen. 741 (B-238953.4), 90-2 CPD ¶ 257 (financial condition was not within the scope of a subfactor "ability to meet the published schedule requirements of the Government at an acceptable level of risk").

2. Avoidance of Factor

Once an evaluation factor has been included in the RFP, the agency may not ignore that factor. In *Cardkey Sys., Inc.*, Comp. Gen. Dec. B-239433, 90-2 CPD ¶ 159, an evaluation was found improper because it did not consider a feature of the system being procured that had been designated as "desirable" in the RFP. The Comptroller General found that the protester had increased its price to provide the feature and was prejudiced by the fact that the feature was not considered during the evaluation. See also *Cenci Powder Prods., Inc.*, 68 Comp. Gen. 387 (B-234030), 89-1 CPD ¶ 381 (seven factors not considered); *Labat-Anderson*, 71 Comp. Gen. 252

(B-246071), 92-1 ¶ 193 (institutional experience and quality of proposal not evaluated); *Data General Serv.*, GSBCA 9236-P, 88-1 BCA ¶ 20,458 (agency failed to adequately determine awardee's technical acceptability).

The same rule applies to past performance. When it is designated as an evaluation factor, a source selection official may not ignore information regarding poor past performance of an offeror, *G. Marine Diesel*, 68 Comp. Gen. 577 (B-236622), 89-2 CPD ¶ 101 (agency failed to use data within agency regarding poor performance of ongoing contract), or good past performance, *Univox California, Inc.*, Comp. Gen. Dec. B-210941, 83-2 CPD ¶ 395 (agency failed to use data furnished by offeror); *Inlingua Schools of Languages*, Comp. Gen. Dec. B-229784, 88-1 CPD ¶ 340 (agency failed to use data within agency relating to performance as incumbent contractor).

3. Subfactors

When a subfactor is specified in the RFP, it is subject to the same rule applying to factors — it may not be ignored in the evaluation. Thus, it was improper for an agency to fail to consider six of twelve specified evaluation subfactors where the effect was to increase the relative importance of price from 30 percent to 50 percent, *Dynalectron Corp.*, Comp. Gen. Dec. B-187057, 77-1 CPD ¶ 95. If subfactors are listed without any indication of relative importance, they will be treated as equally important. Thus, giving such a subfactor "predominant" importance is improper, *Isratex, Inc. v. United States*, 25 Cl. Ct. 223 (1992).

When a subfactor is not specified in the RFP, it may be used in the evaluation of offers if it meets the relationship rule discussed above. The Comptroller General has been liberal in applying this rule. See, for example, *Bendix Field Eng'g Corp.*, Comp. Gen. Dec. B-241156, 91-1 CPD ¶ 44, where the past performance factor listed two subfactors, "technical performance" and "schedule performance," yet the Comptroller General ruled that it was proper to downgrade past performance because of a cost overrun on a prior contract. See also *Barnes & Reinecke, Inc.*, Comp. Gen. Dec. B-236622, 89-2 CPD ¶ 572, where past efforts in designing tracked vehicles were found to be reasonably related to a subfactor covering "knowledge of Tracked Armored Vehicles." In *Stewart-Warner Elecs. Corp.*, Comp. Gen. Dec. B-235774.3, 89-2 CPD ¶ 598, the Comptroller General permitted the evaluation of 31 technical subfactors where the RFP called for "paying appropriate premiums for measured increments of quality."

4. Changing Factors or Subfactors

As discussed earlier, FAR 15.206 provides specific guidance governing changes to Government requirements. These rules also apply to changes to the evaluation factors. Thus, if an agency determines during the evaluation process that different evaluation factors will yield a more sound source selection decision, it may amend the RFP to ensure that the offerors have an opportunity to respond to the new evaluation factors. For example, the Comptroller General has held that changes in evaluation factors are ordinarily permitted during the course of a negotiated procurement so long as the offerors are given the opportunity to respond to them, *Consulting & Program Management*, 66 Comp. Gen. 229 (B-225369), 87-1 CPD ¶ 229 (Comptroller recommended a resolicitation relaxing experience requirements so as not to deprive any offeror of a chance of award). Similarly, in *H.J. Group Ventures, Inc.*, Comp. Gen. Dec. B-246139.3, 92-2 CPD ¶ 116, it was found proper to add an evaluation factor for performance risk and permit new proposals.

One result of this rule is that a relaxation of requirements for the winning offeror without informing the other competitors is improper, *Barents Group, L.L.C.*, Comp. Gen. Dec. B-276082, 97-1 CPD ¶ 164 (relaxation of requirement to submit resumes in specific labor category); *Armour of America, Inc.*, Comp. Gen. Dec. B-237690, 90-1 CPD ¶ 304 (relaxation of technical specifications); *MTS Sys. Corp.*, Comp. Gen. Dec. B-238137, 90-1 CPD ¶ 434 (relaxation of domestic source requirement). In *Minnesota Mining & Mfg. Co. v. Shultz*, 583 F. Supp. 184 (D.D.C. 1984), the court found an improper deviation from the technical requirements by the offeror that had been selected for award and noted that any change in factors must be communicated to every offeror. See also *Paper Corp. of the United States*, Comp. Gen. Dec. B-229785, 88-1 CPD ¶ 388, where the agency was found to have improperly relaxed a testing requirement in evaluating the sample submitted by the awardee, and *Management Sys. Designers, Inc.*, Comp. Gen. Dec. B-244383.4, 91-2 CPD ¶ 518, where the agency was required to inform offerors of a significant change in quantity. In extreme cases, substantial and significant changes in the evaluation factors will require an amended solicitation in order to allow other offerors the opportunity to submit proposals, *United Telephone Co.*, Comp. Gen. Dec. B-246977, 92-1 CPD ¶ 374.

The requirement that offerors be advised of changes in evaluation factors does not apply to changes in subfactors that are reasonably related to stated evaluation factors but which are not themselves listed in the RFP, *Dynalectron Corp.*, Comp. Gen. Dec. B-199741, 81-2 CPD ¶ 70. In that case, the Comptroller General held that the unlisted subcriterion which was changed "was devised in order to assist the technical evaluators in their internal deliberations."

The same procedures must be used when an agency changes the evaluation scheme. Thus, it is not improper for an agency to issue an amended solicitation altering the relative importance of the evaluation factors, *Unisys Corp.*, 67 Comp. Gen. 512 (B-230019.2), 88-2 CPD ¶ 35 (clarifying the importance of cost), or the overall evaluation scheme, *Galler Assocs., Inc.*, Comp. Gen. Dec. B-210204, 83-1 CPD ¶ 515 (changing from low cost acceptable offer scheme to best value scheme), *American Lawn Serv., Inc.*, Comp. Gen. Dec. B-267715, 95-2 CPD ¶ 278 (changing from best value scheme to lowest priced, technically acceptable basis). It is also proper to amend the evaluation scheme in the solicitation to accommodate a method of performance suggested by an offeror, *Loral Terracom*, 66 Comp. Gen. 272 (B-224908), 87-1 CPD ¶ 182 (different technical approach). Of course, such changes are only permissible if all offerors still under consideration are informed of the change, *Labat-Anderson Inc.*, 71 Comp. Gen. 252 (B-246071), 92-1 CPD ¶ 193 (change required by issuance of amendment to RFP or by raising issue in discussions); *Hughes STX Corp. v. NASA*, GSBCA 11665-P, 92-3 BCA ¶ 25,035 (change only allowed with amendment).

The Comptroller General will not overturn an award in which the agency has changed the evaluation criteria without notifying the offerors if the losers are not prejudiced by the change, *FKW Inc. Sys.*, Comp. Gen. Dec. B-235989, 89-2 CPD ¶ 370; *Akal Security, Inc.*, Comp. Gen. Dec. B-261996, 96-1 CPD ¶ 33.

D. Disqualification of an Offeror

There is a growing body of law holding that an offeror should be disqualified from the procurement if the agency learns during the evaluation that the offeror has violated a criminal statute or committed some other serious impropriety. Such disqualification is not a determination of lack of responsibility and thus need not be referred to the Small Business Administration if the offeror is a small business, *NKF Eng'g, Inc. v. United States*, 805 F.2d 372 (Fed. Cir. 1986); *Compliance Corp. v. United States*, 22 Cl. Ct. 193 (1990), *aff'd*, 960 F.2d 157 (Fed. Cir. 1992). The result of this rule is that an offeror may be immediately dropped from the evaluation when the agency learns of the impropriety.

One type of violation that has led to such disqualification is fraud in the form of material misrepresentation. See, for example, *Sterling Fed. Sys., Inc.*, GSBCA 10381-P, 90-2 BCA¶ 22,802, *recons. denied*, 90-3 BCA ¶ 22,962, *mot. denied*, 90-3 BCA ¶ 22,990, where the board disqualified an offeror who had quoted labor rates that were approximately 67 percent of the actual salaries of the key personnel to be used on a cost-reimbursement contract. The board concluded that this was a material misrepresentation of the probable cost to the Government. Other cases disqualifying offerors for material misrepresentation include *University Sys., Inc. v. Department of Health & Human Servs.*, GSBCA 12039-P, 93-2 BCA ¶ 25,646 (false certification that tested product was same as product called for by specifications); *ManTech Advanced Sys. Int'l, Inc.*, Comp. Gen. Dec. B-255719.2, 94-1 CPD ¶ 326 (submission of resumes of personnel with no intent to use those workers); *PPATHI, Inc.*, Comp. Gen. Dec. B-249182.4, 93-1 CPD ¶ 64 (multiple nondisclosures and false certifications); *Electronic Data Sys. Fed. Corp.*, GSBCA 9869-P, 89-2 BCA ¶ 21,655, *recons. denied*, 89-2 BCA ¶ 21,778, *aff'd sub. nom. Planning Research Corp. v. United States*, 971 F.2d 736 (Fed. Cir. 1992) (submission of resumes of 101 personnel to be employed on contract with no intent to use those workers); *Ultra Technology Corp.*, Comp. Gen. Dec. B-230309.6, 89-1 CPD ¶ 42 (proposing person as "lead technician" without obtaining his permission); and *Informatics, Inc.*, 57 Comp. Gen. 217 (B-188566), 78-1 CPD ¶ 53 (misstating the availability of proposed personnel).

Disqualification is not proper when the misrepresentation is inadvertent rather than intentional, *Universal Technologies, Inc.*, Comp. Gen. Dec. B-248808.2, 92-2 CPD ¶ 212 (false certification not made in bad faith); *Tucson Mobilephone, Inc.*, Comp. Gen. Dec. B-258408.3, 95-1 CPD ¶ 267 (record did not support a finding that offeror intentionally misrepresented that it had lead technician's permission to use his credentials). In *Mantech Field Eng'g Corp.*, Comp. Gen. Dec. B-245886.4, 92-1 CPD ¶ 309, *recons. denied*, 92-2 CPD ¶ 89, although the offeror made no attempt to determine whether personnel were available prior to submitting its BAFO, the Comptroller General did not find an intentional misrepresentation and recommended that discussions be reopened.

Offerors have also been disqualified for violating or appearing to violate the conflict of interest laws barring retired Government employees from participating in certain Government procurements, 18 U.S.C. § 207 (representation of contractor in matter where there has been substantial prior involvement). For example, in *Naddaf Int'l Trading Co.*, Comp. Gen. Dec. B-238768.2, 90-2 CPD ¶ 316, the Comptroller General ruled that the contracting officer had properly disqualified an offeror that employed a retired military officer who had contacted the Small Business Administration to argue for the issuance of a Certificate of Competency. Offerors have also been disqualified for conducting employment discussions with a current Government employee, 18 U.S.C. § 208 (engaging in discussion of future employment with Government official); 41 U.S.C. § 423 (engaging in any discussion of future employment with a procurement officer). For example, in *NKF Eng'g, Inc. v. United States*, 805 F.2d 372 (Fed. Cir. 1986), the court ruled that the contracting officer had properly disqualified an offeror who hired a member of the Navy source selection board after the initial evaluation and prior to the submission of the best and final offer. The contracting officer had concluded that this gave an appearance of impropriety even though the offeror claimed that the Government employee had been carefully screened from the people in the company handling the procurement.

Conflicts of interest involving current Government employees will disqualify offerors from the procurement, 18 U.S.C. § 208 (participation in procurement involving offeror in which employee had financial interest); FAR Subpart 3.6 (award of contract to company owned or controlled by Government employee). For example, in *United Tel. Co.*, GSBCA 10031-P, 89-3 BCA ¶ 22,108, an offeror was disqualified because its subcontractor had used a Government employee participating in the procurement as a consultant during the competition. Similarly, in *Revnet Env't & Analytical Lab., Inc.*, Comp. Gen. Dec. B-221002.2, 86-2 CPD ¶ 102, the contracting officer disqualified an offeror that had submitted an offer developed by a Government employee who had attempted to disassociate himself from his company by turning it over to his wife.

The responsibility for determining whether an offeror should be disqualified due to a conflict of interest rests with the agency and will be upheld by the Comptroller General so long as the decision is reasonable, *Cygnus Corp.*, Comp. Gen. Dec. B-275957, 97-1 CPD ¶ 202. In *Cygnus*, the protester asserted that the offeror should have been disqualified from the competition because the offeror's spouse was a Government employee. The protester argued that by virtue of having vested marital property rights, the Government employee possessed substantial ownership or control of the offeror such that the matter constituted a conflict of interest. The Comptroller General denied the protest finding no evidence of substantial control or interest such as to warrant disqualification.

Improperly obtaining information during the procurement process will also serve as a grounds for disqualify offerors. For example, in *Litton Sys., Inc.*, 68 Comp. Gen. 422 (B-234060), 89-1 CPD ¶ 450, *recons. denied*, 68 Comp. Gen. 677 (B-234060.2) 89-2 CPD ¶ 228, the Comptroller General ordered a contractor disqualified for obtaining Government information through a marketing consultant. See also *AT&T Communications, Inc.*, GSBCA 9252-P, 88-2 BCA ¶ 20,805, where the board disqualified an offeror that had been given the range of its competitor's prices by a Government employee with whom it had conducted employment discussions and to whom it had given gratuities. Similarly, in *Compliance Corp.*, Comp. Gen. Dec. B-239252, 90-2 CPD ¶ 126, *recons. denied*, Comp. Gen. Dec. 239252.3, 90-2 CPD ¶ 435, the contracting officer properly disqualified an offeror who had obtained Government information from an incumbent service contractor through the use of "industrial espionage." The Federal Circuit agreed with this decision in *Compliance Corp. v. United States*, 22 Cl. Ct. 193 (1990), *aff'd*, 960 F.2d 157 (Fed. Cir. 1992), holding that industrial espionage was a valid ground for disqualification (even though no Government personnel were involved) because such activity puts the integrity of the procurement system at risk.

In reviewing the reasonableness of an agency's decision on disqualification, the Comptroller General will examine both the nature of the information to which the offeror had access, *Textron Marine Sys.*, Comp. Gen. Dec. B-255580.3, 94-2 CPD ¶ 63 (information disclosed did not give an unfair competitive advantage), and the conditions under which access was gained, *KPMG Peat Marwick*, Comp. Gen. Dec. B-251902.3, 93-2 CPD ¶ 272, *recons. denied*, 94-1 CPD ¶ 201 (received information through Freedom of Information Act). For example, in *IGIT, Inc.*, Comp. Gen. Dec. B-271823, 96-2 CPD ¶ 51, the Comptroller General sustained a protest challenging a contracting officer's decision to disqualify the protester from the competition on the basis that the protester had possessed a page from the installation's solicitation register which included a lump-sum Government estimate for the cost of the solicited work. The Comptroller General found that there was no basis to conclude that the offeror obtained the information improperly. The information was taped to the offeror's door apparently to advise IGIT of the agency's decision to resolicit the laundry services rather than to exercise the options. The Comptroller General also found that the information could be given to the other offerors to ameliorate any competitive advantage.

Offerors that give bribes or gratuities to Government employees will also be disqualified. See *Litton Sys., Inc.*, 68 Comp. Gen. 422 (B-234060), 89-1 CPD ¶ 450, *recons. denied*, 68 Comp. Gen. 677 (B-234060.2), 89-2 CPD ¶ 228, where the Comptroller General ordered termination of a major contract due to bribery of a high ranking Government employee by the awardee. See also *Howema Bau-GmbH*, Comp. Gen. Dec. B-245356, 91-2 CPD ¶ 214 (excluding protester from contract consideration due to suspected bribery of Government officials); and *National Roofing & Painting Corp.*, ASBCA 36,551, 90-2 BCA ¶ 22,936 (voiding contract because it was "tainted with fraud from its inception as well as during performance").

E. Assessment of Strengths, Weaknesses and Risks

The most important part of the evaluation process is the assessment of the strengths, deficiencies, significant weaknesses and risks of each proposal and the assessment of their relative qualities, FAR 15.305(a). This is the critical information that is used to make the source selection decision and serves as the documentation supporting that decision. The FAR contains no guidance on the timing of these assessments but it has been common practice to direct the evaluators to make their initial evaluation by only assessing each proposals' quality in meeting the requirements of the RFP and its evaluation factors and then to have the evaluators or some other group make the assessment of the relative merits of the competing proposals. In a case where the Air Force regulation required this two-step procedure, the Court of Federal Claims held that permitting the evaluators to make the comparative assessment was a "harmless regulatory violation," *Aero Corp. v. United States*, 38 Fed. Cl. 237 (1997). See also *Food Servs. of Am.*, Comp. Gen. Dec. B-276860, 97-2 CPD ¶ 55, and *ASR Management & Technical Servs.*, Comp. Gen. Dec. B-244862.3, 92-1 CPD ¶ 383, where the Comptroller General noted that comparative assessments were made by technical evaluators but did not comment on the use of the procedure. Thus, it appears that agencies can use a two-step evaluation process or evaluate the proposals by making a comparative assessment in the initial evaluation. Whatever system is used, it should be clear that the end result of the evaluation process is a comparative assessment of the relative merits of the proposals because that must be the basis for the ultimate source selection decision, FAR 15.308.

1. Documenting the Assessment

FAR 15.305(a) requires documentation as follows:

> The relative strengths, deficiencies, significant weaknesses, and risks supporting proposal evaluation shall be documented in the contract file.

This documentation is generally prepared in narrative form simultaneously with the scoring and describes the reasons that the evaluators have assigned the scores to each proposal. Thus, these narratives identify the "strengths, weaknesses, and risks" of each proposal that have led to the score that has been assigned. A fully documented evaluation will contain such narratives for each score — generally at the lowest level of scoring in the evaluation scheme. It is very helpful if these narratives contain a reference to the specific pages of the proposal that contain the information on which the evaluation is based.

The preparation of these narrative statements can be prepared by each individual evaluator or as a summary evaluation by all of the evaluators that have assessed the element of the proposals being evaluated. Preparation of these narratives at the same time the proposals are scored provides an excellent discipline for the evaluators because it forces them to justify their scores. If the narratives are prepared by the entire evaluation team, this will also force evaluators to reconcile disparate scores or at least to focus on the reason for the disparities. Thus, this part of the narratives can improve the scoring as well as flow valuable information to the source selection official.

Although the FAR gives no guidance on the extent of documentation required, it is clear that the Comptroller General bases the level of documentation required by the agency on the specific complexity of each source selection. In *Champion-Alliance, Inc.*, Comp. Gen. Dec. B-249504, 92-2 CPD ¶ 386, the Comptroller General held that relatively little documentation was required from the agency because the requirements under the RFP were fairly unambiguous and the proposals were very similar. See also *Quality Elevator Co.*, Comp. Gen. Dec. B-276750, 97-2 CPD ¶ 28, where inadequate documentation was overlooked because the proposals were very similar. It has also been held that there is no need for narrative statements when the proposal was acceptable with no notable advantages or disadvantages, *PRC, Inc.*, Comp. Gen. Dec. B-274698.2, 97-1 CPD ¶ 115. See also *Delta Dental Plan v. Perry*, ___ F. Supp. __ (N.D. Cal. 1996) (no need for narrative supporting a rating of "satisfactory"). However, when the technical scores of the two top offerors were within one percentage point of each other, the Comptroller General sustained a protest because the scores were not adequately supported by written narratives, *Universal Shipping Co.*, Comp. Gen. Dec B-223905.2, 87-1 CPD ¶ 424. For other protests that have been sustained because of insufficient documentation, see *Matrix Int'l Logistics, Inc.*, Comp. Gen. Dec. B-272388.2, 97-2 CPD ¶ 89 (summary evaluation results with no narrative supporting changed scores on BAFOs); *JW Assocs., Inc.*, Comp. Gen. Dec. B-275209, 97-1 CPD ¶ 57 (one-paragraph summary of each proposal with no supporting narrative for low scores); *Engineering & Computation, Inc.*, Comp. Gen. Dec. B-261658, 95-2 CPD ¶ 176 (summary decision memorandum but no narrative for individual subfactors where significant risks had been found); *Deployable Hospital Sys., Inc.*, Comp. Gen. Dec. B-260778, 95-2 CPD ¶ 65 (preaward survey showed significant distinctions between the two offerors that did not support an equal rating on their quality control factors and subfactors and the ratings were not otherwise explained or justified); *Arco Management of Washington, D.C., Inc.*, Comp. Gen. Dec. B-248653, 92-2 CPD ¶ 173 (no narratives supporting point scores); *Northwest EnviroService, Inc.*, 71 Comp. Gen. 453 (B-247380.2), 92-2 CPD ¶ 38 (no documentation to support evaluation that competing offerors were equal in past performance); and *Beckman Instruments, Inc.*, Comp. Gen. Dec. B-246195.3, 92-1 CPD ¶ 365 (no documentation showing that agency evaluated changes in BAFO). When the agency's source selection apparently deviates in any way from the stated evaluation criteria, the Comptroller General will require comprehensive documentation explaining the apparent deviation, *Dewberry & Davis*, Comp. Gen. Dec. B-247116, 92-1 CPD ¶ 421 (award to low priced, technically acceptable offer where evaluation scheme provided that technical merit was more important than price).

Agencies have been permitted to destroy the worksheets of individual evaluators if the documentation that is retained is sufficient to justify the source selection decision. See *Dimensions Int'l/QSOFT, Inc.*, Comp. Gen. Dec. B-270966, 96-1 CPD ¶ 257, stating:

> While an agency is not required to retain every document or worksheet generated during its evaluation of proposals, the agency's evaluation must be sufficiently documented to allow review of the merits of a protest. *Southwest Marine, Inc.*; *American Sys. Eng'g Corp.*, [Comp. Gen. Dec. B-265865.3, 96-1 CPD ¶ 56]; *KMS Fusion, Inc.*, B-242529, May 8, 1991, 91-1 CPD ¶ 447. In this regard, evaluators' notes and workpapers may or may not be necessary to determine the reasonableness of the agency's evaluation. *KMS Fusion, Inc.*, *supra*; see *Department of the Army-Recon.*, B-240647.2, Feb. 26, 1991, 91-1 CPD ¶ 211. Where an agency fails to document or retain evaluation materials, it bears the risk that there is inadequate supporting rationale in the record for the source selection decision and that we will not conclude that the agency had a reasonable basis for the decision. *Southwest Marine, Inc.*; *American Sys. Eng'g Corp.*, *supra*; *Engineering and Computation, Inc.*, B-261658, Oct. 16, 1995, 95-2 CPD ¶ 176; *American President Lines, Ltd.*, B-236834.3, July 20, 1990, 90-2 CPD ¶ 53. We find no basis to object to the Navy's evaluation and subsequent rejection of Dimension's proposal. While we think the Navy's destruction of the individual evaluators' worksheets may have been premature, this is insufficient reason to disturb a procurement where, as here, the protest record is otherwise adequate for our review.

See also *Dynalantic Corp.*, Comp. Gen. Dec. B-274944.2, 97-1 CPD ¶ 101, where the Comptroller General permitted the agency to attempt to justify the evaluation of the protester in a hearing after it had destroyed the evaluators' work papers. In sustaining the protest because of the lack of rationale supporting the decision, the Comptroller General granted protest costs and noted that they were higher because of the need for a hearing. It was also noted that the agency had decided to discontinue the practice of destroying work papers.

2. Comparison of Proposals

The other part of the narratives is the statement of the "relative qualities of the proposals." As noted above, this comparison of the proposals has generally been done as a second step in the evaluation process and is frequently done by the evaluation board or the evaluation team leaders. In many ways, this is the most important part of the narratives because it summarizes the information needed by the source selection official to make the selection decision.

This comparison of proposals should be prepared in sufficient detail to identify each area where there is a significant difference between proposals.

Ideally, the narrative will contain a concise description of the difference and an assessment of the *value of the difference* or the *impact* that the difference will have on the procuring agency. This value/impact statement in the areas of technical and management provides the key information needed by the source selection official in making the tradeoff with the cost/price differences among offerors. Thus, such narratives provide the source selection official clear information concerning the relative advantages or disadvantages of proposals in a way that scores, such as numbers, colors, or adjectives obviously cannot. See *Alliant Techsystems, Inc.*, Comp. Gen. Dec. B-276162, 97-1 CPD ¶ 141, stating:

> Evaluating the relative merits of competing proposals is a matter within the discretion of the contracting agency since the agency is responsible for defining its needs and the best method of accommodating them, and it must bear the burden resulting from a defective evaluation. *Advanced Tech. and Research Corp.*, B-257451.2, Dec. 9, 1994, 94-2 CPD ¶ 230 at 3. Consequently, in reviewing an evaluation we will not reevaluate proposals but instead will examine the agency's evaluation to ensure that it was reasonable and consistent with the stated evaluation criteria.

See also *Suncoast Assocs., Inc.*, Comp. Gen. Dec. B-265920, 95-2 CPD ¶ 268, where the Comptroller General held that the agency's explanation of why it determined two proposals to be technically equivalent, despite the protester's two-point advantage in technical scoring, was reasonable and consistent with the documentation which showed the relative strengths and weaknesses of the proposals. Compare *Northwest EnviroService, Inc.*, 71 Comp. Gen. 453 (B-247380.2) 92-2 CPD ¶ 38, where the Comptroller General sustained a protest because the record lacked sufficient documentation to show that the source selection was reasonably based on the announced evaluation criteria.

F. Scoring

After assessment of proposals, agencies generally score some or all of the evaluation factors as a means of summarizing the evaluations to assist the source selection official in making the tradeoff decision between the competing proposals. Thus, scoring systems are notational devices which provide a rough means of measuring differences between proposals. However, it is clear that, in almost all cases, the scores alone will not support a source selection decision. See *JW Assocs., Inc.*, Comp. Gen. Dec. B-275209, 97-1 CPD ¶ 57, stating:

> While both adjectival ratings and point scores are useful as guides to decision-making, they generally are not controlling, but rather, must be supported by documentation of the relative differences between proposals, their weaknesses and risks, and the basis and reasons for the selection decision.

In general, an agency's scoring system cannot be challenged, *BRC Assocs., Inc.*, Comp. Gen. Dec. B-237156, 90-1 CPD ¶ 145 (numerical scoring of subfactors permitted even though the RFP stated that subfactors did not have assigned points).

Most scoring systems do not score all of the factors and subfactors. Technical factors appear to be the most frequently scored while price or cost is the least frequently scored. This is logical because the marginal difference in price or cost between the proposals, which will be used to make the source selection decision, is clearly apparent in dollar amounts and scoring tends to obscure rather than illuminate this difference.

Scoring systems are particularly useful when there are a large number of evaluation factors and subfactors. However, as the number of factors decreases, there is less need for scoring. For example, there have been a number of procurements were the only factors were past performance and price. In that case, there would appear to be no need to score the proposals.

Any system can be used as long as it provides meaningful differentiation among proposals of various merit. The most frequently used systems are adjectival rating systems, color coding, numerical scoring, and ranking. These are the systems identified in FAR 15.305(a).

1. Adjectival Ratings

Adjectival rating systems are widely used and generally call for the use of four or five ratings such as excellent, good, fair and poor or outstanding, highly acceptable, acceptable, marginally acceptable and unacceptable. They have the disadvantage of providing very few gradations to distinguish between proposals — making the scoring somewhat imprecise as a tool to measure the marginal differences between proposals. However, the Comptroller General has accepted the use of these systems — finding that they can give the source selection official a clear understanding of the relative merit of the proposals, *Dynamics Research Corp.*, Comp. Gen. Dec. B-240809, 90-2 CPD ¶ 471. See also *Metropolitan Contract Servs., Inc.*, Comp. Gen.

Dec. B-191162, 78-1 CPD ¶ 435, *recons. denied*, 78-2 CPD ¶ 43, where the Comptroller General rejected the argument that the use of an adjectival rating system precluded offerors from access to the rationale employed in the decision-making process. The acceptance of such systems is justified because they do not form the basis for the ultimate source selection decisions. See *Able-One Refrigeration, Inc.*, Comp. Gen. Dec. B-244695, 91-2 CPD ¶ 384, where the Comptroller General commented that adjectival scores "are useful only as guides to intelligent decision making, and are not generally controlling for award because they often reflect the disparate, subjective judgments of the evaluators."

Adjectival rating will not be accepted, however, if the system distorts the relationship between the proposals. See, for example, *Redstone Technical Servs.*, Comp. Gen. Dec. B-259222, 95-1 CPD ¶ 181, where the Comptroller General sustained a protest finding that the contracting officer had mechanically applied the adjectival scoring system without documenting whether the relative differences represented any meaningful qualitative differences justifying award to higher technically rated, significantly higher cost offeror. See also *Deployable Hosp. Sys., Inc.*, Comp. Gen. Dec. B-260778, 95-2 CPD ¶ 65, where the Comptroller General sustained a protest when two offerors with significantly different levels of experience were scored as "acceptable." Compare *Akal Sec., Inc.*, Comp. Gen. Dec. B-261996, 96-1 CPD ¶ 33, where the Comptroller General disagreed with the protester's contention that the use of the adjectival rating "acceptable" was too broad to allow for differences in technical superiority.

2. Color Coding

A scoring system very similar to adjectival scoring is the color coding system. See paragraph 304 of AFFARS Appendix AA, which sets forth the following description of this type of system:

Color	Rating	Definition
Blue	Exceptional	Exceeds specified performance or capability in a beneficial way to the Air Force, and has no significant weakness.
Green	Acceptable	Meets evaluation standards and weaknesses are readily corrected.

Yellow	Marginal	Fails to meet evaluation standards; however, any significant deficiencies are correctable.
Red	Unacceptable	Fails to meet a minimum requirement of the RFP and the deficiency is uncorrectable without a major revision of the proposal.

This regulation also describes the use of a symbol system which is used less frequently. A plus (+) sign is used for proposals which exceed minimum requirements, a check (✓) for those offers which meet the requirements, and a minus (-) sign for proposals which do not meet the requirements.

The use of four colors without the plus and minus symbols is essentially the same as a four adjective system in that it provides minimal gradations to distinguish between proposals. However, the Comptroller General has agreed with the use of color coding, holding that such a system does not produce "an artificial equality in the ratings," *Ferguson-Williams, Inc.*, 68 Comp. Gen. 25 (B-231827), 88-2 CPD ¶ 344. The Comptroller General has also held that a color rating system does not prevent the agency from gaining a clear understanding of the relative merits of the proposals, *Bendix Field Eng'g Corp.*, Comp. Gen. Dec. B-241156, 91-1 CPD ¶ 44. See also *Peterson Builders, Inc.*, Comp. Gen. Dec. B-244614, 91-2 CPD ¶ 419, where the Comptroller General denied a protest that the color coding system obscured the fact that the technical proposals were essentially equal. However, the Comptroller General has questioned a color coding system which gives a "green" to all factors and subfactors which are acceptable, *Trijicon, Inc.*, 71 Comp. Gen. 41 (B-244546), 91-2 CPD ¶ 375. The Comptroller General rejected this system because it did not differentiate between proposals that were merely acceptable and those with superior technical features — thus converting a tradeoff decisional scheme into a low-price/technically acceptable proposal scheme.

3. *Numerical Systems*

Numerical systems have typically assigned 100 or 1000 points to the factors being scored numerically. Most agencies that have used numerical scoring have scored only the technical and management factors. However, a few agencies have used total numerical systems — scoring price or cost as well as the other factors.

a. Partial Systems

The advantage of numerical scoring systems is that they generally contain a large number of gradation which permits greater differentiation between proposals. However, the Comptroller General has approved systems which reduce the number of gradations by prohibiting the use of certain scores. See *Hoffman Management, Inc.*, 69 Comp. Gen. 579 (B-238752), 90-2 CPD ¶ 15 (10-5-0 scoring system with 0 points given for meeting minimum requirements); *American Sys. Corp.*, Comp. Gen. Dec. B-247923.3, 92-2 CPD ¶ 158 (10-4-2-0 system); and *Fox & Co.*, Comp. Gen. Dec. B-197272, 80-2 CPD ¶ 340 (10-8-5-2-0 system). These systems tend to distort the differences between proposals but the Comptroller General has not seen the distortion as a serious problem — probably because the scores are not used as the basis of the source selection decision.

Numerical systems that do not provide similar scores for similar proposals will be rejected. See, for example, *Arco Management of Washington, D.C., Inc.*, Comp. Gen. Dec. B-248653, 92-2 CPD ¶ 173. See also *SDA, Inc.*, Comp. Gen. Dec. B-248528.2, 93-1 CPD ¶ 320, where the Comptroller General granted a protest because the numerical scores given for experience were irrational. The agency had used a system where an offeror was given a zero score if over half of the prior projects it listed were under an undisclosed size — even if many of the projects indicated substantial experience.

b. Totally Numerical Systems

Some agencies have used totally numerical systems to select sources. There are three systems of this nature that have been commonly used.

(1) TOTAL POINT SCORING

This system assigns point scores to each evaluation factor and makes the source selection decision based on the total point scores. In such a system all criteria, including price or cost, are numerically scored. Generally, price is scored by giving the lowest price proposal the total points assigned to the criteria and computing the number of points for the other proposals in accordance with their relationship to the lowest price. Although this evaluation technique totally obscures the tradeoff between price and the other evaluation factors, the Comptroller General has ruled that an evaluation that one offeror has achieved the highest number of points will validly support the selection of that offeror for award. See *Barnard Constr., Co.*, Comp. Gen. Dec. B-271644, 96-2 CPD ¶ 18, stating:

> Our Office has specifically recognized the propriety of using such a formula in selecting an offeror. See *Stone & Webster Eng'g Corp.*, B-255286.2, Apr. 12, 1994, 94-1 CPD ¶ 306; *Management Sys. Designers, Inc.*, B-244383.3, Sept. 30, 1991, 91-2 CPD ¶ 310. Because the awardee's proposal earned the highest combined price/technical score under the specified formula, the agency was not required to perform price/technical tradeoff analysis to justify the selection decision.

The same result was reached in *Tulane Univ.*, Comp. Gen. B-259912, 95-1 CPD ¶ 210, and *Securigard, Inc.*, Comp. Gen. Dec. B-248584, 92-2 CPD ¶ 156.

An illustration of the difficulties created by this system is found in *Harrison Sys., Ltd.*, 63 Comp. Gen. 379 (B-212675), 84-1 CPD ¶ 572, where price was assigned 30 points and the proposals were:

A $1,150,782

B $1,392,293

Offeror A was given 30 points and Offeror B was given 24.79 points derived from the following formula:

$$\frac{\$1{,}150{,}782}{\$1{,}392{,}293} \times 30 = 24.79 \text{ points}$$

After completing the technical evaluation, the agency computed the results of the total evaluation as follows:

PROPOSAL	COST	TECHNICAL	TOTAL
A	30 points	59.88 points	89.88 points
B	24.79 points	70 points	94.79 points

However, the source selection official was unwilling to blindly follow the RFP and award to Offeror B on the basis of the highest point score. The source selection official made an independent analysis and determined that the technical proposals were of equal merit. The contract was therefore awarded to Offeror A based on its low price. The Comptroller General upheld this decision but stated that he would have granted the protest if the source selection official had independently analyzed whether the difference in technical merit was worth the difference in price. This example demonstrates the pitfalls inherent in the total point evaluation system. The simple summation of points to obtain a total score gives the appearance of mathematical exactitude but there is no assurance that points assigned to one set of criteria have the same value to the Government as points assigned to another set of criteria. Thus, award on the sole basis of the total points may not provide the Government with the best value.

Some agencies have used the total point evaluation system but have not stated in the RFP that award would be made to the offeror earning the most points. In that situation, it is proper to make a normal tradeoff analysis and award to the offeror with the best value, *DATEX, Inc.*, Comp. Gen. Dec. B-270268.2, 96-1 CPD ¶ 240; *Paxson Elec. Co. v. United States*, 14 Cl. Ct. 634 (1988). However, it is not clear what is added to the evaluation process by giving point scores to price when a full tradeoff analysis is going to be made.

The use of numerical scoring methods which produce "distorted" scores has been discouraged. In *Custom Janitorial Serv.*, Comp. Gen. Dec. B-205023, 82-2 CPD ¶ 163, the Comptroller General criticized the use of "spread scoring," in which the proposal with the lowest realistic cost received the maximum number of points and that with the highest cost received zero. The Comptroller General concluded that this system produced distorted results when applied to the two offerors in the competitive range. See also *Tennessee Wholesale Drug Co.*, Comp. Gen. Dec. B-243018, 91-2 CPD ¶ 9, holding that a system which improperly reduced the importance of price as an evaluation factor unfairly distorted the scores. In *Lingtec, Inc.*, Comp. Gen. Dec. B-208777, 83-2 CPD ¶ 279, a form of mathematical analysis in which prices closest to the Government estimate received maximum points and deviations from the estimate were penalized was held improper, as it penalized lower prices more than higher ones. It can be argued that any system which assigns scores by formula will potentially produce distorted results and thus should not be used.

(2) Conversion to Dollar Values

Another completely numerical system determines the relative value of all evaluation factors according to their expected impact on the life cycle cost of the item being procured. An example of this method is found in *Storage Tech. Corp.*, Comp. Gen. Dec. B-215336, 84-2 CPD ¶ 190, in which the Comptroller General described the method as follows:

> Section IV.3 of the RFP, "Evaluation of Proposals" . . . states that award will be "made to that responsible offeror whose proposal is in the best interests of the VA, cost and other factors considered." Section H.1.3 of the RFP lists the additional factors that the VA would consider. These factors were ranked in order of importance based on their maximum dollar impact on ESLC and listed in descending order of importance . . . . For each of these factors, the VA assigned a dollar credit or assessment commensurate with the cost savings/avoidance or added cost to be incurred by the VA with each proposal system. The VA indicates that the technical evaluation "dollars" are not intended to be precise indicators of actual value, but, rather, like a point score, will serve as a guide to the selecting official. The VA states that the dollar figures arrived at for these additional factors will be compared to the ESLC to determine which proposal is in the VA's best interests and award will be made on that basis.

See also *C.M.P., Inc.*, Comp. Gen. Dec. B-216508, 85-1 CPD ¶ 156, where the agency made the entire evaluation in dollars by assigning dollar amounts for the value of three years of previous performance, guarantee of performance, and remedial and preventive maintenance services.

Assigning dollar values to all evaluation factors is an extremely rare form of proposal evaluation. However, it is not uncommon to assign dollar values to some of the evaluation factors. See, for example, *Cessna Aircraft Co.*, Comp. Gen. Dec. B-261953.5, 96-1 CPD ¶ 132, where this occurred. The Comptroller General indicated that he would accept the judgment of the agency in such cases stating that life-cycle cost analysis "involves the exercise of informed judgment and . . . [its use] will not [be] question[ed] . . . unless it clearly lacks a reasonable basis." See also *Global Assocs., Ltd.*, Comp. Gen. Dec. B-275534, 97-1 CPD ¶ 129 (quantified values of non-price factors properly used to determine best value); *Continential Airlines, Inc.*, Comp. Gen. Dec. B-258271.4, 97-1 CPD ¶ 81 (adjusted prices based on monetary benefits of non-price factors properly used in making selection decision).

(3) Dollars Per Point

The third numerical system is the dollars per point system. In this system all of the criteria other than cost are scored numerically and the prices proposed are used to compute a mathematical relationship. An earlier version of DARCOM Pamphlet 1715-3 described this system as follows:

> (3) *Evaluation of lowest dollar per technical quality point ($/q.p.).* The concept of selecting the best technical proposal for the dollar is supportable by the dollar/technical point relationships. This factor can be determined by dividing the cost of the proposal by the total unweighted raw score developed for "technical." With the knowledge contained in the RFP that this relationship will be given consideration and will force offerors to tradeoff between cost and technical factors in order to prepare the best possible proposal at a fair and reasonable price, $/q.p. relationship by itself is not justification for selection; but is only considered an additional factor to offer to the SSA in making the decision. An example area is below:

Proposal	Cost	Technical	$ / q.p.
1	$30,000	374	$80.21
2	$28,500	355	$80.28
3	$42.500	385	$110.38
4	$32,670	362	$90.24

In some instances, a dollar per quality point system has been used as the sole basis for source selection. The Comptroller General has approved this method even when a losing competitor submitted a lower priced proposal that was technically acceptable, *Shapell Gov. Hous., Inc.*, 55 Comp. Gen.

839 (B-183830), 76-1 CPD ¶ 161. See *Management Sys. Designers, Inc.*, Comp. Gen. Dec. B-244383.3, 91-2 CPD ¶ 310, where the Comptroller General accepted the use of this technique as the sole basis for the source selection even though the RFP reserved the right to make an independent cost/technical tradeoff decision. See also *Frank E. Basil, Inc.*, Comp. Gen. Dec. B-208133, 83-1 CPD ¶ 91, allowing such an award even though the protester's price was significantly lower.

This technique gives an appearance of greater precision than is justified by the point scores assigned because point scoring inherently is less precise than price, yet the use of a ratio between the scores assumes that they are of equal precision. Thus, it is better to use this technique as one method of evaluating the merits of the proposals. See *Moran Assocs.*, Comp. Gen. Dec. B-240564.2, 91-2 CPD ¶ 495, where the agency did this and the Comptroller General stated:

> We have recognized that such a cost/technical ratio formula can be a proper tool for the government to utilize in determining which proposal is the most advantageous to the government. See *Morrison-Knudsen Co., Inc.*, B-237800.2, 90-1 CPD ¶ 443. Here, the ratio was only one tool utilized to assure that the government was getting the best buys, given relative technical rankings and costs. The record shows that awards were not made to the offerors with the best ratios.

4. Ranking

The direct ranking of proposals, without the aid of scores, has also been upheld, as numerical scoring does not "transform the technical evaluation into a more objective process," *Development Assocs., Inc.*, Comp. Gen. Dec. B-205380, 82-2 CPD ¶ 37. The Comptroller General has even stated that "ranking proposals may be a more direct and meaningful method" than numerical scoring, *Maximus*, Comp. Gen. Dec. B-195806, 81-1 CPD ¶ 285. However, ranking is infrequently used because it bypasses the scoring of proposals in terms of how well they meet the RFP requirements. Thus, ranking runs the risk of not identifying the key deficiencies in the proposals — unless the agency has prepared very thorough narratives evaluating the details of each proposal.

G. Evaluation of Specific Factors

While agencies must be diligent in ensuring fair evaluations of all evaluation factors, specific concerns have been raised in regard to the evaluation of cost to the Government and past performance.

1. Price or Cost to the Government

In every procurement, price or cost to the Government is an evaluation factor. In fixed-price contracts, the agency must make a price reasonableness determination as part of the evaluation process. In cost-reimbursement contracts, the evaluation factor must be probable cost to the Government which must be determined by making a cost realism analysis. This critical part of the evaluation process is discussed in detail in Chapter 9.

2. Evaluation of Past Performance

Past performance has become a major evaluation factor, and it has become common to see agencies using only two evaluation factors — price and past performance. See *USA Elecs.*, Comp. Gen. Dec. B-275389, 97-1 CPD ¶ 75, where the Comptroller General agreed that it was rational to award to an offeror with a good past performance but a higher price. Thus, a fair and even-handed assessment of the past performance of each offeror is vital. Although there have been numerous protests, the Comptroller General has accorded agencies considerable discretion in the evaluation of contractor past performance. In *HLC Indus., Inc.*, Comp. Gen. Dec. B-274374, 96-2 CPD ¶ 214, the Comptroller General stated:

> Evaluation of an offeror's past performance is a matter within the discretion of the contracting agency, and we will not substitute our judgment for the agency's, so long as the rating is reasonably based and documented. *PMT Servs., Inc.*, B-270538.2, Apr. 1, 1996, 96-2 CPD ¶ 98. Mere disagreement with the agency's evaluation does not itself render the evaluation unreasonable, *Macon Apparel Corp.*, B-272162, Sept. 4, 1996, 96-2 CPD ¶ 95.

This broad discretion permits agencies to refuse to accept an offeror's explanation for a poor past performance rating, *H.F. Henderson Indus.*, Comp. Gen. Dec. B-275017, 97-1 CPD ¶ 27; and *Continental Serv. Co.*, Comp. Gen. Dec. B-274531, 97-1 CPD ¶ 9. See *MAC's General Contractor*, Comp. Gen. Dec. B-276755, 97-2 CPD ¶ 29, where the Comptroller

General denied a protest that the agency had given a poor evaluation based on a default termination that was still in litigation, stating that such an evaluation may be based on a "reasonable perception of inadequate prior performance."

One of the major tasks in evaluating contractor past performance information is to distinguish between a few inconsequential problems and a significant record of inferior performance. For example, in *Cubic Applications, Inc.*, Comp. Gen. Dec. B-274768, 97-1 CPD ¶ 98, the contracting officer evaluated the performance reports on the competitors, considered the negative comments, but concluded that the overall positive nature of the reports indicated that the winning offeror was entitled to an excellent rating. The Comptroller General found that this was reasonable. The same result was reached in *CH2M Hill, Ltd.*, Comp. Gen. Dec. B-259511, 95-1 CPD ¶ 203. However, when contracting officers received a significant number of negative comments on an offeror's past performance, they have properly been given lower ratings. See, for example, *AAC Assocs., Inc.*, Comp. Gen. Dec. B-274928, 97-1 CPD ¶ 55, where the contracting officer gave a moderate past performance rating based on a number of negative comments from references; and *SEAIR Transport Servs., Inc.*, Comp. Gen. Dec. B-274162, 96-2 CPD ¶ 198, where the contracting officer concluded that the overall ratings given by references adequately reflected the severity of the problems that they had identified. In *Quality Fabricators, Inc.*, Comp. Gen. Dec. B-271431, 96-2 CPD ¶ 22, there were so many past performance problems that the contracting officer properly dropped the offeror out of the competitive range.

Care must also be exercised in determining responsibility for past performance problems. See *CDA Investment Technologies, Inc.*, Comp. Gen. Dec. B-272093, 97-1 CPD ¶ 102, where the Comptroller General affirmed the evaluation of a prime contractor and a subcontractor on a prior contract that were competing for a new contract and there had been performance problems on the prior contract. The evaluators took the time to make a careful analysis of which problems should be attributable to each of the two companies and gave them past performance ratings in accordance with this assignment of responsibility.

a. Reliability of Past Performance Information

Past performance information is obtained in two ways. Most agencies have obtained the information from offerors and from references submitted by the offerors or other organizations that have dealt with the offeror. FAR 15.305(a)(2)(ii) requires that offerors be permitted to identify all such organizations to whom they have sold similar goods or services. Agencies must carefully assess this information to ensure that it is a reliable measure of the past performance of the offeror. While there may be some question as to the reliability of such information, the practice of calling references and other organizations for whom the offeror has worked has not been challenged. Some agencies have used questionnaires to obtain past performance information and this practice has been approved by the Comptroller General, *Continental Serv.*, Co., Comp. Gen. Dec. B-274531, 97-1 CPD ¶ 9; *SWR, Inc.*, Comp. Gen. Dec. B-276878, 97-2 CPD ¶ 34.

The other way to obtain past performance information is through data collection systems. FAR Subpart 42.15 provides guidance on such systems. FAR 42.1502(a) requires the preparation of performance evaluation reports on all contracts over $1 million. FAR 42.1503(e) limits the retention and use of the information to three years after the completion of contract performance. Under this regulation, contractors are given a minimum of 30 days to submit comments, rebut statements, or provide additional information. The completed evaluated information cannot be released to other than Government personnel and the contractor whose performance is being evaluated during the period the information is being used for source selection purposes. It is generally believed that this type of information that has been carefully reviewed by the contractor is more reliable than the less formally developed information.

The earliest system of collecting performance information on contractors is the current system applicable to all construction contracts over $500,000, FAR 36.201, and all architect-engineer contracts over $25,000, FAR 36.604. These systems were all incorporated in the FAR in 1984. The Air Force adopted a system in 1988 called the Contractor Performance Assessment Reporting System (CPARS) to assess performance risk on current systems acquisitions greater than $5 million, AFSC Regulation 800-54, Aug. 11, 1988. This system is now implemented by AFMC Instruction 64-107, July 15, 1996. It rates contractor performance in one of the following categories:

(1) Blue (Exceptional) — Indicates performance clearly exceeds contractual requirements. The area of evaluation contains few minor problems for which corrective action appears highly effective.

(2) Green (Satisfactory) — Indicates performance clearly meets contractual requirements. The area of evaluation contains some minor problems for which the corrective actions appear satisfactory.

(3) Yellow (Marginal) — Indicates performance meets contractual requirements. The area of evaluation contains a serious problem for which corrective actions have not yet been identified, appear only marginally effective, or have not been fully implemented.

(4) Red (Unsatisfactory) —Indicates the contractor is in danger of not being able to satisfy contractual requirements and recovery is not likely in a timely manner. The area of evaluation contains serious problems for which the corrective action appears ineffective.

(5) N/A (Not Applicable) — Area of evaluation does not pertain to the contract under evaluation.

The data collected are submitted to the contractor for review and comment before being entered into the system. Thereafter, evaluators use the data in accordance with their relevance to each specific procurement. The Comptroller General has upheld the use of this system, *Rockwell Int'l Corp.*, Comp. Gen. Dec. B-261953.2, 96-1 CPD ¶ 34; *Questech, Inc.*, Comp. Gen. Dec. B-236028, 89-2 CPD ¶ 407; *Pan Am World Servs., Inc.*, Comp. Gen. Dec. B-235976, 89-1 CPD ¶ 283.

The subjectivity of some past performance information has led to questions about its reliability. FAR 42.1501 defines "past performance information" as follows:

> Past performance information is relevant information, for future source selection purposes, regarding a contractor's action under previously awarded contracts. It includes, for example, the contractor's record of conforming to contract requirements and to standards of good workmanship; the contractor's record of forecasting and controlling costs; the contractor's adherence to contract schedules, including the administrative aspects of performance; the contractor's history of reasonable and cooperative behavior and commitment to customer satisfaction; and generally, the contractor's business-like concern for the interest of the customer.

Although the elements of this definition dealing with "reasonable and cooperative behavior" and "customer satisfaction" allow a great deal of subjectivity in the evaluations, the Comptroller General has denied a protest that these elements permit contracting officers to rely on "gossip and innuendo," *RMS Indus.*, Comp. Gen. Dec. B-247229, 92-1 CPD ¶ 451. In that procurement the agency used the FAR definition but changed "history of" to "reputation for." The Comptroller General stated:

> [W]e find nothing unlawful in the agency's taking into account, as one element of past performance, an offeror's reputation for reasonable and cooperative behavior and commitment to customer satisfaction. In the context of this [Request for Proposals], we understand the term "reputation" to refer to fact-based evaluations rather than mere hearsay. We note that [the protester] does not challenge the propriety of the agency's seeking references from prior contracts. Indeed, where, as here, the solicitation informs offerors that the references will be considered as part of the evaluation process, relying on such references is a common and proper part of proposal evaluation.

The Department of Defense has adopted a performance rating system which was initiated on February 1, 1998. This system classifies contracts in one of eight areas: systems, services, information technology, operations support, health care, fuels, construction and architect-engineer services, and science and technology. In each of these areas, specified elements of performance will be assessed and placed in an automated data bank for use in the source selection process.

b. Relevance of the Data

Another difficult problem is determining what prior work will yield a meaningful assessment of the competence of the offeror to perform the contract being awarded. While agencies have considerable discretion in making this determination, *Roy F. Weston, Inc.*, Comp. Gen. Dec. B-274945, 97-1 CPD ¶ 92, the Comptroller General has held that it was unreasonable to fail to obtain past performance information on the prior contract with the agency for the same services, *International Bus. Sys., Inc.*, Comp. Gen. Dec. B-275554, 97-1 CPD ¶ 114. The Comptroller General granted the protest in part because of the fact that the contracting officer had also been the contracting officer on the prior contract and had recently written a letter stating that the offeror's performance on the prior contract had been "exemplary." The Comptroller General stated the rule that "some information is simply too close at hand to require offerors to shoulder the inequities that spring from an agency's failure to obtain, and consider, the information." Compare, however, *Northport Handling, Inc.*, Comp. Gen. Dec. B-274615, 97-1 CPD ¶ 3, where the contracting officer excluded performance on the prior contract in evaluating the past performance of the incumbent contractor. The Comptroller General denied the protest because there was no prejudice. The Comptroller General concluded that including a high performance rating on that contract would not have significantly changed the past performance rating of the offeror because the contracting officer had averaged the scores on a number of contracts to arrive at the overall rating.

In rating past performance with the same agency, it is proper for the evaluators to use their personal knowledge of an offeror's performance of contracts with the agency. See *Omega World Travel, Inc.*, Comp. Gen. Dec. B-271262.2, 96-2 CPD ¶ 44; and *HLC Indus., Inc.*, Comp. Gen. Dec. B-274374, 96-2 CPD ¶ 214. In these cases, the Comptroller General commented that the agency was, in effect, using itself as a reference. *In Systems Integration & Dev., Inc.*, Comp. Gen. Dec. B-271050, 96-1 CPD ¶ 273, the Comptroller General also denied a protest that using the past performance of an incumbent gave the incumbent an unfair competitive advantage.

Random sampling has been permitted, *MilTech, Inc.*, Comp. Gen. Dec. B-275078, 97-1 CPD ¶ 208, and an agency has been permitted to contact a different number of sources for different offerors, *IGIT, Inc.*, Comp. Gen. Dec. B-275299.2, 97-2 CPD ¶ 7, or only a single reference, *Neal R. Gross & Co.*, Comp. Gen. Dec. B-275066, 97-1 CPD ¶ 30; *HLC Indus., Inc.*, Comp. Gen. Dec. B-274374, 96-2 CPD ¶ 214. The Comptroller General has also denied protests when the agency determined that dissimilar work was relevant, *All Star Maintenance, Inc.*, Comp. Gen. Dec. B-271119, 96-1 CPD ¶ 278; *Hughes Missile Sys. Co.*, Comp. Gen. Dec. B-272418, 96-2 CPD ¶ 221. Compare *Ogden Support Servs., Inc.*, Comp. Gen. Dec. B-270012.2, 96-1 CPD ¶ 137, where the Comptroller General granted a protest where the agency had considered dissimilar work relevant but the RFP had used an evaluation factor of "demonstrated successful performance on similar efforts." See also *PMT Servs., Inc.*, Comp. Gen. Dec. B-270538.2, 96-2 CPD ¶ 98, where the Comptroller General granted a protest because it had no prior contracts of the same size as the current procurement. The Comptroller General found that complexity of the work on prior contracts was more important than dollar value of the contracts.

FAR 15.305(a)(2)(ii) requires that offerors be permitted to submit information on corrective action that has been taken to overcome past performance problems but agencies have been given broad discretion in refusing to adjust past performance ratings to reflect such corrective action, *Laidlaw Envtl. Servs. (GS), Inc.*, Comp. Gen. Dec. B-271903, 96-2 CPD 75; *Macon Apparel Corp.*, Comp. Gen. Dec. B-272162, 96-2 CPD ¶ 95. In *Hughes Missile Sys. Co.*, Comp. Gen. Dec. B-272418, 96-2 CPD ¶ 221, the Comptroller General denied a protest where the agency had adjusted a rating of one competition based on corrective action but had refused to adjust the rating of another competitor that had overcome some of the problems encountered on a development contract by taking action on a follow-on productions contract.

One way to ensure relevancy is to evaluate past performance on only those contracts that were performed by the group that is proposed for the current procurement and that were for similar work. In *Robbins-Gioia, Inc.*, Comp. Gen. Dec. B-274318, 96-2 CPD ¶ 222, the agency only considered contracts performed by the same division of the company. In *TESCO*, Comp. Gen. Dec. B-271756, 96-1 CPD ¶ 284, the scope of work was narrowly defined. Similarly, in *Israel Aircraft Indus.*, Comp. Gen. Dec. B-274389, 97-1 CPD ¶ 41, the RFP stated that the agency would focus its evaluation of past performance risk on the offerors' and proposed subcontractors' histories of past performance relevant to the proposed effort, and stated detailed instructions regarding the information that offerors were to provide. In *EastCo Building Servs., Inc.*, Comp. Gen. Dec. B-275334, 97-1 CPD ¶ 83, the Comptroller General denied a protest where the agency had limited its evaluation of past performance to contracts of a comparable size to the procurement being undertaken. Compare *Computer Sys. Dev. Co.*, Comp. Gen. Dec. B-275356, 97-1 CPD ¶ 91, where the Comptroller General denied a protest where the agency gave the winning offeror high past performance ratings based on much smaller contracts than the one under consideration.

c. *Offerors With No Past Performance*

41 U.S.C. § 405 states the following rule with regard to evaluating offerors where the agency has no past performance information:

> (j)(2) In the case of an offeror with respect to which there is no information on past contract performance or with respect to which information on past

> contract performance is not available, the offeror may not be evaluated favorably or unfavorably on the factor of past contract performance.

Initially the FAR implemented this statute by requiring a "neutral" evaluation of past performance in this situation. However, in the process of the FAR Part 15 Rewrite, the FAR was altered to adopt the statutory language. FAR 15.305(a)(2)(iv) now provides:

> In the case of an offeror without a record of relevant past performance or for whom information on past performance is not available, the offeror may not be evaluated favorably or unfavorably on past performance.

The Comptroller General has accorded agencies wide discretion in implementing this rule. Thus, the Comptroller General has agreed that an "excellent" rating on past performance can be considered superior to a "neutral" rating, *Engineering & Computation, Inc.*, Comp. Gen. Dec. B-275180.2, 97-1 CPD ¶ 47. The Comptroller General also stated that an evaluation of "good" past performance may be considered to be superior to an evaluation of "neutral" past performance. See *Excalibur Sys., Inc.*, Comp. Gen. Dec. B-272017, 96-2 CPD ¶ 13, where the Comptroller General stated:

> Thus, where an RFP identifies past performance and price as the evaluation criteria and indicates that an offeror with good past performance can expect a higher rating than an offeror without such a record of performance, proposals must be evaluated on that basis, and ultimately the selection official must decide, if the offeror with the better past performance rating is not the low-cost offeror, whether the more costly offeror represents the best value to the government in light of the better past performance rating.
>
> In general, we do not view RFP evaluation schemes that specify a "neutral" rating for vendors with no past performance record, see, e.g., *Quality Fabricators, Inc.*, B-271431; B-271431.3, June 25, 1996, 96-2 CPD ¶ [22]; *Caltech Serv. Corp.*, B-261044.4, Dec. 14, 1995, 95-2 CPD ¶ 285, as precluding this same type of source selection decision-making. That is, we think that the use of a neutral rating approach, to avoid penalizing a vendor without prior experience and thereby enhance competition, does not preclude, in a best value procurement, a determination to award to a higher-priced offeror with a good past performance record over a lower-cost vendor with a neutral past performance rating. Indeed such a determination is inherent in the concept of best value.

Unfortunately, in the *Excalibur* procurement, the contracting officer had stated in the RFP that offerors with no past performance record would be evaluated "solely on the basis of price." The Comptroller General did not object to this questionable evaluation technique but affirmed the agency's award on the basis of price alone.

VII. DECISION TO AWARD

Upon the completion of the evaluation of offers, the agency must decide, circumstances permitting, whether to make an award without negotiations or to establish a competitive range and conduct negotiations with all the offerors within the competitive range. Whether award without negotiations is permissible depends upon a number of factors, including the provisions included in the solicitation, the offers received, and the nature of communications between the agency and the offerors. Within these parameters, the agency has broad discretion in deciding whether to award or to negotiate. It also has broad discretion in establishing the competitive range. The statutory and regulatory requirements concerning the exercise of these discretionary determinations have evolved over the years.

Although the statutes use the phrase "award without discussions," the phrase "award without negotiations" is more descriptive of the concept and avoids use of the same term to describe two different types of communications. The statutory provisions authorizing award "based on the proposals received," give two different meanings to the word "discussions." It is used to describe both the communications which are permitted prior to award on the basis of proposals received and the communications which are to occur after the competitive range is established. See 10 U.S.C. § 2305(b)(4)(A)(ii) and 41 U.S.C. § 253b(d)(1)(B) stating that award can be made on the basis of proposals received "without discussions with the offerors (other than discussions conducted for the purpose of minor clarifications)." The same different meanings of "discussions" are contained in 10 U.S.C. § 2305(a)(2)(B)(ii)(I) and 41 U.S.C. § 253a(b)(2)(B)(i). In addition, the FAR Part 15 Rewrite removed the definition of "discussions" which had previously appeared in the FAR. It envisions that the exchanges between the agency and the offerors after establishment of the competitive range will constitute "negotiations" which "may include bargaining," FAR 15.306(d).

A. Background

The Government policy concerning whether to award without negotiations or to establish a competitive range and conduct discussions has changed several times over the years. The original statutory standard permitted award on an "initial proposal . . . where it can be clearly demonstrated from the existence of adequate competition or accurate prior cost experience that acceptance of an initial proposal without discussion would result in fair and reasonable prices," 10 U.S.C. § 2304(g) (1964). However, CICA changed the standard substituting "full and open competition" for "adequate competition" and "lowest overall cost to the Government" for "fair and reasonable prices." These changes were interpreted by the Comptroller General to mean that award would have to be made on the basis of the lowest evaluated price unless the proposal was technically unacceptable and that price/quality/capability tradeoffs where not permitted. See, e.g., *Information Spectrum, Inc.*, Comp. Gen. Dec. B-233208, 89-1 CPD ¶ 187. Congress recognized that the "lowest overall cost" standard was too restrictive, causing unnecessary competitive range determinations thereby increasing the cost and time of procurements. In 1990 it removed the "lowest overall cost" language and made related changes for defense contracts, Section 802 of the National Defense Authorization Act for 1991, P.L. 101-510. Four years later, the same changes were adopted for non-defense agencies by the Federal Acquisition Streamlining Act of 1994, P.L. 103-355.

B. Solicitation Provisions

While recognizing that award without negotiations would be preferable in many situations, Congress was concerned that competitors would not submit their best offers if they believed that the agency would likely conduct negotiations. Thus, 10 U.S.C. § 2305(a)(2)(B)(ii)(I) and 41 U.S.C. § 253a(b)(2)(B)(i) require that the solicitation indicate whether the agency intends to award without negotiations or intends to conduct negotiations, stating that the solicitation shall include:

> [E]ither a statement that the proposals are intended to be evaluated with, and award made after, discussions with the offerors, or a statement that the proposals are intended to be evaluated, and award made, without discussions with the offerors (other than discussions conducted for the purpose of minor clarification) unless discussions are determined to be necessary.

Neither the statute nor the regulations provide any directions related to selecting the appropriate provision. FAR 15.209(a) merely requires that once this determination is made, the appropriate solicitation provision is to be adopted.

1. Award Without Negotiations Intended

Paragraph (f)(4) of the standard FAR 52.215-1 Instructions to Offerors — Competitive Acquisition solicitation provision permits award without negotiations as follows:

> The Government intends to evaluate proposals and award a contract without discussions with offerors (except clarifications as described in FAR 15.306(a)). Therefore, the offeror's initial proposal should contain the offeror's best terms from a cost or price and technical standpoint. The Government reserves the right to conduct discussions if the Contracting Officer later determines them to be necessary. If the Contracting Officer determines that the number of proposals that would otherwise be in the competitive range exceeds the number at which an efficient competition can be conducted, the Contracting Officer may limit the number of proposals in the competitive range to the greatest number that will permit an efficient competition among the most highly rated proposals.

While indicating that award without negotiation is intended, this provision gives the agency the option to conduct negotiations when they are determined to be "necessary." However, FAR 15.306(a)(2) requires that when such a determination is made, "the rationale for doing so shall be documented in the contract file." This provision apparently reflects the congressional concern that offerors might not make their best offers in their original submission if they expect negotiations to take place. Thus, the Government should not avail itself of this option as a matter of course.

Incorporation of the substance of this notice into solicitations has been held to put offerors on notice that they should not expect to have an opportunity to revise their offers. See, e.g., *Robotic Sys. Technology*, Comp. Gen. Dec. B-278195.2, 98-1 CPD ¶ ___, stating:

> [S]ince the RFP advised offerors that the agency intended to make award without discussions, RST could not reasonably presume that it would have a chance to improve its proposal through discussions. *Scientific-Atlanta, Inc.*, B-255343.2, B-255343.4, Mar. 14, 1994, 94-1 CPD ¶ 325 at 8-9.

An offeror does not have a *right* to award on the basis of an initial proposal, *Kisco Co.*, Comp. Gen. Dec. B-216953, 85-1 CPD ¶ 334.

2. Negotiations Intended

When the agency has determined that it intends to conduct negotiations, the following Alternate I to the FAR 52.215-1 paragraph (f)(4) solicitation provision is to be used:

> The Government intends to evaluate proposals and award a contract after conducting discussions with offerors whose proposals have been determined to be within the competitive range. If the Contracting Officer determines that the number of proposals that would otherwise be in the competitive range exceeds the number at which an efficient competition can be conducted, the Contracting Officer may limit the number of proposals in the competitive range to the greatest number that will permit an efficient competition among the most highly rated proposals. Therefore, the offeror's initial proposal should contain the offeror's best terms from a price and technical standpoint.

When this provision is used, the Government may not make award without negotiations, *American Native Medical Transport, LLC*, Comp. Gen. Dec. B-276873, 97-2 CPD ¶ 73.

C. Deciding Whether or Not to Negotiate

Neither the statutes nor the FAR specify criteria for determining whether or not to hold negotiations. 10 U.S.C. § 2305(b)(4)(A) merely states:

> The head of an agency shall evaluate competitive proposals in accordance with paragraph (1) and may award a contract —
>
> > (i) after discussions with the offerors, provided that written or oral discussions have been conducted with the responsible offerors who submit proposals within the competitive range; or
> >
> > (ii) based on the proposals received, without discussions with the offerors (other than discussions conducted for the purpose of minor clarification) provided that the solicitation included a statement that pro-

> posals are intended to be evaluated, and award made, without discussions, unless discussions are determined necessary.

The same substance is contained in 41 U.S.C. § 253b(d)(1).

Under the CICA standard, negotiations appeared to have been the favored procedure. However, the statutory changes have served to make award without negotiations, at least, an equally appropriate procedure. House Report 101-665, 101st Cong., 2d Sess. (accompanying P.L. 101-510) discussed some of the factors to consider in making the selection. However, it did not go so far as indicating a preference for either procedure, stating, "The committee does not recommend a preference for conducting discussions or not conducting discussions, believing that this is more appropriately dealt with in regulation." The FAR has not adopted any guidance implementing these statutes. Thus, the lack of statutory or regulatory direction leaves the agency with broad discretion in determining whether or not negotiations should be conducted either in advance or after offers are received.

1. Award Without Negotiations

Award without negotiations is one of the most important techniques that agencies have adopted to streamline their procurements. House Report 101-665 recognized the advantages of this process by noting the following benefits of making awards without negotiations:

- Significant reduction of acquisition lead-time
- Permitting award on technical superiority when discussions are not needed
- Lessening the chances of wrongful disclosure of source selection information
- Reduction of the Government's overall acquisition costs by reducing the amount a contractor is spending on bid and proposal costs

An additional benefit is the avoidance of final proposal revisions which include arbitrary price reductions. Such reductions have resulted in excessively low prices which can create serious difficulties during contract performance.

In *International Data Prods. Corp.*, Comp. Gen. Dec. B-274654.5, 97-1 CPD ¶ 34, the Comptroller General recognized the broad discretion the statutes and the FAR afford the agency:

> With respect to the general decision to award without discussions, we addressed this issue in response to IDP's protest and need not revisit it here. However, we will address two of Dunn's contentions that unique factors here required the agency to open discussions. First, Dunn argues that our prior decision in *The Jonathan Corp.*; *Metro Machine Corp.*, B-251698.3; B-251698.4, May 17, 1993, 93-2 CPD ¶ 174, *recon. denied, Moon Eng'g Co., Inc.*, B-251698.6, Oct. 19, 1993, 93-2 CPD ¶ 233, mandates overturning the agency's decision not to hold discussions in this case. Dunn claims that the agency and intervenor failed to distinguish this case because it cannot be distinguished. We disagree.
>
> As an initial matter, Dunn correctly notes that a contracting officer's decision to make award on initial proposals is not unfettered. *The Jonathan Corp.*; *Metro Machine Corp.*, *supra* at 14. We will review the exercise of such discretion to ensure that it was reasonably based on the particular circumstances of the procurement, including consideration of the proposals received and the basis for the selection decision. *Lloyd-Lamont Design, Inc.*, B-270090.3, Feb. 13, 1996, 96-1 CPD ¶ 71 at 6; *Facilities Management Co., Inc.*, B-259731.2, May 23, 1995, 95-1 CPD ¶ 274 at 8. On the other hand, this discretion is quite broad, and in recent years has been expanded. For example, Congress has deleted the requirement originally set forth in the Competition in Contracting Act that an agency could only make award without discussions to the offeror with the lowest price or evaluated cost. Compare 10 U.S.C. § 2305(b)(4)(A)(ii) (1988) with 10 U.S.C. § 2305(b)(4)(A)(ii) (1994) (showing deletion of requirement applicable to defense agencies) and 41 U.S.C. § 253b(d)(1)(B) (1988) with 41 U.S.C. § 253(d)(1)(B) (1994) (showing deletion of requirement applicable to civilian agencies). In addition, the FAR now provides that once the government has stated its intent to award without discussions, "the rationale for reversal of this decision shall be documented in the contract file." FAR 15.610(a)(3) (FAC 90-31, Oct. 1, 1995).

See also *Inter-Con Sec. Servs., Inc.*, Comp. Gen. Dec. B-270828, 96-1 CPD ¶ 233; *Faison Office Prods. Co.*, Comp. Gen. Dec. B-260259, 95-2 CPD ¶ 116; *Energy & Envtl. Research Corp.*, Comp. Gen. Dec. B-261422,

95-2 CPD ¶ 81; and *Professional Safety Consultants Co.*, B-247331, 92-1 CPD ¶ 404.

The mere possibility that lower prices or better technical solutions might result from negotiations is not sufficient to overcome the agency's determination that negotiations are not "necessary." Agency decisions to award without negotiations were found to be reasonable in the following cases: *Richard M. Milburn High School*, Comp. Gen. Dec. B-277018, 97-2 CPD ¶ 53 (award on initial proposals reasonable given deficiencies in protester's proposal and overall technical superiority of awardee's proposal); *OMNIPLEX World Servs. Corp.*, Comp. Gen. Dec. B-278105.3, 97-2 CPD ¶ ___ (although proposal received marginal rating, awardee's proposal was responsive from a technical/management prospective and contained no deficiencies and thus reasonable to award on initial proposals); *Harry A. Stroh Assocs., Inc.*, Comp. Gen. Dec. B-274335, 97-1 CPD ¶ 18 (award on initial proposals to offeror submitting technically superior proposal at a fair price reasonable even though protester argued that a possibility existed that its inferior proposal could become best value through discussions); *Lloyd-Lamont Design, Inc.*, Comp. Gen. Dec. B-270090.3, 96-1 CPD ¶ 71 (award on initial proposals reasonable where awardee was best value and agency had advised offerors of intent to award without conducting discussions); *Cornet, Inc.*, Comp. Gen. Dec. B-270330, 96-1 CPD ¶ 189 (award on initial proposals reasonable given technical superiority of awardee's proposal and determination that no other offeror could improve its proposal to the level of awardee's); *Southwest Marine, Inc.*, Comp. Gen. Dec. B-265865.3, 96-1 CPD ¶ 56 (award on initial proposals reasonable where proposal was evaluated as clearly best value); and *Federal Sys. Group*, GSBCA 11461-P, 92-1 BCA ¶ 24,591 (award without discussions to next lower offeror reasonable because contracting officer concluded that protester's cost would become higher priced when deficiencies were corrected).

2. Decision to Negotiate

The nature of the specifications and the extent to which technical merit is to be considered in a tradeoff strategy procurement will be critical in determining whether to indicate in the solicitation that negotiations are intended. This was noted in H.R. Rep. 101-665, which stated:

> The committee believes that when technical characteristics that cannot be quantified in cost terms are so critical that they are weighed more than low-

> est overall cost, the government may need discussions to ensure a clear understanding by both the government and the contractor of what the government truly needs and can get.

Where the solicitation indicates that award without negotiations is anticipated, the decision to negotiate will depend on the facts and circumstances of the procurement. Even though the criteria for such an award are present, negotiations would be called for if circumstances indicate that the Government could obtain a significantly better bargain. This would be the case where one or more otherwise favorable offers contain defects. This is particularly so where the defects are readily correctable. See *Computer Literacy World, Inc. v. Department of the Air Force*, GSBCA 13438-P, 96-1 BCA ¶ 28,119. See also *Day & Zimmermann Servs. v. United States*, 38 Fed. Cl. 591 (1997), where the court stated at 608:

> [Despite not addressing relevant issues that could have explained the disparity between DZS's proposal and the undisclosed and apparently inaccurate independent Government cost estimate,] the Army ultimately decided not to conduct discussions solely because J & J outranked all offerors in all three award factors. At first blush, such a statement would seem to be sufficient justification for the Army's definitive actions. However, as noted previously, this justification is suspect, because defendant's curious conduct at trial, resulting in the court's finding that DZS's MPCE [most probable cost estimate] is not sustainable on this record, brings into substantial doubt any award decision premised upon [the cost analyst's narrative report] and the MPCE purportedly computed therefrom.
>
> Furthermore, upon a careful review of the Army's evaluation results, it is patently clear that DZS, in fact, was a very close second to J & J. More specifically, the MPCE for J & J's proposal was only $432,361 less than DZS's evaluated cost, and J & J's quality rating was merely 2.42 points higher than that of DZS's proposal. Had J & J enjoyed a significant advantage over DZS, our conclusion might be different. But, on this record, that is not a fact. Rather, in light of the small margin, the undisclosed Government estimate, and the discussible issues identified by the evaluators, we find that, had the Army brought the evaluators' concerns to DZS's attention, it "would have generated answers which could have significantly changed the nature and extent of the cost adjustments [and the quality ratings made by the Army] and therefore could have changed the outcome of the procurement."

In *Veda Inc. v. United States*, Civ. Action No. 93-0518-LFO (D.D.C. 1993), the court found that the decision to conduct discussions was reasonable because the contracting officer had serious problems with Veda's Small Business and Small Business Subcontracting Plan and deemed it unacceptable. Negotiations may also be called for when offers vary substantially from Government estimates, *Jonathan Corp.*, Comp. Gen. Dec. B-251698.3, 93-2 CPD ¶ 174. In deciding whether to negotiate in such situations, the agency should balance the delay and expense involved in conducting negotiations with the potential benefits which might be obtained. It should also consider the effect on competitors, such as unduly increasing bid and proposal expense.

D. Determining the Competitive Range

Determination of the competitive range is of extreme importance to both the Government and competitors. Nevertheless, neither of the statutes provided any guidance for contracting agencies in establishing the range. Former FAR 16.609(a) contained the following statement:

> The competitive range shall be determined on the basis of cost or price and other factors that were stated in the solicitation and shall include all proposals that have a reasonable chance of being selected for award. When there is doubt as to whether a proposal is in the competitive range, the proposal should be included.

Following this guidance many agencies were including a large number of offerors in the competitive range, with the result that they were unable to conduct meaningful negotiations with these offerors. This practice also increased the costs of the competition by requiring many competitors to continue to participate in the process when only one would be awarded a contract. In one case, such a competitor recovered the costs of remaining in the competition because it was placed in the competitive range without any real chance for award, *SMS Data Prods., Group, Inc.*, GSBCA 8589-P, 87-1 BCA ¶ 19,496. These negative effects of broad inclusion of offerors in the competitive range were recognized as detrimental to the competitive negotiation process; and, in 1995, Congress was requested to amend the procurement statutes to permit more limited competitive range determinations.

As discussed below, the statutes and regulations now contain completely different standards for determining the competitive range. As a result, the large number of decisions dealing with this issue are no longer applicable or are of questionable authority.

1. Standards for Inclusion

The standards for inclusion in the competitive range and for determining its size were changed significantly with the passage of the Clinger-Cohen Act of 1996, P.L. 104-106, and the promulgation of the FAR Part 15 Rewrite.

a. Statutory Changes

In passing the Clinger-Cohen Act, Congress recognized that the inclusion of large numbers of offers in the range can unnecessarily increase the time and cost of procurements and considered a number of ways in which the size of the range could be limited. Alternatives aimed at replacing the requirement for "full and open competition" were rejected because of concerns that they would lead to noncompetitive practices. However, two provisions were adopted which the FAR Council has relied upon to change the standards for determining inclusion in the competitive range. First, 10 U.S.C. § 2304(j) and 41 U.S.C. § 253(h) require that "full and open competition" be conducted "efficiently" as follows:

> The Federal Acquisition Regulation shall ensure that the requirement to obtain full and open competition is implemented in a manner that is consistent with the need to efficiently fulfill the Government's requirements.

More specifically, 10 U.S.C. § 2305(b)(4)(B) and 41 U.S.C. § 253b(d)(2) permit the contracting officer to limit the competitive range:

> If the contracting officer determines that the number of offerors that would otherwise be included in the competitive range . . . exceeds the number at which an efficient competition can be conducted, the contracting officer may limit the number of proposals in the competitive range, in accordance with the criteria specified in the solicitation, to the greatest number that will permit an efficient competition among the offerors rated most highly in accordance with the criteria.

b. FAR Part 15 Rewrite

The FAR Part 15 Rewrite drastically changed the standards for inclusion in the competitive range and implemented the statutory authority for limiting the size for purposes of efficiency. As quoted above, the FAR had required that an offer be included in the competitive range if it had a "reasonable chance of being accepted for award," and had stated that, "When there is doubt as to whether a proposal is in the competitive range, the proposal should be included." These standards were removed and replaced with a two step process. First, the agency is required to establish a competitive range which is to include, "all of the most highly rated proposals," FAR 15.306(c)(1). Then, the agency must decide if the number of such proposals is too large for an "efficient competition." If so, FAR 15.306(c)(2) permits the number to be limited as follows:

> After evaluating all proposals in accordance with 15.305(a) and paragraph (c)(1) of this section, the contracting officer may determine that the number of most highly rated proposals that might otherwise be included in the competitive range exceeds the number at which an efficient competition can be conducted. Provided the solicitation notifies offerors that the competitive range can be limited for purposes of efficiency (see 52.215-1(f)(4)), the contracting officer may limit the number of proposals in the competitive range to the greatest number that will permit an efficient competition among the most highly rated proposals (10 U.S.C. § 2305(b)(4) and 41 U.S.C. § 253b(d)).

c. Most Highly Rated Offers and Efficient Competition

Neither the statutes nor the final FAR Part 15 Rewrite attempt to define these terms. Draft versions of the Rewrite had listed factors to be considered in limiting the competitive range but were deleted from the final Rewrite to permit "the facts of the instant acquisition to guide the contracting officer" in limiting the competitive range, 62 Fed. Reg. 51228 (1997). Similarly, the Rewrite does not contain a definition of "efficiency." However, the promulgation comments make it clear that the cost and time involved in conducting negotiations were the primary factors in rejecting the prior "when in doubt leave them in" rule.

The determination of which offers are the "most highly rated" will depend upon the facts and circumstances of each procurement. Under the FAR

Rewrite, as under the prior regulations, the determination will be based on a comparison of the proposals. Thus, a break or gap in the evaluation scores might be the basis for determining the most highly rated offerors. However, the comparative approach to determining the competitive range generally precludes the use of a predetermined cut-off score as a means of determining the range, *DOT Sys., Inc.*, Comp. Gen. Dec. B-186192, 76-2 CPD ¶ 3. In 50 Comp. Gen. 59 (B-169645) (1970), the RFP contained a minimum score, 75, below which proposals would be deemed outside the competitive range. As a result of this cut-off score, five proposals with point scores between 71.4 and 74.8 were excluded. The Comptroller General held that these five proposals could not be excluded from the competitive range solely because of failure to meet the cut-off score. In *National Veterans Law Ctr.*, 60 Comp. Gen. 223 (B-198738), 81-1 CPD ¶ 58, the contracting agency established an evaluation score of 80 points, arguing that the score was only a "qualifying score" meant to inform the offerors of the relative importance of each area of evaluation. The Comptroller General found no difference between this "qualifying score" and a "predetermined cut-off score . . . used to establish the competitive range" and reiterated the impropriety of its use. Nevertheless, the Comptroller General has upheld the exclusion of an offeror based on a predetermined cut-off score when the score of the excluded proposal was so low in comparison with scores on other proposals that no prejudicial effect could be said to exist, 52 Comp. Gen. 382 (B-174870) (1972); *PRC Computer Ctr., Inc.*, 55 Comp. Gen. 60 (B-178205), 75-2 CPD ¶ 35; *Monarch Enters., Inc.*, Comp. Gen. Dec. B-233303, 89-1 CPD ¶ 222.

Reduction of the competitive range on the basis for efficiency is more problematic. Whether reduction should occur does not depend upon mere numbers. For example, where negotiations are not anticipated to be complex or time consuming, a relatively large number of offerors might not result in inefficiency. In contrast, where the nature of the procurement and the offers require substantial negotiations and complex offer revisions, limiting the competitive range would be desirable. If, as the FAR seems to indicate, reduction requires the elimination of "most highly rated" offers, it is difficult to see what rationale would support the elimination of offerors from the competitive range when other offerors that had similar evaluations were included in the range. It would seem that instead of attempting to draw extremely fine distinctions for purposes of limitation, drawing lots or some similar fair technique would be called for.

2. Discretion to Include or Exclude

Under the FAR Part 15 Rewrite, as under the prior regulations, the agencies continue to have broad discretion in determining whether to include or exclude an offer within the competitive range. Thus, it can be anticipated that their decisions will not be disturbed unless they are clearly shown to be arbitrary or unreasonable. See, for example, *Arsenault Acquisition Corp.*, Comp. Gen. Dec. B-276959, 97-2 CPD ¶ 74; *Atlantic Coast Contracting, Inc.*, Comp. Gen. Dec. B-270645.2, 96-1 CPD ¶ 252; *Resource Applications, Inc.*, Comp. Gen. Dec. B-271079, 96-1 CPD ¶ 244; *Interactive Communication Technology, Inc.*, Comp. Gen. Dec. B-271051, 96-1 CPD ¶ 260. However, contracting officers must treat all offerors fairly. Thus, they are not free to treat similarly situated offerors differently, *Isometrics, Inc. v. United States*, 5 Cl. Ct. 420 (1984); *RMI, Inc.*, Comp. Gen. Dec. B-203652, 83-1 CPD ¶ 423, *recons. denied*, 84-1 CPD ¶ 630. In *Isometrics*, the exclusion of a proposal which might legitimately have been excluded due to a failure to comply with RFP requirements was nullified because a similarly situated offeror was included in the competitive range and given an opportunity to cure the problems.

a. Factors to be Considered

The statutes require that the competitive range be established "solely on the factors specified in the solicitation," 10 U.S.C. § 2305(b)(1) and (4)(A) and 41 U.S.C. § 253b(a) and (d). This requirement is repeated in the final Rewrite, FAR 15.306(c)(1) and FAR 15.305(a). Previously, the regulations required that "cost or price and other factors, be considered" in establishing the competitive range, pre-Rewrite FAR 15.609(a). The same language was also included in an earlier draft of FAR 15.306(c)(1) but it was removed in the final draft.

The deletion of the language concerning consideration of cost does not necessarily mean that cost is not to be considered. Cost, with all the other evaluation factors would ordinarily be considered in establishing the range. However, in some instances a complete evaluation of each element of each offer would not appear to be necessary prior to determining the competitive range. If one or more aspects of an offer is so inferior to other offers as to make it unlikely that it could be improved through negotiations, it would not be reasonable to invest more time and effort into evaluating other aspects of the offer. While an offeror has a right to have its offer fairly evaluated, the

Government should not be required to perform expensive and useless exercises.

There is support for this interpretation in decisions under the prior rules. Under the pre-Rewrite rules (requiring consideration of cost) it was held to be proper to exclude offers without considering price or cost when the technical proposal is clearly unacceptable, *Regional Envtl. Consultants*, 66 Comp. Gen. 67 (B-223555), 86-2 CPD ¶ 476, *recons. denied*, 66 Comp. Gen. 388 (B-223555.2), 87-1 CPD ¶ 428; *Aid Maintenance Co.*, Comp. Gen. Dec. B-255552, 94-1 CPD ¶ 188; *Telestar Corp.*, Comp. Gen. Dec. B-275855, 97-1 CPD ¶ 150. For an analysis of this rule, see *Paul & Gordon*, 52 Comp. Gen. 382 (B-174870) (1972), where the Comptroller General explained that the procedure was compatible with the prior statutory requirement in 10 U.S.C. § 2304(g) that "proposals, including price, shall be solicited." However, technically inferior but acceptable proposals may not be rejected without considering cost or price, *HSI-CCEC*, Comp. Gen. Dec. B-240610, 90-2 CPD ¶ 465; *Bay Tankers, Inc.*, 69 Comp. Gen. 403 (B-238162), 90-1 CPD ¶ 389. See also *SCIENTECH, Inc.*, Comp. Gen. Dec. B-277805.2, 98-1 CPD ¶ ___, holding it improper to exclude an acceptable offer without considering cost.

A technically acceptable proposal may be properly determined to be outside the competitive range because the contracting officer believes that the prospective costs of performance are too high and cannot be reduced sufficiently without detracting from the proposal's technical acceptability, *Tracor Marine, Inc.*, Comp. Gen. Dec. B-222484, 86-2 CPD ¶ 150 (denying protest even though protester's technical score was highest). See also *Radio Sys., Inc.*, Comp. Gen. Dec. B-255080, 94-1 CPD ¶ 9 (price 350 percent higher than the low offeror); *Everpure, Inc.*, Comp. Gen. Dec. B-226395.2, 88-2 CPD ¶ 264 (sustaining exclusion of higher priced proposal even though that left only one offeror in the competitive range); *Systems Integrated*, Comp. Gen. Dec. B-225055, 87-1 CPD ¶ 114 (30 percent higher proposed costs); and *Jack Faucett Assocs.*, Comp. Gen. Dec. B-224414, 86-2 CPD ¶ 310 (35 percent higher costs).

The lower the technical rating, the less the cost differential must be to properly exclude an offeror from the competitive range. For example, in *Emerald Maintenance, Inc.*, Comp. Gen. Dec. B-221353, 86-1 CPD ¶ 308, an offeror only 14 percent higher in probable cost was properly excluded when its technical rating was 30 percent lower. In *JDR Sys. Corp.*, Comp. Gen. Dec. B-214639, 84-2 CPD ¶ 325, the Comptroller General concurred in a procedure which excluded from the competitive range all but the three proposals with the highest technical ratings and the lowest proposed costs. In *Bollam, Sheedy, Torani & Co.*, Comp. Gen. Dec. B-270700, 96-1 CPD ¶ 185, the Comptroller General held that the agency properly excluded the protester's proposal from the competitive range because it was ranked tenth out of 34 and the protester's price was higher than seven of the eight proposals with higher technical scores that were included in the competitive range. See also *Documentation Assocs.*, Comp. Gen. Dec. B-190238, 78-1 CPD ¶ 228, where the Comptroller General found that an offer which was considered by evaluation officials to be so costly as to be noncompetitive was improperly placed within the competitive range. Compare *Monitor Int'l, Inc.*, Comp. Gen. Dec. B-200756, 81-2 CPD ¶ 214, *recons. denied*, 81-2 CPD ¶ 370, where the Comptroller General found it improper to exclude all offerors but the one offering the lowest price from the competitive range because the agency had not performed a satisfactory cost realism analysis.

A low cost proposal is not guaranteed inclusion in the competitive range by virtue of its low cost. See, for example, *Forecasting Int'l, Ltd.*, Comp. Gen. Dec. B-220622.3, 86-1 CPD ¶ 306, where the Comptroller General agreed that a very poor technical proposal should be excluded from the competitive range even though that left only one offeror. See also *Hydro-science, Inc.*, Comp. Gen. Dec. B-227989, 87-2 CPD ¶ 501, where a proposal with three major technical deficiencies was properly excluded even though it was considerably lower in cost than the four proposals placed in the competitive range.

b. Inclusion of Defective or Unacceptable Offers

Since negotiations are conducted for the purpose of giving offerors the opportunity to cure weaknesses or deficiencies or to modify other aspects of their proposals, an offer need not be excluded from the competitive range solely because it fails to conform to the RFP. In this respect, the competitive range decision is very different from the "nonresponsiveness" determination in sealed bid contracting. See *Construcciones Aeronauticas, S.A.*, Comp. Gen. Dec. B-244717, 91-2 CPD ¶ 461, where the Comptroller General stated that "the concept of competitive range — whether the proposal is or can be readily made acceptable — is incompatible with responsiveness." See also *DeMat Air, Inc. v. United States*, 2 Cl. Ct. 197 (1983). In *National Ass'n of State Directors of Special Educ., Inc.*, Comp. Gen. Dec. B-227989, 89-1 CPD ¶ 189, the Comptroller General affirmed a contracting officer's decision to keep a technically unacceptable proposal in the competitive range because it was only one of two proposals. In one decision, which is at variance with the regulatory and decisional principles for establishing the competitive range, the Comptroller General held that the Army should have rejected a proposal which substantially failed to conform to the RFP, *Computer Mach. Corp.*, 55 Comp. Gen. 1151 (B-185592), 76-1 CPD ¶ 358. In that decision, the Comptroller General stated that when an agency uses the term "responsive" in its RFP, the offeror should understand that any terms referenced thereby are considered to be material requirements, and that a proposal failing to conform to such terms will be considered unacceptable.

c. *Exclusion for Offer Deficiencies*

While proposals with significant offer deficiencies may be included in the competitive range, they may also be excluded if the contracting officer determines that the offeror does not stand a chance of winning the competition. Thus, it is proper to exclude from the competitive range a proposal which could be made acceptable only if major modifications or revisions were undertaken, *Orincon Corp.*, Comp. Gen. Dec. B-276704, 97-2 CPD ¶ 26; *Orbit Advanced Technologies, Inc.*, Comp. Gen. Dec. B-271293, 96-1 CPD ¶ 254; *Hines-Ike Co.*, Comp. Gen. Dec. B-270693, 96-1 CPD ¶ 158; *Eastern Technical Enters., Inc.*, Comp. Gen. Dec. B-259844, 95-1 CPD ¶ 232. Proposals are also properly excluded for failure to meet a mandatory nonnegotiable specification, *Radix II, Inc.*, Comp. Gen. Dec. B-184913, 76-1 CPD ¶ 37, and where the proposal was rated so low that "any attempt to upgrade . . . to an acceptable level would require an unreasonable and unfair degree of assistance on the part of the Government," *Energy Research Corp.*, Comp. Gen. Dec. B-185018, 76-2 CPD ¶ 37. See also *Pyramid Servs., Inc.*, Comp. Gen. Dec. B-257085, 94-2 CPD ¶ 79, finding it proper to exclude the protester where the proposal failed to propose sufficient staffing, proposed using older, used equipment and lacked experience. The Comptroller General held that it was reasonable to conclude that the protester was not capable of performing the requirement.

A proposal was also found properly excluded when the offeror did not respond to a request for clarification of the technically unacceptable proposal in a timely manner, *Data Resources, Inc.*, 65 Comp. Gen. 125 (B-220079), 85-2 CPD ¶ 670. The exclusion of a proposal which was not "grossly deficient" was upheld where inclusion would not have enhanced competition, as the protester was the sole offeror, *Magnavox Advanced Prods. & Sys. Co.*, Comp. Gen. Dec. B-215426, 85-1 CPD ¶ 146. The agency decided to exclude the proposal from the competitive range and resolicited with relaxed specifications.

d. Informational Deficiencies

Many RFPs require the submission of information relating to the offeror's capability to perform or to establish that the products or services offered meet the specifications. In the past, the contracting agency has been permitted to exclude offers from the competitive range for material failures to provide the information requested. In determining whether an informational deficiency is "material," the Comptroller General has considered (1) the detail called for in the RFP, (2) whether the omissions make the proposal unacceptable or merely inferior, (3) the scope and range of omissions, and (4) whether the proposal offers significant cost savings, *XYZTEK Corp.*, Comp. Gen. Dec. B-214704, 84-2 CPD ¶ 204. Offerors have been held to bear the risk of submitting proposals which do not comply with the RFP's informational requirements, *Pace Data Sys., Inc.*, Comp. Gen. Dec. B-236083, 89-2 CPD ¶ 429. Proposal page limitations are not excuses for failing to provide required information. In *Infotec Dev., Inc.*, Comp. Gen. Dec. B-238980, 90-2 CPD ¶ 58, a proposal was properly excluded for lack of information after the agency rejected 49 pages of the proposal which exceeded the page limitations in the RFP. Similarly, in *Management & Indus. Technologies Assocs.*, Comp. Gen. Dec. B-257656, 94-2 CPD ¶ 134, an RFP had a 20-page limit and the protester submitted over 200 pages of material. The agency removed the pages which exceeded the page limit and found the remaining pages deficient and excluded the protester from the competitive range.

The discretion to exclude proposals for informational deficiencies is reduced when there is only one offeror left in the competitive range, *Falcon Sys., Inc.*, Comp. Gen. Dec. B-213661, 84-1 CPD ¶ 658. In that case, the Comptroller General stated that it is "incumbent upon an agency . . . to keep an informationally deficient proposal in the competitive range unless further discussions . . would be truly meaningless."

Where the information sought is for the purpose of verifying whether the offered products or services conform to specifications, exclusion from the competitive range has been held to be justified. In *Amperif Corp.*, Comp.

Gen. Dec. B-211992, 84-1 CPD ¶ 409, the exclusion of a proposal was upheld where the proposal "parroted" the specifications and merely stated it would meet or exceed the minimum requirements. The solicitation required detailed discussion of plans for satisfying or taking exception to the requirements, although it also cautioned that "unnecessarily elaborate brochures" or other representations might be taken as evidence of a lack of cost consciousness. The Comptroller General stated that where the solicitation includes specific instructions to address mandatory requirements, "offerors are put on notice that they risk rejection if they fail to do so." See also *Ensign-Bickford Co.*, Comp. Gen. Dec. B-211790, 84-1 CPD ¶ 439; and *S&Q Corp.*, Comp. Gen. Dec. B-219420, 85-2 CPD ¶ 471, *recons. denied*, 85-2 CPD ¶ 628, where proposals were excluded from the competitive range for failing to include detailed information establishing the feasibility of the proposed approach. However, in *Moxon Inc.*, Comp. Gen. Dec. B-179160, 74-1 CPD ¶ 134, the Comptroller General held that although a "blanket promise" to conform is not normally an adequate response to an RFP, the proposal was improperly excluded where the RFP clearly stated the Government's exact requirements in a technically detailed manner and did not request offerors to explain their proposals. It has also been held that a "proposal cannot be excluded from the competitive range for lack of substantiating information called for by the RFP if the agency has independently obtained the information," *Integrated Sys. Group, Inc.*, GSBCA 11156-P, 91-2 BCA ¶ 23,961. In that case, other competitors had proposed using the same equipment as the protester and had submitted the required information substantiating that it met the specifications. Thus, the contracting officer knew that the equipment offered by the protester met the requirements of the RFP even though the protester had not submitted data demonstrating compliance.

Information related to the capability of the offeror has also been held to be material and the failure to furnish such information has been held to be a valid reason for exclusion from the competitive range. See *Chant Eng'g Co.*, Comp. Gen. Dec. B-257125.2, 94-2 CPD ¶ 247 (informational deficiencies rendered proposal so deficient that it would require a major rewrite in order to be made acceptable). See also *Pace Data Sys., Inc.*, Comp. Gen. Dec. B-236083, 89-2 CPD ¶ 429. stating:

> While Pace contends that many of its deficiencies resulted from poor proposal draftsmanship, rather than a misunderstanding of the requirements, an offeror is responsible for preparing its proposal in a manner which establishes that what is offered will best meet the government's needs. A techni-

> cal evaluation must be based on the information submitted with the proposal and no matter how capable an offeror may be, if it does not submit an adequately written proposal, it will not be considered in the competitive range.

See also *Global Engr. & Constr. J.V.*, Comp. Gen. Dec. B-275999.4, 97-2 CPD ¶ 125 (lack of information showing understanding of the work and experience of offeror and proposed subcontractor); *American Overseas Book Co.*, Comp. Gen. Dec. B-266297, 96-1 CPD ¶ 60 (RFP called for sufficient information to determine whether offeror understood scope of work; protester had several informational deficiencies leading evaluators to conclude that it failed to understand nature and complexity of work).

Given the increased latitude provided by the FAR Part 15 Rewrite, the contracting agencies will continue to have broad discretion in this area. In exercising this discretion, the number and nature of the other proposals should be considered. If the substantive portions of the proposal (the offer) place it within the proposals "most highly rated," the failure to provide material information would not call for exclusion unless the number of proposals is to be limited for purposes of efficiency. In exercising the authority to reduce the size of the range for purposes of efficiency, the agency must treat the offerors fairly. Thus, it would be improper to exclude such an offer if other offers included in the reduced range had similar informational deficiencies.

e. Only One Offeror

An agency's decision to include only one offeror in the competitive range will be subject to close scrutiny due to the elimination of competition, *Apt Corp.*, GSBCA 9237-P, 88-1 BCA ¶ 20,411. In *Comten-Comress*, Comp. Gen. Dec. B-183379, 75-1 CPD ¶ 400, the Comptroller General stated that any of the following factors may provide a basis for overturning such a decision:

> If there is a close question of acceptability; if there is an opportunity for significant cost savings; if the inadequacies of the solicitation contributed to the technical deficiency of the proposal; if the informational deficiency could be reasonably corrected by relatively limited discussions.

See also *Besserman Corp.*, Comp. Gen. Dec. B-237327, 90-1 CPD ¶ 191. A competitive range of one has been overturned in a number of cases.

See *Dynalantic Corp.*, Comp. Gen. Dec. B-274944.2, 97-1 CPD ¶ 101 (deficiencies were minor and easily correctable and price was lower); *Coastal Gov't Servs., Inc.*, Comp. Gen. Dec. B-250820, 93-1 CPD ¶ 167 (inadequacies were minor which could have been easily resolved during discussions); *Stay, Inc.*, Comp. Gen. Dec. B-247606, 92-1 CPD ¶ 481 (reasons for exclusion of protester were minor and some deficiencies were also found in awardee's proposal); *Corporate Strategies, Inc.*, Comp. Gen. Dec. B-239219, 90-2 CPD ¶ 99 (lower priced proposals that were eliminated were rated excellent or good and had weaknesses which could have been resolved by discussions); *Laser Photonics, Inc.*, Comp. Gen. Dec. B-214356, 84-2 CPD ¶ 470 (deficiencies in eliminated proposals were caused by deficiencies in the RFP); and *Falcon Sys., Inc.*, Comp. Gen. Dec. B-213661, 84-1 CPD ¶ 658 (major deficiencies in other proposals were informational in nature).

Notwithstanding the Comptroller General's policy against including only one offeror in the competitive range, he has upheld such a decision when it is reasonably made. For cases upholding the decision to include only one offeror within the competitive range, see *EER Sys. Corp.*, Comp. Gen. Dec. B-256383, 94-1 CPD ¶ 354 (proposal was substantially inferior in demonstrating an understanding of requirements and no appreciable cost difference between the two proposals to justify inclusion in competitive range); *Novel Pharmaceutical, Inc.*, Comp. Gen. Dec. B-255374, 94-1 CPD ¶ 149 (proposal had no reasonable chance for award because it did not show that protester had the required experience or capability to perform the contract); *HITCO*, 68 Comp. Gen. 10 (B-232093), 88-2 CPD ¶ 337 (excluded proposal had numerous informational deficiencies rated "unacceptable"); *Rice Servs., Ltd.*, 68 Comp. Gen. 112 (B-232610), 88-2 CPD ¶ 514 (lack of required explanatory information after clarification request); *Optical Data Sys.— Tex., Inc.*, Comp. Gen. Dec. B-227755, 87-2 CPD ¶ 393 (protester's proposal not close to being acceptable and deficiencies not easily correctable); *Systems Integrated*, Comp. Gen. Dec. B-225055, 87-1 CPD ¶ 114 (protester's proposal priced 30 percent higher and offered no technical advantages); *Commission on Professional & Hosp. Activities*, Comp. Gen. Dec. B-228924, 87-2 CPD ¶ 637 (protester's proposal did not contain essential required information and was quite inferior); and *Regional Envtl. Consultants*, 66 Comp. Gen. 67 (B-223555), 86-2 CPD ¶ 476, *recons. denied*, 66 Comp. Gen. 388 (B-223555.2), 87-1 CPD ¶ 428 (protester's technical proposal significantly inferior even though scores quite similar).

3. Changes in the Competitive Range

The competitive range is dynamic rather than static. Thus, as an agency learns more about an offer, through communications, negotiations or reevaluation, the competitive range may be altered to reflect the current status of the offerors.

a. Removal from the Competitive Range

Procuring agencies are not bound by initial determinations to include offers within the competitive range, *Intown Properties, Inc.*, Comp. Gen. Dec. B-250232, 93-1 CPD ¶ 43. In this regard, FAR 15.306(c)(3) provides that an offer originally included in the competitive range may be removed, as follows:

> If the contracting officer, after complying with paragraph (d)(3) of this section, decides that an offeror's proposal should no longer be included in the competitive range, the proposal shall be eliminated from consideration for award. Written notice of this decision shall be provided to unsuccessful offerors in accordance with 15.503.

If it subsequently becomes clear that a proposal should not have been included in the competitive range or no longer belongs in that range, the offeror may be precluded from further written or oral discussions, *Shel-Ken Properties, Inc.*, Comp. Gen. Dec. B-277250, 97-2 CPD ¶ 79; *MAR Inc.*, Comp. Gen. Dec. B-246889, 92-1 CPD ¶ 367; *Scientific Management Assocs., Inc.*, Comp. Gen. Dec. B-238913, 90-2 CPD ¶ 27. In *Travel Co.*, Comp. Gen. Dec. B-249560.2, 93-1 CPD ¶ 76, the protester was initially found to be within the competitive range but after the agency requested and received supplementary and clarifying information, it determined that the protester was only at a minimally acceptable level and therefore no longer within the competitive range. See also *Herley Indus., Inc.*, Comp. Gen. Dec. B-237960, 90-1 CPD ¶ 364, *recons. denied*, 90-2 CPD ¶ 173, where the Comptroller General held it was proper to drop an offeror from the competitive range when there remained "significant deficiencies" after the first round of discussions; *BASIX Controls Sys. Corp.*, Comp. Gen. Dec. B-212668, 84-2 CPD ¶ 2, where the Comptroller General found a proposal properly removed from the competitive range without further discussions after tests revealed weaknesses not identified in the proposal; and *Westinghouse Elec. Corp.*, Comp. Gen. Dec. B-197768, 80-1 CPD ¶ 378, where the

Comptroller General agreed with the decision of the contracting agency to drop one of two proposals from the competitive range because the other proposal was so technically superior that the other proposal no longer stood a chance of acceptance.

An offer may be dropped from the competitive range once negotiations have begun without affording the offeror an opportunity to submit a revised offer. FAR 15.306(d)(4) stating:

> If, after discussions have begun, an offeror originally in the competitive range is no longer considered to be among the most highly rated offerors being considered for award, that offeror may be eliminated from the competitive range whether or not all material aspects of the proposal have been discussed, or whether or not the offeror has been afforded an opportunity to submit a proposal revision (see 15.307(a) and 15.503(a)(1)).

Conducting discussions with all offerors does not obligate the agency to conduct further discussions with all offerors or to allow all to submit proposal revisions, *All State Boiler Work, Inc.*, Comp. Gen. Dec. B-277362, 97-2 CPD ¶ 144; *ALM, Inc.*, Comp. Gen. Dec. B-217284, 85-1 CPD ¶ 433; *Informatics Gen. Corp.*, Comp. Gen. Dec. B-210709, 83-2 CPD ¶ 47, *recons. denied*, 83-2 CPD ¶ 580. In *Cotton & Co.*, Comp. Gen. Dec. B-210849, 83-2 CPD ¶ 451, the Comptroller General approved the agency's making a revised competitive range determination after receiving clarifications although the protester did not have an opportunity to submit a revised proposal. The removal was justified by the facts that (1) technical merit, rather than cost, was the primary evaluation factor; (2) the protester's lower rating was in large part a result of its low experience rating, a factor which could not be improved in a best and final offer; and (3) it did not appear that the protester could reduce its costs sufficiently to offset the other offerors' technical superiority. Similarly, in *A. T. Kearney, Inc.*, Comp. Gen. Dec. B-237731, 90-1 CPD ¶ 305, an offeror was properly dropped from the competitive range when additional cost realism analysis indicated that its probable costs were not as low as originally thought and its technical score was far below the other offeror. In *Systems Integrated*, Comp. Gen. Dec. B-225055, 87-1 CPD ¶ 114, it was held proper to drop one of two competitors with almost equal technical scores from the competitive range because its cost proposal was almost 30 percent higher. See also *DuVall Servs. Co.*, Comp. Gen. Dec. B-265698.2, 96-1 CPD ¶ 133, where the Comptroller General found proper an agency's decision to drop a protester from the revised competitive range because it did not have a reasonable chance for award. The protester's explanation and analysis of the staffing requirement during discussions indicated to the contracting officer that it would not be likely to perform well.

b. Addition or Reinstatement to the Competitive Range

Offerors excluded or removed from the competitive range are required to be given prompt "preaward" notice of exclusion, FAR 15.503(a)(1) and may request a "preaward debriefing," FAR 15.505. Following notice or debriefing the agency may discover that the offer was mistakenly excluded. Under such circumstances, it would be appropriate for the agency to include or reinstate the offer in the range. However, the inclusion would have to be based on the offer as originally submitted. FAR 15.307(a) prohibits the agency from accepting or considering revisions to offers once they are excluded:

> If an offeror's proposal is eliminated or otherwise removed from the competitive range, no further revisions to that offeror's proposal shall be accepted or considered.

A similar provision was in the pre-Rewrite FAR (FAR 15.603). While this provision affords the agency protection against having to cope with a flurry of proposal revisions and a never ending evaluation process, there may be circumstances where consideration of a revision would be desirable. It is difficult to see the harm in considering an unsolicited revision which did not require significant evaluation effort and did not result in unfair treatment of the other offerors.

VIII. NEGOTIATIONS

The procurement statutes require written or oral discussions with all offerors in the competitive range, but do not indicate the purpose of the discussion process, the matters to be discussed, or the procedures to be followed in conducting negotiations. The pre-Rewrite FAR was also silent on the purpose of discussions. In addition, under the pre-Rewrite rules, contracting agencies were significantly limited in the type of exchanges which could take place in the discussion process (former FAR 15.610). The Rewrite made a number of substantial changes in the rules for discussions and recognized that discussions means negotiation which includes bargaining with the view to "allowing the offeror to revise its proposal," 62 Fed. Reg. 51229 (1997). FAR 15.306(d) states:

> *Exchanges with offerors after establishment of the competitive range*. Negotiations are exchanges, in either a competitive or sole source environment, between the Government and offerors, that are undertaken with the intent of allowing the offeror to revise its proposal. These negotiations may include bargaining. Bargaining includes persuasion, alteration of assumptions and positions, give-and-take, and may apply to price, schedule, technical requirements, type of contract, or other terms of a proposed contract. When negotiations are conducted in a competitive acquisition, they take place after establishment of the competitive range and are called discussions.

This new description of the process of discussions with offerors in the competitive range encourages contracting officers to conduct in-depth negotiations with each offeror. However, if such negotiations alter the contract requirements or terms and conditions included in the RFP, all offerors still in the competition must be informed of the alteration by an amendment to the RFP, FAR 15.206(a) and (c). Furthermore, if the alteration is "so substantial as to exceed what prospective offerors reasonably could have anticipated," the contracting officer must cancel the solicitation and issue a new one, FAR 15.206(e).

A. Purpose of Negotiations

Among the stated purposes of the Rewrite were to increase the "scope of discussions," 62 Fed. Reg. 51225 (1997), and to "require a more robust exchange of information during discussions," 62 Fed. Reg. 51229 (1997). Implementing the policy favoring enhanced discussions, FAR 15.306(d)(2) states that the primary purpose of negotiations is to obtain best value for the Government:

> The primary objective of discussions is to maximize the Government's ability to obtain best value, based on the requirement and the evaluation factors set forth in the solicitation.

This is consistent with the view expressed by the Comptroller General that discussions should be conducted "to the end that competition is maximized and the Government is assured of receiving the most favorable contract," 51

Comp. Gen. 621 (B-173677) (1972). See also 52 Comp. Gen. 466 (B-177008) (1973), where the Comptroller General stated at 468:

> Since one of the primary purposes of conducting negotiations with offerors is to raise to an acceptable status those proposals which are capable of being made acceptable, and thereby increase competition for the procurement, we believe it is incumbent upon Government negotiators to be as specific as practical considerations will permit in advising offerors of the corrections required in their proposals.

Although there is no express statement requiring the agencies to "assist" an offeror in improving an offer, other changes in the FAR support the propriety of appropriately assisting an offeror to improve its offer. Under the pre-Rewrite rules, agencies were prohibited from "helping an offeror" to improve its proposal under certain conditions (former FAR 15.610(d)). Such coaching was erroneously labeled as "technical leveling." However, this prohibition was removed in the Rewrite. Thus, it would appear that assistance would be appropriate if all offerors are treated fairly, the rules against improper disclosure of source selection information are observed, and the assistance is not a response to an offeror's incompetence. Care should be taken so that the assistance does not result in a superior offer from an offeror with inferior capabilities, *Raytheon Ocean Sys. Co.*, Comp. Gen. Dec. B-218620.2, 86-1 CPD ¶ 134. Award to an incapable or less capable offeror would not be in the Government's interest.

B. Matters for Negotiation

Do not auction

FAR 15.306(d)(3) makes it clear that *all* matters relating to an offer are proper subjects for negotiation, providing:

> The contracting officer shall, subject to paragraphs (d)(4) and (e) of this section and 15.307(a), indicate to, or discuss with, each offeror still being considered for award, significant weaknesses, deficiencies, and other aspects of its proposal (such as, cost, price, technical approach, past performance, and terms and conditions) that could, in the opinion of the contracting officer, be altered or explained to enhance materially the proposal's potential for award. The scope and extent of discussions are a matter of contracting officer judgment. In discussing other aspects of the proposal, the Government may, in situations where the solicitation stated that evaluation credit would be given for technical solutions exceeding any mandatory minimums, negotiate with offerors for increased performance beyond any mandatory minimums, and the Government may suggest to offerors that

have exceeded any mandatory minimums (in ways that are not integral to the design), that their proposals would be more competitive if the excesses were removed and the offered price decreased.

1. *Deficiencies and Weaknesses*

The terms "deficiency" and "weakness" have been at the center of much confusion in the discussion process. Under the pre-Rewrite FAR, "deficiency" was defined in FAR 15.601, and contracting officers were directed to "advise the offeror of deficiencies" in FAR 15.610(c)(2), but no statement requiring notice of "weaknesses" was present. The only reference to "weaknesses" was in a provision directing the contracting officer not to engage in "technical leveling (i.e., helping an offeror to bring its proposal up to the level of other proposals . . . by pointing out weaknesses," FAR 15.610(d). This language was generally interpreted as not requiring disclosure of areas in which the offer was acceptable but contained an approach that was relatively less desirable than the approach proposed by another offeror, *Data Sys. Analysts, Inc.*, Comp. Gen. Dec. B-255684, 94-1 CPD ¶ 209. In *Fairchild Space & Defense Corp.*, Comp. Gen. Dec. B-243716, 91-2 CPD ¶ 190, the Comptroller General stated:

> [T]here is no requirement on the part of an agency to identify relative weaknesses in a proposal which is technically acceptable, but presents a relatively less desirable approach than others received.

Nevertheless, the procuring agencies and the Comptroller General tended to use the terms "deficiency" and "weakness" interchangeably when not dealing with comparisons to other offers. See, for example, *Crowley Maritime Salvage*, Comp. Gen. Dec. B-234555, 89-1 CPD ¶ 555. In such cases, the distinction between "deficiencies" and "weaknesses" sometimes led contracting officers to omit necessary items from the discussions and the rule evolved that an agency could not avoid discussing a correctable element in a proposal by calling it a weakness. See, for example, *RGI, Inc. v. Department of the Navy*, GSBCA 11348-P, 92-1 BCA ¶ 24,737, where the board found that inadequate discussions had been held where the agency omitted discussion of "weaknesses" but could not adequately distinguish between "deficiencies" and "weaknesses" in defending against the protest. Similarly, in *Eldyne, Inc.*, Comp. Gen. Dec. B-250158, 93-1 CPD ¶ 430. The Comptroller General found inadequate discussions where the contracting officer failed to discuss areas of an offeror's technical and management proposals where it had received low scores because of lack of detail in the proposal. The Comptroller General explained this ruling in *Department of the Navy — Recons.*, Comp. Gen. Dec. B-250158.4, 93-1 CD ¶ 422, as follows:

> The Navy's contention that contracting officers are never required to discuss aspects of a proposal that do not make it unacceptable is simply wrong. As we stated in our decision sustaining Eldyne's protest, discussions conducted with offerors in the competitive range must be meaningful. FAR 15.610; *Jaycor*, B-240029.2 et al., Oct. 31, 1990, 90-2 CPD ¶ 354. The FAR explicitly recognizes that, in conducting meaningful discussions, a contracting officer must use his or her judgment based on the facts of each acquisition (except that deficiencies and other matters listed in FAR 15.610(c) must always be discussed). Substitution of the mechanical approach suggested by the Navy for this exercise of judgment can, as it did in this case, frustrate the fundamental requirement of the Competition in Contracting Act of 1984 (CICA), 41 U.S.C. § 253b(d)(2) (1988), for meaningful discussions. As reflected in FAR 15.610, CICA effectively requires agencies to point out weaknesses, deficiencies or excesses in proposals necessary for an offeror to have a reasonable chance of being selected for award, which is, after all, the basis for including a proposal in the competitive range in the first place. See FAR 15.609(a); *Price Waterhouse*, B-222562, Aug. 18, 1986, 86-2 CPD ¶ 190.
>
> * * *
>
> Here, Eldyne was not advised during discussions of any concerns about its technical proposal except in regard to its initial proposal of an individual who subsequently became unavailable for employment. Yet, each evaluator supported his individual determination to significantly downgrade Eldyne's technical evaluation score (primarily for technical approach, but also for management approach) on the basis of the proposal's lack of detail. Our review of the record showed that this lack of detail raised concerns regarding Eldyne's level of understanding and ability to address certain technical problems and, in at least one management area, whether or not Eldyne's "vague" approach met the requirements.
>
> Regardless of the agency's description of its concerns with Eldyne's proposal as constituting a weakness rather than a deficiency, the record shows that Eldyne's proposal was significantly downgraded in these areas of its proposal. We believe the agency was required to discuss the matter with Eldyne; the firm should have been allowed the opportunity to amplify its approach to confirm its understanding of the RFP's requirements and satisfy the agency's serious concerns.

Following this decision, the Comptroller General stated that agencies "must point out weaknesses that, unless corrected, would prevent an offeror from having a reasonable chance for award," *Gutierrez-Palmenberg, Inc.*, Comp. Gen. Dec. B-255797.3, 94-2 CPD ¶ 158; *Docusort, Inc.*, Comp. Gen. Dec. B-254852, 94-1 CPD ¶ 38. See also *Alliant Techsystems, Inc.*, Comp. Gen. Dec. B-260215.4, 95-2 CPD ¶ 79, finding that the agency could not avoid its obligation to conduct discussions by labeling significant weaknesses as something less than a deficiency.

The FAR Part 15 Rewrite made a number of important changes in this area designed to eliminate some of this confusion. First, FAR 15.301 defines *both* terms:

> "Deficiency," as used in this subpart, is a material failure of a proposal to meet a Government requirement or a combination of significant weaknesses in a proposal that increases the risk of unsuccessful contract performance to an unacceptable level.
>
> "Weakness," as used in this subpart, is a flaw in the proposal that increases the risk of unsuccessful contract performance. A "significant weakness" in the proposal is a flaw that appreciably increases the risk of unsuccessful contract performance.

More importantly, FAR 15.306(d)(3) requires the disclosure in negotiations of not only "deficiencies" but also "significant weaknesses" and "other aspects of its proposal that could . . . be altered or explained to enhance materially the proposal's potential for award." In addition, the prohibition against "technical leveling" was removed. Coupled with the broad endorsement of bargaining in FAR 15.306(d) these changes should make it clear that concerns about "leveling" and "coaching" offerors should not result in limiting negotiations.

While the changes made by the Rewrite should considerably reduce the confusion and result in more effective negotiations, the remaining distinction between "deficiencies" and "weaknesses" is problematic. Attempting to draw distinctions between these terms and to determine when a "weakness" is "significant," would be difficult, at best, and of questionable benefit. Thus, contracting officers should fully explore the offers which are in the competitive range and conduct meaningful negotiations on all elements of the proposal which could be altered to improve the chance of the offeror winning the competition.

2. Information

In many cases, there is uncertainty as to exactly what performance is being offered. This may result from an offeror's failure to provide required information or from questions as to the meaning of terms in the offer. To the extent that these matters were not cleared up in pre-competitive range communications, they must be addressed in the negotiation. When this informational inadequacy results from a lack of clarity in the RFP, discussion of the matter is required. In *Logistic Sys. Inc.*, 59 Comp. Gen. 548 (B-196254), 80-1 CPD ¶ 442, *recons. denied*, 80-2 CPD ¶ 313, the Comptroller General stated at 553:

> Where, as here, a proposal in the competitive range is informationally inadequate so that the agency evaluators cannot determine the extent of the offeror's compliance with its requirements, the agency should use the discussion process to attempt to ascertain exactly what the offeror is proposing. In this connection, we have recognized that where a solicitation specifically calls for certain information, the agency should not be required to remind the offeror to furnish the necessary information with its final proposal. *Value Engineering Company*, Comp. Gen. Dec. B-182421, July 3, 1975, 75-2 CPD ¶ 10. But here the solicitation was not so specific in calling for information on the offeror's personnel and laboratory facilities.

See also *Sperry Corp.*, 65 Comp. Gen. 195 (B-220521), 86-1 CPD ¶ 28, where discussions of price alone were held improper because there were correctable informational deficiencies in lower priced offers. Since it is frequently difficult to determine whether an informational deficiency is due to lack of clear guidance in the RFP, contracting officers should normally point out such deficiencies during discussions.

Agencies have also been required to resolve uncertainties as to whether an offeror is submitting an alternate proposal. See *Peirce-Phelps, Inc.*, Comp. Gen. Dec. B-238520.2, 91-1 CPD ¶ 385, where the Comptroller General stated:

> Where there are uncertainties with respect to proposals, attempts should be made to resolve the problem with meaningful discussions which point out the uncertainties and give the offeror an opportunity to resolve them. . . . The requirement for meaningful discussions extends to alternate, acceptable proposals within the competitive range. *San/Bar Corp.*, B-219644.3, Feb. 21, 1986, 86-1 CPD ¶ 183.

See also *Analytical Servs., Inc.*, Comp. Gen. Dec. B-202473, 82-1 CPD ¶ 214, *recons. denied*, 82-2 CPD ¶ 502, in which discussions were found inadequate where the protester was not informed that the agency could not ascertain the extent to which research associate services were included in the proposal's indirect cost pool, and consequently could not accurately compare the protester's proposed costs with those of other offerors. In *American Combustion Indus*, Comp. Gen. Dec. B-275057.2, 97-1 CPD ¶ 105, the Comptroller General held that the agency improperly downgraded the protester when the agency, without discussing the matter with the protester, assumed that one of the protester's personnel would initially substitute for the proposed project manager. In *Peter N.G. Schwartz Companies Judiciary Square Ltd.*, Comp. Gen. Dec. B-239007.3, 90-2 CPD ¶ 353, *aff'd*, Civ. Action No. 90-2951 (D.D.C. 1991), the Comptroller General held that it was improper to downgrade a proposal based on a lack of clarity of the role of certain employees when the matter could have been cleared up through discussions. Similarly, in *ST Aerospace Engines Pte. Ltd.*, Comp. Gen. Dec. B-275725, 97-1 CPD ¶ 161, the Comptroller General held that the agency improperly downgraded the protester's proposal based on the protester's affiliate company's poor past performance when the agency should have verified the relationship between the two companies during discussions with the firm. The Comptroller General has also held that a call for best and final offers alone does not constitute meaningful discussions when there are still unresolved uncertainties concerning the proposals, *Decision Sciences Corp.*, 60 Comp. Gen. 36 (B-196100), 80-1 CPD ¶ 357.

3. Failure to Comply With Requirements

The purpose of discussions is to disclose proposal deficiencies to offerors in such a way as to permit correction. This results in better proposals for the Government and maximizes competition. In *Essex Electro Eng'rs, Inc.*, Comp. Gen. Dec. B-211053.2, 84-1 CPD ¶ 74, the Comptroller General stated that "[t]he essence of meaningful discussions is that the agency point out the offeror's deficiencies and permit it to revise its proposal to attempt to correct those deficiencies." See *Huff & Huff Serv. Corp.*, Comp. Gen. Dec. B-235419, 89-2 CPD ¶ 55, stating:

> The contracting officer is required to advise an offeror of deficiencies in its proposal so that the offeror is given an opportunity to satisfy the government's requirements. . . . In evaluating whether there has been sufficient disclosure of deficiencies, the focus is not on whether the agency described

the deficiencies in such detail that there could be no doubt as to their identification and nature, but whether the agency imparted sufficient information to the offeror to afford it a fair and reasonable opportunity in the context of the procurement to identify and correct the deficiencies in its proposal. *Eagan, McAllister Assocs., Inc.*, B-231983, Oct. 28, 1988, 88-2 CPD ¶ 405. The degree of specificity necessary in the disclosure of deficiencies to meet the requirement for meaningful discussions varies with the context of individual procurements. Where certain information is specifically requested in the solicitation, an agency is not necessarily required to remind an offeror to submit that information with its final offer. *Id.* Further, we will not disturb the award of a contract to another offeror even where the contracting agency improperly fails to point out a deficiency to the protester during discussions in the absence of material prejudice to the protester. *Checchi & Co.*, 56 Comp. Gen. 473 (1977), 77-1 CPD ¶ 232.

Deficiencies can include such matters as failures to meet specifications, failures to submit information, or questionable technical or management approaches. Such matters may raise doubts concerning the possibility of accurate evaluation of the proposal or may indicate that it is or may be unacceptable. Thus, agencies must disclose the principal deficiencies that led to the low score during the evaluation of the proposal, *Columbia Research Corp.*, Comp. Gen. Dec. B-247631, 92-1 CPD ¶ 539. A failure to hold meaningful discussions was found where several offerors were not told during discussions that various proposed personnel were considered unqualified, 52 Comp. Gen. 466 (B-177008) (1973).

4. Cost and Price Negotiations

Under the pre-Rewrite FAR, there was a hesitancy on the part of some agencies to conduct meaningful cost or price negotiations. This was caused partly by the admonition in pre-Rewrite FAR 15.610(e)(2) that the contracting officer not use:

Auction techniques, such as —

(i) Indicating to an offeror a cost or price that it must meet to obtain further consideration;

(ii) Advising an offeror of its price standing relative to another offeror (however, it is permissible to inform an offeror that its cost or price is considered by the Government to be too high or unrealistic); and

(iii) Otherwise furnishing information about other offerors' prices.

The reference to auction techniques and subsections (i) and (ii) were removed in the Rewrite and replaced with the following language in FAR 15.306(e):

> Government personnel engaged in the acquisition shall not engage in conduct that —
>
> (3) Reveals an offeror's price without that offeror's permission. However, the contracting officer may inform an offeror that its price is considered by the Government to be too high, or too low, and reveal the results of the analysis supporting that conclusion. It is also permissible, at the Government's discretion, to indicate to all offerors the cost or price that the Government's price analysis, market research, and other reviews have identified as reasonable (41 U.S.C. 423(h)(1)(2)).

In addition FAR 15.306(d)(3) includes cost and price among examples of "other aspects of [a] proposal" which might be enhanced through negotiations. Thus, the FAR now permits full price negotiation with each offeror in the competitive range. See *Price Waterhouse*, 65 Comp. Gen. 205 (B-220049), 86-1 CPD ¶ 54, where the Comptroller General sustained a protest because the agency failed to inform the protester during discussions that its estimated level of effort and proposed price were considered unreasonably high.

Even when auctioning was prohibited, the practice was narrowly defined as occurring when there was "direct price bidding between two competing offerors," *Washington School of Psychiatry*, Comp. Gen. Dec. B-192756, 79-1 CPD ¶ 178. See also 52 Comp. Gen. 425 (B-176334) (1973); and *General Eng'g Serv., Inc.*, Comp. Gen. Dec. B-242618.2, 92-1 CPD ¶ 266. Since the language prohibiting auctions was removed, it would not be improper for the agency to conduct an auction provided that it received the permission of all offerors to have their prices disclosed, FAR 15.306(e)(3). Whether such permission could be obtained and whether it would be wise to conduct auctions are another matter.

Under the pre-Rewrite rules, the Comptroller General upheld the propriety of price discussions in which the agency has revealed its own conception of price reasonableness to all offerors. See, e.g., *M.W. Kellogg Co./Siciliana Appalti Costruzioni, S.p.A., J.V. v. United States*, 10 Cl. Ct. 17 (1986), disclosing the amount of funds available for the project; *Bethlehem Steel*

Corp., Baltimore Marine Div., Comp. Gen. Dec. B-231923, 88-2 CPD ¶ 438, disclosing current contract prices. In *Ikard Mfg. Co.*, 63 Comp. Gen. 239 (B-213891), 84-1 CPD ¶ 266, the contracting officer reopened negotiations after both best and final offers contained prices considered too high and told both offerors that the Army's negotiating goal was a $1,740 unit price. The Comptroller General indicated that this procedure was proper because the point of the auction prohibition was to prevent direct price bidding between offerors, not to prevent the Government from negotiating price when it had not otherwise disclosed the competitive standing of offerors. See also *Printz Reinigung GmbH*, Comp. Gen. Dec. B-241510, 91-1 CPD ¶ 143, where the Comptroller General considered the disclosure of a desired price range to be a permissible negotiation tool for achieving a fair and reasonable price.

The Government may have different price objectives for each offer. See *Racal Guardata, Inc.*, 71 Comp. Gen. 218 (B-245139.2), 92-1 CPD ¶ 159, where the Comptroller General reasoned that no unfairness occurred where the price objectives were based on the technical proposals of each competitor and were not stated as mandatory figures. In *Griggs & Assocs., Inc.*, Comp. Gen. Dec. B-205266, 82-1 CPD ¶ 458, the Comptroller General upheld the agency's disclosure of individual cost objectives developed for each offeror's proposal based on separate appraisals of each offeror's costs as a valid basis for negotiations. In *Newport News and Drydock Co.*, Comp. Gen. Dec. B-254969, 94-1 CPD ¶ 198, the Comptroller General stated:

> NNS and Ingalls contend that the agency improperly coached NASSCO by providing that firm during written discussions with the government estimate, including both the overall estimated overrun ([deleted]) and the estimate in critical areas (*e.g.*, "your proposed manhours for SWBS groups 100 and 500 are unrealistically low by approximately 40%, and 50% respectively"), such that NASSCO knew by how much it had to increase its price and profit in order to avoid having its price be found unrealistically low. NNS and Ingalls note that, in contrast, NAVSEA never advised them of the detailed government estimate for their proposals.
>
> A contracting agency properly may disclose a price objective to an offeror as a negotiation tool for reaching an agreement as to a fair and reasonable price, *Racal Guardata, Inc.*, 71 Comp. Gen. 219 (1992), 92-1 CPD ¶ 159, although where the agency discloses the Government estimate to only some offerors it runs the risk that the discussions will be rendered unfair and prejudicial to the other offerors. *Cf. Bank Street College of Education*, 63 Comp. Gen. 393 (1984), 84-1 CPD ¶ 607 (not improper to discuss govern-

ment cost estimate with awardee but not protester where only the awardee's proposed costs were above the government estimate).

Here, even if NNS and Ingalls are correct that it was improper to inform only NASSCO of the detailed government estimate, had the agency provided NNS and Ingalls with the equivalent information for their proposals, the outcome would have been the same. In this regard, the benefit NASSCO arguably obtained from the specific information it received was being able — unlike NNS and Ingalls — roughly to calculate the price at which its proposal would be found unrealistically low. Based on this figure, it was able to modify (*i.e.*, increase) its BAFO target price precisely enough that the agency would not find the price unreasonably low and thus discard that price and use the higher "Estimated Final Price to the Government" in evaluating NASSCO's proposal. If the protesters had been furnished equivalent information, it would have provided them with the same benefit — it would have allowed them roughly to calculate the price below which their proposals would be deemed unrealistically low. Since (the record shows) the lowest realistic prices for the protesters under the original government estimate were higher than NASSCO's BAFO price (because both protesters' costs of performance were inherently higher than NASSCO's), neither would have moved into line for award basing their BAFO prices on this calculation. *See Racal Guardata, Inc.*, *supra* (where alleged improper discussions did not prejudice the protester, protest will not be sustained).

C. Conduct of Negotiations

Contracting agencies have broad discretion in conducting negotiations. See FAR 15.306(d)(3) stating that "the scope and extent of discussions are a matter of contracting officer judgment." See also *Dimensions Travel Co.*, Comp. Gen. Dec. B-224214, 87-1 CPD ¶ 52 (agency is given broad discretion in determining content of discussions because it is most familiar with its needs); and *Pioneer Contract Servs., Inc.*, Comp. Gen. Dec. B-197245, 81-1 CPD ¶ 107, where the Comptroller General stated:

> As to the exact content and extent of the discussions, we have held that this is essentially a matter of judgment primarily for decision by the agency and not subject to question by our Office unless the judgment is clearly arbitrary.

Given broad discretion

However, within this discretion, negotiations must be meaningful and must be conducted in a way that offerors are treated fairly. See 51 Comp. Gen. 621 (B-173677) (1972); and *Wetlands Research Assocs., Inc.*, Comp. Gen.

Dec. B-246342, 92-1 CPD ¶ 251. The "burden to conduct meaningful discussions is on the contracting officer and not on individual offerors," *Teledyne Lewisburg Okl. Aerotronics, Inc.*, Comp. Gen. Dec. B-183704, 75-2 CPD ¶ 228. In evaluating whether there has been sufficient disclosure of deficiencies, the primary focus is on whether there has been a reasonable communication of specific deficiencies rather than requiring any specific form of communication. Thus, discussions must fairly and reasonably lead an offeror into areas of its offer requiring change or amplification, *Creative Management Technology, Inc.*, Comp. Gen. Dec. B-266299, 96-1 CPD ¶ 61; *Research Analysis & Maintenance, Inc.*, Comp. Gen. Dec. B-242836.4, 91-2 CPD ¶ 387.

1. Meaningful Negotiations

The FAR Rewrite emphasizes that negotiations with each offeror in the competitive range includes bargaining to obtain the best offer. Thus, FAR 15.306(d)(3) permits bargaining about the optimum technical solution that can be offered by each offeror as well as price and the terms and conditions of the contract. This new guidance encourages agencies to conduct in-depth negotiations and may increase the scope of the contracting officer's obligation to conduct meaningful negotiations.

Prior to the FAR Rewrite the emphasis was on *the minimum standards* that a contracting officer had to meet to conduct meaningful negotiations. In *Boeing Sikorsky Aircraft Support*, Comp. Gen. Dec. B-277263.3, 97-2 CPD ¶ 91, the Comptroller General made the following observations concerning meaningful negotiations:

> Discussions cannot be meaningful unless they lead an offeror into those aspects of its proposal that must be addressed in order for it to have a reasonable chance of being selected for award, and afford an offeror an opportunity to revise its proposal to satisfy the government's requirements. *Global Indus., Inc.*, B-270592.2 et al, Mar. 29, 1996, 96-2 CPD ¶ 85 at 4-5; *Stone & Webster Eng'g Corp.*, B-255286.2, Apr. 12, 1994, 94-1 CPD ¶ 306 at 10-11. An agency may not consciously coerce or mislead an offeror during discussions (see *Eagle Tech., Inc.*, B-236255, Nov. 16, 1989, 89-2 CPD ¶ 468 at 3-4), nor may it inadvertently mislead an offeror through the framing of discussion questions into responding in a manner that does not address the agency's concerns. *Peckham Vocational Indus., Inc.*, B-257100, Aug. 26, 1994, 94-2 CPD ¶ 81 at 6.

a. Specific Identification

The Comptroller General has stated that "it is incumbent upon Government negotiators to be as specific as practical considerations will permit in advising offerors of the corrections required in their proposals," 52 Comp. Gen. 466 (B-177008) (1973). Thus, at a minimum, discussions must lead the offeror "into the areas of [its] proposal which require amplification," *Price Waterhouse*, Comp. Gen. Dec. B-222562, 86-2 CPD ¶ 190. In *International Underwriters, Inc.*, Comp. Gen. Dec. B-198109, 80-2 CPD ¶ 410, the deficiency in question, lack of details of the offeror's experience, was held to be "particularly suitable to cure through discussions." The protest was granted because the agency had not informed the offeror that it was unable to contact the offeror's references. Similarly, inadequate discussions were found in *Sperry Corp.*, GSBCA 8208-P, 86-1 BCA ¶ 18,704, *recons. denied*, 86-2 BCA ¶ 18,821, where the agency failed to reveal that it had received negative information from users of the offeror's equipment. In *Delta Data Sys. Corp. v. Webster*, 744 F.2d 197, 240 App. D.C. 182 (D.C. Cir. 1984), the court found a failure to conduct meaningful discussions when the agency did not inform the offeror that the agency had concluded that the proposal evidenced insufficient financing for the contract. In *General Elec. Co. v. Seamans*, 340 F. Supp. 636 (D.D.C. 1972), inadequate discussions were found where the offeror was not informed that its price was considered unrealistically low.

The Comptroller General has also stated that, in general, once discussions are opened, the agency is required to point out all deficiencies in the offeror's proposal, not merely selected areas, *Checchi & Co.*, 56 Comp. Gen. 473 (B-187982), 77-1 CPD ¶ 232; *TM Sys., Inc.*, Comp. Gen. Dec. B-228220, 87-2 CPD ¶ 573. Thus, partial discussions have also been found inadequate. For example, in *Tracor Marine, Inc.*, Comp. Gen. Dec. B-207285, 83-1 CPD ¶ 604, it was found improper to disclose to the offeror that its proposed schedule was unrealistic, while disclosing only one out of five bases for this conclusion. Offerors should not be left with the impression that there are no remaining problem areas. See *E-Systems, Inc.*, Comp. Gen. Dec. B-191346, 79-1 CPD ¶ 192, where the Comptroller General stated:

> We have regarded as deficient negotiations which led an offeror reasonably to believe that a problem area had been cleared up during oral discussions because of the lack of specific identification of a proposal weakness.

In *Dynalectron Corp.*, Comp. Gen. Dec. B-193604, 79-2 CPD ¶ 50, the Comptroller General found that Dynalectron had not been sufficiently alerted to remaining deficiencies in its proposal when, after revisions had been made, it was shown a list of five deficiencies with the words "cleared by amendment" written after the first three deficiencies. Dynalectron misinterpreted this to mean these deficiencies had been cleared up by its revisions and made no further changes in these areas.

b. Lack of Identification Excused

In a number of cases, the Comptroller General has found that factors surrounding a procurement may excuse the agency from specifically identifying areas where offers should be amplified or changed. However, it would seem that agencies should err on the side of greater communication rather than relying on these rulings to win a protest.

A lack of specific identification will not be fatal if the offeror has been given sufficient information to provide notice of the deficiency. In *Broomall Indus., Inc.*, Comp. Gen. Dec. B-193166, 79-1 CPD ¶ 467, the Comptroller General found that a broad request that the offeror "discuss in detail" one aspect of the required work was sufficient to disclose that the proposal was deficient in that area. The Comptroller General stated:

> We have held that requests for clarification or amplification or other statements made during discussions which lead offerors into areas of their proposals that are unclear are sufficient to alert offerors to deficiencies in their proposals. *Serv-Air, Inc.*, B-189884, September 25, 1978, 78-2 CPD ¶ 223; *Houston Films, Inc.*, B-184402, December 22, 1975, 75-2 CPD ¶ 404.

Similarly, where the agency was concerned about the analytic model used by the protester, and questioned the protester's low proposed level of effort which was primarily attributable to the model, this was enough to alert the protester of the real concern, *CRC Sys., Inc.*, Comp. Gen. Dec. B-207847, 83-1 CPD ¶ 462. See also *Richard S. Carson & Assocs., Inc.*, GSBCA 9411-P, 88-2 BCA ¶ 20,778, finding that the substance of letters from the agency sufficiently identified the deficiencies, and *Okaw Indus., Inc.*, Comp. Gen. Dec. B-197306, 80-2 CPD ¶ 228, holding that an agency's request for samples was reasonable notice of deficiencies and hence was a meaningful discussion. Discussions were also found sufficient where the list of questions was "reasonably related" to deficiencies identified by the agency in evaluating the proposal, *Earth Technology Corp.*, Comp. Gen.

Dec. B-230980, 88-2 CPD ¶ 113; *WASSKA Technical Sys. & Research Co.*, Comp. Gen. Dec. B-189573, 79-2 CPD ¶ 110.

Although meaningful discussions require disclosure of deficiencies, there is considerable discretion in deciding which deficiencies are of sufficient significance to warrant disclosure and discussion. Thus, the Comptroller General has frequently stated that an agency "is under no obligation to discuss every aspect of the proposal which received less than the maximum score," *ADP Network Servs., Inc.*, Comp. Gen. Dec. B-200675, 81-1 CPD ¶ 157; *Communications Int'l, Inc.*, Comp. Gen. Dec. B-246076, 92-1 CPD ¶ 194. See also *SEAIR Transport Servs.*, Inc., Comp. Gen. Dec. B-274436, 96-2 CPD ¶ 224, where the Comptroller General held that the protester was not entitled to discussions which would essentially have been conducted solely to permit it to achieve a perfect score in all areas. In *TRW, Inc.*, Comp. Gen. Dec. B-243450.2, 91-2 CPD ¶ 160, the Comptroller General stated this rule very liberally holding that the agency was required to disclose deficiencies in subfactors only when the subfactor had received a score of less than four on a ten point rating scale. This ruling was based on the fact that the agency defined a score of four as "satisfactory." Compare *Technical & Management Servs. Corp.*, Comp. Gen. Dec. B-242836.3, 91-2 CPD ¶ 101, where the protester was rated unacceptable in several subcategories, but received acceptable ratings in every category because high scores in other subcategories raised the averages. The Comptroller General held that the agency must discuss every rating that is less than acceptable, and hence was required to discuss these inadequate ratings. See also *Software Eng'g, Inc.*, Comp. Gen. Dec. B-272820, 96-2 CPD ¶ 193 (agency not required to pinpoint instances that result from the offeror's own lack of diligence, such as typographical errors in the proposal); and *TRI-COR Indus., Inc.*, Comp. Gen. Dec. B-259034.2, 95-1 CPD ¶ 143 (agency not required to pinpoint each specific instance in which the protester's proposal exhibited a lack of technical understanding).

The Comptroller General has held that an agency may limit discussions of a deficiency when the deficient score relates to the offeror's general understanding of the technical aspects of the work as demonstrated by its submission of a solution to a sample task, *Syscon Servs., Inc.*, 68 Comp. Gen. 698 (B-235647), 89-2 CPD ¶ 258. In *Technology Applications, Inc.*, Comp. Gen. Dec. B-238259, 90-1 CPD ¶ 451, the Comptroller General stated:

> Where an offeror's responses to sample tasks are used to test its understanding of the technical requirements of a contemplated contract, as opposed to being used to evaluate the adequacy of its technical approach to the contract work, an agency need not specify during discussions all identified deficiencies in the offeror's approach to the tasks.

The Comptroller General reasoned that if the purpose of the task is to determine whether the offeror has the background and understanding to identify and resolve the technical issues that would arise during contract performance, to require the agency to discuss weak sample task results would defeat the purpose of using the response to a sample task to determine the offeror's understanding of the work. See also *NDI Eng'g Co.*, Comp. Gen. Dec. B-245796, 92-1 CPD ¶ 113, where the Comptroller General upheld the agency's decision not to discuss low scores on responses to a sample task when the responses were used to determine the offerors' understanding of the contract work.

2. Fairness

Fair treatment of offerors is a cornerstone of effective competition. Thus, assuring that all offerors are treated fairly is a major concern when conducting negotiations. In 51 Comp. Gen. 621 (B-173677) (1972), the Comptroller General stated at 622:

> [T]he statute [now 10 U.S.C. § 2305(b)(4)(A)] should not be interpreted in a manner which discriminates against or gives preferential treatment to any competitor. Any discussion with competing offerors raises the question as to how to avoid unfairness and unequal treatment.

Fairness requires that offerors be treated equally and that the agency not engage in prohibited conduct.

a. Equal Treatment

One of the most common examples of unequal treatment is where the agency gives information to one or more offerors but fails to provide the same information to other offerors who might be able to use it to their advantage. See, for example, *SeaSpace*, 70 Comp. Gen. 268 (B-241564), 91-1 CPD ¶ 179, where the agency improperly suggested that one offeror use a more powerful computer that had recently come on the market without providing the same suggestion to other offerors. Similarly, in *Cylink Corp.*, Comp. Gen. Dec. B-242304, 91-1 CPD ¶ 384, it was improper to inform only one competitor that the agency would accept performance that seemed to be out of compliance with the specifications.

Fairness also requires the agency to ensure that offerors compete on an equal basis. The Comptroller General held in *Perkin-Elmer Corp.*, Comp. Gen. Dec. B-204082, 82-1 CPD ¶ 315, that, where the specifications are ambiguous and it becomes clear during discussions that offerors are proposing on different bases, the agency has a duty to conduct further discussions to assure competition on the same basis. In *MSI, Div. of Bionetics Corp.*, Comp. Gen. Dec. B-233090, 89-1 CPD ¶ 185, discussions were required where the proposals indicated that the offerors did not understand the quantity of work required. Unfairness was found in *EMS Dev. Corp.*, 70 Comp. Gen. 459 (B-242484), 91-1 CPD ¶ 427, *recons. denied*, 91-2 CPD ¶ 131, where an agency provided clarifications of the solicitation requirements to an offeror under a sole source solicitation, but did not provide the same clarifications to the protester when the solicitation was resolicited on a competitive basis. Unfairness was also found where the agency answered questions of one offeror but disclosed answers without the corresponding questions to the other offerors, *Grumman Data Sys. Corp. v. Stone*, 37 CCF ¶ 76,179 (D.D.C. 1991). In *Morrison Knudsen Corp.*, Comp. Gen. Dec. B-270703, 96-2 CPD ¶ 86, the Comptroller General held that an agency conducted unequal discussions when it did not adequately inform the protester that it needed to list the equipment that would be used, but explicitly told the awardee that it should list the equipment it planned to use. Competition on an unequal basis was also found where the agency inaccurately informed all offerors how much higher their proposed costs were than the Government estimate and the information given to the protester involved a significantly larger percentage error than the mistaken figures provided to other offerors, *Northwest Regional Educ. Lab.*, Comp. Gen. Dec. B-213464, 84-1 CPD ¶ 357, and where the agency told only one offeror that it had decided to delete a significant portion of the work, *Management Sys. Designers, Inc.*, Comp. Gen. Dec. B-244383.4, 91-2 CPD ¶ 518.

While fairness requires equal treatment of offerors with similar deficiencies, it does not require the agency to spend an equal amount of time with all offerors, or to discuss the same areas. See FAR 15.306(d)(1):

> Discussions are tailored to each offeror's proposal, and shall be conducted by the contracting officer with each offeror within the competitive range.

In *Trident Sys., Inc.*, Comp. Gen. Dec. B-243101, 91-1 CPD ¶ 604, the Comptroller General made the following observations concerning tailoring the negotiations:

> [I]nsofar as Trident alleges the Navy did not hold equal discussions because the offerors were not asked the same questions, the only additional question Trident was asked concerned its relationship with its subcontractor; SPA was not asked this question because SPA did not propose to use a subcontractor. In any case, in order for discussions to be meaningful, contracting agencies must furnish information to all offerors in the competitive range as to the areas in which their proposals are believed to be deficient so that the offerors have a chance to revise their proposals to fully satisfy the agency requirements. *Pan Am World Servs., Inc.*; *Base Maintenance Support Group; Holmes & Narver Servs, Inc.*, B-231840 et al., Nov. 7, 1988, 88-2 CPD ¶ 446. In other words, since the number and type of proposal deficiencies will vary among offerors the agency should tailor the discussions for each offeror, based on the offerors' evaluated deficiencies. *Holmes & Narver, Inc.*, B-239469.2; B-239469.3, Sept. 14, 1990, 90-2 CPD ¶ 210.

See also *CBIS Fed. Inc.*, 71 Comp. Gen. 319 (B-245844.2), 92-1 CPD ¶ 308 (more extensive discussions with one offeror was proper because that offeror's proposal contained more deficiencies); *Holmes and Narver, Inc.*, Comp. Gen. Dec. B-239469.2, 90-2 CPD ¶ 210 (issues to be discussed vary among proposals). Since the content and extent of negotiations with each offeror will be determined by the deficiencies in the particular proposal, *Drexel Heritage Furnishings, Inc. v. United States*, 7 Cl. Ct. 134 (1984), an agency may properly conduct "extensive discussions with offerors whose initial proposals contain technical deficiencies while conducting more limited discussions with offerors whose proposals contain fewer weaknesses or deficiencies," *Pacific Architects & Eng'rs, Inc.*, Comp. Gen. Dec. B-236432, 89-2 CPD ¶ 494. Thus, it is proper to conduct detailed discussions with offerors whose proposals contain technical deficiencies while affording those with technically acceptable proposals only an opportunity to submit a final proposal, *Weinschel Eng'g Co.*, 64 Comp. Gen. 524 (B-217202), 85-1 CPD ¶ 574. The agency may also reveal the Government's cost estimate to an offeror proposing a cost considered too high without disclosing the estimate to an offeror submitting an acceptable proposed cost, *Bank Street College of Educ.*, 63 Comp. Gen. 393 (B-213209), 84-1 CPD ¶ 607, *recons. denied*, 84-2 CPD ¶ 445. See also *Ralph G. Moore & Assoc.*, Comp. Gen. Dec. B-270686, 96-1 CPD ¶ 118, holding that an agency did not conduct unequal discussions when it discussed the awardee's unreasonably low price and did not discuss the protester's reasonable price.

b. Prohibited Conduct

The FAR Part 15 Rewrite made significant changes in specifying the conduct which is proper. FAR 15.306(e) provides the following limitations on communications:

> Government personnel involved in the acquisition shall not engage in conduct that —
>
> (1) Favors one offeror over another;
>
> (2) Reveals an offeror's technical solution, including unique technology, innovative and unique uses of commercial items, or any information that would compromise an offeror's intellectual property to another offeror;
>
> (3) Reveals an offeror's price without that offeror's permission. However, the contracting officer may inform an offeror that its price is considered by the Government to be too high, or to low, and reveal the results of the analysis supporting that conclusion. It is also permissible, at the Government's discretion, to indicate to all offerors the cost or price that the Government's price analysis, market research, and other reviews have identified as reasonable (41 U.S.C. 423(h)(1)(2));
>
> (4) Reveals the names of individuals providing reference information about an offeror's past performance; or
>
> (5) Knowingly furnishes source selection information in violation of 3.104 and 41 U.S.C. 423(h)(1)(2).

The statutory reference to conduct prohibited by this provision is the Procurement Integrity Act. In addition, there are criminal statutes broadly prohibiting disclosure of certain types of information, e.g., 18 U.S.C. § 1905. Thus, violation of these statutory provisions could result in criminal liability. See *Panafax Corp.*, Comp. Gen. Dec. B-201176, 81-1 CPD ¶ 515, *recons. denied*, 81-2 CPD ¶ 220, where a disclosure to another offeror of Panafax's identity as an offeror and the fact that Panafax was offering a newly developed machine enabled the offeror to lower its price 27 percent, $1 below Panafax's price. A referral was made to the Department of Justice and the Comptroller General sustained the protest, stating that the disclosure of information enabled the other offeror to determine what equipment its competitor was offering and at approximately what price. See Chapter 1, Section VII for a discussion of these statutory provisions.

The practice of improving an offer through the use of information gained from another offer has been described as "technical transfusion." In addition to being illegal, there is a procurement policy reason for refraining from such conduct. In 51 Comp. Gen. 621 (B-173677) (1972), the Comptroller General gave a further reason for avoidance of this practice, stating that if the Government disclosed technical innovations to other offerors, offerors would tend to hold back technical innovation from the negotiation process. Thus, the Government would lose the benefits accruing from contractor innovation during negotiation. See also 52 Comp. Gen. 870 (B-177542) (1973), stating at 872:

> However, in 51 Comp. Gen. 621 (1972), we recognized that the statute should not be interpreted in a manner which discriminates against or gives preferential treatment to a competitor and that the disclosure to other offerors of one offeror's innovative solution to a problem is unfair. Thus, where there is a research and development procurement and the offeror's independent approach to solving a problem is the essence of the procurement, technical negotiations must be curtailed to the extent necessary to avoid technical "transfusion."

It has been very difficult for a protester to establish that technical transfusion has taken place because the Comptroller General requires proof "that the contracting agency either directly or indirectly disclosed one offeror's technical approach to another offeror," *Northwest Regional Educ. Lab.*, Comp. Gen. Dec. B-222591.3, 87-1 CPD ¶ 74. Thus, even if the protester can prove similarities to its technical approach in a competitor's BAFO, the lack of actual evidence of disclosure will lead to a denial of the protest, *Le Don Computer Servs., Inc.*, Comp. Gen. Dec. B-225451.2, 87-1 CPD ¶ 441. Similarly, speculative protests of possible technical transfusion are summarily denied, *Sparta, Inc.*, Comp. Gen. Dec. B-228216, 88-1 CPD ¶ 37.

If one offeror proposes a technical approach not permitted by the RFP but which the agency would like to consider, it is not improper to disclose to other offerors that the agency is willing to consider alternative approaches (as long as the specific technical approach proposed is not disclosed), *Rix Indus., Inc.*, Comp. Gen. Dec. B-241498, 91-1 CPD ¶ 165; *Loral Terracom*,

66 Comp. Gen. 272 (B-224908), 87-1 CPD ¶ 182. In addition, if the procuring agency is aware of a technical concept prior to the submission of a proposal incorporating that concept, conveying the concept to another offeror is not technical transfusion, *Dynalectron Corp.*, Comp. Gen. Dec. B-216201, 85-1 CPD ¶ 525. See also *Litton Sys., Inc.*, Comp. Gen. Dec. B-239123, 90-2 CPD ¶ 114, where the Comptroller General found no technical transfusion when the procuring agency discussed with all offerors the need for testing which was first identified by the protester. The Comptroller General accepted the procuring agency's explanation that all the offerors had identified the need to verify that the various proposed techniques met the contract requirement and the discussions of specific testing flowed from this mutual identification of a gap in the RFP. It is also not improper to permit an offeror for a follow-on service contract to visit the Government site where the incumbent contractor is performing the work, *Contact Int'l Corp.*, 70 Comp. Gen. 115 (B-237122.3), 90-2 CPD ¶ 442.

c. Procedure Following Improper Disclosure

When there has been an improper disclosure of pricing or technical information, the contracting officer must decide on a course of action to minimize the harm. The general rule stated by the Comptroller General is that the requirement for full and open competition overrides the prohibitions against improper disclosure — with the result that the proper course of action may be to reopen the competition permitting all offerors to compete. See *Pan Am Support Servs., Inc.*, 66 Comp. Gen. 457 (B-225964.2), 87-1 CPD ¶ 512, stating at 460:

> [C]oncerns as to technical leveling or technical transfusion do not necessarily overcome the need to remedy a procurement which has failed to satisfy the statutory requirement for full and open competition. See *Roy F. Weston, Inc.— Request for Reconsideration*, B-221863.3, Sept. 29, 1986, 86-2 CPD ¶ 324. Similarly, the risk of an auction is generally viewed as secondary to the preservation of the integrity of the competitive procurement system through the taking of appropriate corrective action. *Environmental Tectonics Corp. — Reconsideration*, B-225474.2 et al., Apr. 9, 1987, 87-1 CPD ¶ [96].

This rule has been followed in *Logicon, Inc. v. United States*, 22 Cl. Ct. 776 (1991), and *IMS Servs., Inc. v. United States*, 33 Fed. Cl. 167 (1995). In both of these cases, the court emphasized the difficult burden — not met by either plaintiff — of showing that an offeror's individual prejudice resulting from the disclosure of pricing information outweighed the harm to the procurement process that would occur if the agency were denied the ability to take corrective action by reopening the solicitation. See also *Unisys Corp.*, 67 Comp. Gen. 512 (B-230019.2), 88-2 CPD ¶ 35 (holding that "where the reopening of negotiations is properly required, the prior disclosure of an offeror's proposal does not preclude reopening"); *Faxon Co.*, 67 Comp. Gen. 39 (B-227835.3), 87-2 CPD ¶ 425 (reopening negotiations after an improper award was neither technical leveling nor an improper auction, although original awardee's proposal had been disclosed). An exception to this rule occurs when the offeror obtains information by illegal means. See *Litton Sys., Inc.*, 68 Comp. Gen. 422 (B-234060), 89-1 CPD ¶ 450, *recons. denied*, 68 Comp. Gen. 677, 89-2 CPD ¶ 228, where the Comptroller General ordered the termination of a contract because of evidence that the contractor had obtained proprietary information concerning the procurement through bribery of a Government official.

In following the general rule, the Comptroller General has approved actions in which the agency did not attempt to remedy the effects of the improper disclosure. For example, in *Computer Sciences Corp.*, Comp. Gen. Dec. B-231165, 88-2 CPD ¶ 188, negotiations were continued with an offeror that had inadvertently been given access to another's costing data. The Comptroller General stated that the agency would be justified in removing the offeror from the procurement if its BAFO indicated that it had made use of the data. Note also that the FAR prohibition in this regard is limited to the *knowing* disclosure by Government personnel of source selection information in violation of the law, FAR 15.406(e)(5).

On the other hand, several methods have been used to avert an auction or unfair competitive advantage. A commonly used method is for the agency to make an award on the basis of initial proposals and permit no modifications, Comp. Gen. Dec. B-171015, July 13, 1971, *Unpub.* For instance, in *M. Bennett, Ltd.*, Comp. Gen. Dec. B-198316, 80-1 CPD ¶ 363, the Comptroller General recommended that an award on initial proposals be made where the offerors' prices were improperly revealed at a public opening of proposals. See also *American Elec. Labs., Inc.*, 65 Comp. Gen. 62 (B-219582), 85-2 CPD ¶ 545, concurring with award on BAFOs where pricing information had been revealed in a protest because reopening negotiations would constitute auctioning, which would impugn the integrity of the competitive system.

Another technique is to cancel the RFP after an improper disclosure has been made, *Neomed, Inc.*, Comp. Gen. Dec. B-186930, 76-2 CPD ¶ 434; *Ford Aerospace & Communications Corp.*, Comp. Gen. Dec. B-224421.2, 86-2 CPD ¶ 582. Compare *Apex Int'l Management Servs., Inc.*, 60 Comp. Gen. 172 (B-200008), 81-1 CPD ¶ 24, where the Comptroller General found it improper for the agency to have cancelled a solicitation due to an improper award, but because low prices had been disclosed, recommended reinstatement of the solicitation and award based on a new responsibility determination. In *Franklin Inst.*, 55 Comp. Gen. 280 (B-182560), 75-2 CPD ¶ 194, an employee of one competitor was allowed to sit in on discussions conducted with another offeror. The Comptroller General recommended that the agency either revise its RFP to eliminate possible advantages or, if a revision would be detrimental to the agency's needs, to exclude the recipient of the information from the competition.

The Comptroller General has also approved remedies which attempt to eliminate an improper advantage one offeror may have as a result of the disclosure, although not averting an auction. For instance, in *T M Sys., Inc.*, 55 Comp. Gen. 1066 (B-185715), 76-1 CPD ¶ 299, one offeror submitted a revised price, claiming a mistake on its initial proposal, after it was erroneously informed of the only other offeror's initial price. It was held that it was proper for the contracting officer to disclose both offerors' proposed prices and call for BAFOs. See also *Federal Data Corp.*, GSBCA 9732-P, 89-1 BCA ¶ 21,414, *aff'd*, 911 F.2d 699 (Fed. Cir. 1990), finding that the Government's disclosure of all competitors' prices after one offeror's price was prematurely disclosed was a good faith effort to place all competitors on an equal footing during the second round of BAFOs, and any auction concerns were overridden by the need for such corrective action. Compare *University Sys., Inc. v. Defense Nuclear Agency*, GSBCA 11813-P, 92-3 BCA ¶ 25,173, where the board sustained the agency's decision not to reveal all prices after the winning offeror's price had been disclosed in the notice of award. The board reasoned that there was no need to reveal all prices to equalize the competition because the revealed price had been the high price and thus the other offerors' knowledge of the price did not pose a significant competitive harm. See also *International Bus. Machs. Corp.*, GSBCA 11324-P, 92-1 BCA ¶ 24,439, holding that this technique of disclosing all information is not allowed to be used if the improper disclosure was not the result of a "procurement error." In that case, the agency had disclosed pricing data during a debriefing. It is highly questionable whether this type of mass disclosure of pricing information is proper in view of the Clinger-Cohen Act of 1996, 41 U.S.C. § 423(a).

3. Form of Negotiations

The form of negotiations should be structured to permit sufficient communication to ensure that offerors are fairly and equally informed of information necessary to decide whether to revise their offers. The actual form of discussions will not be questioned as long as it achieves these objectives. Thus, discussions in the form of written questions have been permitted. See *American Dist. Tel. v. Department of Energy*, 555 F. Supp. 1244 (D.D.C. 1983), finding that a list of requested "explanations" and "clarifications" met the requirement because a reasonable offeror would have recognized the items as deficiencies; *SRS Technologies*, Comp. Gen. Dec. B-270341.2, 96-1 CPD ¶ 120, finding that two written discussion items reasonably led the protester into the areas of its proposal that needed amplification; *Gutierrez-Palmenberg, Inc.*, Comp. Gen. Dec. B-255797.3, 94-2 CPD ¶ 158, finding that a written list of items sufficiently alerted the protester to specific areas of its proposal considered weak or requiring further explanation; and *Johnson, Basin & Shaw, Inc.*, Comp. Gen. Dec. B-240265, 90-2 CPD ¶ 371, where the Comptroller General found sufficient discussion in the form of written questions submitted to the offeror. In *Joule Technical Corp.*, Comp. Gen. Dec. B-197249, 80-2 CPD ¶ 231, the Comptroller General commented on this written listing-of-deficiencies procedure as follows:

> The real question here is not whether the October 19 letter, standing alone, described the deficiencies perceived in Joule's proposal in such intimate detail that there could be no doubt as to their identification and nature, but whether the letter imparted sufficient information to Joule to afford it a fair and reasonable opportunity in the context of this procurement to identify and correct the deficiencies in its proposal. We believe that it did.

See also *KPMG Peat Marwick*, Comp. Gen. Dec. B-258990, 95-1 CPD ¶ 116, where the Comptroller General held that there was no requirement that the agency conduct face-to-face discussions in addition to, or in lieu of, written discussions; and *Austin Elecs.*, 54 Comp. Gen. 60 (B-180690), 74-2 CPD ¶ 61, where the Comptroller General rejected the protester's assertion that the agency was required to conduct "give and take" oral discussions. The Comptroller General held that the agency's decision to disclose deficiencies by letter was not an abuse of discretion.

In spite of the numerous decisions permitting written discussions, it is doubtful that this procedure is an adequate form of communication when there are significant deficiencies. See *Logistic Sys., Inc.*, 59 Comp. Gen. 548 (B-196254), 80-1 CPD ¶ 442, where the Comptroller General found that there had been inadequate communication of the deficiencies when the agency sent the offeror an elaborate list of deficiencies and conducted no oral discussions. Oral discussions can be held over the telephone, Comp. Gen. Dec. B-157156, Nov. 8, 1965, *Unpub.*, or in a face-to-face meeting. However, meetings are normally called for procurements where there are significant deficiencies. When meetings are held, there is no requirement that agreement be reached on each issue. See 52 Comp. Gen. 161 (B-176223) (1972), where the Comptroller General stated at 164:

> The duration per se of a negotiation session is by no means determinative of whether meaningful discussions have been held. Moreover, while recognizing that the term negotiation (which we equate to discussions) generally implies a series of offers and counter-offers we have not concluded that the presence of such offers and counter-offers is essential for compliance with 10 U.S.C. § 2304(g).

The description in FAR 15.306(d) of negotiation as including bargaining makes it likely that discussions in the future will include more face-to-face meetings where the contracting officer and the offeror conduct negotiations until they reach an understanding of the best offer that the offeror can make. See FAR 15.307(b) which reflects this process of reaching understandings during negotiations.

D. Offer Revisions

Under the pre-Rewrite FAR, changes to offers following negotiations were termed "best and final offers." The Rewrite not only changed the name of the term, it also gave it a new meaning. See FAR 15.001 defining revisions:

> "Proposal revision" is a change to a proposal made after the solicitation closing date, at the request of or as allowed by a contracting officer, as the result of negotiations.

Thus, revisions of offers will occur only during or after negotiations with offerors within the competitive range. FAR 15.307(b) contains the following coverage of offer revisions:

> The contracting officer may request or allow proposal revisions to clarify and document understandings reached during negotiations. At the conclusion of discussions, each offeror still in the competitive range shall be given an opportunity to submit a final proposal revision. The contracting officer is required to establish a common cut-off date only for receipt of final proposal revisions. Requests for final proposal revisions shall advise offerors that the final proposal revisions shall be in writing and that the Government intends to make award without obtaining further revisions.

Some contracting agencies call for revisions during the process of negotiations. This is usually done in relatively complex procurements. However, the protest decisions focus on the final revision process where the agency is bound to permit all offerors remaining in the competitive range to submit final revisions if they so desire. The process was previously known as "requests" for best and final offers.

1. Requesting Revisions

Requests for final revisions should specifically address the matters to be revised and, if agreement has been reached during negotiations, should include those agreements. The aim should be to receive an offer which the Government can accept if it is determined to be most advantageous to the Government. In addition, while oral requests may be necessary under some procurements, they should be followed up in writing. See *Woodward Assocs., Inc.*, Comp. Gen. Dec. B-216714, 85-1 CPD ¶ 274, where, under prior regulations, the protester misinterpreted an ambiguous oral request for a second round of BAFOs as a request for reconfirmation of its price. The Comptroller General ruled that another round of discussions should be held to correct the confusion that had occurred as a result of the unclear nature of the oral request and the lack of a written confirmation. When oral requests for BAFOs are followed up by a written confirmation, no relief is granted if the offeror misconstrues the request, *KMS Fusion, Inc.*, Comp. Gen. Dec. B-242529, 91-1 CPD ¶ 447; *Israel Aircraft Indus., Ltd.*, Comp. Gen. Dec. B-239211, 90-2 CPD ¶ 84. If an amendment does not specifically request offerors to submit BAFOs, "language giving notice to all offerors of a common cutoff date for receipt of offers has the intent and effect of a request for BAFOs," *Cleveland Telecommunications Corp. v. National Aeronautics & Space Admin.*, GSBCA 12586-P, 94-2 BCA ¶ 26,620.

a. Reasonable time

To foster fair competition, the established common cut-off date should allow sufficient time for all offerors in the competitive range to submit their final offer revisions. When discussions are conducted sequentially, this means that the closing date should give adequate time to the last offeror with whom discussions were conducted. However, the amount of time is highly dependent on the circumstances. In *Morris Guralnick Assocs., Inc.*, Comp. Gen. Dec. B-218353, 85-2 CPD ¶ 50, the Comptroller General held that allowing one day for submission of BAFOs was reasonable when both competitors were able to submit proposals within that time period. In *Evergreen Landscaping, Inc.*, Comp. Gen. Dec. B-239241, 90-2 CPD ¶ 36, the Comptroller General held that six days were reasonable for submission of BAFOs where both offerors were given the same amount of time and both offerors were located in the same city. In *FRC Int'l, Inc.*, Comp. Gen. Dec. B-255345, 94-1 CPD ¶ 125, the Comptroller General held that two hours and fifteen minutes was reasonable for submission of BAFOs where there was decreasing availability and increasing price of the item needed and the offerors' proposals were scheduled to expire within two days. The Comptroller General also noted that since the offerors revised their proposals quickly during discussion it was reasonable for the agency to presume that the offerors could quickly submit BAFOs.

b. Common Cut-off Date

The FAR 15.307(b) requirement for a common cut-off date for the receipt of final revisions has been justified as necessary to preserve the integrity of the competition in order to minimize the possibility of information in one proposal "leaking" to another offeror with a later closing date. See *Federal Data Corp.*, Comp. Gen. Dec. B-236265.4, 90-1 CPD ¶ 504; and *Kleen-Rite Corp.*, Comp. Gen. Dec. B-209474, 83-1 CPD ¶ 512, stressing the need for such a common cutoff date as an essential part of the competitive negotiation process. The purpose of establishing a common cutoff date is to prevent offerors from being treated unfairly or being prejudiced. However, prejudice does not necessarily occur because there is no common cutoff date. See *Gas Turbine Corp.*, Comp. Gen. Dec. B-251265, 93-1 CPD ¶ 400, where the Comptroller General stated:

> We agree that the Coast Guard's failure to set a common cut-off date caused no prejudice here. There is no allegation that any aspect of GTC's

> proposal was disclosed to Turbo. Moreover, as noted above, there is no basis to conclude that, even if the agency had afforded GTC the few extra days provided to Turbo, the protester could have obtained the seven parts which it did not propose to provide in its BAFO. On the current record, it appears implausible that an additional few days would have enabled GTC to obtain the missing seven parts from the OEM (Turbo) or any other source. Accordingly, GTC was not prejudiced by the absence of a common cut-off date for the submission of BAFOs, and we therefore deny this ground of protest.

See also *Atlantic Terminal Co.*, Comp. Gen. Dec. B-160976, May 29, 1967, *Unpub.*, where the Comptroller General found no prejudice, although the successful offeror was permitted to revise its price on February 6, and the unsuccessful offeror was last contacted regarding its price on January 31. In *Canaveral Port Servs., Inc.*, Comp. Gen. Dec. B-211627.3, 84-2 CPD ¶ 358, the Comptroller General found no prejudice where the agency used staggered closing dates but kept all offers sealed until a common opening date. Mistaken notification to one offeror of a common closing date one week in advance of the date supplied to other offerors was not prejudicial since the Government offered to extend the offeror's time to enable resubmission of the BAFO, *Alan-Craig, Inc.*, Comp. Gen. Dec. B-202432, 81-2 CPD ¶ 263. In *B.F. Goodrich Co.*, Comp. Gen. Dec. B-230674, 88-1 CPD ¶ 471, the Comptroller General criticized the agency for not establishing a common cutoff date but denied the protest. The common cutoff date applies to written offers, or written confirmation of oral offers, unless oral BAFOs are authorized in the RFP, *Gregory A. Robertson*, Comp. Gen. Dec. B-213351, 84-1 CPD ¶ 592.

Generally, the request for a BAFO is open-ended in permitting alterations to the original proposals. However, if it contains restrictions on the permissible alterations, the agency must abide by those restrictions and not consider additional alterations submitted by offerors, *DynaLantic Corp.*, 68 Comp. Gen. 413 (B-234035), 89-1 CPD ¶ 421 (technical alterations should not have been considered when agency had called for "best and final price and delivery schedule" and had stated "negotiations have been concluded").

The contracting officer may extend the closing date for receipt of final proposal revisions if such extension will enhance competition, *Solar Resources, Inc.*, Comp. Gen. Dec. B-193264, 79-1 CPD ¶ 95. In *Institute for Advanced Safety Studies*, Comp. Gen. Dec. B-221330.2, 86-2 CPD ¶ 110, it was held proper to extend the closing date for BAFOs three days after the closing date because none of the offerors were prejudiced by this extension. In addition, an agency may extend the closing date for BAFOs upon request of an offeror. See also *Fort Biscuit Co.*, Comp. Gen. Dec. B-247319, 92-1 CPD ¶ 440, where extension of the closing date was proper to permit a competitor to submit a proposal that would not have otherwise been submitted, and *TRS Design & Consulting Servs.*, Comp. Gen. Dec. B-218668.2, 85-2 CPD ¶ 370, where the agency properly extended the closing date after it misinformed one of two offerors, causing it to miss the original closing date. The decision to extend the closing date to accept late BAFOs is within the contracting officer's discretion and will not be reviewed by the Comptroller General, *Scientific Sys., Inc.*, Comp. Gen. Dec. B-225574, 87-1 CPD 19.

c. Late Final Revisions

late is late

The Instructions to Offerors — Competitive Acquisition solicitation provision at FAR 52.215-1 defines "late" proposals, modifications, or final revisions as those received after the designated time for receipt. Thus, late final proposal revisions are normally rejected unless they meet one of the exceptions to these rules.

Under the late proposal rules contained in paragraph (c)(3) of FAR 52.215-1, a late final proposal revision may be considered for award only if:

> (i) The Contracting Officer extends the due date for all offerors; or
>
> (ii) The Contracting Officer determines in writing on the basis of a review of the circumstances that the lateness was caused by actions, or inactions, of the Government; or
>
> (iii) In the judgment of the Contracting Officer, the offeror demonstrates by submission of factual information that the circumstances causing the late submission were beyond the immediate control of the offeror.

The Comptroller General has strictly construed the FAR definition of lateness. For example, the Comptroller General held that a BAFO which was received six minutes late was properly rejected where none of the exceptions to the late offer rule applied, *Potomac Sys. Resources, Inc.*, Comp. Gen. Dec. B-219896, 85-2 CPD ¶ 393. In *Fishermen's Boat Shop, Inc.*, Comp. Gen. Dec. B-223366, 86-2 CPD ¶ 389, the Comptroller General held that a BAFO received in the agency's central mail depot 25 minutes before the closing time was properly rejected as late because receipt at the mail depot does not constitute receipt at the designated contracting facility, and an agency cannot reasonably be expected to convey the mail to the contracting facility in 25 minutes. Similarly, in *SYS v. National Aeronautics & Space Admin.*, GSBCA 12154-P, 93-2 BCA ¶ 25,582, *recons. denied*, 93-2 BCA ¶ 25,652, a BAFO was properly held to be late when it was delivered by courier on the morning of the closing day but was not received by the contracting officer until the next day. The board stated the reason that the BAFO was not given to the contracting officer on the closing day was because the BAFO was addressed to the contracting officer rather than, as required by the request for BAFOs, to the agency bid room.

When a BAFO is submitted by facsimile transmission, the facsimile must be received in its entirety by the Government with a reasonable time remaining for the Government to carry the BAFO from the facsimile room to the contracting office, *Phoenix Research Group, Inc.*, Comp. Gen. Dec. B-240840, 90-2 CPD ¶ 514. Thus, a BAFO which is received in the facsimile room several minutes before the deadline may still be rejected if the Government could not reasonably relay the BAFO to the contracting office before the deadline. See also *Cyber Digital, Inc.*, Comp. Gen. Dec. B-270107, 96-1 CPD ¶ 20 (where entire BAFO was not received until after deadline, agency was not required to consider that portion of the BAFO received before the deadline since it did not constitute the entire offer).

FAR 52.215-1(c)(6) allows offers to submit modifications "at any time before award" if the modification is made in response to an amendment or for the purpose of correcting a mistake. Thus the Government may elect to consider a late BAFO which modifies an otherwise acceptable low offer and other offerors may not complain because their relative standing is not affected, *Woodward Assocs., Inc.*, Comp. Gen. Dec. B-216714, 85-1 CPD ¶ 274.

2. Procedure Following Receipt of Final Revision

After receipt of final proposal revisions, the agency must reevaluate the proposals as quickly as possible. It is then in a position to proceed to source selection and award of a contract. However, under some circumstances, it may be necessary to reopen negotiations.

a. Reevaluation

The first step after receipt of final proposal revisions is the reevaluation of each BAFO to determine its current status in the competition. The failure to correctly assess the changes an offeror made in a BAFO can lead to the granting of a protest, *Jaycor*, Comp. Gen. Dec. B-240029.2, 90-2 CPD ¶ 354. See, for example, *Intown Properties, Inc.*, Comp. Gen. Dec. B-262236.2, 96-1 CPD ¶ 89 (agency unreasonably evaluated BAFO where protester, in response to discussions about lack of qualifications of certain personnel, proposed different personnel in its BAFO but the agency did not consider this); and *Jack Faucett Assocs.*, Comp. Gen. Dec. B-233224, 89-1 CPD ¶ 115, *recons. denied*, 89-1 CPD ¶ 551 (agency could not explain its failure to upgrade a BAFO when the offeror included more manpower in response to an agency statement that too little manpower was a deficiency). This reevaluation must, of course, follow the original evaluation criteria in the RFP, *Hattal & Assocs.*, 70 Comp. Gen. 632 (B-243357), 91-2 CPD ¶ 90.

Agency evaluators have the same discretion in evaluating final proposal revisions that they have in evaluating proposal revisions. Thus, an agency may use information in a cost proposal to downgrade a technical proposal, *Cygna Project Management*, Comp. Gen. Dec. B-236839, 90-1 CPD ¶ 21. Similarly, a BAFO may be downgraded for failing to specifically elaborate on how the work will be performed, *Northwestern Travel Agency, Inc.*, Comp. Gen. Dec. B-244592, 91-2 CPD ¶ 363.

There is no requirement that each BAFO be totally rescored. Thus, it has been found proper for agency evaluators to assess the changes which a BAFO has made to the original proposal and report them to the source selection official, *Northwest Regional Educ. Lab.*, Comp. Gen. Dec. B-222591.3, 87-1 CPD ¶ 74; *VSE Corp.*, Comp. Gen. Dec. B-224397, 86-2 CPD ¶ 392, or to take the BAFO changes "into consideration" in making the source selection decision, *Scientex Corp.*, Comp. Gen. Dec. B-238689, 90-1 CPD ¶ 597. See also *Aircraft Porous Media, Inc.*, Comp. Gen. Dec. B-241665.2, 91-1 CPD ¶ 356, *recons. denied*, 91-1 CPD ¶ 613, where the Comptroller General found that it was proper for an agency to not bother rescoring because the changes in the BAFO could not have altered the original determination that two proposals were technically equal.

There is no requirement that the BAFOs be evaluated by the same evaluators that scored the original proposals, *Data Flow Corp.*, 62 Comp. Gen. 506 (B-209499), 83-2 CPD ¶ 57. However, the reevaluation must be reasonable in applying the evaluation criteria, *Bauer Assocs., Inc.*, Comp. Gen. Dec. B-229831.6, 88-2 CPD ¶ 549. The Comptroller General has stated that the fact that new evaluators reached different conclusions than the original evaluators does not automatically indicate an impropriety, *Chemonics Int'l*, Comp. Gen. Dec. B-222793, 86-2 CPD ¶ 161. See also *Magnavox Advanced Prods. & Sys. Co.*, Comp. Gen. Dec. B-215426, 85-1 CPD ¶ 146 (finding differences among individual evaluators as insufficient to discredit a technical evaluation).

b. Reopening Negotiations

Reopening negotiations is not a desirable course of action. It adds time and expense to the procurement and extends the time when information may be improperly disclosed. See *Mine Safety Appliances Co.*, Comp. Gen. Dec. B-242379.5, 92-2 CPD ¶ 76 holding that the conduct of another round of negotiations in the absence of a valid reason tends to undermine the integrity of the competitive negotiation process. In this regard, Pre-Rewrite FAR 15.611(c) stated that negotiations should not be reopened "unless it is clearly in the Government's best interests to do so." In addition, DFARS 215.611 prohibits contracting officers from reopening negotiations unless higher level approval is obtained. However, the FAR Part 15 Rewrite removed the coverage, leaving the matter to the contracting officer's discretion under the circumstances surrounding each procurement. Similarly, DOD has indicated that it will remove the DFARS requirement for higher approval, 62 Fed. Reg. 63050 (Nov. 26, 1997).

The Comptroller General has held it proper to reopen discussions if substantial questions requiring discussions are raised by one of the BAFOs, *Ocean Technology, Inc.*, Comp. Gen. Dec. B-183749, 75-2 CPD ¶ 262; previously existing ambiguities are not discovered until after submission of BAFOs, 52 Comp. Gen. 409 (B-176913) (1973), *Swedlow, Inc.*, 53 Comp. Gen. 564 (B-178212), 74-1 CPD ¶ 55; additional technical information is needed to evaluate the proposals, *Introl Corp.*, Comp. Gen. Dec. B-194570, 80-1 CPD ¶ 41; Government estimates are discovered to be in error, *Dyneteria, Inc.*, Comp. Gen. Dec. B-181707, 75-1 CPD ¶ 86; Government requirements change, *Simulators Ltd., Inc.*, Comp. Gen. Dec. B-208418, 82-2 CPD ¶ 473; incorrect information was provided to one offeror during discussions, *Computer Related Servs., Inc.*, Comp. Gen. Dec. B-244638, 91-2 CPD ¶ 420; specifications not clear, *ES, Inc.*, Comp. Gen. Dec. B-258911.2, 95-1 CPD ¶ 168; or deficiencies in initial BAFO prevented offeror's acceptance, *Dube Travel Agency & Tours, Inc.*, Comp. Gen. Dec. B-270438, 96-1 CPD ¶ 141. Also upheld was a decision to reopen discussions and request a second round of BAFOs after the recommended awardee's place of performance had become unavailable and the quality of materials required by the Government had changed, *Hayes Int'l Corp. v. United States*, 7 Cl. Ct. 681 (1985). See also *M.W. Kellogg Co./Siciliana Appalti Costruzioni S.p.A. (J.V.) v. United States*, 10 Cl. Ct. 17 (1986), permitting multiple BAFOs.

While the agency has the discretion to call for another offer, it also has the discretion to refuse to do so. Thus, the agency is not obligated to bring up deficiencies remaining from the initial proposal when the offeror has already been informed of the deficiency, *Phoenix Safety Assocs., Ltd.*, Comp. Gen. Dec. B-216504, 84-2 CPD ¶ 621. Offerors also cannot rely on further discussions to clarify or amplify newly introduced aspects of the BAFO. See *RCA Serv. Co.*, Comp. Gen. Dec. B-197752, 80-1 CPD ¶ 407, where the Comptroller General concurred in the decision of the procuring agency not to reopen discussions with an offeror that had included a cost ceiling in its BAFO on a CPAF support services contract. The agency awarded the contract to another offeror because of grave doubts raised by the cost ceiling proposal without discussing it with the protester. The Comptroller General stated:

> In reviewing whether the Army acted properly in not reopening discussions with offerors, we cannot ignore the length of time that this procurement was in process — more than 1 year from the issuance of the RFP to receipt of best and final offers. Clearly, the time for innovative suggestions and approaches was over when RCA presented its price ceiling proposal. In this regard, our decision in *Electronic Communications, Inc.*, 55 Comp. Gen. 636 [B-183677] (1976), 76-1 CPD 15, cited by the Army, presented a similar situation. There, an offeror's best and final offer appeared to be inconsistent with the RFP and its initial acceptable offer. We held that the contracting officer's determination not to reopen discussions with all offerors in the competitive range was proper as not being in the best interests of the Government. We also noted that when an offeror submits in its best and final offer unexplained or incomplete revisions to its otherwise acceptable proposal, it has the burden of affirmatively demonstrating the acceptability of its proposal. Here, RCA did not meet its burden.

The same result was arrived at in *Nova Research Co.*, Comp. Gen. Dec. B-270092, 96-1 CPD ¶ 52, where the agency was not required to reopen discussions to allow the protester to cure a deficiency which had been introduced in its BAFO; *Saco Defense, Inc.*, Comp. Gen. Dec. B-252066, 93-1 CPD ¶ 395, where the agency was not required to conduct new tests on a redesigned item that was proposed as a solution to deficiencies identified in discussions; and in *Integrated Sys. Analysts, Inc.*, GSBCA 10750-P, 91-1 BCA ¶ 23,383, where the board held that it was proper for the agency not to seek to determine if an offeror was stating that it would not meet a mandatory requirement of the specification when it's BAFO said that price was contingent on purchasing a noncomplying component by a certain date. See also *Analysis & Computer Sys., Inc.*, 57 Comp. Gen. 239 (B-188787), 78-1 CPD ¶ 75, where the agency downgraded an offeror's technical score because it appeared that manpower had been reduced when the price proposal was significantly reduced. Thus, an offeror takes the risk that aspects of its proposal, included in the BAFO for the first time, will be found unacceptable to the agency, *General Elec. Co.*, 55 Comp. Gen. 1450 (B-186372), 76-2 CPD ¶ 269; *Management & Technical Servs. Co.*, Comp. Gen. Dec. B-209513, 82-2 CPD ¶ 571 (new management technique rendered proposal unacceptable); *Aircraft Porous Media, Inc.*, Comp. Gen. Dec. B-241665.2, 91-1 CPD ¶ 356 (reduced cost adjusted upward because not realistic — rationale for reduction not sufficiently explained); *Logicon RDA*, Comp. Gen. Dec. B-261714.2, 95-2 CPD ¶ 286 (unsupported cost reduction introduced for first time in BAFO); *Suntron Corp.*, Comp. Gen. Dec. B-270456, 96-1 CPD ¶ 143 (unexplained cost reduction rendered proposal unacceptable).

This rule has been carried to the extreme in holding that an agency need not reopen discussions to permit correction of a mistake in the BAFO, *Standard Mfg. Co.*, 65 Comp. Gen. 451 (B-220455), 86-1 CPD ¶ 304; *American Elec. Lab., Inc.*, 65 Comp. Gen. 62 (B-219582), 85-2 CPD ¶ 545. See also *International Bus. Machs. Corp.*, GSBCA 11324-P, 92-1 BCA ¶ 24,439, holding that it was improper to reopen discussions after disclosure of the award price when the agency found that the next offeror had been misled by an ambiguity in the RFP. Compare *FCC.O&M, Inc.*, Comp. Gen. Dec. B-238610.2, 91-1 CPD ¶ 26, where it was found proper to conduct another round of discussions in order to correct a mistake in the winning offeror's proposal. Thus, an agency may, but is not required to, reopen discussions after submission of BAFOs and the agency's decision will not be disturbed unless it is found to be unreasonable.

The rule permitting the contracting officer not to reopen discussions when an offeror has included newly introduced material in a BAFO does not apply to information which the agency learns from other sources that appears to modify a BAFO. See *AAA Eng'g & Drafting, Inc.*, Comp. Gen. Dec. B-250323, 93-1 CPD ¶ 287, where the contracting officer gave a BAFO a low evaluation based on a manning table obtained in a preaward survey which appeared to conflict with the manning table that had been included in the BAFO. The Comptroller General ruled that the contracting officer should have sought clarification since the offeror did not state that the new manning table modified its BAFO.

IX. SOLE SOURCE PROCUREMENTS

In a sole source procurement an actual negotiation will usually occur before award of a contract. Thus, there is little need for the Government to obtain a formal offer from the prospective contractor. However, FAR 15.002(a) appears to contemplate the use of an RFP in this situation, stating:

> Sole source acquisitions. When contracting in a sole source environment, the request for proposals (RFP) should be tailored to remove unnecessary information and requirements, e.g., evaluation criteria and voluminous proposal preparation instructions.

Since this guidance is not mandatory, agencies can follow other procedures to initiate a sole source procurement such as the issuance of a Request for Quotations (RFQ). The regulations are silent on the use of an RFQ for this purpose.

The use of an RFP would be particularly appropriate when the agency had never acquired the product or services before but had concluded from market research that only one source was able to perform the work. In that case, the preparation of the RFP would give the prospective contractor all of the specifications and terms and conditions that the agency intended to use — providing the basis for the company to estimate the costs of performance and prepare an offer of the price or cost plus fee for the contract.

In contrast, when the sole source procurement was a follow-on to an existing contract, the use of an RFQ might speed the acquisition process. In that case, the parties will already have a relatively complete understanding of the specifications and the terms and conditions and the company will have thorough knowledge of how to price the follow-on work. In such cases, all that is needed to permit the beginning of negotiations is a price proposal and suggestions as to any desirable changes to the specifications or terms and conditions. This information can be obtained through the issuance of a very simple RFQ or by less formal communication.

In either case, there is no need to obtain most of the information that is required in a competitive negotiation. This is recognized in FAR 15.300 which states that FAR Subpart 15.3 is only applicable to competitive procurements. Thus, information demonstrating the capability of the contractor, such as past performance or experience information, should not be obtained in a sole source environment. The goal should be to use the most streamlined procedure possible to arrive at a formal contract document.

Once the agency has obtained a proposed price from the sole source contractor, the parties will usually enter into a comprehensive negotiation of all of the elements of the pricing, as described in FAR 15.405. In the course of this negotiation the parties usually will discuss the details of the work that are necessary to perform the contract and will identify elements of the specification that should be changed to better reflect the Government's requirements. They may also bargain about the terms and conditions of the contract. This in-depth negotiation process generally permits both the contractor and the Government agency to obtain a relatively clear understanding of the work that must be done to satisfy the requirement and to arrive at a balanced contract that contains sufficient funds to perform the work.

When this negotiation is concluded and agreement has been reached, the Government almost always takes the responsibility for preparing the format contract document. Generally, this is sent to the contractor for signature and subsequently signed by the contracting officer.

This process can be compressed to the extent necessary. It can be initiated by a telephone call or an oral RFP, FAR 15.203(f). Work can be started by the issuance of a letter contract in accordance with FAR 16.603. See Chapter 8. The lack of guidance in the procurement regulations gives the contracting officer and the contractor almost complete flexibility to follow the most efficient and effective process to arrive at a sole source contract.

X. SELECTION, AWARD, NOTICES AND DEBRIEFINGS

Upon completion of evaluation of offers, the winner must be selected and award made. The process of selecting the source, making the award, providing required notices and giving requested debriefings is essentially the same whether award is made on initial offers or after negotiations. The procurement statutes contain minimal requirements concerning selection and award, leaving the decisions in these areas to the discretion of the agencies. On the other hand, the statutes deal specifically with notices of procurement actions and debriefings. The FAR deals with all of these matters in varying degrees of detail.

A. Source Selection Authority

While the procurement statutes provide that the "agency," 41 U.S.C. § 253b(d)(3), or the "head of the agency," 10 U.S.C. § 2305(b)(4)(C), shall award the contract, the FAR provisions focus on the individual who will make the selection and award decisions. This individual is called the source selection authority (SSA). FAR 15.303(a) provides that the contracting officer is the SSA "unless the agency head appoints another individual for a particular acquisition or group of acquisitions." In many agencies, particularly in large dollar value procurements, the SSA is a high level agency official.

1. Responsibilities

The source selection responsibilities of the SSA are set out in FAR 15.303(b), as follows:

> (4) Ensure that proposals are evaluated based solely on the factors and subfactors contained in the solicitation (10 U.S.C. 2305(b)(1) and 41 U.S.C. 253b(d)(3));
>
> (5) Consider the recommendations of advisory boards or panels (if any); and
>
> (6) Select the source or sources whose proposal is the best value to the Government (10 U.S.C. 2305(b)(4)(B) and 41 U.S.C. 253b(d)(3)).

In addition, the SSA must make a determination of whether to award without negotiation or whether to award after receiving final offer revisions or to call for further revisions.

Another responsibility of the SSA is to determine whether to cancel the solicitation. Under some circumstances, it would not be appropriate to continue a procurement and make an award. In this regard, the procurement statutes provide that "all . . . proposals . . . may be rejected if the head of the agency determines that such action is in the public interest," 10 U.S.C. § 2305(b)(2) and 41 U.S.C. § 253b(b). FAR 15.305 vests the authority to make this determination in the SSA. Pre-Rewrite FAR 15.608(b) dealt with this subject and contained a number of examples where rejection of all offers would be justified. It also required a determination, in writing, that one of the identified factors was present. However, this provision was deleted in the Rewrite which merely authorizes rejection if the SSA determines rejection to be in the "public interest." The SSA has broad discretion in making such determinations, *Atlantic Scientific & Technology Corp.*, Comp. Gen. Dec. B-276334.2, 97-2 CPD ¶ 116 (cancellation of procurement appropriate when protest led agency to reassess its needs); and *Rotary Furnishing Co.*, Comp. Dec. B-277704, 97-2 CPD ¶ 140 (cancellation appropriate when one offeror submitted a high price and the other offeror was nonresponsible). However, rejection of all offers and requiring resubmission or cancellation of the solicitation is a serious matter, particularly where substantial effort is required in the submission and evaluation of offers. Thus, rejection and cancellation would not be appropriate where concerns with the procurement could be addressed through negotiations, *A&W Flamar GmbH*, Comp. Gen. Dec. B-278486, 98-1 CPD ¶ ___.

2. Independent Judgment

FAR 15.308 requires that, while the SSA may use the analyses of other participants in the process, the source selection decision must represent the SSA's independent judgment:

> The source selection authority's (SSA) decision shall be based on a comparative assessment of proposals against all source selection criteria in the solicitation. While the SSA may use reports and analyses prepared by others, the source selection decision shall represent the SSA's independent judgment.

The information furnished to the SSA can vary in nature and detail. It may consist only of evaluation results or may also contain further analyses and recommendations for award. The SSA must make an assessment of the information and determine whether it conforms to the evaluation factors specified in the solicitation and whether it is sufficient to make a rational selection for award. If not, the SSA must see that corrective action is taken.

a. Evaluations or Recommendations

Procedures which communicate summaries of the evaluations to the SSA have been sustained as fully adequate to ensure rational source selection decisions. See, for example, *Sabreliner Corp.*, Comp. Gen. Dec. B-242023, 91-1 CPD ¶ 326, where the Comptroller General stated:

> The SSA is not required to personally review the proposals or the complete evaluation documentation, but can rely upon a briefing that presents the results of the proposal evaluation. *See Systems & Processes Eng'g Corp.*, B-234142, May 10, 1989, 89-1 CPD ¶ 441. Here, the SSA, in addition to receiving a technical evaluation briefing, reviewed the proposal analysis report, which set forth, among other things, a description of the evaluation standards and criteria; a description of the competing proposals; a comparative evaluation analysis of the proposal; the offerors' proposed prices/costs; and the performance risk assessment.

Thus, in most cases the SSA can rely on the scores of the evaluators and the evaluation board's conclusions. See *ICF Kaiser Engr's*, Comp. Gen. Dec. B-271079, 96-2 CPD ¶ 15 (source selection official based award decision on information set forth in the SEB and TEP reports).

b. Reliance Not Justified

The SSA is not entitled to rely upon faulty evaluations. See, for example, *Programmatics, Inc.*, Comp. Gen. Dec. B-228916.2, 88-1 CPD ¶ 35, where a review of the narrative statements prepared by two evaluators indicated that there was no rational support for the scores given by the evaluators and adopted by the source selection official. Thus, the SSA is ultimately responsible for any mistakes made in the evaluation process. In *J.A. Jones Management Servs., Inc.*, Comp. Gen. Dec. B-276864, 97-2 CPD ¶ 47, the Comptroller General observed:

> While an agency's initial review of proposals may be done independently, it is necessary for the agency at some point to make a rational comparison of the relative merits of directly competing proposals. The agency's SSA cannot make a rational comparison where the evaluators' point scores do not accurately reflect the relative strengths and weaknesses of the competing

proposals and the record lacks adequate documentation in support of such technical point scores. Here, the dearth of evaluation narratives or other explanations in this evaluation record and the SSA's summary reliance on the point scores, which have been sufficiently shown by the protester to be inaccurate in numerous areas, lead us to the conclusion that the SSA could not and did not make a reasonable selection decision. *See Adelaide Blomfield Management Co.*, [Comp. Gen. Dec. B-253128.2, 93-2 CPD ¶ 197], at 4-6. In sum, on the evaluation record furnished to our Office — consisting of point scores and cursory narratives — we find the absence of a consistent, reasonable and accurate evaluation scoring as well as the absence of supporting narrative documentation; moreover, the agency has offered no substantive response to the protester's concerns in response to the protest, and our review shows none. Here, we simply are unable to assess the reasonableness of the agency's selection decision. Accordingly, we sustain the protest.

c. Ordering Reevaluation

The SSA can order a complete reevaluation if there are doubts about the validity of the initial evaluation, *PRC, Inc.*, Comp. Gen. Dec. B-233561.8, 92-2 CPD ¶ 215. In that case, a new evaluation panel was constituted after questions were raised about the propriety of the initial evaluation. The Comptroller General stated:

> Contracting officials in negotiated procurements have broad discretion to take corrective action where the agency determines that such action is necessary to ensure fair and impartial competition. *Oshkosh Truck Corp.; Idaho Norland Corp.*, B-237058.2; B-237058.3, Feb. 14, 1990, 90-1 CPD ¶ 274. An agency may convene a new selection board and conduct a new evaluation where the record shows that the agency made the decision in good faith, without the specific intent of changing a particular offeror's technical ranking or avoiding an award to a particular offeror. *Burns & Roe Servs. Corp.*, B-248394, Aug. 25, 1992, 92-2 CPD ¶ [124]; *Loschky, Marquardt & Nesholm*, B-222606, Sept. 23, 1986, 86-2 CPD ¶ 336. We will not object to proposed corrective action where the agency concludes that award was not necessarily made on a basis most advantageous to the government, so long as the corrective action taken is appropriate to remedy the impropriety. See *Oshkosh Truck Corp.; Idaho Norland Corp.*, *supra*; *Power Dynatec Corp.*, B-236896, Dec. 6, 1989, 89-2 CPD ¶ 522.

See also *Pro-Mark, Inc.*, Comp. Gen. Dec. B-247248, 92-1 CPD ¶ 448 (Comptroller affirmed a decision of an agency to reevaluate proposals using a more experienced evaluation panel); and *EBA Eng'g, Inc.*, Comp. Gen.

Dec. B-275818, 97-1 CPD ¶ 127 (Comptroller found proper an agency's decision to replace panel members in order to avoid the appearance of impropriety).

d. Rescore or Conduct Own Evaluation

The SSA is not bound by the rankings, scores, or recommendations of either the evaluators, boards or other intermediate groups, as long as the official has a rational basis for the differing evaluation. In some cases, source selection officials merely ignore the scores and make the source selection decision based on the narratives. However, in most instances, an attempt is made to make the scores an accurate reflection of the merits of the proposals.

There have been numerous protest decisions upholding rescoring by source selection officials, either explicitly or implicitly. See *Grey Advertising, Inc.*, 55 Comp. Gen. 1111 (B-184825), 76-1 CPD ¶ 325, where the Comptroller General stated at 1120:

> [W]hile point scores, technical evaluation narratives, and adjective ratings may well be indicative of whether one proposal is technically superior to another and should therefore be considered by source selection officials, see *EPSCO, Incorporated*, B-183816, November 21, 1975, 75-2 CPD ¶ 338, we have recognized that selection officials are not bound by the recommendations made by evaluation and advisory groups. *Bell Aerospace Company*, 55 Comp. Gen. 244 (1975), 75-2 CPD ¶ 168; *Tracor Jitco, Inc., supra*; 51 Comp. Gen. 272 (1971); B-173137(1), *supra*. This is so even though it is the working level procurement officials and evaluation panel members who may normally be expected to have the technical expertise relevant to the technical evaluation of proposals. Accordingly, we have upheld source selection officials' determinations that technical proposals were essentially equal despite an evaluation point score differential of 81 out of 1000, see 52 Comp. Gen. 686, *supra*, and despite contracting officer recommendations that award be made to the offeror with the highest technical rating. See 52 Comp. Gen. 738, *supra*.

Rescoring is often performed by the SSA to correct errors or poor judgment of subordinate evaluation personnel. In the *Grey* case, for instance, Navy officials determined that two proposals were technically equal, although the evaluation panel rated the protester's technical proposal 47 points higher — out of a possible 1000 points. The Comptroller General found this judgment had a rational basis, as the officials had concluded that the protester's higher score was based too much on the advantages of incumbency rather than actual technical superiority. Similarly, in *Polaris, Inc.*, Comp. Gen. Dec. B-220066, 85-2 CPD ¶ 669, the Comptroller General approved a rescoring by an SSA based on his view that the evaluation panel had misinterpreted the RFP requirement; and in *L&E Assocs.*, Comp. Gen. Dec. B-224448, 86-2 CPD ¶ 568, the contracting officer properly altered the protester's technical score when he found that the evaluating committee had based their technical evaluations solely on cost and later had performed only cursory and insufficient analysis in the reevaluation. See also *Pro-Mark, Inc.*, Comp. Gen. Dec. B-247248, 92-1 CPD ¶ 448, in which the Comptroller General approved the contracting officer's lowering of incongruous quality control scores as given by an inexperienced review panel. But see *Morrison Knudsen Corp.*, Comp. Gen. Dec. B-270703, 96-2 CPD ¶ 86, where the Comptroller General found that the SSA's decision to disregard the evaluation scores of the source evaluation board was not reasonably based. The Comptroller General stated that the significant reason relied on by the SSA for disregarding the protester's higher evaluation score was the superior subcontract approach of the other offeror. The Comptroller General found that the two proposals were not fundamentally different in this regard.

In a number of cases, a source selection decision has been upheld on the basis that the SSA implicitly rescored some aspect of the evaluation. For example, in *PRC Kentron, Inc.*, Comp. Gen. Dec. B-230212, 88-1 CPD ¶ 537, rescoring was permitted to overcome the over reliance on incumbency by the evaluators, but "no formal rescoring was performed." In *CRC Sys., Inc.*, Comp. Gen. Dec. B-207847, 83-1 CPD ¶ 462, the Comptroller General approved the contracting officer's implicit lowering of the protester's high score because its offer did not satisfy all the RFP requirements. In *Bank St. College of Educ.*, 63 Comp. Gen. 393 (B-213209), 84-1 CPD ¶ 607, *recons. denied*, 84-2 CPD ¶ 445, the agency director overturned a finding of technical superiority made by a technical evaluation panel without actually altering the technical scores. The Comptroller General approved this intervention into the selection process finding that the director properly concluded that the awardee's proposal was actually technically superior because the level of effort in the protester's proposal deviated significantly from the RFP's estimated level of effort. In *NKF Eng'g, Inc.*, Comp. Gen. Dec. B-232143, 88-2 CPD ¶ 497, the Comptroller General found that the contracting officer properly considered the protester's score an exaggeration of its technical superiority because the evaluation committee did not consider relevant factors in management and employee transition when giving the scores. Implicit rescoring is not sound practice and should be avoided. When the source selection official concludes that rescoring is necessary, the contract file should contain a clear indication of the rescoring that has occurred and the justification for that rescoring.

The SSA is also permitted to conduct a completely independent evaluation if the original evaluation is not acceptable, *Benchmark Sec., Inc.*, Comp. Gen. Dec. B-247655.2, 93-1 CPD ¶ 133. In that case, the Comptroller General affirmed the decision of the SSA after he completely altered the evaluation of the offerors, determined that two best proposals were technically equal and that costs of performance would be equivalent, and selected the incumbent contractor. The Comptroller General commented that the evaluation and source selection were well reasoned and thoroughly documented. See also *Calspan Corp.*, Comp. Gen. Dec. B-258441, 95-1 CPD ¶ 28, upholding the SSA's decision to raise the awardee's score on past performance. The Comptroller General found that the decision was rationally based on the knowledge of agency personnel familiar with the prior successful performance of the awardee. Similarly, in *Loral Aeronutronic*, Comp. Gen. Dec. B-259857.2, 95-2 CPD ¶ 213, after review and discussion of the SSEB's findings, the SSAC changed the risk assessment of one of the awardee's subfactor from medium to low. The SSAC also upgraded the other awardee's technical rating from satisfactory to exceptional. The Comptroller General held that the SSAC acted reasonably and in a manner consistent with the evaluation scheme.

The SSA is permitted to use information in one of the segments of a proposal to alter an evaluation of another segment. For example, in a procurement which precluded the technical evaluators from seeing the pricing proposal, the source selection evaluation board made substantial adjustments to the technical evaluation based on information in the pricing proposal. The Comptroller General denied a protest — ruling that this procedure was entirely proper, *Cygna Project Management*, Comp. Gen. Dec. B-236839, 90-1 CPD ¶ 21. It can be argued that failure to correlate the information in the segments of an offeror's proposal can lead to an irrational evaluation or at least to a poor selection of the source. Hence, SSAs should ensure that such correlation is made, with commensurate adjustments to the scores, before the source selection decision is made.

3. Allegations of Bias

Offerors are entitled to fair and impartial treatment in the source selection process and have a right to an unbiased determination of which source should receive the award. In a number of cases, charges have been made that the selection was based upon favoritism. However, it has been very difficult to overcome a decision through the allegation of bias of the SSA. In *Conax Fla. Corp. v. United States*, 641 F. Supp. 408 (D.D.C. 1986), *aff'd*, 824 F.2d 1124 (D.C. Cir. 1987), the court held that even if a protester establishes some degree of bias, it cannot win unless it can show that the source selection decision was unreasonable. In addition, in *Howard Cooper Corp. v. United States*, 763 F. Supp. 829, 841 (E.D. Va. 1991), the court, quoting *Arrowhead Metals, Ltd. v. United States*, 8 Cl. Ct. 703, 712 (1985), stated that claims of bias must be established by "well-nigh irrefragable proof." In *GE Gov't Servs., Inc. v. United States*, 788 F. Supp. 581 (D.D.C. 1992), a protester attempted to establish bias by providing statements about the SSA that demonstrated he was prejudiced against the protester. The protester also submitted evidence of sexual improprieties with a contractor employee. The court denied any relief because there was no proof that the source selection decision was affected by any alleged bias. It based its decision, to a large extent, on the fact that other agency officials that had participated in the procurement had also arrived at the decision that the selected contractor had offered the "best value" to the Government.

In *Aumann, Inc.*, Comp. Gen. Dec. B-251585.3, 93-1 CPD ¶ 423, the protester argued that the SSA improperly influenced the technical evaluation panel resulting in the downgrading of the protester's score. After having reviewed the evaluators' worksheets, the SSA found numerous instances where the narrative assessments were inconsistent with the numerical scores and the proposals. The SSA prepared detailed comments on the affected factors and subfactors and explained the inconsistencies and failures to follow the stated evaluation criteria. The evaluators again reviewed the proposals and provided the SSA with a revised assessment. The Comptroller General found that there was no evidence that the evaluators' independent judgment was improperly swayed by the SSA. In *Centra Technology, Inc.*, Comp. Gen. Dec. B-27477, 97-1 CPD ¶ 35, the protester asserted that the personal relationship between the director of the Johnson Space Center and the president of the awardee firm improperly influenced the SSA's decision because the SSA was in a subordinate position to the director. The Comptroller General found no evidence of improper influence. The Comptroller

General pointed out that although the director appointed the SSA prior to the SSA's selection of the SSEB members, the director was not involved in the evaluation nor was there any evidence that the director had any contact with the SSA or the SSEB during the course of the procurement.

B. Selection Decision

Neither the procurement statutes nor the FAR specify detailed standards for the source selection decision. The statutes merely require that the award is to be made "to the responsible source whose proposal is most advantageous to the United States, considering only cost or price and the other factors included in the solicitation," 10 U.S.C. § 2305(b)(4)(C) and 41 U.S.C. § 253b(d)(3). The FAR adds little, simply stating that the selection decision "shall be based upon a comparative assessment of proposals against all source selection criteria in the solicitation," FAR 15.308. Thus, the rules governing the source selection decision have been derived from decisions in contract award controversies.

The elements of the source selection decision are the comparative assessment of the proposals against the evaluation criteria and the ultimate tradeoff decision if the lowest price proposal is not rated most highly on the nonprice factors. The SSA has broad discretion in making the tradeoff decision but must make the decision consistent with the description of the evaluation factors and evaluation scheme in the solicitation.

1. *Broad Discretion in Tradeoff Decision*

If the selection decision is based on the evaluation factors enumerated in the RFP, the selection official has broad discretion in determining which offer is most advantageous to the Government. See *Lockheed Missiles & Space Co. v. Bentsen*, 4 F.3d 955 (Fed. Cir. 1993), stating that, "effective contracting demands broad discretion." The court illustrated the breadth of this discretion by stating at 960:

> Neither the FAR nor the broad language of the RFP requires that evaluation points be proportional to cost. Accordingly, a proposal which is one point better than another but costs millions of dollars more may be selected if the agency can demonstrate within a reasonable certainty that the added value of the proposal is worth the higher price. Here, as we have already noted,

> the IRS tradeoff analysis revealed that the dollar value of the two technical subfactors together with the value of the nonquantified discriminators justified the additional price to the AT&T proposal. Thus use of the IRS's evaluation method did not constitute an abuse of discretion because the method did not skew the importance of the two technical subfactors.

Thus, the selection will be upheld so long as there is a coherent and reasonable explanation for the selection, *Latecoere Int'l, Inc. v. Department of the Navy*, 19 F.3d 1342 (11th Cir. 1994). To be successful, a protester must show the selection to be "irrational or unreasonable," *Analytical & Research Technology, Inc. v. United States*, 39 Fed. Cl. 34 (1997). In *Brisk Waterproofing Co.*, Comp. Gen. Dec. B-276247, 97-1 CPD ¶ 195, the Comptroller General stated:

> [S]ource selection officials in negotiated procurements have broad discretion in determining the manner and extent to which they will make use of the technical and price results subject only to the tests of rationality and consistency with the RFP's evaluation factors. *Grey Advertising, Inc.*, 55 Comp. Gen. 1111, 1120–1121 (1976), 76-1 CPD ¶ 325 at 12.

See also *Research Triangle Inst.*, Comp. Gen. Dec. B-278254, 98-1 CPD ¶ ___; and *LTR Training Sys., Inc.*, Comp. Gen. Dec. B-274996, 97-1 CPD ¶ 71. In *J.A. Jones Management Servs., Inc.*, Comp. Gen. Dec. B-276864, 97-2 CPD ¶ 47, the Comptroller General stated the following limits used in reviewing selection decisions:

> In considering protests against an agency's evaluation of proposals, we will not reevaluate the proposals in order to make our own determination as to their acceptability or relative merits. *Technical Servs. Corp.*, B-216408.2, June 5, 1985, 85-1 CPD ¶ 640 at 6. However, we will examine the record to determine whether the evaluation was fair, reasonable and consistent with the evaluation criteria. *Bendix Field Eng'g Corp.*, B-219406, Oct. 31, 1985, 85-2 CPD ¶ 496 at 3.

2. Consistency With the Solicitation

While the SSA has a great deal of discretion in making the ultimate tradeoff decision, he or she must follow the guidance in the RFP as to the way the selection decision will be made.

a. Factors Used

The SSA may not introduce new factors or subfactors into the process. See *Contel Fed. Sys., Inc.*, GSBCA 9743-P, 89-1 BCA ¶ 21,458, *recons. denied*, 89-1 BCA ¶ 21,510, where the board overturned an award based on superiority of an offeror in a minor evaluation factor, stating at 108,134:

> A source selection official's discretion does not extend so far as to permit the making of a selection decision which is so completely at variance with the evaluation criteria set out in the solicitation. The motivation for the procurement, and the source selection official's personal view of the ultimate goal of the acquisition, are not criteria on which a selection decision may be based if they are not reflected in the solicitation. If the rule were otherwise, the entire evaluation process could be dominated by personal whim, making a mockery of statutory requirements for full and open, and fair and equal, competition in Government procurements.

See also *Bendix Field Eng'g Corp.*, Comp. Gen. Dec. B-219406, 85-2 CPD ¶ 496, where a protest was sustained when the SSA did not consider over half of the technical factors listed in the evaluation scheme. The Comptroller General stated that the official was clearly incorrect in believing that a source selection official had the power to substitute different source selection factors from the evaluation factors stated in the RFP.

The evaluation criteria in the RFP must be followed even if this produces an irrational result. See *Unified Indus., Inc.*, Comp. Gen. Dec. B-237868, 90-1 CPD ¶ 346, *recons. denied*, 90-2 CPD ¶ 120, where the agency was required to follow the RFP statement that all offerors would be evaluated using "the same number of hours" even though this meant evaluating the incumbent contractor on labor hours that it would not incur in performing the proposed contract. The Comptroller General dismissed the Navy's argument that this would be "irrational and unrealistic" holding that the rule requiring evaluation in accordance with the RFP was firm. Clearly, in this case, the agency should have amended the evaluation criteria in the RFP when it found that the stated criteria produced an irrational result.

As discussed in Section II, this rule does not prevent evaluation using any matters within the scope of the factors and subfactors set forth in the RFP, and there are numerous cases giving a broad interpretation of scope.

b. Relative Importance

The source selection official is not free to alter the relative importance of the factors stated in the RFP when the relationship of the factors is stated in a mathematical formula. However, as discussed in Section II.C., this statement of relative importance is generally not set forth in a formula but is stated in very general terms. Thus, the degree of discretion in this area depends on the degree of specificity of this statement in the RFP.

(1) SPECIFIC STATEMENT OF RELATIVE IMPORTANCE

The SSA has virtually no discretion, other than the ability to rescore, in cases where each factor is numerically scored, factor weights are numerical, and the RFP states that award will be made to the proposal receiving the highest number of points. In such a case, there can be no question as to whether RFP criteria have been adhered to, and the Comptroller General will uphold an award based on such a formula despite the apparent irrationality of the result. For example, in *Eaton-Kenway*, Comp. Gen. Dec. B-212575.2, 84-1 CPD ¶ 649, the agency paid $16 million more for a 17 percent higher technical score. The Comptroller General found that the agency "properly adhered to the results of the evaluation formula" in making the award without analyzing whether the difference in technical scores was worth the substantial amount of money paid for it. See also *Stone & Webster Eng'g Corp.*, Comp. Gen. Dec. B-255286.2, 94-1 CPD ¶ 306, where the Comptroller General held that the agency was not required to perform a tradeoff analysis because the "formula already accounted for both technical merit and proposed costs."

In this type of specific evaluation scheme, if the selection official does not follow the RFP decisional scheme, the decision will be rejected. See *Harrison Sys., Ltd.*, 63 Comp. Gen. 379 (B-212675), 84-1 CPD ¶ 572, for a case where the Comptroller General stated this rule but denied the protest by the offeror with the highest point score because the SSA implicitly rescored the technical proposals by finding that they were equal in value.

This strict rule does not apply to procurements where total numerical scores are computed for each offeror but the RFP gives the source selection official discretion to make a best value decision. In that case, the SSA can either award to the offeror with the highest total score or make a tradeoff decision to determine the offeror with the best value. See, for example,

ICOS Corp. of Am., 66 Comp. Gen. 246 (B-225392), 87-1 CPD ¶ 146, stating at 248:

> While the RFP did contain a formula for point scoring proposals, it did not state that award would be made to the offeror receiving the highest total score, but instead stated that the offeror representing the best combination of technical merit and price would be selected for award. Accordingly, the point scores were merely guides for decision making by the source selection official, who had the discretion to determine whether the technical advantage associated with ICOS's proposal was worth the extra cost associated with the proposal.

The same result was reached in *Resource Management Int'l, Inc.*, Comp. Gen. Dec. B-278108, 98-1 CPD ¶ __. However, in *Management Sys. Designers, Inc.*, Comp. Gen. Dec. B-244383.3, 91-2 CPD ¶ 310, the Comptroller General affirmed a source selection decision in a procurement with this type of evaluation scheme where the SSA merely awarded to the offeror with the highest point score without making a tradeoff analysis. See also *Halifax Security Servs., Inc.*, Comp. Gen. Dec. B-248584, 92-2 CPD ¶ 156; and *Tulane Univ.*, Comp. Gen. Dec. B-259912, 95-1 CPD ¶ 210.

(2) General Statement of Relative Importance

In procurements where the source selection official is given discretion to select the offeror proposing the "best value," it is more difficult to determine if a selection decision is consistent with the relative importance stated in the RFP. The tradeoff between cost/price and technical factors made by the selection official must still be based on the established criteria, but, whatever the stated relative importance of the factors, the ultimate decision will be based on an assessment of whether the difference in technical and management merit of the proposals is worth the difference in price, *TRW, Inc.*, GSBCA 11309-P, 92-1 BCA ¶ 24,389; *Barron Builders & Management Co.*, Comp. Gen. Dec. B-225803, 87-1 CPD ¶ 645. In such cases, a reasonable tradeoff between cost and other factors is generally supported.

(A) Technical/Management More Important Than Price

If the RFP states that technical and management factors are more important than price, the SSA is permitted to select an offeror that has proposed a significantly higher price if the technical and management benefits can be identified. See *EDG Eng'g of Texas, Inc.*, Comp. Gen. Dec. B-218540, 85-2 CPD ¶ 32, where the RFP stated that primary emphasis would be placed on technical factors, a lesser degree of importance would be placed on the management/personnel area, and an even lesser degree on the cost/price area; and *Fairchild Weston Sys., Inc.*, Comp. Gen. Dec. B-218470, 85-2 CPD ¶ 39, where the RFP stated that technical proposals "were significantly more important" than cost proposals. In *Suddath Van Lines, Inc.*, Comp. Gen. Dec. B-274285.2, 97-1 CPD ¶ 204, the Comptroller General affirmed a decision to award a contract for moving services to an offeror with higher technical ratings at a price 18 percent and 31 percent above the prices of the protesters. See also *Israel Aircraft Indus., Inc.*, Comp. Gen. Dec. B-274389, 97-1 CPD ¶ 41, where the SSA selected an offeror with higher technical scores and lower performance risk even though its price was approximately $4 million more than the protester's offer to perform for $23 million. The most striking decision of this type is *Lockheed Missile & Space Co. v. Department of the Treasury*, GSBCA 11776-P, 93-1 BCA ¶ 25,401, *aff'd*, 4 F. 3d 995 (Fed. Cir. 1993), where the board affirmed the award to an offeror that had submitted a superior technical proposal at a price of $1.4 billion, which was over $500 million higher than its next competitor. The board would not affirm the award until the agency had submitted a detailed analysis of the discriminators between the proposals — showing that the difference in technical merit was worth the difference in price by quantifying some of the major technical factors.

Award to the higher priced offeror has been overturned in a few cases where the benefits could not be demonstrated. See *Sturm, Ruger & Co.*, Comp. Gen. Dec. B-250193, 93-1 CPD ¶ 42, where the Comptroller General overturned a $1,366,550 award to an offeror receiving a technical score of 94 points when the protester had received a score of 89 points and had proposed a price of $768,012. The Comptroller General rejected the agency's contention that price should only be considered when the technical scores were equal and held that, in such a best value procurement, award to the higher priced offer "should be supported by a specific, documented determination that the technical superiority of the higher-priced offer warrants the additional cost involved, even where, as here, cost is stated to be the least important factor." Similarly, in *System Dev. Corp.*, Comp. Gen. Dec. B-213726, 84-1 CPD ¶ 605, the Comptroller General found an award to a higher technically rated, higher price firm to have been improper where the awardee's offer was only scored eight points higher than the protester's proposal (on a scale of 100 possible points), but the awardee's proposed price was more than 50 percent higher and the record contained no justification for paying a much greater cost for a proposal only slightly better in terms of quality. See also *Ball Technical Prods. Group*, Comp. Gen. Dec. B-224394, 86-2 CPD ¶ 465, where it was held improper to award to an offeror with an "excellent" technical proposal when its price was 53 percent higher than another offeror with an "acceptable" technical proposal. It appears that protests were sustained in these cases because the agency did not present detailed evaluations of the technical benefits that justified paying the higher prices.

Selection of a lower priced proposal is justified if the SSA determines that the technical and management benefits offered by the high priced offeror are not worth the higher cost. See, for example, *United Eng'rs & Constructors, Inc.*, Comp. Gen. Dec. B-240691, 90-2 CPD ¶ 490, where the Comptroller General agreed with a decision to award to an offeror that was $11 million lower in probable cost even though a competitor had submitted a clearly superior technical and management proposal. The RFP had stated that management and technical factors were more important than cost but that award would be made to the most advantageous proposal. The Comptroller General stated:

> [E]ven if cost is the least important evaluation criterion, an agency may properly award to a lower-cost, lower-scored offeror if it determines that the cost premium involved in awarding to a higher-rated, higher-cost offeror is not justified given the acceptable level of technical competence available at the lower cost. *Carrier Joint Venture*, B-233702, Mar. 13, 1989, 89-1 CPD ¶ 268, *aff'd*, B-233702.2, June 23, 1989, 89-1 CPD ¶ 594. The determining element is not the difference in technical merit, per se, but the contracting agency's judgment concerning the significance of the difference. *Dayton T. Brown, Inc.*, B-229664, Mar. 30, 1988, 88-1 CPD ¶ 321. Cost/technical tradeoffs may be made, and the extent to which one may be sacrificed for the other is governed only by the test of rationality and consistency with the established evaluation criteria.

Similarly, in *Ecology & Env't, Inc.*, Comp. Gen. Dec. B-209516, 83-2 CPD ¶ 229, the Comptroller General held that a selection official, finding a particular percentage differential in technical scores insignificant, was not compelled to find a lower percentage cost differential insignificant, stating: "Contracting agencies generally need a degree of discretion in weighing the significance of the relationship between technical scores and cost differentials, and reserve to themselves such discretion by not including rigid evaluation formulas in the RFP." See also *Wyle Lab., Inc.*, 69 Comp. Gen.

648 (B-239113), 90-2 CPD ¶ 107, finding reasonable a determination that the difference in technical merit was not worth the difference in price; *ERC Envtl. & Energy Servs. Co.*, Comp. Gen. Dec. B-241549, 91-1 CPD ¶ 155, holding that an award to the low cost proposal was rational when the difference in price was significant and the difference in technical factors was relatively small; *Ares Corp.*, Comp. Gen. Dec. B-275321, 97-1 CPD ¶ 82, affirming an award to the lower cost offeror when the protester had a slightly higher technical rating; *Creative Apparel Assocs.,* Comp. Gen. Dec. B-275139, 97-1 CPD ¶ 65, finding the award rational when the SSA determined that the slightly higher price was not worth the modest difference in technical rating; *PRC, Inc.*, Comp. Gen. Dec. B-274698.2, 97-1 CPD ¶ 115, finding reasonable a determination to award to the lower cost proposal even though the protester's proposal was scored higher on all technical factors; and *Crown Clothing Corp.*, Comp. Gen. Dec. B-277505.2, 97-2 CPD ¶ 127, affirming an award to a low price offeror because the difference in technical scores, even if the protest of an improper evaluation was sustained, would not be worth the difference in price.

Award to a lower priced offeror will be overturned if the source selection official cannot state a reasonable basis for giving up the technical benefits offered by the higher priced, technically superior offeror. For instance, in *Dewberry & Davis*, Comp. Gen. Dec. B-247116, 92-1 CPD ¶ 421, a protest was sustained because the agency did not provide justification of its selection of the lower priced proposal where the RFP had stated that technical was more important than cost. The Comptroller General stated that it would uphold such a decision only if the agency provided a "cogent rationale" in the documentation for such a decision. Similarly, in *Pharm-Chem Lab., Inc.*, Comp. Gen. Dec. B-244385, 91-2 CPD ¶ 317, the Comptroller General sustained a protest where the source selection official had determined two technical proposals equal and awarded to the low cost offeror in the face of evaluations which indicated that the high cost offeror was clearly superior. The Comptroller General reasoned that the small difference in cost was not worth the difference in technical merit and recommended award to the high cost, technically superior offeror. See also *Hattal & Assocs.*, 70 Comp. Gen. 632 (B-243357), 91-2 CPD ¶ 90, where an award was overturned because it was made to a lower cost offeror when the two competitors were both determined to be "technically acceptable." The Comptroller General stated at 637:

> When an RFP provides that the technical factors will be considered more important than cost, a procuring agency may not make its award decision as

> though the RFP provided for award to the lowest cost, technically acceptable offeror. *RCA Serv. Co.*, B-219406.2, Sept. 10, 1986, 86-2 CPD ¶ 278. It is improper for an agency to induce an offeror to prepare and submit a proposal emphasizing technical excellence, then fail to consider technical factors and award solely on the basis of cost. Such action clearly disregards the RFP's evaluation criteria. . . . *Kempter-Rossman Int'l*, B-220772, Feb. 4, 1986, 86-1 CPD ¶ 127; *Applied Financial Analysis, Ltd.*, B-194388.2, Aug. 10, 1979, 79-2 CPD ¶ 113.

In some cases involving cost-reimbursement contracts, the Comptroller General has stressed the "extremely strong justification" necessary to support award to a lower cost proposal which is ranked lower in technical and management. For example, in *DLI Eng'g Corp.*, Comp. Gen. Dec. B-218335, 85-1 CPD ¶ 742, *recons. denied*, 65 Comp. Gen. 34 (B-218335.2), 85-2 CPD ¶ 468, the Comptroller General indicated that, where the selection official does not rescore proposals or otherwise indicate that the technical point differential is not an accurate measure of the difference in technical quality of the proposals, primary emphasis may not be placed on cost in the selection decision when the RFP stated that cost was the least important criterion. The Navy justified selection of the lower cost offeror by claiming that, although the lower cost proposal was technically inferior, the inferiority could be overcome by the application of additional contractor and Government hours, and that the total Government expenditure would still be less after these additional amounts were added to the awardee's costs. The Comptroller, however, found that the awardee would not be able to offer several unique technical features offered by the protester even with the additional hours, and thus the selection was inconsistent with the RFP criteria. See also *RCA Serv. Co.*, Comp. Gen. Dec. B-219406.2, 86-2 CPD ¶ 278, where it was found improper to award to a lower cost proposal with only an adequate technical rating where technical merit was the most important criteria. Similarly, in *AAA Eng'g & Drafting, Inc.*, Comp. Gen. Dec. B-202140, 81-2 CPD ¶ 16, the Comptroller General upheld a protest where the agency recommended award to the low cost offeror submitting the lowest rated technical proposal when the RFP stated that the evaluation criteria were listed in descending order of importance and cost was ranked third out of four evaluation factors. The Comptroller General held that cost could not account for more than 20-25 percent of the total evaluation.

(B) PRICE MORE IMPORTANT THAN TECHNICAL/MANAGEMENT

When the RFP states that price is more important than the other factors, the SSA can award the contract to the offeror with the lowest price as long as the price advantage outweighs the technical advantage of higher priced offerors, *GTE Hawaiian Tel. Co.,* Comp. Gen. Dec. B-276487.2, 97-2 CPD ¶ 21.

In this situation, the SSA is also permitted to award the contract to an offeror with a higher price if the differences in technical and management merit are worth paying the higher costs. Thus, in *Frequency Eng'g Lab. Corp.*, Comp. Gen. Dec. B-225606, 87-1 CPD ¶ 393, award at a price of $57.6 million was permitted when the protester had offered a price of $51.2 but had proposed to use less qualified personnel whom the agency evaluated as posing a much higher risk that performance would not be successfully accomplished. See also *Centex Constr. Co.*, Comp. Gen. Dec. B-238777, 90-1 CPD ¶ 566 (award to offeror with slightly higher price justified by strong technical rating); *Oklahoma Aerotronics, Inc.*, Comp. Gen. Dec. B-237705.2, 90-1 CPD ¶ 337 (award to an offeror with 2 percent higher price justified by the lower technical risk obtained); and *F.A.S. Sys. Corp.*, Comp. Gen. Dec. B-236344, 89-2 CPD ¶ 512 (award to offeror with $1,100,000 higher price justified when detailed agency evaluation indicated significantly stronger technical ability).

(C) PRICE AND TECHNICAL/MANAGEMENT EQUAL

When the price factor and the technical/management factors are stated to be equal, the source selection official probably has the greatest discretion to make a "best value" source selection decision. In 52 Comp. Gen. 686 (B-176763) (1973), the Comptroller General held that, under the RFP, cost could be deemed equally as important as technical merit and that the agency had discretion to assess cost ceilings and cost realism considerations in determining which offer was most advantageous to the Government. In *IBI Sec. Serv., Inc.*, Comp. Gen. Dec. B-216799, 85-2 CPD ¶ 85, the Comptroller General approved the agency's award of a contract for security services to a higher priced offeror where the lower priced offeror had deficient technical facilities and staff, stating that this was acceptable when the technical concerns were reasonable and the selection decision was made "in the best interest of the government." In *EER Sys. Corp.*, 69 Comp. Gen. 207

(B-237054), 90-1 CPD ¶ 123, a selection decision for a higher priced, higher technically rated offeror was affirmed because it provided the best value to the Government. The protester's offer was found to represent inferior personnel and quality of work and was judged to be not worth the monetary difference. In *Martech USA, Inc.*, Comp. Gen. Dec. B-250284.2, 93-1 CPD ¶ 110, award to a 15 percent higher priced offer was affirmed when the protester had been rated lowest technically because of poor past performance. In *SWR, Inc.*, Comp. Gen. Dec. B-276878, 97-2 CPD ¶ 34, the Comptroller General denied a protest of a decision to award to a higher priced offer to obtain better past performance. However, the tradeoff that is made between cost and technical/management proposals must still be justified as being rational. See, for example, *Kempter-Rossman Int'l*, Comp. Gen. Dec. B-220772, 86-1 CPD ¶ 127, finding it unreasonable to award to a 2 percent lower priced offer when the competitive offer had a 25 percent technical superiority and the RFP gave equal weight to the price and technical factors. Similarly, in *Mechanical Contractors, S.A.*, Comp. Gen. Dec. B-277916, 97-2 CPD ¶ 121, a protest was sustained when the Comptroller General found multiple errors in the evaluation which was used by the SSA to make the selection decision.

3. *Determinations of Relative Technical Merit*

There are a large number of cases where the SSA exercises discretion by ignoring differences in technical scoring by evaluators and determining that the technical merit of competing offers is relatively equal, thus, allowing contracts to be awarded to the lower cost offeror. In *Verify, Inc.*, 71 Comp. Gen. 158 (B-244401.2), 92-1 CPD ¶ 107, for example, the contracting personnel and evaluators agreed that the original technical scores given to Verify were an overstatement of merit and that rescoring was necessary to achieve accuracy. The final score given by the contracting officer was actually lower than the original score and supported a finding of technical equality between Verify and the lower cost awardee. In most cases, such determinations of equality are made without explicitly rescoring the proposals. For example, in *Jack Faucett Assocs. — Request for Recons.*, Comp. Gen. Dec. B-233224.2, 89-1 CPD ¶ 551, the contracting officer properly awarded the contract to the low priced offeror after concluding that Faucett's higher price offer, with a technical score of 8.63 out of 10 points, was substantially equal to the lower priced offeror's technical score of 8.22. See also *Systems Integrated*, Comp. Gen. Dec. B-225055, 87-1 CPD ¶ 114, where the low priced awardee's technical score of 66.7 out of 80 points was properly considered by the contracting officer to be equal to the 68.1 technical score of the higher priced offer; *General Offshore Corp.*, Comp. Gen. Dec. B-246824, 92-1 CPD ¶ 335, where the contracting officer properly found that a nine percent higher technical score did not represent any actual technical superiority and awarded to the lower cost offeror; *LTR Training Sys., Inc.*, Comp. Gen. Dec. B-274996, 97-1 CPD ¶ 71, where the contracting officer found the proposals technically equal although the evaluators had scored the protester's proposal substantially higher; and *EBA Eng'g, Inc.*, Comp. Gen. Dec. B-275818, 97-1 CPD ¶ 127, where the Comptroller General found proper the SSA's determination that the technical proposals were basically equal even though the source selection panel rated the protester higher on every evaluation factor.

Such a determination of equality has also been supported in a case where the RFP called for precise numerical scores for technical and cost factors and stated that award would be made to the offeror with the highest number of points. The Comptroller General stated that the source selection official would not have been permitted to alter the cost/technical tradeoff announced in the RFP but was entitled to rescore the proposals by determining that the technical proposals were equal, *Harrison Sys., Ltd.*, 63 Comp. Gen. 379 (B-212675), 84-1 CPD ¶ 572. See also *Crowley Maritime Salvage*, Comp. Gen. Dec. B-234555, 89-1 CPD ¶ 555 (award to lower point total permissible where contracting officer determined that a 14.4 percent difference in technical score was not significant).

The Comptroller General has permitted determinations of equality even though the technical factors are weighted more heavily than cost, *E.J. Richardson Assocs., Inc.*, Comp. Gen. Dec. B-250951, 93-1 CPD ¶ 185 (technical scores of 93.3 and 90.0 found substantially equal when technical factor "slightly more important" than cost); *WB, Inc.*, Comp. Gen. Dec. B-250954, 93-1 CPD ¶ 173 (technical scores of 88 and 87 found essentially equal when technical factor was "primary" and price/cost was "least important"); *Systems Research Corp.*, Comp. Gen. Dec. B-237008, 90-1 CPD ¶ 106 (technical scores of 48.15 and 54.63 found equal where technical factors had weight of 60 percent); *DDL Omni Eng'g*, Comp. Gen. Dec. B-220075, 85-2 CPD ¶ 684 (technical scores of 6.61 and 6.96 found equal where the technical score was "of paramount importance" but variable).

A frequently upheld reason for finding equality of technical scores is where technical evaluators can give no cogent reasons explaining the technical point differential between two proposals. This was permitted in

DLM&A, Inc. v. United States, 6 Cl. Ct. 329 (1984), where the selection official determined on this basis that the proposals were "substantially equal" and, therefore, awarded to the low cost proposal.

Determinations of equality will be overturned if they are not supported by reasoned analysis. See, for example, *DynCorp*, Comp. Gen. Dec. B-232999, 89-1 CPD ¶ 152 (no rational explanation for ignoring evaluators' concerns); *University Found., Cal. State Univ., Chico*, Comp. Gen. Dec. B-200608, 81-1 CPD ¶ 54 (no indication given as to why the evaluation point scores were not followed in awarding the contract). See also *Tracor Jitco, Inc.*, 54 Comp. Gen. 896 (B-182213), 75-1 CPD ¶ 253, where the source selection was based on the conclusion of one evaluator that the proposals were technically equal, but no reasoning was advanced to support the conclusion, and it conflicted with the factually supported views of two other evaluators and the technical evaluation committee. The selection decision was later found to be supportable, after a review of the selection process by the procuring agency showed that the evaluator had judged the proposals technically equal on the basis of additional information from the awardee which cleared up deficiencies, *Tracor Jitco, Inc.*, 55 Comp. Gen. 499 (B-182213), 75-2 CPD ¶ 344.

The selection official is not required to find the proposals equal when the point differential is small. In *Bell & Howell Corp.*, Comp. Gen. Dec. B-196165, 81-2 CPD ¶ 49, the protester argued that the competing proposals should have been considered technically equal since there was a difference of only 3.6 points between them, and consequently, that cost should have been the determinative evaluation factor. In denying the protest, the Comptroller General held that "[t]he dispositive element in a case such as this is not the technical scores per se but the considered judgment of the procuring agency concerning the significance of that difference." See also *Super Teams Operating Co.*, Comp. Gen. Dec. B-260100, 95-1 CPD ¶ 246, where the protester received a technical score of 83.3, the awardee received a score of 86.7, and a third, high-cost offeror received a technical score of 91.1. The source selection official considered the 86.7 and 91.1 scores to be technically equal. The protester argued that if a 4.4-point difference makes two proposals technically equal, its smaller 2.9-point difference must make its proposal equal to the awardee's technical proposal. The Comptroller General denied the protest, stating that "closeness of point scores does not necessarily indicate that proposals are essentially equal." The source selection official determined that there were significant differences in the technical merit between the proposals and this difference was reflected in the narrative summaries.

4. Quantification of Technical Ratings

Quantification of technical ratings is not required when a tradeoff decision is made, FAR 15.308. This rule was established by the Court of Appeals for the Federal Circuit in *Lockheed Missiles & Space Co. v. Bentsen*, 19 F.3d 955 (1993). See also *EG&G Team*, Comp. Gen. Dec. B-259917, 95-2 CPD ¶ 175, stating that "the source selection authority has discretion to determine how to balance cost and technical advantages in making an award decision in a best value procurement." Quantification was not required in *Sudath Van Lines, Inc.*, Comp. Gen. Dec. B-274285.2, 97-1 CPD ¶ 204; *Ingalls Shipbuiding, Inc.*, Comp. Gen. Dec. B-275830, 97-1 CPD ¶ 180; and *Kay & Assocs., Inc.*, Comp. Gen. Dec. B-258243.7, 96-1 CPD ¶ 266.

When quantification of the benefit of making an award to a higher priced offer is practical, the tradeoff should be justified in terms of dollars. See, for example, *Continental Airlines, Inc.*, Comp. Gen. Dec. B-258271.4, 97-1 CPD ¶ 81, where the Comptroller General held that the agency had made a valid tradeoff decision by quantifying most of the nonprice evaluation factors; and *Global Assocs., Ltd.*, Comp. Gen. Dec. B-275534, 97-1 CPD ¶ 129, where quantification of many of the nonprice factors was found to be proper.

5. Documentation

Agencies must prepare documentation demonstrating that the source selection decision was reasonable and consistent with the solicitation. Prior to the FAR Rewrite, the FAR was somewhat unclear as to the documentation required to support selection decisions. However, the Comptroller General required agencies to submit documentation when awards were protested. See *Quality Elevator Co.*, Comp. Gen. Dec. B-276750, 97-2 CPD ¶ 28, stating:

> While judgments concerning the evaluation of proposals are by their nature subjective, they must be reasonable; such judgments must bear a rational relationship to the announced criteria upon which proposals were to be evaluated. *Management Technology, Inc.*, B-257269.2, Nov. 8, 1994, 95-1

> CPD ¶ 248 at 6-7. Implicit in the foregoing is that the rationale for these judgments must be documented in sufficient detail to show that they are not arbitrary and that there was a reasonable basis for the selection decision. *Id.* Federal Acquisition Regulation (FAR) 15.608(a)(3) requires documentation to support the evaluation of proposals, including the basis for evaluation and an analysis of the technically acceptable and unacceptable proposals, an assessment of each offeror's ability to accomplish the technical requirement, and a summary of findings. FAR 15.612(d)(2) requires supporting documentation for the source selection decision, stating the basis and reasons for the decision and showing the relative differences among proposals and their strengths, weaknesses, and risks in terms of the evaluation criteria. Numerical point scores, while useful as guides to decision-making, do not of themselves supply the basis and reason for the award decision. *U.S. Defense Sys., Inc.*, B-245563, Jan. 17, 1992, 92-1 CPD ¶ 89 at 3; *S&M Property Management*, B-243051, June 28, 1991, 91-1 CPD ¶ 615 at 4. Where there is inadequate supporting documentation for an award decision, we cannot conclude that the agency had a reasonable basis for the decision. *Hattal & Assocs.*, 70 Comp. Gen. 632, 637 (1991), 91-2 CPD ¶ 90 at 7.

The FAR Rewrite adopted a more rigorous documentation requirement following the guidance established by the Comptroller General. See FAR 15.308 stating the following requirement:

> The source selection decision shall be documented, and the documentation shall include the rationale for any business judgments and tradeoffs made or relied on by the SSA, including benefits associated with additional costs. Although the rationale for the selection decision must be documented, that documentation need not quantify the tradeoffs that led to the decision.

See also FAR 15.305(a) which includes the following statement:

> (3) *Technical evaluation.* When tradeoffs are performed (see 15.101-1), the source selection records shall include —
>
> > (i) An assessment of each offeror's ability to accomplish the technical requirements; and
> >
> > (ii) A summary, matrix, or quantitative ranking, along with appropriate supporting narrative, of each technical proposal using the evaluation factors.

If an agency's documentation does not demonstrate that the source selection decision is rational, a protest will be granted. See *Matrix Int'l*

Logistics, Inc., Comp. Gen. Dec. B-272388.2, 97-2 CPD ¶ 89, where the determination of the SSA that two technical proposals were "essentially equal" was not supported in the documentation submitted by the agency. The Comptroller General stated:

> An agency which fails to adequately document its evaluation of proposals or [the] source selection decision bears the risk that its determinations will be considered unsupported, and absent such support, our Office may be unable to determine whether the agency had a reasonable basis for its determinations.

See also *J.A. Jones Management Services, Inc.*, Comp. Gen. Dec. B-276864, 97-2 CPD ¶ 47 (inadequate documentation to support decision when agency submitted "point scores and cursory narratives" with no "consistent, reasonable and accurate evaluation scoring" or "supporting narrative documentation"); *J.W. Assocs., Inc.*, Comp. Gen. Dec. B-275209, 97-1 CPD ¶ 57 (point scores plus one paragraph "evaluation summary" inadequate to explain the evaluation of technical proposals); *Cygnus Corp.,* Comp. Gen. Dec. B-275181, 97-1 CPD ¶ 63 (documentation contained only point scores for technical factors with no explanation of basis for scores); *Engineering & Computation, Inc.*, Comp. Gen. Dec. B-261658, 95-2 CPD ¶ 176 (no explanation of agency analysis that protester's proposal posed risks); *Arco Management of Washington, D.C., Inc.*, Comp. Gen. Dec. B-248653, 92-2 CPD ¶ 173 (no documentation explaining rescoring of BAFOs); *U.S. Defense Sys., Inc.*, Comp. Gen. Dec. B-245563, 92-1 CPD ¶ 89 (final technical scores, accompanied by no narrative explanation of any kind, inadequate to justify selection decision).

While documentation compiled contemporaneously with the evaluation and the source selection decision is preferable, the lack of contemporaneous documentation will not be fatal if the evaluation and selection can be shown to be reasonable and in conformance with the evaluation criteria. Thus, documentation supporting the source selection decision may be created by the agency after the filing of a protest. See *Network Solutions, Inc. v. Department of the Air Force*, GSBCA 11498-P, 92-3 BCA ¶ 25,083, where the board stated at 125,044 that the "record created in the course of the Board's de novo review could support the selection actually made despite the SSA's failure to articulate the cost/technical tradeoff analysis at the time." The Comptroller General has also followed this rule — even in the extreme case where the agency has destroyed the original documentation.

See *Southwest Marine, Inc.*, Comp. Gen. Dec. B-265865.4, 96-1 CPD ¶ 56, stating:

> In determining the rationality of an agency's evaluation and award decision, we do not limit our review to contemporaneous evidence, but consider all the information provided, including the parties' arguments, explanations, and hearing testimony. *Benchmark Sec., Inc.*, [Comp. Gen. Dec. B-247655, 93-1 CPD ¶ 133]; *KMS Fusion, Inc.*, [Comp. Gen. Dec. B-242529, 91-1 CPD ¶ 447]; *Hydraudyne Sys. and Eng'g B.V.*, [Comp. Gen. Dec. B-241236, 91-1 CPD ¶ 88]. While we consider the entire record, including the parties' later explanations and arguments, we accord greater weight to contemporaneous evaluation and source selection material than to arguments and documentation prepared in response to protest contentions. *Dyn-Corp*, 71 Comp. Gen. 129 (1991), 91-2 CPD ¶ 575.
>
> Here, the Navy's destruction of the evaluators' notes and workpapers left a written record that did not meet the requirements of FAR 15.608(a)(3)(ii). The contemporaneous documentation retained by the Navy — the TEC's final report, the TEC chair's cost/technical tradeoff document, and source selection decision — did not adequately explain why BAV's proposal was judged to be technically superior to SWM's and AMSEC's. Specifically, while the TEC report described BAV's proposal's strengths and advantages to justify its "highly acceptable" rating, it did not explain why the protesters' proposals, which appeared from this document to have similar strengths, were not essentially technically equivalent. Accordingly, the retained documentation was not sufficient to support the evaluation results. Indeed, a hearing was convened at our request, in part, because of the inadequacy of the evaluation documentation in the record, which did not fully explain the agency's evaluation . . . and the hearing testimony revealed that a number of identified strengths and weaknesses for all offerors' proposals were not recorded in the TEC's final evaluation report. . . .
>
> While the Navy's document destruction was improper, we will not disrupt an agency's procurement on this basis alone where the protest record is otherwise adequate for our review. See *Hydraudyne Sys. and Eng'g B.V.*, *supra*. SWM and AMSEC assert that the evaluators' notes and workpapers are necessary here to allow for our review of the procurement; they correctly note that the evaluators could not recall in their hearing testimony all the details of the lengthy evaluation process and that there were some minor inconsistencies in the evaluators' testimony. This, however, does not establish the inadequacy of the protest record. The testimony of the agency's evaluators, TEC chair, and SSA explained the basis of the agency's evaluation conclusions, and, more specifically, why BAV's proposal was determined to be technically superior to SWM's and AMSEC's; they agreed on

> the major aspects of the evaluation and the evaluated differences among the parties' proposals. Looking at the record as a whole, we believe that it adequately explains the agency's actions so as to allow the parties to present their arguments concerning the reasonableness of the agency's source selection and to allow our Office to effectively review the matter. *Id.*
>
> From our detailed review of this record, we conclude that the agency's evaluation of technical proposals and its cost/technical tradeoff decision were reasonable.

See also *AT&T Corp.*, Comp. Gen. Dec. B-260447.4, 96-1 CPD ¶ 200 (source selection decision affirmed based on the agency protest report which presented extensive and detailed narratives concerning the strengths of the awardee's technical and management proposals when this information was consistent with the less detailed contemporaneous documentation); *Sociometrics, Inc.*, Comp. Gen. Dec. B-261367.2, 95-2 CPD ¶ 201 (although the details of the cost realism analysis were not spelled out in a contemporaneous document, the contracting officer adequately explained the details of the analysis in an agency protest report); and *Hydraudyne Sys. & Eng'g B.V.*, Comp. Gen. Dec. B-241236, 91-1 CPD ¶ 88 (source selection decision sustained based on its after-the-fact explanations of the scoring of individual evaluators after the documentation created by these evaluators had been "discarded"). In *Universal Shipping Co.*, Comp. Gen. Dec. B-223905.2, 87-1 CPD ¶ 424, *recons. denied*, 87-2 CPD ¶ 125, the protester won the initial protest based on a finding of inadequate documentation but ultimately lost the protest on the basis of documentation created by the agency after the initial decision by the Comptroller General.

The Comptroller General has stated that, though the entire record would be considered in protest resolutions, he will "accord greater weight to contemporaneous source selection materials rather than documents . . . prepared in response to protest contentions," *DynCorp*, 71 Comp. Gen. 129 (B-245289), 91-2 CPD ¶ 575. This logic was followed in *United Int'l Eng'g, Inc.*, 71 Comp. Gen. 177 (B-245448.3), 92-1 CPD ¶ 122, in which the source selection official's post-selection testimony regarding his reluctance to award to the protester was inconsistent with the evaluation criteria and contemporaneous evidence. The Comptroller General sustained the protest "giving due weight to the contemporaneous source selection documents."

The Comptroller General has not demanded that the documentation cover every element of the selection decision as long as it supports the overall rationale used by the SSA. See *SEAIR Transport Servs., Inc.*, Comp. Gen. Dec. B-274436, 96-2 CPD ¶ 224, stating:

> SEAIR challenges the agency's documentation of its award decision, characterizing the record as "devoid of any real rationale for the decision to award the contract to EAST," and alleging that the source selection decision does not address the relative differences between SEAIR's and EAST's proposals. While the selection official's judgment must be documented in sufficient detail to show it is not arbitrary, *KMS Fusion, Inc.*, B-242529, May 8, 1991, 91-1 CPD ¶ 447, a source selection official's failure to specifically discuss every detail regarding the relative merit of the proposals in the selection decision document does not affect the validity of the decision if the record shows that the agency's award decision was reasonable. See *McShade Gov't Contracting Servs.*, B-232977, Feb. 6, 1989, 89-1 CPD ¶ 118. Here, the record documents the evaluation process, the color coding, and the risk assessments, concluding with the agency's determination that SEAIR's and EAST's proposals were essentially equal technically. The source selection document refers to this determination and concludes that, taking price into consideration, EAST's lower-priced offer represented the best overall value to the government. We see no basis to object to the source selection document, which very clearly sets forth the basis for the agency's award decision.

The documentation need not comply literally with the requirement of the FAR that it contain a statement of the "strengths, weaknesses and risks" as long as it explains the selection decision. See *Matrix Int'l Logistics, Inc.*, Comp. Gen. Dec. B-272388.2, 97-2 CPD ¶ 89, stating:

> The form of the documentation is not important if it supports the source selection decision. Thus, sketches of proposed designs were adequate documentation in lieu of narratives where aesthetics was a relevant factor in the construction of a scenic footbridge, *Bell Free Contractors, Inc.*, Comp. Gen. Dec. B-227576, 87-2 CPD ¶ 418.

C. Post Selection Communication

Neither the procurement statutes nor the FAR deal with the subject of communications between the agency and the selected offeror after selection has been made and before award. However, in many cases, it is necessary to clear up uncertainties or to resolve remaining issues before award can be made. In other cases the agency may wish to negotiate more favorable terms or prices with the selected source. Thus, it is essential to determine whether such communications constitute negotiations which would require the agency to negotiate with all those who submitted offers if award was being made on the basis of initial proposals or with all those remaining in the competitive range if final offer revisions have been requested.

1. Negotiations Not Permitted

The general rule is that negotiation with only one offeror is prohibited. Such negotiations would occur if an offeror were given the opportunity to revise its offer to establish that the offer is acceptable. See *SmitKline Beecham Pharmaceuticals, N.A.*, Comp. Gen. Dec. B-252226.2, 93-2 CPD ¶ 79, stating:

> It is a fundamental principle of federal procurement that all offerors must be treated equally. *Loral Terracom*; *Marconi Italiana*, 66 Comp. Gen. 272 (1987), 87-1 CPD ¶ 182. Thus, the conduct of discussions with one offeror generally requires that discussions be conducted with all offerors whose offers are within the competitive range and that offerors have an opportunity to submit revised offers. *Microlog Corp.*, B-237486, Feb. 26, 1990, 90-1 CPD ¶ 227. This rule applies even to post-selection negotiations that do not directly affect the offerors' relative standing, because all offerors are entitled to an equal opportunity to revise their proposals. *PRC Information Sciences Co.*, 56 Comp. Gen. 768 (1977), 77-2 CPD ¶ 11. Discussions occur when an offeror is given an opportunity to revise or modify its proposal, or when information provided by an offeror is essential for determining the acceptability of its proposal. Federal Acquisition Regulation (FAR) 15.601; *Motorola. Inc.*, 66 Comp. Gen. 519 (1987), 87-1 CPD ¶ 604.

See also *Global Assocs., Ltd.*, Comp. Gen. Dec. B-271693.2, 96-2 CPD ¶ 100 (offer as received could not have been accepted). *In Matrix Int'l Logistics, Inc.*, Comp. Gen. Dec. B-272388.2, 97-2 CPD ¶ 89, the Comptroller General held that correction of a mistake in awardee's price after receipt of best and final offers required "discussions" with all offerors where the intended price was not ascertainable from the offer and the solicitation. In assessing the post selection communication cases, the Comptroller General focuses on whether there is a "reasonable possibility of prejudice" to the other offerors, *Labat-Anderson Inc.*, 71 Comp. Gen. 252 (B-246071.2), 92-1 CPD ¶ 193.

2. Communications and Nonmaterial Changes

Communications which would be permissible under FAR 15.306(a) do not require communications with other offerors. See Section V, above for a discussion of this type of communications. Thus, "touch up negotiations" have been permitted, *Medical Care Dev., Inc.*, Comp. Gen. Dec. B-227848.3, 87-2 CPD ¶ 371. In addition, discussing or requiring changes in nonmaterial aspects of an offer would not require negotiations with other offerors. See *Assets Recovery Sys., Inc.*, Comp. Gen. Dec. B-275332, 97-1 CPD ¶ 67 (change in payment provision did not increase or decrease overall value of offer); *Optimum Sys., Inc.*, Comp. Gen. Dec. B-194984, 80-2 CPD ¶ 32 (substitution of computer would have had same effect on all offerors); and *Information Sys. & Networks Corp.*, Comp. Gen. Dec. B-220661, 86-1 CPD ¶ 30 (negotiations to obtain a small reduction in price). See also *L.G. Lefler v. United States*, 6 Cl. Ct. 514 (1984), where the offer would have been lowest even without the negotiated price change.

3. Negotiations Permitted

There are several situations in which negotiations with only the selected source will be permitted.

a. Alternate Source Selection Procedures

In the past, several agencies adopted alternate source selection procedures which permit a degree of negotiation with only the selected offeror. These procedures were authorized by pre-Rewrite FAR 15.613 as follows:

> (a) The National Aeronautics and Space Administration (NASA) and the Department of Defense (DOD) have developed, and use in appropriate situations, source selection procedures that limit discussions with offerors during the competition and that differ from other procedures described in Subpart 15.6. The procedures are the NASA Source Evaluation Board procedures and the DOD "Four Step" Source Selection Procedures. Detailed coverage of these procedures is in the respective agency acquisition regulations.
>
> (b) Other agencies may use either the NASA or DOD procedures as a model in developing their own procedures, including applicability criteria, consistent with mission needs.

Under the NASA procedure and the DOD "Four Step" procedure set forth in DFARS 215.613-70, the agency conducted limited communications with all offerors within the competitive range and then negotiated the final contract price, terms, and conditions with the selected offeror. However, the negotiations could not permit any changes in the Government's requirements or the offer which would affect the source selection decision. The Comptroller General recognized that such procedures met the statutory requirements for conducting oral or written discussions with all offerors within the competitive range. See *Ogden Logistics Servs.*, Comp. Gen. Dec. B-257731.3, 95-1 CPD ¶ 3, stating:

> [T]he FAR expressly acknowledges that NASA and DOD have developed alternate "source selection procedures that limit discussions with offerors during the competition, and that differ from other procedures prescribed in [FAR] Subpart 15.6." FAR § 15.613(a). In essence, NASA's alternate procedures, set forth at 48 C.F.R. § 18-15.613-71, limit discussions to clarification of proposals. Our Office has recognized NASA's alternate procedures as one legitimate approach to the statutory requirement for holding discussions with competitive range offerors. *Taft Broadcasting Corp.*, B-222818, July 29, 1986, 86-2 CPD ¶ 125; *Support Sys. Assocs., Inc.*, B-215421, Sept. 4, 1984, 84-2 CPD ¶ 249; *Program Resources, Inc.*, B-192964, Apr. 23, 1979, 79-1 CPD ¶ 281.

See also *Sperry Rand Corp.*, 54 Comp. Gen. 408 (B-181460), 74-2 CPD ¶ 276; *Dynalectron Corp.*, 54 Comp. Gen. 562 (B-181738), 75-1 CPD ¶ 17; *Management Servs., Inc.*, 55 Comp. Gen. 715 (B-184606), 76-1 CPD ¶ 74; *GTE Sylvania*, 57 Comp. Gen. 715 (B-188272), 77-2 CPD ¶ 422; and *Taft Broadcasting Corp.*, Comp. Gen. Dec. B-222818, 86-2 CPD ¶ 125.

The Comptroller General has also recognized the validity of similar procedures adopted by the Department of Energy, *Holmes & Narver, Inc.*, Comp. Gen. Dec. B-239469.2, 90-2 CPD ¶ 210, *recons. denied*, 91-1 CPD ¶ 51. The Department of Health and Human Services alternate procedure at HHSAR 315.670 provides for a "limited negotiation with the selected offeror." It prohibits introduction of any "factor which could have any effect on the selection process." The agency's requirements cannot be changed without reopening negotiations with all sources and the negotiations are not to prejudice the competitive interests of the unsuccessful offerors. The subjects for negotiation are described as follows:

> Negotiations with the selected offeror shall be restricted to definitizing the final agreement on terms and conditions; e.g., assuming none of these fac-

> tors were involved in the selection process, negotiation could include such topics as payment provisions, patent rights, rights in data, property provisions, labor rates, indirect cost rates, and fees.

In *Prospect Assocs., Inc.,* Comp. Gen. Dec. B-260696, 95-2 CPD ¶ 53, the agency, using this procedure, conducted negotiations with the selected offeror on labor and indirect cost rates and other "minor issues." The negotiations resulted in a "relatively minor reduction" in the offered cost. The Comptroller General held that there was no need to negotiate with other offerors since the purpose of the negotiation was to "definitize" the terms "not to obtain more competitive pricing." That case should be contrasted with *SmithKline Beecham Pharmaceuticals, N.A.*, Comp. Gen. Dec. B-252226.2, 93-2 CPD ¶ 79, where the agency negotiated a "concession" from the selected offeror and the Comptroller General held that this required negotiations with other offerors. The Comptroller General's rationale was that the agency was "reluctant" to award a contract to the selected source without the concession.

The former FAR 15.613 authorizing these alternative procedures was removed in the FAR Part 15 Rewrite. However, FAR 15.101 permits agencies considerable latitude in designing source selection methods:

> An agency can obtain best value in negotiated acquisitions by using any one or a combination of source selection approaches.

See also FAR 15.504(a) which appears to recognize that some communications may occur after source selection by stating:

> If the award document includes information that is different than the latest signed proposal, as amended by the offeror's written correspondence, both the offeror and the contracting officer shall sign the contract award.

The Department of Defense has indicated that FAR 15.101 permits contracting agencies to develop selection procedures which permit negotiation after source selection. See 62 Fed. Reg. 63050 (1997), stating:

> DFARS guidance on the four-step source selection process and the alternate source selection process have been removed, as the new guidance at FAR 15.101, best value continuum, clearly allows such source selection processes.

The proposed removal of the four-step procedure indicates that alternative procedures can be adopted by contracting officers without the necessity of regulatory coverage. However, in doing so the procedures to be followed must be spelled out in the solicitation so that offerors will be able to compete on a common basis. In addition, negotiations must not (1) change the Government's requirements, (2) make an unacceptable offer acceptable, (3) change the basis for selection or (4) otherwise prejudice other offerors.

b. Competitive Range of One

Post selection negotiations have been held to be appropriate where only one offeror was found to be in the competitive range. See *HITCO*, 68 Comp. Gen. 10 (B-232093), 88-2 CPD ¶ 337 (all but one offeror excluded from the competitive range when others were found to have deficiencies); *Rice Servs., Ltd.*, 68 Comp. Gen. 112 (B-232610), 88-2 CPD ¶ 514 (the sum of both major and minor deficiencies in the protester's offer justified its exclusion from the competitive range, which was narrowed to one); and *Regional Envtl. Consultants*, 66 Comp. Gen. 67 (B-223555), 86-2 CPD ¶ 476, *recons. denied*, 66 Comp. Gen. 388 (B-22355.2), 87-1 CPD ¶ 428 (one of two offerors excluded from the competitive range because of its undesirable approach to the contracted-for work).

In these cases, however, the Comptroller General has made it clear that source selection decisions which result in competitive ranges of one will be carefully scrutinized in the interest of achieving full and open competition. In *NITCO*, Comp. Gen. Dec. B-246185, 92-1 CPD ¶ 212, the Comptroller General thoroughly studied the evaluation committee's scoring and rationale which had led it to exclude all offerors but the awardee from the competitive range and concluded that the protester should have been included in the competitive range and should also have been involved in discussions following that determination.

The statutory and regulatory changes in describing the competitive range raise the question of whether this line of cases is still valid. Previously, those sources which had a reasonable chance of receiving award were included in the competitive range. Thus, one offer might be so superior that no other has a reasonable chance for award. The new standard requires inclusion of all the "most highly rated" offers in the competitive range. While this might suggest that more than one offer is to be included in the competitive range, it could also be argued that only one offer is highly rated.

It would appear that the standard for determining a competitive range of one would be that, even with the matters needed for negotiation, there is a clear winner and there is no reason to believe than other offers could be improved in negotiations to displace the winner.

D. Award

Once a source selection decision has been made, the contracting officer is to make the award with "reasonable promptness" by transmitting the notice of award "in writing or by electronic means," 10 U.S.C. § 2305(b)(4)(C) and 41 U.S.C. § 253b(d)(3). The procedures for making awards are outlined in FAR 15.504:

> The contracting officer shall award a contract to the successful offeror by furnishing the executed contract or other notice of the award to that offeror.
>
>> (a) If the award document includes information that is different than the latest signed proposal, as amended by the offeror's written correspondence, both the offeror and the contracting officer shall sign the contract award.
>>
>> (b) When an award is made to an offeror for less than all of the items that may be awarded and additional items are being withheld for subsequent award, each notice shall state that the Government may make subsequent awards on those additional items within the proposal acceptance period.
>>
>> (c) If the Optional Form (OF) 307, Contract Award, Standard Form (SF) 26, Award/Contract, or SF 33, Solicitation, Offer and Award, is not used to award the contract, the first page of the award document shall contain the Government's acceptance statement from Block 15 of that form, exclusive of the Item 3 reference language, and shall contain the contracting officer's name, signature, and date. In addition, if the award document includes information that is different than the signed proposal, as amended by the offeror's written correspondence, the first page shall include the contractor's agreement statement from Block 14 of the OF 307 and the signature of the contractor's authorized representative.

In some cases, the notice of award might constitute an acceptance by the Government of the winning offeror's BAFO (final proposal revision) or initial proposal. This would occur, for example, in a situation where the

Government was fully in agreement with all of the terms of that offer and merely desired to enter into a binding contract immediately. However, in most cases, the contracting officer will want to prepare an integrated contractual document and obtain the signature of both parties to that document. In such cases, the notice of award may merely notify the offeror that it has been selected for award and that the integrated document will be forwarded in due course. Offerors should be aware that there are varying procedures used in this area and should ensure that they have a legally binding document before beginning work.

The Comptroller General has enforced the FAR requirement that award of the contract be in written form. In *Litton Sys., Inc.*, Comp. Gen. Dec. B-229921, 88-1 CPD ¶ 448, the Comptroller General held that the protester's argument that partial award had been orally made over the phone was irrelevant in light of an actual written award made to another offeror, as was required. In *G. McMillan & Co.*, Comp. Gen. Dec. B-239805, 90-2 CPD ¶ 214, the Comptroller General stated, in reference to an argument that a protester was due expenses it incurred in anticipation of receiving a contract award, that "[s]ince the law and regulations require written notice of award, we think it unlikely that the protester could establish that a contract resulted from the alleged oral advice."

Telegraphic notices of award are frequently used by the Government to speed up the award process. In 49 Comp. Gen. 295 (B-167473) (1969), where an offeror was notified of award of a negotiated contract telegraphically and only later sent the formal contract documents, the Comptroller General remained silent on the issue as to what point the Government was bound. In many cases involving sealed bidding, however, the Comptroller General has explicitly held that the Government was bound by telegraphic notices of award. In *S.J. Groves*, 55 Comp. Gen. 936 (B-184260), 76-1 CPD ¶ 205, the Comptroller General held that because Groves protested after the agency had sent a telegraphic notice of award to the winner, its protest was a postaward protest. In *Wolverine Diesel Power Co.*, 57 Comp. Gen. 468 (B-189789), 78-1 CPD ¶ 375, telegraphic notices of award of two contracts were sent several days before the awardee attempted to withdraw its erroneous bids. The Comptroller General held that the telegrams made the contract effective and, therefore, that the awardee had made its allegations of mistake in bidding after award. See also *Niedenthal Corp.*, ASBCA 48159, 96-2 BCA ¶ 28,572, where the agency sent notice of award to the offeror on July 20, 1994, via facsimile transmission. Niedenthal informed the agency of a mistake in its bid on July 26, and later tried to claim that award could not be made by facsimile. The board held that the mistake-in-bid claim was a postaward claim under the Contract Disputes Act. Although these cases primarily refer to sealed bid procurements, their reasoning would be applicable to negotiated procurements where the telegraphic notice was framed in terms of acceptance of an offeror's BAFO or initial proposal with no alteration in terms. Technically, award can also be made by the signing of the cover page of the offer on one of the standard forms prescribed by the Government. However, if there have been alterations to the RFP during the procurement process, this can lead to confusion. See *F & F Lab., Inc.*, ASBCA 33007, 89-1 BCA ¶ 21,207, where the contracting officer signed Standard Form (SF) 26 after the contractor had stated in its offer that it would supply a candy bar at variance with that called for by the specifications. The board held the Government bound on the theory that the offer was incorporated by reference into the contract by the terms of the standard form. The listing of provisions on the standard form can also have consequences when these forms are used for acceptance. For example, in *Codex Corp.*, GSBCA 8186-P, 86-1 BCA ¶ 18,590, the contracting officer and the awardee signed the cover page of SF 26, where the table of contents indicated which sections of the contract were to be incorporated. In actuality, one of the sections was missing from the contract due to a clerical error. The board found that the parties had entered into a binding contract and that, despite its absence from the actual contract, the section in question was incorporated into the contract by reference on the cover page.

As a general rule, when written or oral discussions have been held and BAFOs requested, award is made by acceptance of a BAFO (in one of the forms described above). However, award has been permitted on the basis of an original offer where the offeror did not submit a BAFO in response to the request for BAFOs, *MR&S/AME*, Comp. Gen. Dec. B-250313.2, 93-1 CPD ¶ 245. In this case, the Comptroller General reasoned that the offeror had agreed to an extension that kept its original offer open beyond the award date and the submission of a BAFO was permissible, not mandatory. The Comptroller General also ruled that contacting the offeror to find out why no BAFO had been submitted was not a post-BAFO discussion.

1. Time of Award

Award may be made within a reasonable time after receipt of a proposal or BAFO. However, once a reasonable time has expired, the offer will no longer be open for award. See *Western Roofing Serv.*, 70 Comp. Gen. 323

(B-232666.4), 91-1 CPD ¶ 242, where the agency had delayed action on a procurement for over a year and then reopened the procurement by requesting another round of BAFOs. When one of the original offerors protested because it had never received the request for a BAFO, the Comptroller General denied the protest holding that the agency was correct in assuming that the earlier BAFO had expired and hence award could only be made to an offeror that had submitted a new BAFO. The Comptroller General reasoned that the offer had expired in view of the statutory mandate for agencies to award promptly, 41 U.S.C. § 253b(d)(4), and the *Uniform Commercial Code's* rule that offers without expiration dates remain open only for a reasonable time, U.C.C. § 2-205. The Comptroller General found that the thirteen months which had passed between the submission of the BAFO and the award was too long a period to constitute a reasonable time. See *M.J.S., Inc.*, Comp. Gen. Dec. B-244410, 91-2 CPD ¶ 344, where the Comptroller General held that a BAFO with no expiration date could clearly be accepted one month after submission.

The standard solicitation forms, SF 33 (Solicitation, Offer, and Award) and SF 1442 (Solicitation, Offer, and Award (Construction, Alteration, or Repair)), used to solicit both sealed bids and competitive proposals, contain statements that offerors agree to be bound by their offers if they are accepted within a stated number of days. While these provisions were written to require bidders on sealed bid procurements to submit firm bids, they also appear to limit the time in which a competitive proposal can be accepted. The Comptroller General has ruled, however, that this is not the case, *Fletcher Constr. Co.*, Comp. Gen. Dec. B-248977, 92-2 CPD ¶ 246, reasoning:

> Even assuming that protester's interpretation of the acceptance period clause on the SF 1442 on which BAFOs were submitted is correct, and that all offers including the protester's had expired by the time of award, it is not improper for an agency to accept an expired offer for a proposed award without reopening negotiations. *Protective Materials Co., Inc.*, B-225495, Mar. 18, 1987, 87-1 CPD ¶ 303. Where the acceptance period has expired on all offers, the contracting officer may allow the successful offeror to waive the expiration of its proposal acceptance period without reopening negotiations to make an award on the basis of the offer as submitted, since waiver under these circumstances is not prejudicial to the competitive system. *Sublette Elec., Inc.*, B-232586, Nov. 30, 1988, 88-2 CPD ¶ 540.

See also *CDA Investment Technologies, Inc.*, Comp. Gen. Dec. B-272093.3, 97-1 CPD ¶ 103; and *Krug Life Sciences, Inc.*, Comp. Gen. Dec. B-258669.2, 95-1 CPD ¶ 111.

Generally, contracting officers obtain proposal extensions from offerors when they find that there will be substantial delays in awarding the contract. The Comptroller General has found this to be proper when the agency has valid reasons for extending the time of award, *Saco Def., Inc.*, Comp. Gen. Dec. B-240603, 90-2 CPD ¶ 462 (eleven-month delay to permit a small business reasonable time to cure a responsibility problem and to conduct discussions); *Trim-Flite, Inc.*, 67 Comp. Gen. 550 (B-229926.4), 88-2 CPD ¶ 124 (eight-month delay to correct agency errors); *American Identification Prods., Inc.*, Comp. Gen. Dec. B-227599, 87-2 CPD ¶ 42 (six-month delay to evaluate samples).

If an offeror agrees to hold its offer open and is later awarded the contract, it takes the risk of cost increases that may have occurred in the intervening period, *Ordnance Parts & Eng'g Co.*, ASBCA 44327, 93-2 BCA ¶ 25,690. In that case, the contractor was properly terminated for default when it failed to perform because of significant price increases that had occurred in the year that it held its offer open.

2. Delay of Award By Protest

When a preaward protest is filed, the award is generally delayed until the protest is resolved. This imposes the burden on the winning offeror if such delayed award increases its costs of performance or otherwise makes it more difficult to perform the work. However, a winning offeror is not required to remain available for award in the face of a protest.

If an agency decides to withhold award pending the outcome of a protest, the selected offeror, as well as other offerors that might be in line for award, will normally be requested to keep their offers open. In addition, the protester's offer will be held to have remained open by virtue of the protest, 50 Comp. Gen. 357 (B-170178) (1970). Thus, upon conclusion of the protest, the agency will normally be able to make award in accordance with the original procurement if that is the proper course of action. The Comptroller General has permitted this outcome by holding that expiration dates may be waived and offers revived by the offeror in negotiated procurements because the only right conferred by expiration dates is upon the offeror,

Riggins & Williamson Mach. Co., 54 Comp. Gen. 783 (B-182801), 75-1 CPD ¶ 168. The Comptroller General has specified that revival of offers or waiver of expiration dates for the purpose of awarding the contract must be done "on the basis of the offer as submitted," *Donald N. Humphries & Assocs.*, 55 Comp. Gen. 432 (B-183292), 75-2 CPD ¶ 275. Under these circumstances, the Comptroller General has repeatedly held that, because the offer was not altered, no reopening of negotiations was necessary as it was not prejudicial to the competitive system. See *Medical Coaches, Inc.*, Comp. Gen. Dec. B-196339.2, 79-2 CPD ¶ 308, and *Protective Materials Co.*, Comp. Gen. Dec. B-225495, 87-1 CPD ¶ 303, where the offers were not altered and, therefore, no further discussions were found to have been held by the agency. In *Data Technology Indus., Inc.*, Comp. Gen. Dec. B-197858, 80-2 CPD ¶ 2, the Comptroller General specifically noted that the actual request that an offeror waive the expiration date of its offer did not constitute discussions requiring the reopening of negotiations with all offerors.

Offerors that elect to keep their offers open during the protest period and are subsequently awarded the contract have no recourse thereafter. Thus, the Comptroller General has refused to grant delay damages in such circumstances. See *Trim-Flite, Inc.*, 67 Comp. Gen. 550 (B-229926.4), 88-2 CPD ¶ 124, stating at 550:

> A delay in meeting procurement milestones generally is a procedural deficiency which does not provide a basis of protest because it has no effect on the validity of the procurement. *American Identification Products, Inc.*, B-227599, July 13, 1987, 87-2 CPD ¶ 42. While an agency is required to award a contract with reasonable promptness, the 8-month period here from closing date to award is not unreasonable per se given the attempts by the agency to correct the matters raised in offerors' complaints and protests through reevaluations. See *Id.* The fact that the delays may have been the result of initial agency errors in the procurement is irrelevant; once the errors occurred . . . the [agency's] proper course of action was to take steps to correct the errors. The award delay was merely an unfortunate, but necessary, by-product of the [agency's] proper action.

3. Date of Award

The forums are in disagreement on when the precise date of award occurs for purposes of determining issues such as the timeliness of notification of protest or the expiration of the ten days in which the filing of a protest will require a stay of performance. The Comptroller General follows the common law, or "mailbox," rule that the contract is binding when acceptance of the offer is dispatched. See *Wolverine Diesel Power Co.*, Comp. Gen. Dec. B-189789, 78-1 CPD ¶ 375, and 45 Comp. Gen. 700 (B-158862) (1966), where the award was said to have taken effect at the time the notice was mailed. Likewise, the boards have followed this common law reasoning. See *Adaptive Concepts, Inc.*, ASBCA 73123, 96-1 BCA ¶ 28,248; *Singleton Contracting Corp.*, IBCA-1770-1-84, 86-2 BCA ¶ 18,800; and *IMCO Precision Prods., Inc.*, ASBCA 17572, 73-2 BCA ¶ 10,250, where the boards held that award was effective when the acceptance documents were dispatched. The Court of Claims, however, reached the opposite conclusion, stating that award by mail forms a binding contract when the awardee receives the notification. See *Emeco Indus., Inc. v. United States*, 202 Ct. Cl. 1006, 485 F.2d 652 (1973), and *Rhode Island Tool Co. v. United States*, 130 Ct. Cl. 698, 128 F. Supp. 417 (1955), where the court, relying on postal regulations allowing the retrieval of acceptances from the mail by the Government, reasoned that award does not occur until the offeror receives the dispatch.

The parties may agree to an effective date of contract award other than the date of execution of the contract document. In *Northrop Worldwide Aircraft Servs., Inc.*, ASBCA 45216, 96-2 BCA ¶ 28,574, the agency amended Standard Form 26 to read "conditional/award," whereby the parties agreed that the contract effective date would be the date on which it received approval from the secretary of the agency. The approval occurred subsequent to the date the form was executed, and it was this later date that the board recognized as the effective date of the contract.

E. Notices and Debriefings

Agencies are required to notify offerors when they are eliminated from the competition and to provide debriefings when requested. Section 1014 of FASA, amending 10 U.S.C. § 2305(b), and Section 1064 of FASA, amending 41 U.S.C. § 253b, added new guidance on postaward debriefings. Section 4104 of the Clinger-Cohen Act of 1996, further amended 10 U.S.C. § 2305(b) and 41 U.S.C. § 253b to add a new provision on preaward debriefings. These statutes are implemented in FAR 15.605 and FAR 15.606.

1. *Preaward Notices and Debriefings*

Preaward notices and debriefings serve a number of purposes. Early notice of exclusion from the competition will permit excluded offerors to turn their attention to other contracting opportunities. It will also conserve resources since offerors will be on notice that investing further expense on the procurement would not be productive. These purposes were noted in the promulgation comments of the FAR Part 15 Rewrite at 62 Fed. Reg. 51226 (1997):

> This final rule insures that offerors with little probability of success are advised early on that their competitive position does not merit additional expense in a largely futile attempt to secure the contract.
>
> This knowledge will benefit both large and small entities, but will be especially beneficial to small entities that have constrained budgets. These entities will be able to conserve scarce bid and proposal funds and employ their resources on more productive business opportunities.

Another function of the preaward notice is that it provides an offeror an opportunity to challenge its elimination from the competition by requesting a preaward debriefing and determining whether to file a preaward protest or request alternative dispute resolution of its objection to the exclusion. While additional effort may be required of procurement personnel and delays in the procurement result if protests are filed, early resolution will be to the public's advantage if the exclusion was not appropriate. Corrective action is less time consuming and expensive to all parties if undertaken while the procurement is in process than after award.

a. *Preaward Notices*

Although the procurement statutes do not specifically state that preaward notice of exclusion from competition is to be given, the requirement for such notice is implicit in the offeror's right to request a preaward debriefing. Thus, FAR 15.503(a) requires preaward notices of exclusion as follows:

> *Preaward notices* — (1) Preaward notices of exclusion from competitive range. The contracting officer shall notify offerors promptly in writing when their proposals are excluded from the competitive range or otherwise

eliminated from the competition. The notice shall state the basis for the determination and that a proposal revision will not be considered.

The term "or otherwise eliminated from the competition" is not defined. It apparently is meant to implement the statutory phrase "or otherwise excludes such an offeror from further consideration prior to the final source selection decision" providing for preaward debriefing, 10 U.S.C. § 2305(b)(6)(A) and 41 U.S.C. § 253b(f)(1). Determinations of exclusion which would qualify for such notice would include determinations that an offeror is not responsible or otherwise not eligible for award or that an offer is inexcusably late (FAR 15.208(c)) or is unacceptable. It might also be argued that an offeror is "eliminated from the competition" when another offeror is selected for award. Contradicting such an interpretation is the statutory language providing for preaward debriefing for an excluded offeror "prior to the final source selection decision." While the FAR would be free to go beyond the statutory mandate, it is doubtful if this is the correct interpretation because FAR 15.503(a)(2) specifically provides for post-selection, preaward notice for small business setasides, as follows:

> Preaward notices for small business set-asides. In addition to the notice in paragraph (a)(1) of this section, when using a small business set-aside (see Subpart 19.5), upon completion of negotiations and determinations of responsibility, but prior to award, the contracting officer shall notify each offeror in writing of the name and location of the apparent successful offeror. The notice shall also state that
>
> > (i) The Government will not consider subsequent revisions of the offeror's proposal; and
> >
> > (ii) No response is required unless a basis exists to challenge the small business size status of the apparent successful offeror. The notice is not required when the contracting officer determines in writing that the urgency of the requirement necessitates award without delay or when the contract is entered into under the 8(a) program (see 19.805-2).

b. Preaward Debriefings

The statutory provisions for preaward debriefings at 10 U.S.C. § 2305(b)(6)(A) and 41 U.S.C. § 253b(f) are implemented in FAR 15.505, as follows:

Offerors excluded from the competitive range or otherwise excluded from the competition before award may request a debriefing before award (10 U.S.C. 2305(b)(6)(A) and 41 U.S.C. 253b(f)–(h)).

(a)(1) The offeror may request a preaward debriefing by submitting a written request for debriefing to the contracting officer within 3 days after receipt of the notice of exclusion from the competition.

(2) At the offeror's request, this debriefing may be delayed until after award. If the debriefing is delayed until after award, it shall include all information normally provided in a postaward debriefing (see 15.506(d)). Debriefings delayed pursuant to this paragraph could affect the timeliness of any protest filed subsequent to the debriefing.

(3) If the offeror does not submit a timely request, the offeror need not be given either a preaward or a postaward debriefing. Offerors are entitled to no more than one debriefing for each proposal.

(b) The contracting officer shall make every effort to debrief the unsuccessful offeror as soon as practicable, but may refuse the request for a debriefing if, for compelling reasons, it is not in the best interests of the Government to conduct a debriefing at that time. The rationale for delaying the debriefing shall be documented in the contract file. If the contracting officer delays the debriefing, it shall be provided no later than the time postaward debriefings are provided under 15.506. In that event, the contracting officer shall include the information at 15.506(d) in the debriefing.

(c) Debriefings may be done orally, in writing, or by any other method acceptable to the contracting officer.

(d) The contracting officer should normally chair any debriefing session held. Individuals who conducted the evaluations shall provide support.

(e) At a minimum, preaward debriefings shall include —

(1) The agency's evaluation of significant elements in the offeror's proposal;

(2) A summary of the rationale for eliminating the offeror from the competition; and

(3) Reasonable responses to relevant questions about whether source selection procedures contained in the solicitation, applicable regulations, and other applicable authorities were followed in the process of eliminating the offeror from the competition.

(f) Preaward debriefings shall not disclose —

(1) The number of offerors;

(2) The identity of other offerors;

(3) The content of other offerors' proposals;

(4) The ranking of other offerors;

(5) The evaluation of other offerors; or

(6) Any of the information prohibited in 15.506(e).

(g) An official summary of the debriefing shall be included in the contract file.

The Comptroller General has held that it would not review an agency's decision in a particular procurement that it is in the Government's best interests to delay the debriefing until after award, *Global Eng'g & Constr.*, Comp. Gen. Dec. B-275999.3, 97-1 CPD ¶ 77. In that case, Global requested a preaward debriefing after the agency excluded its proposal from the competitive range. The agency denied Global's request on the ground that preaward debriefings in the procurement would not be in the Government's best interest. The agency also stated that a preaward debriefing would require redirecting the agency's resources "which would not best serve our customers' needs or be a wise expenditure of U.S. tax dollars." The Comptroller General stated that Global presented several "valid reasons" why preaward debriefings should be encouraged but still denied the protest, stating:

> The arguments Global makes all are valid reasons why preaward debriefings should be encouraged no matter what the procurement circumstances. For example, honest exchange of information in a preaward debriefing may well obviate the need for, or discourage, a bid protest; competitive range evaluation results for excluded offerors always are "fresher" in the preaward than in the postaward timeframe; and since a protest potentially could

> result in a disruption to correct a procurement deficiency it generally would be better to correct the problem at an earlier time whenever possible.
>
> Nevertheless, we will not review the [agency's] determination that it is not in the government's best interest to provide preaward debriefings in this procurement. In adding the preaward debriefing requirement to 10 U.S.C. § 2305 through section 4104 of the Clinger-Cohen Act the Congress also expressly recognized that it may not be in the government's best interests to conduct a debriefing until after award. In other words, the Congress determined that despite the considerations that make preaward debriefings important elements of government procurements, agencies need to retain the discretion to decide that the government's interests may warrant delaying debriefings in certain circumstances.

The same agency indicated its intention not to grant a preaward debriefing in another decision, *Siebe Envtl. Controls*, Comp. Gen. Dec. B-275999.2, 97-1 CPD ¶ 70. In *Global*, the Comptroller General defended its position claiming that the offeror would not be prejudiced by the denial of the preaward debriefing since it would be entitled to receive a postaward debriefing and, if it filed a protest after award, work on the procurement would be stayed. In the Comptroller General's view, an agency postponing the debriefing "may find it difficult to marshall the resources to defend its earlier decision" and that "simply may prejudice the agency in defending the protest." The Comptroller General's refusal to review such actions would appear to permit the agency to arbitrarily deny a preaward debriefing. Whether that is consistent with the intent of the statute is questionable.

FAR 15.505(a)(2) permits an offeror to elect a postaward debriefing in lieu of a preaward debriefing. In cases where the offeror does not intend to challenge its exclusion from the competition but desires to learn how to improve its competitive position in future procurements, this is a sensible election because far more information can be obtained in a postaward debriefing. This election also benefits the procuring agency because it permits debriefing at a time when the workload of the contracting officer is likely to be less than prior to award.

2. Postaward Notices and Debriefings

Postaward notices and debriefings serve a number of functions in addition to those served by preaward notices and debriefings. In addition to advising offerors that their offers are no longer under consideration and providing them with information to challenge the selection, postaward debriefings can provide offerors with "an indication of how those offerors can improve their chances for success in future procurements," Sen. Rep. 103-258 accompanying FASA, PL 103-355. By identifying the source selected, postaward notices also provide information which other offerors may use for subcontracting opportunities.

a. Postaward Notices

The procurement statutes require notice of contract award to be given to "all other offerors within 3 days after date of contract award in writing or by electronic means of the rejection of their proposals," 10 U.S.C. § 2305(b)(4)(C) and 41 U.S.C. § 253b(d)(3). This requirement is implemented in FAR 15.503(b) as follows:

> *Postaward notices.* (1) Within 3 days after the date of contract award, the contracting officer shall provide written notification to each offeror whose proposal was in the competitive range but was not selected for award (10 U.S.C. 2305(b)(5) and 41 U.S.C. 253b(c)) or had not been previously notified under paragraph (a) of this section. The notice shall include —
>
> (i) The number of offerors solicited;
>
> (ii) The number of proposals received;
>
> (iii) The name and address of each offeror receiving an award;
>
> (iv) The items, quantities, and any stated unit prices of each award. If the number of items or other factors makes listing any stated unit prices impracticable at that time, only the total contract price need be furnished in the notice. However, the items, quantities, and any stated unit prices of each award shall be made publicly available, upon request; and
>
> (v) In general terms, the reason(s) the offeror's proposal was not accepted, unless the price information in paragraph (b)(1)(iv) of this section readily reveals the reason. In no event shall an offeror's cost breakdown, profit, overhead rates, trade secrets, manufacturing processes and techniques, or other confidential business information be disclosed to any other offeror.

(2) Upon request, the contracting officer shall furnish the information described in paragraph (b)(1) of this section to unsuccessful offerors in solicitations using simplified acquisition procedures in Part 13.

(3) Upon request, the contracting officer shall provide the information in paragraph (b)(1) of this section to unsuccessful offerors that received a preaward notice of exclusion from the competitive range.

b. Postaward Debriefings

The statutory requirements for postaward debriefings, 10 U.S.C. § 2305(b)(5) and 41 U.S.C. § 253b(e), are implemented in FAR 15.506 which provides:

(a)(1) An offeror, upon its written request received by the agency within 3 days after the date on which that offeror has received notification of contract award in accordance with 15.503(b), shall be debriefed and furnished the basis for the selection decision and contract award.

(2) To the maximum extent practicable, the debriefing should occur within 5 days after receipt of the written request. Offerors that requested a postaward debriefing in lieu of a preaward debriefing, or whose debriefing was delayed for compelling reasons beyond contract award, also should be debriefed within this time period.

(3) An offeror that was notified of exclusion from the competition (see 15.505(a)), but failed to submit a timely request, is not entitled to a debriefing.

(4)(i) Untimely debriefing requests may be accommodated.

(ii) Government accommodation of a request for delayed debriefing pursuant to 15.505(a)(2), or any untimely debriefing request, does not automatically extend the deadlines for filing protests. Debriefings delayed pursuant to 15.505(a)(2) could affect the timeliness of any protest filed subsequent to the debriefing.

(iii) Debriefings of successful and unsuccessful offerors may be done orally, in writing, or by any other method acceptable to the contracting officer.

(c) The contracting officer should normally chair any debriefing session held. Individuals who conducted the evaluations shall provide support.

(d) At a minimum, the debriefing information shall include —

(1) The Government's evaluation of the significant weaknesses or deficiencies in the offeror's proposal, if applicable;

(2) The overall evaluated cost or price (including unit prices) and technical rating, if applicable, of the successful offeror and the debriefed offeror, and past performance information on the debriefed offeror;

(3) The overall ranking of all offerors, when any ranking was developed by the agency during the source selection;

(4) A summary of the rationale for award;

(5) For acquisitions of commercial items, the make and model of the item to be delivered by the successful offeror; and

(6) Reasonable responses to relevant questions about whether source selection procedures contained in the solicitation, applicable regulations, and other applicable authorities were followed.

(e) The debriefing shall not include point-by-point comparisons of the debriefed offeror's proposal with those of other offerors. Moreover, the debriefing shall not reveal any information prohibited from disclosure by 24.202 or exempt from release under the Freedom of Information Act (5 U.S.C. 552) including —

(1) Trade secrets;

(2) Privileged or confidential manufacturing processes and techniques;

(3) Commercial and financial information that is privileged or confidential, including cost breakdowns, profit, indirect cost rates, and similar information; and

(4) The names of individuals providing reference information about an offeror's past performance.

(f) An official summary of the debriefing shall be included in the contract file.

A post-debriefing protest must be timely filed. See *Professional Rehabilitation Consultants, Inc.*, Comp. Gen. Dec. B-275871, 97-1 CPD ¶ 94, where the Comptroller General dismissed a post-debriefing protest because the protester waited until two months after it was informed that it had not received the award to request a debriefing. See also *Fumigadora Popular, S.A.*, Comp. Gen. Dec. B-276676, 97-1 CPD ¶ 151, where the Comptroller General found a post-debriefing protest to be untimely where the protester filed more than ten days after the protester received written notice from the agency of the basis for rejection of its bid.

Inadequate debriefings have not, in the past, created a protestable issue, *CACI Field Servs., Inc.*, Comp. Gen. Dec. B-234945, 89-2 CPD ¶ 97; *Haworth, Inc.*, Comp. Gen. Dec. B-215638.2, 84-2 CPD ¶ 461. However, Congress has given protesters more rights by making the stay from proceeding with performance of an awarded contract in the event of a protest dependent on the debriefing. Prior to FASA, this stay was put in effect (absent urgency) only if the protest was received no more than 10 days from contract award. Under § 1402 of FASA, the stay will go into effect if a protest is received within five days after the debriefing is conducted. This provision penalizes agencies that do not conduct their debriefings in a timely fashion. Although agencies can wait, by doing so they lengthen the time that a protester has to evaluate the merits of any projected protest. In contrast, if a protester delays the debriefing, it may lose its right to the statutory stay. See *Pentec Envtl., Inc.*, Comp. Gen. Dec. B-276874.2, 97-1 CPD ¶ 199, where a protest was found untimely because the protester delayed the debriefing one month after the date offered by the agency. See also FAR 33.103(f)(3) calling for suspension of performance of the contract if a protest is received within five days after a debriefing date *offered* by the agency.

An inadequate debriefing can extend the time that an offeror has to protest even if the time to stay the performance of the contract has passed. For example, in *Geo-Centers, Inc.*, Comp. Gen. Dec. B-276033, 97-1 CPD ¶ 182, the Comptroller General sustained a protest that was filed three months after contract award and two months after a debriefing which did not contain sufficient details to disclose the basis for the protest. The Comptroller General ruled that the protest was timely because it was filed within 10 days after the protester learned of the grounds for protest by receiving the information in response to a request for the information pursuant to the Freedom of Information Act, 5 U.S.C. § 552.

CHAPTER 7

SPECIAL NEGOTIATION PROCEDURES

In addition to the standard negotiation procedure discussed in Chapter 6, a number of special procedures are used in various classes of negotiated procurements. The procurement statutes contain provisions permitting the use of these special procedures in order to simplify the procurement process or adapt it to the unique conditions that are encountered in specific markets. This chapter covers eight such procedures. The first is the procurement of supplies or services that are designated as "commercial items." The second is the procurement of work with a value of $100,000 or less following simplified acquisition procedures. The following two procedures cover the procurement of architect-engineer services and the use of a two-step design-build contract for the procurement of construction work. Next, the chapter addresses the broad agency announcement procedures used to procure research work in general and under the small business innovative research program. This is followed by a discussion of special procedures for the procurement of information technology and for the establishment of multiple award schedules. The chapter concludes with a discussion of the major special procedures that have been adopted by specific agencies to enhance their ability to carry out their procurement missions.

I. COMMERCIAL ITEMS

In recent years, there have been a number of initiatives in Government procurement designed to take advantage of products and services available in the commercial marketplace. These initiatives have focused on the use of commercial product or service descriptions rather than Government-unique specifications. They have also been aimed at using commercial buying practices and eliminating statutory and regulatory provisions that either discourage commercial firms from competing for Government business or unnecessarily increase the costs of performance. As a result, a number of provisions were adopted by the Federal Acquisition Streamlining Act of 1994 (FASA), P.L. 103-355, and the Clinger-Cohen Act of 1996, P.L. 104-106. These provisions, designed to promote and facilitate the procurement of commercial items, include 10 U.S.C. § 2377(b) and 41 U.S.C. § 264(b), which require that:

> The head of an agency shall ensure that procurement officials in that agency, to the maximum extent practicable —
>
> (1) acquire commercial items or nondevelopmental items other than commercial items to meet the needs of the agency;
>
> (2) require prime contractors and subcontractors at all levels under the agency contracts to incorporate commercial items or nondevelopmental items other than commercial items as components of items supplied to the agency;
>
> (3) modify requirements in appropriate cases to ensure that the requirements can be met by commercial items or, to the extent that commercial items suitable to meet the agency's needs are not available, nondevelopmental items other than commercial items;
>
> (4) state specifications in terms that enable and encourage bidders and offerors to supply commercial items or, to the extent that commercial items suitable to meet the agency's needs are not available, nondevelopmental items other than commercial items in response to the agency solicitations;
>
> (5) revise the agency's procurement policies, practices, and procedures not required by law to reduce any impediments in those policies, practices, and procedures to the acquisition of commercial items; and
>
> (6) require training of appropriate personnel in the acquisition of commercial items.

In addition, agency competition advocates are responsible for "promoting the acquisition of commercial items," 41 U.S.C. § 418. Other provisions dealing with the procurement of commercial items are scattered throughout various statutes that are discussed in the following material.

FAR Part 12 is the primary regulation implementing the commercial item statutes, while FAR Part 13 covers the procurement of commercial items using simplified acquisition procedures. In addition, a number of different FAR Parts deal with commercial items. For example, requirements for market research, the drafting of specifications and the solicitation of offers are covered in FAR Parts 10, 11, and 5, respectively. The rules applicable to pricing commercial items are contained in FAR Part 15. See Chapter 9. This section deals with the special rules applicable to contracts for commercial items in excess of $5,000,000. Contracts for commercial items with a value of $5,000,000 or less are covered in the following section dealing with simplified acquisition procedures.

A. Definitions

The term "commercial item," as defined in 41 U.S.C. § 403(12) and FAR 2.101, includes both commercial supplies and commercial services. However, supplies and services are given disparate treatment, with the definition of commercial supplies being much broader than the definition of commercial items. The terminology is further complicated by the fact that when used alone, the term "item" most often refers to supplies only. In addition, nondevelopmental items and commercial-off-the-shelf items are distinct subcategories of supplies. The following material deals with the definitions of the various types of commercial items and the critical elements of the definition of services and commercial-off-the-shelf items.

1. Supplies

The statutes and the FAR contain a general definition of supplies and special definitions of nondevelopmental items and commercial-off-the-shelf items.

a. General Definition

The following general definition of supplies is contained in FAR 2.101, which is identical to the definition contained in 41 U.S.C. § 403(12):

> "Commercial item" means —
>
> (a) Any item, other than real property, that is of a type customarily used for nongovernmental purposes and that —
>
> (i) Has been sold, leased, or licensed to the general public; or
>
> (ii) Has been offered for sale, lease, or license to the general public;
>
> (b) Any item that evolved from an item described in paragraph (a) of this definition through advances in technology or performance and that is not yet available in the commercial marketplace, but will be available in the

commercial marketplace in time to satisfy the delivery requirements under a Government solicitation;

(c) Any item that would satisfy a criterion expressed in paragraphs (a) or (b) of this definition, but for —

(1) Modifications of a type customarily available in the commercial marketplace; or

(2) Minor modifications of a type not customarily available in the commercial marketplace made to meet Federal Government requirements. "Minor" modifications means modifications that do not significantly alter the nongovernmental function or essential physical characteristics of an item or component, or change the purpose of a process. Factors to be considered in determining whether a modification is minor include the value and size of the modification and the comparative value and size of the final product. Dollar values and percentages may be used as guideposts, but are not conclusive evidence that a modification is minor;

This broad definition of commercial items includes a large number of supplies, as long as they meet the key test of being "of a type customarily used for nongovernmental purposes." Thus, the Government can be the first purchaser of such an item even though it is not being sold commercially at the time of the procurement. The definition also includes modified products as long as they are of the type customarily available in the marketplace or the modifications are minor. Under prior DOD policy, certifications from offerors that their products met the definition were sufficient to justify award using the commercial item procedures, *Coherent, Inc.*, Comp. Gen. Dec. B-270998, 96-1 CPD ¶ 214 (product had been offered for sale); *Canberra Indus., Inc.*, Comp. Gen. Dec. B-271016, 96-1 CPD ¶ 269 (modifications in offered product were minor).

b. Nondevelopmental Items

Nondevelopmental items are covered by the statutes and regulations in two different ways. First, they are considered to be commercial items if they meet the following requirements contained in FAR 2.101 and 41 U.S.C. § 403(12):

> A nondevelopmental item, if the procuring agency determines that the item was developed exclusively at private expense and sold in substantial quantities, on a competitive basis, to multiple State and local governments.

Second, nondevelopmental items are treated as a separate category of item subject to the Congressional policies encouraging the purchase of commercial items *or* nondevelopmental items discussed earlier. For this purpose, the term "nondevelopmental item" is given a broader definition in 41 U.S.C. § 403(13). This definition, with minor modifications, is set forth in FAR 2.101 as follows:

> (a) Any previously developed item of supply used exclusively for governmental purposes by a Federal agency, a State or local government, or a foreign government with which the United States has a mutual defense cooperation agreement;
>
> (b) Any item of supply described in paragraph (a) of this definition that requires only minor modification or modifications of a type customarily available in the commercial marketplace in order to meet the requirements of the procuring department or agency; or
>
> (c) Any item of supply being produced that does not meet the requirements of paragraph (a) or (b) solely because the item is not yet in use.

Care must be exercised in using these two definitions because some of the policies discussed in this section apply only to commercial items, while other policies apply as well to nondevelopmental items (as defined in the broader sense). If a solicitation permits proposals for either commercial items or nondevelopmental items, the second definition will be used and minor modifications will be acceptable, *Tremble Navigation, Ltd.*, Comp. Gen. Dec. B-271882, 96-2 CPD ¶ 102 (award on the basis of a proposed nondevelopmental item improper because modifications were major).

c. Commercially Available Off-the-Shelf Items

This following definition is contained in 41 U.S.C. § 431(c) but has not yet been incorporated into the FAR:

> As used in this section, the term "commercially available off-the-shelf item" means, except as provided in paragraph (2), an item that —

(A) is a commercial item (as described in section 4(A)(12) [41 U.S.C. § 403(12)(A)]);

(B) is sold in substantial quantities in the commercial marketplace; and

(C) is offered to the Government, without modification, in the same form in which it is sold in the commercial marketplace.

(2) The term "commercially available off-the-shelf item" does not include bulk cargo, as defined in section 3 of the Shipping Act of 1984 (46 U.S.C. App. 1702), such as agricultural products and petroleum products.

2. Services

The statute and the FAR include two types of services within the definition of commercial items.

a. Services in Support of Commercial Supplies

FAR 2.101 contains the following definition, which is the same as the definition included in 41 U.S.C. § 403(12):

(e) Installation services, maintenance services, repair services, training services, and other services if such services are procured for support of an item referred to in paragraphs (a), (b), (c), or (d) of this definition, and if the source of such services —

(1) Offers such services to the general public and the Federal Government contemporaneously and under similar terms and conditions; and

(2) Offers to use the same work force for providing the Federal Government with such services as the source uses for providing such services to the general public.

b. stand-alone Services

The stand-alone services that constitute commercial items are defined in FAR 2.101 as follows:

(f) Services of a type offered and sold competitively in substantial quantities in the commercial marketplace based on established catalog or market

> prices for specific tasks performed and under standard commercial terms and conditions. This does not include services that are sold based on hourly rates without an established catalog or market price for a specific service performed.

The first sentence of this definition substantially adopts the definition contained in 41 U.S.C. § 403(12). The last sentence is not contained in the statute but is derived from the legislative history, House Conf. Rep. 103-712. The definition is very difficult to understand because a number of the terms are undefined and, as discussed below, some of the definitions have been removed from the FAR. However, it seems clear that to fall within this category of services, the precise services need not have been specifically sold but merely must be "*of a type* offered and sold competitively . . . in the commercial marketplace." In addition, such sales must have been based on "prices for *specific tasks*." There is no guidance on the breadth of a specific task under this definition, but some agencies have interpreted it to include all the work called for under a contract, such as performing janitorial services on a building. Nor is there any guidance as to whether an hourly rate can constitute a price if the services are sold commercially on that basis and the rates can be established through catalogs or market research. See *Nalco Forwarding, Inc.*, Comp. Gen. Dec. B-277241.8, 97-2 CPD ¶ 110, where the Comptroller General held that an agency properly determined that household goods moving services for military personnel could be acquired under commercial item procedures because such services were a "type" offered and sold in the commercial marketplace.

3. Combinations

The statute and FAR 2.101 permit combinations of supplies and services in support of commercial supplies as follows:

> (d) Any combination of items meeting the requirements of paragraphs (a), (b), (c), or (e) of this definition that are of a type customarily combined and sold in combination to the general public.

4. Transfers Between Organizations

The statute and FAR 2.101 permit transfers between organizations with a contractor to be treated as commercial items as follows:

(g) Any item, combination of items, or service referred to in paragraphs (a) through (f), notwithstanding the fact that the item, combination of items, or service is transferred between or among separate divisions, subsidiaries, or affiliates of a contractor.

5. Key Terms

The statutory and regulatory definitions of commercial items use a number of key terms that are not defined. The following definitions of these terms and related terms were previously incorporated into FAR 15.804-3, but were removed from the FAR by Federal Acquisition Circular (FAC) 90-32, September 18, 1995.

a. General Public

(5) The "general public" is a significant number of buyers other than the Government or affiliates of the offeror; the item involved must not be for Government end use. For the purpose of this subsection 15.804-3, items acquired for "Government end use" include items acquired for foreign military sales.

b. Substantial Quantities

The phrase "sold in substantial quantities" is applicable only to stand-alone services and commercially available off-the-shelf supplies. The previous FAR definition stated:

(4) An item is "sold in substantial quantities" only when the quantities regularly sold are sufficient to constitute a real commercial market. Nominal quantities, such as models, samples, prototypes, or experimental units, do not meet this requirement. For services to be sold in substantial quantities, they must be customarily provided by the offeror, using personnel regularly employed and equipment (if any is necessary) regularly maintained solely or principally to provide the services.

c. Established Catalog Prices

(1) "Established catalog prices" must be recorded in a form regularly maintained by the manufacturer or vendor. This form may be a catalog, price list, schedule, or other verifiable and established record. The record

must (i) be published or otherwise available for customer inspection and (ii) state current or last sales price to a significant number of buyers constituting the general public (see subparagraph (5) below).

d. Established Market Prices

(2) "Established market prices" are current prices that (i) are established in the course of ordinary and usual trade between buyers and sellers free to bargain and (ii) can be substantiated by data from sources independent of the manufacturer or vendor.

B. Solicitation, Evaluation, and Award

The statutory goal is to use procurement procedures that "reduce any impediments . . . to the acquisition of commercial items," 10 U.S.C. § 2377(b)(5) and 41 U.S.C. § 264(b)(5). Such impediments should be identified by the contracting officer in the course of performing the required market research to determine the availability of commercial items as discussed in Chapter 3. See FAR 12.202. In general, it can be expected that the major impediments will be excessive requirements for proposal information and data during contract performance. Based on an understanding of the impact of such requirements on the Government's ability to attract offers from commercial sellers, the procurement should be structured to minimize the affect of such impediments by streamlining the source selection process. The procedural guidance discussed in this section contains sufficient flexibility to permit contracting with commercial sources in most situations.

FAR 12.207 requires that contracts for commercial items be either firm-fixed-price or fixed-price with economic price adjustment. This provision provides that indefinite-delivery contracts can be used if they call for the establishment of prices on one of these two bases. FAR 12.301(e)(2) permits the use of options in commercial item procurements.

1. Specifications

FAR 12.202(b) requires that the Government's needs be described in "sufficient detail for potential offerors of commercial items to know which commercial products or services to offer." In *National Aeronautics & Space Admin.*, Comp. Gen. Dec. B-274748.3, 97-1 CPD ¶ 159, the Comptroller General held that, while the use of functional or performance specifications is appropriate, the agency must advise offerors of its "specific ideas" of what features would satisfy its needs.

2. Solicitation

The FAR contains general guidance on the solicitation procedures to be followed in acquiring commercial items, as well as a "streamlined" solicitation procedure. The contracting officer has complete discretion as to the procedure to be used.

a. General Guidance

The initial guidance states that the contracting officer "shall use" the policies in FAR Part 12 "in conjunction with the policies and procedures" in FAR Parts 13, 14, and 15 "as appropriate for the particular acquisition," FAR 12.203. This appears to give the contracting officer complete freedom in selecting the solicitation procedure — including the use of sealed bidding or competitive negotiation procedures. However, the balance of the guidance makes it clear that simplification is desirable. Thus, it can be expected that sealed bidding or standard negotiation procedures will be used very rarely in the procurement of commercial items.

Unless the streamlined procedure is used, the contracting officer must use Standard Form 1449, Solicitation/Contract/Order for Commercial Items, when issuing written solicitations and awarding contracts and placing orders for commercial items. This form may also be used for documenting receipt, inspection, and acceptance of commercial items, FAR 12.204. FAR 12.205 provides the following guidance for solicitations for commercial items:

> (a) Where technical information is necessary for evaluation of offers, agencies should, as part of market research, review existing product literature generally available in the industry to determine its adequacy for purposes of evaluation. If adequate, contracting officers shall request existing product literature from offerors of commercial items in lieu of unique technical proposals.
>
> (b) Contracting officers should allow offerors to propose more than one product that will meet a Government need in response to solicitations for commercial items. The contracting officer shall evaluate each product as a separate offer.

> Consistent with the requirements at 5.203(b) and (h), the contracting officers may allow fewer than 30 days response time for receipt of offers for commercial items.

FAR 12.301(b) provides two standard solicitation provisions, described as follows:

> To implement [the FASA], the contracting officer shall insert the following provisions in solicitations for the acquisition of commercial items, and clauses in solicitations and contracts for the acquisition of commercial items:
>
> (1) The provision at 52.212-1, Instructions to Offerors — Commercial Items. This provision provides a single, streamlined set of instructions to be used when soliciting offers for commercial items and is incorporated in the solicitation by reference (see Block 27a, SF 1449). The contracting officer may tailor these instructions or provide additional instructions tailored to the specific acquisition in accordance with 12.302;
>
> (2) The provision at 52.212-3, Offeror Representations and Certifications — Commercial Items. This provision provides a single, consolidated list of certifications and representations for the acquisition of commercial items and is attached to the solicitation for offerors to complete and return with their offer. This provision may not be tailored except in accordance with Subpart 1.4.

FAR 12.302 provides the following guidance on the permissible tailoring of the FAR 52.212-1 solicitation provision:

> The provision and clauses established in this subpart are intended to address, to the maximum extent practicable, commercial market practices for a wide range of potential Government acquisitions of commercial items. However, because of the broad range of commercial items acquired by the Government, variations in commercial practices, and the relative volume of the Government's acquisitions in the specific market, contracting officers may, within the limitations of this subpart, and after conducting appropriate market research, tailor the provision at 52.212-1, Instructions to Offerors—Commercial Items.

FAR 12.301 also provides for a standard solicitation provision describing the evaluation process. This is discussed below.

b. Streamlined Procedures

The FAR also permits the use of a "streamlined" procedure combining the synopsis and solicitation into a single document with a response time no longer than is necessary to give potential offerors a reasonable opportunity to respond to the solicitation. This allows greatly shortening the statutory requirements for standard procurement that require a 15-day synopsis period and a 30-day offer period. The guidance on the use of this fast procedure is set forth in FAR 12.603, as follows:

> (a) When a written solicitation will be issued, the contracting officer may use the following procedure to reduce the time required to solicit and award contracts for the acquisition of commercial items. This procedure combines the Commerce Business Daily (CBD) synopsis required by 5.203 and the issuance of the solicitation into a single document with the following limitations:
>
> (1) Section 5.207 limits submissions to the CBD to 12,000 textual characters (approximately 3 :1/2 single-spaced pages).
>
> (2) This combined CBD synopsis/solicitation is only appropriate where the solicitation is relatively simple and is not recommended for use when lengthy addenda to the solicitation are necessary.
>
> (b) When using the combined synopsis/solicitation procedure, the SF 1449 is not used for issuing the solicitation.
>
> (c) To use these procedures, the contracting officer shall —
>
> (1) Prepare the synopsis as described at 5.207 for items 1-16.
>
> (2) In item 17, Description, include the following additional information:
>
> (i) The following statement:
>
> This is a combined synopsis/solicitation for commercial items prepared in accordance with the format in FAR Subpart 12.6, as supplemented with additional information included in this notice. This announcement constitutes the only solicitation; proposals are being requested and a written solicitation will not be issued.

(ii) The solicitation number and a statement that the solicitation is issued as an invitation to bid (IFB), request for quotation (RFQ) or request for proposal (RFP).

(iii) A statement that the solicitation document and incorporated provisions and clauses are those in effect through Federal Acquisition Circular ___.

(iv) A notice regarding any set-aside and the associated standard industrial classification code and small business size standard. Also include a statement regarding the Small Business Competitiveness Demonstration Program, if applicable.

(v) A list of contract line item number(s) and items, quantities and units of measure, (including option(s), if applicable).

(vi) Description of requirements for the items to be acquired.

(vii) Date(s) and place(s) of delivery and acceptance and FOB point.

(viii) A statement that the provision at 52.212-1, Instructions to Offerors — Commercial, applies to this acquisition and a statement regarding any addenda to the provision.

(ix) A statement regarding the applicability of the provision at 52.212-2, Evaluation — Commercial Items, if used, and the specific evaluation criteria to be included in paragraph (a) of that provision. If this provision is not used, describe the evaluation procedures to be used.

(x) A statement advising offerors to include a completed copy of the provision at 52.212-3, Offeror Representations and Certifications — Commercial Items, with its offer.

(xi) A statement that the clause at 52.212-4, Contract Terms and Conditions — Commercial Items, applies to this acquisition and a statement regarding any addenda to the clause.

(xii) A statement that the clause at 52.212-5, Contract Terms and Conditions Required To Implement Statutes Or Executive Orders — Commercial Items, applies to this acquisition and a statement regarding which, if any, of the additional FAR clauses cited in the clause are applicable to the acquisition.

(xiii) A statement regarding any additional contract requirement(s) or terms and conditions (such as contract financing arrangements or warranty requirements) determined by the contracting officer to be necessary for this acquisition and consistent with customary commercial practices.

(xiv) A statement regarding the Defense Priorities and Allocations System (DPAS) and assigned rating, if applicable.

(xv) A statement regarding any applicable Commercial Business Daily numbered notes.

(xvi) The date, time and place offers are due.

(xiii) The name and telephone number of the individual to contact for information regarding the solicitation.

(3) Allow response time for receipt of offers as follows:

(i) Because the CBD synopsis and solicitation are contained in a single document, it is not necessary to publish a separate CBD synopsis 15 days before the issuance of the solicitation.

(ii) When using the combined CBD synopsis/solicitation, contracting offerors shall establish a response time in accordance with 5.203(b).

(4) Publish amendments to solicitations in the same manner as the initial synopsis/solicitation.

3. Evaluation

The general guidance on the evaluation scheme to be used in the acquisition of commercial items indicates that the contracting officer has broad latitude in selecting the evaluation factors and may conduct commercial item procurement without evaluation factors. This would entail the procurement of commercial items on the basis of price alone. When evaluation factors are used, FAR 12.206 strongly urges that past performance be one of the factors. FAR 12.301(c) provides a standard solicitation provision in FAR 52.213-2 when evaluation factors are used. This provision calls for the insertion of the evaluation factors and their relative importance. It would be expected that, in furtherance of the goal of simplification of these procurements, the number of evaluation factors would be kept to a minimum.

When evaluation factors are used, the agency must conduct the evaluation and source selection in accordance with the listed factors, *Access Logic, Inc.*, Comp. Gen. Dec. B-274748, 97-1 CPD ¶ 36, *recons. denied*, 97-1 CPD ¶ 159 (proposed commercial product may not be rejected on the basis of technical requirements not set forth in the solicitation). It is permissible to cancel the procurement after receipt of proposals if the evaluation factors are inadvertently omitted from the solicitation, *Nidek, Inc.*, Comp. Gen. Dec. B-272255, 96-2 CPD ¶ 112.

FAR 12.602 provides for the following guidance on the evaluation of offers when the streamlined procedure is used:

> (a) When evaluation factors are used, the contracting officer may insert a provision substantially the same as the provision at 52.212-2, Evaluation—Commercial Items, in solicitations for commercial items or comply with the procedures in 13.106-2 if the acquisition is being made using simplified acquisition procedures. When the provision at 52.212-2 is used, paragraph (a) of the provision shall be tailored to the specific acquisition to describe the evaluation factors and relative importance of those factors. However, when using the simplified acquisition procedures in part 13, contracting officers are not required to describe the relative importance of evaluation factors.
>
> (b) Offers shall be evaluated in accordance with the criteria contained in the solicitation. For many commercial items, the criteria need not be more detailed than technical (capability of the item offered to meet the agency need), price and past performance. Technical capability may be evaluated by how well the proposed products meet the Government requirement instead of predetermined subfactors. Solicitations for commercial items do not have to contain subfactors for technical capability when the solicitation adequately describes the item's intended use. A technical evaluation would normally include examination of such things as product literature, product samples (if requested), technical features and warranty provisions. Past performance shall be evaluated in accordance with the procedures in section 13.106-2 or subpart 15.6, as applicable. The contracting officer shall ensure the instructions provided in the provision at 52.212-1, Instructions to Offerors—Commercial Items, and the evaluation criteria provided in the provision at 52.212-2, Evaluation—Commercial Items, are in agreement.

4. Award

The only guidance on the award of contracts for commercial items is found in FAR 12.602(c), as follows:

> Select the offer that is most advantageous to the Government based on the factors contained in the solicitation. Fully document the rationale for selection of the successful offeror including discussion of any tradeoffs considered.

C. Terms and Conditions

One of the major elements of the policy favoring the procurement of commercial items was the elimination of as many contract clauses as was practicable. The FASA amended a number of laws to state that they did not apply to the procurement of commercial items and added 41 U.S.C. § 430 requiring the FAR to include a list of laws that were not applicable to contracts and subcontracts for commercial items. Subsequently, Section 4203 of the Clinger-Cohen Act of 1996 enacted 41 U.S.C. § 431 requiring that the FAR list laws that are not applicable to the procurement of commercial-off-the-shelf items.

1. Standard Commercial Items

FAR 52.212-4 provides a standard contract clause, Contract Terms and Conditions — Commercial Items, which contains 19 specific provisions to be used in contracts for commercial items. These provisions are greatly shortened versions of the standard clauses used in Government procurement such as the termination clauses, the inspection clauses, the changes clause, and the disputes clause. The contracting officer is authorized to "tailor" certain of these provisions, but only to reflect commercial practices, FAR 12.302. However, the following clauses, which implement statutory requirements may not be tailored:

> (1) Assignments;
>
> (2) Disputes;
>
> (3) Payment (except as provided in subpart 32.11);

(4) Invoice;

(5) Other compliances; and

(6) Compliance with laws unique to Government contracts.

FAR 12.213 contains the following guidance to contracting officers on the subject of tailoring:

> It is a common practice in the commercial marketplace for both the buyer and seller to propose terms and conditions written from their particular perspectives. The terms and conditions prescribed in this Part 12 seek to balance the interests of both the buyer and seller. These terms and conditions are generally appropriate for use in a wide range of acquisitions. However, market research may indicate other commercial practices that are appropriate for the acquisition of the particular item. These practices should be considered for incorporation into the solicitation and contract if the contracting officer determines them appropriate in concluding a business arrangement satisfactory to both parties and not otherwise precluded by law or Executive order.

FAR 52.212-5 provides a standard clause, Contract Terms and Conditions Required to Implement Statutes or Executive Orders — Commercial Items, that sets forth the mandatory clauses that must be included in these procurements. The contracting officer must check the appropriate provisions in this clause in accordance with the instructions in FAR 12.503. This clause also contains a list of the four statutes and executive orders that must be passed down to subcontractors. See the guidance in FAR 12.504 which includes a list of some of the statutes that remain applicable even though they are not listed in the clause. Contractors should be aware that there are other statutes that are of general applicability in the United States that are also not listed in this clause. See **Figure 7-1** for a comprehensive list giving the applicability of these statutes and executive orders and the standard FAR clause that is used to implement them.

2. Commercial Off-the-Shelf Items

The Clinger-Cohen Act of 1996 included the following provision:

> (a) Lists of inapplicable provisions of law. — (1) The Federal Acquisition Regulation shall include a list of provisions of law that are inapplicable to contracts for the procurement of commercially available off-the-shelf items.

(2) A provision of law that, pursuant to paragraph (3), is properly included on a list referred to in paragraph (1) may not be construed as being applicable to contracts referred to in paragraph (1). Nothing in this section shall be construed to render inapplicable to such contracts any provision of law that is not included on such list.

(3) A provision of law described in subsection (b) shall be included on the list of inapplicable provisions of law required by paragraph (1) unless the Administrator for Federal Procurement Policy makes a written determination that it would not be in the best interest of the United States to exempt such contracts from the applicability of that provision of law. Nothing in this section shall be construed as modifying or superseding, or as being intended to impair or restrict authorities or responsibilities under —

(A) section 15 of the Small Business Act (15 U.S.C. 644);

(B) bid protest procedures developed under the authority of subchapter V of chapter 35 of title 31, United States Code; subsections (e) and (f) of section 2305 of title 10, United States Code; or subsections (h) and (I) of section 303B of the Federal Property and Administrative Services Act of 1949 (41 U.S.C. 253b).

(b) Covered Law. — Except as provided in subsection (a)(3), the list referred to in subsection (a)(1) shall include each provision of law that, as determined by the Administrator, imposes on persons who have been awarded contracts by the Federal Government for the procurement of commercially available off-the-shelf items Government-unique policies, procedures, requirements, or restrictions for the procurement of property or services, except the following:

(1) A provision of law that provides for criminal or civil penalties.

(2) A provision of law that specifically refers to this section and provides that, notwithstanding this section, such provision of law shall be applicable to contracts for the procurement of commercial off-the-shelf items.

This provision has not yet been implemented in the FAR.

II. SIMPLIFIED ACQUISITION PROCEDURES

Known for many years as "small purchases," simplified acquisition procedures now encompass three different classes of procurement — micro-purchases ($2,500 or less), purchases over $2,500 but not more than $100,000, and commercial purchases not in excess of $5,000,000. The rules governing these procurements are promulgated in the FAR under authority granted by the Federal Acquisition Streamlining Act of 1994 (FASA), P.L. 103-355, and the Clinger-Cohen Act of 1996, P.L. 104-106. Neither the statutes nor the regulations provide any detailed procedures for these purchases. Rather, they relieve contracting officers from most of the procedures required for sealed bidding and conventional negotiation.

The statutory provisions authorizing simplified procedures are contained in 41 U.S.C. § 427. Directions for agencies to use them are provided in 10 U.S.C. § 2302b and 41 U.S.C. § 252b. The Government's policy is that simplified acquisition procedures are to be used to the "maximum extent practicable," Exec. Order No. 12931, 59 Fed. Reg. 52387, Oct. 13, 1994; FAR 13.003(a). Purchases over $2,500 but not more than $100,000 must be set aside exclusively for small business concerns in accordance with FAR Subpart 19.5, FAR 13.003(b)(1). It should be noted that the authority to use simplified acquisition procedures does not relieve agencies of their obligation to use the required sources of supply specified in Part 8 of the FAR.

FAR 13.002 specifies the following purposes of simplified acquisition procedures:

(a) Reduce administrative costs;

(b) Improve opportunities for small, small disadvantaged, and women-owned small business concerns to obtain a fair proportion of Government contracts;

(c) Promote efficiency and economy in contracting; and

(d) Avoid unnecessary burdens for agencies and contractors.

A. Dollar Values

The simplified acquisition threshold is for procurements not exceeding $100,000, 41 U.S.C. § 403(11). 41 U.S.C. § 252a(a) adopts that amount for civilian executive agencies. The same amount is adopted for military departments, NASA, and the Coast Guard by 10 U.S.C. § 2302(7), which increases the amount by two times for "any contract to be awarded and performed, or purchase to be made, outside the United States in support of a contingency operation or a humanitarian or peacekeeping operation."

1. Thresholds Applicable to Both Solicitation Estimates and Award Values

The dollar values apply to *both* the amount estimated for the procurement as well as resulting contract values, FAR 13.003(d). Thus, if a procurement is begun using other than simplified procedures based on an estimate that exceeds the applicable threshold, simplified procedures may not be used even though the price of the source selected is lower than the threshold. Conversely, even though a solicitation was issued under simplified procedures, award may not be made above the applicable threshold. However, award on the basis of simplified procedures would be proper if the selected source reduced its price to come within the threshold. See *TLC Sys.*, Comp. Gen. Dec. B-277095, 97-2 CPD ¶ 62, finding proper an agency's use of simplified acquisition procedures because the estimated value of the procurement was beneath the simplified acquisition threshold of $100,000.

Once an award is properly made using simplified acquisition procedures, there is no requirement that the actual amount paid under the contract be below the threshold. The contract may be modified to an amount above the threshold to cover unforeseen circumstances such as a change order or an unexpected overrun in the quantity of work, *Jones Seeding & Sprigging Co.*, 63 Comp. Gen. 497 (B-215260), 84-2 CPD ¶ 87.

2. Breaking Down Purchases to Fit Within Thresholds Prohibited

Agencies are prohibited from "breaking down" procurements that aggregate more than the thresholds to permit use of the procedures within the applicable threshold, 41 U.S.C. § 427(b) and FAR 31.003(d). Thus, an $125,000 procurement could not be properly acquired using five $25,000 purchase orders. Similarly, if an agency has an identified recurring need for supplies or services, it is improper to enter into a series of small purchases to fulfill this need.

In *L.A. Sys. v. Department of the Army*, GSBCA 13472-P, 96-1 BCA ¶ 28,220, the board held that the determination of whether a "fragmentation" or breaking down of a quantity occurs depends upon the knowledge of the user, not the contracting officer. The board stated at 140,915–16:

> That the contracting officer had no "advance knowledge of the megacenter's total requirements" is not dispositive of the issue. The prohibition in FAR 13.103(c) against breaking down requirements into several purchases that are less than the simplified acquisition threshold does not excuse fragmentation merely because the contracting officer is unaware that a series of orders is actually one requirement. To read the regulation as respondent suggests would allow a contracting officer to receive orders for a fragmented requirement and circumvent the regulation as long as the contracting officer is not told of the true nature of the requirement by individuals who had such knowledge.

FAR 13.100(d) states that requirements should not be broken down "merely" to take advantage of the threshold. While that language is not contained in 41 U.S.C. § 427(b), it appears that fragmentation would be appropriate if there were a valid reason to do so. One reason might be to permit small businesses to take advantage of the procurement. Another possible reason might be lack of funding. In *L.A. Systems*, the Government argued that it could not "consolidate" the procurement because of a lack of available funding and that to allow funds to accumulate would result in a loss of funding. However, the board found that sufficient funds were available for the total requirement before the first order was placed.

B. Micro-Purchases

The term "micro-purchase" is defined in FAR 2.101 to mean an acquisition of supplies or services (except construction), the aggregate amount of which does not exceed $2,500. In the case of construction, the amount is limited to $2,000. Purchases under the micro-purchase threshold may be conducted using any of the simplified acquisition procedures in FAR Subpart 13.3. Micro-purchases do not require the incorporation of provisions or clauses. Section 848 of the National Defense Authorization Act for Fiscal Year 1998, P.L. 105-85, requires that at least 60 percent of all eligible purchases made by DOD for an amount less than the micro-purchase threshold must be made through streamlined micro-purchase procedures by October 1, 1998. This requirement increases to 90 percent of all eligible purchases by October 1, 2000.

The authority to make micro-purchases is frequently delegated to non-procurement personnel. See FAR 1.603-3, stating:

> (b) Agency heads are encouraged to delegate micro-purchase authority to individuals who are employees of an executive agency or members of the Armed Forces of the United States who will be using the supplies or services being purchased. Individuals delegated this authority are not required to be appointed on an SF 1402, but shall be appointed in writing in accordance with agency procedures.

These purchases are generally made using the Government-wide commercial purchase card.

1. Sources

Micro-purchases are not reserved exclusively for small businesses, and the Buy American Act is not applicable. However, the requirements in FAR Part 8, Required Sources of Supplies and Services, apply to purchases within the micro-purchase threshold.

2. Procedures

Based on the authority granted in 41 U.S.C. § 428, the following purchase guidelines are set forth in FAR 13.202:

> (a) Solicitation, evaluation of quotations, and award.
>
> (1) To the extent practicable, micro-purchases shall be distributed equitably among qualified suppliers.
>
> (2) Micro-purchases may be awarded without soliciting competitive quotations if the contracting officer or individual appointed in accordance with 1.603-3(b) considers the price to be reasonable.
>
> (3) The administrative cost of verifying the reasonableness of the price for purchases may more than offset potential savings from detecting instances of overpricing. Therefore, action to verify price reasonableness need only be taken if —
>
> (i) The contracting officer or individual appointed in accordance with 1.603-3(b) suspects or has information to indicate that the

price may not be reasonable (e.g., comparison to the previous price paid or personal knowledge of the supply or service); or

(ii) Purchasing a supply or service for which no comparable pricing information is readily available (e.g., a supply or service that is not the same as, or is not similar to, other supplies or services that have recently been purchased on a competitive basis).

(b) Documentation. If competitive quotations were solicited and award was made to other than the low quoter, documentation to support the purchase may be limited to identification of the solicited concerns and an explanation for the award decision.

See *Michael Ritschard*, Comp. Gen. Dec. B-276820, 97-2 CPD ¶ 32 (protest that agency improperly refused to solicit a potential source denied where agency conducted the acquisition in accordance with micro-purchase procedures). See also *Navistar Marine Instrument Corp.*, Comp. Gen. Dec. B-278075, 97-2 CPD ¶ ___ (acquisition was micro-purchase not subject to competition requirements and therefore unpriced purchase order was properly awarded on a sole source basis).

C. Commercial or Non-Commercial Over $2,500 but Not Over $100,000

The Comptroller General views the statutory and regulatory requirements to use these procedures "to the maximum extent practicable" as *mandatory*, *Southeast Technical Servs.*, Comp. Gen. Dec. B-272374.2, 97-1 CPD ¶ 107. The Comptroller General indicated that a contracting officer must justify why simplified procedures are not practicable in order to use sealed bidding or conventional negotiation.

1. Competition Requirements

In contrast to micro-purchases, agencies are expected to obtain competition on these simplified acquisitions.

a. Degree of Competition

The statutes and regulations require that competition be promoted "to the maximum extent practicable," 41 U.S.C. § 427(c) and FAR 13.104. As long as the agency makes a reasonable effort to obtain competition and does not intentionally and improperly exclude an interested source from competing, it will be found to have met this standard. In *S.D.M. Supply, Inc.*, Comp. Gen. Dec. B-271492, 96-1 CPD ¶ 288, *recons. denied*, 96-2 CPD ¶ 203, the Comptroller General indicated that this encompasses both the obtaining and consideration of quotes, stating:

> In meeting this requirement, agencies must make reasonable efforts, consistent with efficiency and economy, to afford all eligible and interested vendors an opportunity to compete. *RMS Indus.*, B-247074, Mar. 18, 1992, 92-1 CPD ¶ 290. Agencies have a fundamental obligation to have procedures in place not only to receive quotations, but also to reasonably safeguard quotations actually received and to give them fair consideration. *East West Research, Inc.*, B-239565, B-239566, Aug. 21, 1990, 90-2 CPD ¶ 147, *aff'd, Defense Logistics Agency — Recons.*, B-239565.2, B-239566.2, Mar. 19, 1991, 91-1 CPD ¶ 298.

The Comptroller General found that the agency failed to meet this standard when it lost quotations due to a previously identified "systemic" failure of its computer system. In doing so, the Comptroller General distinguished those cases where "the occasional negligent loss of a quotation by an agency does not entitle the supplier to any relief."

FAR 13.104(b) provides that if using simplified acquisition procedures and not using FACNET, maximum practicable competition ordinarily can be obtained by soliciting quotations or offers from at least three sources within the local trade area. However, if the contracting officer is aware of additional sources that wish to participate in the competition, they should be accorded an opportunity to submit offers or quotations.

Whether an interested source has been intentionally and improperly excluded from the competition will be determined on a case-by-case basis. See *Omni Elevator Co.*, 71 Comp. Gen. 308 (B-246393), 92-1 CPD ¶ 264, stating at 309:

> Generally, a solicitation of three vendors is sufficient. *J. Sledge Janitorial Serv.*, [70 Comp. Gen. 307 (B-241843), 91-1 CPD ¶ 225]; FAR 13.106(b)(5). It is not sufficient merely to solicit three vendors where another responsible source requests the opportunity to compete — in those circumstances, such sources should be afforded a reasonable opportunity to compete. *J. Sledge Janitorial Serv.*, *supra*; *Gateway Cable Co.*, 65 Comp. Gen. 854 (1986), 86-2 CPD ¶ 333. The determinative issue in such cases is

> whether the agency made a deliberate or conscious attempt to preclude the protester — in this case the incumbent — from competing, knowing the firm's interest in competing, and if it did so, whether that action was reasonable. *CardioMetrix*, B-241344, Jan. 31, 1991, 91-1 CPD ¶ 108; *Omni Elevator*, B-233450.2, Mar. 7, 1989, 89-1 CPD ¶ 248.

The Comptroller General concluded that the failure to solicit Omni was an "unintentional oversight that resulted from VA's use of a bidders list based upon an informal market survey conducted by the contracting officer, instead of the standard bidders list on which Omni was included." The Comptroller General found that this was a reasonable method of identifying prospective offerors and the fact that four firms (two of which responded) were solicited satisfied the maximum practicable competition standard. See also *The Source*, Comp. Gen. Dec. B-266362, 96-1 CPD ¶ 48. There, the contracting officer was not aware of the protester's interest and the supply officer did not advise the contracting officer of the protester's interest in the procurement. The Comptroller General found that there was "simply no basis" to conclude that the contracting officer deliberately excluded the protester from competing. In *SF & Wellness*, Comp. Gen. Dec. B-272313, 96-2 CPD ¶ 122, the Comptroller General found that the purchasing agent's statements that she left a message on the incumbent's answering machine indicated that the incumbent had been solicited. The incumbent denied ever receiving such a message.

These cases should be contrasted with *Bosco Contracting, Inc.*, Comp. Gen. Dec. B-270366, 96-1 CPD ¶ 140, where the protester was found to have been improperly excluded. There, the decision not to solicit the incumbent was based on an alleged record of poor past performance, which the Comptroller General found not to have been supported by the record.

b. Sole Source

Sole source procurement is authorized if the contracting officer makes a determination that "only one source is reasonably available," FAR 13.106-1(b)(1). The decision will be supported if the contracting officer makes a reasonable attempt to find other sources. See *Midwest Dynamometer & Eng'g Co.*, Comp. Gen. Dec. B-252168, 93-1 CPD ¶ 408, where the contracting officer contacted three sources and found that only one would meet the Government's needs.

2. Solicitation and Procurement Notices

Agencies are given broad discretion in determining whether to solicit quotes or offers and in choosing techniques to use for the solicitation.

a. Quote or Offer

The traditional method of solicitation for small purchases has been the Request for Quotations (RFQ), and this method is preserved in the simplified acquisition regulations. This technique places the Government in the position of being the offeror with the quoter having the right either to accept or reject the offer. FAR 13.004(a) states:

> A quotation is not an offer and, consequently, cannot be accepted by the Government to form a binding contract. Therefore, issuance by the Government of an order in response to a supplier's quotation does not establish a contract. The order is an offer by the Government to the supplier to buy certain supplies or services upon specified terms and conditions. A contract is established when the supplier accepts the offer.

Using an RFQ presents a substantially lower risk for the supplier than that which would be incurred if the supplier were making an offer. If the quote contains judgmental errors or costs go up, the supplier can escape a loss contract by simply refusing to accept the Government's offer or by making a counteroffer, *Bloch Lumber Co.*, ASBCA 23512, 79-2 BCA ¶ 14,167. This reduced risk could reduce contingencies and result in lower quoted prices.

Under the broad discretion afforded by FAR Part 13, an agency could request offers (either proposals or bids) rather than quotations. See FAR 13.206-2(b)(1). However, the regulations give no suggestions as to when it would be advantageous to do so. One reason might be that timing is critical and that it is essential to have the contract formed at the time the Government makes the award decision.

b. Method of Solicitation

Solicitations may be made orally, on paper, or electronically. FAR 13.106-1(c)(ii) provides that FACNET must be used "when practicable and cost-effective." In the absence of FACNET, FAR 13.106-1(c)(2) favors oral solicitations for purchases not in excess of $25,000 unless it is not economical or practical to do so. However, "written" solicitations are required for construction contracts over $2,000.

c. Procurement Notices

The requirements for public notice of procurements depends upon the estimated dollar value. The regulations do not prescribe any public notice requirements for procurements not in excess of $10,000. A public display of solicitations over $10,000 but not over $25,000 is required, FAR 5.101(a)(2). For procurements in excess of $25,000, a CBD notice must be published at least 15 days before issuance of a solicitation, FAR 5.101(a)(1). However, the solicitation can be combined with the CBD notice, thus eliminating the 15-day waiting period, FAR 13.105(b).

d. Submission of Quotes or Offers

Contracting officers are given broad discretion to determine the time and manner for the submission of responses. Deadlines for responses to solicitations are required to be set to afford suppliers a reasonable opportunity to respond, FAR 13.003(i)(2). Responses may be required to be oral, on paper, or submitted by electronic means. The needs of the agency will be considered in determining whether the time and method selected is reasonable. See *Arcy Mfg. Co.*, Comp. Gen. Dec. B-261538, 95-2 CPD ¶ 283, where the agency stated that it would consider quotations only if submitted on its electronic bulletin board (EBB). The protester claimed that this placed an undue burden on small businesses. However, the Comptroller General denied the protest based upon the agency's claim that the large volume of purchases it processed made the use of the electronic method cost effective, stating:

> With regard to the burden imposed on the protesters by the requirement that quotes be electronically transmitted, the essential difference between the electronic method of responding to RFQs and the paper method is that under the electronic method the protester is required to have access to a personal computer, certain telecommunications software, and a modem. These items are readily available for purchase in the commercial marketplace, or, as the record demonstrates, should a vendor not desire to purchase such equipment, access to the EBB can be obtained by contacting an EDI service provider. As such, we fail to see how requiring access to the EBB can be considered overly burdensome to a prospective DISC supplier.

> In our view, the record establishes that the agency has a reasonable basis for requiring that quotes be submitted electronically and that this requirement is not overly burdensome on the vendor community. In this regard, we note that no potential vendor is precluded from submitting quotes; only the format of quotes is being restricted. *See Essex Electro Eng'rs, Inc.*, B-252288.2, 93-2 CPD ¶ 47 (protest that proposal format instructions were overly burdensome because they required an unnecessary amount of desktop publishing capabilities was denied where the formatting requirements were determined reasonable and could easily be met using a personal computer). In sum, under the circumstances here, DISC's requirement that quotes be submitted electronically is reasonable and consistent with the mandate that it promote competition to the maximum extent practicable for small purchase acquisitions.

See also *Commonwealth Indusrial Specialties, Inc.*, Comp. Gen. Dec. B-277833, 97-2 CPD ¶ ___, finding proper an agency's requirement that responses to a simplified acquisition request for quotations be submitted electronically through the agency's electronic bulletin board.

e. Standing Quotations

FAR 13.103 permits the use of "standing price quotations" in lieu of the solicitation of specific quotations as follows:

> Authorized individuals do not have to obtain individual quotations for each purchase. Standing price quotations may be used if —
>
> (a) The pricing information is current; and
>
> (b) The Government obtains the benefit of maximum discounts before award.

This procedure is used extensively by the Department of Veterans Affairs.

3. Procedures

The absence of statutory or regulatory procedures does not permit agencies to use arbitrary or unfair selection procedures. The Comptroller General holds that simplified acquisition procedures must be conducted "consistent with the concern for fair and equitable treatment that is inherent in any federal procurement," *General Metals, Inc.*, 72 Comp. Gen. 54 (B-249259), 92-2 CPD ¶ 319.

a. Evaluation Factors

The factors to be evaluated may be price alone or price and other factors, FAR 13.106-1(a)(2). However, best value is encouraged, FAR 13.106-1(a)(2). Solicitations must state the basis upon which award is to be made, but the relative importance of evaluation factors is not required to be in the solicitation and subfactors need not be included, FAR 13.106-1(a)(2). The Comptroller General has indicated that where relative importance had not been indicated, it will be presumed that the factors will be given "approximately equal weight," *Carol Soloman & Assocs.*, Comp. Gen. Dec. B-271713, 96-2 CPD ¶ 28. However, the FAR does not contain such a statement. In *Vocational Resources, Inc.*, Comp. Gen. Dec. B-242396, 91-1 CPD ¶ 414, the Comptroller General held that items required to be addressed in the technical proposal and a specification requirements were to be evaluated even though "not designated as evaluation factors." The Comptroller General found that "quoters could reasonably expect that their technical proposals would be evaluated in these four areas." See, however, *Forestry, Surveys & Data*, Comp. Gen. Dec. B-276802.3, 97-2 CPD ¶ 46, which indicates that requiring a quoter to submit an experience questionnaire but not specifically identifying experience as an evaluation factor was improper.

b. Evaluation

Quotes or offers must be evaluated using the evaluation factors established in the solicitation, FAR 13.106-2(a)(2). Failure to do so will result in the award being improper. See, for example, *Ann Riley & Assocs., Ltd.*, Comp. Gen. Dec. B-241309.2, 91-1 CPD ¶ 142, where the Federal Energy Regulatory Commission (FERC) solicited quotations for stenographic services to be awarded to the firm proposing the most favorable cost to the public. In holding that it was improper to award on the basis of a quote that proposed to make bonus payments to the Government, the Comptroller General stated:

> While small purchases therefore are not governed by normal competition procedures, all procurements, including small purchases, must be conducted consistent with the concern for a fair and equitable competition that is in-

herent in any procurement. *Armour of Am.*, B-237690, Mar. 19, 1990, 90-1 CPD ¶ 304. In this connection, it is fundamental that an agency may not solicit quotations on one basis and then make award on a materially different basis when other vendors would be prejudiced by such an award. *Discount Mach. and Equip., Inc.*, B-220949, Feb. 25, 1986, 86-1 CPD ¶ 193.

The agency clearly did not meet this standard. As indicated, the RFQ stated that the award decision would be based on the cost to the public, that is, on the amount the contractor would charge the public for transcripts. A bonus payment back to the government does not affect the amount the public must pay for a copy of a transcript and a bonus bid therefore clearly is not encompassed by reference to cost to the public. While FERC may have had a legal obligation to consider cost to the government and, thus, to evaluate bonus bids, quoters were aware that FERC would consider cost to the government only to the extent indicated in the RFQ — that FERC did not expect to be charged; there was nothing implicit in this provision indicating that bonus payments would be evaluated. As there was nothing explicit in the RFQ providing for the evaluation of bonus payments and the language of the RFQ in no way suggested that the award determination would be based wholly or in part on offered bonus payments, it was improper for the agency to make award based on Executive's bonus bid; quoters, including Riley, were not on notice that bonus bids would be considered. Exacerbating FERC's improper evaluation is the fact that it advised Executive, but not other quoters, that bonus bids could be offered. FERC correctly notes that the FAR 15.410 requirement that equal information be provided to all offerors does not apply *per se* to small purchases. However, as discussed above, notwithstanding the inapplicability of particular FAR provisions, FERC was required to conduct the competition in a fair and equitable manner. FERC did not meet this standard; communicating the basis for award to only one quoter precluded other quoters, including Riley, from competing on an equal basis. *See Introl Corp.*, 64 Comp. Gen. 672 (1985), 85-2 CPD ¶ 35.

FERC asserts that we previously have held that contracting officers properly may consider evaluation criteria that are not stated in the solicitation. *Hoffman Mgmt., Inc.*, B-238752, July 6, 1990, 69 Comp. Gen. [579] (1990), 90-2 CPD ¶ 15; *Washington Occupational Health Assocs., Inc.*, B-222466, June 19, 1986, 86-1 CPD ¶ 567. However, FERC's reliance on these decisions is misplaced. In those cases the agencies allegedly applied unstated subfactors of stated evaluation factors; we held that agencies may apply unstated subfactors that are reasonably related to the stated factors. Here, FERC did not apply a subfactor of a stated evaluation factor, but rather applied an evaluation factor — amount of a bonus bid — that was not related to the sole stated criterion, cost to the public. Thus, FERC clearly had no

> basis to consider a bonus bid under the terms of the RFQ as issued. We conclude that the evaluation was based on a factor not specified in the solicitation. Had all quoters, including Riley, been advised, as Executive was, that the award would be based on both cost to the public and bonus bids, which apparently is what the agency intended, the outcome of the competition could have been different. Therefore, the award to Executive under the deficient solicitation was improper, and we sustain the protest on this basis.

See also *New Brunswick Scientific Co.*, Comp. Gen. Dec. B-246291, 92-1 CPD ¶ 141 (company may not be selected based on technical criteria not included in solicitation). In *Vocational Resources, Inc.*, Comp. Gen. Dec. B-242396, 91-1 CPD ¶ 414, it was held improper for the agency not to use all of the factors that quoters could reasonably expect to be considered.

c. *Discussions and Consideration of Noncompliant Responses*

The contracting officer is not required to conduct oral or written discussions or to afford quoters an opportunity to submit additional information. See *Rotair Indus.*, Comp. Gen. Dec. B-219994, 85-2 CPD ¶ 683, where the Comptroller General stated:

> [T]he solicitation was issued under the small purchase procedures, which do not contemplate the type of discussions or the opportunity to submit revised proposals that occur in a full scale negotiated procurement. In this context, we do not believe that the agency acted improperly by rejecting Rotair's offer without affording it an opportunity to submit additional information. See *M.F. Services, Inc.*, B-210954, Jan. 20, 1984, 84-1 CPD ¶ 87.

See also *Metropolitan Federal Network*, Comp. Gen. Dec. B-232096, 88-2 CPD ¶ 495.

Although oral or written discussions are not required, the contracting officer is not prohibited from conducting discussions and obtaining modifications of offers or quotations, provided that all offerors are treated fairly and equitably and are not prejudiced. This does not mean that discussions must be conducted with all quoters, *Oregon Innovative Prods.*, Comp. Gen. Dec. B-231767, 88-2 CPD ¶ 110. See *DataVault Corp.*, Comp. Gen. Dec. B-248664, 92-2 CPD ¶ 166, where the Comptroller General stated:

> The government's small purchase procedures establish abbreviated, competitive requirements designed to minimize administrative costs that might otherwise equal or exceed the cost of relatively inexpensive items. An RFQ, unlike an invitation for bids (IFB) or request for proposals (RFP), does not seek offers that can be accepted by the government to form a contract. Rather, the government's purchase order is the offer which the proposed supplier may accept through performance or by a formal acceptance document. FAR 13.108. It follows that, generally, the government may seek and consider revisions to a quotation under small purchase procedures any time prior to the government's issuance of a purchase order. See *Instruments & Controls Serv. Co.*, 65 Comp. Gen. 685 [B-222122] (1986), 86-2 CPD ¶ 16; *Oregon Innovative Prods.*, B-231767, Aug. 2, 1988, 88-2 CPD ¶ 110. Here, since the Army could properly seek additional information regarding a quotation up to the time the purchase order was issued, we find nothing improper in the agency's issuance of a purchase order to FFC after determining that FFC would comply with the RFQ vault temperature requirements.

The contracting officer also has considerable discretion in treating responses that deviate from the solicitation requirements. Since the concept of responsiveness is not applicable, *Memopro*, GSBCA 8264-P, 86-1 BCA ¶ 18,072, the contracting officer is free to consider responses that deviate from the solicitation. However, if a substantial specification change is made, all quoters should be advised, *Uni-Tek Mfg. Co.*, Comp. Gen. Dec. B-208324, 82-2 CPD ¶ 483. Conversely, the contracting officer may decide to reject responses that are technically unacceptable and not to permit modification of the response, *Huntington Valley Indus.*, Comp. Gen. Dec. B-272321, 96-2 CPD ¶ 126.

d. Late Quotations

Late quotations must be considered unless the solicitation contains a late quotations clause, other bidders would be prejudiced, or the agency has begun the award process, *John Blood*, Comp. Gen. Dec. B-274624, 96-2 CPD ¶ 233. In *John Blood*, the Comptroller General stated:

> Under simplified acquisition procedures, agencies generally may seek and consider revisions to a quotation any time prior to award. See *DataVault Corp.*, B-248664, Sept. 10, 1992, 92-2 CPD ¶ 166. Where, as here, an RFQ does not contain a late quotations provision — but merely requests quotations by a certain date — that date is not considered to be a firm closing deadline; consequently, so long as the award process has not begun, an

> agency is not precluded from considering a quotation received after that date. *AFT Constr. Co., Inc.*, B-260829, July 18, 1995, 95-2 CPD ¶ 29.

In *Instruments & Controls Serv. Co.*, Comp. Gen. Dec. B-222122, 65 Comp. Gen. 685, 86-2 CPD ¶ 16, the Comptroller General stated that the "failure to do so would be inconsistent with the statutory requirement for competition to the maximum extent practicable." Two exceptions to this requirement were noted in *Compspace Corp.*, Comp. Gen. Dec. B-274037, 96-2 CPD ¶ 186. Late quotations would not have to be considered if substantial activity had transpired in evaluating quotations or if other firms would be prejudiced. The Comptroller General stated:

> When, as here, the RFQ does not contain a late quotations clause, but merely requests quotations by a certain date, that date is not considered a firm date for purposes of determining whether a quotation may form the basis for an award. *A&B Trash Serv.*, B-250322, Jan. 22, 1993, 93-1 CPD ¶ 53. Rather, the agency is not precluded from considering a quotation received after the announced due date provided that no substantial activity has transpired in evaluating quotations, and the other firms submitting quotations would not be prejudiced. *Id.* Activity is deemed substantial where the agency has begun the award process prior to receiving the late quotation. *Adrian Supply Co.*, 68 Comp. Gen. 575 (1989), 89-2 CPD ¶ 99.

Because a late quotations clause is not prescribed by the regulations, it is unlikely that purchasing agents and contracting officers will include such a clause in a solicitation. The Comptroller General decisions indicate that a late quotations provision must expressly provide that quotations must be received by the specified date to be considered. See, for example, *Instruments & Controls Serv. Co.*, Comp. Gen. Dec. B-222122, 65 Comp. Gen. 685, 86-2 CPD ¶ 16. Thus, language that "merely suggests" the submission of quotes by a specified date would not qualify. Neither would language that advises quoters that failure to submit a quote by a specified date "may result in your quotation not being considered for award," *Adrian Supply Co.*, Comp. Gen. Dec. B-235352, 68 Comp. Gen. 575, 89-2 CPD ¶ 99.

However, if a late quotations clause is included, it will be enforced. See *Alpha Executive Servs., Inc.*, Comp. Gen. Dec. B-246173, 92-1 CPD ¶ 197, where the Comptroller General held that the agency "acted reasonably" in declining to consider a late proposal when the solicitation had included a late quotations clause.

When electronic quotations are submitted, the quote is considered received on the date it is received by the agency, not the date the quoter submits it to a Value Added Network (VAN), *Comspace Corp.*, Comp. Gen. Dec. B-274037, 96-2 CPD ¶ 186. There, the only evidence of Government receipt showed that the quote was received by the Government after award, too late to be considered.

e. Award

Award need not be made to the firm submitting the lowest quotation if the contracting officer makes a good faith finding that award to a different firm is in the best interests of the Government and that the price is reasonable, *Creative Elecs., Inc.*, Comp. Gen. Dec. B-206684, 83-2 CPD ¶ 95; *JCL Servs., Inc.*, Comp. Gen. Dec. B-182994, 75-1 CPD ¶ 364. However, where price was identified as the only evaluation factor, it was improper not to award to the quoter that took no exception to the RFQ and submitted the lowest price, *Cromartie Constr. Co.*, Comp. Gen. Dec. B-271788, 96-2 CPD ¶ 48. The Comptroller General also indicated that where price is the only evaluation factor, the quote may not be rejected because the agency believes that it is too low. In such a situation, the matter is one of responsibility, requiring reference to the Small Business Administration.

If an agency has solicited offers, award will be made by accepting the offer in the same way that this is accomplished in standard negotiated procurement. If an agency has solicited quotations, award will be made by issuance of a purchase order. In such cases, the contracting officer must determine whether the contractor will be required to accept the offer forming a bilateral contract. FAR 13.302-3(a) requires that such acceptance be obtained by signature of the purchase order. FAR 13.004(b) discusses requiring a signed acceptance but gives no guidance as to when this is desirable.

f. Notice and Debriefing

FAR 13.106-3(c) states that notice to "unsuccessful suppliers shall be given only if requested." However, this would not appear to preclude the agency from giving notice as a courtesy. Furthermore, a notice of award is required to be published in the CBD if the award is over $25,000 and "if there is likely to be any subcontract," 41 U.S.C. § 416(a)(1)(C). Once notification is requested, an agency's failure to respond in a timely fashion is improper, *Professional Data Sys.*, GSBCA 8475-P, 86-3 BCA ¶ 19,083.

If a supplier requests information on an award that was based on factors other than price alone, FAR 13.106-3(d) provides that a brief explanation of the basis for the contract award decision must be provided.

D. Commercial Over $100,000 but Not Over $5,000,000

FAR 13.500(a) authorizes contracting agencies to use the simplified procedures of Part 13 "as a test program" if the contracting officer "reasonably expects, based on the nature of the supplies or services sought, and on market research, that offers will include only commercial items." The simplified procedures are to be used to the "maximum extent practicable," FAR 13.500(b). The authority to use the "test program" expires on January 1, 2000, FAR 13.500(d).

FAR 13.501 requires special documentation applicable only to the commercial item test program. For acquisitions over $100,000, the contracting officer must certify that the justification for sole source procurement is accurate and complete, FAR 13.501(a). For procurements in excess of $500,000, the approval must be by the competition advocate of the procuring activity on a non-delegable basis, FAR 13.501(a)(2)(ii).

For all procurements conducted under the test program, the contract file is to include a brief description of the procedures used, the number of offers received, the basis for the award, and any justification required for a sole source procurement, FAR 13.501(b).

E. Laws and Clauses Not Applicable

The Federal Acquisition Streamlining Act (FASA) of 1994 made certain laws inapplicable to procurements at or below the simplified acquisition threshold. This list is set forth in FAR 13.005. FAR 13.006 lists additional provisions and clauses that are inapplicable to contracts and subcontracts at or below the simplified acquisition threshold. The provisions and clauses set forth in FAR 13.005 as inapplicable is not an exclusive list. **Figure 7-1** is a complete list of all socioeconomic clauses from FAR Parts 19–26 and their applicability to simplified acquisitions.

Collateral Policy	Simplified Procedures	Commercial (Less than $100,000)	Commercial (Greater than $100,000 and less than $5 million)	Standard (over $100,000 and not commer-cial)
Small Business and Socially Disadvantaged				
Women-Owned Business (52.204-5)	No	No	Yes	Yes
Small Business Program Representations (52.219-1)	Yes	Yes	Yes	Yes
Utilization of Small, Small Disadvantaged and Women-Owned Small Business Concerns (52.219-8)	No	No	Yes	Yes
Small, Small Disadvantaged and Women-Owned Small Business Subcontracting Plan (52.219.9)	No	No	Yes	Yes over $500,000
Incentive Subcontracting Program (52.219-10)	No	No	Yes	Yes over $500,000
Utilization of Indian Organizations and Indian-Owned Economic Enterprises (52.226-1)	No	No	Yes	Yes over $500,000
Historically Black College or University and Minority Institution (52.226-2)	Yes	Yes	Yes	Yes
Labor and Equal Opportunity				
Convict Labor (52.222-3)	Yes	Yes	Yes	Yes
Contract Work Hours and Safety Standards (52.222-4)	No	No	No	Yes
Balance of Payments Program — Construction Materials — NAFTA (52.225-22)	Yes	Yes	Yes	Yes
Preference for U.S.-Flag Air Carriers (52.247-63)	No	No	No	Yes

Collateral Policy	Simplified Procedures	Commercial (Less than $100,000)	Commercial (Greater than $100,000 and less than $5 million)	Standard (over $100,000 and not commercial)
Preference for Privately Owned U.S.-Flag Commercial Vessels (52.247-64)	Yes	Yes	Yes	Yes
Davis-Bacon Act (52.222-6)	Yes	Yes	Yes	Yes
Walsh-Healey Act (52.222-20)	Yes	No	No	Yes
Certification of Nonsegregated Facilities (52.222-21)	Yes	Yes	Yes	Yes
Affirmative Action Compliance (52.222-25)	Yes	Yes	Yes	Yes
Equal Opportunity (52.222-26)	Yes	Yes	Yes	Yes
Affirmative Action Compliance Requirements for Construction (52.222-27)	Yes	Yes	Yes	Yes
Equal Opportunity Preaward Clearance of Subcontracts (52.222-28)	No	No	No	Yes over $1m
Affirmative Action for Special Disabled and Vietnam-Era Veterans (52.222-35)	Yes	Yes	Yes	Yes
Affirmative Action for Handicapped Workers (52.222-36)	Yes	Yes	Yes	Yes
Service Contract Act (52.222-41)	Yes	Yes	Yes	Yes
Fair Labor Standards Act and Service Contract Act — Price Adjustment (Multiple Year and Option Contracts) (52.222-43)	No	No	Yes	Yes
Fair Labor Standards Act and Service Contract Act—Price Adjustment (52.222-44)	No	No	Yes	Yes
Protection of the Environment				
Clean Air and Water Certification (52.223-1)	No	No	No	Yes

Collateral Policy	Simplified Procedures	Commercial (Less than $100,000)	Commercial (Greater than $100,000 and less than $5 million)	Standard (over $100,000 and not commer-cial)
Clean Air and Water (52.223-2)	No	No	No	Yes
Hazardous Material Identification and Material Safety Data (52.223-3)	Yes	Yes	Yes	Yes
Recovered Material Certification (52.223-4)	Yes	Yes	Yes	Yes
Pollution Prevention Right-to-know Information (52.223-5)	Yes	Yes	Yes	Yes
Drug-Free Workplace (52.223-6)	No	No	No	Yes
Notice of Radioactive Materials (52.223-7)	Yes	Yes	Yes	Yes
Certification of Percentage of Recovered Material Content for EPA-Designated Items Used in Performance of the Contract (52.223-9)	No	No	Yes	Yes
Waste Reduction Program (52.223-10)	Yes	Yes	Yes	Yes
Ozone-Depleting Substances (52.223-11)	Yes	Yes	Yes	Yes
Refrigeration Equipment and Air, Conditioners (52.223-12)	Yes	Yes	Yes	Yes
Certification of Toxic Chemical Release Reporting (52.223-13)	No	No	Yes	Yes
Toxic Chemical Release (52.223-14)	No	No	Yes	Yes
Preferences				
Buy American Act Certificate (52.225-1)	Yes	Yes	Yes	Yes
Balance of Payments Program Certificate (52.225-6)	No	No	Yes	Yes

Collateral Policy	Simplified Procedures	Commercial (Less than $100,000)	Commercial (Greater than $100,000 and less than $5 million)	Standard (over $100,000 and not commer-cial)
Balance of Payments Program (52.225-7)	No	No	Yes	Yes
Buy American Act — Trade Agreements — Balance of Payments Certificate (52.225-8)	Yes	Yes	Yes	Yes
Buy American Act — Trade Agreements — Balance of Payments Program (52.225-9)	Yes	Yes	Yes	Yes
Duty-Free Entry (52.225-10)	No	No	Yes	Yes
Restrictions on Certain Foreign Purchases (52.225-11)	Yes	Yes	Yes	Yes
Buy American Act — North American Free Trade Agreement Implementation Act — Balance of Payments Program (52.225-20)	Yes	Yes	Yes	Yes
Buy American Act — North American Free Trade Agreement Implementation Act — Balance of Payments Certificate (52.225-21)	Yes	Yes	Yes	Yes

F. Forms

1. Solicitation Forms

There is no standard form for request for offers under simplified acquisition procedures. FAR 13.307(b)(1) provides:

> Except when quotations are solicited via FACNET, other electronic means, or orally, the SF 1449; SF 18, Request for Quotations; or other agency form/automated format may be used. Each agency request for quotations form/automated format should conform with the SF 18 or SF 1449 to the maximum extent practicable.

The contracting officer must use SF 1449, Solicitation/Contract/Order for Commercial Items if (1) the acquisition is expected to exceed the simplified acquisition threshold, (2) a paper solicitation or contract is being used, and (3) procedures at 12.603 (streamlined solicitation for commercial items) are not being used, FAR 12.204. Use of SF 1449 is not mandatory but is encouraged for commercial acquisitions not exceeding the simplified acquisition threshold.

2. Award Forms

Normally award will be made by the issuance of a purchase order to the winning contractor. FAR 13.307 contains the following guidance on the forms to be used:

> (a) Commercial items. For use of the SF 1449, Solicitation/Contract/Order for Commercial Items, see 12.204.
>
> (b) Other than commercial items.
>
>> (1) Except when quotations are solicited via FACNET, other electronic means, or orally, the SF 1449; SF 18, Request for Quotations; or an agency form/automated format may be used. Each agency request for quotations form/automated format should conform with the SF 18 or SF 1449 to the maximum extent practicable.
>>
>> (2) Both SF 1449 and OF 347, Order for Supplies or Services, are multipurpose forms used for negotiated purchases of supplies or services, delivery or task orders, inspection and receiving reports, and invoices. An agency form/automated format also may be used.
>
> (c) Forms used for both commercial and other than commercial items.
>
>> (1) OF 336, Continuation Sheet, or an agency form/automated format may be used when additional space is needed.
>>
>> (2) OF 348, Order for Supplies or Services Schedule — Continuation, or an agency form/automated format may be used for negotiated purchases when additional space is needed. Agencies may print on these forms the clauses considered to be generally suitable for purchases.

(3) SF 30, Amendment of Solicitation/Modification of Contract, or a purchase order, unless an agency form/automated format is prescribed in agency regulations.

(d) SF 44, Purchase Order — Invoice — Voucher, is a multipurpose pocket-size purchase order form that may be used as outlined in 13.306.

(e) SF 1165, Receipt for Cash — Subvoucher, or an agency purchase order form may be used for purchases using imprest funds or third party drafts.

For military departments, DD Form 1155, Orders for Supplies or Services, must be used for purchases made using the simplified acquisition procedures of FAR Part 13, DFARS 213.505-1(b). Civilian agencies may also use special forms when using simplified acquisition procedures. For example, the General Services Administration uses GSA Form 3186, Order for Supplies or Services; GSA Form 3186A, Order for Supplies or Services; or GSA Form 3186B, Order for Supplies or Services (EDI), instead of the OF 347, Order for Supplies or Services, when making simplified acquisitions, GSA 513.505-2. The Department of Agriculture uses Form AD-838, Purchase Order, in lieu of Optional Forms 347 and 348. The Environmental Protection Agency permits the use of Form 1900-8, Procurement Request/Order, in lieu of Optional Forms 347 and 348 for simplified acquisitions, EPA 1513.505-2. DOE provides that Optional Forms 347 and 348 or DOE F 4250.3, Order for Supplies or Services, may be used for purchase orders using simplified acquisition procedures, DEAR 913.505-1.

III. ARCHITECT-ENGINEER CONTRACTS

Architectural or engineering services must be procured in accordance with the procedures set forth in the Brooks Act, 40 U.S.C. § 541 et seq. See FAR 36.601-3(b). These procedures meet the Competition in Contracting Act mandate of obtaining "competing proposals," 10 U.S.C. § 2302(2)(A). The Brooks Act was passed in 1972 after the Comptroller General notified Congress in 46 Comp. Gen. 556 (B-152306) (1966) that the existing practices in awarding architect-engineer (A-E) contracts "represent a deviation from the statutory requirements expressed in 10 U.S.C. § 2304(g) that proposals from a maximum number of qualified sources shall be solicited and that written or oral discussions be conducted with all responsible offerors who submit proposals within a competitive range, price and other factors considered." The Act amended the Federal Property and Administrative Services Act by ratifying the longstanding practice of procuring A-E services without price competition. The Act states that the Government's policy is to "publicly announce all requirements for architectural and engineering services, and to negotiate contracts for architectural and engineering services on the basis of demonstrated competence and qualification . . . at fair and reasonable prices," 40 U.S.C. § 542.

A. Definition of Architect-Engineer Services

In 1988, P.L. 100-656 and P.L. 100-679 amended the Brooks Act definition of A-E services at 40 U.S.C. § 541 to establish three independent categories of A-E services. This definition is implemented in FAR 36.102 as follows:

> (1) Professional services of an architectural or engineering nature, as defined by State law, if applicable, which are required to be performed or approved by a person licensed, registered, or certified to provide such services;
>
> (2) Professional services of an architectural or engineering nature performed by contract that are associated with research, planning, development, design, construction, alteration, or repair of real property; and
>
> (3) Such other professional services of an architectural or engineering nature, or incidental services, which members of the architectural and engineering professions (and individuals in their employ) may logically or justifiably perform, including studies, investigations, surveying and mapping, tests, evaluations, consultations, comprehensive planning, program management, conceptual designs, plans and specifications, value engineering, construction phase services, soils engineering, drawing reviews, preparation of operating and maintenance manuals, and other related services.

In *Forest Serv., Dept. of Agriculture*, 68 Comp. Gen. 555 (B-233987), 89-2 CPD ¶ 47, the Comptroller General discussed the reason for the amendment to the A-E services definition, as follows:

> The legislative history of Pub. L. No. 100-656, § 742, 102 Stat. 3853 (1988), indicates that the amendment is intended to clarify the definition of A-E services in response to the General Accounting Office decisions issued since the enactment of the Brooks Act, "which have had the effect of narrowing the application of the law, particularly in the field of surveying and mapping." 134 Cong. Rec. H10058 (daily ed. Oct. 12, 1988) (statement of Mr. Myers).

The Comptroller General stated that the amendment required a modification of the two-prong test enunciated in prior decisions, stating:

> Clause (C) of the 1988 amendment includes in the definition "other professional services of an architectural or engineering nature, or incidental services, which members of the architectural and engineering professions (and individuals in their employ) may logically or justifiably perform . . . ." The statute then lists services such as surveying and mapping which fall into this category. Thus, the revised definition now makes it clear that "incidental services" means types of services which are incidental to (part of) A-E services, and not, as we previously have held, incidental to an A-E project. The test to be applied in making this determination, then, is not whether the service is incidental to a traditional A-E project; rather, it is first, whether the service is the type which is incidental to professional services of an architectural or engineering nature, and if so, whether the service is one which members of the architectural and engineering profession may logically or justifiably perform.

See *White Shield, Inc.*, Comp. Gen. Dec. B-235522, 89-2 CPD ¶ 257; *Fodrea Land Surveys*, Comp. Gen. Dec. B-236413, 89-2 CPD ¶ 364 (traditional surveying and mapping must be acquired under A-E services because logically or justifiably performed by A-E firm). Other types of A-E services include computer-assisted design and drafting services, *EBA Ernest Bland Assocs.*, Comp. Gen. Dec. B-270496, 96-1 CPD ¶ 148; conducting flood studies, *Northwest Hydraulic Consultants, Inc.*, Comp. Gen. Dec. B-266211, 95-2 CPD ¶ 229; inspection and maintenance of work on towers and an antenna, *Fantozzi Co.*, Comp. Gen. Dec. B-265631, 95-2 CPD ¶ 255; and comprehensive long-term environmental services, *ABB Envtl. Servs., Inc.*, Comp. Gen. Dec. B-258258.2, 95-1 CPD ¶ 126.

B. Announcement of Requirements

The Brooks Act provides only that the agency must "publicly announce all requirements for architectural and engineering services," 40 U.S.C. § 542. This has been interpreted as requiring a CBD synopsis for any proposed A-E contract expected to exceed $25,000, FAR 5.205(d)(1). FAR 5.207(c)(2)(xii) states that the synopsis should contain the following information:

> For architect-engineer projects and other projects for which the supply or service codes are insufficient, provide brief details with respect to: location,

scope of services required, cost range and limitations, type of contract, estimated starting and completion dates, and any significant evaluation factors.

After publishing the synopsis, agencies must allow a 30-day response time from the date of publication before taking further action, FAR 5.203(d). A firm that does not respond to this notice is not necessarily excluded from consideration, as A-E firms are selected based on forms on file with the agency. However, the synopsis allows interested firms that have not done so to file the proper forms or to update data already on file. The CBD synopsis also alerts firms which might wish to protest some aspect of the procurement.

C. Selection Criteria

The policy of the Brooks Act is to award A-E contracts on the basis of competence and qualifications. This involves a two-step process: (1) selection based upon demonstrated competence and qualifications, and (2) post selection negotiation of a fair and reasonable price.

Each contractor is evaluated in terms of professional qualifications, specialized experience in the type of work required, capacity to perform on time, past performance, location in the area of the project (provided this criterion leaves an appropriate number of qualified firms), and acceptability under other appropriate evaluation criteria, FAR 36.602-1. Firms may be evaluated on the basis of the project design as well. FAR 36.602-1(b) provides that design competitions may be used, with the approval of the agency head or a designee, when unique situations exist involving prestige projects, sufficient time is available for the production and evaluation of designs, and the design competition will benefit the project after considering its costs.

These criteria are applied at two stages. The information submitted or on file with the agency is reviewed and not less than three firms are chosen for discussions "regarding concepts, the relative utility of alternative methods, and feasible ways to prescribe the use of recovered materials and achieve waste reduction and energy-efficiency in facility design," FAR 36.602-3(c). After these discussions, the top three firms are ranked according to these criteria as well as the merit of each firm's concepts.

When a source selection official is unable to choose between offerors on the basis of the established factors, other "rationally related" factors may be considered, *Group Hosp. Serv., Inc.*, 58 Comp. Gen. 263 (B-190401), 79-1 CPD ¶ 245. However, under no circumstances is cost or price to be considered. In *Mounts Eng'g; Department of the Interior — Request for Advance Decision*, 64 Comp. Gen. 772 (B-218489), 85-2 CPD ¶ 181, because the agency found two A-E firms "equally preferred," it requested cost proposals prior to selection. The Comptroller General sustained the protest, stating at 777:

> [G]iven the legislative mandate to rank A-E firms without reference to compensation, we believe that the fee proposed by a firm is not a factor rationally related to deciding which A-E firm is most highly qualified . . . .

One factor used in evaluation by the Department of Defense that differs from standard negotiated procurement is the volume of work previously awarded. DFARS 236.602-1(a)(6)(A) provides that:

> Consider the volume of work awarded by DOD during the previous 12 months. In considering equitable distribution of work among A-E firms, include small and small disadvantaged business firms and firms that have not had prior DOD contracts.

The Comptroller General has sustained a protest when the Navy failed to consider this factor, *Randolph Eng'g, Inc.*, Comp. Gen. Dec. B-192375, 79-1 CPD ¶ 465.

Since most factors considered in the Brooks Act evaluation process are responsibility-related, determinations of nonresponsibility are rare in this type of procurement. In *Richard Sanchez Assocs.*, 64 Comp. Gen. 603 (B-218404.2), 85-1 CPD ¶ 661, after the firm had been tentatively selected, negotiations were terminated due to the firm having fewer employees than the agency had believed. The Comptroller General held that since A-E selection procedures concern a firm's capabilities and qualifications relative to other firms rather than minimal responsibility, no referral to SBA for a Certificate of Competency was required when assessing relative capability. See also *Nomura Enters., Inc.*, Comp. Gen. Dec. B-236217, 89-2 CPD ¶ 437, where the Comptroller General held that, although certain evaluation criteria encompassed traditional elements of responsibility, this did not convert a technical finding that the protester was less qualified and experienced than other firms into a finding of nonresponsibility.

D. Source Selection Personnel

The required qualifications for source selection personnel differ somewhat from standard negotiated procurement. FAR 36.602-2 provides:

> (a) When acquiring architect-engineer services, an agency shall provide for one or more permanent or ad hoc architect-engineer evaluation boards (which may include preselection boards when authorized by agency regulations) to be composed of members who, collectively, have experience in architecture, engineering, construction, and Government and related acquisition matters. Members shall be appointed from among highly qualified professional employees of the agency or other agencies, and if authorized by agency procedure, private practitioners of architecture, engineering, or related professions. One Government member of each board shall be designated as the chairperson.
>
> (b) No firm shall be eligible for award of an architect-engineer contract during the period in which any of its principals or associates are participating as members of the awarding agency's evaluation board.

E. Appraising Firms' Qualifications

The first step in the selection process is to appraise each firm's qualifications using SF 254, "Architect-Engineer and Related Services Questionnaire" and, when applicable, SF 255, "Architect-Engineer and Related Services Questionnaire for Specific Project," FAR 36.603. Agencies are to maintain offices or permanent evaluation boards to keep files on A-E firms (or arrange to use other agencies' offices or boards) and to review and update these files annually. The updating process includes encouraging firms to submit revisions to SF 254 on an annual basis. When a contract of more than $25,000 is completed, a "performance evaluation report" must be prepared on SF 1421; the firm's file should contain all such pertinent reports, FAR 36.604, FAR 36.603(d)(4). The file should also record any awards to the firm made in the past year. However, where equitable distribution of A-E contracts was an evaluation factor, the Comptroller General criticized a six-month lag in recording information concerning prior contract awards and recommended that the agency update this information between the preselection board's evaluation and the selection board's final recommendation, *Dhillon Eng'rs, Inc.*, Comp. Gen. Dec. B-209687, 83-1 CPD ¶ 268. Where equitable distribution of work is an evaluation factor, it can still be outweighed by other performance- and qualification-based factors,

Liberty Assocs., Inc., Comp. Gen. Dec. B-232650, 89-1 CPD ¶ 29. In *ABB Envtl. Servs., Inc.*, Comp. Gen. Dec. B-258258.2, 95-1 CPD ¶ 126, the fact that equitable distribution of work was not a listed evaluation factor but was nonetheless used to resolve a tie, was deemed not to have prejudiced the protester because (1) it was applied equally to all offerors and (2) it was implausible to believe that the protester would not have competed had it known that this factor would be used. Compare *Fantozzi Co.*, Comp. Gen. Dec. B-265631, 95-2 CPD ¶ 255, where it was noted that unless an A-E synopsis expressly provides that equitable distribution is to be an evaluation criterion, contracting agencies are prohibited from considering this factor in their evaluation decision.

In deciding which firms to hold discussions with, agencies are permitted but not required to use information not included on SF 254 and SF 255, *FACE Assocs., Inc.*, Comp. Gen. Dec. B-211877, 83-2 CPD ¶ 643. The Comptroller General found that 40 U.S.C. § 543, which provides that firms should be encouraged to submit statements of qualifications and performance data annually, evidenced a legislative intent to avoid burdensome investigations into the firms' qualifications for each procurement.

When an agency learns that information on the SF 254 or SF 255 is misleading or inaccurate, it may terminate negotiations with a firm that has been tentatively selected, *Vertrans Design Assocs.*, Comp. Gen. Dec. B-242080, 91-1 CPD ¶ 265; *Richard Sanchez Assocs.*, 64 Comp. Gen. 603 (B-218404.2), 85-1 CPD ¶ 661; *Paul F. Pugh & Associated Professional Eng'rs*, Comp. Gen. Dec. B-198851, 80-2 CPD ¶ 171. The evaluation board is also free to change its ranking upon receipt of new information, *Henderson Design Group*, Comp. Gen. Dec. B-248973.3, 92-2 CPD ¶ 406; *Harding Lawson Assocs., Inc.*, Comp. Gen. Dec. B-230219, 88-1 CPD ¶ 483; *Arix Corp.*, Comp. Gen. Dec. B-195503, 79-2 CPD ¶ 331.

F. Selection and Ranking of Firms

The evaluation board holds discussions with at least three of the most highly qualified firms and prepares a selection report recommending the top three firms in order of preference, FAR 36.602-3(c). The report must include a narrative of the board's discussions and evaluation in order to allow the selection authority to review the recommendation. The Comptroller General sustained a protest where no documentation of the board's reasoning was created, rejecting the contention that because architects and engineers "are called upon to exercise their professional judgment . . . the process is necessarily a highly subjective one which does not lend itself to reasoned statements of the basis on which the selection is made," *Wadell Eng'g Corp.*, 60 Comp. Gen. 11 (B-199171), 80-2 CPD ¶ 269. However, in *ABB Envtl. Servs., Inc.*, Comp. Gen. Dec. B-258258.2, 95-1 CPD ¶ 126, the fact that the evaluation board was orally advised that its report was inadequate and was instructed to revise it (rather than rejecting the report outright and stating the reasons therefor in writing) was deemed to be a deficiency of form that did not affect the validity of the selection decision.

The final ranking is made by the agency head or another designated selection authority. The selection official reviews the board's recommendations with the advice of staff and technical representatives and selects the most qualified firms in order of preference. The selection official may select from only those firms on the board's list, FAR 36.602-4, but exercises an independent evaluation function, *SRG Partnership, PC*, 56 Comp. Gen. 721 (B-188444), 77-1 CPD ¶ 438. However, if the highest-ranked firm is not the firm most highly rated by the evaluation board, a written explanation must be provided, FAR 36.602-4(b).

The Comptroller General has consistently held that it will not upset the A-E selection decision as long as the record shows that the agency reasonably evaluated the protester's qualifications in accordance with the stated evaluation criteria. See *Geographic Resource Solutions*, Comp. Gen. Dec. B-260402, 95-1 CPD ¶ 278; *CH2M Hill, Ltd.*, Comp. Gen. Dec. B-259511, 95-1 CPD ¶ 203; *Environmental Technology Assessment Compliance Serv.*, Comp. Gen. Dec. B-258093, 94-2 CPD ¶ 239; *Shah & Assocs.*, Comp. Gen. Dec. B-257405, 94-2 CPD ¶ 123; *ConCeCo Eng'g, Inc.*, Comp. Gen. Dec. B-250666, 93-1 CPD ¶ 98.

FAR 36.602-5 allows two "short selection processes," consisting of selection by the board or by the chairperson of the board, when the contract is not expected to exceed the simplified acquisition threshold. The agency may also use a longer process including "preselection boards" if it desires. DFARS 236.602-2 requires such boards to prepare preselection lists of the maximum practicable number of qualified firms when the contract is for more than $25,000.

In other cases agencies may use more elaborate procedures. In *URS Consultants*, Comp. Gen. Dec. B-275068, 97-1 CPD ¶ 100, the agency followed a two-stage procedure to make its selection. The process was described as follows:

> The CBD synopsis indicated that GSA would select a contractor through a two-stage process. Stage I would establish the architectural, mechanical and electrical engineering, and industrial hygienist design capabilities of interested A/E firms and their key designers. During Stage I, interested firms were to submit standard forms (SF) 254 and 255 for the A/E design firm only and additional information including: 8 X 10 graphics and written descriptions of relevant prior completed projects; a statement from their key designers regarding the firm's design philosophy and the parameters that apply specifically to the modernization of buildings; their key designers' portfolios; and biographical profiles of their key designers. After the qualifications statements and related materials were evaluated, a short list of at least three firms would be selected for participation in Stage II. The synopsis stated that, during Stage II, each short-list offeror's entire project team — including the A/E design firm, its key designers, and all the consultants that will work on the project — would be evaluated. This evaluation was to be based upon submission of SFs 254 and 255 which reflected the entire project team and would include a face-to-face interview with each project team.

See also *Geonex Corp.*, Comp. Gen. Dec. B-274390-2, 97-1 CPD ¶ 225, where the selection procedure involved site visits, live-test demonstrations, and oral presentations. The solicitation contained 18 evaluation criteria and 38 subcriteria.

G. Negotiations

Final ranking by the selection official authorizes the contracting officer to begin negotiations with the most highly rated firm, FAR 36.606(a). The contracting officer should ordinarily request a proposal from the firm "ensuring that the solicitation does not inadvertently preclude the firm from proposing the use of modern design methods," FAR 36.606(b). Such methods, such as computer-assisted design, should be discussed in negotiations if not covered in the firm's proposal, FAR 36.606(d).

The negotiation process differs significantly from discussions in standard competitive procurement. This is primarily because 40 U.S.C. § 544 requires the agency to negotiate a contract at a "fair and reasonable" price although the statute does not permit the agency to consider price in selecting the contractor. Hence, safeguards must be built into the negotiation process in order to ensure reasonable costs and prices. 10 U.S.C. § 2306(d) and 41 U.S.C. § 254(b) provide that the price or cost plus fee for A-E services for public works or utilities cannot exceed six percent of the estimated construction costs. In addition, the agency must prepare an independent cost estimate for contracts over $25,000 and provide it to the contracting officer prior to negotiations, FAR 36.605. The estimate should be based on a detailed analysis of the work, "as though the Government were submitting a proposal." DFARS 236.606-70 limits the contract preparation of designs, plans, drawings and specifications to six percent of the project's estimated construction costs.

If the contracting officer is unable to negotiate a reasonable price or is otherwise unable to negotiate a satisfactory contract, negotiations should be formally terminated and negotiations should begin with the second-ranked firm, 40 U.S.C. § 544(b); FAR 36.606(f). In *Dworsky Assocs.*, Comp. Gen. Dec. B-248216, 92-1 CPD ¶ 533, the contracting officer's decision to terminate negotiations when after 10 months the parties could not come to a mutually acceptable agreement was not arbitrary or unreasonable. FAR 36.606(f) provides that the contracting officer should request a written best and final offer from a firm prior to terminating negotiations. This procedure continues until a satisfactory contract is negotiated. See *Inca Eng'rs, Inc.*, 69 Comp. Gen. 34 (B-236406), 89-2 CPD ¶ 371.

Negotiation may involve matters other than price. When a design competition is held as a basis for selection, the Government will not be bound to the design proposed by the selected firm unless the solicitation so provides, *Kerry Lindahl*, Comp. Gen. Dec. B-276057, 97-1 CPD ¶ 165.

IV. TWO-PHASE DESIGN-BUILD SELECTION PROCEDURES

Traditionally, the Federal Government has obtained new buildings and other civil works by contracting with an architect-engineering firm (A-E) for design of the project, soliciting competitive bids or proposals for the construction of the project, and awarding a contract to the successful offeror. This is known as the design-bid-build delivery system. Although this system has worked well, it is relatively slow and it separates design responsibility from construction responsibility. The system has been criticized for not bringing sufficient consideration of constructibility into the design process and for subjecting the Government to claims of the construction contractor for design defects. In using detailed construction drawings, the Government is liable to the contractor on a standard that approaches strict liability yet its claims against the A-E for defective design are generally judged by a standard of negligence.

Private owners, finding themselves in this same situation, have increasingly turned to a delivery system known as design-build. Under this system, the owner contracts initially with a single entity for both the design and the construction of the project. This entity is selected by a careful interview process, and the owner then proceeds to work with the design-build contractor for the remainder of the project. Usually, after the full scope of the project is determined (but before the detailed design is developed), the design-build contractor will agree to deliver the entire project within a guaranteed maximum price. The design-build contractor is not a construction contractor. It is a team composed of A-Es and constructors that work together from the beginning of design to the completion of construction to ensure that the owner receives the most cost-effective project that the team is capable of producing.

Federal agencies such as the Postal Service, the General Services Administration, and the Army Corps of Engineers have also used the design-build system, but they have concluded that the contractor should be selected using a competitive negotiation process. See the General Services Administration publication "Design-Build Request for Proposals Guide" (Nov. 1991) and the Corps of Engineers publication "Design-Build Instructions for Military Construction" (Sept. 26, 1994). This procedure has placed a heavy burden on offerors when the agency required extensive design work as a part of the competitive proposal.

Section 4105 of the Clinger-Cohen Act of 1996 amended 10 U.S.C. § 2305a and 41 U.S.C. § 253m to include new "design-build selection procedures." This section of the Act establishes a series of new acquisition rules — known as two-phase selection procedures — that must be followed when an agency decides to use the design-build delivery system and concludes that extensive design proposals will be required. The regulatory implementation adds a new FAR Subpart 36.3.

A. Authorization and Criteria for Use

The following statement on when the new procedure should be used is set forth in 10 U.S.C. § 2305a:

> Authorization — Unless the traditional acquisition approach of design-bid build established under the Brooks Architect-Engineers Act (41 U.S.C. § 541 et seq.) is used or another acquisition procedure authorized by law is used, the head of an agency shall use the two-phase selection procedures for entering into a contract for the design and construction of a public building, facility, or work when a determination is made that the procedures are appropriate for use.

Almost identical language is used in 41 U.S.C. § 253m. FAR 36.104 uses virtually the same language but also includes the following sentence:

> Other acquisition procedures authorized by law include the procedures established in this part and other parts of this chapter and, for DOD, the design-build process described in 10 U.S.C. 2862.

Thus, there are essentially two delivery systems for construction projects — design-bid-build and design-build. If design-bid-build is chosen, the design effort must be done using the Brooks Act procedures. Thereafter, the construction can be procured using sealed bidding, negotiation, or construction management. If design-build is chosen, either a one-step or two-step procedure may be used. The one-step procedure would follow normal competitive negotiation procedures. The two-step procedure would follow this new statutory two-phase procedure.

Contracting officers must consider the following criteria set forth in 10 U.S.C. § 2305a and 41 U.S.C. § 253m to determine whether the two-phase procedure is appropriate:

> (b) Criteria for use. — A contracting officer shall make a determination whether two-phase selection procedures are appropriate for use for entering into a contract for the design and construction of a public building, facility, or work when the contracting officer anticipates that three or more offers will be received for such contract, design work must be performed before an offeror can develop a price or cost proposal for such contract, the offeror will incur a substantial amount of expense in preparing the offer, and the contracting officer has considered information such as the following:

(1) The extent to which the project requirements have been adequately defined.

(2) The time constraints for delivery of the project.

(3) The capability and experience of potential contractors.

(4) The suitability of the project for use of the two-phase selection procedures.

(5) The capability of the agency to manage the two-phase selection process.

(6) Other criteria established by the agency.

These criteria are repeated in FAR 6.301(b). The key criteria are the requirement for design work and the resulting incurrence of cost by offerors. If extensive design work will be required with commensurate high proposal costs, the two-phase design-build procedure should be used. If little design work or proposal costs will be required, the normal competitive negotiation procedure will likely be the most efficient procedure.

Neither the FAR nor the statutes contain any guidance on when the design-build delivery system should be used in preference to the design-bid-build delivery system. Thus, this decision is left entirely to the discretion of each contracting agency.

B. Procedures

The agency develops, either in-house or by contract, a scope of work statement for inclusion in the solicitation that defines the project and provides prospective offerors with sufficient information regarding the Government's requirements (which may include criteria and preliminary design, budget parameters, and schedule or delivery requirements) to enable the offerors to submit proposals that meet the Government's needs. If the agency contracts for development of the scope of the work statement, then it must contract for A-E services in accordance with the Brooks Architect-Engineers Act, 40 U.S.C. § 541 et seq.

A two-phase procurement can utilize a single solicitation covering both phases or sequential solicitations, FAR 36.303. In either case, FAR 36.303-1 provides the following guidance on the solicitation instructions covering phase one:

> (a) Phase One of the solicitation(s) shall include —
>
> (1) The scope of work;
>
> (2) The phase-one evaluation factors, including —
>
> (i) Technical approach (but not detailed design or technical information);
>
> (ii) Technical qualifications, such as
>
> (A) Specialized experience and technical competence;
>
> (B) Capability to perform;
>
> (C) Past performance of the offeror's team (including the architect-engineer and construction members); and
>
> (iii) Other appropriate factors (excluding cost or price related factors, which are not permitted in Phase One);
>
> (3) Phase-two evaluation factors (see 36.303-2); and
>
> (4) A statement of the maximum number of offerors that will be selected to submit phase-two proposals. The maximum number specified shall not exceed five unless the contracting officer determines, for that particular solicitation, that a number greater than five is in the Government's interest and is consistent with the purposes and objectives of two-phase design-build contracting).

The intent of this guidance is to ensure that the phase one competition will not be unduly expensive. Thus, detailed design work and cost or price proposals are *prohibited.* The result is that the phase one competition is primarily based on the evaluation of the capabilities of the competing teams. This is appropriate because success of the entire technique depends on selecting a highly competent team. Two things must be evaluated here — the competence of the individual members of the team (as well as their key employees) and the ability of the team members to work together. The key data that should be used to perform this evaluation are information on the experience and past performance records of both the members of the team and the team itself.

The second phase of this procedure is conducted with the most highly qualified offerors in phase one, FAR 36.303-1(b). In order to carry out the intent of the statute, the number of offerors should be limited to three in most cases (the guidance is no more than five). In this phase, standard competitive negotiation procedures are used. See FAR 36.303-2, which states:

> (a) Phase Two of the solicitation(s) shall be prepared in accordance with part 15, and include phase-two evaluation factors, developed in accordance with 15.605. Examples of potential phase-two technical evaluation factors include design concepts, management approach, key personnel, and proposed technical solutions.
>
> (b) Phase Two of the solicitation(s) shall require submission of technical and price proposals, which shall be evaluated separately, in accordance with part 15.

The key evaluation factors in this phase will be the proposed design, the capability of the offerors, and the guaranteed maximum price. In accordance with FAR Part 15, the solicitation will be required to identify all significant subfactors and the relative importance of the factors. While the guaranteed maximum price will normally be an important factor, the solicitation should make it clear that the agency will not give a high value to a guaranteed maximum price that is too low to permit the contractor to give the agency the level of quality that it needs. Thus, the RFP should state that the agency is looking for a reasonable price and will not make an award at a price that is unreasonably low. An agency may want to include its estimate of the price range of the project in the RFP in order to avoid this problem.

In the past, offerors have been required to include detailed information on all aspects of the proposed project, including conceptual designs, and agencies have then evaluated and scored the numerous elements of each proposal. This has resulted in a lengthy evaluation process. The process can be conducted more efficiently if the design information called for in the phase-two RFP is limited to the amount of design effort necessary to arrive at the guaranteed maximum price. There is no need to evaluate the details of the proposed design if the performance specification is adequately written and the capability of the offerors is an important evaluation factor.

Selection of the contractor on the basis of the proposal with the best value to the Government and award of the contract will be done following the procedures for standard competitive negotiations. See Chapter 6 for a full discussion of these procedures.

V. COMPETITIVE SELECTION OF BASIC RESEARCH

The competitive selection of basic research proposals is recognized as a "competitive procedure" by 10 U.S.C. § 2302(2)(B) and 41 U.S.C. § 259(b)(2), which set out the criteria for such contracting as follows:

> the competitive selection for award of basic research proposals resulting from a general solicitation and the peer review or scientific review (as appropriate) of such proposals.

This competitive procedure differs significantly from sealed bid or competitive proposal procedures. Here the research organizations propose to undertake different research tasks in response to periodic announcements of broad areas of research interest. The agencies then sequentially review these proposals and award contracts until funds run out in a particular area.

There are no standard procedures for making these awards, and there is little published guidance from the agencies, the Comptroller General, or the courts. The lack of agency guidance results in part from the desire to allow for a great deal of flexibility in contracting for basic research.

A. Nature of Work

Although the statutes refer only to "basic research," the FAR implementation of the statute includes "applied research" and "development not related to the development of a specific system or hardware procurement" within the description of "competitive procedures," FAR 6.102(d)(2). The legislative history of this provision, H. Rep. 861, 98th Cong., 2d Sess. 7517, *reprinted in* 1984 U.S.C.C.A.N. 1445, 2111, indicates that the drafters of the statute considered basic research as research "directed toward increasing knowledge of a subject apart from any clear or necessary practical application of that knowledge." It is questionable whether "applied research" and "development," as defined in FAR 31.205-18 and FAR 35.001, fall within the scope described in the legislative history. Nevertheless, in response to a request from the FAR Secretariat, the Comptroller General indicated that it had no objection to the inclusion of "applied research" in the proposed FAR implementation, Comp. Gen. Dec. B-227314, Aug. 6, 1987. However, there was no mention of "development" by the Comptroller General. It should be noted that DEAR 935.016-2(b)(1) precludes the use of this technique to acquire development:

> The use of broad agency announcements for the acquisition of that part of development not related to the development of a specific system or hardware is authorized by FAR 35.016(a). Notwithstanding that authorization, ROAs [Research Opportunity Announcements] shall be used within DOE only to acquire basic and applied research.

B. Announcements

In this form of procurement, an agency publishes its areas of interest and private organizations submit proposals for specific projects within a specified area. Awards are made to proposals that are judged to be promising until the funds have been utilized. Thus, the competition is for funding within an area of interest rather than to perform a task that has been specified by the agency. However, the area of interest may be very narrowly defined, making the procedure much like a normal competitive procurement. See *TRW Inc.*, Comp. Gen. Dec. B-258347, 95-1 CPD ¶ 15, where the Comptroller General sustained a best value type award decision in a narrowly defined area.

The FAR uses the term "broad agency announcements" (BAAs) in its implementation of the statutory requirement for "general solicitations." These announcements are general in nature, identifying areas of research interest, selection criteria, method of evaluation, and period during which proposals may be submitted, FAR 35.016(b). Thus, many awards for different subjects of research within the general area may be made under a single BAA. Individual RFPs are not required. The Comptroller General described the BAA process as follows in *Golden Mfg. Co.*, Comp. Gen. Dec. B-255347, 94-1 CPD ¶ 183:

> A BAA is a contracting method by which government agencies can acquire basic and applied research. BAAs may be used by agencies to fulfill requirements for scientific study and experimentation directed toward advancing the state of the art or increasing knowledge or understanding rather than focusing on a specific system or hardware solution. Unlike sealed bidding and other negotiated procurement methods, a BAA does not contain a

> specific statement of work and no formal solicitation is issued. Under a BAA, the agency identifies a broad area of interest within which research may benefit the government, and organizations are then invited to submit their ideas within a specified period of time. The firms that submit proposals are not competing against each other but rather are attempting to demonstrate that their proposed research meets the agency's requirements. *Avogadro Energy Sys.*, B-244106, Sept. 9, 1991, 91-2 CPD ¶ 229. The agency may decide to award contracts to those offerors who submit ideas which the agency finds suitable. See FAR 35.016.

The nomenclature for BAAs varies from agency to agency. For example, the Department of Energy (DOE) uses the terms "Research Opportunity Announcement" or "Program Research and Development Announcements" (PRDA's) (DEAR 935.016), while NASA uses the terms "Announcement of Opportunity" or "NASA Research Announcements" (NFS 1835.016). NASA also uses contracts for its "NASA Acquisition of Investigations," a special procedure in which researchers propose investigations to be carried out on NASA missions, NFS Subpart 18-72. Another procedure for contracting for basic research is through a "Young Investigator Program." Both the Army and Navy have such a procedure.

1. Contracts or Other Instruments

Not all BAAs result in the award of contracts. Agencies issuing BAAs usually retain the option of funding the research under a contract or using a grant, cooperative agreement, or other form of assistance agreement. The requirements of procurement statutes and the FAR apply only if a contract is used. As discussed in Chapter 1, when the agency decides to use another funding instrument, different statutory or regulatory requirements may be prescribed. See, for example, Grants Management Common Rule, 53 Fed. Reg. 8034, Mar. 11, 1988. In *Energy Conversion Devices, Inc.*, Comp. Gen. Dec. B-260514, 95-2 CPD ¶ 121, the Comptroller General concluded that the principal purpose of the contract was not the acquisition of supplies or services and, therefore, use of a procurement contract was not required.

In the case of the Air Force, NASA, and DOE, the general policy is to use contracts for profitmaking organizations and grants for nonprofit organizations and universities. However, contracts may be used for nonprofit organizations and universities to obtain tighter control over a research project involving substantial acquisition of equipment or considerable subcontracting. Classified research is also usually done under a contract.

2. Requirement for Competition

The legislative history, H. Rep. 861, 98th Cong., 2d Sess. 7517, *reprinted in* 1984 U.S.C.C.A.N. 1445, 2111, makes it clear that the authority of 10 U.S.C. § 2302(2)(B) and 41 U.S.C. § 259(b)(2) may not be used if the general solicitation precludes the participation of capable individuals or firms:

> By recognizing such procurement of basic research as competitive, the conferees intend to promote the participation of all individuals or companies capable of supporting the government's needs in this important area. Any agency procurement which cannot meet this standard and, in fact, restricts participation, must be justified and approved under the requirements in this substitute for other than competitive procurement procedures.

Thus, if a BAA limits the submission of proposals to certain firms or individuals, procurement on the basis of other than full and open competition must be justified. See, for example, *Right Away Foods/Shelf Stable Foods*, Comp. Gen. Dec. B-259859.3, 95-2 CPD ¶ 34 (limitation of competition justified on the need to maintain the mobilization base).

Some agencies evaluate unsolicited proposals under their BAA rather than following the procedures in FAR Subpart 15.3. DEAR 917.7301-1(b) provides that a sole source justification will not be required when DOE handles an unsolicited proposal in this manner.

BAAs may be subject to set asides without violation of the requirement that competition not be limited. See DFARS 235.016:

> To help achieve the goals of Section 1207 of Public Law 99-661 (see part 226), contracting officers shall — (1) Whenever practicable, reserve discrete or severable areas of research interest contained in broad agency announcements for exclusive competition among historically black colleges and universities and minority institutions; (2) Indicate such reservation — (i) In the broad agency announcement; and (ii) In the announcement synopsis (see 205.207(d)(v)).

3. Content and Publication

FAR 35.016 specifies the following requirements for BAAs:

> The BAA, together with any supporting documents, shall —
>
> (1) Describe the agency's research interest, either for an individual program requirement or for broadly defined areas of interest covering the full range of the agency's requirements;
>
> (2) Describe the criteria for selecting the proposals, their relative importance, and the method of evaluation;
>
> (3) Specify the period of time during which proposals submitted in response to the BAA will be accepted; and
>
> (4) Contain instructions for the preparation and submission of proposals.
>
> (c) The availability of the BAA shall be published in the Commerce Business Daily and, if authorized pursuant to Subpart 5.5, may also be published in noted scientific, technical, or engineering periodicals. The notice shall be published no less frequently than annually.

4. Supplemental Information

Many BAAs published in the CBD contain only summary information. Further details are often made available on designated electronic bulletin boards or internet sites. For example, a BAA issued by the Office of Naval Research provided:

> Information regarding areas of interest and points of contact are available without fee through an on-line database service the Federal Information Exchange (FEDIX). Access FEDIX through computer and modem at 1-800-783-3349 or (301) 258-0953, through Internet (Telnet, FTP or Gopher to "fedix.fie.com" and at log-in type "fedix"), or through WorldWide Web at http://www.onr.navy.mil/. The FEDIX helpline is 301-975-0103. For the printed publication, please send a self addressed label to the address above.

The Army's broad agency announcement is a five-part document covering research interests, evaluation factors, proposal preparation, and containing sample proposals and all the necessary proposal forms. The Air Force has a two-part broad agency announcement consisting of the initial notice and a pamphlet entitled "Research Interests of the Air Force Office of Scientific Research," AFOSR Pamphlet 70-1, containing detailed information on areas of research interest as well as instructions for preparing and submitting proposals, AFOSR Pamphlet 64-11 (Nov. 1994).

C. Discussions With Proposers

Agency discussions with proposers occur in several stages. Prior to submitting a proposal the researcher is encouraged to talk informally with agency scientists in order to ascertain the degree of interest in the proposed research. The Army and Air Force will also consider a preliminary proposal or a brief outline of a proposal. These contacts must be initiated by the proposer. The appropriate scientist is usually identified in the broad agency announcement. After a proposal has been submitted, the agency may contact a representative of the proposing institution, usually the principal investigator, for any necessary clarification.

The contacts between the agency and proposer differ considerably from the type of contacts allowed in the standard procedures. There is no guidance on the type or extent of assistance that should be provided during this process. Such guidance is less necessary in this context, as proposers are proposing to do different tasks.

D. Evaluation of Proposals

FAR 35.016(d) specifies the following requirements for evaluating BAA proposals:

> Proposals received as a result of the BAA shall be evaluated in accordance with evaluation criteria specified therein through a peer or scientific review process.

This is generally consistent with the rule applicable to conventional negotiated procurement. The following discussion focuses on some of the unique aspects of this type of contracting, including the requirement for peer or scientific review.

1. Evaluation Factors

FAR 35.016(e) prescribes the following factors and states the primary basis for the evaluation of proposals:

> The primary basis for selecting proposals for acceptance shall be technical, importance to agency programs, and fund availability. Cost realism and reasonableness shall also be considered to the extent appropriate.

The use of unstated criteria is not permitted in evaluating proposals, but criteria that are reasonably related to stated criteria may be used, *Avogadro Energy Sys.*, Comp. Gen. Dec. B-244106, 91-2 CPD ¶ 229. There, the Comptroller General reviewed and approved the evaluation criteria in a BAA for basic research, finding that, to the extent that unstated criteria were present, they were reasonably related to stated criteria and so caused no prejudice to the selection process. See also *ABB Lummus Crest Inc.*, Comp. Gen. Dec. B-244440, 91-2 CPD ¶ 252 (allegation of evaluation based upon an unstated criterion — access to rights in proprietary data — not proved).

Although a formal responsibility determination is not made, responsibility-related factors are taken into account. Particularly important in contracting for basic research are the qualifications of the principal investigator and other key personnel, as the success of the endeavor is likely to depend more on these individuals than on the characteristics of the sponsoring institution. The Air Force's BAA, in fact, provides that the grant or contract may be terminated if the principal investigator leaves the organization or is unable to continue active participation.

2. Peer or Scientific Review

Peer or scientific review is a process of proposal review that utilizes a group of experts in the field represented by the proposal to evaluate the proposal merit. Peer or scientific review can be done by Government or outside scientists and can take a number of forms. The evaluation can be done by assembling panels of scientists, by receiving evaluations by mail, or by hiring a contractor to evaluate all proposals.

The use of outside evaluators is probably the most controversial element of this process. Agencies differ considerably in the extent to which such personnel are used. All agencies notify the offeror of proposed outside review and give the offeror the option of precluding this review if desired. For example, NFS 1872.705-1, Appendix A, General Instructions and Provisions provides:

> IX. Disclosure of Proposals Outside Government
>
> NASA may find it necessary to obtain proposal evaluation assistance outside the Government. Where NASA determines it is necessary to disclose a proposal outside the Government for evaluation purposes, arrangements will be made with the evaluator for appropriate handling of the proposal information. Therefore, by submitting a proposal the investigator and institution agree that NASA may have the proposal evaluated outside the Government. If the investigator or institution desire to preclude NASA from using an outside evaluation, the investigator or institution should so indicate on the cover. However, notice is given that if NASA is precluded from using outside evaluation, it may be unable to consider the proposal.

Note that under NASA's provision, NASA may elect to refuse to consider a proposal if outside review is precluded. The Department of Energy has a similar provision. See DEAR 927.7000.

Once a decision to use outside evaluators is made, FAR 15.609(f) requires that the following safeguards be observed:

> (1) Attach a cover sheet clearly marked with the legend in paragraph (d) of this section;
>
> (2) Change the beginning of this legend to read "All Government and non-Government personnel * * * "; and
>
> (3) Require any non-Government evaluator to agree in writing that data in the proposal will not be disclosed to others outside the Government.

Outside reviewers should be carefully selected. The range of potential conflicts of interest which need to be taken into account is recognized in the following NASA guidance at NFS 1872.403-1(a)(5):

> Care must be taken to avoid conflicts of interest. These include financial interests, institutional affiliations, professional biases and associations, as well as familiar relationships. Conflicts could further occur as a result of imbalance between Government and non-Government appointees or membership from institutions representing a singular school of thought in discipline areas involving competitive theories in approach to an investigation.

See *Herdon Science & Software, Inc.*, Comp. Gen. Dec. B-245505, Jan. 9, 1992, *Unpub.* (allegation of conflict of interest unfounded where evaluators were excluded from review or discussion of any proposal which they submitted as a principal or collaborator or which was supported by an institutional affiliate).

Careful selection of reviewers, however, may not be sufficient to avoid potential conflicts. Where evaluators are selected beforehand, problems may not become apparent until after the receipt of proposals. Special arrangements for review would be necessary in such cases.

E. Award

After the technical and cost evaluations are completed, a designated agency official reviews the information and decides whether to accept the proposal for negotiation. The award decision is discretionary. For example, in *AEC-ABLE Eng'g Co.*, Comp. Gen. Dec. B-257798.2, 95-1 CPD ¶ 37, the Comptroller General reviewed a number of allegations that the agency had improperly selected two other proposals but held that the agency was justified in awarding to those companies.

FAR 35.016(d) provides that in making awards, there is no need to evaluate proposals against each other:

> Written evaluation reports on individual proposals will be necessary but proposals need not be evaluated against each other since they are not submitted in accordance with a common work statement.

However, this may not be the case when proposals are required to be submitted on a common date. Under Army, Navy, and Air Force broad agency announcements, the funding decision is made on the basis of the proposal itself and the available funds. Under the DOE's and NASA's Acquisition Investigation Processes, the selection official is choosing a mix of research projects and a proposal's chances of funding will be affected by the other proposals and by how well it fits into the desired mix. The factors taken into account may be socioeconomic, budgetary, or technical or may involve tradeoffs between research in different disciplines.

NASA's "Acquisitions of Investigations," NFS 1872.405, provides the following guidance:

> A Program Office responsible for the project or program at Headquarters will receive the evaluation of the proposals, and weigh the evaluative data to determine an optimum payload or program of investigation. This determination will involve recommendations concerning individual investigations; but, more importantly, should result in a payload or program which is judged to optimize total mission return within schedule, engineering, and budgetary constraints.

Under NASA's procedures, unsuccessful proposers are notified as soon as their proposal has been rejected, and are provided an opportunity for debriefing under the guidelines of FAR 15.506, NFS 1872.504(a). Under DOE's procedures, the cognizant DOE program official must notify unsuccessful offerors in writing of the source selection decision and state, in general terms, the basis for the determination, DEAR 935.016-8. DOE's regulation does not provide for a debriefing of unsuccessful offerors.

VI. SMALL BUSINESS INNOVATIVE RESEARCH PROGRAM

Another special procedure permitted by 10 U.S.C. § 2302(2)(E) is competitive selection of research proposals resulting from a general solicitation and peer or scientific review solicited pursuant to Section 9 of the Small Business Act, 15 U.S.C. § 638. This section of the Small Business Act, known as the Small Business Innovation Development Act, became effective in October 1982 and created the Small Business Innovation Research (SBIR) program. The purposes of the program are to increase participation in Government-funded research and development by small innovative firms and to provide incentives for the conversion of research into commercial applications. Firms with 500 or fewer employees are eligible for participation in the program, and nonprofit organizations are excluded, 121 C.F.R. § 121.702.

A. Description of SBIR Program

The Act requires federal agencies with research and research and development budgets in excess of $100 million to establish SBIR programs, with funding derived from a fixed percentage of the agency's research and research and development budget. Seventeen federal agencies presently have SBIR programs. The law directed the SBA to issue a SBIR Program Policy Directive to be used as guidance by the participating agencies. The current directive, 58 Fed. Reg. 6144 (1993), constitutes the main source of guidance in this area. The Comptroller General has held that in the absence of an express statutory provision, the policy directive's terms (in this case, providing for payment of a profit) will take precedence over an agency's regulations, *Appropriations/Financial Management*, 71 Comp. Gen. 310 (B-245032) (1992). Other sources of information on the SBIR program include the SBA's SBIR presolicitation announcement and the SBIR solicitations issued by the participating agencies.

The three phases of the program are designed to take an idea through the stages of research, development and demonstration, and commercial application. Phase I primarily involves awards of $100,000 or less to support up to six months of effort to demonstrate the scientific and technical merit and feasibility of a proposed innovation. Only Phase I awardees are eligible to compete for Phase II funding. Phase II awards generally involve a maximum of $750,000 to support up to two years of work to further develop the innovation. Projects with commercial potential receive special consideration for a Phase II award. Phase III is for the commercialization of Phase II results and does not involve SBIR funding. Private or non-SBIR federal funds must be used for this purpose. The dollar amounts for NASA are slightly less, $70,000 for Phase I and $600,000 for Phase II contracts, NASA SBIR/STTR Participation Guide.

The program is designed to assist small businesses by establishing simplified and fairly uniform procedures, while also allowing sufficient flexibility to the participating agencies. Thus, the SBA's Office of Innovation, Research, and Technology establishes certain guidelines, primarily concerning the timing and content of SBIR solicitations. The individual procuring agencies unilaterally determine the categories of research to be included in the SBIR program, issue solicitations, evaluate and select projects, and administer the resulting agreements. Agencies are free to choose the SBIR funding instrument, consistent with the Grants and Cooperative Agreements Act. They are generally expected to make Phase I and Phase II awards within the $100,000 and $750,000 guidelines, but they may make larger awards when necessary.

The SBIR program is not intended to replace research awards to small businesses authorized under statutes or regulations. Thus, unsolicited proposals from small businesses, or any other proposals not submitted in response to the SBIR solicitations, are ineligible for SBIR awards, 58 Fed. Reg. 6148 (1993).

B. SBIR Announcement

When each procuring agency has determined the categories of research in which Phase I proposals are to be solicited, they are furnished to the SBA. The SBA then issues a quarterly presolicitation announcement covering all participating agencies. This announcement is designed to provide small businesses with advance information on upcoming SBIR solicitations. 58 Fed. Reg. 6150 (1993) requires the following information to be included:

> (1) The list of topics upon which research or R&D proposals will be sought. Each research or R&D topic shall have up to 10 words in its title.
>
> (2) Agency address and/or phone number from which SBIR Program Solicitations can be obtained.
>
> (3) Names, addresses, and phone numbers of agency contact points where SBIR-related inquiries may be directed.
>
> (4) Release date(s) of program Solicitations.
>
> (5) Closing date(s) for receipt of proposals.
>
> (6) Estimated number and average dollar amounts or level of effort of Phase I awards to be made under the solicitation.

At the same time, each agency publishes a CBD notice announcing the current research categories. Such notices must be published 15 days prior to issuing the SBIR solicitations pursuant to Section 8(e) of the Small Business Act, 15 U.S.C. § 637(e).

Agency SBIR solicitations must be issued in accordance with a master schedule established by the SBA. The master schedule is designed to avoid bunching of solicitations and proposal due dates so as to allow small firms to prepare more than one SBIR proposal. Agencies may issue annual solicitations or multiple solicitations during the year.

Agency SBIR solicitations must follow a uniform format established by the SBA to minimize the burden on participating businesses. The SBIR solicitation is not allowed to exceed 20 pages, with the exception of the section describing research topics. Solicitations must contain the following sections in the order shown, as listed at 58 Fed. Reg. 6154 (1993):

a. Program Description

b. Definitions

c. Proposal Preparation Instructions and Requirements

d. Methods of Selection and Evaluation Criteria

e. Considerations

f. Submission of Proposals

g. Scientific and Technical Information Sources

h. Research Topics

The agency solicitations basically contain all the information and forms a firm needs in order to submit a proposal. The solicitation must indicate if external review is to be used as part of the evaluation process. The main body of the solicitation is the description of research topics for which proposals are being solicited. The Policy Directive states that topics and subtopics "shall describe the needs in sufficient detail so as to assist small firms in providing on-target responses but shall not involve detailed specifications to prescribed solutions to the problems." Some agency solicitations, from the Department of Defense for example, provide only topics; while others, such as from the Department of Agriculture, provide illustrative subtopics as well. The degree of detail in the DOD topic description differs considerably depending on whether the topic is categorized as research, exploratory development, or advanced/engineering development. Proposals are limited to 25 pages and must respond to only one topic or subtopic.

C. Agency Evaluation and Proposal Selection

Agencies have considerable freedom to develop evaluation and selection procedures under the SBIR program. Unlike the procedure with basic research proposals, most agencies limit contact with proposers during the proposal preparation and evaluation stage. For example, the DOD's SBIR Program Solicitation No. 98-1 prohibits oral communication during the preparation period with two exceptions. Proposers are encouraged to contact the Defense Technical Information Center, which will provide bibliographies of reports that have resulted from prior DOD-funded research, information about current DOD-sponsored work in the relevant area, and references to other sources of scientific and technical information needed to prepare the SBIR proposal. In addition, firms may receive general administrative guidance from small and disadvantaged business utilization specialists located in Defense Contract Administration Services activities. These specialists are available to discuss "general administrative requirements" but are prohibited from taking any action that might give an offeror an unfair advantage such as "discussing or explaining the technical requirements of the solicitation, writing or discussing technical or cost proposals, estimating cost or any other actions which are the offerors' responsibility." These limitations are not required by the SBA Policy Directive.

Evaluation factors differ somewhat between Phase I and Phase II proposals. Agencies are free to develop their own evaluation factors, subject to the following SBA guidance at 58 Fed. Reg. 6156 (1993):

> 1. The agency in its evaluation process shall develop a standardized method that will consider as a minimum the following factors:
>
> a. The technical approach and the anticipated agency and commercial benefits that may be derived from the research.
>
> b. The adequacy of the proposed effort and its relationship to the fulfillment of requirements of the research topic or subtopics.
>
> c. The soundness and technical merit of the proposed approach and its incremental progress toward topic or subtopic solution.
>
> d. Qualifications of the proposed principal/key investigators supporting staff and consultants.
>
> e. In Phase II, evaluations of proposals require, among other things, consideration of a proposal's commercial potential as evidenced by:
>
> (1) The small business concern's record of commercializing SBIR or other research,
>
> (2) The existence of second phase funding commitments from private sector or non-SBIR funding sources,
>
> (3) The existence of third phase follow-on commitments for the subject of the research, and

> (4) The presence of other indicators of commercial potential of the idea.
>
> Phase II proposals may only be submitted by Phase I award winners within the same agency.

Agencies may not consider cost-sharing as a factor, except where required by other statutes, 58 Fed. Reg. 6156 (1993). Program balance can be considered, but only as a secondary factor. The following list of Phase I evaluation factors, from the Department of Energy's SBIR solicitation, is typical:

> Evaluation Criteria — Phase I
>
> DOE plans to select for award those proposals offering the best value to the Government with approximately equal consideration given to each of the following criteria:
>
> 1. The scientific/technical quality of the Phase I research proposal and its relevance to the proposal's stated objectives.
>
> 2. The innovation and originality demonstrated by the proposal.
>
> 3. The qualifications of the Principal Investigator, other key staff, and consultants, if any, and the adequacy of available or obtainable instrumentation and facilities.
>
> 4. The anticipated benefits, technical and/or economic, of the proposed research (Phase I and Phase II), if successful.
>
> 5. The adequacy of the Phase I proposed effort to show progress toward proving the feasibility of the concept.

The results of the Phase I effort are considered as a major factor in Phase II decisions.

The review process generally involves an initial screening followed by an in-depth technical review by inside or outside scientists. The SBA Policy Directive encourages agencies to use their normal review process, whether this involves internal or external evaluation. In *Systems Research Co.*, Comp. Gen. Dec. B-260280.2, 95-2 CPD ¶ 62, the Comptroller General confirmed that, in conducting an SBIR procurement, agencies have wide discretion and, absent a violation of applicable regulations or solicitation provisions or a finding of fraud or bad faith, the agency's decision of which proposals it will fund will not be disturbed. See also *Bostan Research, Inc.*, Comp. Gen. Dec. B-274331, 96-2 CPD ¶ 209 (agency technical evaluation was not unreasonable); *Deborah Bass Assocs.*, Comp. Gen. Dec. B-257958, 94-2 CPD ¶ 180 (failure to hold discussions or request BAFOs is unobjectionable); *Genovation, Inc.*, Comp. Gen. Dec. B-251714, Apr. 1993, *Unpub.* (evaluator's overall evaluation and funding recommendation was not unreasonable); *Quantum Mechanics, Inc.*, Comp. Gen. Dec. B-257968, Nov. 1994, *Unpub.* (no basis to conclude that evaluator acted in bad faith, which requires a showing that official acted with specific and malicious intent to harm the protester); and *Noise Cancellation Technologies, Inc.*, Comp. Gen. Dec. B-246476, 92-1 CPD ¶ 269 (no basis for the contention that agency failed to apply the evaluation criteria properly).

Review procedures are to be formulated so as to minimize potential conflicts of interest. Unlike most basic research proposals, the proposals have a common cutoff date, so that they are considered in relation to one another. Agencies reserve the right to fund no proposals or to fund several proposals falling within a particular topic or subtopic. After award decisions are made, some negotiation with Phase I awardees may occur and more detailed negotiation with Phase II awardees is envisioned. After award decisions are announced, unsuccessful proposers are entitled to receive copies of technical evaluations, with the identity of the evaluator withheld.

VII. INFORMATION TECHNOLOGY

Another new acquisition procedure established by the Clinger-Cohen Act of 1996, P.L. 104-106, relates to information technology. The Act repealed the Brooks Act, 40 U.S.C. § 759, giving the General Services Administration (GSA) central authority over the purchase of information technology for the Federal Government. This effectively abolished the Federal Information Resources Management Regulation (FIRMR), which was the primary regulation on the acquisition of information technology. Although the FIRMR is no longer effective, it is likely that parts of it will be retained and relocated to the FAR or other procurement documents.

The Administrator of the Office of Management and Budget (OMB) has assumed responsibility for the Government's information technology investments, and individual agencies are now permitted to contract directly for information technology. Section 5112 of the Clinger-Cohen Act of 1996 provides that:

> The Director shall promote and be responsible for improving the acquisition, use, and disposal of information technology by the Federal Government to improve the productivity, efficiency, and effectiveness of Federal programs, including through dissemination of public information and the reduction of information collection burdens on the public.

The term "information technology" means any equipment or interconnected system or subsystem that is used in the automatic acquisition, storage, management, movement, display, switching, transmission, or reception of data or information by an executive agency, FAR 2.101. Equipment is "used by an agency" if it is used by the agency directly or is used by a contractor under a contract with the agency which requires the use of such equipment, or requires the use, to a significant extent, of such equipment in the performance of a service or the furnishing of a product, FAR 2.101.

Information technology includes computers, ancillary equipment, software, firmware and similar procedures, services (including support services), and related resources, FAR 2.101. It does not include equipment that is acquired by a contractor incidental to a contract, FAR 2.101.

The Clinger-Cohen Act of 1996 provides that the FAR Council is required to ensure that, to the maximum extent practicable, the acquisition of information technology is accomplished by a simplified, clear, and understandable process that specifically addresses the management of risk, incremental acquisitions, and the need to incorporate commercial information technology.

A. Performance-Based and Results-Based Management

Section 5113 of the Clinger-Cohen Act of 1996 provides that the Director of OMB is required to encourage performance-based and results-based management for agency information technology programs. The Director is required to review an agency's management practices based on the performance and results of its information technology programs and investments, and to issue clear and concise directions to ensure that agencies have effective and efficient capital planning processes that are used to select, control, and evaluate the results of major information systems investments and to ensure that agency information security is adequate.

B. Modular Contracting

Agencies are required to use modular contracting to the maximum extent possible for major systems technology acquisitions. Under modular contracting, an agency's need for a system is satisfied by successive acquisitions of interoperable increments. Each increment complies with common or commercially accepted standards applicable to information technology so that the increments are compatible with other increments of information technology comprising the system.

Section 5202 of the Clinger-Cohen Act of 1996 adds 41 U.S.C. § 434, providing:

> (c) Implementation. The Federal Acquisition Regulation shall provide that —
>
> (1) under the modular contracting process, an acquisition of a major system of information technology may be divided into several smaller acquisition increments that —
>
> (A) are easier to manage individually than would be one comprehensive acquisition;
>
> (B) address complex information technology objectives incrementally in order to enhance the likelihood of achieving workable solutions for attainment of those objectives.
>
> (C) provide for delivery, implementation, and testing of workable systems or solutions in discrete increments each of which comprises a system or solution that is not dependent on any subsequent increment in order to perform its principal functions; and
>
> (D) provide an opportunity for subsequent increments of the acquisition to take advantage of any evolution in technology or needs that occur during conduct of the earlier increments;
>
> (2) a contract for an increment of an information technology acquisition should, to the maximum extent practicable, be awarded within 180 days after the date on which the solicitation is issued and, if the con-

> tract for that increment cannot be awarded within such period, the increment should be considered for cancellation; and
>
> (3) the information technology provided for in a contract for acquisition of information technology should be delivered within 18 months after the date on which the solicitation resulting in award of the contract was issued.

This statute is implemented, without any significant additional guidance, in FAR 39.103. The GSA has issued an *Acquisition White Paper on Modular Contracting* giving additional guidance on this type of contracting. This paper warns that there are risks in using modular contracting because the modules may not be fully compatible. To overcome this problem, the paper recommends that prior to undertaking modular contracting the agency should formulate agency-wide information technology architecture based on common and commercial standards.

C. Acquisition Pilot Programs

The Administrator of the Office of Federal Procurement Policy (OFPP) has authority to conduct pilot programs to test alternative acquisition approaches for information technology. Section 5301 of the Clinger-Cohen Act of 1996 provides that no more than two pilots may be conducted and that each pilot may be carried out in no more than two procuring activities in the selected agency. The pilots cannot exceed $750 million for a period not to exceed five years. The statute also requires agency heads to develop evaluation and test plans, prepare and submit test plans to Congress prior to implementation, report on results within 180 days after completion, and make recommendations for legislation.

The Clinger-Cohen Act of 1996 suggests two specific pilot programs that can be carried out by agencies as authorized by the Administrator of OFPP. The first, described in Section 5311, is a program to test the feasibility of:

> (1) contracting on a competitive basis with a private source to provide the Federal Government with an information technology solution for improving mission-related or administrative processes of the Federal Government; and
>
> (2) paying the private-sector source an amount equal to a portion of the savings derived by the Federal Government from any improvements in mis-

sion-related processes and administrative processes that result from implementation of the solution.

The second pilot, called a "solutions-based contracting" program, is suggested in Section 5312 of the Act, as amended by Section 852 of the National Defense Authorization Act for Fiscal Year 1998, P.L. 105-85. This technique, described in detail, essentially consists of a procurement based on a statement of work identifying only the results that the agency desires. After a simplified source selection, the agency awards a 30-to-60-day program definition contract (or longer if approved by the Administrator) to the winning contractor, evaluates the solution arrived at in this period, and awards a contract to carry out the work if the solution is acceptable. If the solution is not acceptable, the contractor receives no payment for the program definition work and the agency is free to undertake another program definition effort with the next most highly qualified offeror. The Act limits each agency to 10 such pilot programs.

VIII. GSA AWARD SCHEDULES

Award schedules are lists of standard commercial products (often with related services) established by the Federal Supply Service (FSS) of the General Services Administration (GSA). These award schedules contain the discounted commercial prices that the listed offerors will charge Government agencies placing orders under them, GSAR 538.271(a). In the past, awards under Federal Supply Schedules were made under requirements contracts, making them mandatory for use by specified Government agencies. However, in 1994 GSA indicated that it intended to make new schedules nonmandatory, FSS Acquisition Letter FC-94-2. The process of listing offerors on these nonmandatory award schedules and the agencies' ordering procedures differ significantly from standard negotiation procedures and are discussed in the following material.

A. Solicitations and Offers

Proposed schedules are announced in the *Commerce Business Daily,* and interested parties may obtain solicitations either by contacting the issuing office or by downloading them from the FSS Internet site. Solicitations call for certain classes of commercial products and services, allowing offerors to propose differing products that fall within a designated class. In addition to identifying specific products, offerors are required to submit information concerning their catalog prices, dollar value of sales to the general public, discounts and concessions given to customers, explanations of any deviations from its discount and concession policy and other information, GSAR 515.804-6. This provision contains approximately four pages of instructions to offerors on furnishing "information other than cost or pricing data" to be used by the contracting officer in determining reasonableness of proposed discounts. The format to be used in submitting the actual offer is specified in GSAR 552.212-70, Preparation of Offer (Multiple Award Schedule).

Solicitations will normally indicate that it is the Government's intent to place multiple offerors on the schedules, GSAR 552.212-73, Evaluation — Commercial Items (Multiple Award Schedule). However, where it is anticipated that competition will involve identical items, Alternate I to this clause provides that the Government reserves the right to award "only one contract for all or part of a manufacturer's product line." In such a case, award will be made to the offeror proposing the lowest price.

In some solicitations, there is no closing date for submission of offers. Thus, offers may be submitted any time during the time period of the schedule (often five years). In other cases, offers from firms not already on the schedule may be submitted only during an "open season" and there may be a closing date for receipt of offers.

B. Evaluation and Negotiation

GSAR 538.270 contains the following instructions to contracting officers for negotiating prices and placing offerors on schedules:

> (a) The Government will seek to obtain the offeror's best price (the price given to the most favored customer). However, the Government recognizes that the terms and conditions of commercial sales vary and that there may be legitimate reasons why the best price is not achieved.
>
> (b) The contracting officer will establish negotiation objectives based on a review of relevant data and determination of price reasonableness.
>
> (c) When establishing negotiation objectives and determining price reasonableness, contracting officers will compare the terms and conditions of the MAS solicitation with the terms and conditions of agreements with the offeror's commercial customers. The contracting officer will consider the

following factors when determining the Government's price negotiation objectives:

(1) Aggregate volume of anticipated purchases;

(2) The purchase of a minimum quantity or a pattern of historic purchases;

(3) Prices taking into consideration any combination of discounts and concessions offered to commercial customers;

(4) Length of the contract period;

(5) Warranties, training and/or maintenance included in the purchase price or provided at additional cost to the product prices;

(6) Ordering and delivery practices; and

(7) Any other relevant information including differences between the MAS solicitation and commercial terms and conditions that may warrant differentials between the offer and the best prices offered to the most favored commercial customer(s). For example, if it is more expensive for an offeror to sell to the Government than to the customer who receives the offeror's best price or if the customer (e.g., dealer, distributor, OEM, other reseller) who receives the best price performs certain value-added functions for the offeror that the Government does not perform, then some reduction in the discount given to the Government may be appropriate. In cases where the best price is not offered to the Government, the contracting officer should ask the offeror to identify and explain the reason for any differences. Offerors shall not be required to provide detailed cost breakdowns.

(c) The contracting officer may award a contract containing pricing which is less favorable than the best price the offeror extends to any commercial customer for similar purchases, when the contracting officer makes a determination that:

(1) The prices offered to the Government are fair and reasonable even though comparable discounts were not negotiated, and

(2) Award of a contract is otherwise in the best interest of the Government.

C. Award

GSAR 552.212-73, Evaluation — Commercial Items (Multiple Award Schedule), contains the following basis for making multiple awards:

> (a) The Government may make multiple awards for the supplies or services offered in response to this solicitation that meet the definition of a "commercial item" in FAR 52.202-1. Awards may be made to those responsible offerors that offer reasonable pricing, conforming to the solicitation, and will be most advantageous to the Government, taking into consideration the multiplicity and complexity of items of various manufacturers and the differences in performance required to accomplish or produce required end results, production and distribution facilities, price, compliance with delivery requirements, and other pertinent factors. By providing a selection of comparable supplies or services, ordering activities are afforded the opportunity to fulfill their requirements with the item(s) that constitute the best value and that meet their needs at the lowest overall cost.
>
> (b) A written notice of award or acceptance of an offer, mailed or otherwise furnished to the offeror within the time for acceptance specified in the offer, shall result in a binding contract without further action by either party. Before the offer's specified expiration time, the Government may accept an offer (or part of an offer), whether or not there are negotiations after its receipt, unless a written notice of withdrawal is received before award.

Although this provision indicates that contracts are being awarded, from the language of individual solicitations it appears that the nonmandatory schedule awards are merely ordering arrangements. FSS Acquisition Letter FC-94-2 and the individual solicitations indicate that these nonmandatory schedule awards are indefinite-delivery, indefinite-quantity (IDIQ) contracts. For example, a typical CBD notice posted on August 4, 1997, covered a contract period of five years and stated:

> All contracts will be indefinite delivery—indefinite quantity contracts with $100 guaranteed minimum for the contract period.

Similarly, FSS Solicitation FCI-96-DL000001BB contains the following clause:

> The Government is obligated to purchase under each resultant contract a guaranteed minimum of one hundred dollars during the contract term. If at the conclusion of the contract period the contractor has received orders for

> less than $100, the Government will pay (upon request) the difference between the amount ordered and the $100.

These amounts are surely nominal.

In this regard, FAR 16.504(a)(2) states:

> To ensure that the contract is binding, the minimum quantity must be more than a nominal quantity, but it should not exceed the amount that the Government is fairly certain to order.

This FAR provision reflects the case law that holds that a "nominal" amount will not satisfy the minimum quantity requirement, *Tennessee Soap Co. v. United States*, 130 Ct. Cl. 154, 126 F. Supp. 439 (1954) ($10 minimum order held to be nominal). Thus, these nonmandatory awards are not IDIQ contracts and, failing other consideration (none is suggested), are not contracts. By contrast, the mandatory FSS schedules that still remain in effect are binding requirements contracts.

The use of multiple award schedules does not shield an agency from protests. See *L.A. Sys., Inc.*, Comp. Gen. Dec. B-276349, 97-1 CPD ¶ 206; and *Severn Companies, Inc.*, Comp. Gen. Dec. B-275717.2, 97-1 CPD ¶ 181. In *Severn*, the agency argued that the prohibition on protests involving task and delivery order contracts (10 U.S.C. § 2304c(d) and 41 U.S.C. § 253j(d)) applied to MAS awards. The Comptroller General viewed the legislative history of those statutes and concluded that there is "no evidence that that provision is intended to preclude protests" against MAS awards. The Comptroller General also noted that Subpart 16.5 of the FAR treats "FSS contracts as separate from other indefinite-delivery contracts."

D. Ordering

Although the FAR ordering procedures are covered in Part 8, entitled "Required Sources of Supplies and Services," they cover ordering under both mandatory and nonmandatory schedules. FAR 8.404(a) indicates that agencies are relieved from obtaining competition and determining reasonableness of prices when placing orders under schedules, as follows:

> *General.* When agency requirements are to be satisfied through the use of Federal Supply Schedules as set forth in this subpart, the simplified acquisition procedures of part 13 and the small business set-aside provisions of

> subpart 19.5 do not apply except for the provision at 13.202(c)(3). Orders placed pursuant to a Multiple Award Schedule (MAS), using the procedures in this subpart, are considered to be issued pursuant to full and open competition (see 6.102(d)(3)). Therefore, when placing orders under Federal Supply Schedules, ordering offices need not seek further competition, synopsize the requirement, make a separate determination of fair and reasonable pricing, or consider small business set-asides in accordance with subpart 19.5. GSA has already determined the prices of items under schedule contracts to be fair and reasonable. By placing an order against a schedule using the procedures in this section, the ordering office has concluded that the order represents the best value and results in the lowest overall cost alternative (considering price, special features, administrative costs, etc.) to meet the Government's needs.

This policy statement is based on 10 U.S.C. § 2302(2)(C) and 41 U.S.C. § 259(b)(3), which states that competitive procedures have been followed when using —

> the procedures established by the Administrator for the multiple awards schedule program of the General Services Administration if —
>
> > (i) participation in the program has been open to all responsible sources; and
> >
> > (ii) orders and contracts under such procedures result in the lowest overall cost alternative to meet the needs of the Government;

See *National Office Sys.*, Comp. Gen. Dec. B-274785, 97-1 CPD ¶ 12, where the Comptroller General stated:

> [FAR 8.404(b)(2)] requires a procuring agency to review automated pricing and product information, if such is available; it does not require procuring agencies to seek further competition by soliciting quotations. Further, there is no requirement under the regulations governing FSS use that the agency solicit quotes in order to obtain price reductions from schedule contractors. While schedule contractors are allowed to reduce their schedule contract prices to an individual agency for a specific order, there is no requirement that they do so. FAR 8.404(b)(3). Since a formal solicitation process is not contemplated for ordering from an FSS — the purpose of the FSS program is to provide government agencies with "a simplified process" for obtaining commonly used supplies and services at prices associated with volume buying — we have no basis to conclude that the agency erred by not competing its FSS purchase simply to obtain possible price reductions. See *National Mailing Sys.*, B-251932.3, Aug. 4, 1993, 93-2 CPD ¶ 78.

1. Placing Orders

Micro-purchases may be placed with any firm on the schedule, FAR 8.404(b)(1). FAR 8.404(b)(2) provides for orders above the micro-purchase threshold to be placed on a best value basis, as follows:

> (2) *Orders exceeding the micro-purchase threshold but not exceeding the maximum order threshold.* Orders should be placed with the schedule contractor that can provide the supply or service that represents the best value. Before placing an order, ordering offices should consider reasonably available information about the supply or service offered under MAS contracts by using the "GSA Advantage!" on-line shopping service or by reviewing the catalogs/pricelists of at least three schedule contractors and select the delivery and other options available under the schedule that meet the agency's needs. In selecting the supply or service representing the best value, the ordering office may consider —
>
> > (i) Special features of the supply or service that are required in effective program performance and that are not provided by a comparable supply or service;
> >
> > (ii) Trade-in considerations;
> >
> > (iii) Probable life of the item selected as compared with that of a comparable item;
> >
> > (iv) Warranty considerations;
> >
> > (v) Maintenance availability;
> >
> > (vi) Past performance; and
> >
> > (vii) Environmental and energy efficiency considerations.

When placing orders above the maximum order limitations contained in the schedule awards, FAR 8.404(b)(3) requires agencies to seek price reductions as follows:

> *Orders exceeding the maximum order threshold.* Each schedule contract has an established maximum order threshold. This threshold represents the point where it is advantageous for the ordering office to seek a price reduction. In addition to following the procedures in paragraph (b)(2) of this sec-

tion and before placing an order that exceeds the maximum order threshold, ordering offices shall —

(i) Review additional schedule contractors' catalogs/pricelists or use the "GSA Advantage!" on-line shopping service;

(ii) Based upon the initial evaluation, generally seek price reductions from the schedule contractor(s) appearing to provide the best value (considering price and other factors); and

(iii) After price reductions have been sought, place the order with the schedule contractor that provides the best value and results in the lowest overall cost alternative (see 8.404(a)). If further price reductions are not offered, an order may still be placed, if the ordering office determines that it is appropriate.

Agencies have substantial discretion in placing delivery orders under MAS contracts. See *EMC Corp.*, Comp. Gen. Dec. B-277133, 97-2 CPD ¶ 64, where the Comptroller General denied a protest of a MAS delivery order because the MAS contractor's proposed solution met the requirements of the agency's RFQ. Agencies also have discretion to terminate MAS delivery orders. See *Severn Companies, Inc.*, B-275717.2, 97-1 CPD ¶ 181.

When agencies become aware of lower prices from nonschedule sources, they are advised to seek price reductions from schedule sources, FAR 8.404(b)(5). Although the FAR does not so state, it would not be appropriate to award to a schedule source at a price higher than that offered by a nonschedule source, unless the agency makes a determination that the features offered by the schedule source warrant the higher price.

Although the FAR permits agencies to make a best value determination when reviewing competing vendors' schedule offerings, vendors must be advised of the basis for the selection. In *COMARK Fed. Sys.*, Comp. Gen. Dec. B-278343, 98-1 CPD ¶ ___, the Comptroller General sustained a protest on the basis that the agency requested quotations from vendors without advising them that it did not require the lowest priced, technically acceptable configuration.

2. *Blanket Purchase Agreements*

Agencies anticipating frequent ordering are permitted to enter into blanket purchase agreements (BPAs) with selected firms, FAR 8.404(b)(4). These BPAs do not obligate the agency to order from the selected firms. Their purpose is to simplify ordering, invoicing, payment, and other administrative matters. FAR 13.202(c)(3) provides:

> (c) BPAs may be established with —
>
> * * *
>
> (3) Federal Supply Service contractors, if not inconsistent with the terms of the applicable schedule contract.

The Comptroller General generally will not disturb an agency's decision to award a BPA to a MAS contractor. See *Pfizer, Inc.*, Comp. Gen. Dec. B-276362, 97-1 CPD ¶ 205, where the Comptroller General found proper the Veteran Administrations' decision to enter into only one BPA even though more than one MAS contractor carried appropriate competing drugs.

In *Intelligent Decisions, Inc.*, Comp. Gen. Dec. B-274626, 97-1 CPD ¶ 19, *recons. denied*, 97-1 CPD ¶ 185, the Comptroller General held that the Department of Justice (DOJ) had entered into a BPA pursuant to the FAR and the terms of the schedule contract. The protester also argued that DOJ had not conducted a MAS buy and, as a result, had violated the provisions of FAR Parts 13 or 15 by holding discussions with only the schedule contractor. In concluding that this was an FSS buy, the Comptroller General stated:

> Non-mandatory, multiple award FSS contracts are indefinite delivery contracts for commercial firms to provide government agencies with a variety of commonly used supplies and services at stated prices for given periods of time. Government ordering activities can order supplies or services under simplified procedures from the FSS contractors to meet their requirements. FAR 8.401(a). Here, the record indicates that DOJ determined that its requirements could be satisfied through the use of the FSS, then reviewed price lists and descriptive literature of competing systems, obtained quotes from FSS vendors, compared the features of [contractor's] offered Pentium 166 processor with those of other FSS vendors, and selected [the contractor] after determining that its Pentium 166 processor represents the best value and meeting the agency's needs at the lowest overall cost.

The Comptroller General stated that because requests for quotations issued to MAS contractors "are merely intended to identify suitable products available on the FSS, the agency can seek additional information from vendors after the submission of quotations."

3. Incidental Nonschedule Items

Agencies often included "incidental" nonschedule items when ordering schedule products under a MAS order. The Comptroller General generally approved of this practice. See, for example, *ViON Corp.*, Comp. Gen. Dec. B-275063.2, 97-1 CPD ¶ 53 (approved purchase of non-FSS items under single FSS procurement because cost of incidentals were small compared to total cost of procurement); *Dictaphone Corp.*, Comp. Gen. Dec. B-254920, 94-1 CPD ¶ 6 (approved purchase of incidental item that was less than 4 percent of total price). The Court of Federal Claims recently ruled, however, that GSA's practice of "bundling" nonschedule products with schedule products under a multiple award schedule purchase order is illegal, *ATA Defense Indus., Inc. v. United States*, 38 Fed. Cl. 489 (1997). In *ATA Defense*, GSA argued that the court should uphold the purchase of the nonschedule products because they were "incidental" to the products being purchased against the schedule and cited a series of Comptroller General decisions. The court rejected this argument, stating at 503:

> It is fundamentally inconsistent with Congress' unambiguous statutory mandate in the CICA to allow a contracting officer, when purchasing products against the FSS, to include in the purchase order "incidental" products that are competitively available, unless the prices charged for these "incidental" products are not product of full and open competition. As noted above, Congress unequivocally states in 10 U.S.C. § 2304(a)(1)(A) that in conducting a procurement, unless an exception applies, an agency "shall obtain full and open competition through the use of competitive procedures." As summarized above, these exceptions are specific and narrow in scope. There is no exception that even arguably covers "incidentals."

E. Documentation

FAR 8.404(b)(7) provides for the following minimum documentation for the placement of orders:

Documentation. Orders should be documented, at a minimum, by identifying the contractor the item was purchased from, the item purchased, and the amount paid. If an agency requirement in excess of the micro-purchase threshold is defined so as to require a particular brand name, product, or a feature of a product peculiar to one manufacturer, thereby precluding consideration of a product manufactured by another company, the ordering office shall include an explanation in the file as to why the particular brand name, product, or feature is essential to satisfy the agency's needs.

IX. OTHER AGENCY PROCEDURES

In addition to the "other procedures" specified in 10 U.S.C. § 2302(2) and 41 U.S.C. § 259(b), some agencies have statutory authority to use special procurement procedures in an effort to streamline the acquisition process.

A. NASA's MidRange Procurement Procedures

Section 5062 of the Federal Acquisition Streamlining Act (FASA) of 1994, P.L. 103-355, authorized NASA to conduct a MidRange procurement test program on procurements up to $500,000. This authority was further extended by the Administrator of the Office of Federal Procurement Policy, NFS 1871.102.

NASA's MidRange procurement procedures are set forth at NFS 1871. Procurements conducted under this part are considered to be full and open competition, NFS 1871.105. NASA's MidRange procurement procedures are intended to "streamline and expedite the acquisition process," NFS 1871.301. MidRange procurement procedures are applicable to all contract actions over the simplified acquisition threshold ($100,000) and not more than $2 million in basic value (not more than $10 million with options) and for commercial items not more than $25 million including options, NFS 1871.103.

Synopses are publicized via the NASA Acquisition Internet Service (NAIS). Synopses are not to be sent to the CBD unless the basic award is expected to exceed $500,000, the total amount of the basic award plus options is expected to exceed $2,500,000, or annual obligations are expected to exceed $500,000 in any one year, NSF 1871.302.

The planning and requirement process involves using a buying team to conduct the procurement. NFS 1871.201 explains the procedure as follows:

> The concept is to designate individuals who are competent in their respective functional areas, provide those individuals with the basic authority to conduct the procurement and hold them accountable for the results. The buying team will normally consist of one technical member and one procurement member, but may be augmented with additional members as necessary. Personnel providing normal functional assistance to the team (e.g., legal financial) will not be considered a part of the team unless so designated. To function properly, the team should be given the maximum decision authority in matters related to the procurement. When higher level management approvals remain essential, it will be incumbent upon the functional team member to obtain such approvals.

Solicitation of sources for MidRange procurements is accomplished by use of a Request for Offer (RFO), NFS 1871.400. The RFO may be used for all types of procurements to which MidRange is applicable, NFS 1871.401. The buying team determines the type of procurement to use depending on the extent of discussion required, the number of non-price factors that will be evaluated, and the amount of competition available, NFS 1871.401. The types of procurement methods include sealed offers (NFS 1871.401-1), two-step competitive procurement (NFS 1871.401-2), competitive negotiated procurement not using qualitative criteria (NFS 1871.401-3), competitive negotiations using qualitative criteria (best-value selection) (NFS 1871.401-4), noncompetitive negotiations (NFS 1871.401-5), and commercial item procedures (NFS 1871.401-6). If the conditions for sealed bidding are met, then sealed offers or two-step sealed bidding must be used, NSF 1871.401. If sealed bid conditions do not exist, then one of the other methods may be used, NSF 1871.401.

The best value selection method eliminates the use of area evaluation factors and highly structured scoring, NFS 1871.601. The offeror is guided in meeting the Government's needs by a separate set of value characteristics that are performance based and permit the selection of the offer that provides better results for a reasonable marginal increase in price, NFS 871.602. The requiring activity will provide a list of value characteristics against which the offers will be judged. NSF 1871.603(a) sets forth the various characteristics that may be used as follows:

> Characteristics may include such factors as improved reliability, innovativeness of ideas, speed of service, demonstrated delivery performance,

> higher speeds, ease of use, qualifications of personnel, solutions to operating problems, level of service provided on previous similar contracts, or any of numerous other characteristics that may be of value to the Government in satisfying its needs.

The best value selection method involves four evaluation phases, NFS 1871.604. The first phase is the initial evaluation. Under this step, offers are reviewed to determine whether all required information has been provided and whether the offeror has made a reasonable attempt to present an acceptable offer, NFS 1871.604-1. Under the next step — determination of "finalists" — all acceptable offers are evaluated against the requirement and the value characteristics, NFS 1871.604-2. Based on this evaluation, the team identifies the finalists. The procurement team then holds discussions with the finalists under the third step, NFS 1871.604-3. Finally, as the last step, the procurement team selects the best value offer, NFS 1871.604-4.

A preaward notice is electronically transferred to all the offerors, NFS 1871.505. This serves as notification to those offerors that were not selected. If requested, a debriefing is provided by a member of the buying team, NFS 1871.505.

B. FAA Procedures

Public Law 104-50 exempted the Federal Aviation Agency (FAA) from the Federal Property and Administrative Services Act, as well as from a number of other designated statutes. As a result, on April 1, 1996, the FAA issued a separate procurement regulation entitled the Federal Aviation Administration Management System (AMS). A revised version of the AMS was issued in June 1997.

Under the AMS, there are two competitive procurement methods available for obtaining products and services through the FAA contracting process. The first method is described under "Complex and Noncommercial Source Selection" and is used for complex, large-dollar, developmental, and noncommercial items and services. The second method is described under "Commercial and Simplified Purchase Method" and is typically used for commercial items and are less complex, small in dollar value, and shorter term.

1. Complex and Noncommercial Source Selection

AMS 3.2.2.3 provides that there are five phases in complex and noncommercial source selection:

- Planning
- Screening
- Selection
- Debriefing (as requested)
- Lessons learned

Procurement planning is required for all FAA procurements except for those procurements using the simplified purchasing methods and those for utilities and is conducted by an integrated product team (IPT), AMS 2.9.5. This team consists of representatives of all "functional disciplines" responsible for the procurement of program needs, AMS 1.11. Evaluators and advisors selected by the IPT to assist in the evaluation are not considered members of the team, but rather support of the IPT. The IPT documents the overall procurement strategy in an acquisition strategy paper and details planning for specific procurement actions in the contracting section of the integrated program plan. The acquisition strategy paper is required for the overall acquisition program and must address individual procurements within the approved program, AMS 2.9.5. The scope of procurement planning should address all significant considerations of the procurement and should be in proportion to the complexity and dollar value of the requirement, AMS 3.2.1.2.2.

The screening process determines which offeror provides the best value to the FAA. A screening information request (SIR) is a request by the FAA for documentation, information, presentations, proposals, or binding offers. Once the public announcement has been released, the SIR may be released to start the competitive process, AMS 3.2.2.3.1.2.1. The number of distinct screening steps for a particular procurement will vary depending on the complexity of the procurement. Three categories of SIRs may be used according to the procurement strategy adopted by the IPT: qualitative information, screening information, and requests for offers, AMS 3.2.2.3.1.2.1. Qualitative information should be used to qualify vendors and establish qualified vendor lists (QVLs). It should be used only if it is intended that the resultant QVL will be used for multiple FAA procurements. Requested qualification information should be tailored to solicit information that will allow the FAA to make a determination as to which vendors meet the FAA's minimum qualification requirements for the required products or services. The qualification information is evaluated in accordance with the evaluation plan. A QVL will then be established for the given product or service. Once the list is established, only qualified vendors may compete for the products or services. This list can be updated at the FAA's discretion.

The second category of SIR calls for screening information, AMS 3.2.2.3.1.2.1. This category allows the FAA to determine which offerors will provide the best value. This SIR focuses on information that directly relates to the key discriminators for the procurement. Types of information that may form the basis of a screening request include equipment/products for FAA testing, capability statements, draft/model contracts, technical proposals (including oral presentations, if appropriate), commercial pricing information, financial information, cost or price information, and cost or price proposals, AMS 3.2.2.3.1.2.1. Each SIR requesting screening information must include some cost or pricing information appropriate to the specific SIR level of detail, AMS 3.2.2.3.1.2.1.

The last category of SIR is the request for offer, which is a request for an offeror to commit formally to provide the products or services required by the acquisition, AMS 3.2.2.3.1.2.1. The request for offer may take the form of a formal solicitation, a proposed contract, or a purchase order. The response to the request for offer is a binding offer and will become a binding contract if signed by the contracting officer, AMS 3.2.2.3.1.2.1.

The selection decision is based on the stated evaluation criteria, including cost or price considerations, AMS 3.2.2.3.1.3. After the IPT briefs the Source Selection Official (SSO) on its evaluation findings, the SSO documents the selection decision in a decision memorandum including the rational basis supporting the screening or selection decision, AMS 3.2.2.3.1.3. The contracting officer then transmits a proposed contract to the selected offeror, AMS 3.2.2.3.1.3.

All offerors that participated in the competitive process are notified of the award and given three working days from receipt of the notification to request a debriefing, AMS 3.2.2.3.1.4.

The last phase in this method is the preparation of a lessons learned memorandum, AMS 3.2.2.3.1.5. The purpose of this memorandum is for the IPT to relay its procurement experiences to other FAA personnel. The memorandum should highlight those issues that had a significant impact on their procurement.

2. *Commercial and Simplified Purchase Method*

This method permits the FAA to acquire commercial products and services from the marketplace using a simplified purchase method and best commercial practices. The purpose of this method, as set forth at AMS 3.2.2.5.1, is to:

- determine whether commercial items meet the FAA's needs;
- identify potential commercial sources; and
- publicly announce requirements in excess of $50,000.

Under this method, the contracting officer "should solicit an appropriate number of vendors to ensure quality products and services are delivered in a timely manner at a fair and reasonable price," AMS 3.2.2.5.2. Requirements are to be stated in commercial terms, AMS 3.2.2.5.2. The contracting officer will determine the appropriate screening approach and format, e.g., electronic, written, oral, use of standard commercial, or FAA forms, AMS 3.2.2.5.3. The contracting officer's selection decision is to be based on the FAA's stated evaluation criteria, AMS 3.2.2.5.4. The selection criteria should include such factors as price, functional specifications, delivery capability, warranty, and payment terms, AMS 3.2.2.5.4. The method of selection and rationale for awards should be documented, as well as a determination that the price is fair and reasonable, AMS 3.2.2.5.4.1.

C. Postal Service

The Postal Reorganization Act of 1970, P.L. 91-375, codified at 39 U.S.C. § 101 et seq., abolished the old Post Office Department and in its place created the U.S. Postal Service as an independent establishment of the executive branch. Under the Act, Congress exempted the Postal Service from most statutes and regulations relating to Government procurement, 39

U.S.C. § 410(a). The Postal Service follows special procedures set forth in the *U.S. Postal Procurement Manual* (PM), January 1, 1997.

The Postal Service does not require full and open competition, but rather requires only "adequate competition whenever feasible," PM 1.7.1.a. This is defined as the "solicitation and participation of a sufficient number of qualified suppliers to ensure that the required quality and quantity of goods and services is obtained when needed, and that the price is fair and reasonable," PM 1.7.1.a.

The standard purchasing method used by the Postal Service is a streamlined version of the process used by other federal agencies when conducting a best value procurement. Solicitations are issued and offerors are given "sufficient time . . . to prepare and submit proposals" (no minimum times are specified), PM 4.2.2.d. Solicitations state the evaluation criteria to be used in selecting the source and the proposals are evaluated comparatively, PM 4.2.5.a. Oral presentations are encouraged in lieu of written technical proposals, PM 4.2.4. Open communication with offerors is permitted throughout the process, culminating in the negotiation of a contract with the selected offeror, PM 4.2.5.c. The contract is awarded to the offeror whose proposal offers the best value to the Postal Service, PM 4.2.5.d. Unsuccessful offerors, upon written request, must be provided a debriefing, PM 4.2.8.

The Postal Service also has special procedures for purchasing commercially available goods and services (PM 4.3.), architect-engineer services (PM 4.4.2), construction (PM 4.4.3), design-build services (PM 4.4.4), construction management services (PM 4.4.5), mail transportation (PM 4.5), and other categories of work (PM 4.6).

CHAPTER 8

TYPES OF CONTRACTS

There are two basic types of pricing arrangements used in Government contracts — the cost-reimbursement contract, where the contractor is reimbursed for the allowable costs incurred in performance of the contract, and the fixed-price contract, where the contractor is paid a price for performing the work. In their purest form, these types of contracts are distinguished by the degree of risk of the cost of performance which is allocated to the contractor. In the firm-fixed-price contract, the contractor must complete the work to receive the price, which is preestablished and is not influenced by the cost of performance. Thus, if the costs are greater than the price, the contractor will suffer a loss; conversely, the lower the costs the greater the profits. Further, if the work is not satisfactorily completed on time, the contractor will be liable to the Government for the breach. In contrast, under a cost-reimbursement contract, the contractor's profit is not affected by the cost of performance because incurred costs will be reimbursed and the amount of the fee is predetermined. Equally as important, if the costs of performance are higher than estimated, the contractor is not obligated to complete the work if the Government does not continue to furnish additional funds. Further, it is extremely unlikely that the contractor would be held liable for defective or untimely work.

Fixed-price and cost-reimbursement contracts are also distinguished by the method of payment of the contractor. Under the fixed-price contract, payment is made for completed and delivered work. If this method of payment imposes financial burdens on the contractor, the Government may agree to provide financing in the form of progress payments. In either case, contractors incur significant financing costs in performing most fixed-price contracts. In contrast, payment is made on cost-reimbursement contracts on the basis of costs incurred during contract performance. Under these contracts, the contractor is assured of reimbursement of costs on a regular basis and needs to provide only a minimal amount of financing.

Refinements and sophistication in contracting techniques have resulted in a variety of types of fixed-price and cost-reimbursement contracts that alter the normal risk distribution and blur the distinctions between these basic contract types. The major category of contract types that fall in this middle ground are called incentive contracts. In these contracts, the parties share the risk by negotiating arrangements that alter the contractor's profit based on the cost or quality of performance. Another means of sharing the risk is the fixed-price contract with economic price adjustment, where the costs of labor and material are adjusted if there are fluctuations in market conditions. In another category of contracts, the Government relieves the contractor of risk by contracting for a level-of-effort or for labor-hours rather than for a completed job or task. These contracts are called time-and-materials, labor-hour, or level-of-effort contracts.

The Government also uses several different types of variable quantity forms of contracts. In some of these instances, the Government uses a form of contract where the contractor is bound to perform but the Government is free to order some or all of the work from another party. Examples of this type of arrangement are simple options and indefinite-quantity contracts with minimum quantities. Other forms of variable quantity contracts bind the Government as firmly as the contractor. The most commonly used contracts of this type are requirements contracts and multiyear contracts. All of these types of contracts are discussed in this chapter.

I. BASIC POLICIES

The statutory guidance on the selection of contracts is simple and direct. 10 U.S.C. § 2306(a) and 41 U.S.C. § 254(a) give broad discretion to use any appropriate type of contract on negotiated procurements but prohibit the use of a cost-plus-a-percentage-of-cost (CPPC) system of contracts. FAR 16.102 implements these statutes by restricting the types of contracts considered appropriate to those described in Part 16, as follows:

> (a) Contracts resulting from sealed bidding shall be firm-fixed-price contracts or fixed-price contracts with economic price adjustment.
>
> (b) Contracts negotiated under Part 15 may be of any type or combination of types that will promote the Government's interest, except as restricted in this part (see 10 U.S.C. § 2306(a) and 41 U.S.C. § 254(a)). Contract types not described in this regulation shall not be used, except as a deviation under Subpart 1.4.
>
> (c) The cost-plus-a-percentage-of-cost system of contracting shall not be used (see 10 U.S.C. § 2306(a) and 41 U.S.C. § 254(b)). Prime contracts (including letter contracts) other than firm-fixed-price contracts shall, by an

> appropriate clause, prohibit cost-plus-a-percentage-of-cost subcontracts (see clauses prescribed in Subpart 44.2 for cost-reimbursement contracts and Subparts 16.2 and 16.4 for fixed-price contracts).

This section addresses several general issues that must be considered in selecting the appropriate type of contract. The first issue is the *broad discretion* granted to contracting officers in selecting the type of contract in negotiated procurements. Second is the scope of the prohibition of CPPC systems of contracting. Finally, the section reviews the policies on undefinitized contractual actions such as letter contracts or letters of intent.

A. Discretion

Since sealed bidding requires the use of either firm-fixed-price contracts or fixed-price contracts with economic price adjustment, FAR 14.104, the broad discretion granted to contracting officers pertains to negotiated procurements. FAR 16.103 balances the need to impose *reasonable risks* on the contractor with the need to use a type of contract that *motivates effective performance*, stating:

> (a) Selecting the contract type is generally a matter for negotiation and requires the exercise of sound judgment. Negotiating the contract type and negotiating prices are closely related and should be considered together. The objective is to negotiate a contract type and price (or estimated cost and fee) that will result in reasonable contractor risk and provide the contractor with the greatest incentive for efficient and economical performance.
>
> (b) A firm-fixed-price contract, which best utilizes the basic profit motive of business enterprise, shall be used when the risk involved is minimal or can be predicted with an acceptable degree of certainty. However, when a reasonable basis for firm pricing does not exist, other contract types should be considered, and negotiations should be directed toward selecting a contract type (or combination of types) that will appropriately tie profit to contractor performance.

FAR 16.104 provides a list of factors to be considered in selecting the contract type with guidance as to the application of each factor. The factors are listed as follows:

a. Price competition

b. Price analysis

c. Cost analysis

d. Type and complexity of the requirement

e. Urgency of the requirement

f. Period of performance or length of production run

g. Contractor's technical capability and financial responsibility

h. Adequacy of the contractor's accounting system

i. Concurrent contracts

j. Extent and nature of proposed subcontracting

The guidance in this paragraph of the FAR makes it quite clear that it is the basic policy of the Government to use the type of contract that imposes sufficient risk on the contractor to motivate good performance yet relieves the contractor of unduly high risks over which it has no control and that are unpredictable.

The contracting officer has broad discretion in selecting the contract type. See, for example, *Master Sec., Inc.*, Comp. Gen. Dec. B-232263, 88-2 CPD ¶ 449, where the Comptroller General denied a protest where the contracting officer had used a firm-fixed-price contract for three years of work. The protester argued that such a contract imposed an inordinate risk of higher labor costs, but the Comptroller General accepted the contracting officer's reasoning that competition would keep the prices from containing too high a contingency and that "practical individual financial considerations would dissuade offerors from proposing unrealistically low prices." Historically, this discretion has occasionally been used to impose very high risks on contractors undertaking major development programs. Congress reacted to this by limiting the use of fixed-price contracts in the following section of the Omnibus Appropriations Act of 1988, P.L. 100-202:

> Section 8118. None of the funds provided for the Department of Defense in this Act may be obligated or expended for fixed-price-type contracts in excess of $10,000,000 for the development of a major system or subsystem unless the Under Secretary of Defense for Acquisition determines, in writing, that program risk has been reduced to the extent that realistic pricing

> can occur, and that the contract type permits an equitable and sensible allocation of program risk between the contracting parties.

This provision has been included in Department of Defense Appropriations Acts since that time and is implemented in DFARS 235.006. In *American Tel. & Tel. Co. v. United States*, 32 Fed. Cl. 672 (1995), a contract in contravention of this provision was held to be void.

This discretion has also been used, on occasion, to impose very low risks on contractors by using cost-reimbursement contracts in situations where fixed-price contracts could be used. This can occur, for example, when the following guidance in FAR 16.103 is not followed:

> (c) In the course of an acquisition program, a series of contracts, or a single long-term contract, changing circumstances may make a different contract type appropriate in later periods than that used at the outset. In particular, contracting officers should avoid protracted use of a cost-reimbursement or time-and-materials contract after experience provides a basis for firmer pricing.

One example of failure to follow this guidance was in the case of support service contracts awarded by the National Aeronautics and Space Administration (NASA) on a cost-plus-award-fee basis for many years. This policy was criticized by Congress in the early 1990s, and NASA was ordered in Section 401 of the NASA Authorization Act for FY 1993, P.L. 102-588, to review its policies to allocate the risk more equitably.

Thus, the discretion conferred on the contracting officer in this area must be exercised with great care — taking into account the interests of both the Government and the contractor. The number of contract types included in the regulations permit the striking of a fair balance between these interests in virtually all contracting situations.

B. Cost-Plus-a-Percentage-of-Cost Contracts

The two major procurement statutes prohibit CPPC contracts. Both 10 U.S.C. § 2306(a) and 41 U.S.C. § 254(b) state simply, with no further statutory guidance, that a "cost-plus-a-percentage-of-cost system of contracting shall not be used." This prohibition applies to both cost-reimbursement and fixed-price contracts. The Supreme Court explained the basis for this statutory prohibition in *Muschany v. United States*, 324 U.S. 49 (1944), at 61-62:

> The purpose of Congress was to protect the Government against the sort of exploitation so easily accomplished under cost-plus-a-percentage-of-cost contracts under which the Government contracts and is bound to pay costs, undetermined at the time the contract is made and to be incurred in the future, plus a commission based on a percentage of these future costs. The evil of such contracts is that the profit of the other party to the contract increases in proportion to that other party's costs expended in the performance. The danger guarded against by the Congressional prohibition was the incentive to a government contractor who already had a binding contract with the Government for payment of undetermined future costs to pay liberally for reimbursable items because higher costs meant a higher fee to him, his profit being determined by a percentage of cost.

In view of the clear statutory prohibition, explicit CPPC contracts are not likely to be encountered. Since, however, the statutory language prohibits a "system of contracting" and not merely a type of contract, numerous sorts of contractual arrangements may become subject to this prohibition. Generally, any contractual arrangement where the contractor is assured of greater profits by incurring additional costs will be held illegal. The Comptroller General has enunciated general criteria for ascertaining whether a contract violates this proscription. These criteria were adopted by the Federal Circuit in *Urban Data Sys., Inc. v. United States*, 699 F.2d 1147 (Fed. Cir. 1983), at 1150:

> We accept, at the outset, the general criteria (adopted by the Board) which were developed by the Comptroller General for determining whether a contract is a cost-plus-a-percentage-of-cost contract: (1) payment is on a predetermined percentage rate; (2) the predetermined percentage rate is applied to actual performance costs; (3) the contractor's entitlement is uncertain at the time of contracting; and (4) the contractor's entitlement increases commensurately with increased performance costs. 55 Comp. Gen. 554, 562 (1975). These standards incorporate the common understanding of the "cost-plus-a-percentage-of-cost system of contracting," an understanding which was undoubtedly in Congress's mind when it enacted the prohibition.

In spite of these clear criteria, there is still some confusion as to the arrangements that will constitute such a system of contracting. See, for example, *General Eng'g & Mach. Works v. O'Keefe*, 991 F.2d 775 (Fed. Cir. 1993), where the court affirmed a board holding that the recovery of a separate material handling charge and the inclusion of material handling costs in the hourly rate of a time-and-materials contract would constitute a violation of the CPPC prohibition because it was double recovery. The board had stated in *General Eng'g & Mach. Works*, ASBCA 38788, 92-3 BCA ¶ 25,055, at 124,872:

> It [the contractor] has already received compensation for its effort in handling material as part of its general overhead, further compensation in the form of a material handling charge would constitute additional profit. The payment of that additional profit, in an amount dependent upon the amount of material costs incurred, would constitute a cost-plus-a-percentage-of-cost contractual payment, and thus be illegal.

Neither the board nor the court found that payment of material handling costs as a percentage of material costs was proscribed as long as the material handling costs were excluded from the contractor's overhead. However, this practice has been dropped from the regulations. See the Payments under Time-and-Materials and Labor-Hour Contracts clause in FAR 52.232-7, which calls for payment of material handling costs either as part of overhead costs or at the amount of costs incurred.

1. Percentage Compensation

To fall within the definition of a CPPC arrangement, the agreement must provide that some element of the contractor's compensation will be computed as a *percentage* of some of the costs of performance. Such an arrangement meets the first, second, and fourth elements of the above criteria. When the element of compensation established on a percentage basis is profit or fee, it is easy to determine that a violation has occurred. See *Michael Weller, Inc.*, GSBCA 10627-NHI, 94-2 BCA ¶ 26,849, where a time-and-materials contract that authorized reimbursement for cost of subcontracts was not to be a CPPC contract because the profit paid was not computed as a percentage of costs.

A violation is somewhat more difficult to see when one element of cost is paid as a percentage of another cost element. However, this is the more common form of violation. Thus, payment of indirect costs on a percentage basis has been held to violate the CPPC proscription. Such violations were found when a contract called for the payment of overhead rates at predetermined percentages of direct costs, 35 Comp. Gen. 434 (B-126794) (1956); 35 Comp. Gen. 63 (B-120714) (1955); *Decision of Assoc. Gen. Counsel Kepplinger*, Comp. Gen. Dec. B-252378, Sept. 21, 1993, *Unpub.*, and when a material handling charge was to be paid at a percentage of subcontract and material costs, *Systems Eng'g Assocs. Corp.*, ASBCA 21846, 77-2 BCA ¶ 12,740. Similarly, a time-and-materials contract calling for payment of overhead and profit at 15 percent and 10 percent of cost, respectively, was held to be unenforceable, 46 Comp. Gen. 612 (B-159713) (1967). The problem created by contracts where one type of costs is paid on a percentage basis is that such compensation may be greater than the actual costs incurred by the contractor, with the result that a part of this compensation will be additional profit. Hence, these contracts contain the same improper motivation — to increase the base costs in order to increase profits — as contracts where profit is paid as a percentage of costs.

The most unusual element of cost included under this proscription is an executive bonus. In *Air Repair, GmbH.*, ASBCA 10288, 67-1 BCA ¶ 6115, a contractor working under a cost-reimbursement contract agreed to pay its principal officer a bonus computed at a percentage of gross billings. The board found that this was a CPPC arrangement since the officer of the company had the ability to increase the amount of the bonus by increasing the costs of performing the contract.

In most cases finding this type of violation, the percentage has been applied evenly to some of the costs of performance. However, a "stepladder" compensation arrangement has also been held to be a violation. For example, in *Department of State Method of Payment Provisions*, Comp. Gen. Dec. B-196556, 80-2 CPD ¶ 87, the Comptroller General found a violation where the contractor was to be paid a management fee based on a sliding scale of actual costs incurred, as follows:

Monthly Total Actual Cost			Management Fee
$ 0	–	5,000	$ 250
5,001	–	10,000	750
10,001	–	15,000	1,250
15,001	–	20,000	1,750
above		20,000	1,750 plus $500 for each additional $5,000 of invoiced costs

The Comptroller General rejected the argument of the agency that this formula was merely a series of fixed fees. A similar result was reached in

Marketing Consultants Int'l Ltd., 55 Comp. Gen. 554 (B-183705), 75-2 CPD ¶ 384.

In contrast, no violation was found in *Grey Advertising, Inc.*, 55 Comp. Gen. 1111 (B-184825), 76-1 CPD ¶ 325, where the contract provided for interim fee payments based on "costs being paid" but the total fee was fixed at the inception of the contract.

Violation can be avoided by removing the percentage basis of compensation. When fee is involved, the remedy is to use a cost-reimbursement contract with a fixed or target fee. When overhead is involved, the remedy is accomplished by compensating contractors at negotiated billing rates until the close of an accounting period, FAR 42.704, at which time final rates are negotiated on the basis of actual cost data and costs are adjusted to reflect these final rates, FAR 42.705. One statutory exception to this rule permits educational institutions to be compensated based on predetermined overhead rates, 41 U.S.C. § 254(a), FAR 42.705-3. Another means of removing the percentage relationship is to include overhead and profit in fixed rates for labor. This is done in time-and-materials and labor-hour contracts where the contractor is paid a single rate for each hour of labor performed, FAR 16.601, FAR 16.602. Since this type of arrangement contains an incentive, similar to the CPPC contract, to increase costs, the regulations require close Government surveillance of such contracts, FAR 16.601(b)(1).

2. Uncertain Entitlement

To fall within the statutory proscription, a contractor's entitlement to compensation must also be uncertain *at the time of contracting*. Conversely, when the amount of entitlement is established at the time of contracting, even though it was computed on a percentage basis, the contract will not be viewed as a CPPC contract. For example, in *Muschany v. United States*, 324 U.S. 49 (1944), the Court ruled that an arrangement permitting a broker, acquiring land on behalf of the Government, to charge vendors of the land a 5 percent commission was not a violation of the statute. The Court reasoned that since the 5 percent was part of the price of the land, certain at the time of purchase, the Government was fully able to determine whether it should pay that price; the arrangement did not motivate the broker to increase its fee by increasing the cost of the land. The Court stated at 63:

> The arrangement may have been improvident from the point of view of the Government. But that question goes to the quality of management by its procurement officers. The fact that the procurement system is improvident obviously does not make it illegal. Illegality does not emerge from inadequate supervision of prices by the Real Estate Branch. Such official failures are not chargeable to a third party dealing with the Government in good faith. It may be unwise for the Government to pay its purchasing agent a commission which is figured on cost of purchases to the Government but there is no statutory prohibition.

Marketing Consultants Int'l Ltd., 55 Comp. Gen. 554 (B-183705), 75-2 CPD ¶ 384, addresses a similar situation. In that case, the contractor was buying work from subcontractors on behalf of the Government, under an agreement providing for a percentage markup to compensate the contractor. For some of the purchases, where the Government reviewed the subcontract prices prior to award of the subcontracts by the contractor, the Comptroller General ruled that there was no violation of the statute. For other purchases, where the contractor was authorized to award the subcontract without prior Government review and approval, the Comptroller General found a violation because the amount of subcontractor compensation was uncertain "at the time of contracting." See also *Tero Tek Int'l Ltd.*, Comp. Gen. Dec. B-228548, 88-1 CPD ¶ 132, where a contract that provided for reimbursement of travel expenses based on actual cost plus an agreed percentage thereof subject to a regulatory guideline was held not to be a CPPC contract because the contractor's entitlement was not uncertain at the time of contracting.

3. Ceilings

The inclusion of a ceiling price in an arrangement that otherwise violates the statute will not cure the violation, 38 Comp. Gen. 38 (B-120546) (1958); *Federal Aviation Admin. — Request for Advance Decision*, 58 Comp. Gen. 654 (B-195173), 79-2 CPD ¶ 34. In these cases, the Comptroller General reasoned that there was a violation because the contractor had the same improper motivation to increase profit by increasing the costs up to the amount of the ceiling. *Urban Data Sys., Inc. v. United States*, 699 F.2d 1147 (Fed. Cir. 1983), follows this reasoning in a more complex transaction. There the parties had agreed to a fixed-price contract that included a clause calling for a downward price adjustment computed as the difference between actual costs and anticipated costs, plus 5 percent. The court reasoned that this was no different from paying actual costs plus

5 percent profit up to a ceiling price. This holding was buttressed by the fact that the parties negotiated the fixed price using the anticipated costs plus the same 5 percent profit rate.

In *Department of Labor — Request for Advance Decision*, 62 Comp. Gen. 337 (B-211213), 83-1 CPD ¶ 429, the Comptroller General applied this rule on ceilings in an unusual way. The agreement provided for markups of a "maximum of . . . 7.5 percent . . . to cover overhead and profit." The Comptroller General reasoned that limiting the markup to a maximum amount was the same as providing for a ceiling price and was thus a statutory violation. This is a highly questionable decision because the contract language can be interpreted more logically as calling for a markup to be negotiated by the parties at the time of pricing new work, with a ceiling on that amount. Such an arrangement would not be a violation of the proscription since the Government would not have agreed to a fixed percentage rate of compensation.

4. Pricing after Incurrence of Costs

After-the-fact pricing is quite common in Government contracting and presents the appearance of CPPC contracting because the profit policy of most Government agencies, adopted pursuant to FAR 15.404-4(b), computes profit largely on the basis of costs of performance. See Chapter 9. Such pricing does not violate the statute, however, when there is no agreement between the contracting parties that any fixed percentage will be applied to incurred costs in negotiating the price. Further, the policy is generally construed as calling for a lower rate of profit if substantial costs have been incurred prior to pricing, because the contractor's risk has been reduced, and contractor risk is one of the key elements considered in arriving at the Government's profit position.

The courts and boards have generally agreed that after-the-fact pricing is not a statutory violation. The Court of Claims held that a contract calling for price revision after completion did not violate the CPPC prohibition; the court concluded that the contract more closely resembled a cost-plus-fixed-fee (CPFF) contract than a CPPC contract, *National Elec. Labs., Inc. v. United States*, 148 Ct. Cl. 308, 180 F. Supp. 337 (1960). In *United Food Servs., Inc.*, 64 Comp. Gen. 880 (B-217211), 85-2 CPD ¶ 326, it was held that a cost-plus-award-fee (CPAF) contract was not a CPPC contract because the amount of fee to which the contractor was entitled decreased as costs increased. In *E.V. Lane Corp.*, ASBCA 9741, 65-2 BCA ¶ 5076, and *J.G. Watts Constr. Co.*, ASBCA 9454, 1964 BCA ¶ 4171, it was held that the pricing of changes following completion of work did not violate the rule. See also *Allison Div., General Motors Corp.*, ASBCA 15528, 72-1 BCA ¶ 9343, stating at 43,382-83:

> The Government also contends that to grant an increase in fixed fee for a "comparatively minor" change in the contract would transform the contract into a cost-plus-percentage-of-cost contract which is prohibited by law. 10 U.S.C. 2306. No argument or reasoning, other than the bare assertion, has been advanced by the Government in support of its contention. The change here, as we have concluded, was not minor. It substantially increased appellant's work under the contract. The fixed fee was earned when appellant had exerted the level of effort specified in the contract (i.e., 173,200 hours) in performing the work called for. ASPR 3-405.6(d)(2). In cost-plus-fixed-fee contracts, the fixed fee once negotiated does not vary with actual cost, but it may be adjusted as a result of any subsequent changes in the work or services to be performed under the contract. ASPR 3-405.6(a), cf. *Martin Marietta Corporation*, ASBCA 10062, 65-2 BCA ¶ 4973. The granting of additional profit in connection with increased work under change orders has never been considered, to our knowledge, a violation of the cost-plus-a-percentage-of-cost system of contracting.

A few questionable cases reach the opposite result. The Comptroller General has held that the conversion of a letter contract to a definitive contract, after the work was substantially completed, violated the rule, 33 Comp. Gen. 291 (B-110609) (1954). See also *Program Resources, Inc.*, ASBCA 21656, 78-1 BCA ¶ 12,867, where the board concluded that allowing the contractor an additional fee for an increase in labor rates, when there was no "change" in the nature of the work, would violate the CPPC proscription. In one unusual case, the Court of Claims held that payment of any profit on Government-caused delay costs would constitute a violation of the CPPC prohibition, *Laburnum Constr. Corp. v. United States*, 163 Ct. Cl. 339, 325 F.2d 451 (1963).

5. *Quantum Meruit Compensation*

While contracts violating the CPPC proscription are illegal and thus unenforceable, the Comptroller General has sometimes permitted contractors to recover the fair value of goods and services provided to the Government on a quantum meruit or quantum valebant basis despite the use of a

CPPC contract, *Federal Aviation Admin. — Request for Advance Decision*, 58 Comp. Gen. 654 (B-195173), 79-2 CPD ¶ 34; 33 Comp. Gen. 533 (B-118109) (1954); Comp. Gen. Dec. B-167790, Apr. 12, 1973, *Unpub*. See also *Yosemite Park & Curry Co. v. United States*, 217 Ct. Cl. 360, 582 F.2d 552 (1978), where the Court of Claims granted quantum meruit relief because the agency had entered into an invalid contract when the fee exceeded the 10 percent statutory limitation. In *Alisa Corp.*, AGBCA 84-193-1, 94-2 BCA ¶ 26,952, the board awarded quantum meruit relief in an amount limited to the lowest price the contractor could have negotiated where the illegal CPPC contract had called for the payment of "actual cost" plus a "fixed fee" computed at a rate of 10 percent of incurred cost.

C. Undefinitized Contractual Actions

Government agencies sometimes encounter situations where they must issue a contract on very short notice with too little time to negotiate all of the terms and conditions of the price. In such cases, it has been common practice to issue a "letter contract" firmly binding the Government to pay for the work but calling for the negotiation of a firm contract at a later date. See FAR 16.603-1, stating:

> A letter contract is a written preliminary contractual instrument that authorizes the contractor to begin immediately manufacturing supplies or performing services.

Congress has placed limitations on "undefinitized contractual actions" by the Department of Defense in 10 U.S.C. § 2326. This statute is implemented by DFARS Subpart 217.74, which contains the following definition in DFARS 217.7401(d):

> *Undefinitized contract action* means any contract action for which the contract terms, specifications, or price are not agreed upon before performance is begun under the action. Examples are letter contracts, orders under basic ordering agreements, and provisioned item orders, for which the price has not been agreed upon before performance has begun.

1. Restrictions on Use

The general policy has been to greatly restrict the use of such transactions because they are open-ended arrangements that place the risk of excessive costs largely on the Government. FAR 16.603-2(a) permits the use of letter contracts when "(1) the Government's interests demand that the contractor be given a binding commitment so that work can start immediately and (2) negotiating a definitive contract is not possible in sufficient time to meet the requirement." FAR 16.603-3 places the following limitations on the use of such contracts:

> A letter contract may be used only after the head of the contracting activity or a designee determines in writing that no other contract is suitable. Letter contracts shall not —
>
> (a) Commit the Government to a definitive contract in excess of the funds available at the time the letter contract is executed;
>
> (b) Be entered into without competition when competition is required by Part 6; or
>
> (c) Be amended to satisfy a new requirement unless that requirement is inseparable from the existing letter contract. Any such amendment is subject to the same requirements and limitations as a new letter contract.

Similar limitations are contained in 10 U.S.C. § 2326 as implemented by DFARS 217.7404. Sole source letter contracts have been approved when properly justified in accordance with the standards discussed in Chapter 3, *Space Vector Corp.*, Comp. Gen. Dec. B-253295.2, 93-2 CPD ¶ 273 (only one company capable of meeting agency needs within time requirements); *Essex Electro Eng'rs, Inc.*, Comp. Gen. Dec. B-250437, 93-1 CPD ¶ 74 (only one firm capable of quickly supplying product needed urgently for military program); *Greenbrier Indus.*, Inc., Comp. Gen. Dec. B-241304, 91-1 CPD ¶ 92 (only one company capable of meeting urgent need). Compare *Jervis B. Webb Co.*, Comp. Gen. Dec. B-211724, 85-1 CPD ¶ 35, where the Comptroller General ruled that a sole source award of a letter contract was improper because the agency had conducted inadequate acquisition planning.

2. *Terms and Conditions*

A letter contract should contain the terms and conditions appropriate for the type of contract that the contracting officer believes will be used for the definitive contract, FAR 16.603-4(a). In addition, special contract clauses must be used in these contracts.

a. Expenditure Limitations and Ceiling Prices

FAR 52.216-24 contains a standard clause limiting the Government's obligations prior to definitization:

LIMITATION OF GOVERNMENT LIABILITY (APR 1984)

(a) In performing this contract, the Contractor is not authorized to make expenditures or incur obligations exceeding __________ dollars.

(b) The maximum amount for which the Government shall be liable if this contract is terminated is __________ dollars.

The amount to be inserted in this clause is the amount of costs expected to be incurred before definitization, and generally, this amount should not be greater than 50 percent of the estimated cost of the contract, FAR 16.603-2(d). The Government is not obligated to pay more than the amount included in the clause, *Magnavox Co.*, ASBCA 17455, 74-1 BCA ¶ 10,495.

Agencies normally obligate the amount of funds set forth in these expenditure limits from current year appropriations and may not obligate any greater amount from an annual appropriation if the contract is definitized in a subsequent fiscal year. Rather, the balance of the contract amount must be obligated from the appropriations current at the time of the contract definitization, *Obligating Letter Contracts*, Comp. Gen. Dec. B-197274, 84-1 CPD ¶ 90.

The Department of Defense is subject to statutory rules calling for the negotiation of a *ceiling price* on undefinitized contractual actions and limiting expenditures to 50 percent of that ceiling, 10 U.S.C. § 2326(b). DFARS 252.217-7027 provides a short clause to implement this requirement. FAR 16.603-4(b)(3) also requires the insertion of a ceiling price in letter contracts that are awarded on the basis of competition. This is to ensure that the contractor is held to the price that was the basis of the source selection. Such ceilings impose a significant risk on a contractor because they necessarily must be determined before all of the elements of the contract have been negotiated. See, for example, *Litton Sys., Inc.*, ASBCA 36976, 93-2 BCA ¶ 25,705, where a contractor that had agreed to a letter contract to become a firm-fixed-price contract was bound by the ceiling price even though its costs were substantially higher than that price. In that case, the board also ruled that the ceiling price was to be adjusted to reflect changes to the work, both additive and deductive.

The DOD procedure also permits the contracting officer to raise the level of the Government's limitation of obligations to 75 percent of the ceiling price if the contractor has submitted a "qualifying proposal" prior to reaching the 50 percent limitation. DFARS 217.7401(c) contains the following definition:

> *Qualifying proposal* means a proposal containing sufficient information for the DoD to do complete and meaningful analyses and audits of the —
>
> (1) Information in the proposal; and
>
> (2) Any other information that the contracting officer has determined DoD needs to review in connection with the contract.

b. Definitization Schedule

FAR 52.216-25 provides the following clause setting forth the procedures for contract definitization:

> CONTRACT DEFINITIZATION (APR 1984)
>
> (a) A ________________ [*insert specific type of contract*] definitive contract is contemplated. The Contractor agrees to begin promptly negotiating with the Contracting Officer the terms of a definitive contract that will include (1) all clauses required by the Federal Acquisition Regulation (FAR) on the date of execution of the letter contract, (2) all clauses required by law on the date of execution of the definitive contract, and (3) any other mutually agreeable clauses, terms, and conditions. The Contractor agrees to submit a ________________ [*insert specific type of proposal (e.g., fixed-price or cost-and-fee)*] proposal and cost or pricing data supporting its proposal.
>
> (b) The schedule for definitizating this contract is [*insert target date for definitization of the contract and dates for submission of proposal, begin-*

ning of negotiations, and, if appropriate, submission of make-or-buy and subcontracting plans and cost or pricing data]:

______________________________,

______________________________,

______________________________,

______________________________,

(c) If agreement on a definitive contract to supersede this letter contract is not reached by the target date in paragraph (b) above, or within any extension of it granted by the Contracting Officer, the Contracting Officer may, with the approval of the head of the contracting activity, determine a reasonable price or fee in accordance with Subpart 15.8 and Part 31 of the FAR, subject to Contractor appeal as provided in the Disputes clause. In any event, the Contractor shall proceed with completion of the contract, subject to only to the Limitation of Government Liability clause.

(1) After the Contracting Officer's determination or price or fee, the contract shall be governed by —

(i) All clauses required by the FAR on the date of execution of this letter contract for either fixed-price or cost-reimbursement contracts, as determined by the Contracting Officer under this paragraph (c);

(ii) All clauses required by law as of the date of the Contracting Officer's determination; and

(iii) Any other clauses, terms, and conditions mutually agreed upon.

(2) To the extent consistent with subparagraph (c)(1) above, all clauses, terms, and conditions included in this letter contract shall continue in effect, except those that by their nature apply only to a letter contract.

FAR 16.603-2(c) requires that the schedule for definitization call for completion of the process "within 180 days after the date of the letter contract or before completion of 40 percent of the work to be performed, whichever occurs first." It permits the granting of additional time "in extreme cases." These provisions reflect the strong policy of the Government to preclude letter contracts from running indefinitely without being firmly priced. If the parties cannot agree to the definitization, the clause permits unilateral action by the contracting officer with appeal under the Disputes clause. In *Litton Sys., Inc.*, ASBCA 36976, 93-2 BCA ¶ 25,705, the Armed Services Board of Contract Appeals (ASBCA) considered such an appeal and ruled that the unilaterally definitized price should have included the costs of extra work performed by the contractor. Earlier versions of the clause did not contain this procedure, but the Court of Claims ruled that it had jurisdiction to make a decision as to the proper definitization of a letter contract where the contractor had completed the work but the parties had been unable to agree to a final price, *Sanders Assocs. v. United States*, 191 Ct. Cl. 157, 423 F.2d 291 (1970).

The clause also binds the parties to the mandatory contract clauses in effect at the time the letter contract was issued and the statutory clauses in effect on the date of definitization, unless the parties agree to other clauses. Thus, a contractor must be sure to obtain agreement prior to contract execution for any variances from FAR clauses or other modifications to the language that may be desired. See *Teledyne Continental Motors*, ASBCA 22571, 85-3 BCA ¶ 18,472, where the Government was bound to a clause that it had included in the modification definitizing the letter contract even though that clause increased the costs chargeable to the contract.

Paragraph (a) of the clause requires the submission of cost or pricing data — a requirement that will substantially increase the time necessary for definitization. FAR 16.603-4(b)(3) permits deletion of this requirement if "at the time of entering into the letter contract, the contracting officer knows that the definitive contract will be based on adequate price competition or will otherwise meet the criteria of 15.804-1 [now 15.403-1] for not requiring submission of cost or pricing data."

c. Payment

In cost-reimbursement letter contracts, FAR 16.603-4(c) requires the use of the Payments of Allowable Costs Before Definitization clause in FAR 52.216-26. This clause is intended to motivate the contractor to definitize the contract quickly by limiting reimbursement as follows:

> (a)(1) One hundred percent of approved costs representing progress payments to subcontractors under fixed-price subcontracts; *provided*, that the

Government's payments to the Contractor shall not exceed 80 percent of the allowable costs of those subcontractors.

(2) One hundred percent of approved costs representing cost-reimbursement subcontracts; *provided*, that the Government's payments to the Contractor shall not exceed 85 percent of the allowable costs of those subcontractors.

(3) Eighty-five percent of all other approved costs.

There is no such clause to be used for fixed-price letter contracts. Thus, if the contractor desires progress payments during performance of a fixed-price letter contract, one of the standard clauses should be used. See Progress Payments, FAR 52.232-16 (fixed-price supply or service contracts) or Payment under Fixed-Price Construction Contracts, FAR 52.232-5 (fixed-price construction).

II. FIXED-PRICE CONTRACTS

The most frequently used type of contract is the fixed-price contract. Such contracts can be either firm-fixed-price or fixed-price subject to adjustment during or after performance. These contracts all have the common characteristic of binding the contractor to complete the work at a fixed amount of compensation, once adjusted, regardless of the costs of performance. To obtain the benefit of the fixed price, the Government must draft and administer the contract in a manner that avoids significant claims for price adjustment. If these conditions exist, the firm-fixed-price contract places the risk of incurring unforeseen costs on the contractor rather than on the Government. Conversely, it provides the contractor the greatest opportunity to earn higher profits by devising ways to reduce the costs of performance.

Since there are many situations where the work can be reasonably well defined but it is unwise to place the entire cost risk on the contractor, a number of variations on the firm-fixed-price contract are commonly used. These variations are of two types: (i) fixed-price contracts with *formula repricing*, such as the fixed-price incentive (FPI) and the fixed-price with economic price adjustment contracts, and (ii) fixed-price contracts with repricing *after some costs have been incurred*, such as the fixed-price redeterminable contracts. Descriptions of the firm-fixed-price contract and its variations follow. FPI contracts are dealt with in the section on incentive contracts.

A. Firm-Fixed-Price Contracts

In the pure fixed-price contract, the bargain is stated in terms of a fixed amount of compensation with no formula or technique for varying the price in the event of unforeseen contingencies. FAR 16.202-2, recognizing that the use of this type contract might place the risk of *too high* a price on the Government, contains the following guidance:

> A firm-fixed-price contract is suitable for acquiring commercial items (see parts 2 and 12) or for acquiring other supplies or services on the basis of reasonably definitive functional or detailed specifications (see part 11) when the contracting officer can establish fair and reasonable prices at the outset, such as when —
>
> (a) There is adequate price competition;
>
> (b) There are reasonable price comparisons with prior purchases of the same or similar supplies or services made on a competitive basis or supported by valid cost or pricing data;
>
> (c) Available cost or pricing information permits realistic estimates of the probable costs of performance; or
>
> (d) Performance uncertainties can be identified and reasonable estimates of their cost impact can be made, and the contractor is willing to accept a firm fixed price representing assumption of the risks involved.

Firm-fixed-price contracts must be used with caution because both parties can lose if the actual costs of performance are greatly at variance with the contract price. If the costs greatly exceed the price, the contractor will incur a substantial loss and may be financially unable or unwilling to complete the work at the contract price. See *Ball Bros. Research Corp.*, NASABCA 1277-6, 80-2 BCA ¶ 14,526, where the Government converted a fixed-price contract to a cost-plus-fixed-fee (CPFF) contract in order to obtain completion of the work. See also *General Dynamics Corp. v. United States*, 229 Ct. Cl. 399, 671 F.2d 474 (1982), where a similar "conversion" to a cost-type contract occurred after the contractor encountered great difficulties in performing a fixed-price-type contract. If the costs are far under the price, the Government will have paid substantially more for the work than might have been possible under some other form of contract. When there is adequate information to assure the parties that the costs are predictable, however, the firm-fixed-price contract is the simplest form of contract to accomplish the work.

Firm-fixed-price contracts are also of questionable value if the work is not well defined and stable in nature. If the scope of the work is unclear or subject to change during performance, the contractor will inevitably assert claims for price adjustment during performance and contract administration will be very complex. These issues are dealt with in detail in Cibinic & Nash, *Administration of Government Contracts* (3d ed., 1995).

B. Fixed-Price Contract with Economic Price Adjustment

This type of contract provides for upward or downward adjustment of the fixed price or incentive target price if economic conditions change during contract performance. Usually, such adjustments are based on changes in material costs or labor rates.

The use of economic price adjustment clauses is a major means of risk allocation. Such clauses place on the Government some or all of the risk of fluctuations in the cost of labor or material. Absent such a clause, these risks are allocated to the contractor by virtue of entering into a firm-fixed-price contract, *McNamara Constr. of Manitoba, Ltd. v. United States*, 206 Ct. Cl. 1, 509 F.2d 1166 (1975) (no mutual mistake as to labor rates when parties used firm-fixed-price contract); *Charles H. Siever Co.*, ASBCA 23968, 80-1 BCA ¶ 14,390, *recons. denied*, 80-2 BCA ¶ 14,589 (contractor not entitled to increase price of firm-fixed-price contract when escalation clause was not included in the contract). See *Southern Dredging Co.*, ENGBCA 5843, 92-2 BCA ¶ 24,886, denying reformation of a contract to account for increased fuel prices where fixed-price contract did not include price escalation clause, and stating at 124,116:

> "It is black letter law that the risk of performance costs in a firm fixed-price contract, absent a clause stating otherwise, are on the contractor." *Chevron U.S.A., Inc.*, ASBCA No. 32323, 90-1 BCA ¶ 22,602. See *Nedlog Co.*, ASBCA No. 26034, 82-1 BCA ¶ 15,519; *D.K.'s Precision and Manufacturing*, ASBCA No. 39616, 90-2 BCA ¶ 22,830. Further, neither abnormal price increases nor unusual trade conditions change this basic principle regarding a contractor's assumption of the risk of increased performance costs in a fixed-price contract. *Anthony P. Miller, Inc. v. United States*

[9 CCF ¶ 72,218], 161 Ct. Cl. 455, *cert. Denied,* 375 U.S. 879 (1963); *Jalaprathan Cement Co., Ltd.*, ASBCA No. 21248, 79-2 BCA ¶ 13,927.

See also *Cobra, S.A.*, ASBCA 28146, 84-3 BCA ¶ 17,535, denying reformation of a contract to include an escalation clause. These cases demonstrate the general understanding that this matter is covered by specific contract language, and absent such specific language, the risk of economic fluctuations is on the contractor.

1. Use of Economic Price Adjustment Clauses

FAR 16.203-2 provides the following brief guidance on the use of this type of contract:

> A fixed-price contract with economic price adjustment may be used when (i) there is serious doubt concerning the stability of market or labor conditions that will exist during an extended period of contract performance, and (ii) contingencies that would otherwise be included in the contract price can be identified and covered separately in the contract. Price adjustments based on established prices should normally be restricted to industry-wide contingencies. Price adjustments based on labor and material costs should be limited to contingencies beyond the contractor's control. For use of economic price adjustment in sealed bid contracts, see 14.408-4.
>
> > (a) In establishing the base level from which adjustment will be made, the contracting officer shall ensure that contingency allowances are not duplicated by inclusion in both the base price and the adjustment requested by the contractor under economic price adjustment clause.
> >
> > (b) In contracts that do not require submission of cost or pricing data, the contracting officer shall obtain adequate information to establish the base level from which adjustment will be made and may require verification of data submitted.

Although most economic price adjustment clauses are used in firm-fixed-price contracts, they may also be used in any fixed-price-type contract, including incentive or redeterminable contracts. On major systems contracts, economic price adjustment provisions have frequently been used in fixed-price incentive contracts. In such cases, the Government bears the risk of increases in labor rates and material prices and the parties share the risk of increases in cost due to other factors.

If there is the possibility of significant economic fluctuation during contract performance, the use of an economic price adjustment clause will probably encourage more companies to participate in the competition and will permit contracting at a price free of the contingencies that would otherwise be included to compensate for such fluctuations. However, the contracting officer may conclude that there is sufficient competition to minimize contingencies in pricing and therefore use firm-fixed-price contracting. If large fluctuations in the economy are possible, it can be argued that it is not in the Government's best interests to contract without economic price adjustment clauses even if it is likely that competition will limit price contingencies. In such cases, a loss contract may result with all of its inherent difficulties.

The discretion of the contracting officer is substantial in this area, and challenges to a decision to omit an economic price adjustment clause from a procurement will invariably fail. See, for example, *B & P Refuse Disposal, Inc.*, Comp. Gen. Dec. B-253661, 93-2 CPD ¶ 177 (contracting officer told offerors of prior increases in price and forced them to include such a contingency in bid to protect against risk); *Master Security, Inc.*, Comp. Gen. Dec. B-232263, 88-2 CPD ¶ 449 (contracting officer determined market conditions were sufficiently stable to enable offerors to make realistic estimates of future costs); *Sentinel Elecs., Inc.*, Comp. Gen. Dec. B-212770, 84-1 CPD ¶ 5 (contracting officer determined that there were sufficient capable producers that could reasonably price work even though last delivery was 43 months after award); *Barker & Williamson*, Comp. Gen. Dec. B-208236, 82-2 CPD ¶ 454 (omission of clause in basic quantity in first year of contract upheld even though it was included in option quantities in subsequent years because contracting officer determined that pricing was sufficiently stable to permit bidders to assume risks for initial requirement); and *Tri-Wall Containers*, Comp. Gen. Dec. B-200702, 81-1 CPD ¶ 277 (omission of clause upheld because market price had been stable for eight months and three bids were received although prior-year pricing had been very volatile). See also *Argus Servs., Inc.*, Comp. Gen. Dec. B-234016.2, 89-2 CPD ¶ 227, where it was held that the contracting officer had the discretion not to use an economic price adjustment provision in order to have "minimum administrative burdens" even though it imposed "maximum risks" on the prospective contractor.

2. Types of Economic Price Adjustment Provisions

FAR 16.203-1 describes three general types of economic price adjustment provisions: (1) adjustments based on established prices, (2) adjustments based on actual costs of labor and material, and (3) adjustments based on cost indexes of labor and material.

FAR 16.203-4 provides standard clauses for use with the first two types. However, there is no standard clause for economic price adjustment based on indexes — requiring each agency to draft its own clause in this area. In addition, FAR 16.203-4 permits the use of "agency prescribed" clauses with the result that great latitude is given in drafting special clauses for different contracting situations. Generally, such specially drafted economic price adjustment clauses should use some basis of measurement of the price fluctuation that is not under the control of the contractor. See FAR 16.203-2, stating that such clauses should cover contingencies that are "industry-wide" or "beyond the contractor's control." This protects the Government from price increases due to contractor inefficiency or intentional overspending and permits evaluation of competitive prices. For example, an economic price adjustment clause providing that the price would be adjusted in an amount equal to higher prices charged by the contractor would be improper unless there were some market constraints limiting the ability of the contractor to manipulate its prices. See *Roarda, Inc.*, Comp. Gen. Dec. B-204524.5, 82-1 CPD ¶ 438, where the Comptroller General found a clause improper because it permitted the contractor to increase the contract price if its market price increased. The Comptroller General objected that the agency had not included any mechanism in the procurement to ascertain that the contractor's price reflected "some objective standard," with the result that the price could be varied at will. In that case, consequently, there was no assurance in a sealed bid procurement that the contractor was actually the low bidder. See also *American Transparents Plastic Corp.*, Comp. Gen. Dec. B-210898, 83-2 CPD ¶ 539, stating the same "objective standard" rule.

In a sealed bid procurement, it is also important that all bidders use substantially the same basis for price adjustment so that the low price can be determined. Thus, a clause should not be used that allows the bidder to select the basis for price adjustment. See *Steuart Petroleum Co. v. United States*, 438 F. Supp. 527 (D.D.C. 1977), enjoining the performance of a contract awarded to a bidder that had selected a volatile basis for price adjustment, which cast great doubt on whether its low bid would actually lead to the low price after economic price adjustment. In *Amarillo Aircraft Sales & Servs., Inc.*, 63 Comp. Gen. 568 (B-214225), 84-2 CPD ¶ 269, the Comptroller General concurred in the termination of a procurement after the procuring agency determined that the contractor had used a basis for price adjustment that was not comparable to that used by other bidders and was subject to the control of the contractor. If the bidder inserts a price adjustment provision in a bid where the Invitation for Bids (IFB) does not call for a clause, an even more restrictive rule will apply. If the clause contains no ceiling, the bid will be held to be nonresponsive, *Joy Mfg. Co.*, 54 Comp. Gen. 237 (B-181136), 74-2 CPD ¶ 183. If the clause contains a ceiling, the bid will be evaluated at the ceiling price, FAR 14.407-4(a)(1). This rule removes all of the bidding advantage that would be obtained from including a clause in the bid.

In negotiated procurement, the Government will be bound if it accepts an offer containing a price adjustment clause. See *United States Steel Corp.*, ASBCA 29111, 85-1 BCA ¶ 17,761, *recons. denied*, 85-1 BCA ¶ 17,921, holding the Government to a provision in a letter responding to a negotiated Request for Proposals (RFP) stating the price would be that "in effect at the time of shipment, subject to a 10 percent maximum escalation" from the price in effect at the time of award. The board reasoned that this type of bargain was permitted in negotiated procurement.

a. Adjustments Based on Established Prices

The first type of economic price adjustment provision provided for in FAR 16.203-1 uses established catalog or market prices as the basis for price adjustment. Standard contract clauses are provided for standard supplies, FAR 52.216-2, and semi-standard supplies, FAR 52.216-3. Standard supplies are those with established catalog or market prices, while semi-standard supplies are those whose "prices can be reasonably related to the prices of nearly equivalent standard supplies," FAR 16.203-4(b)(1)(ii). In the latter situation, the clause requires that the related catalog or market item be identified in the schedule of the contract. Both clauses contain the same provisions calling for upward or downward price adjustments on a pro rata basis following changes in catalog or market prices. The clause for standard supplies provides:

ECONOMIC PRICE ADJUSTMENT—
STANDARD SUPPLIES (JAN 1997)

(a) The Contractor warrants that the unit price stated in the Schedule for ______________ [*offeror insert Schedule line item number*] is not in excess of the Contractor's applicable established price in effect on the contract date for like quantities of the same item. The term "unit price" excludes any part of the price directly resulting from requirements for preservation, packaging, or packing beyond standard commercial practice. The term "established price" means a price that (1) is an established catalog or market price for a commercial item sold in substantial quantities to the general public, (2) is the net price after applying any standard trade discounts offered by the Contractor.

(b) The Contractor shall promptly notify the Contracting Officer of the amount and effective date of each decrease in any applicable established price. Each corresponding contract unit price shall be decreased by the same percentage that the established price is decreased. The decrease shall apply to those items delivered on and after the effective date of the decrease in the Contractor's established price, and this contract shall be modified accordingly.

(c) If the Contractor's applicable established price is increased after the contract date, the corresponding contract unit price shall be increased, upon the Contractor's written request to the Contracting Officer, by the same percentage that the established price is increased, and the contract shall be modified accordingly, subject to the following limitations:

(1) The aggregate of the increases in any contract unit price under this clause shall not exceed 10 percent of the original contract unit price.

(2) The increased contract unit price shall be effective (i) on the effective date of the increase in the applicable established price if the Contracting Officer receives the Contractor's written request within 10 days thereafter or (ii) if the written request is received later, on the date the Contracting Officer receives the request.

(3) The increased contract unit price shall not apply to quantities scheduled under the contract for delivery before the effective date of the increased contract unit price, unless failure to deliver before that date results from causes beyond the control and without the fault or negligence of the Contractor, within the meaning of the Default clause.

(4) No modification increasing a contract unit price shall be executed under this paragraph (c) until the Contracting Officer verifies the increase in the applicable established price.

(5) Within 30 days after receipt of the Contractor's written request, the Contracting Officer may cancel, without liability to either party, any undelivered portion of the contract items affected by the requested increase.

(d) During the time allowed for the cancellation provided for in subparagraph (c)(5) above, and thereafter if there is no cancellation, the Contractor shall continue deliveries according to the contract delivery schedule, and the Government shall pay for such deliveries at the contract unit price, increased to the extent provided by paragraph (c) above.

DFARS 216.203-4-70 provide for two additional bases of price adjustment of this type. See the clauses at DFARS 252.216-7000 for basic steel, aluminum, brass, bronze, or copper mill products and DFARS 252.216-7001 for nonstandard steel products.

These clauses provide the necessary "objectivity" by using catalog or market prices for items that are sold to the general public in "substantial quantities." Elaborate tests for establishing that items fall within this category were contained in FAR 15.804-3(c) prior to 1995, though the current guidance is quite vague. Nonetheless, the theory is that if an item meets these tests, its price will be determined by market forces and the contractor will be unable to manipulate the price to increase the amount paid under the contract containing the economic price adjustment clause.

b. Adjustment Based on Actual Costs

The second type of economic price adjustment provision in FAR 16.203-1 uses the actual costs of the contractor as the basis for the adjustment. A standard contract clause is provided in FAR 52.216-4:

(a) The Contractor shall notify the Contracting Officer if, at any time during contract performance, the rates of pay for labor (including fringe benefits) or the unit prices for material shown in the Schedule either increase or decrease. The Contractor shall furnish this notice within 60 days after the increase or decrease, or within any additional period that the Contracting Officer may approve in writing, but not later than the date of final payment under this contract. The notice shall include the Contractor's proposal for an adjustment in the contract unit prices to be negotiated under paragraph (b) below, and shall include, in the form required by the Contracting Officer, supporting data explaining the cause, effective date, and amount of the increase or decrease and the amount of the Contractor's adjustment proposal.

(b) Promptly after the Contracting Officer receives the notice and data under paragraph (a) above, the Contracting Officer and the Contractor shall negotiate a price adjustment in the contract unit prices and its effective date. However, the Contracting Officer may postpone the negotiations until an accumulation of increases and decreases in the labor rates (including fringe benefits) and unit prices of material shown in the Schedule results in an adjustment allowable under subparagraph (c)(3) below. The Contracting Officer shall modify this contract (1) to include the price adjustment and its effective date and (2) to revise the labor rates (including fringe benefits) or unit prices of material as shown in the Schedule to reflect the increases or decreases resulting from the adjustment. The Contractor shall continue performance pending agreement on, or determination of, any adjustment and its effective date.

(c) Any price adjustment under this clause is subject to the following limitations:

(1) Any adjustment shall be limited to the effect on unit prices of the increases or decreases in the rates of pay for labor (including fringe benefits) or unit prices for material shown in the Schedule. There shall be no adjustment for (i) supplies or services for which the production cost is not affected by such changes, (ii) changes in rates or unit prices other than those shown in the Schedule, or (iii) changes in the quantities of labor or material used from those shown in the Schedule for each item.

(2) No upward adjustment shall apply to supplies or services that are required to be delivered or performed before the effective date of the adjustment, unless the Contractor's failure to deliver or perform according to the delivery schedule results from causes beyond the Contractor's control and without its fault or negligence, within the meaning of the Default clause.

(3) There shall be no adjustment for any change in rates of pay for labor (including fringe benefits) or unit prices for material which would not result in a net change of at least 3 percent of the then-current total contract price. This limitation shall not apply, however, if, after final

delivery of all contract line items, either party requests an adjustment under paragraph (b) above.

(4) The aggregate of the increases in any contract unit price made under this clause shall not exceed 10 percent of the original unit price. There is no percentage limitation on the amount of decreases that may be made under this clause.

(d) The Contracting Officer may examine the Contractor's books, records, and other supporting data relevant to the cost of labor (including fringe benefits) and material during all reasonable times until the end of 3 years after the date of final payment under this contract or the time periods specified in Subpart 4.7 of the Federal Acquisition Regulation (FAR), whichever is earlier.

When this clause is used, FAR 16.203-4(c)(3) requires that a clause be inserted in the schedule of the contract describing the specific types of labor and material subject to price adjustment, the labor rates and material prices to be increased or decreased, and the quantities of labor and material allocable to each contract unit. In the 1980s, DFARS 216.203-4(c)(3) contained a sample provision that contained useful guidance:

The following types of labor and material are subject to price adjustment pursuant to the "Economic Price Adjustment — Labor and Material" clause of this contract.

Type of Labor and Material	Contract Item No. 1 Rates of Pay and Material Prices	Quantities and Direct Costs Per Unit of Procurement
Drill Press Operator	$3.00/hour no fringe benefits included ------------ $3.00	20 min. — $1.00
Welder	$2.75/hour .05/hour — vacation pay .20/hour — pension plan ------------ $3.00	10 min. — $ .50
Copper Sheet	$ .40/lb.	2 lb. — $ .80
Purchased Parts: (1) ABC tube X5721 (2) XYZ part #9348	 $1.00 each $ .50 each	 3 ea. — $3.00 10 ea. — $5.00

This schedule provision is of critical importance because adjustments are made only for listed elements of the price. Thus, no adjustment was granted for a profit-sharing plan that did not appear among the fringe benefits in the labor rates listed in the schedule, *Optic-Electronic Corp.*, ASBCA 24962, 83-2 BCA ¶ 16,677, *recons. denied*, 84-3 BCA ¶ 17,565. Similarly, it was held that this type of economic price adjustment clause applied only to items added to a contract by amendment rather than to all contract items, because the schedule listed only the added items, *Minowitz Mfg. Co.*, ASBCA 23784, 83-1 BCA ¶ 16,324. See also *Arcadia Mfg. Co.*, ASBCA 20764, 76-2 BCA ¶ 12,058, where the board found, in a sealed bid procurement, that the bidder's failure to include the required schedule of items covered eliminated the clause even though it was designated in the IFB. Compare *Transportes Especiales de Automoviles, S.A.*, ASBCA 43851, 93-2 BCA ¶ 25,745, where the board ordered reformation of a negotiated contract because the contract contained the standard economic price adjustment clause but did not have the schedule required by the FAR and illustrated by the DFARS to set rates and quantities of labor. The board concluded that the parties intended to have escalation but had mistakenly omitted the schedule.

At first glance, this type of economic price adjustment appears to contain no objective basis for price increases. However, FAR 16.203-2 states that this technique should "normally be restricted to industry-wide contingencies" and "limited to contingencies beyond the contractor's control." To meet this requirement, the clause should only be used in those situations where the labor covered by the clause is used for a mix of work, some of which is not subject to economic price adjustment, and the material covered by the clause is material bought in a competitive market. In such cases, there would be outside pressures limiting the amount of increases the contractor could pay and subsequently recover under the clause. It is clear when this clause is included that changes in quantity of items or amount of effort will not lead to escalation — only changes in labor rates or prices, *Nuclear Components, Inc.*, ASBCA 22884, 79-2 BCA ¶ 14,006.

This clause is not well suited for use in sealed bid contracts because it requires each bidder to furnish the schedule as part of the bid. This makes evaluation rather speculative, *VBM Corp.*, Comp. Gen. Dec. B-182225, 75-1 CPD ¶ 130, and may motivate bidders to include rates in the schedule that are lower than those actually used in order to obtain greater price adjustments, *Galaxy Custodial Servs., Inc.*, 64 Comp. Gen. 594 (B-215738), 85-1 CPD ¶ 658. In *Galaxy*, the Comptroller General suggested that if the agency found the data inaccurate, the bid should be rejected. The Comptroller

General has agreed to the use of this type provision in two-step sealed bidding, *Norris Indus.*, Comp. Gen. Dec. B-182921, 75-2 CPD ¶ 31.

c. Adjustments Based on Cost Indexes

The third type of economic price adjustment provision in FAR 16.203-1 uses national indexes as the basis for price adjustment. The procurement regulations contain no standard clauses for this type of price adjustment, and the FAR contains virtually no guidance on the structuring of such a clause. However, the drafting of such a clause is highly complex. NFS 1816.203-4(d)(2) requires consultation with NASA Headquarters in drafting such a clause, and GSAR 516.203-4(a) requires obtaining the assistance of counsel and approval of GSA Headquarters. DFARS 216.203-4(d) contains the following elaborate guidance on drafting a clause of this type:

> (i) Do not make the clause unnecessarily complex.
>
> (ii) Normally, the clause should not provide either a ceiling or a floor for adjustment unless adjustment is based on indices below the four digit level of the Bureau of Labor Statistics —
>
>> (A) Producer Price Index;
>>
>> (B) Employment Cost Index for wages and salaries, benefits, and compensation costs for aerospace industries; or
>>
>> (C) Wage and Income Series by Standard Industrial Classification (Labor).
>
> (iii) Normally, the clause should cover all potential economic fluctuations within the original contract period of performance.
>
> (iv) The clause must accurately identify the index(es) upon which adjustments will be based.
>
>> (A) It must provide for a means to adjust for appropriate economic fluctuation in the event publication of the movement of the designated index is discontinued. This might include the substitution of another index if the time remaining would justify doing so and an appropriate index is reasonably available, or some other method for repricing the remaining portion of work to be performed.

(B) Normally, there should be no need to make an adjustment if computation of the identified index is altered. However, it may be appropriate to provide for adjustment of the economic fluctuation computations in the event there is such a substantial alteration in the method of computing the index that the original intent of the parties is negated.

(C) When an index to be used is subject to revision (e.g., the Bureau of Labor Statistics Producer Price Indices), the economic price adjustment clause must specify that any economic price adjustment will be based on a revised index and must identify which revision to the index will be used.

(v) Construct the index to encompass a large sample of relevant items while still bearing a logical relationship to the type of contract costs being measured. The basis of the index should not be so large and diverse that it is significantly affected by fluctuations not relevant to contract performance, but it must be broad enough to minimize the effect of any single company, including the anticipated contractor(s).

(vi) Construction of an index is largely dependent upon three general series published by the U.S. Department of Labor, Bureau of Labor Statistics (BLS). These are the —

(A) Industrial Commodities portion of the Producer Price Index;

(B) Employment Cost Index for wages and salaries, benefits, and compensation costs for aerospace industries; and

(C) Wage and Income Series by Standard Industrial Classification (Labor). Since there is no BLS published series currently available that relates directly to total prices of delivered DoD aircraft, ships, missiles, electronics, etc., it will be necessary to construct composite indices from major portions of the three series identified.

(vii) Normally, do not use more than two indices, i.e., one for labor (direct and indirect) and one for material (direct and indirect).

(viii) The clause must establish and properly identify a base period comparable to the contract periods for which adjustments are to be made as a reference point for application of an index.

(ix) The clause should not provide for an adjustment beyond the original contract performance period, including options. The start date for the adjustment may be the beginning of the contract or a later time, as appropriate, based on the projected rate of expenditures.

(x) The expenditure profile for both labor and material should be based on a predetermined rate of expenditure (expressed as the percentage of material or labor usage as it relates to the total contract price) in lieu of actual cost incurred.

(A) If the clause is to be used in a competitive acquisition, determine the labor and material allocations, with regard to both mix of labor and material and rate of expenditure by percentage, in a manner which will, as nearly as possible, approximate the average expenditure profile of all companies to be solicited so that all companies may compete on an equal basis.

(B) If the clause is to be used in a noncompetitive acquisition, the labor and material allocations may be subject to negotiation and agreement.

(C) For multiyear contracts, establish predetermined expenditure profile tables for each of the annual increments in the multiyear buy. Each of the second and subsequent year tables must be cumulative to reflect the total expenditures for all increments funded through the latest multiyear funding.

(xi) The clause should state that percentage of the contract price subject to price adjustment.

(A) Normally, do not apply adjustments to the profit portion of the contract.

(B) Examine the labor and material portions of the contract to exclude any areas that do not require adjustment. For example, it may be possible to exclude —

(1) Subcontracting for short periods of time during the early life of the contract which could be covered by firm-fixed-priced subcontracting;

(2) Certain areas of overhead, e.g., depreciation charges, prepaid insurance costs, rental costs, leases, certain taxes, and utility charges;

(3) Labor costs for which a definitive union agreement exists; and

(4) Those costs not likely to be affected by fluctuation in the economy.

(C) Allocate that portion of the contract price subject to adjustment to specific periods of time (e.g., quarterly, semiannually, etc.) based on the most probable expenditure or commitment basis (expenditure profile).

(xii) The clause should provide for definite times or events that trigger price adjustments. Adjustments should be frequent enough to afford the contractor appropriate economic protection without creating a burdensome administrative effort. The adjustment period should normally range from quarterly to annually.

(xiii) When the contract contains cost incentives, any sums paid to the contractor on account of economic price adjustment provisions must be subtracted from the total of the contractor's allowable costs for the purpose of establishing the total costs to which the cost incentive provisions apply. If the incentive arrangement is cited in percentage ranges, rather than dollar ranges, above and below target costs, structure the economic price adjustment clause to maintain the original contract incentive range in dollars.

(xiv) The economic price adjustment clause should provide that once the labor and material allocations and the portion of the contract price subject to price adjustment have been established, they remain fixed through the life of the contract and shall not be modified except in the event of significant changes in the scope of the contract. The clause should state that pricing actions pursuant to the Changes clause or other provisions of the contract will be priced as though there were no provisions for economic price adjustment. However, subsequent modifications may include a change to the delivery schedule or significantly change the amount of, or mix of, labor or material for the contract. In such cases, it may be appropriate to prospectively apply economic price adjustment coverage. This may be accomplished by —

(A) Using an economic price adjustment (EPA) clause that applies only to the effort covered by the modification;

(B) Revising the baseline data or period in the EPA clause for the basic contract to include the new work; or

(C) Using an entirely new EPA clause for the entire contract, including the new work.

(xv) Consistent with the factors in paragraphs (d)(i) through (xiv) of this subsection, it may also be appropriate to provide in the prime contract for similar economic price adjustment arrangements between the prime contractor and affected subcontractors to allocate risks properly and ensure that those subcontractors are provided similar economic protection.

(xvi) When economic price adjustment clauses are included in contracts that do not require submission of cost or pricing data as provided in FAR 15.804-1, the contracting officer must obtain adequate information to establish the baseline from which adjustments will be made. The contracting officer may require verification of the data submitted to the extent necessary to permit reliance upon the data as a reasonable baseline.

This type of economic price adjustment is normally the most objective since it is usually based on national indexes prepared by the Bureau of Labor Statistics of the Department of Labor. See *California Microwave, Inc.*, Comp. Gen. Dec. B-202317, 81-1 CPD ¶ 505, concurring that the effect of the clause need not be evaluated when a national index was used since the index would have the same effect on all prices. However, a clause of this type is very difficult to negotiate and draft. First, the parties must agree on an index or a weighted group of indexes that match, with reasonable accuracy, the work on the contract. Second, the parties must agree on an expenditure profile that represents the expenditure of funds in performing the contract. This is to prevent the contractor from influencing the recovery under the clause by varying the incurrence of actual costs. Third, the parties must agree on those portions of the work subject to price adjustment. All of these factors require a detailed analysis of the work called for by the contract. Yet it should be anticipated that the clause finally arrived at will cover no more than a portion of the risk of fluctuations in the economy. This is especially true since the guidance suggests that no adjustments be made for deliveries beyond the scheduled delivery date. This requires the contractor to bear the risk of price fluctuations due to delays for which the Government is not responsible. As a result, the contractor will seek to assure that the contract price reflects the residual pricing risk assumed by the contractor. See *American Transparents Plastic Corp.*, Comp. Gen. Dec. B-210898, 83-2 CPD ¶ 539, for a case upholding the use of a clause based on a national index even though it did not relieve the contractor of many of the risks of fluctuations in the economy. The use of a national index was also approved in *Utah LP Gas, Inc. v. General Servs. Admin.*, GSBCA 12472, 96-1 BCA ¶ 27,960, where the contracting officer chose to use the index in the contract even though the clause permitted amendment "to substitute a more appropriate index" if the contractually specified index did not reflect market conditions. The board reviewed the contracting officer's analysis of the situation and concluded that there had been no abuse of discretion in deciding not to alter the national index.

Contracting officers in the DOD have been held bound to the DFARS guidance on the proper structuring of economic price adjustment clauses using indexes. See *Beta Sys., Inc. v. United States*, 838 F.2d 1179 (Fed. Cir. 1988), where the court ordered reformation of an index in a clause that did not match the work under the contract, and *Craft Mach. Works, Inc.*, ASBCA 35167, 90-3 BCA ¶ 23,095, where the board reformed the portion of the clause that based the price adjustment in each period on the baseline of the prior period. In both cases, it was held that the intent of the DFARS was to provide a price adjustment that fairly compensated the contractor for fluctuations in the economy and that clauses that significantly deviated from this intent were not binding on the contractor because they did not comply with regulations that had the force and effect of law. Compare *Glopak Corp. v. United States*, 851 F.2d 334 (Fed. Cir. 1988), where the court refused to reform a General Services Administration (GSA) contract that contained an index that did not match the contractor's costs. In that case, there was no regulation, such as the DFARS, that bound the contracting officer, and the court reasoned that reformation was only available if the resulting contract was "unconscionable."

3. Common Problems in Structuring Economic Price Adjustment Clauses

Most economic price adjustment clauses are tailored to the individual procurement as permitted or required by the regulations. This places a large burden on the contracting parties to analyze the situation fully and draft a contract clause that provides the intended protection from economic fluctuations. The litigated cases in this area indicate that there are numerous instances where specially drafted clauses do not achieve this goal.

a. Clarity in Contract Language

Probably the most common problem encountered is vague or ambiguous contract language. In most cases, these ambiguities appear to result from a failure of the parties to understand fully the intricacies of the arrangement they have negotiated. For example, in *Firestone Tire & Rubber Co. v. United States*, 195 Ct. Cl. 21, 444 F.2d 547 (1971), an index adjustment clause called for the use of a Steel Products index without specifying any subcategories of the index. The court found that it was not reasonable to use the main index since its fluctuations did not match the fluctuations in the price of the steel components used in the contract. The court therefore "interpreted" the clause to require the use of subcategories of the index that matched the actual work. Interpretation was more appropriately used in several cases where the question was whether the cost was covered by the clause. In *Optic-Electronic Corp.*, ASBCA 24962, 83-2 BCA ¶ 16,677, *recons. denied*, 84-3 BCA ¶ 17,565, the board looked to the negotiations of the parties to determine if they might have intended to include profit-sharing as a fringe benefit even though it had been omitted from the contract schedule in a labor and material adjustment clause. The board found no evidence of such intent and therefore interpreted the contract as omitting the benefit from the price adjustment formula. Similarly, in *ITT Arctic Servs., Inc. v. United States*, 207 Ct. Cl. 743, 524 F.2d 680 (1975), the contractor was denied recovery for increased "labor cost" under the price escalation clause since the increases were due to currency fluctuation. In *Merritt-Chapman & Scott Corp.*, IBCA 240, 61-2 BCA ¶ 3193, the escalation clause provided for increases in wages but not subsistence payments, and the Government unsuccessfully claimed that the portion of the hourly wage paid on a "remote" project in excess of the state average was actually a subsistence payment.

Interpretation was also used to determine the correct method of computing the price adjustment in *Brunswick Corp. v. United States*, 951 F.2d 334 (Fed. Cir. 1991). There the court affirmed the board decision at 91-1 BCA ¶ 23,458 that the Government was correct in adjusting the base for the price adjustment by the factors included in a table in the contract. The contractor had argued that the proper adjustment was the amount it had used in computing its bid, but the court held that this was not in accord with the contract language and would give it an undue advantage over other bidders. See also *United States Steel Corp.*, ASBCA 29111, 85-1 BCA ¶ 17,761, *recons. denied*, 85-1 BCA ¶ 17,921, where the Government was held bound to a contractor's brief description in the proposal of the price adjustment technique to be used even though the RFP had included one of the standard economic price adjustment clauses. Perhaps the most egregious example of lack of clarity is found in *Holland Oil Co.*, ASBCA 26603, 82-2 BCA ¶ 15,908, where the Government was bound to a questionable price due to its inartful draftsmanship and lack of attention to detail in analyzing bids.

Compare *Barry L. Miller Eng'g, Inc.*, ASBCA 20554, 75-2 BCA ¶ 11,567, where an unambiguous response in the contractor's proposal was held to bind the Government to pay costs over the escalation ceiling in the RFP.

b. Ceilings

One of the most troublesome elements of economic price adjustment clauses is the ceiling on the total amount of the adjustment. The three FAR clauses all contain a ceiling of 10 percent of the total contract price with the provision that this ceiling may be modified when drafting the contract with the approval of the "chief of the contracting office," FAR 52.216-2, -3, and -4. See NFS 1816.203-4(a) requiring coordination with finance officers before agreeing to a higher ceiling. The current DOD guidance on index adjustment clauses provides that normally no ceiling will be used although ceilings have been used in the past in such clauses. Whenever a ceiling is used, the parties should carefully review the economic situation to ascertain whether the clause provides the necessary protection since these ceilings are enforced literally. See, for example, *Martin-Copeland Co.*, ASBCA 26551, 83-2 BCA ¶ 16,752, where a 10 percent ceiling covered only one third of the price fluctuation in the price of gold encountered by the contractor. The board held that the parties were bound to the contract agreement and that no further recovery was possible. See also *American Transparents Plastic Corp.*, Comp. Gen. Dec. B-210898, 83-2 CPD ¶ 539, where the Comptroller General dismissed a protest that a 30 percent ceiling was inadequate to cover the risk of price fluctuations. The Comptroller General stated that there was no statutory or regulatory requirement that economic price adjustment clauses fully protect the contractor. In one curious case, the parties left the ceiling provision blank in the executed contract and the contracting officer subsequently inserted 25 percent in the blank, *American Optical Corp. v. United States*, 219 Ct. Cl. 131, 592 F.2d 1149 (1979). The court concluded that the basic guidance in the ASPR called for the ceiling to be "reasonable" and that 25 percent was reasonable in a situation where the escalation provision covered the price of gold over a one-year period.

The use of ceilings creates a problem in price adjustment clauses where the contractor is required to warrant that the contract price does not include any contingency for items subject to escalation. See, for example, the Economic Price Adjustment — Standard Supplies clause set forth above. In *Echelon Serv. Co.*, Comp. Gen. Dec. B-208720.2, 83-2 CPD ¶ 86, the Comptroller General concurred with the agency's use of a ceiling and a warranty against allowances for increased costs in the original contract price and appeared to concur with the agency's view that the warranty did not prevent the inclusion of a contingency for cost elements not covered by the clause. See also *International Business Invs., Inc.*, Comp. Gen. Dec. B-213723, 84-1 CPD ¶ 668, where the Comptroller General reached the same conclusion on the validity of the two provisions without discussion of whether a contingency was permitted.

c. *Pricing Elements Subject to Escalation*

The specific elements of the contractor's price that are subject to escalation must be carefully and accurately described to avoid controversy in the application of escalation provisions. For example, in *VBM Corp.*, ASBCA 23268, 79-2 BCA ¶ 14,037, the clause called for escalation of "direct labor cost" defined as "the hours of work as of the contract date of non-supervisory employees required for the manufacture of each unit of contract supplies times the hourly rate." The board ruled that the tooling costs were within this definition since they had been treated as direct costs by the contractor in its proposal and met accounting definitions of direct costs. See also *Fermont Div., Dynamics Corp.*, ASBCA 21949, 79-1 BCA ¶ 13,774, where the board concluded that an escalation clause covering "delivered items" applied to option quantities. The board held that such escalation was warranted even though the option prices were higher than the base price for the items on the contract. Apparently, the evidence indicated that the contractor had not included a contingency in the option prices to cover higher labor or material costs. The board distinguished *F.W. Faxon Co.*, ASBCA 20925, 76-2 BCA ¶ 12,103, in which the board refused to apply an escalation clause where the Government had exercised an option to extend the performance period of the contract. In that case the board concluded that the clause was clear and that it only applied to the first calendar year of performance of the work.

d. *Timing of Price Adjustments*

It has been common practice to limit adjustments for economic fluctuations to price changes prior to the adjusted delivery or completion dates set forth in the contract. See the standard FAR clauses containing such a provision. Such provisions do not involve substantial risk in stable market periods but can impose unreasonable risks when markets are volatile. See, for example, *Stanwick Corp.*, ASBCA 24010, 80-1 BCA ¶ 14,252, denying any adjustment because the price increase occurred after the contract delivery date. The difficulty with this provision is that the parties are agreeing to such risks without a very clear approximation of the amount of risk that may be encountered. In instances of large inflationary increases, the resulting costs of such agreements may be greater than the contractor can sustain, while in periods of deflation, the Government may pay excessive prices.

There have also been interpretation problems in contract language describing the timing of the adjustment. A contract providing for price adjustment "as of the date of delivery" was interpreted as allowing adjustment based on the scheduled delivery date rather than the actual date of late delivery, *Deloro Smelting & Refining Co. v. United States*, 161 Ct. Cl. 489, 317 F.2d 382 (1963). In *Sears Petroleum & Transp. Corp.*, ASBCA 41401, 94-2 BCA ¶ 26,414, the board held that a clause in which the price was to be that in effect on the "date of delivery" meant the price was to be determined at the date on which the product was actually delivered and not the date when the contractor gave notice of readiness to deliver. Similarly, in *Ssangyong Trading Co.*, ASBCA 21614, 79-1 BCA ¶ 13,810, the board held that a clause calling for price adjustment on all items delivered "on and after" the date of a price change was to be applied literally to the specified delivery dates of items under the contract. In one case, an economic price adjustment clause provided for price increases under the contract to become effective on the date of the issue of the trade journal in which the price increases were published rather than on the date the prices were reported to have become effective, *Sterling Oil Terminal Corp.*, ASBCA 3704, 57-1 BCA ¶ 1265. See also *St. Louis Refrigerator Car Co.*, ASBCA 10837, 65-2 BCA ¶ 5161, in which the board held that the earliest date of price adjustment was the date of delivery of the price adjustment demand to the Government and not before. In *Allis-Chalmers Corp.*, Comp. Gen. Dec. B-186693, 76-2 CPD ¶ 48, the Comptroller General held that the term "latest available indices" meant published indexes rather than preliminary figures available from the Department of Labor. In *Libby Corp.*, ASBCA 40765, 96-1 BCA ¶ 28,255, the board accepted the argument that the Government could not recover a price reduction based on the contract delivery date if it had been responsible for a delay but found no proof of Government responsibility.

e. Effect of Changes

Changes affecting the amount or type of labor or material must be carefully analyzed to determine whether they require modifications to the economic price adjustment provisions. If such changes substantially alter the cost elements subject to price adjustment, the structure of a composite escalation formula can be significantly impacted. The ASBCA has held that because the Government issues a change order that distorts or destroys the adjustment formula, it is not excused from its basic agreement to escalate, *Babcock & Wilcox Co.*, ASBCA 7531, 1962 BCA ¶ 3575. The most appropriate method of overcoming this problem would be for the parties to agree on separate price escalation provisions in any major contract amendments or supplemental agreements, Sharp, "Pricing and Contracting for Inflation," 5 Nat. Cont. Mgt. J. 87 (1971). The parties may also agree that a change requires an economic price adjustment clause even though none had been included in the basic contract, *Minowitz Mfg. Co.*, ASBCA 23784, 83-1 BCA ¶ 16,324.

f. Notice Requirements

Almost all economic price adjustment clauses require that the contractor notify the contracting officer, within a specified period of time, when a price adjustment is due. Such requirements have generally been held to be enforceable only when the Government is prejudiced by lack of notice, and such prejudice has been difficult to demonstrate, *Chemray Coatings Corp.*, GSBCA 10117, 91-1 BCA ¶ 23,356; *Sky Top Plastics*, GSBCA 7000, 91-1 BCA ¶ 23,350; *Interlog Corp.*, ASBCA 21212, 77-1 BCA ¶ 12,362. However, in *Bataco Indus., Inc. v. United States*, 29 Fed. Cl. 318 (1993), the court held that a notice provision was a "time-bar" provision that should be strictly enforced. The clause stated:

> (d) Price increases shall be subject to the following limitations:
>
> * * *
>
> (2) The contractor's entitlement to price increases shall be waived, unless the contractor's written request therefor is received by the contracting officer within 180 days after the date of final shipment of supplies under the contract.

The same result was reached in *Universal Dev. Corp. v. General Servs. Admin.*, GSBCA 12138, 93-3 BCA ¶ 26,100. This strict interpretation of the clause is completely dependent on the language setting forth the notice provision. Thus, some of these provisions may be interpreted to impose only a notice requirement (that will be waived absent prejudice to the Government) while others may be interpreted to bar contractor claims for price adjustment.

C. Fixed-Price Redeterminable

FAR 16.205 and 206 provide for two types of redeterminable contracts where the prices are established during or after performance. Contracts of this type were widely used in the past but are infrequently used at the present since they provide very little incentive for the contractor to control the costs of performance. Thus, the current guidance calls for their use in quite narrow circumstances.

1. Prospective Price Redetermination

FAR 16.205-2 contains the following guidance:

> A fixed-price contract with prospective price redetermination may be used in acquisitions of quantity production or services for which it is possible to negotiate a fair and reasonable firm fixed price for an initial period, but not for subsequent periods of contract performance.
>
> > (a) The initial period should be the longest period for which it is possible to negotiate a fair and reasonable firm fixed price. Each subsequent pricing period should be at twelve months.
> >
> > (b) The contract may provide for a ceiling price based on evaluation of the uncertainties involved in performance and their possible cost impact. This ceiling price should provide for assumption of a reasonable proportion of the risk by the contractor and, once established, may be adjusted only by operation of contract clauses providing for equitable adjustment or other revision of the contract price under stated circumstances.

The redetermination process followed in this type of contract is quite involved. The contractor must prepare and submit a full-price proposal for the new price; this proposal is then audited by the Government; an audit report is submitted to the contracting officer; and the new price is negotiated. The requirement that the pricing periods be at least 12 months in duration reflects the need for a significant amount of time to arrive at a redetermined price and attempts to ensure that the contractor bear a significant degree of risk by leaving some time of performance after the price is redetermined. In this type of contract, the contractor will not have performed very much of the contract under the pressures of a fixed price but will have the opportunity to adjust the prices as cost experience is incurred. FAR 16.205-3 contains the following limitations on the use of this type of contract:

> This contract type shall not be used unless —
>
> (a) Negotiations have established that (1) the conditions for use of a firm-fixed-price contract are not present (see 16.202-2), and (2) a fixed-price incentive contract would not be more appropriate;
>
> (b) The contractor's accounting system is adequate for price redetermination;
>
> (c) The prospective pricing periods can be made to conform with operation of the contractor's accounting system; and
>
> (d) There is reasonable assurance that price redetermination actions will take place promptly at the specified times.

A standard clause for this type of contract is contained in FAR 52.216-5.

2. *Retroactive Redetermination*

An infrequently used type of redetermination is the retroactive redetermination type contract where the final price is negotiated after completion of the work. FAR 16.206-2 provides the following guidance:

> A fixed-ceiling-price contract with retroactive price redetermination is appropriate for research and development contracts estimated at $100,000 or less when it is established at the outset that a fair and reasonable firm fixed price cannot be negotiated and that the amount involved and short performance period make the use of any other fixed-price contract type impracticable.

(a) A ceiling price shall be negotiated for the contract at a level that reflects a reasonable sharing of risk by the contractor. The established ceiling price may be adjusted only if required by the operation of contract clauses providing for equitable adjustment or other revision of the contract price under stated circumstances.

(b) The contract should be awarded only after negotiation of a billing price that is as fair and reasonable as the circumstances permit.

(c) Since this contract type provides the contractor no cost control incentive except the ceiling price, the contracting officer should make clear to the contractor during discussion before award that the contractor's management effectiveness and ingenuity will be considered in retroactively redetermining the price.

Because of the obvious lack of incentive in this type of contract, FAR 16.206-3 permits its use only on research and development contracts under the simplified acquisition threshold. A standard clause for this type of contract is contained in FAR 52.216-6, but it is doubtful if an agency would use this type of contract.

III. COST-REIMBURSEMENT CONTRACTS

When it has been decided that the nature of the work or the unreliability of the cost estimate makes it necessary to use a cost-reimbursement contract, the contracting officer and the contractor have several choices. This section discusses two types of cost-reimbursement contracts. First, the basic type of cost-reimbursement contract — the CPFF contract — will be reviewed. The section then considers the various types of cost-sharing contracts that have been used when the parties desire to share the risks of the contract by entering into an agreement that provides for cost-sharing throughout performance of the work. Cost-plus-incentive-fee (CPIF) and cost-plus-award-fee (CPAF) contracts are dealt with in the section on incentive contracts. Cost-reimbursement term type contracts are covered in the section on level-of-effort contracts.

FAR 16.301-2 contains the following basic guidance on the use of cost-reimbursement contracts:

> Cost-reimbursement contracts are suitable for use only when uncertainties involved in contract performance do not permit costs to be estimated with sufficient accuracy to use any type of fixed-price contract.

FAR 16.301-3 provides limitations on the use of any cost-reimbursement contract as follows:

> (a) A cost-reimbursement contract may be used only when —
>
> (1) The contractor's accounting system is adequate for determining costs applicable to the contract; and
>
> (2) Appropriate Government surveillance during performance will provide reasonable assurance that efficient methods and effective cost controls are used.
>
> (3) See 15.903(d) for statutory limitations on price or fee.
>
> (b) The use of cost-reimbursement contracts is prohibited for the acquisition of commercial items (see parts 2 and 12).

The feature that all cost-reimbursement contracts have in common is the Limitation of Cost clause, FAR 52.232-20. This clause overrides all of the contract requirements by providing that when the contractor has fully expended the funds included in the contract, there is no further obligation to continue performance or incur costs, but that when the Government provides additional funds, the contractor must continue performance as long as funds are available until completion of the specified work. The clause provides, in addition, that the contractor must give notice of overruns and that the Government has no obligation to provide such additional funding or to reimburse the contractor for costs incurred in excess of the contractual amount. This latter provision has been quite strictly enforced to deny contractor's reimbursement of cost overruns not approved in writing by the contracting officer, *ITT Defense Communications Div.*, ASBCA 14270, 70-2 BCA ¶ 8370; *American Standard, Inc.*, ASBCA 15660, 71-2 BCA ¶ 9109. In the most liberal case on this issue, the Court of Claims found that an overrun had been funded when a contracting officer indicated approval of the funding on an internal memorandum that was not communicated to the contractor, *General Elec. Co. v. United States*, 188 Ct. Cl. 620, 412 F.2d 1215, *mot. for reh'g denied*, 189 Ct. Cl. 116, 416 F.2d 1320 (1969). In making the decision on whether to fund the overrun, the contracting officer has great discretion. Hence, a choice can be made either to fund or not to fund the overrun after the costs have been incurred, *Eyler Assocs.*, ASBCA 16804, 75-1 BCA ¶ 11,320; *ARINC Research Corp.*, ASBCA 15861, 72-2 BCA ¶ 9721. However, a decision not to fund the overrun based entirely on the failure of the contractor to give notice of the overrun as required by the clause may lead to difficulty. It has been held to be an abuse of discretion to make such a decision in a situation where the contractor could not have known of the overrun, *General Elec. Co. v. United States*, 194 Ct. Cl. 678, 440 F.2d 420 (1971). However, a stringent test has been used to determine if the contractor could have learned of the overrun in such circumstances, and it has been held that it can meet this test only by showing that a fully adequate accounting system would not have revealed the overrun, *Stanwick Corp.*, ASBCA 14905, 71-1 BCA ¶ 8777, *recons. denied*, 71-2 BCA ¶ 9115. The Government has also been estopped from denying overrun funding where it told the contractor funds were available and observed the occurrence of the overrun, *American Elec. Labs., Inc. v. United States*, 774 F.2d 1110 (Fed. Cir. 1985). For a complete discussion of the Limitation of Cost clause see Cibinic & Nash, *Cost-Reimbursement Contracting* 930–71 (2d ed., 1993).

It has also become quite common practice to include ceiling amounts at the inception or during performance of cost-reimbursement contracts. If such provisions are carefully drafted to provide that they establish ceiling prices and that the contractor is obligated to complete the work, they will be enforced, *LSi Serv. Corp. v. United States*, 191 Ct. Cl. 185, 422 F.2d 1334 (1970); *National Civil Serv. League v. United States*, 226 Ct. Cl. 478, 643 F.2d 768 (1981); *CRC Sys. Inc. v. General Servs. Admin.*, GSBCA 11173, 93-2 BCA ¶ 25,842. However, in less clearly drafted clauses, the contractor has been permitted to avoid the ceiling, *Singer — General Precision, Inc. v. United States*, 192 Ct. Cl. 435, 427 F.2d 1187 (1970) (cost allocated to overhead as bidding expense); *General Dynamics Corp. v. United States*, 229 Ct. Cl. 399, 671 F.2d 474 (1982) (termination clause interpreted with ceiling permitting reimbursement of costs up to ceiling after default termination but making contractor responsible for excess costs of reprocurement). Overhead rate ceilings have also been strictly enforced when clearly drafted, *Metro Mach. Corp.*, ASBCA 47005, 97-1 BCA ¶ 28,723.

A. Cost-Plus-Fixed-Fee Contracts

In the CPFF contract, the parties negotiate an estimated cost of performance and preestablish the fee to be paid to the contractor for performing the work. This fixed fee is stated as a set amount of dollars that will vary only as the contractor is required to perform additional work not included in the original contract or less work than required by the contract. Thus, the contractor bears the risk of the adequacy of the fee while the Government bears the risk of the incurrence of additional costs to permit full performance of the work. FAR 16.306(a) describes this type of contract as follows:

> A cost-plus-fixed-fee contract is a cost-reimbursement contract that provides for payment to the contractor of a negotiated fee that is fixed at the inception of the contract. The fixed fee does not vary with actual cost, but may be adjusted as a result of changes in the work to be performed under the contract. This contract type permits contracting for efforts that might otherwise present too great a risk to contractors, but it provides the contractor only a minimum incentive to control costs.

In the CPFF contract, the estimated cost and the fixed fee are stated separately and, thus, must be negotiated separately. The estimated cost will, ideally, be the amount that the parties agree represents their best estimate of the amount that will be spent in accomplishing the work called for by the contract. It is not uncommon, however, for the estimated cost to be set at an amount less than the best estimate. Two factors appear to account for this practice. First, in a number of Government procurements, agencies have not had sufficient funds in the budget to cover the cost estimate submitted by the contractor. In such cases, contractors have frequently been quite willing to agree to a lower cost estimate in order to obtain the immediate award of the contract. This will generally result in a somewhat lower fixed fee than would have been used if a higher estimated cost had been included. This lower fixed fee has been seen as a small concession compared to the risk of not being awarded the contract.

The second factor that has led to low estimated costs is the presence of competition in the contract award process. In most competitive procurements, the cost of performance is a significant evaluation factor in the source selection decision. As a result, offerors are motivated to make very optimistic estimates of the costs of performance. Although such estimates are adjusted, through cost realism analysis, for the purpose of selecting the winning contractor, contracting officers have a tendency to award contracts based on the cost estimate submitted by the contractor in the competitive process. This is a questionable procedure because it results in a contract funded at too low a level to permit accomplishment of the work. A much better procedure would be to include an estimated cost at a level representing the contracting officer's appraisal of the realistic cost of performance. However, it appears that only a minority of contracting officers follow this procedure, with the result that many CPFF contracts contain estimated costs that are unreasonably low.

The fixed fee in a CPFF contract is established in one of two ways. If the contract is awarded using a competitive negotiation process, the contracting officer may provide in the solicitation that each offeror propose the fixed fee that it will accept to perform the work and that this fixed fee be evaluated in the source selection process. This, of course, will induce some of the offerors to propose low fees and may result in a fixed fee that is quite low, perhaps in the range of 2 to 5 percent. Alternatively, the contracting officer may provide for the fixed fee to be established using the profit formula established in the agency's regulations (see Chapter 9). In this case, the offeror will normally submit an analysis of the elements of the fee, following the agency profit formula, and the fee will be negotiated during written or oral discussions or negotiations depending on the amount of competition. In such cases, fixed fees in the range of 6 to 10 percent can be anticipated. In addition, contractors with unique capabilities have been able in a few instances to negotiate, on a sole source basis, fee levels significantly higher than this range.

B. Cost-Sharing Contracts

When contracting parties expect to receive mutual benefit from the performance of a contract, the most equitable arrangement may be to enter into an agreement at the outset providing for a sharing of costs. There are numerous ways to share costs of Government work. One of the most common is to enter into a fixed-price contract at a price below anticipated costs. Another technique is to enter into a cooperative agreement or "other transaction" as discussed in Chapter 1. Grants also can be used as cost-sharing vehicles. This text discusses cost-sharing only in the context of contracts where a cost-reimbursement contract is used with an agreement by the contractor to bear some portion of the incurred costs. FAR 16.303(b) describes this type of contract giving the following minimal guidance:

> A cost-sharing contract may be used when the contractor agrees to absorb a portion of the costs, in the expectation of substantial compensating benefits.

Prior to issuance of the FAR in April 1984, there was considerably greater guidance on this type of contract. Both the Federal Procurement Regulation and the Defense Acquisition Regulation contained substantive provisions, and the Office of Management and Budget had issued Federal Management Circular (FMC) 73-3 on this topic. The last significant policy initiative in this area occurred in December 1980 when the Office of Federal Procurement Policy circulated a proposed policy letter suggesting significant changes to the cost-sharing policy of the Federal Government, 45 Fed. Reg. 86952 (Dec. 1980). This policy letter would have prohibited cost-sharing on all R&D contracts. It was accompanied, however, by a policy letter suggesting recoupment of R&D costs on contracts where a clear potential for commercial sales resulted from performance of the contract, 45 Fed. Reg. 86953 (1980). Industry objection to these policies apparently resulted in a lack of further action, and no Government-wide guidance appears to be forthcoming.

There has also been sporadic congressional activity in this area. For many years, the Department of Labor — Health and Human Services Appropriation Act contained a provision requiring cost-sharing on research grants. This provision is no longer included in the Act. But since 1970, the Department of Housing and Urban Development — Independent Agencies Appropriation Act has contained a similar provision. See P.L. 98-371, § 407:

> None of the funds provided in this Act may be used for payment, through grants or contracts, to recipients that do not share in the cost of conducting research resulting from proposals not specifically solicited by the Government: *Provided*, That the extent of cost sharing by the recipient shall reflect the mutuality of interest of the grantee or contractor and the Government in the research.

This provision applies to the Department of Housing and Urban Development, NASA, the National Science Foundation, and the Department of Veterans Affairs.

This section discusses three aspects of cost-sharing contracts: their use on research contracts, the counteractive recoupment policies of the Government, and use of cost-sharing contracts for development work.

1. Research Contracts

Congressional interest in cost-sharing has focused on research contracts, and prior to the FAR the major procurement regulations gave guidance in this area. These regulations generally stated that cost-sharing was appropriate when the contractor was expected to derive a significant commercial benefit from the research work. This policy has now been withdrawn, and there is very little guidance in the area. See, however, NASA's policy calling for cost-sharing in research contracts resulting from unsolicited proposals as required by statute and in other contracts when voluntarily offered by the contractor, NFS 1816.303-70. Under this policy NASA does not require cost-sharing from research contracts resulting from unsolicited proposals if the contractor has no commercial interest in the research.

The guidance on the amount of cost-sharing is also minimal at present. NFS 1816.303-70 provides that cost-sharing for educational and nonprofit organizations should be no more than 10 percent, and cost-sharing for other organizations should be at any sharing percentage commensurate with the degree of mutuality of interest. A standard clause is provided in NFS 1852.216-73 for this purpose:

ESTIMATED COST AND COST SHARING (DEC 1991)

(a) It is estimated that the total cost of performing the work under this contract will be $______ .

(b) For performance of the work under this contract, the Contractor shall be reimbursed for not more than ______ percent of the costs of performance determined to be allowable under the Allowable Cost and Payment clause. The remaining ______ percent or more of the costs of performance so determined shall constitute the Contractor's share, for which it will not be reimbursed by the Government.

(c) For purposes of the ______ [insert "Limitation of Cost" or "Limitation of Funds"] clause, the total estimated cost to the Government is hereby established as $______ (insert estimated Government share); this amount is the maximum Government liability.

(d) The Contractor shall maintain records of all contract costs claimed by the Contractor as constituting part of its share. Those records shall be subject to audit by the Government. Cost contributed by the Contractor shall not be charged to the Government under any other grant, contract, or agreement (including allocation to other grants, contracts, or agreements as part of an independent research and development program).

It is also possible to share costs by having the contractor agree to pay all or a part of specified costs. See, for example, *Shale Dev. Corp.*, IBCA 1256-3-79, 81-1 BCA ¶ 15,128, where the board held that a cost-sharing contract existed because the parties had agreed that the Government would pay direct costs and the contractor would pay indirect costs. In contrast, in *General Am. Research Div., Gen. Am. Transp. Corp.*, PSBCA 91, 77-1 BCA ¶ 12,732, the board held that a CPFF contract with a special clause providing for cost-sharing on overruns did not require sharing of costs incurred in a convenience termination settlement.

2. Recoupment on Development Contracts

Another method of sharing costs, after the fact, is recoupment. Recoupment is the recovery of nonrecurring costs of developing and preparing a product for manufacture from other buyers of that product. Recoupment was a standard practice of the DOD from the 1950s until 1992. However, on June 19, 1992, the White House issued a press report announcing that the President had abolished recoupment fees on all products other than "major defense equipment" (MDE) exported for military uses. As a result, recoupment is now only utilized as required by statute in contracts for foreign military sales (FMS).

Recoupment has been implemented in two ways. First, DOD recovers a recoupment charge directly from a foreign government if a product is sold to a foreign government under a FMS arrangement. Second, a contractor adds a recoupment charge to the contract and pays it to the Government if a product is sold by the contractor directly to a foreign or domestic customer, or if a foreign company is licensed to manufacture the product.

The DOD first issued a written policy on recoupment in 1967 — DOD Directive 2140.2, Recovery of Nonrecurring Costs Applicable to Foreign Sales. This directive applied to sales of MDE to foreign buyers. MDE was defined as equipment that had been developed and produced with an expenditure of Research, Development, Test, and Evaluation (RDT&E) funds in excess of $25 million or a production investment in excess of $100 million. The thresholds for MDE doubled in 1972. Subsequently, in 1974, the Directive was revised to split the recoupment charge into two segments, one for nonrecurring development costs and the other for nonrecurring production costs.

Congress first adopted the recoupment policy in the Arms Export Control Act of 1976, P.L. 94-329. The Act contains a provision at 22 U.S.C. § 2761(e)(1)(B), requiring that FMS agreements include

> a proportionate amount of any nonrecurring costs of research, development, and production of major defense equipment (except for equipment wholly paid for either from funds transferred under section 503(a)(3) of the Foreign Assistance Act of 1961 [22 U.S.C. § 2311(a)(3)] or from funds made available on a nonrepayable basis under section 23 of this Act [22 U.S.C. § 2763]).

The Office of Federal Procurement Policy subsequently recognized that recoupment was not a sound policy because it had a negative impact on the competitiveness of American industry in international markets — resulting in the 1992 presidential action. In response to the new policy, DOD issued a revised Directive 2140.2, Jan. 13, 1993, which states that a "recoupment charge shall be imposed for sales of MDE only as required by Act of Congress." In 1996, Section 4303 of the Clinger-Cohen Act, P.L. 104-106, added 22 U.S.C. § 2761(e)(2)(B), which provides for Presidential waiver of recoupment on FMS sales to prevent loss of the sale or to obtain savings on procurement of equipment for the United States.

Recoupment clauses have created some difficult contractual issues. See, for example, *BMY, Div. of Harsco Corp.*, ASBCA 38172, 93-2 BCA ¶ 25,704, where the board held that the Government was entitled to recoupment of nonrecurring costs only in connection with the second of two commercial sales because the Government's investment in the R&D of the product at the time of the first sale was less than the $5 million required for reimbursement in the DAR clause in the contract. In *Hughes Aircraft Co.*, ASBCA 30570, 90-2 BCA ¶ 22,780, the board found the contractor liable for R&D expenditures following a commercial sale of weapons to the United Kingdom despite a subsequent international agreement between the United States and the United Kingdom that stated such costs would be paid by the United Kingdom. The board concluded the contractor was not relieved of its responsibility to pay because the agreement had not been made for the purpose of absolving the contractor of liability. In *General Elec. Co.*, ASBCA 20930, 79-2 BCA ¶ 13,956, the board held that the Government was not entitled to recoupment for nonrecurring program and

R&D costs because the original contractor sold the product to another contractor for use in a separate Government contract. The board reasoned that no commercial sale warranting recoupment had occurred because the Government would ultimately be the end user in both contracts.

3. Support of Commercial Development

The most obvious type of agreement where cost-sharing should be required is the agreement used when the Government supports the work of an organization to develop a product for the commercial market. The Department of Energy (DOE) has issued the most helpful regulation dealing with this type of contract, which requires "cost participation." DEAR 917.7001(a) states:

> When DOE supports performer research, development, and/or demonstration efforts, where the principal purpose is ultimate commercialization and utilization of the technologies by the private sector, and when there are reasonable expectations that the performer will receive present or future economic benefits beyond the instant contract as a result of performance of the effort, it is DOE policy to obtain cost participation. Full funding may be provided for early phases of development programs when the technological problems are still great.

This regulation gives full discretion in establishing the type of cost-sharing required on each contract. DEAR 917.7001(b) gives the following guidance on the amount of "cost participation":

> In making this determination to obtain cost participation, and evaluating present and future economic benefits to the performer, DOE will consider the technical feasibility, projected economic viability, societal and political acceptability of commercial application, as well as possible effects of other DOE-supported projects in competing technologies.

The Environmental Protection Agency has also issued a cost-sharing policy. EPAAR 1516.303-72 states:

> (a) The Agency shall use cost-sharing contracts where the principal purpose is ultimate commercialization and utilization of technologies by the private sector. There should also be a reasonable expectation of future economic benefits for the contractor and the Government beyond the Government's contract.

EPAAR 1516.303-75 gives the following guidance on the amount of cost-sharing:

> (a) Contractors should contribute a reasonable amount of the total project cost covered under the contract. The ratio of cost participation should correlate to the apparent advantages available to performers and the proximity of implementing commercialization, i.e., the higher the potential for future profits, the higher the contractor's share should be.
>
> * * *
>
> (c) The Contracting Officer, with the input of technical experts, may consider the following factors in determining reasonable levels of cost sharing:
>
> (1) The availability of the technology to competitors;
>
> (2) Improvements in the contractor's market share position;
>
> (3) The time and risk necessary to achieve success;
>
> (4) If the results of the project involve patent rights which could be sold or licensed;
>
> (5) If the contractor has non-Federal sources of funds to include as cost participation; and
>
> (6) If the contractor has the production and other capabilities to capitalize the results of the project.
>
> (d) A contractor's cost participation can be provided by other subcontractors with which it has contractual arrangements to perform the contract as long as the contractor's cost-sharing goal is met.

EPAAR 1516.303-74 also contains guidance on in-kind contributions, which can be accepted as part of a contractor's cost-sharing. EPAAR 1552.216-76 contains a standard clause for cost-sharing contracts.

IV. INCENTIVE CONTRACTS

Incentive contracts are used when the other types of fixed-price or cost-reimbursement contracts are inappropriate because the risks are moderate. Thus, they provide a middle alternative that the contracting parties can use to impose some risk on the contractor without requiring a full assumption of pricing risk. There are two distinct types of incentive contracts: the "objective" incentive, where the parties include a *formula* in the contract to determine the profit earned by the contractor based on the actual performance results achieved; and the "subjective" incentive, where the parties agree that the profit earned on the contract will be *determined by the Government* based on an appraisal of the contractor's performance. The two objective incentive contracts are the CPIF contract and the FPI contract. The subjective incentive contract is the CPAF contract.

FAR 16.401 contains the following basic guidance on these forms of contract:

> (a) Incentive contracts as described in this subpart are appropriate when a firm-fixed-price contract is not appropriate and the required supplies or services can be acquired at lower costs and, in certain instances, with improved delivery or technical performance, by relating the amount of profit or fee payable under the contract to the contractor's performance. Incentive contracts are designed to obtain specific acquisition objectives by —
>
>> (1) Establishing reasonable and attainable targets that are clearly communicated to the contractor; and
>>
>> (2) Including appropriate incentive arrangements designed to (i) motivate contractor efforts that might not otherwise be emphasized and (ii) discourage contractor inefficiency and waste.

Numerous kinds of incentives are included in these types of contracts. In all cases, they must include incentives on the cost of performance, FAR 16.402-1(a). Incentives on technical performance and time of performance may be included at the discretion of the procuring agency. This section first discusses the major types of objective incentive contract focusing on the cost incentives. It then addresses technical and delivery incentives. The section concludes with a discussion of the CPAF contract.

A. Cost-Plus-Incentive-Fee Contracts

The CPIF contract is an objective incentive where the parties include a formula in the contract to determine the profit earned by the contractor based on the actual performance results achieved. FAR 16.405-1(a) describes this type of contract, as follows:

> The cost-plus-incentive-fee contract is a cost-reimbursement contract that provides for the initially negotiated fee to be adjusted later by a formula based on the relationship of total allowable costs to total target costs. This contract type specifies a target cost, a target fee, minimum and maximum fees, and a fee adjustment formula. After contract performance, the fee payable to the contractor is determined in accordance with the formula. The formula provides, within limits, for increases in fee above target fee when total allowable costs are less than target costs, and decreases in fee below target fee when total allowable costs exceed target costs. This increase or decrease is intended to provide an incentive for the contractor to manage the contract effectively. When total allowable cost is greater than or less than the range of costs within which the fee-adjustment formula operates, the contractor is paid total allowable costs, plus the minimum or maximum fee.

CPIF contracts can include incentives only on the costs of performance or can include multiple incentives covering, in addition, technical performance and delivery. The following section addresses the cost incentives in the CPIF contract.

1. Elements of the Contract Formula on Costs

There are five elements in the basic formula for CPIF contracts covering the costs of performance:

- Target Cost
- Target Fee
- Maximum Fee
- Minimum Fee
- Sharing Arrangement

The formula is expressed in contract language in the Incentive Fee clause in FAR 52.216-10, as follows:

> (e) *Fee Payable.* (1) The fee payable under this contract shall be the target fee increased by __________ [*Contracting Officer insert Contractor's participation*] cents for every dollar that the total allowable cost is less than the target cost or decreased by __________ [*Contracting Officer insert Contractor's participation*] cents for every dollar that the total allowable cost exceeds the target cost. In no event shall the fee be greater than

__________ [*Contracting Officer insert percentage*] percent or less than __________ [*Contracting Officer insert percentage*] percent of the target cost.

The essence of the cost incentive formula is that the contractor's actual fee *varies inversely* with the amount of costs incurred as long as the actual costs incurred fall within the range of sharing established by the points where the maximum and minimum fees take effect. Once these points are reached, the contract becomes a CPFF contract at either the maximum or minimum fee depending on the circumstances. The range in which the sharing arrangement is effective is commonly called the "range of incentive effectiveness" (RIE). **Figure 8-1** is a graphic illustration of the relationship of these elements of the CPIF contract where the following elements have been negotiated:

Target Cost	$100	
Target Fee	$8	
Maximum Fee	15%	($15)
Minimum Fee	2%	($2)
Sharing Arrangement	80/20	

In this incentive formula, the RIE where sharing occurs is between incurred costs of $65 and $130. If the work is performed at a cost of $65 or less, the contractor is paid the maximum fee of $15, while the minimum fee of $2 is paid if the total costs of performance are $130 or more. This formula is the simplest possible with a single sharing percentage for the entire RIE.

Figure 8-1 presents the CPIF contract in terms of variations in earned fee against variations in incurred cost. This is the normal form of presentation used to depict the outcome of incentives on cost. Both cost and fee are expressed in terms of dollars rather than percentages although the target fee is commonly negotiated in terms of a percentage. The graphic presentation is easy to work with because it clearly shows the extent of the sharing and the outcomes at any projected level of cost incurrence.

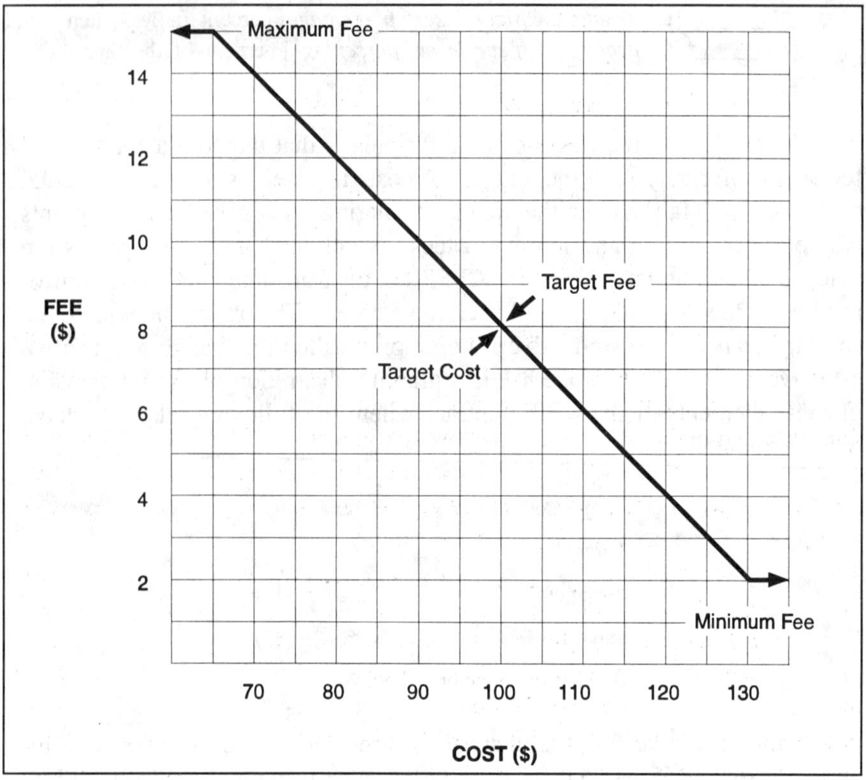

Figure 8-1

2. Negotiating the Cost Incentive Formula

Little general guidance is available on procedures for negotiating the elements of an incentive formula, although a good discussion of some of the factors is included in the DOD and NASA Incentive Contracting Guide, October 1969. In practice, it appears that the most common method of establishing these formulas is to follow past practice in the specific procuring agency negotiating the contract. In this sense, local practice is the major determinant in establishing the elements of the formula. Historically, the range of these elements for most CPIF contracts has been as follows:

Target Cost	$100
Target Fee	6.5% to 9%
Maximum Fee	10% to 15%
Minimum Fee	0% to 4%
Sharing Arrangement	90/10 to 70/30

a. Guidance on Cost Incentive Elements

While the incentive formula is probably best viewed as a single, unified formula for risk allocation, the formula can be established in different ways. In some instances, particularly in procurements with limited or no competition, the contracting officer will follow the guidance of FAR 16.103(a) and establish the elements of the formula through negotiation with the contractor. In such cases, the parties usually conduct negotiations using a step-by-step process beginning with the establishment of the target cost, proceeding to the negotiation of the target fee, and finally factoring in the other elements of the formula. In contrast, when the source is selected competitively, the Government agency may prescribe the elements of the incentive formula in the RFP, permitting the competitors to propose the target cost but maintaining the other elements of the formula at specified percentages or amounts in order to ease the problem of evaluating the proposals. In either case, the tendency has been to arrive at a formula on a mechanical basis without regard to whether or not the formula is a realistic reflection of the possible outcome of the performance of a contract. For example, in the formula depicted in **Figure 8-1** the maximum fee is reached only when actual costs incurred are $65, implying that an underrun of 35 percent is possible. However, the facts of the procurement, including the practices used in establishing the target cost of $100, would almost always show that an underrun of this magnitude would be unlikely, if not impossible.

Although the elements of the incentive formula may be established in a variety of ways, the following guidance can be provided on the considerations applicable to each element.

(1) TARGET COST

The target cost is usually the focal point of the negotiation process since it is the baseline around which the other elements of the formula revolve. This cost is established through the competitive process or after detailed analysis of the contractor's proposal, as discussed in Chapter 9. Although the CPIF contract places greater risk on the contractor than does the CPFF contract, it is generally believed that the target cost should be set at essentially the same level as the estimated cost in the CPFF contract. It is also generally believed that the target cost should be set at the level of costs representing the outcome most likely to be attained through efficient performance of the work. However, strong pressures may be placed upon the contractor to agree to a target cost level lower than this theoretical level, with the result that fee erosion will occur through the application of the incentive formula. Pressure on the contractor is especially strong when the target cost is established in a competitive environment. Pressure also stems from the guidance given to contracting officers that contingencies should not be included in target costs unless they "may arise from presently known and existing conditions, the effects of which are foreseeable within reasonable limits of accuracy," FAR 31.205-7(c)(1). Thus, even if the target cost is negotiated in a noncompetitive environment, the contracting officer may press for a level of cost that is lower than a reasonable prediction of final incurred costs. Another influence working to produce a low target cost is the generally optimistic view of program and technical personnel concerning the level of effort needed to accomplish R&D contracts. Such personnel may not fully recognize or anticipate the pitfalls that are frequently encountered during the course of performance; as a result, they use a low estimate of labor-hours in establishing the target cost.

The same factors that may lead to a low target cost also make it difficult for the contractor and contracting officer to reach agreement on the target cost. When the contractor and contracting officer have such difficulty, the other elements of the formula provide a means of compromise. A common compromising technique is the use of a "plateau" in the sharing formula, whereby the parties agree that in a certain range of cost no sharing will take place. For example, if the contracting officer will agree to a target cost of no more than \$95 and the contractor is adamant that a figure of no less than \$105 is the most valid prediction of the costs of performance, the contract could provide for no sharing between these two amounts. The parties would still have to agree on an intermediate target cost for purposes of making the fee calculation, but this too is susceptible to compromise at a target cost of \$100. The result would be that the middle segment of the formula would contain a CPFF plateau, which would keep either party from encountering windfall profits or losses. Another possible means of compromise is for the contracting officer to accept the contractor's position on the target cost while both parties agree that the target fee will be established using the Government's anticipated target cost as the base. This reduces the target fee somewhat and gives the Government some protection from excessive profits if the contractor performs the contract at a low cost. Thus, the process of establishing the target cost provides the parties with considerable flexibility in arriving at a mutually acceptable incentive formula.

(2) Target Fee

There are two major factors that come into play in establishing the target fee — the competitive situation and the profit policy of the procuring agency, as discussed in Chapter 9. In a procurement with little or no competition, the contracting officer will use the agency profit formula as the starting point for negotiations of the fee. Most contractors are willing to use these profit formulas as the basis for negotiation of the target fee and many will submit their analysis in their original proposal (although FAR 15.404-4(c)(5) prohibits contracting officers from requiring such submission). However, their analysis may well result in a considerably higher fee than that arrived at by the contracting officer. In such cases, the target fee will be determined by vigorous negotiations. In contrast, in highly competitive procurements, some contractors will propose lower target fees in an effort to win the competition, and contracting officers are prone to accept such fees.

Use of the agency profit formula will result in varying levels of target fee in CPIF contracts, depending primarily on the factors of performance risk and investment in facilities in DOD contracts and on contractor effort in contracts with other agencies. In addition, these formulas provide for a small increment of fee for a CPIF contract based on cost risk. The major factor determining this risk in the incentive formula is the sharing arrangement. Thus, a high contractor share should lead to a higher target fee than a low contractor share.

(3) Maximum Fee

The maximum fee should be established at a level that provides a sufficiently wide RIE to reward the contractor for all realistic levels of cost that might be incurred to perform the contract. Thus, assuming that the parties have negotiated a target cost of $100 and have concluded that the lowest possible cost of performance is $85, the maximum fee should be established at a level so that incentive bonuses will be earned in the full range between

$85 and $100. If they have agreed to a 70/30 share for underruns and a target fee of 7 percent, this would require a maximum fee of 11½ percent. Any lower maximum fee would provide no incentive for the contractor to strive to perform the contract for costs of $85.

Prior to 1997, the limiting factor in establishing the maximum fee was the statutory fee limitation on CPFF contracts — 15 percent on R&D contracts and 10 percent on all other contracts. While it is generally agreed that the statutory fee limitation were not applicable to CPIF contracts, FAR 15.903(d)(2) required a deviation from the FAR before the maximum fee on a CPIF contract could exceed the CPFF level. FAC 97-02, September 30, 1997, eliminated this provision from the FAR with the result that contracting officers are now authorized to negotiate maximum fees that provide the necessary incentive to the contractor to reduce the costs of performance.

(4) Minimum Fee

The minimum fee is probably the most contentious element in the CPIF formula because in negotiating this element the parties' goals are diametrically opposed. The contracting officer generally wants a low minimum fee in order to ensure that the sharing continues over a wide range of cost overruns, while the contractor wants a high minimum fee in order to protect against the possibility of a loss contract. It is generally accepted that a minimum fee set at approximately 3 percent of target cost will yield zero profit because this amount of profit is necessary to cover *disallowed costs*. Hence, the contractor will normally argue that the minimum fee should be no less than this amount. In some cases, the Government has agreed to this figure, but there have been many instances where a minimum fee of 2 percent or lower has been used. There are even a few instances where the contracting parties have negotiated a minimum fee of less than zero percent. As with the target fee, the negotiation of the minimum fee will depend on the competitive situation and the bargaining skills of the parties.

It has been quite common for the minimum and maximum fees to be equally distant from the target fee, and FAR 16.404-1(b)(3) requires a low minimum fee when a high maximum fee is negotiated. It is commonly believed that this is the fairest arrangement because it permits the contractor to earn as much in incentive bonuses as it risks losing in incentive penalties. However, this is not necessarily the case. If a uniform sharing arrangement is used for the entire contract, it is possible that the maximum fee will never be attainable, whereas reaching the minimum fee may be quite possible. For example, with the 80/20 sharing arrangement in **Figure 8-1** the contractor could earn $6 of additional fee by performing the work at $70 but would lose $6 of fee by performing at $130. In most development contracting situations, where such a formula would be found, it is far more likely that the actual results will reach $130 than $70 since it is very difficult to achieve significant cost underruns. Thus, it is important that the parties analyze the true potential outcomes of minimum and maximum fees within the sharing arrangement rather than merely negotiate theoretical formulas that have the appearance of symmetry.

(5) Sharing Arrangement

The amount of motivation provided by a CPIF contract is controlled primarily by the level of sharing agreed to by the parties. Clearly, a contract where the contractor shares at a rate of 30 percent of costs incurred over the entire RIE is a more powerful tool than a contract where the contractor's share is only 10 percent. Thus, the sharing arrangement is the major element of the formula reflecting the cost risk imposed by the contract, and the contractor's share will be established, to a large extent, by the parties' appraisal of the amount of risk the procurement entails. If the work is well defined and the cost outcome relatively predictable, imposing more risk by using a higher contractor share would be expected. Conversely, if the work statement is vague and the field of technology not well defined, a lower contractor share would be appropriate. There is very little guidance on which sharing levels are proper in varying circumstances, but it is usually agreed that a contractor share of less than 10 percent is relatively ineffective and a contractor share of over 30 percent is somewhat unusual, with the result that almost all CPIF contracts contain sharing levels within this range. Further, the great majority of the contracts in existence use shares in the middle of the range, from 15 percent to 25 percent. These practices are probably best understood and explained in terms of the traditions within procuring agencies rather than logic. Nevertheless, the establishment of the sharing level is the subject of hard negotiation in many cases and does provide the parties an opportunity to tailor the incentive formula to fit the nature and difficulty of the work called for by the contract.

Widely divergent sharing arrangements have been used in CPIF contracts. The most common is probably the single, straight-line share depicted in **Figure 8-1**, but multiple-line arrangements such as that depicted in **Figure 8-2** have also been quite common. The rationale for this arrangement is that the sharing should increase, with commensurately greater rewards and penalties, as the contractor deviates from the norm of the target cost. This recognizes that the target cost estimate may not be too accurate and that deviations close to target may be desirable as the work progresses. Of course, any other sharing structure that accomplishes the objectives of the parties is equally acceptable, and the contracting officer and the contractor are expected to negotiate a sharing structure that best serves the needs of the specific procurement.

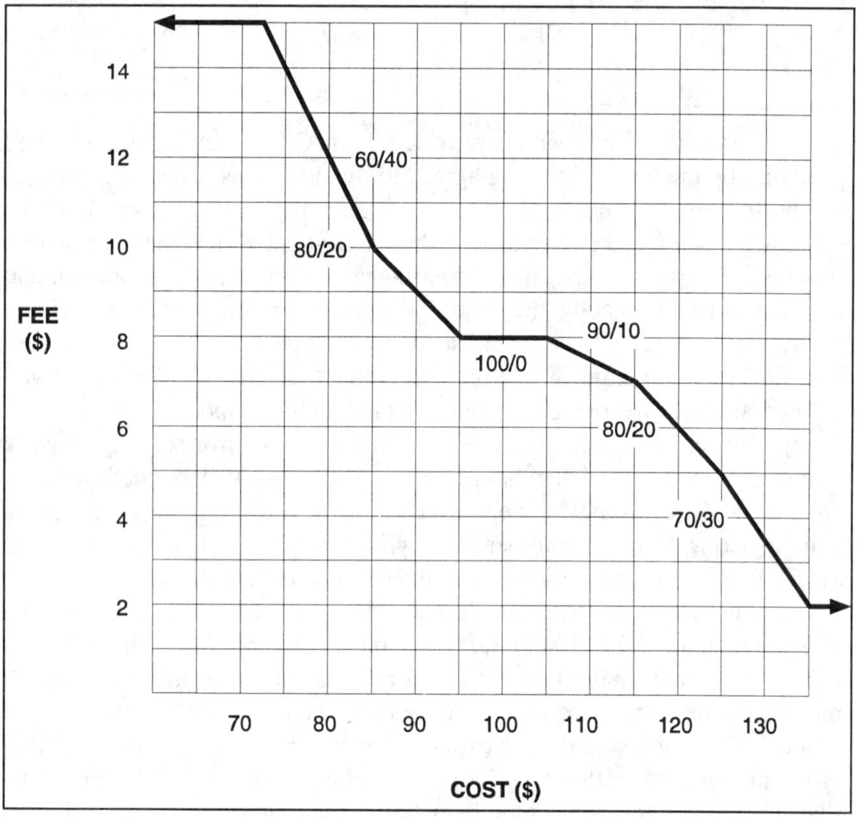

Figure 8–2

b. Use of Range of Incentive Effectiveness

An alternate method of arriving at the elements of the CPIF contract is to use the RIE as the major controlling element in establishing the formula. This technique is depicted in **Figure 8-3**, which reflects parties negotiating three levels of cost: the most likely cost outcome, the best foreseeable cost outcome, and the worst foreseeable cost outcome. The parties also negotiate three levels of profit, reflecting the reasonable profits that a contractor should earn at each of the three cost outcomes. They then structure the sharing arrangement as an outcome of these cost and fee amounts.

For example, in **Figure 8-3** the parties agreed on the following cost levels:

Target Cost	$100
Minimum Possible Cost	$85
Maximum Probable Cost	$135

These levels are reasonably realistic in that significant underruns are very rare, but relatively large overruns are quite common. Thus, they reflect the fact that it is difficult to reduce expenditures while accomplishing the contract goals. They also reflect the fact that target cost levels are commonly set quite optimistically. In **Figure 8-3**, the parties also agreed on the following fee levels:

Target Fee	8%	($8)
Maximum Fee	15%	($15)
Minimum Fee	2%	($2)

The 8 percent target fee represents the fee for a CPIF contract derived from the agency's structured profit policy. The minimum and maximum fees are set at the amount the contracting officer would be willing to agree to at maximum and minimum cost.

Figure 8-3 illustrates that when the three points derived from these numbers are connected, they yield very disparate sharing levels on the overrun and underrun sides of target cost. The sharing arrangements are as follows:

Overrun 82.9/17.1
Underrun 53.3/46.7

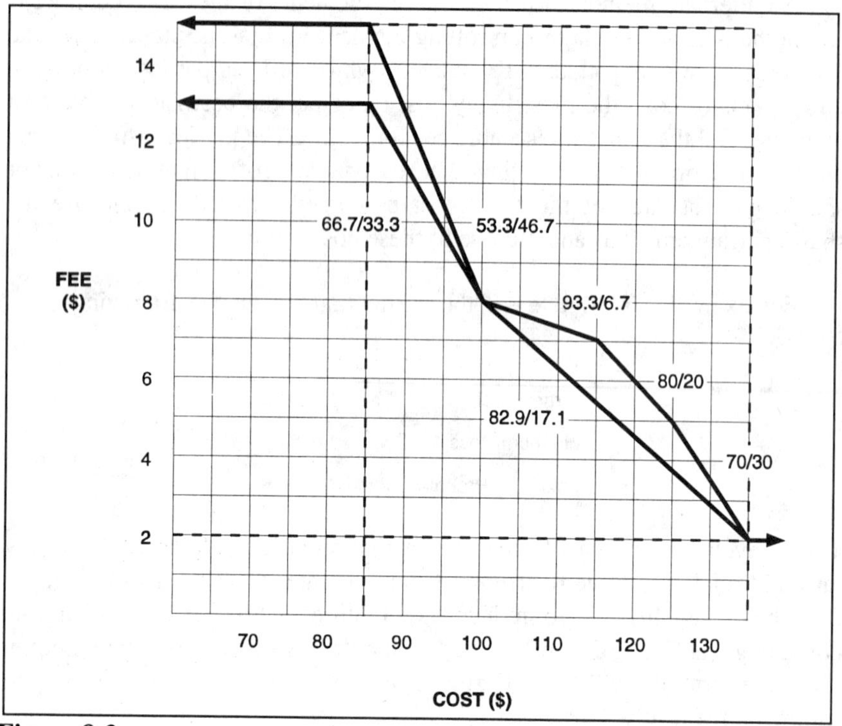

Figure 8-3

While these shares may seem unusual, they reflect the fact that the Government desires sharing over a wide range of overrun, while the parties have agreed that sharing is not realistic over nearly such a wide range of underrun. One way to reduce this disparity is to reduce the maximum fee as depicted in the alternate formula in **Figure 8-3**. Another way to modify this formula is to reduce the overrun sharing for the first part of the overrun and to increase it as the contractor approaches minimum fee. This is also depicted in the alternate formula in **Figure 8-3**. In general, however, the parties should not be disturbed by the higher shares for underruns, since great effort is demanded of contractors to accomplish such cost savings, and the rewards for such efforts should be substantial.

c. *Costs Subject to Incentive Sharing*

Consistent with the theory of the CPIF contract that transferring a portion of the cost risk to the contractor will motivate more efficient performance, the contract language has been carefully drafted to remove certain costs not under the contractor's control from the sharing formula. See the following paragraph in the Incentive Fee clause in FAR 52.216-10:

> (e)(4) For the purpose of fee adjustment, "total allowable cost" shall not include allowable costs arising out of —
>
> (i) Any of the causes covered by the Excusable Delays clause to the extent that they are beyond the control and without the fault or negligence of the Contractor or any subcontractor;
>
> (ii) The taking effect, after negotiating the target cost, of a statute, court decision, written ruling, or regulation that results in the Contractor's being required to pay or bear the burden of any tax or duty or rate increase in a tax or duty;
>
> (iii) Any direct cost attributed to the Contractor's involvement in litigation as required by the Contracting Officer pursuant to a clause of this contract, including furnishing evidence and information requested pursuant to the Notice and Assistance Regarding Patent and Copyright Infringement clause;
>
> (iv) The purchase and maintenance of additional insurance not in the target cost and required by the Contracting Officer, or claims for reimbursement for liabilities to third persons pursuant to the Insurance-Liability to Third Persons clause;
>
> (v) Any claim, loss, or damage resulting from a risk for which the Contractor has been relieved of liability by the Government Property clause; or
>
> (vi) Any claim, loss, or damage resulting from a risk defined in the contract as unusually hazardous or as a nuclear risk and against which the Government has expressly agreed to indemnify the Contractor.

The ASBCA has also held that certain costs not under the contractor's control should be removed from the incentive formula even though they are not enumerated in this clause. See *Federal Elec. Corp.*, ASBCA 9476, 65-1 BCA ¶ 4747, where the board held that the cost incentive formula in a CPIF contract did not cover the increased wages that resulted when the Canadian government disapproved a proposed wage decrease. The parties had negotiated the target cost anticipating that the Canadian government would approve a wage decrease, but the parties knew that such approval had not been granted at the time the contract was signed. The board adjusted the target cost of the contract to reflect the increased wages based on the following questionable reasoning found at 22,573:

> In arriving at these terms, the parties must have been aware of the fact that one of the cost elements — the wage rates to be paid the DEW line employees — was to some extent beyond their control, because it depended on the approval of the Canadian Department of Labour. While the witnesses for the parties at the hearing asserted that they did not doubt that the reduced wage rates would be approved, other testimony in the record leads to the conclusion that they must have been aware of the fact that such approval was not a certainty and might be denied. In any event, the record is clear that both parties negotiated on the basis of the wage rates proposed by the [contractor]. In the light of the goal inherent in incentive contracting it does not seem, therefore, likely or believable that two highly sophisticated parties, such as [the contractor] and ROAMA as representative of the Government, intended to, and did, enter into a cost-plus-incentive-fee contract, which would, upon the occurrence of a particular event beyond the control of either party and prior to commencement of the contract term deprive appellant automatically of a large portion of its proposed target fee.

B. Fixed-Price Incentive Contracts

The FPI contract is very similar in concept to the CPIF contract except that it contains a ceiling price in lieu of the minimum and maximum fees. FAR 16.403(a) describes this type of contract as follows:

> A fixed-price incentive contract is a fixed-price contract that provides for adjusting profit and establishing the final contract price by application of a formula based on the relationship of total final negotiated cost to total target cost. The final price is subject to a price ceiling, negotiated at the outset. The two forms of fixed-price incentive contracts, firm target and successive targets, are further described in 16.403-1 and 16.403-2 below.

Because the ceiling price requires the contractor to complete performance no matter how high the cost, this type of contract should be used only when the contracting parties can predict the costs of performance with a reasonable degree of accuracy. The FAR provides that FPI contracts are normally used to place more cost risk on contractors in order to motivate them to control costs more vigorously than they would on cost-reimbursement contracts. Thus, these regulations discuss the use of the "profit motive" as a fundamental means of inducing lower costs of performance. However, there is another use of the FPI contract — that of protecting the Government from excessive profits when a contractor will not agree to a firm-fixed-price contract at a level that the Government believes represents a fair sharing of the cost risk. See 46 Comp. Gen. 631 (B-159922) (1967), where the Comptroller General upheld a contracting officer's decision to use a FPI contract when a contractor would not agree to a firm-fixed-price at a level deemed to be fair to the Government. In both situations, the incentive contract gives the parties a means of sharing the cost risk so that neither will be seriously impacted by significant cost fluctuations from those costs projected at the outset.

The FPI contract is similar to the CPIF contract in that both provide for sharing of costs on a predetermined percentage basis. However, the FPI contract uses fixed-price clauses and contains no Limitation of Cost clause, with the result that the Government is legally obligated to pay all cost up to the ceiling price without prior notification, and the contractor is obligated to complete the work and is liable for excess costs or reprocurement or other damages if it does not. The final price of the FPI contract is established by negotiation after incurrence and audit of substantially all costs of performance, while the final costs in a CPIF contract are paid through audit determination.

There are two types of FPI contracts: the fixed-price incentive with a firm target price (FPIF) and the fixed-price incentive with successive targets (FPIS).

1. Elements of the Formula

The elements of the basic formula covering the costs of performance in the FPIF contract are:

- Target Cost
- Target Profit
- Ceiling Price
- Sharing Arrangement

The formula is expressed in contract language in the Incentive Price Revision — Firm Target clause in FAR 52.216-16, as follows:

> (a) *General.* The supplies or services identified in the Schedule as Items ________ [*Contracting Officer insert Schedule line item numbers*] are subject to price revision in accordance with this clause; *provided*, that in no event shall the total final price of these items exceed the ceiling price of ________ dollars ($_____). Any supplies or services that are to be (1) ordered separately under, or otherwise added to, this contract and (2) subject to price revision in accordance with the terms of this clause shall be identified as such in a modification to this contract.
>
> * * *
>
> (d) *Price revision.* Upon the Contracting Officer's receipt of the data required by paragraph (c) above, the Contracting Officer and the Contractor shall promptly establish the total final price of the items specified in (a) above by applying to final negotiated cost an adjustment for profit or loss, as follows:
>
> > (1) On the basis of the information required by paragraph (c) above, together with any other pertinent information, the parties shall negotiate the total final cost incurred or to be incurred for supplies delivered (or services performed) and accepted by the Government and which are subject to price revision under this clause.
> >
> > (2) The total final price shall be established by applying to the total final negotiated cost an adjustment for profit or loss, as follows:
> >
> > > (i) If the total final negotiated cost is equal to the total target cost, the adjustment is the total target profit.
> > >
> > > (ii) If the total final negotiated cost is greater than the total target cost, the adjustment is the total target profit, less ________ [*Contracting Officer insert percent*] percent of the amount by which the total final negotiated cost exceeds the total target cost.
> > >
> > > (iii) If the final negotiated cost is less than the total target cost, the adjustment is the total target profit plus _____ [*Contracting Officer insert percent*] percent of the amount by which the total final negotiated cost is less than the total target cost.

As in the CPIF contract, the contracting officer has significant discretion in establishing the elements of this FPIF formula. The range of these elements most commonly encountered is:

Target Cost	$100
Target Profit	0% to 12%
Ceiling Price	$115 to $135
Sharing Arrangement	80/20 to 60/40

Two formulas are compared in **Figure 8-4**. Guidance on negotiating formulas is contained in the DOD and NASA Incentive Contracting Guide, October 1969. See also Nash, "Incentive Contracting, Government Contracts Monograph" 7 (1963).

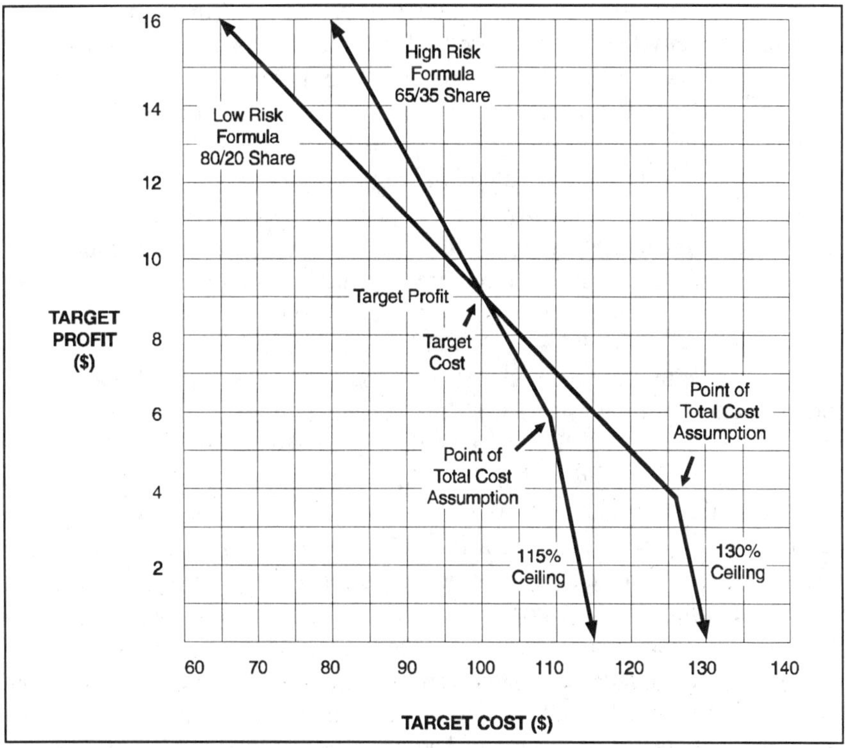

Figure 8-4

2. Negotiation and Analysis of Formulas

The procurement regulations imply that incentive formulas are established by negotiation, and this is generally the case in noncompetitive situations. In competitive procurements, this is less likely because difficulties are encountered in comparing FPI contract proposals with different sharing formulas and ceilings. The result is that in competitive solicitations requesting proposals for FPIF contracts, some procuring activities specify the profit rate, sharing percentages, and ceiling percentage above target cost. This forces all competitors to propose the same basic incentive formula and allows a valid comparison of target costs proposed by the competitors. Notwithstanding the contrary views of the Comptroller General in 46 Comp. Gen. 631 (B-159922) (1967), without such similarity, the use of target costs as the comparative number can greatly distort the comparison and lead to the selection of a contractor that is taking less cost risk than, for example, another company that has proposed a higher target cost but a lower ceiling price. See *General Elec. Co.*, Comp. Gen. Dec. B-186372, 76-2 CPD ¶ 269, for a case where the Comptroller General recognized the validity of the agency's giving more weight in the competitive evaluation to the proposed ceiling prices than to proposed targets. In this regard, it should be noted that the regulations are not directive on the amount of freedom that the RFP may give offerors in structuring their own incentive formulas. Hence, contracting officers are free to establish required formulas if they conclude proper evaluation is not otherwise possible.

Whether either the contractor or the Government establishes the formula independently or they establish it through negotiation, the pertinent considerations are essentially the same as those discussed above in considering CPIF contracts. The only element unique to FPIF contracts is the ceiling price, and this, of course, is the critical element. The first aspect of this ceiling that must be recognized is that it is a ceiling *price* — combining both cost and profit. Thus, except for price adjustments under contract clauses, it imposes an ultimate limitation on the amount the contractor will be paid for the work. As such, it should be established at a level commensurate with the ability of the parties to accurately estimate the costs of performance. In the past, ceiling prices have been negotiated as high as 150 percent of target costs in contracts where the parties had very little confidence in the accuracy of their cost estimates. However, in that situation, use of the CPIF contract is more appropriate. Thus, in normal circumstances, ceiling prices would be expected to range from 115 percent to 135 percent of the target cost.

Figure 8-4 depicts two FPI formulas — a high-risk formula,with a ceiling price of $115, and a low-risk formula, with a ceiling of $130.

In some cases, contracts have used different ceiling prices for different elements of the work. See, for example, *Reflectone, Inc.*, ASBCA 34891, 89-3 BCA ¶ 21,962, where the board ruled that the proper interpretation of contract ceiling prices was that a ceiling on the base work and another ceiling on option work were separate ceilings that were separately enforceable. Compare *Aerojet-General Corp.*, ASBCA 13548, 70-1 BCA ¶ 8245, where the board found that the contract contained a single ceiling for both development and production work. When the contract contains work using two different appropriations, as in *Aerojet-General*, it is better practice to use separate ceilings for those different elements in order to avoid any possibility that work in one area might be charged to the other appropriation.

If the contractor must incur costs exceeding the target cost to complete performance of the contract, the initial overrun will be subject to the sharing arrangement — as is the case in the CPIF contract. However, at some point, the ceiling price will force the contractor to bear *all of the extra costs* being incurred. This point is called the *point of total cost assumption* — and it is generally at a point lower than the ceiling price. This occurs because the ceiling price is usually negotiated as a percentage of target cost, not a percentage of target price. Hence, in a FPI contract such as the high-risk contract in **Figure 8-4**, the ceiling price is 115 percent of target cost but only 105.5 percent of the target price of $109. This provides very little room for the incurrence of unanticipated costs before the contractor will bear the entire burden of overruns. In this formula, the point where the agreed sharing percentage ceases to operate and all additional costs of performance are treated as they would be in a firm-fixed-price contract is at approximately 109 percent of target cost. If the parties do not have the ability to predict costs within a high degree of accuracy, the use of such a formula would impose an inordinate risk on the contractor.

The point of total cost assumption is the most important feature in the FPIF contract because it identifies the point at which the contractor's risk changes from the incentive sharing that has been negotiated to a fixed-price risk — 100 percent responsibility for costs incurred. As depicted on **Figure 8-4**, this point occurs where the share line and the ceiling line intersect, because this is the point where the ceiling overrides the sharing arrangement. Hence, the amount of ceiling is the key determinant of the point of total cost assumption. For example, in the low-risk formula in

Figure 8-4, the point of total cost assumption occurs much further from target cost — at approximately 126 percent of target cost.

3. *Successive Targets*

A less frequently used form of FPI contract is the FPIS contract. This type of contract is described in FAR 16.403-2 as follows:

> (a) *Description.* (1) A fixed-price incentive (successive targets) contract specifies the following elements, all of which are negotiated at the outset:
>
> (i) An initial target cost.
>
> (ii) An initial target profit.
>
> (iii) An initial profit adjustment formula to be used for establishing the firm target profit, including a ceiling and floor for the firm target profit. (This formula normally provides for a lesser degree of contractor cost responsibility than would a formula for establishing final profit and price.)
>
> (iv) The production point at which the firm target cost and firm target profit will be negotiated (usually before delivery or shop completion of the first item).
>
> (v) A ceiling price that is the maximum that may be paid to the contractor, except for any adjustment under other contract clauses providing for equitable adjustment or other revision of the contract price under stated circumstances.
>
> (2) When the production point specified in the contract is reached, the parties negotiate the firm target cost, giving consideration to cost experience under the contract and other pertinent factors. The firm target profit is established by the formula. At this point, the parties have two alternatives, as follows:
>
> (i) They may negotiate a firm fixed price, using the firm target cost plus the firm target profit as a guide.
>
> (ii) If negotiation of a firm fixed price is inappropriate, they may negotiate a formula for establishing the final price using the firm target cost and firm target profit. The final cost is then negotiated at comple-

> tion, and the final profit is established by formula, as under the fixed-price incentive (firm target) contract (see 16.403-1 above).

This type of contract is used when the parties do not have adequate costing or pricing information to establish firm prices at the outset but they believe that sufficiently accurate information will be available early in performance to permit the negotiation of a firm-fixed-price or a FPIF contract, FAR 16.403-2(b). The use of this type of contract is limited since it requires a significant administrative effort to conduct the two or three negotiations required. However, it does provide some flexibility in pricing long-term contracts whose performance period will extend over two or more years. The initial formula in this contract is established using the same logic as that used in negotiating the FPIF contract with a firm target but it is expected that the ceiling price would be quite high and the sharing arrangement would impose a modest share on the contractor, to reflect that the parties do not have the ability to accurately predict the cost of performance at the outset.

C. Performance and Delivery Incentives

Objective incentives have also been applied to contract performance requirements (such as weight of an item, thrust of an engine, or speed of a vehicle) and to contract delivery requirements (such as date of delivery or date of meeting a contract milestone for some intermediate task). When these incentives are used on incentive contracts, that contain must contain an incentive on cost, FAR 16.402-1(a).

Primarily used in development contracts, where they originated, objective performance and delivery incentives can be structured in many different ways. For example, they have been written both to give additional profit and to reduce profit on a single element of performance or delivery. They can also be written to provide for specific dollar bonuses or penalties for accomplishing or failing to accomplish a performance or delivery goal. Objective incentives should be contrasted with other types of provisions used by Government agencies to motivate technical or schedule performances. These other types of provisions are most frequently called "liquidated damages," requiring fixed compensation to the Government for a contractor's failure to meet contract requirements — usually specified delivery or completion dates. See FAR Subpart 11.5 for guidance on the use of such clauses pertaining to the time of delivery or performance. While not termed "incentives," bonuses or rewards are also occasionally used in contracts that may or may not contain required compensation for inferior performance. FAR 16.402-2 gives the following guidance on the use of technical performance incentives:

> (a) Technical performance incentives may be considered in connection with specific product characteristics (e.g., a missile range, an aircraft speed, an engine thrust, or a vehicle maneuverability) or other specific elements of the contractor's performance. These incentives should be designed to tailor profit or fee to results achieved by the contractor, compared with specified target goals.
>
> (b) Technical performance incentives may be particularly appropriate in major systems contracts, both in development (when performance objectives are known and the fabrication of prototypes for test and evaluation is required) and in production (if improved performance is attainable and highly desirable to the Government).

FAR 16.402-3 provides guidance on the use of delivery incentives:

> (a) Delivery incentives should be considered when improvement from a required delivery schedule is a significant Government objective. It is important to determine the Government's primary objectives in a given contract (e.g., earliest possible delivery or earliest quantity production).

Performance and delivery incentives have been used in many contracts. In some instances, they were used to balance cost incentives, attempting to ensure that the contractor did not overemphasize low costs to the detriment of performance. The FAR emphasizes the use of incentives for a different purpose: to focus attention on specific important performance and delivery objectives of the Government.

1. *Enforceability of Clauses*

Traditionally, liquidated damages clauses have been enforceable only if they do not assess a "penalty" for nonperformance. See *Priebe & Sons, Inc. v. United States*, 332 U.S. 407 (1947), applying this rule to a Government contract and stating that such clauses would not be enforced where they were "included not to make a fair estimate of damages to be suffered but to serve only as an added spur to performance." This rule has been uniformly applied to provisions specifically termed "liquidated damages" clauses. The fundamental test that has been used to determine whether the clause provides for a "penalty" is whether the amount assessed was a reasonable forecast of damages at the time of entering into the contract, *DJ Mfg. Corp. v. United States*, 86 F.3d 1130 (Fed. Cir. 1996); *Southwest Eng'g Co. v. United States*, 341 F.2d 998 (8th Cir.), *cert. denied*, 382 U.S. 819 (1965); *International Elec. Corp. v. United States*, 227 Ct. Cl. 208, 646 F.2d 496 (1981).

These principles would appear to be directly applicable to any performance or delivery incentive clause written in terms of a penalty for failure to meet the contract requirement, since in very few cases would the Government be able to show that such penalties were a reasonable approximation of actual damage. No court or board decision has considered this issue concerning performance incentives. However, in *Fairchild Camera & Instrument Corp.*, ASBCA 12291, 68-2 BCA ¶ 7327, the board ruled that a delivery incentive clause has a "distinct legal identity" from a liquidated damages clause. The board stated that no reasonable forecast of damages was necessary and that the clause was enforceable as a binding agreement between the parties.

The penalty rule has been applied to contract clauses that are not termed liquidated damages clauses but that assess compensation for delinquent performance. For example, in *JMNI, Inc. v. United States*, 4 Cl. Ct. 310 (1984), the court refused to enforce a clause calling for a "payment adjustment factor" that reduced the contract payment on a pro rata basis for units of work up to 15 percent delinquent and provided for no payment for a unit that was more than 15 percent delinquent. The court found that this clause was in the nature of a liquidated damages clause and that the nonpayment for over 15 percent delinquency was a penalty and not a reasonable forecast of damages. See also *Work Force Reforestation, Inc.*, AGBCA 90-132-3, 90-3 BCA ¶ 23,233; and *Charley O. Estes*, IBCA 1198-7-78, 84-1 BCA ¶ 17,073. Similarly, in *Linda Vista Indus., Inc.*, Comp. Gen. Dec. B-214447, 84-2 CPD ¶ 380, the Comptroller General applied the liquidated damages rule to a Contractor's Failure to Perform clause that called for nonpayment for an entire cleaning item if the contractor failed to perform any part of the cleaning services required for that item. See also *Environmental Aseptic Servs. Admin.*, 62 Comp. Gen. 219 (B-207771), 83-1 CPD ¶ 194, finding a Performance Requirements Summary clause to be a penalty clause because it permitted nonpayment for the cleaning of an entire room when only one cleaning task was poorly performed, and *Wackenhut Corp.*, IBCA 2311,

91-1 BCA ¶ 23,318, finding a clause assessing a "penalty" of 1 percent of the price per day unenforceable.

2. Structuring Practices

The procurement regulations contain no specific guidance on the structuring of performance and delivery incentives. FAR 16.402-2 contains the following general guidance on writing technical performance incentives:

> (c) Technical performance incentives may involve a variety of specific characteristics that contribute to the overall performance of the end item. Accordingly, the incentives on individual technical characteristics must be balanced so that no one of them is exaggerated to the detriment of the overall performance of the end item.
>
> (d) Performance tests are generally essential in order to determine the degree of attainment of performance targets. Therefore, the contract must be as specific as possible in establishing test criteria such as testing conditions, instrumentation precision, and data interpretation.
>
> (e) Because performance incentives present complex problems in contract administration, the contracting officer should negotiate them in full coordination with Government engineering and pricing specialists.
>
> (f) It is essential that the Government and contractor agree explicitly on the effect that contract changes (e.g., pursuant to the Changes clause) will have on performance incentives.
>
> (g) The contracting officer must exercise care, in establishing performance criteria, to recognize that the contractor should not be rewarded or penalized for attainments of Government-furnished components.

FAR 16.402-3 contains only the following provision on delivery incentives:

> (b) Incentive arrangements on delivery should specify the application of the reward-penalty structure in the event of Government-caused delays or other delays beyond the control, and without the fault or negligence, of the contractor or subcontractor.

See also DFARS 216.402-2, stating that such incentives "should relate to specific performance areas or milestones, such as delivery or test schedules, quality controls, maintenance requirements, and reliability standards."

Since performance and delivery incentives are always used in conjunction with cost incentives, they are usually written in terms of bonuses and penalties for deviations from contractually specified targets. Such a formula is depicted in **Figure 8-5** using the following factors:

Target Weight	100 lbs.
Target Fee	$0
Maximum Fee	$3
Minimum Fee	$3
Sharing Arrangement	$1 fee/3 lb. Weight

In this case, the sharing occurs over a range of 18 pounds of weight (from 91 pounds to 109 pounds), and the bonus or penalty earned is added to or deducted from the profit or fee that results from the application of the incentive formula on costs of performance. The DFARS no longer contains any detailed guidance on the structuring of performance and delivery incentives. Prior to 1991, however, DFARS 16.402-2(S-70) contained the following guidance on the levels of performance that should be used to set the fee levels:

> "Performance," as used in this paragraph, refers not only to the performance of the article being procured, but to the performance of the contractor as well. Performance which is the minimum which the Government will accept shall be mandatory under the terms of the Completion form contract and shall warrant only the minimum profit or fee related thereto. Performance which meets the stated targets will warrant the "target" profit or fee. The incentive feature (providing for increases or decreases, as appropriate) is applied to performance targets rather than performance requirements.

Following this guidance, incentives should never be used in ranges of performance and delivery that the Government is not willing to accept as meeting the contract requirements.

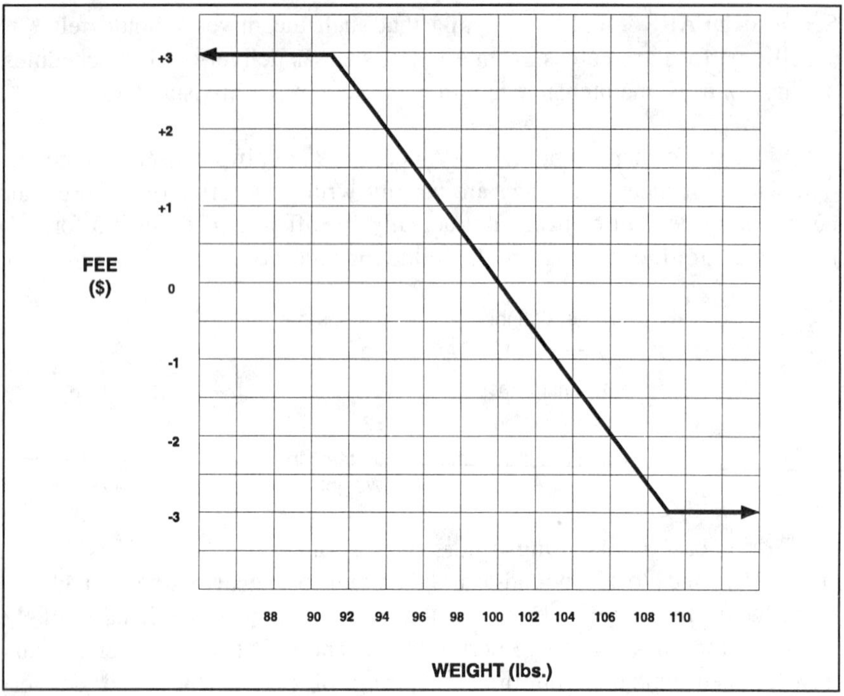

Figure 8-5

NASA requires the use of performance incentives on all contracts for deliverable hardware over $25 million, unless the hardware is commercial, and permits their use on contracts of lesser amounts, NFS 1816.402-270(a). NASA has promulgated the following standard clause for performance incentives in NFS 1852.216-88:

PERFORMANCE INCENTIVE (JAN 1997)

(a) A performance incentive applies to the following hardware item(s) delivered under this contract: (1).

The performance incentive will measure the performance of those items against the salient hardware performance requirement, called "unit(s) of measurement," e.g., months in service or amount of data transmitted, identified below. The performance incentive becomes effective when the hardware is put into service. It includes a standard performance level, a positive incentive, and a negative incentive, which are described in this clause.

(b) Standard performance level. At the standard performance level, the Contractor has met the contract requirement for the unit of measurement. Neither positive nor negative incentives apply when this level is achieved but not exceeded. The standard performance level for (1) __ is established as follows: (2).

(c) Positive incentive. The Contractor earns a separate positive incentive amount for each hardware item listed in paragraph (a) of this clause when the standard performance level for that item is exceeded. The amount earned for each item varies with the units of measurement achieved, up to a maximum positive performance incentive amount of $ (3) __ per item. The units of measurement and the incentive amounts associated with achieving each unit are shown below: (4).

(d) Negative incentive. The Contractor will pay to the Government a negative incentive amount for each hardware item that fails to achieve the standard performance level. The amount to be paid for each item varies with the units of measurement achieved, up to the maximum negative incentive amount of $ (5) __. The units of measurement and the incentive amounts associated with achieving each unit are shown below: (6).

(e) The final calculation of positive or negative performance incentive amounts shall be done when performance (as defined by the unit of measurement) ceases or when the maximum positive incentive is reached.

> (1) When the Contracting Officer determines that the performance level achieved fell below the standard performance level, the Contractor will either pay the amount due the Government or credit the next payment voucher for the amount due, as directed by the Contracting Officer.
>
> (2) When the performance level exceeds the standard level, the Contractor may request payment of the incentive amount associated with a given level of performance, provided that such payments shall not be more frequent than monthly. When performance ceases or the maximum positive incentive is reached, the Government shall calculate the final performance incentive earned and unpaid and promptly remit it to the contractor.

(f) If performance cannot be demonstrated, through no fault of the Contractor, within ______ (*insert number of months or years*) after the date of hardware acceptance by the Government, the Contractor will be paid (*insert percentage*) of the maximum performance incentive.

(g) The decisions made as to the amount(s) of positive or negative incentives are subject to the Disputes clause.

(1) Insert applicable item number(s) and/or nomenclature.

(2) Insert a specific unit of measurement for each hardware item listed in (1) and each salient characteristic, if more than one.

(3) Insert the maximum positive performance incentive amount (see 1816.402 -270(e)(1) and (2)).

(4) Insert all units of measurement and associated dollar amounts up to the maximum performance incentive.

(5) Insert the appropriate amount, in accordance with 1816.402-270(e).

(6) Insert all units of measurement and associated dollar amounts up to the maximum negative performance incentive.

NFS 1816.402-270 provides the following guidance on structuring such performance incentives:

(b) When a performance incentive is used, it shall be structured to be both positive and negative based on hardware performance after delivery and acceptance. In doing so, the contract shall establish a standard level of performance based on the salient hardware performance requirement. This standard performance level is normally the contract's minimum performance requirement. No incentive amount is earned at this standard performance level. Discrete units of measurement based on the same performance parameter shall be identified for performance both above and below the standard. Specific incentive amounts shall be associated with each performance level from maximum beneficial performance (maximum positive incentive) to minimal beneficial performance or total failure (maximum negative incentive). The relationship between any given incentive, both positive and negative, and its associated unit of measurement should reflect the value to the Government of that level of hardware performance. The contractor should not be rewarded for above-standard performance levels that are of no benefit to the Government.

(c) The final calculation of the performance incentive shall be done when performance, as defined in the contract, ceases or when the maximum positive incentive is reached. When the performance ceases below the standard established in the contract, the Government shall calculate the amount due and the contractor shall pay the Government that amount. Once hardware performance exceeds the standard, the contractor may request payment of the incentive amount associated with a given level of performance, provided that such payments shall not be more frequent than monthly. When hardware performance ceases above the standard level of performance, or when the maximum positive incentive is reached, the Government shall calculate the final performance incentive earned and unpaid and promptly remit it to the contractor. The exclusion at FAR 16.405(e)(3) does not apply to decisions made as to the amount(s) of positive or negative incentive.

(d) When the deliverable hardware lends itself to multiple, meaningful measures of performance, multiple performance incentives may be established. When the contract requires the sequential delivery of several hardware items (e.g., multiple spacecraft), separate performance incentive structures may be established to parallel the sequential delivery and use of the deliverables.

It is also possible to create performance and delivery incentives in terms of a single bonus or penalty to be paid or deducted upon the meeting or missing of a target. This type of incentive is used most frequently in the case of performance milestones where the contract contains a series of bonuses to be paid upon the meeting of each milestone. Such an incentive combines both performance and delivery incentives because the bonus is paid only if the contractor performs the required work in accordance with the specifications at the time called for. There has been some criticism of this type of incentive because it gives the contractor additional profit when performance is no better than that called for by the contract. If contract requirements are demanding, however, and if the performance and delivery incentive motivates the contractor to perform well, there should be no objection to this type of incentive.

When performance or delivery incentives are used, the contract should include specific provisions defining conditions that must be met for the contractor to earn the bonus or suffer the loss called for by an incentive clause. One issue that should be addressed is the effect on performance incentives of Government failure to fund an overrun on a CPIF contract. In such a case, for example, the contractor may not be able to conduct a test program to demonstrate that a performance incentive has been earned. See, for example, *North Am. Rockwell Corp.*, ASBCA 14329, 72-1 BCA ¶ 9207, where the board held that because the contractor submitted convincing evidence that the product met the weight requirement earning the maximum bonus on a weight incentive, a pro rata share of that bonus, commensurate with the percentage of completion of the contract, should be paid. The board reasoned at 42,724:

> We find no merit in the Government's argument that the performance incentive provision does not come into operation unless and until the Government accepts the tank as meeting all contract requirements. The performance incentive provision was written in contemplation of full contract performance and does not cover the situation where the contractor exercises its right to stop work before full performance because of the Government's refusal to allot the additional funds necessary for full performance. When the contractor exercises its right to stop work after failure of the Government to add funds necessary for the completion of the contract, this has the practical effect of terminating the contract for the convenience of the Government as to any work remaining to be done under the contract. Under the standard termination clause included in the contract, when the contract is terminated for the convenience of the Government before completion, the contractor is entitled to be paid "the percentage of the fee equivalent to the percentage of the completion of the work contemplated by the contract." The performance incentive provision should be interpreted in conjunction with the termination clause when the contract work is stopped before completion due to the failure of the Government to add sufficient funds for its completion.

There may also be difficulties in specifying the precise tests to be used to determine when each performance incentive has been met. This was an issue in *Western Elec. Co.*, ASBCA 16110, 73-1 BCA ¶ 10,013, where the bonus was to be paid if a missile passed through a point under guidance control. The board ruled that the contractor had earned the bonus even though the missile engine failed prior to reaching the specified point, since the missile did in fact pass through the point and the guidance system functioned sufficiently well before engine failure.

3. Relationship of Incentive to Other Provisions

In drafting CPIF contracts with performance and delivery incentives, great care must be exercised to ensure that the relationship of these incentives to other contract provisions is clearly defined. Thus, the relationship of performance incentives to the inspection and warranty clauses in the contract must be stated. Contractors failing to meet performance goals may also fail to meet specification requirements, but the penalties for these two failures are quite different. The performance incentive formula calls for a profit or fee reduction when performance goals are not met, while other provisions of the contract allow the contracting officer to reject the work, require rework until specifications are met, or even terminate the contract for default. Many contracts containing performance incentives do not spell out the rights of the parties, but in most contracting situations it is clear that the parties do not intend to provide a double remedy for the Government. This issue should be addressed and resolved by specific contract language. In general, such language would state that the *sole remedy* to be assessed when the performance falls in the RIE would be the penalty under the performance incentive clause. This is logical when, as in the case of the DOD, the Government does not include unacceptable ranges of performance within the incentive provision. If, as in the case of NASA, the performance incentive includes failure of an item of hardware, it is logical to conclude that the negative incentive has been calculated to include the damages that the Government will suffer.

In the case of delivery incentives, the contract should include explicit language stating the relationship of the incentive to excusable delays. FAR 16.402-3(b) requires that this issue be addressed in the contract but gives no guidance as to the preferred agreement. In many cases, contracting officers have included contract language providing that the date for calculation of the delivery incentive will be extended for excusable delays. In CPIF contracts, this is generally accomplished by keying the incentive bonus or penalty to the Excusable Delays clause in FAR 52.249-14, which is included in all cost-reimbursement contracts. This clause provides for schedule adjustments for excusable delays; and the contract language would state that such adjustments would occur prior to the computation of the incentive bonus or penalty. In FPI contracts, the incentive bonus or penalty must be keyed to Paragraph (c) of the Default (Fixed-Price Supply and Service) clause in FAR 52.249-8, and the special contract clause should explicitly provide that the contractor will be granted a time extension for excusable delays (the Default clause contains no such language). Even if there is no such contract provision, it may be held that such is the proper interpretation of the total contract, *North Am. Aviation, Inc.*, ASBCA 11603, 68-1 BCA ¶ 6998 (CPIF contract); *General Precision, Inc.*, ASBCA 11071, 66-2 BCA ¶ 5904 (FPI contract). See, however, *Sosedil-Pizzarotti*, ASBCA 31135, 89-2 BCA ¶ 21,807, where the board enforced clear contract language stating that "no time extensions shall be allowed for the purpose of payment under the bonus clause provisions."

4. *Interrelationship With Cost Incentives*

When performance and delivery incentives are used in incentive contracts, any increased costs incurred to achieve better performance or avoid a performance and delivery penalty will be chargeable to the contract and subject to sharing. Thus, if the contractor incurs more labor-hours or uses more expensive labor or material in attempting to enhance performance, such costs will be shared by the Government to the extent that the costs are reasonable and within the RIE. In addition, the contractor has considerable latitude in selecting techniques to motivate employees. See *Celesco Indus., Inc.*, ASBCA 20569, 77-1 BCA ¶ 12,445, *sustained on other grounds*, 77-2 BCA ¶ 12,585, where the contractor established an internal incentive program to motivate its employees that used the entire performance incentive bonus for successful missile flights. After earning $70,500, which was distributed to the employees, the contractor claimed the amount as an allowable cost. The Government argued that the cost was unallowable since it was a distribution of profit, but the board ruled that the employee bonuses were reasonable compensation under the Cost Principles. Compare *Petroleum Operations & Support Servs., Inc.*, EBCA 291-6-83, 85-2 BCA ¶ 18,037, denying the allowability of bonuses paid on a CPAF contract because they did not comply with the Cost Principles.

One important aspect of performance and delivery incentives is that they create a value structure, within the incentive formula, that states the value of each performance and delivery factor in the formula. For example, if the weight incentive in **Figure 8-5** is used on a contract containing the cost incentive in **Figure 8-1**, the two sharing arrangements tell the contractor the value of weight savings. The value is determined by equating each incentive to the fee bonus or penalty to be derived from the formula. Thus, the contractor will incur a fee bonus or penalty of $1 for each three pounds of weight variance and each $5 of cost variance. The result is that the incentive formula tells the contractor that the Government places a value of $5 on a three pound weight savings, as long as each savings occurs within the RIE. From this information the contractor could be expected to make decisions on weight reduction efforts based on the cost of the reduction. If it was probable that a weight reduction of three pounds could be achieved at a cost of less than $5, the contractor would be expected to spend the funds (in an attempt to achieve the weight reduction) and increase its total fee on the contract. Thus, the formula contains an unexpressed tradeoff for each performance and delivery incentive, where fee can be maximized by spending or saving money. In some cases, this tradeoff situation is not fully thought through at the time the formula is written, with the result that the contractor may take actions during contract performance that are not desired by the Government.

FAR 16.402-4 recognizes this issue but gives the following minimal guidance:

> A properly structured multiple-incentive arrangement should —
>
> (a) Motivate the contractor to strive for outstanding results in all incentive areas; and
>
> (b) Compel tradeoff decisions among the incentive areas, consistent with the Government's overall objectives for the acquisition. Because of the interdependency of the Government's cost, the technical performance, and the delivery goals, a contract that emphasizes only one of the goals may jeopardize control over the others. Because outstanding results may not be attainable for each of the incentive areas, all multiple-incentive contracts must include a cost incentive (or constraint) that operates to preclude rewarding a contractor for superior technical performance or delivery results when the cost of those results outweighs their value to the Government.

This requirement is generally implemented in one of two ways. First, in the ideal situation, performance and delivery incentives are structured on the basis of the Government's tradeoff analysis. For example, in the weight incentive discussed above, the contracting officer determines from consultation with agency technical personnel that the value of weight savings is at least $5 for three pounds. The incentive arrangement is then structured to reflect this Government tradeoff judgment. Second, special contract clauses are used to prevent incentive awards when they are not desired by the Government. For example, if the contracting officer has determined that weight savings are of value only if the contractor does not overrun the target cost of the contract, a special clause will provide that no bonuses will be paid for the performance incentive on weight if there is a cost overrun. These clauses should be used judiciously, however, since they cancel out the performance and delivery incentives in the specified range of cost.

Better regulatory guidance would permit use of performance and delivery incentives only when the Government can identify the specific value of enhanced performance or avoidance of performance reductions and has determined that such results are worth additional costs. If this policy were followed, the Government would be assured that the contractor was not being motivated to overrun the contract in situations where the Government did not desire enhanced performance.

D. Cost-Plus-Award-Fee Contracts

The CPAF contract was devised by NASA in the 1960s to introduce incentives for improved performance into major contracts for support services. Since that time it has become one of the major types of contracts used for service contracts including R&D. The CPAF contract provides that the contractor's fee will be determined largely by an award given periodically by a high-ranking official in the procuring agency. While the basic elements to be evaluated in arriving at this award and the evaluation mechanism itself are usually disclosed to the contractor prior to performance, this type of contract is known as a "subjective" incentive since the award official has a significant amount of discretion in establishing the precise amount of award. This subjectivity has led some contractors to question the use of this type of incentive, but experience gathered over the past three decades indicates that CPAF contracts are quite effective in situations where it is not possible to write a contract specification or work statement that contains a precise description of the work the contractor is expected to perform.

FAR 16.405-2(a) describes this type of contract as follows:

> A cost-plus-award-fee contract is a cost-reimbursement contract that provides for a fee consisting of (1) a base amount fixed at inception of the contract and (2) an award amount that the contractor may earn in whole or in part during performance and that is sufficient to provide motivation for excellence in such areas as quality, timeliness, technical ingenuity, and cost-effective management. The amount of the award fee to be paid is determined by the Government's judgmental evaluation of the Contractor's performance in terms of the criteria stated in the contract. This determination is made unilaterally by the Government and is not subject to the Disputes clause.

The major advantage of the CPAF contract is improved communication between the parties. In the course of making periodic awards, the Government gives the contractor a detailed evaluation of performance, pointing out deficiencies and weaknesses. As a result, the contractor is able to improve performance as work proceeds or persuade the Government that the Government's analysis is incorrect. In either case, the contracting parties are forced to analyze performance on a regular basis and communicate with each other regarding any problems. From the contractor's point of view, the CPAF contract has also been advantageous in that it has frequently yielded higher fees than the CPFF contract.

The major disadvantage of the CPAF contract is that substantial administrative costs are incurred through the continual evaluations and the processing of award decisions. Expanding the evaluation periods can ameliorate this situation, but the CPAF contract inherently calls for a significant amount of paperwork. It has been suggested that the internal evaluation effort is not significantly greater than the work a well-staffed program management office does in its regular evaluation of a development contractor's performance, but even when the evaluation is done by a program management office, the paperwork is increased substantially. Of course, this added paperwork leads to the enhanced communication that is the strength of the CPAF contract. An agency should recognize, however, the demands that this type of contract places on its staff and limit the use of CPAF contracts to situations where the size and importance of the work justify the expenditure of such resources.

Another disadvantage noted by some commentators is the potential for the CPAF contractor to follow Government directions without challenge. Evaluators are normally the Government personnel monitoring the contractor's performance, and the contractor's reaction may be to follow an evaluator's direction in order to earn a higher award fee. This disadvantage can be overcome by carefully selecting Government evaluators, ensuring that they have sufficient technical and management expertise and judgment to make sound decisions. Full participation of the contractor in the award process is also helpful in ensuring that sound decisions are made in evaluating the contractor's performance.

A disadvantage identified in the 1990s was the tendency of some Government evaluators to give high ratings to contractors that had not performed the work well. This apparently occurred on long-standing CPAF contracts where the evaluators had become accustomed to working with the contractor over a number of years. This disadvantage may result from the burdensome nature of the administrative effort demanded by this type of contract. One result of this disadvantage was NASA's adoption of more stringent requirements for the use of this type of contract, NFS 1816.404-270. Under this regulation, award fee provisions may be used only when a contractor's effort cannot "be objectively measured in terms of technical and quality achievement, schedule progress or cost performance." In addition, such provisions are to be used only in contracts over $2 million per year with the approval by the procurement officer.

1. Structuring the Award Fee

The elements of a CPAF contract are as follows:

- Estimated Cost
- Base Fee
- Maximum Fee
- Award Periods

The difference between the base fee and the maximum fee is the *award fee pool* available for award to the contractor on the basis of the periodic evaluations of its performance. This award fee pool is allocated to the award periods, and each award is made in accordance with the evaluation criteria provided in the contract.

The estimated cost in the CPAF contract is negotiated in the same manner as the target cost in the CPIF contract, based on the parties' best estimate of the expected cost of performance. The other elements of the CPAF contract are established through negotiation, if the contract is awarded as a sole source contract, or on the basis of competitive proposals, if the contract is awarded under competitive procedures. In the latter case, it is quite common for the Government to permit offerors to propose CPAF structures and consider the adequacy of the proposed structures in evaluating competing sources. It has been held proper for an agency to downgrade a proposal for offering a structure that does not meet the agency's needs as stated in the RFP, *Management & Technical Servs. Co.*, Comp. Gen. Dec. B-209513, 82-2 CPD ¶ 571 (proposed base fee and maximum fee too high); *Management Servs., Inc.*, Comp. Gen. Dec. B-206364, 82-2 CPD ¶ 164 (proposed awards too high for levels of performance, and proposed employee bonuses for very high levels of performance found to be a disincentive for such performance). It has also been held proper for an agency to request assurances of "cost containment," which induced the competitors to propose cost ceilings, *Hughes Space & Communications Co.*, Comp. Gen. Dec. B-266225.6, 96-1 CPD ¶ 199.

a. Base Fee

The base fee is the minimum dollar amount of fee that a contractor can earn on a CPAF contract. By using the concept of a base fee rather than a target fee, the Government has made the decision that all the incentive will be in the form of awards (no penalties). Thus, the base fee is comparable to the minimum fee in the CPIF contract. DFARS 216.404-2(c)(2)(B) states that the base fee shall not exceed 3 percent of estimated cost. NASA used base fees for many years; but in 1993, NFS 1816.404-271 was issued prohibiting base fees where the award fee evaluation was "final," such as on service contracts (in effect, requiring a zero base fee). This regulation further states that on other CPAF contracts the base fee cannot exceed 3 percent. DEAR 915.972 provides that base fees should not exceed 50 percent of the fixed fee that would have been negotiated on a CPFF contract. The regulations of other agencies contain no maximum amount for the base fee, and in the past, base fees have ranged from zero to 5 percent. Many contracts have used base fees of 2 percent of estimated cost.

Base fees in the range of 2 to 3 percent do little more than guarantee the contractor against loss, since such base fees are roughly equivalent to normal cost disallowances. In practice, significant awards are usually earned on CPAF contracts, with the result that there is only modest risk that the contractor will be required to perform the work for the base fee.

b. Maximum Fee

Prior to 1997, the controlling requirement with regard to the maximum fee in a CPAF contract was that this fee could not exceed the statutory limitation on CPFF contracts. This requirement was deleted from the FAR by FAC 97-02, September 30, 1997, with the result that the contracting officer is now permitted to negotiate any maximum fee necessary to accomplish the purpose of the contract. In *CACI, Inc.-Fed.*, 64 Comp. Gen. 439 (B-216516.2), 85-1 CPD ¶ 363, the Comptroller General ruled that the maximum fee should be computed as a percentage of contract estimated cost and not realistic cost as determined by the agency. In *CACI*, the realistic cost was lower, but the agency did not negotiate down the estimated cost to match the realistic cost.

Whether the procurement is sole source or competitive, the base fee and the maximum fee can be established by the procuring agency's either specifying precise percentages in the RFP or permitting the offeror to propose the levels. For example, in *Holmes & Narver Inc.*, Comp. Gen. Dec. B-196832, 80-1 CPD ¶ 134, the Comptroller General affirmed the propriety of an RFP provision permitting offerors to propose any maximum fee up to 10 percent. The maximum fee, of course, is an important competitive factor since it places a ceiling on the Government's expenditures in this part of the contract. In theory, a low maximum fee is disadvantageous to the Government because by reducing the amount of fee available for award purposes, the contractor's incentive to better its performance is also reduced; the Comptroller General did not, however, consider this aspect of the situation. Similarly, in *Management & Technical Servs. Co.*, Comp. Gen. Dec. B-209513, 82-2 CPD ¶ 571, the Comptroller General did not object to an RFP provision permitting offerors to propose both the base fee and the maximum fee and making these elements of the CPAF structure evaluation factors. Compare *CACI, Inc.-Fed.*, Comp. Gen. Dec. B-216516, 84-2 CPD ¶ 542, where the agency also permitted the offerors to propose any level of base and award fees within the regulatory maximum but stated that fee levels would not be evaluated in the source selection process. The Comptroller affirmed this procedure even though the competitors offered different base and award fee levels. Not surprisingly, all of the competitors proposed a maximum fee of 10 percent since the level was not to be evaluated. This gave the agency the maximum amount of incentive fee on the contract and provided significant award fee pools for the competing contractors.

c. Award Periods

FAR 16.405-2(b)(3) contains the following guidance on the evaluation periods:

> Cost-plus-award-fee contracts shall provide for evaluation at stated intervals during performance, so that the contractor will periodically be informed of the quality of its performance and the areas in which improvement is expected. Partial payment of fee shall generally correspond to the evaluation periods. This makes effective the incentive which the award fee can create by inducing the contractor to improve poor performance or to continue good performance.

Originally, NASA used three-month evaluation periods, but the administrative effort necessary for evaluations was too great to be performed satisfactorily in such short periods. Subsequently, agencies have normally used either four- or six-month evaluation periods. See, for example, NFS 1816.404-272, calling for periods of at least six months but permitting shorter periods when the "additional administrative costs . . . are balanced by benefits accruing to the Government." Clearly, the period should be long enough to permit fee award well before the end of the next evaluation period. This permits the contractor to use the agency evaluation of its performance to better its performance in the following period. It is also possible to use award periods of varying length if the amount of work done in some periods of performance is substantially less than in others. For example, in an R&D contract where the initial effort is small, the contracting officer might specify a six-month award period for the initial period, followed by four-month periods thereafter. In service contracts, since the work is usually level over the life of the contract, the award periods are generally of the same duration.

Evaluation periods can also be established in terms of contractual milestones rather than calendar periods. See NFS 1816.404-272(a), suggesting this technique but stating that such periods must be no longer than 12 months. This would be appropriate in a situation where the contractor was performing critical tests or design reviews on the work under the contract and the evaluation would not be accurate until completion of the tests or reviews.

d. Allocation of Award Fee

The award fee pool must be allocated to award periods to provide a maximum award fee for each period. See NFS 1816.405-272(b), stating:

> A portion of the total available award fee shall be allocated to each of the evaluation periods. This allocation may result in either an equal or unequal distribution of fee among the periods. The contracting officer should consider the nature of each contract and the incentive effects of fee distribution in determining the appropriate allocation structure.

Several agencies have adopted clauses on this issue. See the following clause at TAR 1252.216-73:

DISTRIBUTION OF AWARD FEE (OCT 1994)

(a) The total amount of award fee available under this contract is assigned according to the following evaluation periods and amounts:

Evaluation Period:

Available Award Fee

(insert appropriate information)

(b) Payment of the base fee and award fee shall be made, provided that after payment of 85 percent of the base fee and potential award fee, the Government may withhold further payment of the base fee and award fee until a reserve is set aside in an amount that the Government considers necessary to protect its interest. This reserve shall not exceed 15 percent of the total base fee and potential award fee or $100,000, whichever is less.

(c) In the event of contract termination, either in whole or in part, the amount of award fee available shall represent a prorata distribution associated with evaluation period activities or events as determined by the Government.

(d) The Government will promptly make payment of any award fee upon the submission by the contractor to the contracting officer's authorized representative, of a public voucher or invoice in the amount of the total fee earned for the period evaluated. Payment may be without using a contract modification.

A similar clause is included in HUDAR 2452.216-74 and was included in DEAR 916.405(e) until 1996.

The total award fee is generally distributed to the award periods in rough proportion to the amount of costs to be spent in each period. However, the importance of the work in each period should also be considered in making this allocation. The NASA Guidance on Award Fee Contracting, June 1989 (NASA 1989 Guidance), suggested that a portion of the award fee pool could be allocated to specific events such as tests or demonstrations and that this portion need not be put in a specific award period:

Tests, demonstrations, and other milestones or events are subject to possible slippage. To eliminate the need for a reallocation of award fee potential, it may be a good idea to allocate any portion of the award fee earmarked for

> such milestones or events to whatever evaluation periods the milestones or events ultimately occur, rather than allocating to a specific period.

Some agencies have followed a practice of supplementing the award fee pool by adding award fees not earned in earlier periods to the pool available for awards in later periods. The NASA 1989 Guidance called this technique "rollover" or "rollforward" and gave the following guidance:

> The determination whether to permit a rollover of unearned award fee should be based upon an analysis of the work effort, the planned allocation of the award fee potential, and the likely effect on contractor motivation. Generally speaking, an automatic rollover of unearned award fee from one evaluation period to the next should be avoided, because it tends to reduce the effectiveness of the incentive in the current period. Instead, when rollover authority is desired, consideration should be given to providing in the evaluation plan for the exercise of that authority at the discretion of the designated Fee Determination Official.

The use of this technique in service contracts has now been prohibited by NASA, NFS 1816.404-273(a), but authority to use it is provided in the Determination of Award Fee Earned clause (used by DOT and HUD), which is discussed below. Caution must be exercised to ensure that use of this procedure does not produce excessively large amounts of award fee in the later award periods.

NASA uses provisional interim award fees when the final outcome of performance cannot be determined until completion of the work under the contract. See NFS 1816.405-273, stating:

> (a) Award fee evaluations are either interim or final. On contracts where the contract deliverable is the performance of a service over any given time period, contractor performance is often definitively measurable within each evaluation period. In these cases, all evaluations are final, and the contractor keeps the fee earned in any period regardless of the evaluations of subsequent periods. Unearned award fee in any given period in a service contract is lost and shall not be carried forward, or "rolled-over," into subsequent periods.
>
> (b) On other contracts, such as those for end item deliverables where the true quality of contractor performance cannot be measured until the end of the contract, only the last evaluation is final. At that point, the total contract award fee pool is available, and the contractor's total performance is evaluated against the award fee plan to determine total earned award fee. In ad-

dition, interim evaluations are done to monitor performance prior to contract completion and provide feedback to the contractor on the Government's assessment of the quality of its performance. Interim evaluations are also used to establish the basis for making interim award fee payments. These interim payments are superseded by the fee determination made in the final evaluation at contract completion. The Government will then pay the contractor, or the contractor will refund to the Government, the difference between the final award fee determination and the cumulative interim fee payment.

(c) Provisional award fee payments, i.e., payments made within evaluation periods, may be included in the contract and should be negotiated on a case-by-case basis. The amount of the provisional award fee payment is determined by applying the lesser of the prior period's interim evaluation score (see 1816.405-275) or 80 percent of the fee allocated to the current period. The provisional award fee payments are superseded by the fee determinations made at the conclusion of each award fee performance period.

(d) The Fee Determination Official's rating for both interim and final evaluations will be provided to the contractor within 45 calendar days of the end of the period being evaluated. Any fee, interim or final, due to the contractor will be paid no later than 60 calendar days after the end of the period being evaluated.

(e) Interim and final evaluations may be used to provide past performance information during the source selection process and should be marked and controlled as "Source Selection Information."

These provisional award fees are implemented in the Award Fee for Non-Service Contracts clause in NFS 1852.216-77.

e. Payment of Fee

No standard FAR clause governs the payment of base and award fees. However, FAR 16.405(e) directs agencies to use "appropriate" award fee clauses. Thus, the agencies follow different policies on the payment of these fees. The NASA 1989 Guidance called for monthly payment of a pro rata share of the base fee and prompt payment of award fees as soon as the award was made. The current NASA clauses, Award Fee for Service Contracts at NFS 1852.216-76 and Award Fee for Non-Service Contracts at NFS 1852.216-77, contain procedures to ensure prompt payment of award fees. See also the Payments and Advances clause at DEAR 970.5204-16, the

Distribution of Award Fee clause at TAR 1252.216-73 and the Payment of Base and Award Fee clause at HUDAR 2452.216-71.

2. Performance Evaluation Plan

Although the CPAF contract is intrinsically subjective, the evaluation is done in a very methodical way. Agencies carefully spell out in a performance evaluation plan the areas of performance that will be evaluated, the rating system that will be used, and the way in which these ratings will be translated into fee awards. See TAR 1252.216-72 describing this process in the following clause:

> PERFORMANCE EVALUATION PLAN (OCT 1994)
>
> (a) A Performance Evaluation Plan shall be unilaterally established by the Government based on the criteria stated in the contract and used for the determination of award fee. This plan shall include the criteria used to evaluate each area and the percentage of award fee (if any) available for each area. A copy of the plan shall be provided to the contractor _____ (insert number) calendar days prior to the start of the first evaluation period.
>
> (b) The criteria contained within the Performance Evaluation Plan may relate to (1) Technical (including schedule) requirements if appropriate; (2) Management; and (3) Cost.
>
> (c) The Performance Evaluation Plan may, consistent with the contract, be revised unilaterally by the Government at any time during the period of performance. Notification of such changes shall be provided to the contractor ______ (insert number) calendar days prior to the start of the evaluation period to which the change will apply.

A similar clause is set forth in HUDAR 2452.216-73.

These clauses are explicit in giving the agency full flexibility to issue and change the evaluation plan during contract performance. This is a major advantage to both parties because, particularly in the case of R&D contracts being performed over a period of time, the parties may learn of changed circumstances, making it advisable to redirect the contractor's efforts and, thus, bringing about changes in award criteria. Of course, if such changes are made, the contractor should be fully informed of the new evaluation plan prior to the beginning of the award period.

a. *Award Criteria*

The award criteria set forth elements of the contractor's performance that will be evaluated by the agency in determining the amount of award fees and the relative weight of these fees.

(1) Selecting the Criteria

A great deal of flexibility is given to contracting officers in selecting the award criteria, and it is important that the criteria be tailored to the specific procurement. See FAR 16.405-2(b)(2), stating:

> The number of evaluation criteria and the requirements they represent will differ widely among contracts. The criteria and rating plan should motivate the contractor to improve performance in the areas rated, but not at the expense of at least minimum acceptable performances in all other areas.

The NASA 1989 Guidance contained the following suggestions in the selection of the award criteria:

> Fragmentation of the award fee potential over a large number of performance areas and factors dilutes emphasis. Instead, broad performance areas should be selected, such as technical and business management, supplemented by a limited number of subfactors describing significant evaluation elements over which the contractor has effective management control. Project history and past performance can be helpful in identifying those key problem or improvement areas that should be subject to award fee evaluations.

Agencies disagree about whether award criteria should focus on *contractual results* or *methods of performance*. See the NASA 1989 Guidance, which gave considerable discretion in this area:

> Depending upon the procurement situation, performance evaluation factors may include outputs, inputs or a combination of both. Output factors relate to the end results of contract performance, such as the quality of the end items delivered or services rendered, the actual time of their delivery or completion, and the actual costs incurred. Their use has obvious advantages, but there are potential disadvantages as well. In certain situations, end results of this type may not be discernible until it is too late for an award fee evaluation process to have any appreciable effect on the direction in which the results are heading. Also, given the uncertainties that made it

> necessary to use a cost reimbursement contract, an evaluation limited to output factors may not provide a true or complete picture of actual accomplishments. To illustrate, the incurrence of a cost underrun or overrun may reflect less on the contractor's cost control accomplishments than on the uncertainties existing at the time the contract cost estimate was negotiated.
>
> For these reasons, input factors often are used instead of or as a supplement to the use of output factors. Input factors relate to those intermediate processes, procedures, actions or techniques that experience and analysis indicate will be key elements influencing successful contract performance.

The current NASA regulation, NFS 1816.404-274, does not contain this guidance but emphasized that the "predominant consideration" should be the contractor's performance against the negotiated estimated cost of the contract (an output criterion).

As a general rule, the better the work is defined, the more desirable it is to use output criteria. Thus, output criteria would likely be used on service contracts for repetitive services. Input criteria would more likely be used on R&D contracts where the parties are not sure of their projections of end results and the Government desires to encourage the best performance, even if the parties have originally agreed to erroneous goals. Of course, the use of input criteria makes the entire evaluation considerably more subjective.

The NASA 1989 Guidance contained the following specific examples of the types of award criteria commonly used:

> (i) *Technical Achievement.* Accomplishment achieved in the areas of:
>
> - Design: Approach in design concepts, analysis, detailed execution, and low cost design and manufacturing. Design of test specimens, models, and prototypes.
> - Development: Conception/execution of manufacturing process, test plans, and techniques.
> - Technical: Ability to meet technical requirements for design, performance and processing, e.g., weight control, quality assurance, maintainability, reliability design reviews, test procedures, equipment, performance, etc.
> - Schedule: Ability to meet program key milestones, contractual delivery dates, and ability to anticipate and resolve problems.

(ii) *Business Management*

- Program Planning and Organization and Management: Assignment and utilization of manpower; recognition of critical problem areas, cooperation and effective working relationships with other contractors and Government personnel to assure integrated operation efficiency; support to interface activities; technology utilization; use of resources; labor relations; planning, organizing, and managing all program elements; formulations of business and technical decisions; management actions to achieve and sustain a high level of productivity.

- Compliance with contract provisions: Effectiveness of property and material control, Small Business Subcontracting Program, Equal Employment Opportunity Program, Minority Business Enterprise Program, system and occupational safety, security.

- Subcontracting: Subcontract direction and coordination, purchase order and subcontractor administration.

- Schedule: Promptness of delivery, reaction time and appropriateness of response to changes, recovery from delays, response to emergencies and other unexpected situations.

(iii) *Cost Control.* The contractor's skill and ability to control, adjust, and project the cost aspects of the contract.

- Budgeting, accuracy of funding projections, and control of costs.

- Economies in use of manpower, energy, materials, computer utilization, facility utilization, etc.

- Cost reduction through study and use of alternate arrangements, motivation programs, cost saving programs, cost avoidance programs, designs, processes, methods, etc.

- "Make versus buy" program.

- Purchasing effectiveness through competition, material inspection, etc.

- Control of overhead and overtime.

- Final allowable cost.

There is some disagreement as to whether the award criteria should be made a part of the contract document. Prior to 1991, DFARS 216.404-2(b)(S-72)(ii) stated that this information should be set forth in the contract (there is no statement on this issue in the current DFARS), but a number of agencies reserve the right to unilaterally issue the criteria to the contractor after contract award.

(2) WEIGHTING THE CRITERIA

In most CPAF contracts, the award criteria are assigned relative weights as a means of establishing the priorities of the agency in the elements of performance. Most weighting systems assign points to each evaluation criterion, generally using a total of 100 points. The NASA 1989 Guidance suggested that this weighting be done in a two-step process. First, the major areas of performance are given relative weights in accordance with the agency's priorities. Thus, the agency might decide, on an R&D contract, that the weights should be as follows:

Factor	Assigned Weight
Technical	55
Business Management	35
Cost Control	10

The NASA 1989 Guidance then suggested weighting the subfactors within each factor in the same manner. Thus, within the technical factor there might be three subfactors:

Subfactor	Assigned Weight
Design	55
Quality	30
Schedule	15

After the subfactors for business management and cost control are weighted in a similar manner, the agency has a complete matrix of relative weights for calculating the final evaluation of the award fee.

b. Rating System

Since the FAR contains no guidance on techniques used to rate the performance of a contractor working on a CPAF contract, there is broad discretion in establishing the rating system. Generally, adjectival ratings such as *superior*, *excellent*, *good*, *fair*, and *poor* are used, along with corresponding numerical ratings and guidance on the level of performance necessary to earn these grades. NFS 1816.405-275 contains the following guidance on the award fee factors and their use:

> (a) A scoring system of 0–100 shall be used for all award fee ratings. Award fee earned is determined by applying the numerical score to the award fee pool. For example, a score of 85 yields an award fee of 85 percent of the award fee pool. No award fee shall be paid unless the total score is 61 or greater.
>
> (b) The following standard adjectival ratings and the associated numerical scores shall be used on all award fee contracts.
>
> > (1) *Excellent* (100–91): Of exceptional merit; exemplary performance in a timely, efficient, and economical manner; very minor (if any) deficiencies with no adverse effect on overall performance.
> >
> > (2) *Very good* (90–81): Very effective performance; fully responsive to contract requirements accomplished in a timely, efficient, and economical manner for the most part; only minor deficiencies.
> >
> > (3) *Good* (80–71): Effective performance; fully responsive to contract requirements; reportable deficiencies, but with little identifiable effect on overall performance.
> >
> > (4) *Satisfactory* (70–61): Meets or slightly exceeds minimum acceptable standards; adequate results; reportable deficiencies with identifiable, but not substantial, effects on overall performance.
> >
> > (5) *Poor/Unsatisfactory* (less than 61): Does not meet minimum acceptable standards in one or more areas; remedial action required in one or more areas; deficiencies in one or more areas which adversely affect overall performance.
>
> (c) As a benchmark for evaluation, in order to be rated "Excellent," the contractor must be under cost, on or ahead of schedule, and have provided excellent technical performance.

> (d) A scoring system appropriate for the circumstances of the individual contract requirement should be developed. Weighted scoring is recommended. In this system, each evaluation factor (e.g., technical, schedule, cost control) is assigned a specific percentage weighting with the cumulative weightings of all factors totaling 100. During the award fee evaluation, each factor is scored from 0–100 according to ratings defined in 1816.405-275(b). The numerical score for each factor is then multiplied by the weighting for that factor to determine the weighted score. For example, if the technical factor has a weighting of 60 percent and the numerical score for that factor is 80, the weighted technical score is 48 (80 x 60 percent). The weighted scores for each evaluation factor are then added to determine the total award fee score.

A table with a similar grading system is included in the DOE CPAF Contracting Guide at 2-5.1 See **Figure 8-6**.

These rating systems give a grade of 61 for minimally acceptable performance, and the NASA system applies these grades directly to the award fee pool for the period to determine the award fee — with no award for grades below 61. The DOE CPAF Contracting Guide at 2-5.2 achieves the same result but gives less award fee for acceptable grades by converting the grades to percentages of the award fee pool using the conversion chart in **Figure 8-7**. Other agencies have used grading systems that give grades from zero to 100 points and have avoided the use of conversion charts. Most agencies disclose the grading system to the contractor but it has been held proper to use an undisclosed grading system, *Burnside-Ott Aviation Training Ctr.*, ASBCA 43184, 96-1 BCA ¶ 28,102, *aff'd*, 107 F.3d 854 (Fed. Cir. 1997). Contractors should request that the system be disclosed in order to understand fully what fees will be awarded for different levels of performance.

The key problem in establishing any rating system is ensuring that it yields awards commensurate with the actual performance of the contractor. Since most of the contractor's fee is earned through awards above the base fee, awards must be given for any effort that is better than minimally acceptable (assuming that "minimally acceptable" is the performance level commensurate with the base fee level). With low base fees, this means that any award system must yield fee awards for normal performance as well as for outstanding performance. This can be seen in the NASA and DOE

ATTACHMENT 2-5.1
GRADING TABLE ILLUSTRATION

Grading Table

Symbolic Grade	Description	Range of Performance Points
A	Performance exceeds standard by a substantial margin; with few elements for improvement, all of which are minor.	96 – 100
B	Performance exceeds standard; and, although there may be several elements for improvement, these are more than offset by better performance in other elements.	86 – 95
C	Performance is standard; and elements for improvement are approximately offset by better performance in other elements.	76 – 85*
D	Performance is less than standard; and, although there are elements of standard-or-better performance, these are more than offset by lower-graded performance in other elements.	66 – 75
E	Performance is less than standard by a substantial margin; and there are many elements for improvement which are not offset by better performance in other elements.	61 – 65
F	Performance is below minimum acceptable; and is sufficiently below standard as to indicate that improvement in overall contract performance is required to avoid possible termination action.	60 and below

* A grade of 80 performance points is the numerical median between minimum acceptable of 61 and 100, and corresponds to what is normally expected of the contractor.

Figure 8-6

ATTACHMENT 2-5.2
AWARD FEE CONVERSION CHART ILLUSTRATION

Award Fee Conversion Chart

Performance Points	% of Available Award Fee	Performance Points	% of Available Award Fee
100	100.0	80	50.0
99	97.5	79	47.5
98	95.0	78	45.0
97	92.5	77	42.5
96	90.0	76	40.0
95	87.5	75	37.5
94	85.0	74	35.0
93	82.5	73	32.5
92	80.0	72	30.0
91	77.5	71	27.5
90	75.0	70	25.0
89	72.5	69	22.5
88	70.0	68	20.0
87	67.5	67	17.5
86	65.0	66	15.0
85	62.5	65	12.5
84	60.0	64	10.0
83	57.5	63	7.5
82	55.0	62	5.0
81	52.5	61	2.5
		60	0.0

Figure 8-7

systems where average performance would yield a grade in the range of approximately 75, with an award fee of 75 percent of the award fee pool in the NASA system and 37.5 percent of the award fee pool in the DOE system. Assuming base fees of zero on the NASA contract and 3 percent on the DOE contract, and maximum fees of 10 percent on both, this would yield a final fee of 7.5 percent on the NASA contract (75 percent of the award fee pool of $10) and 5.625 percent on the DOE contract (37.5 percent of the award fee pool of $7 plus the base fee of $3). These fees are roughly equivalent to the fixed fee that would be negotiated on a CPFF contract, although the DOE fee seems low. This means, of course, that a contractor with well above average performance will earn a substantially higher fee. The NASA 1989 Guidance stated that this was entirely proper and that, in fact, award fee rating systems should be structured so that they provide the contractor "with a reasonable opportunity to earn the maximum award fee available." However, the current NASA system and most other systems make this improbable. Conversely, both the NASA and DOE systems impose severe penalties on contractors that perform below acceptable levels — with the current NASA system being the most harsh because it uses base fees of zero.

c. Award Procedure

The amount of the award is usually determined by a three-step procedure within the contracting agency. The first step consists of evaluation and preliminary scoring of the contractor's performance by personnel within the procuring agency who are familiar with the contractor's performance. Generally, the personnel used for this task are the technical and business personnel who are monitoring the contractor's work on a regular basis. In cases where there is a Government program manager, this function will be performed primarily by personnel in the program office. The goal of this part of the process is to obtain an evaluation by the most knowledgeable people in the agency on each aspect of the contractor's performance. Most of the guidance on CPAF contracting contains instructions calling for very detailed monitoring of contractor performance and full documentation of perceived strengths and weaknesses. Detailed documentation is essential because these evaluations form the basis of the entire award process.

The second step consists of a review of these evaluations by a board of higher-level personnel. This step is optional and unnecessary on smaller procurements. On larger procurements, however, this step is advisable in order to ensure that the evaluations are internally consistent and that they reflect an overall view of the contractor's accomplishments. A board of this type would be expected to discern, for instance, not only that one evaluator has downgraded a contractor, but also that the contractor's performance was marginal because of a conscious decision to devote effort to some other important task.

The third step is the award by the award official, generally called the "fee determination official." In major procurements, this official should be at the management level of the procuring agency, while in small contracts, the contracting officer might perform this task. The contract clauses generally provide that awards are not subject to the disputes procedures in the contract. See the following clause in TAR 1252.216-71:

> DETERMINATION OF AWARD FEE EARNED (OCT 1994)
>
> (a) The Government shall, at the conclusion of each specified evaluation period(s), evaluate the contractor's performance for a determination of award fee earned. The contractor agrees that the determination as to the amount of award fee earned will be made by the Government Fee Determination Official (FDO) and such determination is binding on both parties and shall not be subject to appeal under the "Disputes" clause or to any board or court.
>
> (b) It is agreed that the evaluation of contractor performance shall be in accordance with a Performance Evaluation Plan and that the contractor shall be promptly advised in writing of the determination and reasons why the award fee was or was not earned. It is further agreed that the contractor may submit a self-evaluation of performance of each period under consideration. While it is recognized that the basis for determination of the fee shall be the evaluation by the Government, any self-evaluation which is received within ______ (insert number) days after the end of the period being evaluated may be given such consideration, if any, as the FDO shall find appropriate.
>
> (c) The FDO may specify in any fee determination that fee not earned during the period evaluated may be accumulated and be available for allocation to one or more subsequent periods. In that event, the distribution of award fee shall be adjusted to reflect such allocations.

A similar clause is included in HUDAR 2452.216-72.

The provision precluding appeal of award fee determinations under the Disputes clause is not enforceable under the Contract Disputes Act of 1978,

Burnside-Ott Aviation Training Ctr. v. Dalton, 107 F.3d 854 (Fed. Cir. 1997). However, the review of an award decision is a very narrow one, focusing only on whether it is arbitrary or capricious. Thus, the court affirmed *Burnside-Ott Aviation Training Ctr.*, ASBCA 43184, 96-1 BCA ¶ 28,102, where the board ruled that the use of a conversion table was not arbitrary or capricious but was within the contracting officer's discretion even though its use was not disclosed to the contractor. The ASBCA has also taken jurisdiction over a dispute concerning the "availability" of the award fee, *Technical Support Servs., Inc.*, ASBCA 37976, 89-2 BCA ¶ 21,861; the board noted that it was not ruling that it had jurisdiction over the "amount" of the award. The sufficiency of awards was considered in *Nash Janitorial Servs., Inc.*, GSBCA 6390, 84-1 BCA ¶ 17,135, *recons. denied*, 84-2 BCA ¶ 17,355. In *Nash*, the board found that a contract modification agreeing to a total amount of cost and fee (including award fees) due on a services contract was void because of economic duress by the contracting officer. The conduct constituting duress was the manner in which the contracting officer administered the contract, including granting very low award fees that penalized the contractor for Government actions.

One major issue in the award process is the degree of participation that should be granted to the contractor. In the past, some contracts have greatly limited the contractor's participation, giving the contractor no opportunity to submit information or see evaluations and limiting its role to a thorough debriefing after the award has been made. Earlier versions of DFARS 216.404-2(a) provided that evaluations should be furnished to the contractor for comment, but the current regulation merely states that the agency "may . . . afford the contractor an opportunity to present information on its own behalf." The DOT/HUD clauses discussed above and the NASA Award Fee clauses in NFS 1852.216-76 and -77 also provide that the contractor is entitled to submit a self-evaluation as part of the evaluation process. Another option is to permit the contractor to make an independent presentation to the board or award official, either in writing or orally. This was included in an earlier edition of the DFARS but has been removed from the current version of the regulation. Whatever system is selected, the agency must eventually give the contractor detailed information on the basis of the award so that it can fully understand what aspects of performance were downgraded and how performance can be improved in subsequent award periods. Since the CPAF contract will function best when the contractor has a high degree of confidence in the reliability, accuracy, and fairness of the evaluations and awards, the process selected should engender such confidence.

3. Relationship of Award Fee to Other Provisions

As with CPIF contracts, it is important that CPAF contracts state the relationship of the award fee provisions to other provisions of the contract that provide the Government with remedies for less than specified performance. Since most award fee provisions call for awards only if the performance reaches the minimally acceptable level, it would be logical to state that the Government could make fee adjustments under no other contract clauses as long as the award fee provisions were in effect. Similarly, clauses providing remedies other than fee adjustment, such as the Termination clause, would be applied without regard to the award fee provisions. This is a reasonable interpretation of the standard clauses, if the relationship between clauses is not well stated in the contract, since it is not reasonable to conclude that the Government is providing itself a choice of remedies or overlapping remedies. The best solution, of course, is to include clear language in the contract.

Unfortunately, this issue is not adequately addressed in many CPAF contracts. A good example of the problems that can ensue is found in *Holmes & Narver Servs., Inc.*, ASBCA 33025, 88-3 BCA ¶ 20,932, where the contract contained an award fee provision on cost and technical performance and an Inspection of Services clause similar to the clause in FAR 52.246-5. The Inspection of Services clause gave the Government the right to "reduce any fee payable" if the services were defective and could not be corrected. The contracting officer's attempt to reduce the base fee because of poor cost control was held to be improper because cost control was not a specified service under the contract. The board would have faced a more difficult issue if the reduction in base fee had occurred because of poor performance of the technical work called for by the contract, but it would seem that a proper interpretation would be that the award fee provisions are the stated mechanism for making such fee reductions. See also *UNC Nuclear Indus., Inc.*, EBCA 412-4-88, 90-1 BCA ¶ 22,463, interpreting a DOE contract clause stating that "in the event of contract termination . . . the amount of award fee available shall represent a pro rata distribution associated with evaluation period activities or events, and allowable costs." The board ruled that the Government was wrong in using a share of the base and award fees computed by prorating (based on the number of days of performance prior to the convenience termination) the fee assigned to the evaluation period. Here the Government attempted to draft a clause dealing with the possibility of convenience termination but failed to state the result with sufficient clarity. Contrast *Grumman Space Station Integration Div.*, ASBCA 48719, 97-1 BCA ¶ 28,843, where the parties omitted any contract language on the effect of a convenience termination on award fee that had been accumulated over the total period of contract performance. The board ruled that the contractor had no entitlement to such award fee because the termination prevented complete performance of the contract.

The contract should also spell out the consequences of any plan to give employee bonuses if high levels of award fee are earned. As noted in the discussion of CPIF contracts, such bonuses are potentially allowable costs of performance, if they comply with the cost principle in FAR 31.205-6(f). See *Petroleum Operations & Support Servs., Inc.*, EBCA 291-6-83, 85-2 BCA ¶ 18,037, denying compensation of the cost of an award fee-based bonus because it was not given in accordance with a "good faith agreement" between the contractor and its employees. If the bonuses had been recognized as allowable costs, the contractor's costs would have been higher, with the possibility that its award fee would have been lower. It is this interrelationship that should be addressed in the negotiation of the contract.

4. CPAF/CPIF Contracts

It has become quite common practice to combine CPAF and CPIF contracting techniques in a single contract. Most often, this involves using a CPIF formula for the cost incentive and adding CPAF awards in the areas of performance and delivery. The fee is then generally divided into its constituent parts and the incentive provisions structured accordingly. For example, if it were decided to assign 40 percent of the fee to cost incentives and the balance to the award areas, the cost incentive would be structured at this level. Thus, if the normal CPIF contract would have a target fee of 8 percent, with minimum and maximum fees of 2 percent and 14 percent, the parties would use 40 percent of the total fee pool (12 percentage points of fee) to structure the cost incentive in the CPAF/CPIF contract. This would yield:

Target Fee	4.4%
Minimum Fee	2.0%
Maximum Fee (on costs)	6.8%

The balance of the total fee pool (7.2 percentage points of fee) would be assigned to the award fee pool available for awards in the performance and delivery areas, and the maximum fee on the total contract would be set at 14 percent.

There are many variations of this structuring technique. For example, the Government may decide that the above formula does not provide sufficient incentive in the cost area. In that case, it is possible to overlap the different areas using, for example, CPIF elements as follows:

Target Fee	6%
Minimum Fee	2%
Maximum Fee (on costs)	10%

The award fee pool for performance and delivery would be kept at 7.2 percentage points, and the maximum fee for the total contract would be kept at 14 percent. This might result in no fee being available for awards in the final periods of contract performance, but it would increase the motivation for reducing costs and would allow the cost incentive to be spread over a broader RIE.

NASA uses a different combination of objective and subjective incentives. NFS 1816.404-276(a) requires the use of an objective performance incentive on all CPAF contracts over $25 million where the primary deliverable is hardware. This policy includes in the contract the Performance Incentive clause discussed earlier and rewards or penalizes the contractor for the specific results achieved in accordance with a formula contained in the clause.

5. Award Fee Provisions in Fixed-Price Contracts

In 1997 the following provision was added in FAR 16.404, giving guidance on award fee provisions in fixed-price contracts:

> (a) Award-fee provisions may be used in fixed-price contracts when the Government wishes to motivate a contractor and other incentives cannot be used because contractor performance cannot be measured objectively. Such contracts shall —
>
> > (1) Establish a fixed price (including normal profit) for the effort. This price will be paid for satisfactory contract performance. Award fee earned (if any) will be paid in addition to that fixed price; and

(2) Provide for periodic evaluation of the contractor's performance against an award-fee plan.

(b) A solicitation contemplating award of a fixed-price contract with award fee shall not be issued unless the following conditions exist:

(1) The administrative costs of conducting award-fee evaluations are not expected to exceed the expected benefits;

(2) Procedures have been established for conducting the award-fee evaluation;

(3) The award-fee board has been established; and

(4) An individual above the level of the contracting officer approved the fixed-price-award-fee incentive.

This technique was proper prior to the FAR language. See *Diversified Contract Servs., Inc.*, Comp. Gen. Dec. B-224152, 86-2 CPD ¶ 675, where an agency used a stand-alone award fee provision to motivate the contractor to increase the quality of the services being performed. The Comptroller General ruled that this was well within the power of an agency and was a valid method of obtaining the quality of work required. For another case where an award fee provision was included in a fixed-price contract, see *Technology Applications, Inc.*, Comp. Gen. Dec. B-238259, 90-1 CPD ¶ 451.

DFARS 216.470 contains rather cryptic guidance on "other applications of award fees," as follows:

The "award amount" portion of the fee may be used in other types of contracts under the following conditions —

(1) The Government wishes to motivate and reward a contractor for management performance in areas which cannot be measured objectively and where normal incentive provisions cannot be used. For example, logistics support, quality, timeliness, ingenuity, and cost effectiveness are areas under the control of management which may be susceptible only to subjective measurement and evaluation.

(2) The "base fee" (fixed amount portion) is not used.

(3) The chief of the contracting office approves the use of the "award amount."

(4) An award review board and procedures are established for conduct of the evaluation.

(5) The administrative costs of evaluation do not exceed the expected benefits.

V. LEVEL-OF-EFFORT CONTRACTS

The standard types of contracts discussed above describe the work in terms of the end product to be delivered or the services to be performed. This section covers an alternate method of describing the work — in terms of the level of effort to be expended by the contractor. In this type of contract, the contractor receives the compensation called for by the contract upon expenditure of the required hours of effort, regardless of whether the anticipated work is completed. As a result, this type of contract is used infrequently since it imposes significantly less risk on the contractor than contracts calling for completion of a specified task.

In these types of contracts, the Government is primarily buying hours of labor from a contractor. Hence, the most important consideration is the quality of the labor, and negotiated procurement procedures are generally used to permit the evaluation of the capabilities of each offerors' employees. Frequently, agencies evaluate an offeror's relative experience, *Wickman Spacecraft & Propulsion Co.*, Comp. Gen. Dec. B-219675, 85-2 CPD ¶ 690 (1985) (failure to include a small, new firm in competitive range was acceptable); *DDL Omni Eng'g*, Comp. Gen. Dec. B-220075.2, 85-2 CPD ¶ 684 (an agency was allowed to take into consideration personnel and corporate experience in evaluating the proposals). Agencies need not choose a contractor with the most specific experience but may infer that the contractor has the ability to perform the work, *U.S. Defense Sys., Inc.*, Comp. Gen. Dec. B-260702, 95-2 CPD ¶ 22 (award of a contract concerning guard services at embassies given to a contractor with comparable, but not the specific, guard experience); *Research Analysis & Maintenance, Inc.*, Comp. Gen. Dec. B-239223, 90-2 CPD ¶ 129 (award to contractor without experience on the specific missile at issue). An agency cannot, however, require experience to the extent that it is "unduly restrictive." See *Daniel H. Wagner, Assocs.*, 65 Comp. Gen. 305 (B-220633), 86-1 CPD ¶ 166, where the Navy had to revise its solicitation because its requirements for experience were so restrictive that competition was limited to a sole source of supply. The Comptroller General also noted that sealed bidding would be appropriate when routine services were being acquired.

There are two techniques used to contract for a level of effort. First, the parties can agree to fixed hourly rates for specified classes of labor with payment based on the number of actual hours incurred. These rates include the contractor's indirect costs and profit. If this type of contract calls for labor only, it is called a "labor-hour" contract, FAR 16.602. If it includes the purchase of materials as well as the incurrence of labor effort, it is called a "time-and-materials" contract, FAR 16.601. The second technique provides a stated amount of compensation for the incurrence of a specified number of labor-hours over a fixed period of time. This type of contract is generally called a "term" type contract and can be written as a "firm-fixed-price, level-of-effort term contract," FAR 16.207, or a CPFF term contract, FAR 16.306(d). In the former contract, the contractor is paid the price upon the incurrence of the labor-hours, while in the latter contract, the contractor is paid the fixed fee plus the costs upon the incurrence of the labor-hours.

A. Time-and-Materials and Labor-Hour Contracts

Although time-and-materials and labor-hour contracts have been used for many years, they are not regarded as contracts that are beneficial to the Government since they provide "no positive profit incentive to the contractor for cost control or labor efficiency," FAR 16.601(b)(1). This lack of incentive is due to the difficulty of controlling the number of hours that will be expended to perform any assigned task. Thus, FAR guidance on use of these types of contracts is minimal. FAR 52.300 does include these types of contracts in the matrix of contract clauses — providing guidance as to the clauses that are appropriate for these types of contract.

FAR 16.601(c) contains the following limitations on the use of time-and-materials contracts:

> A time-and-materials contract may be used (1) only after the contracting officer executes a determination and findings that no other contract type is suitable and (2) only if the contract includes a ceiling price that the contractor exceeds at its own risk. The contracting officer shall document the contract file to justify the reasons for the amount of any subsequent change in the ceiling price.

These same requirements are applicable to labor-hour contracts, FAR 16.602. The determination and findings is not required by statute but is an additional safeguard called for by the regulation. The FAR provides that it can be executed by the contracting officer, but many regulations call for approval of higher authority, AFARS 16.601(c). FAR 16.601(b)(1) also requires "appropriate Government surveillance" of contractor performance of these types of contract "to give reasonable assurance that efficient methods and effective cost controls are being used." See *Midwest Maintenance & Constr. Co.*, GSBCA 6225, 85-1 BCA ¶ 17,716, commenting on the use of this type of contract without adequate Government surveillance.

Time-and-materials and labor-hour contracts can be awarded for a single specified amount of work, but they are more frequently used as the basis for pricing tasks to be specified after contract award. In that situation, they are subject to the limitations imposed on "task order contracts" — as discussed in the following section on indefinite-delivery contracts.

The initial step required in preparing a time-and-materials or labor-hour contract is to determine the classes or types of labor that will be required to perform the work. Since an agreed rate will be included in the contract for each type of labor, classifications should not include disparate types of employees or disparate skill levels. The contract schedule sets forth these rates. A payments clause for time-and-materials and labor-hour contracts is included in FAR 52.232-7. It provides for payment for labor as follows:

> (a) *Hourly rate.* (1) The amounts shall be computed by multiplying the appropriate hourly rates prescribed in the Schedule by the number of direct labor hours performed. The rates shall include wages, indirect costs, general and administrative expense, and profit. Fractional parts of an hour shall be payable on a prorated basis.
>
> * * *
>
> (3) Unless the Schedule prescribes otherwise, the hourly rates in the Schedule shall not be varied by virtue of the Contractor having performed work on an overtime basis. If no overtime rates are provided in the Schedule and overtime work is approved in advance by the Contracting Officer, overtime rates shall be negotiated. Failure to agree upon these overtime rates shall be treated as a dispute under the Disputes clause of this contract. If the Schedule provides rates for overtime, the premium portion of those rates will be reimbursable only to the extent the overtime is approved by the Contracting Officer.

When competitive proposals are received for these types of contract, the contracting officer should closely analyze the elements of the proposal to determine that the price and estimated costs are fair and reasonable. However, the contracting officer need not obtain cost or pricing data and perform a detailed cost analysis if adequate competition has been obtained, *Milcom Sys. Corp.*, Comp. Gen. Dec. B-255448.2, 94-1 CPD ¶ 339; *Research Management Corp.*, 69 Comp. Gen. 368 (B-237865), 90-1 CPD ¶ 352.

Lack of clarity in the contract can lead to serious disputes over the proper billing of labor-hours. See *Software Research Assocs.*, ASBCA 33578, 88-3 BCA ¶ 21,046, where the contractor was permitted to bill the hourly rates for consultants. The Government had argued that consultants were in the nature of material to be paid at actual cost, but the board reasoned that the consultants did the same work as employees of the contractor. See also *Emerson-Sack-Warner Corp.*, Comp. Gen. Dec. B-206123, 82-2 CPD ¶ 488, where the original IFB was unclear as to whether the contractor could bill the hourly rate for travel time. The procurement was canceled and readvertised under a solicitation that made it clear that such time was not to be reimbursed. A contractor may not recover underestimated indirect costs by billing for extra hours, *Progressive Mach. Works, Inc.*, ASBCA 28785, 85-2 BCA ¶ 18,018. Contractors must also have adequate records to substantiate the hours billed, *JANA, Inc. v. United States*, 936 F.2d 1265 (Fed. Cir. 1991), *cert. denied*, 502 U.S. 1030 (1992) (Government recovered payments made to contractor that could not be substantiated in subsequent audit).

If the contract requires the contractor to purchase materials, their costs are reimbursed on the basis of incurred costs. The FAR 52.232-7 clause contains the following provisions:

> (b) *Materials and subcontracts.* (1) Allowable costs of direct materials shall be determined by the Contracting Officer in accordance with Subpart 31.2 of the Federal Acquisition Regulation (FAR) in effect on the date of this contract. Reasonable and allocable material handling costs may be included in the charge for material to the extent they are clearly excluded from the hourly rate. Material handling costs are comprised of indirect costs, including, when appropriate, general and administrative expense allocated to direct materials in accordance with the Contractor's usual accounting practices consistent with Subpart 31.2 of the FAR.
>
> * * *

> (2) The cost of subcontracts that are authorized under the subcontracts clause of this contract shall be reimbursable costs under this clause; *provided,* that the costs are consistent with subparagraph (3) below. Reimbursable costs in connection with subcontracts shall be limited to the amounts paid to the subcontractor for items and services purchased directly for the contract and only when cash, checks, or other form of payment has been made for such purchased items or services; however, this requirement shall not apply to a Contractor that is a small business concern. Reimbursable costs shall not include any costs arising from the letting, administration or supervision of performance of the subcontract, if the costs are included in the hourly rates payable under (a)(1) above.
>
> (3) To the extent able, the Contractor shall —
>
>> (i) Obtain materials at the most advantageous prices available with due regard to securing prompt delivery of satisfactory materials; and
>>
>> (ii) Take all cash and trade discounts, rebates, allowances, credits, salvage, commissions, and other benefits. . . .

The major issue that has arisen in this area is the treatment of material handling costs. Since the clause permits contractors to include such costs in labor rates or as material costs in accordance with their usual accounting practices, the Comptroller General held that an unequal bidding situation is created, *Beta Indus., Inc.*, 60 Comp. Gen. 487 (B-200121), 81-1 CPD ¶ 391. The Comptroller General suggested that bidders be required to state in the bid which method they would use. There is no FAR guidance on this issue. See also *Ray Serv. Co.*, 64 Comp. Gen. 528 (B-217218), 85-1 CPD ¶ 582, holding that there is nothing intrinsically improper about including material handling costs in the hourly rate. In *General Eng'g & Mach. Works v. Sean C. O'Keefe*, 991 F.2d 775 (Fed. Cir. 1993), the court affirmed a board decision at 92-3 BCA ¶ 25,055 that the contractor was not entitled to charge a 15 percent material handling rate because it did not collect its material handling costs in a separate cost pool, as required by the contract. The court reasoned that this was a proper interpretation in order to avoid the possibility that the contractor could obtain double compensation for material handling in both the labor and material charges.

FAR 16.601(c) requires that each time-and-materials or labor-hour contract contain a "ceiling price." However, the payments clause at FAR

52.232-7 contains the following language making it clear that this "ceiling" is actually a limitation of cost with no further contractor obligation once the amount has been reached:

> (c) *Total cost.* It is estimated that the total cost to the Government for the performance of this contract shall not exceed the ceiling price set forth in the Schedule and the Contractor agrees to use its best efforts to perform the work specified in the Schedule and all obligations under this contract within such ceiling price.
>
> * * *
>
> (d) *Ceiling price.* The Government shall not be obligated to pay the Contractor any amount in excess of the ceiling price in the Schedule, and the Contractor shall not be obligated to continue performance if to do so would exceed the ceiling price set forth in the Schedule, unless and until the Contracting Officer shall have notified the Contractor in writing that the ceiling price has been increased and shall have specified in the notice a revised ceiling that shall constitute the ceiling price for performance under this contract.

This provision contains notice requirements similar to those in the cost-reimbursement contract Limitation of Cost clause. Thus, the same legal rules barring contractor recovery for unreported overruns should apply to this type of contract. A claim for a constructive change in the work would permit a price adjustment to the ceiling under the FAR 52.243-3 Changes clause for time-and-materials or labor-hour contracts. See *Bendix Field Eng'g Corp.*, ASBCA 10124, 66-2 BCA ¶ 5959.

B. Cost-Reimbursement Term Contracts

The cost-reimbursement term type contract describes the work to be performed in terms of a level of effort. FAR 16.306(d) provides the following guidance on this form of contract:

> (2) The term form describes the scope of work in general terms and obligates the contractor to devote a specified level of effort for a stated time period. Under this form, if the performance is considered satisfactory by the Government, the fixed fee is payable at the expiration of the agreed-upon period, upon contractor statement that the level of effort specified in the contract has been expended in performing the contract work. Renewal for

> further periods of performance is a new acquisition that involves new cost and fee arrangements.
>
> * * *
>
> (4) The term form shall not be used unless the contractor is obligated by the contract to provide a specific level of effort within a definite time period.

Contracting agencies have a great deal of latitude in deciding how to express the required level of effort. The principal objective should be to state the desired effort in sufficient detail so as to assure that the Government gets the type and amount of effort it wants while leaving contractors enough flexibility to adjust to new circumstances without the need for repeated contract amendments. The required effort can be expressed in the amount of time to be devoted to performance through the use of terms such as labor-hours, labor-days, or labor-months. In addition, different types of effort can be specified by stating that amount of effort required of different categories of personnel. However, too much detail may greatly limit the flexibility of the contractor in performing the work. Maximum flexibility is achieved under clauses that specify a range of required effort as in the following:

> Level of Effort
>
> Recognizing that this contract is a term form within the meaning of DAR 3-405.6(d)(2), the contractor shall devote to the research hereunder not less than 1,250,000 direct man-hours nor more than 1,360,000 direct man-hours.

The Government also builds flexibility into Level of Effort clauses through provisions stating that deviations in effort up to certain limits will be acceptable and will not effect other contract provisions.

Most cost type level-of-effort contracts are for a specified amount of work, but some of these contracts may call for work to be done as tasks are ordered up to a ceiling number of labor-hours. Such contracts are subject to the limitations on task order contracts discussed below in the section on indefinite-delivery contracts.

When a cost-reimbursement level-of-effort contract is awarded competitively, the contracting officer must make a cost realism analysis, as discussed in Chapter 9, to determine the probable costs of performance of the contract. See, for example, *Delta Research Assocs.*, Comp. Gen. Dec. B-254006.2, 94-1 CPD ¶ 47, where the Comptroller General sustained the contracting officer's determination that the most realistic probable cost of performance was at the proposed indirect cost rates rather than at the ceiling on those rates that had been proposed by the offeror.

Since this type of level-of-effort contract is a cost-reimbursement contract, the contractor need not expend effort when its actual costs reach the cost estimate, and the Government is not bound to compensate for costs incurred above the estimate. However, the level-of-effort clause is controlling as to the fee to be paid and can be controlling as to the contractor's entitlement to incurred costs. See *Space Technology Labs., Inc.*, ASBCA 7676, 1962 BCA ¶ 3609, where the board disallowed costs attributable to labor-hours in excess of the stated monthly maximum level of effort. In *Booz, Allen & Hamilton, Inc.*, EBCA 116-3-80, 80-2 BCA ¶ 14,796, the board held that the fact that the Government added funds to the contract in order to permit the contractor to continue to provide labor-hours up to the stated maximum level of effort did not entitle the contractor to additional fee. In reaching this result, the board relied upon the following clause:

> In the event that during the period of this contract, the Contracting Officer shall issue Task Assignments requiring an effort of greater than *48,635* DPMH but less than *59,440* DPMH, the fixed fee of this contract shall not be adjusted. However, in the event that the contractor shall be required to furnish effort greater than *59,440* DPMH or less than *48,635* the estimated cost and fixed fee shall be adjusted.

Compare *International Space Corp.*, ASBCA 13883, 70-2 BCA ¶ 8519, where the board found that the only "practicable effect" of a generally worded level-of-effort clause was to establish the minimum effort that the contractor had to expend in order to earn the contract's fixed fee. See also *Falcon Research & Dev. Co.*, ASBCA 26678, 83-1 BCA ¶ 16,437, where the board granted a pro rata reduction in fee when the level of effort was not attained, and *PRC Info. Sciences Co.*, EBCA 171-5-81, 82-2 BCA ¶ 15,866, where the board disagreed with the contractor's contention that the full fee was earned when the estimated costs were fully expended.

C. Fixed-Price, Level-of-Effort Term Contract

A fixed-price, level-of-effort term contract is similar to a cost-reimbursement term type contract except that the price is paid upon the incurrence of the specified number of labor-hours. FAR 16.207-2 provides the following guidance:

> A firm-fixed-price, level-of-effort term contract is suitable for investigation or study in a specific research and development area. The product of the contract is usually a report showing the results achieved through application of the required level of effort. However, payment is based on the effort expended rather than on the results achieved.

FAR 16.207-3 places the following limitations on the use of this type of contract:

> This contract type may be used only when —
>
> (a) The work required cannot otherwise be clearly defined;
>
> (b) The required level of effort is identified and agreed upon in advance;
>
> (c) There is reasonable assurance that the intended result cannot be achieved by expending less than the stipulated effort; and
>
> (d) The contract price is $100,000 or less, unless approved by the chief of the contracting office.

No clauses are included in the FAR for this type of contract. However, the contract should contain a schedule of the types of effort required. Failure to expend the effort should lead to a pro rata reduction in payment while complete expenditure of the required labor-hours should result in full payment without regard to the level of accomplishment of the task called for by the contract.

VI. VARIABLE QUANTITY CONTRACTS

Variable quantity contracts obligate the contractor to furnish articles or services in quantities to be ordered by the Government within specified maximum amounts. While the contractor is firmly obligated, the Government's obligation is more malleable and depends upon the technique used. The techniques discussed in this section are contained in two parts of the procurement regulations. FAR 16.5 describes the requirements contract and the indefinite-quantity contract with stated minimum and maximum quantities. FAR 17.1 permits the use of the multiyear contract providing for firm contractual commitments over a number of years if there are both continued need and appropriations to cover the later years. FAR 17.2 permits the use of options by Government procuring activities.

While there is no single clearly enunciated Government policy with regard to the use of these forms of contracting, it is apparent that a fundamental goal of the Government should be to buy articles or services in sufficient quantities to permit efficient performance of the contract. This policy with regard to supplies is contained in 10 U.S.C. § 2384(a) and 41 U.S.C. § 253f(a) and implemented in FAR Subpart 7.2. The latter statute states:

> Each executive agency shall procure supplies in such quantities as (A) will result in the total cost and unit cost most advantageous to the United States, where practicable, and (B) does not exceed the quantity reasonably expected to be required by the agency.

In many cases, the agency may not have identified current requirements to support an immediate procurement of economic quantities yet it may be aware, from past experience, that such requirements will become available over time. In other cases, an agency may be aware that it has requirements over a number of years but will not have immediate funding to place those requirements on contract because appropriations are made for only one year's requirements. In such cases, the use of a variable quantity contract may enable the agency to obtain reduced prices for the goods or services being procured as well as reduce the administrative costs of issuing numerous contracts as requirements become firm. These forms of contracting *should not be used* when the Government has firm requirements and available funding.

In some of the forms of contract discussed below, the Government legally binds itself to purchase the goods or services during a given period of time if the need materializes and is funded. In others, the Government obligates itself to purchase an initial quantity but makes no further legally binding commitment to the contractor. The basic ordering agreement, FAR 16.703, is not discussed in this section since neither party is contractually bound in this arrangement. Such agreements can constitute open offers which would form a contract upon acceptance by the Government but which have no legal effect until that time.

It can be argued that a lower price will be obtained when the Government is obligated to buy a significant amount from the contractor. However, since almost all Government contracts contain a Termination for the

Convenience of the Government clause, giving the Government the right to terminate the contract in many situations, there is much less distinction among the actual Government obligation under the various forms of variable quantity contract than would appear at first glance. Thus, any given agency will use one variable quantity form of contract in preference to another primarily because it has used that form successfully in the past and secondarily because that form may be well adapted to dealing with that agency's peculiar problems such as fiscal or administrative requirements.

These variable quantity contracts can state the contractor's obligation in terms of firm requirements or open-ended commitments to perform work in the future. If they are structured in an open-ended manner, they become subject to the provisions of the Federal Acquisition Streamlining Act of 1994 (FASA), P.L. 103-355, dealing with "task order contracts" and "delivery order contracts," 10 U.S.C. §§ 2304a–2304d and 41 U.S.C. §§ 235h–235k. The following definitions are contained in 10 U.S.C. § 2304d and 41 U.S.C. § 253k:

> (1) The term "task order contract" means a contract for services that does not procure or specify a firm quantity of services (other than a minimum or maximum quantity) and that provides for the issuance of orders for the performance of tasks during the period of the contract.
>
> (2) The term "delivery order contract" means a contract for property that does not procure or specify a firm quantity of property (other than a minimum or maximum quantity) and that provides for the issuance of orders for the delivery of property during the period of the contract.

These statutory provisions are implemented in FAR Subpart 16.5, covering requirements contracts and indefinite-quantity contracts. Other types of contracts, such as level-of-effort contracts, may also provide for the ordering of work by tasks without calling for a "firm quantity" of work. If so, they would be subject to these statutes even though the FAR does not specify that they are covered.

One major purpose of these statutes is to ensure that these types of contracts will be sufficiently precise to enable offerors to ascertain the scope of the work to be ordered so that they can submit meaningful offers, as set forth at 10 U.S.C. § 2304a and 41 U.S.C. § 253h:

> (b) Solicitation. The solicitation for a task or delivery order contract shall include the following:

(1) The period of the contract, including the number of options to extend the contract and the period for which the contract may be extended under each option, if any.

(2) The maximum quantity or dollar value of the services or property to be procured under the contract.

(3) A statement of work, specifications, or other description that reasonably describes the general scope, nature, complexity, and purposes of the services or property to be procured under the contract.

In order to ensure that competition is maximized, these statutes favor the award of *multiple contracts* over single contracts for a designated series of task orders or delivery orders. See 10 U.S.C. § 2304a(d) and 41 U.S.C. § 253h(d), which grant authority to make single awards but state:

(3) The regulations implementing this subsection shall —

(A) establish a preference for awarding, to the maximum extent practicable, multiple task or delivery order contracts for the same or similar services or property under the authority of paragraph (1)(B); and

(B) establish criteria for determining when award of multiple task or delivery order contracts would not be in the best interest of the Federal Government.

10 U.S.C. § 2304b(e) and 41 U.S.C. § 253i(e) contain special limitations on task order contracts for "advisory and assistance services" if the contract period exceeds three years and the estimated contract amount is over $10 million. In such cases, a single contract can be awarded only if the head of the executive agency determines that because the services required under the contract are unique or highly specialized, it is not practicable to award more than one contract. "Advisory and assistance services" are defined in 31 U.S.C. § 1105(g) as follows:

[T]he term "advisory and assistance services" means the following services when provided by nongovernmental sources:

(i) Management and professional support services.

(ii) Studies, analyses, and evaluations.

(iii) Engineering and technical services.

A more complete definition is included in FAR 37.201. See *Nations, Inc.*, Comp. Gen. Dec. B-272455, 96-2 CPD ¶ 170, holding that, pursuant to this expansive FAR definition, training services were included in management and professional support services.

A. Requirements Contracts

A requirements contract is a contract where one party promises to buy all or a designated part of its requirements from another party. FAR 16.503(a) contains the following definition:

> A requirements contract provides for filling all actual purchase requirements of designated Government activities for supplies or services during a specified contract period, with deliveries or performance to be scheduled by placing orders with the contractor.

This definition only contemplates requirements contracts covering *the entire Government quantity* for some class of supplies or services. However, as discussed below, requirements contracts can also be used for designated parts of a Government requirement.

FAR 16.506(d) instructs contracting officers to include the Requirements clause at FAR 52.216-21, or one of its four alternates, in all requirements contracts. The basic clause states:

> REQUIREMENTS (OCT 1995)
>
> (a) This is a requirements contract for the supplies or services specified, and effective for the period stated, in the Schedule. The quantities of supplies or services specified in the Schedule are estimates only and are not purchased by this contract. Except as this contract may otherwise provide, if the Government's requirements do not result in orders in the quantities described as "estimated" or "maximum" in the Schedule, that fact shall not constitute the basis for an equitable price adjustment.
>
> (b) Delivery or performance shall be made only as authorized by orders issued in accordance with the Ordering clause. Subject to any limitations in the Order Limitations clause or elsewhere in this contract, the Contractor shall furnish to the Government all supplies or services specified in the Schedule and called for by orders issued in accordance with the Ordering clause. The Government may issue orders requiring delivery to multiple destinations or performance at multiple locations.

> (c) Except as this contract otherwise provides, the Government shall order from the Contractor all the supplies or services specified in the Schedule that are required to be purchased by the Government activity or activities specified in the Schedule.
>
> (d) The Government is not required to purchase from the Contractor requirements in excess of any limit on total orders under this contract.
>
> (e) If the Government urgently requires delivery of any quantity of an item before the earliest date that delivery may be specified under this contract, and if the Contractor will not accept an order providing for the accelerated delivery, the Government may acquire the urgently required goods or services from another source.
>
> (f) Any order issued during the effective period of this contract and not completed within that period shall be completed by the Contractor within the time specified in the order. The contract shall govern the Contractor's and Government's rights and obligations with respect to the order to the same extent as if the order were completed during the contract's effective period; *provided*, that the Contractor shall not be required to make any deliveries under this contract after _________ [insert date].

If the contract is for less than the full requirements of the Government, as discussed below, the clause must be tailored to fit the precise circumstances of the procurement.

FAR 52.216-18 provides an Ordering clause to be inserted in all requirements contracts as well as other indefinite-delivery contracts. In addition to stipulating the time period during which orders may be issued, the clause provides that the order is binding when issued:

> (c) If mailed, a delivery order or task order is considered "issued" when the Government deposits the order in the mail. Orders may be issued orally, by facsimile, or by electronic commerce methods only if authorized in the Schedule.

Boards have upheld this provision in both *Canadian Commercial Corp.*, ASBCA 20067, 75-2 BCA ¶ 11,441, and *Victory Container Corp.*, GSBCA 5596, 81-2 BCA ¶ 15,346.

1. Nature of Requirements Contracts

A requirements contract provides the contractor with both the legal right and the legal duty to supply goods or services in an amount that is determined by *the Government's need* rather than by a fixed quantity. See *Torncello v. United States*, 231 Ct. Cl. 20, 681 F.2d 756 (1982); and *Mason v. United States*, 222 Ct. Cl. 436, 615 F.2d 1343 (1980). The consideration of the Government that makes this a legally binding contract is *its promise to satisfy its needs by buying from the contractor or contractors with contracts*. A contract containing language that abrogates this promise is not an enforceable requirements contract, *Sea-Land Serv., Inc.*, Comp. Gen. Dec. B-266238, 96-1 CPD ¶ 49 (Limitation of Government Liability clause giving Government the blanket right to obtain the services from other companies overrides requirements promise).

Any contract under which an agency of the Government undertakes to order all, or any specified portion, of its needs for a product or service during a designated period of time from a single contractor will be classified as a requirements contract. The key feature is that the legal obligation of the Government is defined by its *needs* rather than by a fixed amount. See *East Bay Auto Supply, Inc.*, ASBCA 25542, 81-2 BCA ¶ 15,204, stating that the "good faith duty to order all requirements from the contractor renders the contract enforceable, and not illusory." Accord *A-Transport Northwest Co.*, 27 Fed. Cl. 206 (1992), *aff'd*, 36 F.3d 1576 (1994); *Hilton's Cleaners, Inc.*, ASBCA 18213, 74-1 BCA, ¶ 10,433; *Export Packing & Crating Co.*, ASBCA 16133, 73-2 BCA ¶ 10,066. Under this type of contract, the Government is bound to order its requirements from the contractor but is under no obligation to have requirements as long as the absence of requirements is in good faith.

Whether a contract is in fact a requirements contract depends not upon the label attached to it by the parties but, rather, upon the nature of the rights and duties created by the contract, *Ceredo Mortuary Chapel, Inc.*, 29 Fed. Cl. 346 (1993); *Ralph Constr., Inc. v. United States*, 4 Cl. Ct. 727 (1984). In the event that the issue is litigated, the court or board will look first to the terms of the contract to determine its type. For example, in *Torncello v. United States*, 231 Ct. Cl. 20, 681 F.2d 756 (1982), the court held that when the Navy contracted for an indefinite quantity of ground maintenance services, with no guaranteed minimum amount, implicit in the terms was a promise to forgo diverting work to other contractors. In contrast, in *Modern Sys. Technology Corp. v. United States*, 24 Cl. Ct. 360 (1991), *aff'd*, 979 F.2d 200 (Fed. Cir. 1992), the court found that a Basic Purchasing Agreement was not a requirements contract because it contained no express promise by the Government to obtain its needs from the contractor. Similarly, in *Ann Riley & Assocs.*, DOTBCA 2418, 93-3 BCA ¶ 25,963, the board found that an indefinite-quantity contract was not a requirements contract because it did not include the "essential ingredient of a requirements contract, a statement that the [agency] was obligated to satisfy all of its requirements . . . from this source and no other." The board rejected Government testimony that it had intended to enter into a requirements contract and had used such contracts for these services in the past.

The court or board may also consider both facts known to the parties at the time of contracting and prior course of dealing between the parties, even where these are not explicitly mentioned in the contract, *Stanley F. Horton*, DOTCAB 1231, 82-2 BCA ¶ 15,967. In *Crown Laundry & Dry Cleaners, Inc. v. United States*, 29 Fed. Cl. 506 (1993), the court looked to the intentions of the parties to determine that the contract was a requirements contract — even though the contract was labeled an indefinite-quantity contract (with no stated minimum quantity) and did not contain the Requirements clause in FAR 52.216-21.

Requirements contracts should be distinguished from variable quantity contracts where the amount of work may vary but can be identified by some independent criterion other than the needs of the Government. In *Brawley v. United States*, 96 U.S. 168 (1877), the Supreme Court held that a requirements contract resulted when the contractor was obligated to deliver 880 cords of wood, "more or less, as shall be determined to be necessary . . . for the regular supply . . . of the troops." The Court stated at 171–72:

> Where a contract is made to sell or furnish certain goods identified by reference to independent circumstances, such as an entire lot deposited in a certain warehouse, or all that may be manufactured by the vendor in a certain establishment, or that may be shipped by his agent or correspondent in certain vessels, and the quantity is named with the qualification of "about," or "more or less," or words of like import, the contract applies to the specific lot; and the naming of the quantity is not regarded as in the nature of a warranty, but only as an estimate of the probable amount, in reference to which good faith is all that is required of the party making it. . . .
>
> If, however, the qualifying words are supplemented by other stipulations or conditions which give them a broader scope or a more extensive signifi-

> cancy, then the contract is to be governed by such added stipulations or conditions. As, if it be agreed to furnish so many bushels of wheat, more or less, according to what the party receiving it shall require for the use of his mill, then the contract is not governed by the quantity named, nor by that quantity with slight and unimportant variations, but by what the receiving party shall require for the use of his mill; and the variation from the quantity named will depend upon his discretion and requirements, so long as he acts in good faith.

The most common form of these variable quantity contracts where the quantity is identified by "independent circumstances" is the construction contract with unit prices to be paid on the basis of actual work performed. See FAR 36.207, permitting the procurement of construction work on the basis of fixed-unit prices. Although both contracts obligate the Government to pay only for the work that is done, the requirements contract is for needs that may arise in the future and will be ordered as they are identified, while the unit-price contract covers work that can be identified by a physical description such as excavation within specified boundaries (requiring no subsequent orders). In other respects, these contracts are quite similar. Although this material is directed to requirements contracts, it uses cases dealing with unit price contracts when the legal principles are the same.

Brawley also distinguishes another form of contract that indicates that the quantity of work may vary from a stated amount using terms such as "more or less" or "about." If the contract specifies no other criteria for determining quantity, such as requirements or a physical description, the contract will be construed to permit only slight variation. See *Brawley*, stating at 171–72:

> But when no such independent circumstances are referred to, and the engagement is to furnish goods of a certain quality or character to a certain amount, the quantity specified is material, and governs the contract. The addition of the qualifying words, "about," "more or less," and the like, in such cases, is only for the purpose of providing against accidental variations arising from slight and unimportant excesses or deficiencies in number, measure, or weight.

In determining which form of contract has been entered into, the court will look to all surrounding circumstances as well as the contract language. Thus, a contract to supply "six hundred thousand pounds, more or less, of oats . . . or such other quantity, more or less, as may be required . . . for the wants of said station" was found not to be a requirements contract because the contractor knew that another contract for oats had been awarded simultaneously, *Merriam v. United States*, 107 U.S. 437 (1882). In *Shader Contractors, Inc. v. United States*, 149 Ct. Cl. 535, 276 F.2d 1 (1960), the court looked to the contract terms to find a requirements contract where the contract called for the contractor to collect the amount ordered by the contracting officers as "may be needed." The contract contained an estimated quantity of coal of 5,500 tons and an estimated quantity of refuse of 4,000 tons and contained the provision, "The quantity may vary from 75 percent to 125 percent of the figure." The court ruled that the variation provision did not override the requirements language.

2. *Use of Requirements Contracts*

FAR 16.503(b) contains very general guidance stating that it is appropriate to use a requirements contract

> for acquiring any supplies or services when the Government anticipates recurring requirements but cannot predetermine the precise quantities of supplies or services that designated Government activities will need during a definite period.

While it is clearly less burdensome for a Government agency to issue a single requirements contract than to conduct a series of small, individual purchases, the requirements contract is not always preferable to a definite-quantity contract. Thus, although the regulations give no guidance on this issue, the contracting officer should carefully review the agency's needs before issuing a requirements contract. If those needs can be accumulated into an economic ordering quantity, a definite-quantity contract is usually preferable. See FAR Subpart 7.2 implementing 10 U.S.C. § 2384(a) and 41 U.S.C. § 253f(a), which require the use of economic quantities in purchasing supplies. See also Comp. Gen. Dec. B-170544, Jan. 22, 1971, *Unpub.*, where the Comptroller General recommended to the DOD that where appropriated funds were available and the agency's needs had been ascertained with reasonable certainty, with only the allocation of funds remaining, the regulations should express a preference for a more definite type of contract in order to achieve more realistic and reasonable bid prices.

While it is clear that a requirements contract is a task order or delivery order contract, the FAR contains no general guidance on the statutory preference for multiple contracts — which could be achieved by issuing two requirements contracts for a share of the agency's requirements. The working group that drafted the present FAR explained this omission as follows:

> The working group believes multiple awards are inconsistent with the requirements contracts which require a contractor to receive the buyer's entire requirement to establish legal consideration for the contract. See *Appeal of R.C. Swanson Printing & Typesetting Company*, GPOBCA No. 15-90, 1993 WL 668317 (1973). The working group is aware of no legal authority that recognizes the legitimacy of multiple award requirements contracts where a requirement is continuously competed. However, the working group is also aware that some individuals advocate the use of "multiple award requirements contracts."
>
> The prior draft rule attempted to reach a compromise position by including certain elements of secs 1004 and 1054 of FASA in 16.503 while remaining silent on the issue of whether multiple awards may be made. That draft rule was criticized for its ambiguity.
>
> The proposed rule has been revised to essentially retain the current FAR language in 16.503. The proposed rule also includes a limitation on the use of requirements contracts for advisory and assistance services in excess of 3 years and $10,000,000. This limitation is necessary to close a "loophole" so that agencies cannot escape the mandate to make multiple awards for CAAS in excess of the threshold by defining the acquisition as a requirements contract.
>
> Although the proposed rule does not apply the multiple award preference to requirements contracts, the proposed rule does not preclude agencies from experimenting with a multiple award requirements contract if the agency believes it can overcome the legal problems (i.e. illusory promise) related to a multiple award requirements contract.

This intentional ambiguity in the FAR raises the possibility that issuing a single requirements contract may be a statutory violation when the multiple award preference applies. See *Nations, Inc.*, Comp. Gen. Dec. B-272455, 96-2 CPD ¶ 170, where the Comptroller General found such a violation when the agency proposed to issue a single requirements contract for simulation training services with a value of over $10 million.

The limitation in FAR 16.503 for advisory and assistance services reads as follows:

> (d) Limitations on use of requirements contracts for advisory and assistance services. (1) Except as provided in paragraph (d)(2) of this section, no solicitation for a requirements contract for advisory and assistance services in excess of three years and $10,000,000 (including all options) may be issued unless the contracting officer or other official designated by the head of the agency determines in writing that the services required are so unique or highly specialized that it is not practicable to make multiple awards using the procedures in 16.504.
>
> (2) The limitation in paragraph (d)(1) of this section is not applicable to an acquisition of supplies or services that includes the acquisition of advisory and assistance services, if the contracting officer or other official designated by the head of the agency determines that the advisory and assistance services are necessarily incident to, and not a significant component of, the contract.

3. Pricing Arrangement

FAR 16.501-2(c) provides that requirements contracts may use any "cost or pricing arrangement" permitted by the FAR. Thus, these contracts can use any fixed-price, cost-reimbursement, or incentive arrangement or can be a time-and-materials or labor-hour contract. FAR 16.501-2(c) warns:

> Cost or pricing arrangements that provide for an estimated quantity of supplies or services (e.g., estimated number of labor hours) must comply with the appropriate procedures of this subpart.

If the Government's requirements are for well-defined supplies or tasks, arrangements with fixed-unit prices are the most desirable. This permits the most balanced competition and assures the Government that it will obtain performance of the contract at the costs that it anticipated. If the contract is for supplies that are not well defined, cost-reimbursement or incentive contracts can be used to ensure that undue risk is not being placed on the contractor. If the contract is for services that are not well defined, a time-and-materials or labor-hour contract can be used to hold the contractor to fixed labor rates while permitting flexibility as to the amount of work that needs to be done to meet the Government requirement. These latter types of pricing arrangements, of course, place much of the risk of increased costs on the Government.

4. Length of Requirements Contracts

Requirements contracts may be for a single year or for multiple years. In most cases, requirements contracts for more than one year include options for a specified number of additional years where appropriations are not available at the time of contracting. See, for example, *Free State Reporting, Inc.*, Comp. Gen. Dec. B-259650, 95-1 CPD ¶ 199 (requirements for support services for base year and two option years); *Tulane Univ.*, Comp. Gen. Dec. B-259912, 95-1 CPD ¶ 210 (requirements for services for two base years and three option years). Multiyear requirements contracts could also be issued as a single document, including later years not covered by current appropriations, if there is no possibility that the contractor could obligate the Government by performing work prior to the issuance of a requirement. See 42 Comp. Gen. 272 (B-144641) (1962), where the Comptroller General ruled that a requirements contract was in violation of appropriations law because the Government would be obligated to pay for work in a later year not covered under the contract. See also 67 Comp. Gen. 190 (B-224081) (1988), and 48 Comp. Gen. 494 (B-164908) (1969). In cases where a requirement contract is used in this way, an agency will normally include an "availability of funds" clause stating that the Government will not be liable to pay the contractor until funds for future years have been made contractually available. See *Funding of Maintenance Contract Extending Beyond Fiscal Year*, Comp. Gen. Dec. B-259274, 96-1 CPD ¶ 247, where the Comptroller General approved a requirements contract where the requirement covered two fiscal years with the second year restricted by an Availability of Funds clause. The Comptroller General stated that "a naked contractual obligation that carries with it no financial exposure to the government does not violate the Anti-Deficiency Act."

Agencies have also used multiyear requirements contracts when multiyear or no-year funds are being used for the procurement. This practice was explicitly permitted by FAR 17.104-4 until 1996, when the provision was deleted from the regulation. It is still legally permissible even though the FAR is silent on the subject. For examples of multiyear requirements contracts, see *Liebert Corp.*, 70 Comp. Gen. 448 (B-232234.5), 91-1 CPD ¶ 413 (agency issued firm-fixed-price requirements contract for services and materials over a five-year period); *CDI Marine Co.*, Comp. Gen. Dec. B-219934.2, 86-1 CPD ¶ 242 (agency issued a CPFF requirements contract for services performed over a three-year period).

5. Structuring the Requirement

The contracting officer has great flexibility in tailoring a requirements contract to fit the circumstances of each procurement. The Government attempts to obtain the best possible price by defining the requirement in such a way that competition can be maximized and risks to the contractor minimized. The Government also endeavors to structure such contracts to provide maximum assurance that its needs will be met in a timely manner and that it has the operating flexibility that it needs. The most important aspect of a requirements contract is the statement of the "requirement."

There are a number of ways in which the requirement can be stated to achieve these purposes. FAR 16.503(a) gives the following guidance on limitations on the requirement:

> (2) The contract shall state, if feasible, the maximum limit of the contractor's obligation to deliver and the Government's obligation to order. The contract may also specify maximum or minimum quantities that the Government may order under each individual order and the maximum that it may order during a specified period of time.

There is no guidance on limitations on the timing of ordering requirements, and the contractor bears the risk if the Government clusters its orders in one period, *Asfaltos Panamenos, S.A.*, ASBCA 41657, 92-3 BCA ¶ 25,141.

The Government may also wish to obtain only a part of its overall requirements from one contractor and to obtain the balance from others either through another requirements contract or some other form of contract. In some cases, the requirement may be structured to accommodate performance by Government personnel.

a. Limiting the Requirement

Two types of limitations are commonly used in requirements contracts. First, minimum and maximum order limitations are included in almost all such contracts. Second, limitations are sometimes included to divide the work between among two or more contractors.

(1) Minimums and Maximums

The Government includes minimums and maximums on individual orders and maximums for specified periods of time, FAR 16.503(a). FAR 16.506(b) instructs contracting officers to insert a clause in all requirements contracts that is substantially the same as the following Order Limitations clause at FAR 52.216-19:

> (a) *Minimum order.* When the Government requires supplies or services covered by this contract in an amount of less than ________ [*insert dollar figure or quantity*], the Government is not obligated to purchase, nor is the Contractor obligated to furnish, those supplies or services under the contract.
>
> (b) *Maximum order.* The Contractor is not obligated to honor —
>
> > (1) Any order for a single item in excess of ________ [*insert dollar figure or quantity*];
> >
> > (2) Any order for a combination of items in excess of ________ [*insert dollar figure or quantity*]; or
> >
> > (3) A series of orders from the same ordering office within _____ days that together call for quantities exceeding the limitation in subparagraph (1) or (2) above.
>
> (c) If this is a requirements contract (i.e., includes the Requirements clause at subsection 52.216-21 of the Federal Acquisition Regulation (FAR)), the Government is not required to order a part of any one requirement from the Contractor if that requirement exceeds the maximum-order limitations in paragraph (b) above.
>
> (d) Notwithstanding paragraphs (b) and (c) above, the Contractor shall honor any order exceeding the maximum order limitations in paragraph (b), unless that order (or orders) is returned to the ordering office within _____ days after issuance, with written notice stating the Contractor's intent not to ship the item (or items) called for and the reasons. Upon receiving this notice, the Government may acquire the supplies or services from another source.

Although inartfully drafted, this clause appears to cover only individual orders in the case of minimums, and both individual orders and a series of orders within a specified period in the case of maximums. The FAR contains no guidance on how to determine maximum or minimum order limitations. However, it is clear that the major advantage of minimum order limitations is to assure the contractor that orders will not be placed in such a manner as to be administratively burdensome. These minimum order limitations should not be confused with guaranteed minimums which are used in indefinite-quantity contracts. Maximum order limitations are apparently intended to permit the contractor to determine the maximum resources that must be committed to the contract at any time during performance. These limitations are essential if performance is required within a short period of time after placement of orders. If more flexibility in the time of performance is granted, these limitations should be stated in terms of a maximum amount of work over a period of time rather than in terms of individual orders or a series of orders. Maximum order limitations also permit the Government to avoid its requirements obligation if "one requirement" exceeds the limitations in the clause. Neither the clause nor the FAR provides any guidance as to how to determine when one requirement exists. The Government has been permitted to program its requirements to issue orders within a monthly maximum order limitation. In *Victory Container Corp.*, GSBCA 5596, 81-2 BCA ¶ 15,346, the contracting officer ordered the maximum quantity permitted each month in order to build the inventory of the items called for by the contract. The board held that this practice was a good faith use of the requirements contract since the contractor was aware that the items were normally carried in inventory by the Government.

While the Order Limitations clause contains no provision for total contract maximum quantities, FAR 16.503(a)(2) instructs the contracting officer to state the maximum quantity or dollar value of the entire contract. Such a contract maximum defines the scope of the original competition and assists the contractor by placing an outside limit on the resources it must commit to the contract. It also benefits the Government by permitting it the freedom to seek lower prices after the maximum is reached. Such provisions must be included in the contract schedule or by separate clause. Note, however, that orders placed in excess of the maximum order limitation are not necessarily considered to be outside the scope of the contract. See *Exide Corp.*, Comp. Gen. Dec. B-276988, 97-2 CPD ¶ 51, where the Comptroller General held that a delivery order issued under an existing requirements contract for a quantity in excess of the maximum order limitation was not beyond the scope of the contract because the contract permitted orders in excess of maximum quantity and the total quantity ordered under the contract did not significantly exceed the estimated quantity.

(2) DIVIDING THE REQUIREMENT

In some cases the Government can obtain more competition by dividing the requirement among two or more contractors. This technique is particularly useful when the goods or services are normally furnished by smaller contractors and the Government's requirements are large. FAR 52.216-21 contains Alternate III for the Requirements clause that covers the situation where the contracting officer decides to divide the requirement between a small business set-aside contractor and a non-set-aside contractor. This provision states, in part:

> The Government may choose between the set-aside Contractor and the non-set-aside Contractor in placing any particular order. However, the Government shall allocate successive orders, in accordance with its delivery requirements, to maintain as close a ratio as is reasonably practicable between the total quantities ordered from the two Contractors.

The FAR does not address the potential advantages of dividing requirements between contractors without using set-aside techniques. However, there is no prohibition of such practice, and it is clear that the Government might benefit in some circumstances by dividing a requirement geographically, mathematically, or by prescribing the mode of competition to be used in selecting the contractor for each requirement. Dividing the requirement and issuing two or more requirements contracts would also meet the statutory preference for multiple task order or delivery order contracts.

b. Allowing In-House Work

The Government may structure the requirement by limiting it to only those requirements in excess of the quantities that the Government activity may itself furnish within its own capabilities. The Government is thereby obligated to obtain from the contractor only that work "required to be purchased." Alternate I of the Requirements clause at FAR 52.216-21 provides the following provision for this purpose:

> (c) The estimated quantities are not the total requirements of the Government activity specified in the Schedule, but are estimates of requirements in excess of the quantities that the activity may itself furnish within its own capabilities. Except as this contract otherwise provides, the Government shall order from the Contractor all of that activity's requirements for sup-

> plies and services specified in the Schedule that exceed the quantities that the activity may furnish within its own capabilities.

The Government can also structure such a contract to provide for specific situations where Government employees will perform the work. For example, in *Tuscon Mobilephone, Inc.*, Comp. Gen. Dec. B-247687, 92-1 CPD ¶ 487, the Comptroller General approved a requirements contract that provided for work by Government employees when the contractor's personnel were not available or when the work could be done by agency personnel with the equipment on hand.

There is discord among the various courts and boards concerning both the adequacy of consideration where the Government retains the right to perform work in-house and the degree of discretion that the Government may exercise in performing under such contracts. The confusion stems, in part, from the language in FAR 16.503(a) which states, "A requirements contract provides for filling all actual purchase requirements of designated Government activities for specific supplies or services." This occasionally leads to the incorrect conclusion that a requirements contract must obligate the Government to buy all of its needs from the contractor. For example, in *Ralph Constr., Inc. v. United States*, 4 Cl. Ct. 727 (1984), the court ruled that because a requirements contract gives the contractor the right to "fill all of the government's needs," and yet the instant contract permitted the Government to assign work in-house, the contract was unenforceable because of a lack of mutuality of consideration. This analysis begs the question of what the "requirements" were. The contract itself clearly stated that the supplies and services covered by the contract were not all the Government needs but only those "in excess of the quantities which the activity may itself furnish within its own capabilities." Because the contract bound the Government to order from the contractor if it ordered at all, there appears to have been sufficient consideration to support the contractor's promise to perform. See also *Modern Sys. Technology Corp. v. United States*, 24 Cl. Ct. 360 (1991), *aff'd*, 979 F.2d 200 (Fed. Cir. 1992), stating that a requirements contract is one calling for the contractor to fulfill *all* of the Government's requirements. In *Dynamic Science, Inc.*, ASBCA 29510, 85-1 BCA ¶ 17,710, the board did not follow the view adopted by the Claims Court in *Ralph Construction* but held that such a contract was legally binding. After noting that the Government's only obligation was to procure, from the contractor alone, "such requirements as did arise during the contract term that were not to be satisfied by in-house capabilities," the board discussed the validity of "limited form" requirements contracts:

> We characterized the contract as a "limited form" requirements type. The limitation of the requirement to that portion that the Government did not choose to meet from its own capabilities did not render the promise illusory particularly because the Government was precluded from expanding its capabilities during contract performance at the expense of the contractor.

See also *Operational Serv. Corp.*, ASBCA 37059, 93-3 BCA ¶ 26,190, where the board again reviewed a "limited form" requirements contract, stating that it did not agree with the *Ralph Construction* reasoning and did not believe that the concurrence of the Federal Circuit on the *Modern Systems* decision was an adoption of that reasoning. In *D.M. Summers, Inc.*, VABCA 2750, 89-3 BCA ¶ 22,123, the board held that the Government had not breached a requirements contract by using some in-house services because the contractor was aware of this practice when it entered into the contract.

After entering into such a requirements contract, the Government may use its discretion in making ordering decisions, subject to a duty to act in good faith. See *Henry Angelo & Sons, Inc.*, ASBCA 15082, 72-1 BCA ¶ 9356, where the contract was for painting services beyond the capability of the Army's own forces, but because of budgetary considerations, the Government decided to apply funds to other projects even though the painting was still needed. Further, the Government expanded the painting work that was to be accomplished by its own forces. The board held that these actions constituted arbitrary reasons for not placing orders, did not comply with the Government's duty of good faith, and constituted a partial termination. See also *Maya Transit Co.*, ASBCA 20186, 75-2 BCA ¶ 11,552, where, although the Government undertook to buy only those bus services "in excess of the quantities which the activity may itself furnish within its own capabilities," it was not permitted to reduce the services ordered by reordering its budget priorities and redistributing its capabilities to assume more bus routes for its own drivers. In contrast, in *Export Packing & Crating Co.*, ASBCA 16133, 73-2 BCA ¶ 10,066, the Government's decision to assign work to civilian employees, rather than order from the contract, was approved and the contract for services "which are required to be purchased by the Government" was upheld. In *Arcon-Pacific Contractors*, ASBCA 25057, 82-2 BCA ¶ 15,838, the board held that "[a]bsent bad faith, the Government had discretion to determine what painting was 'required to be purchased.' " In exercising that discretion, the Government was permitted to consider the most economical way of meeting its needs and to assign work in-house in a cost-effective manner.

c. Measuring the Work Required

Another aspect of structuring the requirement is selecting the units of measure that will be used in ordering. When the Government procures goods, choosing the appropriate measure is simple. When the Government structures a requirements contract for services, however, it may choose to order by either unit of work actually completed or by unit of time. This choice affects the risks that each party bears.

The most common approach is to estimate, order, and pay for services on the basis of units of work supplied. The Government may, for example, contract for painting services on a per-square-foot basis, *Arcon-Pacific Contractors*, ASBCA 25057, 82-2 BCA ¶ 15,838; for renovation services based on multiple descriptions of renovation work with separate prices, *MDP Constr., Inc.*, ASBCA 49527, 96-2 BCA ¶ 28,525; or for motor vehicle maintenance on a per-vehicle-serviced basis, *S & W Tire Servs., Inc.*, GSBCA 6376, 82-2 BCA ¶ 16,048. Under this type of contract, the contractor assumes the risk that each unit of work can be performed profitably at the contract unit prices without regard to variations between actual and estimated quantities. In addition, both parties assume the risk of quantity variations when such variations increase or decrease the unit costs of performance.

The Government also contracts for services by unit of time. One way to do this is on an hourly basis using a labor-hour or time-and-materials pricing arrangement. For example, in *Stanley F. Horton*, DOTCAB 1231, 82-2 BCA ¶ 15,967, the Government ordered snow removal services at an hourly rate. The consequences of structuring the requirement on an hourly basis are similar to those of the unit of work situation except that there is significantly less contractor risk since the contractor is paid for the hours actually incurred in performing the work. Nevertheless, this type of contract is useful in situations where the work is not easily quantifiable in other units and is also subject to fluctuation in requirements.

6. Government Estimates

To provide equal information to all offerors as to the expected amount of supplies or services required and to provide a basis for evaluating the proposals, the Government includes estimated quantities of the work in the solicitation and uses these estimates to evaluate the offers. FAR 16.503(a) states:

> (1) For the information of offerors and contractors, the contracting officer shall state a realistic estimated total quantity in the solicitation and resulting contract. This estimate is not a representation to an offeror or contractor that the estimated quantity will be required or ordered, or that conditions affecting requirements will be stable or normal. The contracting officer may obtain the estimate from records of previous requirements and consumption, or by other means, and should base the estimates on the most current information available.

a. Liability for Incorrect Estimate

The Government is obligated to use care in calculating estimated quantities. However, a variation between the estimated quantity and the actual quantity does not in itself establish a basis for contractor relief, *Special Waste, Inc.*, ASBCA 36775, 90-2 BCA ¶ 22,935; *Standard-Southern Corp.*, ASBCA 20964, 77-1 BCA ¶ 12,359, *aff'd*, 223 Ct. Cl. 669 (1980). See also *Willamette Indus., Inc.*, Comp. Gen. Dec. B-188548, 79-2 CPD ¶ 338, holding that discrepancies between estimated and actual quantities of up to 80 percent were insufficient to afford a legal basis for relief. The Government's estimate of its needs is not generally regarded as a warranty that such amounts will be required, *Shader Contractors, Inc. v. United States*, 149 Ct. Cl. 535, 276 F.2d 1 (1960).

The decisions granting relief to contractors for faulty Government estimates have varied in their statement of the standard of conduct to which the Government is to be held. Some early cases stated that the Government's only obligation was to use good faith in its estimates, *Wheeler Bros.*, ASBCA 13089, 69-2 BCA ¶ 7861 (good faith error in estimating spare parts on hand); *Sponge Fishing Co.*, GSBCA 1386, 65-1 BCA ¶ 4627 (22,000 estimated, 53,967 ordered, but no recovery because estimate made in good faith). Thus, it was believed that in order to support recovery, the Government's estimate had to be made in bad faith. See Comp. Gen. Dec. B-169037, May 4, 1970, *Unpub.*, where the Comptroller General approved the contracting officer's settlement of a breach of contract claim based on bad faith.

More recently, the Government has been held to a somewhat higher degree of care. The rationale supporting these decisions is based upon

Womack v. United States, 182 Ct. Cl. 399, 389 F.2d 793 (1968), which, although not involving a requirements contract, held the Government liable on a misrepresentation theory for faulty estimates furnished for bidding purposes. See *Clearwater Forest Indus., Inc. v. United States*, 227 Ct. Cl. 386, 650 F.2d 233 (1981), stating that in making estimates, the Government "must act in good faith and use reasonable care." Applying this reasoning in *Integrity Management Int'l, Inc.*, ASBCA 18289, 75-1 BCA ¶ 11,235, *aff'd on recons.*, 75-2 BCA ¶ 11,602, the board reviewed the prior decisions and granted relief because of *Government negligence* in preparing estimates. See also *Datalect Computer Servs., Ltd. v. United States*, ___ Fed. Cl. ___ (1997) (relief granted because Government was negligent in that it knew of several facts that would likely affect estimate); *Crown Laundry & Dry Cleaners, Inc. v. United States*, 29 Fed. Cl. 506 (1993) (relief granted because Government was negligent in not checking estimates whose accuracy had been questioned by Government personnel during preparation of solicitation); *Travel Centre v. General Servs. Admin.*, GSBCA 14057, 98-1 BCA ¶ 29,422, *recons. denied*, 98-1 BCA ¶ ____ (relief granted because GSA knew or should have known that the estimates provided were vastly overstated); *Ambulance Serv. & Transp. of Marlin*, VABCA 3485, 94-2 BCA ¶ 26,729 (relief granted because Government failed to adequately utilize available information when making estimate); *Viktoria Fit Internationale Spedition*, ASBCA 39703, 92-2 BCA ¶ 24,968 (relief granted when contracting officer provided no convincing rationale for arriving at the estimate); *McCotter Motors, Inc.*, ASBCA 30498, 86-2 BCA ¶ 18,784 (relief granted when Government used disproportionately high prior-year quantity without determining whether that figure was an accurate forecast); *Pied Piper Ice Cream, Inc.*, ASBCA 20605, 76-2 BCA ¶ 12,148 (adopting reasonable care standard and finding Government grossly negligent); *American Maintenance & Management Servs., Inc.*, ASBCA 18756, 75-2 BCA ¶ 11,407, *recons. denied*, 75-2 BCA ¶ 11,572 (stating contractor is entitled to honest and informed estimate, but finding no negligence). In *Atlantic Garages, Inc.*, GSBCA 5891, 82-1 BCA ¶ 15,479, where the Government's solicitation for large-scale engine repair was restricted to contractors in a geographical area where large-scale organizations could not be expected to be operating, the Government was held to an enhanced duty to consider the potential effect of faulty estimates on smaller contractors. Compare *Medart, Inc.*, GSBCA 8939, 91-2 BCA ¶ 23,741, *aff'd*, 967 F.2d 579 (Fed. Cir. 1992), finding no liability for very inaccurate estimates because the agency had used the prior-year quantities, as suggested by

FAR 16.503(a)(1), as the basis for the estimate. In affirming, the Federal Circuit stated at 582:

> The government may go beyond the requirements of the regulations, of course. And it might be well advised to do so if it wants to secure the best prices and avoid contractors raising their bids to cover the uncertainties. But we are in no position to impose such a requirement either in this case or as a general proposition in the face of the regulations promulgated by competent authority. The regulations explicitly say that estimates may be based on the most current information about previous requirements available; Medart knew this, as well as who bore the risks of variances in quantity. It should have factored the risks into its bid . . . just as the regulation was factored into the contract.

See also *Apex Int'l Management Servs., Inc.*, ASBCA 37813, 94-1 BCA ¶ 26,299, where the board found no negligence because the agency had used historical workload figures to compile its estimates, and *American Marine Decking Servs., Inc.*, ASBCA 44440, 97-1 CPD ¶ 28,821, where the board found no negligence where the agency had based its estimate on work in another location because it had no experience at the location covered by the contract.

Where the Government acts in good faith and without negligence but the estimate is grossly inaccurate, the contractor may be entitled to relief if the resulting contract is unconscionable. That result was reached in *Operational Serv. Corp.*, ASBCA 37059, 93-3 BCA ¶ 26,190.

The most common type of faulty estimate occurs when the agency fails to consider all relevant, available information, *Grover Contracting Corp.*, GSBCA 4115, 75-2 BCA ¶ 11,550. See *Contract Management, Inc.*, ASBCA 44885, 95-2 BCA ¶ 27,886 (contractor granted equitable adjustment because Government estimate was not adjusted for anticipated budget shortfall); *Pruitt Energy Sources, Inc.*, ENGBCA 6134, 95-2 BCA ¶ 27,840 (contractor given additional compensation because estimate was not adjusted for shorter contract base period than those of prior contracts); *Fa. Kammerdiener GmbH & Co., KG*, ASBCA 45248, 94-3 BCA ¶ 27,197 (contractor entitled to additional costs because Government had information rendering its estimate inaccurate well before award); and *Crown Laundry & Dry Cleaners, Inc.*, ASBCA 28889, 85-2 BCA ¶ 18,003 (contractor entitled to equitable adjustment in price where Government ignored available workload figures in estimating its requirements). The Comptroller General has also stated that relief in the form of contract reformation can be granted when the Government has not based its estimate "on all relevant information that is reasonably available to it," *Lone Star Energy Co.*, Comp. Gen. Dec. B-199049, 80-2 CPD ¶ 98; *Union Carbide Corp.*, Comp. Gen. Dec. B-188426, 77-2 CPD ¶ 204, and that the estimates must be "reasonably accurate representations of anticipated actual needs," *CardioMetrix*, Comp. Gen. Dec. B-252758.3, 94-1 CPD ¶ 316; *Richard M. Walsh Assocs.*, Comp. Gen. Dec. B-216730, 85-1 CPD ¶ 621; *Yamas Constr. Co.*, Comp. Gen. Dec. B-217459, 85-1 CPD ¶ 599.

The Court of Claims has held that in making its estimate, the Government must give consideration to all potential work, whether or not "firm" requirements exist, *Chemical Technology, Inc. v. United States*, 227 Ct. Cl. 120, 645 F.2d 934 (1981). A possible way for the Government to avoid this problem is to provide estimates based on firm data and to inform the offerors of additional data that may indicate greater or fewer requirements. See *International Bus. Invs., Inc.*, Comp. Gen. Dec. B-215081, 85-1 CPD ¶ 228, where the Comptroller General denied a protest alleging that workload estimates in the IFB were not based upon the best available information. The Comptroller General reasoned, in part, that because the information that the protester asserted to be more accurate was provided by letter to all of the bidders prior to their response to the solicitation, no prejudice had occurred to the protester.

Where the contractor fills Government orders far exceeding the estimates without objecting to the validity of the estimates, the contractor will be estopped from later challenging the estimates, *Standard-Southern Corp.*, ASBCA 20964, 77-1 BCA ¶ 12,359, *aff'd*, 223 Ct.Cl. 669 (1980).

b. Contractor Obligation to Fulfill Requirements Exceeding Government Estimate

Subject to any contract or order maximums in the schedule, the requirements contractor must supply the full requirement regardless of the extent to which it may exceed the estimate, *Kasehagen Sec. Servs., Inc.*, ASBCA 25629, 86-2 BCA ¶ 18,797; *Sponge Fishing Co.*, GSBCA 1386, 65-1 BCA ¶ 4627. Where the contractor fails to fulfill that obligation, it will be held liable for excess costs incurred by the Government in reprocurement of any items that the Government would have been entitled to order under the contract, irrespective of whether orders had actually been placed with the defaulted contractor, *Interroyal Corp.*, GSBCA 5439, 83-1 BCA ¶ 16,339.

This same result would not be reached under the *Uniform Commercial Code* (U.C.C.) § 2-306(1), which excludes quantities "unreasonably disproportionate to any stated estimate." In *Miltex Indus., Inc.*, ASBCA 19449, 77-2 BCA ¶ 12,768, the board rejected the application of this provision, holding that federal precedent in this area consistently limited contractor liability only when the Government made a bad faith estimate. Accord *Machlett Labs., Inc.*, ASBCA 16194, 73-1 BCA ¶ 9929.

Commercial impracticability has been used to avoid the contractor's obligation to supply required services. In *Selectronix Communications*, ASBCA 20981, 77-1 BCA ¶ 12,547, a default termination was converted to a termination for the convenience of the Government when the inventory requirements necessary for contractor compliance with an Air Force communications system repair schedule were deemed commercially impracticable.

c. *Relief for Faulty Government Overestimate*

Contractors have frequently submitted claims for relief when quantity underruns were the result of faulty estimates. While the promulgation of such estimates are breaches of contract, *Atlantic Garages, Inc.*, GSBCA 5891, 82-1 BCA ¶ 15,479, the boards have sometimes dealt with such claims as terminations for convenience, *Integrity Management Int'l, Inc.*, ASBCA 18289, 75-1 BCA ¶ 11,235, *aff'd on recons.*, 75-2 BCA ¶ 11,602; *Pied Piper Ice Cream, Inc.*, ASBCA 20605, 76-2 BCA ¶ 12,148. Whichever legal theory applies, the relief has been measured by repricing the contract quantities based on an accurate estimate of the quantities of work. Such repricing places the contractor in the position it would have occupied but for the Government breach.

7. Variations in Estimated Quantities Clauses

The Government often uses clauses that provide for price adjustment when Government requirements vary from the estimate by more than stated percentages. There is no standard variation in quantity clause prescribed for requirements contracts. FAR 52.212-11 provides a Variations in Estimated Quantities clause for use in construction contracts. Many requirements contracts contain similar clauses calling for price adjustments for quantities varying from the estimate by more than a stated percentage.

The Government has unsuccessfully argued that these clauses protect it from liability for faulty estimates or improper actions during performance. In *Integrity Management Int'l, Inc.*, ASBCA 18289, 75-1 BCA ¶ 11,235, *aff'd on recons.*, 75-2 BCA ¶ 11,602, the board found that the Government had made a faulty estimate and reasoned that the clause did not bind the contractor to assume the burden of the first 25 percent of the Government's negligence. In *Chemical Technology, Inc. v. United States*, 227 Ct. Cl. 120, 645 F.2d 934 (1981), the court granted relief even though the deviation from the estimated quantity fell within the range of the Volume Variation clause, stating, "In its dealings with contractors, the Government cannot provide inaccurate data in this manner and then be allowed to bar an equitable recovery by arguing that the resulting damages . . . fall within the 25% Volume Variation clause." It has also been held that a variation in quantity clause will not apply if the original Government estimate is negligently made, *Marine Constr. & Dredging, Inc.*, ASBCA 38538, 95-1 BCA ¶ 27,286; *John Murphy Constr. Co.*, AGBCA 418, 79-1 BCA ¶ 13,836.

Clauses of this type will not prevent the contractor from obtaining a price adjustment under the Differing Site Conditions clause when the variation in quantity occurs because of a condition that falls within the bounds of that clause. For example, in *Continental Drilling Co.*, ENGBCA 3455, 75-2 BCA ¶ 11,541, a changed condition was found when the contractor had to use a substantially larger quantity of a drill hole casing than the estimated quantity. The board reasoned that the Government estimate of a small amount of drill hole casing was an indication that a certain type of subsurface material would be encountered, whereas the need to use a large quantity of the casing indicated that a different type of material was actually present at the site. In *A.S. Horner, Inc.*, ASBCA 76-145, 79-1 BCA ¶ 13,561, a changed condition was found when the contractor had to use different methods to excavate a trench deeper than had been anticipated, and in *Brezina Constr., Inc.*, ENGBCA 3215, 75-1 BCA ¶ 10,989, a changed condition was found where the contractor was required to dispose of a large amount of material off-site although the parties had anticipated that there would be an approximate balance between the excavated material and the material used for fill. In *Brezina*, the board found a changed condition rather than a variation in quantity because the contractor had encountered an "entirely different job" than anticipated. Similarly, in *Dunbar & Sullivan Dredging Co.*, ENGBCA 3165, 73-2 BCA ¶ 10,285, the board found a changed condition when the contractor encountered an unforeseen rock ledge in the river being dredged even though the contract contained a unit price for dredging rock. The board reasoned that since the unusual methods required to remove the rock ledge were not those included in the price of dredging loose rock, a changed condition had been encountered even though the amount of rock in the ledge was less than 1 percent of the estimated quantity of rock.

The Changes clause has also been held to override the Variations in Estimated Quantities clause in situations where the Government orders the contractor to perform unit priced work in excess of that contemplated when the quantity estimates were established. For example, in *Morrison-Knudsen Co. v. United States*, 184 Ct. Cl. 661, 397 F.2d 826 (1968), the court found the contractor entitled to a price adjustment under the Changes clause when the Government overcame unforeseen conditions by ordering the contractor to perform the work in a different manner. See also *C.H. Leavell & Co.*, ENGBCA 3492, 75-2 BCA ¶ 11,596, where a contracting officer's order to change the concrete mixtures was held to be a change rather than a variation in quantity although there was a unit price in the contract for cement. In *Maya Transit Co.*, ASBCA 20186, 75-2 BCA ¶ 11,552, the board held that the clause was not intended to apply to a constructive change.

Normally, such clauses provide that the unit prices set forth in the contract are to apply to all quantities of work within the range specified in the clause. Thus, price adjustments on overruns will be made only to that quantity above the stated percentage. In *N. Fiorito Co. v. United States*, 189 Ct. Cl. 215, 416 F.2d 1284 (1969), it was held that this type of clause binds the parties to the unit prices for quantities of work up to the full extent of the variation range (110 percent of the estimated quantity in the clause in question) with repricing to occur only as to the quantities in excess of the range.

These clauses do not provide for complete repricing of the work above or below the range. The clause in FAR 52.212-11 provides that any equitable adjustment under the clause will be based on increases or decreases in cost "due solely to the variation." In *Victory Constr. Co. v. United States*, 206 Ct. Cl. 274, 510 F.2d 1379 (1975), the court held that the party demanding the adjustment had the burden of proof that the costs had varied because of the difference in quantity. The court further stated that the amount of the equitable adjustment was to be determined solely on the basis of differences in cost because of the larger or smaller quantity rather than on a complete repricing of the work based on actual incurred costs for the excess quantity. The Federal Circuit followed this reasoning in *Foley Co. v. United States*, 11 F.3d 1032 (Fed. Cir. 1993). See also *Clement-Mtarri Cos.*,

ASBCA 38170, 92-3 BCA ¶ 25,192, *aff'd*, 11 F.3d 1072 (Fed. Cir. 1993); *Burnett Constr. Co. v. United States*, 26 Cl. Ct. 296 (1992); *Oneida Constr., Inc./David Boland, Inc. (JV)*, ASBCA 47915, 94-3 BCA ¶ 27,222; and *Ronald Adams Contractor, Inc.*, AGBCA 91-155-1, 94-3 BCA ¶ 27,018. Compare *Bean Dredging Corp.*, ENGBCA 5507, 89-3 BCA ¶ 22,034, and *Carvel Walker*, ENGBCA 3744, 78-1 BCA ¶ 13,005, adjusting the price of an overrun quantity based on the total costs of the additional quantity rather than the increased costs due to the additional quantity. One of the most common reasons for a price adjustment is that the increase or decrease in quantity will alter the amount of fixed costs allocable to each unit. In *Henry Angelo & Co.*, ASBCA 43669, 94-1 BCA ¶ 26,484, the board included in the adjustment for a severe underrun in estimated quantity an amount for indirect costs that would have been recovered if the estimated quantity had been ordered. In *Cottrell Eng'g Corp.*, ENGBCA 3038, 70-2 BCA ¶ 8462, the board found a difference in cost due to the larger quantity based on the full recovery of nonrecurring costs in the unit prices for the estimated quantity. The board therefore granted a downward equitable adjustment removing the nonrecurring costs from the unit prices for the purposes of paying for the overrun quantity.

8. Government Failure to Order Its Requirements under the Contract

The contractor is not entitled to compensation if the Government's failure to place orders results from either risks assumed by the contractor or good faith decisions of the Government to reduce its activity because of unanticipated changes in its situation. The contractor must demonstrate that the Government has breached its obligations or changed the requirement.

a. Obtaining Needs from Alternate Source

Relief has been granted to contractors when the Government has improperly failed to order its requirements under the contract and has obtained its needs from another source or has accomplished the work in-house. In *C&S Park Serv., Inc.*, ENGBCA 3624, 78-1 BCA ¶ 13,134, the contractor was allowed to recover for losses incurred due to the reduction in work caused by Government personnel performing the lawn maintenance services covered by a contract that made no allowances for in-house performance. See also *Inland Container, Inc. v. United States*, 206 Ct. Cl. 478, 512 F.2d

1073 (1975) (Government requisitioned most of the goods from the GSA); *Vehicle Maintenance Servs. v. General Servs. Admin.*, GSBCA 11663, 94-2 BCA ¶ 26,893 (work diverted to other vendors); *Erwin v. United States*, 19 Cl. Ct. 47 (1989) (work bought from other vendors); *Arcon-Pacific Contractors*, ASBCA 25057, 82-2 BCA ¶ 15,838 (Government ordered another contractor to do work); *North Chicago Disposal Co.*, ASBCA 25535, 82-1 BCA ¶ 15,488 (Government had no right to retroactively recoup an amount paid to a contractor where the bulk of the job was actually performed by Navy personnel ignorant of the contract); *Maya Transit Co.*, ASBCA 20186, 75-2 BCA ¶ 11,552 (Government performed work in-house because of budget considerations); and *Pacific Technical Enters., Ltd.*, ASBCA 17087, 74-2 BCA ¶ 10,679 (Government diverted some of its requirements to another contractor). In *MDP Constr., Inc.*, ASBCA 49527, 96-2 BCA ¶ 28,525, the Government breached a requirements contract for renovation of bathrooms by including bathroom renovation in a larger contract for renovation of total buildings. Similarly, in *S & W Tire Servs., Inc.*, GSBCA 6376, 82-2 BCA ¶ 16,048, the board held that the Government was in breach of a requirements contract for tire recapping when, during the contract period, it hired a new contractor to run its entire motor pool, thereby depriving the original contractor of the recapping business. But where the contractor had actual knowledge, prior to bidding, of the Government's capacity for performing work in-house and of its intent to do so, the contractor was held to have bid in full realization that it would only be called upon to perform in the event that the Government's capability proved inadequate to meet its requirements, *Stanley F. Horton*, DOTCAB 1231, 82-2 BCA ¶ 15,967. See also *Pegasus Aviation, Inc. v. General Servs. Admin.*, GSBCA 10112, 93-3 BCA ¶ 25,944, where the board held that the Government had not diverted work where the contract provided six exceptions in which services would be sought elsewhere.

In determining whether a breach has occurred, the court or board will review the specification to ensure that the work obtained from another contract is the same work as that under the requirements contract. In *Cleek Aviation v. United States*, 19 Cl. Ct. 552 (1990), the court found no breach of a requirements contract for supplying aviation fuel directly into airplanes when the agency ordered aviation fuel for storage tanks from another contractor. The court reasoned that the two types of services were essentially different. See also *Eastern Ambulance Servs., Inc.*, VABCA 2078, 86-2 BCA ¶ 18,852, where the board found that award of a contract with a company to transport "stretcher" patients did not violate a requirements contract to provide ambulance services. The board compared the two types of services and found them dissimilar even though the "stretcher" patients could receive some medical services in transit.

b. Government Change in Work

The contractor may also be entitled to relief on a theory that a Government change in work has occurred. In *Desco Serv. Contractors*, ASBCA 21856, 77-2 BCA ¶ 12,752, a change occurred when the Government decreased the frequency of vehicle maintenance inspections under the contract. See also *California Bus Lines*, ASBCA 19732, 75-2 BCA ¶ 11,601 (change in work plan reducing amount of work necessary to meet Government's unchanged requirements constituted a constructive change); and *Del Rio Flying Serv.*, ASBCA 15304, 71-1 BCA ¶ 8744 (Government change in definition of "students," resulting in decreased work is compensable if increased costs result). The changes theory will not cover reductions in the Government's needs that occur because of changed circumstances, *East Bay Auto Supply, Inc.*, ASBCA 25542, 81-2 BCA ¶ 15,204 (reduction of fleet at base contractor was servicing caused a decline in demand for spare vehicle parts); *Solano Aircraft Serv., Inc.*, ASBCA 20677, 77-2 BCA ¶ 12,584 (military commitments in Southeast Asia reduced the number of available domestic aircraft to be serviced); *Gulf Coast Aviation Co.*, ASBCA 10189, 65-2 BCA ¶ 4928 (base closing eliminated the requirement for food services). Neither is it a change if the Government cancels an order after it is issued, *California Bus Lines, Inc.*, ASBCA 42181, 91-3 BCA ¶ 24,341. However, the contractor will be entitled to compensation for costs incurred if the cancellation order is received too late to permit it to avoid the costs, *California Bus Lines, Inc.*, ASBCA 19571, 76-1 BCA ¶ 11,655.

It is not a change to the contract when the Government orders uneven quantities, *Asfaltos Panamenos, S.A.*, ASBCA 41657, 92-3 BCA ¶ 25,141. The board held that the contractor should not have relied on even ordering because there was no contract clause requiring orders to be placed uniformly. See also *Tennessee Valley Auth. v. Imperial Professional Coatings*, 599 F. Supp. 436 (E.D. Tenn. 1984), where construction of nuclear power plants was deferred because demand for electricity was less than anticipated. The court held that the requirements contractor for painting services had assumed the risk of a good faith decision to cancel the construction of the plant.

c. Measuring Contractor Relief

As discussed above, the Government's failure to perform its obligations under a requirements contract has been alternatively treated as a breach of contract or a constructive change. Government breaches are generally treated as constructive terminations for convenience when the contract contains a Termination for Convenience clause, *Nesbitt v. United States*, 170 Ct. Cl. 666, 345 F.2d 583 (1965); *Inland Container, Inc. v. United States*, 206 Ct. Cl. 478, 512 F.2d 1073 (1975); *Kalvar Corp. v. United States*, 211 Ct. Cl. 192, 543 F.2d 1298 (1976), *cert. denied*, 434 U.S. 830 (1977). Breaches will not be converted to convenience terminations if the failure to order was in bad faith, *Kalvar Corp. v. United States*, 211 Ct. Cl. 192, 543 F.2d 1298 (1976), *cert. denied*, 434 U.S. 830 (1977), or if it was based on circumstances known to the Government at the time of award, *Torncello v. United States*, 231 Ct. Cl. 20, 681 F.2d 756 (1982). In *Torncello*, the Government obtained a requirement at a lower price about which it had known at the time of award of the contract. The court reasoned that the Termination for Convenience clause was not properly usable in such circumstances. See also *S & W Tire Servs., Inc.*, GSBCA 6376, 82-2 BCA ¶ 16,048, where the board found that contracting out an entire operation, of which the requirements contract was a part, was a breach and not a constructive termination, because the Government knew of the decision to contract out at the time of award of the requirements contract. In *Erwin v. United States*, 19 Cl. Ct. 47 (1989), the court refused to find a constructive termination when the Government ordered all of the services from other vendors because the termination for convenience clause limited compensation to the price of completed work. The court reasoned that use of this clause would amount to "illusory consideration" for the requirements contract. In *Viktoria Transp. GmbH & Co.*, ASBCA 30371, 88-3 BCA ¶ 20,921, the board treated a failure to order all requirements as a termination for convenience rather than as a breach because there was no bad faith. This rule will also prevent the agency from issuing a termination for convenience order to avoid a requirements contract when no changed circumstances are present, *Tamp Corp.*, ASBCA 25692, 84-2 BCA ¶ 17,460.

The measure of recovery can vary significantly depending on the characterization of the Government's action in failing to order under the contract. If a breach is found, the contractor will be awarded damages including anticipated profits. See *Tamp Corp.*, ASBCA 25692, 84-2 BCA

¶ 17,460, stating that changes must be calculated to put the contractor in "as good a position as if it had been permitted to fully perform the contract." The board held that this required compensation for profits that would have been earned plus "expenses reasonably incurred as the result of the premature termination."

Recovery may be significantly less if an actual or constructive termination for convenience is found. In addition to nonrecovery of anticipated profits in termination pricing, the contractor will be bound by the special cost principle applicable to this type pricing. The major advantage for terminated contractors is the ability to recover settlement costs incurred after the termination. See *Kalvar Corp. v. United States*, 211 Ct. Cl. 192, 543 F.2d 1298 (1976), *cert. denied*, 434 U.S. 830 (1977), where the prohibition of anticipated profits was broadly construed to preclude recovery for the difference between the contract price and a profitable resale price and for higher unit costs on subsequent sales of terminated items. The court also disallowed financing costs and administrative costs associated with the alleged breach on the theory that these were not recoverable under termination cost principles. The court did permit the recovery of some of the contractor's legal fees as settlement costs. Appeals boards have been somewhat more liberal in computing termination costs. See *Drain-A-Way Sys.*, GSBCA 7022, 84-1 BCA ¶ 16,929, where the board held that the unit prices should be recomputed to reflect lower volumes because of the termination. Similarly, in *Wheeler Bros.*, ASBCA 20465, 79-1 BCA ¶ 13,642, where there was a partial termination for convenience, the board permitted repricing to include the entire increase in overhead costs resulting from the reduced volume. See also *Inland Container, Inc. v. United States*, 206 Ct. Cl. 478, 512 F.2d 1073 (1975), where the court permitted recovery of losses incurred in running a manufacturing plant for six months awaiting Government orders under the requirements contract. The court reasoned that this loss was a reasonable approximation of initial and preparatory expenses since the plant would probably not have incurred losses had the Government properly issued orders. However, profits have been limited to those earned on the completed work. See *Adams Mfg. Co.*, GSBCA 5747, 82-1 BCA ¶ 15,740, *aff'd*, 714 F.2d 161 (Fed. Cir. 1983), precluding anticipated profits where failure to order constituted a total termination for convenience, and *Arcon-Pacific Contractors*, ASBCA 25057, 82-2 BCA ¶ 15,838, where the board limited recovery to actual incurred costs plus profit on those costs in the case of a constructive partial convenience termination.

A different pricing theory applies when the Government's failure to honor its requirements obligation is construed as a constructive change. There, the proper measure of the equitable adjustment is the difference between the cost of the work originally called for and the changed work. See *Desco Serv. Contractors*, ASBCA 21856, 77-2 BCA ¶ 12,752, using this technique to compute the adjustment. In *Maya Transit Co.*, ASBCA 20186, 75-2 BCA ¶ 11,552, the board stated that the unit prices of the work should be recomputed following this theory. See also *Pacific Technical Enters., Ltd.*, ASBCA 17087, 74-2 BCA ¶ 10,679, where the equitable adjustment was computed by granting the contractor payment for work diverted to another company.

B. Multiyear Contracts

The multiyear contract is a specialized type of requirements contract that creates a slightly different relationship between the contractor and the Government. It is defined in FAR 17.103 as follows:

> Multiyear contract means a contract for the purchase of supplies or services for more than 1, but not more than 5, program years. A multiyear contract may provide that performance under the contract during the second and subsequent years of the contract is contingent upon the appropriation of funds, and (if it does so provide) may provide for a cancellation payment to be made to the contractor if appropriations are not made. The key distinguishing difference between multiyear contracts and multiple year contracts is that multiyear contracts, defined in [10 U.S.C. § 2306b and 41 U.S.C. § 254c] buy more than 1 year's requirement (of a product or service) without establishing and having to exercise an option for each program year after the first.

Thus, the FAR distinguishes between the multiyear contract and the other types of variable quantity contracts (requirements contracts and indefinite-quantity contracts) that frequently cover multiple years by including option clauses.

This form of contract was devised by the DOD in the 1960s to allow its contracting activities to procure supplies for several years in spite of the fact that appropriated funds were available for such supplies for only one year. The goal was to achieve lower unit prices by permitting the contractor to spread start-up costs over more work, to introduce cost-saving methods of performing the work, and to realize the economies of continuous manufacture of goods. In 1969, the regulations were amended to include service contracts. See FAR 17.105-2, which lists the following objectives for both types of multiyear contracting:

> Use of multiyear contracting is encouraged to take advantage of one or more of the following:
>
> (a) Lower costs.
>
> (b) Enhancement of standardization.
>
> (c) Reduction of administrative burden in the placement and administration of contracts.
>
> (d) Substantial continuity of production or performance, thus avoiding annual startup costs, preproduction testing costs, make-ready expenses, and phaseout costs.
>
> (e) Stabilization of contractor work forces.
>
> (f) Avoidance of the need for establishing quality control techniques and procedures for a new contractor each year.
>
> (g) Broadening the competitive base with opportunity for participation by firms not otherwise willing or able to compete for lesser quantities, particularly in cases involving high startup costs.
>
> (h) Providing incentives to contractors to improve productivity through investment in capital facilities, equipment, and advanced technology.

The Comptroller General has held that multiyear contracting is not unduly prejudicial to small business, 43 Comp. Gen. 657 (B-152766) (1964). See also 46 Comp. Gen. 749 (B-160815) (1967).

In order to use multiyear procurement, an agency must comply with the Anti-Deficiency Act, 31 U.S.C. § 1341, which prohibits the making of contracts in advance of appropriations. This is accomplished by entering into a firm commitment for one year and making the Government's liability for future years' quantities contingent on funds becoming available. The contractor is protected in the event the Government fails to order all of the program years' quantities by the inclusion of a Cancellation under Multiyear Contracts clause in FAR 52.217-2, providing for reimbursement of unrecovered start-up costs. Since these are long term contracts, the use of economic price adjustment provisions is also permitted, FAR 17.109(b).

1. Legal Authority

There has been considerable confusion over the legal authority of agencies to use multiyear contracts. However, it seems clear that agencies have the inherent authority to use multiyear contracts because, for a number of years, Congress acquiesced to the DOD's use of multiyear contracts for the procurement of supplies without statutory authority when multiyear or no-year funds were being used. Ultimately, a limit was imposed on cancellation ceilings of $5 million, Section 810 of the DOD Authorization Act of 1976, P.L. 94-106. This effectively precluded the use of multiyear procurements on major systems. Subsequently, in 1982, the Armed Services Committees concluded that multiyear contracts were a means of obtaining lower prices for major weapon systems. The Armed Services Procurement Act was therefore amended to encourage the DOD to use multiyear contracting under the surveillance of Congress, 10 U.S.C. § 2306(h) (pre-1994). This provision placed a limitation on such contracts by requiring notification of Congress if a cancellation ceiling of more than $100 million was included in such a contract. Further limitations were included in the Authorization and Appropriations Acts of the DOD. See Section 8010 of the 1995 Appropriations Act which required notification of Congress of any multiyear contract with a cancellation ceiling over $20 million and precluded the use of multiyear contracting for systems or components with a contract price over $500 million, P.L. 103-335, 108 Stat. 2618-19. This Act also authorized multiyear contracts on four specific systems. Thus, the DOD has been required to obtain specific statutory authorization for the use of this technique on all major systems. This authorization is initiated by submitting detailed justifications on each system to the Armed Services Committees of the Congress, which obtain assistance in reviewing such proposed actions from the General Accounting Office. See, for example, Comptroller General Reports, GAO/NSIAD-90-270BR, Aug. 1990, GAO/NSIAD-89-224BR, Sept. 1989, GAO/NSIAD-86-1, Nov. 1985, GAO/NSIAD-85-9, Oct. 1984. These oversight provisions are currently found in 10 U.S.C. § 2306b(i) as well as in specific Appropriations Acts. The National Defense Authorization Act for Fiscal Year 1988, P.L. 105-85, added additional approval requirements to Section 2306b(i) for defense multiyear contracts or advance procurements leading to a multiyear contract that employ economic order quantity procurement in excess of $20,000,000, or that include an unfunded contingent liability in excess of $20,000,000, as follows:

(1) Congressional defense committees must be notified of the proposed contract at least 30 days in advance of award.

(2) The economic order quantity advance procurement must be funded to the limit of the Government's liability.

(3) The value of the multiyear contract must not exceed $500,000,000, unless authority for the contract is specifically provided in an appropriations act.

(4) A multiyear procurement contract may not be terminated until 10 days after the date on which notice of the proposed termination is provided to the congressional defense committees.

(5) In executing multiyear contracting authority, present value analysis must be used to determine lowest cost compared to an annual procurement.

During this same period, Congress authorized the DOD, NASA, and the Coast Guard to enter into multiyear service contracts. This was permitted for contracts outside of the United States by the enactment of 10 U.S.C. § 2306(g) in 1968. This statute was broadened in 1981 to permit such contracts within the United States and now permits multiyear contracts using any type of funds if they are for the following types of services:

(A) operation, maintenance, and support of facilities and installations;

(B) maintenance or modification of aircraft, ships, vehicles, and other highly complex military equipment;

(C) specialized training necessitating high quality instructor skills (for example, pilot and aircrew members; foreign language training); and

(D) base services (for example, ground maintenance; in-plane refueling; bus transportation; refuse collection and disposal);

When the FAR was issued in 1984, FAR 17.102-1 reflected the fact that multiyear contracting could be used on both supply and service contracts containing multiyear or no-year funds without statutory authority by stating:

> (a) Multiyear contracting may be used when no-year or multiyear funds are available or, in the case of 1-year funds, when multiyear contracting is specifically authorized by statute. (Specific statutory authority is needed for an agency to make financial commitments for amounts greater than those appropriated annually by the Congress. See 31 U.S.C. § 1341(a)(1).)
>
> (b) The multiyear contracting method may be used for the acquisition of services or supplies (including, but not limited to systems, subsystems, major equipment, components, parts, materials, supplies, and the advance acquisition thereof, and commercial and noncommercial items).

The perceived necessity of statutory authority for multiyear contracting using annual ("1-year") funds was based on the fear that such contracting would be construed as a procurement of more than the bona fide needs of the Government for the single year for which the funds were appropriated, in violation of 31 U.S.C. § 1341, 43 Comp. Gen. 657 (B-152766) (1964). See also *Defense Logistics Agency Multiyear Contract for Storage & Rotation of Sulfadiazine Silver Cream*, 67 Comp. Gen. 190 (B-224081) (1987), and 42 Comp. Gen. 272 (B-144641) (1962), discussing this issue. In *Army's Multiple Launch Rocket Sys. Multiyear Contract*, 64 Comp. Gen. 163 (B-215825) (1984), the Comptroller General implies that the bona fide needs rule, 31 U.S.C. § 1502, also precludes multiyear contracts using multiyear funds without explaining the reasoning.

The Federal Acquisition Streamlining Act of 1994, P.L. 103-355, broadened the statutory coverage of multiyear contracting. First, it moved the provision on multiyear contracting for *supplies* in 10 U.S.C. § 2306(h) to 10 U.S.C. § 2306b and brought the NASA and the Coast Guard within its coverage. In so doing, Congress imposed some of the restrictive provisions in the prior statute on these two agencies and continued to impose some special requirements on the DOD. This statute also states that it is inapplicable to contracts under 40 U.S.C. § 759 for information resource management supplies, 10 U.S.C. § 2306b(k). Second, the Act added a new multiyear statute for both *supplies and services* procured by civilian agencies, 41 U.S.C. § 254c. This is a short statute that permits the use of multiyear contracts with any type of funds (annual, multiyear, or no-year) with fewer congressional restrictions. These new statutes giving authority to use multiyear contracts without regard to the type of funds clear up the issue of whether there is legal authority to use multiyear contracts with annual funds. The FAR is now silent on this issue.

2. Use

The statutes provide criteria that must be met to use a multiyear contract, 10 U.S.C. § 2306b(a); 41 U.S.C. § 254c(a). FAR 17.105-1 states these criteria as follows:

> (a) Except for DoD, NASA and the Coast Guard, the contracting officer may enter into a multiyear contract if the head of the contracting activity determines that —
>
> > (1) The need for the supplies or services is reasonably firm and continuing over the period of the contract; and
> >
> > (2) A multiyear contract will serve the best interests of the United States by encouraging full and open competition or promoting economy in administration, performance, and operation of the agency's programs.
>
> (b) For DoD, NASA, and the Coast Guard, the head of the agency may enter into a multiyear contract for supplies if —
>
> > (1) The use of such a contract will result in substantial savings of the total estimated costs of carrying out the program through annual contracts;
> >
> > (2) The minimum need to be purchased is expected to remain substantially unchanged during the contemplated contract period in terms of production rate, procurement rate, and total quantities;
> >
> > (3) There is a stable design for the supplies to be acquired, and the technical risks associated with such supplies are not excessive;
> >
> > (4) There is a reasonable expectation that, throughout the contemplated contract period, the head of the agency will request funding for the contract at a level to avoid contract cancellation; and
> >
> > (5) The estimates of both the cost of the contract and the cost avoidance through the use of a multiyear contract are realistic.

The guidance in Paragraph (b) applies only to contracts for supplies — implementing 10 U.S.C. § 2306b. The FAR contains no guidance on the criteria applicable to the separate statute for services, 10 U.S.C. § 2306(g). However, DFARS 217.103-1(b) contains the following guidance:

(iii) Award of a multiyear contract for services requires a written determination by the head of the contracting activity (10 U.S.C. § 2306(g)(1)) that —

(A) There will be a continuing need for the services and incidental supplies;

(B) Furnishing the services and incidental supplies will require —

(1) A substantial initial investment in plant or equipment;

(2) The upfront commitment of substantial financial resources for the assembly, training or transportation of a specialized work force; or

(3) Other substantial startup costs; and

(C) Using a multiyear contract will be in the best interest of the United States by encouraging effective competition and promoting economical business operations.

The new FAR provisions reflect the fact that the civilian agency statute imposes very few limitations on use of multiyear contracts. For example, it contains no requirement for an estimate of savings in order to justify the use of a multiyear contract, whereas the statute applying to the DOD, NASA, and the Coast Guard requires "substantial" savings. Under the prior statute, the Comptroller General stated that savings should be "significant," but no fixed standard was adopted. In deciding whether projected savings were significant enough to justify multiyear procurement, cost savings were balanced against added risks. See Comptroller General Report, GAO/NSIAD-86-1, Nov. 1985, stating at 6:

Each proposed multiyear contract should be evaluated on its own merits, weighing the margin of savings against added risks and any other uncertainties. The savings should be high enough to offset any additional risks of entering into a multiyear contract. For example, a candidate with no risks in terms of requirement, funding, or design stability, and in which a high degree of confidence in the cost estimate does exist, may provide only a small percentage or amount of savings. If the savings are essentially ensured, they may be judged substantial enough to take advantage of them. In contrast, a candidate with high projected savings may be inappropriate for multiyear contracting if the design, funding, and/or requirement is unstable or if the cost estimate is not based on sound information and logic.

> Accordingly, savings should be assessed in relation to the risk or absence of risk which is reflected in (1) the confidence in the cost estimate, (2) requirement stability, (3) funding stability, and (4) configuration or design stability.

Congress has been less than clear in enunciating the required degree of cost savings for multiyear procurement of weapons systems. The 1986 DOD Authorization Act, P.L. 99-145, 99 Stat. 583, declared that multiyear contracts authorized for the Army "may not be entered into unless the total anticipated cost over the period of the contract is no more than 90 percent of the total anticipated cost of carrying out the same program through annual contracts," 99 Stat. 591. The Act simultaneously authorized the Army to enter into multiyear contracts for both Bradley fighting vehicle transmissions and M1A1 tank chassis for which the estimated contract cost savings were 8.9 and 9.5 percent respectively, Comptroller General Report, GAO/NSIAD-86-1, Nov. 1985. The 1986 Authorization Act contained no parallel provision for minimum cost savings for Navy multiyear contracts, 99 Stat. 594. The Act did, however, bar the use of multiyear contracting for the procurement of P-3C aircraft following the GAO's report that "savings are relatively small at 5.5 percent and there is a risk that cost estimates are not sound," Comptroller General Report, GAO/NSIAD-86-1, Nov. 1985. Both the DOD and the Comptroller General discount to present value when projecting cost savings for multiyear candidates, though different interest rates are applied in calculating present value, Comptroller General Report, GAO/NSIAD-90-270BR, Aug. 1990, at 8.

In some cases, the savings associated with multiyear procurement are achieved by entering into multiyear subcontracts under multiyear contracts. See discussion of "Source of Savings" in Comptroller General Report, GAO/NSIAD-86-1, Nov. 1985, at 13; and Comptroller General Report, GAO/NSIAD-88-125, May 1988, at 42. FAR 17.106-3 encourages the use of multiyear subcontracts by contractors of the DOD, NASA and the Coast in order to "broaden the defense industrial base, to the maximum extent practicable."

Two of the criteria for the use of multiyear procurement deal with program stability in the areas of the Government requirement and the design. Program stability has been considered to be a necessary element of multiyear procurement because significant changes during contract performance jeopardize the projected savings. Both the GAO Analysis of Multiyear Candidates and the DOD Appropriations Acts have stressed that multiyear contracting should be used only for systems with stable designs. The GAO report states that implementation of multiyear procurement should not occur until successful R&D, operational tests and evaluation, and one or two production runs have been completed.

The final criterion listed in FAR 17.105-1(b)(5) for the use of multiyear contracts by the DOD, NASA and the Coast Guard is a measure of confidence in estimates of costs and savings. In its report on 1986 Multiyear Candidates, GAO/NSIAD-86-1, the Comptroller General stated:

> Confidence in the cost estimates may be increased by receiving firm proposals . . . on an annual and multiyear basis, and then comparing and analyzing these proposals. . . . However, this is not always practical, and DOD officials stated that the additional administrative effort and the cost to negotiate both proposals must be considered.

Cost-savings estimates are usually based on prior history, information received informally from contractors, or in-house estimates by the procuring activity, Comptroller General Report, GAO/NSIAD-85-9, Oct. 1984, Appendix II at 5.

The use of multiyear contracts is further limited by restricting their term to a maximum of five years, absent specific statutory authority, 10 U.S.C. § 2306b(l); 41 U.S.C. § 254c(d); FAR 17.103, except for service contracts issued by the DOD, NASA, or the Coast Guard, where 10 U.S.C. § 2306(g)(2)(B) encourages the use of options for three additional years. Because of the five-year limitation on multiyear contracting, the exercise of an option for advance procurement of economic order quantities to be ordered in the sixth or seventh program year has been held to be unauthorized, *Multiple Launch Rocket Sys. Multiyear Contract*, 64 Comp. Gen. 163 (B-215825) (1984). Compare *Freightliner Corp.*, ASBCA 42982, 94-1 BCA ¶ 26,538, where the board held that an option in the fifth year of a multiyear contract could be used to require the contractor to furnish items that were included in the agency's sixth budget year. Similarly, in accordance with the provision in 10 U.S.C. § 2306(g)(2)(B), options for additional services in program years six through eight were treated as proper options in *Cessna Aircraft Co.*, ASBCA 43196, 93-3 BCA ¶ 25,912.

The statutes also contain monetary restrictions on the use of multiyear contracts. Governing DOD, NASA, and the Coast Guard, 10 U.S.C. § 2306b(g) requires notification and a 30-day waiting period before award of a multiyear contract for supplies with a cancellation ceiling over $100 million. The civilian agency statute, 41 U.S.C. § 254c(c), contains a similar notice and waiting period requirement for any supply or service contract with a cancellation ceiling over $10 million.

The Comptroller General has upheld the use of multiple award schedule (MAS) multiyear agreements because, unlike multiyear contracts, the MAS agreement does not obligate the Government to purchase the items on the schedule, *GSA — Multiple Award Schedule Multiyear Contracting*, 63 Comp. Gen. 129 (B-199079), 84-1 CPD ¶ 46. Thus, even though funds for the purchase of MAS agreement items are generally one-year appropriations, there is no violation of the Anti-Deficiency Act since each agency must make a specific determination that funds are available before issuing an order under the schedule.

3. Procurement Technique

The multiyear contract is probably the most complex contract used by the Government. This requires that the solicitation be carefully structured to ensure that the parties fully understand their respective rights and obligations.

a. Sharing the Risk

In the past, almost all multiyear supply contracts have been written on a fixed-price basis. Multiyear service contracts have been written using a variety of types of pricing arrangements, including cost-reimbursement contracts. When fixed-price contracts are used, the contractor may be induced to spend funds in the first year of performance to reduce the overall contract costs and may be expected to recover such funds over the full contract period. This means that if the contract is not carried to its full term, the contractor will have not recovered such "nonrecurring costs," defined in FAR 17.103 as follows:

> Nonrecurring costs means those costs which are generally incurred on a one-time basis and include such costs as plant or equipment relocation, plant rearrangement, special tooling and special test equipment, preproduction engineering, initial spoilage and rework, and specialized work force training.

See also FAR 17.106-1(c)(2), which describes nonrecurring costs to include

> initial rework, . . . pilot runs, allocable portions of the costs of facilities to be acquired or established for the conduct of the work, costs incurred for the assembly training and transportation to and from the job site of a specialized work force, and unrealized labor learning.

This risk of nonrecovery is mitigated by the inclusion in the multiyear contract of a Cancellation under Multiyear Contracts clause in FAR 52.217-2 which promises the contractor reimbursement, up to a cancellation ceiling, for enumerated costs if the Government does not order the full quantities called for by the contract. This provision is the major distinguishing feature of the multiyear contract and is discussed in full below.

Also inherent in fixed-price multiyear contracts is the risk of changes in the cost of materials and labor over the extended period of contract performance. To mitigate this risk, FAR 17.106-1(b) suggests the use of economic price adjustment clauses. FAR 17.109(b) contains the following guidance on the clauses to be used:

> Economic price adjustment clauses. Economic price adjustment clauses are adaptable to multiyear contracting needs. When the period of production is likely to warrant a labor and material costs contingency in the contract price, the contracting officer should normally use an economic price adjustment clause (see 16.203). When contracting for services, the contracting officer —
>
> > (1) Shall add the clause at FAR 52.222-43, Fair Labor Standards Act and Service Contract Act-Price Adjustment (Multiple Year and Option Contracts), when the contract includes the clause at FAR 52.222-41, Service Contract Act of 1965, as amended;
> >
> > (2) May modify the clause at FAR 52.222-43 in overseas contracts when laws, regulations, or international agreements require contractors to pay higher wage rates; or
> >
> > (3) May use an economic price adjustment clause authorized by FAR 16.203, when potential fluctuations require coverage and are not included in cost contingencies provided for by the clause at FAR 52.222-43.

In selecting the clause to be used in service contracts, the issue is whether the work includes a significant amount of material and whether the contractor is willing to take the risk that its labor rates will fluctuate at the same rates of fluctuation as the prevailing wages determined by the Department of Labor. The clause at FAR 52.222-43 only includes such fluctuations in prevailing wages, whereas an economic price adjustment clause can use indexes or other measures of wage fluctuation and can also include fluctuations in material prices.

The use of an economic price adjustment clause is at the contracting officer's discretion. Thus, the Comptroller General rejected a protest that the contracting officer was arbitrary in not including such a clause in a solicitation, *Kings Point Mfg. Co.*, Comp. Gen. Dec. B-220224, 85-2 CPD ¶ 680.

b. *Ensuring Government Flexibility*

Although multiyear contracts are generally not used unless there is a reasonable belief that the requirements for the multiyear period will remain in effect, there is always a significant risk that program requirements will change. Reduced requirements can be implemented by use of the Termination for the Convenience of the Government clause, as discussed below. Increased requirements are frequently dealt with by the inclusion of options for additional quantities in the contract. See FAR 17.107, which states:

> Benefits may accrue by including options in a multiyear contract. In that event, contracting officers must follow both the requirements of subpart 17.2. Options should not include charges for plant and equipment already amortized, or other nonrecurring charges which were included in the basic contract.

This guidance is to ensure that the contractor does not obtain double recovery for nonrecurring costs that have already been fully included in the base prices and would be paid in cancellation charges if all of the base quantities were not ordered. Inclusion of option quantities is a discretionary decision of the contracting officer, *Kings Point Mfg. Co.*, Comp. Gen. Dec. B-220224, 85-2 CPD ¶ 680.

Options are generally included for each year of the multiyear contract. However, the fact that they are identified as an option for a designated year does not preclude the Government from using an option for one year to buy quantities needed to meet the requirements of the next year, *Freightliner Corp.*, ASBCA 42982, 94-1 BCA ¶ 26,538. In that case, the board ruled that a fifth-year option could be used to buy products needed to meet the sixth year's requirements. This imposes some pricing risk on the contractor since the price of the subsequent year may be higher due to costs increases during that year.

Options in multiyear contracts would normally not be evaluated as part of the initial award. Thus, the solicitation should include the Evaluation Exclusive of Options clause in FAR 52.217-3.

c. Competition Requirements

Multiyear contracting may be accomplished on a competitive or noncompetitive basis, and competition may be obtained through sealed bidding, two-step sealed bidding, or negotiation, FAR 17.106-1(a). However, as in the case of any other type of procurement, the use of noncompetitive procurement must be justified. Thus, where competitive procurement would have been feasible in two to three years, a protest of a noncompetitive award of a five-year contract for telephone services was sustained, *Rolm Intermountain Corp.*, Comp. Gen. Dec. B-206327.4, 82-2 CPD ¶ 564. Similarly, in *Lear Siegler Inc.*, Comp. Gen. Dec. B-209524, 83-2 CPD ¶ 285, the fact that a limited initial quantity of F-16 fuel tanks was urgently needed and could only be obtained from a particular contractor did not justify the award of a multiyear contract for more items than were urgently needed at the time of the award. See also *Command, Control & Communications Corp.*, Comp. Gen. Dec. B-210100, 83-2 CPD ¶ 448.

After submission of proposals, if a contracting officer finds that more competition is available on a multiyear procurement, it is proper to cancel the procurement and resolicit, *JRW Management Co.*, Comp. Gen. Dec. B-260396.2, 95-1 CPD ¶ 276; *Maytag Aircraft Corp.*, Comp. Gen. Dec. B-250628, 93-1 CPD ¶ 93. On reconsideration of the *Maytag* case, the Comptroller General rejected the protester's contention that the proper course of action was to have contracted for the single year's quantity and recompeted for the future years, Comp. Gen. Dec. B-250628.2, 93-1 CPD ¶ 456.

d. Evaluation of Offers

On multiyear contracts the Government solicits offers on a single-year basis as well as on a multiyear basis in order to ensure that it will obtain lower prices by buying on a multiyear basis. Administrative costs of buying annually can be included in this evaluation if they are included in the solicitation. If multiyear unit prices are not lower than single-year prices, award for a single year could be anticipated. FAR 17.106-2 provides the following general guidance on the solicitation provisions alerting offerors to these procedures:

> Solicitations for multiyear contracts shall reflect all the factors to be considered for evaluation, specifically including the following:
>
> (a) The requirements, by item of supply or service, for the —
>
> (1) First program year; and
>
> (2) Multiyear contract including the requirements for each program year.
>
> (b) Criteria for comparing the lowest evaluated submission on the first program year requirements to the lowest evaluated submission on the multiyear requirements.
>
> (c) A provision that if the Government determines before award that only the first program year requirements are needed, the Government's evaluation of the price or estimated cost and fee shall consider only the first year.
>
> (d) A provision specifying a separate cancellation ceiling (on a percentage or dollar basis) and dates applicable to each program year subject to a cancellation (see 17.106-1 (c) and (d)).
>
> (e) A statement that award will not be made on less than the first program year requirements.
>
> (f) The Government's administrative costs of annual contracting may be used as a factor in the evaluation only if they can be reasonably established and are stated in the solicitation.
>
> (g) The cancellation ceiling shall not be an evaluation factor.

FAR 17.106-3 permits the DOD, NASA, and the Coast Guard to solicit only multiyear prices, as follows:

> (f) Annual and multiyear proposals. Obtaining both annual and multiyear offers provides reduced lead time for making an annual award in the event

> that the multiyear award is not in the Government's interest. Obtaining both also provides a basis for the computation of savings and other benefits. However, the preparation and evaluation of dual offers may increase administrative costs and workload for both offerors and the Government, especially for large or complex acquisitions. The head of a contracting activity may authorize the use of a solicitation requesting only multiyear prices, provided it is found that such a solicitation is in the Government's interest, and that dual proposals are not necessary to meet the objectives in 17.105-2.

When the Government selects the contractor by comparing multiyear unit prices with single-year unit prices, it has no assurance that buying single-year quantities will actually be cheaper even when the single-year price is lowest. It cannot prevent yearly price increases when buying one year at a time. Nevertheless, this evaluation procedure has been approved by the Comptroller General, *Mil-Tech Sys., Inc.*, Comp. Gen. Dec. B-212385.4, 84-1 CPD ¶ 632. The Comptroller General has also rejected a protest that it was irrational to evaluate the first year against a five-year price without including an inflation factor for future years if the award is made for only the single year, *Engineered Air Sys., Inc.*, Comp. Gen. Dec. B-220392.4, 86-2 CPD ¶ 43. In one case, the low bidder on the first-year quantity challenged the right of the Government to award the contract to the low bidder on the multiyear (three-year) quantity on the grounds that to do so would be the same as evaluating option quantities. The Comptroller General held that multiyear quantities were not like options in that they did not create the same degree of uncertainty since the Government was binding itself to buy the second- and third-year quantities if funds were available, 43 Comp. Gen. 215 (B-152286) (1963). In another case, a disappointed bidder argued that the decision to use the multiyear alternative, based on the price comparison, was improper since some of the bidders had deliberately overpriced their single-year bids, 46 Comp. Gen. 749 (B-160815) (1967). In denying the protest, the Comptroller General noted that offerors were not precluded from submitting noncompetitive bids on the single-year part of a solicitation to ensure that they did not receive a single-year award. The Comptroller General also held that in this case, the multiyear bids were, in fact, competitive. In another case, the Comptroller General held that it was proper for a contracting officer to award on a single-year basis since the IFB permitted the Government to select either the multiyear or single-year bid, *VBM Corp.*, Comp. Gen. Dec. B-182225, 75-1 CPD ¶ 130.

The bid evaluation process becomes even more involved if the multiyear contract is also a small business or labor-surplus area set-aside, or involves application of the Buy American Act. See 45 Comp. Gen. 735 (B-158525) (1966).

4. Level Pricing Requirement

In the early use of multiyear contracting, the DOD adopted a policy of requiring that unit prices be the same for all program years in order to eliminate the evaluation difficulties created by unbalanced bidding, as discussed in Chapter 5. When the FAR was adopted in 1984, this requirement was included in FAR 17.103-2(e). It has been deleted from the general guidance in the FAR implementing the FASA but is discussed as follows in the special procedures applicable to the DOD, NASA, and the Coast Guard in FAR 17.106-3:

> (g) Level unit prices. Multiyear contract procedures provide for the amortization of certain costs over the entire contract quantity resulting in identical (level) unit prices (except when the economic price adjustment terms apply) for all items or services under the multiyear contract. If level unit pricing is not in the Government's interest, the head of a contracting activity may approve the use of variable unit prices, provided that for competitive proposals there is a valid method of evaluation.

Thus, all agencies appear to have discretion to require level unit pricing or to permit offerors to propose variable unit prices for the program years covered by the procurement. The major advantage of requiring level pricing is that it greatly simplifies the evaluation of offers by eliminating the possibility of unbalancing the prices between the program years.

There are several disadvantages to level pricing. The most serious is that a contractor must incur higher financing costs on such multiyear contracts because it cannot invoice for the high costs in early years, such as starting and learning costs, which must be spread over the entire quantity of supplies or services covered in the procurement. This may be counterbalanced by the fact that high costs of later years, such as the estimated costs of inflation in labor rates and material prices, would also be spread over the prices of all years. However, the Government generally avoids this by using economic price adjustment provisions, FAR 17.109(b). Another disadvantage is that level pricing forces a large amount of costs into the cancellation cost pool, which can lead to difficulties in establishing the cancellation ceiling, as discussed below.

Under the prior mandatory level pricing requirement, contracting officers were permitted to waive the requirement where there was no prejudice to other bidders. In *Keco Indus., Inc.*, 54 Comp. Gen. 967 (B-183114), 75-1 CPD ¶ 301, variable prices were permitted in a case where the IFB contained no warning to bidders that failure to comply with the level pricing requirement would result in a nonresponsive bid. In *International Harvester Co.*, Comp. Gen. Dec. B-212341, 83-2 CPD ¶ 313, variable prices were permitted in a procurement where the IFB contained an explicit warning. See also *InterTrade Indus., Ltd.*, Comp. Gen. Dec. B-225702, 87-1 CPD ¶ 567; and *Everett Dykes Grassing Co.*, Comp. Gen. Dec. B-210223.4, 84-1 CPD ¶ 176.

Some difficulties have been encountered in determining whether the level pricing requirement applies to preproduction items. In one case where a bid was rejected because of higher prices for preproduction items, the Comptroller General ruled that the bid was responsive but that the procurement was ambiguous and should be canceled, Comp. Gen. Dec. B-169205, May 22, 1970, *Unpub*. Taking the case to the district court, the bidder obtained an order directing that it be awarded the contract, *A.G. Schoonmaker Co. v. Resor*, 319 F. Supp. 933 (D.D.C. 1970). This decision was reversed by the circuit court on the grounds that the procuring agency had not acted arbitrarily or capriciously in following the view of the Comptroller General that it should reject all bids and resolicit, *A.G. Schoonmaker Co. v. Resor*, 445 F.2d 726 (D.C. Cir. 1971). In *Keco Indus., Inc.*, 64 Comp. Gen. 48 (B-216396.2), 84-2 CPD ¶ 491, the Comptroller General ruled that the contracting officer properly waived a failure to level price a bid by submitting a lower price on two preproduction items. The Comptroller General found no prejudice to other bidders.

Options in multiyear contracts are not normally subject to the level pricing requirement because it is expected that they will not include nonrecurring costs. See FAR 17.107, warning that option prices should not include "charges for plant and equipment already amortized, or other nonrecurring charges which were included in the basic contract." In *Keco Indus., Inc.*, 64 Comp. Gen. 48 (B-216396.2), 84-2 CPD ¶ 491, the IFB explicitly stated that although unit prices for base quantities in the multiyear procurement had to be level priced, varying prices could be offered for option quantities.

5. *Orders for Future Years*

Since the multiyear contract is funded one year at a time, it should contain a provision establishing the procedure that will be used to order quantities of work subsequent to the first year and the limitations on the obligations of the parties. However, the FAR implementing the FASA contains no such provision. Thus, contracting officers will have to include special provisions in each multiyear contract covering these issues. FAR 17.106-1 contains the following partial guidance:

> (g) Payment limit. The contracting officer shall limit the Government's payment obligation to an amount available for contract performance. The contracting officer shall insert the amount for the first program year in the contract upon award and modify it for successive program years upon availability of funds.
>
> (h) Termination payment. If the contract is terminated for the convenience of the Government in whole, including requirements subject to cancellation, the Government's obligation shall not exceed the amount specified in the Schedule as available for contract performance, plus the cancellation ceiling.

The prior FAR contained a Limitation of Price and Contractor Obligations clause in FAR 52.217-1 for use in this type of contract. This clause made it clear that the Government was making no legal obligation for quantities not covered by firm contractual orders. It also required the contracting officer to notify the contractor, in writing, when additional funds became available for the full requirements of the next succeeding program year. Conversely, this clause provided that the contractor was only obligated to honor the contract as to future-year quantities if the Government gave written notification by the contractually specified date. The Court of Claims has held that the clause should be interpreted to require strict compliance, *International Tel. & Tel. v. United States*, 197 Ct. Cl. 11, 453 F.2d 1283 (1972) (written order received several hours after stated cutoff date did not bind the contractor even thought oral notice was given before the cutoff date). See, however, *Cessna Aircraft Co.*, ASBCA 43196, 93-3 BCA ¶ 25,912, where the board held that the Government could properly exercise an option for three additional years of services at the end of a five-year multiyear contract even though the funds for the second and third years had not been appropriated. The board reasoned that, in accordance with the legislative history of 10 U.S.C. § 2306(g), this was *renewing* the multiyear contract for three years, not ordering the work for three years.

6. Cancellation of Items

The major legal problems in multiyear procurements arise in formulating and administering the cancellation provisions of this type of contract.

a. Costs Included in Ceiling

The initial use of multiyear contracts included only nonrecurring costs in the cancellation ceiling. The original DOD multiyear contracting statute, 10 U.S.C. § 2306(h)(2)(B), recognized the use of such cancellation provisions and also permitted the inclusion of recurring costs:

> [R]egulations may provide for cancellation provisions in such multiyear contracts to the extent that such provisions are necessary and in the best interests of the United States. Such cancellation provisions may include consideration of both recurring and nonrecurring costs of the contractor associated with the production of the items to be delivered under the contract.

Since there was no similar statute applicable to civilian agencies, there was some question as to whether they could include recurring costs in the ceiling. FAR 17.102-3(d)(3) (pre-1996) restricted the inclusion of recurring costs in cancellation ceilings by stating:

> The inclusion of recurring costs in cancellation ceilings is an exception to normal contract financing arrangements and requires approval by the agency head or a designee.

This provision permitted civilian agencies to include recurring costs in ceilings if the proper approvals were obtained. However, the issue was largely resolved by including a very broad definition of "nonrecurring costs" in the standard Cancellation of Items clause of FAR 52.217-2 (which only provided for the recovery of nonrecurring costs). This confusing use of terminology has been continued under the FASA. 10 U.S.C. § 2306b(c) continues to permit recovery of "both recurring and nonrecurring costs," while 41 U.S.C. § 254c is silent on the subject. The Cancellation under Multiyear Contracts clause in FAR 52.217-2 resolves this issue by giving detailed guidance on the costs that may be included in the cancellation claim. Paragraphs (f) and (g) of the clause state:

> (f) The Contractor's claim may include —
>
> (1) Reasonable nonrecurring costs (see Subpart 15.8 of the Federal Acquisition Regulation) which are applicable to and normally would have been amortized in all supplies or services which are multiyear requirements;
>
> (2) Allocable portions of the costs of facilities acquired or established for the conduct of the work, to the extent that it is impracticable for the Contractor to use the facilities in its commercial work, and if the costs are not charged to the contract through overhead or otherwise depreciated;
>
> (3) Costs incurred for the assembly, training, and transportation to and from the job site of a specialized work force; and
>
> (4) Costs not amortized solely because the cancellation had precluded anticipated benefits of Contractor or subcontractor learning.
>
> (g) The claim shall not include —
>
> (1) Labor, material, or other expenses incurred by the Contractor or subcontractors for performance of the canceled work;
>
> (2) Any cost already paid to the Contractor;
>
> (3) Anticipated profit or unearned fee on the canceled work; or
>
> (4) For service contracts, the remaining useful commercial life of facilities. Useful commercial life means the commercial utility of the facilities rather than their physical life with due consideration given to such factors as location of facilities, their specialized nature, and obsolescence.

In spite of this broad coverage, FAR 17.106-3 contains the following special procedure applicable to the DOD, NASA, and the Coast Guard:

> (e) *Recurring costs in cancellation ceilings.* The inclusion of recurring costs in cancellation ceilings is an exception to normal contract financing arrangements and requires approval by the agency head.

The ASBCA has followed the principle that costs included in cancellation ceilings should be broadly construed. For example, in *Continental Elecs. Mfg. Co.*, ASBCA 14749, 71-2 BCA ¶ 9108, the board held that cancellation costs properly included (i) higher costs of early units (computed with the use of a learning curve), (ii) costs charged to a preproduction unit above the contract unit price, and (iii) engineering costs incurred and measured after cancellation. In dealing with this issue, the board took a broad view of the matter since the contractor was forced to bid the same price for all units and had no means of recovering uneven costs other than through the cancellation charge. See also *Bermite Div. of Tasker Indus.*, ASBCA 18280, 77-1 BCA ¶ 12,349, *modified on recons.*, 77-2 BCA ¶ 12,731.

b. Computation of Ceiling

A separate cancellation ceiling is included in the contract for each program year after the first year, FAR 17.106-1(c)(1). Thus, the ceiling decreases in amount as each year's requirement is ordered. The cancellation ceiling is estimated by the contracting officer and included in the solicitation to be applicable to all competitors, FAR 17.106-2(d). It must be established based upon a reasonable estimate of nonrecurring costs (broadly defined) of an "average" contractor, FAR 17.106-1(c)(2). The regulations permit the contracting officer to adjust the cancellation ceiling prior to award "if necessary," FAR 17.106-1(d). In a sealed bid procurement, this would be done by amendment to the solicitation, while in a negotiated procurement, it could be done during the negotiation process. Such adjustment would appear to be mandatory since the Court of Claims reformed a cancellation ceiling that was not reasonable in *Applied Devices Corp. v. United States*, 219 Ct. Cl. 109, 591 F.2d 635 (1979). The court concluded that the regulations calling for inclusion of a reasonable ceiling were for the benefit of potential contractors and increased the ceiling to a reasonable amount in spite of the fact that the contractor had not protested the inadequacy of the ceiling before bid opening. A similar adjustment to the cancellation ceiling was made in *Technical & Management Servs. Corp.*, ASBCA 39999, 93-2 BCA ¶ 25,681.

Because the purpose of the cancellation charge is normally to reimburse the contractor for unamortized costs in the event the contract is canceled, where no such costs are involved in the procurement there is no need to include a cancellation ceiling. See FAR 17.104(b), permitting agency heads to modify cancellation terms to fit the conditions of an individual procurement. In *Big Bud Tractors, Inc.*, Comp. Gen. Dec. B-209858, 83-1 CPD ¶ 127, the Comptroller General held that the Army's RFP for the multiyear procurement of a standard commercial unit of equipment was not defective despite the fact that it did not include a cancellation ceiling where there were no unamortized nonrecurring costs.

c. *Failure to Order Full Quantity*

The Cancellation under Multiyear Contracts clause provides that cancellation may occur when *funds are not available* for "contract performance for any subsequent program year." If the Government does not order the full requirement for some other reason, a termination for convenience will have occurred and the contractor will be entitled to compensation without regard to the cancellation ceiling. In *Varo, Inc.*, ASBCA 13739, 70-1 BCA ¶ 8099, the board held that the cancellation provisions of the contract applied not only when funds were not appropriated but also when the agency decided that it no longer had a requirement for the items. The board reached this conclusion by looking to the agency's records documenting the formulation of the multiyear contracting policy. This reasoning was subsequently adopted by the Court of Claims in *Applied Devices Corp. v. United States*, 219 Ct. Cl. 109, 591 F.2d 635 (1979). The court held that the Cancellation of Items clause was properly used in a situation where the agency obtained the funds necessary for the procurement from Congress but decided, based on an analysis of agency needs, that the requirement should be met by procuring different equipment. The court reasoned that in such a case, the requirement no longer existed. The court further concluded that lack of funding included a lack of requirements, stating that it "is a fallacy to suppose that requirements and funds availability exist in two separate universes of discourse." This questionable reasoning deprives the contractor of the benefits of the Termination for the Convenience of the Government clause when the Government agency makes an internal decision to alter its requirements.

Contractors have been given the protection of the Termination for the Convenience of the Government clause in other circumstances. Thus, when an agency ordered the items from another contractor, a termination for convenience was found, *Maxson Elecs. Corp.*, ASBCA 12983, 72-2 BCA ¶ 9543. This result might not occur under the current clause because it also includes in the definition of "cancellation" the situation where the contracting officer "fails to notify the Contractor that funds are available for performance of the succeeding program year requirement."

A termination for convenience will also be found if work is deleted during a program year. See FAR 17.103, stating:

> Termination for convenience means the procedure which may apply to any Government contract, including multiyear contracts. As contrasted with cancellation, termination can be effected at any time during the life of the contract (cancellation is effected between fiscal years) and can be for the total quantity or a partial quantity (whereas cancellation must be for all subsequent fiscal years' quantities).

See *Aeronca, Inc.*, ASBCA 13040, 70-1 BCA ¶ 8278, where the board held that a partial termination for convenience had occurred when the Government funded only some of the items in the second and third program years. Similarly, the ceiling was held not to apply to a future year when the Government did not completely order all prior years' quantities. In *Condec Corp.*, ASBCA 14234, 73-1 BCA ¶ 9808, the Government issued a notice of convenience termination during the second year and argued that the contract price for purposes of computing the termination costs was the price for two years' quantity (with the third-year quantity being subject to the cancellation ceiling). The board disagreed, holding that the Government had not proved that there was no requirement for the third year's quantity and that its action therefore constituted a termination of the total multiyear quantity. It has been suggested that this holding obligates the Government agency with reduced requirements to order those requirements under the multiyear contract and to reprice as if there had been a partial termination of the year's quantity, Latham, "Multi-Year Procurement," Federal Publications Briefing Paper 73-2 (1973).

d. Legal Validity of Cancellation Provisions

Under normal appropriations law, agencies would be required to obligate current-year funds to cover cancellation costs within the contractual ceiling. However, 10 U.S.C. § 2306b(f) provides:

> In the event funds are not made available for the continuation of a contract made under this subsection into a subsequent fiscal year, the contract shall be canceled or terminated, and the costs of cancellation or termination may be paid from —

(A) appropriations originally available for the performance of the contract concerned;

(B) appropriations currently available for procurement of the type of property concerned, and not otherwise obligated; or

(C) funds appropriated for those payments.

See also 10 U.S.C. § 2306(g)(3), which includes the same language applying to service contracts.

These provisions were apparently written to permit these agencies to incur the legal liability for paying cancellation costs without obligating funds to cover that liability. However, it appears that the statutory language was written omitting any reference to a firm obligation of the Government covering cancellation costs in order to avoid any implication that Congress was granting "contract authority" pursuant to the Anti-Deficiency Act. This was in recognition that 31 U.S.C. § 1341 precludes the creation of contract authority for procurement. See House Report 97-311, the Conference Committee Report on the 1982 Defense Authorization Act (including this language in the provision giving multiyear contracting authority for major systems), stating at 126:

> The provisions agreed to by the conferees limit the authority to enter into multiyear contracts to cases where "funds are otherwise available for obligation." This language was adopted to make clear that the provision does not, by itself, provide contract authority. Rather the authority to enter into contracts is provided subject to funds being available for obligation through other actions of the Congress or other provisions of law. In adopting this language, the conferees did not intend to restrict the authority to enter into multiyear contracts solely to those cases where funds are appropriated for that purpose. On the contrary, the conferees envision that funds could be available for obligation for a multiyear contract from, for example, annually made appropriations, including funds made available through reprogramming or transfer; proceeds from sales of goods and services which under current provision of law would be available for obligation; and funds available for obligation in connection with foreign military sales.

In spite of this confusing situation, which seems to require agencies to violate the Anti-Deficiency Act, funds have not been obligated by the military services to cover cancellation ceilings. See DOD Authorization

Act, 1985, P.L. 98-525, 98 Stat. 2492, directing this course of action at 2498:

> [Multiyear] contracts may include an unfunded cancellation ceiling. If funds are not made available for the continuation of such a contract in subsequent fiscal years, the contract shall be cancelled and the costs of cancellation shall be paid as provided in section 2306(h)(5) of title 10, United States Code.

Apparently, Congress intends that this policy be continued by the DOD, NASA, and the Coast Guard, because the same statutory language was included in the FASA in 10 U.S.C. § 2306b(f) (covering supply contracts).

It would appear that civilian agencies are required to obligate funds to cover cancellation ceilings. See 41 U.S.C. § 254c(b), stating:

> Termination Clause — A multiyear contract entered into under the authority of this section shall include a clause that provides that the contract shall be terminated if funds are not made available for the continuation of such contract in any fiscal year covered by the contract. Amounts available for paying termination costs shall remain available for such purpose until the costs associated with termination of the contract are paid.

FAR 17.104(c) appears to ignore the legislative history of the DOD statutes. It requires that funds covering cancellation costs be obligated at the time of contracting, as follows:

> Agency funding of multiyear contracts shall conform to the policies in OMB Circulars A-11 (Preparation and Submission of Budget Estimates) and A-34 (Instructions on Budget Execution) and other applicable guidance regarding the funding of multiyear contracts. As provided by that guidance, the funds obligated for multiyear contracts must be sufficient to cover any potential cancellation and/or termination costs; and multiyear contracts for the acquisition of fixed assets should be fully funded or funded in stages that are economically or programmatically viable.

7. Distinguishing Requirements Contracts

Requirements contracts are used to procure supplies or services where precise quantities are not fully known. They may be entered into for several years without following the procedures prescribed for multiyear contracts, *Mills Mfg. Corp.*, Comp. Gen. Dec. B-224004, 86-2 CPD ¶ 679, *recons.*

denied, 87-1 CPD ¶ 393. The fact that a requirements contract contemplates performance over a period of years will not transform it into a multiyear contract, *Solar Turbines Int'l v. United States*, 3 Cl. Ct. 489 (1983). In *Solar Turbines*, the Government used a requirements contract containing a Cancellation Ceiling Cost clause entitling the contractor to increased compensation for shortfalls in actual orders. The contractor unsuccessfully argued that Best Estimated Quantities (BEQ) were actually firm orders for minimum quantities under a multiyear contract.

Prior to the enactment of the FASA, the FAR in effect set forth procedures in FAR 17.104-4 (pre-1996) for the multiyear acquisition of supplies and services under modified requirements contracts, to be used only when anticipated annual requirements could be projected with reasonable certainty. Anticipated requirements expressed as BEQ were set forth in the contract. Nonrecurring costs were to be amortized on the BEQ, FAR 17.104-4(a)(2). If actual orders fell short of BEQ, the contractor was reimbursed in accordance with the Cancellation of Items clause. The current FAR is silent on these issues.

C. Indefinite-Quantity Contracts

The indefinite-quantity contract is the other form of variable quantity, indefinite-delivery contract in Subpart 16.5 of the FAR. In this type of contract, the Government obligates itself to buy at least a stated minimum quantity of the goods or services, and the contract will also contain a maximum quantity beyond which the contractor is not bound, FAR 16.504(a)(1). This type of contract is very similar to a contract for a firm quantity with options for additional quantities, the major difference being that the indefinite-quantity contract can be issued initially without any firm orders being placed as long as the Government is obligated to order an adequate minimum quantity.

The following Indefinite Quantity clause in FAR 52.216-22 is used in all indefinite-quantity contracts:

INDEFINITE QUANTITY (OCT 1995)

(a) This is an indefinite-quantity contract for the supplies or service specified, and effective for the period stated, in the Schedule. The quantities of supplies and services specified in the Schedule are estimates only and are not purchased by this contract.

(b) Delivery or performance shall be made only as authorized by orders issued in accordance with the Ordering clause. The Contractor shall furnish to the Government, when and if ordered, the supplies or services specified in the Schedule up to and including the quantity designated in the Schedule as the "maximum." The Government shall order at least the quantity of supplies or services designated in the Schedule as the "minimum."

(c) Except for any limitations on quantities in the Order Limitations clause or in the Schedule, there is no limit on the number of orders that may be issued. The Government may issue orders requiring delivery to multiple destinations or performance at multiple locations.

(d) Any order issued during the effective period of this contract and not completed within that period shall be completed by the Contractor within the time specified in the order. The contract shall govern the Contractor's and Government's rights and obligations with respect to that order to the same extent as if the order were completed during the contract's effective period; *provided*, that the Contractor shall not be required to make any deliveries under this contact after ______________ [*insert date*].

1. Adequate Minimum Quantity

As discussed in Chapter 2, to be binding on the contractor, an indefinite-quantity contract must contain a minimum quantity that is more than "nominal," FAR 16.504(a)(2). In *Tennessee Soap Co. v. United States*, 130 Ct. Cl. 154, 126 F. Supp. 439 (1954), a $10 minimum order was held to be nominal. See also *Goldwasser v. United States*, 163 Ct. Cl. 450, 325 F.2d 722 (1963), where the court found that a contract with a minimum quantity of $100 compared to an estimated price of $40,000 "would have been a one-sided bargain, bordering upon lack of mutuality." The court did not decide this issue since it held the contract to be a requirements contract.

The minimum quantity need not be ordered at the time the contract is issued as long as the Government promises to buy a meaningful minimum amount of goods or services, *Federal Elec. Corp.*, ASBCA 11726, 68-1 BCA ¶ 6834; Comp. Gen. Dec. B-160063, Feb. 10, 1967, *Unpub.* In *Federal Elec. Corp. v. United States*, 202 Ct. Cl. 1028, 486 F.2d 1377 (1973), the Court of Claims upheld the board decision but stated that the contractor was bound to the contract because the minimum quantity had been ordered at the same time the parties entered into the contract. Since the minimum was a substantial quantity, the time the first order was placed would appear to be irrelevant to the issue of whether the contractor was bound to perform the contract.

In an indefinite-quantity contract containing no specified minimum quantities, the contractor was held to be entitled to assume that the estimated quantities were the minimum quantities that would be ordered, *Apex Int'l Management Servs., Inc.*, ASBCA 38087, 94-2 BCA ¶ 26,842. The standard Indefinite Quantity clause in FAR 52.216-22 calls for the inclusion in the contract schedule of both minimum quantities and estimated quantities, but the board held that the absence of minimum quantities was an ambiguity for which the Government was responsible as the drafter of the contract. Compare *Delfour, Inc.*, PSBCA 3333, 95-1 BCA ¶ 27,524, *recons. denied*, 95-2 BCA ¶ 27,908, *aff'd*, 95 F.3d 1163 (Fed. Cir. 1996), where a contract stating that it was an indefinite-quantity contract and containing a minimum quantity of $10,000 was held to constitute an indefinite-quantity contract even though it also stated that it had an "initial contract value" of $1 million.

Indefinite-quantity contracts contain a Termination for the Convenience of the Government clause which permit the Government to terminate the contract before ordering the minimum quantity. In *Southwest Lab. of Okla., Inc.*, Comp. Gen. Dec. B-251778, 93-1 CPD ¶ 368, the Comptroller General held that a special clause stating this proposition did not destroy the consideration supporting the contract because the promise of the Government to pay termination costs and profit was sufficient consideration. The Comptroller ruled, however, that a further provision of the clause making a failure to order the minimum an automatic termination for convenience was improper because it was an attempt to convert a Government breach into a termination for convenience — in conflict with the holding in *Maxima Corp. v. United States*, 847 F.2d 1549 (Fed. Cir. 1988).

When a combination fixed-price/indefinite-quantity contract specifies that the fixed-price component is to be used as the guaranteed minimum, the Government is not obligated to guarantee an additional minimum amount of work under the indefinite-quantity component, *Mac's Cleaning & Repair Serv.*, ASBCA 49652, 97-1 BCA ¶ 28,748, *aff'd*, __ F.3d __ (Fed. Cir. 1997).

2. *Distinguishing Requirements Contracts*

There have been several disputes as to whether a contract is a requirements contract or an indefinite-quantity contract. In such cases, the courts and boards have carefully analyzed the contract language to determine the type of contract intended. In *Goldwasser v. United States*, 163 Ct. Cl. 450, 325 F.2d 722 (1963), the court resolved a conflict between the Indefinite Quantity clause and the specifications listing the items to be procured by concluding that the latter showed an intent to create a requirements contract. In contrast, in *Mason v. United States*, 222 Ct. Cl. 436, 615 F.2d 1343 (1980), the court found that the stated minimum quantity in the contract indicated that the parties had entered into an indefinite-quantity contract because otherwise that clause was superfluous. In *Maintenance Eng'rs v. United States*, 749 F.2d 724 (Fed. Cir. 1984), a conflict between a term in the solicitation identifying the contract as one for an indefinite quantity and a term in the General Provisions stating "this is a requirements contract" was resolved by the Order of Precedence clause giving priority to the solicitation language. In *Stanley F. Horton*, DOTCAB 1231, 82-2 BCA ¶ 15,967, the board considered both course of dealing and the knowledge of the parties at the time of contract formation and found that the contract was a requirements contract despite the absence of an explicit term barring the Government from obtaining snow removal services elsewhere. In contrast, in *Ann Riley & Assocs.*, DOTBCA 2418, 93-3 BCA ¶ 25,963, the board found an indefinite-quantity contract based on the contract language even though the Government argued that it intended to create a requirements contract. Where course of dealing or other circumstances do not imply a requirements contract, the absence of Government obligation to satisfy all needs under the contract will render the contract an indefinite-quantity contract, *Hemet Valley Flying Serv. Co. v. United States*, 7 Cl. Ct. 512 (1985). In *Hemet Valley*, the court was able to find a binding indefinite-quantity contract despite the fact that no stated minimum quantity of flying hours was promised because the Government paid a nonnominal amount for contractor's promise to maintain "availability" to fly. In *Export Packing & Crating Co.*, ASBCA 16133, 73-2 BCA ¶ 10,066, the board looked to the underlying contractual relationship to find a requirements contract and stated that there was no ambiguity despite clauses identifying the contract as both an indefinite-quantity and requirements contract.

Where the language of a contract permits it to be interpreted as either an indefinite-quantity agreement lacking a minimum quantity or a "limited form" requirements contract, the latter interpretation is preferable and avoids a finding that the contract is void for lack of consideration. See *Dynamic Science, Inc.*, ASBCA 29510, 85-1 BCA ¶ 17,710.

3. Multiple Award Preference

The statutory multiple award preference for task order and delivery order contracts, discussed at the beginning of this section, has been incorporated in the FAR coverage of indefinite-quantity contracts. See FAR 16.504(c), which states:

> Multiple award preference — (1) General preference. Except for indefinite-quantity contracts for advisory and assistance services as provided in paragraph (c)(2) of this section, the contracting officer shall, to the maximum extent practicable, give preference to making multiple awards of indefinite-quantity contracts under a single solicitation for the same or similar supplies or services to two or more sources. In making a determination as to whether multiple awards are appropriate, the contracting officer shall exercise sound business judgment as part of acquisition planning. No separate written determination to make a single award is necessary when the determination is contained in a written acquisition plan or when a class determination has been made in accordance with subpart 1.7. Multiple awards should not be made if the contracting officer determines that —
>
> (i) Only one contractor is capable of providing performance at the level of quality required because the supplies or services are unique or highly specialized;
>
> (ii) Based on the contracting officer's knowledge of the market, more favorable terms and conditions, including pricing, will be provided if a single award is made;
>
> (iii) The cost of administration of multiple contracts may outweigh any potential benefits from making multiple awards;
>
> (iv) The tasks likely to be ordered are so integrally related that only a single contractor can reasonably perform the work;
>
> (v) The total estimated value of the contract is less than the simplified acquisition threshold; or

(vi) Multiple awards would not be in the best interests of the Government.

(2) Contracts for advisory and assistance services. (i) Except as provided in paragraph (c)(2)(ii) of this section, if an indefinite-quantity contract for advisory and assistance services will not exceed three years and $10,000,000, including all options, a contracting officer may, but is not required to, give preference to making multiple awards. If an indefinite-quantity contract for advisory and assistance services exceeds three years and $10,000,000, including all options, multiple awards shall be made unless —

(A) The contracting officer or other official designated by the head of the agency determines in writing, prior to the issuance of the solicitation, that the services required under the task order contract are so unique or highly specialized that it is not practicable to award more than one contract. This determination may also be appropriate when the tasks likely to be issued are so integrally related that only a single contractor can reasonably perform the work;

(B) The contracting officer or other official designated by the head of the agency determines in writing, after the evaluation of offers, that only one offeror is capable of providing the services required at the level of quality required; or

(C) Only one offer is received.

(ii) The requirements of paragraph (c)(2)(i) of this section are not applicable to an acquisition of supplies or services that includes the acquisition of advisory and assistance services, if the contracting officer or other official designated by the head of the agency determines that the advisory and assistance services are necessarily incident to, and not a significant component of, the contract.

The criteria for not issuing multiple indefinite-quantity contracts give the contracting officer considerable discretion. However, when an agency is obtaining a significant amount of supplies or services over long periods of time through the use of such contracts, there are substantial benefits to be obtained through the issuance of more than one contract. The major benefits of the continuous competition that can be achieved under multiple contracts are the ability to control the prices of individual task and delivery orders and the ability to award such orders based on the past performance of the contractors. Multiple contracts also permit the agency to award indefinite-quantity contracts to contractors with varying skills — giving the Government access to a broader range of competence than would be possible with only a single contract. It has been held permissible to restrict multiple awards to affiliates when there was a risk that failure of performance of affiliated contractors would jeopardize the agency's program, *District Moving & Storage, Inc.*, Comp. Gen. Dec. B-272070, 96-2 CPD ¶ 60.

When the agency intends to award multiple contracts, the following Single or Multiple Awards solicitation provision in FAR 52.216-27 is used to alert offerors of this intention:

SINGLE OR MULTIPLE AWARDS (OCT 1995)

> The Government may elect to award a single delivery order contract or task order contract or to award multiple delivery order contracts or task order contracts for the same or similar supplies or services to two or more sources under this solicitation.

4. Structuring the Contract

The major elements of the indefinite-quantity contract are the minimum quantities, the maximum quantities, the inclusion of multiple years, and the ordering procedures. The minimums and maximums can be stated in dollars or units of work.

a. Minimum Quantities

As discussed above, the minimum quantity must be more than a nominal quantity to ensure that the contract is legally binding. The only other guidance contained in FAR 16.504(a) is that the minimum quantity should not exceed the amount "that the Government is fairly certain to order," that minimums for individual task or delivery orders may be specified, and that a "total minimum . . . quantity or dollar value of supplies or services to be acquired under the contract" shall be specified. The minimum order limitation is to be included in Paragraph (a) of the mandatory Order Limitations clause in FAR 52.216-19. All other information on minimum quantities must be included in the contract schedule.

There may be a tendency for the contracting officer to specify very low contract minimums in order to limit the Government's liability in the event its requirements change during the life of the contract. However, better prices may be obtained if higher minimum quantities are specified. When multiple contracts are awarded and orders will be placed competitively, the ordering process should control the prices, and there will be little need for concern about the impact of low minimum quantities.

In multiple item, indefinite-quantity contracts, minimum quantities can also be stated for each item or type of services. This gives the offerors assurance that the Government intends to order each item and may provide some inducement for the offerors to avoid unbalanced pricing. However, it is proper to use only a single contract minimum, *C.W. Over & Sons, Inc.*, Comp. Gen. Dec. B-274365, 96-2 CPD ¶ 223; *Sunbelt Properties, Inc.*, Comp. Gen. Dec. B-249307, 92-2 CPD ¶ 309.

b. Maximum Quantities

FAR 16.504(a) provides that the contract should contain a maximum quantity that should be "realistic" and "based on the most current information available." It also permits maximum quantities for any single task or delivery order and maximum quantities that may be ordered during any specified period of time. The Order Limitations clause in FAR 52.216-19 contains the following paragraph, which is to be filled in by the contracting officer to specify such maximums:

> (b) *Maximum order.* The Contractor is not obligated to honor —
>
> (1) Any order for a single item in excess of __________ [*insert dollar figure or quantity*];
>
> (2) Any order for a combination of items in excess of __________ [*insert dollar figure or quantity*]; or
>
> (3) A series of orders from the same ordering office within _____ days that together call for quantities exceeding the limitation in subparagraph (1) or (2) above.

This paragraph should be carefully tailored to fit the circumstances of each procurement. In addition, the contract maximum quantity should be stated in the contract schedule.

Paragraph (d) of the Order Limitations clause requires the contractor to honor an order above the maximums stated in the clause if timely notice is not given of its intention not to fill the order. In *General Cutlery v. General Servs. Admin.*, GSBCA 13154, 96-1 BCA ¶ 27,957, the board affirmed the default termination of a contractor that had not filled an order above the maximum quantity but had not given notice of its intention not to fill the order.

Where the indefinite-quantity contract fails to set maximum amounts for a portion of the work to be performed, the Government may not order unlimited quantities of work, and the amount ordered will be measured by the standard of reasonableness under the circumstances, *Computer Sciences Corp.*, ASBCA 24035, 82-2 BCA ¶ 15,923.

c. Length of the Contract

FAR 16.504(a)(4) requires an indefinite-quantity contract to

> (i) Specify the period of the contract, including the number of options and the period for which the contract may be extended under each option, if any.

This would imply that all such contracts for a period of longer than one year would be written as a contract for the base year plus a series of options. However, the same result can be achieved by writing the contract for a minimum quantity in the first year and for additional quantities, as called for by the Government, subject to the availability of appropriations. This would avoid the need to follow the regulatory rules on the exercise of options.

If the indefinite-quantity contract is written for a period longer than one year by the inclusion of options, the contracting officer has the choice of several standard clauses — the Option for Increased Quantities clause in FAR 52.217-6, the Option to Extend Services clause in FAR 52.217-8, or the Option to Extend the Term of the Contract clause in FAR 52.217-9. If this last clause is used, exercise of the option does not procure additional work but merely extends the period when work can be ordered, *Five Star Elecs., Inc.*, ASBCA 44984, 96-2 BCA ¶ 28,421.

If the contract is for a period of longer than one year without options, Paragraph (a) of the mandatory Ordering clause in FAR 52.216-18 will include an end date for ordering that corresponds to the final day of the last year covered by the contract. If such a contract contains firm prices, the contracting officer should ensure that the prices are still in line with current prices that are available from other vendors. This would not be of concern if multiple contracts have been awarded and the prices of each task or delivery order are to be established by competition between the contractors.

The Indefinite Quantity clause also provides for the insertion in Paragraph (d) of a date after which no "deliveries" are to be made. When this clause is used for services, this is presumably the final date that services may be performed.

There is no general guidance on the permissible length of indefinite-quantity contracts. However, 10 U.S.C. § 2304b(b) and 41 U.S.C. § 253i(b) limit task or delivery order contracts for advisory and assistance services to five years, unless a specific statute permits a longer period.

5. Evaluation and Award

The FAR gives very little guidance on the evaluation and award of indefinite-quantity contracts. However, it would be expected that normal best value techniques would be used in most cases. The evaluation of prices is the most difficult part of the evaluation process. If only one type of supplies or services is included in the contract, evaluation would be based on the unit prices quoted. If more than one type of supplies or services is included in the contract, the FAR gives no guidance as to the basis for evaluation. If prices for the elements of work under such a contract can be established during the contracting process, offers can be evaluated using minimum quantities, estimated quantities, or maximum quantities. If the minimum quantities are set at low levels, use of these quantities for evaluation purposes will not provide a very realistic appraisal of the actual price that will be paid. In such a case, estimated quantities are sometimes used to obtain a more realistic evaluation. These estimates should be based on the best information available to the agency at the time of contracting, but it appears that the Government may not have the same liability for the accuracy of such estimates as it does in requirements contracts. See *DOT Sys., Inc.*, IBCA 1197-6-78, 80-2 BCA ¶ 14,694, stating that the Government would not be liable for a negligent estimate in such a contract because it had no obligation, such as was present in a requirements contract, to purchase more than the minimum quantity. In *DOT Sys., Inc. v. United States*, 231 Ct. Cl. 765

(1982), the court affirmed, stating that the Government will be held to a less stringent standard of accuracy for estimates in indefinite-quantity contracts than in requirements contracts. See *Tracer Technology Resources, Inc.*, ASBCA 44759, 93-2 BCA ¶ 25,616, where the contractor attempted to recover for a very high Government estimated quantity on the grounds that the Government had acted in bad faith. The board rejected this argument because "well nigh irrefragable proof" was necessary to show bad faith. It also stated at 127,515:

> By ordering $197,553 worth of work, the Government substantially exceeded its obligation to order a minimum of $50,000 worth of work. Even if the Government's estimate of 45,000 samples was negligently made, under this indefinite quantity contract [the contractor] assumed that risk.

See also *C.F.S. Air Cargo, Inc.*, ASBCA 40694, 91-2 BCA ¶ 23,985; and *Deterline Corp.*, ASBCA 33090, 88-3 BCA ¶ 21,132, *recons. denied*, 89-3 BCA ¶ 22,069.

There have also been instances where the solicitation called for evaluation at the maximum quantity level, *Radionics, Inc.*, ASBCA 20796, 77-1 BCA ¶ 12,448. In that case, the maximum quantity was set at the Government's estimated requirement, and the contractor claimed a price adjustment when the Government failed to order the maximum quantity. The board recognized that evaluation at the maximum had a tendency to induce the offerors to submit lower prices but held that no recovery was appropriate under the facts of the case, because no negligence was found in preparing the estimate.

There may also be cases where the Government is unable to describe the work to be done in sufficient specificity so that unit prices can be arrived at during the contract formation process. In such cases, the agency can evaluate the rate structure (labor and indirect costs) of the competing offerors and select the winning contractors on that basis. In any event, the solicitation should inform the offerors which quantity should be used for evaluation purposes. See *Fabrics Plus, Inc.*, Comp. Gen. Dec. B-218546, 85-2 CPD ¶ 46, holding that a solicitation providing only minimum order quantity of $100,000 and a maximum order quantity of $1.5 million was too broad a range to permit intelligent bidding.

6. *Ordering Work under Indefinite-Quantity Contracts*

The ordering of work under indefinite-quantity contracts is subject to different rules than the award of contracts. The general procedures for ordering are contained in the following mandatory Ordering clause in FAR 52.216-18.

ORDERING (OCT 1995)

(a) Any supplies and services to be furnished under this contract shall be ordered by issuance of delivery orders or task orders by the individuals or activities designated in the Schedule. Such orders may be issued from ____ through ______ [insert dates].

(b) All delivery orders or task orders are subject to the terms and conditions of this contract. In the event of conflict between a delivery order or task order and this contract, the contract shall control.

(c) If mailed, a delivery order or task order is considered "issued" when the Government deposits the order in the mail. Orders may be issued orally, by facsimile, or by electronic commerce methods only if authorized in the Schedule.

When a single contract is to be awarded, there is no need to insert additional ordering procedures in the contract schedule. When multiple contracts are to be awarded, however, the contract schedule should contain a detailed description of the procedures that will be followed in issuing task or delivery orders under the contracts.

a. *Verification of Prices*

The regulations contain no guidance on whether the contracting officer should verify the reasonableness of prices before placing orders under indefinite-quantity contracts; it would appear that, as in the case of options, such orders should not be placed until a determination has been made that it is the most advantageous course of action available to the Government. This determination will be relatively straightforward when multiple award contracts are being used and prices are obtained on each task or delivery order. In the case of single award contract, the determination will become more difficult as market conditions change. Certainly, if market research revealed that better prices were available, the continued use of an indefinite-quantity contract would be questionable.

It can be argued that there should be no testing of the market until the Government has honored its promise to purchase the minimum quantity of work specified in the contract. Thereafter, market testing would be legally permissible because indefinite-quantity contracts contain no promise to purchase additional quantities from the contractor. However, there is no requirement for obtaining competition by means of a solicitation. In addition, orders under indefinite-quantity contracts are not subject to the synopsis requirement, FAR 5.202(a)(6).

b. Ordering under Multiple Award Contracts

FAR 16.505 contains the following guidance on the procedures for ordering work on multiple award contracts:

> (b) Orders under multiple award contracts. (1) Except as provided for in paragraph (b)(2) of this section, for orders issued under multiple delivery order contracts or multiple task order contracts, each awardee shall be provided a fair opportunity to be considered for each order in excess of $2,500. In determining the procedures for providing awardees a fair opportunity to be considered for each order, contracting officers shall exercise broad discretion. The contracting officer, in making decisions in the award of any individual task order, should consider factors such as past performance on earlier tasks under the multiple award contract, quality of deliverables, cost control, price, cost, or other factors that the contracting officer believes are relevant to the award of a task order to an awardee under the contract. In evaluating past performance on individual orders, the procedural requirements in subpart 42.15 are not mandatory. The procedures and selection criteria that will be used to provide multiple awardees a fair opportunity to be considered for each order must be set forth in the solicitation and contract. The procedures for selecting awardees for the placement of particular orders need not comply with the competition requirements of part 6. However, agencies shall not use any method (such as allocation) that would not result in fair consideration being given to all awardees prior to placing each order. Formal evaluation plans or scoring of quotes or offers are not required. Agencies may use oral proposals and streamlined procedures when selecting an order awardee. In addition, the contracting officer need not contact each of the multiple awardees under the contract before selecting an order awardee if the contracting officer has information available to ensure

that each awardee is provided a fair opportunity to be considered for each order.

(2) Awardees need not be given an opportunity to be considered for a particular order in excess of $2,500 under multiple delivery order contracts or multiple task order contracts if the contracting officer determines that —

(i) The agency need for such supplies or services is of such urgency that providing such opportunity would result in unacceptable delays;

(ii) Only one such contractor is capable of providing such supplies or services required at the level of quality required because the supplies or services ordered are unique or highly specialized;

(iii) The order should be issued on a sole-source basis in the interest of economy and efficiency as a logical follow-on to an order already issued under the contract, provided that all awardees were given a fair opportunity to be considered for the original order; or

(iv) It is necessary to place an order to satisfy a minimum guarantee.

This FAR guidance permits the use of a number of procedures in ordering work under multiple award, indefinite-quantity contracts, and the procedures should be clearly stated in the schedule of each contract. For normal orders for major amounts of work, an agency would be expected to use competitive procedures with very streamlined techniques. This might entail obtaining competitive prices and evaluating past performance on prior task or delivery orders. On larger orders, the agency might also require an oral presentation by each competitor. Smaller orders might be awarded using a rotation technique. Specialized orders might be awarded to the contractor with unique capabilities to perform that work.

10 U.S.C. § 2304c(d) and 41 U.S.C. § 253j(d) prohibit protests of the issuance of task or delivery orders. This is implemented in FAR 16.505(a), as follows:

(7) No protest under subpart 33.1 is authorized in connection with the issuance or proposed issuance of an order under a task order contract or delivery order contract except for a protest on the grounds that the order increases the scope, period, or maximum value of the contract.

To ensure that multiple award contractors have a forum to hear grievances about the way that orders are being issued, 10 U.S.C. § 2304c(e) and

41 U.S.C. § 253j(e) require agencies to have a task and delivery order ombudsman. This is implemented in FAR 16.505(b), as follows:

> (4) The head of the agency shall designate a task order contract and delivery order contract ombudsman who shall be responsible for reviewing complaints from contractors on task order contracts and delivery order contracts. The ombudsman shall review complaints from the contractors and ensure that all contractors are afforded a fair opportunity to be considered, consistent with the procedures in the contract. The ombudsman shall be a senior agency official who is independent of the contracting officer and may be the agency's competition advocate.

c. Time of Effectiveness

The Ordering clause in FAR 52.216-18 states that orders will be effective when deposited in the mail. If this clause is not used, the legal rules for issuing orders under indefinite-quantity contracts will likely be governed by the law of options. For example, *Dynamics Corp. of Am. v. United States*, 182 Ct. Cl. 62, 389 F.2d 424 (1968), involved a dispute as to whether certain orders, placed under a fixed-price, indefinite-quantity contract with a specified minimum and maximum, were issued within the time period specified in the contract. The court stated at 74:

> In analyzing this contract, it cannot be seriously disputed that the portion in question is most accurately characterized as an option contract. As related above, Part VIII ("Orders") of the Special Provisions provides:
>
> The Contractor agrees to furnish to the Government, when ordered, the supplies or services set forth in the Schedule up to and including the quantity designated in the Schedule as the "maximum quantity."

The court concluded that orders were effective only if they were received within the time specified in the contract.

d. Failure to Order Minimum Quantity

Unless the Government terminates the minimum quantity before the end of the performance period, its failure to order the minimum quantity will constitute a breach of contract with compensation based on appropriate damages reflecting the injury to the contractor. In *Maxima Corp. v. United States*, 847 F.2d 1549 (Fed. Cir. 1988), the court awarded damages in the amount of the contract price for the unordered elements of the minimum quantity on the theory that this minimum dollar amount had been promised in return for the contractor's maintenance of the *capability* to perform the minimum quantity. In *PHP Healthcare Corp.*, ASBCA 39207, 91-1 BCA ¶ 23,647, the board refused to award the entire price for the unordered work, holding that the contract was not for the maintenance of a capability. Thus, it required the contractor to prove damages — the amount of costs incurred plus anticipated profits on the minimum quantity. See also *Apex Int'l Management Servs., Inc.*, ASBCA 38087, 94-2 BCA ¶ 26,842; and *Golden West Builders*, PSBCA 3378, 93-3 BCA ¶ 26,195, following the same reasoning. In *Merrimac Management Inst., Inc.*, ASBCA 45291, 94-3 BCA ¶ 27,251, the board stated that damages should be computed by deducting the costs that would have been incurred from the price of the minimum quantity. Prior to *Maxima*, damages for not ordering the minimum quantity had been limited by the Termination for the Convenience of the Government clause if it was in the contract, *Manuals, Inc.*, ASBCA 24123, 80-2 BCA ¶ 14,579; *Charles Bainbridge, Inc.*, ASBCA 19949, 75-2 BCA ¶ 11,414. This rule was also applied to each item in a multiple item, indefinite-quantity contract, *Unified Eng'g, Inc.*, ASBCA 21565, 81-1 BCA ¶ 14,940. These cases are no longer applicable to situations where the Government lets the contract run out without ordering the minimum quantity. They are still applicable if the Government orders a termination for convenience during the contract performance period, *ITT Communications Servs., Inc.*, GSBCA 9072, 91-3 BCA ¶ 24,337 (short form Termination for the Convenience of the Government clause yields no recovery). In that case, the compensation should include repricing of unit prices necessary to recover fixed costs that were spread over the minimum quantity, *SteelCare, Inc.*, GSBCA 5491, 81-1 BCA ¶ 15,143. In *Montana Refining Co.*, ASBCA 44250, 94-2 BCA ¶ 26,656, the board remanded the case to the parties to compute "damages" even though the contracting officer had issued a termination for convenience for most of the unordered minimum quantity 18 days before the end of the contract period. The board did not discuss whether such "damages" should include anticipated profit.

D. Options

Another method of obtaining firm commitments from contractors to perform additional work is the inclusion of option clauses in contracts procuring the initial quantities. Options can be for additional quantities of work or for longer periods of performance. FAR 17.201 contains the following definition:

> Option means a unilateral right in a contract by which, for a specified time, the Government may elect to purchase additional supplies or services called for by the contract, or may elect to extend the term of the contract.

The major difference between options and requirements contracts or multiyear contracts is that the Government makes *no binding commitment* when an option provision is used. Thus, the key characteristic of option clauses is that they give the Government a unilateral right to order the additional quantities if that order is issued by a prescribed time. An option for additional quantities of work is very similar to an indefinite-quantity contract, but the obligation of the Government is stated differently. Option clauses state that the Government has the right to order specified additional quantities, while indefinite-quantity contracts state that the Government has the right to purchase quantities within a specified range. It has been held that regulations pertaining to indefinite-quantity contracts are not applicable to options, *International Transducer Corp. v. United States*, 30 Fed. Cl. 522 (1994); *Schmid Labs., Inc.*, Comp. Gen. Dec. B-214333, 84-2 CPD ¶ 411.

1. Use

Because the Government is not bound by options for additional quantities of supplies or services, there is no fiscal or legal impediment to their use. Thus, they are widely used in Government procurement — in spite of the fact that an effort to strictly limit their use was made by the Comptroller General in the 1960s. See 41 Comp. Gen. 682 (B-148019) (1962), where the Comptroller General stated that option quantities should be limited to 25 percent of the contract quantity and should be exercised no more than 90 days after award.

FAR Subpart 17.2 prescribes general policies for the use of options, stating in FAR 17.200 that these regulations do not apply to contracts for construction, architect-engineer services, R&D services, automatic data processing equipment, or telecommunications equipment and services; but that options may be used for such procurements. FAR 17.202 provides:

> (a) Subject to the limitations of paragraphs (b) and (c) of this section, for both sealed bidding and contracting by negotiation, the contracting officer may include options in contracts when it is in the Government's interest.

When using sealed bidding, the contracting officer shall make a written determination that there is a reasonable likelihood that the options will be exercised before including the provision at 52.217-5, Evaluation of Options, in the solicitation. (See 17.207(f) with regard to the exercise of options.)

(b) Inclusion of an option is normally not in the Government's interest when, in the judgment of the contracting officer —

(1) The foreseeable requirements involve —

(i) Minimum economic quantities (i.e., quantities large enough to permit the recovery of startup costs and the production of the required supplies at a reasonable price); and

(ii) Delivery requirements far enough into the future to permit competitive acquisition, production, and delivery; or

(iii) An indefinite quantity or requirements contract would be more appropriate than a contract with options. However, this does not preclude the use of an indefinite quantity contract or requirements contract with options.

(c) The contracting officer shall not employ options if —

(1) The contractor will incur undue risks; e.g., the price or availability of necessary materials or labor is not reasonably foreseeable;

(2) Market prices for the supplies or services involved are likely to change substantially; or

(3) The option represents known firm requirements for which funds are available unless (i) the basic quantity is a learning or testing quantity and (ii) competition for the option is impracticable once the initial contract is awarded.

(d) In recognition of (1) the Government's need in certain service contracts for continuity of operations and (2) the potential cost of disrupted support, options may be included in service contracts if there is an anticipated need for a similar service beyond the first contract period.

The regulations also provide that the total coverage of a contract with options, including the initial quantity and the option quantities, shall not exceed the requirements of the agency for five years, FAR 17.204(e).

The most important limitation on the use of options is the provision that they should not be used if adequate competition can be obtained when the future requirements are ascertained. See *Altron Iron Works, Inc.*, Comp. Gen. Dec. B-179212, 74-1 CPD ¶ 121, where the Comptroller General urged the procuring agency to go forward with a new procurement of standard commercial supplies rather than using option provisions. See also *Safemasters Co.*, 58 Comp. Gen. 255 (B-192941), 79-1 CPD ¶ 38, where options were found improper when realistic competition was available for subsequent procurements.

Another important limitation is that options cannot be used to procure known requirements for which funds are available. In *East Wind Indus., Inc.*, 58 Comp. Gen. 586 (B-193720), 79-1 CPD ¶ 404, the Comptroller General held that this provision precluded the testing of a currently available option by the addition of an option for the same quantity to a new procurement. The Comptroller General suggested that the proper technique was to test the option by advertising the entire new requirement as a fixed quantity.

2. Structuring and Evaluation of Options

Option provisions must be carefully structured to induce offerors to propose the most advantageous prices. The key considerations are the time the option can be exercised and whether the option prices will be evaluated in the selection of the winning offeror.

The period during which an option may be exercised must be stated in the contract, FAR 17.204(b). In the case of supply contracts, it must be set "so as to provide the contractor adequate lead time to ensure continuous production," FAR 17.204(c). In *Aerojet Techsystems Co.*, Comp. Gen. Dec. B-220033, 85-2 CPD ¶ 636, the Comptroller General reasoned that because this regulation ensures the contractor's continuous production, the Government erred in rejecting as nonresponsive a bid that conditioned third-year option prices on exercise of second-year options. In the case of service contracts, continuity of service should also be provided for, but the FAR is silent on this requirement. The Option to Extend Services clause in FAR 52.217-8 permits the contracting officer to select a period during which that option can be exercised, and this period should be clearly stated. See *American Contract Servs., Inc.*, ASBCA 46788, 94-2 BCA ¶ 26,855, where the contracting officer used the ambiguous language "within 15 days," and the board held that this had to mean within 15 days of contract expiration.

FAR 17.204(d) permits the period for exercise of the option to "extend beyond the contract completion date" when funds would not be available on the completion date. This allows the contracting officer to structure the option to permit its exercise on the first day of the fiscal year (or year when funds are available) when the period of services ends on the previous day. It should not be used to permit longer gaps in service. See *Cessna Aircraft Co.*, ASBCA 43196, 96-1 BCA ¶ 27,966, where the board held that a clause permitting exercise of an option on the first day of the fiscal year was legally binding even though it extended beyond the contract completion date.

The other key consideration in structuring options is the determination of whether option prices will be evaluated. The goal is to give the offerors the greatest possible incentive to propose prices that are realistic and competitive. If the option quantities are included in the evaluation, the offerors will have the incentive to offer competitive prices but may be inclined to unbalance the prices between the years. This could lead to unnecessarily high prices for early years if the later years' requirements do not materialize. If the option quantities are not included in the evaluation, offerors may be inclined to inflate option prices in the hope that the agency will be forced by circumstances to exercise the options. While the FAR contains some minimal guidance on evaluation of options, it contains no guidance on structuring options to achieve the best prices. Methods of structuring and evaluation are dealt with in this section.

a. *Evaluation of Option Quantities*

The regulations call for the evaluation of options when the Government is likely to exercise them in the course of the contract. FAR 17.206 provides:

> (a) In awarding the basic contract, the contracting officer shall, except as provided in paragraph (b) of this section, evaluate offers for any option quantities or periods contained in a solicitation when it has been determined prior to soliciting offers that the Government is likely to exercise the options. (See 17.208.)
>
> (b) The contracting officer need not evaluate offers for any option quantities when it is determined that evaluation would not be in the best interests of the Government and this determination is approved at a level above the contracting officer. An example of a circumstance that may support a determination not to evaluate offers for option quantities is when there is a

reasonable certainty that funds will be unavailable to permit exercise of the option.

When the options are to be evaluated, the Evaluation of Options clause in FAR 52.217-5 is used, and the Comptroller General has upheld this method of evaluation, *S.A.F.E. Export Corp.*, Comp. Gen. Dec. B-204718, 82-1 CPD ¶ 62. This clause permits the Government not to evaluate the options when it is "not . . . in the Government's best interests." In *Foley Co.*, Comp. Gen. Dec. B-245536, 92-1 CPD ¶ 47, the Comptroller General concurred with a decision not to evaluate options when the base price of the low bidder including the options exceeded the available funding. This permitted the agency to award the contract to the bidder whose base price was within the Government funding limit. However, the Comptroller General has found that the FAR states a "clear preference" for the evaluation of options, *Crowley Co.*, Comp. Gen. Dec. B-258967, 95-1 CPD ¶ 105, and has affirmed the propriety of evaluating options after the contracting officer confirmed that funds would likely be available for their exercise, *Merlo, Inc.*, Comp. Gen. Dec. B-277384, 97-2 CPD ¶ 39. In *Occu-Health, Inc.*, Comp. Gen. Dec. B-270228.3, 96-1 CPD ¶ 196, the Comptroller General ruled that an agency was required to inform offerors that it was not going to evaluate options if it made that decision prior to the submission of best and final offers. The Comptroller General stated:

> To read FAR 17.206(a) as broadly as [the agency] suggests — as granting an agency essentially unfettered discretion to decide not to evaluate options without advising offerors of this change under the circumstances when the agency could reasonably provide that advice — would be inconsistent with the agency's fundamental obligations to allow offerors the opportunity to respond to the government's actual needs and to obtain the offer that is most advantageous to the government.

When the clause calling for evaluation of options is used in an IFB, bidders must submit unequivocal offers. In *Sess Constr. Co.*, 64 Comp. Gen. 355 (B-216924), 85-1 CPD ¶ 319, a bid in which prices for option periods included the statement "plus rate of inflation, fuel, labor and gravel" was properly rejected for failure to offer a firm-fixed-price. It is also proper to refuse to evaluate a bid where the prices are conditioned upon exercise of the options. Thus, option price bids should not include separate "all or none" price discounts for option items. In *Telex Communications, Inc.*, Comp. Gen. Dec. B-211236, 83-2 CPD ¶ 122, the Comptroller General concluded that where an IFB reserves the right to exercise only a portion of the options, to require evaluation of options at the bidder's "all or none" discounted price would improperly introduce uncertainty as to whether the bid was actually the lowest received.

The regulations state that the Government may reject unbalanced bids if they pose an unacceptable risk to the Government, FAR 14.404-2; FAR 15.504-1(g)(3), and this right of the Government is stated in the standard provisions in FAR 52.214-10 and FAR 52.215-1. Guidance on determining whether an unbalanced bid poses such a risk states only that the contracting officer should consider "whether award of the contract will result in paying unreasonably high prices." FAR 15.504-1(g)(2)(ii). See Chapter 5 and Chapter 6 for a detailed discussion of unbalanced bidding.

b. Nonevaluation of Option Quantities

Although FAR 17.206(a) states that the normal procedure is to structure options so that both the base quantity and option quantities are evaluated in making the initial award, FAR 17.206(b) states that a contracting officer may decide not to evaluate option quantities when that is "in the best interests of the Government" and is approved by a superior. The Comptroller General has also held that "[t]here is no legal or regulatory requirement that an agency evaluate options in a particular procurement," *International Business Invs., Inc.*, 63 Comp. Gen. 463 (B-215530), 84-1 CPD ¶ 693. This is consistent with the reasoning of the Comptroller General that bid bonds or bid guarantees should cover only base quantities, *Madison Servs., Inc.*, Comp. Gen. Dec. B-245420, 91-2 CPD ¶ 345; *Pacific Coast Utilities Serv., Inc.*, Comp. Gen. Dec. B-209003.2, 83-1 CPD ¶ 73; *Consolidated Technologies, Inc.*, Comp. Gen. Dec. B-215723, 84-2 CPD ¶ 639.

When it is decided not to evaluate options, the Evaluation Exclusive of Options clause at FAR 52.217-3 is used. The regulations give no guidance on how to deal with unusually high option prices where the option quantities are not to be evaluated, but it has been held that significantly higher unevaluated option prices, as compared to prices offered on the basic quantity, are not a sufficient reason for rejecting a bid, *R&R Inventory Serv., Inc.*, 54 Comp. Gen. 206 (B-181264), 74-2 CPD ¶ 163 (prices for second- and third-year options were 700 to 900 percent more than basic quantity prices, but bid was accepted as lowest on basic quantity). See also *SeaArk Marine, Inc.*, Comp. Gen. Dec. B-248755, 92-2 CPD ¶ 193, where it was held that the agency was not required to consider unevaluated option quantity prices when deciding whether a bid was materially unbalanced. Compare *Gracon Corp. v. United States*, 6 Cl. Ct. 497 (1984), where the court held that the contracting officer had discretion to accept or reject a bid containing significantly higher unevaluated option prices in accordance with a solicitation clause permitting the rejection of materially unbalanced bids. In *Gracon*, the court agreed with the contracting officer's decision to award the contract to the low bidder on the base quantity assuming that the Government would not exercise the option but would meet its requirements in some other way. If a subsequent separate procurement were not possible, the proper course of action would arguably have been to reject the bid and award to the next low bidder. In solicitations calling for nonevaluation of options and containing no clause permitting rejection of materially unbalanced bids, the contracting officer would have to cancel the solicitation to avoid awarding to the low base bid with a high option price. The FAR contains no guidance on this issue.

c. Limited Evaluation

Another technique is to evaluate only those options that are exercised at the time of award. FAR 17.208(b) requires the use of the clause at FAR 52.217-4 when this technique is used. This is the one method provided in the regulations that does not give the bidder definite information as to whether options will be evaluated. The result may be that it is the technique most likely to result in balanced bidding. In *National Council for Urban Economic Dev., Inc.*, Comp. Gen. Dec. B-213434, 84-2 CPD ¶ 140, the Comptroller General held that where the Government's RFP both provided for evaluation of option quantities and stated that options could not be exercised at the time of award, the Government's decision to nevertheless exercise options at the time of award, in light of unexpected availability of funds, was valid.

d. Level Pricing

Another technique used to avoid unbalanced bidding is to require that option prices be the same as base prices. This technique is used in multiyear procurement, but the regulations are silent on its use in options. The FAR does permit the use of a solicitation clause preventing unbalanced bidding by low base prices. FAR 17.203 states:

(f) Solicitations may, in unusual circumstances, require that options be offered at prices no higher than those for the initial requirement, e.g., when (1) the option cannot be evaluated under 17.206 or (2) future competition for the option is impracticable.

(g) Solicitations that require the offering of an option at prices no higher than those for the initial requirement shall —

(1) Specify that the Government will accept an offer containing an option price higher than the base price only if the acceptance does not prejudice any other offeror; and

(2) Limit option quantities for additional supplies to not more than 50 percent of the initial quantity of the same contract line item. In unusual circumstances, an authorized person at a level above the contracting officer may approve a greater percentage of quantity.

The Comptroller General has permitted award to a bidder that violated the invitation by bidding option prices higher than the base price but was the low bidder on both the base and option prices, 44 Comp. Gen. 581 (B-155847) (1965). See also Comp. Gen. Dec. B-176356, Nov. 8, 1972, *Unpub.* In cases where prejudice to other bidders has been found, however, the Comptroller General has agreed with decisions to reject the bids. See 51 Comp. Gen. 439 (B-172978) (1972), and *Bristol Elecs., Inc.*, 54 Comp. Gen. 16 (B-180247), 74-2 CPD ¶ 23, where the low bidder on the base quantity violated the solicitation instructions on level pricing, and the aggregate prices (base price plus all options) were higher than another bidder whose option prices did not exceed the base price; the Comptroller General ruled that it was improper to award to the low bidder on the base quantity. See also *Keco Indus., Inc.*, Comp. Gen. Dec. B-216396.2, 84-2 CPD ¶ 491. In *ABL Gen. Sys., Corp.*, 54 Comp. Gen. 476 (B-182066), 74-2 CPD ¶ 318, the Comptroller General ruled that a bid that was low on the base quantity, high on the option prices, but low in the aggregate should not be considered since it had violated the level bidding requirement and it was not clear that it would have been low had other bidders been permitted to submit higher option prices. Additionally, where the IFB advised prospective bidders that offers "containing an option price higher than the lowest basic price for the same item may be accepted only if such acceptance does not prejudice any other offeror," the Comptroller General upheld the rejection of a bid that was low on the base quantity but scaled option prices according to volumes ordered; exercise of the entire option quantity would have resulted in level option pricing, but limited exercise of the option resulted in higher prices, *Numax Elecs. Inc.*, Comp. Gen. Dec. B-206127.2, 82-2 CPD ¶ 317.

In cases where there are significant nonrecurring costs, the contractor takes a large risk when level pricing is required. See *Contact Int'l Corp.*, ASBCA 44636, 95-2 BCA ¶ 27,887, where the board rejected a claim that the failure to exercise the options on a five-year requirements contract was a termination for convenience of the Government. The board found that the Government had full rights not to exercise the options and that the contractor "bears the attendant risks" of spreading nonrecurring costs over the five-year period. The same result was reached in *D&S Mfg. Co.*, ASBCA 32865, 87-1 BCA ¶ 19,351. See also *Metro Mach. Corp.*, ASBCA 47005, 97-1 BCA ¶ 28,723, where the contractor had agreed to overhead rate ceilings on cost-reimbursement contract with multiple options because it assumed that the options would be ordered and that it could spread its overhead costs over the large quantity of work covered by the options. When no options were ordered, the board ruled that the contractor has assumed the risk of this type of pricing and was bound by the ceilings.

e. Prohibition of Nonrecurring Costs in Option Prices

Another method of controlling the pricing of options is to attempt to prohibit the inclusion of nonrecurring start-up costs in option prices. This forces the inclusion of all such costs in the base price. This can readily be accomplished in negotiated procurement. However, it may not be feasible in sealed bidding. See *Hitachi Denshi Am., Ltd.*, Comp. Gen. Dec. B-212925, 84-1 CPD ¶ 342, where the Comptroller General held that a bid that contained the same price for base and option quantities was responsive because bidders were not required to submit cost breakdowns, and inflation during the five-year period could account for the fact that the option prices were the same as the base price.

f. Discounting to Present Value

The most straightforward technique that could be used for evaluating options is to provide that all option-year prices be discounted to present value. This would remove most of the incentive for offerors to front-load their prices in order to obtain the free use of the money in the early years. However, the FAR is silent on the use of this technique. The Government has used a Present Value Method (PVM) of evaluation on ADPE procurements, having recognized a necessity to consider the time value of money in evaluating bids, Federal Information Resources Management Regulations, 41 C.F.R. § 201-32.205-3. See also *Linolex Sys., Inc.*, 53 Comp. Gen. 895 (B-179047), 74-1 CPD ¶ 296. There appears to be no reason why this evaluation method could not be used in evaluating options on other types of procurement. See Chapter 5 for a discussion of the time value of money.

3. Failure to Bid Options

If option prices are not to be evaluated, failure to bid option prices will not result in the bid being nonresponsive unless such failure deprives the Government of a "substantive and valuable right," 51 Comp. Gen. 528 (B-174575) (1972). The Comptroller General reasoned that there was no such deprivation in a case where the solicitation contained no requirement limiting the amount of option prices since the bidder could have bid excessive option prices and been eligible for award if it was low bidder on the base quantity. Compare 46 Comp. Gen. 434 (B-160051) (1966), where the Comptroller General sustained the rejection of a bid omitting an unevaluated option quantity because the IFB required all options to be bid. The Comptroller General reasoned that the Government was deprived of a valuable right.

If option quantities are to be evaluated, failure to bid an option will result in rejection of the bid, *Huff & Huff Serv. Corp.*, Comp. Gen. Dec. B-233740.5, 90-1 CPD ¶ 167; *Rozier, Sidbury & Co.*, Comp. Gen. Dec. B-216741, 85-1 CPD ¶ 58; *Ainslie Corp.*, Comp. Gen. Dec. B-190878, 78-1 CPD ¶ 340. In *E.H. Morrill Co.*, 63 Comp. Gen. 348 (B-214556), 84-1 CPD ¶ 508, the Comptroller General held that a bid that did not provide prices for option work added by an amendment and whose receipt was acknowledged was nonresponsive. Subsequently, in a case that did not involve options, the Comptroller explicitly clarified the *E.H. Morrill* decision and stated that "where an omitted item is divisible from the contract requirements, is de minimis as to total cost, and would not affect the competitive standing of the bidders, it may be waived," *Leslie & Elliott Co.*, 64 Comp. Gen. 279 (B-216676), 85-1 CPD ¶ 212.

There is another limited exception to this rule, stating that the omission of the option price can be corrected by the contracting officer if it can be determined from the face of the bid that the omission is the result of a clerical error, *Con-Chen Enters.*, Comp. Gen. Dec. B-187795, 77-2 CPD ¶ 284; 52 Comp. Gen. 604 (B-187795) (1973). In both of these cases, the Comptroller General reasoned that a clerical error was apparent because, while some options were omitted, the final option was priced in each case. Further, the pricing pattern was uniform, indicating the amount that the bidder had intended to bid. In contrast, in *Ainslie Corp.*, Comp. Gen. Dec. B-190878, 78-1 CPD ¶ 340, it was found that correction was not possible since no option prices had been bid. See also *Goldco Int'l*, Comp. Gen. Dec. B-248059, 92-2 CPD ¶ 59, where the Government properly accepted a bid including a fifth option year when only four years were called for in the IFB.

4. Exercise of Options

If the Government can fulfill its needs by exercise of an option, significant savings in time and administrative costs can be realized. However, exercise of an option could be very disadvantageous to the Government if the work can be obtained from another source at a lower price. Traditionally, the contracting officer has been given broad discretion in deciding whether to exercise an option, *National Cash Register Co.*, Comp. Gen. Dec. B-179045, 74-1 CPD ¶ 116; 36 Comp. Gen. 62 (B-179045) (1956) ("options . . . purely for the interest and benefit of the Government"). Thus, a bankruptcy court has refused to order a Government agency to exercise an option when it was demonstrated that the decision not to exercise was not based on the fact the company was bankrupt, *In re Plum Run Serv. Corp.*, 159 B.R. 496 (S.D. Ohio 1993). Similarly, the ASBCA has held that it will not review a decision not to exercise an option unless it is demonstrated that the decision is made in bad faith or is an abuse of discretion, *Pennyrile Plumbing, Inc.*, ASBCA 44555, 96-1 BCA ¶ 28,044; *Sample Enters.*, ASBCA 44564, 94-3 BCA ¶ 27,105.

The Comptroller General will no longer consider contractor contentions that their options should be exercised, *C.G. Ashe Enters.*, 56 Comp. Gen. 387 (B-188043), 77-1 CPD ¶ 166; *Lanson Indus., Inc.*, 60 Comp. Gen. 661 (B-202942), 81-2 CPD ¶ 176; *Digital Sys. Group, Inc.*, Comp. Gen. Dec. B-252080.2, 93-1 CPD ¶ 228. In *Albert G. Gricoski Private Detective Agency*, Comp. Gen. Dec. B-214179, 84-1 CPD ¶ 157, the Comptroller General reiterated this rule and noted that the contractor's need to be reimbursed for costs not included in base prices did not require the Government to exercise options. The Comptroller General will consider cases where the contracting officer is selecting among options in the contracts of competing firms, *Fjellestad, Barrett & Short*, Comp. Gen. Dec. B-248391, 92-2 CPD ¶ 118; *Mine Safety Appliance Co.*, 69 Comp. Gen. 562 (B-238597.2), 90-2 CPD ¶ 11.

It would be poor business practice to lose the opportunity of an advantageous purchase by failure to exercise an option. Thus, in all cases, the contracting officer should check market prices before failing to exercise an option. See *A.C. Elecs., Inc.*, Comp. Gen. Dec. B-185553, 76-1 CPD ¶ 295, where a decision not to exercise an option was upheld because there had been recent procurements at prices lower than the option price.

a. Determining That Exercise Is Advantageous to the Government

Before exercising an option, the contracting officer must analyze the situation and make a number of determinations. FAR 17.207 provides:

> (b) When the contract provides for economic price adjustment and the contractor requests a revision of the price, the contracting officer shall determine the effect of the adjustment on prices under the option before the option is exercised.
>
> (c) The contracting officer may exercise options only after determining that —
>
> > (1) Funds are available;
> >
> > (2) The requirement covered by the option fulfills an existing Government need;
> >
> > (3) The exercise of the option is the most advantageous method of fulfilling the Government's need, price and other factors (see paragraphs (d) and (e) below) considered; and
> >
> > (4) The option was synopsized in accordance with Part 5 unless exempted by 5.202(a)(11) or other appropriate exemptions in 5.202.
>
> (d) The contracting officer, after considering price and other factors, shall make the determination on the basis of one of the following:
>
> > (1) a new solicitation fails to produce a better price or a more advantageous offer than that offered by the option. If it is anticipated that the

best price available is the option price or that this is the more advantageous offer, the contracting officer should not use this method of testing the market.

(2) An informal analysis of prices or an examination of the market indicates that the option price is better than prices available in the market or that the option is the more advantageous offer.

(3) The time between the award of the contract containing the option and the exercise of the option is so short that it indicates the option price is the lowest price obtainable or the more advantageous offer. The contracting officer shall take into consideration such factors as market stability and comparison of the time since award with the usual duration of contracts for such supplies or services.

(e) The determination of other factors under (c)(3) of this section should take into account the Government's need for continuity of operations and potential costs of disrupting operations.

(f) Before exercising an option, the contracting officer shall make a written determination for the contract file that exercise is in accordance with the terms of the option, the requirements of this section, and Part 6. To satisfy requirements of Part 6 regarding full and open competition, the option must have been evaluated as part of the initial competition and be exercisable at an amount specified in or reasonably determinable from the terms of the basic contract, e.g. —

(1) A specific dollar amount;

(2) An amount to be determined by applying provisions (or a formula) provided in the basic contract, but not including renegotiation of the price for work in a fixed-price type contract;

(3) In the case of a cost-type contract, if —

(i) The option contains a fixed or maximum fee; or

(ii) The fixed or maximum fee amount is determinable by applying a formula contained in the basic contract (but see 16.102(c));

(4) A specific price that is subject to an economic price adjustment provision; or

> (5) A specific price that is subject to change as the result of changes to prevailing labor rates provided by the Secretary of Labor.
>
> (g) The contract modification or other written document which notifies the contractor of the exercise of the option shall cite the option clause as authority.

This regulation incorporates two changes reflecting the requirements of the Competition in Contracting Act of 1984 (CICA). First, Paragraph (c)(4) was added to require synopses of all prospective option exercises unless the original contract was synopsized with sufficient clarity to inform offerors of that possibility. Second, Paragraph (f) was amended to cross-reference Part 6 of the FAR, calling for "full and open competition." The requirement for full and open competition appears to apply to the exercise of options that have not been evaluated in the award, since such exercise can be considered to be a form of sole source contracting. See *Kollsman Instrument Co.*, 68 Comp. Gen. 303 (B-233759), 89-1 CPD ¶ 243, where the Comptroller General denied a protest that an option had been exercised without competition on a contract where the option prices had not been evaluated. The Comptroller General found that the agency had properly justified the lack of competition on the basis of urgency and also found that the agency had performed a sufficient check of market conditions before exercising the option.

It appears that the competition requirement does not apply to evaluated options, because they were part of the original competition. However, FAR 17.207(d) requires some analysis of the reasonableness of the price before exercising options, *Ross & McDonald Contracting, GmbH*, ASBCA 38154, 94-1 BCA ¶ 26,316 (improper to exercise option on reprocurement contract without checking validity of prices); *Banknote Corp. of Am.*, Comp. Gen. Dec. B-250151, 92-2 CPD ¶ 413 (improper to rely on original bid prices, especially when quantities were increasing); *AAA Eng'g & Drafting, Inc.*, Comp. Gen. Dec. B-236034.2, 92-1 CPD ¶ 307 (current market price must be checked to ensure that option price is reasonable). The Comptroller General has been quite lenient in enforcing this requirement. See *Sippican, Inc.*, Comp. Gen. Dec. B-257047.2, 95-2 CPD ¶ 220, where the protester, a firm that had lost the competition, had informed the agency that it could offer the option quantities at lower prices because it had reduced its costs. The Comptroller General held that the contracting officer had properly exercised his discretion in failing to conduct a competition for the option quantity, stating:

As a general rule, option provisions in a contract are exercisable at the discretion of the government. See Far 17.201. An informal analysis of prices or an examination of the market which indicates "that the option price is better than prices available in the market or that the option is the more advantageous offer" is one of three methods specifically set forth in FAR 17.207(d) as a basis for determining whether to exercise an option. *Person-System Integration, Ltd.*, B-246142; B-246142.2, Feb. 19, 1992, 92-1 CPD ¶ 204. The form of such examination is largely within the discretion of the contracting officer, so long as it is reasonable. See *Kollsman Instrument Co.*, 68 Comp. Gen. 303 (1989), 89-1 CPD ¶ 243; *Action Mfg. Co.*, 66 Comp. Gen. 463 (1987), 87-1 CPD ¶ 518. The FAR also permits a determination that the option price is the most advantageous based upon a finding that the time between contract award and option exercise is short enough and the market stable enough that the option price remains most advantageous. FAR 17.207(d).

Our Office will not question an agency's exercise of an option under an existing contract unless the protester shows that the agency failed to follow applicable regulations or that the determination to exercise the option, rather than conduct a new procurement, was unreasonable. *Tycho Technology, Inc.*, B-222413.2, May 25, 1990, 90-1 CPD ¶ 500. The intent of the regulations is not to afford a firm that offered high prices under an original solicitation an opportunity to remedy this business judgment by undercutting the option price of the successful offeror. *Person-System Integration, Ltd., supra.* We find no basis to question the agency's determination to exercise the option.

The record shows that the contracting officer considered (1) the prices offered in the original competition and the fact that [the contractor's] high technical score and low price had made its proposal more advantageous than the protester's proposal; (2) that only a relatively short period of time had passed since the original competition and the agency's requirements for the third option year remained the same as stated in the original competition; (3) that agency information showed that [the protester] had recently charged substantially more for EMATT units in a foreign procurement than [the contractor's] option price; (4) that there was no known change in the current EMATT market; (5) that since [the protester] did not provide any financial data to support its allegations of more advantageous pricing, and since prior prices known to the agency for required materials were substantial, it remained unlikely that [the protester] could reduce its material costs to the extent stated to be below those of [the contractor]; and (6) the need for continuity of operations and the cost of disruption, as well as the costs of a new competition (which would involve additional costs of proposal evaluation, start-up costs and the possible requalification of a vendor or qualification of a new contractor).

The same result was reached in *Bulova Technologies, Inc.*, Comp. Gen. Dec. B-252660, 93-2 CPD ¶ 23, and *Valentec Wells, Inc.*, Comp. Gen. Dec. B-239499, 90-2 CPD ¶ 177.

Since option prices are generally a matter of public record, they should be disclosed when examining the market or soliciting offers. The Comptroller General has held that disclosure of the option price in a solicitation is permissible, *JL Assocs.*, Comp. Gen. Dec. B-239790, 90-2 CPD ¶ 261; *Milwaukee Valve Co.*, Comp. Gen. Dec. B-206249, 82-1 CPD ¶ 135.

Under the prior statutes and regulations, the Comptroller General held that where option prices have been evaluated in the initial award, the requirement that the exercise of options be advantageous to the Government was not intended to require a new solicitation that would permit a firm that had an opportunity to compete under the original solicitation to displace the incumbent contractor by undercutting the option price, *Jaxon, Inc.*, Comp. Gen. Dec. B-213998, 84-2 CPD ¶ 33; *A.J. Fowler Corp.*, Comp. Gen. Dec. B-205062, 82-1 CPD ¶ 582. In addition, the contracting officer was permitted to consider the satisfactory performance of the incumbent contractor and administrative budget constraints that might cause lack of personnel to process a new solicitation, *Humanics, Ltd.*, Comp. Gen. Dec. B-202418.2, 82-1 CPD ¶ 514. Note that FAR 17.207(e) still permits consideration of continuity of operations and disruption costs. The Comptroller General has affirmed the exercise of an option where, "due to time constraints, procuring competitively would disrupt services and create substantial costs to the Government," *A. Lee Parker*, Comp. Gen. Dec. B-206735, 82-2 CPD ¶ 259. See also *Cerberonics, Inc.*, Comp. Gen. Dec. B-199924, 81-1 CPD ¶ 351, where the Comptroller General held that a contracting officer had properly decided to exercise an option rather than conduct a new competition in a case where the option was on a cost-reimbursement basis and the agency determined that it needed the continuity of the contractor that was performing the job well. In this case, the protesting competitor had submitted an unsolicited proposal to perform the work for less than the option price. See also *Silent Hoist & Crane Co.*, Comp. Gen. Dec. B-186006, 76-1 CPD ¶ 392 (exercise of option upheld when repeated IFBs for additional quantity did not result in lower prices); and *Oscar Holmes & Sons, Inc.*, Comp. Gen. Dec. B-183897, 75-2 CPD ¶ 339 (survey of market supported exercise of option even though other firms claimed that competitive bidding would result in lower prices).

The GSA has adopted special procedures calling for the contractor's past performance to be one of the considerations in deciding whether to exercise an option, GSAR Subpart 517.2. This procedure is intended to motivate the contractor to give better performance in an effort to induce the Government to exercise an option. However, comparative prices are still a major consideration in the exercise of such options.

Prior to the CICA, the Comptroller General limited the discretion of the contracting officer in instances where the option prices were not evaluated in the original procurement. See *KET Inc.*, 58 Comp. Gen. 38 (B-191949), 78-2 CPD ¶ 305, holding that the procedures followed in determining whether to exercise the option should "comport, as much as possible, with the competitive norm of federal procurement." The Comptroller General has also held that where an option is included in a sole source contract, it may be exercised despite the possibility that competition may become feasible at a future date; the Comptroller did also advise that exercise should be delayed where practicable, *Bird Elecs. Corp.*, Comp. Gen. Dec. B-205155, 82-1 CPD ¶ 519. However, where options were not evaluated and prior to exercise of the option a competitor unambiguously declared that it was willing to perform at a price lower than the option price, the Government may not renegotiate any terms of the option without issuing a new solicitation, *Department of the Army-Recons.*, Comp. Gen. Dec. B-208281.2, 83-2 CPD ¶ 78.

Where an option contract was awarded under the Small Business Administration's 8(a) program, the Government may exercise the option, subject to other regulatory requirements, irrespective of the fact that the company outgrows its small business status during the time of the contract, *Vantex Serv. Corp.*, Comp. Gen. Dec. B-251102, 93-1 CPD ¶ 221; *Gallegos Research Corp.*, Comp. Gen. Dec. B-209992.2, 83-2 CPD ¶ 597.

It has been held that the Government may exercise an option as part of a litigation settlement, even when a minor increase in price was allowed and the agency relied on an informal market survey in its determination that exercise was in the best interests of the Government, *Gulton Indus., Inc.*, Comp. Gen. Dec. B-203265, 82-2 CPD ¶ 59.

b. Negotiation of Options

In some cases, the contracting officer has negotiated with the contractor extending the option to obtain more favorable terms. The Comptroller General has held that this is permissible if it is done as part of a negotiated procurement to test the option price, *Interscience Sys., Inc.*, Comp. Gen. Dec. B-194497, 79-2 CPD ¶ 306, *recons. denied*, 81-1 CPD ¶ 61. However, an incumbent contractor may not undermine the integrity of the competitive bidding system by reducing the option price subsequent to bid opening if the option-testing competition is accomplished using sealed bid procedures, Comp. Gen. Dec. B-173504, Sept. 12, 1972, *Unpub.*

The Comptroller General has also held that negotiation of the terms of the option prior to testing the market is, in effect, a new procurement requiring negotiation with all competitors, *Varian Assocs.*, Comp. Gen. Dec. B-208281, 83-1 CPD ¶ 160, *modified on other grounds*, 83-2 CPD ¶ 78. In circumstances where the market included only two eligible contractors, informal negotiations on price and delivery schedules were sufficient because both eligible offerors were afforded an equal opportunity to compete, *Nuclear Metals, Inc.*, 64 Comp. Gen. 290 (B-216319), 85-1 CPD ¶ 217.

c. Method of Exercising an Option

The Government must exercise options in a timely manner and in exact compliance with the option terms, *Lockheed Martin IR Imaging Sys., Inc. v. West*, 108 F.3d 319 (Fed. Cir. 1997); *New England Tank Indus. of New Hampshire, Inc. v. United States*, 861 F.2d 685 (Fed. Cir. 1988); *Chemical Technology, Inc.*, ASBCA 21863, 80-2 BCA ¶ 14,728; *Holly Corp.*, ASBCA 24975, 83-1 BCA ¶ 16,327.

(1) Strict Compliance

The strict compliance requirement governing the exercise of options has been imposed because options give the party with the right to exercise unique power over the other party. FAR 17.207 provides minimal guidance in this regard, stating:

> (a) When exercising an option, the contracting officer shall provide written notice to the contractor within the time period specified in the contract.

However, it has consistently been held that for the Government's exercise of an option to be effective, the election must be positive, unambiguous, and in exact compliance with the terms of the option, 51 Comp. Gen. 119 (B-172586) (1971). Thus, exercise of an option is invalid if the option reduces the quantity of work, *Grumman Technical Servs., Inc.*, ASBCA 46040, 95-2 BCA ¶ 27,918, unless the option contains flexible quantities, *Raven Indus., Inc.*, Comp. Gen. Dec. B-185052, 76-1 CPD ¶ 90 (clause permitting option "up to" 100 percent enables Government to order partial quantity). Adding new contract clauses in conjunction with an option exercise will also invalidate the exercise, *Varo, Inc.*, ASBCA 47945, 96-1 BCA ¶ 18,161. An option exercise is also improper if it is sent to an official of the contractor without authority to receive such communications, *Western States Management Servs., Inc.*, ASBCA 37490, 89-2 BCA ¶ 21,803.

Exercise of an option before funds are made available, contingent of the availability of funds, is an invalid exercise, *J.E.T.S., Inc.*, ASBCA 26135, 82-2 BCA ¶ 15,986; *Lear Siegler Inc.*, ASBCA 30224, 86-3 BCA ¶ 19,155. However, exercise of an option contingent on the availability of funds is proper if that is called for in the option clause of the contract, *Western States Management Servs., Inc.*, ASBCA 37504, 92-1 BCA ¶ 24,663; *Cessna Aircraft Co.*, ASBCA 43196, 93-3 BCA ¶ 25,912. See also *Freightliner Corp.*, ASBCA 42982, 94-1 BCA ¶ 26,538, where the board held that the agency could obtain its requirements for a sixth year by exercising an option on the fifth year of a multiyear contract.

If a contractor leads the Government to believe that it can exercise the option without strictly complying with the clause, it will be estopped from asserting the strict compliance rule, *Ampex Corp.*, GSBCA 5913, 82-1 BCA ¶ 15,738, *recons. denied*, 82-2 BCA ¶ 15,858 (authorized contractor told the Government that the option notice could be sent by TWX). For another case not requiring strict compliance with the terms of the option exercise, see *Contel Page Servs., Inc.*, ASBCA 32100, 87-1 BCA ¶ 19,540. There, the board found that an option was properly exercised when the contracting officer sent the contractor an unsigned bilateral modification exercising the option. The board reasoned that the cover letter, signed by the contracting officer, was a proper exercise of the option. In *TECOM, Inc.*, IBCA 2970a-1, 95-2 BCA ¶ 27,607, the board required exact compliance with the option terms distinguishing *Contel Page Services* and holding that the mailing of a draft bilateral modification was not a proper option exercise. Where the period for option exercise is established by reference to the date of final delivery, amendments changing that date should specify whether the option period is also changed. See *Damascus Hosiery Mills, Inc.*, ASBCA 18776, 74-2 BCA ¶ 10,961; and Comp. Gen. Dec. B-176386, Oct. 24, 1972, *Unpub.* (contractor allowed to recover for untimely exercise of the option where a modification of the delivery schedule was the direct result of Government-caused delay).

Although the strict compliance rule is generally adhered to closely, there are a few cases interpreting ambiguous option clauses. See, for example, *International Transducer Corp. v. United States*, 30 Fed. Cl. 522 (1994), where the court interpreted an option for "a part of" any line item to include an option to order parts of subline items — finding that this was a patent ambiguity for which the contractor should have sought clarification. See also *BMY-Combat Sys.*, ASBCA 39495, 95-2 BCA ¶ 27,809, where the board permitted exercise of an option after the full documentation of the results of the "testing process" when the contract called for exercise of the option "within 30 days after completion of initial production testing." The board used contract interpretation principles to give the Government additional time to exercise the option.

There are also cases finding proper exercise of options where the language purporting to exercise the option is not completely clear. For example, in *Technical Servs. Corp.*, ASBCA 36505, 93-1 BCA ¶ 25,310, the board found a proper option exercise where a letter stated that "the Government shall exercise the second option year" and contained an incorrect line item number and an incorrect initial date for the option work. Similarly, in *Mills Mfg. Corp.*, ASBCA 10416, 66-1 BCA ¶ 5450, the board found a proper exercise where a telegram stated that "the government proposes to exercise the option." In both cases, the board found that the total import of the communications was that the option was being exercised and that it would not require the Government to be grammatically correct.

(2) Sequential Options

If options are sequential, failure to exercise the option properly for one year will preclude the Government from exercising future year options, *Grumman Technical Servs., Inc.*, ASBCA 46040, 95-2 BCA ¶ 27,918. There the board reasoned that the contract "came to an end" when an annual option was not exercised; in effect, no options then remained for future years. Similarly, where a contract contained several options that both parties understood were priced on a learning curve, they were required to be exercised sequentially, *Motorola, Inc.*, ASBCA 39782, 93-3 BCA ¶ 26,081 (exercise of second option improper when first option had been permitted to expire). The same reasoning was followed in *Texas Instruments, Inc.*, ASBCA 25942, 88-1 BCA ¶ 20,421 (parties understood options were based on continuous production). FAR 52.217-7 contains a clause calling for options for "separately priced line items." Prior to 1990, this clause stated that such items were "independent of each other" and that the Government could exercise the options independently. See *Knights' Piping, Inc.*, ASBCA 46989, 94-3 BCA ¶ 27,023, following this clause. This language has now been omitted from the FAR clause, but it appears that the contractor would be bound to "independent" options if the contract clearly gave the Government this right.

(3) Time of Effectivity

The time of exercise of an option is calculated based on the time of *receipt* of the notice not on the time of transmission. Thus, one aspect of the strict compliance rule is that, to be timely, a notice of exercise of an option must be received prior to the expiration of the contractual time for exercise. Comment f. of *Restatement, Second, Contracts* § 63, states:

> Option contracts are commonly subject to a definite time limit, and the usual understanding is that the notification that the option has been exercised must be received by the offeror before that time. Whether or not there is such a time limit, in the absence of a contrary provision in the option contract, the offeree takes the risk of loss or delay in the transmission of the acceptance and remains free to revoke the acceptance until it arrives. Similarly, if there is such a mistake on the part of the offeror as justifies the rescission of his unilateral obligation, the right to rescind is not lost merely because a letter of acceptance is posted.

Thus, exercise of an option is effective upon receipt unless a contrary intent is shown, *Dynamics Corp. of Am. v. United States*, 182 Ct. Cl. 62, 389 F.2d 424 (1968). In *Cessna Aircraft Co.*, ASBCA 43196, 96-1 BCA ¶ 27,966, the board found receipt of a facsimile on the nonworking day it was sent, even though no contractor employee picked it up for two days. When a contact provision alters the basic rule, that provision will govern. See *USD Technologies, Inc.*, ASBCA 31305, 87-2 BCA ¶ 19,680, where the contract contained a special provision stating that the option would be "considered to have been exercised at the time the Government deposits [it] in the mails."

The board held that the Government had the burden of proof that the option exercise was actually mailed before the option expired.

There have been a number of instances where the contract clause is rather vague as to the final date for exercising the option. In such cases, the boards have looked to the entire agreement to determine the date. For example, in *TECOM, Inc.*, IBCA 2970a-1, 94-2 BCA ¶ 26,787, the board interpreted a clause calling for exercise of an option "within 30 calendar days of expiration date" to require exercise of the option at least 30 days *before* final date of contract performance. See also *American Contract Servs., Inc.*, ASBCA 46788, 94-2 BCA ¶ 26,855, where the board held that "within 15 days" inserted in the Option to Extend the Term of the Contract clause in FAR 52.217-9 meant within 15 days of the expiration of the contract, not within 15 days of contract award.

(4) Requirement for Written Notice

Almost all option clauses call for exercise of the option by written notice, and it has been held that oral notice will not suffice, *International Tel. & Tel. v. United States*, 197 Ct. Cl. 11, 453 F.2d 1283 (1972) (exercise of right to purchase quantities in a subsequent program year under multiyear procurement where the court decided the case using the legal principles applicable to options); *Maintenance, Inc.*, Comp. Gen. Dec. B-215619.3, 84-2 CPD ¶ 263 (oral advice that an option will be exercised is not binding on the Government). See, however, *American Mach. & Foundry Co.*, ASBCA 8862, 65-1 BCA ¶ 4654, where the Government was held bound to an oral agreement extending the date on which the option could be exercised. In *Diversified Marine Tech, Inc.*, DOTBCA 2455, 93-2 BCA ¶ 25,720, the board refused to compensate the contractor for work done on an option that had been orally discussed with the captain of a ship (indicating a high probability that the option would be exercised) but which had not been exercised in writing.

(5) Performing after Improper Option Exercise

There have been a number of instances where a contractor has asserted that an option was not properly exercised but has agreed to perform the option work "under protest." In such cases, relief for the added costs of option work done pursuant to untimely exercises of options has been granted on the theory that a constructive change has occurred, *Lockheed Martin IR*

Imaging Sys., Inc. v. West, 108 F.3d 319 (Fed. Cir. 1997); *Lear Siegler Inc.*, ASBCA 12164, 69-1 BCA ¶ 7563; *Keco Indus., Inc.*, ASBCA 16645, 73-2 BCA ¶ 10,056. See also *Holly Corp.*, ASBCA 24975, 83-1 BCA ¶ 16,327, where the exercise of an option without adequate funds was held to be a constructive change order because a Government employee stated funds were available and the contractor could not reasonably have known of the lack of funds. The Comptroller General has refused to consider such allegations because they are "appropriate for handling under the Disputes clause," *Murdock Mach. & Eng'g Co.*, Comp. Gen. Dec. B-183098, 75-1 CPD ¶ 98.

If the contractor honors an improper option exercise by performing without objection, it is normally estopped from later contesting the validity of the option exercise. In *E. Walters & Co. v. United States*, 217 Ct. Cl. 254, 576 F.2d 362 (1978), the court held that the contractor had lost the right to an equitable adjustment for improper exercise of an option because it had performed the option work without challenge and had not raised the issue until six months after completion of performance. See also *CARAM v. General Servs. Admin.*, GSBCA 12773, 95-1 BCA ¶ 27,488, where the contractor was estopped from asserting an improper option exercise when it failed to raise the issue at any time during the option year. Similarly, in *USD Technologies, Inc.*, ASBCA 31305, 87-2 BCA ¶ 19,680, the board found that the contractor was estopped from denying that an option was properly exercised when it had signed a bilateral modification "restating" the terms of the option exercise. In *TECOM, Inc.*, IBCA 2970a-1, 95-2 BCA ¶ 27,607, the board found no estoppel where the contractor performed the option work for four and one half months without protest but did not realize that the option had been improperly exercised until it hired an attorney.

(6) Unconscionability

The ASBCA has considered allegations of unconscionability in the Government's decision to exercise options, but these protests have been unsuccessful, *United Serv. Corp.*, ASBCA 25786, 82-2 BCA ¶ 15,985; *Mercantile Servs., Ltd.*, ASBCA 26386, 82-1 BCA ¶ 15,767, absent evidence that the entire contract had become commercially senseless and that the Government had superior knowledge regarding inflation at the time it exercised the options. In *McGrail Equip. Co.*, ASBCA 20555, 76-1 BCA ¶ 11,723, where prices had increased substantially after a Government price freeze had been lifted, the exercise of an option was held not to be unconscionable. The Comptroller General has written that the concept of unconscionability is inapplicable to the exercise of options since the exercise of an option does not constitute the making of a new contract, *Heirs of Kim Xum*, Comp. Gen. Dec. B-189121, 83-1 CPD ¶ 408.

5. Soft Options

The traditional option used in Government contracts has been on a firm-fixed-price basis with definitive specifications and a firm delivery schedule. Such options have been referred to as "hard" options. Procuring agencies also use options with less definite terms, referred to as "soft" options. See, for example, *Aviation Contractor Employees, Inc. v. United States*, 945 F.2d 1568 (Fed. Cir. 1991) (option to extend contract period with no agreement on how additional work would be priced); and *Fox Int'l, Inc.*, Comp. Gen. Dec. B-181675, 75-1 CPD ¶ 126 (option price to be negotiated in good faith). Because the contractor's obligations under such soft options are uncertain, the major purpose for using options — that of protecting the Government from future uncertainties — is absent. It appears that the major benefits to be gained from such options are administrative convenience in the option procurement and any advantage accruing from the contractor's obligation to negotiate in good faith. In *Electronic Sys. USA, Inc.*, ASBCA 26063, 82-1 BCA ¶ 15,521, the board held that performance of work in accordance with the Government's exercise of an unpriced option is compensable as a constructive change.

CHAPTER 9

CONTRACT PRICING

The Government's policy is to purchase supplies and services at reasonable prices. See 41 U.S.C. § 401(2), providing for procurement at the "lowest reasonable cost." In this regard, FAR 14.408-2 requires the contracting officer to determine that bid prices are reasonable before awarding the contract, and FAR 14.404-1(c)(6) permits cancellation of sealed bid solicitations if all acceptable bids are at unreasonable prices or if only one bid is received and the reasonableness of the price cannot be established. With respect to negotiated procurement, FAR 15.402(a) requires the contracting officer to "[p]urchase supplies and services . . . at fair and reasonable prices." Reasonableness of price is also a concept applicable to contract modifications. Thus, as a part of the vast majority of contract actions, the contracting officer is required to determine that the proposed contract price is reasonable before an award is made.

The primary focus of these requirements is to ensure that the Government does not pay *unreasonably high* prices. However, prices that are *unreasonably low* must also be dealt with before an award is made. Such prices may place the contracting officer on notice of a possible mistake in the bid or proposal requiring that the offeror be requested to verify the price, FAR 14.407-1 and FAR 15.508. Unreasonably low prices may also constitute evidence that the offeror is not responsible, FAR 9.103(c). In negotiated procurement, an unreasonably low price may indicate that the offeror does not understand the work, FAR 15.305(a)(1), resulting in a reduced scoring of the offeror's technical proposal. Finally, proposing an unreasonably low price that is below cost may constitute "buying in," alerting the contracting officer to take precautions to prevent the contractor from obtaining improper relief from the underpricing. See FAR 3.501.

This chapter considers the process that is followed by the contracting parties in analyzing and negotiating contract prices. The techniques used by the Government to determine reasonableness of price are price analysis and cost analysis. Price analysis looks at an offeror's proposed unit or total price and uses data external to the offeror's anticipated costs of performance to make a judgment as to its reasonableness. In contrast, cost analysis reviews the offeror's proposed estimated costs to ascertain the reasonableness of each cost element. The first section deals with the selection of the analytical technique that is appropriate for use in a procurement and the data necessary to use that technique. The second section considers the roles and functions of the various personnel involved in cost analysis and price analysis. The third section covers the process of price analysis, while the fourth section deals with the process of cost analysis. The fifth section addresses the methods prescribed for the negotiation of profit where the parties have negotiated the costs of performance. The last section reviews the procedures to be followed in price negotiations.

I. SELECTING THE ANALYTICAL TECHNIQUE

Some form of price analysis is *required* in all procurement actions, FAR 14.408-2 and FAR 15.404-1(a). Thus, the contracting officer should obtain data to permit such analysis on all but the unique procurements. However, as discussed in Section III, this data need not necessarily be obtained from offerors because it may be available in the agency or obtainable through market research.

Cost analysis must be conducted when it is necessary to examine individual cost elements, such as estimated labor hours or material prices, to determine the reasonableness of price, FAR 15.404-1(a)(3). Traditionally, cost analysis was performed by obtaining cost element breakdowns and supporting factual data. This factual data is referred to by the statutes and regulations as "cost or pricing data" and is required to be submitted by contractors and subcontractors in certain specified types of procurement actions over the statutory threshold ($500,000 at the current time), 10 U.S.C. § 2306a and 41 U.S.C. § 254b (often called the "Truth in Negotiations Act"). Cost analysis can also be performed by obtaining cost element breakdowns or other information regarding the estimated costs of performance of the contract with limited or no cost or pricing data. This type of cost analysis is frequently called *cost realism analysis*. Such analysis is required when awarding a cost-reimbursement contract, *KPMG Peat Marwick, LLP*, Comp. Gen. Dec. B-259479.2, 95-2 CPD ¶ 13. Cost analysis is *never* performed on sealed bid procurements, but on negotiated procurements the contracting officer must determine whether cost analysis is necessary and, if so, what type of data is necessary to perform such analysis.

Cost analysis is *required* to be performed on all procurement actions where cost or pricing data are required, FAR 15.404-1(a)(3). However, the

Comptroller General has made it clear that this requirement applies only when applicable statutes require obtaining cost or pricing data. Thus, in those instances where offerors have been required to submit cost or pricing data by an RFP but it is later determined that one of the statutory exceptions applies, cost analysis is not required, *Research Management Corp.*, 69 Comp. Gen. 368 (B-237865), 90-1 CPD ¶ 352 (adequate price competition precluded need for cost analysis). Prior to 1994, contracting officers had substantial discretion to require the submission of cost or pricing data and to perform detailed cost analysis using that data. However, the Federal Acquisition Streamlining Act of 1994 (FASA), P.L. 103-355, as amended by the Clinger-Cohen Act of 1996, P.L. 104-106, *prohibited* obtaining cost or pricing data when one of the statutory exceptions applies. See 10 U.S.C. § 2306a(b) and 41 U.S.C. § 254b(b) stating:

> (1) In General. — Submission of certified cost or pricing data shall not be required under subsection (a) in the case of a contract, a subcontract, or modification of a contract or subcontract —
>
> > (A) for which the price agreed upon is based on —
> >
> > > (i) adequate price competition; or
> > >
> > > (ii) prices set by law or regulation.
> >
> > (B) for the acquisition of a commercial item; or
> >
> > (C) in an exceptional case when the head of the procuring activity, without delegation, determines that the requirements of this section may be waived and justifies in writing the reasons for such determination.
>
> (2) Modifications of Contracts and Subcontracts for Commercial Items. — In the case of a modification of a contract or subcontract for a commercial item that is not covered by the exception to the submission of cost or pricing data in paragraph (1)(A) or (1)(B), submission of certified cost or pricing data shall not be required under subsection (a) if —
>
> > (A) the contract or subcontract being modified is a contract or subcontract for which submission of certified cost or pricing data may not be required by reason of paragraph (1)(A) or (1)(B); and
> >
> > (B) the modification would not change the contract or subcontract, as the case may be, from a contract or subcontract for the acquisition of a

> commercial item to a contract or subcontract for the acquisition of an item other than a commercial item.

Under this statutory mandate, the contracting officer must determine whether any of these exceptions applies and, if so, select the appropriate technique to be used and the data to be obtained. FAR 15.402 contains the following guidance — suggesting that contracting officers should obtain only the minimum amount of data necessary to make a determination of price reasonableness:

> Contracting officers shall —
>
> (a) Purchase supplies and services from responsible sources at fair and reasonable prices. In establishing the reasonableness of the offered prices, the contracting officer shall not obtain more information than is necessary. To the extent that cost or pricing data are not required by 15.403-4, the contracting officer shall generally use the following order of preference in determining the type of information required:
>
> > (1) No additional information from the offeror, if the price is based on adequate price competition, except as provided by 15.403-3(b).
> >
> > (2) Information other than cost or pricing data:
> >
> > > (i) Information related to prices (e.g., established catalog or market prices or previous contract prices), relying first on information available within the Government; second, on information obtained from sources other than the offeror; and, if necessary, on information obtained from the offeror. When obtaining information from the offeror is necessary, unless an exception under 15.403-1(b) (1) or (2) applies, such information submitted by the offeror shall include, at a minimum, appropriate information on the prices at which the same or similar items have been sold previously, adequate for evaluating the reasonableness of the price.
> > >
> > > (ii) Cost information, that does not meet the definition of cost or pricing data at 15.401.
> >
> > (3) Cost or pricing data. The contracting officer should use every means available to ascertain whether a fair and reasonable price can be determined before requesting cost or pricing data. Contracting officers shall not require unnecessarily the submission of cost or pricing data, because it leads to increased proposal preparation costs, generally ex-

tends acquisition lead time, and consumes additional contractor and Government resources.

(b) Price each contract separately and independently and not —

(1) Use proposed price reductions under other contracts as an evaluation factor; or

(2) Consider losses or profits realized or anticipated under other contracts.

(c) Not include in a contract price any amount for a specified contingency to the extent that the contract provides for a price adjustment based upon the occurrence of that contingency.

This guidance combines both price information and cost information (other than cost or pricing data) into a broad category of data called "information other than cost or pricing data." FAR 15.401 defines this category of data:

> *Information other than cost or pricing data* means any type of information that is not required to be certified in accordance with 15.406-2 and is necessary to determine price reasonableness or cost realism. For example, such information may include pricing, sales, or cost information, and includes cost or pricing data for which certification is determined inapplicable after submission.

The result of this statutory and regulatory scheme is that the contracting officer is given broad discretion to select the analytical technique to be used on a procurement but is encumbered with numerous limitations on the information that can be obtained to make the analysis. The critical first step is to determine whether the Truth in Negotiations Act (TINA) applies or the procurement falls under the monetary threshold or within one of the statutory exceptions. The contracting officer can then decide on the analytical technique that will be used and the data that will be needed to carry out the necessary analysis. This section discusses these issues separately for each of the categories of procurement described in TINA.

A. Where Cost or Pricing Data Is Required

The *mandatory* requirement for the submission of cost or pricing data was placed in the Armed Services Procurement Act in 1962 by P.L. 87-653.

It was later applied to civilian agencies by the Federal Procurement Regulations. Subsequently, the Competition in Contracting Act (CICA) added the requirement to the Federal Property and Administrative Services Act in 1984. The submission requirements for cost or pricing data are now contained in virtually identical language in 10 U.S.C. § 2306a(a) and 41 U.S.C. § 254b(a).

1. When Cost or Pricing Data Is Mandatory

Cost or pricing data is required to be submitted and cost analysis is mandatory when the procurement action (a) is a negotiated contract or contract modification or a subcontract or subcontract modification under such a contract or contract modification; (b) is over the statutory dollar threshold; and (c) is not within one of the statutory exceptions. Since each of the statutory exceptions is a separate class of procurement action, they will be dealt with individually in the following subsections.

a. Type of Procurement Action

The statutes require the submission of certified cost or pricing data only on negotiated procurement actions. Thus, no cost or pricing data is submitted in the initial award of a sealed bid contract or a subcontract under such a contract. However, amendments or modifications to sealed bid contracts, as well as those to negotiated contracts, are covered because they are negotiated procurement actions, FAR 15.403-4(a)(1)(iii). The regulations provide that final negotiated pricing actions, such as termination settlements or final pricing of fixed-price incentive or redeterminable contracts, are contract modifications to which the procedures apply, FAR 15.403-4(a)(1)(iii). Prior regulations applied this rule to final negotiated overhead rate settlements, but the current regulations are silent on this issue.

Subcontracts under negotiated contracts are covered by the statute as long as the contract and all higher-tier subcontracts are not exempted from coverage, FAR 15.403-4(a)(1)(ii). Amendments to such subcontracts are also covered, FAR 15.403-4(a)(1)(iii).

b. Dollar Threshold

The original Truth in Negotiations Act in 1962 contained a $100,000 threshold. In 1981, this threshold in the Armed Services Procurement Act was raised to $500,000, P.L. 97-86. This change was effective on December 1, 1981, but was not implemented in the Defense Acquisition Regulation until December 27, 1982. The Competition in Contracting Act (CICA), P.L. 98-369, reduced the threshold to $100,000, effective with solicitations issued after March 31, 1985. This Act also added this requirement to the Federal Property and Administrative Services Act — with a $100,000 threshold. In 1990, the threshold in the Armed Services Procurement Act was again raised to $500,000, effective December 5, 1990, P.L. 101-510. This Act called for the threshold to revert to $100,000 on December 31, 1995. However, the FASA repealed this reversion and raised the threshold in the Federal Property and Administrative Services Act to $500,000. This increased threshold became effective October 13, 1994, but was not incorporated in the FAR until December 5, 1994, Federal Acquisition Circular 90-22, 59 Fed. Reg. 62498 (1994).

With these numerous changes in the threshold and the accompanying delays in implementation of the statutes, it can be expected that some contracts will contain contract requirements that differ from the statutory requirements. Generally, the contract provisions dealing with contract modifications will govern over statutory provisions. However, the FASA contains a provision, 41 U.S.C. § 254b(a)(6), permitting contractors to obtain contract amendments adopting the new $500,000 threshold for civilian agency contracts:

> Upon the request of a contractor that was required to submit cost or pricing data . . . in connection with a prime contract entered into on or before the date of the enactment of the Federal Acquisition Streamlining Act of 1994, the head of the executive agency that entered into such contract shall modify the contract to [change the threshold to $500,000]. All such modifications shall be made without requiring consideration.

The FAR did not implement this provision. However, FAR 43.102(c) contains an omnibus provision permitting the inclusion of any part of FASA or the Clinger-Cohen Act into an existing contract without consideration, pursuant to Section 4402 of the Clinger-Cohen Act of 1996. Thus, the new statutory provisions can be implemented by inserting the new contract clauses into particular contracts and providing that such clauses shall be applicable only to contract modifications and subcontracts for which agreement on price is reached after the date of enactment of the Act (October 13, 1994).

For the purpose of applying the statute, the dollar value of a price adjustment is calculated by totaling the costs added and the costs deleted by the adjustment, FAR 15.403-4(a)(1)(iii). Thus, a modification adding $255,000 and deleting $250,000 would be subject to the statutory requirement. The regulation notes that this rule should not be followed when "unrelated and separately priced" changes are included in the modification "for administrative convenience."

2. *Obtaining the Data*

When the contracting officer determines that a procurement will be over the $500,000 threshold and none of the exceptions apply, cost or pricing data must be obtained. However, the standard solicitation provisions do not permit the contracting officer to call for the mandatory submission of such data with the proposal. Rather, the Requirements for Cost or Pricing Data or Information Other Than Cost or Pricing Data solicitation provision in FAR 52.215-20 gives the offeror the opportunity to defer the submission of cost or pricing data by claiming that either the commercial item exception or the prices set by law or regulation exception applies. Paragraph (a) of the provision states that if the offeror believes that it qualifies for either of these exceptions to the requirement for the submission of cost or pricing data, it may submit a written request for exception with the data pertinent to that exception. The provision is silent as to what action an offeror may take if it believes that the adequate price competition exception applies or if it wants the agency to give a statutory waiver. However, offerors would be well advised to request either of these exceptions if they believe they are applicable. Paragraph (b) states that the offeror must submit cost or pricing data if it "is not granted an exception." In addition, if no exception applies — as in the case of a sole source procurement of an item or service that is not a commercial item — the offeror should submit the cost or pricing data with the proposal and the provision requires that it be submitted in accordance with the instructions in Table 15-2 in FAR 15.408. FAR 52.215-20 also provides for three alternate provisions that can be used to (1) require the data to be delivered in a different format than required by Table 15-2, (2) require copies of the offeror's proposal to be submitted to the Administrative

Contracting Officer and the contract auditor, and (3) require the data to be submitted by electronic media. See the instructions in FAR 15.408.

Similar procedures are prescribed for contract modifications. FAR 15.408(m) permits the contracting officer to insert the Requirements for Cost or Pricing Data or Information Other Than Cost or Pricing Data — Modifications clause in FAR 52.215-21 in contracts "if it is reasonably certain that [such] data will be required for modifications" to the contract. This clause also permits the contractor to apply for an exception in lieu of submitting cost or pricing data to support a modification over the statutory threshold and contains the same alternate provisions for varied submissions of data. Since some data will be required for modifications over the statutory threshold, it is anticipated that this clause will be used in all contracts where there is any possibility that a modification over $500,000 might be issued.

B. Actions under the Dollar Threshold

The contracting officer has considerable discretion in selecting the analytical technique when the procurement action is under the $500,000 threshold because the FAR is totally silent on this issue. However, the contracting officer would be expected to use the same analytical technique for procurements in this category as would be appropriate for larger procurements of the same type. Thus, if, for example, a procurement was for a commercial item with a contract price of less than $500,000, it could be anticipated that the contracting officer would use the same analytical techniques that would be appropriate for procurement of commercial items over $500,000.

The statutes permit the obtaining of cost or pricing data in procurements under the threshold in *extremely limited circumstances*. See 10 U.S.C. § 2306a(c) and 41 U.S.C. § 254b(c) as follows:

> Cost or Pricing Data on Below Threshold Contracts. —
>
> (1) Authority to Require Submission. — Subject to paragraph (2), when certified cost or pricing data are not required to be submitted . . . for a contract, subcontract, or modification of a contract or subcontract, such data may nevertheless be required to be submitted by the head of the procuring activity, but only if the head of the procuring activity determines that such data are necessary for the evaluation by the agency of the reasonableness of the price of the contract, subcontract, or modification of a contract or sub-

> contract. In any case in which the head of the procuring activity requires such data to be submitted under this subsection, the head of the procuring activity shall justify in writing the reason for such requirement.
>
> (2) Exception. — The head of the procuring activity may not require certified cost or pricing data to be submitted under this paragraph for any contract or subcontract, or modification of a contract or subcontract, covered by the exceptions [for adequate price competition, prices set by law or regulation or commercial items].
>
> (3) Delegation of Authority Prohibited. — The head of a procuring activity may not delegate the functions under this paragraph.

FAR 15.403-1(a) prohibits obtaining cost or pricing data on acquisitions at or below the $100,000 simplified acquisition threshold, while FAR 15.403-4(a)(2) implements this statutory provision for acquisitions between $100,000 and $500,000. Since it precludes contracting officers from obtaining cost or pricing data without getting the approval of the head of the contracting activity and may not be used when the major exceptions apply, it will probably be used sparingly. Its major application will be to contract modifications where there is little or no pricing information. Under the prior statute, agencies frequently required the submission of cost or pricing data when the price was determined to be not reasonable. See *Sperry Rand Corp. v. United States*, 212 Ct. Cl. 329, 548 F.2d 915 (1977), where the court affirmed the exercise of this discretion under the Defense Acquisition Regulation (which gave considerably greater discretion to the contracting officer). In contrast, when the contracting officer did not request the data because it was determined that an exemption applied, the board held that no submission was required, *J.W. Bateson Co.*, GSBCA 4133, 76-1 BCA ¶ 11,751, *recons. denied*, 76-2 BCA ¶ 12,109.

The FAR is silent on obtaining information other than cost or pricing data in below threshold procurements. However, it would appear that the general guidance in FAR 15.403-3(a) would apply for these acquisitions. This guidance states that the contracting officer must obtain "information that is adequate for evaluating the reasonableness of the price of determining cost realism" but may not obtain "more information than is necessary" for these purposes.

C. Actions Where There Is Adequate Price Competition

The statutes and the regulations prohibit the obtaining of cost or pricing data and restrict the other data that can be obtained for this type of procurement action. Thus, when adequate price competition exists, the contracting officer must rely heavily on the competitive prices to ascertain the reasonableness of the price.

1. Definition of Adequate Price Competition

The statute does not define "adequate price competition," but FAR 15.403-1(c) contains the following guidance to be used in determining whether there is adequate price competition:

> (1) Adequate price competition. A price is based on adequate price competition if —
>
> (i) Two or more responsible offerors, competing independently, submit priced offers that satisfy the Government's expressed requirement and if —
>
> (A) Award will be made to the offeror whose proposal represents the best value (see 2.101) where price is a substantial factor in source selection; and
>
> (B) There is no finding that the price of the otherwise successful offeror is unreasonable. Any finding that the price is unreasonable must be supported by a statement of the facts and approved at a level above the contracting officer;
>
> (ii) There was a reasonable expectation, based on market research or other assessment, that two or more responsible offerors, competing independently, would submit priced offers in response to the solicitation's expressed requirement, even though only one offer is received from a responsible offeror and if —
>
> (A) Based on the offer received, the contracting officer can reasonably conclude that the offer was submitted with the expectation of competition, e.g., circumstances indicate that —

(1) The offeror believed that at least one other offeror was capable of submitting a meaningful offer; and

(2) The offeror had no reason to believe that other potential offerors did not intend to submit an offer; and

(B) The determination that the proposed price is based on adequate price competition, is reasonable, and is approved at a level above the contracting officer; or

(iii) Price analysis clearly demonstrates that the proposed price is reasonable in comparison with current or recent prices for the same or similar items, adjusted to reflect changes in market conditions, economic conditions, quantities, or terms and conditions under contracts that resulted from adequate price competition.

This regulation was revised in 1995 to permit a finding of adequate price competition, under limited circumstances, when *only one offer* is received by the Government. Prior regulations required that at least two responsible offerors compete independently for the award. Under this earlier, more restrictive rule, determinations of adequate price competition were upheld even though only a small number of competitors were involved in serious consideration for award. See *Ogden Plant Maintenance Co.*, Comp. Gen. Dec. B-255156.2, 94-1 CPD ¶ 275 (adequate price competition when two offerors were in competitive range; offeror downgraded on capability factors not a nonresponsible offeror); *Family Realty*, Comp. Gen. Dec. B-247772, 92-2 CPD ¶ 6 (adequate price competition where two offerors were in competitive range); *Adrian Supply Co.*, Comp. Gen. Dec. B-241502, 91-1 CPD ¶ 138 (adequate price competition on second solicitation when two price-competitive proposals received; no adequate price competition on first solicitation when only one proposal received); *D-K Assocs., Inc.*, Comp. Gen. Dec. B-213417, 84-1 CPD ¶ 396 (adequate price competition where only two of seven proposals were technically acceptable); and *Uniflite, Inc.*, ASBCA 27818, 85-1 BCA ¶ 17,813 (determination of adequate price competition based upon prices of three offerors and Government estimate). In one case, the contracting officer's determination of adequate price competition was found to be reasonable, although one of two offerors thought that the Government might not receive any other proposals, *ABA Electromechanical Sys., Inc.*, NASABCA 1081-13, 85-3 BCA ¶ 18,225. The other proposal and the Government estimate were held to have demonstrated the reasonableness of the proposed price. However, in 53 Comp. Gen. 5 (B-177847) (1973), it was held that price competition did not exist when only one acceptable proposal was received. In *Litton Sys., Inc.*, ASBCA 35914, 96-1 BCA ¶ 28,201, the board rejected a motion for summary judgment based on the argument that the contractor had no liability for defective data because there had been adequate price competition. The board ruled that the presence of only one "responsive" offeror precluded the applicability of the exception.

In best value procurements, where there are multiple evaluation factors, adequate price competition will be found where price is a *substantial evaluation factor* and is so evaluated. This rule applies to both fixed-price contracts and cost-reimbursement contracts. It is derived from decisions of the Comptroller General and has now been incorporated in FAR 15.403-1(c)(1)(i)(A). See *Serv-Air, Inc. — Recons.*, 58 Comp. Gen. 362 (B-189884), 79-1 CPD ¶ 212, where cost to the Government was held to be a "substantial" factor even though it was considerably less important than the other factors. The case involved the award of a fixed-price incentive contract where price was stated to be 30 percent of the total evaluation, with 15 percent for the comparative level of the price (which increased the score for prices that were low) and 15 percent for "cost realism" (which reduced the score for prices that were considered to be too low). The Comptroller General ruled that price was a substantial factor even though the components of the evaluation might cancel out the factor. In *Dynalectron, Corp.*, 52 Comp. Gen. 346 (B-176217) (1972), cost to the Government was found to be a substantial factor in a cost-plus-award-fee contract even though it was 20 percent of the total evaluation. In *U.S. Nuclear, Inc.*, 57 Comp. Gen. 185 (B-187716), 77-2 CPD ¶ 511, adequate price competition was found on a cost-plus-fixed-fee contract. The contracting officer also has the discretion to determine that price is not a substantial factor in these circumstances. See *Cubic Defense Sys.*, Comp. Gen. Dec. B-229884, 88-1 CPD ¶ 395, where the Comptroller General affirmed such a decision where price on a fixed-price contract was a minor factor (stating that *Serv-Air* holds that "the contracting officer has broad discretion to make that determination"). When the final award decision is made by a tradeoff analysis between the differences in price and the difference in the other factors (as is the case in almost all best value procurements), it would appear that price would always be a substantial factor and the contracting officer would have little discretion in this regard.

Adequate price competition also exists when the RFP provides for award on the basis of the "lowest-priced, technically acceptable offer," *D-K Assocs., Inc.*, Comp. Gen. Dec. B-213417, 84-1 CPD ¶ 396. This rule is now included in FAR 15.403-1(c)(1)(i)(A) because this type of procurement is defined as a best value procurement by FAR 15.101-2.

Adequate price competition can exist where offerors propose to furnish different products to satisfy a Government performance specification. See *Prudential-Maryland (J.V.) Co. v. Lehman*, 590 F. Supp. 1390 (1984), where the contracting officer's determination that adequate price competition existed was found to be reasonable in a procurement of hospital ships in which the competitors were proposing different designs. Similarly, in *ABA Electromechanical Sys., Inc.*, NASABCA 1081-13, 85-3 BCA ¶ 18,225, the board found the contracting officer's determination that adequate price competition existed to be reasonable. In that procurement, two offerors submitted proposals for different hardware configurations in response to the Government's performance specification.

The fact that oral and written discussions are conducted does not preclude a finding of adequate price competition. See *UTL Corp.*, Comp. Gen. Dec. B-185832, 76-1 CPD ¶ 209, holding that conducting oral and written discussions and calling for "best and final offers" supported a finding of adequate price competition because competition was, in fact, enhanced. Further, adequate price competition can exist though full and open competition does not occur, *International Sys. Mktg., Inc.*, GSBCA 7948-P, 85-3 BCA ¶ 18,196.

Adequate price competition can also be found on the basis of price analysis alone, FAR 15.403-1(c)(1)(iii). Under prior regulations this guidance was under the category of situations where a price was "based on" adequate price competition. See DFARS 215.804-1 giving the following additional guidance, which appears applicable to the new regulations as well:

> (b)(1)(A) An example of a price "based on" adequate price competition is exercise of a priced option in a contract where adequate price competition existed, if the contracting officer has determined that the option price is reasonable in accordance with FAR 17.207(d);

In the one litigated case on this issue, the board construed the definition narrowly and held that the procurement did not meet the test, *Norris Indus., Inc.*, ASBCA 15442, 74-1 BCA ¶ 10,482. In *Norris*, the contractor argued that its prices were based on adequate price competition in view of two prior competitive procurements of the items. The board held that the two prior procurements provided too meager a basis for price comparison under the circumstances.

The Department of Defense also provides guidance as to when adequate price competition can be found in dual or multiple source programs. See DFARS 215.804-1(b)(1) stating:

> (B) Dual or multiple source programs.
>
> (1) In dual or multiple source programs, the determination of adequate price competition must be made on a case-by-case basis. Contracting officers must exercise deliberation and thorough review in making the determination. Even when adequate price competition exists, in certain cases it may be appropriate to obtain additional information to assist in price analysis.
>
> (2) Adequate price competition normally exists when —
>
> (i) Prices are solicited across a full range of step quantities, normally including a 0-100 percent split, from at least two offerors that are individually capable of producing the full quantity; and
>
> (ii) The reasonableness of all prices awarded is clearly established on the basis of price analysis (see FAR 15.805-2).

In the past the determination of whether adequate price competition exists has been held to be a discretionary decision of the contracting officer. A contracting officer's determination that adequate price competition exists was not disturbed if it was reasonably based, *Fraass Surgical Mfg. Co. v. United States*, 215 Ct. Cl. 820, 571 F.2d 34 (1978). See also *Sperry Rand Corp. v. United States*, 212 Ct. Cl. 329, 548 F.2d 915 (1977), recognizing that sound pricing depends upon the exercise of sound judgment. The contracting officer was required to first determine whether adequate price competition existed before the mandatory exemption would apply. However, see *Libby Welding Co.*, ASBCA 15084, 73-1 BCA ¶ 9859, holding that a contracting officer's internal notation that there was adequate price competition could have no effect when there was actually no competition at all in the procurement.

2. Technique and Data

In most cases when there is adequate price competition, the contracting officer will be able to determine that the price is reasonable by making a price analysis. When there are two or more competitors that have submitted competitive prices, the prices submitted will frequently be sufficient to demonstrate that the award price is fair and reasonable. If the supplies or services have been procured in the past, the contracting officer will also have those prices to be used in a price analysis. Normally, such data would be sufficient in fixed-price contracting situations. In contrast, in cost-reimbursement contracts where there is adequate price competition, the contracting officer will generally need some cost data to evaluate the cost realism of the proposals. FAR 15.403-3(b) gives the following guidance on these issues:

> When adequate price competition exists (see 15.403-1(c)(1)), generally no additional information is necessary to determine the reasonableness of price. However, if there are unusual circumstances where it is concluded that additional information is necessary to determine the reasonableness of price, the contracting officer shall, to the maximum extent practicable, obtain the additional information from sources other than the offeror. In addition, the contracting officer may request information to determine the cost realism of competing offers or to evaluate competing approaches.

Obtaining pricing information from an offeror, such as the prices charged to other customers, is viewed by the statutes and regulations as a circumstance that will occur rarely. When cost data is required to perform a cost realism analysis in these situations, the contracting officer is *prohibited* from obtaining cost or pricing data.

When the contracting officer decides to obtain data in these circumstances, FAR 15.408(l)(4) calls for the use of an alternate solicitation provision to obtain "information other than cost or pricing data." This provision (Alternate IV in FAR 52.215-20) provides:

> (a) Submission of cost or pricing data is not required.
>
> (b) Provide information described below: *[Insert description of the information and the format that are required, including access to records necessary to permit an adequate evaluation of the proposed price in accordance with 15.403-3.]*

D. Actions Where There Are Prices Set by Law or Regulation

FAR 15.403-1(c)(2) contains the following brief statement on this exception:

> Prices set by law or regulation. Pronouncements in the form of periodic rulings, reviews, or similar actions of a governmental body, or embodied in the laws are sufficient to set a price.

The Requirements for Cost or Pricing Data or Information Other Than Cost or Pricing Data solicitation provision in FAR 52.215-20 requires that offerors submit supporting data when this exception applies:

> (a) Exceptions from cost or pricing data. (1) In lieu of submitting cost or pricing data, offerors may submit a written request for exception by submitting the information described in the following subparagraphs. The Contracting Officer may require additional supporting information, but only to the extent necessary to determine whether an exception should be granted, and whether the price is fair and reasonable.
>
>> (i) Identification of the law or regulation establishing the price offered. If the price is controlled under law by periodic rulings, reviews, or similar actions of a governmental body, attach a copy of the controlling document, unless it was previously submitted to the contracting office.

This guidance appears to allow the use of this exception and a determination of price reasonableness if the data submitted demonstrates that the proposed price meets the requirements of the law or regulation by which it is governed. However, FAR 15.403-3(a)(1) gives the contracting officer discretion to seek additional information to determine price reasonableness or cost realism. The contracting officer is prohibited from obtaining cost or pricing data in these circumstances.

E. Actions Where There Are Commercial Items

The FASA added a new exception to the requirements of the Truth in Negotiations Act to permit the Government to follow commercial buying practices with a wide variety of commercial items. This created considerable confusion because there was already an exception for "catalog or market price items." The Clinger-Cohen Act of 1996 clarified this situation by deleting the "catalog or market price items" exception. Thus, there is now a single exception prohibiting the obtaining of cost or pricing data when procuring a commercial item, 10 U.S.C. § 2306a(b)(1)(B); 41 U.S.C. § 254b(b)(1)(B).

The term "commercial item" is defined in 41 U.S.C. § 403(12) and FAR 2.101 to include both products and services. See the discussion and analysis in Chapter 7.

The statutes and regulations appear to contemplate that price analysis will be used to ascertain the reasonableness of prices for commercial items. However, FAR 15.403-3(a)(1) permits contracting officers to obtain data necessary to determine cost realism when procuring a commercial item. Presumably, this is applicable to the rare situation where the commercial item was being procured on a cost-reimbursement contract.

The guidance on the data that may be obtained when procuring commercial items is varied and confusing. 10 U.S.C. § 2306a(d)(2) and 41 U.S.C. § 254b(d)(2) require that the regulations contain limitations on the data that can be obtained when procuring a commercial item. These limitations are set forth in FAR 15.403-3(c) as follows:

> (1) Requests for sales data relating to commercial items shall be limited to data for the same or similar items during a relevant time period.
>
> (2) The contracting officer shall, to the maximum extent practicable, limit the scope of the request for information relating to commercial items to include only information that is in the form regularly maintained by the offeror as part of its commercial operations.
>
> (3) Information obtained relating to commercial items that is exempt from disclosure under 24.202(a) or the Freedom of Information Act (5 U.S.C. 552(b)) shall not be disclosed outside of the Government.

10 U.S.C. § 2306a(d)(1) and 41 U.S.C. § 254b(d)(1) also contains the following mandatory requirement to obtain data:

> Authority to Require Submission. When certified cost or pricing data required to be submitted under this section for a contract, subcontract, or modification of a contract or subcontract, the contracting officer shall require submission of data other than certified cost or pricing data to the extent necessary to determine the reasonableness of the price of the contract,

> subcontract, or modification of the contract or subcontract. Except in the case of a contract or subcontract covered by the exceptions [for adequate price competition and prices set by law or regulation], the data submitted shall include, at a minimum, appropriate information on the prices at which the same item or similar items have previously been sold that is adequate for evaluating the reasonableness of the price for the procurement.

The Requirements for Cost or Pricing Data or Information Other Than Cost or Pricing Data solicitation provision at FAR 52.215-20 also contains the following guidance on the type of data that should be submitted to support a request for application of the commercial item exception:

> (ii) Commercial item exception. For a commercial item exception, the offeror shall submit, at a minimum, information on prices at which the same item or similar items have previously been sold in the commercial market that is adequate for evaluating the reasonableness of the price for this acquisition. Such information may include —
>
> > (A) For catalog items, a copy of or identification of the catalog and its date, or the appropriate pages for the offered items, or a statement that the catalog is on file in the buying office to which the proposal is being submitted. Provide a copy or describe current discount policies and price lists (published or unpublished), e.g., wholesale, original equipment manufacturer, or reseller. Also explain the basis of each offered price and its relationship to the established catalog price, including how the proposed price relates to the price of recent sales in quantities similar to the proposed quantities.
> >
> > (B) For market-price items, the source and date or period of the market quotation or other basis for market price, the base amount, and applicable discounts. In addition, describe the nature of the market.
> >
> > (C) For items included on an active Federal Supply Service Multiple Award Schedule contract, proof that an exception has been granted for the schedule item.

Alternatively, the contracting officer can use the Alternate IV provision in FAR 52.215-20 and describe the specific data that each offeror is required to provide.

It would appear that the key issue in ascertaining the reasonableness of prices of commercial items is the amount of competition that will be achieved. If there will be substantial competition, the competitive prices should provide sufficient information without the need for additional data. On the other hand, if the commercial item is a sole source item or the competition is very limited, the contracting officer will need additional data. If such data is available through market research, there may be no need to require offerors to submit the data. If not, sales data will have to be obtained from offerors. The goal of the statutes and regulations is to obtain necessary data in the least burdensome manner possible in the circumstances of each procurement. While the guidance in the FAR is confusing, it is sufficiently permissive to permit the contracting officer to obtain necessary information without placing burdensome data requirements on offerors of commercial items.

F. Actions Where There Are Agency Waivers

Originally, this exception permitted the waiver of the requirement for submission of cost or pricing data by the agency head. The FASA granted this waiver authority to "the head of the procuring activity, without delegation." The statutes require that waivers be supported by written documentation. FAR 15.403-1(c) provides the following guidance on the use of waivers:

> (4) Waivers. The head of the contracting activity (HCA) may, without power of delegation, waive the requirement for submission of cost or pricing data in exceptional cases. The authorization for the waiver and the supporting rationale shall be in writing. The HCA may consider waiving the requirement if the price can be determined to be fair and reasonable without submission of cost or pricing data. For example, if cost or pricing data were furnished on previous production buys and the contracting officer determines such data are sufficient, when combined with updated information, a waiver may be granted. If the HCA has waived the requirement for submission of cost or pricing data, the contractor or higher-tier subcontractor to whom the waiver relates shall be considered as having been required to provide cost or pricing data. Consequently, award of any lower-tier subcontract expected to exceed the cost or pricing data threshold requires the submission of cost or pricing data unless an exception otherwise applies to the subcontract or the waiver specifically includes that subcontract.

The format used by the DOD for such waivers is set forth in DFARS 215.804-1.

While the above waiver guidance is stated in permissive language, FAR 15.402(a)(3) appears to encourage the use of waivers by stating that contracting officers should "use every means available to ascertain whether a fair and reasonable price can be determined before requesting cost or pricing data." This guidance implies that when this determination can be made using data other than cost or pricing data, a waiver should be sought.

Initially, the Comptroller General permitted an informal waiver, *Televiso Elecs.*, 46 Comp. Gen. 631 (B-159922) (1967), but subsequent decisions stated that this requirement must be formally complied with to justify not obtaining data, Comp. Gen. Dec. B-161448, Feb. 7, 1968, *Unpub.*; 53 Comp. Gen. 5 (B-177847) (1973). It has also been held that an agency may refuse to waive the cost or pricing data requirement and contract with another offeror on a sole source basis, *Telectro-Mek, Inc.*, Comp. Gen. Dec. B-185892, 76-2 CPD ¶ 81.

In *M-R-S Mfg. Co. v. United States*, 203 Ct. Cl. 551, 492 F.2d 835 (1974), the Court of Claims held that the contracting officer could not agree to nonsubmission of data. The court stated at 562:

> Since the Government chose to ignore any data developed between March 23 and August 17, the plaintiff says the obligation to furnish accurate, complete, and current data was waived. The most basic flaw in this argument is the assumption that the obligation to furnish proper data can be waived by a Government agent. The duty to furnish accurate, complete, and current data is a duty imposed on Government contractors by a statute, and, therefore, that duty cannot be waived by a Government agent. *United States v. Stewart*, 311 U.S. 60 (1940); *Utah Power & Light Co. v. United States*, 243 U.S. 389 (1917); *see Federal Crop Ins. Corp. v. Merrill*, 332 U.S. 380 (1947); *Montilla v. United States*, 198 Ct. Cl. 48, 457 F.2d 978 (1972).

The court omitted any discussion of statutory waiver by the agency head since that was not an issue in the case. The same result was reached in *Conrac Corp. v. United States*, 214 Ct. Cl. 561, 558 F.2d 994 (1977), where the court noted that a "reasonable" cutoff date for establishing the timeliness of data submissions would not have constituted an improper waiver. In *Numax Elecs., Inc.*, ASBCA 29186, 85-3 BCA ¶ 18,396, the board found that the submission of data could not be waived by the contracting officer. See also *Southwest Marine, Inc.*, DOTBCA 1577J, 95-2 ¶ 27,760, where the board held that the contracting officer's failure to request cost and pricing data did not waive the Government's right to reduce the contract proceeds for defective pricing. The board stated that the contractor had a statutory duty to disclose and certify all relevant cost and pricing data regardless of whether the contracting officer asked for it.

G. Modifications to Commercial Items

10 U.S.C. § 2306a(b)(2) and 41 U.S.C. § 254b(b)(2) prohibit the obtaining of cost or pricing data for modifications to contracts for commercial items. FAR 15.403-1(b)(5) implements this prohibition and FAR 15.403-1(c)(3) states that it applies to any modification "that does not change the item from a commercial item to a noncommercial item."

As discussed in Chapter 7, modifications that meet this requirement must be either "minor" or "customarily available in the commercial marketplace." The FAR contains no guidance on the data that should be obtained to ascertain that the price for such modifications is fair and reasonable. However, FAR 52.215-21 contains a standard contract clause for modifications that permits the contractor to request an exception to the submission of cost or pricing data and submit information on prices at which the same or similar items have been sold to demonstrate that the modification is reasonably priced. This appears to assume that the prices for such modifications can be evaluated without the use of cost or pricing data and that obtaining cost or pricing data would be done only in unusual cases.

II. ROLES OF GOVERNMENT PERSONNEL

The regulations provide that the determination of the reasonableness of the contract price is the responsibility of the contracting officer. FAR 15.404-1(a)(1) states that the contracting officer "is responsible for evaluating the reasonableness of the offered prices." See also FAR 14.408-2(a) stating that the "contracting officer shall determine . . . that prices offered are reasonable before awarding the contract." This responsibility is carried out through detailed analysis of the contract price on all procurements. FAR 15.404-1 gives the following guidance on the extent of the proposal analysis that the contracting officer is required to conduct and the process that is used to make this analysis:

> (a) *General.* The objective of proposal analysis is to ensure that the final agreed-to price is fair and reasonable.
>
> > (1) The contracting officer is responsible for evaluating the reasonableness of the offered prices. The analytical techniques and procedures described in this section may be used, singularly [sic] or in combination with others, to ensure that the final price is fair and reason-

> able. The complexity and circumstances of each acquisition should determine the level of the analysis required.
>
> (2) Price analysis shall be used when cost or pricing data are not required (see paragraph (b) of this subsection and 15.404-3).
>
> (3) Cost analysis shall be used to evaluate the reasonableness of individual cost elements when cost or pricing data are required. Price analysis should be used to verify that the overall price offered is fair and reasonable.
>
> (4) Cost analysis may also be used to evaluate information other than cost or pricing data to determine cost reasonableness or cost realism.
>
> (5) The contracting officer may request the advice and assistance of other experts to ensure that an appropriate analysis is performed.
>
> (6) Recommendations or conclusions regarding the Government's review or analysis of an offeror's or contractor's proposal shall not be disclosed to the offeror or contractor without the concurrence of the contracting officer. Any discrepancy or mistake of fact (such as duplications, omissions, and errors of computation) contained in the cost or pricing data or information other than cost or pricing data submitted in support of a proposal shall be brought to the contracting officer's attention for appropriate action.

Prior guidance had made it clear that the contracting officer frequently coordinated a team of experts that participated in the analysis of costs or prices. However, the regulations have always made it clear that the ultimate responsibility for the adequacy of the price analysis or cost analysis rested with the contracting officer and his or her immediate staff. However, initial analysis is done by many other employees, depending on the agency and the resources available. In many instances, the initial assistance that is available is from employees working at locations close to the contractor's place of business or the site of the work. FAR 15.404-2 provides the following guidance on obtaining this "field pricing assistance."

> (a)(1) Field pricing assistance. The contracting officer should request field pricing assistance when the information available at the buying activity is inadequate to determine a fair and reasonable price. Such requests shall be tailored to reflect the minimum essential supplementary information needed to conduct a technical or cost or pricing analysis.

(2) Field pricing assistance generally is directed at obtaining technical, audit, and special reports associated with the cost elements of a proposal, including subcontracts. Information on related pricing practices and history may also be obtained. Field pricing assistance may also include information relative to the business, technical, production, or other capabilities and practices of an offeror. The type of information and level of detail requested will vary in accordance with the specialized resources available at the buying activity and the magnitude and complexity of the required analysis.

(3) When field pricing assistance is requested, contracting officers are encouraged to team with appropriate filed experts throughout the acquisition process, including negotiations. Early communication with these experts will assist in determining the extent of assistance required, the specific areas for which assistance is needed, a realistic review schedule, and the information necessary to perform the review.

(4) When requesting field pricing assistance on a contractor's request for equitable adjustment, the contracting officer shall provide the information listed in 43.204(b)(5).

(5) Field pricing information and other reports may include proprietary or source selection information (see 3.104-4(j) and (k)). Such information shall be appropriately identified and protected accordingly.

This guidance gives the contracting officer broad discretion as to the amount of field pricing assistance to obtain. The prior guidance had made the obtaining of field pricing support mandatory for procurement over $500,000 when cost or pricing data was obtained. It also contained considerable guidance on the types of information that was generally obtained from field pricing personnel.

These provisions assume that agencies have fully staffed field offices capable of providing the type of cost analysis discussed in this regulation. However, most civilian agencies have no such capability, with the result that such assistance cannot be obtained. See, for example, DEAR 915.805-5, stating that field pricing reports are not required in the Department of Energy, and GSAR 515.805-5 stating that within the General Services Administration (GSA) field pricing support is provided by the Assistant Inspector General — Auditing, or the Regional Inspector General — Auditing, as appropriate. The National Aeronautics and Space Administration (NASA) does not require a field pricing report for procurements of less than $1 million, NFS 1815.805-5.

A. Field Contracting Offices

Some agencies, such as the DOD and NASA, have fully staffed field offices that are available to provide field pricing support when requested. Other agencies can obtain such assistance from field personnel on only a portion of their acquisitions. These agencies can often obtain assistance from the field offices of other agencies that are familiar with the offeror. Field pricing assistance is also available from Government auditors familiar with the offeror's organization, as discussed below.

When field pricing assistance is obtained, the field personnel should coordinate their work with the offeror. DFARS 215.805-5(e) encourages such close coordination, as follows:

> (8) The administrative contracting officer and auditor shall confer with the contractor during the course of the field pricing review to fully understand the basis for each item in the proposal and to remove any doubts as to the validity and accuracy of their conclusions and findings.

In many cases, the factual data supporting the offeror's estimate are submitted to these personnel in the field rather than to the contracting officer negotiating the contract. Since it is expected that the data will be subsequently transmitted to the contracting officer in the field pricing report, such submission meets the statutory requirements for the submission of cost or pricing data, *Singer Co. v. United States*, 217 Ct. Cl. 225, 576 F.2d 905 (1978). In *Singer*, however, the court noted that submission required physical delivery of the data and disclosure of their significance to the pricing action. Thus, the furnishing of monthly reports of labor cost information to Government field personnel was held not to be an adequate submission of data to support a specific pricing action. See also *Sylvania Elec. Prods., Inc. v. United States*, 202 Ct. Cl. 16, 479 F.2d 1342 (1973), where the court held that submission of relevant data on another contract pricing action was not a proper submission. In *M-R-S Mfg. Co. v. United States*, 203 Ct. Cl. 551, 492 F.2d 835 (1974), the court clarified this requirement by stating that the submission requirement could be met by either physically submitting the data or making known its significance to the pricing action. In *M-R-S*, the submission was not met by giving the Government auditor the bill of materials and open access to all of the offeror's purchasing records. This requirement is spelled out in FAR 15.408, which states:

Note 1: There is a clear distinction between submitting cost or pricing data and merely making available books, records, and other documents without identification. The requirement for submission of cost or pricing data is met when all accurate cost or pricing data reasonably available to the offeror have been submitted, either actually or by specific identification, to the Contracting Officer or an authorized representative. As later information comes into your possession, it should be submitted promptly to the Contracting Officer in a manner that clearly shows how the information relates to the offeror's proposal. The requirement for submission of cost or pricing data continues up to the time of agreement on price, or an earlier data agreed upon between the parties if applicable.

A proper submission was found in *Texas Instruments, Inc.*, ASBCA 30836, 89-1 BCA ¶ 21,489, where the offeror submitted data correcting an error in the previous data to the administrative contracting officer one day before it signed its certificate, and in *FMC Corp.*, ASBCA 30069, 87-1 BCA ¶ 19,544, where the offeror followed a standard practice of submitting supporting data for its incurred labor rates to the administrative contracting officer. See also *McDonnell Douglas Corp.*, ASBCA 12786, 69-2 BCA ¶ 7897, and *Boeing Co.*, ASBCA 32753, 90-1 BCA ¶ 22,270, *recons. denied*, 90-1 BCA ¶ 22,426, stating that the submission requirement would be met if Government field personnel had "actual knowledge" of the data.

When the personnel providing field pricing assistance find that the offeror is unable to provide sufficient information to permit them to provide the necessary assistance to the contracting officer, they must address this problem immediately. FAR 15.404-2 states:

(d) Deficient proposals. The ACO or the auditor, as appropriate, shall notify the contracting officer immediately if the data provided for review is so deficient as to preclude review or audit, or if the contractor or offeror has denied access to any records considered essential to conduct satisfactory review or audit. Oral notifications shall be confirmed promptly in writing, including a description of deficient or denied data or records. The contracting officer immediately shall take appropriate action to obtain the required data. Should the offeror/contractor again refuse to provide adequate data, or provide access to necessary data, the contracting officer shall withhold the award or price adjustment and refer the contract action to a higher authority, providing details of the attempts made to resolve the matter and a statement of the practicability of obtaining the supplies or services from another source.

B. Auditors

All contracting agencies have access to audit services and can therefore obtain prepricing audit reviews of proposals even when they have no field contracting personnel. The contracting officer has considerable discretion in determining when to request an audit, *Del-Jen Inc.*, Comp. Gen. Dec. B-216589, 85-2 CPD ¶ 111. The major contract audit agency is the Defense Contract Audit Agency (DCAA), which performs all contract audit work for the DOD and NASA, Defense Contract Audit Manual (DCAM) 1-201, 15-106. Other agencies can sometimes obtain audit assistance from their Inspectors General who have this responsibility pursuant to the Inspector General Act of 1978, 5 U.S.C. App. § 1-11. When a contracting officer cannot obtain audit assistance within the agency, assistance can be obtained from another audit group under a cross-servicing arrangement. See OMB Circular A-73 and DCAM 1-303 for guidance in this area.

FAR 15.404-2 contains the following guidance on prepricing audits:

> (c) Audit assistance for prime contracts or subcontracts. (1) The contracting officer may contact the cognizant audit office directly, particularly when an audit is the only field pricing support required. The audit office shall send the audit report, or otherwise transmit the audit recommendations, directly to the contracting officer.
>
> > (i) The auditor shall not reveal the audit conclusions or recommendations to the offeror/contractor without obtaining the concurrence of the contracting officer. However, the auditor may discuss statements of facts with the contractor.
> >
> > (ii) The contracting officer should be notified immediately of any information disclosed to the auditor after submission of a report that may significantly affect the audit findings and, if necessary, a supplemental audit report shall be issued.
>
> (2) The contracting officer shall not request a separate preaward audit of indirect costs unless the information already available from an existing audit, completed within the preceding 12 months, is considered inadequate for determining the reasonableness of the proposed indirect costs (41 U.S.C. 254d and 10 U.S.C. 2313).

> (3) The auditor is responsible for the scope and depth of the audit. Copies of updated information that will significantly affect the audit should be provided to the auditor by the contracting officer.
>
> (4) General access to the offeror's books and financial records is limited to the auditor. This limitation does not preclude the contracting officer or the ACO, or their representatives from requesting that the offeror provide or make available any data or records necessary to analyze the offeror's proposal.

See DCAM Chapter 9 for detailed guidance on audits evaluating pricing proposals.

As indicated in FAR 15.404-2(c) above, prepricing audits can also be obtained on subcontracts if the contracting officer concludes that an audit is necessary. There is no separate guidance in the FAR as to when such audits should be requested. The following guidance was contained in FAR 15.806-3, stating:

> (a) When obtaining field pricing support on a prime contractor proposal in accordance with 15.805-5, the contracting officer should request audit or field pricing support to analyze and evaluate the proposal of a subcontractor at any tier (notwithstanding availability of data or analyses performed by the prime contractor) if the contracting officer believes that such support is necessary to ensure reasonableness of the total proposed price. This step may be appropriate when, for example —
>
> (1) There is a business relationship between the contractor and subcontractor not conducive to independence and objectivity;
>
> (2) The contractor is a sole source and the subcontract costs represent a substantial part of the contract cost;
>
> (3) The contractor has been denied access to the subcontractor's records; or
>
> (4) The contracting officer determines that, because of factors such as the size of the proposed subcontract price, audit or field pricing support for a subcontract or subcontracts at any tier is critical to a fully detailed analysis of the prime contract proposal.

The current FAR gives the contracting officer complete discretion as to when prepricing audits are required on major contracts. This should obviate the problem under the prior FAR where a waiver was required when certain audits were not obtained. Under such regulations, it was held that a settlement agreed to by the parties was not binding because the contracting officer did not obtain a mandatory prepricing audit and did not follow the waiver procedure, *Bromley Contracting Co.*, DOTCAB 1284, 84-2 BCA ¶ 17,233.

When Government auditors work with contractors on a regular basis, they become very conversant with contractors' estimating and pricing practices. In such cases, they can be expected to know the impact of cost or pricing data given to them during prepricing audits, with the result that a contractor may meet the submission requirement more easily than when data are submitted to less experienced personnel. See, for example, *Motorola, Inc.*, ASBCA 48841, 96-2 BCA ¶ 28,465, where a valid data submission to the contracting officer was found where a subcontractor submitted its data to a DCAA auditor; *Motorola, Inc.*, ASBCA 41528, 94-2 BCA ¶ 26,596, where a valid submission by a subcontractor was found when the subcontractor disclosed data to its cognizant DCAA auditor with whom the prime contractor was conferring; *Litton Sys., Inc.,* ASBCA 34435, 93-2 BCA ¶ 25,707, where a valid submission of indirect cost data was found when the contractor submitted monthly actuals to the resident DCAA auditor; *Texas Instruments, Inc.*, ASBCA 23678, 87-3 BCA ¶ 20,195, where a valid data submission was found when the contractor submitted detailed data on the costs incurred in manufacturing parts to the DCAA auditor and to a Government price analyst; *Hardie-Tynes Mfg. Co.*, ASBCA 20717, 76-2 BCA ¶ 12,121, where a valid data submission was found when the offeror gave the auditor the file containing the record of purchases of a part without stating which purchases were relevant to the current procurement; and *Whittaker Corp.*, ASBCA 17267, 74-2 BCA ¶ 10,938, where a valid submission was found when a purchase order was available to an auditor during a prepricing audit and the auditor specifically knew of its relevance to the audit through prior correspondence. The contractor cannot, however, mislead the auditor and escape liability. For example, in *Aerojet-General Corp.*, ASBCA 16988, 73-2 BCA ¶ 10,242, a failure of submission was found where the contractor gave the auditor all of the current factual data but incorrectly told him it would be fruitless to analyze them because they were commingled with other data. In addition, submission to an auditor may not suffice if the offeror later finds that the auditor has not included the data in the audit report, *American Mach. & Foundry Co.*, ASBCA 15037, 74-1 BCA ¶ 10,409. There the offeror learned during contract negotiations that the contracting officer did not know of an additional quotation that had been received from a vendor and furnished to the auditor. The board held that the offeror had a duty to inform the contracting officer about the quotation even though it had been submitted to the auditor.

Auditors obtain access to a firm's books and records in several ways. If the offeror has had no previous negotiated contracts with the Government, it is generally believed that the auditor has no legal right of access to the firm's books and records. See, however, *Aerospatiale Helicopter Corp.*, DOT-CG-80513-A, 89-1 BCA ¶ 21,559, where the board granted access to the contractor's books and records to audit data submitted to support a contract modification — based on the board's interpretation of the contract's Audit clause. Generally, offerors permit access to their records voluntarily because failure to cooperate can result in the contracting officer's refusal to negotiate with the firm. In addition, Table 15-2, Instructions for Submitting Cost or Pricing Data, in FAR 15.408 contains the following statement:

> Note 2: By submitting your proposal, you grant the Contracting Officer or an authorized representative the right to examine records that formed the basis for the pricing proposal. That examination can take place at any time before award. It may include those books, records, documents, and other types of factual information (regardless of form or whether the information is specifically referenced or included in the proposal as the basis for pricing) that will permit an adequate evaluation of the proposed price.

The enforceability of this regulatory statement is subject to question.

Offerors that have had negotiated Government contracts are generally required to give access to their books and records. While no contract clause gives the Government the specific right to audit for purposes of determining reasonableness of proposed prices, information relating to incurred costs or other data under existing contracts might be subject to audit and could be useful in analyzing proposed costs. The Audit — Negotiation clause in FAR 52.215-2 gives the procuring agency the right to audit the following three types of data:

> (b) Examination of costs. If this is a cost-reimbursement, incentive, time-and-materials, labor-hour, or price redeterminable contract, or any combination of these, the Contractor shall maintain and the Contracting Officer, or an authorized representative of the Contracting Officer, shall have the right to examine and audit all records and other evidence sufficient to reflect properly all costs claimed to have been incurred or anticipated to be incurred directly or indirectly in performance of this contract. This right of

examination shall include inspection at all reasonable times of the Contractor's plants, or parts of them, engaged in performing the contract.

(c) Cost or pricing data. If the Contractor has been required to submit cost or pricing data in connection with any pricing action relating to this contract, the Contracting Officer, or an authorized representative of the Contracting Officer, in order to evaluate the accuracy, completeness, and currency of the cost or pricing data, shall have the right to examine and audit all of the Contractor's records, including computations and projections, related to —

(1) The proposal for the contract, subcontract, or modifications;

(2) The discussions conducted on the proposal(s), including those related to negotiating;

(3) Pricing of the contract, subcontract, or modification; or

(4) Performance of the contract, subcontract or modification.

(d) Comptroller General — (1) The Comptroller General of the United States, or an authorized representative, shall have access to and the right to examine any of the Contractor's directly pertinent records involving transactions related to this contract or a subcontract hereunder.

* * *

(e) Reports. If the Contractor is required to furnish cost, funding, or performance reports, the Contracting Officer or an authorized representative of the Contracting Officer shall have the right to examine and audit the supporting records and materials, for the purpose of evaluating (1) the effectiveness of the Contractor's policies and procedures to produce data compatible with the objectives of these reports and (2) the data reported.

This clause implements the audit requirements of 10 U.S.C.§ 2313 and 41 U.S.C. § 254d.

A broad right to audit negotiated contracts is granted to the Comptroller General by the Examination of Records by Comptroller General clause in FAR 52.215-2(d), which is required to be included in all negotiated contracts by 10 U.S.C. § 2313(c) and 41 U.S.C. § 254d(c). However, the Comptroller General is not normally involved in prepricing audits. When using this audit authority, the Comptroller is permitted to audit "directly pertinent . . . records of the Contractor involving transactions related to this contract." In *Hewlett-Packard Co. v. United States*, 385 F.2d 1013 (9th Cir. 1967), *cert. denied*, 390 U.S. 988 (1968), the court interpreted this provision to include production costs of a catalog-priced item for which the Government had not required the submission of cost or pricing data. In *United States, v. McDonnell Douglas Corp.*, 751 F.2d 220 (8th Cir. 1984), the Comptroller General was granted access to estimates of tooling and design engineering costs. *Bowsher v. Merck & Co.*, 460 U.S. 824 (1983), held that records relating to costs of independent research and development, marketing and promotion, distribution and administration are not directly pertinent records unless the contractor "allocated these costs as attributable to the particular contract." The Court was apparently distinguishing between situations where a contractor allocates these general costs of overhead to individual contracts or products, in which case they would be directly pertinent, and those cases where the costs are collected in a general pool and charged against total sales for the year. See also *Bristol Labs. v. Staats*, 428 F. Supp. 1388 (S.D. N.Y. 1977), *aff'd*, 620 F.2d 17 (2d Cir. 1980), *aff'd*, 451 U.S. 400 (1981).

Inspectors General have the right to subpoena books and records necessary to carry out their functions, Inspector General Act of 1978, 5 U.S.C. App. § 6; 41 U.S.C. § 254d(b). This broad right is available in the civilian agencies to support an agency's analysis of proposed costs. Because the DOD Inspector General's duties do not include contract pricing audits (5 U.S.C. App. § 8), there is some question whether that organization's subpoena powers can be used for such purposes. See *United States v. Westinghouse Elec. Corp.*, 788 F.2d 164 (3d Cir. 1986), where the DOD Inspector General issued a subpoena to obtain records for the DCAA. The court held that the subpoena was valid based on the district court's finding that the Inspector General had an independent investigative purpose in issuing the subpoena. The court also held that this subpoena power is extremely broad, extending to documents such as a company's internal audit reports.

The DCAA has subpoena powers of its own, 10 U.S.C. § 2313(b). This power is granted only for books and records subject to audit under the FAR 52.215-2 Audit — Negotiation clauses. In *United States v. Newport News Shipbuilding & Dry Dock Co.*, 837 F.2d 162 (4th Cir. 1988), the court denied access to reports by the company's internal auditors because they were not "cost or financial data." However, in *United States v. Newport News Shipbuilding & Dry Dock Co.*, 862 F.2d 464 (4th Cir. 1988), the court granted access to a wide variety of financial data, including state and federal income tax returns, because they were "objective factual material useful in verifying actual costs." Subsequently, access was granted for estimates, projections, and accompanying work papers on the ground that they would assist in verifying claimed costs, *United States v. Newport News Shipbuilding & Dry Dock Co.*, 737 F. Supp. 897 (E.D. Va. 1989), *aff'd*, 900 F.2d 257 (4th Cir. 1990).

III. PRICE ANALYSIS

FAR 15.404-1(b) defines "price analysis" as follows:

> (1) Price analysis is the process of examining and evaluating a proposed price without evaluating its separate cost elements and proposed profit.

The most desirable method of negotiating the price of a fixed-price-type contract is by determining through the use of price analysis that a negotiated price is fair and reasonable without a detailed analysis of its cost and profit elements. This technique is faster and requires much less accumulation of detailed data by both parties.

The price analysis techniques that are usable in this process are described in FAR 15.404-1(b)(2):

> The Government may use various price analysis techniques and procedures to ensure a fair and reasonable price, given the circumstances surrounding the acquisition. Examples of such techniques include, but are not limited to the following:
>
> > (i) Comparison of proposed prices received in response to the solicitation.
> >
> > (ii) Comparison of previously proposed prices and contract prices with current proposed prices for the same or similar end items, if both the validity of the comparison and the reasonableness of the previous price(s) can be established.
> >
> > (iii) Use of parametric estimating methods/application of rough yardsticks (such as dollars per pound or per horsepower, or other units) to highlight significant inconsistencies that warrant additional pricing inquiry.

(iv) Comparison with competitive published price lists, published market prices of commodities, similar indexes, and discount or rebate arrangements.

(v) Comparison of proposed prices with independent Government cost estimates.

(vi) Comparison of proposed prices with prices obtained through market research for the same or similar items.

Price analysis is generally based on data obtained from sources other than the prospective contractor. See the preferences set forth in FAR 15.403-3. This information is gathered by the Government negotiating team from as many sources as possible and should be accumulated as a product or service is repeatedly purchased. Generally, to assure that the proposed contract price is reasonable, a sound price analysis will be based on several different types of data.

Very few protest cases discuss the use of price analysis for negotiated procurements. However, there is considerable guidance on this topic in protests involving sealed bid procurements where the contracting officer has used price analysis to make a determination as to the reasonableness of the price. Almost all of these cases deny the protest that the agency has performed an improper price analysis, finding instead that there is great discretion in this area. See *Family Realty*, Comp. Gen. Dec. B-247772, 92-2 CPD ¶ 6, stating that "[t]he depth of an agency's price analysis is a matter within the sound exercise of the agency's discretion." But see *Crawford Labs.*, Comp. Gen. Dec. B-277069, 97-2 CPD ¶ 63, where the Comptroller General sustained a protest finding that the agency provided no rational basis for its determination of price reasonableness of contract awards for primer coatings at prices more than double the award prices under the prior procurement for the same items.

A. Competitive Prices

Prices proposed by competitors are the most important data used in price analysis. They are based on the identical specifications for the work and are submitted in the same time period, thus reflecting current economic conditions. Competitors' prices are particularly useful when the contract will be fixed-price or fixed-price with economic price adjustment. In these cases, the competitors are motivated to estimate their costs accurately, yet are subject to competitive pressures to propose a price that is low enough to win the competition. For example, it has been held proper to cancel IFBs based on unreasonableness of prices (1) when the price of a nonresponsive bidder was significantly lower than the lowest responsive bid, *McCarthy Mfg. Co.*, 56 Comp. Gen. 369 (B-186550), 77-1 CPD ¶ 116; and (2) when the prices in a post-bid opening quotation were lower than the timely bids, *Mil-Base Indus.*, Comp. Gen. Dec. B-218015, 85-1 CPD ¶ 421. In *Mil-Base*, the Comptroller General recognized that such a situation could establish price unreasonableness but questioned the reliability of the quote under the facts of that case. Similarly, prices from small businesses have been found unreasonable (and set-asides canceled) based on proposed prices from large business firms, *Western Filter Corp.*, Comp. Gen. Dec. B-247212, 92-1 CPD ¶ 436; *Stacor Corp.*, 57 Comp. Gen. 234 (B-189987), 78-1 CPD ¶ 68; and on prices from foreign companies, *General Metals, Inc.*, Comp. Gen. Dec. B-248446.3, 92-2 CPD ¶ 256. But see *Airborne Servs., Inc.*, Comp. Gen. Dec. B-221894, 86-1 CPD ¶ 523, where the Comptroller General held that an informal telephone quotation from a firm was not sufficiently reliable to support a determination of unreasonable price.

The mere presence of competition is inadequate to assure that the prices proposed are fair and reasonable. For example, if the low offeror has such a decided advantage gained from past performance of the work that it is practically immune from competition, other competitive prices would not provide a valid basis for comparison. Similarly, competitive prices may be suspect when there are a very limited number of competitors. In such cases, the relative experience and sophistication of the offerors must be closely scrutinized. The contracting officer must also assess whether the market conditions are the same for the various competitors. In a period of high economic activity when the competitors are working close to their levels of capacity, competitive prices are not nearly as good an indicator of reasonable price as are prices submitted when competitors are actively seeking more work.

Much less credence should be given to competitive prices when the contract is to be awarded on a cost-reimbursement basis. In such cases, the cost estimates of the various competitors may be established with very different goals in mind than predicting the actual costs of performance. Because the Government will bear the risk of underestimates of the performance costs, competitors are not as fully motivated to predict the costs accurately. This is why cost realism analysis is required for such procurements. Comparisons of cost-reimbursement proposals are made in cost realism analysis, but they must be done very carefully, as discussed below.

B. Prior Pricing Information

The second type of information that can be used to assess proposed prices is pricing information from prior procurements. Both contract prices and other available price information should be reviewed. See, for example, *Crawford Labs.*, Comp. Gen. Dec. B-277069, 97-2 CPD ¶ 76 (prices double those of prior procurement unreasonable); *TAAS Israel Indus., Ltd.*, Comp. Gen. Dec. B-260733, 95-2 CPD ¶ 23 (prior prices paid to other contractors on recent competitive procurements showed that price was reasonable); *California Scaffold Corp.*, Comp. Gen. Dec. B-220082.2, 85-2 CPD ¶ 729 (prior prices of an incumbent contractor were used to show unreasonable price); and *Century Metal Parts Corp.*, Comp. Gen. Dec. B-194421.3, 79-2 CPD ¶ 437 (past procurement history demonstrated that price was reasonable). In some cases, prior prices have been used along with the Government estimate to demonstrate that the price was unreasonable, *Western Filter Corp.*, Comp. Gen. Dec. B-247212, 92-1 CPD ¶ 436; *Freund Precision, Inc.*, Comp. Gen. Dec. B-207426, 82-2 CPD ¶ 509; *Society Brand, Inc.*, 55 Comp. Gen. 475 (B-183963), 75-2 CPD ¶ 327.

There are several variables that must be accounted for when using prior pricing information. One of the most important of these variables is changes in economic conditions between the times of the prior procurements and the current procurement. See *Honolulu Disposal Serv., Inc. — Recons.*, 60 Comp. Gen. 642 (B-200753.2), 81-2 CPD ¶ 126, finding a price unreasonable because it was 14 percent higher than prior years' prices, whereas the agency believed a 3 percent inflation adjustment was reasonable. This type of adjustment is particularly important in a period of sharply rising prices. Another important variable is differences in quantity. As a general rule, it is expected that higher quantities will yield lower prices, but this may not hold true when a company is exceeding its capacity. It is also important to determine the total quantities involved when the product or service is being produced or performed for other customers as well as the procuring agency. A third factor is the inclusion of nonrecurring costs in the prices. If the offeror has been forced to discontinue the work since the performance of the prior contract, startup costs may necessarily be included in the new price. This also raises the question of whether nonrecurring costs have been included in the prior prices. In order to make a fair comparison, such nonrecurring costs should be removed from both prices and assessed separately. See *General Fire Extinguisher Corp.*, 54 Comp. Gen. 416 (B-181796), 74-2 CPD ¶ 278, where prior prices from a contractor were used to demonstrate reasonableness of prices including startup costs. The source of the prior price may also be a factor. See *W.H. Compton Shear Co.*, Comp. Gen. Dec. B-208626.2, 83-2 CPD ¶ 404, where the fact that the prior price was obtained from a foreign company was validly considered in finding reasonableness of price.

If the same work has not been done in the past, comparative prices of *similar work* can be used as a rough means of price analysis. In such cases, adjustments must be made to account for the dissimilarities between the two types of work. If the differences in the work are minor, such adjustments may not be too difficult to determine. However, at a minimum, this will require a detailed analysis of the product to ascertain its specific differences from prior products. See *Family Realty*, Comp. Gen. Dec. B-247772, 92-2 CPD ¶ 6, where prices received on another solicitation for similar services were used, along with the competitive prices on the instant procurement and the Government estimate, to determine that the proposed price was reasonable.

When data is available for several years, price analysis can be very valuable. Detailed analysis will disclose pricing trends that may indicate that significant learning has occurred and should be expected to continue through the current purchase. This type of information is a valuable cross-check for the competitive pricing information discussed above.

C. Parametric Data

Some industries compile and use very general data relating prices of products to characteristics of the product such as weight, electrical or electronic circuits, or other units of measurement. One of the oldest types of this information is the data compiled by the aircraft manufacturing industry relating labor hours in manufacturing to aircraft weight. Such data is a useful tool in making a price analysis — especially if the database is sufficiently large to demonstrate a consistent relationship. There is very little published guidance on the use of parametric data. However, the DCAA Contract Audit Manual (DCAM 9-1003.1 (1997)) contains five criteria for judging the reliability of this type of data when submitted by a contractor:

1. Do the procedures clearly establish guidelines for when parametric techniques would be appropriate?

2. Are there guidelines for the consistent application of estimating techniques?

3. Is there proper identification of sources of data and the estimating methods and rationale used in developing cost estimates?

4. Do the procedures ensure that relevant personnel have sufficient training, experience, and guidance to perform estimating tasks in accordance with the contractor's established procedures?

5. Is there an internal review of and accountability for the adequacy of the estimating system, including the comparison of projected results to actual results and an analysis of any differences?

If these criteria are met, parametric data submitted by contractors can provide another indication of the reasonableness of a proposed price. Such data can also be compiled and used by Government agencies in analyzing prices.

D. Published Prices

If the product or service is sold to the public, the offeror may have published prices or standard pricing techniques that are used for these sales. Such information will frequently demonstrate that the price is reasonable — especially if the product or service is sold in a competitive market. For example, in *Logics, Inc.*, Comp. Gen. Dec. B-237412, 90-1 CPD ¶ 189, a protest was sustained where the agency failed to consider pricing information contained in a Government catalog which indicated that the fair market prices of an item in question were much higher than the agency estimates. When using this type of information, care must be used in determining what discounts are given for quantity purchases and what other types of special arrangements are made for preferred customers. See *Interscience Sys., Inc.*, 59 Comp. Gen. 658 (B-195773), 80-2 CPD ¶ 106, where the Comptroller General found that discounts were not sufficiently large to permit a determination of reasonableness based on market prices. The volume of sales to the general public will also be a factor in assessing the validity of this type of data. Thus, a large volume of sales at a published price in a competitive market would make such data highly reliable, while a low volume of sales in a narrow market would render the data less reliable.

Published prices for similar products or services may also be useful in performing a price analysis. Of course, adjustments have to be made to reflect dissimilarities, but if the differences are minor, this may be a valid source of information. See, for example, *Eclipse Sys., Inc.*, Comp. Gen. Dec. B-216002, 85-1 CPD ¶ 267, where reasonableness of price was determined based on a "market survey" of prices of comparable products.

E. Independent Government Cost Estimates

Although the current FAR contains no requirement that agencies prepare an independent cost estimate for each procurement, this has been very common practice. Prior to FAC 97-02, September 30, 1997, FAR 15.803(b) required the development of such an estimate as follows:

> Before issuing a solicitation, the contracting officer shall (when it is feasible to do so) develop an estimate of the proper price level or value of the supplies or services to be purchased. Estimates can range from simple budgetary estimates to complex estimates based on inspection of the product itself and review of such items as drawings, specifications, and prior data.

Paragraph 3.5.1 of DOD Instruction 5000.2-R, *Mandatory Procedures for Major Defense Acquisition Programs and Major Automated Information System Acquisition Programs*, March 15, 1996, requires "life-cycle cost estimates" for all major programs in the Department of Defense.

Such independent estimates are based on all of the types of data that are discussed above plus any cost or pricing data that may be available from past procurements. They represent the agency's best estimate of the most reasonable current price for the products or services being procured. Thus, they can serve as a sound basis for finding a price unreasonable, *Northern Va. Van Co. v. United States*, 3 Cl. Ct. 237 (1983) (approving cancellation of solicitation because of a large discrepancy between the bid and the Government estimate because the cancellation would prevent "a misapplication of public funds"); *Kinetic Structures Corp. v. United States*, 6 Cl. Ct. 387 (1984) (permitting cancellation of IFB because all prices were unreasonable when compared to Government estimate); *Clark Bros. Contractors*, Comp. Gen. Dec. B-189625, 78-1 CPD ¶ 11 (upholding cancellation of IFB because sole bid was 13.67 percent higher than Government estimate); *Trebor Indus., Inc.*, Comp. Gen. Dec. B-228906, 87-2 CPD ¶ 446 (denying protest of cancellation when the sole bidder's price was 38 percent higher than a Government estimate based on data from a reliable incumbent supplier).

Since Government estimates are made early in the procurement process, it may be necessary to update them for use in the price analysis. See, for example, *Adam Elec. Co.*, Comp. Gen. Dec. B-207782, 82-2 CPD ¶ 576, where all bid prices were determined to be unreasonable based on a Government estimate that was revised after bid opening. The Comptroller General upheld the cancellation of the IFB even though the bid prices were lower than the original Government estimate. Of course, the competitive prices that are proposed may also demonstrate that market conditions have overridden the basic logic used in making the Government estimate. The proper procedure is to consider both the Government estimates and other proposed prices. See *Francis & Jackson, Assocs.*, 57 Comp. Gen. 244 (B-190023), 78-1 CPD ¶ 79, where a price was found reasonable by comparing it to both the Government estimate and competitive prices; *Mid-Atlantic Forestry Servs., Inc.*, Comp. Gen. Dec. B-217334, 85-2 CPD ¶ 279, where competitive prices and the Government estimate were used to demonstrate that the proposed price was not only reasonable but also quite low; and *Hughes Advanced Sys. Co.*, GSBCA 9601-P, 89-1 BCA ¶ 21,276, where the Government estimate was used to suggest price reasonableness, and competitive prices supported the decision. In one interesting case, an agency was allowed to cancel a procurement after a specification change rendered the Government estimate unreliable and left the contracting officer uncertain as to the reasonableness of the protester's price, *Adrian Supply Co.*, Comp. Gen. Dec. B-241502, 91-1 CPD ¶ 138. Verifying the price would have required an audit which could not have been completed before the end of the fiscal year, when the funds for the project expired.

F. Market Prices

Prices of the same or similar items that are available in the commercial market provide an excellent comparison to prices proposed for Government contracts. See *Sea-Land Serv., Inc.*, Comp. Gen. Dec. B-246784.6, 93-2 CPD ¶ 84, where the Comptroller General agreed with the use of this type of information for price analysis before this category was added to the FAR in 1995.

Care must be exercised in using this type of information because of the large differences that may exist between commercial transactions and

Government procurements. In some cases, the undue complexity of Government procurements may justify a significantly higher price than that being offered in the commercial market. On the other hand, there may be situations where the Government is buying such large quantities of the supplies or services that it will expect to pay a lower price than the commercial market price.

IV. COST ANALYSIS

FAR 15.404-1(c)(1) defines "cost analysis" as follows:

> Cost analysis is the review and evaluation of the separate cost elements and profit in an offeror's or contractor's proposal (including cost or pricing data or information other than cost or pricing data), and the application of judgment to determine how well the proposed costs represent what the cost of the contract should be, assuming reasonable economy and efficiency.

Cost analysis differs intrinsically from price analysis in that cost analysis focuses on the reasonableness of the estimated costs of performance, not the reasonableness of the contract price. Thus, cost analysis reviews each element of cost to ascertain whether the contractor's estimate contains an accurate and reasonable prediction of the costs that will be incurred during performance of the work. The contract price is then arrived at by adding a rate of profit that is determined to be fair in accordance with the profit guidelines that will be discussed in the next section. The fundamental theory of pricing using cost analysis is that a price is fair if it includes all reasonable costs of performance plus a fair profit. This theory, of course, ignores the fact that the price may be far out of line with the market value or intrinsic value of the work. FAR 15.812 recognized this problem, to some extent, by precluding the inclusion of costs other than manufacturing or acquisition costs in unit prices if such costs would result in unit prices greatly out of line with the value of the item.

The fact that costs and profit are analyzed separately does not mean that they must be negotiated separately. See the basic guidance in FAR 15.405(a), which states:

> The purpose of performing cost or price analysis is to develop a negotiation position that permits the contracting officer and the offeror an opportunity to reach agreement on a fair and reasonable price. A fair and reasonable price does not require that agreement be reached on every element of cost,

> nor is it mandatory that the agreed price be within the contracting officer's initial negotiation position. Taking into consideration the advisory recommendations, reports of contributing specialists, and the current status of the contractor's purchasing system, the contracting officer is responsible for exercising the requisite judgment needed to reach a negotiated settlement with the offeror and is solely responsible for the final price agreement. However, when significant audit or other specialist recommendations are not adopted, the contracting officer should provide rationale that supports the negotiation result in the price negotiation documentation.

Thus, in firm-fixed-price contracts and contracts with economic price adjustment clauses, the parties merely need to agree on a price to consummate the negotiation. In cost-reimbursement and fixed-price incentive contracts, this is not true. There the cost estimate and the profit or fee are stated separately in the contract document and must therefore be separately negotiated. However, even in these types of contracts, there is no need for the parties to agree on each element of the costs. Compromises are frequently made among elements of cost in order to arrive at an agreement on the estimated cost of performing the contract. Note that FAR 15.405(a) does not reflect 10 U.S.C. § 2324(f)(4) and 41 U.S.C. § 256(f)(4), which require identification of the treatment accorded specific costs included in indirect cost proposals that have been questioned by auditors, as follows:

> The Federal Acquisition Regulation shall require that all categories of costs designated in the report of the contract auditor as questioned with respect to a proposal for settlement [of indirect costs] be resolved in such a manner that the amount of the individual questioned costs that are paid will be reflected in the settlement.

While this provision requires internal documentation of the results of negotiations of indirect cost rates, it does not appear to require specific agreement on individual costs.

Cost analysis requires a complete review of the offeror's proposed costs to assure that they reflect an accurate projection of the costs of performance of the work to be placed under the contract. The elements of cost analysis are described in FAR 15.404-1(c) as follows:

> (2) The Government may use various cost analysis techniques and procedures to ensure a fair and reasonable price, given the circumstances of the acquisition. Such techniques and procedures include the following:

(i) Verification of cost or pricing data and evaluation of cost elements, including —

(A) The necessity for, and reasonableness of, proposed costs, including allowances for contingencies;

(B) Projection of the offeror's cost trends, on the basis of current and historical cost or pricing data;

(C) Reasonableness of estimates generated by appropriately calibrated and validated parametric models or cost-estimating relationships; and

(D) The application of audited or negotiated indirect cost rates, labor rates, and cost of money or other factors.

(ii) Evaluating the effect of the offeror's current practices on future costs. In conducting this evaluation, the contracting officer shall ensure that the effects of inefficient or uneconomical past practices are not projected into the future. In pricing production of recently developed complex equipment, the contracting officer should perform a trend analysis of basic labor and materials, even in periods of relative price stability.

(iii) Comparison of costs proposed by the offeror for individual cost elements with —

(A) Actual costs previously incurred by the same offeror;

(B) Previous cost estimates from the offeror or from other offerors for the same or similar items;

(C) Other cost estimates received in response to the Government's request;

(D) Independent Government cost estimates by technical personnel; and

(E) Forecasts or planned expenditures.

(iv) Verification that the offeror's cost submissions are in accordance with the contract cost principles and procedures in Part 31 and, when applicable, the requirements and procedures in 48 CFR Chapter 99 (Appendix of the FAR loose-leaf edition), Cost Accounting Standards.

(v) Review to determine whether any cost or pricing data necessary to make the contractor's proposal accurate, complete, and current have not been either submitted or identified in writing by the contractor. If there are such data, the contracting officer shall attempt to obtain them and negotiate, using them or making satisfactory allowance for the incomplete data.

(vi) Analysis of the results of any make-or-buy program reviews, in evaluating subcontract costs (see 15.407-2).

The following material discusses three types of cost analysis: (1) analysis of the offeror's proposed costs using cost or pricing data, (2) analysis of the proposed costs without using cost or pricing data, and (3) should-cost analysis. While the above FAR guidance is primarily concerned with the first type of cost analysis, it also recognizes the other two types. Thus, Paragraph (iii) reflects the analysis of the cost elements proposed by an offeror using data other than cost or pricing data. Similarly, Paragraph (ii) reflects the need for should-cost analysis.

A. Analysis of Proposed Costs Using Cost or Pricing Data

In conventional cost analysis, the contracting officer reviews the offeror's cost estimate to assure that the proposed costs are as accurately projected as is possible under the circumstances of the procurement. Summaries of cost estimates (cost element breakdowns) are submitted in a format that depicts the manner that the offeror accumulates costs, and cost or pricing data is submitted to support this summary information. Detailed guidance on the required submission is set forth in Table 15-2 of FAR 15.408. Instruction 4 of Table 15-2 calls for the submission to be organized by contract line item as follows:

> D. You must show the relationship between contract line item prices and the total contract price. You must attach cost-element breakdowns for each proposed line item, using the appropriate format prescribed in the "Formats for Submission of Line Item Summaries" section of this table. You must furnish supporting breakdowns for each cost element, consistent with your cost accounting system.

Cost analysis considers two types of information — *the factual data* in the possession of the offeror that are reasonably pertinent to the determination of the price and *the judgmental factors* used by the offeror to arrive at the submitted estimate. Table 15-2 requires the submission of both of these types of information, as well as additional relevant information. See the following instructions in Table 15-2:

> C. As part of the specific information required, you must submit, with your proposal, cost or pricing data (that is, data that are verifiable and factual and otherwise as defined at FAR 15.401). You must clearly identify on your cover sheet that cost or pricing data are included as part of the proposal. In addition, you must submit with your proposal any information reasonably required to explain your estimating process, including —
>
> (1) The judgmental factors applied and the mathematical or other methods used in the estimate, including those used in projecting from known data; and
>
> (2) The nature and amount of any contingencies included in the proposed price.
>
> * * *
>
> F. Whenever you have incurred costs for work performed before submission of a proposal, you must identify those costs in your cost/price proposal.
>
> G. If you have reached an agreement with Government representatives on use of forward pricing rates/factors, identify the agreement, including a copy, and describe its nature.

The factual data to be submitted are called "cost or pricing data" and will vary in amount depending on the element of cost being considered and the work being procured. Because this data must be submitted in accordance with the procurement statutes, the parties should always have this data available during cost analysis and price negotiation. The offeror's projections will also be the subject of analysis and negotiations although there is no penalty if they are not submitted to the Government since they are not cost or pricing data. The Government team will also make independent projections in most cases, and much of the ultimate price negotiation will consist of a comparison and evaluation of these different projections.

The offeror's estimate is normally broken down into categories of cost, such as labor, material, and indirect costs, which are listed in the cost element breakdowns. In accordance with Cost Accounting Standard 401, 48 C.F.R. § 99.401, each contractor's estimating practices must be consistent with its cost accounting practices used in accumulating and reporting actual costs. Thus, while each contractor has substantial freedom in establishing its cost accounting system, the costs accumulated must be directly relatable to the cost elements in estimates. Table 15-2 reflects this freedom by prescribing no specific cost breakdown by elements of cost. The following discussion addresses the requirement for the submission of cost or pricing data, the broad types of costs that are common to almost all systems, and the requirement that such data be certified at the conclusion of negotiations.

1. Cost or Pricing Data

The statutes require that, when required, offerors must submit cost or pricing data that are "*accurate, complete, and current.*" Thus, contractors must know what data fall within the definition of "cost or pricing data," what will constitute "complete" data, and how recent their records must be in order to comply fully with the requirement that the data be "current."

The submission requirement is a strict requirement. Hence, available data that are significant must be submitted even if the offeror does not use the data in arriving at the proposed price of the contract, *Rosemount, Inc.*, ASBCA 37520, 95-2 BCA ¶ 27,770; *Hardie-Tynes Mfg. Co.*, ASBCA 20717, 76-2 BCA ¶ 12,121. However, the Government has the burden of proving that the data was reasonably available to the contractor before the close of negotiations, *Litton Sys., Inc.*, ASBCA 34435, 93-2 BCA ¶ 25,707.

a. Definition of Cost or Pricing Data

The regulations contain a comprehensive definition of "cost or pricing data," emphasizing that such data are factual in nature but including some illustrations that are less than clear. See FAR 15.401, which states:

> Cost or pricing data (10 U.S.C. 2306a(h)(1) and 41 U.S.C. 254b) means all facts that, as of the date of price agreement or, if applicable, an earlier date agreed upon between the parties that is as close as practicable to the date of agreement on price, prudent buyers and sellers would reasonably expect to affect price negotiations significantly. Cost or pricing data are data requiring certification in accordance with 15.406-2. Cost or pricing data are factual, not judgmental; and are verifiable. While they do not indicate the accuracy of the prospective contractor's judgment about estimated future costs or projections, they do include the data forming the basis for that

> judgment. Cost or pricing data are more than historical accounting data; they are all the facts that can be reasonably expected to contribute to the soundness of estimates of future costs and to the validity of determinations of costs already incurred. They also include such factors as: vendor quotations; nonrecurring costs; information on changes in production methods and in production or purchasing volume; data supporting projections of business prospects and objectives and related operations costs; unit-cost trends such as those associated with labor efficiency; make-or-buy decisions; estimated resources to attain business goals; and information on management decisions that could have a significant bearing on costs.

The statutes contain a much shorter definition at 10 U.S.C. § 2306a(i) and 41 U.S.C. § 254b(i):

> [T]he term "cost or pricing data" means all facts that, as of the date of agreement on the price of a contract (or the price of a contract modification) or, if applicable consistent with subsection (e)(1)(B) [requiring the data to be as close to the data of agreement on price "as is practicable"], another date agreed upon between the parties, a prudent buyer or seller would reasonably expect to affect price negotiations significantly. Such term does not include information that is judgmental, but does include the factual information from which a judgment was derived.

It has been very difficult to arrive at a precise distinction between factual data and judgmental information. However, it is very clear that recorded costs are factual — with the result that they are cost or pricing data. Thus, the term includes labor rates paid in prior periods, *Boeing Co.*, ASBCA 32753, 90-1 BCA ¶ 22,270, *recons. denied*, 90-1 BCA ¶ 22,426; *Kaiser Aerospace & Elecs. Corp.*, ASBCA 32098, 90-1 BCA ¶ 22,489, *recons. denied*, 90-2 BCA ¶ 22,695; incurred labor hours, *Grumman Aerospace Corp.*, ASBCA 35188, 90-2 BCA ¶ 22,842; and incurred indirect costs, *Norris Indus., Inc.*, ASBCA 15442, 74-1 BCA ¶ 10,482. Information in the offeror's purchasing department relating to the prices of materials is also factual in nature. Thus, the term includes purchase orders, *Grumman Aerospace Corp.*, ASBCA 35188, 90-2 BCA ¶ 22,842, and vendor quotations, *Cutler-Hammer, Inc. v. United States*, 189 Ct. Cl. 76, 416 F.2d 1306 (1969). Accounting adjustments to actual cost data are also cost or pricing data, *Hughes Aircraft Co.*, ASBCA 46321, 97-1 BCA ¶ 28,972.

Accounting information on the costs of prior work on different projects may also be cost or pricing data if the information is sufficiently relevant to be usable in the analysis of proposed costs. Thus, prices paid for "similar" items were held to be cost or pricing data, *Hardie-Tynes Mfg. Co.*, ASBCA 20717, 76-2 BCA ¶ 12,121.

In some cases, a mixture of factual data and judgmental information has been held to be cost or pricing data. For example, in *Lambert Eng'g Co.*, ASBCA 13338, 69-1 BCA ¶ 7663, labor-hour estimates derived from actual information were held to be cost or pricing data even though they were not technically "actual" cost data. In *Aerojet-General Corp.*, ASBCA 12264, 69-1 BCA ¶ 7664, *modified*, 70-1 BCA ¶ 8140, the underlying factual data in an internal company report analyzing a subcontractor's pricing proposal were held to be cost or pricing data. See also *Grumman Aerospace Corp.*, ASBCA 27476, 86-3 BCA ¶ 19,091, holding that an internal company report analyzing a subcontractor's proposal was cost or pricing data, and *Texas Instruments, Inc.*, ASBCA 23678, 87-3 BCA ¶ 20,195, holding that a computer-generated report containing an estimate of the costs of future work that was derived from actual cost data but manipulated using complex estimating formulas was cost or pricing data. All of these cases seem to find that a document is cost or pricing data because it is the most readily available document and contains some factual data.

A contractor's management decisions are cost or pricing data if (1) they have a substantial relationship to a cost element and (2) they are made by an official with the authority to approve the action under consideration, *Lockheed Corp.*, ASBCA 36420, 95-2 BCA ¶ 27,722. In *Lockheed*, the board found that a decision to adopt a new strategy in collective bargaining negotiations met the first test because it would have a substantial effect on wage rates to be paid in the future. The board found, however, that this decision did not meet the second test because it had not been approved by senior corporate management as required by the policies of the company. In *Motorola, Inc.*, ASBCA 41528, 94-2 BCA ¶ 26,596, and *Motorola, Inc.*, ASBCA 48841, 96-2 BCA ¶ 28,465, a manufacturing policy memorandum directing that certain costs not be charged to Government contracts was held to be cost or pricing data. In *Aerojet Ordnance Tenn.*, ASBCA 36089, 95-2 BCA ¶ 27,922, a management decision to proceed "with all possible haste" to close a waste containment pond was not cost or pricing data because the cost consequences of the decision could not be determined until the action was approved by the state of Tennessee. In contrast, *Millipore Corp.*, GSBCA 9453, 91-1 BCA ¶ 23,345, held that a decision to change the company's discount policy did constitute cost or pricing data. The board did not address the question of whether a decision to alter the discount policy had been made at a level of management with the authority to approve the decision. It would seem that, to fall within the scope of this rule, the decision would have to impact the resources expected to be used to perform the work, such as a decision to change work methods or to buy from a different vendor. Thus, it is doubtful that a management decision to project costs differently would fall within this rule since such a decision is purely judgmental.

Factual data submitted by a subcontractor on a prior contract to support the prices of "long lead" items were held to be cost or pricing data on a current contract because the items were transferred to the current contract, *General Dynamics Corp.*, ASBCA 39866, 94-1 BCA ¶ 26,339. Similarly, a cost analysis made by a subcontractor to test the validity of the price of a sub-subcontractor was cost or pricing data when it demonstrated that the subcontractor's quoted price, that had been submitted to the Government, was too high, *McDonnell Aircraft Co.*, ASBCA 44504, 97-1 BCA ¶ 28,977.

Data containing only judgments are not cost or pricing data. In *Litton Sys., Inc.,* ASBCA 36509, 92-2 BCA ¶ 24,842, the board held that the estimated standard labor hours (ESLH) used by the contractor were not cost or pricing data even though there were internal reports listing these hours for parts manufactured by the contractor. The board found that the reports were not in themselves factual in nature because they contained no facts. The board distinguished these reports from documents containing mixed fact and judgment, stating at 123,944–45:

> The ESLH report is not mixed fact and judgment. In this appeal, we have no underlying document that is verifiable. The ESLH report is based on estimates made by [the contractor's] industrial engineers or test engineers and, as we have found above, no two industrial engineers or test engineers would estimate either the task or the frequency of the task the same. The ESLH report is therefore pure judgment and is, accordingly, not data and need not be disclosed.

b. Insignificant Data

In a few cases, contractors have escaped liability for nonsubmission of cost or pricing data by demonstrating that the data were not the type that prudent buyers and sellers would have believed to have a significant effect on the pricing. For example, in *Plessey Indus., Inc.*, ASBCA 16720, 74-1 BCA ¶ 10,603, a rejected vendor quotation was found not to be significant, and in *Boeing Co.*, ASBCA 20875, 85-3 BCA ¶ 18,351, incurred labor costs at the beginning of the contract were held to be the type of information that would not have been used by prudent buyers and sellers in the pricing process. The same logic would apply to old information in the nature of cost or pricing data. For example, contractors have labor rate and overhead rate information going back many years. Only the data relating to recent years are useful in estimating future costs. Reasonable buyers and sellers might disagree over how many years' information is significant, but all would agree that obsolete information would be of no use. The rule that all significant data must be disclosed has on occasion been interpreted very strictly. In *Sylvania Elec. Prods., Inc. v. United States*, 202 Ct. Cl. 16, 479 F.2d 1342 (1973), the Court of Claims held that if there is a "logical nexus between the nondisclosed pricing data and the possibility of a lower negotiated contract price, then the data is to be considered significant and subject to disclosure." Offerors should exercise care in deciding to use this logic to withhold data that the Government may believe are necessary to evaluate the proposed costs.

c. Submission Techniques

A notice in Table 15.2 provides that there are two techniques for the submission of cost or pricing data — *physical submission* or *specific identification*:

> Note 1: There is a clear distinction between submitting cost or pricing data and merely making available books, records, and other documents without identification. The requirement for submission of cost or pricing data is met when all accurate cost or pricing data reasonably available to the offeror have been submitted, either actually or by specific identification, to the Contracting Officer or an authorized representative. As later information comes into your possession, it should be submitted promptly to the Contracting Officer in a manner that clearly shows how the information relates to the offeror's proposal. The requirement for submission of cost or pricing data continues up to the time of agreement on price, or an earlier data agreed upon between the parties if applicable.

There is little guidance in the regulations or the litigated cases as to how specific identification of data is accomplished. See *M-R-S Mfg. Co. v. United States*, 203 Ct. Cl. 551, 492 F.2d 835 (1974), requiring communication of the specific data that are relevant to the pricing action. Volume 1 of the Armed Services Pricing Manual (1986) contains the following statement at 3-39:

> The identified data will be the details behind the proposal. There will be several layers of data, each more detailed than the preceding.

This would indicate that the specific identification requirement is met if the offeror includes a matrix of all data related to each element of performance. This matrix should contain specific information on where the data are located at the offeror's site and which of the offeror's employees have custody of the data. Instruction 2 in Table 15-2 contains guidance on the preparation of an index of data that may meet part or all of this requirement, as follows:

> B. In submitting your proposal, you must include an index, appropriately referenced, of all the cost or pricing data and information accompanying or identified in the proposal. In addition, you must annotate any future additions and/or revisions, up to the date of agreement on price, or an earlier date agreed upon by the parties, on a supplemental index.

While these specific identification requirements are somewhat cryptic, there is a clear rule that merely making the data available without specific identification is insufficient. Thus, giving complete access to all contractor data does not meet the submission requirement, *Hughes Aircraft Co.*, ASBCA 46321, 97-1 BCA ¶ 28,972 (making cost ledgers available for audity); *Aerojet-General Corp.*, ASBCA 12873, 69-1 BCA ¶ 7585 (submitting data to the Government plant representative); *McDonnell Douglas Corp.*, ASBCA 12786, 69-2 BCA ¶ 7897 (making data available to Government auditor and resident price analyst); *Grumman Aerospace Corp.*, ASBCA 35188, 90-2 BCA ¶ 22,842 (giving contractor complete access to subcontractor data but not identifying relevant data). However, if the Government pricing personnel have actual knowledge of the data, the submission requirement is satisfied, *Texas Instruments, Inc.*, ASBCA 23678, 87-3 BCA ¶ 20,195; *Boeing Co.*, ASBCA 32753, 90-1 BCA ¶ 22,270, *recons. denied*, 90-1 BCA ¶ 22,426. In one case, *Motorola, Inc.*, ASBCA 41528, 94-2 BCA ¶ 26,596, the board inferred that current indirect cost data of a subcontractor had been submitted to a resident auditor because that auditor gave the contractor a recommendation for an overhead rate that was apparently based on knowledge of that data.

d. Explaining the Significance of the Data

In a number of cases, submission of cost or pricing data without an explanation of their significance has been held to be a failure to meet the statutory requirement. Thus, a contractor must make efforts to tell the Government pricing personnel how the data are relevant to the cost estimate in instances when this is not readily apparent. This obligation occurs in two distinct situations — when the data are complex or unusual in nature and when they are submitted to update previously submitted data.

Complexity of the data is determined on a case-by-case basis. For example, in *Grumman Aerospace Corp.*, ASBCA 35188, 90-2 BCA ¶ 22,842, the subcontractor had not explained the significance of labor-hour data submitted to the contractor in computerized form. The board determined that the relevance of the data was not readily apparent to the contractor's pricing personnel and that the subcontractor had failed to meet the submission requirement when it did not explain the data. In contrast, in *Boeing Co.*, ASBCA 32753, 90-1 BCA ¶ 22,270, *recons. denied*, 90-1 BCA ¶ 22,426, the contractor was found to have met the submission requirement when it submitted raw data on labor rates without explanation. The board found that the Government personnel were fully able to use the data in their raw form and, therefore, that no further explanation of the data was required. Similarly, in *Rosemount, Inc.*, ASBCA 37520, 95-2 BCA ¶ 27,770, the contractor was found to have met the submission requirement when it gave the Government its incurred labor hours for the product being procured. The board rejected the argument that the contractor was required to plot the hours on a learning curve in order to meet the submission requirement, finding that the agency's negotiators could easily have plotted the data. These cases illustrate the basic proposition that the Truth in Negotiations Act does not require the offeror to perform routine analysis of cost or pricing data for the Government.

This rule requiring explanation of the data will also apply if the data contain information that is unusual in nature. For example, in the *Grumman* case, the subcontractor submitted information on an interdivisional order but did not disclose that the price of the order included profit. The board ruled that this nondisclosure was a failure to meet the submission requirement because the subcontractor knew that the inclusion of profit in such orders was generally against Government policy.

The rule is also applied in cases where the contractor updates prior data. For example, in *Singer Co. v. United States*, 217 Ct. Cl. 225, 576 F.2d 905 (1978), the court held that the contractor's mailing of monthly labor-hour reports to Government field pricing personnel and auditors did not meet the submission requirement. The court was critical of the offeror's failure to specifically identify the relationship of this information to the cost estimate. Similarly, cost or pricing data submitted in connection with other procurements do not meet the submission requirement on a contract to which the data have not been related, *Sylvania Elec. Prods., Inc. v. United States*, 202 Ct. Cl. 16, 479 F.2d 1342 (1973).

e. Currency of the Data

Until 1995, the certificate required to be executed by the offeror before award of the contract stated that the date of currency of the data was to be the date when price negotiations were concluded. See *Arral Indus., Inc.*, ASBCA 41493, 96-1 BCA ¶ 28,030, where the board found that the date when price negotiations were concluded was best determined by the date on the certificate. This made the data used in the negotiation defective because they had not been updated.

To preclude this result offerors performed "sweeps" making a total review of their cost or pricing data after the conclusion of price negotiations and submitting all new data to the contracting officer. This delayed the award of the contract and led to difficult decisions as to what the Government should do with the new data.

In 1995, the FAR was revised to permit the parties to agree on variable dates of currency. This is now relocated in Table 15-2 as quoted above. The Certificate of Current Cost or Pricing Data, in FAR 15.406-2(a) was also revised to contain the following instruction on the date of currency of the data:

> ** Insert the day, month, and year when price negotiations were concluded and price agreement was reached or, if applicable, an earlier date agreed upon between the parties that is as close as practicable to the date of agreement on price.

In addition, FAR 15.406-2(c) contains the following guidance:

> The contracting officer and contractor are encouraged to reach a prior agreement on criteria for establishing closing or cutoff dates when appropriate in order to minimize delays associated with proposal updates. Closing or cutoff dates should be included as part of the data submitted with the proposal and, before agreement on price, data should be updated by the contractor to the latest closing or cutoff dates for which the data are available. Use of cutoff dates coinciding with reports is acceptable, as certain

data may not be reasonably available before normal periodic closing dates (e.g., actual indirect costs). Data within the contractor's or a subcontractor's organization on matters significant to contractor management and to the Government will be treated as reasonably available. What is significant depends upon the circumstances of each acquisition.

This new policy reflects the fact that in order to be in compliance with the currency requirement, the offeror must continually update the data until the price is agreed upon, and this requirement may not be waived by a Government employee, *Singer Co. v. United States*, 217 Ct. Cl. 225, 576 F.2d 905 (1978). If there is insufficient time to compile the data in a usable form, the requirement can arguably be met by submitting raw data as they exist in the contractor's records, *Conrac Corp. v. United States*, 214 Ct. Cl. 561, 558 F.2d 994 (1977); *Lambert Eng'g Co.*, ASBCA 13338, 69-1 BCA ¶ 7663.

The best way to ensure that the currency requirement is met is for the contracting officer and the offeror to agree on the closing dates for various types of data at the conclusion of the negotiation and to attach this agreement to the certificate. In most cases, these closing dates correspond to the labor rate and indirect cost rate information already furnished to the Government. The contractor then conducts a "sweep" to check for any material cost or labor-hour information that has been accumulated during the negotiation. Such information would be furnished to the contracting officer with the signed certificate. By following this procedure, the contractor fully complies with the currency requirement of the Truth in Negotiations Act.

In the absence of an agreement on cutoff dates, there is a significant question as to whether an offeror is permitted any "lag time" for the transmission of cost or pricing data within the corporate structure. In *Sylvania Elec. Prods., Inc. v. United States*, 202 Ct. Cl. 16, 479 F.2d 1342 (1973), the Court of Claims established a strict rule that the data must be "current" as of the time of the price negotiation. The court held that data received by the contractor's purchasing department approximately one week prior to price negotiations were required to be furnished to the Government. This decision raises the question as to whether any period of time is permitted for processing the information through a company. The original board decisions allowed such a time lag, *American Bosch Arma Corp.*, ASBCA 10305, 65-2 BCA ¶ 5280, and one later case permitted a substantial time lag (as much as six months) in a situation where the contracting officer concurred in the nonsubmission of current data, *LTV Electrosystems, Inc.*,

ASBCA 16802, 73-1 BCA ¶ 9957, *recons. denied*, 74-1 BCA ¶ 10,380. However, it is clear from the language in *Sylvania* that the court will not tolerate a time lag of any significant length. See, however, *Boeing Co.*, ASBCA 20875, 85-3 BCA ¶ 18,351, where the board permitted a three-week lag in the preparation of labor-cost data because this was the period required by the contractor's accounting system. In *Aerojet Ordnance Tenn.*, ASBCA 36089, 95-2 BCA ¶ 27,922, labor-hour information through the month of February was required to be submitted for a negotiation completed on March 2, 1983.

2. *Types of Costs*

The types of data provided and the analytical techniques available vary considerably depending on the types of cost being evaluated.

a. *Material Costs*

This category encompasses all work purchased by the contractor from raw materials to major subcontracts. Table 15-2 contains guidance on the information desired for each purchased item, including the degree of competition or other information demonstrating the reasonableness of the price. In all cases, the critical information necessary to estimate the costs of any material category is the past purchases, if any, of the material, the anticipated source(s) of the material for the proposed procurement, and any pricing information that has been obtained from those sources.

(1) VENDOR DATA

If the work to be performed on a contract is reasonably understood, the offeror will have decided which part of that work will be purchased. Generally, the offeror also will have prepared a list of such items or services. For manufacturing contracts involving items that are fully designed, the contractor normally prepares a bill of materials that lists each material item with quantities, estimated prices, and source data. A typical bill of materials is set forth in **Figure 9-1**. See *Sylvania Elec. Prods., Inc. v. United States*, 202 Ct. Cl. 16, 479 F.2d 1342 (1973), where the court held that, in spite of the fact that the Truth in Negotiations Act does not normally require contractor's to create data, a bill of materials must be submitted because it is the basic factual tool necessary for estimating and analyzing the cost of materials. See also *Lockheed Aircraft Corp. v. United States*, 193 Ct. Cl. 86,

The prices of material items frequently consist of a combination of factual data and projections. The most reliable data would be fully negotiated **SCHEDULE A**

(See Bill of Materials 1523, June 19X2)

PART NO.	NOMENCLATURE	QUANTITY PER ITEM	SCRAP FACTOR* (%)	TOTAL QUANTITY	UNIT PRICE	TOTAL
9876543	Housing casting. (Vendor — Pic Corp. PO 351522, issued 12/20 to lowest of three proposals.)	1	4	468	$ 84.72	$ 39,648.96
9876542	Bearing, X design. (Vendor — Sun Co. PO 351480, issued 12/5 to only qualified source. Cost analysis performed.)	2	4	936	14.89	13,937.04
9876541	Gear, 14-tooth. (Vendor — Autoco. Two proposals. Autoco's the lower and its price used here. Bid file BB 442.)	4	4	1,872	418.00	7,824.96
9876540	Cable assembly. (Vendor — Rockaway Corp. Only proposal received. Completed 1411 attached.)	1	4	468	328.00	153,504.00
9876539	Bracket, main. (Vendor — Cee Cee Corp. Bracket is same as that used on earlier model of this system. Prior price was $22.19 each (PO 341110). 8% added in making estimate, two years since last buy.)	3	4	1,404	23.97	33,653.88
9876538	Race assembly. (Similar assembly bought 5/25 from Hup, Inc., for $150 each. Engineering estimates P/N 9876538 will cost 1/3 more to make.)	1	4	468	200.00	93,600.00
9876537	Solenoid. (Engineer estimate (estimate file — Eng-47).)	1	4	468	90.00	42,120.00
9876536	Gear, drive. (Engineer estimate, review of drawing (estimate file — Eng-487).)	1	4	468	24.00	11,232.00
	TOTAL MATERIAL					$395,520.84

Figure 9-1

432 F.2d 801 (1970), where a subcontractor had furnished raw data containing all of the purchasing records of the company but had not created a bill of materials indicating which purchased items were applicable to the contract being negotiated. The court held that this was an inadequate submission because it did not factually relate the data to the pricing action at hand. Compare *Conrac Corp. v. United States*, 214 Ct. Cl. 561, 558 F.2d 994 (1977), where the contractor argued that *Lockheed* stood for the proposition that when there was insufficient time to prepare a bill of material, raw data need not be furnished. The court rejected this argument, holding that raw purchasing data must be submitted if there is no time to prepare a bill of materials. The court stated at 569–70:

> The rule in *Lockheed* is that the best price data must be furnished, not that data in less than prime form, because of time or other constraints, may handily be hidden from the Government.

Thus, the contractor is normally expected to furnish the material data in the form of a priced bill of materials referencing all of the available cost or pricing data relevant to the items listed, yet must present the raw data if the bill of materials cannot be compiled for some reason.

The quantities on a bill of materials are derived from an analysis of the detailed drawings for the item, and any mistake in the quantities will constitute defective cost or pricing data. In the *Sylvania* case, discussed above, a defective submission was found when an offeror duplicated the quantities of two items on the bill of materials. The court dismissed the contractor's contention that the contracting officer should have recognized the error by comparing the bill of materials with other data.

The prices of material items frequently consist of a combination of factual data and projections. The most reliable data would be fully negotiated purchase orders or subcontracts for the work under the contract. However, FAR 15.404-3(a) does not permit a determination that prices are fair and reasonable on the basis of that fact alone. Thus, contracting officers must analyze such prices before making a determination.

Normally, an offeror will not have entered into purchase orders or subcontracts with prospective vendors at the time of negotiation with the Government; such prices will therefore not be available. If there have been past purchases of an item, however, the price paid will be available and will almost always be considered to be cost or pricing data, *Grumman Aerospace*

Corp., ASBCA 35188, 90-2 BCA ¶ 22,842. Similarly, quotations from vendors for the current work are generally held to be facts that must be disclosed to the Government, *Cutler-Hammer, Inc. v. United States*, 189 Ct. Cl. 76, 416 F.2d 1306 (1969); *Bell & Howell Co.*, ASBCA 11999, 68-1 BCA ¶ 6993. See also *Aydin Monitor Sys.*, NASABCA 381-1, 84-2 BCA ¶ 17,297, holding that a vendor quote for a quantity greater than that to be supplied under the contract was factual data and was therefore required to be submitted. The board reasoned that the quote was significant since its total price, including the greater quantity, was less than the contractor's estimated total price for the smaller quantity actually being purchased. Similarly, the cost of items held in inventory that have a reasonable chance of being used on the contract must be disclosed, *Hardie-Tynes Mfg. Co.*, ASBCA 20367, 76-1 BCA ¶ 11,827. See also *Etowah Mfg. Co.*, ASBCA 27267, 88-3 BCA ¶ 21,054, where the board granted a price reduction when the contractor submitted vendor quotations but failed to submit subsequent purchase orders entered into with the vendors at the quoted prices. The board reasoned that there had been a violation of the submission requirement and that the purchase orders provided a more certain basis for estimating the costs of performance.

If the offeror is actively negotiating with a proposed vendor at the same time it is negotiating the contract price with the Government, any significant changes of position by the vendor are cost or pricing data and must be disclosed. See *TGS Int'l, Inc.*, ASBCA 31120, 87-2 BCA ¶ 19,683, *recons. denied*, 87-3 BCA ¶ 19,989, where the contractor failed to submit information specifying that the vendor had agreed to alter the work to be done and had failed to give the subcontractor's new proposal to the contracting officer. See also *McDonnell Aircraft Co.*, ASBCA 44504, 97-1 BCA ¶ 28,977, where nondisclosure of cost or pricing data was found when a subcontractor developed additional information about the validity of the price of a sub-subcontractor but did not disclose it to the contractor in time for it to be disclosed to the Government. Changes in the offeror's negotiating position with a subcontractor may also be cost or pricing data. See *Boeing Military Airplane Co.*, ASBCA 33168, 87-2 BCA ¶ 19,714, where the company was held liable for failing to furnish all of the information relating to a dispute with a vendor on the proper price of work that had already been performed on a letter contract.

Vendor quotations and other vendor data must be included in the submission of cost or pricing data only if they would have a significant effect on the pricing action. Thus, outdated data or data not relevant to the pricing action need not be submitted or evaluated. For example, a contractor has been permitted to omit data pertaining to a vendor quotation that had been rejected although the contractor subsequently decided to purchase the item from that vendor, *Chu Assocs., Inc.*, ASBCA 15004, 73-1 BCA ¶ 9906, *recons. denied*, 73-2 BCA ¶ 10,120. Similarly, in *Plessey Indus., Inc.*, ASBCA 16720, 74-1 BCA ¶ 10,603, the contractor was not required to submit a vendor quotation when the contractor had decided prior to price negotiation to manufacture the item in-house. See also *Boeing Co.*, ASBCA 20875, 85-3 BCA ¶ 18,351, where the board held that the price of an undisclosed purchase order signed after data submission but before negotiation of the price was so close to the price of a submitted quotation from another vendor that the undisclosed data did not have a significant effect on price.

If the parties have agreed that the pricing should be based on data other than the cost or pricing data accumulated by the contractor, the requirement for submission of the data will not be enforced. See *Texas Instruments, Inc.*, ASBCA 30836, 89-1 BCA ¶ 21,489, where all of the current vendor data — purchase order prices, quotations, and subcontractor negotiations — were found not to constitute cost or pricing data because the parties had agreed that material costs would be computed using average prices of each item based on accumulated costs after the material had been used in the manufacturing process. The board found that since this pricing system made no use of the normal vendor data, the data could have no significant effect on the pricing.

The projections from the factual data are much more difficult to evaluate. If vendor quotations for the instant procurement are being used, the projection is relatively simple. There the key issue is whether the quotation was obtained under conditions that assure that it reflects a reasonable price. Normal price analysis techniques can be used to make this judgment. In most material pricing, however, the offeror is not required to obtain vendor quotes. In such cases, the data will consist of past purchase prices and the analysis will have to consider the length of time between purchases, the number of items purchased, the economic trends, and other relevant data in order to arrive at an appraisal of the reasonableness of the projection of the estimated price. See Chapter 5 of the Armed Services Pricing Manual (1986) (ASPM) for detailed guidance on the techniques that should be used in making this analysis.

(2) MAJOR SUBCONTRACTS

There is one special situation where offerors are required to submit detailed cost or pricing data relating to material purchases. FAR 15.404-3(c) requires contractors to submit subcontractor cost or pricing data for each subcontract cost estimate that is (1) $10 million or more or (2) both more than the cost or pricing data threshold ($500,000 at the current time) and more than 10 percent of the total price. Failure to submit such data will constitute a violation of the statutory submission requirement, *Martin Marietta Corp.*, ASBCA 43223, 96-2 BCA ¶ 28,270. In addition, the contracting officer is authorized by these regulations to require the submission of subcontractor data for subcontracts of lesser amounts if it is "necessary for adequately pricing the prime contract." When such data is submitted, it becomes the offeror's data with consequent liability for price reduction if it is inaccurate, incomplete, or not current, *Lockheed Aircraft Corp. v. United States*, 193 Ct. Cl. 86, 432 F.2d 801 (1970); *EDO Corp.*, ASBCA 41448, 93-3 BCA ¶ 26,135. The offeror is also required to submit an analysis of the subcontractor's cost or pricing data in these circumstances, FAR 15.806-1(a).

Subcontractor cost or pricing data above the thresholds need not be submitted if the subcontract falls within one of the statutory exceptions to the submission of data, FAR 15.404-3(c). The regulation contains no guidance on whether the contractor or the contracting officer is empowered to decide whether an exception applies. Prior to the issuance of FAC 97-02, September 30, 1997, FAR 15.806-2(c) appeared to state that the contracting officer had to make this determination.

When a subcontractor is a competitor of the contractor, contracting officers have permitted the subcontractor to submit required cost or pricing data directly to the Government. In such cases, a Government administrative contracting officer or auditor will analyze the data and provide the analysis to the contractor. See *Motorola, Inc.*, ASBCA 41528, 94-2 BCA ¶ 26,596, where the board found that a subcontractor had properly submitted data to a Government auditor because the auditor gave the contractor up-to-date information on an indirect cost rate that was applicable to the subcontract.

(3) NEW ITEMS

When work that has not previously been performed is purchased, cost estimating and analysis are much less precise. The specific material that will be used on the contract may not have been fully ascertained, yet the contractor will be forced to make the best possible estimate of material costs. In this situation, the most relevant data may be prices for similar work, and this information may be determined to be factual data which must be submitted to the Government. See *Hardie-Tynes Mfg. Co.*, ASBCA 20717, 76-2 BCA ¶ 12,121, where the board found that the price of items similar to those that were to be designed for the contract were cost or pricing data. The board also held that a vendor quote for an item that the offeror was considering using on the contract had to be submitted as part of the proposal. The contractor had made its own estimate on a very broad basis without regard to prior data, but the board held, nonetheless, that the data, if available, had to be furnished to the Government so that it could be used in the cost analysis. See also *Aerojet-General Corp.*, ASBCA 12264, 69-1 BCA ¶ 7664, *modified*, 70-1 BCA ¶ 8140, where the board held that a contractor's analysis of a subcontractor proposal was cost or pricing data.

b. Direct Labor Costs

This category covers all of the types of labor — manufacturing, engineering, tooling, etc. — that will be directly charged to the contract. The contractor is free to group labor in any categories that assist in managing the company, as long as the costs are accumulated for the same categories that are used for estimating purposes. The instructions to Table 15-2 calls for a "time-phased breakdown" of labor hours and labor rates, reflecting the fact that the process of estimating and analyzing labor costs normally considers hours and rates separately.

(1) Labor-Hours

Labor-hours present the greatest difficulty in the analysis of costs. In cases where the contractor has performed the same or similar work in the past, the number of labor-hours incurred will be factual data which must be presented in the proposal or disclosed during the negotiations. See *McDonnell Douglas Corp.*, ASBCA 12786, 69-2 BCA ¶ 7897 (tapes containing labor-hours incurred in months prior to price negotiation); *Singer Co. v. United States*, 217 Ct. Cl. 225, 576 F.2d 905 (1978) (labor-hour data adjusting standard labor-hour information to actual costs incurred in prior period); *Grumman Aerospace Corp.*, ASBCA 35188, 90-2 BCA ¶ 22,842 (reports of labor-hour lot costs containing data collected prior to conclusion of negotiations); and *Limpiezas Corona S.A.*, ASBCA 45504, 96-1 BCA ¶ 28,137 (number of employees on current janitorial services contract).

When the contractor must analyze the data in order to use it for estimating purposes, it is entitled to the time necessary to make the analysis, *Litton Sys., Inc.,* ASBCA 34435, 93-2 BCA ¶ 25,707. Even if the offeror does not record labor-hours, derivative data providing approximate labor-hours must be disclosed, *Lambert Eng'g Co.*, ASBCA 13338, 69-1 BCA ¶ 7663. In *Lambert*, the board held that an offeror must disclose labor-hour information derived by dividing the recorded labor dollars by average labor rates to arrive at the approximate labor hours used by the offeror on past work. Internal company work authorizations permitting departments to incur a specified number of labor-hours of work need not be disclosed to the Government because they are not factual in content, *Kaiser Aerospace & Elecs. Corp.*, ASBCA 32098, 90-1 BCA ¶ 22,489, *recons. denied*, 90-2 BCA ¶ 22,695. Similarly, pure estimates made by industrial engineers or test engineers need not be disclosed because they contain no factual element, *Litton Sys., Inc.*, ASBCA 36509, 92-2 BCA ¶ 24,842.

If an offeror uses an estimating system that factors actual labor-hours through pricing formulas, it may be necessary to disclose the entire system to the Government. See *Texas Instruments, Inc.*, ASBCA 23678, 87-3 BCA ¶ 20,195, where the board found that such a system was cost or pricing data because disclosure was necessary for the Government to fully understand the labor-hour data contained in the estimating system. However, there is no requirement to disclose a learning curve analysis of labor-hours because this technique is so well understood that any competent price analyst can plot the curve using the raw data, *Rosemount, Inc.*, ASBCA 37520, 95-2 BCA ¶ 27,770. Further, there is no requirement to present the labor-hour data in the form of a learning curve when the contractor does not use learning curve analysis, *Aerojet Ordnance Tenn.*, ASBCA 36089, 95-2 BCA ¶ 27,922.

If the contractor has begun work on the contract before the price is negotiated, incurred labor-hours would be factual data that would be expected to be disclosed, *Aerojet Ordnance Tenn.*, ASBCA 36089, 95-2 BCA ¶ 27,922; *University of Calif., San Francisco*, VABCA 4661, 97-1 BCA ¶ 28,642. Nondisclosure might not create contractor liability, however, if the data are so incomplete that they are not helpful in arriving at a meaningful estimate of the price. See *Boeing Co.*, ASBCA 20875, 85-3 BCA ¶ 18,351, holding that labor-hours incurred early in the performance of a developmental contract would not have been useful to the negotiators even if such data had been disclosed.

The projections made from labor-hours from prior contracts present far more difficult problems. In some cases, the offeror will use an accepted technique for projecting labor-hours, such as a learning curve analysis, and the Government will in turn analyze this projection technique using its own calculations. In other cases, an offeror will base the projection on an estimate of the variance that can be expected from standard costs. In all cases, volume and continuity of work will be major factors affecting the projection. See Chapters 5.2 and 5.3 of ASPM for a discussion of the various techniques that can be used to analyze labor-hour estimates. The most difficult situation occurs when the offeror has no previous experience in performing the work to be purchased. In such cases, the estimate of labor-hours must be made by breaking down the projected work into its constituent parts and estimating the labor-hours necessary to perform each part of the work. In most cases, each part of the work can be compared to similar work that the contractor has performed in the past, and this data can be used to support the estimate. Nevertheless, this process requires the application of a large amount of judgment, and analysis of this judgmental process is quite difficult. In such cases, parametric estimating techniques may be useful in checking the estimate.

(2) LABOR RATES

Labor rate determination is considerably easier. Even if the offeror has never performed the specific work being contracted for, there will be factual information regarding the labor rates that have been paid to the various categories of employees to be used on the contract. This information must be included as part of the offeror's cost or pricing data and must be updated as new data are accumulated, *Boeing Co.*, ASBCA 32753, 90-1 BCA ¶ 22,270, *recons. denied*, 90-1 BCA ¶ 22,426; *Kaiser Aerospace & Elecs. Corp.*, ASBCA 32098, 90-1 BCA ¶ 22,489, *recons. denied*, 90-2 BCA ¶ 22,695. Management decisions affecting labor rates must also be disclosed, *Lockheed Corp.*, ASBCA 36420, 95-2 BCA ¶ 27,722. There the board ruled that a management decision to utilize a new bargaining strategy in collective bargaining negotiations would have been cost or pricing data if it had been made by a corporate officer with authority to adopt the policy.

Based on the historical data on labor rates and any decisions as to future plans affecting the workforce, the cost analyst can make a projection of the rates that will be paid during contract performance. This projection involves determining the rate of increase or decrease in the wages or salaries and the length of time between the date of the actual data and the time of contract performance. The estimate usually will be based on the midpoint of projected contract performance, which can be determined by analyzing the rate of usage of labor over the contract performance period. The changes in labor rate are dependent on economic conditions over the long run and may be easily determinable by reviewing the terms of the offeror's labor agreements. The other factor that must be assessed is the number of workers the contractor expects to employ during the contract performance period. If the number is increasing, average labor rates will normally decrease, while a reduction in the number of employees will normally increase the rate. See Chapter 7 of ASPM for a discussion of techniques for analyzing labor rate projections.

c. Other Direct Costs

Contractors charge a variety of costs directly to contracts to obtain more accurate cost allocation. Such costs are frequently sporadic in nature varying greatly from one contract to another. They are therefore difficult to analyze based on past incurred costs. It is clear, however, that offerors must submit past data on such costs. The contracting officer will usually have to assess each type of direct cost in terms of its relationship to the work on the contract to determine if the offeror is estimating a level of cost that is reasonable under the circumstances. See Chapter 5.5 of the ASPM for a discussion of this area.

d. Indirect Costs

Contractors maintain pools of indirect costs in a variety of categories depending on the nature of their work and the size of the organization. Common groupings of indirect costs are manufacturing overhead, engineering overhead, and general and administrative (G&A) expense. However, any logical grouping is proper, FAR 31.203. A typical indirect cost pool for manufacturing overhead is set forth in **Figure 9-2**. Indirect costs are accumulated over a period of time, usually the contractor's fiscal year, and are uniformly charged as a percentage of an allocation base to all of the contractor's work during that period. See Cost Accounting Standard 406, 48 C.F.R. § 99.406, for guidance on the selection of these accounting periods. Cost Accounting Standards 410, 48 C.F.R. § 99.410, and 418, 48 C.F.R. § 99.418, provide guidance on the selection of allocation bases and allocation methods. Normally, allocation bases for manufacturing and engineering overhead are direct labor dollars in these categories, while the

EXHIBIT 1 — MANUFACTURING OVERHEAD

ACCOUNT TITLE	YEAR ENDED DEC 31, X3	YEAR ENDED DEC 31, X4*	PROJECTED YEAR ENDING DEC 31, x5
Salaries and wages:			
Indirect labor	$1,338,330	$1,395,245	$1,472,160
Additional compensation	80,302	83,950	88,000
Overtime premium	13,214	11,296	4,500
Sick leave	63,575	67,742	72,130
Holidays	79,164	83,006	87,080
Suggestion awards	310	423	500
Vacations	140,272	147,891	154,3000
Personnel expense:			
Compensation insurance	25,545	26,304	27,500
Unemployment insurance	50,135	52,692	51,500
FICA tax	70,493	73,907	77,850
Group insurance	153,755	161,401	169,130
Travel expense	11,393	12,725	13,900
Dues and subscriptions	175	175	175
Recruiting and relocation — new employees	897	574	250
Relocation — transferees	4,290	3,562	1,825
Employees pension fund:			
Salary	25,174	26,350	27,500
Hourly	62,321	65,497	64,200
Training, conferences, and technical meetings	418	539	575
Educational loans and scholarships	400	400	400
Supplies and services:			
General operating	495,059	509,839	545,000
Maintenance	9,102	12,318	15,700
Stationery, printing, and office supplies	23,052	24,125	25,500
Material O/H on supplies	56,566	62,071	62,500
Maintenance	9,063	10,875	15,000
Rearranging	418	3,523	500
Other	3,314	2,635	2,500
Heat, light, and power	470,946	489,123	517,200
Telephone	32,382	33,874	35,000
Fixed charges:			
Depreciation	187,118	175,641	439,850
Equipment rental	7,633	7,633	7,633
Total manufacturing expense (A)	$3,416,816	$3,545,336	$3,979,858
Total manufacturing direct labor dollars (B)	$1,340,887	$1,407,931	$1,267,200
Manufacturing overhead rate (A) + (B)	254.8%	251.8%	314.1%

* Includes budgetary estimate for last two months.

Figure 9-2

allocation base for G&A expense is total costs before G&A. However, the contractor has significant discretion to select an accounting system that most accurately allocates indirect costs to work being performed, *Ford Aerospace & Communications Corp.*, ASBCA 23833, 83-2 BCA ¶ 16,813.

Analysis of indirect costs involves analysis of the individual costs in the overhead pool and the allocation base. Except in the case of new businesses, there will always be a substantial amount of factual data on the costs in each indirect cost pool. The offeror's accounting system will contain such data for past years, and if the estimate is for work commencing during the year, there will be some data for that current year. See *Rose, Beaton & Rose*, PSBCA 459, 80-1 BCA ¶ 14,242, where incorrect inclusion of an item of cost in the indirect cost pool was held to be a violation of the obligation to disclose accurate cost or pricing data, and *Norris Indus., Inc.*, ASBCA 15442, 74-1 BCA ¶ 10,482, where failure to submit past indirect costs was a violation of the obligation to submit complete cost or pricing data. See also *PAE Int'l*, ASBCA 20595, 76-2 BCA ¶ 12,044, where inclusion of other direct costs in a G&A pool was held to be a violation of the requirement to disclose accurate data. Contractors normally collect indirect cost data on a monthly or quarterly basis, and FAR 15.406-2(c) encourages agreement on closing or cutoff dates for submission of cost or pricing data that match these periodic cost collection dates. All of this actual cost data serves as the base for evaluation of the offeror's projection of the costs in the indirect cost pool for the years of contract performance. Each cost element of the pool should be analyzed to assure that the projection is reasonable in view of the current and projected business situation of the offeror. See Section 9-700 of DCAA (1997) for further discussion of this evaluation process.

Analysis of the indirect cost allocation bases is considerably more difficult. These bases are estimated by forecasting the sales that the offeror will make in the accounting periods during which the contract work will be performed. Such forecasting is inherently imprecise although some of the sales will be factual, i.e., in accordance with signed contracts. See *Universal Restoration, Inc. v. United States*, 798 F.2d 1400 (Fed. Cir. 1986), where newly recorded sales were held to be cost or pricing data required to be disclosed during negotiations. Current negotiation of contracts with other customers might also be thought to be factual information which must be furnished by the offeror. See *E-Systems, Inc.*, ASBCA 17557, 74-2 BCA ¶ 10,782, *recons. denied*, 74-2 BCA ¶ 10,943, for a case dealing with this type of information and holding that an offeror's study of this type of data was not cost or pricing data because the underlying factual information had been furnished to the Government. In addition to the factual data on sales during the contract performance period, an estimate must be made of other sales that will be booked. Analysis of this estimate is very difficult, but information can often be obtained from other procuring activities on future contracts that will likely be awarded to the offeror.

3. *Certification*

When cost or pricing data is required to be furnished by statute, the offeror is required to certify that the data is accurate, current, and complete. The certificate is furnished after completion of negotiations, *not at the time of submission of the data.* FAR 15.406-2(a) contains the following certificate to be used in such cases:

CERTIFICATE OF CURRENT COST OR PRICING DATA

This is to certify that, to the best of my knowledge and belief, the cost or pricing data (as defined in section 15.401 of the Federal Acquisition Regulation (FAR) and required under FAR subsection 15.403-4) submitted, either actually or by specific identification in writing, to the Contracting Officer or to the Contracting Officer's representative in support of ____________* are accurate, complete, and current as of ____________**. This certification includes the cost or pricing data supporting any advance agreements and forward pricing rate agreements between the offeror and the Government that are part of the proposal.

Firm ________________________________

Signature ____________________________

Name ________________________________

Title ________________________________

Date of Execution*** __________________

*Identify the proposal, request for price adjustment, or other submission involved, giving the appropriate identifying number (e.g., RFP No.).

**Insert the day, month, and year when price negotiations were concluded and price agreement was reached or, if applicable, an earlier date agreed upon between the parties that is as close as practicable to the date of agreement on price.

***Insert the day, month, and year of signing, which should be as close as practicable to the date when the price negotiations were concluded and the contract price was agreed to.

This certificate is to be furnished as soon as practicable after price agreement is reached. In order to avoid major updating of data after the conclusion of negotiations (with resulting delay in furnishing the certificate), FAR 15.406-2(c) encourages reaching agreement on cutoff dates for specific categories of data.

In some cases, cost or pricing data may be called for by an RFP, but it may be subsequently determined that there is an exception to the submission requirement, such as adequate price competition or a commercial item. In such cases, cost or pricing data may have already been submitted by the offeror and reviewed by the Government. Under these circumstances, the question arises as to whether the data must be certified by the successful offeror. FAR 15.403-4(c) states that such data "shall not be considered cost or pricing data . . . and shall not be certified." This regulatory policy follows *ABA Electromechanical Sys., Inc.*, NASABCA 1081-13, 85-3 BCA ¶ 18,225, where data were submitted and audited but not certified because the contracting officer determined that adequate price competition was present, and *Intermountain Research*, Comp. Gen. Dec. B-209827, 83-2 CPD ¶ 103, where neither cost analysis nor a certificate was necessary since adequate price competition was present even though cost and pricing data were required to be submitted by the RFP.

B. Cost Analysis Without Cost or Pricing Data

A significant amount of cost analysis can be performed on proposals submitted in negotiated procurements without obtaining full cost or pricing data. The FAR now recognizes that "information other than cost or pricing data" may be requested. FAR 15.403-3(a)(1) permits obtaining no more data "than is necessary for determining the reasonableness of the price or evaluating cost realism." The contracting officer can specify the type of information needed for the analysis by including in the RFP the Requirements for Cost or Pricing Data or Information Other Than Cost or Pricing Data clause, FAR 52.215-20, with Alternate IV. No further guidance is provided on how the data should be used.

The most common form of cost data of this nature will be *cost element breakdowns* for the work that is required by the contract. These breakdowns show the types of cost (material, labor, indirect costs, etc.) that the offeror anticipates will be required to perform the work. They are not cost or pricing data but are merely summary estimates that have been made by the offeror. However, they provide sufficient information to allow the contracting officer to perform a cost analysis — obtaining additional information (such as prior labor or indirect cost rates) from Government auditors or from internal files documenting prior negotiations with the offeror. See *Research Management Corp.*, 69 Comp. Gen. 368 (B-237865), 90-1 CPD ¶ 352, for a case where this technique was used.

When contracting officers include a requirement for cost element breakdowns in the RFP, they should specify in the "work breakdown structure" the level that should be supported by such cost breakdowns. A work breakdown structure separates the contract work into its separate parts in a logical manner in order to ensure that all necessary tasks are considered in planning the job. See Military Standard (MIL-STD) 881B, Mar. 25, 1993, containing the following definition:

> 3.4 Work Breakdown Structure. A work breakdown structure (WBS) is a product-oriented family tree composed of hardware, software, services, data and facilities which results from systems engineering efforts during the acquisition of a defense materiel item. A work breakdown structure displays and defines the product(s) to be developed and/or produced and relates the elements of work to be accomplished to each other and to the end product(s). The work breakdown structures prescribed by this standard have been organized within the seven categories of defense materiel items and consist of the upper three levels of the work breakdown structure.

MIL-STD 881B calls for work breakdown structures to be organized into three levels as follows:

> Level 1: Level 1 is the entire defense materiel item; for example, the Minuteman ICBM System or the LHA Ship System. Level 1 is usually directly identified in the DoD programming/budget system either as an integral program element or as a project or subprogram within an aggregated program element.
>
> Level 2: Level 2 elements are major elements of the defense material item and are subordinate to Level 1; for example, a ship, an air vehicle, a tracked vehicle, and aggregations of services (such as system test and evaluation, and systems engineering/program management) and data.

> Level 3: Level 3 elements are elements subordinate to Level 2 major elements; for example, an electric plant, an airframe, the power package/drive train, or type of service (such as development test and evaluation, contractor technical support, training services), or type of data (such as technical publications). Lower levels follow the same process.

It can be seen that Level 1 corresponds, in general, to an entire contract, while Level 2 is normally used to identify the specific line items in a contract. Contractual documents do not normally contain any breakdowns that correspond to Level 3 in the DOD cost breakdown structure.

Cost breakdowns can be obtained for any level in the cost breakdown structure — with the understanding that the lower the level the more detailed the information that will be available to the contracting officer to use for evaluation purposes. In general, the size of the procurement will indicate which level is appropriate. Level 1 — providing only a single cost element breakdown for the entire contract — will generally be sufficient for contracts with one major task. Level 2 — providing cost element breakdowns for each contract line item — will be sufficient for many contracts. Level 3 or lower — providing cost element breakdowns for parts of the work — will be called for in contracts for major systems or complex services.

1. Cost Realism Analysis

Cost realism analysis is required on cost-reimbursement contracts to determine *the probable cost of performance* that will be used as the evaluation factor, FAR 15.404-1(d)(2); *KPMG Peat Marwick, LLP*, Comp. Gen. Dec. B-259479.2, 95-2 CPD ¶ 13. However, such analysis is also a valuable tool on both cost-reimbursement and fixed-price contracts to evaluate the offeror's understanding of the work required to carry out the contract tasks. See the following definition in FAR 15.404-1(d):

> (1) Cost realism analysis is the process of independently reviewing and evaluating specific elements of each offeror's proposed cost estimate to determine whether the estimated proposed cost elements are realistic for the work to be performed; reflect a clear understanding of the requirements; and are consistent with the unique methods of performance and materials described in the offeror's technical proposal.

Cost realism analysis is accomplished by determining the amount of resources (labor-hours and material) that the offeror proposes to use to accomplish each contract task and by ascertaining whether this amount of resources is a realistic estimate of those that will actually be required. A low estimate of resources could indicate a lack of understanding of the complexity of the work, but it might also indicate that the offeror has devised a more efficient way to perform. A low estimate of resources on a fixed-price contract could also raise questions as to whether the contractor will have the ability to complete the contract at the offered price. In an extreme case, this might lead to a determination of nonresponsibility. A high estimate of resources could also indicate a lack of understanding of the work and, on a fixed-price contract, could indicate that the price is not fair and reasonable.

The best regulatory guidance on cost realism analysis is contained in NFS 1815.608(a)(1), ¶ 302, as follows:

> (C) When contracting on a basis other than firm fixed price, the contracting officer shall perform price and cost realism analyses to assess the reasonableness and realism of the proposed costs. A cost realism analysis will determine if the costs in an offeror's proposal are realistic for the work to be performed, reflect a clear understanding of the requirements, and are consistent with the various elements of the offeror's technical proposal. The analysis should include:
>
> > (a) The probable cost to the Government of each proposal, including any recommended additions or reductions in materials, equipment, labor hours, direct rates and indirect rates. The probable cost should reflect the best estimate of the cost of any contract which might result from the offeror's proposal.
> >
> > (b) The differences in business methods, operating procedures, and practices as they impact cost.
> >
> > (c) A level of confidence in the probable cost assessment for each proposal.
>
> (D) The cost realism analysis may result in adjustments to Mission Suitability scores in accordance with the procedure described in 18-15.608(a)(3)(B).

The contracting officer must specify the data necessary to perform a cost realism analysis, FAR 15.403-3(a)(1). See, however, FAR 15.403-5(b)(2) stating that such information "may be submitted in the offeror's own format unless the contracting officer decides that use of a specific format is essential." The key information that is needed is estimated labor hours and material costs for designated elements of the work. Generally, each contractor should be permitted to identify the labor categories to be used and the specific material to be acquired. Labor rate and indirect cost rate information is also needed but may be readily available from the cognizant Government auditor when the offeror is subject to regular audit. It is also possible that such information will be available in the contracting agency. All available information should be used in this type of analysis.

Cost realism analysis has been most widely used in the selection of cost-reimbursement contractors, where it has been regularly challenged by losing offerors. In these protests, the Comptroller General, the General Services Board of Contract Appeals, and the courts, in determining whether the agency has followed a rational process in arriving at the probable cost of performance, have reviewed the analytical processes used by contracting officers.

Agencies are accorded substantial discretion in making a cost realism analysis but they must meet the test of *rationality*. See *Science Applications Int'l Corp.*, Comp. Gen. Dec. B-238136.2, 90-1 CPD ¶ 517, where the Comptroller General stated:

> [A]n agency is not required to conduct an in-depth cost analysis or to verify each and every item in conducting its cost realism analysis. Rather, the evaluation of competing cost proposals requires the exercise of informed judgment by the contracting agency involved, since it is in the best position to assess "realism" of cost and technical approaches and must bear the difficulties of additional expenses resulting from a defective cost analysis. *Burns & Roe Indus. Servs. Co.*, B-233561, Mar. 7, 1989, 89-1 CPD ¶ 250. Since the cost realism analysis is a judgmental function on the part of the contracting agency, our review is limited to a determination of whether an agency's cost evaluation was reasonably based. *OptiMetrics, Inc.; NU-TEK Precision Optical Corp.*, [68 Comp. Gen. 714], B-235646; B-235646.2, Sept. 22, 1989, 89-2 CPD ¶ 266.

See *Halifax Technical Servs., Inc. v. United States*, 848 F. Supp. 240 (D.D.C. 1994), and *Program Resources, Inc.*, GSBCA 8879-P, 87-2 BCA ¶ 19,816, following the same standard. Thus, a cost realism analysis need not identify every adjustment that might be made to an offeror's cost of performance. However, the adjustments that are made must be supported by sufficient data to permit analysis of the validity of the adjustments, *Day & Zimmermann Servs. v. United States*, 38 Fed. Cl. 591 (1997). In *Raytheon*

Support Servs. Co., 68 Comp. Gen. 566 (B-234920), 89-2 CPD ¶ 84, the Comptroller General found that the agency's cost realism analysis was satisfactory even though it did not make some possible adjustments. In a footnote, the Comptroller General stated:

> We find no merit to Raytheon's argument that the Navy should have made downward adjustments to its cost proposal for Raytheon's "inadvertent" failure to take into consideration any "productivity" or "learning curve" reductions in its cost proposal. The burden is on the offeror to submit a cost proposal that takes into consideration all aspects of its technical approach and the agency has no duty to prepare or revise an offeror's proposal.

See also *PAE GmbH Planning & Constr.*, 68 Comp. Gen. 358 (B-233823), 89-1 CPD ¶ 336, where the Comptroller General denied a protest that the contracting officer should have seen a mistake in the offeror's cost proposal in the process of making the cost realism analysis. The Comptroller General concluded that the mistake was neither readily apparent in the data included in the protester's proposal nor made any clearer by comparison with other proposals.

In order to be rational, the cost realism analysis has to be performed on a contractor-by-contractor basis. The contracting officer must consider both the work the contractor proposes to do and the contractor's cost structure in order to determine whether the proposed costs are an accurate projection of the costs of that work. Thus, a mechanical approach that applies the same factors to all offerors is likely to fail the test of rationality. In *Jonathan Corp.*, Comp. Gen. Dec. B-251698.3, 93-2 CPD ¶ 174, the protesters argued that the Navy's cost realism analysis was arbitrary and irrational because it mechanically adjusted the offerors' proposed labor-hour and material cost estimates based on an undisclosed Government estimate. The Comptroller General summarized the Navy approach as follows:

> The computer was programmed to accept an offeror's labor hour and material costs for a work item if the number was within plus or minus [deleted] percent of the government's estimate for that item.
>
> For those work items where an offeror's proposed labor hour and material cost estimates were outside the [deleted] percent range, the source selection plan proposed a two-pronged approach. The first approach provided that if an "offeror's estimate is not adequately supported with data and rationale," the estimate would be rejected and the government's labor hour or material cost estimate would be used instead to calculate the projected cost to the

government. The second approach provided that if an "offeror's estimate is well supported with an equal probability of [g]overnment or [o]fferor being correct," the following predetermined mathematical formula would be used to determine an adjusted labor hour or material cost estimate:

> "One half of the difference between the [g]overnment estimate and the offeror's proposed cost [will be] added to (or subtracted from) the offeror's estimate after first reducing or increasing the [g]overnment estimate by [deleted] % in the direction of the difference (reduce the difference) in order to establish projected cost and adjustment dollars."

In other words, the computer program approximately "split the difference" between the government's labor hour or material cost estimate and the offeror's proposed labor hours and material cost for each of the 100 work items in the notional package.

The Comptroller General sustained the protest, finding that the agency failed to consider each offeror's individualized approach and instead mechanically adjusted costs. The Comptroller General stated that the agency's cost evaluation "did not satisfy the requirement for an independent analysis of each offeror's cost proposal based upon its particular approach, personnel, and other circumstances." The Court of Claims reached the same conclusion in *Day & Zimmermann*.

If an offeror places a contractually binding "cap" on an element of cost, that amount can be determined by a cost realism analysis to be the probable cost of performance, *BNF Technologies, Inc.*, Comp. Gen. Dec. B-254953.3, 94-1 CPD ¶ 274 (contracting officer improperly adjusted capped overhead and G&A costs above the amount of the cap); *Unisys Corp. v. National Aeronautics & Space Admin.*, GSBCA 13247-P, 95-2 BCA ¶ 27,818 (contracting officer properly used cap on phase-out costs but was entitled to adjust cap on overhead based on information in proposal); *Halifax Technical Servs., Inc. v. United States*, 848 F. Supp. 240 (D.D.C. 1994) (contracting officer properly used capped labor costs in making cost realism analysis). However, if the contracting officer concludes that a realistic estimate of the rates to be incurred is below the cap, that estimate can be used in lieu of the cap, *Delta Research Assocs., Inc.*, Comp. Gen. Dec. B-254006.2, 94-1 CPD ¶ 47. When the capped costs are used as the probable costs, the contracting officer must still consider whether the amount imposes a constraint on the offeror significant enough to hamper its ability to perform the work under contract.

The cost realism analysis is normally done by analyzing each major cost element: material, direct labor, indirect costs, and other direct costs.

a. Material

Most of the cost realism analysis of material costs appears to occur in reviewing the proposed subcontracts in competing offers. See, for example, *Electronic Data Sys. Fed. Corp.*, Comp. Gen. Dec. B-207311, 83-1 CPD ¶ 264, where the offeror's proposed subcontract costs were found to be too low because they did not reflect the need for a subcontractor during the entire life of the contract. Subcontractors' labor and indirect cost rates should also be checked for cost realism when the subcontracts will be performed on a cost-reimbursement basis, *General Marine Indus. of N.Y., Inc.*, Comp. Gen. Dec. B-240059, 90-2 CPD ¶ 311; *OptiMetrics, Inc.*, 68 Comp. Gen. 714 (B-235646), 89-2 CPD ¶ 266. See also *Dayton T. Brown, Inc.*, Comp. Gen. Dec. B-229664, 88-1 CPD 321, where material costs were determined to be realistic even though they appeared low; the reasoning was that the material costs would not impact the ultimate cost to the Government because they were included in indirect costs of performance.

b. Direct Labor

Cost realism analysis of direct labor costs is performed by reviewing the labor-hours proposed by the offeror, as well as the labor rates that will be applied to the various categories of direct labor to be used.

Perhaps the major area where discrepancies are found in proposals is the estimated number of labor hours required for performance. One cost realism analysis technique that is commonly used is to compare the labor-hours in the cost proposal with the labor hours in the technical proposal. If they vary, it is logical to conclude that the cost proposal is incorrect and to rely on the hours in the technical proposal, *TechDyn Sys. Corp.*, Comp. Gen. Dec. B-237618, 90-1 CPD ¶ 264; *Complere, Inc.*, Comp. Gen. Dec. B-227832, 87-2 CPD ¶ 254. See, however, *DLM&A, Inc. v. United States*, 6 Cl. Ct. 329 (1984), where this type of discrepancy in the two proposals was resolved during the analysis.

The cases have sustained other reasons for determining that labor-hour estimates are incorrect. See, for example, *TRW Inc.*, Comp. Gen. Dec. B-234558.2, 89-2 CPD ¶ 560 (use of new personnel would require more labor-hours than estimated); and *Range Technical Servs.*, 68 Comp. Gen. 81 (B-231968), 88-2 CPD ¶ 474 (past staffing levels indicated that the labor-hours were underestimated). See also *Aircraft Porous Media, Inc.*, Comp. Gen. Dec. B-241665.2, 91-1 CPD ¶ 356, where it was held proper to conclude that the estimate of labor-hours was too low when the offeror had reduced the labor-hours in its best and final offer (BAFO) because of savings that could be achieved through simultaneous performance of similar work on another contract. The Comptroller General found that the contracting officer had the discretion to question the offeror's ability to achieve such savings. In *Fairchild Weston Sys., Inc.*, Comp. Gen. Dec. B-229568.2, 88-1 CPD ¶ 394, the agency was permitted to make major changes in the labor-hours proposed by both offerors based on the technical expertise of agency personnel. See, however, *Aurora Assocs., Inc.*, Comp. Gen. Dec. B-215565, 85-1 CPD ¶ 470, where the Comptroller General found improper an assumption that all offerors' direct costs would be the same, despite the agency's claim that this assumption was necessary: the contracts were indefinite-quantity contracts for the design and evaluation of agricultural projects, and the agency did not know what tasks each contractor would be asked to perform and for what period of time.

A number of cases support an agency's failure to question low estimates of labor-hours because it has determined that the offeror's approach to the work will likely require fewer hours than have been used in the past, *Consolidated Safety Servs., Inc.*, Comp. Gen. Dec. B-252305.2, 93-2 CPD ¶ 225; *Research Analysis & Maintenance, Inc.*, Comp. Gen. Dec. B-239223, 90-2 CPD ¶ 129; *SRS Technologies*, Comp. Gen. Dec. B-238403, 90-1 CPD ¶ 484; *OptiMetrics, Inc.*, 68 Comp. Gen. 714 (B-235646.2), 89-2 CPD ¶ 266. See also *Unisys Corp. v. National Aeronautics & Space Admin.*, GSBCA 13247-P, 95-2 BCA ¶ 27,818, where the board agreed that the agency had made a valid analysis of the staffing levels required for support services even though they were lower than the incumbent contractor's staffing levels. Compare *PRC Kentron, Inc.*, Comp. Gen. Dec. B-230212, 88-1 CPD ¶ 537, where the Comptroller General did not object to a solicitation provision calling for automatic adjustment of labor-hours that did not conform to the agency's prescribed staffing levels.

Labor rates can also be questioned when the rates included in a proposal are not realistic. For example, in *Computer Sciences Corp.*, Comp. Gen. Dec. B-210800, 84-1 CPD ¶ 422, the agency properly concluded that the offeror's proposed labor rates were too low because they were below the rates being paid by an incumbent service contractor. The agency assumed that the winning contractor would hire most of the incumbent employees at their current salaries. In *A. T. Kearney, Inc.*, Comp. Gen. Dec. B-237731, 90-1 CPD ¶ 305, rates were properly analyzed as being low because they were under the current average rates being paid on a similar contract, while in *Associates in Rural Dev., Inc.*, Comp. Gen. Dec. B-238402, 90-1 CPD ¶ 495, both salaries and fringe benefits were properly found to be low by comparing them to earlier costs. In *ManTech Envtl. Technology, Inc.*, Comp. Gen. Dec. B-271002, 96-1 CPD ¶ 272, a protest was granted when the agency failed to adjust very low labor rates and it was doubtful the offeror would be able to hire qualified personnel at those rates. In *Radian, Inc.*, Comp. Gen. Dec. B-256313.2, 94-1 CPD ¶ 299, it was proper to make an upward adjustment in labor rates based on a "rate check" furnished by the cognizant DCAA auditors. See also *Sabre Sys., Inc.*, Comp. Gen. Dec. B-255311, 94-1 CPD ¶ 129, and *NKF Eng'g, Inc.*, Comp. Gen. Dec. B-232143, 88-2 CPD ¶ 497, where labor rates after the first year of performance were found to be low because they did not reflect normal escalation, and *Bendix Field Eng'g Corp.*, Comp. Gen. Dec. B-230076, 88-1 CPD ¶ 437, where rates were found low because they were under the rates prescribed by the Service Contract Act. Compare *Ares Corp.*, Comp. Gen. Dec. B-275321, 97-1 CPD ¶ 82, where an adjustment of only 1 percent for future years was found to be reasonable based on analysis of the specific company. In *Unified Indus. Inc.*, Comp. Gen. Dec. B-237868, 90-1 CPD ¶ 346, it was held improper not to question proposed wages that were less than the required wage rates under the Service Contract Act.

It is improper to question labor rates based on past experience without making a detailed analysis of the offeror's specific approach to performance and the personnel expected to be hired, *United Int'l Eng'g, Inc.*, 71 Comp. Gen. 177 (B-245448.3) (1992). In that case, the contracting officer had mechanically questioned the labor rates without making such an analysis. See *Bendix Field Eng'g Corp.*, Comp. Gen. Dec. B-246236, 92-1 CPD ¶ 227, where the Comptroller General also ruled that a labor rate adjustment was improper when the agency's application of a projected inflation factor resulted in labor rates in excess of those called for by the collective bargaining agreement that the offeror had with its union. The Comptroller General also rejected adjustments to management salaries because they were made "mechanically" without considering the specifics of the offeror's situation.

When labor rates are questioned, the contracting officer must be certain that the adjustments are based on the offeror's accounting practices. For example, an adjustment of rates to reflect a 40-hour workweek was overturned in *General Research Corp.*, Comp. Gen. Dec. B-241569, 91-1 CPD ¶ 183, because the offeror had an established accounting practice (disclosed in its Cost Accounting Standards Disclosure Statement) that charged for labor based on the full hours worked by each employee. The Comptroller General stated that the contracting officer should not have relied on the incorrect advice of the Defense Contract Audit Agency (DCAA) auditor, who stated that the Disclosure Statement did not deal with this issue, but should have been familiar with the offeror's accounting practices. Compare *PAI, Inc.*, 67 Comp. Gen. 516 (B-230610), 88-2 CPD ¶ 36, where the Comptroller General sustained a protest that the contracting officer had not adjusted labor rates to comply with a solicitation provision prohibiting use of rates based on uncompensated overtime. The Comptroller General did not address the issue of whether such rates were in accordance with the offeror's accounting practices. Similarly, in *Hardman (J.V.),* Comp. Gen. Dec. B-224551, 87-1 CPD ¶ 162, the Comptroller General agreed with an adjustment to remove the effect of uncompensated overtime, pursuant to a solicitation provision, without addressing the accounting practices of the offeror.

In *Compuware Corp.*, GSBCA 9533-P, 88-3 BCA ¶ 21,109, the board rejected an upward adjustment of labor rates that conflicted with the findings of the auditor reviewing the proposals. The auditor had determined that the contractor reasonably concluded that an imminent turnover in employees would lower its labor costs because the new workers would be paid less than those with seniority. The board found that the contracting officer had no evidence that the audit finding was incorrect.

c. *Indirect Costs*

Contracting officers also frequently question proposed costs in the indirect cost area. In *Polaris, Inc.*, Comp. Gen. Dec. B-220066, 85-2 CPD ¶ 669, the Comptroller General held that an agency was correct in concluding that the offeror's proposed overhead rates were too low. The offeror had projected a gradual reduction in overhead rates over a five-year period, but the agency had rejected this possibility based on the recommendations of the DCAA. Similarly, in *Signal Corp.*, Comp. Gen. Dec. B-241849, 91-1 CPD ¶ 218, and *Purvis Sys., Inc.*, Comp. Gen. Dec. B-245761, 92-1 CPD ¶ 132, the contracting officer properly used prior-year indirect cost rates when the offeror had included substantially lower rates in the proposal based on its theory that additional work would reduce its rates; the offeror had failed to submit sufficient evidence to support this theory. See also *Mandex, Inc.*, Comp. Gen. Dec. B-241841, 91-1 CPD ¶ 253, *recons. denied*, 91-2 CPD ¶ 83, where an offeror's G&A rate was found to be low because it was based on an accounting system change that had not been fully approved by the administrative contracting officer at the time of award (the change had been approved by the DCAA subject to correction of deficiencies in the accounting system). Compare *Aurora Assocs., Inc.*, Comp. Gen. Dec. B-215565, 85-1 CPD ¶ 470, where a conclusion that the rate was too low was found to be improper because the agency used only the highest indirect cost multiplier when three different multipliers, corresponding to different categories of employees, were applicable to the proposed costs.

In making the cost realism analysis of indirect costs, the contracting officer may rely entirely on the computations of the cognizant auditor, *SRS Technologies*, Comp. Gen. Dec. B-238403, 90-1 CPD ¶ 484. Conversely, an auditor's recommendations may be disregarded entirely if the contracting officer believes that the information is invalid, *Electronic Warfare Integration Network*, Comp. Gen. Dec. B-235814, 89-2 CPD ¶ 356.

FAR 15.407-3(b) requires contracting officers to use forward pricing rates as the basis for pricing "all contracts" during the period an agreement on such rates is in effect, unless the ACO determines that a "changed condition invalidates the agreement." It is proper to use such labor and indirect cost rates in performing a cost realism analysis, *Hoboken Shipyards, Inc.*, Comp. Gen. Dec. B-219428, 85-2 CPD ¶ 416, *recons. denied*, 85-2 CPD ¶ 582. In *Jonathan Corp.*, Comp. Gen. Dec. B-230971, 88-2 CPD ¶ 133, the contracting officer used such rates in concluding that the estimated costs were too low even though the offeror attempted to demonstrate that the forward pricing rates were invalid due to changed conditions. The Comptroller General agreed with the contracting officer's conclusion, finding that the offeror had not clearly demonstrated that the rates were invalid.

d. Other Direct Costs

Cost realism analysis has also been used to question other direct costs proposed by offerors. For example, in *Amtec Corp.*, Comp. Gen. Dec. B-240647, 90-2 CPD ¶ 482, the contracting officer properly found the estimate of travel costs too low because the discount fares proposed by an offeror would probably not be obtainable during performance. See, however, *Science Applications Int'l Corp.*, Comp. Gen. Dec. B-238136.2, 90-1

CPD ¶ 517, where it was found proper to accept a low rate for other direct costs when the agency, after discussions, agreed with the offeror's rationale for the low rate.

e. Use of Analysis

As discussed above, the most common use of cost realism analysis is to determine the probable cost of performance of a cost-reimbursement contract in order to use that cost in the evaluation of the proposals and the selection of the source. It is also proper to use such analysis to reduce the probable cost of performance in a cost-reimbursement contract by negotiating a cap on G&A expenses where the cost realism analysis indicates that this element of the costs is far below expected costs, *Vitro Corp.*, Comp. Gen. Dec. B-247734.3, 92-2 CPD ¶ 202.

The cost realism analysis can also be used as a negotiating tool. If the analysis indicates that the proposed price of a fixed-price contract or the estimated cost of a cost-reimbursement contract is low, the offeror can be alerted to the problem in the written or oral discussion. This provides a better understanding of the basis for the price or estimated cost and may identify problems such as mistakes or lack of understanding of the requirements of the RFP. It may also lead to a revised price or estimated cost in the offeror's BAFO.

When a cost realism analysis indicates that the probable costs of performance are significantly higher that the offeror's estimate, the agency can also downgrade the technical evaluation. The low cost estimate might demonstrate a lack of understanding of the work, *Chesapeake & Potomac Tel. Co.*, GSBCA 9297-P, 90-1 BCA ¶ 22,335. It could also signal significant risks in terms of future performance, *Cubic Field Servs., Inc.*, Comp. Gen. Dec. B-247780, 92-1 CPD ¶ 525 (proposed cap on costs of performance of cost-reimbursement contract created risk of nonperformance); *Modern Technologies Corp.*, Comp. Gen. Dec. B-236961.4, 90-1 CPD ¶ 301 (extended workweek created substantial risk offeror would be unable to hire and retain stable workforce); *Culver Health Corp.*, Comp. Gen. Dec. B-242902, 91-1 CPD ¶ 556 (low rates of compensation of proposed employees created risk of poor performance). Compare *Harris Corp. v. United States*, 628 F. Supp. 813 (D.D.C. 1986), where the court held that it was improper to downgrade a proposal merely because the offeror had made a decision to absorb some costs of performance. See also *VSE Corp.*, Comp. Gen. Dec. B-247610.2, 92-2 CPD ¶ 81, where the Comptroller General held that the contracting officer had acted properly in not downgrading an offeror's technical and management proposal; the proposed labor rates were lower than the Government's estimate, but analysis indicated that they did not detract from the offeror's ability to perform the work.

2. Determining Price Reasonableness

Cost analysis using cost element breakdowns and other data on the offeror's prospective costs of performance can also be used to determine if the price of a fixed-price contract is fair and reasonable. The analysis in these circumstances is substantially the same as that made for cost realism. Here, however, the focus is on whether the price is too high. See *TAAS Israel Indus., Ltd.*, Comp. Gen. Dec. B-260733, 95-2 CPD ¶ 23, agreeing that a valid price reasonableness determination was made when the contracting officer used detailed cost element breakdowns from two competitors to perform the analysis. A similar result was reached in *Family Realty*, Comp. Gen. Dec. B-247772, 92-2 CPD ¶ 6. Cost data can also be used to make a performance risk assessment. See *General Elec. Co.*, 55 Comp. Gen. 1450 (B-186372), 76-2 CPD ¶ 269, where the source selection official concluded that there was performance risk because the contractor had not submitted detailed cost data supporting the reduced price in its BAFO, and *Systems Processes Eng'g Corp.*, Comp. Gen. Dec. B-234142, 89-1 CPD ¶ 441, where cost data indicated a low price and, thus, a risk of inability to perform.

The contracting officer enjoys considerable discretion in deciding how much cost data to obtain and how to make use of such cost data in these circumstances. See, for example, *Allied-Signal Aerospace Co.*, Comp. Gen. Dec. B-249214.4, 93-1 CPD ¶ 109, where the Comptroller General held that an agency was not required to make a comparative analysis of each element of each offeror's detailed cost estimates. The Comptroller General stated that instructing the offerors to submit cost estimates at the work breakdown level did not obligate the agency to analyze that information "in any greater detail than was necessary to assure the realism of the cost proposals." See also *Communications Int'l, Inc.*, Comp. Gen. Dec. B-246076, 92-1 CPD ¶ 194, where the sum of work element cost estimates, rather than the total cost estimate, was properly used in the evaluation and the contracting officer was not required to reopen discussions to reconcile disparity between the two.

C. Should-Cost Analysis

A selective form of cost analysis used primarily on major procurements is should-cost analysis. This process is described in FAR 15.407-4(a), as follows:

> (1) Should-cost reviews are a specialized form of cost analysis. Should-cost reviews differ from traditional evaluation methods because they do not assume that a contractor's historical costs reflect efficient and economical operation. Instead, these reviews evaluate the economy and efficiency of the contractor's existing workforce, methods, materials, facilities, operating systems, and management. These reviews are accomplished by a multi-functional team of Government contracting, contract administration, pricing, audit, and engineering representatives. The objective of should-cost reviews is to promote both short and long-range improvements in the contractor's economy and efficiency in order to reduce the cost of performance of Government contracts. In addition, by providing rationale for any recommendations and quantifying their impact on cost, the Government will be better able to develop realistic objectives for negotiation.

See also DFARS 215.810(b), requiring a should-cost review on systems acquisitions exceeding $100 million. Should-cost analysis has been used most often on major contracts for the manufacture of high-priced equipment. It requires a detailed industrial engineering analysis of the specific methods used by the contractor to manufacture the product and a determination of more cost-effective methods that will reduce the costs. In this regard, it is significantly different than conventional cost analysis because it challenges not the offeror's projections of current costs but, rather, the necessity for incurring those costs. Congress has expressed considerable interest in increasing the use of should-cost analysis. See Section 915 of the Defense Procurement Improvement Act of 1985, P.L. 99-145, requiring a report to Congress on the amount of should-cost analysis performed on sole source manufacturing contracts for weapon systems.

D. Methods for Expediting Analysis

In the case of contractors performing numerous Government contracts, proposals are being submitted and analyzed on a regular basis. Since many of the elements of cost, such as labor and indirect cost rates, are the same regardless of the contract for which the costs are incurred, repetitive analysis is unnecessary. Cost analysis can also be greatly expedited if the parties are in agreement on the basic estimating system used by the contractor. The regulations give guidance on these techniques for expediting cost analysis.

1. Forward Pricing Rate Agreements

FAR 15.407-3 recognizes that major contractors frequently enter into forward pricing rate agreements with elements of the Department of Defense. These agreements are negotiated by administrative contracting officers and may cover indirect cost rates or labor rates. FAR 15.407-3(b) requires contracting officers to use the rates in these agreements "as the bases for pricing all contracts, modifications, and other contractual actions" and to report conditions that would affect the agreement's validity to the administrative contracting officer.

Because the labor and indirect cost rates covered by these agreements are subject to fluctuation at any time based on the costs being incurred by the contractor, these agreements must be closely monitored to assure that they contain valid rates. However, if the administrative contracting officer and the cognizant auditor regularly monitor them and renegotiate the rates quickly when new data call for such modification, these agreements can greatly reduce the effort needed to complete a cost analysis and negotiate a price. If the agreement covers all labor and indirect cost elements of the contractor's estimating system, only direct labor hours and material will require analysis on an individual basis. This can greatly expedite the procurement process.

2. Estimating System Reports

FAR 15.407-5 provides that "cognizant audit activities" will establish regular programs for reviewing estimating systems used by contractors. The purpose of such a review is to identify deficiencies in contractor's estimating systems so that they can be addressed and corrected. Ultimately, this process is intended to lead to complete agreement on an estimating system with resultant reduction in the audit necessary on any proposal. Each estimating system review is to be documented by a report from the audit activity.

FAR 15.407-5(b) calls for the following procedure:

> The auditor shall send a copy of the estimating system survey report and a copy of the official notice of corrective action required to each contracting office and contract administration office having substantial business with

> that contractor. Significant deficiencies not corrected by the contractor shall be a consideration in subsequent proposal analyses and negotiations.

DFARS 215.811-70(b)(2)(i) requires all large business contractors with DOD prime contracts or subcontracts of $50 million or more for which cost or pricing data are required to meet detailed estimating system requirements. The details of this program are contained in the Cost Estimating System Requirements clause in DFARS 252.215-7002. The intent of this requirement is to ensure that such contractors have estimating systems that produce accurate, documented estimates of the cost of future work. See DCAM 9-1100 for additional guidance in this area.

V. NEGOTIATION OF PROFIT

In negotiated procurements where cost is negotiated separately, the parties must also negotiate the profit that will be included in the price. In cost-reimbursement contracts, this profit will be stated separately in the contract as a fixed fee, an award fee (including a base fee), or an incentive target fee and will be subject to statutory or regulatory limitations on the amount that may be negotiated. In fixed-price contracts, this profit will either be included in the price or stated as a target fee in incentive contracts, and in neither case will the profit be subject to prescribed limitations. In all cases where the profit is to be negotiated, the contracting officer is subject to specific regulatory guidance on the techniques that are to be used to determine the proper level of profit acceptable to the Government.

A. Fee Limitations

There are similar statutory limitations on the rates of fee that can be negotiated in cost-plus-fixed-fee contracts in both the Armed Services Procurement Act, 10 U.S.C. § 2306(d), and the Federal Property and Administrative Services Act, 41 U.S.C. § 254(b). The latter states:

> [I]n the case of a cost-plus-a-fixed-fee contract the fee shall not exceed 10 percent of the estimated cost of the contract, exclusive of the fee, as determined by the agency head at the time of entering into such contract (except that a fee not in excess of 15 percent of such estimated cost is authorized in any such contract for experimental, developmental, or research work and that a fee inclusive of the contractor's costs and not in excess of 6 percent of the estimated cost, exclusive of fees, as determined by the agency head at the time of entering into the contract, of the project to

> which such fee is applicable is authorized in contracts for architectural or engineering services relating to any public works or utility project).

These statutes have several features. First, the provision uses "fee" to mean both *profits* of contractors on cost-plus-fixed-fee contracts and *total charges* of architects and engineers for their services on all types of contracts. This is confusing, but the 6 percent limitation has no direct relationship to the negotiation of fees on cost-reimbursement contracts. Second, the statute applies to the rate of fee *negotiated*, not the rate of fee actually *earned* by the contractor through performance of the contract. In this regard, the rate is limited in terms of a percentage of the estimated cost of the contract as determined by the parties at the outset, *CACI, Inc. — Federal*, Comp. Gen. Dec. B-216516, 85-1 CPD ¶ 363. The Comptroller General has ruled that when a settlement of an aborted cost-reimbursement contract is negotiated, the statute must be applied to limit the total fee paid in settlement, but the agency is not required to impose the percentage limitation on each part of the work performed, *National Visitors Ctr.*, Comp. Gen. Dec. B-158792, 80-1 CPD ¶ 121. Third, the statute applies by its precise terms to only cost-plus-fixed-fee contracts and not to other types of cost-reimbursement contracts. Thus, the provisions do not apply to cost-plus-incentive-fee contracts. This rule is set forth in DOD/NASA Incentive Contracting Guide, October 1959. For many years, the FAR imposed 10 percent and 15 percent limitations on the maximum fees computed as a percentage of estimated or target cost of cost-plus-award-fee and cost-plus-incentive-fee contracts but these limitations were deleted by FAC 97-02, September 30, 1997.

In one case, the Court of Claims applied this statute in an unusual way in holding that the Government was not bound by a contract containing a fee arrangement that violated the statute. In *Yosemite Park & Curry Co. v. United States*, 217 Ct. Cl. 360, 582 F.2d 552 (1978), the parties had entered into a transportation contract that compensated the contractor for the cost of providing bus service plus a fee at the rate of 12½ percent of the contractor's gross investment in equipment to perform the contract. The court held that the contract was a cost-plus-fixed-fee contract that was invalid because the fee resulted in an amount greater than 10 percent of the estimated costs of performance of the contract. Thus, a fee not based directly on costs of performance but yielding a rate higher than permitted by the statute may be found to be in violation of the statute. In *Yosemite Park*, the court further held that the contractor was entitled to be paid for the value of the services rendered to the Government not exceeding "the entire, total, provable costs" of performance plus 10 percent of these costs. It is interesting to note that this judgment permitted a larger payment than is permitted by the fee limitation statute.

B. Profit Negotiation Techniques

The techniques used to establish profit have varied among the procuring agencies. In the 1950s and 1960s, contracting officers were given complete discretion to negotiate profits with contractors; the regulations merely contained a list of the factors that should be considered in such negotiation. In 1964, the DOD adopted the "weighted guidelines" approach to profit negotiation, requiring their contracting officers to follow a prescribed formula in analyzing the profit to be negotiated and arriving at a prenegotiation position. The weighted guidelines formula was revised extensively in the 1970s to give greater recognition to facilities employed by contractors in the performance of contracts. During this period, the civilian agencies continued to give their contracting officers greater latitude. In December 1980, OFPP issued Policy Letter 80-7, 45 Fed. Reg. 82,593 (1980), requiring that all agencies making noncompetitive awards over $100,000 adopt a "structured approach" to profit negotiation when these awards total $50 million or more each year. This policy letter was subsequently canceled, but the policy is now included in FAR Subpart 15.404-4. These policies require all agencies with significant procurement functions to follow an approach similar to the DOD's weighted guidelines but permit each agency to tailor its formula to the particular programs of the agency. The DOD subsequently conducted another profit study, the Defense Financial and Investment Review (DFAIR), June 1985, and adopted a new weighted guidelines formula in August 1987. This newer formula departs from the FAR guidance in significant ways but has never been challenged.

1. Goal of Structured Approach

The original weighted guidelines approach was based on a detailed study of the negotiation of profit in the DOD. The study found that the rates of profit and fee negotiated were almost the same regardless of the complexity of the work, the past performance of the contractor, or variations in other elements that might be considered relevant to the amount of profit included in the contract. It was concluded that a new procedure was needed to force contracting officers to use a profit negotiation process that recognized these different aspects of procurements. A major goal was to use profit to encourage good performance and penalize bad performance. FAR 15.404-4(a) now contains the following general guidance:

> (1) Profit or fee prenegotiation objectives do not necessarily represent net income to contractors. Rather, they represent that element of the potential total remuneration that contractors may receive for contract performance over and above allowable costs. This potential remuneration element and the Government's estimate of allowable costs to be incurred in contract performance together equal the Government's total prenegotiation objective. Just as actual costs may vary from estimated costs, the contractor's actual realized profit or fee may vary from negotiated profit or fee, because of such factors as efficiency of performance, incurrence of costs the Government does not recognize as allowable, and the contract type.
>
> (2) It is in the Government's interest to offer contractors opportunities for financial rewards sufficient to stimulate efficient contract performance, attract the best capabilities of qualified large and small business concerns to Government contracts, and maintain a viable industrial base.
>
> (3) Both the Government and contractors should be concerned with profit as a motivator of efficient and effective contract performance. Negotiations aimed merely at reducing prices by reducing profit, without proper recognition of the function of profit, are not in the Government's interest. Negotiation of extremely low profits, use of historical averages, or automatic application of predetermined percentages to total estimated costs do not provide proper motivation for optimum contract performance.

Since each structured approach imposes a formula on contracting officers, their discretion is significantly limited. The goal is to make profit determination considerably more objective than it has been in the past. However, there is no indication in any of the regulations that the objective is binding on either the contractor or the Government. The fee to be used in the contract is subject to free bargaining and is ultimately determined in the negotiation process, where the contracting officer has a substantial amount of discretion. Some regulations require that contracting officers document their profit analysis in the price negotiation memorandum (PNM). See, for example, DFARS 215.903(b)(5) and DEAR 915.970-3.

Agencies also retain considerable flexibility under the FAR policy. Thus, they may accommodate different policy objectives by varying the elements of their formula and the weights given to each element.

2. Applicability of Structured Approach

The structured approach to profit determination is generally applicable to all procurements where cost analysis is required, FAR 15.404-4(b)(1)(i). Contracts are not subject to these regulations where the price is justified by price analysis or where competition controls the price. See DFARS 215.903(a), which states that the weighted guidelines method shall not be used when cost analysis is being used to assess cost realism on competitive acquisitions. From the outset, it has been recognized that a structured approach is not applicable to all types of procurements, and FAR 15.404-4(b)(1)(ii) permits agencies to make exceptions to their policies. DFARS 215.903(b)(3) states that the contracting officer may use an alternate structured approach (see 215.973) when

> (i) The contract action is —
>
> (A) Under $500,000;
>
> (B) For architect-engineer or construction work;
>
> (C) Primarily for delivery of material from subcontractors; or
>
> (D) A termination settlement; or
>
> (ii) The weighted guidelines method does not produce a reasonable overall profit objective and the head of the contracting activity approves use of the alternate approach in writing.

This regulation requires the use of an alternate structured approach in these types of procurements and in unusual situations where the weighted guidelines method "may not produce a reasonable overall profit objective." Such exceptions must be justified in writing and be authorized by the head of the contracting activity.

A similar list of exceptions is included in NFS 1815.902, DEAR 915.970-4, GSAR 515.902(b), and TAR 1215.902(a).

3. Procedure

The structured approach to profit determination is a procedure used by the contracting officer to arrive at a "prenegotiation objective" on the profit that will be used in negotiations with the contractor, FAR 15.404-4(a). The regulations require the contracting officer to calculate this objective but contain very little guidance on the procedures to be used to obtain the information necessary to make this calculation. See GSAR 515.902(a), which states:

> The contracting officer's analysis of these profit factors is based on information available to the Government before negotiations. Such information is furnished in proposals, audit data, performance reports, preaward surveys and the like.

DFARS 215.903(e) permits contractors to furnish specific information in proposals:

> [T]he contracting officer may encourage the contractor to —
>
> (1) Present the details of its proposed profit amounts in the weighted guidelines format or similar structured approach; and
>
> (2) Use the weighted guidelines format in developing profit objectives for negotiated subcontracts.

See FAR 15.404-4(c)(5), which prohibits contracting officers from *requiring* contractors to submit such information.

In all of the structured profit approaches, the profit objective is determined by separately analyzing each factor in the formula and computing the dollars of profit for that factor. The contracting officer then totals the dollars of profit for each factor to arrive at the profit objective. This computation is performed using standard forms provided by each agency that uses a structured approach. The following forms are currently in use:

Agency	Form
Department of Defense	DD Form 15474-4
National Aeronautics & Space Administration	NASA Form 634
General Services Administration	GSA Form 1766
Department of Energy	DEAR Form F 4220.234-7
Department of Transportation	DOT Form 4220.324-8

Most of the computations in the structured approaches that have been used in the past are based on the costs of performance of the work. FAR 15.404-4(c)(3) provides that the contracting officer will use the Government prenegotiation cost objective amounts as the basis for calculating the profit objective. The result is that the contracting officer's profit objective is based on the Government's analysis of the costs of performance rather than the contractor's proposed costs. If the costs are changed significantly during negotiation, an adjustment in the negotiated profit is appropriate.

4. Profit Factors

While the FAR contains no prescribed formula, it does require all agencies to include, at a minimum, six factors in their structured approach:

(1) contractor effort;

(2) contract cost risk;

(3) federal socioeconomic programs;

(4) capital investments;

(5) cost control and other past accomplishments; and

(6) independent development.

While almost all of these factors are included in the existing formulas, as set forth in the agency forms in **Figures 9-3** through **9-7**, they are not all broken out under these classifications. For ease of discussion, however, the following detailed analysis of the application of the profit formulas is divided into these categories.

In general, civilian agencies of the Government have implemented the requirement for a structured profit approach by following the DOD techniques that were in effect in the early 1980s. In many cases, the only detailed guidance on the application of these techniques was in the ASPM, which was revised in 1986. The new DOD profit policy, adopted in 1987, dropped a number of these techniques and substituted new techniques. The current DOD profit policy is set forth in DFARS 215.971. The following

Defense Federal Acquisition Regulation Supplement

Part 253--Forms

RECORD OF WEIGHTED GUIDELINES APPLICATION

REPORT CONTROL SYMBOL DD-P&L(Q)1751

1. REPORT NO.	2. BASIC PROCUREMENT INSTRUMENT IDENTIFICATION NO. a. PURCHASING OFFICE	b. FY	c. TYPE PROC INST CODE	d. PRISN	3. SPIIN	4. DATE OF ACTION a. YEAR	b. MONTH

		ITEM	COST CATEGORY	OBJECTIVE
5. CONTRACTING OFFICE CODE				
6. NAME OF CONTRACTOR		13.	MATERIAL	
		14.	SUBCONTRACTS	
7. DUNS NUMBER	8. FEDERAL SUPPLY CODE	15.	DIRECT LABOR	
		16.	INDIRECT EXPENSES	
9. DOD CLAIMANT PROGRAM	10. CONTRACT TYPE CODE	17.	OTHER DIRECT CHARGES	
		18.	SUBTOTAL COSTS *(13 thru 17)*	
11. TYPE EFFORT	12. USE CODE	19.	GENERAL AND ADMINISTRATIVE	
		20.	TOTAL COSTS *(18 + 19)*	

WEIGHTED GUIDELINES PROFIT FACTORS

ITEM	CONTRACTOR RISK FACTORS	ASSIGNED WEIGHTING	ASSIGNED VALUE	BASE (ITEM 18)	PROFIT OBJECTIVE
21.	TECHNICAL	%			
22.	MANAGEMENT	%			
23.	COST CONTROL	%			
24.	PERFORMANCE RISK (COMPOSITE)				
25.	CONTRACT TYPE RISK				
		COSTS FINANCED	LENGTH FACTOR	INTEREST RATE	
26.	WORKING CAPITAL			%	
	CONTRACTOR FACILITIES CAPITAL EMPLOYED		ASSIGNED VALUE	AMOUNT EMPLOYED	
27.	LAND				
28.	BUILDINGS				
29.	EQUIPMENT				
30.	TOTAL PROFIT OBJECTIVE				

NEGOTIATION SUMMARY

		PROPOSED	OBJECTIVE	NEGOTIATED
31.	TOTAL COSTS			
32.	FACILITIES CAPITAL COST OF MONEY *(DD Form 1861)*			
33.	PROFIT			
34.	TOTAL PRICE *(Line 31 + 32 + 33)*			
35.	MARKUP RATE *(Line 32 + 33 divided by 31)*	%	%	%

CONTRACTING OFFICER APPROVAL

36. TYPED/PRINTED NAME OF CONTRACTING OFFICER *(Last, First, Middle Initial)*	37. SIGNATURE OF CONTRACTING OFFICER	38. TELEPHONE NO.	39. DATE SUBMITTED *(YYMMDD)*

OPTIONAL USE

96.	97.	98.	99.

DD Form 1547, AUG 87 *Previous editions are obsolete.* 184/298

Figure 9-3

NASA
National Aeronautics and Space Administration

Structured Approach Profit/Fee Objective

CONTRACTOR	RFP/CONTRACT NO.
BUSINESS UNIT	CONTRACT TYPE
ADDRESS	

1. CONTRACTOR EFFORT

COST CATEGORY	GOVERNMENT'S COST OBJECTIVE (a)	WEIGHT RANGE (b)	ASSIGNED WEIGHT (c)	WEIGHTED PROFIT/FEE ((a) × (c)) (d)
MATERIAL ACQUISITION				
		1% TO 4%		
DIRECT LABOR				
		4% TO 12%		
OVERHEAD				
		3% TO 8%		
OTHER COSTS				
		1% TO 3%		
GENERAL MANAGEMENT (G & A)		4% TO 8%		
1. A TOTAL				

2. OTHER FACTORS

FACTOR	MEASUREMENT BASE (a)	WEIGHT RANGE (b)	ASSIGNED WEIGHT (c)	WEIGHTED PROFIT/FEE 1.A (a) × (c) (d)
COST RISK	TOTAL COST OBJECTIVE 1.A (a)	0% TO 7%		
INVESTMENT		−2% TO +2%		
PERFORMANCE		−1% TO +1%		
SUBCONTRACT PROGRAM MANAGEMENT		−1% TO +1%		
SOCIO-ECONOMIC PROGRAMS		−.5% TO +.5%		
SPECIAL SITUATIONS				
2.A TOTAL OTHER FACTORS				

3.	SUBTOTAL PROFIT/FEE LINES (1.A) + (2.A)	
4.	*LESS FACILITIES CAPITAL COST OF MONEY*	−
5.	TOTAL PROFIT/FEE OBJECTIVE LINE (3) − (4)	

NASA FORM 634 SEP 91 PREVIOUS EDITION IS OBSOLETE.

Figure 9-4

STRUCTURED APPROACH PROFIT/FEE OBJECTIVE

CONTRACTOR	RFP/CONTRACT NO.
BUSINESS UNIT	CONTRACT TYPE
ADDRESS	

CONTRACTOR EFFORT

1. COST CATEGORY	GOVERNMENT'S COST OBJECTIVE (a)	WEIGHT RANGE (b)	ASSIGNED WEIGHT (c)	WEIGHTED PROFIT/FEE ((a) x (c)) (d)
MATERIAL ACQUISITION		1% TO 4%		
DIRECT LABOR		4% TO 12%		
OVERHEAD		3% TO 8%		
OTHER COSTS		1% TO 3%		
GENERAL MANAGEMENT (G & A)		4% TO 8%		
1A. TOTAL				

OTHER FACTORS

2. FACTOR	MEASUREMENT BASE (a)	WEIGHT RANGE (b)	ASSIGNED WEIGHT (c)	WEIGHTED PROFIT/FEE 1.A (a) x (c) (d)
COST RISK	TOTAL COST OBJECTIVE 1.A(a)	0 TO 7%		
INVESTMENT		-2% TO +2%		
PERFORMANCE		-2% TO +2%		
SOCIO-ECONOMIC PROGRAMS		-5% TO +5%		
SPECIAL SITUATIONS		-2% TO +2%		
2A. TOTAL OTHER FACTORS				
3. SUBTOTAL PROFIT/FEE LINES (1.A) + (2.A)				
4. LESS FACILITIES CAPITAL COST OF MONEY				-
5. TOTAL PROFIT/FEE OBJECTIVE LINE (3) - (4)				

GENERAL SERVICES ADMINISTRATION GSA FORM 1766 (11-82)

Figure 9-5

DOE F 4220.23
(7-83)
(Formerly PR-336)

U.S. DEPARTMENT OF ENERGY

WEIGHTED GUIDELINES PROFIT/FEE OBJECTIVE

1. CONTRACTOR IDENTIFICATION — a. Name; b. Division *(If any)*; c. Street address; d. City; e. State; f. Zip code

2. TYPE OF ACQUISITION ACTION *(REFER TO OFPP MANUAL, FEDERAL PROCUREMENT DATA SYSTEMS PRODUCT AND SERVICE CODES, APRIL 1980)*

a. ___ SUPPLIES & EQUIPMENT b. ___ RESEARCH & DEVELOPMENT

c. ___ SERVICES: (1) ___ ARCHITECT-ENGINEER: (2) ___ MANAGEMENT SERVICES: (3) ___ MEDICAL: (4) ___ OTHER *(e.g., SUPPORT SERVICES)*

3. ACQUISITION INFORMATION — a. Purchasing Offices; b. Contract type; c. RFP/RFQ No.; d. FY; e. Contract No.

PROFIT/FEE OBJECTIVE COMPUTATION

PROFIT/FEE CONSIDERATIONS a.	MEASUREMENT BASE b.	PROFIT/FEE WEIGHT RANGES % c.	ASSIGNED WEIGHT (%) d.	PROFIT/FEE DOLLARS *(Col. b. x d.)* e.
4. CONTRACTOR EFFORT:	(Acquisition Costs)			
a. MATERIAL ACQUISITIONS:				
(1) Purchased parts		1 to 3		
(2) Subcontracted items		1 to 4		
(3) Other materials		1 to 3		
b. LABOR SKILLS:	(Labor Costs)			
(1) Technical & managerial				
(a) Scientific		10 to 20		
(b) Project management/administration		8 to 20		
(c) Engineering		8 to 14		
(2) Manufacturing		4 to 8		
(3) Support services		8 to 14		
c. OVERHEAD:	(Overhead Costs)			
(1) Technical & managerial		5 to 8		
(2) Manufacturing		3 to 6		
(3) Support services		3 to 7		
d. OTHER DIRECT COSTS	(O.D. Costs)	3 to 8		
e. G&A EXPENSE	(G&A Exp.)	5 to 7		
f. TOTAL CONTRACTOR EFFORT BASE COSTS & PROFIT DOLLARS *(Total of Lines 4.a. thru 4.e.)*				
5. CONTRACTOR RISK	(Base Costs: Line 4.f., Col. b.)	0 to 8		
6. CAPITAL INVESTMENT (FACILITIES)	(NBV of Allocated Facilities Cost)	5 to 20		
7. INDEPENDENT RESEARCH & DEVELOPMENT:	(Allocated IR&D Costs)			
a. PROGRAM INVESTMENT		5 to 7		
b. USE OF ITEMS DEVELOPED	(Base Profit $: Line 4.f. Col. e.)	0 to 20		
8. SPECIAL PROGRAM PARTICIPATION	(Base Profit $: Line 4.f. Col. e.)	5 to +5		
9. OTHER CONSIDERATIONS	(Base Profit $: Line 4.f., Col. e.)	5 to + 5		
10. PRODUCTIVITY/PERFORMANCE ADJUSTMENT				
11. TOTAL PROFIT/FEE OBJECTIVE				

12. SUMMARY CONTRACT PRICE OBJECTIVE:

a. Contractor Effort Base Costs *(Line 4.f., Col. b.)* $________
b. IR&D Cost *(Line 7.a., Col. b.)* ________
c. Subtotal of Base Costs + IR&D Cost $________
d. Facilities Capital Cost of Money – CAS 414 *(Separately Computed)* ________
e. Total Prospective Cost $________
f. Total Profit/Fee Objective *(Line 11, Col. e.)* ________
g. Total Contract Price Objective $________

13. REMARKS

14. DATE | 15. PREPARED BY: | 16. SIGNATURE

Figure 9-6

WEIGHTED GUIDELINES PROFIT/FEE OBJECTIVE

1. CONTRACTOR IDENTIFICATION	a. COMPANY NAME		b. DIVISION NAME *(If any)*		
	c. STREET ADDRESS		d. CITY	e. STATE	f. ZIP CODE
2. WEIGHTED GUIDELINES CATEGORY *(Check one)* a. ☐ MANUFACTURING b. ☐ RESEARCH AND DEVELOPMENT c. ☐ SERVICES			3. TYPE OF CONTRACT		
4. BASIC PROCUREMENT INSTRUMENT IDENTIFICATION NO.				5. SPECIALIST NAME	
a. PURCHASING OFFICE	b. FY	c. C/S PROD/SVCS CODE	d. PR NO.		

6. WEIGHTED GUIDELINES PROFIT FACTORS

PROFIT/FEE FACTOR OR SUBFACTOR *(a)*	MEASUREMENT BASE *(b)*	PROFIT WEIGHT RANGES MFG (%) *(c)*	R&D (%) *(d)*	SVCS (%) *(e)*	ASSIGNED WEIGHT (%) *(f)*	PROFIT/FEE DOLLARS *(g)*
PART I – CONTRACTOR EFFORT						
7. MATERIAL ACQUISITION a. SUBCONTRACTED ITEMS		1 TO 5	1 TO 5	1 TO 5		
b. PURCHASED PARTS		1 TO 4	1 TO 4	1 TO 4		
c. OTHER MATERIAL		1 TO 4	1 TO 4	1 TO 4		
8. ENGINEERING a. DIRECT LABOR		9 TO 15	9 TO 15			
b. OVERHEAD		6 TO 9	6 TO 9			
9. MANUFACTURING a. DIRECT LABOR		5 TO 9	5 TO 9			
b. OVERHEAD		4 TO 7	4 TO 7			
10. SERVICES a. DIRECT LABOR				5 TO 15		
b. OVERHEAD				4 TO 8		
11. OTHER COSTS						
12. GENERAL MGMT – G & A		6 TO 8	6 TO 8	6 TO 8		
13. SUBTOTAL PROFIT/FEE						
14. TOTAL EFFORT						
PART II – CONTRACTOR RISK						
15. COST RISK	*(Total from Col. b)*	0 TO 8	0 TO 7	0 TO 4		
PART III – FACILITIES INVESTMENT						
16. CAPITAL EMPLOYED	*(Line 8, DD Form 1861)*	16 TO 20				
17. BASIC PROFIT/FEE OBJECTIVE *(Items 14 + 15 + 16, Col. g)*						
PART IV – SPECIAL FACTORS						
18. SPECIAL PROFIT/FEE OBJ a. PRODUCTIVITY						
b. INDEPENDENT DEVELOPMENT		1 TO 4	1 TO 4			
c. OTHER	*(Total from Item 17)*	-5 TO +5	-5 TO +5	-5 TO +5		
d. TOTAL SPECIAL PROFIT/FEE OBJECTIVE						
19. SUBTOTAL PROFIT/FEE OBJECTIVE *(Items 17 + 18, col. g)*						
PART V – COST OF MONEY OFFSET *(Applicable to Research and Development and Services Weighted Guidelines only.)*						
20. LESS: FACILITIES CAPITAL COST OF MONEY						
21. TOTAL PROFIT/FEE OBJECTIVE *(Items 19 – 20, col. g)*						

Form DOT F 4220.32 (2-82)

Figure 9-7

discussion uses the ASPM guidance, when it is applicable, without regard to which agency's policy is being considered.

a. Contractor Effort

The first major element in the profit computation measures the value of the work to be performed on the contract. Intrinsic to this valuation process is the concept that a contractor is entitled to a higher rate of profit on its own efforts than on the efforts of others. In addition, the formulas provide higher profits on managerial and technological effort than on other more routine types of work. FAR 15.404-4(d)(1) gives the following guidance:

> *Contractor effort.* This factor measures the complexity of the work and the resources required of the prospective contractor for contract performance. Greater profit opportunity should be provided under contracts requiring a high degree of professional and managerial skill and to prospective contractors whose skills, facilities, and technical assets can be expected to lead to efficient and economical contract performance. The subfactors in paragraphs (d)(1)(i)(A) through (D) of this subsection shall be considered in determining contractor effort, but they may be modified in specific situations to accommodate differences in the categories used by prospective contractors for listing costs:
>
> > (A) *Material acquisition.* This subfactor measures the managerial and technical effort needed to obtain the required purchased parts and material, subcontracted items, and special tooling. Considerations include the complexity of the items required, the number of purchase orders and subcontracts to be awarded and administered, whether established sources are available or new or second sources must be developed, and whether material will be obtained through routine purchase orders or through complex subcontracts requiring detailed specifications. Profit consideration should correspond to the managerial and technical effort involved.
> >
> > (B) *Conversion direct labor.* This subfactor measures the contribution of direct engineering, manufacturing, and other labor to converting the raw materials, data, and subcontracted items into the contract items. Considerations include the diversity of engineering, scientific, and manufacturing labor skills required and the amount and quality of supervision and coordination needed to perform the contract task.
> >
> > (C) *Conversion-related indirect costs.* This subfactor measures how much the indirect costs contribute to contract performance. The labor

> elements in the allocable indirect costs should be given the profit consideration they would receive if treated as direct labor. The other elements of indirect costs should be evaluated to determine whether they merit only limited profit consideration because of their routine nature, or are elements that contribute significantly to the proposed contract.
>
> (D) *General management.* This subfactor measures the prospective contractor's other indirect costs and general and administrative (G&A) expense, their composition, and how much they contribute to contract performance. Considerations include how labor in the overhead pools would be treated if it were direct labor, whether elements within the pools are routine expenses or instead are elements that contribute significantly to the proposed contract, and whether the elements require routine as opposed to unusual managerial effort and attention.

This FAR guidance reflects the logic in the original DOD weighted guidelines. However, in 1987, the DOD adopted an entirely different approach to calculating this element of the formula while the civilian agencies continued to use the old approach set forth in the weighted guidelines. The following discussion reviews the approaches separately and uses the prior DOD guidance when it provides the most helpful explanation of how the computation should be made.

(1) Civilian Agency Calculation

The weighted guidelines "value added" approach is implemented in the agencies' profit formulas by assigning varying weights to the elements of cost in the estimated cost. See the forms set forth in **Figures 9-3** through **9-7**. In these forms, purchased effort is given a weight of 1 percent to 5 percent, and direct labor is given a weight of 4 percent to 20 percent. All agencies give engineering or scientific labor a higher weight (9 percent to 20 percent) than manufacturing or support labor (4 percent to 9 percent), reflecting the higher value given technological effort. Indirect costs are assigned weights by analyzing the specific elements of cost in the contractor's indirect cost pools and applying a weight to each element of cost in accordance with the general value-added theory. Chapter 4 of the ASPM suggests at 4-7 that indirect cost pools not be analyzed for each procurement since the weight would not change until the composition of the pool changed significantly. While the ranges of weights to be used for each cost element are prescribed by the profit formula of the agency issuing the contract, the contracting officer is given considerable discretion in selecting the weight within the range. The ASPM gives the following guidance on assigning weights to material costs at 4-4:

> Weight ranges for material are lower than the ranges for other costs because material represents the lowest investment of resources per sales dollar. Analysis of direct material costs will show variations in the managerial and technical effort needed to obtain the material. A direct material cost of $1 million could represent a single subcontract with an established source for standard material, or it could include several subcontracts that require the contractor to find suppliers to develop difficult items to complex performance specifications. Obviously, the amount of managerial and technical effort is much greater in the second case than in the first.
>
> The contractor that obtains maximum competition in procuring direct materials exerts greater effort than the contractor that routinely places repeat orders with established vendors. Subcontracts for professional or consulting services should be assigned a weight commensurate with the management liaison involved.
>
> The normal low weight for direct materials is 2 percent. A lesser weighting should be used only in unusual circumstances where the contractor makes only a minimum contribution. You might use a weighting of less than 2 percent, for instance, if the material represents a large part of the total contract costs, is a follow-on order with an existing vendor, and is to be shipped directly from the vendor to the Government.

The ASPM guidance on labor costs is set forth at 4-5 as follows:

> There are two basic rules in assigning weights to the labor categories. First, all labor must be rated within minimum and maximum DFARS weights. For instance, all engineering labor must carry weights within the 9-to-15 percent range, and services labor must carry weights within ranges of 5-to- 15 percent for direct labor and 4 to 8 percent for overhead. Second, except for services, labor carries the same weight whether it is classified as direct or indirect.
>
> One way to arrive at an appropriate weight is to use the contractor's job designations to classify labor into the categories shown in [the following table:]

Engineering	Manufacturing	Administrative
Top scientist or engineer	Department head	Top management
Senior engineering or project manager	Supervisor	Executive assistants
Engineer	Engineer	Professional staff
Junior engineer	Skilled	Clerical
Draftsman	Semi-skilled	Support
Technical writer	Unskilled	
Clerical	Support	
Support		

> Next, [an agency] might assign weights to the classes of labor. The assigned weights remain the same whether the salary cost represented by the job designation is treated as a direct or an indirect cost. [The agency] would determine the approximate dollar amounts attributable to salaries of personnel with these job designations and would multiply the amounts by the assigned weights.
>
> Assignment by job designations is only one method of arriving at an appropriate weight assignment. Another is to find the total scale of labor rates within the labor pool of the contractor's organization, determine the average labor rate for the particular contract, and assign the weight that bears the same relationship to the DFARS range of weights that the average labor rate for the contract bears to the total scale of labor rates in the labor pool.
>
> For example, if the scale of labor rates within the contractor's engineering organization is from $5 to $20 per hour, and the average engineering labor in the particular contract is $12 per hour, [an agency] could determine that $12 falls within the scale of $5 to $20 as 11.8 percent falls within the 9-to-15 percent range. As a result, [an agency] might assign a weight of 11.8 percent to the direct engineering labor input.

The same technique is used for indirect costs, except that the contracting officer has the discretion to assign weights to individual items of cost outside the prescribed ranges as long as the final weight given to the total indirect cost pool falls within the range in the formula, ASPM at 4-6.

All costs of performance are included in the cost base for purposes of making this profit calculation, except that the facilities capital cost of money provided for in FAR 31.205-10(a) is specifically required to be excluded from this base, FAR 15.404-4(d).

(2) Department of Defense Calculation

In the DOD profit calculation, the contractor effort factor is now called the "performance risk" factor. See DFARS 215.971-2(a), which states:

> This profit factor addresses the contractor's risk in fulfilling the contract requirements. The factor consists of three parts —
>
> (1) Technical — the technical uncertainties of performance.
>
> (2) Management — the degree of management effort necessary to ensure that contract requirements are met.
>
> (3) Cost control — the contractor's efforts to reduce and control costs.

This calculation is accomplished by applying gross percentages (rather than percentages by cost element) to the estimated costs of performance excluding (1) general and administrative expense, (2) independent research and development and bid and proposal expense, and (3) facilities capital cost of money. The DFARS contains two ranges of percentages to be applied in this calculation:

Calculation	Normal Value	Designated Range
Standard calculation	4%	2% to 6%
Alternate calculation	6%	4% to 8%

The standard calculation is used in most types of procurements. The alternate calculation is provided for those research and development and service contracts where the contractor has made a relatively low capital investment in facilities. It provides the 2 percent higher profit *in lieu of* the facilities-capital-employed factor.

This profit calculation is made on three different criteria — technical, management, and cost control. The first step in the calculation is the determination by the contracting officer of the weight to be assigned to each of these criteria. These weights are determined on the basis of the importance of the criteria to the Government in the performance of the contract. For example, if the contract is for research and development work requiring the use of new technology on a cost-plus-fixed-fee contract, the following weights might be appropriate:

- Technical 50%
- Management 35%
- Cost Control 15%

In contrast, if the contract is for the manufacture of an item with a stable design on a fixed-price type contract, the contracting officer might assign weights as follows:

- Technical 20%
- Management 35%
- Cost Control 45%

The next step in the calculation is the assignment of values to each criterion. The DFARS contain considerable guidance on the logic of assigning these values. With regard to technical and management criteria, values are assigned on the basis of the difficulty of the task in the specific contract. Thus, if the contract requires the contractor to perform development work using advanced technologies, a value above normal would be assigned. In contrast, a contract calling for routine technical effort would be assigned a value below normal. Similarly, a contract requiring complex management effort would get an above-normal value while a contract requiring minimal management effort would get a below-normal value. The logic is somewhat different with regard to the cost control criterion, where value is assigned in accordance with the contracting officer's evaluation of the effectiveness of the contractor's efforts to control and reduce costs. This can be determined by analyzing the past performance of the contractor or the contractor's proposed efforts.

The final step in the calculation is to arrive at a composite percentage. This is done using the assigned weights and values. For example, in the research and development contract calling for use of new technology, the calculation would be as follows:

Criterion	Weight Assigned	Value Assigned	Weighted Value
Technical	50%	5.4%	2.7%
Management	35%	5.0%	1.75%
Cost Control	15%	4.0%	0.6%
Composite Value			5.05%

If it were determined that the contractor did not have significant facilities in the division performing the contract, the alternate calculation would be used. With the same type of contract, that calculation would be as follows:

Criterion	Weight Assigned	Value Assigned	Weighted Value
Technical	50%	7.4%	3.7%
Management	35%	7.0%	2.45%
Cost Control	15%	6.0%	0.9%
Composite Value			7.05%

b. Contract Cost Risk

The second major factor included in structured approaches to profit is the risk assumed by the contractor in the pricing arrangement. This factor *does not measure economic risk* assumed by the contractor in undertaking the contract, but merely the pricing risk as determined by the pricing arrangement. FAR 15.404-4(d)(1) contains the following discussion of this factor:

> (ii) *Contract cost risk.* (A) This factor measures the degree of cost responsibility and associated risk that the prospective contractor will assume as a result of the contract type contemplated and considering the reliability of the cost estimate in relation to the complexity and duration of the contract task. Determination of contract type should be closely related to the risks involved in timely, cost-effective, and efficient performance. This factor should compensate contractors proportionately for assuming greater cost risks.

Since the Government assumes almost all of the risk of cost overruns on cost-reimbursement contracts, this factor is insignificant on such contracts (and quite significant on fixed-price contracts). However, it varies somewhat between the profit policies of the different agencies. The normal values and the designated ranges used by the DOD are set forth in DFARS 215.971-3(c), as follows:

Contract type	Notes	Normal value (percent)	Designated range (percent)
Firm-fixed-price, no financing	(1)	5	4 to 6
Firm-fixed-price, with financing	(2)	3	2 to 4
Fixed-price-incentive, no financing	(1)	3	2 to 4
Fixed-price with redeterminable provision	(3)		
Fixed-price-incentive, with financing	(2)	1	0 to 2
Cost-plus-incentive-fee	(4)	1	0 to 2
Cost-plus-fixed-fee	(4)	.5	0 to 1
Time and material contracts (including overhaul contracts priced on time and material basis)	(5)	.5	0 to 1
Labor-hour contracts	(5)	.5	0 to 1
Firm fixed-price-level-of-effort-term	(5)	.5	0 to 1

(1) *No financing* means that the contract either does not provide progress payments, or provides them only on a limited basis, such as financing of first articles. Do not compute a working capital adjustment.

(2) *With financing* means progress payments. When progress payments are present, compute a working capital adjustment (Block 26).

(3) For the purposes of assigning profit values, treat a fixed-price contract with redeterminable provisions as if it were a fixed-price-incentive contract with below normal conditions.

(4) Cost-plus contracts shall not receive the working capital adjustment.

(5) These types of contracts are considered cost-plus-fixed-fee contracts for the purposes of assigning profit values. They shall not receive the working capital adjustment in Block 26. However, they may receive higher than normal values within the designated range to the extent that portions of cost are fixed.

When assigning a profit value for this factor, the contracting officer should consider elements that affect contract risk such as length of contract, adequacy of cost data for projections, economic environment, nature and extent of subcontracting activity, protection provided to the contractor under contract provisions (e.g., economic price adjustment clauses), the ceilings and share lines contained in incentive provisions, and risks associated with contracts for foreign military sales not funded by U.S. appropriations. See DFARS 215.971-3(d).

Civilian agencies use higher weightings for this factor, as follows:

CONTRACTOR COST RISK (%)				
	AGENCY			
Contract Type	NASA	GSA	DOE	DOT
Fixed-price	3 to 7	3 to 7		
Cost-reimbursement	0 to 3	0 to 3		
Cost-plus-fixed-fee	*	0 to 1		
Cost-plus-incentive-fee	**	0 to 3		

* CPFF normally would not justify a reward for risk in excess of 0 percent, unless the contract contains cost risk features such as ceiling on overheads, etc. In such cases, up to 0.5 percent may be justified

** CPIF contracts fill the remaining portion of the range with weightings directly related to such factors as confidence in target cost, share ratio of fees, etc.

The regulations of the civilian agencies place the major emphasis on the reliability of the contractor's cost estimate and on the difficulty of the contract task, DEAR 915.970-8(c)(4). However, they also provide for lower profit factors when risk has been transferred to subcontractors, DEAR 915.970-8(c)(6)(iii); GSAR 515.905-1(c)(3)(ii), and when the work has been started on a contract (for example, a letter contract) that does not contain firm cost estimates, NFS 1815.970-2(a)(3)(ii); DEAR 915.970-8(c)(6)(iv); GSAR 515.905-1(c)(3)(iii). The elements of the incentive formula in an incentive contract will also be important in determining the range of profit. For example, a higher contractor share of overruns would indicate a higher profit rate. See also DEAR 915.970-8(c)(6)(i), stating:

> [I]f a cost-plus-incentive-fee contract includes an unlimited downward (negative) fee adjustment on cost control, it could be comparable to a fixed-price-incentive contract. In such a pricing environment, the negotiating official may determine that the Government has transferred a greater amount of cost responsibility to the contractor than is typical under a normal cost-plus-incentive-fee contract.

c. Federal Socioeconomic Programs

This factor has been included in the weighted guidelines since its inception. FAR 15.404-4(d)(1) contains the following guidance:

> (iii) *Federal socioeconomic programs*. This factor measures the degree of support given by the prospective contractor to Federal socioeconomic programs, such as those involving small business concerns, small business concerns owned and controlled by socially and economically disadvantaged individuals, women-owned small business concerns, handicapped sheltered workshops, and energy conservation. Greater profit opportunity should be provided contractors that have displayed unusual initiative in these programs.

This factor is not considered separately in the DOD formula but is made a part of the management evaluation in the performance risk area. In the formulas of the civilian agencies, it is treated as a separate factor and handled in one of two ways. In the Departments of Energy and Transportation, the factor has a range of –5 percent to 5 percent of the basic profit objective derived from adding all of the other profit factors, DEAR 915.970-8(f). In NASA and the GSA, the factor is weighted at –0.5 percent to 0.5 percent of the costs used as the base for the contractor effort factor, NASA Form 634 and GSAR 515.905(a). In either case, the regulations provide that "merely satisfactory" effort in implementing these programs is entitled to no weight, that "energetic" support is entitled to a plus weight, and that "poor" support should receive a minus weight. See DEAR 915.970-8(f).

d. Capital Investments

Originally, OFPP Policy Letter 80-7 required that all structured profit approaches consider capital investment in *both facilities and working capital*. However, the DOD weighted guidelines never included investment in working capital because the DOD did not agree with this guidance. As a result, FAR 15.404-4(d)(1), issued in 1984, states this requirement in very general language, as follows:

> (iv) *Capital Investments*. This factor takes into account the contribution of contractor investments to efficient and economical contract performance.

Agencies have adopted a wide variety of techniques to calculate the amount of profit/fee under this factor. They have also adopted different approaches to the correlation of this profit factor to the allowability of the cost of facilities capital (imputed interest on the cost of facilities).

(1) Discretionary Determination

The GSA and NASA provide that a weight of –2 percent to 2 percent of the cost base should be included in the profit for this factor. The following guidance is provided at NFS 1815.970-2:

> (b) Investment. NASA encourages its contractors to perform their contracts with a minimum of financial, facilities, or other assistance from the Government. As such, it is the purpose of this factor to encourage the contractor to acquire and use its own resources to the maximum extent possible. Evaluation of this factor should include an analysis of the contractor's facilities and the frequency of payments:
>
> > (1) To evaluate how facilities contribute to the profit objective requires knowledge of the level of facilities utilization needed for contract performance, the source and financing of the required facilities, and the overall cost effectiveness of the facilities offered. Contractors furnishing their own facilities that significantly contribute to lower total contract costs should be provided additional profit. On the other hand, contractors that rely on the Government to provide or finance needed facilities should receive a correspondingly lower profit. Cases between the above examples should be evaluated on their merits, with either a positive or negative adjustment, as appropriate, in the profit objective. However, where a highly facilitized contractor is to perform a contract which does not benefit from this facilitization, or when a contractor's use of its facilities has a minimum cost impact on the contract, profit need not be adjusted.
> >
> > (2) In analyzing payments, consider the frequency of payments by the Government to the contractor and unusual payments, i.e., advance payments or milestone payments. The key to this weighting is proper consideration of the impact the contract will have on the contractor's cash flow. Generally, negative consideration should be given for payments more frequent than monthly, with maximum reduction being given as the contractor's working capital approaches zero. Positive consideration should be given for payments less frequent than monthly.

See also GSAR 515.905-1(c)(4), which contains essentially the same guidance.

(2) Precise Measurement of Facilities Capital

In contrast to the above system, the DOD weighted guidelines contain a rather precise mathematical method of determining the amount of profit to be given for facilities capital. Thus, DFARS 215.971-4(c) calls for use of a factor that is computed based on the following percentages of the net book value of capital assets employed on the contract:

Asset Type	Normal Value	Designated Range
Land	0%	N/A
Buildings	15%	10% to 20%
Equipment	35%	20% to 50%

The goal of this relatively large profit factor is to motivate the contractor to invest in labor-saving equipment. Thus, DFARS 215.971-4(d) provides the following guidance on selection of the percentage within the designated range:

> (2) *Above normal conditions.* (i) The contracting officer may assign a higher than normal value if the facilities capital investment has direct, identifiable, and exceptional benefits. Indicators are —
>
> > (A) New investments in state-of-the-art technology which reduce acquisition cost or yield other tangible benefits such as improved product quality or accelerated deliveries;
> >
> > (B) Investments in new equipment for research and development applications; or
> >
> > (C) Contractor demonstration that the investments are over and above the normal capital investments necessary to support anticipated requirements of DOD programs.
>
> (ii) The contracting officer may assign a value significantly above normal when there are direct and measurable benefits in efficiency and significantly reduced acquisition costs on the effort being priced.

Maximum values apply only to those cases where the benefits of the facilities capital investment are substantially above normal.

(3) *Below normal conditions.* (i) The contracting officer may assign a lower than normal value if the facilities capital investment has little benefit to DOD. Indicators are —

(A) Allocations of capital apply predominantly to commercial product lines;

(B) Investments are for such things as furniture and fixtures, home or group level administrative offices, corporate aircraft and hangars, gymnasiums; or

(C) Facilities are old or extensively idle.

(ii) The contracting officer may assign a value significantly below normal when a significant portion of defense manufacturing is done in an environment characterized by outdated, inefficient, and labor-intensive capital equipment.

The net book value of facilities employed on the contract is calculated using a two-step process. The first step is to compute the cost of money factors for each overhead pool of the contractor's organizations performing work on the contract. This calculation is made using Form CASB-CMF and following the procedures set forth in CAS 414, FAR 9904.414. Form CASB-CMF is set forth in **Figure 9-8**. These cost-of-money factors are percentages (like overhead rates) reflecting the ratio of the imputed cost of capital (imputed interest) to the cost base (normally direct labor dollars) for the overhead pool for any fiscal period. They provide a mechanism for allocating the imputed cost of capital to any specific contract, and they are also used to calculate the net book value of assets employed in the performance of a contract. This second step of the profit calculation is made using DD Form 1861, set forth in **Figure 9-9**. Here the imputed cost of interest attributable to each overhead pool is calculated by multiplying the cost-of-money factor for each pool by the estimated expenditure of effort on the contract in that pool (direct labor dollars in most cases). The total imputed cost of capital obtained from this calculation is divided by the cost of money rate (interest rate) to provide the net book value of facilities used on the contract. This amount is then entered on DD Form 1547 (see **Figure 9-3**) as the measurement base, and the weight determined to be applicable for buildings and equipment is applied to compute this profit factor.

Form CASB-CMF

TABLE XI

FACILITIES CAPITAL
COST OF MONEY FACTORS COMPUTATION
("Regular" Method - Cost of Money Excluded from Total Cost Input)

CONTRACTOR: ABC Corp. | ADDRESS:

BUSINESS UNIT: A Division

COST ACCOUNTING PERIOD: Y.E. 12/31/75		1. APPLICABLE COST OF MONEY RATE 8 %	2. ACCUMULATION & DIRECT DISTRIBUTION OF N.B.V.	3. ALLOCATION OF UNDISTRIBUTED	4. TOTAL NET BOOK VALUE	5. COST OF MONEY FOR THE COST ACCOUNTING PERIOD	6. ALLOCATION BASE FOR THE PERIOD	7. FACILITIES CAPITAL COST OF MONEY FACTORS
BUSINESS UNIT FACILITIES CAPITAL	RECORDED	Table IX	8,270,000	BASIS OF ALLOCATION	COLUMNS 2 + 3	COLUMNS 1 x 4	IN UNIT(S) OF MEASURE	COLUMNS 5 ÷ 6
	LEASED PROPERTY							
	CORPORATE OR GROUP	Table VI	450,000	Worksheet Table X			Table VII	
	TOTAL		8,720,000					
	UNDISTRIBUTED		3,450,000					
	DISTRIBUTED		5,270,000					
OVERHEAD POOLS	Engineering	Table IX	320,000	756,000	1,076,000	86,080	$ 2,000,000	.04304
	Manufacturing	Table IX	4,500,000	2,250,000	6,750,000	540,000	$ 3,000,000	.18
	Technical Computer			444,000	444,000	35,520	2,280 hr	15.57895
G & A EXPENSE POOLS	G&A Expense	Table VI	450,000		450,000	36,000	$36,700,000	.00098
TOTAL			5,270,000	3,450,000	8,720,000	697,600	//////////////	//////////////

101

Figure 9-8

CONTRACT FACILITIES CAPITAL COST OF MONEY

Form Approved
OMB No. 0704-0267
Expires Feb 28, 1995

Public reporting burden for this collection of information is estimated to average 10 hours per response, including the time for reviewing instructions, searching existing data sources, gathering and maintaining the data needed, and completing and reviewing the collection of information. Send comments regarding this burden estimate or any other aspect of this collection of information, including suggestions for reducing this burden, to Washington Headquarters Services, Directorate for Information Operations and Reports, 1215 Jefferson Davis Highway, Suite 1204, Arlington, VA 22202-4302, and to the Office of Management and Budget, Paperwork Reduction Project (0704-0267), Washington, DC 20503

PLEASE DO NOT RETURN YOUR COMPLETED FORM TO EITHER OF THESE ADDRESSES.
RETURN COMPLETED FORM TO YOUR CONTRACTING OFFICIAL.

1. CONTRACTOR NAME	2. CONTRACTOR ADDRESS
3. BUSINESS UNIT	
4. RFP / CONTRACT PIIN NUMBER	5. PERFORMANCE PERIOD

6. DISTRIBUTION OF FACILITIES CAPITAL COST OF MONEY

POOL a.	ALLOCATION BASE b.	FACILITIES CAPITAL COST OF MONEY c.	
		FACTOR (1)	AMOUNT (2)
d. TOTAL			
e. TREASURY RATE			%
f. FACILITIES CAPITAL EMPLOYED (TOTAL DIVIDED BY TREASURY RATE)			

7. DISTRIBUTION OF FACILITIES CAPITAL EMPLOYED

	PERCENTAGE a.	AMOUNT b.
(1) LAND	%	
(2) BUILDINGS	%	
(3) EQUIPMENT	%	
(4) FACILITIES CAPITAL EMPLOYED	100%	

DD Form 1861, MAR 93 PREVIOUS EDITION IS OBSOLETE

Figure 9-9

There are special provisions for service or research and development contracts. First, if the contractor performs such work in locations where there is little or no need for capital equipment (where use of this formula would yield a profit factor of less than 2 percent of the cost base), the contracting officer is permitted to use the alternate performance risk calculation (with no factor for facilities capital) as discussed earlier. Second, if the contractor will be performing such work in a "highly facilitized manufacturing" operation, the contracting officer is directed to use the following alternate set of values found in DFARS 215.971-4(c) to avoid paying too high a profit:

Asset Type	Normal Value	Designated Range
Land	0%	N/A
Buildings	5%	0% to 10%
Equipment	20%	15% to 25%

The Department of Energy has adopted the DOD policy with regard to facilities capital, DEAR 915.970-8(d), using a range of 5 percent to 20 percent of facilities employed on the contract. The Department of Transportation has also adopted this technique in computing the profit objective for manufacturing contracts (not service or research and development contracts), using a range of 16 percent to 20 percent of net book value of facilities employed on the contract, DOT Form F 4220.32 (see **Figure 9-7**).

(3) WORKING CAPITAL TECHNIQUES

The DOD has adopted a "working capital adjustment" factor to compensate for the use of working capital in fixed-price type contracts with a very long period of performance and providing for progress payments, DFARS 215.971-3. This factor also compensates for unusual increases in interest rates. The factor is only applicable when cost-based progress payments are included in a fixed-price type contract and is computed by the following calculation:

costs financed x contract length factor x current interest rate

The costs financed are the amount of costs not paid through progress payments. Thus, if the contract contains a provision for progress payments at the rate of 75 percent of costs incurred, the costs financed would be 25 percent of the total estimated costs of performance excluding facilities capital cost of money, DFARS 215.971-3(e). This regulation calls for reduction of this amount "as appropriate" in the following circumstances:

(i) The contractor has little cash investment (e.g., subcontractor progress payments liquidated late in period of performance);

(ii) Some costs are covered by special financing provisions, such as advance payments; or

(iii) The contract is multiyear and there are special funding arrangements.

The contract length factor is computed using the following table:

Period to perform substantive portion (in months)	Contract length factor
21 or less	.40
22 to 27	.65
28 to 33	.90
34 to 39	1.15
40 to 45	1.40
46 to 51	1.65
52 to 57	1.90
58 to 63	2.15
64 to 69	2.40
70 to 75	2.65
76 or more	2.90

DFARS 215.971-3(f) provides that the contract period should exclude periods where only minimum performance is called for (usually at the beginning of the contract) and should average the end date of contract performance when multiple deliveries are required. It also provides for exclusion from the calculation of option years and multiyear contract years beyond the initial program year.

The interest rate to be used is the rate established by the Secretary of the Treasury that is used to calculate the cost of facilities capital.

As an example of this calculation, assume a $10 million fixed-price contract calls for progress payments of 75 percent and deliveries of three aircraft in months 36, 38, and 40 after award of the contract. This factor would be derived by the following calculation:

costs financed		contract length factor		current interest rate		factor
$2,500,000	x	1.15	x	7%	=	$201,250

The Department of Energy has a much broader factor for working capital, requiring the discretionary consideration of the amount of "operating capital" needed to perform the contract under a broad factor called "other considerations," DEAR 915.970-8(g). This regulation suggests that a negative profit rate would be appropriate for cost-reimbursement contracts.

As discussed above, NASA permits contracting officers to consider working capital as part of their discretionary profit determination.

e. Cost Control and Other Past Accomplishments

FAR 15.404-4(d)(1) gives the following guidance on cost control and other past accomplishments:

> (v) *Cost-control and other past accomplishments.* This factor allows additional profit opportunities to a prospective contractor that has previously demonstrated its ability to perform similar tasks effectively and economically. In addition, consideration should be given to measures taken by the prospective contractor that result in productivity improvements, and other cost-reduction accomplishments that will benefit the Government in follow-on contracts.

It can be seen that this factor covers several different aspects of the contractor's past or prospective performance. Contractor performance, in general, was a factor in the original weighted guidelines adopted by the DOD in 1964 but was deleted from the formula in 1976. The remaining elements of this factor were deleted from the DOD weighted guidelines in 1987.

The civilian agencies have adopted a variety of approaches under this factor. NASA uses a broad factor on the contractor's performance with a weight of –1 percent to 1 percent of the cost base. NFS 1815.970-2(c) states:

> *Performance.* The contractor's past and present performance should be evaluated in such areas as product quality, meeting performance schedules, efficiency in cost control (including the need for and reasonableness of costs incurred), accuracy and reliability of previous cost estimates, degree of cooperation by the contractor (both business and technical), timely processing of changes and compliance with other contractual provisions.
>
> (d) *Subcontract program management.* Subcontract program management includes evaluation of the contractor's commitment to its competition program and its past and present performance in competition in subcontracting. If a contractor has consistently achieved excellent results in these areas in comparison with other contractors in similar circumstances, such performance merits a proportionately greater opportunity for profit or fee. Conversely, a poor record in this regard should result in a lower profit or fee.

The Department of Energy has adopted a broad factor called "other considerations" with a weight of –5 percent to 5 percent of the basic profit objective. This factor includes (1) cost control and other past accomplishments, (2) complexity of research and development or services assignment, and (3) operating capital. DEAR 915.970-8(g)(2)(i) provides the following guidance on the cost control element of this factor:

> This factor allows additional profit opportunities to a prospective contractor that has previously demonstrated its ability to perform similar tasks effectively and economically. In addition, consideration should be given to (A) measures taken by the prospective contractor that result in productivity improvements and (B) other cost-reduction accomplishments that will benefit Government contracts. Among other things, consideration should be given to the contractor's efforts to explore additional production opportunities or to improve or develop new product, manufacturing or performance technologies to reduce production cost.

The Department of Transportation includes a similar factor on DOT Form F 4220.32.

The GSA has a separate factor covering cost control and other past accomplishments with a weight of –2 percent to 2 percent of the cost base, GSAR 515.905(a). However, the regulation contains no guidance on the application of this factor.

f. Independent Development

FAR 15.404-4(d)(1) contains the following guidance on independent development:

> (vi) *Independent development.* Under this factor, the contractor may be provided additional profit opportunities in recognition of independent development efforts relevant to the contract end item without Government assistance. The contracting officer should consider whether the development cost was recovered directly or indirectly from Government sources.

The original DOD weighted guidelines contained this factor with a weight of 1 percent to 4 percent of the cost base, but it was deleted from the DFARS in 1987. However, it is included in most of the civilian agency policies.

NFS 1815.970-2(f) provides for the independent development factor as an unweighted part of the formula. This gives the contracting officer total discretion as to the amount of profit to be included for such contributions to the agency's program. This regulation also permits the contracting officer to include a negative factor in this area in situations where "the contractor is expected to obtain spin-off benefits as a direct result of the contract, for example, products with commercial application."

The Department of Energy has two factors in this category. A factor for a "viable" independent research and development program is included in DEAR 915.970-8(e)(1) at a weight of 5 percent to 7 percent of allowable independent research and development costs allocable to the contract. An independent development factor is included in DEAR 915.970-8(e)(2) with a weight of zero to 20 percent of the basic profit dollars. This factor applies only when contractors develop "items with energy program applications on their own initiative with no direct Government assistance and little or no indirect Government assistance."

The GSA has a factor for "special situations and independent development" with a weight of –2 percent to 2 percent of the cost base, GSAR 515.905(a). The regulations contain no guidance on the application of this factor.

The Department of Transportation has a factor of 1 percent to 4 percent for independent development, which is applicable to manufacturing and research and development contracts (not service contracts), DOT Form F 4220.32.

g. Other Factors

FAR 15.404-4(d)(1) also permits agencies to include additional factors in their structured approaches to profit. Several of the civilian agencies have included such factors. For example, NFS 1815.970-2(f)(1) contains the following guidance with regard to unusual pricing agreements:

> Occasionally, unusual contract pricing arrangements are made with the contractor under which it agrees to accept a lower profit or fee for changes or modifications within a prescribed dollar value. In such circumstances, the contractor should receive favorable consideration in developing the profit objective.

See also DEAR 915.970-8(h), which provides for a "productivity/ performance adjustment" to be added to the profit objective for follow-on contracts in cases where the contractor has taken special steps to reduce the costs of performance of an entire program. This factor is designed to overcome the reluctance of contractors to reduce costs when they anticipate follow-on contracts that would benefit from such cost reductions but would yield commensurately lower profits. The Department of Transportation also uses this factor, DOT Form F 4220.32.

5. Facilities Capital Cost of Money Adjustment

FAR 31.205-10(a)(2) provides that the facilities capital cost of money will be an allowable cost of performance of Government contracts if it is "specifically identified or proposed in cost proposals," but FAR 15.404-4(d) provides that it will not be included in the cost base for computation of the fee. FAR 15.404-4 also provides that a contractor can waive this cost, and FAR 52.215-16 provides a Waiver of Facilities Capital Cost of Money clause to be used when the contractor makes this election.

If the contractor does not waive this cost, the FAR is silent on any profit adjustment for this cost element. However, OFPP Policy Letter 80-7 (canceled in 1984 but replaced by FAR policy) addressed this issue as follows:

> (2) Agencies shall ensure that contractors are not compensated for facilities capital cost of money both as a direct or indirect cost and in profit or fee. Before the allowability of facilities capital cost of money, this cost was included in profits and fees. Therefore, profit and fee prenegotiation objectives shall be reduced if necessary to reflect this refinement in cost accounting practices. This reduction may be accomplished by means of offsets; that is, by (i) using a dollar-for-dollar offset in the Government's prenegotiation profit or fee objective or (ii) incorporating a common offset factor under an agency's structured approach. No offset is necessary when the profit rates applied to the profit analysis factors under an agency's structured approach already take into account the allowability of facilities capital cost of money.

The agencies have split on which of these two techniques to use. NASA uses the "dollar-for-dollar offset" technique by providing that any facilities capital cost of money included in the estimated cost will be deducted from the profit objective, NFS 1815.970-3. The other agencies (DOD, DOE, GSA, and DOT) require no such reduction because *they have incorporated the offset into the standard profit formula.* In such cases, it would be improper for the contracting officer to take any additional offset when recognizing the cost of facilities capital cost of money. Similarly, it would be unwise for the contractor to waive the recovery of such costs in these circumstances since no profit offset is required. Unfortunately, most of the agency regulations are silent on this issue. See, however, DFARS 215.973, which permits contracting officers to use alternate formulas in lieu of the weighted guidelines formula but requires such alternate formulas to include an offset in the amount of 1 percent or the amount of the facilities capital cost of money. The regulation explains the need for this adjustment as follows:

> (b)(2)(ii) This adjustment is needed for the following reason: The values of the profit factors used in the weighted guidelines method were adjusted to recognize the shift in facilities capital cost of money from an element of profit to an element of contract cost (FAR 31.205-10) and reductions were made directly to the profit factors for performance risk. In order to ensure that this policy is applied to all DOD contracts which allow facilities capital cost of money, similar adjustments shall be made to contracts which use alternate structured approaches.

DFARS 215.974 also requires contracting officers to apply this offset to the base fee on cost-plus-award-fee contracts.

6. Application to Nonprofit Organizations

Although the structured profit approaches currently in use were devised to determine the profits negotiated with commercial organizations, a number of agency regulations provide that they will also be used to calculate the profits paid to nonprofit organizations with certain prescribed adjustments. For example, DFARS 215.972 calls for the following adjustments:

> a. Performance risk factor — a reduction of this factor by 1 percent of the cost base if the standard factor is used or 2 percent if the alternate factor is used.
>
> b. Contract cost risk — the use of a range of –1 percent to 0 of the cost base.

Since the alternate performance risk factor would be used in almost all contracts with nonprofit organizations, the net result of this policy is the use of a profit factor that is 3 percent (of the cost base) lower than that used with profit-making organizations.

Similarly, NFS 1815.970(f)(2) provides for the use of a structured approach for nonprofit organizations other than educational institutions. This regulation states:

> (2) For contracts with nonprofit organizations under which fees are involved, an adjustment of up to 3 percent shall be subtracted from the total profit/fee objective. In developing this adjustment, it will be necessary to consider —
>
> (i) Tax position benefits;
>
> (ii) Granting of financing through letters of credit;
>
> (iii) Facility requirements of the nonprofit organization; and
>
> (iv) Other pertinent factors that may work to either the advantage or disadvantage of the contractor in its position as a nonprofit organization.

See also GSAR 515.905-70, containing the same guidance, and TAR 1215.905-71, containing similar guidance.

DEAR 915.970-5 also calls for the use of the structured approach for nonprofit organizations other than educational institutions with a reduction in the fee objective of "at least 25 percent."

VI. PRICE NEGOTIATION PROCEDURES

The extent of negotiation will vary from one procurement to another depending on the nature of the procurement, the type of analysis done by the Government, and the past business dealings of the parties. If price analysis is used on a commercial item, there may be little need for negotiation. In contrast, if cost analysis is done on a new item where the Government agency has had little experience with the contractor, protracted negotiations may be necessary to permit the contracting officer to gain confidence in the offeror's estimating system and the price to be paid. In all cases, sufficient negotiations must be conducted to permit the contracting officer to determine that the price to be paid is fair and reasonable, FAR 15.404-1(a).

While the extent of negotiation is left to the discretion of the contracting officer, there are two procedures relating to the negotiation process that are mandatory. First, prior to entering into a price negotiation, the contracting officer must establish a prenegotiation objective. Second, after completing the negotiation, the contracting officer must prepare and circulate a price negotiation memorandum (PNM). These procedures are discussed in this section.

A. Prenegotiation Objectives

FAR 15.406-1 requires the determination of prenegotiation objectives as follows:

> (a) The prenegotiation objectives establish the Government's initial negotiation position. They assist in the contracting officer's determination of fair and reasonable price. They should be based on the results of the contracting officer's analysis of the offeror's proposal, taking into consideration all pertinent information including field pricing assistance, audit reports and technical analysis, fact-finding results, independent Government cost estimates and price histories.
>
> (b) The contracting officer shall establish prenegotiation objectives before the negotiation of any pricing action. The scope and depth of the analysis supporting the objectives should be directly related to the dollar value, im-

> portance, and complexity of the pricing action. When cost analysis is required, the contracting officer shall document the pertinent issues to be negotiated, the cost objectives, and a profit or fee objective.

This process forces the contracting officer to assimilate all of the data prepared by the offeror, the Government auditor, the administrative contracting officer, and all other specialists who have reviewed the proposed pricing action. The result should be a Government negotiating position that represents the Government's best estimate of a fair and reasonable price.

A number of agencies require the contracting officer to obtain approval from a higher authority before the negotiation of major contracts. See, for example, NFS 1815.807-71, requiring each field center to establish a formal system for the review of prenegotiation memoranda, and NFS 1815.807-72, requiring approval of the prenegotiation position by the assistant administrator for procurement before negotiations on any procurement action selected for headquarters review. See also AFARS 15.807, requiring that prenegotiation objectives be documented in a business clearance memorandum and be prepared, reviewed, and approved in accordance with the procedures set forth in AFARS 15.890-2. This provision provides that "[a]s a minimum, the PreBCM shall be approved at a level higher than that of the individual assigned to the negotiations."

B. Negotiation

FAR 15.404-1 provides that the contracting officer is "solely responsible" for the final decision on price. See also FAR 15.306(d), requiring the contracting officer to "control all discussions" with the contractor. In carrying out this responsibility, the contracting officer may include other Government specialists such as price analysts, technical personnel, or lawyers in the negotiation sessions. Auditors may also be included in negotiations and are required to be included in DOD negotiations involving indirect costs. See 10 U.S.C. § 2324(f)(3), stating:

> The Federal Acquisition Regulation shall provide that, to the maximum extent practicable, the contract auditor be present at any negotiation or meeting with the contractor regarding a determination of the allowability of indirect costs of the contractor.

A detailed discussion of negotiation procedures and technique is contained in Chapter 8 of the ASPM.

C. Price Negotiation Memorandum

FAR 15.406-3 requires the preparation of a PNM on each negotiated procurement as follows:

(a) The contracting officer shall document in the contract file the principal elements of the negotiated agreement. The documentation (e.g., price negotiation memorandum (PNM)) shall include the following:

(1) The purpose of the negotiation.

(2) A description of the acquisition, including appropriate identifying numbers (e.g., RFP No.).

(3) The name, position, and organization of each person representing the contractor and the Government in the negotiation.

(4) The current status of any contractor systems (e.g., purchasing, estimating, accounting, and compensation) to the extent they affected and were considered in the negotiation.

(5) If cost or pricing data were not required in the case of any price negotiation exceeding the cost or pricing data threshold, the exception used and the basis for it.

(6) If cost or pricing data were required, the extent to which the contracting officer —

(i) Relied on the cost or pricing data submitted and used them in negotiating the price;

(ii) Recognized as inaccurate, incomplete, or noncurrent any cost or pricing data submitted; the action taken by the contracting officer and the contractor as a result; and the effect of the defective data on the price negotiated; or

(iii) Determined that an exception applied after the data were submitted and, therefore, considered not to be cost or pricing data.

(7) A summary of the contractor's proposal, any field pricing assistance recommendations, including the reasons for any pertinent variances from them, the Government's negotiation objective, and the negotiated position. Where the determination of price reasonableness is

based on cost analysis, the summary shall address the amount of each major cost element. When determination of price reasonableness is based on price analysis, the summary shall include the source and type of data used to support the determination.

(8) The most significant facts or considerations controlling the establishment of the prenegotiation objectives and the negotiated agreement including an explanation of any significant differences between the two positions.

(9) To the extent such direction has a significant effect on the action, a discussion and quantification of the impact of direction given by Congress, other agencies, and higher-level officials (i.e., officials who would not normally exercise authority during the award and review process for the instant contract action).

(10) The basis for the profit or fee prenegotiation objective and the profit or fee negotiated.

(11) Documentation of fair and reasonable pricing.

(b) Whenever a field pricing assistance has been obtained, the contracting officer shall forward a copy of the negotiation documentation to the office(s) providing assistance. When appropriate, information on how advisory field support can be made more effective should be provided separately.

The parties to the negotiation are not required to agree on each element of cost in the ultimate negotiated price, FAR 15.405(a). As a result, it is very likely that the memorandum of each party will contain a different explanation of the way the final cost estimate was calculated. If there is a subsequent dispute over the adequacy of the contractor's submission of cost or pricing data, it would be expected that the memorandum of the contracting officer would be the best evidence of whether the price was significantly altered by the data deficiency, *McDonnell Douglas Corp.*, ASBCA 12786, 69-2 BCA ¶ 7897. See, however, *Sperry Rand Corp.*, DOTCAB 1144, 82-2 BCA ¶ 15,812, *recons. denied*, 84-1 BCA ¶ 16,968, where the contractor was able to persuade the board that no price reduction should be made because its negotiation memorandum reflected the fact that it had reduced its negotiating position to reflect the undisclosed data. See 10 U.S.C. § 2306a(e)(3)(C) and 41 U.S.C. § 254b(e)(3)(C), stating that it is *not a defense* to a Government claim for a price reduction because of defective cost or pricing data that "the contract was based on an agreement between the contractor and the United States about the total cost of the contract and there was no agreement about the cost of each item procured under such contract."

CHAPTER 10

COLLATERAL POLICIES

The primary focus of this book is on how the Federal Government achieves the primary goal of any procurement: obtaining timely satisfaction of its needs at fair prices and terms. However, the Government also uses the acquisition process to implement policies that have little or no direct relationship to, and are often in tension with, the primary goals of procurement. For example, in choosing a contractor, the Government may give weight to the size of the contractor (i.e., is it a small business?); the place of performance (i.e., is work being done in a labor surplus area?); the ownership of the contractor (i.e., is it women-owned?); and the compliance of the contractor with a variety of other federal standards (e.g., minimum wage and hour requirements). This chapter examines the major collateral policies, particularly those that have social or economic goals as their primary focus.

Implementing these collateral policies through the acquisition process sometimes conflicts with the Government's policy of full and open competition and may increase the total costs of a procurement. However, the prevailing view is that these negative features are offset by the benefits that flow to many contractors that would otherwise be excluded from the process.

There are a number of ways in which collateral policies impact on the Government procurement function. The contract price may be increased by excluding from award an offeror with a potentially lower price. For example, to implement a collateral policy, an agency may specify that award will be made only to offerors in a preferred group, even though entities outside that group may be able to offer lower prices. Contractors' administrative costs of implementing collateral programs also lead to higher overall prices. Agencies also incur additional costs in implementing the policies. They need to prepare, maintain, and enforce extensive regulations and may become involved in "bid protests" over whether particular awards are consistent with the rules concerning collateral policies. Some observers have also suggested that collateral policies sometimes result in awards to firms that are more likely to default, thereby seriously impeding the procurement process and ultimately causing added expense and delays to the involved agencies.

In view of these factors, there has been constant debate over whether the Government should use the procurement process to implement collateral policies. Proponents of implementation argue that it is reasonable and effective to use the Government's purchasing power to carry out policies aiding disadvantaged persons, reducing unemployment, reducing pollution, conserving energy, and accomplishing other beneficial purposes. These proponents also argue that the policies broaden the base of suppliers, thereby ultimately increasing competition for federal contracts.

Opponents contend that since the costs of implementing collateral policies are high and may be hidden, there rarely is any conclusive determination that the costs are justified by the benefits. They argue further that the collateral policies are often difficult to reconcile with one another and frequently become outmoded, that the acquisition process is slowed and made more complicated by the collateral policies, and that some potentially excellent contractors become discouraged by the preferences and by the complex regulations that their enforcement requires.

There is a view that collateral policies can be implemented only when authorized by statute. The Comptroller General has ruled that an executive agency needs a clear grant of authority from Congress to implement a collateral policy that limits those who are eligible for award of contracts, 10 Comp. Gen. 294 (A-34106) (1931); 42 Comp. Gen. 1 (B-148930) (1962). The Comptroller General also has held that a particular executive agency's rules for collateral policies must be consistent with higher-level executive branch regulations, *Educational Servs. Group (ESG), Management Concepts Inc.*, 62 Comp. Gen. 353 (B-210420), 83-1 CPD ¶ 466.

Statutory authority for collateral policies may be explicit or implicit. Examples of explicit statutory authority are the Buy American Act, 41 U.S.C. §§ 10a–d, and the Small Business Act, 15 U.S.C. § 631 et seq. Implicit authority can be found in the general language of the procurement statutes, particularly in the Federal Property and Administrative Services Act (FPASA), 40 U.S.C. § 481(a), which requires procurement of goods and services in a manner "advantageous to the Government in terms of economy, efficiency, or service." See *American Fed'n of Labor & Congress of Indus. Orgs. v. Kahn*, 618 F.2d 784 (D.C. Cir.), *cert. denied*, 443 U.S. 915 (1979), where the court sustained the power of the President to deny contract awards to companies that were in violation of presidentially imposed wage and price standards; and *Contractors Ass'n of E. Pa. v. Secretary of Labor*, 442 F.2d 159 (3d Cir.), *cert. denied*, 404 U.S. 854

(1971), where the court sustained equal employment contract provisions promulgated under Exec. Order No. 11,246. Compare *Liberty Mut. Ins. Co. v. Friedman*, 639 F.2d 164 (4th Cir. 1981), where the court held that this statutory authority did not authorize the imposition of equal employment obligations on a workers' compensation insurer. In *Chamber of Commerce v. Reich*, 74 F.3d 1322 (D.C. Cir. 1996), the court reversed the district court's finding that the President had authority under the FPASA to issue an executive order authorizing the Secretary of Labor to disqualify workers with federal contracts exceeding $100,000 who hire permanent replacement workers during a lawful economic strike. The court stated that although the broad contract management authority under the FPASA generally permits the President to draw on policy views directed beyond immediate concerns with the quality and price of purchased goods, labor relations are viewed differently because of the NLRA and its broad field of preemption.

The Comptroller General also has upheld some collateral policies where authorization was found in broad statutory language, *Fairplain Dev. Co.*, 59 Comp. Gen. 409 (B-192483), 80-1 CPD ¶ 293 (policy dealing with preference for location of federal facilities in urban areas).

I. POLICIES ASSISTING SMALL BUSINESSES

Congress has authorized a number of programs the are designed to assist small businesses in the procurement process. These programs are under the general supervision and control of the Small Business Administration (SBA) and are promulgated by the Small Business Act, 15 U.S.C. § 631 et seq. Under this Act, the SBA establishes small business size standards, rules on size appeals, and is solely authorized to make determinations that a small business is not a responsible contractor. The Act also establishes a number of business preferences for small businesses, including "set-aside" programs and programs to assist in small business subcontracting. These various programs are discussed in this section.

A. Size Determination

The Small Business Act defines a "small business concern" as one that is independently owned and operated and that is not dominant in its field of operation, 15 U.S.C. § 632(a)(1). The statute provides that a concern's number of employees and dollar business volume criteria determine whether it qualifies as a small business. The SBA has established size criteria for numerous classes of businesses, as listed in the Standard Industrial Classification (SIC) Manual issued by the Office of Management and Budget. See 13 C.F.R. § 121.201 for a listing of size standards by SIC industry, SIC code, and description. Most size determinations are based on average gross receipts or number of employees, 15 U.S.C. § 632(a)(2), 13 C.F.R. Part 121. The standards vary from one industry to another, depending on the number and sizes of firms within the industry, but they "may utilize number of employees, dollar volume of business, net worth, net income, a combination thereof, or other appropriate factors," 15 U.S.C. § 632(a)(2)(B). A company whose stock is publicly traded, as opposed to a corporation whose stock is privately held, can qualify as a small business concern if it meets the size standard designated in the solicitation, *Geo-Seis Helicopters, Inc.*, SIZ-94-3-23-32, May 10, 1994, *Unpub.*

In terms of determining annual receipts, 13 C.F.R. § 121.104 states:

> (1) Receipts means "total income" (or in the case of a sole proprietorship, "gross income") plus the "cost of goods sold" as these terms are defined or reported on Internal Revenue Service (IRS) Federal tax return forms (Form 1120 for corporations; Form 1120S for Subchapter S corporations; Form 1065 for partnerships; and Form 1040, Schedule F for farm or Schedule C for other sole proprietorships). However, the term receipts excludes net capital gains or losses, taxes collected for and remitted to a taxing authority if included in gross or total income, proceeds from the transactions between a concern and its domestic or foreign affiliates (if also excluded from gross or total income on a consolidated return filed with the IRS), and amounts collected for another by a travel agent, real estate agent, advertising agent, or conference management service provider.

See *Kittrell Garlock & Assocs.*, SIZ-94-10-26-142, Apr. 20, 1995, *Unpub.* (consultants' fees of an architectural and engineering firm must be included in calculating average annual receipts).

Annual receipts for a concern that has been in business for three or more completed fiscal years means the receipts of the concern over its last three completed fiscal years divided by three, 13 C.F.R. § 121.104(b)(1). For a concern that has been in business for less than three completed fiscal years, annual receipts means the receipts for the period the concern has been in business divided by the number of weeks in business, multiplied by 52, 13 C.F.R. § 121.104(b)(2). See *Dun-Well Servs., Inc.*, SIZ-94-4-21-55, July 12, 1994, *Unpub.*, where a size determination was remanded to a regional office because incorrect fiscal years were used by that office to calculate the challenged firm's average annual receipts.

1. Affiliates

An offeror's size is determined by considering not only the offeror itself, but by aggregating the annual receipts and number of employees of the offeror and all "affiliates," regardless of industrial classification. FAR 19.101 provides that "[b]usiness concerns are affiliates of each other if, directly or indirectly, either one controls or has the power to control the other, or another concern controls or has the power to control both." In determining affiliation, all pertinent facts may be considered, including common ownership, common management, and contractual relationships, 13 C.F.R. § 121.103; FAR 19.101. Note that not all affiliation factors need be considered — only those appropriate or relevant under the specific facts of the case. Moreover, equal weight need not be given to each factor; the presence of one or more of these factors may be sufficient to constitute affiliation, *Agrigold Juice Prods.*, SIZ-95-7-19-72, Jan. 24, 1996, *Unpub.* In addition, these factors are not intended to be exhaustive. Affiliation has been a controversial issue, particularly where a finding of affiliation has the effect of disqualifying a concern that would otherwise be able to compete as a small business, *Aloha Dredging & Constr. Co. v. Heatherly*, 661 F. Supp. 738 (D.D.C. 1987). See also Reeder and Vergilio, "Small Business Set-Asides and Corporate Affiliation — A Billion Dollar Business," 15 Pub. Contract L.J. 279 (1985).

Common ownership is often considered in determining affiliation. For instance, affiliation has been found to exist among firms owned by brothers and a cousin and uncle, based not on family ties but rather on the common investments and ownership, *Agrigold Juice Prods.*, SIZ-95-7-19-72, Jan. 24, 1996, *Unpub.* Similarly, where a franchiser controlled 60 percent of the franchisee's voting stock, the franchiser's chairman of the board was also the franchisee's chairman of the board, the franchiser provided ongoing management and assistance to the franchisee, and there were excessive restrictions on the sale of the franchisee's stock, the two firms were considered affiliates, *ERM-South, Inc.*, SIZ-95-4-12-33, Aug. 22, 1995, *Unpub.* On the other hand, in *ROH, Inc.*, SIZ-94-11-25-156, May 25, 1995, *Unpub.*, the SBA found no affiliation between firms where the challenged firm's owner had sold all its stock in a large firm and divested any interest prior to the challenged firm's self-certification as a small business, and there was no evidence to show that any ties remained between the two firms. See also *Shiloh Indus. Contractors, Inc.*, SIZ-95-9-22-90, Jan. 31, 1996, *Unpub.* (although both firms were owned by the same family, no affiliation existed because the alleged large firm had no ownership or other interest in the other firm, and the firms did not share officers, directors, shareholders, employees, or facilities); and *Griffin Servs., Inc.*, SIZ-95-10-28-110, Jan. 23, 1996, *Unpub.* (no affiliation where alleged affiliates no longer shared family ties, and the challenged firm's owner had given up his executive position and sold his stock in the alleged affiliate nine years prior to the challenge).

Common management is another factor often considered when examining affiliation. For example, where the overall management of a contract is only nominally in the control of the prime contractor and actual control resides in a large subcontractor and there is no demarcation of the tasks that would be performed by each participant, the relationship will be regarded as a joint venture and the firms will be considered affiliates, *Fortier & Assocs., Inc.*, SIZ-95-2-22-15, June 27, 1995, *Unpub.* Similarly, where the ostensible subcontractor will perform the vital and primary requirements of the solicitation, the relationship will be regarded as a joint venture and the firms will be considered affiliates under the solicitation, *CardioMetrix, Inc.*, SIZ-95-1-11-4, June 15, 1995, *Unpub.*

Affiliation may be found based upon a contractual relationship between parties. For example, where an agreement between the challenged firm and a large firm provides that the large firm has total management authority over the challenged firm's contracts, the businesses will be considered affiliates, *Picazo Constructors, Inc.*, SIZ-94-7-19-95, Nov. 21, 1994, *Unpub.*

A determination of affiliation through stock ownership is provided in 13 C.F.R. § 121.103(c). This provision states that a person is "an affiliate of a concern if the person owns or controls, or has the power to control 50 percent or more of its voting stock, or a block of stock which affords control because it is large compared to other outstanding blocks of stock." This is a change from the predecessor regulation, which stated that there was a "presumption of control for persons that own, control, or have the power to control 50 percent or more of a concern's voting stock." This presumption of control was permitted to be negated by specific facts in a particular case, e.g., person may own over 50 percent of voting stock, but through voting agreements or proxies may have divested control of the company. The change in the regulation was due to the SBA belief that a person owning

50 percent of a concern should be deemed to control that concern regardless of any voting arrangements.

Although "common facilities" was eliminated as a separate basis for finding affiliation in the revised regulations, it was not the SBA's intent to prohibit SBA from considering all appropriate factors, including "common facilities," in determining whether affiliation exists, 61 Fed. Reg. 3281, Jan. 31, 1996.

An affiliation may arise where officers, directors, or other key employees serve as the majority or otherwise as the controlling element of another concern. See *SA Technologies, Inc.*, SIZ-95-4-28-40, Sept. 5, 1995, *Unpub.*, where because key employees of a large firm organized a new firm in the same industry and the large firm's purchase orders amounted to 80 percent of the new firm's annual receipts, the two firms were considered affiliated. But see *Ferg-N-Sons Plastics, Inc.*, SIZ-94-2-22-12, Mar. 21, 1994, *Unpub.* (individual was the comptroller but not an officer or director of the business entity and thus not considered a key employee).

13 C.F.R. § 121.103(b) provides for exclusion from affiliation coverage for small business investment companies and development companies, as well as concerns owned by certain capital firms, pension funds, and tax-exempt charitable entities. This exclusion was added under the revised regulations issued in 61 Fed. Reg. 3280, Jan. 31, 1996. In addition to the existing exclusion from affiliation for Small Business Investment Companies (SBICs) and Development Companies, the revised regulations added an exclusion, for purposes of SBIC assistance only, for concerns owned by certain venture capital firms, pension funds, and charitable entities exempt from federal taxation under Section 501(c) of the Internal Revenue Code.

Where a different party is involved in a later protest involving that firm, the doctrines of res judicata and collateral estoppel do not apply, and a regional office or area office may reach a contrary result as to affiliation as long as it adequately explains the legal and factual basis for that result, *Agrigold Juice Prods.*, SIZ-95-7-19-72, Jan. 24, 1996, *Unpub.* In this case, an area office determined that Agrigold was other than a small business based on affiliation. Agrigold argued that the area office failed to give proper weight to the prior regional office determination that it was small. The SBA stated that because the regional office determination was not appealed, the Office of Hearings and Appeals had no opportunity to consider the question and, thus, the prior regional office determination did not constitute precedent.

2. Subcontracts to Large Firms

Unless prohibited by statute, the terms of a solicitation, or an applicable regulation, small businesses awarded set-aside contracts may subcontract to large businesses, *Shelf Stable Foods, Inc.*, Comp. Gen. Dec. B-215763.3, 85-1 CPD ¶ 605; *O.V. Campbell & Sons Indus., Inc.*, Comp. Gen. Dec. B-216585, 85-1 CPD ¶ 385. Since the statutes are silent with respect to subcontracts, the Comptroller General "may do no more than insist that the contracting agency conduct its small business procurement in a manner which is not inconsistent with existing law, regulation, and proper contract provisions," Comp. Gen. Dec. B-148155, May 17, 1962, *Unpub.* Consequently, the Comptroller General's office has adopted the policy that "so long as the small business firm, which has subcontracted a major portion of the work to large business, makes some significant contribution to the manufacture or production of the end item, the contractual requirement that the 'end item' be manufactured or produced by a small business concern has been met," *Southwest Tool & Die Co.*, 49 Comp. Gen. 41 (B-166727) (1969) (painting, dipping, and packaging of the product by the small business is a significant contribution); *Culligan, Inc.*, 58 Comp. Gen. 307 (B-192581), 79-1 CPD ¶ 149 (fact that large business will manufacture, inspect, package, and ship supplies indicates that small business will not make a significant contribution).

The Comptroller General has consistently held that subcontracting up to 49 percent of the contract dollar volume is not against the policy of the Small Business Act, *M.D. Oppenheim & Co.*, 70 Comp. Gen. 213 (B-241252), 91-1 CPD ¶ 98; *Science Sys. & Applications, Inc.*, Comp. Gen. Dec. B-240311, 90-2 CPD ¶ 381. See also *Tonya, Inc. v. United States*, 28 Fed. Cl. 727 (1993), *aff'd without op.*, 31 F.3d 1176 (Fed. Cir. 1994), where the court held that an agency's expectation that a prospective contractor would subcontract a portion of its work to a large contractor did not violate the Small Business Act. However, in a total small business set-aside, a bid that indicated that the end item would not be manufactured or produced by a small business was considered nonresponsive, *American Amplifier & Tel. Corp.*, 53 Comp. Gen. 463 (B-179149), 74-1 CPD ¶ 10. In contrast, where a non-set-aside procurement is involved, a small business bidder that certifies itself as a manufacturer of the offered supplies for purposes of the Walsh-

Healey Act may subcontract the entire work to a large business manufacturer, *Stellar Indus., Inc.*, 64 Comp. Gen. 748 (B-218287.2), 85-2 CPD ¶ 127.

3. *Self-Certification*

The initial determination of size is made by the small business, which is required to "self-certify" with its offer that it is small, 13 C.F.R. § 121.405(a). Thus, each offeror must determine whether it qualifies as a small business. In order to facilitate self-certification, federal procuring agencies are required to classify the products and services being procured and specify an applicable size standard in each solicitation, FAR 19.102(b) and FAR 19.303. The self-certification is made by checking the appropriate blank in the solicitation provision in FAR 52.219-1, thereby representing and certifying whether the offeror is a small business concern. In sealed bid procurement, failure to self-certify at the time of bidding may not be cured after opening, *Covenant Indus., Inc.*, Comp. Gen. Dec. B-218091.2, 85-1 CPD ¶ 372; *Julie Cades*, Comp. Gen. Dec. B-248218, 92-2 CPD ¶ 18. Further, the failure of a bidder to self-certify is not cured by completion of the Place of Performance clause, which relates to responsibility of the bidder and not responsiveness of the bid, *Delta Concepts, Inc.*, 67 Comp. Gen. 522 (B-230632), 88-2 CPD ¶ 43.

An offeror may represent that it is "small" if it meets the definition of a small business concern in the solicitation and the SBA has made no adverse determination regarding its size status, FAR 19.301(a). This certification must be made in accordance with a high standard of good faith because of the potential for abuse inherent in a self-certification procedure, *Bancroft Cap Co.*, 55 Comp. Gen. 469 (B-182569), 75-2 CPD ¶ 321. Lack of good faith is "not necessarily limited to an incident of intentional misrepresentation" but can also be found in a failure to exercise prudence and care in ascertaining size under prescribed guidelines, 51 Comp. Gen. 595 (B-174807) (1972). A bidder's self-certification was held to be not prepared in good faith when it certified itself as small although it knew the SBA had questioned that status, 41 Comp. Gen. 47 (B-144621) (1961). However, in 49 Comp. Gen. 369 (B-167353) (1969), the Comptroller General found no basis for imputing bad faith even though the successful bidder changed its management structure between the filing of the protest and the SBA size determination and it was held not to be a small business at the time of award. In *Vantex Serv. Corp.*, Comp. Gen. Dec. B-251102, 93-1 CPD

¶ 221, a contractor properly certified as a small business was awarded a contract and later was acquired by a large business. The Comptroller General found that the agency was not required to reexamine the contractor's size status in order to exercise an option under the contract because the size determination at the time of self-certification controls.

A knowingly false certification may create liability under criminal statutes including 18 U.S.C. § 1001, or invite a civil suit. See, for example, *Iconco v. Jensen Constr. Co.*, 622 F.2d 1291 (8th Cir. 1980). In addition, state law may provide a remedy for fraud, unjust enrichment, or interference with a business relationship caused by a lowest bidder who misrepresents itself as a small business, *Tectonics, Inc. v. Castle Constr. Co.*, 753 F.2d 957 (11th Cir.), *cert. denied*, 474 U.S. 848 (1985). Obviously, to receive such a remedy, the plaintiff must demonstrate that the firm that received the award does not qualify as a small business under the Act, *Ferguson-Williams, Inc. v. BAMSI, Inc.*, 782 F.2d 940 (11th Cir. 1986) (SBA determined that low bidder qualified as a small business; therefore, no recovery was allowed).

An offeror's self-certification is normally accepted without any further inquiry, unless it is challenged, FAR 19.301(b); *Otis Steel Prods. Corp. v. United States*, 161 Ct. Cl. 694, 316 F.2d 937 (1963). Challenges may be made by the contracting officer, offerors in the same procurement, or other interested parties. Although such challenges are often filed with the procuring agency, the investigation and determination of whether the offeror is in fact "small" will be made by the SBA, FAR 19.103(c). An initial determination is ordinarily made by a regional office of the SBA. Any appeal must be taken to the SBA Office of Hearings and Appeals in Washington, D.C., "within the time limits and in strict accordance with the procedures contained in 13 C.F.R. 121.11," FAR 19.302(i). The procedures for protesting the self-certification of an offeror are set forth in 13 C.F.R. §§ 121.1001 – 121.1009.

Where a timely size protest is filed after a small business award, and the awardee is found by the SBA to be other than small, the agency, in the absence of legitimate countervailing reasons, should terminate the contract. In *Diagnostic Imaging Technical Educ.*, Comp. Gen. Dec. B-257590, 94-2 CPD ¶ 148, the protester timely protested the size status of the awardee to the contracting officer, who referred the matter to the SBA. The SBA found the awardee to be other than a small business. In spite of this finding, the agency did not terminate the contract. The Comptroller General held that the agency should not have permitted the award to stand when it was apprised by the SBA that the awardee was not small, stating:

> While FAR § 19.302(j) treats post-award size protests as having no applicability to the current contract, awards under set-aside procurements to other than small businesses should be terminated if possible, and SBA's regulations provide that such timely-filed size protests "shall apply to the procurement in question even though the contracting officer may have awarded the contract prior to receipt of the protest." 13 C.F.R. § 121.1603(a)(2); *see also* FAR § 19.302(d)(1)(ii). Further, RSTI did not defend its adverse size certification by appealing SBA's determination. Thus, in the absence of countervailing reasons, it would be inconsistent with the integrity of the competitive procurement system, and the intent of the Small Business Act, to permit a large business, which under the terms of the solicitation was ineligible for award, to continue to perform the contract. *American Mobilphone Paging, Inc.*, [69 Comp. Gen. 392 (B-238027), 90-1 CPD ¶ 366].

The Comptroller General views the SBA as having conclusive authority to determine whether a particular business is "small" for purposes of federal procurement, *Arbor Indus., Inc.*, B-231515, 88-1 CPD ¶ 564. Therefore, the Comptroller General will not make such a determination, or review SBA determinations, *NJCT Corp.*, Comp. Gen. Dec. B-216919, 85-1 CPD ¶ 33. Once an offeror has been found not to be small, the offeror may not, unless the SBA has issued a later decision finding the firm to be small, certify itself as small under the same or lower standards as those under which it had been found not to be small, 13 C.F.R. § 121.1009(g)(3); *Choctaw Mfg. Co. v. United States*, 761 F.2d 609 (11th Cir. 1985); *Propper Int'l, Inc.*, 55 Comp. Gen. 1188 (B-185302), 76-1 CPD ¶ 400. See *Timothy S. Graves*, Comp. Gen. Dec. B-253813, 93-2 CPD ¶ 244, *aff'd*, 94-1 CPD ¶ 19, where award was denied to a firm that was in fact small at the time of award. In this case, the bidder on a timber sale had been determined not to be a small business by the SBA regional office. The bidder appealed the determination to the SBA's Office of Hearings and Appeals (OHA), and while the matter was being considered by the OHA, the bidder submitted a bid on a subsequent timber sale and certified itself to be a small business. Subsequently, the OHA reversed the regional office's determination on the previous contract, and the agency proposed to award the contract to the bidder. However, the award was appealed to the OHA, which held that the bidder could not qualify as small because the regional office determination had not been reversed at the time that the bidder signed its self-certification, even though by OHA's own determination, the bidder was small at the time. The

Comptroller General denied the subsequent protest on the grounds that the SBA size determination was conclusive.

Once a business is found to be other than small, it is required to recertify prior to bidding on any Government procurement, 13 C.F.R. § 121.1010. In *Evans Cooperage Co.*, SIZ-94-11-2-145, May 5, 1995, *Unpub.*, the appellant was found to be other than small for the applicable 500-employee size standard in a particular solicitation. The appellant did not recertify but stated that it had intended to do so and that it now had fewer than 500 employees. The SBA found that this argument had no merit.

B. Certificates of Competency

The SBA has the authority to issue certificates of competency (COCs) for all elements of responsibility of small businesses. In the original Small Business Act, Congress authorized the SBA to certify as to the "capacity and credit" of small businesses to perform particular contracts. If a small business were found by a contracting officer not to be responsible, the firm could seek a COC from the SBA. If granted, such a certificate was conclusive on the procuring agency as to the "capacity and credit" of the small business for performance of the particular contract. However, the Comptroller General later ruled that since "responsibility" determinations included elements — such as perseverance, integrity, and tenacity — that were separable from "capacity and credit," contracting officers could still find a small business not responsible, even though the SBA had issued a COC, 43 Comp. Gen. 257 (B-151121) (1963).

As a result of complaints about this "dilution" of the COC authority, Congress expanded the reach of such certificates in 1977 to cover "all elements of responsibility, including, but not limited to, capability, competency, capacity, credit, integrity, perseverance, and tenacity," 15 U.S.C. § 637(b)(7). Such a certificate is conclusive on a procuring agency, *J.R. Youngdale Constr. Co.*, Comp. Gen. Dec. B-219439, 85-2 CPD ¶ 473; *International Business Invs., Inc.*, 60 Comp. Gen. 275 (B-198894), 81-1 CPD ¶ 125. The scope of the SBA's review authority is not limited to those factors specified by a contracting officer as deficient in a referral letter, but rather includes all elements of responsibility, *C & G Excavating, Inc. v. United States*, 32 Fed. Cl. 231 (1994) (contracting officer based nonresponsibility finding on capacity, whereas SBA based nonresponsibility on financial condition). Neither the SBA nor the procuring agency may create exceptions to the statutory requirement for referral to the SBA for determination regarding whether a COC should be issued, 15 U.S.C. § 637(b)(7); *Sess Constr. Co.*, 64 Comp. Gen. 355 (B-216924), 85-1 CPD ¶ 319; *Small Business Admin. — Request for Recons.*, Comp. Gen. Dec. B-219654.3, 86-1 CPD ¶ 420.

COC's are issued on a contract-by-contract basis. If a contracting officer determines that a small business that submitted the most favorable acceptable offer lacks responsibility, contract award must be withheld and the matter referred to the "cognizant SBA Regional Office," FAR 19.602-1(a)(2). The SBA then offers the small business an opportunity to apply for a COC, FAR 19.602-2(a)(1). If the small business provides the detailed information required by the application, the SBA will investigate the matter and issue or deny issuance of the COC. If the SBA has not issued a COC within 15 business days, or a longer period agreed to by the contracting officer, the agency proceeds with the acquisition, FAR 19.602-4(c). See *General Painting Co.*, Comp. Gen. Dec. B-219449, 85-2 CPD ¶ 530, holding that award should have been made when the SBA delayed issuing a COC without an agreement with the contracting officer. If an agency rejects a proposal as technically unacceptable on the basis of factors not related to responsibility as well as responsibility-related ones, the agency is not required to refer the matter to the SBA under its COC procedure, *Paragon Dynamics, Inc.*, Comp. Gen. Dec. B-251280, 93-1 CPD ¶ 248.

Prior to issuance of a COC, the SBA is required to notify the contracting officer, FAR 19.602-2(c). If the contracting officer disagrees with the proposed issuance of a COC, and the controversy cannot be resolved through further communications, the procuring agency may request referral of the matter to the SBA Central Office, FAR 19.602-3. A contractor otherwise eligible for the COC program is entitled to have the involved agency notify the SBA prior to terminating negotiations, so that the contractor could have the SBA's assistance in responding to the deficiencies perceived by the agency, *CelTech, Inc. v. United States*, 24 Cl. Ct. 269 (1991).

The Comptroller General will not review the denial of a COC unless the procurement agency makes a showing of fraud or bad faith, for example, where information vital to the determination of responsibility has not been considered, or where the SBA has disregarded its own published regulations, *West State, Inc.*, Comp. Gen. Dec. B-255692, 94-1 CPD ¶ 211;

Tomko, Inc., 63 Comp. Gen. 218 (B-210023.2), 84-1 CPD ¶ 202; *Skillens Enters.*, 61 Comp. Gen. 142 (B-202508.2), 81-2 CPD ¶ 472.

FAR 19.602-1(a)(2) provides that the COC procedure does not apply to issues of eligibility covered in FAR 9.104-1(g) or to suspended or debarred contractors. The Comptroller General has held that the COC procedure does not apply to an agency's determination that certain technical requirements are essential even though the effect of such a determination may be to exclude a small business from the procurement, *Aero Corp.*, 59 Comp. Gen. 146 (B-194445.3), 79-2 CPD ¶ 430. In addition, the COC procedure does not apply to findings that a proposal is technically unacceptable or that a bid is nonresponsive, *Trading Atlanta Ltd.*, Comp. Gen. Dec. B-238978, 90-2 CPD ¶ 52; *Vac-Hyde Corp.*, 64 Comp. Gen. 658 (B-216840), 85-2 CPD ¶ 2; *Pacific Sky Supply, Inc.*, 64 Comp. Gen. 194 (B-215189), 85-1 CPD ¶ 53.

The COC procedure does not apply when an agency is evaluating offers in a negotiated procurement if the evaluation factors are scored on a comparative basis, *Smith of Galeton Gloves, Inc.*, Comp. Gen. Dec. B-271686, 96-2 CPD ¶ 36. Thus, the COC procedure is not applicable in deciding whether a small business concern comes within the "competitive range" in a negotiated procurement, even if some of the factors used in determining the "competitive range" are related to responsibility, *Electro-Methods, Inc. v. United States*, 7 Cl. Ct. 755 (1985); *C.M.P. Corp.*, Comp. Gen. Dec. B-211371, 83-2 CPD ¶ 238; *Electrospace Sys., Inc.*, 58 Comp. Gen. 415 (B-192574), 79-1 CPD ¶ 264. In an earlier decision, the Comptroller General indicated that exclusion of a small business during a competitive range determination might be subject to the COC procedure if the exclusion of the small business was tantamount to a determination of nonresponsibility, 52 Comp. Gen. 47 (B-174012) (1972).

If an agency is evaluating offers on a go/no go basis, and the solicitation includes a criterion that is traditionally a responsibility-type factor, then the matter must be referred to the SBA, *Tri-Servs., Inc.*, Comp. Gen. Dec. B-256196.4, 94-2 CPD ¶ 121. The Comptroller General explained this rule in *Federal Support Corp.*, 71 Comp. Gen. 152 (B-245573), 92-1 CPD ¶ 81, stating:

> While traditional responsibility factors may be used as technical evaluation criteria in a negotiated procurement, *see, e.g.*, *CORVAC, Inc.*, B-244766, Nov. 13, 1991, 91-2 CPD ¶ 454; and 87-1 CPD ¶ 292, the factors may be used only if circumstances warrant a comparative evaluation of those areas.

> *Flight Int'l Group, Inc.*, 69 Comp. Gen. 741 (1990), 90-2 CPD ¶ 257; *Sanford and Sons Co.*, 67 Comp. Gen. 612 (1988), 88-2 CPD ¶ 266. Otherwise, an agency effectively would be determining the responsibility of an offeror under the guise of making a technical evaluation of proposals. Under the Small Business Act, agencies may not find that a small business is nonresponsible without referring the matter to the SBA, which has the ultimate authority to determine the responsibility of small business concerns. See *Cleqq Indus., Inc.*, B-242204.3, Aug 14, 1991, 70 Comp. Gen. 679, 91-2 CPD ¶ 145; 52 Comp. Gen. 47 (1972); *Antenna Prods. Corp.*, B-227116.2, Mar. 23, 1988, 88-1 CPD ¶ 297.
>
> Here, the Air Force did not use the responsibility-related technical evaluation criterion "corporate experience" for the purpose of making a comparative evaluation of proposals received; rather, it determined technical acceptability solely on a "go-no go" basis, and the record shows that FSC's proposal was found technically unacceptable and incapable of being made acceptable solely because of the firm's purported lack of 3 years of corporate experience in the area of operating civil engineering supply stores. Thus, regardless of how the corporate experience criterion was characterized in the RFP or the evaluation, the determination that FSC was technically unacceptable was, in effect, a determination by the contracting officer that FSC was not a responsible contractor and the rejection of FSC's proposal without a referral to SBA for complete consideration under the COC procedures was improper.

SBA issuance of a COC was properly reversed because the bidder lacked the personnel, space, and equipment needed to produce marine propulsion systems; the overwhelming portion of the assembly work was subcontracted; and the bidder's leases were not binding within the meaning of Walsh-Healey regulations, *Ulstein Maritime, Ltd. v. United States*, 646 F. Supp. 720 (D.C. R.I. 1986). The court concluded that no COC should have been issued because both the Navy and the SBA failed to make a sincere inquiry into whether the bidder was capable of complying with the contract specifications.

C. Business Preferences

It is federal policy that a "fair proportion" of Government contracts and subcontracts be placed with small businesses, 15 U.S.C. § 631(a). See also 41 U.S.C. § 252(b), and 50 U.S.C. App. § 468(a). In order to assure that small businesses receive a "fair proportion" of federal procurements, it has been recognized that small businesses must receive more smaller dollar contracts than they would obtain in full and open competition with large businesses since major systems contracts require greater funds and capability than small businesses possess. In seeking comment on a regulation dealing with small businesses, the Office of Federal Procurement Policy (OFPP) has stated at 49 Fed. Reg. 40135 (1984) that:

> The bulk of Federal expenditures are for major systems which, at the prime contract level, are unavailable to small business. Therefore, ensuring that small business receives a fair proportion of the total Government contracts practically dictates that a disproportionate share must be awarded to small business outside of the major systems.

A court of appeals has stated that Congress has sought to protect small business from unlimited competition, and that the term "fair proportion" of federal contracts is to be determined on the basis of total awards, not awards within a particular industry, *J.H. Rutter Rex Mfg. Co. v. United States*, 706 F.2d 702 (5th Cir.), *cert. denied*, 464 U.S. 1008 (1983).

Advocates of small business interests have periodically urged Congress to establish by statute the percentage of contract awards that would constitute a "fair proportion." Congress has made the President responsible for establishing annual Government-wide goals for participation by small business concerns. These goals may not fall below the congressionally mandated minimums of 20 percent of the total value of all prime contract awards for small businesses, and 5 percent of the total value of all prime contract and subcontract awards for both small businesses owned and controlled by socially and economically disadvantaged individuals and small business concerns owned and controlled by women, 15 U.S.C. § 644(g)(1). In addition, each agency must have an annual goal that presents the maximum practicable opportunity for small business concerns to participate in agency procurements. The goals are to be set jointly by the head of the procuring agency and the SBA. If the procuring agency and SBA disagree, the Administrator of OFPP is empowered to resolve the dispute, 15 U.S.C. § 644(g)(2).

After each fiscal year, the procuring agency must inform the SBA of the extent to which the goals have been met; and the SBA must forward the information, along with any SBA comments, to the President who, in turn, includes the information in the annual report to Congress on the state of small business, 15 U.S.C. § 644(h).

1. Set Asides

One form of preference given to small businesses in the award of federal contracts is through "set-asides," a term applied to the reservation of contracts for award only to a designated group. Congress has authorized federal agencies to restrict entire procurements ("total set-asides") or portions of procurements ("partial set-asides") for award to small businesses, 15 U.S.C. § 644.

The Federal Acquisition Streamlining Act of 1994 (FASA), P.L. 103-355, § 7101, eliminated those sections of the Small Business Act that established the priority for award of partial and total set-asides. Contracting officers are required to set aside individual acquisitions or classes of acquisitions in order to assure that a fair proportion of Government contracts in each four-digit SIC category is placed with small business concerns. A contract may not be awarded under a small business set-aside if the cost of that contract exceeds a fair market price (15 U.S.C. § 644(a)) as determined by the price analysis techniques set forth in FAR 15.404-1, FAR 19.202-6(a).

a. Total Set-Asides

Certain purchases from domestic sources are subject to being "set aside" for performance solely by small business concerns. Congress has mandated that each contract that has an anticipated value greater than $2,500 but not greater than $100,000 awarded for goods and services must be reserved exclusively for small businesses unless the contracting officer determines there is not a reasonable expectation of obtaining offers from two or more responsible small business concerns that are competitive, FAR 19.502-2.

Procurements valued at over $100,000 must be totally set aside for performance by small businesses if there is a reasonable expectation that offers will be made by at least two responsible small businesses, offering the products of different small business concerns, and award will be made at "fair market prices," FAR 19.502-2(b). Such a price need not be as low as the price obtainable in full and open competition, *Society Brand, Inc.*, 55 Comp. Gen. 475 (B-183963), 75-2 CPD ¶ 327. The Comptroller General has ruled that receipt of only one reasonable bid is not a valid basis to challenge a set-aside because there was a reasonable expectation of at least two reasonable bids, *NJCT Corp.*, Comp. Gen. Dec. B-219455, 85-2 CPD

¶ 70. In making this determination, the past acquisition history of the item or items being procured, while important, is not the only factor to be considered. For example, in making research and development (R&D) set-asides, there must also be a reasonable expectation of obtaining from small businesses the best scientific and technical sources consistent with the requirements of the acquisition, FAR 19.502-2(b).

Contracting officers have broad discretion in determining whether particular procurements should be set aside for small businesses or whether set-asides that have been established should be withdrawn, *Louisiana-Pacific Corp. v. Block*, 694 F.2d 1205 (9th Cir. 1982); *Kinnett Dairies, Inc. v. Farrow*, 580 F.2d 1260 (5th Cir. 1978); *McGhee Constr., Inc.*, B-249235, 92-2 CPD ¶ 318; *FACE Assocs., Inc.*, 63 Comp. Gen. 86 (B-211877), 83-2 CPD ¶ 643; *Fermont Div., Dynamics Corp. of Am.*, 59 Comp. Gen. 533 (B-195431), 80-1 CPD ¶ 438. In *Peterson Builders, Inc.*, Comp. Gen. Dec. B-251695, 93-1 CPD ¶ 342, the Comptroller General found that an agency's determination not to set aside a procurement was reasonable where it involved the development of a craft that had never been attempted by the shipbuilding industry. The Comptroller General stated that the agency could not reasonably expect to receive the best mix of cost, performance, and schedules from the small business shipbuilding community. See also *CardioMetrix*, Comp. Gen. Dec. B-261327, 95-2 CPD ¶ 96, where the Comptroller General found that an agency reasonably concluded that, based on the prior procurement history for the solicited services, it could not reasonably expect to receive at least two offers from small business concerns.

The Comptroller General will sustain a protest if it determines that an agency's decision not to set aside is unreasonable. In *Thermal Solutions, Inc.*, Comp. Gen. Dec. B-259501, 95-1 CPD ¶ 178, the Comptroller General found that an agency's decision not to set aside a procurement for small disadvantaged business (SDB) was unreasonable. The Comptroller General stated that the agency received expressions of interest from five undisputed SDBs. The decision not to set aside the procurement was based on prior SDB set-aside procurements for dissimilar work, and prior procurements for similar work that were not set aside for SDBs. The Comptroller General stated that SDBs often cannot effectively compete with non-SDB firms, and thus may not bid on contracts that they are otherwise capable of performing. See also *Kato Corp.*, 69 Comp. Gen. 374 (B-237965), 90-1 CPD ¶ 354 (agency decision not to set aside was unreasonable because it made no effort to ascertain SDB interest and capabilities, and the agency reasonably should have expected offers from at least two responsible SDBs); *Bollinger Mach. Shop & Shipyard, Inc.*, Comp. Gen. Dec. B-258563, 95-1 CPD ¶ 56 (protest of failure to set procurement aside for small businesses was sustained because agency expected bids from at least two small businesses and did not have a reasonable basis for concluding that award at a fair market price could not be expected); *ACCU-Lab Med. Testing*, Comp. Gen. Dec. B-270259, 96-1 CPD ¶ 106 (agency improperly withdrew set-aside by relying on the prior procurement history instead of investigating the numerous small business responses to the CBD announcement and performing a current market study). However, the Comptroller General may object to a set-aside when the evidence strongly indicates that only one small business is likely to submit an offer, *DISA Elecs.*, 62 Comp. Gen. 271 (B-206798), 83-1 CPD ¶ 306.

b. Partial Set-Asides

An agency may determine that small businesses cannot furnish the entire quantity that is needed but may be able to supply a portion. FAR 19.502-3 provides that a partial set-aside is appropriate when:

> (1) A total set-aside is not appropriate (see 19.502-2);
>
> (2) The requirement is severable into two or more economic production runs or reasonable lots;
>
> (3) One or more small business concerns are expected to have the technical competence and productive capacity to satisfy the set-aside portion of the requirement at a fair market price;
>
> (4) The acquisition is not subject to simplified acquisition procedures; and
>
> (5) A partial set-aside shall not be made if there is a reasonable expectation that only two concerns (one large and one small) with capability will respond with offers unless authorized by the head of a contracting activity on a case-by-case basis. Similarly, a class of acquisitions, not including construction, may be partially set aside. Under certain specified conditions, partial set-asides may be used in conjunction with multiyear contracting procedures.

A "partial set-aside" reserves for award to small businesses only a portion — called the "set-aside" portion — of the quantity being procured. Any firm, regardless of size, is eligible for award of the balance — the non-set-aside portion. Partial small business set-asides may be conducted using sealed bids, competitive proposals, or procedures for acquisition of commercial items, FAR 19.502-4(a).

Both small and large offerors may submit offers on the non-set-aside portion, which is awarded first, following normal contracting procedures, FAR 19.502-3(c)(1). The set-aside portion is then awarded through negotiation with small business offerors that submitted responsive offers on the non-set-aside portion. The priority in which small business offerors will be asked to negotiate on the set-aside portion is determined by the terms of the solicitation, FAR 19.502-3(c)(2)(i). Under the standard solicitation provision in FAR 52.219-7, negotiations are conducted first with the small business concern that submitted the lowest responsive offer on the non-set-aside portion. If the negotiations are not successful or if only part of the set-aside portion is awarded to that concern, negotiations are conducted with the concern that submitted the second low responsive offer. This process continues until a contract (or contracts) are awarded for the entire set-aside portion.

The set-aside portion is awarded at the highest unit price(s) on which the non-set-aside portion was awarded, adjusted to reflect transportation and similar factors. For example, assume that an agency needs 1 million units and believes that small businesses may be able to supply at least 400,000 units but not the entire requirement, and that 100,000 units is a reasonable production run. The agency should use a small business partial set-aside, with 600,000 units as the non-set-aside portion and 400,000 units reserved for award to small businesses. As stated above, both large and small offerors may bid on the non-set-aside portion. Assume the following simplified results of bidding:

Offeror	Size	Price	No. of Units
A	Large	$1.00	400,000 max.
B	Large	1.03	unlimited
C	Large	1.05	unlimited
D	Small	1.06	unlimited

E	Large	1.08	unlimited
F	Small	1.09	unlimited
G	Small	1.11	500,000 max.

Assume further that all offers are responsive, that all offerors are responsible, and that all of the small business concerns are either all in labor-surplus areas or not in labor-surplus areas. The non-set-aside portion would be awarded as follows:

A	Large	400,000 at $1.00 each
B	Large	200,000 at $1.03 each

The agency should then ask D, whose offer was the lowest small-business offer on the non-set-aside portion, whether it is willing to accept award for all or any portion of the 400,000 set-aside units at $1.03, the maximum price paid on the non-set-aside units. If D will accept award at $1.03 each, award should be made to it. If D will not take all 400,000 units, any remaining units should be offered to F, and then, if necessary, to G, at $1.03 per unit. If any of the 400,000 set-aside units cannot be awarded through this procedure, they may only be awarded through negotiation or sealed bidding in an entirely new procurement.

c. *Small Business Innovation Research Set-Asides*

Congressional hearings have produced evidence that small businesses are the nation's most efficient innovators, but that only a small proportion of federal R&D funds go to them, S. Rep. No. 97-194, 97th Cong., 1st Sess. (1984). As a result, Congress passed the Small Business Innovation Development Act, P.L. 97-219 (1982). Under that Act, federal agencies with budgets over certain amounts for outside R&D must direct specified percentages of such funds to small businesses, 15 U.S.C. § 638(f). The Small Business Innovation Development Act of 1992, Title I of P.L. 102-564, reauthorized the program through the year 2000. See Chapter 7 for a discussion of the procedures for such procurements.

2. Subcontracting to Small Businesses

The Government recognizes that many of its acquisitions require resources that are beyond the capability of any small business to serve as the prime contractor. However, small businesses may be able to participate as subcontractors. There are mechanisms designed to increase awards of subcontracts to small businesses.

Under procedures established in 1978 by P.L. 95-507, most federal contracts that exceed the simplified acquisition threshold ($100,000) must contain a clause stating that it is federal policy that small businesses have the "maximum practicable opportunity to participate in the performance of" federal contracts, 15 U.S.C. § 637(d)(1). Under the clause in FAR 52.219-8 the contractor agrees "to carry out this policy in the awarding of subcontracts to the fullest extent consistent with efficient contract performance," and the contractor also agrees to cooperate with the contracting agency and the SBA in studies to determine the extent of compliance with the statute.

P.L. 95-507 imposes far more extensive requirements for contracts of $500,000 or more ($1 million or more for contracts for construction of a public facility) awarded to any entity other than a small business, 15 U.S.C. § 637(d)(4). See FAR 19.702. The clause in FAR 52.219-9 requires that the contractor must provide a subcontracting plan that, as approved by the contracting officer, is incorporated into the contract. Paragraph (i) of the clause provides that failure to comply with the plan in good faith is a material breach. See also 15 U.S.C. § 637(d)(8). FAR 19.704(a) provides that each such plan must include:

> (1) Separate percentage goals for using small business concerns, small disadvantaged business concerns and women-owned small business concerns as subcontractors;
>
> (2) The name of an individual employed by the offeror who will administer the offeror's subcontracting program, and a description of the duties of the individual;
>
> (3) A description of the efforts the offeror will make to ensure that small business concerns, small disadvantaged business concerns and women-owned small business concerns will have an equitable opportunity to compete for subcontracts;

(4) Assurances that the offeror will include the clause at 52.219-8, Utilization of Small, Small Disadvantaged and Women-Owned Small Business Concerns (see 19.708(b)), in all subcontracts that offer further subcontracting opportunities, and that the offeror will require all subcontractors (except small business concerns) that receive subcontracts in excess of $500,000 ($1,000,000 for construction) to adopt a plan similar to the plan required by the clause at 52.219-9, Small, Small Disadvantaged and Women-Owned Small Business Subcontracting Plan (see 19.708(c));

(5) Assurances that the offeror will (i) cooperate in any studies or surveys as may be required, (ii) submit periodic reports in order to allow the Government to determine the extent of compliance by the offeror with the subcontracting plan, and (iii) submit Standard Form (SF) 294, Subcontracting Report for Individual Contracts, and SF 295, Summary Subcontract Report, in accordance with the instructions on the forms;

(6) A recitation of the types of records the offeror will maintain to demonstrate procedures adopted to comply with the requirements and goals in the plan, including establishing source lists; and a description of the offeror's efforts to locate small, small disadvantaged and women-owned small business concerns and to award subcontracts to them.

In negotiated procurements, the successful offeror must submit a proposed plan and negotiate its terms with the contracting officer, and "[i]f the apparently successful offeror fails to negotiate a subcontracting plan acceptable to the contracting officer within the time limit prescribed by the contracting officer, the offeror will be ineligible for award," FAR 19.702(a)(1). Such negotiation is required to ensure that the plan included in the contract provides "the maximum practicable opportunity" for small businesses to participate in the performance of the contract. See *Columbia Research Corp.*, 61 Comp. Gen. 194 (B-202762), 82-1 CPD ¶ 8, where the Comptroller General approved a plan stating "zero percent of the estimated costs would be subcontracted to small business." The Comptroller General noted that the statute required only the offeror's best efforts in subcontracting to small business.

In sealed bid procurements, the firm selected for award must submit its plan regarding subcontract awards to small businesses, FAR 19.702(a)(2), but the plan is not subject to negotiation because such negotiation would be inconsistent with sealed bidding. Subcontracting plans required by P.L. 95-507 are a matter of responsibility, not responsiveness, and thus may be submitted after bids are received and opened, *Devcon Sys. Corp.*, 59 Comp.

Gen. 614 (B-197935), 80-2 CPD ¶ 46; *CH2M Hill, Ltd.*, Comp. Gen. Dec. B-259511, 95-1 CPD ¶ 203.

Contractors may establish, for either plants or divisions, a master subcontracting plan that, after approval by the contracting officer, can be incorporated into individual contracts, eliminating the need for separate plans for each individual contract, FAR 19.704(b).

Under P.L. 95-507, federal agencies have authority to include in negotiated contracts an incentive clause under which the contractor may increase its profit by a percentage based upon the extent to which the actual awards to small businesses exceed the percentage negotiated and included in the clause, 15 U.S.C. § 637(d); FAR 19.708(c)(1). FAR 52.219-10 provides a clause for this purpose.

3. *Equal Low Bids*

FAR 14.408-6 provides that when two or more low bids are equal in all respects, agencies must "break the tie" by awarding contracts in the following order of priority:

(1) Small business concerns that are also labor surplus area concerns;

(2) Other small business concerns;

(3) Other business concerns.

When an award is to be made using this order of priority, a clause should be included in the contract requiring that the contract be performed in accordance with the circumstances justifying the priority used to break the tie, FAR 14.408-6(c).

II. SMALL DISADVANTAGED BUSINESSES

Starting in the late 1960s, the executive branch of the Government began several programs to increase awards of federal contracts to "minority-owned" businesses. In 1978, most of those programs were revised and expanded by amendments to the Small Business Act, P.L. 95-507. Those amendments used the expression "small businesses owned and controlled by socially and economically disadvantaged persons" to describe the businesses aided by such programs. The shortened expression, "small disadvantaged businesses" (SDBs), and the older term, "minority-owned businesses" are used interchangeably.

A 1995 Supreme Court decision has cast a cloud over the entire SDB program. In *Adarand Constructors, Inc. v. Pena*, 515 U.S. 200 (1995), the Supreme Court significantly limited the Federal Government's authority to implement programs that favor racial minorities. In this decision, the Supreme Court held that federal affirmative action programs that use racial classifications are subject to a high level of judicial scrutiny, must serve a compelling Government interest, and must be narrowly tailored to further that interest. The impact of *Adarand* on Government contracting programs designed to assist SDBs has not yet been fully determined. Reacting to *Adarand*, the President issued a directive to federal agencies ordering officials to review existing affirmative action programs and to eliminate or reform any program that creates a quota, creates preferences for unqualified individuals, creates reverse discrimination, or continues even after its equal opportunity purposes have been achieved, Memorandum for Heads of Executive Departments and Agencies, Evaluation of Affirmative Action Programs 1, July 19, 1995.

The Comptroller General has dismissed bid protest challenges to the constitutionality of the DOD's SDB set-aside program based on *Adarand*, citing a lack of clear judicial precedent, *Elrich Contracting Inc.*, Comp. Gen. Dec. B-262015, 95-2 CPD ¶ 71. Noting that *Adarand* set forth the standard to be applied by the federal courts in determining the constitutionality of such programs but did not actually decide whether the challenged program was unconstitutional, the Comptroller General stated that "[t]here must be clear judicial precedent before we will consider a protest based on the asserted unconstitutionality of the procuring agency's actions."

As a result of the *Adarand* decision, in October 1995, the DOD issued a directive suspending the Section 1207 set-aside program. The directive provided that until further notice, contracting officers should not set aside acquisitions for SDBs. It further ordered that contracting officers should amend already issued solicitations to remove set-asides that were based on the suspended sections of the DFARS "where the amendment of the solicitation will not unduly delay a procurement." The Comptroller General has concluded that deletion of an SDB preference provision from an Air Force RFP in accordance with the DOD's directive was proper even though proposals had already been received and evaluated, *PI Constr. Corp.*, Comp. Gen. Dec. B-270576.2, 95-2 CPD ¶ 270.

A. Direct Award by Procuring Agencies

An early step in assisting SDBs to obtain federal contracts was the establishment of "minority business enterprise programs." At least in part because of legal questions about whether preferences in award of contracts could be created without statutory authority, these programs did not use set-aside procedures as the sole means of directing contracts to minority-owned businesses. See *Aurora Assocs., Inc.*, Comp. Gen. Dec. B-215565, 85-1 CPD ¶ 470. Such programs sought to reduce what were perceived as possible barriers to competition by minority-owned businesses for contracts awarded through normal competitive procedures. Among the steps included in minority business enterprise programs were efforts (i) to seek out minority-owned concerns and to help place them on agency bidders lists; (ii) to solicit offers whenever possible from such concerns; and (iii) to set bidding times, specifications, quantities, and delivery schedules to facilitate competition by minority-owned concerns. The FAR contains no guidance on such efforts.

B. "8(a) Program

The primary program designed to assist minority-owned businesses is commonly known as the "8(a)" program. The program takes its name from Section 8(a) of the Small Business Act. Section 8(a) authorizes the SBA to enter into contracts with other federal agencies and to perform such contracts by subcontracting to small businesses, 15 U.S.C. § 637(a). However, once a solicitation is issued and publicized as a small business set-aside, the SBA cannot, absent extraordinary circumstances, accept the procurement into the 8(a) program, *John Blood*, Comp. Gen. Dec. B-261477, 95-2 CPD ¶ 147. Beginning in the late 1960s, the SBA employed the 8(a) procedure to increase the amount of federal contract work performed by minority-owned businesses by taking contracts from procuring agencies and awarding subcontracts to minority-owned businesses. The SBA invested considerable resources in the 8(a) program, and it grew quickly. By the late 1970s, contracts valued at hundreds of millions of dollars were being awarded annually under the 8(a) program.

The 8(a) program has been the subject of constant criticism. Nondisadvantaged small businesses complained that many 8(a) contracts had formerly been reserved for small businesses in general and that the 8(a) program discriminated in favor of minority-owned small businesses. The program was also challenged as unconstitutional because of racial or ethnic discrimination. The courts have upheld the program against such charges, e.g., *Ray Baillie Trash Hauling, Inc. v. Kleppe*, 477 F.2d 696 (5th Cir. 1973), *cert. denied*, 415 U.S. 914 (1974). In one instance, nonminority competing contractors were granted declaratory relief because a total set-aside of all 1981 Corps of Engineers small business contracts in the Mississippi market was found to be an overly broad exercise of statutory power and, therefore, discriminatory to non-SDBs in violation of 42 U.S.C. § 2000d, *Fordice Constr. Co. v. Marsh*, 773 F. Supp. 867 (S.D. Miss. 1990).

In 1988, Congress enacted the Business Opportunity Development Reform Act, P.L. 100-656, which sought to curb abuses in the 8(a) program and make SDBs more competitive. The Act included reforms of the program which (1) require competition among 8(a) firms for manufacturing contracts exceeding $5 million and for service contracts and nonmanufacturing contracts exceeding $3 million, (2) require the SBA to establish business activity targets for businesses that have been in the program for five years, (3) authorize contracting officers to assess "liquidated damages" against prime contractors that fail to meet SDB subcontracting goals, and (4) prohibit SBA employees from holding stock in 8(a) firms for two years after leaving the SBA.

1. Participants

15 U.S.C. § 637(a)(4) provides:

> For purposes of this section, the term "socially and economically disadvantaged small business concern" means any small business concern which meets the requirements of subparagraph (B) and —
>
> (i) which is at least 51 per centum unconditionally owned by —
>
> (I) one or more socially and economically disadvantaged individuals,
>
> (II) an economically disadvantaged Indian tribe (or a wholly owned business entity of such tribe), or

(III) an economically disadvantaged Native Hawaiian organization, or

(ii) in the case of any publicly owned business at least 51 per centum of the stock of which is unconditionally owned by —

(I) one or more socially and economically disadvantaged individuals,

(II) an economically disadvantaged Indian tribe (or a wholly owned business entity of such tribe), or

(III) an economically disadvantaged Native Hawaiian organization.

(B) A small business concern meets the requirements of this subparagraph if the management and daily business operations of such small business concern are controlled by one or more —

(i) socially and economically disadvantaged individuals described in subparagraph (A)(i)(I) or subparagraph (A)(ii)(I),

(ii) members of an economically disadvantaged Indian tribe described in subparagraph (A)(i)(II) or subparagraph (A)(ii)(II), or

(iii) Native Hawaiian organizations described in subparagraph (A)(i)(III) or subparagraph (A)(ii)(III).

The statute also contains separate definitions of "socially disadvantaged" and "economically disadvantaged" individuals, 15 U.S.C. § 637(a)(5) and (6). Participation requires that the individuals meet both of these tests, *Autek Sys Corp.*, 835 F. Supp. 13 (D.D.C. 1993), *aff'd*, 43 F.3d 712 (D.C. Cir. 1994).

As part of P.L. 95-507, Congress sought in 1978 to strengthen the 8(a) program by prescribing standards of eligibility for 8(a) contracts and requiring that determinations about such eligibility be the responsibility of a designated high official within SBA. Further, Congress required that before any business is admitted to the 8(a) program, the SBA must find that the firm has "reasonable prospects for success in competing in the private sector," 15 U.S.C. § 637(a)(7). The SBA is responsible for determining which of these firms are eligible for the 8(a) program. The SBA's regulations on this point are in 13 C.F.R. Part 124. The SBA has reasonable discretion to deny participation in the 8(a) program to clearly unqualified firms as long as applications receive thorough and careful review. See *Neuma Corp. v. Abdnor*, 713 F. Supp. 1 (D.D.C. 1989). The SBA also has a "Standard Operating Procedure," designated 80-05 2 (1990), on the 8(a) program. In order to qualify for this program, a contractor must certify at the time it submits its initial offer, including price, that it is a small business for purpose of that particular contract. Size status is determined in accordance with 13 C.F.R. Part 121.

SBA responsibility determinations for SDBs seeking contracts under the 8(a) program are covered exclusively by 15 U.S.C. § 637(a)(16) and do not involve the COC procedures required by § 637(b)(7). In *DAE Corp. v. Small Bus. Admin.*, 958 F.2d 436 (D.C. App. 1992), the court distinguished § 637(a) and § 637(b), stating at 439:

> Section 637(b)(7) no doubt does mean what it plainly says — but only where it applies. It is part of the § 8(b) program, and any small business proceeding under § 8(b) is entitled to its protections and its disadvantages. As the Comptroller General has affirmed, § 637(b)(7) is designed to help small businesses overcome the hesitance a procuring agency may have in awarding an ordinary contract to a small business. See *Custom Research, Inc.*, Comp. Gen. Dec. B-238976.2, 90-1 Comp. Gen. Dec. ¶ 567 (1990) (explaining that the COC process "is provided by law to protect small businesses from arbitrary nonresponsibility determinations made by procurement agencies.").
>
> The disadvantaged small business seeking a sole source contract under § 8(a), such as DAE, faces a vastly different situation. There, the procuring agency has asked the SBA to obtain the services of a specified disadvantaged small business — no passport is necessary because the contractor has already been admitted. Under § 637(a)(16), the SBA, not the procuring agency's contracting officer, assesses the responsibility of the prospective contractor. See 13 C.F.R. §§ 124.308 & 124.313. Thus, the § 637(a)(16) procedures are triggered as a matter of course whenever a disadvantaged small business is being considered for a § 8(a) contract, and not, as under the COC program, when a procuring agency contracting officer questions the responsibility of a small business. In this way, the SBA's role in a § 8(a) contract is analogous to an agency contracting officer's duty to make a responsibility determination for prospective contractors bidding to perform government work. See 48 C.F.R. Subpart 9.1 (providing policy and guidance to contracting officers who must assess whether a prospective contractor meets the responsibility standards).

Firms participating in the 8(a) program must have an approved business plan, 15 U.S.C. § 636(j)(10)(D). Enacted in 1988, P.L. 100-656 established the maximum period of time a disadvantaged firm could remain in the program as nine years, and divided the time into two stages: a "developmental" stage and a "transitional" stage, 13 C.F.R. § 124.303. For firms approved for 8(a) participation after November 15, 1988, the developmental stage is four years and the transitional stage is five years. The two stages are described in 13 C.F.R. § 124.303(a) as follows:

> The developmental stage is designed to assist participants to overcome their economic disadvantage by providing such assistance as may be necessary and appropriate to enable them to access relevant markets and strengthen their financial and managerial skills. The transitional stage of program participation follows the developmental stage and is designed to assist Participants to overcome, insofar as practicable, the remaining elements of economic disadvantage and to prepare Participants for leaving the 8(a) program.

The SBA regulations limiting the period that firms can participate in the 8(a) program were upheld in *Minority Bus. Legal Defense & Educ. Funds, Inc. v. Small Bus. Admin.*, 557 F. Supp. 37 (D.D.C. 1982). A court did not abuse its discretion by refusing to extend an 8(a) contractor's eligibility beyond nine years, even though the SBA had acted unlawfully in preventing the contractor from receiving full 8(a) benefits, *Woerner v. United States*, 934 F.2d 1277 (App. D.C. 1991).

The Comptroller General will not review SBA decisions on a firm's eligibility for the 8(a) program, unless there are strong allegations of fraud, bad faith, or the SBA's violation of its own regulations, *Forway Indus.*, Comp. Gen. Dec. B-217046, 84-2 CPD ¶ 573. One court has also ruled that egregious procedural violations by SBA of its own regulations in terminating a firm's participation in the 8(a) program justify court review, *Oklahoma Aerotronics, Inc. v. United States*, 661 F.2d 976 (D.C. Cir. 1981).

2. *Assistance*

The SBA assists SDBs both in the making and the performance of contracts. The SBA participates with the procuring agencies to identify potential 8(a) contracts, to match the needs of 8(a) firms as effectively as practicable with the available contracts, and to promote continuity of awards, 15 U.S.C. § 636(j). Further assistance is provided by establishing the fair market price of the work to be performed by the 8(a) contractor in accordance with FAR 19.807.

The Business Opportunity Development Act of 1988, P.L. 100-656, abolished the concept of assisting disadvantaged firms through providing "business development expense" (an amount added to contract prices to compensate for the firm's disadvantages). Assistance is now provided directly to the firm outside of specific contracts. The statute specifies a number of specific types of assistance, including: (1) loans and loan guarantees, (2) two exemptions from the "manufacturer or regular dealer" requirements of the Walsh-Healey Act, (3) five exemptions from the bond requirements of the Miller Act, (4) training or upgrading employees with SBA funds, (5) transfer of technology or surplus Government property to the firm, (6) training conducted by the SBA to assist 8(a) concerns in the development of business principles and strategies, and (7) transitional management business planning training and technical assistance, 15 U.S.C. § 636(j)(13).

3. *Contractual Relationships*

Although the 8(a) arrangement is technically a contract between the procuring agency and the SBA, and a subcontract between the SBA and the disadvantaged small business, the procuring agency and the disadvantaged small business normally deal directly with each other. With respect to the contract with the procuring agency, 15 U.S.C. § 637(a)(3)(A) provides that, when practicable, the concern shall "participate in any negotiation of the terms and conditions of such contract."

After award, the relationships under an 8(a) contract are principally between the 8(a) firm and the procuring agency; the SBA is no longer directly involved. The SBA does not "insure" performance of its 8(a) subcontractors, *ATC Petroleum, Inc. v, Sanders*, 860 F.2d 1104 (App. D.C. 1988). The subcontract between the 8(a) firm and the SBA contains a clause stating that the SBA has delegated responsibility for administering the subcontract to the procuring agency, which will act for the Government, FAR 52.219-12. In such circumstances, the procuring agency may properly terminate an 8(a) contract for default and the termination need not come from the SBA, *Philadelphia Regent Builders, Inc. v. United States*, 225 Ct. Cl. 234, 634 F.2d 569 (1980).

C. Government Contractor Responsibilities

In passing P.L. 95-507, Congress prescribed certain provisions intended to maximize the award of subcontracts to minority-owned businesses, 15 U.S.C. § 637(d). In 1994, the Federal Acquisition Streamlining Act (FASA), P.L. 103-355, amended the statute to substitute the term "small business concerns owned and controlled by socially and economically disadvantaged individuals" for "small business concerns owned and controlled by socially and economically disadvantaged individuals and small business concerns owned and controlled by women," 15 U.S.C. § 637(d). Most contracts over $2,500 must include a clause requiring the contractor to implement this policy. The statute and the clause in FAR 52.219-8(a) include references to small businesses, small disadvantaged businesses, and small businesses owned and controlled by women:

> It is the policy of the United States that small business concerns, small business concerns owned and controlled by socially and economically disadvantaged individuals, and small business concerns owned and controlled by women, shall have the maximum practicable opportunity to participate in the performance of contracts let by any Federal agency.

Federal contracts for more than $500,000 ($1 million for contracts for construction of public facilities) are subject to requirements under P.L. 95-507 for subcontracting "plans" parallel to those prescribed to aid small, non-minority-owned businesses. The "incentive" provision that may be included in contracts to encourage increases in awards of small business subcontracts may also cover small disadvantaged businesses.

Congress has made a form of the self-certification procedure applicable to subcontracting procedures under P.L. 95-507. That statute, as amended, provides that the contract clause used shall state that "[c]ontractors acting in good faith may rely on written representations by their subcontractors regarding their status as either a small business concern, a small business concern owned and controlled by socially and economically disadvantaged individuals, or a small business concern owned and controlled by women," 15 U.S.C. § 637(d)(3)(E).

D. Proposed Evaluation Preference for Small Disadvantaged Businesses

In order to facilitate attainment of SDB contract goals, the FASA amended the Small Business Act to permit the civilian agencies to restrict competition to SDBs and to provide a 10 percent price evaluation preference when evaluating offers from such firms received as a result of an unrestricted solicitation, P.L. 103-355, § 7101. The evaluation preference was proposed to be used in unrestricted, competitive acquisitions where award is based on price and price-related factors.

The implementation of this program in FAR Part 19 has been postponed pending the Government-wide review of all racial preference programs resulting from the *Adarand Constructors* decision.

III. POLICIES FOR ASSISTING WOMEN-OWNED ENTERPRISES

The FASA amended the Small Business Act to establish a Government-wide goal for participation by women-owned and controlled small business concerns in prime contracts and subcontracts of not less than 5 percent of the total value of all prime contract and subcontract awards for each fiscal year, 15 U.S.C. § 644(g). A small business is owned and controlled by women if 51 percent or more of the business is owned by one or more women, or 51 percent of stock in a publicly traded company is owned by one or more women, and the management and daily business operation of the concern are controlled by one or more women, 15 U.S.C. § 637(d)(3)(D).

IV. DOMESTIC PREFERENCE POLICIES

The Government has a variety of policies favoring the acquisition of articles of domestic origin or acquisition from domestic sources. The major policy is the Buy American Act, but there are numerous additional policies that also favor the use of domestic products or sources.

A. Buy American Act

The Buy American Act establishes a general preference for the acquisition of domestic "articles, materials, and supplies" when they are being acquired for public use in the United States, 41 U.S.C. §§ 10a–d. The Act was passed during the Depression of the 1930s and was designed to save and create jobs for American workers. The central consideration under the Act has consistently been the place of manufacture; the nationality of the contractor is not relevant, *E-Systems, Inc.*, 61 Comp. Gen. 431 (B-206209), 82-1 CPD ¶ 533; *Patterson Pump Co.*, Comp. Gen. Dec. B-200165, 80-2 CPD ¶ 453. The term "acquired for public use" applies to leases as well as purchases, *National Office Equip. Co.*, Comp. Gen. Dec. B-191003, 78-1 CPD ¶ 413.

The Buy American Act has separate provisions governing supply and construction contracts. The rules for determining whether articles, materials, or supplies are foreign or domestic are the same for both types of procurement, the differences being the terminology used and the juncture in the total manufacturing or construction process at which the test is applied. Under supply contracts, the proscriptions of the Act fall on the articles, materials, or supplies delivered to the Government; whereas, under construction contracts, they apply to the articles, materials, and supplies used by the contractor and subcontractors in constructing, altering, or repairing the building or work.

The articles, materials, and supplies covered by the Act are discussed in the FAR using different nomenclature for supply and construction contracts. FAR 25.101 defines an "end product" for purposes of supply contracts, as "those articles, materials and supplies to be acquired for public use under the contract," while FAR 25.201 defines them as "construction materials" for purposes of construction contracts. Items delivered to the construction site simply for the use of the contractor that are not to be incorporated into the building or work, such as construction shacks and trailers, are not construction materials subject to the Buy American Act, *Mico Mobile Sales & Leasing Co.*, 51 Comp. Gen. 538 (B-174851) (1972).

The Buy American Act applies similar distinct requirements to unmanufactured and manufactured articles, materials, or supplies.

1. Unmanufactured Articles

For unmanufactured articles, materials, or supplies acquired by the Government for use in the United States, the Buy American Act requires that they must have been "mined" or "produced" in the United States, unless one of the exceptions discussed below applies, 41 U.S.C. § 10a and § 10b.

2. Manufactured Articles

The Buy American Act requires that manufactured articles, materials, or supplies acquired by the Government for public use in the United States or incorporated into domestic construction projects must have been manufactured in this country "substantially all" (more than 50 percent) from components that have themselves been "mined, produced, or manufactured" within the United States, unless one of the exceptions discussed below is applicable, 41 U.S.C. § 10a and § 10b. Hence, for an end product or construction material to be domestic, it must meet two tests: it must have been manufactured in the United States, and more than 50 percent of its components must have been mined, produced, or manufactured in the United States. In contrast, components must meet only one test — manufacture in the United States. For example, a watch movement that was domestically manufactured (assembled) entirely from foreign-made parts is a domestic component of the watch into which it is incorporated, *Hamilton Watch Co.*, Comp. Gen. Dec. B-179939, 74-1 CPD ¶ 306. Thus, an end product or construction material is of domestic origin only (1) if manufactured domestically and (2) if the costs of the foreign components do not exceed 50 percent of the costs of all the components. A component, however, qualifies as being of domestic origin if it has been manufactured domestically.

The three major issues concerning manufactured products are (a) what constitutes manufacturing, (b) the distinction between end products and construction materials versus components, and (c) the application of the "substantially all" rule.

a. Manufacturing

The meaning of "manufacturing" is important because it will determine whether an end product, construction material, or component is domestic. The term "manufacture" has been interpreted broadly to include the assembly of parts, *Hamilton Watch Co.*, Comp. Gen. Dec. B-179939, 74-1 CPD ¶ 306, but does not include packaging, testing, and evaluation operations, 48 Comp. Gen. 727 (B-166008) (1969). However, the Comptroller General has also held that disassembly and reassembly in the United States of a product that was manufactured outside the United States to a condition almost ready to use before the disassembly do not constitute domestic "manufacture," *Ampex Corp.*, Comp. Gen. Dec. B-203021, 82-1 CPD ¶ 163. Compare *Textron, Inc. v. Adams*, 493 F. Supp. 824 (D.D.C. 1980), where foreign disassembly and domestic reassembly was held to constitute domestic manufacture. In *DynAmerica, Inc.*, Comp. Gen. Dec. B-248237, 92-2 CPD ¶ 210, the Comptroller General held that the packing in Mexico of domestically manufactured ammunition links into feeder sleeve cartons was merely packaging that made the end product easier to use and did not constitute manufacturing. "Processing" of magnetic tape for computer use was held not to constitute manufacturing since it was a service analogous to translation, *Blodgett Keypunching Co.*, 54 Comp. Gen. 18 (B-153751), 76-2 CPD ¶ 331. The Comptroller General has drawn some fine distinctions in this area resulting in considerable confusion. Compare 45 Comp. Gen. 658 (B-158869) (1966) with 48 Comp. Gen. 727 (B-166008) (1969), both involving sequential manufacturing processes, from which the Comptroller General drew different conclusions. The basic test is whether the operations performed on the foreign item create a basically new material or result in a fundamental change in the item. See *A. Hirsh, Inc.*, Comp. Gen. Dec. B-237466, 90-1 CPD ¶ 247, where the Comptroller General ruled that domestic processing of foreign-bought horsehair — including sterilization, sorting, cutting, inspecting, blending with oil, wrapping, and trimming — was not "manufacturing," because after all the processing, the horsehair was still horsehair.

Construction cases are equally fact-sensitive. For example, where contract specifications required the construction of a water pump unit, and the complete, operable unit was delivered to the construction site, the entire unit, rather than simply its motor, was considered to be the construction material, 46 Comp. Gen. 813 (B-161061) (1967). In contrast, where circuit breakers and switchgear were brought to the site separately and installed in a building as a unit, they were each held to be construction material, *George Hyman Constr. Co.*, ASBCA 13777, 69-2 BCA ¶ 7830.

Once it is determined that an end product, construction material, or component has been "manufactured," the actual place the "manufacturing" occurred — not the relative costs of manufacturing — will control the Buy

American determination. Thus, if an end product is assembled (manufactured) outside of the United States from domestic components, it is not a domestic product even though substantially all of the costs of the product are incurred domestically, 52 Comp. Gen. 13 (B-175526) (1972). In this case, the Comptroller General reasoned that manufacture had occurred outside of the United States, even though only 3 percent of the costs were incurred for foreign work. An interesting controversy over the application of this rule occurred where a company performed final assembly and testing in the United States after 85 to 90 percent of the manufacture was accomplished in Mexico using American components, *Cincinnati Elecs. Corp.*, 55 Comp. Gen. 1479 (B-185842), 76-2 CPD ¶ 286. The Comptroller General denied a protest against this procedure because this issue was under consideration at a policy level in the agency. However, the regulations are still silent on whether early stages of the final assembly process can be performed outside of the United States within the requirement for domestic manufacture.

The Comptroller General has noted that the meaning of "manufacture" is difficult to ascertain and has recommended that the procurement regulations be amended to provide a precise definition, *Davis Walker Corp.*, Comp. Gen. Dec. B-184672, 76-2 CPD ¶ 182. The Comptroller General suggested that a procuring agency formulate a general definition of "manufacture." The agency replied that such a rigid approach to a fluid concept was undesirable, 654 FCR A-5 (1976). The FAR does not provide a general definition of "manufacture" for Buy American purposes, FAR 25.101.

b. *End Products and Construction Materials versus Components*

FAR 25.101 contains the following definitions for supply contracts:

> "End product," as used in this subpart, means those articles, materials, and supplies to be acquired for public use under the contract.
>
> "Components," as used in this subpart, means those articles, materials, and supplies incorporated directly into the end products.

FAR 25.201 contains the following definitions for construction contracts:

> "Construction materials," as used in this subpart, means an article, material, or supply brought to the construction site for incorporation into the building or work.
>
> "Components," as used in this subpart, means those articles, materials, and supplies incorporated directly into construction materials.

These definitions provide little guidance regarding the distinctions between supply and construction contracts. Yet this is a major issue, since the origin of parts assembled into components need not be domestic, 45 Comp. Gen. 658 (B-158869) (1966). In view of the lack of regulatory guidance, the definitions primarily rest on the exercise of procurement judgment, 48 Comp. Gen. 384 (B-165634) (1968).

There have sometimes been conflicting results. In *Bell Helicopter Textron*, 59 Comp. Gen. 158 (B-195268), 79-2 CPD ¶ 431, the Comptroller General ruled that the end product was a helicopter rather than the total work performed on the contract including the helicopter. In *Textron, Inc. v. Adams*, 493 F. Supp. 824 (D.D.C. 1980), the court disagreed, ruling that the contract end product was a helicopter system consisting of five components: a helicopter, system test and evaluation, system engineering/management, data, and integrated logistics support. The court reasoned that deference should be given to the agency's contractual statement of its need for a "system" without regard to the fact that the helicopter constituted the predominant element of the procurement. This decision concludes that an end product may be composed of various discrete products, so long as it is being procured as, and will be used as, a single unit, such as a "tool kit," *Imperial Eastman Corp.*, 53 Comp. Gen. 726 (B-177865), 74-1 CPD ¶ 153, or a modification kit, 47 Comp. Gen. 21 (B-161325) (1967). Occasionally, a solicitation will specify what items will be considered end products for Buy American Act purposes. Compare *Ampex Corp.*, Comp. Gen. Dec. B-203021, 82-1 CPD ¶ 163, where operation and maintenance manuals were held not to be components. This follows the more prevalent Comptroller General view that an end product is the item being manufactured, in the form in which it is required by the Government, as distinguished from such things as packaging and services or tests performed after the item has been manufactured, *Patterson Pump Co.*, Comp. Gen. Dec. B-200165, 80-2 CPD ¶ 453. See also 46 Comp. Gen. 784 (B-160627) (1967), where sulfa tablets, not the bottled sulfa tablets actually delivered, were held to be the end products.

c. *Substantially All Rule*

An end product is considered to have been manufactured "substantially all" from components of domestic origin if the cost of all components mined, manufactured, or produced in the United States is more than 50 percent of the cost of all of its components, FAR 25.101; Exec. Order No. 10582, 19 Fed. Reg. 8723 (1954). In applying the over-50 percent test, the boards and the Comptroller General have addressed two issues: what constitutes a component and what costs are included in the computation.

The term "component" is applied only to those articles, materials, and supplies directly used in the manufacture of the end product. For example, in the procurement of clothing, yarn used in the manufacture of the cloth was not considered a component because it was not directly incorporated into the clothing, 45 Comp. Gen. 658 (B-158869) (1966). See also *Ampex Corp.*, Comp. Gen. Dec. B-203021, 82-1 CPD ¶ 163 (operation and maintenance manuals were merely tools to provide instructions and not components incorporated into the end product).

In *General Kinetics, Inc.*, 70 Comp. Gen. 473 (B-242052.2), 91-1 CPD ¶ 445, the Government was purchasing both "Tempest" (used for secure messages) and "non-Tempest" fax systems. The major component of each system was a commercial fax machine of foreign origin. Each of the fax machines was disassembled in the United States, certain operations were conducted, and the machines were reassembled in the United States. The Comptroller found that the operations conducted on the Tempest fax machine, which included replacement of the programmable memory chips, addition of Tempest-required insulation, and the addition and integration of a protocol converter, were sufficient to make it a domestic component, and the "Tempest" system a domestic end product. However, the operations conducted on the non-Tempest machine, which consisted of disassembly, removal of circuit board and replacement of memory chips, and reassembly, were not sufficient to alter the essential nature of the machine, so that it remained a foreign component. Thus, the non-Tempest system was a foreign end item subject to the Act's evaluation differential.

In applying the substantially-all test, only the cost of components is considered. Domestic component costs are comprised of the purchase price of the component or the full cost of manufacture if the contractor manufactured the component, *Avantek, Inc.*, 50 Comp. Gen. 697 (B-170498) (1973). The total cost of the end product — what it would sell for, minus profit — is irrelevant, since that figure includes cost elements other than components. For example, labor, packaging, testing, and evaluation costs incurred in manufacturing the end product would not be included as part of the costs of the components of the end product. Thus, transportation costs of ready-mixed concrete were not assignable as a cost of the components because the concrete was an identifiable end item at the time it was transported to the job site, *Dick Hollan, Inc.*, ASBCA 21304, 77-1 BCA ¶ 12,540. Similarly, in 53 Comp. Gen. 259 (B-179029) (1973), engineering costs were excluded from the computation because such services were not directly incorporated into the end product.

3. Solicitation and Contract Provisions

The procuring agency is required to include Buy American provisions in each solicitation and contract that may be affected, FAR 25.109 and FAR 25.205. The Buy American Certificate provision in FAR 52.225-1 is included in each solicitation for a supply contract. This provision requires the offeror to certify that each end product, other than those specifically identified in the certificate, is of domestic origin, and that components of unknown origin have been considered to have been mined, produced, or manufactured outside the United States. If the offeror leaves the certificate blank, the offeror will be deemed to be offering only products of domestic origin, *Consolidated Devices, Inc.*, Comp. Gen. Dec. B-214469, 84-1 CPD ¶ 383; *Lanier Business Prods., Inc.*, Comp. Gen. Dec. B-196736, 81-1 CPD ¶ 186. See *Designware, Inc.*, Comp. Gen. Dec. B-221423, 86-1 CPD ¶ 181, where the fact that a listed product was manufactured only in Korea was held irrelevant where the bidder left the certificate blank and the contracting officer did not know that the product was foreign. See, however, *Airpro Equip., Inc.*, 62 Comp. Gen. 154 (B-209612), 83-1 CPD ¶ 105, where the product was treated as foreign when the bidder left the certificate blank but identified the country of manufacture as "USA/England" in the schedule.

The standard Buy American Act contract clauses for supply and construction require that the contractor deliver domestic end products, unless one of the specified exceptions to the Act's provisions is applicable,

FAR 52.225-3 and FAR 52.225-5. Whether an offeror will, in fact, comply with the Buy American Act is viewed by the Comptroller General as a matter of contract administration and not a basis for a bid protest, *Autoclave Eng'rs, Inc.*, Comp. Gen. Dec. B-217212, 84-2 CPD ¶ 668. If the contractor does not comply with the Act, the contract may be terminated for default, *Sunox, Inc.*, ASBCA 30025, 85-2 BCA ¶ 18,077.

4. Exceptions

Congress has recognized that application of the Buy American Act might severely restrict an agency's ability to meet its needs. For example, many specific products are not manufactured, mined, or produced in the United States or, if they are available domestically, their prices might be far higher than the price of equivalent items of foreign origin. Congress has established a number of exceptions to give procuring agencies flexibility.

a. Unreasonable Costs

The head of an agency is authorized to permit procurement of foreign items if the cost of the lowest-priced domestic item is "unreasonable," 41 U.S.C. § 10a and § 10b. The President has established uniform standards for agencies to use in determining when prices of foreign supplies are considered "unreasonable," and those standards have been incorporated into the FAR, Exec. Order No. 10582, 19 Fed. Reg. 8723 (1954); FAR 25.105.

Under these standards, agencies add a percentage to the price, inclusive of duty, of the low acceptable offer of a foreign item and then compare that increased price to the price for an item of domestic origin, FAR 25.105(a). The percentage is 6 percent for large businesses and 12 percent for small businesses, FAR 25.105. If, for example, the low responsive bid offering a foreign item is $100, the 6 percent differential would be $6, and the agency would, solely for evaluation purposes, treat the price of the offeror of a foreign item as $106. If the low responsive offeror of a domestic item is a small business, the differential would be 12 percent, and the evaluated price of the offeror of the foreign item would be treated as $112. If an award for more than $250,000 would be made to a domestic concern at a price more than 6 percent above the foreign price, the head of the procuring agency must determine whether award to the domestic concern would be at an "unreasonable cost," FAR 25.105(c).

The differential is applied only to the material delivered under the contract and not necessarily to the total bid price. Thus, post-delivery services such as installation, testing, and training are exempted from the surcharge applicable to foreign end products, *Dynatest Consulting, Inc.*, Comp. Gen. Dec. B-257822.4, 95-1 CPD ¶ 167. See *STD Research Corp.*, 72 Comp. Gen. 211 (B-252073.2), 93-1 CPD ¶ 406 (agency should not apply the surcharge to an offeror's total evaluated price for a high-technology power generator, which included not only the price of foreign hardware but also post-delivery services); and *Allis-Chalmers Corp. v. Friedkin*, 635 F.2d 248 (3d Cir. 1980) (costs of installation and post-delivery services were excluded from the price of the foreign item to which the 12 percent differential was applied).

The evaluation procedure ordinarily is applied on an item-by-item basis, or to any group of items on which award may be made as specifically provided in the solicitation, FAR 25.105(b). Absent such a provision, each item or group of closely related items will be treated separately for evaluation purposes, even though award may be made on an all-or-nothing basis, 47 Comp. Gen. 676 (B-163740) (1968); *Essex Assocs., Inc.*, 63 Comp. Gen. 503 (B-213279), 84-2 CPD ¶ 97.

b. *Unavailability*

The requirements of the Buy American Act do not apply to products that have been determined not to be reasonably available in commercial quantities and of a satisfactory quality, 41 U.S.C. § 10a; FAR 25.108. A list of such products is set forth in FAR 25.108(d). See *Midwest Dynamometer & Eng'g Co.*, Comp. Gen. Dec. B-252168, 93-1 CPD ¶ 408, where the Comptroller General held that the Buy American Act was not applicable to the purchase of a dynamometer from a foreign firm because the item was not manufactured in the United States in sufficient and reasonably available commercial quantities.

c. *Use Abroad*

The Buy American Act exempts articles purchased "for use outside the United States," 41 U.S.C. § 10a. See *Systems & Defense Servs. Int'l*, Comp. Gen. Dec. B-254254.2, 94-1 CPD ¶ 91 (contract not subject to Buy American Act because the work was to be performed outside the United States); and *Maremont Corp.*, 55 Comp. Gen. 1362 (B-186276), 76-2 CPD ¶ 181

(Act held not to apply to the purchase of machine guns for installation in vehicles deployed outside the United States, or to the procurement of steel towers for installation as part of a communications system in West Germany). This exception permits any foreign-made product to be offered for such procurements and does not require the furnishing of products manufactured in the country of use.

d. Public Interest

The Buy American Act allows the head of a procuring agency to waive application of the Act upon a determination that such application would be "inconsistent with the public interest," 41 U.S.C. § 10a. The DOD has used this authority to grant a broad exemption from foreign acquisition restrictions for procurements of defense equipment from certain countries with which the United States has entered into Memoranda of Understanding (MOU) or other relevant agreements, DFARS 225.872. A list of qualifying countries is provided in DFARS 225.872-1. See *Self-Powered Lighting, Ltd. v. United States*, 492 F. Supp. 1267 (S.D.N.Y. 1980), where the court ruled that a MOU created a blanket exemption for all United Kingdom defense products and *American Hosp. Supply, Equipping & Consulting*, Comp. Gen. Dec. B-221357, 86-1 CPD ¶ 70, where the Comptroller General found proper use of an exemption under a MOU with Italy. Such exemptions extend to nondefense products procured by the DOD, *Allis-Chalmers Corp. v. Arnold*, 619 F.2d 44 (9th Cir. 1980). See also *Air Plastics, Inc.*, Comp. Gen. Dec. B-199307, 80-2 CPD ¶ 141 (exemption for Denmark by MOU); and *Baganoff Assocs., Inc.*, 54 Comp. Gen. 44 (B-179607), 74-2 CPD ¶ 56 (broad Canadian exemption).

The head of a procuring agency has considerable discretion in determining whether to invoke the public interest exception. The Comptroller General has held that this exception may be invoked after bid opening, *E-Systems, Inc.*, 61 Comp. Gen. 431 (B-206209), 82-1 CPD ¶ 533. An agency has also been permitted to invoke this exception after contract award when the only domestic price is unreasonable, *John T. Brady & Co. v. United States*, 693 F.2d 1380 (Fed. Cir. 1982). In *John T. Brady & Co.*, VACAB 1300, 84-1 BCA ¶ 16,925, *recons. denied*, 84-1 BCA ¶ 17,161, the board, on remand, held that the failure of the agency to grant the exception was an abuse of discretion since the Government would have incurred no additional costs by granting the exception. The board, therefore, granted the contractor a price adjustment for the difference in price between the domestic and foreign material. However, a contractor should generally request waiver of the Buy American Act before contract award or at least before contract performance, *C. Sanchez & Son, Inc. v. United States*, 24 Cl. Ct. 14 (1991), *aff'd in part, vacated in part*, 6 F.3d 1539 (Fed. Cir. 1993). In *C. Sanchez*, a contractor sought an equitable adjustment to compensate for certain increased costs in using domestic wire and cable. Although the contractor complained during performance about the cost to a contracting officer's technical representative (COTR), it never submitted a waiver of the Buy American Act. The Claims Court held that the contractor should have requested a waiver of the Buy American Act before contract performance, and since it did not do so, it was not entitled to an equitable adjustment.

e. Trade Agreements Act of 1979

A major objective of the "Tokyo Round" of international trade negotiations during the 1970s was to reduce "nontariff barriers," such as the Buy American Act, to international trade. The Tokyo Round resulted in a series of "international codes," one of which is known as the "Government Procurement Code." That code includes provisions designed to reduce the effect of buy-national practices of the signatory nations.

The United States joined in the agreements that resulted from the Tokyo Round, including the Government Procurement Code. To implement those agreements, Congress enacted the Trade Agreements Act of 1979, 19 U.S.C. § 2501 et seq. One provision of that Act authorized the President to waive any otherwise applicable "law, regulation, procedure or practice regarding Government procurement" that would accord foreign products less favorable treatment than that given to domestic products, 19 U.S.C § 2511(a). That provision of the Trade Agreements Act has been implemented by the President, Exec. Order No. 12260, 46 Fed. Reg. 1653 (1981). Thus, the Buy American Act and at least some other federal restrictions favoring domestic products have been superseded as to the specific products and countries covered by the President's action, FAR Subpart 25.4. FAR 25.401 lists all countries designated under the Trade Agreements Act. This exemption covers contracts for the acquisition of products through purchase, lease, rental or lease-purchase agreement for amounts above a specified figure (which is periodically revised and published in the *Federal Register*). See *Presto Lock, Inc.*, Comp. Gen. Dec. B-218766, 85-2 CPD ¶ 183 (padlocks from Hong Kong); and *Qualimetrics, Inc.*, Comp. Gen. Dec. B-222726,

86-1 CPD ¶ 519 (use of Finnish components raises no Buy American issue since Trade Agreement Act applies). See also *Olympic Container Corp.*, Comp. Gen. Dec. B-250403, 93-1 CPD ¶ 89 (no application of the Buy American Act's differential to offers of products from non-designated countries is permitted); *Trading Atlanta Ltd.*, Comp. Gen. Dec. B-239056, 90-2 CPD ¶ 88 (since the Trade Agreements Act prohibits the acceptance of South African products, the protester was not prejudiced by the award to a higher-priced domestic competitor); and *Puerto Rico Marine Management, Inc.*, Comp. Gen. Dec. B-247975.5, 92-2 CPD ¶ 275 (items indispensable to the national defense is not subject to the Trade Agreements Act; in such cases the Buy American Act applies).

An article is considered to be a "designated country end product" under the Trade Agreements Act if it is "wholly the growth, product, or manufacture of the designated country," FAR 25.401. In some cases, an article in a designated country may consist "in whole or in part of materials from another country or instrumentality." Whether such an article is deemed to be a "designated country end product" depends upon whether the product

> has been substantially transformed into a new and different article of commerce with a name, character, or use distinct from that of the article or articles from which it was so transferred.

The same definition is used in the definition of the terms "Canadian end product" and "Caribbean Basin country end product."

There are very few decisions defining "substantial transformation." In *Becton Dickinson AcuteCare*, Comp. Gen. Dec. B-238942, 90-2 CPD ¶ 55, the Comptroller General held that parts manufactured and sterilized in the United States and then shipped to Mexico for assembly into "tracheal suction sets" were not "substantially transformed" in Mexico. Thus, they could be considered for award because they did not become the product of a "non-designated country" (Mexico) and retained their status as a "domestic end product."

The concept of substantial transformation is derived from U.S. Customs Regulations. Thus, there are a number of Customs cases decided by the Court of International Trade dealing with the matter. See *Ferrostaal Metals Corp. v. United States*, 664 F. Supp. 535 (N.D. Ill. 1987) (full-hard cold rolled steel sheet substantially transformed by continuous annealing and hot-dip galvanizing operation in New Zealand); *Superior Wire v. United States*,

669 F. Supp. 472 (1987 Ct. Intl. Trade), *aff'd*, 867 F.2d 1409 (Fed. Cir. 1989) (wire rod from Spain made into wire in Canada did not constitute substantial transformation); and *Madison Galleries, Ltd. v. United States*, 688 F. Supp. 1544 (1988 Ct. Intl. Trade), *aff'd*, 870 F.2d 627 (Fed. Cir. 1989) (blank porcelain pieces produced in Taiwan substantially transformed by decoration in Hong Kong).

f. Caribbean Basin Recovery Act

The Caribbean Basin Recovery Act, P.L. 98-67, codified at 19 U.S.C. § 2701 et seq., was passed to further economic and political stability in countries in this region. Regulations adopted under this statute waive the Buy American Act for certain products from listed countries.

g. North American Free Trade Agreement

The North American Free Trade Agreement (NAFTA), as enacted by the North American Free Trade Agreement Implementation Act, P.L. 103-182, codified at 19 U.S.C. § 3301 et seq., contains provisions which effect domestic preference rules in federal procurements. NAFTA applies to procurements by specified federal agencies of goods, services, and construction services above certain monetary thresholds. For acquisition of supplies, the threshold is $25,000 for Canadian end products and $50,000 for Mexican end products, FAR 25.402(a)(3)(ii). For construction contracts, the threshold is $6.5 million, FAR 25.402(a)(3)(i).

The main effect of NAFTA on U.S. procurements is that it obligates the United States to afford Mexican products and services the same treatment as domestic products, FAR 25.402(a)(3). Mexico is thus equivalent to a designated country, and the preferences under the Buy American Act and the Balance of Payments Program do not apply to Mexican supply, services, or construction contracts.

The United States had been obligated to afford Canadian products and services domestic-products status under the United States-Canada Free Trade Agreement, which had been approved by the United States-Canada Free Trade Agreement Implementation Act of 1988, P.L. 100-449, codified at 19 U.S.C. § 2112 note. NAFTA supersedes the United States-Canada Free Trade Agreement.

B. Other Domestic Preferences

The Government has a number of policies, besides the Buy American Act, favoring acquisition of articles of domestic origin. These policies either impose restrictions on the purchase of specific articles or services or require the use of price differentials in evaluating the price of foreign articles or services.

1. Statutory Restrictions

There are a number of statutory restrictions. The oldest originated in 1941 when the military services were prohibited from using appropriated funds to procure foreign food or clothing, *A&P Surgical Co.*, 62 Comp. Gen. 256 (B-206111.2), 83-1 CPD ¶ 263. DFARS Subpart 225.70 contains detailed guidance on Appropriation or Authorization Act restrictions applying to food, clothing, fabrics, specialty metals, hand or measuring tools, machine tools, valves, shipyard construction or repair of vessels, buses, R&D, aircraft ejection seats, chemical weapons antidotes, ballistic missile defense R&D, anchor and mooring chain, polyacrylonitrile-based carbon fiber, night-vision image intensifier tubes and devices, air circuit breakers, steel plate, dolly jacks, antifriction bearings, coal and petroleum-pitch carbon fiber, aircraft fuel cells, and lifeboat survival systems.

Additional restrictions are found in the transportation field. See FAR Subpart 47.5, implementing the numerous statutes giving preference to U.S. flag vessels for the transportation of supplies. Another statute affecting transportation is the Surface Transportation Assistance Act, P.L. 97-424.

The provisions of such specific statutes may bar purchase of foreign materials even if the Buy American Act would not, *Penthouse Mfg. Co.*, Comp. Gen. Dec. B-217480, 85-1 CPD ¶ 487; 49 Comp. Gen. 606 (B-168791) (1970).

2. Balance of Payments Differentials

The executive branch has adopted an additional technique favoring domestic supplies and services called the Balance of Payments Program. FAR 25.300 makes this program applicable to acquisitions of supplies, services, or construction for use outside the United States. DFARS 225.302

makes the program applicable to acquisitions for foreign military sales but not applicable to services, except for those that are incidental to the acquisition of supplies. Certain purchases under the Trade Agreements Act of 1979 and the NAFTA Implementation Act are exempted from this program, FAR 25.402. FAR 25.305(b) also lists nine instances in which the program is not applicable, including small purchases and the acquisition of perishable items.

The Balance of Payments program uses the same definitions of foreign and domestic supplies as the Buy American program and adds a definition for domestic services when 25 percent or less of the total cost is attributable to services performed outside the United States, FAR 25.301. The program is implemented by requiring the addition of a 50 percent factor to each foreign offer in the evaluation process, FAR 25.303(b). Illustrations of the evaluation procedure for acquisitions for use outside of the United States are contained in DFARS 225.105.

In the case of DOD procurements of supplies to be used in the United States, both the Buy American Act and the Balance of Payments program differentials must be used. DFARS 225.105(72) gives examples of the use of these factors. It provides for the use of the higher evaluation price. The 50 percent balance of payments factor is applied to the foreign price, less any applicable duty, while the Buy American 6 percent or 12 percent factor is applied to the price including duty. See *Training, Operations & Procedures Video Corp.*, Comp. Gen. Dec. B-219825, 85-2 CPD ¶ 615, *recons. denied*, 86-1 CPD ¶ 453.

V. POLICIES ON THE ENVIRONMENT AND ENERGY

Since the 1960s, Congress has passed a number of statutes concerning the environment and energy. These statutes and the regulations implementing them contain a variety of provisions that use federal contracts to foster the policies established for environment and energy.

A. National Environmental Policy Act

The National Environmental Policy Act, passed in 1969, "authorizes and directs that, to the fullest extent possible . . . the policies, regulations and public laws of the United States" shall be interpreted and administered in accordance with the environmental policies set out in the Act, 42 U.S.C. § 4332. The Act also requires that an environmental impact statement be prepared in connection with all "major Federal actions significantly affecting the quality of the human environment," 42 U.S.C. § 4332(2)(C). Examples of regulations implementing this requirement include 24 C.F.R. Part 50 (Department of Housing and Urban Development) and 14 C.F.R. Part 1216.3 (National Aeronautics and Space Administration). In certain circumstances, award of a federal contract might be a "major federal action" that triggers the need for an environmental impact statement. Sometimes contract award acts as a signal that prompts opponents of a federal project (e.g., a dam or new military installation) to seek an injunction delaying the project on grounds that no environmental impact statement, or an inadequate one, has been prepared; see Nash & Linden, "Federal Procurement and the Environment, in Environmental Law Institute," Federal Environmental Law 476-87 (1974).

B. Energy Policy and Conservation Act

The Energy Policy and Conservation Act, P.L. 94-163, codified at 42 U.S.C. § 6361(a)(1), passed in 1975, directs that

> [t]he President shall, to the extent of his authority under other law, establish or coordinate Federal agency actions to develop mandatory standards with respect to energy conservation and energy efficiency to govern the procurement policies and decisions of the Federal Government and all Federal agencies, and shall take such steps as are necessary to cause such standards to be implemented.

Although this section has some broad language, it is subject to the limitations inherent in the provision that the President's power to carry out duties under the section is only what is granted "under other law." This subordinates consideration of energy conservation and efficiency to other policies, including those requiring full and open competition. Executive agency implementation of the Energy Policy and Conservation Act has been limited accordingly. The implementation emphasizes that energy efficiency and conservation are to be considered in procurement decisions "along with estimated cost and other relevant factors," FAR 23.203(a). OFPP Policy Letter 92-4, 57 Fed. Reg. 53362, Nov. 9, 1992, provides executive branch guidance for the acquisition and use of environmentally sound, energy-efficient products and services and employs life cycle cost analysis in making product and service selections. The principal application of the Act has been to products such as air conditioners and furnaces for which energy efficiency ratings are established by the Department of Energy. Federal agencies are expected to review those ratings when purchasing included products, FAR Subpart 23.2.

C. Preferences for Low-Pollution Products

Several statutes require federal procuring agencies to give preference to products that emit comparatively low amounts of environmental pollution. However, stringent standards must be met by any product before it is entitled to such a preference.

Under the Noise Control Act of 1972, P.L. 92-574, codified at 42 U.S.C. § 4901 et seq., federal agencies must give preference to products that meet several prerequisites. The Environmental Protection Agency must determine through appropriate testing that the product is a "low-noise emission" product, 42 U.S.C. § 4914(b). The product must be found to be a "suitable substitute" for articles that the Government is procuring. The General Services Administration must determine that the cost of the product is not more than 125 percent of the retail price of the least expensive article for which it is a substitute, 42 U.S.C. § 4914(c)(1).

In the Resource Conservation and Energy Act of 1976, P.L. 94-580, codified at 42 U.S.C. § 6901 et seq., Congress required procuring agencies to modify their traditional policy of "buying new." Congress required that agencies examine their specifications and remove requirements for "new" materials to the extent such requirements could not be justified, 42 U.S.C. § 6962(c)(1). Congress also required that the Office of Federal Procurement Policy designate items that can be produced with "recovered material" and whose procurement would carry out the objectives of the Act. Agencies are required to procure such items "composed of the highest percentage of recovered material practicable . . . consistent with maintaining a satisfactory level of competition," 42 U.S.C. § 6962. The term "recovered material" includes most material recovered from "any garbage, refuse, sludge from a waste treatment plant, water supply treatment plant, or air pollution control facility and other discarded material," 42 U.S.C. § 6903(19) and (27). Agencies must require vendors to certify that the percentage of "recovered materials" to be used in contract performance will be at least the amount required by applicable specifications or contract requirements, 42 U.S.C.

§ 6962(d)(2). Agencies may decide not to procure items composed of the highest percentage of recovered materials practicable consistent with maintaining a satisfactory level of competition if they determine that such items are not reasonably available in a reasonable time, or that they will not meet applicable performance standards, or are available only at an unreasonable price, 42 U.S.C. § 6962(c)(1). Regulations designed to implement these provisions are contained in FAR Subpart 23.4.

The Comptroller General has criticized the Office of Federal Procurement Policy and others for delays in implementing the procurement provisions of the Resource Conservation and Recovery Act, *Federal Industrial Targets and Procurement Guidelines Programs Are Not Encouraging Recycling and Have Contract Problems*, Comp. Gen. Rep. EMD 81-7, Dec. 5, 1980. Where a potential bidder protested against specifications that did not require recovered materials, the Comptroller General relied upon the absence of agency guidelines as one ground for denying the protest, *Sunbelt Indus., Inc.*, Comp. Gen. Dec. B-214414.2, 85-1 CPD ¶ 113.

D. Clean Air and Water

The Clean Air Amendments of 1970, P.L. 91-604, codified at 42 U.S.C. § 7401 et seq., and the Water Pollution Control Act Amendments of 1972, P.L. 92-500, codified at 33 U.S.C. § 1251 et seq., established a procedure to use federal contract awards to help implement the pollution control aspects of those statutes. The Environmental Protection Agency is authorized to list facilities if they are found liable for violations of air and water pollution standards. Offerors on certain federal contracts must certify that their performance will not take place at any of these listed facilities, 42 U.S.C. § 7606; 33 U.S.C. § 1368; 40 C.F.R. Part 32; FAR Subpart 23.1. FAR 23.105 requires that the Clean Air and Water clause at FAR 52.223-2 be inserted in solicitations and contracts if (1) the contract is expected to exceed $100,000, (2) the contracting officer believes that orders under an indefinite-quantity contract in any year will exceed $100,000, or (3) a facility to be used has been the subject of conviction under the applicable portion of the Air Act or Water Act and is listed by the EPA as a violating facility. The Clean Air and Water Certification clause at FAR 52.223-1 is required to be inserted in solicitations when FAR 52.223-2 is applicable. Commercial items are exempted from FAR 23.105.

VI. EQUAL EMPLOYMENT

Nondiscrimination provisions have been required in Government contracts by a series of executive orders commencing with Exec. Order No. 8802, 6 Fed. Reg. 3109 (1941). This section deals first with the current executive orders requiring equal opportunity in employment. It then reviews other sources of equal employment policies.

A. Executive Order No. 11246

The major source of the equal employment opportunity requirements for federal contractors is Exec. Order No. 11246, 30 Fed. Reg. 12319 (1965), as amended by Exec. Order No. 11375, 32 Fed. Reg. 14303 (1967); Exec. Order No. 11478, 34 Fed. Reg. 12985 (1969); and Exec. Order No. 12086, 43 Fed. Reg. 46501 (1978). These orders provide that the Secretary of Labor will administer this program and promulgate regulations. This is done through the Office of Federal Contract Compliance Programs (OFCCP). See 41 C.F.R. Part 60. At the same time, Exec. Order No. 11246, as amended, makes each contracting agency primarily responsible for ensuring that its contractors comply with the applicable regulations, rules, and orders. FAR Subpart 22.8 contains the general regulations for these procedures.

The legal authority of the President to issue Exec. Order No. 11246, has been sustained. See *Contractors Ass'n of E. Pa. v. Secretary of Labor*, 442 F.2d 159 (3d Cir.), *cert. denied*, 404 U.S. 854 (1971). But note that the two grounds on which the court in *Contractors Association* based its decision were questioned by another court in *AFL-CIO v. Kahn*, 618 F.2d 784 (D.C. Cir.), *cert. denied*, 443 U.S. 915 (1979). Other cases supporting the executive order's validity include *Farkas v. Texas Instrument, Inc.*, 375 F.2d 629 (5th Cir.), *cert. denied*, 389 U.S. 977 (1967); *Legal Aid Society of Alameda County v. Brennan*, 381 F. Supp. 125 (N.D. Cal. 1974), *aff'd in part*, 608 F.2d 1319 (9th Cir. 1979), *cert. denied*, 447 U.S. 921 (1980); and *United States v. Local 189, United Papermakers & Paperworkers*, 282 F. Supp. 39 (E.D. La. 1968). The Comptroller General has held that including nondiscrimination provisions in a federal contract does not violate the requirements of statutes requiring maximum feasible competition, 40 Comp. Gen. 592 (B-145475) (1961).

1. Equal Opportunity Clause

Executive Order No. 11246, prescribes a clause that is mandatory in all contracts exceeding $10,000, absent a special exemption from the Secretary of Labor. The clause is also required for contracts under $10,000 if the contractor has, or reasonably can expect to have, contracts or subcontracts with the Government exceeding $10,000 in a 12-month period, FAR 22.807(b)(1). The required clause is set forth in FAR 52.222-26. The clause can be applicable even if it is not included in a contract. See *United States v. New Orleans Pub. Serv., Inc.*, 553 F.2d 459 (5th Cir. 1977), *vacated & remanded on other grounds*, 436 U.S. 942 (1978), where the court held that a utility supplying electricity to the Government was subject to the provisions of the executive order even though the company had refused to sign a contract because of the inclusion of this clause. Compare *Liberty Mut. Ins. Co. v. Friedman*, 639 F.2d 164 (4th Cir. 1981), invalidating Labor Department regulations requiring sureties to comply with the requirements of the executive order. The court reasoned that a surety could not reasonably be construed to be a subcontractor.

Under the required Equal Opportunity clause at FAR 52.222-26, the contractor agrees not to discriminate against any employee or applicant for employment because of race, color, religion, sex, or national origin. Paragraph (b)(2) of the clause further requires that "[t]he Contractor shall take affirmative action to ensure that applicants are employed, and that employees are treated during employment, without regard to their race, color, religion, sex, or national origin." The clause also commits the contractor to furnish certain information and reports and to permit access to records by the contracting agency and the Department of Labor to ascertain compliance with the applicable requirements. Unless an exemption applies, Paragraph (b)(10) of the clause provides that a prime contractor must flow down the requirements of the clause in its subcontracts and purchase orders.

Affirmative action is described in detail in 41 C.F.R. Part 60-2. Initially the contractor must make a utilization analysis to determine if the composition of its workforce is in conformity with the composition of people living in its labor area. This requires a determination of the appropriate labor area serving the contractor, the availability of minority groups in categories of labor in that area, and the number of minority employees working in each job category. If this analysis indicates that the contractor's percentage of minority employment is less than those available in any labor category, "underutilization" is required to be found. In such cases, the contractor must establish a series of "goals and timetables: to attain percentages of minority employment comparable to the availability of minorities in the labor area. The contractor must also adopt policies for recruitment and training that will aid in achieving these goals." The affirmative action requirement applies to promotion as well as employment. See *Legal Aid Society of Alameda County v. Brennan*, 381 F. Supp. 125 (N.D. Cal. 1974), *aff'd in part*, 608 F.2d 1319 (9th Cir. 1979), *cert. denied*, 447 U.S. 921 (1980), for a decision analyzing and finding deficient an agency's efforts to ensure that its contractors are complying with the affirmative action requirement.

2. Affirmative Action Programs

Each nonconstruction prime contractor or subcontractor with 50 or more employees and prime contracts or subcontracts for $50,000 or more (or cumulatively expected to total $50,000 or more in any 12-month period) is required to develop a written affirmative action program, FAR 22.804-1. These programs are reviewed and approved by the OFCCP regional office and must be developed within 120 days from the commencement of the first contract or subcontract for $50,000 or more. The regulations require an affirmative action program for each establishment of a contractor, 41 C.F.R. § 60-1.40. This requirement has been interpreted as applying to every establishment of a contractor regardless of whether such establishment performs work for the Government. An OFCCP Policy Interpretation issued in the 1970s contained the following statement regarding the meaning of "establishment":

> Revised Order No. 4 requires that a written affirmative action program be developed for each of the contractor's establishments. The question has arisen as to whether this means that a contractor must develop such plans for an "establishment" where it may have a few employees, such as a sales outlet. We have defined "establishment" for purposes of Revised Order No. 4 as a facility at which hiring takes place and/or personnel actions are instituted. If such authority exists at the facility, it would be required to have a written affirmative action program as specified in Revised Order No. 4. If such authority does not exist at the facility, the location that has the hiring authority and handles personnel actions for the facility would have to develop and implement an affirmative action plan. In the latter case, the personnel at the facility would be covered by the plan maintained at the hiring and personnel location.

A subsidiary not performing Government work is considered an "establishment" only if the parent exercises actual control, 50 Comp. Gen. 627 (B-170536) (1971). The lack of an approved affirmative action program by a nonconstruction concern is grounds for a determination that the company is not a responsible offeror. However, the OFCCP regulations do not require the contracting officer to ascertain whether such a program exists in smaller procurements. For example, the regulations provide that if "it comes to the contracting officer's attention" in the preaward period that there is no approved affirmative action program, the offeror must be declared nonresponsible unless the contracting officer "can otherwise affirmatively determine that the contractor is able to comply with his equal employment obligations," 41 C.F.R. § 60-2.2(b).

Requirements become more stringent as dollar amounts increase. For instance, contracts or subcontracts over $1 million may not be awarded unless a compliance review of the contractor has been conducted within 12 months prior to the award and the contractor is found to be in compliance, 41 C.F.R. § 60-1.20(d). See FAR 22.805(a), providing that compliance reviews should be requested from OFCCP in such circumstances and award should be withheld for 45 days while the review is conducted. This procedure is intended to prevent the award of major contracts without an affirmative determination by the compliance agency that the contractor's program meets the requirements of Revised Order No. 4. A prospective contractor may be determined nonresponsible twice without a hearing, but is entitled to a hearing after the second determination of nonresponsibility, 41 C.F.R. § 60-2.2(b). In *Commercial Envelope Mfg. Co. v. Dunlop*, 21 Cont. Cas. Fed. (CCF) ¶ 84,097 (S.D.N.Y. 1975), the court held that this procedure did not violate any of the prospective contractor's rights and found that a contractor was properly determined nonresponsible a fifth time based on employment practices, even though the four prior determinations were based on other grounds. The Comptroller General has stated that similar procedures violate the requirement for open and competitive bidding because they do not contain sufficiently definitive requirements to enable all bidders to compete on an equal basis, *Illinois Equal Employment Opportunity Regulations for Public Contracts*, 54 Comp. Gen. 6 (B-167015), 74-2 CPD ¶ 1.

Construction contractors are not required to develop affirmative action programs since many do not perform work in fixed geographic areas. However, they must comply with any "hometown plan" covering a geographic area in which they work, FAR 22.804-2(a). These hometown plans are affirmative action programs covering specific geographic areas that have been agreed to by unions, contractor associations, and governmental units in that area. See 41 C.F.R. § 60-4.5. Each contracting agency is required to maintain a list of such plans, FAR 22.804-2(b), and contracting officers are required to include the goals and timetables from such plans in solicitations for work to be performed in geographic areas with plans in effect. The clause used for this purpose is set forth in FAR 52.222-23. If the construction is to be performed in an area not covered by a plan, the contractor is not obligated to attempt to meet any goals and timetables. However, all construction contracts over $10,000 must contain the Affirmative Action Compliance Requirements for Construction clause at FAR 52.222-27, which contains 16 affirmative action steps that the contractor must take during contract performance.

All of the affirmative action program requirements are matters of responsibility not responsiveness. Thus, bidders can furnish information demonstrating that they are in compliance after bid opening, *A&C Bldg. & Indus. Maintenance Corp.*, Comp. Gen. Dec. B-218035, 85-1 CPD ¶ 195.

3. Compliance Procedures

If an individual employee has a grievance regarding a contractor's compliance with Exec. Order No. 11246, requirements, the employee may file a complaint with OFCCP. That office may investigate and may, in appropriate circumstances, refer the complaint to the Equal Employment Opportunity Commission, 41 C.F.R. § 60-1.21 et seq.; FAR 22.808. As to lawsuits against the employer under Exec. Order No. 11246, courts are in disagreement about whether there is a private cause of action. Compare *Rogers v. Frito-Lay*, 611 F.2d 1074 (5th Cir.), *cert. denied*, 449 U.S. 889 (1980) and cases cited therein with *Lewis v. Western Airlines, Inc.*, 379 F. Supp. 684 (N.D. Cal. 1974). See Annot., 31 A.L.R. Fed. 108, 122 et seq. (1977). See also *Banks v. Jacksonville Shipyards*, 55 Fair Empl. Prac. Cas. 151 (M.D.Fla. 1988), where the court stated at 156:

> In fact, neither the United States Supreme Court, nor the Eleventh Circuit Court of Appeals has ever decided the question whether Executive Order 11246 affords employees of, and applicants for employment with, federal contractors a private right of action to combat discrimination by such contractors.

The OFCCP may without any complaint by an employee or applicant review a contractor's compliance with executive order requirements. If it concludes that a violation exists, the OFCCP will ordinarily seek to resolve the matter through discussions and a "conciliation agreement" with the contractor. The OFCCP may institute administrative enforcement proceedings and may refer the matter to the Department of Justice for initiation of a lawsuit, 41 C.F.R. 60-1 Subpart B. The Government may sue seeking an order barring the defendant from violating or interfering with rights of employees under the order, *United States v. Local 189, United Papermakers & Paperworkers*, 301 F. Supp. 906 (E.D. La.), *aff'd*, 416 F.2d 980 (5th Cir. 1969), *cert. denied*, 397 U.S. 919 (1970).

4. Sanctions

Among the sanctions available for violation of the requirements of the order are cancellation of the contract and debarment of the contractor from eligibility for future Government contracts, FAR 22.809. In *Timken Co. v. Vaughan*, 413 F. Supp. 1183 (N.D. Ohio 1976), the Government's efforts to debar a contractor for an alleged violation of the order were unsuccessful. Upon consideration of the population surrounding the contractor's facility, the court held that the failure of the contractor's affirmative action program to include a city with a higher minority population did not violate the executive order. The court reasoned that, although the city was within a reasonable commuting distance, the population's habits indicated that residents were unlikely to seek work in the contractor's facility.

B. Other Sources of Equal Employment Opportunity Requirements

Most prime contractors and subcontractors are likely to be subject to some of the provisions of the Civil Rights Act of 1964, as amended by the Equal Employment Opportunity Act of 1972, 42 U.S.C. §§ 2000e – 2000e(17). Title VII of this Act prohibits employers with 15 or more employees and employment entities of labor organizations affecting interstate commerce to discriminate because of race, color, religion, sex, or national origin. An aggrieved employee or applicant for employment may sue the employer in a district court. The Equal Employment Opportunity Commission has power to investigate charges of discrimination under the Act and to sue if efforts to secure voluntary compliance fail.

Under Exec. Order No. 11141, federal contractors and subcontractors may not discriminate against employees or potential employees based on age, except upon the basis of a bona fide occupational qualification, retirement plan, or statutory requirement, 29 Fed. Reg. 2477 (1964). FAR 22.901(c) provides that agencies are to bring this policy to the attention of contractors, but that no implementing contract clause is required.

Unless exempted by the Secretary of Labor, contractors awarded contracts for supplies or services, including construction, of $10,000 or more must agree not to discriminate against qualified special disabled veterans of the Vietnam Era based on their disability or their status as veterans, 38 U.S.C. § 4212; Exec. Order No. 11701, 38 Fed. Reg. 2675 (1973); 41 C.F.R. 60-250; FAR Subpart 22.13. This policy does not apply to contracts to be performed outside the United States. A standard contract clause on this subject is prescribed for contracts and subcontracts over $10,000, FAR 52.222-35.

All federal contracts and subcontracts over $2,500 for supplies and services, including construction, except where the Secretary of Labor grants a waiver, must include requirements barring discrimination against any employee or applicant because of physical or mental handicaps. Contractors under such contracts and subcontracts are also required to agree to take affirmative action with respect to such individuals, 29 U.S.C. § 793; Exec. Order No. 11758, 39 Fed. Reg. 2075 (1974); 41 C.F.R. 60-741; FAR Subpart 22.14. The contract clause prescribed for use is set forth at FAR 52.222-36.

VII. LABOR STANDARDS

For many years there has been extensive statutory coverage of the labor standards to be observed by Federal Government contractors. These statutes have imposed minimum wage levels, overtime wage restrictions, and provisions governing working conditions on various classes of work. This section considers the minimum wage provisions governing contracts for construction, supplies, and services.

A. Davis-Bacon Act

The Davis-Bacon Act, 40 U.S.C. § 276a, establishes minimum wages, including fringe benefits, to be paid to laborers and mechanics on contracts of over $2,000 for the construction, alteration, or repair of public buildings and public works. Department of Labor regulations implementing this statute are found in 29 C.F.R. Part 1. FAR regulations are contained in Subpart 22.4.

The purpose of this Act is not to guarantee contractors that specified wage levels will be applicable, but rather to protect employees from substandard earnings by fixing a minimum wage on Government projects, *United States v. Binghamton Constr. Co.*, 347 U.S. 171, *reh'g denied*, 347 U.S. 940 (1954). Therefore, the contractor has no right under the Act for recovery if the wage that must be paid to obtain employees is higher than the prevailing wage rate set forth in the contract. But see *Sunswick Corp. v. United States*, 109 Ct. Cl. 772, 75 F. Supp. 221, *cert. denied*, 334 U.S. 827 (1948), where a contractor was allowed recovery for payment of wages higher than the wage determination when the higher payment was the result of a directive and the contract clause prohibited payment of more or less than the wage determination.

1. Determination That Contract Is a Construction Contract

It is the procuring agency's responsibility to determine initially whether the Davis-Bacon Act is applicable to a particular contract, 29 C.F.R. § 5.5(a). The Comptroller General has held that the procuring agency's good faith determination should not be overturned, 44 Comp. Gen. 498 (B-150828) (1965).

The Act applies only to federal contracts that essentially or substantially contemplate construction, alteration, or repair, 40 Comp. Gen. 565 (B-144901) (1961). Contracting officers must determine the extent of construction, alteration, or repair work that will be involved, *D.E. Clarke*, Comp. Gen. Dec. B-146824, 75-1 CPD ¶ 317. A contract for the furnishing and installing of a mechanized materials handling system for which 30 percent of the work and 40 percent of the dollar value of the equipment represented construction work was properly included in the provisions of the Davis-Bacon Act, Comp. Gen. Dec. B-178159, June 6, 1973, *Unpub.* FAR

37.301 provides that if a contract for dismantling, demolition, or removal of improvements also requires construction, alteration, or repair, the Davis-Bacon Act will apply.

It is sometimes difficult to ascertain whether the contract is for construction, services, or manufacturing. In one situation, the Secretary of Labor held that the construction of a mobile nuclear reactor was work covered by the Act while the Comptroller General held it was not, Opinion Letter of the Solicitor of Labor, Oct. 14, 1966, DB-52, C.C.H. Labor Law Transfer Binder, Wages, Hours and Administrative Rulings, ¶ 30,997.49; 47 Comp. Gen. 192 (B-161858) (1967).

2. Employees Covered

The Act covers the minimum wages "to be paid various classes of laborers and mechanics." FAR 22.401 defines laborers and mechanics as workers "whose duties are manual or physical in nature (including those workers who use tools or who are performing the work of a trade), as distinguished from mental or managerial." The definition includes apprentices, trainees, and helpers, but not workers whose duties are primarily executive, supervisory, administrative, or clerical.

The Act applies to all "mechanics and laborers employed directly upon the site of the work." 29 C.F.R. § 5.2(k)(1)(2) defines the "site of the work" as including "fabrication plants, mobile factories, batch plants, borrow pits, job headquarters, tool yards" that are "dedicated exclusively, or nearly so, to the performance of the contract or project, and are located in proximity to the actual construction location." There seems to be a disagreement between the courts and the Department of Labor as to what constitutes "site of the work." In *Ball, Ball & Brosamer v. Secretary of Labor*, 24 F.3d 1447 (D.C. Cir. 1994), the court held that a contractor was not obligated to pay Davis-Bacon Act wages to workers at a batch plant and borrow pit two miles from the construction site because those locations were not directly on the site of the work within the meaning of the Act. In reviewing the Act, the court stated at 1448:

> The statutory phrase "employed directly upon the site of the work," means "employed directly upon the site of the work." Laborers and mechanics who fit that description are covered by the statute. Those who don't are not.

See also *L.P. Cavett Co. v. Department of Labor*, 101 F.3d 1111 (6th Cir. 1996). In this case, the prime contractor established an asphalt plant approximately three miles from the midpoint of the highway site. The prime contractor then hired a subcontractor to haul materials, supplies, and equipment from the batch plant to the highway. The subcontract did not contain Davis-Bacon Act prevailing wage provisions. The Department of Labor's Wage Appeals Board ruled that the subcontractor's truck drivers hauling asphalt to the batch plant should have been paid Davis-Bacon Act wages because the plant was located on "the site of the work." The Sixth Circuit reversed, relying on the reasoning in *Ball, Ball & Brosamer*. In *Building & Constr. Trades Dept., AFL-CIO v. Department of Labor Wage Appeals Bd.*, 932 F.2d 985 (D.C. Cir. 1991), the court held that material delivery truck drivers were not covered under the Act because the truck drivers came on to the site only to deliver materials. The court stated that the truck drivers spent 90 percent of their workday on the highway driving to and from commercial supply sources and stayed on the work site only long enough to drop off their loads, usually for not more than 10 minutes. In *Bechtel Constructors*, DOL-ARB, No. 95-45A, July 15, 1996, the board held that workers at sites providing concrete for a nearby federal project were subject to Davis-Bacon wage requirements. The board stated that the D.C. Circuit's ruling in *Ball, Ball & Brosamer* does not bar application of prevailing rates for all off-site plants and that "work performed in actual or virtual adjacency to one portion of a long continuous project is to be considered adjacent to the entire project."

The Federal Acquisition Streamlining Act amended the Davis-Bacon Act by waiving the application of prevailing wage-setting requirements to volunteer workers. The purpose of this waiver is to promote and provide opportunities for volunteers to provide their services in the construction, repair, or alteration of public buildings and works, 40 U.S.C. § 276d. Under 40 U.S.C. 276d-1(a)(1)(A), Davis-Bacon wage-setting provisions are waived for persons who volunteer their services to state, local, or federal projects, and payment of expenses and nominal fees to such volunteers is authorized. Under 40 U.S.C. § 276d-2, Davis-Bacon applicability is waived for volunteers who work for nonprofit organizations supported with federal funds.

3. Obtaining Wage Determinations

The Department of Labor is responsible for issuing wage determinations reflecting prevailing wages, including fringe benefits, FAR 22.404. There are two types of wage determinations — general and project.

A general wage determination contains prevailing wage rates for the types of construction designated in the determination and is used in contracts performed within a specified geographical area, FAR 22.404-1. General wage determinations are published weekly by the General Printing Office in a document entitled "General Wage Determinations Issued Under the Davis-Bacon and Related Acts." Notices of general wage determinations are published in the *Federal Register* and are effective on the publication date of the notice or upon receipt of the determination by the agency, whichever occurs first, FAR 22.404-1(a)(1). Such wage determinations contain no expiration date and are valid until modified, superseded, or canceled by a notice in the *Federal Register.* If there is a general wage determination applicable to the project, the agency may use it without notifying the Department of Labor, FAR 22.404-3. Once incorporated into a contract, a general wage determination normally remains effective for the life of the contract, FAR 22.404-1(a)(1). These determinations must be used whenever possible.

A project wage determination is issued at the specific request of a contracting agency, FAR 22.404-1(b). It is used only when no general wage determination applies. A contracting officer must submit requests for project wage determinations on SF 308 to the Department of Labor, FAR 22.404-3(b). The contracting officer must include a sufficiently detailed description of the work to indicate the type of construction involved, FAR 22.404-3(b). The wage determination is effective for 180 calendar days from the date of issuance and applies only to contract awards made within that time period, FAR 22.404-3(d). Once incorporated into a contract, a project wage determination is normally effective for the entire contract.

If it appears that a project wage determination may expire between bid opening and contract award, the contracting officer must request a new wage determination sufficiently in advance of bid opening, FAR 22.404-5(b)(1). If a wage determination expires after opening but prior to award, the contracting officer should request that the administrator extend the expiration date, FAR 22.404-5(b)(2). If the request is granted, the contracting officer will award the contract and modify it to apply the extended expiration date to the already incorporated project wage determination, FAR 22.404-5(b)(2). If the request is denied, the administrator will issue a new project wage determination. If a new determination changes any wage rates for classifications to be used in the contract, the contracting officer may cancel the solicitation only for compelling reasons in accordance with FAR 14.404-1, FAR 22.404-5(b)(2)(i). Otherwise, the contracting officer must award the contract and incorporate the new wage determination. The new determination is to be effective on the date of contract award. The contractor must equitably adjust the contract price for any increased or decreased cost of performance resulting from any changed wage rates, FAR 22.404-5(b)(2)(i). If the new determination does not change any wage rates, the contracting officer must award the contract and modify it to include the number and date of the new determination, FAR 22.404-5(b)(2)(ii).

4. Procedures for Making Wage Determinations

The Act requires that the minimum wages included in wage determinations be based upon the "prevailing wages" paid to various classes of employees on projects of a similar character in the "city, town, village or other civil subdivision of the State in which the work is to be performed." The prevailing wage is the wage paid to more than 50 percent of the laborers or mechanics in the classification on similar projects in the area during the period in question, 29 C.F.R. § 1.2(a)(1). If the same wage is not paid to a majority in the class, the wage is calculated by taking the average wage paid to all the employees, 29 C.F.R. § 1.2(a)(1). The Labor Secretary's authority to make wage determinations in such a manner is based on the broad language employed in the Act delegating the authority, *Building & Constr. Trades' Dep't, AFL-CIO v. Donovan*, 712 F.2d 611 (D.C. Cir. 1983), *cert. denied*, 464 U.S. 1069 (1984). The geographic reference point for wage determinations is normally the county in which the work is to be performed, 29 C.F.R. § 1.7(a). If there has not been sufficient similar construction in the area within the past year, the wage determination may be based upon wages paid on similar construction sites in surrounding counties, 29 C.F.R. § 1.7(b). However, the wages paid on projects in metropolitan counties may not be used as a source of data to be paid on projects in rural counties and vice versa, 29 C.F.R. § 1.7(b). In *Building & Construction Trades' Department*, the court upheld this regulation as furthering the intention of the statute. If no similar construction in the surrounding counties or in the state was performed within the past year, wages paid on projects completed more than one year prior to the beginning of the survey period may be considered, 29 C.F.R. § 1.7(c).

The Secretary of Labor's wage determinations are final and unreviewable by the Comptroller General, unless they are found to be arbitrary, capricious, or not supported by substantial evidence, 50 Comp. Gen. 103 (B-160778) (1970). The courts are also precluded from reviewing wage determinations, *United States v. Binghamton Constr. Co.*, 347 U.S. 171, *reh'g denied*, 347 U.S. 940 (1954). Thus, questions about the applicability or interpretation of a wage determination must be submitted to the Secretary of Labor, *North Ga. Building & Constr. Trades Council v. Goldschmidt*, 621 F.2d 697 (5th Cir. 1980).

The contract must include the clause set forth in 29 C.F.R. § 5.5(a)(1). This clause requires the payment of employees' wages at "rates not less than those contained in the wage determination of the Secretary of Labor which is attached hereto and made a part hereof." If the Davis-Bacon provisions are omitted from the contract but are included in the IFB, they are incorporated in the contract by reference, *International Bd. of Elec. Workers*, Comp. Gen. Dec. B-183271, 75-1 CPD ¶ 201. The wage rate may be corrected after award if the error is a clerical one as opposed to an error of judgment, *Dawson Constr. Co.*, Comp. Gen. Dec. B-189036, 78-1 CPD ¶ 108. In *Dawson*, the Comptroller General held that if a wage rate was incorrect through an error in judgment, the contract should not be corrected.

B. Walsh-Healey Act

The Walsh-Healey Act, 41 U.S.C. § 35 et seq., is the supply contract counterpart of the Davis-Bacon Act. It establishes "minimum" wages for contracts in excess of $10,000 for the manufacturing or furnishing of materials, supplies, articles, and equipment. Department of Labor regulations implementing this statute are found in 41 C.F.R. Part 50-201. The Walsh-Healey Act was part of a package of New Deal legislation in the 1930s. The Act sought to provide worker protection in order to alleviate two major problems faced by workers during the Depression — the number of hours worked and minimum wages. The protections of the Act have been superseded by subsequent legislation, i.e., the Fair Labor Standards Act.

C. Service Contract Act

The Service Contract Act of 1965, 41 U.S.C. §§ 351–58, as amended by P.L. 92-473, and P.L. 94-489, establishes minimum wage rates and fringe benefits based on those prevailing in the locality to be paid service employees for contracts over $2,500 which are principally for services and are furnished by service employees, 41 U.S.C. § 351(a)(1). It prohibits employment under hazardous or unsanitary working conditions and requires the contractor to provide notice of required compensation to all covered service employees on the first day of employment, 41 U.S.C. § 351(a)(3) and (4). The Act also provides remedies for noncompliance including debarment (§ 354), contract termination (§ 352(c)), and withholding of contract funds (§ 352(a)).

The Act applies only when the services are performed in the United States, 41 U.S.C. § 351(a). Both prime contractors and subcontractors are subject to the Act, 41 U.S.C. § 351(b)(1).

All contractors and subcontractors subject to the Act are required to pay their service employees no less than the minimum wage specified by the Fair Labor Standards Act, as amended, 29 U.S.C. § 201 et seq. This requirement applies to contracts under $2,500 where no wage determination is required and to contracts over $2,500 where no wage determination has been issued. It has been held that this requirement is applicable even though the contract contains no applicable contract clause, Comp. Gen. Dec. B-167287, Sept. 4, 1969, *Unpub.*

The Secretary of Labor has responsibility for administering and implementing the Act, 41 U.S.C. § 353. Enforcement authority is vested in both the Secretary of Labor and the head of the procuring agency, 41 U.S.C. § 352(b). Pursuant to this authority, the Secretary has issued regulations governing the administration and interpretation of the Act in 29 C.F.R. Part 4. In addition, the Secretary has established the Board of Service Contract Appeals to provide administrative appellate review, 29 C.F.R. Part 8. FAR regulations are contained in Subpart 22.10. A supplementary regulation is provided by FAR 37.301 for the contracts involving dismantling, demolition, or removal of improvements.

1. Scope of the Act

Rulings by the Department of Labor on coverage of the Act are binding on the procuring agencies and the Comptroller General, 48 Comp. Gen. 22 (B-164338) (1968). See also 57 Comp. Gen. 501 (B-190505) (1978) (an agency must comply with the Labor Department's regulations implementing the Act unless the regulation is clearly contrary to law). However, the procuring agency makes the initial determination as to whether a contract falls within the Act; it has been held that if the contracting officer believes in good faith that the Act is not applicable, there is no duty to notify the Department of Labor or to include the Service Contract Act provisions in the contract, 53 Comp. Gen. 412 (B-178773) (1973); *Curtiss-Wright Corp. v. McLucas*, 381 F. Supp. 657 (D.N.J. 1974). The Comptroller General subsequently modified this ruling, finding that if the contracting officer is on notice that the Department of Labor may regard the procurement as subject to the Act, the matter must be referred to that Department whose decision on the question will be binding, *Hewes Eng'g Co.*, Comp. Gen. Dec. B-179501, 74-1 CPD ¶ 112.

In general, the Service Contract Act is construed liberally by the Labor Department. Thus, the Act has been applied to a referral service even though the service had neither control over its nominal employees nor interest in the work they performed, *Menlo Serv. Corp. v. United States*, 765 F.2d 805 (9th Cir. 1985).

a. Services

The Act does not define the type of service that it covers, but the Department of Labor regulations at 29 C.F.R. § 4.130 provide examples of the types of services covered. Such services include repair and maintenance, aircraft flight services, stenographic reporting, food service, trash and garbage removal, and warehousing or storage services. See also FAR 22.1003-5. In addition, interpretations regarding the coverage of the Act are issued by the Wage and Hour Administrator of the Labor Department. The Act's apparent legislative intent, according to 29 C.F.R. § 4.111(b), was to include "those contracts which have as their principal purpose the procurement of something other than the construction activity described in the Davis-Bacon Act or the materials, supplies, articles, and equipment described in the Walsh-Healey Act." If a contract involves both end products and services, it will be covered by the Act as long as the facts demonstrate that the contract is chiefly for services and that the furnishing of products is secondary, 29 C.F.R. § 4.131(a).

Department of Labor regulations interpret "principal purpose" to mean that the Act applies to all contracts that are primarily for services unless the contractor's use of service employees is incidental to the performance of the contract, 29 C.F.R. § 4.111(a) and § 4.113(a)(3). For example, timber sale contracts are not generally subject to the Act because many of the services provided, such as land clearing, are incidental to the contractor's principal purpose, 29 C.F.R. § 4.131(f). Although the regulation fails to define "incidental," the Department of Labor has considered the use of service employees incidental only when they have constituted less than 20 percent of the contract's workforce, 48 Fed. Reg. 49743 (1983). This broad interpretation of "principal purpose" has prevailed, as evidenced by the Department of Labor's rejection of a proposed change to its regulations that would have limited the scope of the Act to contracts that were principally for service and principally performed by service employees, 48 Fed. Reg. 49743 (1983).

Confusion has arisen concerning whether the Act applies to specific tasks within a contract where the contract as a whole is not principally for service. Until 1983, the Department of Labor applied the Act to any line item for services in a contract, such as maintenance and repair of automated data processing equipment. After persistent objections by the GSA and the computer industry and recommendations by the Comptroller General (Comp. Gen. Report Nos. HRD-80-102, Sept. 16, 1980, and HRD-80-102(A), Mar. 25, 1981) the Department of Labor revised its regulations to provide that the Act applies only if services are the principal part of the contract as a whole, 29 C.F.R. § 4.132.

b. Service Employees

Although the Act originally applied only to blue collar workers, *Descomp, Inc. v. Sampson*, 377 F. Supp. 254 (D. Del. 1974); *Federal Elec. Corp. v. Dunlop*, 419 F. Supp. 221 (M.D. Fla. 1976), Congress amended the Act in 1976 to include some white collar workers, P.L. 94-489, 90 Stat. 2358 (1976). 41 U.S.C. § 357(b) states:

> The term "service employee" means any person engaged in the performance of a contract entered into by the United States and not exempted under

> section 7 [41 U.S.C. § 356], whether negotiated or advertised, the principal purpose of which is to furnish services in the United States (other than any person employed in a bona fide executive, administrative, or professional capacity, as those terms are defined in part 541 of title 29, Code of Federal Regulations, as of July 30, 1976, and any subsequent revision of those regulations); and shall include all such persons regardless of any contractual relationship that may be alleged to exist between a contractor or subcontractor and such persons.

The Department of Labor has found several classes of white collar workers to be service employees. For example, 29 C.F.R. § 4.152 considers stenographers to be service employees, and wage determinations have been issued covering marine engineers, priests, ministers, librarians, and radio announcers.

2. *Wage Determinations*

The principal purpose of the Act is to specify the minimum wages and benefits to be paid to service employees in accordance with prevailing rates in the locality, 41 U.S.C. § 351. When a procuring agency determines that a prospective contract is subject to the Act, it must file Standard Form 98, FAR 53.301-98 and Standard Form 98a, FAR 53.301-98a, "Notice of Intention to Make Service Contract and Response to Notice" and "Attachment A" with the Department of Labor not less than 30 days prior to the solicitation, FAR 22.1007. This allows time to provide a wage determination to be attached to the solicitation so that all offerors will be informed of the minimum wages applicable to the contract. The Department of Labor has encountered great difficulty in providing wage determinations for all types of services; consequently, numerous service contracts have been awarded without such determinations. The discretion of the Department to decide not to issue a wage determination has been upheld, *Kentron Hawaii, Ltd. v. Warner*, 480 F.2d 1166 (D.C. Cir. 1973). See also *International Ass'n of Machinists & Aerospace Workers v. Hodgson*, 515 F.2d 373 (D.C. Cir 1975). As a result, Congress amended the Act in 1972 to state that its intention was that wage determinations be made for all service contracts over $2,500 as soon as administratively feasible, 41 U.S.C. § 358, and to limit the power of the Secretary to create variations on or exemptions from the Act, 41 U.S.C. § 353(b).

Since it is extremely difficult to prepare a wage determination for each service contract, the Department of Labor has established a register of wage determinations for various types of services in different localities in the United States, 29 C.F.R. § 4.3. If the contract is to be performed in one of these localities, the contracting officer is authorized to select the appropriate class of service employees from the descriptions and wage rate determinations provided by the Department of Labor, *IBI Security Servs., Inc.*, Comp. Gen. Dec. B-218565, 85-2 CPD ¶ 7, *recons. denied*, 85-2 CPD ¶ 136. If a procuring agency does not receive a wage determination from the Department of Labor in response to its SF 98, it is required to use the most current wage determination in the register for the procurement. In sealed bid procurements, any revisions to the determination received by the procuring agency earlier than 10 days prior to bid opening must be incorporated in the procurement by amendment to the solicitation. Revisions received later than this time may be ignored by the procuring agency if found that reasonable time is not available to notify bidders, 29 C.F.R. 4.5(a)(2). In negotiated procurement, revisions received by the agency after contract award will not be effective if the contract start of performance is within 30 days of such award, 29 C.F.R. § 4.5(a)(2). If the contract does not specify a start of performance and if contract performance does not commence within 30 days of the award, the Department of Labor must be notified and any revision received by the contracting agency not less than 10 days before commencement will be effective, 29 C.F.R. § 4.5(a)(2). Where a wage determination that is included in the contract omits one or more categories of service employees, the contractor must classify such employees and pay them wages and fringe benefits as determined by agreement of the contracting agency, the contractor, and the employees, 29 C.F.R. § 4.6(b)(2). A contractor can rely on a wage determination for the life of the contract, but new wage determinations are required in the event of a modification or change to the contract or use of an option clause, 29 C.F.R. § 4.143.

There are two major obstacles confronting the Secretary of Labor in exercising the authority to make wage determinations: (1) defining what is meant by "locality" and (2) deciding between prevailing wages and higher wages under a collective bargaining agreement.

a. Determining Locality

Wage determinations must include wages for the "locality" where the work will be performed. When a contract requires services to be performed at a Government site, locality has been defined as the area in which the facility is located. However, some controversy has ensued in identifying the appropriate locality when the place of contract performance is unknown at the time of solicitation. It has been held that locality in such cases refers to the area where the services are actually performed, *Descomp, Inc. v. Sampson*, 377 F. Supp. 254 (D. Del. 1974). The Department of Labor, however, refused to adopt this position and instead defined locality as the site of the procuring activity, 41 Fed. Reg. 5388 (1976). Under this approach, wages from one locality were applied to all localities in which offerors were located. The Comptroller General was dissatisfied with the Department of Labor's interpretation of locality, *Descomp, Inc.*, 53 Comp. Gen. 522 (B-178956), 74-1 CPD ¶ 44; *Cage Co. of Abilene, Inc.*, 57 Comp. Gen. 549 (B-187665), 78-1 CPD ¶ 430, but refused to overturn the Department of Labor because the language of the Act did not prohibit its interpretation. Finally, in *Southern Packaging & Storage Co. v. United States*, 458 F. Supp. 726 (D.S.C. 1978), *aff'd*, 618 F.2d 1088 (4th Cir. 1980), the court required the Department of Labor to issue separate wage determinations for each potential contractor's locality. The court also noted that nationwide determinations would discourage competitive bidding by requiring a bidder to pay its employees higher wages than those prevailing in the geographic region where the contract would actually be performed.

In compliance with the court's decision, the Department of Labor has adopted a two-step procedure for making wage determinations, 29 C.F.R. § 4.3(c) and § 4.4(a)(2)(i). Under the first step, the contracting agency identifies the prospective offerors and their localities in its notice to make a service contract. In the second step, a wage determination is issued for the locality of each offeror. When award is made, the appropriate wage determination is incorporated into the contract and is applicable even if the contractor subsequently changes the place of contract performance. If the contracting agency can show extraordinary circumstances for which the two-step procedure is not practicable, it may request that wage determinations be issued for one or more composite localities, 29 C.F.R. § 4.4(a)(2)(ii). Detailed guidance on the two-step procedure is found in FAR 22.1009.

The two-step procedure was challenged in *AFL-CIO v. Donovan*, 757 F.2d 330 (D.C. Cir. 1985). The union argued that this approach would cause a disproportionate amount of contract awards to be made to low-wage areas, and a nationwide determination was therefore needed to provide the kind of wage protection intended by Congress. In response, the court stated, "To read 'locality' to mean 'Nation' conflicts squarely with the term's ordinary, common meaning." Finding no expression of congressional intent for a nationwide wage determination, the court upheld the two-step procedure.

b. Collective Bargaining Agreements

The Service Contract Act originally allowed the Department of Labor to find a prevailing wage lower than the wage being paid by an incumbent contractor under a collective bargaining agreement. This provision was amended at 41 U.S.C. § 353(c), making the prior collective bargaining agreement rates applicable to subsequent contracts without regard to any wage determination that has been issued unless one of the statutory exceptions applies. See *Eastern Serv. Management Co.*, SCA-352-355, 22 WH Cases 796 (1975). The Department of Labor has issued procedures to implement this requirement in 29 C.F.R. § 4.1b(b). Under these procedures, the contracting officer is required to give the incumbent contractor and the collective bargaining representative of the incumbent's employees prior notice of the proposed procurement at least 30 days before issuance of a solicitation. If the contracting officer does not receive timely notice of a collective bargaining agreement, the procurement is allowed to proceed without regard to the wage rates in the collective bargaining agreement. Otherwise, such wages are binding on the new contractor.

This "successor" contract rule does not apply if the Department of Labor makes a determination that a collective bargaining agreement was not entered into as a result of arm's-length negotiations, or the negotiated wages and benefits substantially vary from those prevailing in the locality. Determination that the predecessor contractor's collective bargaining agreement resulted from arm's-length negotiations may be made through investigation, hearing, or pursuant to the Secretary's authority, FAR 22.1002-3(a). The regulations are also quite complete in setting forth the procedures to be followed for making a determination that the rates in the collective bargaining agreement are substantially at variance with prevailing rates, 29 C.F.R. § 4.10. In the past, if a substantial variance decision was made after the contract had been awarded, the Labor Department applied the new wage determination retroactively to the start of contract performance if it increased the workers' wages, but applied the determination prospectively when it decreased those wages. Since 1983, the Labor Department has made these determinations solely on a prospective basis, 48 Fed. Reg. 49737 (1983).

3. Exemptions to Service Contract Act

The Secretary of Labor has authority to exempt contracts from the Service Contract Act under 41 U.S.C. § 353(c). Exempted from the provisions of the Act are contracts for transportation (§ 356(3)), communications (§ 356(4)), public utilities (§ 356(5)), individual personal services (§ 356(6)), and contracts with the Postal Service (§ 356(7)). Contracts covered by the Walsh-Healey Act are also exempt from the Act (§ 356(2)), but the Department of Labor has ruled that the Act will cover some contracts that would otherwise be subject to Walsh-Healey but for the fact that they are for amounts less than $10,000, SCA Op. 303.4, 302.4, 302.3, Feb. 1, 1968. For example, the Act has been held to apply to storage of household goods, SCA Op. 401, May 21, 1969, and a contract to furnish, stock, and maintain vending machines, SCA Op. 302.3, 303.4, Jan. 22, 1968. See also *Williams v. Department of Labor*, 697 F.2d 842 (8th Cir. 1983), where military "pack and crate" contracts were not exempted from the Act because the contracts were not primarily for carriage of freight.

Similarly, contracts subject to the Davis-Bacon Act are exempt (§ 356(1)). For dismantling, demolition, or removal of improvements contracts, FAR 37.301 requires the use of the Davis-Bacon Act only if "further work which will result in the construction, alteration, or repair of a public building or public work at that location is contemplated." Otherwise, the Service Contract Act applies. See also 29 C.F.R. § 4.131(f). For other contracts containing both services and construction, the Comptroller General has permitted broad discretion by contracting officers, loosely following the rule that the Davis-Bacon Act will apply if the contract contains substantial amounts of construction work, *D.E. Clarke*, Comp. Gen. Dec. B-146824, 75-1 CPD ¶ 317.

In 1983, the Department of Labor promulgated 29 C.F.R. § 4.123(e)(1)(i)(A), (B), and (C), which permit exemption of contracts for the maintenance and repair of automated data processing equipment and office information systems, office and business machines, and high-technology scientific and medical apparatus. To qualify for the exemption, the contractor is required to certify that it will maintain the same compensation plan for employees on both Government and commercial equipment contracts. See *AFL-CIO v. Donovan*, 757 F.2d 330 (D.C. Cir. 1985), where the court found proper an exemption for contracts for commercial products support services of high-technology companies in view of the industry's established merit pay systems and the significant impairment of Government operations which would result if computers were not available because manufacturers refused to accept service contracts.

The Department of Labor has declined a proposal to exempt R&D contracts from the Act after concluding that such an exemption is unnecessary and would be extremely difficult to define, 48 Fed. Reg. 49751 (1983).

VIII. OTHER EMPLOYEE-RELATED STATUTES

Congress has enacted two statutes that have direct impact on the manner in which contractor employees are treated at the workplace. This section discusses the Americans with Disabilities Act of 1990 (ADA), 42 U.S.C. § 12101 et seq., and the Drug-Free Workplace Act of 1988 (DFWA), 41 U.S.C. § 701. Although the main purposes of these two laws are not related, they share the common goals of attempting to make the contract work environment more accessible to all qualified personnel, more acceptable as a "good" place to work, and more productive.

A. Americans with Disabilities Act

The ADA seeks to protect "individuals with a disability" if they are qualified to perform job requirements. It defines an "individual with a disability" as someone with a physical or mental impairment that substantially limits one or more major life activities, 42 U.S.C. § 12102(2). It prohibits discrimination against such individuals and requires "reasonable accommodation" for them, 42 U.S.C. § 12112.

1. Prohibited Discrimination

The ADA prohibits all employers (not only Government contractors) from discriminating in all aspects of employment against any "qualified individual with a disability" because of that person's disability. The ADA specifically bars discrimination in job application procedures, hiring, promotion, termination, compensation, training, and other "terms, conditions, and privileges of employment," 42 U.S.C. § 12112(a).

The statute defines the term "qualified individual with a disability" to mean an "individual with a disability who, with or without reasonable accommodation, can perform the essential functions of the employment position that such individual holds," 42 U.S.C. § 12111(8). In *Floyd E. McDaniel v. AlliedSignal, Inc.*, 896 F. Supp. 1482 (1995), the court found that a security clearance was an essential function of an individual's employment position. An employee of AlliedSignal claimed that the company was obligated under the ADA to provide him a reasonable accommodation that would cure or mitigate his disability so that his required security clearance would not be revoked by the Government. The court stated that to make a prima facie case under the ADA, an employee must be able to perform the essential functions of the job in spite of the disability with no need for accommodation or with reasonable accommodation. The employee conceded that he could not perform the essential functions of the job unless AlliedSignal provided some sort of accommodation. The court held that because the decision to revoke a security clearance is solely the Government's, no amount of accommodation by AlliedSignal would render the employee able to perform the essential functions of the position.

The ADA expressly forbids any preemployment medical examination or other inquiry of a job applicant about the existence or extent of any disability, 42 U.S.C. § 12112(d). However, if all employees are subject to a medical examination, then an individual with a disability can properly be subject to the same requirement so long as the results are maintained in confidence and used only as otherwise permitted under the statute, 42 U.S.C. § 12112(d)(3). Employers are further forbidden from discriminating against an otherwise-qualified individual because of the disability of another person with whom the qualified individual has a relationship, 42 U.S.C. § 12112(b)(4). Finally, the ADA requires that the job application process be accessible to people with different disabilities, and it prohibits the use of standards or tests if they tend to screen out individuals with disabilities, unless the selection criteria are job related for the position in question and consistent with business necessity, 42 U.S.C. § 12112(b)(6).

2. Reasonable Accommodation

The ADA requires employers to make "reasonable accommodation" for the physical or mental impairments of the employee or applicant, that is, changes in the work environment or in the way things are customarily done that enable a person with a disability to enjoy equal employment opportunities, 29 C.F.R. Part 1630 App. 1630(2)(o).

Employers are required to make only accommodations that are reasonable. An accommodation is not reasonable if the employer can demonstrate that it would impose undue hardship on the conduct of its business. This would include accommodations that are unduly costly, extensive, substantial, or disruptive, or that would fundamentally alter the nature or operation of the business, 29 C.F.R. Part 1630 App. 1630(2)(o).

3. Defenses

Employers have several defenses available. First, accommodations need not be made if they would impose an undue hardship on the employer's business. Second, qualification standards may be used, even those that tend to screen out people with disabilities, if the standards are job related and consistent with business necessity. Furthermore, employers are not obligated to hire anyone who poses a direct threat to the health or safety of himself or herself or to others in the workplace, 42 U.S.C. § 12113(b). Protection under the ADA does not extend to any employee or applicant who is currently engaging in the illegal use of drugs, 42 U.S.C. § 12114(a).

4. Enforcement

The ADA is enforced by the EEOC in the same manner used to enforce Title VII of the Civil Rights Act of 1964, 42 U.S.C. § 12117(a). Any job applicant or employee who believes that discrimination has occurred can file a charge with the nearest EEOC office. The complaining party, once its administrative remedies have been exhausted, is free to file suit in federal court.

The remedies available to a successful complainant in an ADA proceeding are the same remedies available under Title VII of the Civil Rights Act of 1964, 42 U.S.C. § 12117(a). Available remedies may include hiring, reinstatement, promotion, back or front pay, reasonable accommodation, attorney fees, expert witness fees, and court costs, 42 U.S.C. § 1981a(a). Compensatory and punitive damages also may be available where intentional discrimination is found, 42 U.S.C. § 1981a(a). These damages are capped at a level corresponding to the size of the employer. For example, employers of between 15 and 100 employees will not pay damages in excess of $50,000, 42 U.S.C. § 1981a(b)(3).

The ADA expressly prohibits retaliation against an individual who makes a charge of discrimination or who participates in any resulting investigation, proceeding, or hearing, 42 U.S.C. § 12203.

B. Drug-Free Workplace Act of 1988

The DFWA requires most Government contractors to establish and maintain a drug-free workplace as a condition of their current contracts and in order to maintain eligibility for future contracts. The DFWA is implemented by FAR Subpart 23.5.

1. Policy

The Act prohibits award of contracts except those under the simplified acquisition threshold or for commercial items, unless the contractor has certified that it will provide a drug-free workplace and adhere to several specific practices, FAR 23.504. Contractors must:

- Publish a policy statement that prohibits any unlawful activity involving controlled substances in the workplace and specifying the actions that will be taken with respect to violations of the policy.
- Establish a drug-free awareness program that will inform employees about the drug-free workplace, the availability of counseling and employee assistance programs, and the sanctions that will be imposed for drug abuse violations occurring in the workplace.
- Notify the contracting agency in writing of any employee conviction for a drug statute violation within 10 calendar days after being made aware of the conviction.
- Impose sanctions (up to and including termination) on the involved employee or require the employee to participate in an approved drug abuse assistance or rehabilitation program.
- Make a "good faith" effort to maintain a drug-free workplace.

The Act is implemented by a Drug-Free Workplace clause at FAR 52.223-6.

2. *Drug Testing*

The DFWA does not require drug testing of employees by contractors. However, Exec. Order No. 12564, issued by President Reagan in 1986, did provide for random drug testing in sensitive positions. The FAR is silent on drug testing procedures. Individual agencies have issued drug testing procedures that vary depending upon the duties of the agency and the "sensitivity" of the work being performed by contractors. The DOD and NASA offer representative examples of these rules.

The drug testing protocol required of DOD contractors is found in the Drug-Free Work Force clause, DFARS 252.223-7004. This clause requires as part of a contractor's drug-free program "provisions for identifying illegal drug users on a controlled and carefully monitored basis." The clause goes on to discuss the extent of and criteria for such testing. As important considerations it mentions the nature of the work being performed; the employee's duties; the efficient use of contractor resources; and the risks to health, safety, and national security that could result from the failure of employees to adequately perform their work. In addition, the clause provides that testing is appropriate (1) when there is a reasonable suspicion that an employee uses illegal drugs, (2) when an employee has been involved in an accident or unsafe practice, (3) as part of a follow-up to counseling or rehabilitation, or (4) as part of a voluntary employee drug testing program.

NASA has initiated a drug and alcohol testing program to implement the Civil Space Employee Testing Act of 1991, 48 C.F.R. §§ 1823 & 1852, 61 Fed. Reg. 7224, Feb. 27, 1996. Among other things, the proposed rules require NASA contractors to provide preemployment, reasonable suspicion, random, postaccident, and periodic follow-up testing of contractor employees "responsible for safety-sensitive, security, or national security functions."

The Department of Health and Human Services has issued "Guidelines for Federal Workplace Drug Testing Programs," 59 Fed. Reg. 29908, June 6, 1994, which, as revised, became effective in September 1994. Among other things, these Guidelines seek to establish (1) scientific and technical rules for federal agencies' workplace drug testing programs, and (2) a certification program for laboratories engaged in urine drug testing for federal agencies.

3. Sanctions

FAR 23.504(a) provides that no offeror will be considered a responsible source in the absence of certification regarding a drug-free workplace. Similarly, under FAR 23.504(b), an individual will be denied award of a contract of any dollar amount unless that individual certifies that he or she "will not engage in the unlawful manufacture, distribution, dispensing, possession, or use of a controlled substance in the performance of a covered contract."

FAR 23.506 provides that the contracting officer may suspend contract payments if an offeror has submitted a false certification, if a contractor has failed to comply with the certification, or if the number of contractor employees convicted of criminal drug violations throws into question the contractor's good faith effort to provide a drug-free workplace. The contracting officer also has the discretion to terminate a contract for default, or to debar or suspend a contractor under appropriate circumstances, FAR 23.506(e).

CHAPTER 11

CONTRACT AWARD CONTROVERSIES

Contract award controversies have become a substantial part of the procurement process. Offerors, prospective offerors, and other parties often seek to challenge procurement actions. For a long time, these challenges were heard without specific statutory authority. However, beginning in 1982, Congress began to take an active role in formalizing the process by adopting a number of statutes dealing with award controversies. Presently, there are four forums where contract award controversies may be heard — the procuring agencies, the Comptroller General (the head of the General Accounting Office (GAO)), the Court of Federal Claims (COFC), and the U.S. district courts. **Figure 11-1** summarizes the major features of each of these forums.

The boards of contract appeals have not generally been involved in contract award controversies, *Coastal Corp. v. United States*, 713 F.2d 728 (Fed. Cir. 1983) (board's jurisdiction under the Contract Disputes Act of 1978, 41 U.S.C. § 601 et seq., does not extend to implied contract to consider bids and proposals fairly). A notable exception was the General Services Administration Board of Contract Appeals (GSBCA). In 1984, the GSBCA was granted authority to hear protests on Brooks Act automatic data processing equipment (now, information technology) procurements, 40 U.S.C. § 759(h). However, Section 5101 of the Clinger-Cohen Act of 1996, P.L. 104-106, took away that authority by repealing 40 U.S.C. § 759. During this tenure, the board rendered numerous decisions dealing with various phases of the award process. Those decisions and the decisions of the Court of Appeals for the Federal Circuit dealing with them can be helpful in resolving current award controversies. The Department of Housing and Urban Development Board of Contract Appeals has been delegated authority by the Secretary to hear protests on contracts for procurement or sale under the National Housing Act, 24 C.F.R. § 20.1 et seq.

The following material first deals with the distinction between contract award controversies that may be brought by a third party and contract performance disputes. It then considers, in detail, the features of each of the four forums.

CONTRACT AWARD CONTROVERSIES				
Forum	**Procuring Agency**	**Court of Federal Claims (COFC)**	**District Courts**	**GAO**
Who May Protest	Interested parties	Persons with implied contract for good faith consideration of offer and interested parties	Persons adversely affected or aggrieved by agency action and interested parties	Interested parties
Jurisdiction	FAR 33.103	28 U.S.C. §1491(a)(1) and (b)(2)	5 U.S.C. §702, 28 U.S.C. §1346(2), and 28 U.S.C. § 1491(b)(2)	31 U.S.C. §3551, with deference to actions in other forums
Time for Protest	Pre- and postaward	Pre- and postaward	Pre- and postaward	Pre- and postaward
Time of Decision	No designated time	No designated time	No designated time	100 calendar days (65 calendar days — express option)
Procedures	Various agency procedures; Informal in nature	Evidentiary trial, including discovery	Evidentiary trial, including discovery	Submission of written reports and optional hearing
Burden of Proof	Probably same as GAO	Clear and convincing evidence of violation	Preponderance of evidence	Presumption of correctness of agency action
Standard s of Review	Violation of statute or regulation	No rational basis or clear violation of statute or regulation	No rational basis or clear violation of statute or regulation	Violation of statute or regulation
Interim Remedies	Agency must delay award or suspend performance unless CICA override	Discretionary temporary restraining order or preliminary injunction	Discretionary temporary restraining order or preliminary injunction	Agency must delay award or suspend performance unless CICA override
Remedies	Any appropriate actions	Injunction or declaratory judgment if consistent with national defense; bid or proposal costs	Injunction or declaratory judgment, unless inconsistent with overriding public interest; bid or proposal costs (limited to $10,000 under § 1346(2))	Recommend that agency recompete, terminate, or award; contract costs; attorneys' fees; bid or proposal costs
Appeals	If within jurisdictional time period, begin action again in either GAO, COFC, or district court	Federal circuit	Applicable circuit	Indirectly through suit in the COFC or district court

Figure 11-1

I. AWARD VERSUS PERFORMANCE CONTROVERSIES

Contract award controversies must be distinguished from controversies arising during contract performance. As a general rule, performance controversies occur between the parties to a contract, and third parties cannot challenge actions that occur during the performance of a contract. See, for example, *Gull Airborne Instruments, Inc. v. Weinberger*, 694 F.2d 838 (D.C. Cir. 1982), denying a competitor a right to obtain an injunction ordering the contracting officer to terminate the contract for default based on the contractor's alleged failure to perform as proposed. This rule has been incorporated in the protest regulations of the Comptroller General at 4 C.F.R. § 21.5(a), which states, "The administration of an existing contract is within the discretion of the contracting agency." Other cases denying jurisdiction because the issue was a matter involving contract administration include *Control Data Sys., Inc. v. United States*, 32 Fed. Cl. 520 (1994) (decision not to exercise an option); *Dial Page, Inc.*, Comp. Gen. Dec. B-256210, 94-1 CPD ¶ 311 (whether awardee can successfully implement a paging system and bring it into compliance with the specifications); *American Instrument Corp.*, Comp. Gen. Dec. B-239997, 90-2 CPD ¶ 287 (whether awardee complies with Buy American Act certification); *Digital Sys. Group, Inc.*, Comp. Gen. Dec. B-252080.2, 93-1 CPD ¶ 228, and *AVW Elec. Sys., Inc.*, Comp. Gen. Dec. B-252399, 93-1 CPD ¶ 386 (exercise of an option); *Anderson Columbia Co.*, Comp. Gen. Dec. B-249475.3, 92-2 CPD ¶ 288 (whether awardee may violate contract requirement for use of U.S. flag vessels); *Sierra Technologies, Inc.*, Comp. Gen. Dec. B-251460, 92-2 CPD ¶ 427 (failure to continue making dual awards on acquisition program); *RGI, Inc.*, Comp. Gen. Dec. B-243387.2, 91-2 CPD ¶ 572 (use of less qualified individuals by the awardee than originally proposed to fill positions under the contract); *C.M.P., Inc. v. United States*, 8 Cl. Ct. 743 (1985) (exercise of an option in competitor's contract); and *Willow Beach Resort, Inc. v. United States*, 5 Cl. Ct. 241 (1984) (refusal of agency to treat "preferential right" in contract as a promise to buy only from protester).

Where, however, the contract action is considered to clearly compromise the competition that led to the award, it will be considered a contract award controversy, *Webcraft Packaging, Div. of Beatrice Foods Co.*, Comp. Gen. Dec. B-194087, 79-2 CPD ¶ 120 (agency should have resolicited rather than relax specifications in contract for specialty product produced by only a few sources). Thus, the contract award controversy process will be available where a contract modification alters the contract requirement to the extent that the modified contract is outside the scope of the original competition, *AT&T Communications, Inc. v. Wiltel, Inc.*, 1 F.3d 1201 (Fed. Cir. 1993). This is determined by analyzing the entire contract to determine whether the original competitors would have anticipated that the modification would be issued under the contract. See *American Air Filter Co.*, 57 Comp. Gen. 567 (B-188408), 78-1 CPD ¶ 443 (modification requiring units to operate on diesel fuel rather than gasoline was outside scope of original competition); *Avtron Mfg., Inc.*, 67 Comp. Gen. 404 (B-229972), 88-1 CPD ¶ 458 (modifying the speed drive of the equipment would materially alter the terms of the original contract); and *Neil R. Gross & Co.*, Comp. Gen. Dec. B-237434, 90-1 CPD ¶ 212 (modification adding new court reporting services with substantial increased costs was outside scope of original competition). But see *Arjay Elecs. Corp.*, Comp. Gen. Dec. B-243080, 91-2 CPD ¶ 3 (contract price was not adjusted, period of time for delivery was not extended, and there was no evidence that changes in the item descriptions were significant; thus, no evidence that field of competition changed due to contract modification).

II. PROCURING AGENCIES AND OMBUDSMEN

Persons seeking to contest a procurement have always had the option of lodging a complaint with the procuring agency. Some agencies adopted procedures to handle these protests. Until recently, however, there were no Governmentwide regulations dealing with agency protests. On October 25, 1995, President Clinton issued Exec. Order No. 12979, 60 Fed. Reg. 55171, requiring all agencies to establish administrative procedures for resolving bid protests. These procedures are required to:

> (a) emphasize that whenever conduct of a procurement is contested, all parties should use their best efforts to resolve the matter with agency contracting officers;
>
> (b) to the maximum extent practicable, provide for inexpensive, informal, procedurally simple, and expeditious resolution of protests, including where appropriate and as permitted by law, the use of alternative dispute resolution techniques, third party neutrals, and another agency's personnel;
>
> (c) allow actual or prospective bidders or offerors whose direct economic interests would be affected by the award or failure to award the contract to request a review, at a level above the contracting officer, of any decision by

> a contracting officer that is alleged to have violated a statute or regulation and, thereby, caused prejudice to the protester.

The provisions of the executive order are implemented in FAR 33.103. This section considers the various ways in which the agencies have responded to the executive order and the FAR.

A. Jurisdiction

There are no jurisdictional limitations on agency protests because any agency of the Government has inherent authority to consider a protest alleging some defect in one of its procurements. The agency protest procedures mandated by FAR Subpart 33.1 apply to all "executive agencies," FAR 1.101. The meaning of this term is discussed in the next section on protests to the Comptroller General.

B. Who May Protest

The FAR contains no rule limiting the parties that may file a protest with an agency. Thus, agencies may consider protests from any party that raises legitimate concerns about the conduct of a procurement, and it is clear that some agency officials, such as the NASA ombudsman, will consider such protests. To determine the scope of an agency's protest procedures, each agency regulation must be reviewed.

FAR 33.102(e) does "encourage" an "interested party" wishing to protest to seek resolution within the procuring activity. FAR 33.101 defines "interested party" as "an actual or prospective offeror whose direct economic interest would be affected by the award of a contract or by the failure to award a contract." This is the same definition as used by the Comptroller General.

C. Time for Protest

FAR 33.103(e) states very formal rules, patterned on the GAO rules, on the time for submitting protests to an agency. Protests based on alleged improprieties in a solicitation that are apparent prior to bid opening or the closing date for receipt of proposals must be filed prior to bid opening or the closing date for receipt of proposals. In all other cases, protests must be filed not later than 10 days after the basis of the protest is known or should have been known, whichever is earlier. The agency may, for good cause shown or where the protest raises issues significant to the agency's acquisition system, consider the merits of any protest that is not timely filed. In addition, there is nothing in the FAR that precludes an agency from considering untimely protests on other bases.

The FAR provides some assurance to protesters that an executive agency will not moot a protest by permitting contract performance during the consideration of the protest. FAR 33.103(f)(1) provides that if an agency protest is filed before award, award will not be made unless it is justified in writing for "urgent and compelling reasons or is determined, in writing, to be in the best interest of the Government." This decision to award in the face of a protest must be made "at a level above the contracting officer, or by another official pursuant to agency procedures." With respect to agency protests received within 10 days after award, the contracting officer is not required to suspend performance or terminate the awarded contract unless it appears likely that the award may be invalidated.

D. Procedures

Protests to the contracting agency should be submitted to the person designated in the solicitation. Under the standard Service of Protest clause in FAR 52.233-2, this is generally expected to be the contracting officer, but each agency may designate the official to which protests may be sent. When the protester sends in its protest, it may "request an independent review at a level above the contracting officer," FAR 33.103(d)(4).

Agency-level protests should include a complete statement of the complaint that the protester has with the procurement. In adopting procedures for agency-level protests, FAR 33.103(d) set forth the following legalistic guidance modeled on the GAO protest procedures:

> The following procedures are established to resolve agency protests effectively, to build confidence in the Government's acquisition system, and to reduce protests outside of the agency:
>
>> (1) Protests shall be concise and logically presented to facilitate review by the agency. Failure to substantially comply with any of the requirements of subparagraph (d)(2) of this section may be grounds for dismissal of the protest.

(2) Protests shall include the following information:

(i) Name, address, and fax and telephone numbers of the protester.

(ii) Solicitation or contract number.

(iii) Detailed statement of the legal and factual grounds for the protest, to include a description of resulting prejudice to the protester.

(iv) Copies of relevant documents.

(v) Request for a ruling by the agency.

(vi) Statement as to the form of relief requested.

(vii) All information establishing that the protester is an interested party for the purpose of filing a protest.

(viii) All information establishing the timeliness of the protest.

Agencies are encouraged to resolve agency protests within 35 days after the protest is filed, FAR 33.103(g). Written protest decisions should be sent to the protester and should contain reasoning and "sufficient factual detail explaining the agency position," FAR 33.103(h).

The Army Materiel Command (AMC) has successfully used agency-level protests since 1991. Under the AMC's protest procedures, a protest may be filed with either the contracting officer or the AMC Office of Command Counsel. Within 10 working days after the protest is filed, the contracting officer, with the assistance of legal counsel, is required to file an administrative report responsive to the protest to the AMC Office of Command Counsel. The AMC Protest Decision Authority will issue a written decision within 20 working days after the filing of the protest, regardless of whether the administrative report is timely filed. For good cause, the AMC Protest Decision Authority may grant an extension of time for filing the administrative report and for the issuance of the written decision. The written decision is binding on the AMC and the contractor.

One technique used to resolve an agency protest is to appoint an ombudsman. NASA has created an ombudsman program, 60 Fed. Reg. 47099 (1995), and the following clause must be included in NASA solicitations:

> An ombudsman has been appointed to hear concerns from offerors, potential offerors, and contractors during the preaward and postaward phases of this acquisition. The purpose of the ombudsman is not to diminish the authority of the contracting officer, the Source Evaluation Board, or the selection official, but to communicate concerns, issues, disagreements, and recommendations of interested parties to the appropriate Government personnel and to work to resolve them. When requested, the ombudsman will maintain strict confidentiality as to the source of the concern. The ombudsman does not participate in the evaluation of proposals, the source selection process, or the adjudication of formal contract disputes. Interested parties are invited to call the installation ombudsman ________ [insert name] at ________ [insert telephone number]. Concerns, issues, disagreements, and recommendations which cannot be resolved at the installation may be referred to the NASA ombudsman _______ [insert name] at _______ [insert telephone number].

The scope of this ombudsman's duties extends beyond protests orders — covering all matters concerning contracts with the agency.

The Federal Acquisition Streamlining Act of 1994 (FASA), P.L. 103-355, task and delivery order authority precludes protests concerning the issuance of orders under task and delivery order contracts. See 10 U.S.C. § 2304c(d) and 41 U.S.C. § 303J(d), stating:

> Protests. — A protest is not authorized in connection with the issuance or proposed issuance of a task or delivery order except for a protest on the ground that the order increases the scope, period, or maximum value of the contract under which the order is issued.

In lieu of protests, the legislation provides a new type of agency "protest" forum. A task and delivery order ombudsman will review complaints from contractors holding multiple award task order or delivery order contracts to ensure that they are afforded a fair opportunity to be considered for task or delivery orders. 10 U.S.C. § 2304c(e) and 41 U.S.C. § 303J(e) provide:

> Each head of an agency who awards multiple task or delivery order contracts . . . shall appoint or designate a task and delivery order ombudsman who shall be responsible for reviewing complaints from the contractors on such contracts and ensuring that all of the contractors are afforded a fair opportunity to be considered for task or delivery orders when required. . . . The task and delivery order ombudsman shall be a senior agency official

> who is independent of the contracting officer for the contracts and may be the agency's competition advocate.

FAR 16.505(b)(4) incorporates this requirement with slightly different wording. While the statute appears to limit the ombudsman's role to multiple award situations, the FAR seems to extend it to all aspects of all task and delivery order contracts, whether single or multiple.

E. Standards of Review

The FAR is not clear on the standards of review that will be used in dealing with agency-level protests. Its initial guidance is the broad statement that contracting officers "shall consider all protests," FAR 33.102(a). See also FAR 33.103(b), stating:

> Prior to submission of an agency protest, all parties shall use their best efforts to resolve concerns raised by an interested party at the contracting officer level through open and frank discussions.

This guidance indicates that a potential offeror can obtain the contracting officer's review of any concern regarding the procurement. In particular, this type of "protest" would be appropriate when a potential offeror has questions about the meaning of a solicitation or concerns that a solicitation is not properly drafted.

If the more formal "agency protest" procedure is used, FAR 33.102(b) and FAR 33.103(d)(4) state that the standard of review will be whether a solicitation, proposed award, or award complies with "the requirements of law and regulation." It appears that this is too narrow a statement of the standard of review that will be applied to formal agency protests, because such protests will also consider whether the actions of the contracting agency are reasonable (as that requirement is construed by the Comptroller General and the courts). In addition, agencies may adopt broader standards of review in accordance with their own internal procedures.

F. Prejudice

As discussed below, the Comptroller General and the courts have refused to grant relief on a protest unless they find that the protester has been prejudiced by the improper agency action. There is no reason why this rule should be followed in an agency protest because agencies should correct a problem that has occurred in the procurement process as soon as they are aware of the problem.

G. Remedies

The contracting officer or an agency protest authority with broad powers, such as the NASA ombudsman, can take any action necessary to resolve a protest that is brought to it. If a protest is brought to the head of an agency using the FAR agency protest procedures, the FAR provides that the agency can take any action that could have been recommended by the Comptroller General had the protest been filed with the GAO. FAR 33.102(b) states:

> If, in connection with a protest, the head of an agency determines that a solicitation, proposed award, or award does not comply with the requirements of law or regulation, the head of the agency may —
>
> > (1) Take any action that could have been recommended by the Comptroller General had the protest been filed with the General Accounting Office; and
> >
> > (2) Pay appropriate costs as stated in 33.104(h).
> >
> > (3) Require the awardee to reimburse the Government's costs, as provided in this paragraph, where a postaward protest is sustained as the result of an awardee's intentional or negligent misstatement, misrepresentation, or miscertification. In addition to any other remedy available, and pursuant to the requirements of Subpart 32.6, the Government may collect this debt by offsetting the amount against any payment due the awardee under any contract between the awardee and the Government.
> >
> > > (i) When a protest is sustained by GAO under circumstances that may allow the Government to seek reimbursement for protest costs, the contracting officer will determine whether the protest was sustained based on the awardee's negligent or intentional misrepresentation. If the protest was sustained on several issues, protest costs shall be apportioned according to the costs attributable to the awardee's actions.
> > >
> > > (ii) The contracting officer shall review the amount of the debt, degree of the awardee's fault, and costs of collection, to determine

> whether a demand for reimbursement ought to be made. If it is in the best interests of the Government to seek reimbursement, the contracting officer shall notify the contractor in writing of the nature and amount of the debt, and the intention to collect by offset if necessary. Prior to issuing a final decision, the contracting officer shall afford the contractor an opportunity to inspect and copy agency records pertaining to the debt to the extent permitted by statute and regulation, and to request review of the matter by the head of the contracting activity.

Because this provision is permissive, there appear to be no restrictions preventing the agency from granting other requested relief following review of an agency-level protest. This includes the authority to allow correction or withdrawal in mistake cases, *Unico Constr. Co.*, Comp. Gen. Dec. B-258862, 95-1 CPD ¶ 42; *National Heat & Power Corp.*, Comp. Gen. Dec. B-212923, 84-1 CPD ¶ 125. However, the granting of relief from mistakes in sealed bid procurements is subject to a number of restrictions within the executive agencies. Contracting officers are permitted to correct clerical mistakes apparent on the face of the bid, FAR 14.407-2, but relief for other types of mistakes must be granted by the agency heads who may delegate their authority to a limited number of central authorities, FAR 14.407-3(e). In all mistake cases, the concurrence of legal counsel within the agency is required before a determination is made, FAR 14.407-3(f). Numerous subsidiary regulations implement the FAR and contain delegations of authority to grant relief for mistakes prior to award. See, e.g., DFARS 214.406-3, NFS 1814.407, and GSAR 514.407. Mistakes in negotiated procurements are processed substantially in accordance with FAR 14.407-4, FAR 15.508.

III. GENERAL ACCOUNTING OFFICE

For many years, the only forum to consider contract award controversies was the GAO, headed by the Comptroller General of the United States. It began to hear protests from disappointed bidders early in its existence, e.g., 10 Comp. Gen. 480 (A-36067) (1931); 11 Comp. Gen. 220 (A-39095) (1931). The Comptroller General took these protests and issued decisions under the predecessors of 31 U.S.C. §§ 3526 and 3529. These statutes give the Comptroller General the authority to settle and adjust the accounts of accountable officers and the obligation to render advance decisions to certifying and disbursing officers on questions concerning the legality of payments. The procuring agencies generally acquiesced in the decisions, with the result that the Comptroller General protest procedure became firmly embedded in the procurement process.

It was not until 1984 that the Comptroller General was given specific statutory authority to hear protests, 31 U.S.C. § 3551 et seq. As originally enacted, this statute gave the Comptroller General the authority to order a stay of performance longer than the period specified in the statute, 31 U.S.C. § 3554(a)(1). This raised questions as to the constitutionality of the provision given that the GAO is an office in the legislative branch and procurement is an executive function. However, this provision was deleted by Section 8139 of the 1989 Department of Defense Appropriations Act, P.L. 100-463. As a result, *United States Army Corps of Eng'rs v. Ameron, Inc.*, 809 F.2d 979 (3d Cir. 1986), *cert. granted*, 485 U.S. 958 (1988), *mot. denied*, 488 U.S. 809 (1988), *cert. dismissed*, 488 U.S. 918 (1988), which had been scheduled for argument to determine the constitutionality of the statute, was dismissed at the request of the Solicitor General.

A. Jurisdiction

The Comptroller General has slightly different authority to hear protests under 31 U.S.C. § 3551 et seq. and under its prior nonstatutory authority.

1. *Statutory Authority*

The jurisdiction of the Comptroller General under its statutory authority depends on the status of the agency conducting the procurement and the nature of the transaction. 31 U.S.C. § 3551 defines "protest" as a written objection to a "procurement of property or services" by a "federal agency" as defined in 40 U.S.C. § 472.

a. *Status of Agency*

The term "federal agency" covers virtually all agencies of the Government that operate with appropriated funds. Thus, protests have been taken on procurement of the Tennessee Valley Authority, *Monarch Water Sys., Inc.*, 64 Comp. Gen. 756 (B-218441), 85-2 CPD ¶ 146, *recons. denied*, 85-2 CPD ¶ 335; the Federal Housing Administration Fund, *CoMont, Inc.*, 65 Comp. Gen. 66 (B-219730), 85-2 CPD ¶ 555; the Bonneville Power Administration, *International Line Builders*, 67 Comp. Gen. 8 (B-227811),

87-2 CPD 345, *recons. denied*, 87-2 CPD ¶ 472; and the Federal Reserve Board, *Computer Support Sys., Inc.*, 69 Comp. Gen. 644 (B-239034), 90-2 CPD ¶ 94. See, however, *P.O.M., Inc.*, 64 Comp. Gen. 488 (B-218178), 85-1 CPD ¶ 467, where the Comptroller General held that the District of Columbia government is not a federal agency for purposes of the statute, citing 40 U.S.C. § 472. Mixed-ownership corporations are not considered federal agencies, *Kennan Auction Co.*, Comp. Gen. Dec. B-248965, 92-1 CPD ¶ 503 (Resolution Trust Corporation); *Chas. G. Stott & Co.*, Comp. Gen. Dec. B-220302, 85-2 CPD ¶ 333 (Federal Deposit Insurance Corporation). Nonappropriated fund instrumentalities, as well, are not considered federal agencies, *LDDS Worldcom*, Comp. Gen. Dec. B-270109, 96-1 CPD ¶ 45.

The Comptroller General's protest jurisdiction does not depend on the intended use of the items being acquired or on the source of the funds for the acquisition, *CPT Text-Computer GmbH*, Comp. Gen. Dec. B-222037.2, 86-2 CPD ¶ 29. The key factor in determining applicability is that the procurement is conducted by a federal agency. See *Artisan Builders*, 65 Comp. Gen. 240 (B-220804), 86-1 CPD ¶ 85, holding that the statutory bid protest authority is applicable to a procurement that the Air Force conducted for a base golf course, a nonappropriated fund activity. In *Professional Pension Termination Assocs.*, Comp. Gen. Dec. B-230007.2, 88-1 CPD ¶ 498, the Comptroller General found that it had jurisdiction over a protest even though the procurement was partially funded with trust funds, because the Pension Benefit Guaranty Corporation, which conducted the procurement, was a federal agency. Similarly, a procurement by a federal agency for a foreign government is subject to the statute, *Cosmos Eng'rs, Inc.*, Comp. Gen. Dec. B-220000.3, 86-1 CPD ¶ 186 (procurement by Agency for International Development for foreign government). But see *Environmental Tectonics Corp.*, 65 Comp. Gen. 504 (B-222483), 86-1 CPD ¶ 377, where the Comptroller General denied jurisdiction because, although the contract was financed by a federal agency, the solicitation was issued and award made by the government of Egypt.

The Comptroller General will consider a protest when a nonappropriated fund instrumentality is acting only as a mere conduit for an agency, *Premiere Vending*, Comp. Gen. Dec. B-256560, 94-2 CPD ¶ 8 (protester alleged that agency was diverting vending machine requirements to employees' association in order to avoid applicable procurement statutes and regulations). In *Americable Int'l, Inc.*, Comp. Gen. Dec. B-251614, 93-1 CPD ¶ 336, the Comptroller General dismissed a protest holding that the award of franchise contracts for cable television services and telephone services by a nonappropriated fund instrumentality was beyond the scope of the GAO's jurisdiction. The protester argued that the nonappropriated fund activity was acting as an agent for the Navy. The Comptroller General found that there was no evidence of significant Navy participation in the procurement process, stating:

> [T]here was no participation by Navy contracting officials in the agreements finally ratified, and no suggestion that the Navy was ever intending to sign the agreement. Nor is there any evidence to suggest that agency contracting officials dictated the terms of the franchise contracts.
>
> In our view, this evidence does not constitute the kind of pervasive involvement required for our Office to conclude that an entity that is not a federal agency has become a mere conduit for the agency. *See St. Mary's Hosp. and Med. Center of San Francisco, Cal.*, [70 Comp. Gen. 579 (B-243061, 91-1 CPD ¶ 597]; *Perkin-Elmer Corp., Metco Div.*, [Comp. Gen. Dec. B-237076, 89-2 CPD ¶ 604]. Without evidence of such involvement by a federal agency, and since there is no question that the franchise contracts were awarded by a NAFI, we have no jurisdiction over the procurements here.

Agencies may be exempted from the protest statute by provisions in their own statutes. See *Falcon Sys., Inc.*, 65 Comp. Gen. 584 (B-222549), 86-1 CPD ¶ 462, finding that United States Postal Service contracts were not subject to the protest statute based upon 39 U.S.C. § 410(a), which states that the Postal Service is exempted from any federal law dealing with public or federal contracts except those listed. Because the protest statute is not listed, it does not apply. Under P.L. 104-50, § 348, codified at 49 U.S.C. § 106, Congress directed the Federal Aviation Administration (FAA) to develop and implement a new acquisition management system and exempted the FAA from most provisions of federal acquisition law, one being the procurement protest system. Under the new FAA management system, protesters can choose between internal FAA procedures or the current protest forums in resolving protests.

b. Nature of Transaction

The Comptroller General, in considering protests concerning the "procurement of property or services," will not take jurisdiction of protests over the procedures used in other types of transactions. Thus, jurisdiction will be denied over protests concerning grants or cooperative agreements as defined in 31 U.S.C. § 6303, *SBMA, Inc.*, Comp. Gen. Dec. B-255780, 93-2 CPD ¶ 292; cooperative research and development agreements under 15 U.S.C. § 3710a, *Spice Corp.*, Comp. Gen. Dec. B-258267, 94-2 CPD ¶ 257; and "other transactions" under 10 U.S.C. § 2371, *Energy Conversion Devices, Inc.*, Comp. Gen. Dec. B-260514, 95-2 CPD ¶ 121. The Comptroller General will review a protest that an agency is improperly using one of these instruments instead of a procurement contract. See, for example, *Sprint Communications Co., L.P.*, Comp. Gen. Dec. B-256586, 94-1 CPD ¶ 300, holding that a cooperative agreement was properly used and that the agency did not use it to avoid the requirements of procurement statutes and regulations.

The Comptroller General will not exercise jurisdiction over subcontractor procurement unless specifically requested to do so by the agency, 4 C.F.R. § 21.5(h). This rule is derived from *U.S. West Communications Servs., Inc. v. United States*, 940 F.2d 622 (Fed. Cir. 1991). In that case, the court of appeals, construing language similar to that applicable to the GAO, held that the GSBCA did not have jurisdiction over subcontract procurements that were conducted "for" a federal agency. In light of this decision, the Comptroller General stated in *Compugen, Ltd.*, Comp. Gen. Dec. B-261769, 95-2 CPD ¶ 103, that the GAO will not exercise jurisdiction over subcontract procurements for the Government without a written request from the agency that awarded the prime contract. See also *Geo-Centers, Inc.*, Comp. Gen. Dec. B-261716, 95-2 CPD ¶ 69, where the Comptroller General stated that the GAO will no longer review protests of procurements by the Department of Energy's management and operating prime contractors unless specifically requested to do so by the Department. Previously, the Comptroller General reviewed subcontractor procurements in cases where the prime contractor was acting "by or for the government," *St. Mary's Hosp. & Medical Ctr. of San Francisco, Cal.*, 70 Comp. Gen. 579 (B-243061), 91-1 CPD ¶ 597; *Ocean Enters., Ltd.*, 65 Comp. Gen. 585 (B-221851), 86-1 CPD ¶ 479.

2. Nonstatutory Authority

The Comptroller General's nonstatutory protests are conducted under its advance decision statute, 31 U.S.C. § 3529. This statute authorizes the Comptroller General to issue a decision on a question involving a payment the disbursing officer or head of agency will make or a voucher presented to a certifying official for certification. Pursuant to 4 C.F.R. § 21.13, the Comptroller General will hear procurement protests from a Government agency not included in the definition of "federal agency" and protests involving sales of property from any Government agency only if the agency agrees in writing to have the Comptroller General decide its protests. See, for example, *Total Spectrum Mfg., Inc.*, Comp. Gen. Dec. B-225400, 86-2 CPD ¶ 673 (procurements by the Architect of the Capitol, which is not a federal agency under the definition); and *Victory Salvage Co.*, Comp. Gen. Dec. B-253006, 93-2 CPD ¶ 92 (protest involving surplus property sales).

B. Who May Protest

The Comptroller General is required to decide protests submitted by an "interested party," 31 U.S.C. § 3553(a). 31 U.S.C. § 3551(2) states that an interested party is "an actual or prospective bidder or offeror whose direct economic interest would be affected by the award of the contract or by failure to award the contract." This definition is the same as that under the repealed GSBCA protest authority statute, 40 U.S.C. § 759(h)(9). Because the General Services Board applied the same definition and used the same rationale as that of the Comptroller General, GSBCA cases are included in this section for illustrative purposes. The key phrases in the definition are "actual or prospective bidder or offeror" and "direct economic interest." The protester must meet both tests. The protest must relate to a particular solicitation or to the proposed award or award of a particular contract, *A. Moe & Co.*, 64 Comp. Gen. 755 (B-219762), 85-2 CPD ¶ 144 (protest against the denial of its application for a Master Agreement for Repair and Alteration of Vessels does not pertain to a particular solicitation or to the proposed award or award of a particular contract and, thus, does not constitute a protest within CICA).

1. Actual or Prospective Bidder or Offeror

Because *actual* bidders or offerors are determined by those who submit bids or proposals to the Government, the major difficulties in this area have arisen in determining whether a party is a *prospective* bidder or offeror. The term has been taken to mean a potential competitor for the type of work being procured, *Tumpane Servs. Corp.*, Comp. Gen. Dec. B-220465, 86-1 CPD ¶ 95 (protester did not bid but would have if specifications were not defective). Parties are not potential competitors and, thus, are not interested parties if they do not participate or do not have the capacity to participate in the market involved, *Polycon Corp.*, Comp. Gen. Dec. B-218304.2, 85-1 CPD ¶ 714 (firm's mere characterization of itself as a "prospective prime contractor" ineffective when it was a material supplier and had not bid for construction contract awards); *Julie Research Labs., Inc.*, Comp. Gen. Dec. B-219370, 85-2 CPD ¶ 185, *recons. denied*, 85-2 CPD ¶ 294 (contractor was required to do more than provide manufactured equipment, which was the only function the party contended it could perform); *Signal Corp.*, 69 Comp. Gen. 659 (B-240450), 90-2 CPD ¶ 116, *recons. denied*, 69 Comp. Gen. 725 (B-240450.2), 90-2 CPD ¶ 236 (party voluntarily released its proposed team and unequivocally asserted that it did not want to be further considered in the procurement). In *Federal Data Corp. v. United States*, 911 F.2d 699 (Fed. Cir. 1990), the court held that Federal Data was not an interested party because it knowingly removed itself from the bidding. The court also stated that the protester's desire to compete in a later solicitation if the board found the Government's conduct unlawful was not sufficient to make Federal Data an interested party. See also *Robotic Sys. Technology*, Comp. Gen. Dec. B-271760, 96-1 CPD ¶ 229.

Prospective suppliers or subcontractors are not considered interested parties, *PPG Indus., Inc.*, Comp. Gen. Dec. B-272126, 96-1 CPD ¶ 285 (protester did not manufacturer or sell equipment and thus was not an interested party); *U.S. Polycon Corp.*, Comp. Gen. Dec. B-254655.3, 94-2 CPD ¶ 53 (protester was a potential supplier to the ultimate awardee and, therefore, not an interested party); *Allied Tube & Conduit*, Comp. Gen. Dec. B-252371, 93-1 CPD ¶ 345 (prospective supplier of pipe did not qualify as an interested party); *Control Technologies, Inc.*, Comp. Gen. Dec. B-251335, 93-1 CPD ¶ 16 (mechanical and electrical subcontractor not an interested party); *Industrial Combustion*, Comp. Gen. Dec. B-222043, 86-1 CPD ¶ 201 (manufacturer that may supply its product to bidders not an interested party); *Polycon Corp.*, 64 Comp. Gen. 523 (B-218304), 85-1 CPD ¶ 567, *recons. denied*, 85-1 CPD ¶ 714 (protester was solely a subcontractor/supplier rather than a prime contractor and, therefore, not an actual or prospective interested party); *ADB-ALNACO, Inc.*, 64 Comp. Gen. 577 (B-218541), 85-1 CPD ¶ 633 (manufacturer that supplied equipment to potential bidders or offerors not an interested party).

Associations or organizations that do not perform contracts are not interested parties and cannot bring protests in their own name, *American Fed'n of Gov. Employees*, Comp. Gen. Dec. B-219590.3, 86-1 CPD ¶ 436 (Government employees' union, protesting contracting-out cost comparison, was not an interested party); *Northwest Forest Workers Assocs.*, Comp. Gen. Dec. B-218097.2, 85-2 CPD ¶ 131, and Comp. Gen. Dec. B-218891.2, 85-1 CPD ¶ 685 (association representing organizations, some of which submitted bids, was not interested party to protest in its own name); *Don Strickland's Consultant & Advisory Serv.*, Comp. Gen. Dec. B-217178, 85-1 CPD ¶ 141 (consultant who refused to identify prospective bidders it was representing was not an interested party). Compare *Windet Hotel Corp.*, Comp. Gen. Dec. B-220987, 86-1 CPD ¶ 138, accepting a protest filed by a representative on behalf of an identified interested party. Although an agent may represent an interested party in a protest where it files the protest on behalf of a specified party and has been authorized to act for that party, *E&R, Inc.*, Comp. Gen. Dec. B-255868, 94-1 CPD ¶ 218, the agent is not itself a prospective bidder or offeror and thus is not an interested party to protest on its own behalf, *Bulloch Int'l*, Comp. Gen. Dec. B-265982, 96-1 CPD ¶ 5; *Priscidon Enters., Inc.*, Comp. Gen. Dec. B-220278, 85-2 CPD ¶ 549. See *Total Procurement Servs., Inc.*, Comp. Gen. Dec. B-272343.2, 96-2 CPD ¶ 92, holding that a value-added network used to submit quotes by trading partners via FACNET was not an actual or prospective supplier because it did not submit quotes on its own behalf. Persons acting as private attorneys general are not interested parties, *Julie Research Labs., Inc.*, GSBCA 8070-P-R, 86-2 BCA ¶ 18,881.

2. Direct Economic Interest

In order to have a direct economic interest, an actual or prospective bidder or offeror must be in line for award or be able to compete for award if its position in the protest is upheld. Whether a person would be in line for award on a procurement depends upon the type of competitive procedure being used and the stage of the competition. Thus, once bids have been opened in a sealed bid procurement, the low bidder is in line for award. The second low bidder is next in line for award if a protest against the low bidder is upheld, *Tektronix, Inc.*, Comp. Gen. Dec. B-219981, 85-2 CPD ¶ 611 (protester challenging mistake correction of low bidder would receive award if correction was denied). However, a third low bidder protesting against award to the low bidder was held not to be an interested party because the second low bidder was next in line for award, *Eastman Kodak Co.*, Comp. Gen. Dec. B-220646, 86-1 CPD ¶ 113, *recons. denied*, 86-1 CPD ¶ 289 (supposition that the second low bidder would be held nonresponsible was too tenuous to support a protest against the low bidder). See also *Bracket Aircraft Radio Co.*, Comp. Gen. Dec. B-244831.3, 92-1 CPD ¶ 131 (fourth low bidder that does not challenge the three higher bidders' eligibility for award would not be in line for award even if protest were sustained). In *International Business Machs. Corp.*, GSBCA 9703-P, 89-1 BCA ¶ 21,367, IBM was ranked fourth lowest in a sealed bid procurement. Although it did not challenge either the solicitation or the eligibility of the intervening bidders, the board summarily found that it had a direct economic interest in the award. The Federal Circuit reversed in *United States v. International Business Machs. Corp.*, 892 F.2d 1006 (Fed. Cir. 1989), finding that "Congress intended the phrase 'interested party' to be a meaningful limitation on the authority of the board to entertain" a protest. The court stated at 1011:

> The board was troubled by the "logic" that would allow the award of a questionable procurement to go unchallenged if the second-lowest bidder did not file a protest. It believed this result would be "contrary to the notions of full and open and fair and equal competition and would significantly undermine the integrity of the procurement and protest processes." *Id.* But, as the Supreme Court has said in an analogous context,
>
> > the requirement that a party seeking review must allege facts showing that he is himself adversely affected does not insulate executive action from judicial review, nor does it prevent any public interests from being protected through the judicial process. It does serve as at least a rough attempt to put the decision as to whether review will be sought in the hands of those who have a direct stake in the outcome.
>
> *Sierra Club*, 405 U.S. at 740. Congress has decided that the coincidence of a disappointed bidder's "direct economic" interest with the public interest adequately accommodates both. By striking a different balance more solicitous of the latter, the board has upset this congressional scheme. Congress simply did not intend for the board to entertain the protests of innumerable disappointed bidders who have little or no chance of receiving the contract.

In negotiated procurement, it is much more difficult to determine whether the protester has a direct economic interest in the award. The Comptroller General defined the problem in *Meridian Management Corp.*, Comp. Gen. Dec. B-271557, 96-2 CPD ¶ 64, as follows:

> Determining whether a party is interested involves consideration of a variety of factors, including the nature of the issue raised, the benefit of relief sought by the protester, and the party's status in relation to the procurement. *Black Hills Refuse Serv.*, 67 Comp. Gen. 261 (1988), 88-1 CPD ¶ 151. A

protester is not an interested party where it would not be in line for contract award were its protest to be sustained. *ECS Composites, Inc.*, B-235849.2, Jan. 3, 1990, 90-1 CPD ¶ 7.

It is easy to establish that a protester is an interested party if the relief being requested is to permit all of the offerors to submit revised proposals. For example, in *Meridian*, the protester was held to be an interested party because it was arguing that the agency had improperly waived a mandatory contract requirement in selecting the winner. The Comptroller General reasoned that because the proper relief was notifying all offerors of the waiver and permitting them to submit revised proposals, all offerors were interested parties. Similarly, in *Loral Infrared & Imaging Sys., Inc.*, Comp. Gen. Dec. B-247127.3, 92-2 CPD ¶ 52, the protester was found to be an interested party because it claimed that the agency should have established a competitive range and conducted discussions instead of awarding without discussions, and the Comptroller found that Loral's proposal would have been in the competitive range.

A protester will also be found to be an interested party if it claims that its proposal was improperly evaluated and that proper evaluation would have put it in line for award, *Pan Am World Servs., Inc.*, Comp. Gen. Dec. B-231840, 88-2 CPD ¶ 446. See *Northwest EnviroService, Inc.*, 71 Comp. Gen. 453 (B-247380.2), 92-2 CPD ¶ 38 (contention that had its past performance been properly assessed, protester would have been the best value for the agency); *Rome Research Corp.*, Comp. Gen. Dec. B-245797.4, 92-2 CPD ¶ 194 (contention that proper evaluation of management experience and technical qualifications would have made protester the best value because it was the lowest cost offeror); *A.G. Personnel Leasing, Inc.*, Comp. Gen. Dec. B-238289, 90-1 CPD ¶ 416 (contention that proper evaluation of its proposal would have placed protester in competitive range); and *SAMCA*, Comp. Gen. Dec. B-237981.3, 90-1 CPD ¶ 413 (contention that protester should have been placed in competitive range because deficiencies in its proposal were easily correctable.

If an offeror is challenging the evaluation of the winning offeror and not claiming that its proposal was improperly evaluated, it must challenge all higher ranked offerors to be an interested party. In *Government Technology Servs., Inc.*, Comp. Gen. Dec. B-258082.2, 94-2 CPD ¶ 93, the protesters were not interested parties because they did not challenge the agency's evaluation of the proposals of the higher ranked offerors vis-à-vis their own rankings. The Comptroller General held that even if the protests were sustained, the second ranked offeror would be in line for award, not the protesters. In *Panhandle Venture V; Sterling Inv. Properties, Inc.*, Comp. Gen. Dec. B-252982.3, 93-2 CPD ¶ 142, the protesters were fourth and sixth lowest offerors. Neither protester challenged the eligibility of the intervening offerors for award. Thus, even if the protests were sustained, the protesters were not interested parties because each lacked the direct economic interest. See also *Abre Enters., Inc.*, Comp. Gen. Dec. B-251569.2, 93-1 CPD ¶ 239, where the contracting officer's price analysis/source selection document showed that the protester was the lowest technically rated, second lowest priced offeror. The protester did not challenge the evaluation of its own proposal nor the evaluation of the second rated proposal, and had the third highest combined total score for technical and price. The Comptroller General found that even if the protester's allegations against the awardee were sustained, the protester was not next in line for award based on the evaluation results and, therefore, not an interested party. Where there are intermediate parties that have a greater interest than the protester, the Comptroller General finds that the protester's interests are too remote to be considered an interested party, *Charles Redwood Ltd, Partnership*, Comp. Gen. Dec. B-241050, 91-1 CPD ¶ 32. See also *Trataros/Basil, Inc.*, Comp. Gen. Dec. B-260321, 95-1 CPD ¶ 265 (protester did not challenge intervening offeror, which would precede the protester in eligibility under the solicitation, and, therefore, lacked direct economic interest). However, if an offeror not only challenges the award but also claims that evaluation of other proposals was inconsistent with stated evaluation factors and that its proposal represented the best value to the Government, it will be found to be an interested party, *Wyle Labs., Inc.*, 69 Comp. Gen. 648 (B-239113), 90-2 CPD ¶ 107.

Parties that are ineligible for award do not have a direct economic interest in the award. Thus, they will normally not be interested parties unless they are contesting their ineligibility, *Endure-A-Lifetime Prods., Inc.*, Comp. Gen. Dec. B-219529.2, 85-2 CPD ¶ 404 (protester's bid was nonresponsive because it offered a nonconforming model); *LBCO, Inc.*, Comp. Gen. Dec. B-254995, 94-1 CPD ¶ 57 (protester's bid was materially unbalanced and therefore unacceptable even if the agency rejected the low bid); *Innovative Refrigeration Concepts*, Comp. Gen. Dec. B-252357, 93-1 CPD ¶ 448 (protester's bid was nonresponsive and there were other responsive bidders in line for award if awardee were found ineligible). See also *Southern Atl. Servs., Inc.*, Comp. Gen. Dec. B-252419, 93-1 CPD ¶ 418; and *FeinFocus, USA, Inc.*, Comp. Gen. Dec. B-245119, 91-2 CPD ¶ 502. However, a nonresponsive bidder was found to be an interested party in *Big State*

Enters., 64 Comp. Gen. 482 (B-218055), 85-1 CPD ¶ 459. In that case, the nonresponsive bidder was contesting the award on the basis of defective specifications and would have been able to submit another bid if the contract was terminated and the requirement resolicited. Where a firm submits a bid or proposal extension conditioned upon a change to a material term of the solicitation, the firm is ineligible for award and will not be considered an interested party, *Bencor-Petrifond (J.V.)*, Comp. Gen. Dec. B-254205, 93-2 CPD ¶ 208.

Winners of multiple award contracts are not interested parties because their economic interest is too speculative, *Recon Optical, Inc.*, Comp. Gen. Dec. B-272239, 96-2 CPD ¶ 21. The Comptroller General concluded that because each offeror had received award of the specific contract that they proposed, they could obtain no additional stake in the procurement by winning a protest.

Ineligibility for a procurement may result from the bidder's or offeror's suspension or debarment, *S.A.F.E. Export Corp.*, Comp. Gen. Dec. B-215022, 84-2 CPD ¶ 58 (protester was debarred and ineligible to receive any contract under the protested procurements and, therefore, was not an interested party). It may also result from the restrictive nature of the procurement, *Cable Antenna Sys.*, 65 Comp. Gen. 313 (B-220752), 86-1 CPD ¶ 168, *recons. denied*, 86-1 CPD ¶ 298 (incumbent was not permitted to participate in a procurement intended to establish a second source for future competition and therefore was not an interested party); *Precision Kinetics*, Comp. Gen. Dec. B-249975.2, 93-1 CPD ¶ 226 (protester was not eligible for award because it was not an approved source and, therefore, not an interested party); *S.A. SABER*, Comp. Gen. Dec. B-249874, 92-2 CPD ¶ 403 (where procurement is set aside for a small disadvantaged business (SDB) and protester does not qualify as an SDB, protester not an interested party to challenge the proposal evaluation); *Hospital Klean, Inc.*, Comp. Gen. Dec. B-249391.4, 93-1 CPD ¶ 96 (protester not an interested party because its offer was the second lowest acceptable offer submitted by a non-SDB firm and the third lowest of all acceptable offers received). In *Lewis & Smith Constr. Co.*, Comp. Gen. Dec. B-253382, 93-2 CPD ¶ 150, the protester's proposal under an SDB set-aside was found technically unacceptable and, therefore, ineligible for award. The agency determined that the remaining two acceptable proposals exceeded the fair market price by 10 percent when compared to the Government estimate. Thus, the agency decided to cancel the solicitation and resolicit on an unrestricted basis. The protester argued that the other two SDB offerors were improperly rejected for failure to offer an acceptable price. The Comptroller General found that the protester was not an interested party because if the two firms' proposals were not excessively priced, as the protester contended, one of those firms would be entitled to the award under the original solicitation and, thus, the protester was not in line for award.

A potential competitor is an interested party in challenging the propriety of a sole source procurement, *Julie Research Labs., Inc.*, GSBCA 8070-P, 85-3 BCA ¶ 18,375. However, once the sole source procurement has been held to be proper, the potential competitor is no longer an interested party, *Julie Research Labs., Inc.*, GSBCA 8070-P, 85-3 BCA ¶ 18,375. See also *International Training, Inc.*, Comp. Gen. Dec. B-272699, 96-2 CPD ¶ 132, where the Comptroller General ruled that a protester was not an interested party to protest the failure of a contracting agency to follow sole source acquisition procedures: the solicitation contained restrictive requirements that made the protester ineligible for award, and the protester did not challenge these restrictive provisions.

C. Time for Protest

Prior to the enactment of the statutory protest authority, the Comptroller General had adopted very restrictive time limitations on the filing of protests in order to ensure that the impact of protests on the procurement process was minimized. Although these time limitations remain in effect under the statutory protest authority, the statutes also contain additional protections when protests are timely filed — providing for limitations on contract award when a protest is filed before award and a stay of performance if the protest is filed quickly after award.

1. Restrictive GAO Rules

Protests of improprieties in solicitations are required to be filed before bid opening or the closing date for receipt of proposals, 4 C.F.R. § 21.2(a)(1). See, for example, *Neal R. Gross & Co.*, Comp. Gen. Dec. B-275066, 97-1 CPD ¶ 30 (postaward protest that solicitation failed to provide for adequate evaluation of price untimely); *Paging Network of Wash., Inc.*, Comp. Gen. Dec. B-274052, 96-2 CPD ¶ 63 (concern over specification requirement should have been raised before bid opening); *Agriculture Technology Partners*, Comp. Gen. Dec. B-272978, 96-2 CPD

¶ 226 (allegation that RFP failed to define the term "complexity," which was used to evaluate each offeror's corporate experience, untimely); and *Executive Court Reporters, Inc.*, Comp. Gen. Dec. B-272981, 96-2 CPD ¶ 227 (failure of RFP to include estimate quantities of the various types of transcripts untimely).

Protests on any other ground are required to be filed at the GAO within 10 calendar days after the basis of the protest is known or should have been known, whichever is earlier, 4 C.F.R. § 21.2(a)(2). See, for example, *General Physics Fed. Sys. Inc.*, Comp. Gen. Dec. B-274795, 97-1 CPD ¶ 8 (protester's argument against the acceptance of an offer that included a particular subcontractor could and should have been made shortly after debriefing); *Learjet, Inc.*, Comp. Gen. Dec. B-274385, 96-2 CPD ¶ 215 (protest over the interpretation of solicitation requirements untimely because it was not raised within 10 days after the protester was informed in writing during discussions of the agency's interpretation); and *Harris Corp.*, Comp. Gen. Dec. B-274566, 96-2 CPD ¶ 205 (postaward complaint untimely because protester was challenging a defect in the procurement process that should have been raised well before discussions were concluded and an award was made).

There is an exception for protests challenging a procurement conducted on the basis of competitive proposals where a debriefing is requested and, when requested, is required. In this case, with respect to any protest basis that is known or should have been known either before or as a result of the debriefing, the initial protest cannot be filed before the debriefing date offered to the protester but must be filed not later than 10 calendar days after the date on which the debriefing is held, 4 C.F.R. § 21.2(a)(2). In *Real Estate Ctr.*, Comp. Gen. Dec. B-274081, 96-2 CPD ¶ 74, the Comptroller General ruled that it would not consider a protest challenging a procurement conducted on a competitive basis under which a debriefing is requested and required if filed before the debriefing date offered to the protester. The Comptroller General stated that the protest should be filed not later than 10 days after the date on which the debriefing is held. This rule is designed to encourage early and meaningful debriefings and to preclude strategic or defense protests. See also *Minotaur Eng'g*, Comp. Gen. Dec. B-276843, 97-1 CPD ¶ 194.

Protests originally filed with an agency must be filed at the GAO within 10 days of actual or constructive knowledge of initial adverse agency action, 4 C.F.R. § 21.2(a)(3); *IBP, Inc.*, Comp. Gen. Dec. B-275259, 96-2 CPD

¶ 169; *Orbit Advanced Technologies, Inc.*, Comp. Gen. Dec. B-275046, 96-2 CPD ¶ 228. In *Timothy J. Penny*, Comp. Gen. Dec. B-221710, Feb. 20, 1986, *Unpub.*, the Comptroller General held that these time limitations could not be avoided by having the protest filed through a member of Congress.

The GAO regulations permit consideration of late protests for "good cause" or if the protest raises "issues significant to the procurement system," 4 C.F.R. § 21.2(c). The Comptroller General, in order to maintain the value of the time limitations, will construe these exceptions strictly. See, for example, *Merck & Co.*, Comp. Gen. Dec. B-248655, 92-1 CPD ¶ 454, where the Comptroller General, refusing to decide on a protest issue raised late, stated that "we strictly construe and seldom use the exception, limiting it to protests that raise issues of widespread interest to the procurement community." See also *Source Diversified, Inc.*, Comp. Gen. Dec. B-259034, 95-1 CPD ¶ 119 (issue of whether a delegation of procurement authority should have been obtained for a particular procurement not one of widespread interest to the procurement community); *International Science & Technology Inst., Inc.*, Comp. Gen. Dec. B-259648, 95-1 CPD ¶ 16 (untimely protest alleging organizational conflict of interest on the part of awardee was not a significant issue of widespread interest); *Pardee Constr. Co.*, Comp. Gen. Dec. B-256414, 94-1 CPD ¶ 372 (propriety of solicitation provisions that were incorporated by amendment neither unique nor of widespread interest); *American Material Handling, Inc.*, Comp. Gen. Dec. B-255467.2, 94-1 CPD ¶ 158 (protest involving the solicitation specifications not significant issue of widespread interest); *Julie Research Labs., Inc.*, Comp. Gen. Dec. B-219364, 85-2 CPD ¶ 222 (no significant issue because there were numerous decisions on the issue).

The good cause exception is available only for a compelling reason beyond the protester's control, *Oracle Corp.*, Comp. Gen. Dec. B-260963, 95-1 CPD ¶ 231 (argument that dismissal of protest would be "particularly unfair" did not meet good cause exception); *John Cuneo, Inc.*, Comp. Gen. Dec. B-227983.2, 87-2 CPD ¶ 147 (protester's lack of awareness of the bid protest timeliness requirements not a good cause); *Arian Fashions, Inc.*, Comp. Gen. Dec. B-247314.3, 92-1 CPD ¶ 223 (fact that basis of protest arose during a holiday was not a good cause).

For cases where the Comptroller General has found a significant issue and thus considered a late protest, see *Gene Quigley, Jr.*, 70 Comp. Gen. 273 (B-241565), 91-1 CPD ¶ 182 (protests involving newly promulgated regulations on individual sureties); *Discount Mach. & Equip., Inc.*,

70 Comp. Gen. 108 (B-240525), 90-2 CPD ¶ 420 (failure of an agency to refer an adverse agency nonresponsibility determination on a small business to Small Business Administration (SBA)); *Golden North Van Lines, Inc.*, 69 Comp. Gen. 610 (B-238874), 90-2 CPD ¶ 44 (failure to specify whether option prices would be evaluated); *Baszile Metal Serv.*, Comp. Gen. Dec. B-237925, 90-1 CPD ¶ 378 (DOD's regulatory requirements that SDB regular dealers provide a product manufactured by a small business concern when there is no SDB manufacturer in order to be eligible for an SDB evaluation preference in unrestricted procurements); *Cincinnati Milacron Mktg. Co.*, Comp. Gen. Dec. B-237619, 90-1 CPD ¶ 241 (interpretation of a congressional restriction on the use of appropriated funds); *F.J. O'Hara & Sons, Inc.*, 69 Comp. Gen. 274 (B-237410), 90-1 CPD ¶ 197 (statutory restriction on the purchase of food); *Department of the Navy; Fairchild Weston Sys, Inc.*, Comp. Gen. Dec. B-230013.2, 88-2 CPD ¶ 100 (unreasonable exclusion of a protester from the competitive range); *Sinclair Radio Labs, Inc.*, 67 Comp. Gen. 66 (B-227474.2), 87-2 CPD ¶ 470 (exclusion of a small business from competition); *Adrian Supply Co.*, 66 Comp. Gen. 367 (B-225440.2), 87-1 CPD ¶ 357 (actions by the contracting agency that are inconsistent with statute and regulation); and *Topley Realty Co.*, 65 Comp. Gen. 510 (B-221459), 86-1 CPD ¶ 398 (questionable application of definitive responsibility criteria).

2. Statutory Stay

Although the statutes do not limit the filing times for jurisdictional purposes, they do contain provisions that delay award or suspend contract performance pending the decision on a protest. These provisions were enacted to ensure that effective relief could be obtained by successful protesters. If a protest is filed before award, 31 U.S.C. § 3553(c) provides that while a protest is pending, "a contract may not be awarded in any procurement after the federal agency has received notice of the protest" from the Comptroller General. If a protest is filed after award but within specified time limitations, 31 U.S.C. § 3553(d) provides that the federal agency shall, on receipt of notice of the protest from the Comptroller General, "immediately direct the contractor to cease performance under the contract." Both of these stay provisions have exceptions based on urgency or compelling circumstances, 31 U.S.C. § 3553(c)(2) and (d)(3)(C). In addition, performance of a contract awarded prior to receipt of a protest may be continued during a protest based on a finding that it is "in the best interests of the United States," 31 U.S.C. § 3553(d)(3)(C). These findings must be made by "the head of the procuring activity," and the authority to make such findings may not be delegated, 31 U.S.C. § 3553(e).

The time limitations imposed on the postaward stay were altered by the FASA. Prior to its passage, for the postaward stay provision to become effective, the agency must have received notice of the protest within 10 working days (14 calendar days) of contract award. The FASA amended 31 U.S.C. § 3553 to change the time limitations and now provides that the period for notice of the protest begins "on the date of contract award and ends on the later of — (A) the date that is 10 [calendar] days after the date of the contract award; or (B) the date that is 5 [calendar] days after the debriefing date offered to an unsuccessful offeror for any debriefing that is requested and, when requested, is required." Thus, an agency must suspend contract performance if it receives notice of a protest by the tenth calendar day following contract award or the fifth calendar day following a timely requested debriefing, whichever is later.

Under 31 U.S.C. § 3553, an agency is required to suspend performance of a contract only if the agency receives notice *from the Comptroller General* within 10 days of contract award. See *BDM Management Servs. Co.*, Comp. Gen. Dec. B-228287, 88-1 CPD ¶ 93, holding that there was no duty to suspend contract performance where protest was filed on the tenth calendar day after award but the agency received GAO notification of the protest on the eleventh calendar day. See also *Florida Professional Review Org.*, Comp. Gen. Dec. B-253908.2, 94-1 CPD ¶ 17, finding no duty to suspend performance where the protest was filed on the eighth day after award (a Friday) and the agency was notified within one working day, on the eleventh day after award (a Monday). The Comptroller General is required to notify the agency of a protest within one calendar day of the receipt of the request, but there is no recourse if this is not done. Notice by the protester to the agency is insufficient to trigger suspension of contract performance, *Technology for Communications Int'l v. Garrett*, 783 F. Supp. 1446 (D.D.C. 1992) (although protester notified Navy of protest, GAO did not notify the agency until the fourteenth day after contract award).

An agency can override a stay on a finding of urgent and compelling circumstances or, in the case of postaward protests, on a finding of urgent and compelling circumstances *or* if the override is in the Government's best interests, 31 U.S.C. § 3553(c)(2) and (d)(3)(C). If an agency decides to award a contract or to proceed with performance in spite of the statutory stay, the Comptroller General has no authority to challenge this action.

However, a protester can challenge the agency's decision to override the stay requirement by filing a suit in federal district court under the Administrative Procedure Act (APA), 5 U.S.C. § 706(2)(a). The district court will determine whether the agency's override of the statutory stay was "arbitrary, capricious, an abuse of discretion, or otherwise not in accordance with law."

In reviewing the use of the urgent and compelling circumstances standard, the district courts focus on whether the type of work is urgently needed. See *Litton Sys., Inc. v. Carlucci*, No. 88-0652 (D.D.C. Mar. 14, 1988), which concerned a contract for the manufacture of night vision goggles (NVG). In overriding the statutory stay, the agency had stated that "any further delays in this procurement will significantly delay the manufacture and delivery of critically needed, mission safe [NVG]." The court held that the agency's findings were rationally based.

Where an incumbent contractor is available to perform follow-on work during a protest, the urgent and compelling circumstances standard may be more difficult to meet. Some courts have reasoned that an agency with an incumbent contractor has no grounds for urgency. For example, in *Dairy Maid Dairy, Inc. v. United States*, 837 F. Supp. 1370 (E.D. Va. 1993), the incumbent contractor challenged the Army's decision to award a follow-on contract to the successful offeror. The Army focused its determination that urgent and compelling circumstances justified the override on the item being purchased — milk products needed in Korea. Dairy Maid did not dispute the Army's findings but argued that those findings were insufficient to override a stay, contending that the Army failed to consider extending its contract rather than proceeding with the new contract. The court agreed with Dairy Maid. In *DTH Management Group v. Kelso*, 844 F. Supp. 251 (E.D.N.C. 1993), involving a Navy contract for housing maintenance and repair services, the court found that the Navy "completely ignore[d] the availability of plaintiff to continue in the interim while plaintiff's protest is pending before the GAO." Because the Navy failed to explain why it could not continue to use the incumbent's services during the pendency of the Comptroller General protest, the court held that the Navy's action in overriding the stay was "contrary to law and not rational or reasonable." See also *Taylor Group, Inc. v. Johnson*, 915 F. Supp. 295 (D. Ala. 1995), where the court held that the agency failed to explain why it could not have continued to employ the plaintiff's services pending the decision of the Comptroller General. The court stated that the plaintiff was "ready, willing and able to continue its services until the GAO issued a determination on its protest."

If the agency can show that the incumbent contractor cannot satisfy the urgency, the court will uphold the agency's decision to override the stay. For example, in *Superior Servs., Inc. v. Dalton*, 851 F. Supp. 381 (S.D. Cal. 1994), the agency specifically considered the extension of the incumbent's contract and rejected it. The court was satisfied with the agency's justification for the override, noting that the findings addressed why the incumbent's contract could not be extended during the pendency of the Comptroller General protest. See also *Commercial Energies, Inc. v. Cheney*, 745 F. Supp. 647 (D. Colo. 1990), where the agency, as part of its determination to override the stay, concluded that it would save an estimated $463,000 by overriding the stay and awarding the contract to the low bidder rather than extending the incumbent's contract.

Some district courts do not appear to consider whether an incumbent contractor would be available to perform follow-on work when assessing the urgency. For example, in *Burnside-Ott Aviation Training Ctr., Inc. v. Department of the Navy*, No. 88-3056 (D.D.C. Nov. 4, 1988), the incumbent contractor protested the Navy's decision to award a pilot training contract to a competitor. The Navy lifted the stay with a finding of urgent and compelling circumstances, and the protester sought to enjoin further performance in district court. The court denied the request for a preliminary injunction because the Navy's decision had a rational basis and the protester could not show irreparable injury. Similarly, in *Northern Management Servs., Inv. v. United States*, No. 92-2104 (D.D.C. 1992), the incumbent contractor on a Navy maintenance contract for fuel recovery systems filed a bid protest prior to bid opening. The Navy overrode the stay based on a determination of urgent and compelling circumstances. The court held that the necessity of continued operation of the fuel recovery system provided a rational basis for the decision to lift the stay. The court also found that failure to operate the system could subject the agency to penalties under the Clean Water Act. Thus, the determination of urgent and compelling circumstances was rationally based.

In a postaward situation, an agency can choose to override a stay based on either the urgent and compelling circumstances standard or the best interests standard. Under the best interests standard, 31 U.S.C. § 3553(d)(3)(C) requires that the agency make a finding that "performance of the contract is in the best interests of the United States" to override the stay. Some courts have determined that an agency's decision to override a stay based on the best interests of the United States is not subject to judicial review, *Topgallant Group, Inc. v. United States*, 704 F. Supp. 265 (D.D.C.

1988) (Administrative Procedures Act bars review of agency action that is "committed to agency discretion by law," and there is no law to apply to determine what constitutes the best interests of the United States); *Foundation Health Fed. Servs. v. United States*, 39 Cont. Cas. Fed. (CCH) ¶ 76,681 (D.D.C. 1993). However, if the courts conduct a review, they recognize that an agency has broad discretion under the best interests standard and give the agency substantial deference, *Universal Shipping Co. v. United States*, 652 F. Supp. 668 (D.D.C. 1987); *Ingram Barge Co. v. United States*, 34 Cont. Cas. Fed. (CCH) ¶ 75,486 (D.D.C. 1988).

D. Intervenors

4 C.F.R. § 21.0 defines the term "intervenor" as

> an awardee if the award has been made or, if no award has been made, all bidders or offerors who appear to have a substantial prospect of receiving an award if the protest is denied.

Potential intervenors become aware of a protest by the fact that the contracting agency must immediately give notice of a protest to the awardee, if award has been made or, if award has not been made, to all bidders or offerors who appear to have a reasonable prospect of receiving an award, 4 C.F.R. § 21.3(a). Most often it is the awardee that files as an intervenor, e.g., *Alliant Techsystems, Inc.*, Comp. Gen. Dec. B-276162, 97-1 CPD ¶ 141 (awardee filed as intervenor when protester challenged the technical evaluation of awardee's proposal); *EBA Eng'g, Inc.*, Comp. Gen. Dec. B-275818, 97-1 CPD ¶ 127 (awardee filed as intervenor when protester alleged that awardee used bait-and-switch tactics with proposed key personnel). However, bidders or offerors that are likely to win an award may also file as intervenors, e.g., *Ryan Co.*, Comp. Gen. Dec. B-275304, 97-1 CPD ¶ 62 (intervenor next lower bidder). Upon receiving notification of a protest, any intervenor may file a request for dismissal, it if believes that a protest or specific protest allegations should be dismissed before submission of an agency report, 4 C.F.R. § 21.3(b). If the protest is not dismissed, the agency must prepare the agency report and, subject to any protective order, simultaneously furnish a copy to the protester and any intervenors, 4 C.F.R. § 21.3(e). As with protesters, intervenors have 10 days after receipt of the agency report to provide comments, 4 C.F.R. § 21.3(i). These comments must be given to the contracting agency and all other participating parties, 4 C.F.R. § 21.3(i).

Sometimes a party will find itself in the position of filing as an intervenor after having been a protester on the procurement. In *Executive Conference Ctr., Inc.*, Comp. Gen. Dec. B-275882.2, 97-1 CPD ¶ 138, the intervenor, Howard Johnson, had previously protested the procurement because its bid was deemed nonresponsive for failing to acknowledge an amendment. In considering Howard Johnson's protest, the contracting officer concluded that the amendment was not material and waived Howard Johnson's failure to properly acknowledge the amendment. The award to Executive Conference Center was terminated, and the contract awarded to Howard Johnson. As a result, Howard Johnson withdrew its protest. Following the award to Howard Johnson, Executive Conference protested, asserting that the amendment was material. The Comptroller General agreed and sustained the protest. In *Alice Roofing & Sheet Metal Works, Inc.*, Comp. Gen. Dec. B-275477, 97-1 CPD ¶ 86, the intervenor, Port Enterprises, had previously filed a protest, asserting that the bid of the awardee, Alice Roofing, had been unbalanced. In preparing a response to the protest, the contracting officer reviewed the pricing and determined that the bid was, in fact, unbalanced. The agency terminated Alice's contract and awarded the contract to Port Enterprises. Alice Roofing filed a protest with the Comptroller General challenging the decision that its bid was unbalanced. The Comptroller General denied the protest.

E. Procedures

Protests in the GAO are governed by its Protest Procedures, 4 C.F.R. Part 21. The procedures were revised on July 26, 1996, 61 Fed. Reg. 39039, to incorporate the statutory requirements in the Clinger-Cohen Act of 1996, P.L. 104-106.

1. Filing a Protest

Protests are filed directly with the GAO, not with the contracting agency. A copy of the protest, however, should be sent to the contracting agency at the time the protest is filed.

a. Manner of Protest

Protests must be filed in writing, 4 C.F.R. § 21.1(b). They may be hand delivered or sent by mail, commercial carrier, or facsimile. If they are sent by facsimile, the protester is responsible for ensuring that the GAO's equipment is operational. Protests are properly filed on a day if they are received by 5:30 p.m., eastern time, 4 C.F.R.§ 21.0(g).

Protests should be addressed to:

General Counsel
General Accounting Office
441 G Street, N.W.
Washington, D.C. 20548
Attention: Procurement Law Control Group

4 C.F.R. § 21.1(c) provides that the protest must:

(1) Include the name, address, and telephone and facsimile numbers of the protester,

(2) Be signed by the protester or its representative,

(3) Identify the contracting agency and the solicitation and/or contract number,

(4) Set forth a detailed statement of the legal and factual grounds of protest including copies of relevant documents,

(5) Set forth all information establishing that the protester is an interested party for the purpose of filing a protest,

(6) Set forth all information establishing the timeliness of the protest,

(7) Specifically request a ruling by the Comptroller General of the United States, and

(8) State the form of relief requested.

Failure to specifically request a ruling by the Comptroller General or to state the form of relief requested has not been considered a fatal defect to the consideration of the protest on the merits, *Carolina Auto Processing*, Comp. Gen. Dec. B-226841, 87-2 CPD ¶ 8; *Container Prods. Corp.*, 64 Comp. Gen. 641 (B-218556), 85-1 CPD ¶ 727.

b. Copy to Contracting Agency

The protester must furnish a copy of the protest to the agency official designated in the solicitation — or if there is no such designation, to the contracting officer — within one day of filing at the GAO, 4 C.F.R. § 21.1(e). A delay in providing a copy to the agency will not be considered prejudicial to the merits of the protest if the delay is not unreasonable and does not delay the preparation of the procuring agency's report to the GAO, 4 C.F.R. § 21.1(i). For cases where notification to the agency was delayed but was not deemed prejudicial, see *Container Prods. Corp.*, 64 Comp. Gen. 641 (B-218556), 85-1 CPD ¶ 727 (delay of one day); and *Land Mark Realty, Inc.*, Comp. Gen. Dec. B-224323, 86-2 CPD ¶ 620 (delay of two working days). But see *Alan Scott Indus.*, Comp. Gen. Dec. B-226012, 87-1 CPD ¶ 338, where a protest was dismissed because the copy to the procuring agency was received four working days after it was filed at the GAO.

c. Detailed Statement

The protest must include a detailed statement of its legal and factual grounds, 4 C.F.R. § 21.1(c). In *Mercer Prods. & Mfg. Co.*, Comp. Gen. Dec. B-251126, 92-2 CPD ¶ 385, the Comptroller General dismissed a request for reconsideration because the protester did not provide a detailed statement as to why it believed the awards to be improper. In *Image Contracting, Inc.*, Comp. Gen. Dec. B-245599, 91-2 CPD ¶ 588, the Comptroller General found that a detailed statement of the protest was insufficient because it merely stated that the technical specifications for the project were inadequate. In discussing the importance of the detailed statement, the Comptroller General stated:

> This requirement is intended to provide us and the agency with a sufficient understanding of the grounds for the protest and with an opportunity to consider and resolve the matter without disrupting the orderly process of government procurement.

See also *Herley Indus., Inc.*, Comp. Gen. Dec. B-242903, 91-1 CPD ¶ 449 (allegation that item did not meet salient characteristics of brand name or equal specification without identifying the particular characteristics not met was insufficient); *Blackhorse Servs. Co.*, Comp. Gen. Dec. 244545, 91-2 CPD ¶ 30 (protest by a low bidder against a higher bidder without setting out and responding to the agency's basis for rejection was insufficient);

Imaging Equip. Servs., Inc., Comp. Gen. Dec. B-247201, 92-1 CPD ¶ 50 (unsupported assertion that agency's stated requirements were overly restrictive was insufficient); *TAAS — Israel Indus., Inc.*, Comp. Gen. Dec. B-251789, 94-1 CPD ¶ 197 (mere allegation that the agency's determination was wrong was insufficient); *Federal Computer Int'l Corp.*, Comp. Gen. Dec. B-257618, 94-2 CPD ¶ 24 (protest that evaluation of proposals was improper without an explanation was insufficient); *Automated Power Sys., Inc.*, Comp. Gen. Dec. B-257178, 95-1 CPD ¶ 76 (protest that merely listed allegedly ambiguous specifications without details or explanation was insufficient); and *Tidewater Marine, Inc.*, Comp. Gen. Dec. B-270602.5, 96-2 CPD ¶ 2 (protest that failed to articulate how or why the proposed work commencement date was unduly restrictive was insufficient).

2. Actions Following Receipt of Protest

The Clinger-Cohen Act of 1996 shortened the time for the Comptroller General to decide a protest to 100 calendar days. To comply with this requirement, the GAO protest procedures specify the precise times when the parties must take actions or deliver documents. These times are set to permit the parties adequate time to prepare documents while giving the Comptroller General time to decide the protest.

a. Notification

The Comptroller General has one day to notify the contracting agency of the GAO's receipt of the protest, 31 U.S.C. § 3553(b)(1); 4 C.F.R. § 21.3(a). As discussed above, the time for invoking a suspension of contract performance under 31 U.S.C § 3553(d) continues to run until the agency receives notice of the protest from the GAO, and there is no recourse if the GAO fails to comply with this one-day notification requirement.

b. Requests for Dismissal

The Comptroller General may summarily dismiss a protest because the protest is untimely, the protester does not qualify as an interested party, or the protest fails to meet the requirement of specificity, 4 C.F.R. § 21.5. In addition, the GAO rules specifically state that the Comptroller General will not consider the following issues:

1. A matter of contract administration

2. A matter that is in the purview of the SBA

3. Affirmative determinations of responsibility not involving definitive responsibility criteria

4. Procurements by other than federal agencies as defined in Section 3 of the Federal Property and Administrative Services Act of 1949

5. Protests of procurements or proposed procurements by agencies such as the U.S. Postal Service, the Federal Deposit Insurance Corporation, and nonappropriated fund activities

6. Subcontract protests

c. Early Request for Documents

A protest may include a request for the early release of documents relevant to the protest, 4 C.F.R. § 21.1(d)(2). In such cases, the agency should send the documents to the protester as quickly as possible or arrange for an on-site review of documents. When such a request is made, the contracting agency must provide to all parties and the Comptroller General a list of the documents released and the documents that the agency intends to withhold from the protester, as well as the reasons for such withholding, 4 C.F.R. § 21.3(c). Objections to any proposed withholdings must be submitted to the Comptroller General within two days of the receipt of the list.

This procedure is intended to facilitate the resolution of disputes about the release of documents and to enable the protester to more easily meet the time limitations imposed after receipt of the agency report, 61 Fed. Reg. 39041. However, the procedure is required only when the protester submits a specific request for release of documents at the time the protest is filed.

d. Agency Report

31 U.S.C. § 3553(f) requires that a protest file be made available to the parties to the protest. The contracting agency must file its report within 30 calendar days from the date it receives telephone notification from the Comptroller General of receipt of protest, 4 C.F.R. § 21.3(c). The agency

must simultaneously send a copy of the report to the protester and any intervenors, 4 C.F.R. § 21.3(e). If a protective order has been issued, parties under the protective order will receive the entire file. Those not under the protective order will receive only a redacted version. If no protective order has been issued, only the Comptroller General will receive protected documents.

4 C.F.R. § 21.3(d) provides that the agency report should include

> the contracting officer's statement of the relevant facts, including a best estimate of the contract value, a memorandum of law, and a list and a copy of all relevant documents, or portions of documents, not previously produced, including, as appropriate: the protest; the bid or proposal submitted by the protester; the bid or proposal of the firm which is being considered for award, or whose bid or proposal is being protested; all evaluation documents; the solicitation, including the specifications; the abstract of bids or offers; and any other relevant documents. In appropriate cases, the contracting agency may request that the protester produce relevant documents, or portions of documents, that are not in the agency's possession.

The procuring agency may request an extension of time for submission of the agency report, 4 C.F.R. § 21.3(f). The Comptroller General will grant an extension of time on a case-by-case basis, *Land Mark Realty, Inc.*, Comp. Gen. Dec. B-224323, 86-2 CPD ¶ 620; *Adrian Supply Co.*, Comp. Gen. Dec. B-227022.6, 88-1 CPD ¶ 417.

e. Additional Documents

If a protester becomes aware of the existence of relevant documents after submission of the initial protest, it has two days from the time it first knew or should have known of the existence of additional documents to submit a written request for them to the Comptroller General and the agency, 4 C.F.R. § 21.3(g). This provision further provides that the agency must then respond within five days with either the documents and an index or an explanation for why it is not required to produce the documents.

The Comptroller General will decide any dispute that arises concerning the release of withheld documents and whether this should be done under a protective order, 4 C.F.R. § 21.3(h). When withheld documents are provided, the protester's comments on the agency report must be filed within 10 calendar days after its receipt of such documents, 4 C.F.R. § 21.3(i).

f. Comments on Agency Report

Comments on the agency report must be filed with the GAO within 10 calendar days after receipt of the report, with a copy provided to the contracting agency and other participating parties, 4 C.F.R. § 21.3(i). Under this provision, if the protester fails to file comments or a written statement expressing continuing interest within the deadline, the Comptroller General will dismiss the protest, *Carmon Constr., Inc.*, Comp. Gen. Dec. B-271316.2, 96-2 CPD ¶ 3. In addition, if the protester fails to respond to the rebuttal of any protest issue, the Comptroller General will consider that the protester has abandoned that issue, *J.M. Yurick Assocs.*, Comp. Gen. Dec. B-243806.2, 91-2 CPD ¶ 245; *The Big Picture Co.*, Comp. Gen. Dec. B-220859.2, 86-1 CPD ¶ 218.

g. Further Submissions

Although no further submissions are specifically provided for in the rules, the Comptroller General may permit or request further submissions by the parties, 4 C.F.R. § 21.3(j).

3. Protective Orders

The Comptroller General is authorized by statute to issue protective orders, 31 U.S.C. § 3553(f)(2). 4 C.F.R. § 21.4(a) provides:

> At the request of a party or on its own initiative, GAO may issue a protective order controlling the treatment of protected information. Such information may include proprietary, confidential, or source-selection-sensitive material, as well as other information the release of which could result in a competitive advantage to one or more firms. The protective order shall establish procedures for application for access to protected information, identification and safeguarding of that information, and submission of redacted copies of documents omitting protective information. Because a protective order serves to facilitate the pursuit of a protest by a protester through counsel, it is the responsibility of protester's counsel to request that a protective order be issued and to submit timely applications for admission under that order.

If there is no protective order, proprietary and procurement-sensitive documents must be furnished to the Comptroller General but not to nongovernmental parties, 4 C.F.R. § 21.4(b).

a. *Admissible Parties*

Three kinds of parties may be admitted under the protective order: (1) outside counsel, (2) in-house counsel, and (3) experts or consultants.

In determining whether counsel should be admitted under a protective order, the Comptroller General will look to whether the attorney is involved in the competitive decision-making process, *Allied-Signal Aerospace Co.*, Comp. Gen. Dec. B-250822, 93-1 CPD ¶ 201. Where an attorney is involved in competitive decision making, the attorney will not be granted access to proprietary data of another company, because there is an unacceptable risk of inadvertent disclosure of protected material, *U.S. Steel Corp. v. United States*, 730 F.2d 1465 (Fed. Cir. 1984).

Although it is often easier to establish that outside counsel is not involved in the decision-making process, *International Tech. Corp.*, GSBCA 9967-P, 89-2 BCA ¶ 21,746, the Comptroller General will determine the admission of counsel on a case-by-case basis, *U.S. Steel Corp. v. United States*, 730 F.2d 1465 (Fed. Cir. 1984). See *Allied-Signal Aerospace Co.*, Comp. Gen. Dec. B-250822, 93-1 CPD ¶ 201, where the Comptroller General excluded outside counsel because they were also officials involved in competitive decision making for the firms they represented. In *Colonial Storage Co.*, Comp. Gen. Dec. B-253501.5, 93-2 CPD ¶ 234, the Comptroller General did not admit an interested party's counsel under a protective order because the counsel had represented the interested party at a presolicitation conference and had also participated in price discussions between the interested party and the agency. Although an individual outside counsel may be excluded from admission under the protective order, other attorneys from the same law firm may be admitted if adequate procedures are in place to guarantee access by only those attorneys admitted, *Mine Safety Appliances Co.*, Comp. Gen. Dec. B-242379.2, 91-2 CPD ¶ 506.

In-house counsel who are not involved in competitive decision making may be admitted under a protective order when the risk of inadvertent disclosure of proprietary or procurement-sensitive information is small, *Robbins-Gioia, Inc.*, Comp. Gen. Dec. B-274318, 96-2 CPD ¶ 222. In *Earle Palmer Brown Companies*, Comp. Gen. Dec. B-243544, 91-2 CPD ¶ 134, the Comptroller General stated:

> In determining whether to grant access to protected material, we consider such factors as whether counsel primarily advises on litigation matters or

> also advises on pricing and production decisions, including the review of bids and proposals, the degree of physical separation and security with respect to those who participate in competitive decision-making and level of supervision to which in-house counsel is subject.

Here, the Comptroller General denied admittance under the protective order, stating that the direct relationship between the chief executive officer of the company and in-house counsel made the risk of inadvertent disclosure too high. Similarly, in *McDonnell Douglas Corp.*, Comp. Gen. Dec. B-259694.2, 95-2 CPD ¶ 51, the Comptroller General denied admittance under the protective order because the in-house counsel were in the position of advising the firm's competitive strategists. See also *TRW, Inc.*, Comp. Gen. Dec. B-243450.2, 91-2 CPD ¶ 160, where in denying admittance under the protective order, the Comptroller General stated that there were only two attorneys in the office and, thus, the general legal counsel would likely be relied upon to render legal advice on many subjects, including business-related decisions.

Similarly, with regard to experts or consultants, if the risk of inadvertent disclosure is too high, the Comptroller General will not admit such individuals under a protective order. *Bendix Field Eng'g Corp.*, Comp. Gen. Dec. B-246236, 92-1 CPD ¶ 227, is an interesting case where the agency requested that admission of experts to a protective order be made contingent upon a promise to avoid participation in future procurements for prepositioning for a period of five years. The Comptroller General found this to be reasonable given the large dollar value of the contract and the competition-sensitive nature of the information to be made available to the experts.

Even if there is little risk of inadvertent disclosure, if the information is highly sensitive, the Comptroller General may decline to admit experts or consultants, *EER Sys. Corp.*, Comp. Gen. Dec. B-256383, 94-1 CPD ¶ 354 (information contained highly sensitive and proprietary engineering approaches and solutions that would be invaluable to any practicing engineer).

b. Procedure

An individual seeking admission under a protective order must submit an application to the GAO with copies furnished to all other parties, 4 C.F.R. § 21.4(c). See *Bid Protests at GAO: A Descriptive Guide*, GAO/OGC-96-24 (1996) for sample forms. Although there is no time limit for filing an application, it should be done as soon as possible. Parties have two days to object to the applicant's admission, 4 C.F.R. § 21.4(c). The Comptroller General may, however, consider objections raised after that time.

4. Hearings

In 1991, the GAO revised its bid protest regulations to permit a hearing on the protest at the request of one of the parties or on its own initiative, 4 C.F.R. § 21.7(a). The hearing replaced the former administrative conference proceedings. A hearing is not automatic but, rather, is held at the discretion of the Comptroller General, *Jack Faucett Assocs.*, Comp. Gen. Dec. B-254421, 94-2 CPD ¶ 72. A hearing may be requested by any party or conducted at the initiative of the Comptroller General, 4 C.F.R. § 21.7(a). Requests must set forth the reasons why a hearing is necessary.

A prehearing conference (usually by telephone) is generally conducted prior to the hearing to decide on the timing, the procedures to be followed, the issues to be considered, and the witnesses who will be called to testify, 4 C.F.R. § 21.7(b).

Generally, hearings are conducted as soon as practicable after receipt by the parties of the agency report and relevant documents, 4 C.F.R. § 21.7(c). Hearings are usually limited to one day and are conducted at the GAO in Washington, D.C., or, at the discretion of the Comptroller General, at other locations, 4 C.F.R. § 21.7(c).

Witnesses are not sworn but are reminded that false testimony may subject them to criminal penalties. If a witness fails to appear or to answer a question, the Comptroller General may draw inferences unfavorable to the party for whom the witness would have testified, 4 C.F.R. § 21.7(f).

Posthearing comments are to be submitted within five calendar days of the hearing unless the Comptroller General sets a different time, 4 C.F.R. § 21.7(g).

5. Time for Decision

Under the original statute in the CICA establishing GAO protest authority, the Comptroller General was given 90 working days to resolve a protest. The FASA restated this time as 125 calendar days. The Clinger-Cohen Act of 1996 shortened this time to 100 calendar days.

a. Statutory Deadline

The statutorily prescribed deadline for a Comptroller General decision on a protest is 100 calendar days after the date the protest is submitted to the Comptroller General, 31 U.S.C. § 3554(a)(1). Although there is no specific exception authorizing an extension of time, where supplemental protests have been filed, the Comptroller General may "roll over" a protest — that is, dismiss the earlier protest and incorporate it into the last supplemental protest, 31 U.S.C. § 3554(a)(2). This, in effect, can extend the time taken to have the protest decided well beyond the 100-calendar-day period.

b. Express Option

In cases that can be decided on an expeditious basis, the Comptroller General may decide to use the "express option procedures." The FASA amended the express option process to require completion within 65 working days, P.L. 103-355, § 1403(a). The Clinger-Cohen Act of 1996 shortened this to 65 calendar days. A request for use of the express option may be submitted by any party in writing and must be received by the Comptroller General within five days after the protest or supplemental protest is filed, 4 C.F.R. § 21.10(c). When the express option is used, the following schedule applies, as set forth in 4 C.F.R. § 21.10(d):

> (1) The contracting agency shall file a complete report with GAO and the parties within 20 days after it receives notice from GAO that the express option will be used.
>
> (2) Comments on the agency report shall be filed with GAO and the other parties within 5 days after receipt of the report.
>
> (3) If a hearing is held, no separate comments on the agency report under paragraph (d)(2) of this section should be submitted unless specifically requested by GAO. Consolidated comments on the agency report and hearing shall be filed within 5 days after the hearing was held or as specified by GAO.

(4) Where circumstances demonstrate that a case is no longer suitable for resolution using the express option, GAO shall establish a new schedule for submissions by the parties.

c. *Summary Decision and Accelerated Schedule*

At the request of a party or on its own initiative, the Comptroller General may set up an accelerated schedule for deciding a protest and may issue a summary decision on a protest, 4 C.F.R. § 21.10(e).

d. *Decision Distribution*

A hard copy of the decision is to be made available to each of the parties as well as to the public, unless the decision is protected. If the decision is protected, only the parties under the protective order and the contracting agency will receive copies. Protected decisions are redacted and then made available to the public. Protest decisions are available electronically, 4 C.F.R. § 21.12, at <http://www.gao.gov/decisions/bidpro/bidpro.htm>.

6. *Reconsiderations*

The Comptroller General will reconsider a bid protest decision at the request of a protester, an intervenor, or a federal agency involved in the protest, 4 C.F.R. § 21.14. Copies of the request must be sent to all parties that participated in the protest.

The request for reconsideration must be filed within 10 calendar days of the date the basis for the request for reconsideration was or should have been known, 4 C.F.R. § 21.14(b). Normally, that is 10 days after receipt of the decision, but if the protester learns of the decision in some other way, the 10-day rule will be enforced strictly. See *Speedy Food Serv., Inc.*, Comp. Gen. Dec. B-274406.2, 97-1 CPD ¶ 5, where the request for reconsideration was dismissed as untimely because it was not filed within 10 days of the time the protester saw the decision on the Internet.

The request for reconsideration must do more than restate the arguments in the initial protest. 4 C.F.R. § 21.14(a) provides:

> GAO will not consider a request for reconsideration that does not contain a detailed statement of the factual and legal grounds upon which reversal or

modification is deemed warranted, specifying any errors of law made or information not previously considered.

In *Tri-Star Indus.*, Comp. Gen. Dec. B-254767.3, 94-1 CPD ¶ 388, the Comptroller General stated that the request for reconsideration must be based on (1) the failure to consider evidence that should have been considered, (2) newly discovered evidence that the party could not reasonably have furnished for the initial consideration, or (3) errors of law. See *Department of the Navy*, Comp. Gen. Dec. B-237342.2, 90-2 CPD ¶ 39 (Comptroller misread agency record); *Gracon Corp.*, Comp. Gen. Dec. B-236603.2, 90-1 CPD ¶ 496 (man-hours for electrical work considered in prior protest was in error); *Richards Painting Co.*, Comp. Gen. Dec. B-232678.2, 89-1 CPD ¶ 481 (agency submitted new evidence that protester was in different room from the bid opening room at the time of bid opening); *Orkand Corp.*, Comp. Gen. Dec. B-224466.2, 87-1 CPD ¶ 88 (Comptroller applied conventional rules of sealed bid procurement rather than two-step sealed bidding). More often, the protester fails to provide a basis for reconsideration. See *Deployable Hosp. Sys., Inc.*, Comp. Gen. Dec. B-260778.4, 96-2 CPD ¶ 6 (request for reconsideration was insufficient because it consisted largely of quotations from prior filings); *Saturn Indus.*, Comp. Gen. Dec. B-261954.4, 96-2 CPD ¶ 25 (request for reconsideration denied because party merely reiterated arguments raised during initial protest); *Schleicher Community Corrections Ctr.*, Comp. Gen. Dec. B-270499.6, 96-2 CPD ¶ 68 (request for reconsideration denied because protester did not show that prior decision contained any errors of fact or law); and *Dyna-Air Eng'g Corp.*, Comp. Gen. Dec. B-271587.2, 96-2 CPD ¶ 93 (request for reconsideration denied because no errors of fact or law). The Comptroller General rarely finds that the protester is offering newly discovered evidence that could not possibly have been furnished upon the initial consideration, *Allstate Van & Storage, Inc.*, Comp. Gen. Dec. B-270744.2, 96-2 CPD ¶ 72 (information proffered seven months after the protester had learned of the evidence not new).

There is no statutory deadline for issuing a decision on reconsideration. Also, there is no requirement to withhold award or suspend performance during the pendency of the reconsideration, 4 C.F.R. § 21.14(c).

F. Standards of Review

31 U.S.C. § 3554(b)(1) provides that the Comptroller General will review an agency action to determine if it "complies with statute or regulation." Under this standard, a protester must establish that the contracting agency has prejudicially violated a statute or regulation or has taken a discretionary action without a rational basis. The Comptroller General has given agencies considerable latitude in applying this rational basis standard to discretionary actions. This contrasts with the GSBCA, which was far more willing to find agency decisions lacking a rational basis. See *B3H Corp. v. Department of the Air Force*, GSBCA 12813-P, 94-3 BCA ¶ 27,068, *rev'd*, 75 F.3d 1577 (Fed. Cir. 1996) (board had held that source selection determination lacked credible support and failed to demonstrate with reasonable certainty that the added value was worth the higher price); and *Unisys Corp. v. Department of the Air Force*, GSBCA 13129-P, 95-2 BCA ¶ 27,622, *rev'd*, 98 F.3d 1325 (Fed. Cir. 1996) (board had held that the best value source selection decision was "fundamentally flawed" because it did not reasonably establish that the awardee's superior technical proposal was worth its higher price). In reversing these GSBCA decisions, the Federal Circuit has made it clear that administrative protest authorities are not permitted to substitute their judgment for that of the contracting agency.

The Comptroller General traditionally acted in accordance with this guidance of the court, as shown by standard language in Comptroller General decisions in protests challenging the rationality of discretionary decisions of contracting agencies. See, for example, *Red River Serv. Corp.*, Comp. Gen. Dec. B-253671.2, 94-1 CPD ¶ 385, stating:

> Where, as here, the RFP provides that technical considerations will be more important than cost, source selection officials have broad discretion in determining the manner in which they will make use of the technical and cost evaluation results in arriving at a source selection decision. *University of Dayton Research Inst.*, B-245431, Jan. 2, 1992, 92-1 CPD ¶ 6. Such cost/technical tradeoffs are governed only by the test of rationality and consistency with the RFP's stated evaluation criteria. *Miller Bldg. Corp.*, B-245488, Jan. 3, 1992, 92-1 CPD ¶ 21.

See also *JB Indus.*, Comp. Gen. Dec. B-251118.2, 93-1 CPD ¶ 297 (award to offeror with 13 percent higher price to obtain lower risk of unsuccessful performance); *University of Dayton Research Inst.*, Comp. Gen. Dec. B-245431, 92-1 CPD ¶ 6 (award to offeror with 27 percent higher cost and fee to obtain lower risk of technical failure). In none of these three cases was there any quantification of the technical and management evaluations. The Comptroller General stated a slightly different formulation of the standard in *Technology Vectors, Inc.*, Comp. Gen. Dec. B-252518.2, 94-1 CPD ¶ 345:

> Since the RFP here stated that award would be made to the offeror whose proposal was determined to be most advantageous to the government, considering price and other factors, the agency had the discretion to determine whether the technical advantages associated with [the winning offeror's] proposal was worth its higher price. Our Office will not object to that determination if the agency reasonably determined that the price premium involved is justified by the technical superiority of the proposal.

See *Ameriko Maintenance Co.*, Comp. Gen. Dec., B-253274.2, 93-2 CPD ¶ 121 (award to higher-priced offeror to obtain more extensive experience); *D'Wiley's Servs., Inc.*, Comp. Gen. Dec., B-251912, 93-1 CPD ¶ 377, *DynCorp*, Comp. Gen. Dec. B-257037.2, 95-1 CPD ¶ 34, and *Scheduled Airlines Traffic Offices, Inc.*, Comp. Gen. Dec. B-257292.9, 95-2 CPD ¶ 113 (award to higher-priced offeror to obtain better staffing); *Centro Management, Inc.*, Comp. Gen. Dec., B-249411.2, 92-2 CPD ¶ 387, and *Hornet Joint Venture*, Comp. Gen. Dec. B-258430.2, 95-1 CPD ¶ 55 (award to higher-priced offeror to obtain better staffing and lower risk of poor performance); *EG&G Team*, Comp. Gen. Dec. B-259917.2, 95-2 CPD ¶ 138 (award to higher-price offeror to obtain benefits of higher-rated proposal); *TRW, Inc.*, Comp. Gen. Dec. B-260623, 95-2 CPD ¶ 92 (award to higher-priced offeror to obtain lower risk). However, in *Strum, Ruger & Co.*, Comp. Gen. Dec. B-250193, 93-1 CPD ¶ 42, the Comptroller General overturned an award that required the agency to pay a large premium to an offeror that was rated only marginally superior to the protester. The source selection authority had selected the offeror with the highest technical score without making any tradeoff analysis. The Comptroller General stated that the source selection authority had "misapprehended applicable law" and sent the matter back to the agency to "document a reasoned source selection decision."

G. Prejudice

Competitive prejudice is an essential element of every viable protest, 51 Comp. Gen. 678 (B-174367) (1972); *Lithos Restoration Ltd.*, 71 Comp. Gen. Dec. 367 (B-247003.2), 92-1 CPD ¶ 379. The protester must establish that but for the agency's actions, it would have had a substantial chance of receiving the award, *McDonald-Bradley*, Comp. Gen. Dec. B-270126, 96-1 CPD ¶ 54; *Unified Indus. Inc.*, Comp. Gen. Dec. B-212996.2, 84-2 CPD ¶ 139; *University Research Corp.*, Comp. Gen. Dec. B-186311.2, 81-2 CPD ¶ 428. This is the same test as used in the courts, *Statistica, Inc. v. United States*, 102 F.3d 1577 (Fed. Cir. 1996). In some instances, the Comptroller General states the test as a "reasonable possibility that the protester would have otherwise been the successful offeror as a sufficient basis for sustaining a protest," *CDA Investment Technologies, Inc.*, Comp. Gen. Dec. B-272093.3, 97-1 CPD ¶ 103. The court in *Statistica, Inc.* stated that "reasonable likelihood" should be interpreted to be the same as "substantial chance."

General allegations of prejudice will not suffice. See *MCI Constructors, Inc.*, Comp. Gen. Dec. B-274347, 96-2 CPD ¶ 210, where the Comptroller General found a failure to show prejudice when the protester failed to present information showing how it could reduce its price by the nearly $7 million dollar margin with the low offeror. See also *Labrador Airways Ltd.*, Comp. Gen. Dec. B-241608, 91-1 CPD ¶ 167, where the protester did not demonstrate to the Comptroller General that it was prejudiced because the agency relaxed specifications for commercial flight services for one offeror. The protester alleged in general terms that on past contracts this requirement resulted in a net cost to the protester, but failed to provide any information showing how it calculated this cost or how much of this cost was included in its offer.

Protesters have most readily demonstrated prejudice when they have been denied the opportunity to revise their proposals in the same manner as a competitor. For example, in *Global Assocs. Ltd.*, Comp. Gen. Dec. B-271693, 96-2 CPD ¶ 100, the Comptroller General found that the protester was prejudiced when the agency conducted discussions with only the awardee after the submission of best and final offers (BAFOs). Similarly, the failure to conduct meaningful discussions may be prejudicial. In *Ogden Support Servs., Inc.*, Comp. Gen. Dec. B-270354, 96-1 CPD ¶ 175, the Comptroller General sustained a protest because the agency did not inform the protester of the evaluated weaknesses and deficiencies in its proposal. The Comptroller General concluded that the protester was prejudiced because it would have had an opportunity to improve its score to a level approaching the awardee's score and its proposal may well have remained low in cost. See also *Alliant Techsystems, Inc.*, Comp. Gen. Dec. B-260215.4, 95-2 CPD ¶ 79, where the Comptroller General stated that in these circumstances, it would "resolve any doubts concerning the prejudicial effect of the agency's action in favor of the protester." But see *McDonald-Bradley*, Comp. Gen. Dec. B-270126, 96-1 CPD ¶ 54, where an allegation that the protester was misled during discussions was denied because the protester did not demonstrate a reasonable possibility that it was prejudiced. The protester argued that the agency misled the firm during discussions into believing that its proposed wages had to be consistent with the Service Contract Act requirements, but the Comptroller General found no proof that the protester would have lowered its wages further in its BAFO or that an adjustment to the protester's price would have made its price competitive.

Prejudice has also been demonstrated when the agency makes errors in initiating the procurement. In *Comint Sys. Corp.*, Comp. Gen. Dec. B-274853, 97-1 CPD ¶ 14, the agency's letter offering a requirement to the SBA for acceptance into the 8(a) program failed to give complete and accurate information regarding the proposed offering. The Comptroller General found prejudice because the failure to provide the information deprived the SBA of the opportunity to make a fully informed decision with respect to the acquisition and deprived the protester of a potential opportunity to participate in the procurement.

Prejudice has been found where an agency relaxes its requirements. See *George Hyman Constr. Co.*, Comp. Gen. Dec. B-265798, 95-2 CPD ¶ 173, where the agency relaxed a go/no-go key personnel experience evaluation criterion. The Comptroller General noted that the key personnel experience requirements were very restrictive and that a prospective offeror had requested that the requirements be amended to be less restrictive, which the agency declined to do. Additionally, one offeror was rejected as technically unacceptable for failing to meet this requirement. Thus, the Comptroller General held that there was a reasonable possibility of prejudice by relaxing this requirement for the awardee. But prejudice will not be found in these circumstances if the protester does not demonstrate that it could have won the competition. See *Brown & Root, Inc.*, Comp. Gen. Dec. B-270505.2, 96-2 CPD ¶ 143, where no prejudice was found because there was no evidence that, had the protester been aware of the waiver of the security clearance requirement, it would have submitted a different proposal. See also *Safety-Kleen Corp.*, Comp. Gen. Dec. B-274176, 96-2 CPD ¶ 200, where the Army had improperly waived a provision requiring a certificate of environmental impairment liability insurance when it awarded the contract to a firm that did not meet the requirement. The Comptroller General denied the protest, holding that the waiver did not place the protester at a competitive disadvantage because the protester did not assert that it would have refrained from providing the insurance coverage had it known that the Army did not consider the coverage necessary.

When the procurement defect is a failure to evaluate proposals properly, the protester must show that proper evaluation would have given it a chance to win the competition. This test was met in *Labat-Anderson, Inc.*, 71 Comp. Gen. 252 (B-246071), 92-1 CPD ¶ 193, where the agency had so significantly deviated from its evaluation scheme that it was not clear how a reevaluation would have scored the competitors. However, when the evaluation errors are minor, prejudice is difficult to prove. See *Northport Handling, Inc.*, Comp. Gen. Dec. B-274615, 97-1 CPD ¶ 3 (no prejudice by any errors that may have occurred during evaluation because even if agency assigned the highest rating to protester's performance as the incumbent it would have no impact on past performance rating); *Agriculture Technology Partners*, Comp. Gen. Dec. B-272978, 96-2 CPD ¶ 226 (even if agency improperly evaluated staff evaluation factor, there were several superior proposals and protester had no reasonable chance for award); *Executive Court Reporters, Inc.*, Comp. Gen. Dec. B-272981, 96-2 CPD ¶ 227 (the slightly unequal weighting of the three factors in the evaluation did not have a material effect on protester's proposal score and resulting competitive position); *PADCO, Inc.*, Comp. Gen. Dec. B-270445, 96-1 CPD ¶ 142 (protester's own nominee had a similar deficiency and was found acceptable); and *Lithos Restoration Ltd.*, 71 Comp. Gen. Dec. 367 (B-247003.2), 92-1 CPD ¶ 379 (even if key personnel factor was evaluated under most important factor, as contemplated by RFP, protester's proposal would not have improved vis-à-vis the awardee's technically superior proposal).

Prejudice cannot be proved if the protester is ineligible for award. See *Wyeth-Lederle Vaccines & Pediatrics*, Comp. Gen. Dec. B-274490, 96-2 CPD ¶ 229, where the protester was found to have suffered no prejudice as a result of the agency's inclusion of the single award clause in the solicitation because even if the single award clause were removed, the protester would still be ineligible for award because it did not possess the required license.

In cases finding prejudice, the protester is often entitled to its costs of filing and pursuing its protest, as well as reasonable attorneys' fees, *Global Assocs. Ltd.*, Comp. Gen. Dec. B-271693, 96-2 CPD ¶ 100; *Ogden Support Servs., Inc.*, Comp. Gen. Dec. B-270354, 96-1 CPD ¶ 175.

H. Remedies

The Comptroller General can make recommendations to the agency but does not have the authority to direct the agency to take action or to refrain from doing so. Only in rare cases, however, do agencies fail to follow these recommendations. The Comptroller General is required to report annually to Congress all cases in which procuring agencies do not fully implement the Comptroller General's recommendations, 31 U.S.C. § 3554(e)(2). See Comptroller General Report B-158766, Jan. 31, 1996, indicating that there was no instance in 1996 where a federal agency failed to implement the Comptroller General's recommendations.

1. Nonmonetary Remedies

The Comptroller General can recommend a variety of nonmonetary remedies. 31 U.S.C. § 3554(b)(1) states:

> If the Comptroller General determines that the solicitation, proposed award, or award does not comply with a statute or regulation, the Comptroller General shall recommend that the Federal agency —
>
> (A) refrain from exercising any of his options under the contract;
>
> (B) recompete the contract immediately;
>
> (C) issue a new solicitation;
>
> (D) terminate the contract;
>
> (E) award a contract consistent with the requirements of such statute and regulation;
>
> (F) implement any combination of recommendations under clauses (A), (B), (C), (D), and (E); or
>
> (G) implement such other recommendations as the Comptroller General determines to be necessary in order to promote compliance with procurement statutes and regulations.

If award has already been made, the Comptroller General, in making recommendations, is prohibited from considering any cost or disruption resulting from the termination, recompetition, or reaward of the contract, 31 U.S.C. § 3554(b)(2). In *Price Waterhouse*, Comp. Gen. Dec. B-220049, 86-1 CPD ¶ 333, an agency requested reconsideration of a decision that sustained a protest and recommended possible contract termination. The Comptroller General held that its decision would not be reconsidered based upon the estimated costs of termination where the agency proceeded with performance of the contract upon a finding that to do so would be in the best interests of the Government. See also *World-Wide Sec. Serv., Inc.*, 66 Comp. Gen. 195 (B-224277) (1987); and *Department of the Navy*, Comp. Gen. Dec. B-274944.4, 97-2 CPD ¶ 16.

A common remedy in negotiated procurement is to conduct a new round of discussions and solicit new BAFOs, *Gardiner, Kamya & Assocs.*, Comp. Gen. Dec. B-258915.2, 95-1 CPD ¶ 193; *National Med. Staffing, Inc.*, Comp. Gen. Dec. B-259402, 95-1 CPD ¶ 163.

For cases where the Comptroller General recommended that award be made to the protester, see *L&E Assocs.*, Comp. Gen. Dec. B-258808.4, 95-1 CPD ¶ 288; and *Special Sys. Servs., Inc.*, Comp. Gen. Dec. B-259865.2, 95-1 CPD ¶ 241.

2. Monetary Remedies

The monetary remedies that protesters have been able to recover are the costs of pursuing the protest, including attorneys' fees and the costs of preparing the bid or proposal. Recovery of anticipated profits has been uniformly denied, *Baker Support Servs., Inc.*, Comp. Gen. Dec. B-256192.3, 95-1 CPD ¶ 75.

When the Comptroller General recommends payment of protest costs and/or bid or proposal preparation costs, it leaves it to the parties to agree on the amount. The protester is required to submit to the procuring agency a detailed and certified claim within 60 calendar days after receipt of the Comptroller General recommendation that the costs be paid, 4 C.F.R. § 21.8(f)(1). The protester seeking to recover the costs of pursuing its protest must submit sufficient evidence to support its monetary claim, *Consolidated Bell, Inc.*, 70 Comp. Gen. 358 (B-220425.4) (1991). In *Wind Gap Knitwear, Inc.*, Comp. Gen. Dec. B-251411.2, 95-2 CPD ¶ 94, the Comptroller General denied a claim for costs where the protester failed to file an adequately detailed claim with the agency within 60 days after the protester received a copy of the decision awarding protest costs. See also *Custom Production Mfg., Inc.*, Comp. Gen. Dec. B-235431.8, 95-2 CPD ¶ 40 (protester submitted its claim four and a half years after it was entitled to such costs).

The procuring agency must decide the claim "as soon as practicable after the claim is filed" and notify the Comptroller General within 60 calendar days after the Comptroller General decision recommending the payment of costs, 4 C.F.R. § 21.8(f)(3). If the parties cannot reach agreement on the amount within a reasonable time, the protester may refer the matter to the Comptroller General for decision, 4 C.F.R. § 21.8(f)(2). The Comptroller General will not ordinarily recommend the amount of costs to be paid for pursuing the claim, *Princeton Gamma-Tech, Inc.*, 68 Comp. Gen. 401 (B-228052.5), 89-1 CPD ¶ 401, except where the parties cannot agree on the amount, 4 C.F.R. § 21.8(f)(2). See *ViON Corp.*, Comp. Gen. Dec. B-256363.3, 95-1 CPD ¶ 219, where the Comptroller General determined the amount of protest costs because the protester and the agency were unable to reach agreement. The Comptroller General, if determining the amount of costs to be paid, may also recommend that the agency pay the costs of pursuing this claim for costs before the GAO, 4 C.F.R. § 21.8(f)(2).

a. Bid or Proposal Preparation Costs

31 U.S.C. § 3554(c)(1)(B) permits the Comptroller General to award the costs of preparing a bid or proposal to a successful protester. However, bid or proposal costs are not awarded merely if a protest is sustained; rather, recovery is appropriate only when a protester is unreasonably excluded from the competition and no other remedy is appropriate. This is often the case when performance of the contract is complete or when it is impractical to terminate the contract because performance has reached its latter stages. See *Bush Painting, Inc.*, Comp. Gen. Dec. B-239904.3, 91-2 CPD ¶ 159, where the protester was entitled to its bid preparation costs because it was impracticable to terminate performance of a contract that was 90 percent complete. See also *Adelaide Blomfield Management Co.*, Comp. Gen. Dec. B-253128.4, 95-1 CPD ¶ 7, where the protester was entitled to its bid preparation and protest costs because the Comptroller General was unable to recommend termination of the awarded lease contract because the lease did not contain a termination for convenience clause.

The Comptroller General will not award proposal costs if the protester would not have been in line for the award, *Temps & Co.*, 65 Comp. Gen. 819 (B-221846.2), 86-2 CPD ¶ 236. But see *EHE Nat'l Health Servs.*, Inc., 65 Comp. Gen. 1 (B-219361.2), 85-2 CPD ¶ 362, where the Comptroller General found that a protester had a substantial chance of receiving the award when the protester was one of three firms in line for award.

If a solicitation is canceled for valid reasons not related to the protest, no bid or proposal preparation costs will be awarded. In *Orange Personnel Servs., Inc.*, Comp. Gen. Dec. B-256164.2, 95-1 CPD ¶ 26, cancellation precluded the award of bid preparation costs although the protester was in line for award. See also *Fischer and Porter Co.*, Comp. Gen. Dec. B-227941.3, 88-1 CPD ¶ 327 (no bid preparation costs awarded where legislation passed subsequent to a Comptroller General decision sustaining a protest had the effect of rendering moot the decision).

A protester is not entitled to award of bid preparation costs if it will have an opportunity to compete for award of the contract under a resolicitation conducted as a result of its protest, *KIME Enters.*, Comp. Gen. Dec. B-241996.5, 91-2 CPD ¶ 523; 65 Comp. Gen. 268 (B-219667.2) (1986).

The Comptroller General has awarded bid preparation costs where a protester bid was improperly rejected even though the agency's subsequent review of the bid determined that it was not eligible for award, *Industrial Storage Equipment-Pacific*, Comp. Gen. Dec. B-228123.2, 88-1 CPD ¶ 328.

b. Protest Costs

The Comptroller General has the authority to grant protest costs, including reasonable attorneys' fees, 31 U.S.C. § 3554(c). Protest costs can be granted even when other corrective action is taken in a sustained protest, *Norse Inc.*, Comp. Gen. Dec. B-233534, 89-1 CPD ¶ 293 (protester was both reinstated into the contract competition and granted protest costs).

Generally, no protest costs will be granted if the Comptroller General has not made a decision on the merits, *Signal Corp.*, 69 Comp. Gen. 659 (B-240450), 90-2 CPD ¶ 116. However, 4 C.F.R. § 21.8(e) states that the GAO may recommend payment of protest costs when the procuring agency takes corrective action on the basis of the protest without waiting for a Comptroller General decision. The Comptroller General has stated that such costs will be awarded if the procuring agency has unduly delayed taking corrective action in a clearly meritorious protest, *Commercial Energies, Inc.*, 71 Comp. Gen. 97 (B-243718.2), 91-2 CPD ¶ 499; *Tucson Mobilephone, Inc.*, Comp. Gen. Dec. B-252659.3, 94-1 CPD ¶ 12; *GVC Cos.*, Comp. Gen. Dec. B-254670.4, 94-1 CPD ¶ 292; *Multi-Bloc, Inc.*, Comp. Gen. Dec. B-259182.2, 95-1 CPD ¶ 217; *Custom Printing Co.*, Comp. Gen. Dec. B-275798.3, 97-2 CPD ¶ 9; *Chant Eng'g Co.*, Comp. Gen. Dec. B-274871.2, 97-2 CPD ¶ 58. For cases finding that the protester was not entitled to award of costs of filing and pursuing its protest because the agency took prompt corrective action, see *Oklahoma Indian Corp.*, 70 Comp. Gen. 558 (B-243785.2), 91-1 CPD ¶ 558 (agency took corrective action within two weeks of protest being filed); *Metters Indus., Inc.*, B-240391.5, 91-2 CPD ¶ 535 (agency promptly initiated an investigation and, in conjunction with the preparation of a lawsuit filed by another offeror during the investigation, discovered potential regulatory and statutory violations, which led to the cancellation of the solicitation two days after the agency report was due to be filed); *Locus Sys., Inc.*, 71 Comp. Gen. 243 (B-241441.5), 92-1 CPD ¶ 177 (agency promptly investigated the protester's allegations and subsequently resolicited the requirement after determining that the protester was correct); *Boaz Towing, Inc.*, Comp. Gen. Dec. B-257883.2, 95-1 CPD ¶ 109 (initiation of corrective action took place approximately when agency report was due); *Carlson Wagonlit Travel*, Comp. Gen. Dec. B-266337.3, 96-2 CPD ¶ 99 (38 working days before corrective agency action not unreasonable where four separate protests were filed against the agency); and *DuraMed Enters., Inc.*, Comp. Gen. Dec. B-271793.2, 96-2 CPD ¶ 135 (corrective action taken on day agency report was due). See also *Veda Inc.*, Comp. Gen. Dec. B-265809.2, 96-2 CPD ¶ 27; *Bionetics Corp.*, Comp. Gen. Dec. B-270323.3, 96-2 CPD ¶ 70; and *Carlson Wagonlit Travel*, Comp. Gen. Dec. B-266337.3, 96-2 CPD ¶ 99. Note that as a prerequisite to entitlement to costs where a protest has been settled by corrective action, not only must the agency have unduly delayed taking corrective action, but also the protest must have been meritorious, *J.F. Taylor, Inc.*, Comp. Gen. Dec. B-266039.3, 96-2 CPD ¶ 5. See also *Baxter Healthcare Corp.*, Comp. Gen. Dec. B-259811.3, 95-2 CPD ¶ 174 (protest that the contracting agency's technical evaluation was flawed because it erroneously determined that the firm's demonstration failed to show that it met the solicitation requirements was not clearly meritorious).

To be eligible for protest costs when the agency takes corrective action, the protester is required to file with the GAO within 15 calendar days after being advised of the procuring agency's decision to take corrective action,

4 C.F.R. § 21.8(e). The protester must also file a copy with the procuring agency, which then has 15 calendar days to respond.

Where an agency's decision to cancel a solicitation is not the result of corrective action taken in response to a protest, the protester will not be entitled to recover the costs of filing and pursuing its protest, *H. Watt & Scott Gen. Contractors, Inc.*, Comp. Gen. Dec. B-257776.3, 95-1 CPD ¶ 183 (cancellation based on inability to proceed with work due to weather conditions); *Digital Sys. Group, Inc.*, Comp. Gen. Dec. B-257835.2, 95-1 CPD ¶ 173 (agency did not receive any proposals that satisfied requirement); *Red River Serv. Corp.*, Comp. Gen. Dec. B-259462.2, 95-2 CPD ¶ 106 (bid acceptance period had expired).

The Comptroller General will award only those protest costs that are related to the protest. Related costs have included the salaries of the protester's president and other employees for the time they worked on the protest, *Ultraviolet Purification Sys., Inc.*, Comp. Gen. Dec. B-226941.3, 89-1 CPD ¶ 376. See, however, *Berkshire Computer Prods.*, Comp. Gen. Dec. B-240327.3, 95-1 CPD ¶ 6, where the Comptroller General denied the award of protest costs because the protester did not establish that the costs claimed to have been paid to an unsalaried consultant and an attorney were related to the protest. A protester's time spent soliciting help from members of Congress is not related to the protest and, thus, the cost is not recoverable, *Omni Analysis*, 69 Comp. Gen. 433 (B-233372.4), 90-1 CPD ¶ 436. The Comptroller General will not award attorneys' fees associated with seeking injunctive relief from a federal district court pending the Comptroller General's decision.

The Comptroller General will not allow the recovery of costs that may be related to the protest but are not properly documented, *W. S. Spotswood & Sons*, 69 Comp. Gen. 622 (B-236713.3), 90-2 CPD ¶ 50. The burden is on the protester to adequately document the costs incurred, and the protester cannot rely on standard rates to substantiate its claim. See *John Peeples*, 70 Comp. Gen. 661 (B-233167.2), 91-2 CPD ¶ 125. The Comptroller General will also disallow legal expenses or fees that are not adequately documented by the law firm, *Diverco, Inc.* (B-240639.5), 92-2 CPD ¶ 460. In *W. S. Spotswood & Sons*, 69 Comp. Gen. 622 (B-236713.3), 90-2 CPD ¶ 50, the Comptroller General disallowed costs due to data insufficiency. The protester submitted evidence showing the type and amount of work performed by the employees, but did not demonstrate how the hourly rates were calculated or whether the rates claimed reflected actual compensation plus reasonable overhead and fringe benefits. See also *McNeil Technologies, Inc.*, Comp. Gen. Dec. B-254909.3, 95-1 CPD ¶ 207; and *Innovative Refrigeration Concepts*, Comp. Gen. Dec. B-258655.2, 97-2 CPD ¶ 19. In *Custom Production Mfg., Inc.*, Comp. Gen. Dec. B-235431.7, 95-1 CPD ¶ 236, the protester's claim was denied because it consisted of lump-sum figures that prevented both the agency and the Comptroller General from reviewing the reasonableness of the amount claimed.

A prevailing protester is entitled to recover reasonable attorneys' fees, *KPMG Peat Marwick*, Comp. Gen. Dec. B-259479.4, 96-2 CPD ¶ 43. A cost is reasonable if, in nature and amount, it does not exceed the costs a prudent person would incur pursuing the protest, *Bay Tankers, Inc.*, Comp Gen. Dec. B-238162.4, 91-1 CPD ¶ 524. See *Bush Painting, Inc.*, Comp. Gen. Dec. B-239904.3, 91-2 CPD ¶ 159 (protester was not entitled to attorneys' fees where it retained the attorney after its protest was filed and the agency had submitted its comments); and *ViON Corp.*, Comp. Gen. Dec. B-256363.3, 95-1 CPD ¶ 219 (protester not entitled to reimbursement for attorney hours expended to review third-party intervention that was based entirely on unsuccessful protest issue). However, an agency's generalized objection that hours are excessive is not a sufficient basis for rejecting a properly documented and certified claim for attorneys' fees, *Omni Analysis*, 69 Comp. Gen. 433 (B-233372.4), 90-1 CPD ¶ 436; *Data Based Decisions, Inc.*, 69 Comp. Gen. 122, 89-2 CPD ¶ 538. But see *Armour of Am., Inc.*, B-237690.2, 92-1 CPD ¶ 257, where the Comptroller General determined that legal fees were excessive even though well documented. There, the Comptroller General disallowed all 36 hours of the attorneys' billed time for pursuit of issues that were clearly untimely, disallowed one-fourth of Armour's attorneys' hours attributable to legal research and writing, and disallowed one-third of the total time claimed by Armour's attorneys for travel to and from the informal bid protest conference held at the GAO offices. In *Price Waterhouse*, Comp. Gen. Dec. B-254492.3, 95-2 CPD ¶ 38, the Comptroller General reviewed each hour billed to determine the reasonableness of the attorney hours claimed. The Comptroller General found that although 13.5 hours seemed to be high in preparing a protective order, it was not excessive. However, 4.5 hours to review the agency's notice to authorize contract performance pursuant to statutory best interest clause was considered excessive by the Comptroller General.

The FASA placed a cap on attorneys' fees and expert and consultant fees. The top rate reimbursable to large businesses for attorneys' fees is $150 per hour unless the procuring agency determines, on the recommendation of the Comptroller General, that a higher fee is justified, 31 U.S.C. § 3554(c)(2)(B). The top rate for consultants and expert witnesses for large businesses is the "highest rate of compensation for expert witnesses paid by the Federal Government." Prior to the FASA, the Comptroller General had rejected the argument that reasonable attorneys' fees should be limited, and stated that the prevailing rate in the area for similar services would determine reasonableness. See *Princeton Gamma-Tech, Inc.*, 68 Comp. Gen. 400 (B-228052.5), 89-1 CPD ¶ 401 (the reasonable and normally charged hourly rates for Washington, D.C., were $185 to $195 for partners and $90 for associates).

IV. COURT OF FEDERAL CLAIMS

The Court of Federal Claims and its predecessors initially relied upon the Tucker Act, 28 U.S.C. § 1491(a)(1), to take jurisdiction over contract award controversies. This statute gives the court jurisdiction over claims "founded either upon the Constitution, or any Act of Congress or any regulation of an executive department, or upon any express or implied contract with the United States." As early as 1956, the Court of Claims used the Government's "implied contract to consider bids" in holding that a disappointed bidder would be entitled to bid preparation costs if it could show that its bid had not been evaluated in good faith, *Heyer Prods. Co. v. United States*, 135 Ct. Cl. 63, 140 F. Supp. 409 (1956). The court again held that its jurisdiction extends to implied contracts to consider bids and proposals fairly and honestly in *Keco Indus., Inc. v. United States*, 203 Ct. Cl. 566, 492 F.2d 1200 (1974). However, lacking general equitable powers, the court could not grant injunctive relief.

Injunctive relief became available in 1982, when the following provision was added to 28 U.S.C. § 1491(b)(3), granting the following equitable powers to the Claims Court:

> To afford complete relief on any contract claim brought before the contract is awarded, the court shall have exclusive jurisdiction to grant declaratory judgments and such equitable and extraordinary relief as it deems proper, including but not limited to injunctive relief. In exercising this jurisdiction, the court shall give regard to the interests of national defense and national security.

The Administrative Dispute Resolution Act of 1996 (ADRA), P.L. 104-320, repealed this provision but gave new "bid protest" jurisdiction to the court by enacting 28 U.S.C. § 1491(b), stating:

> (1) [T]he United States Court of Federal Claims . . . shall have jurisdiction to render judgment on any action by an interested party objecting to a solicitation by a Federal agency for bids or proposals for a proposed contract or to a proposed award or the award of a contract or any alleged violation of statute or regulation in connection with a procurement or a proposed procurement. . . . [T]he United States Court of Federal Claims . . . shall have jurisdiction to entertain such an action without regard to whether suit is instituted before or after award.

The court's new bid protest jurisdiction is available to a broader class of protesters and encompasses expanded grounds for protest as compared with its implied contract jurisdiction. Under the implied contract jurisdiction, the plaintiff (usually described as a "disappointed bidder") must have actually responded to the Government's solicitation and its response must have complied with the provisions of the solicitation, e.g., *Yachts Am., Inc. v. United States*, 3 Cl. Ct. 447 (1983), *aff'd*, 779 F.2d 656 (Fed. Cir. 1985). By contrast, the bid protest jurisdiction is available to an "interested party," thereby allowing suits by other than actual bidders.

This new statute permits monetary relief (limited to bid and proposal costs) as well as equitable relief (injunctions and declaratory judgments), 28 U.S.C. § 1491(b)(2). Thus, the court now has two statutes permitting monetary relief, 28 U.S.C. § 1491(a)(1) and 28 U.S.C. § 1491(b)(2).

Although the court also has jurisdiction under 28 U.S.C. § 1491(a)(1) over money claims "founded upon the Constitution, or any Act of Congress or any regulation," such suits have not proved to be a useful basis for preaward controversies for those without a contractual relationship arising from their participation in the procurement process. The court has jurisdiction to hear claims based solely on statutes or regulations. However, the statute or regulation sued upon must "confer a substantive right to recover money damages from the United States" before any recovery may be had, *United States v. Testan*, 424 U.S. 392 (1976). In that case, the Court found that the statutes in question did not create such a right because they contained no express provisions for recovery of money. The Court stated that a "grant of a right of action must be made with specificity" and then quoted *Eastport S.S. Corp. v. United States*, 178 Ct. Cl. 599, 606, 372 F.2d 1002

(1967), that such a right depends upon whether a statute or regulation "can fairly be interpreted as mandating compensation." Such rights are not found in statutes and regulations for the guidance of Government personnel, such as procurement statutes, *Eagle Constr. Corp. v. United States*, 4 Cl. Ct. 470 (1984); regulations dealing with employee conduct, *Dynalectron Corp. v. United States*, 4 Cl. Ct. 424, *aff'd*, 758 F.2d 665 (Fed. Cir. 1984); or regulations dealing with the SBA, *Stellacom, Inc. v. United States*, 24 Cl. Ct. 213 (1991).

The Court of Federal Claims' jurisdiction over claims based upon the Constitution has also proved not to be a significant basis for relief in the area of contract award controversies. See *Prevado Village Partnership v. United States*, 3 Cl. Ct. 219 (1983) (no taking of an "expectancy" interest that the parties would follow applicable regulations in their dealings); *Airborne Data, Inc. v. United States*, 702 F.2d 1350 (Fed. Cir. 1983) (no taking where agency disclosed trade secrets contained in a proposal). When the taking claim is for rights arising under a contract, the claim will be treated as contractual rather than Constitutional, *Sun Oil Co. v. United States*, 215 Ct. Cl. 716, 572 F.2d 786 (1978).

A. Procurement Activities Covered

The court's statute uses different terms to describe the procuring activities covered.

1. Contract of the United States

The language of 28 U.S.C. § 1491(a)(1) permitting monetary relief is extremely broad, extending to "any contract of the United States." The following nonappropriated fund activities are included within the definition of the United States:

Army and Air Force Exchange Service

Navy Exchanges

Marine Corps Exchanges

Coast Guard Exchanges

Exchange Councils of the National Aeronautics and Space Administration

The only Government agency excluded from coverage is the Tennessee Valley Authority, 28 U.S.C. § 1491(c). Cases considering whether an entity is covered under the statute include *McDonald's Corp. v. United States*, 926 F.2d 1126 (Fed. Cir. 1991) (Navy Resale and Services Support Office was covered even though it was not specifically listed in the statute because the legislative history showed that Congress intended to waive sovereign immunity for military organizations funded by resale activities); *Wolverine Supply, Inc. v. United States*, 17 Cl. Ct. 190 (1989) (Eielson AFB Central Base Fund not covered because it was not included in the NAFI military exchanges set forth in the statute); *Eubanks v. United States*, 25 Cl. Ct. 131 (1992) (United States was not a party to the contract between housing authority and property owner, and its funding and regulating program did not establish any contractual obligation).

2. Federal Agency

The court's "bid protest" jurisdiction is stated in somewhat narrower terms than its "contract" jurisdiction. 28 U.S.C. 1491(b)(1) gives the court jurisdiction to hear protests involving the procurement of a "federal agency." While the bid protest statute does not define the term, it is defined in 40 U.S.C. § 472 as

> any executive agency or any establishment in the legislative or judicial branch of the Government, including any wholly owned Government corporation.

The term "federal agency" is defined in other statutes, as well. Some definitions seem to be very broad. For example, 22 U.S.C. § 4802 states that "federal agency" "includes any department or agency of the United States Government." Some definitions do not include the legislative or judicial branches of the Government within the definition. For example, 40 U.S.C. § 304e defines "federal agency" as "any executive department, independent establishment, commission, board, bureau, or office in the executive branch, or other agency of the United States." See also 5 U.S.C. § 804, which states that "federal agency" means any agency as is defined in § 551(1). This section defines "agency" as "each authority of the Government of the United States, whether or not it is within or subject to review by another agency, but does not include such entities as Congress, the courts, territories or possessions of the United States, the government of the District of Columbia, and courts martial and military commissions." Other statutory definitions include the legislative and judicial branches of the Government. For example, 5 U.S.C. § 7901 defines "federal agency" as "an Executive agency as defined under section 105 of title 5, United States Code, and shall include any agency of the legislative or judicial branch of Government." 40 U.S.C. § 612 is similarly defined but excludes the Senate, the House of Representatives, and the Architect of the Capitol and any activities under his direction. 40 U.S.C. § 762 and 41 U.S.C. § 423 state that "federal agency" "has the meaning given such term by section 3(b) of the Federal Property and Administrative Services Act of 1949" (40 U.S.C. § 472). It may be argued that the 28 U.S.C. § 451 definition of the term "agency" should be used in bid protest cases. In *Butz Eng'g, Corp. v. United States*, 204 Ct. Cl. 561, 499 F.2d 619 (1974), the court, applying the 28 U.S.C. § 451 definition, determined that the Postal Service was subject to Tucker Act jurisdiction. However, it is questionable whether § 451 applies to 28 U.S.C. § 1491(b) because the protest statute covers "federal agency" while 28 U.S.C. § 451 defines "agency" without the modifier "federal."

B. Who May Protest

There are significant differences among the parties that may assert claims for money damages under 28 U.S.C. § 1491(a)(1) and those that may assert claims for equitable and monetary relief under 28 U.S.C. 1491(b)(2).

1. Disappointed Bidders

There was extensive litigation over the parties that could obtain relief under the 1982 implied contract jurisdiction. The most common form of implied contract in contract award cases arose when the Government issued a solicitation, thereby making an offer to honestly and fairly consider responses, and the prospective contractor accepted this offer by submitting a bid or proposal, *Keco Indus., Inc. v. United States*, 192 Ct. Cl. 773, 428 F.2d 1233 (1970); *United States v. John C. Grimberg Co.*, 702 F.2d 1362 (Fed. Cir. 1983); *National Forge Co. v. United States*, 779 F.2d 665 (Fed. Cir. 1985). Such cases are usually characterized as "disappointed bidder" cases. In order to obtain jurisdiction on the basis of such implied contracts, the "disappointed bidder" must plead that it has accepted the Government's offer contained in the solicitation. Thus, a party that did not submit a bid or proposal has no contract claim because it did not furnish the Government the consideration requested for its promise, *Hero, Inc. v. United States*, 3 Cl. Ct. 413 (1983). In that case, the plaintiff expended effort in preparing a bid but did not submit the bid, contending that the specifications were defective. The court refused to grant an injunction preventing award under the solicitation, reasoning that the mere expenditure of effort and money in preparing a bid without actually submitting it is not sufficient consideration for the Government's implied promise. In *Harris Sys. Int'l, Inc. v. United States*, 5 Cl. Ct. 253 (1984), the court found no jurisdiction in an action by a small business minority firm that had not submitted a proposal because the procuring agency had demanded that the SBA nominate another firm under the 8(a) set-aside. The court also held that the fact that the SBA had originally nominated the plaintiff to the Air Force did not establish an implied contract. In *Eagle Constr. Corp. v. United States*, 4 Cl. Ct. 470 (1984), the court found that the Government's cancellation of a solicitation after technical proposals were received was not improper under the circumstances. Thus, the plaintiff who submitted a proposal under that solicitation but failed to submit one under the new solicitation for the same work had no disappointed bidder status under the new solicitation. See also *Control Data Sys., Inc. v. United States*, 32 Fed. Cl. 520 (1994) (incumbent contractor did not submit a bid for follow-on contract, and the plaintiff's claim was therefore not a preaward protest within the jurisdiction of the court); *Howard v. United States*, 21 Cl. Ct. 475 (1990) (bid submitted after closing date for receipt of proposals; thus, no valid offer to contract that the Government could accept); *Durable Metals Prods., Inc. v. United States*, 27 Fed. Cl. 472 (1993) (no jurisdiction because bidder withdrew from bidding process); and *Data Transformation Corp. v. United States*, 13 Cl. Ct. 165 (1987) (informal presentation made to an agency of the plaintiff's technical ability to perform the work called for under the planned program was not the same as a response to a solicitation and did not create an implied-in-fact contract). While the court's rationale in nonbidder cases is clearly supportable where the plaintiff has not expended effort in reliance on the solicitation or decides to forgo the procurement, it is questionable where expenditures have been made in reliance on a solicitation that contains defective specifications or is otherwise improper.

Other interested parties are likewise unable to invoke the Court of Federal Claims jurisdiction because they are not disappointed bidders, *Indian Wells Valley Metal Trades Council v. United States*, 1 Cl. Ct. 43, 553 F. Supp. 397 (1982) (federal employees seeking injunction against contracting-out had not bid on work, and court, therefore, had no jurisdiction); *Omega World Travel, Inc. v. United States*, 9 Cl. Ct. 623 (1986) (protest against sole source awards to be made in the future was dismissed because the would-be competitors had not bid on an outstanding solicitation).

The mere submission of a bid or proposal will not establish the necessary contractual relationship; the submission must be responsive to the invitation for bids. In *Yachts Am., Inc. v. United States*, 3 Cl. Ct. 447 (1983), *aff'd*, 779 F.2d 656 (Fed. Cir. 1985), the documents and letter submitted to the agency were found to be wholly nonresponsive and, thus, failed to give the plaintiff the status of a disappointed bidder. However, the court will review the bid and the solicitation to determine whether it is responsive and, if it so finds, will exercise its jurisdiction, *Olympia USA, Inc. v. United States*, 6 Cl. Ct. 550 (1984). See also *Blount, Inc. v. United States*, 22 Cl. Ct. 221 (1990) (court exercised jurisdiction to determine whether a clause in the IFB not addressed by the bid related to bidder responsiveness or responsibility). The disappointed bidder must also be able to show actual or threatened injury. In *Caddell Constr. Co. v. United States*, 9 Cl. Ct. 610 (1986), the court held that an offeror ranked sixth had no substantial chance for award and thus had no standing to sue. In addition, the firm submitting the offer must be eligible to receive the award, *ATL, Inc. v. United States*, 735 F.2d 1343 (Fed. Cir. 1984) (bids following a firm's suspension or debarment could not create implied contract because such firms are ineligible for award); *Gibraltar Indus., Inc. v. United States*, 2 Cl. Ct. 589 (1983), *vacated as moot*, 726 F.2d 747 (Fed. Cir. 1984) (bidder determined not to be a small business could not create implied contract by bidding on small business set-aside). However, a suspension or debarment issued after a bid or proposal has been submitted does not deprive the disappointed offeror of jurisdiction over such a previous bid or proposal, *Sterlingwear of Boston, Inc. v. United States*, 11 Cl. Ct. 517 (1987); *Electro-Methods, Inc. v. United States*, 728 F.2d 1471 (Fed. Cir. 1984). The court will take jurisdiction over claims alleging that the agency has improperly applied responsibility standards to an offeror, *Hayes Int'l Corp. v. United States*, 7 Cl. Ct. 681 (1985). See also *Skytech Aero, Inc. v. United States*, 26 Cl. Ct. 251 (1992), where an unsuccessful bidder alleged that the Army acted arbitrarily and capriciously by awarding a contract to a bidder that was not responsible and whose bid was nonresponsive. The court exercised jurisdiction and held that a preaward survey conducted by the Army allowed a reasonable conclusion to be made that the bidder was responsible. The Court of Federal Claims has jurisdiction to review certificate of competency determinations by the SBA, *Related Indus., Inc. v. United States*, 2 Cl. Ct. 517 (1983); *Cavalier Clothes, Inc. v.*

United States, 810 F.2d 1108 (Fed. Cir. 1987); *Stapp Towing, Inc. v. United States*, 34 Fed. Cl. 300 (1995).

In several rare cases, the court has found preaward implied contracts to exist in situations other than disappointed bidder cases. See *Western Pioneer, Inc. v. United States*, 8 Cl. Ct. 291 (1985), where the court held that a letter requesting that the plaintiff submit its proposed operating plan constituted "a sufficient request . . . such as to form an implied contract to fairly and honestly consider [the] responding proposal." See also *Standard Mfg. Co. v. United States*, 7 Cl. Ct. 54 (1984), where the plaintiff alleged that it responded to a *Commerce Business Daily* (CBD) notice in which the Air Force stated its intention to award a sole source contract and invited interested parties to identify interests in the procurement or to submit proposals for the work. The court held that such facts are sufficient to create an implied promise for the Air Force to give fair and impartial consideration to the response. See also *Magnavox Elec. Sys. Co. v. United States*, 26 Cl. Ct. 1373 (1992), where the court also held that the CBD notice of intent to conduct a sole source procurement and plaintiff's response resulted in an implied contract to give plaintiff's response fair and impartial consideration. However, in *Motorola, Inc. v. United States*, 988 F.2d 113 (Fed. Cir. 1993), the court affirmed a decision of the Court of Federal Claims denying jurisdiction over a suit filed by a company that assisted the Government in drafting the procurement specification but did not submit an offer because a bid sample was required. The Federal Circuit adopted the Court of Federal Claims decision, which disagreed with the rationale in *Standard Manufacturing*, stating that Government requests for information and responses from prospective bidders are not the equivalents of offer and acceptance. The Federal Circuit quoted the Court of Federal Claims at 116, as follows:

> Such exchanges are not carried on with an expectation to presently affect legal relations. Rather, the parties are dealing — as they were here — exclusively with an eye to the future, each being free, in the meantime, to withdraw from the dialogue.
>
> The situation, therefore, is quite unlike that encountered where a bid has been submitted. In that circumstance there is a promise — the contractor's bid — which empowers the Government, upon acceptance, to bind the contractor to the terms of the solicitation. The essence of the contractor's engagement — the manifestation of an intention to be bound — warrants reading into the situation a reciprocal commitment from the Government, *i.e.*, a promise to fairly and honestly consider the contractor's bid. *Heyer*

Products Co. v. United States, 135 Ct. Cl. 63, 69, 140 F. Supp. 409, 412 (1956).

See also *Garchik v. United States*, 37 Fed. Cl. 52 (1996).

In *American Hoist & Derrick, Inc. v. United States*, 3 Cl. Ct. 198 (1983), the plaintiff was a large business that was precluded from bidding on a solicitation because the procurement was set aside for small businesses. However, the court took jurisdiction on the basis of an implied contract alleged to have been formed when the plaintiff released its proprietary data to the Government in exchange for an agreement that it would be permitted to bid on the procurement. See also *Yachts Am., Inc. v. United States*, 3 Cl. Ct. 447 (1983), *aff'd*, 770 F.2d 656 (Fed. Cir. 1985). In *Airborne Data, Inc. v. United States*, 702 F.2d 1350 (Fed. Cir. 1983), the court held that an implied contract was formed when an unsolicited proposal was received in response to regulations inviting the submittal of such proposals. In *Pressman v. United States*, 33 Fed. Cl. 438 (1995), the court held that the agency's regulations prohibiting the release of confidential information did not give rise to an implied contract not to disclose confidential information contained in unsolicited proposals. The court distinguished *Airborne Data*, stating that in that case the text of the regulations contained an explicit promise of confidentiality, whereas in *Pressman* the regulations, although binding on the agency, could not be construed as suggesting that the agency was directing an offer to the general public to confidentially consider unsolicited proposals.

2. Interested Party

The new statute in 28 U.S.C. § 1491(b) provides that bid protest suits may be brought by "an interested party." In the Court Approved Guidelines, issued on December 11, 1996, the Court of Federal Claims referred to that definition contained in 31 U.S.C. § 3551(2), which states that an interested party is

> an actual or prospective bidder or offeror whose direct economic interest would be affected by the award of the contract or by failure to award the contract.

Subsequently, the court adopted the definition of "interested party" used at the GAO in *C C Distributors Inc. v. United States*, 38 Fed. Cl. 771 (1997). In its discussion, the court stated at 793–94:

> The decision by the Congress when it drafted 28 U.S.C.A. § 1491(b)(1) to reference 5 U.S.C. § 706 of the APA, but not the APA standing requirement in 5 U.S.C. § 702, while at the same time to explicitly include the term "interested party" (the standing requirement term used in the GAO protest legislation), appears to the court to be significant on the question of how to determine the definition of "interested party" for post-award bid protest cases filed in this court. In GAO parlance, the term "interested party" can be considered a term of art. Plaintiff, however, proposes that the term "interested party" have one meaning when a contractor protests to the GAO, and another when it protests before this court. Such a definitional scheme is not per se impossible. If Congress had expressed an intention to have the same words defined differently in different fora, that would be within the prerogative of the Congress, and the courts would carry out that Congressional intent. However, in the absence of evidence of a Congressional intent to deviate from the settled use and interpretation of a term of art, the effect of which would be to potentially expand significantly the population of protesters, this court is reluctant to embrace the proposed regime of dual definitions. In the absence of a contrary indication, the court finds it appropriate to conclude that Congress intended the amendments in 28 U.S.C.A. § 1491(b)(1) to follow the established, or term of art, meaning of "interested party" as defined by the Congress in the GAO statute, and as reaffirmed by the Congress just six months prior to the enactment of the amendments to 28 U.S.C. 1491.

Contrast this decision with *CCL, Inc.*, ___ Fed. Cl. __ (1997), where the court stated that while "it makes sense to use [the GAO's interested party] definition as a means of informing the discussion, it does not follow that it necessarily represents the four corners of potential standing under [the ADRA]. Here, the Government argued that the court should apply the interested party definition that CICA established for the Comptroller General bid protest jurisdiction. The Government then asserted that since the protester decided not to compete for the original contract, it cannot be considered to be an "actual or prospective bidder," and, therefore, is not an interested party. The court stated that it was hesitant to adopt GAO's interested party definition for two reasons, as follows:

> The first is obvious. The GAO enforces a different statute. The standing question cannot be divorced entirely from the precise nature of the challenge brought and hence from the jurisdictional waiver. See *Bennett v. Spear*, 137 L. Ed. 2d 281, 117 S. Ct. 1154, 1161 (1997). In this case, the plaintiff is alleging a violation of a statute or regulation in connection with a procurement that should have been the subject of competition. Because

> the court has jurisdiction to hear such a claim, see 28 U.S.C.A. § 1491(b)(1), the test of standing must be applied in that context.
>
> The second reason is that the language enforced by GAO is not identical. The GAO is permitted to hear protests as defined in 31 U.S.C. § 3551(1). The preamble to the GAO definition limits the terms to use in connection with contracts, solicitations, or requests for offers. See 31 U.S.C. § 3551(2). As explained above, because the language of the Tucker Act contemplates a claim that a procurement should have been the subject of competition, there is not a perfect joinder between the GAO's definition of interested party and the Tucker Act's jurisdictional waiver. While as a practical matter there normally will be no difference in the grants of authority, the differences in language warrant some caution about presumptively limiting standing to the GAO definition of "interested party." That is particularly the case in view of Congress's apparent intent to have this court dispense with its historical and somewhat quixotic search for the fictional "implied contract of good faith and fair dealing," which only arose in the presence of a bid. See *Ships Deck Works, Inc. v. United States*, 1997 U.S. Claims LEXIS 284 (Fed. Cl. 1997). The court notes, in any event, that the GAO definition has been judicially construed to apply to persons who would have submitted a bid if given the opportunity. See *Rapides Regional Med. Ctr. v. Department of Veterans Affairs*, 974 F.2d 565 (5th Cir. 1992).

The court further stated that GAO's definition is clearly relevant. The plaintiff must stand in some connection to the procurement and it must have an economic interest in it. The court found that CCL met this test.

The Federal Circuit has considered whether a protester is an "interested party" in several cases, see *Durable Metal Prods., Inc. v. United States*, 11 F.3d 1073 (Fed. Cir. 1993) (contractor that withdrew bid not an interested party); *Morton Management, Inc.*, 954 F.2d 733 (Fed. Cir. 1992) (contractor that did not submit bid not an interested party); *Federal Data Corp. v. United States*, 911 F.2d 699 (Fed. Cir. 1990) (bidder that withdrew from the procurement not an interested party); *United States v. IBM*, 892 F.2d 1006 (Fed. Cir. 1989) (bidder fourth in line for award not an interested party because contractor had no direct economic interest in the award of the contract); *MCI Telecoms. Corp. v. United States*, 878 F.2d 362 (Fed. Cir. 1989) (contractor that is "neither an actual nor prospective bidder" not an interested party). These decisions would appear to be binding on the Court of Federal Claims.

Decisions of the Comptroller General and the General Services Board of Contract Appeals (during the period of its authority to hear protests) deal extensively with the term "interested party." While these decisions are not necessarily binding on the Court of Federal Claims, they may carry significant weight in court determinations. See Section II, above, for a discussion of Comptroller General decisions. Any decisions by the Court of Appeals for the Federal Circuit construing the term "interested party" would be binding on the Court of Federal Claims.

C. Time for Protest

Under the previous statutes, the time for protest depended on whether equitable or solely monetary relief was sought. The earlier Section 1491(a)(3) provided that in order for the Court of Federal Claims and its predecessor, the Claims Court, to decide a protest requesting equitable relief, a complaint had to have been filed in the court before the relevant contract was awarded, *John C. Grimberg Co. v. United States*, 702 F.2d 1362 (Fed. Cir. 1983); *Howard v. United States*, 21 Cl. Ct. 475 (1990). This rule was changed, however, by 28 U.S.C. § 1491(b), which states:

> Both the United States Court of Federal Claims and the district courts of the United States shall have jurisdiction to entertain such an action without regard to whether suit is instituted before or after the contract is awarded.

The statute does not set forth specific rules on the filing of bid protests. Such rules are to be developed by the Court of Federal Claims. See *CC Distributors, Inc. v. United States*, 38 Fed. Cl. 771 (1997), where the court adopted GAO's rule that requires contractors to protest before proposals are due, if the terms of the solicitation are clearly objectionable. See also *Allied Technology Group v. United States*, 39 Fed. Cl. 125 (1997), referencing GAO's timeliness rules, the court held that challenges to the terms of a solicitation must be filed prior to the due date for proposals. The court denied the protest because the protest was filed more than four months after the contract award.

D. Intervenors

Intervenors are permitted under the Rules of the United States Court of Federal Claims (RCFC) 24, which states:

> (a) Intervention of Right. Upon timely application anyone shall be permitted to intervene in an action: (1) when a statute of the United States confers an unconditional right to intervene; or (2) when the applicant claims an interest relating to the property or transaction which is the subject of the action and the applicant is so situated that the disposition of the action may as a practical matter impair or impede the applicant's ability to protect that interest, unless the applicant's interest is adequately represented by existing parties.
>
> (b) Permissive Intervention. Upon timely application anyone may be permitted to intervene in an action: (1) when a statute of the United States confers a conditional right to intervene; or (2) when an applicant's claim or defense and the main action have a question of law or fact in common. In exercising its discretion the court shall consider whether the intervention will unduly delay or prejudice the adjudication of the rights of the original parties.

This rule thus provides for both intervention of right and permissive intervention.

The application to intervene must be timely. In *TRW Envtl. Safety Sys., Inc. v. United States*, 16 Cl. Ct. 516 (1989), the Claims Court held that an unsuccessful bidder's motion to intervene in another unsuccessful bidder's suit for injunctive relief was untimely: the bidder waited 84 days from knowing of the suit before moving to intervene.

E. Procedures

The Court of Federal Claims follows the rules set forth in the Rules of the United States Court of Federal Claims (RCFC). These rules are based upon the Federal Rules of Civil Procedure.

1. Commencement of Action

a. Complaint and Service of Summons

A civil action in the Court of Federal Claims is commenced by filing a complaint with the clerk of court, RCFC 3(a). A claim is considered to be filed when it is received by the clerk, RCFC 3(b). Upon receipt, the clerk date stamps the complaint. This date stamp serves as final and conclusive evidence of the date on which the complaint was filed, absent corrective order from the court by means of a motion. The plaintiff must file an original and seven copies of the complaint with the court, RCFC 3(c). Service of summons must be made by the clerk of the court upon the United States by serving the Attorney General of the United States. This can be accomplished by delivering or by mailing a copy of the summons to the attorney-in-charge, International Trade Field Office, Commercial Litigation Branch, Department of Justice, RCFC 4(a).

b. Filing Fee

A $120 filing fee must be paid to the clerk of the court when the action is commenced.

2. Pleadings and Motions

a. Claim for Relief

Rule 8(a) states that the complaint must contain:

> (1) a short and plain statement of the grounds upon which the court's jurisdiction depends, unless the court already has jurisdiction and the claim needs no new grounds to support it, (2) a short and plain statement of the claim showing that the pleader is entitled to relief, and (3) a demand for judgment for the relief to which the pleader is entitled.

In all averments of fraud or mistake, the circumstances constituting fraud or mistake must be stated with particularity, RCFC 9(b). See *Keco Indus., Inc. v. United States*, 203 Ct. Cl. 566, 492 F.2d 1200 (1974), where the court held that a disappointed bidder's pleadings lacked particularity. In reaching this finding, the court stated that alleging general violations of the Armed Services Procurement Regulations fell far short of the specificity called for in the rule. See also *Baskett v. United States*, 2 Cl. Ct. 356 (1983) (although the Claims Court has adopted the notice pleading system found in the federal courts, this system does not do away with the requirement of particularity; unclear allegations of fraud and misrepresentation in pleadings of plaintiff are dismissed).

b. *Preliminary Hearings*

Evidentiary hearings may be conducted by the Court of Federal Claims, RCFC 12(d). This rule provides that the following defenses must be heard and determined at a preliminary hearing, unless the court orders deferral until trial:

(1) lack of jurisdiction over the subject matter;

(2) lack of jurisdiction over the person;

(3) insufficiency of process; or

(4) failure to state a claim upon which relief can be granted.

3. *Depositions and Discovery*

Parties may conduct discovery by one or more of the following methods: "depositions upon oral examination or written questions; written interrogatories; production of documents or things or permission to enter upon land or other property, for inspection and other purposes; physical and mental examinations; requests for admission; and calls," RCFC 26(a).

The scope of discovery is set forth in RCFC 26(b)(1), as follows:

> Parties may obtain discovery regarding any matter, not privileged, which is relevant to the subject matter involved in the pending action, whether it relates to the claim or defense of the party seeking discovery or to the claim or defense of any other party, including the existence, description, nature, custody, condition, and location of any books, documents, or other tangible things and the identity and location of persons having knowledge of any discoverable matter. It is not ground for objection that the information sought will be inadmissible at the trial if the information sought appears reasonably calculated to lead to the discovery of admissible evidence.

Discovery must be conducted in a timely fashion early in the proceedings. If a party finds that unforeseen discovery is necessary during the argument of a case, it must request discovery at that time. In *Vanguard Sec., Inc. v. United States*, 20 Cl. Ct. 90 (1990), the plaintiff found, while arguing summary judgment motions, that the Government was asserting new grounds to support the cancellation of a solicitation. The plaintiff did not indicate at the time that it needed discovery but made the request in its post-argument brief. The court denied this request, holding that it was untimely.

It is very difficult to obtain sanctions for failing to comply with discovery requests. In *ViON Corp. v. United States*, 906 F.2d 1564 (Fed. Cir. 1990), the court reversed the board's dismissal of a protest on the grounds that it was frivolous because the protester had not provided good faith answers to the Government's interrogatories. The court quoted the board's reasoning, 90-1 BCA ¶ 22,287 at 111,941, as follows:

> Since this protest was filed, however, we have had the opportunity to observe the actions of protester first hand. We have reviewed in detail the answers ViON has provided to critical discovery requests. We have concluded that they were inadequate. We have likewise seen protester disregard important provisions in the Board's order authorizing discovery, with the result that the Board's control over the discovery process was diminished and the discovery accomplished was less efficient and less productive. In the absence of some redress from the Board, all of these actions on the part of ViON make it increasingly difficult for the agency to prepare a timely defense and, to that extent, provide ViON with an unfair advantage in pursuing the protest.

The court found that the interrogatories for which the board considered ViON nonresponsive did not relate to a matter that ViON had the burden to prove and held that a protest cannot be dismissed as frivolous unless the protest lacks an arguable basis in fact or law. The court held that noncompliance with a discovery order on issues that the protester did not have to prove and a finding by the board that the motive of the protester was not genuine did not make the protest frivolous. However, the court added in a footnote at 1566:

> This is not to say that the refusal to respond promptly and adequately to proper discovery request might not, in this or some other case, give rise to an inference that the protester's case lacks merits because the protester does not have the facts required for an arguable case.

In postaward bid protest cases, the court will look at the state of the record at the GAO in determining whether to permit discovery. In *Cubic Applications, Inc. v. United States*, 37 Fed. Cl. 345 (1997), the court permitted only one deposition for purposes of developing an issue that was not raised before the GAO. In *Cincom Sys., Inc. v. United States*, 37 Fed. Cl.

663 (1997), the court denied all requests for discovery on the basis that the record as established at the GAO was complete.

F. Standards of Review

28 U.S.C. § 1491(b)(4) states that the court's standards of review for its bid protest jurisdiction is to be "pursuant to the standards set forth in section 706 of title 5." Section 706 provides that the reviewing court shall

> (2) hold unlawful and set aside agency action, findings, and conclusions found to be —
>
>> (A) arbitrary, capricious, an abuse of discretion, or otherwise not in accordance with law.

This appears to be essentially the same standards that the court uses in its contract jurisdiction. In cases alleging that the Government has violated its implied promise to honestly and fairly consider bids or proposals, the standard of review used by the Court of Federal Claims is to determine if the Government's conduct toward the protester was arbitrary or capricious, *Keco Indus., Inc. v. United States*, 192 Ct. Cl. 773, 428 F.2d 1233 (1970); *Contract Custom Drapery Serv., Inc. v. United States*, 6 Cl. Ct. 811 (1984). This standard applies to both claims for equitable and monetary relief, *United States v. John C. Grimberg Co.*, 702 F.2d 1362 (Fed. Cir. 1983). In *Keco Indus., Inc. v. United States*, 203 Ct. Cl. 566, 492 F.2d 1200 (1974), the court indicated that arbitrary or capricious action would not result from mere negligence by the Government, but may be proved in a number of ways, stating at 574:

> One is that subjective bad faith on the part of the procuring officials, depriving a bidder of the fair and honest consideration of his proposal, normally warrants recovery of bid preparation costs. *Heyer Products Co. v. United States*, 135 Ct. Cl. 63, 140 F. Supp. 409 (1956). A second is that proof that there was "no reasonable basis" for the administrative decision will also suffice, at least in many situations. *Continental Business Enterprises v. United States*, 196 Ct. Cl. 627, 637-38, 452 F.2d 1016, 1021 (1971). The third is that the degree of proof of error necessary for recovery is ordinarily related to the amount of discretion entrusted to the procurement officials by applicable statutes and regulations. *Continental Business Enterprises v. United States*, *supra*, 196 Ct. Cl. at 637, 452 F.2d at 1021 (1971); *Keco Industries, Inc. v. United States*, *supra*, 192 Ct. Cl. at 784,

> 428 F.2d at 1240. The fourth is that proven violation of pertinent statutes or regulations can, but need not necessarily, be a ground for recovery.

In considering whether the Government acted in bad faith, the court requires the protester to prove that the Government acted with specific intent to injure it, *Contract Custom Drapery Serv., Inc. v. United States*, 6 Cl. Ct. 811 (1984). In commenting on the degree of proof to establish such bad faith, the court stated at 817:

> Further, in considering a claim of bad faith against the government, there is a strong presumption that government officials acted properly. See *Eagle Constr. Corp. v. United States*, 4 Cl. Ct. 470, 479 (1984); *P. Francini & Co. v. United States*, 2 Cl. Ct. 7 (1983); *Burroughs Corp. v. United States*, 223 Ct. Cl. 53, 64-65, 617 F.2d 590, 597 (1980); *Sun Oil Co. v. United States*, 215 Ct. Cl. 716, 746, 572 F.2d 786, 805 (1978). To overcome this presumption, the law requires "well-nigh irrefragable proof." See *American General Leasing v. United States*, 218 Ct. Cl. 367, 374, 587 F.2d 54, 59 (1978); *Knotts v. United States*, 128 Ct. Cl. 489, 492, 121 F. Supp. 630, 631 (1954). See also *P. Francini & Co. v. United States*, *supra*, 2 Cl. Ct. at 11; *Baird Corp. v. United States*, 1 Cl. Ct. 662, 664 (1983).

See also *Aviation Enters., Inc. v. United States*, 8 Cl. Ct. 1 (1985) (refusing to find bad faith on the basis of "speculation and innuendo"); and *Shields Enters., Inc. v. United States*, 28 Fed. Cl. 615 (1993) (no evidence that the Government specifically intended to injure the plaintiff or that the Government operated with any prejudice toward the plaintiff). However, in *Parcel 49C Limited Partnership v. United States*, 39 Cont. Cas. Fed. (CCH) ¶ 76,689, *aff'd*, 31 F.3d 1147 (Fed. Cir. 1994), the court held that the General Services Administration (GSA) abused its discretion when it canceled a solicitation for the lease of office space allegedly based on changes in the needs of the using agency. The court found that the using agency's needs did not change until five years in the future and concluded that the GSA had relied upon this interpretation merely as a pretext for ridding itself of the procurement. In a fact pattern similar to *Parcel 49C*, the court in *126 Northpoint Plaza L.P. v. United States*, 34 Fed. Cl. 105 (1995), found bad faith when GSA officials canceled a solicitation in an effort to accommodate the Immigration and Naturalization Service, which was trying to avoid contracting with a particular offeror.

Absent bad faith, the protester must establish with clear and convincing evidence that the agency's determination lacked any rational basis or violated applicable statutes or regulations, *Vanguard Sec., Inc. v. United*

States, 20 Cl. Ct. 90 (1990); *Northern Telecom, Inc. v. United States*, 8 Cl. Ct. 376 (1985). In finding that there was no rational basis for the action, the court in *Rockwell Int'l Corp. v. United States*, 4 Cl. Ct. 1 (1983), stated that "[t]o have a reasoned or rational basis, there must be a rational connection between the facts established and the choice made." See also *Prineville Sawmill Co. v. United States*, 859 F.2d 905 (Fed. Cir. 1988) (decision by Forest Service to reject all bids in timber sale had no reasonable basis). In *R.R. Donnelly & Sons, Co. v. United States*, 38 Fed. Cl. 518 (1997), the court rejected that a postaward protester must prove a case by "clear and convincing" evidence and held that the burden was only "high." The court applied the standards traditionally applied in bid protests under *Keco Industries*, but denied summary judgment because of unresolved factual issues between the parties.

If the procurement is negotiated, the court will take a more deferential view of whether an agency's actions were rational or reasonable than it will in sealed bidding, *Logicon, Inc. v. United States*, 22 Cl. Ct. 776 (1991). There, the court found that the Government had a rational basis for reopening negotiations on a contract after having initially decided to award the contract to the plaintiff. See also *IMS Servs., Inc. v. United States*, 33 Fed. Cl. 167 (1995) (Navy did not act arbitrarily, capriciously, or contrary to law when it reopened procurement competition and conducted new round of BAFOs); *Compubahn, Inc. v. United States*, 33 Fed. Cl. 677 (1995) (offeror not entitled to relief because there was no evidence that the evaluators acted in bad faith or without a reasonable basis, notwithstanding the fact that four of the five evaluators were incapable of assessing the proposed technology); *Cincom Sys., Inc.*, 37 Fed. Cl. 993 (1997) (Government's award of software contract was supported by rational basis); *Delbert Wheeler Constr., Inc. v. United States*, 39 Fed. Cl. 239 (1997) (contracting officer's award to offeror who, in his opinion, provided best value, was reasonable).

G. Prejudice

In order for a protester to prevail in a bid protest, it must show not only that there was a significant error in the procurement process but also that the error was prejudicial, *Data General Corp. v. United States*, 78 F.3d 1556 (Fed. Cir. 1996). In this case, the court stated that the test was whether there was a "reasonable likelihood" that the protester would obtain award. In *Statistica, Inc. v. United States*, 102 F.3d 1577 (Fed. Cir. 1996), the court stated that to establish competitive prejudice, a protester must demonstrate that but for the alleged error, there was a "substantial chance" that it would receive an award. It concluded, however, that there was no difference between the "reasonable likelihood" test in *Data General* and the "substantial chance" test that had been used in older cases such as *CACI, Inc.—Fed. v. United States*, 719 F.2d 1567 (Fed. Cir. 1983) and *Morgan Bus. Assocs. v. United States*, 223 Ct. Cl. 325, 619 F.2d 892 (1980). See also *Cubic Applications, Inc. v. United States*, 37 Fed. Cl. 345 (1997), where the court held that the agency's failure to follow statutory procedures in awarding the contract was not prejudicial and thus nullification of the award was not warranted; and *Analytical & Research Technology, Inc. v. United States*, 39 Fed. Cl. 34 (1997), where the court found that there was no reasonable likelihood that a disappointed offeror would have been awarded the contract absent the alleged statutory violations by the Army and thus the offeror could not demonstrate prejudice.

H. Remedies

The ultimate remedy sought by a protester is to receive award of the contract. However, such relief is granted in only the rarest of cases. More often, the agency will be directed to cure a defect in the procurement, and pending the action, the award of a contract will be delayed or the work under a contract will be suspended. In some cases, the remedy may involve declarations of the rights of the parties or directions to recompete the contract. Monetary relief may also be granted.

1. Nonmonetary Remedies

The court has authority to issue declaratory and injunctive relief under its bid protest jurisdiction pursuant to new Section 1491(b)(2). The authority "to grant declaratory judgments and such equitable and extraordinary relief as it deems proper" under its contract jurisdiction pursuant to 28 U.S.C. § 1491(a)(3) has been taken away by the ADRA. Note that the Court of Federal Claims also has limited authority to issue declaratory judgments pursuant to 28 U.S.C. § 1507 (actions under Section 7425 of the Internal Revenue Code).

The types of nonmonetary remedies that a protester may obtain in the Court of Federal Claims are either provisional (temporary restraining order (TRO) or preliminary injunction) or final relief (declaratory relief or permanent injunction). The Court of Federal Claims did not often hear cases for injunctive relief under Section 1491(a)(3). There were two reasons for this. First, few disappointed bidders brought an action before the Court of Federal Claims for nonmonetary remedies. Second, the court did not often grant such relief. Thus, most court actions for nonmonetary remedies have been brought in the district courts, which provide the same nonmonetary remedies as the Court of Federal Claims. Whether interested parties will bring a significant number of actions before the Court of Federal Claims under new Section 1491(b)(2) remains to be seen.

The rules for granting a TRO or preliminary injunction are identical to that followed by the district courts. See RCFC 65. The four factors the court examines when determining whether a preliminary injunction should be granted are the same as in the district courts: (1) reasonable likelihood of success on the merits, (2) irreparable harm if the injunction is not granted, (3) substantial harm to the other parties if the stay is granted, and (4) consideration of the public interest, *Hydro Eng'g, Inc. v. United States*, 37 Fed. Cl. 448 (1997). The court does not often grant either a TRO or a preliminary injunction. In *Magellan Corp. v. United States*, 27 Fed. Cl. 446 (1993), the court denied a request for preliminary injunction, stating that the disruption to the ongoing procurement process would not be justified in view of the unlikelihood of success on the merits. In discussing its review of requests for preliminary injunctions, the court stated at 447:

> The court has the authority to enter an injunction blocking the award to any bidder other than Magellan. 28 U.S.C. § 1491(a)(3) (1988). The limited question is whether the status quo ante should be maintained while the plaintiff undertakes discovery and proofs on its request for permanent relief. Prior decisions of this court and of the United States Court of Appeals for the Federal Circuit, however, make it clear that such authority should not be routinely exercised. As the Federal Circuit wrote in *United States v. John C. Grimberg Co.*, 702 F.2d 1362 (Fed. Cir. 1983), equitable powers "should be exercised in a way which best limits judicial interference in contract procurement." *Id.* at 1372.

In *Logicon, Inc. v. United States*, 22 Cl. Ct. 776 (1991), the court denied injunctive relief, finding that the agency's decision to reopen negotiations and conduct another round of BAFOs was not irrational or unreasonable, and thus the bidder did not establish by clear and convincing evidence a strong likelihood of success on the merits. However, in *Isratex, Inc. v. United States*, 25 Cl. Ct. 223 (1992), the court granted a TRO upon finding a strong likelihood of success on the merits. The offeror was excluded from further participation in a negotiated procurement on the ground that its demonstration model did not satisfy one of the factors listed in the RFP, but the court found no indication in the RFP that automatic exclusion would follow from test failure.

When an appeal is taken, an appellant may request a stay of injunction pending appeal under RCFC 62(c). This test mirrors the TRO test: "(1) a strong likelihood that the movant will prevail on the merits of the appeal; (2) irreparable injury to the movant unless the stay is granted; (3) no substantial harm to the other parties if the stay is granted; and (4) consideration of the public interest," *Aerolease Long Beach & Satsuma Inv., Inc. v. United States*, 39 Cont. Cas. Fed. (CCF) ¶ 76,656 (Fed. Cl. 1994).

The final relief by the Court of Federal Claims may take the form of a declaratory judgment or a permanent injunction. The injunction may prohibit the agency from undertaking some activity or it may be mandatory, directing that certain actions be taken. See *126 Northpoint Plaza L.P. v. United States*, 34 Fed. Cl. 105 (1995), where the court ordered that the original solicitation be reinstated. In granting final injunctive relief, the courts are required to balance the interests of the parties and give due consideration to public policy, including national defense, *B.K. Instrument, Inc. v. United States*, 715 F.2d 713 (2d Cir. 1983).

2. *Monetary Remedies*

The monetary remedies that protesters have been able to recover are generally limited to the costs of preparing the bid or proposal. In some instances, the protester may receive attorneys' fees and expenses under the Equal Access to Justice Act (EAJA). Recovery of anticipated profits (or lost profits) has been uniformly denied. See *Keco Indus., Inc. v. United States*, 203 Ct. Cl. 566, 492 F.2d 1200 (1974) (improper to award lost profits in the absence of a contract and no certainty that protester would have received award); *Rockwell Int'l Corp. v. United States*, 8 Cl. Ct. 662 (1985) (prior precedent flatly precludes such an award); *La Strada Inn, Inc. v. United States*, 12 Cl. Ct. 110 (1987) (disappointed bidder may not recover anticipated profits on a contract improperly awarded to another); and *Finley v. United States*, 31 Fed. Cl. 704 (1994) (lost profits are speculative in nature and have consistently been denied).

Monetary damages will not be awarded where the protester has already received injunctive relief in district court, *Grumman Data Sys. Corp. v. United States*, 28 Fed. Cl. 803 (1993). In *Grumman*, the court explained that both equitable and legal remedies are available to aggrieved protesters, stating at 809:

> Each form of redress available to contract protesters has particular advantages and disadvantages, which protesters should assess carefully before filing an action against the government. In the instant case, plaintiff could have sought monetary damages in lieu of an equitable remedy. By bringing an action for its proposal preparation costs, plaintiff would have stood to obtain a fixed, certain damage award, but would have relinquished the opportunity to win a new contract.
>
> Instead, plaintiff chose to seek equitable relief. The injury that plaintiff asserts in the instant case is that the Army's unequal treatment of another offeror deprived plaintiff of the opportunity to have its proposal fairly and honestly considered. The district court's injunction barring the Army's award corrected this injury by requiring the Army "to repeat the [procurement] process under circumstances that . . . eliminate[d] the alleged taint of the prior proceedings." *CACI, [Inc. — Fed. v. United States*, 719 F.2d 1567, 1575 (Fed. Cir. 1983)]. In exchange for the opportunity to win a new contract, however, plaintiff assumed the risk that the government either would change its contract requirements or would choose not to resolicit the contract at all, thereby rendering futile some or all of plaintiff's original preparation costs. Plaintiff cannot now seek to recover its preparation costs in this court, however, where it already received a chance for a new contract award.

a. *Bid or Proposal Preparation Costs*

Bid or proposal preparation costs can be recovered under either 28 U.S.C. § 1491(a)(1) or § 1491(b)(2). All the litigated cases to date have been decided under the first section. The successful protester that has not received award may recover the costs of preparing its bid or proposal if it had a substantial chance for award, *Morgan Bus. Assocs. v. United States*, 223 Ct. Cl. 325, 619 F.2d 892 (1980). See also *AT&T Technologies, Inc. v. United States*, 18 Cl. Ct. 315 (1989).

In *Keco Indus., Inc. v. United States*, 203 Ct. Cl. 566 (1974), the court described four factors to consider in assessing a claim for bid or proposal preparation costs: (1) whether the agency acted in bad faith, (2) whether there was a reasonable basis for the agency's decision or action, (3) the amount of discretion the agency is afforded in the area being questioned, and (4) whether a procurement statute or regulation was violated. See also *Crux Computer Corp. v. United States*, 24 Cl. Ct. 223 (1991). If the court finds that an agency breached its obligation to fairly and honestly consider a bid or proposal, or that it violated a procurement statute or regulation, the court may award bid or proposal preparation costs. Such actions on the part of the Government are considered to be arbitrary and capricious. However, the protester must demonstrate by clear and convincing proof that the agency's evaluation of bids and/or award of the contract was arbitrary and capricious, *Paxson Elec. Co. v. United States*, 14 Cl. Ct. 634 (1988). See *Finley v. United States*, 31 Fed. Cl. 704 (1994), where the court held that because there was no evidence of bad faith in the evaluation process, the protester had no basis for the award of bid preparation costs. In *Stapp Towing, Inc. v. United States*, 34 Fed. Cl. 300 (1995), the court held that the bidder was not entitled to bid preparation costs because there was no showing that the SBA's decision denying a certificate of competency was arbitrary and capricious. Even if an agency violates a procurement statute or regulation, a bidder will not necessarily receive bid preparation costs unless it can show that it was prejudiced, *E.W. Bliss Co. v. United States*, 33 Fed. Cl. 123 (1995), 77 F.3d 445 (Fed. Cir. 1996).

Once a plaintiff establishes that it was injured, it is entitled to recover the incurred bid or proposal preparation costs that it would have recovered had it been awarded the contract, *AT&T Technologies, Inc. v. United States*, 18 Cl. Ct. 315 (1989). In *AT&T Technologies*, the court held that an offeror could not recover the costs incurred to purchase equipment to meet the requirements of the anticipated contract because those costs were not incurred by the offeror in preparing its proposal. In assessing what costs should be recovered, the court looked to the solicitation, stating at 321:

> [T]he solicitation itself, which incorporates by reference the FAR and CAS, is the very genesis of the implied contract for fair and honest consideration of proposals. The plaintiff asserts that the solicitation should have no bearing on its recovery under the implied-in-fact contract. If the court were to accept this assertion, the question would still remain: What are the terms of the implied-in-fact contract, and from where are they derived? The plaintiff provides no answer. Clearly, the terms of the implied-in-fact contract must be derived from the solicitation. Only by reference to the terms of the solicitation may the government's duty to fairly and honestly deal with offerors be fully defined. A determination of whether this duty was breached

> must necessarily be made with reference to these terms. As the Federal Circuit Court of Appeals stated, the implied contract arising from a solicitation "defines the way the government must deal with bids in the process of selecting a contractor." *Coastal Corporation v. United States*, 713 F.2d 728, 730 (Fed. Cir. 1983).

It is not clear if this reasoning will apply if the claim for bid or proposal preparation costs is filed under 28 U.S.C. § 1491(b)(2).

In *Coflexip & Servs., Inc. v. United States*, 961 F.2d 951 (Fed. Cir. 1992), the court stated that costs incurred as a precondition to final award of a contract may be recovered. In reversing the Claims Court, the court of appeals stated that the court had used the wrong standard in denying recovery on the ground that the solicitation had not required offerors to develop a prototype. The court distinguished between postsubmission costs that are incurred as a result of ongoing negotiations and those incurred in anticipation of contract award, stating at 953:

> [I]n a negotiated procurement, the costs a contractor incurs *pursuant to ongoing negotiations* with the government and in support of a revised proposal, i.e., post-submission costs, can be proposal preparation costs. However, costs which do not support an initial or revised proposal are costs which a contractor incurs in an effort to better position itself to perform any contract it should be awarded. These latter costs, incurred in *anticipation of* contract award, are not proposal preparation costs. The contractor assumes the risk that it will not be awarded the contract, and, accordingly, these contract preparation costs will not be recoverable.

The court distinguished *AT&T Technologies*, stating that none of the plaintiff's costs in that case had been incurred for the purpose of preparing its proposal but, rather, to place it in a position to perform the contract had it received the award. Because the court could not determine whether the prototype was built pursuant to ongoing negotiations or in anticipation of contract award, the court remanded the case to the Claims Court.

b. Protest Costs

Protest costs are not recoverable in the Court of Federal Claims, *Grumman Data Sys. Corp. v. United States*, 28 Fed. Cl. 803 (1993). See also *Coflexip & Servs., Inc. v. United States*, 20 Cl. Ct. 412 (1990) (court is without jurisdiction to award protest costs in the absence of a waiver of sovereign immunity); and *AT&T Technologies, Inc. v. United States*, 18 Cl. Ct. 315 (1989) (damages for breach of the implied contract to fairly and honestly consider offers are limited exclusively to bid and proposal preparation costs). But see *Crux Computer Corp. v. United States*, 24 Cl. Ct. 223 (1991) (court stated in dicta that only profits are excluded as too speculative; protest costs are easily ascertainable and thus can be awarded).

As a general rule, attorneys' fees are not recoverable in court actions, *AT&T Technologies, Inc. v. United States*, 18 Cl. Ct. 315 (1989). However, the EAJA provides that prevailing individuals with a net worth of less than $2 million or prevailing firms with a net worth of less than $7 million and fewer than 500 employees may recover fees and other expenses, including reasonable attorneys' fees, unless the court finds that the position of the Government was substantially justified, 28 U.S.C. § 2412(d)(1)(A). The Court of Federal Claims has authority to award attorneys' fees under this statute, *Essex Electro Eng'rs, Inc. v. United States*, 757 F.2d 247 (Fed. Cir. 1985). In *M.A. Mortenson Co. v. United States*, 996 F.2d 1177 (Fed. Cir. 1993), the court of appeals affirmed the Claims Court judgment awarding attorneys' fees and costs against the United States as a sanction for failure to comply with discovery orders. To avoid an award of fees and costs to the prevailing protester, the Government must prove it was substantially justified in litigating its case, *Cox Constr. Co. v. United States*, 17 Cl. Ct. 29 (1989).

V. DISTRICT COURTS

For a long time, the district courts were not available to protesters. The Supreme Court ruled in 1940 in *Perkins v. Lukens Steel Co.*, 310 U.S. 113 (1940), that no one had a right to a Government contract, and as a result, it was held that disappointed bidders were not entitled to have their protests heard in court. Then, in *Scanwell Labs., Inc. v. Shaffer*, 424 F.2d 859 (D.C. Cir. 1970), the court held that the Administrative Procedure Act (APA), 5 U.S.C. § 702, gave bidders a right to bring an action challenging agency action. This statute states that a "person suffering legal wrong because of agency action, or adversely affected or aggrieved by agency action within the meaning of a relevant statute, is entitled to judicial review thereof." However, because it does not provide for monetary relief, only injunctions or declaratory judgments are available when its provisions are involved.

The ADRA, adding 28 U.S.C. § 1491(b), gave to the district courts the same new protest jurisdiction given the Court of Federal Claims. This permits these courts to give equitable relief as well as limited monetary relief to "interested parties" that filed suit either before or after award.

The district courts also have jurisdiction over suits for monetary relief under 28 U.S.C. § 1346(a) (the "little Tucker Act"), but the amount of relief is limited to $10,000.

A. Procurement Activities Covered

Whether a contract award controversy of a specific Government agency may be litigated in the district courts depends upon whether relief is sought under the APA, 5 U.S.C. § 702; contract jurisdiction, 28 U.S.C. § 1346(a); or "bid protest" jurisdiction, 28 U.S.C. § 1491(1)(b). The APA permits review of "agency action." "Agency" is defined by 5 U.S.C. § 701(b) as follows:

> (1) "agency" means each authority of the Government of the United States, whether or not it is within or subject to review by another agency, but does not include —
>
> (A) the Congress;
>
> (B) the courts of the United States;
>
> (C) the governments of the territories or possessions of the United States;
>
> (D) the government of the District of Columbia;
>
> (E) agencies composed of representatives of the parties or of representatives of organizations of the parties to the disputes determined by them;
>
> (F) courts martial and military commissions;
>
> (G) military authority exercised in the field in time of war or in occupied territory; or
>
> (H) functions conferred by sections 1738, 1739, 1743, and 1744 of title 12; chapter 2 of title 41; subchapter II of chapter 471 of title 49; or

> sections 1884, 1891–1902, and former section 1641(b)(2), of title 50, appendix.

When a district court's jurisdiction to award money damages is invoked under 28 U.S.C. § 1346(a)(2), a somewhat broader definition of "agency" applies. When the new protest jurisdiction is asserted under 28 U.S.C. § 1491(b)(1), it is identical to that applicable to the Court of Federal Claims under 28 U.S.C. § 1491(b)(1), discussed above, except that the Tennessee Valley Authority is not excluded.

B. Who May Protest

1. Person Aggrieved

Suits for equitable relief under the APA, 5 U.S.C. § 702, may be brought by "[a] person suffering legal wrong because of agency action, or adversely affected or aggrieved by agency action within the meaning of a relevant statute." This statute grants the aggrieved person standing to sue the Government. It has been interpreted as requiring the person seeking relief to establish both that it has suffered or will suffer *injury in fact* from the contested action and that its interests are within the *zone of interests* protected by a statute, *Control Data Corp. v. Baldridge*, 655 F.2d 283 (D.C. Cir.), *cert. denied*, 454 U.S. 881 (1981).

a. Injury in Fact

The most common form of injury in Government contract cases is the economic loss that would result from loss of the contract. This test is more easily satisfied than the zone of interests test. Injury in fact is clearly present in the case of a person submitting a bid or a proposal. In *Hayes Int'l Corp. v. McLucas*, 509 F.2d 247 (5th Cir.), *cert. denied*, 423 U.S. 864 (1975), the court stated at 255:

> Unlike the type of delicate question which arises when a plaintiff alleges an injury of a non-economic nature to interests which are widely shared, see, e.g., *Sierra Club v. Morton*, [405 U.S. 727 (1972)]; *United States v. Students Challenging Regulatory Procedures (S.C.R.A.P.)*, 412 U.S. 669, 93 S. Ct. 2405, 37 L. Ed. 2d 254 (1973), the economic injury suffered by a losing bidder in seeking a government procurement contract is manifest. No

> serious doubt exists that Hayes International suffered economic loss by virtue of its inability to obtain the contract at issue in this case.

Sufficient injury is also suffered by a potential competitor that is denied the opportunity to compete, *Abel Converting, Inc. v. United States*, 679 F. Supp. 1133 (D.D.C. 1988); *Aero Corp. v. Department of the Navy*, 540 F. Supp. 180 (D.D.C. 1982), or whose products or services are precluded from consideration by the Government's specifications, *Honeywell Info. Sys., Inc. v. Devine*, Civ. Action 84-2967 (D.D.C. 1984). In *Ray Baillie Trash Hauling, Inc. v. Kleppe*, 477 F.2d 696 (5th Cir. 1973), *cert. denied*, 415 U.S. 914 (1974), the court held that a nonminority small business concern in direct competition for the work in question had standing to challenge the statutory and constitutional basis of the program because it was, in fact, injured by the award of the work to a minority contractor. However, this nonminority concern was found to have no standing to challenge the manner in which the program was being administered (alleging reverse discrimination) because it had not applied for participation in the program and hence could not show that it had been injured in fact by such alleged reverse discrimination. The same result was reached in *Fortec Constructors v. Kleppe*, 350 F. Supp. 171 (D.D.C. 1972). In *Massey Servs., Inc. v. Fletcher*, 348 F. Supp. 171 (N.D. Cal. 1972), it was held that a large company had no standing to challenge the section 8(a) program because it had no injury in fact. However, in *Onan Corp. v. United States*, 476 F. Supp. 428 (D. Minn. 1979), the court held that a large business had standing to challenge the propriety of a small business set-aside absent specific federal definitions and guidelines.

Although the injury need not be substantial, it must be real and not merely theoretical. See *Public Citizen v. Lockheed Aircraft Corp.*, 565 F.2d 708 (D.C. Cir. 1977), holding that machinery dealers did not show that their economic interests were injured through the sale of a Government surplus plant to Lockheed. That case also held that neither machinery dealers nor citizens nor legislators suffered the type of concrete injury from violation of statutes to permit suit in their own name.

In *Kennedy v. Sampson*, 511 F.2d 430 (D.C. Cir. 1974), a senator was found to have standing to challenge a pocket veto of legislation on the grounds that he was asserting a sufficient interest in protecting his affirmative vote on the bill. However, in *Public Citizen v. Sampson*, 379 F. Supp. 662 (D.D.C. 1974), *aff'd*, 515 F.2d 1018 (D.C. Cir. 1975), standing was denied a group of members of Congress challenging the issuance of regulations by the executive branch — apparently on the grounds that they had no real interest in the regulations because they could introduce legislation at any time to override such executive action. See also *Metzenbaum v. Brown*, 448 F. Supp. 538 (D.D.C. 1978), holding that a United States senator had no standing to challenge a DOD decision to award contracts through negotiation rather than sealed bidding.

b. Zone of Interests

In addition to establishing that it has suffered or will suffer an injury in order to have standing, a party must show that the interest sought to be protected is within the zone of interests to be protected or regulated by some statute. In *Control Data Corp. v. Baldridge*, 655 F.2d 283 (D.C. Cir.), *cert. denied*, 454 U.S. 881 (1981), the court rejected the argument that *Scanwell Labs., Inc. v. Shaffer*, 424 F.2d 859 (D.C. Cir. 1970), the seminal case in the use of the APA in a contract award controversy, and *Merriam v. Kunzig*, 476 F.2d 1233 (3d Cir.), *cert. denied*, 414 U.S. 911 (1973), eliminated the need for a statute protecting the plaintiff's interests. These cases maintained that allowing an aggrieved bidder to bring suit vindicated the public's interest in the observance of statutes. Thus, in *Control Data*, a party that satisfied the injury test could not bring suit for violation of a statute acting as a "private attorney general" because the statute sued upon was not intended to protect its interests. See also *Peoples Gas, Light & Coke Co. v. United States Postal Serv.*, 658 F.2d 1182 (7th Cir. 1981), rejecting the argument that the zone of interests test was met because the plaintiff was acting as a private attorney general for the public at large.

Generally, the procurement statutes will be held to protect the interests of disappointed offerors. Even this view, however, has been challenged. See *Cincinnati Elecs. Corp. v. Kleppe*, 509 F.2d 1080 (6th Cir. 1975), where the court stated at 1086:

> We cannot infer a congressional intent to preclude judicial review of agency actions which are alleged to have subverted a clearly stated declaration of policy. In reaching this conclusion, we do not hold that Section 10 of the APA confers standing on every disappointed bidder for government contracts to seek review of agency action. Indeed, in view of the underlying reasons given by Mr. Justice Black for the holding in *Lukens Steel*, we are unable to discover a basis for departure from it. Rather, we view the present case as dealing with an exception recognized in *Lukens Steel*, 310 U.S. at 125, 60 S. Ct. 869, where Congress has by "constitutional legislation" rec-

> ognized the legal right of a bidder for government contracts to benefit from the policy of granting a fair share of such contracts to small business concerns. Standing is conferred by Section 10 only when a relevant statute indicates congressional intent that the person or firm seeking review comes within the zone of interests sought to be regulated or protected. Absent such a congressionally created exception, the general rule of *Perkins v. Lukens Steel, supra*, that a disappointed bidder has no legally enforceable right against the government's award of a procurement contract retains its validity.

The courts have had a more difficult time deciding whether prospective offerors are within the zone of interests of the procurement statutes. In *Control Data Corp. v. Baldridge*, 655 F.2d 283 (D.C. Cir.), *cert. denied*, 454 U.S. 881 (1981), the court held that prospective offerors lacked standing to challenge a determination by the Secretary of Commerce under the Brooks Act establishing mandatory specifications for use in ADPE procurements. The court concluded that these parties were not within the zone of interests: the Brooks Act was intended to foster competition for the benefit of the Government rather than potential ADPE suppliers. The court noted that Control Data was not an actual offeror and, therefore, did not stand in the special relationship existing between an offeror and the Government. The court stated at 293:

> We find, in addition, a more important distinction between this case and those in the bidder area: these circumstances offer the potential for impermissible intrusion upon the government's prerogative to dictate the specifications for the products it wishes to purchase. Characterized by the Supreme Court in *Reeves, Inc. v. Stake*, 447 U.S. 429, 100 S. Ct. 2271, 2278 n.12, 65 L. Ed. 2d 244 (1980) as the "unrestricted power . . . to fix the terms and conditions upon which it [the Government] will make needed purchases," quoting *Perkins v. Lukens Steel Co.*, 310 U.S. 113, 127, 60 S. Ct. 869, 876, 84 L. Ed. 1108 (1940), this prerogative is one traditionally exercised by the legislative and executive branches rather than the judiciary. As this court recently noted in *American Federation of Labor v. Kahn*, 618 F.2d 784, 794 n. 55 (D.C. Cir.) (en banc), *cert. denied*, 443 U.S. 915, 99 S. Ct. 3107, 61 L. Ed. 2d 879 (1970), "nothing has undercut [this] view of the Government's contracting power." Accordingly, we cannot allow appellants to challenge, on the basis of the *Scanwell* rationale, the government specifications embodied in the I/O interface standards absent some demonstration by appellants that they meet the zone standard.

In *Honeywell Info. Sys., Inc. v. Devine*, Civ. Action 84-2967 (D.D.C. 1984), the court applied the *Control Data* rationale to reject a protest by a nonbidder against the award under a solicitation containing these specifications. Compare *Hero, Inc. v. Orr*, 31 Cont. Cases Fed (CCF) ¶ 71,713 (D.D.C. 1983), holding that a nonbidder was within the zone of interests protected by the applicable procurement statute, 10 U.S.C. § 2305(b). Thus, the bidder was permitted to challenge the specifications. The court did not cite *Control Data*. In *Aero Corp. v. Department of the Navy*, 540 F. Supp. 180 (D.D.C. 1982), the court granted relief to a potential offeror that had been denied the opportunity to compete for a contract by the Navy's decision to conduct a sole source procurement. The court found that the potential offeror came within the zone of interests protected by the procurement statutes requiring competition. *Control Data* was distinguished because there was a total denial of the opportunity to compete as opposed to a denial of the opportunity to compete on favorable terms.

In a non-Government contracts case, *Clarke v. Securities Indus. Ass'n*, 479 U.S. 388 (1987), the Court indicated that the zone of interests test was not meant to be applied in a restrictive fashion, stating at 399–400:

> The "zone of interest" test is a guide for deciding whether, in view of Congress' evident intent to make agency action presumptively reviewable, a particular plaintiff should be heard to complain of a particular agency decision. In cases where the plaintiff is not itself the subject of the contested regulatory action, the test denies a right of review if the plaintiff's interests are so marginally related to or inconsistent with the purposes implicit in the statute that it cannot reasonably be assumed that Congress intended to permit the suit. The test is not meant to be especially demanding; in particular, there need be no indication of congressional purpose to benefit the would-be plaintiff.

In *Clarke*, the Court stated that it was not limited to considering the statute under which suit was brought, but rather could consider any provision that helped it to understand Congress's overall purposes in the relevant statute. The court of appeals in *Chem Serv., Inc. v. Environmental Monitoring Sys. Lab.*, 12 F.3d 1256 (3d Cir. 1993), used this logic, holding that a district court erred in ruling that a potential recipient of an agreement lacked standing under the APA to challenge a cooperative research and development agreement (CRADA) awarded to a competing firm pursuant to the Federal Technology Transfer Act (FTTA), 15 U.S.C. § 3710 et seq. The court found that the interests of the potential recipient were within the zone of interests that the relevant statute was designed to protect. In reaching this conclusion, the court stated at 1265–67:

> The district court found that "nowhere in the legislative history or the Act is there any indicia of a Congressional concern for the interests of individual businesses qua competitors. Rather the Act is concerned with improving the nation as a whole so that it may compete globally, not with ensuring the competitive rights of individual domestic companies." There is no doubt, as the district court found, that Congress intended the FTTA to be used to transfer technology from the laboratories and increase the nation's economic competitiveness. Nowhere in the Act did Congress specifically confer a right on private entities to bring suit to challenge a CRADA. But this is not the standard we are required to use in determining whether Chem Service has standing. In a series of cases, the Supreme Court has recognized that Congress does not need to specifically confer a right to bring suit for agency disregard of the law. *See Clarke*, 479 U.S. at 395 n.9. All that we must find is that Congress intended for entities possessing interests such as those of Chem Service to be relied upon to challenge the EPA's disregard for the law. *Id.* at 399.
>
> It is clear from the statute that Congress did not intend that CRADAs be used to circumvent the nation's procurement laws. In our view, the district court did not fully consider the specific language Congress used in defining a CRADA. The FTTA defines a CRADA as an agreement between the laboratory and non-federal party under which each agrees to provide resources "toward the conduct of specific research or development efforts which are consistent with the missions of the laboratory; *except that such term does not include a procurement contract or cooperative agreement as those terms are used in sections 6303, 6304, and 6305 of Title 31.*" 15 U.S.C. § 3710a(d)(1) (emphasis added).
>
> * * *
>
> In this instance, we do not believe that it is a substantial extension to consider the federal procurement laws as relevant in our analysis. The FTTA, in its definition of a CRADA, provides the critical "integral relationship" between the FTTA and the procurement laws that we find sufficient to hold that standing exists. To the extent that a CRADA is used to circumvent the statutory and regulatory requirements of the federal procurement laws, we find that Congress intended potential bidders to such a contract to be within the zone of interests protected under the FTTA.

Subcontractors have been held to have standing in *Lombard Corp. v. Resor*, 321 F. Supp. 687 (D.D.C. 1970) (subcontractor to a contractor operating a Government plant on a cost-reimbursement management-fee basis) and *Optimum Sys., Inc. v. Weinberger*, 21 CCF ¶ 84,000 (D.D.C. 1975) (subcontractor to a contractor administering the Medicare program on a cost-reimbursement basis). In neither of these cases did the court discuss the zone of interests test. See, however, *Contractors Eng'rs Int'l, Inc. v. United States*, 947 F.2d 1298 (5th Cir. 1991), where the court held that a subcontractor lacked standing to challenge a procuring agency's award of a subcontract. The court found that the procuring agency did not have sufficient direct and active control over the selection process for the subcontractor to satisfy the test for disappointed subcontractor standing.

For nonprocurement cases examining the zone of interests test, see *Hoke Co. v. T.V.A.*, 854 F.2d 820 (6th Cir. 1988) (nonunion coal producer did not come within any zone of interests protected or regulated by statute and therefore did not have standing); and *National Fed'n of Fed. Employees v. Cheney*, 883 F.2d 1038 (D.C. Cir. 1989), *cert. denied*, 496 U.S. 936 (1990) (Government employee union's interest in protecting its members' jobs was not within the zone of interests of statutes it alleged were violated by agency decision to contract-out). For nonprocurement cases finding that the plaintiff met the zone of interests test see, *First Nat'l Bank & Trust Co. v. National Credit Union Admin.*, 988 F.2d 1272 (D.C. Cir. 1993) (banks and banking association had standing to bring action to enforce Federal Credit Union Act requirement that membership in federal credit unions be limited to groups having common bond of occupation or association); and *MCI Telecommunications Corp. v. Federal Communications Comm'n*, 917 F.2d 30 (D.C. Cir. 1990) (dominant carrier's competitors fell within zone of interests protected by the Communications Act and thus had standing to challenge carrier's tariff on integrated service packages).

2. Little Tucker Act

The "little Tucker Act," 28 U.S.C. § 1346(a)(2), allows suits "founded either upon the Constitution, or any Act of Congress, or any regulation of an executive department, or upon any express or implied contract with the United States." However, because such suits are limited to claims for $10,000 or less, they are rare. The few cases that have been brought fall within the "implied contract" reasoning of *Heyer Prods. Co. v. United States*, 135 Ct. Cl. 63, 140 F. Supp. 409 (1956), as discussed above. See *Armstrong & Armstrong, Inc. v. United States*, 356 F. Supp. 514 (E.D. Wash. 1973), *aff'd*, 514 F.2d 402 (9th Cir. 1975), permitting recovery under an implied contract obligating the Government to consider bids fairly and honestly.

3. Interested Party

The Administrative Dispute Resolution Act of 1996 (ADRA) provides that bid protest suits may be brought by

> an interested party objecting to a solicitation by a Federal agency for bids or proposals for a proposed contract or to a proposed award or the award of a contract or any alleged violation of statute or regulation in connection with a procurement or a proposed procurement.

The statute does not define "interested party." See the Comptroller General section for a discussion of the term. Any decisions by the Court of Appeals for the Federal Circuit construing the term "interested party" would carry significant weight on the district courts, but would not be binding.

C. Time for Protest

In the early cases under the APA, the district courts made no distinction as to whether the suit had been filed before or after award. However, the 1982 Act giving the Claims Court jurisdiction in this area appeared to limit the jurisdiction of the district courts to postaward appeals (a minority of the circuits had held that the district courts had authority to hear contract award controversies brought before award of the contract). The ADRA has removed this difficulty by repealing the 1982 Act and clearly stating that the district courts and the Court of Federal Claims have concurrent jurisdiction to hear both pre- and postaward protests. A protester has six years to file suit in district court from the date on which its cause of action arose, 28 U.S.C. § 2401(a).

D. Intervenors

Intervenors are permitted under Rule 24 of the Federal Rules of Civil Procedure. As with the Court of Federal Claims, this rule provides for both permissive and mandatory intervention.

E. Procedures

The district courts follow the Federal Rules of Civil Procedure. These rules are similar to the Rules of the Court of Federal Claims. For a discussion of procedures, see Section III.E., above.

F. Standards of Review

Under the APA jurisdiction, district courts are authorized to grant relief upon a finding that there was no rational basis for the agency action, *M. Steinthal & Co. v. Seamans*, 455 F.2d 1289 (D.C. Cir. 1971). In addressing the no rational basis test, the courts that have granted injunctive relief have generally looked to the violation of a procurement regulation as the basis for meeting the test. For example, in *Air Terminal Servs., Inc. v. Department of Transp.*, 515 F.2d 1014 (D.C. Cir. 1975), the court affirmed a holding that it was irrational conduct to defer an award because the offeror's subsidiary had been convicted of criminal activity and was subject to debarment. The district court found that the procurement regulations required a hearing on the debarment issue and such hearing had never been proffered to the offeror. In *Rudolph F. Matzer & Assocs. v. Warner*, 348 F. Supp. 991 (M.D. Fla. 1972), the court noted that a decision is without rational basis if "there is no rational basis in applicable law" or the official has exercised his discretion "in an abusive, unlawful or irrational manner." Basically, the court considered whether any applicable regulation or statute was violated and whether there was substantial evidence in the record on which the official could base his determination. In *Latecoere Int'l, Inc. v. Department of the Navy*, 19 F.3d 1342 (11th Cir. 1994), the court stated at 1356:

> "While contracting officers may not opt to act illegally, they are entitled to exercise discretion upon a broad range of issues confronting them, including 'considerations of price, judgment, skill, ability, capacity, and integrity' in the selection of businesses with whom the government will enter into contracts." *Id.* at 1277 (quoting *Scanwell Laboratories, Inc. v. Shaffer*, [20 CCF ¶ 83,394,] 424 F.2d 859, 869 n.10, 874 (D.C. Cir. 1970)). Accordingly, reviewing courts should be concerned with whether the contracting agency provided a coherent and reasonable explanation of its exercise of discretion. See, e.g., *MCI Telecommunications Corp. v. FCC*, 675 F.2d 408, 413 (D.C. Cir. 1982); *Environmental Defense Fund, Inc. v. Costle*, 657 F.2d 275, 283 (D.C. Cir. 1981). Proof that the award lacked a reasonable basis generally establishes arbitrary and capricious action. *Keco Industries, Inc. v. United States*, [19 CCF ¶ 82,861,] 492 F.2d 1200, 1203–04 (Ct. Cl.

> 1974). Thus, if a reviewing court finds a reasonable basis for the agency's action, the court should stay its hand even though it might, as an original proposition, have reached a different conclusion as to the proper administration and application of the procurement regulations. . . . Only when the court concludes that there has been a clear violation of duty by the procurement officials should it intervene in the procurement process and proceed to a determination of the controversy on the merits.

The same standard of review is enunciated in *Minnesota Mining & Mfg. Co. v. Shultz*, 583 F. Supp. 184 (D.D.C. 1984).

The new protest jurisdiction under the ADRA calls for relief when the court finds a "violation of statute or regulation in connection with a procurement or proposed procurement," 28 U.S.C. § 1491(b)(1). It can be assumed that the district courts will continue to use the no rational basis test in applying this statute.

G. Prejudice

Like the other forums, the court must find that the irrational conduct or violation of the procurement laws or regulations prejudiced the unsuccessful bidder, *Latecoere Int'l, Inc. v. Department of the Navy*, 19 F.3d 1342 (11th Cir. 1994). Prejudice is determined on a case-by-case basis. See *Saratoga Dev. Corp. v. United States*, 777 F. Supp. 29 (D.D.C. 1991) (no prejudice found where agency changed evaluation criteria without informing offerors but protester did not demonstrate that its competitive position would have improved had it been allowed to alter its position); *Strategic Analysis, Inc. v. Department of the Navy*, 939 F. Supp. 18 (D.D.C. 1996) (prejudice found where agency held discussions with only one offeror and did not request BAFOs, because protester could have reduced price had it been permitted to submit a BAFO); *J.G.B. Enters., Inc. v. United States*, 921 F. Supp. 91 (N.D.N.Y. 1996) (no prejudice where agency failed to forward Walsh-Healey question to SBA, because the substance of the question was included in the responsibility determination); *Delta Dental Plan v. Perry*, ___ F. Supp. ___ (N.D. Cal. 1996) (no prejudice where agency awarded contract to lower-priced offeror after determining that protester's technical enhancements were not worth its higher price, because no proof that protester would have reduced its price sufficiently to win competition had it known the enhancements would not be highly valued).

H. Remedies

Unsuccessful bidders and offerors that protest the Government's award of a contract have two potential avenues of recovery in district court. First, unsuccessful bidders and offerors may seek equitable relief; second, unsuccessful bidders and offerors may attempt to recover bid or proposal expenses.

1. Nonmonetary Remedies

Nonmonetary remedies are available under the Administrative Procedure Act (APA). In addition, 28 U.S.C. § 1491(b)(2) permits the recovery of nonmonetary remedies "including declaratory and injunctive relief." Nonmonetary relief is prohibited under the little Tucker Act.

Provisional relief granted by the district courts will be either a TRO or a preliminary injunction ordering a delay in award or the suspension of work under a contract that has already been awarded. Final relief by a district court may take the form of a declaratory judgment or a permanent injunction. These remedies are the same as those available in the Court of Federal Claims.

a. Provisional Relief

Rule 65(b) of the Federal Rules of Civil Procedure gives the court broad discretion to grant a TRO if it appears that irreparable injury will be done to the plaintiff unless the court intervenes. Some courts have conducted a more formal analysis and employed a four-part test that is similar to the test for a preliminary injunction: "(1) a substantial likelihood of success on the merits; (2) irreparable injury in the absence of the requested relief; (3) no other parties will be harmed if the TRO is granted; and (4) the public interest favors entry of a TRO," *Honeywell Fed. Sys., Inc. v. United States*, Civ. A. No. 88-3320 (D.D.C. Nov. 10, 1988), citing *Washington Metro. Area Transit Comm'n v. Holiday Tours*, 559 F.2d 841 (D.C. Cir. 1977).

Notice to the Government is generally required, although the rule permits the granting of a TRO without notice, e.g., *Rental Equip. Co. v. Meridian Eng'g Co.*, 374 F. Supp. 892 (D.V.I. 1974). This rule also allows the granting of a TRO without a hearing, and this sometimes occurs, e.g.,

Pace Co. v. Department of the Army, 344 F. Supp. 787 (W.D. Tenn. 1971). The purpose of a TRO is to maintain the status quo during the time required for a hearing on a preliminary injunction, and Rule 65(b) of the Federal Rules of Civil Procedure provides that a TRO shall expire in a time not to exceed 10 days unless it is extended for good cause shown or with the consent of the other party.

An aggrieved bidder or offeror may also ask the court to issue a preliminary injunction to maintain the status quo during the litigation. Under Rule 65 of the Federal Rules of Civil Procedure, a preliminary injunction may be issued for an indefinite length of time at the discretion of the court, but the other party must be given notice and the right to a hearing prior to the court order. The tests for granting a preliminary injunction are stated in *Virginia Petroleum Jobbers Assocs. v. Federal Power Comm'n*, 259 F.2d 921, 925 (D.C. Cir. 1958), as: (1) substantial probability that the plaintiff will prevail on the merits; (2) irreparable harm to plaintiff unless the injunction is granted; (3) absence of substantial harm to other interested parties; and (4) absence of harm to the public interest. The decision to grant a preliminary injunction involves a balancing of the interests of the parties, *International Controls Corp. v. Vesco*, 490 F.2d 1334 (2d Cir.), *cert. denied*, 417 U.S. 932 (1974). In one award controversy, the aggrieved offeror was required to show that it would suffer irreparable harm absent the injunction and that there was a reasonable probability of success on the merits, *Ainslie Corp. v. Middendorf*, 381 F. Supp. 305 (D. Mass. 1974). In that case, the court ruled that the prospective loss of a contract award was irreparable harm in spite of the fact that there might be a damages remedy for the costs of preparing the bid, citing *General Elec. Co. v. Seamans*, 340 F. Supp. 636 (D.D.C. 1972).

In a number of cases, courts have considered whether preliminary injunctions should be granted to prevent contract performance during the time that the Comptroller General is considering a protest and the agency has refused to stay performance. In *United Power Corp. v. United States Defense Mapping Agency*, 736 F. Supp. 354 (D.D.C. 1990), the district court granted an injunction, finding that the protester would suffer irreparable harm if contract performance continued pending the protest. Although the court acknowledged that, normally, a party seeking a preliminary injunction is required to show that it is likely to succeed on the merits, the court stated that it was unwilling to review the merits of an issue pending before the Comptroller General because a court decision issued prior to the Comptroller's decision would be inappropriate. Compare *Foundation Health Fed.*

Servs. v. United States, 39 Cont. Cas. Fed. (CCH) ¶ 76,681 (D.D.C. 1993), where the court denied a preliminary injunction because the unsuccessful bidder did not show that it would suffer irreparable harm. The bidder alleged that proceeding with contract performance would permit the new contractor to become so entrenched that the Comptroller General would become wary of recommending termination of the contract even if the bidder's protests were valid. The bidder also claimed that it would be damaged by the loss of experienced workers who were being either lured from their present jobs by the new contractor or were seeking other work on the assumption that the new contractor was taking over. The court found these arguments of injury to be speculative and therefore too uncertain to justify injunctive relief. Similarly, in *TEAC Am., Inc. v. Department of the Navy*, 876 F. Supp. 289 (D.D.C. 1995), a disappointed bidder sought a preliminary injunction. The court stated that although design meetings and testing and the manufacture of a limited number of items would proceed before the Comptroller General decision, none of the items would have been delivered by the time of the decision. The court found that the disappointed bidder retained the possibility of having the contract canceled or the bidding process reopened as a result of the imminent Comptroller General decision, making the bidder's injury speculative or, at most, minimal. If the agency agrees not to continue with contract performance, there is little likelihood that a court will issue a preliminary injunction pending the outcome of a GAO protest. See *Diverco, Inc. v. Cheney*, 745 F. Supp. 739 (D.D.C. 1990), where the court held that a bidder was not entitled to a preliminary injunction pending the outcome of a protest before the Comptroller General alleging that the awardee intended to provide foreign spur forgings in violation of the solicitation. In response to the protest, the agency issued a stop-work order and proposed to resolicit the gearshift without the domestic-source requirement. The court found that the bidder failed to show that it would suffer irreparable harm in the absence of an injunction, stating that the bidder could protest to the Comptroller General the award of a contract under either the present solicitation or the proposed amended solicitation. See also *Abel Converting, Inc. v. United States*, 679 F. Supp. 1133 (D.D.C. 1988), where the district court, using the standard four-part test, granted a preliminary injunction barring the agency from following a decision of the Comptroller General.

Rule 65(c) of the Federal Rules of Civil Procedure requires that security be given prior to the issuance of any TRO or preliminary injunction, but it has been held that security may be waived at the discretion of the district court "where there has been no proof of likelihood of harm to the party enjoined," *International Controls Corp. v. Vesco*, 490 F.2d 1334, 1356 (2d

Cir.), *cert. denied*, 417 U.S. 932 (1974). In award controversies, the district courts have exercised broad discretion in the amount of the bond. For example, in *General Elec. Co. v. Seamans*, 340 F. Supp. 636 (D.D.C. 1972), the court issued a preliminary injunction upon the posting of security of $100 although the contract in question was for approximately $35 million; and in *Hayes Int'l Corp. v. Seamans*, 13 G.C. ¶ 414 (D. Ala. 1971), a bond of $20,000 was required when a preliminary injunction was issued prohibiting the Government from taking any action on the disputed, recently awarded contract.

b. Final Relief

The final relief by a district court may take the form of a declaratory judgment or a permanent injunction. The injunction may prohibit the agency from undertaking some activity or it may be mandatory, directing that certain actions be taken. In granting final injunctive relief, the courts are required to balance the interests of the parties and give due consideration to public policy, including national defense, *B.K. Instrument, Inc. v. United States*, 715 F.2d 713 (2d Cir. 1983). In addition, equitable relief will be granted only if the protester has no adequate remedy at law. In several cases, the Government has asserted that a bidder's right to sue for damages, to recover bid preparation costs, constitutes an adequate remedy at law that would bar issuance of an injunction. In *General Elec. Co. v. Seamans*, 340 F. Supp. 636 (D.D.C. 1972) and *Ainslie Corp. v. Middendorf*, 381 F. Supp. 305 (D. Mass. 1974), the court held that the recovery of bidding costs does not adequately compensate a bidder's losses because it does not include lost profits. Some courts have, however, relied on the availability of this damages remedy in support of a refusal to grant the preliminary injunction, e.g., *Cincinnati Elecs. Corp. v. Kleppe*, 509 F.2d 1080 (6th Cir. 1975); *Simpson Elec. Co. v. Seamans*, 317 F. Supp. 684 (D.D.C. 1970). Note that in *M. Steinthal & Co. v. Seamans*, 455 F.2d 1289 (D.C. Cir. 1971), the court specifically rejected the conclusion that the damages available to a disappointed bidder are "automatically an 'adequate' legal remedy as to warrant dismissal" of injunction actions. The granting of a mandatory injunction directing the award of a contract is not considered to be the same as an order directing specific performance, which action is beyond the jurisdiction of district courts in protest cases, *B.K. Instrument, Inc. v. United States*, 715 F.2d 713 (2d Cir. 1983).

2. *Monetary Remedies*

a. *Bid and Proposal Costs*

Under the little Tucker Act, 28 U.S.C. § 1491(a)(1), the district courts may award monetary remedies only up to $10,000. Monetary damages are not permitted under the APA. Because of the low monetary award under Section 1491(a)(1) and the lack of monetary remedy under the APA, protesters traditionally chose another forum over the district court when recovery of proposal costs was a primary objective. However, the district courts may now award monetary damages greater than $10,000 under the ADRA; thus, more cases may be heard by this forum.

b. *Protest Costs*

In district court, protest costs are not available and attorneys' fees are not generally recoverable. However, fees and other expenses, including attorneys' fees, may be recovered under the Equal Access to Justice Act (EAJA). As with the Court of Federal Claims, such fees and other expenses may be recovered, unless the court finds that the position of the Government was substantially justified, 28 U.S.C. § 2412(d)(1)(A). See *Enplanar, Inc. v. Marsh*, 11 F.3d 1284 (5th Cir. 1994), where the court denied recovery under the EAJA because the Government's decision to suspend the 8(a) program pending further guidance was based on an adverse court action and was substantially justified.

I. Federal Tort Claims Act

Unsuccessful offerors and bidders may obtain relief in district court under the Federal Tort Claims Act (FTCA), 28 U.S.C. § 1346(b), but such actions have generally not been successful. In *Scanwell Labs., Inc. v. Thomas*, 521 F.2d 941 (D.C. Cir. 1975), *cert. denied*, 425 U.S. 910 (1976), an unsuccessful bidder bought an FTCA action in district court while its claim for recovery of bid preparation costs was pending in the Court of Claims, alleging in both actions that the Government had violated its procurement regulations by awarding the contract to a nonresponsive bidder. The court first concluded that it need not decide the question of whether the plaintiff would be limited to proceeding under "one theory or the other," but stated that its "solution" would be "merely to prevent a double recovery."

Turning then to the merits of the tort action, the court held that the plaintiff's claim was based upon alleged negligent misrepresentation and was therefore barred by the FTCA exceptions under 28 U.S.C. § 2680(h). The court in *Scanwell* also held that the Government's action in evaluating the bids fell within the discretionary function exception to the Act, 28 U.S.C. § 2680(a), even though it had held in prior litigation that there was "no discretion to ignore the regulations regarding responsiveness of bids," 521 F.2d at 948.

In *Edelman v. Federal Housing Admin.*, 382 F.2d 594 (2d Cir. 1967), the Second Circuit found that a claim by a disappointed bidder alleging that the Government had failed to fairly consider its bid was barred by the misrepresentation exception. In *Covington v. United States*, 303 F. Supp. 1145 (N.D. Miss. 1969), a claim alleging that the Government had fraudulently misrepresented the amount of funds available for the solicited work, causing the bid to be rejected as nonresponsive for exceeding the funding limitation, was held to fall within this same exception. See also *Armstrong & Armstrong, Inc. v. United States*, 356 F. Supp. 514 (E.D. Wash. 1973), *aff'd*, 514 F.2d 402 (9th Cir. 1975), where the court held that a claim by an unsuccessful bidder that the Bureau of Reclamation had acted "negligently, arbitrarily, and capriciously" in denying it award of a contract was a claim based upon interference with contract rights and was thus barred under 28 U.S.C. § 2680(h), which expressly excepts claims based upon interference with contract rights from the waiver of sovereign immunity under 28 U.S.C. § 1336(b). It is evident from these decisions that even where disappointed bidders have succeeded in convincing a court that claims arising out of contract award decisions sound in tort, the breadth of the exceptions to the waiver of immunity set forth in 28 U.S.C. 2680(a)–(m) has effectively precluded that class of plaintiffs from obtaining relief under the FTCA. See, however, *Myers & Myers, Inc. v. United States Postal Serv.*, 527 F.2d 1252 (2d Cir. 1975), where the Second Circuit held that refusal to renew a contract based upon a nonresponsibility determination might be a de facto debarment requiring a hearing and remanded the case to the district court for decision under the FTCA, with instructions that the discretionary function exception to the Act would not apply if it was found that the procurement official had "behave[d] unconstitutionally or outside the scope of . . . authority." In *Cecile Indus., Inc. v. United States*, 793 F.2d 97 (3d Cir. 1986), the court held that the Government's failure to follow debarment regulations did not constitute actionable fraud.

VI. INTERRELATIONSHIP OF FORUMS AND APPEALS

The current system gives protesters more than one available forum to hear protests; thus, protesters are able to select the forum best suited to their needs. This freedom of choice is recognized in the GAO bid protest statute, 31 U.S.C. § 3556, which states that it "does not give the Comptroller General exclusive jurisdiction over protests" and that nothing "shall affect the right of any interested party" to bring suit in the Court of Federal Claims or in a district court. However, care must be taken in selecting the forum because the filing of a protest may be held to be a binding election of that forum by the protester. There are a number of statutory provisions dealing with this issue.

A. Court of Federal Claims and District Courts

28 U.S.C. § 1500 provides that the Court of Federal Claims has no jurisdiction over any claim that is pending against the United States in any other court. Thus, the protester must make an election between the Court of Federal Claims and a district court; and if a protest is first filed in a district court, the Court of Federal Claims is without jurisdiction, *A.C. Seeman, Inc. v. United States*, 5 Cl. Ct. 386 (1984); *UNR Indus., Inc. v. United States*, 962 F.2d 1013 (Fed. Cir. 1992) (Court of Federal Claims dismissed claims by asbestos manufacturers because the manufacturers had filed essentially identical suits against the Government in various district courts, and those suits were still pending at the time the manufacturers filed in the Court of Federal Claims). See also *National Steel & Shipbuilding, Co. v. United States*, 8 Cl. Ct. 274 (1985), where a district court, doubting its jurisdiction over the protest, ordered the protester to bring an action in the Claims Court (now the Court of Federal Claims). The Claims Court dismissed the action because it concluded that the district court did have jurisdiction and that 28 U.S.C. § 1500 precluded the Claims Court from taking jurisdiction of an action still pending in the district court.

Jurisdiction is established at the time suit is filed and not at some later time, such as when a motion to dismiss is considered, *Keene Corp. v. United States*, 508 U.S. 200 (1993). Keene filed two complaints in the Court of Federal Claims. At the time of filing, Keene had similar complaints pending in district court. The district court's complaints were dismissed before the Court of Federal Claims ordered dismissal of the two complaints pursuant to 28 U.S.C. § 1500. Keene argued that jurisdiction should be determined at the time of the district court's ruling on the motion to dismiss, rather than at the time the complaints were filed. The Court found no convincing reason to dispense with the long-standing principle that a court's jurisdiction depends upon the facts at the time of filing.

A later-filed district court action will not divest the Court of Federal Claims of jurisdiction under Section 1500 when both actions involve the same claim, *Hardwick Bros. Co. v. United States*, 72 F.3d 883 (Fed. Cir. 1995). See also *Tecon Eng'rs, Inc. v. United States*, 170 Ct. Cl. 389, 343 F.2d 943 (1965), *cert. denied*, 382 U.S. 976 (1966).

If the protester has filed a protest in either a district court or the Court of Federal Claims and that forum does not, in fact, have jurisdiction over the protest, the action may be transferred to the court having jurisdiction if it is in the interests of justice, 28 U.S.C. § 1631. See *Omega World Travel, Inc. v. United States*, 9 Cl. Ct. 623 (1986), where the Claims Court found that the action was not a claim for preaward relief, as the plaintiff had characterized, and transferred the claim to the United States District Court for the District of Columbia. See also *International Mailing Sys. v. United States*, 6 Cl. Ct. 762 (1984), where the district court transferred a preaward protest to the Claims Court. The advantages of the transfer statute are that the suit is no longer pending in the transferring court, and the filing date in the transferring court is used as the filing date for the action in the court to which the action has been transferred.

B. General Accounting Office

The GAO protest regulations provide that the Comptroller General will dismiss any protest where "the matter involved" is before a court of competent jurisdiction or where the matter has been decided on the merits by a court, unless the court requests a decision by the Comptroller General, 4 C.F.R. § 21.11(b). This rule applies to both initial protests and requests for reconsideration. 4 C.F.R. § 21.11(a) requires a protester to immediately notify the GAO of any court proceedings that involve the subject matter of a protest and to file all relevant documents with the GAO.

A later-filed court action will also divest the Comptroller General of jurisdiction. In *Prince George's Contractors, Inc.*, 64 Comp. Gen. 786 (B-218640.2), 85-2 CPD ¶ 195, the protest was dismissed because the protester filed suit in the district court after filing a protest with the Comptroller General. In addition, the Comptroller General will not consider a request for costs and attorneys' fees for an action that was adjudicated in a court decision, *Pitney Bowes, Inc.*, 64 Comp. Gen. 623 (B-218241), 85-1 CPD ¶ 696. In that case, the protest was first filed at the GAO, but when the agency refused to suspend contract performance, the protester went to court and obtained an injunction. The Comptroller General ruled that its authority to award such remedies was ancillary to its jurisdiction to rule on the protest and that the district court injunction ousted it from jurisdiction in the case.

In determining whether the matter involved is before a court, the Comptroller General has ruled that it will not consider a protest where the court proceeding pertains to a matter that "might have been decided" by the court, even though it was not decided, *Santa Fe Corp.*, 64 Comp. Gen. 429 (B-218234.2), 85-1 CPD ¶ 361, *recons. denied*, 85-1 CPD ¶ 499; *Affiliated Textiles, Inc.*, Comp. Gen. Dec. B-242970.2, 91-2 CPD ¶ 127; *Techniarts Eng'g — Recons.*, Comp. Gen. Dec. B-238520.7, 92-1 CPD ¶ 504. In *Meisel Rohrbau GmbH & Co.*, 67 Comp. Gen. 380 (B-228152.3), 88-1 CPD ¶ 371, the Comptroller General concluded that a pending court case requesting reinstatement of a prior solicitation was relevant to the current protest contesting the cancellation of the replacement solicitation. See also *North Shore Strapping Co.*, Comp. Gen. Dec. B-248003, 92-1 CPD ¶ 532, where the Comptroller General dismissed a protest alleging the use of restrictive specifications because it was within the scope of a pending court suit alleging unfair treatment of the protester by the procuring agency. But if the matter before the court is not relevant to the protest, the Comptroller General will not dismiss the protest. See *Rix Indus., Inc.*, Comp. Gen. Dec. B-241498, 91-1 CPD ¶ 165, where the Comptroller General found that a pending litigation involving an offeror's alleged theft of trade secrets concerning the product to be manufactured under the contract was not relevant to the issue of whether that offeror could perform the pending contract.

The Comptroller General enforces this rule even if a party other than the protester files the court suit. See, for example, *Dawson Constr. Co.*, Comp. Gen. Dec. B-208547.2, 83-1 CPD ¶ 327, where the Comptroller General dismissed a protest of the cancellation of a procurement because a competitor had filed a suit in the Claims Court concerning the same procurement. This can result in a protest being dismissed because another party filed a subsequent suit in a court. *Test Sys. Assocs.* Comp. Gen. Dec. B-256813.6, 96-2 CPD ¶ 161, is a good example of the peculiar nature of these cases. In this case, the agency awarded a contract to TSAI. The unsuccessful offeror filed a protest at the GAO and shortly thereafter in district court. On its own initiative, the agency took corrective action and terminated TSAI's contract. The agency notified TSAI of its intention to award to Dixon. TSAI filed its first protest with GAO (B-256813.3) on the basis of an ambiguous clause and for terminating its contract and rejecting its offer. In the meantime, Dixon choose not to withdraw its civil action in district court. The Comptroller General advised TSAI to intervene in Dixon's court action, but it did not. The Comptroller General then dismissed TSAI's protest, stating that the dispository issue was before the district court. In *Geronimo Serv. Co.*, Comp. Gen. Dec. B-242331.3, 91-1 CPD ¶ 321, the agency made award to Global, and an unsuccessful offeror, Emerald, protested at the GAO and in district court. The court requested an advisory opinion from the GAO. Subsequently, the other unsuccessful offeror, Geronimo, filed a protest at the GAO. The Comptroller General stated that Geronimo chose not to intervene in the district court action and that GAO was therefore precluded from issuing an advisory opinion. Geronimo requested the Comptroller General to reconsider its position, stating that the court could not review the merits of Geronimo's case and that dismissal of the protest would effectively preclude Geronimo from obtaining any relief on its protest. The Comptroller General disagreed and dismissed the protest, stating that "[i]f the court agrees with Emerald's position that the Air Force improperly awarded the contract to Global, the court could direct that award be made to another firm." An action filed in court will also deprive the Government of the ability to obtain reconsideration by the Comptroller General if the protester files a suit in court after winning the protest, *Department of the Navy — Recons.*, Comp. Gen. Dec. B-253129.4, 96-1 CPD ¶ 175.

A court may specifically request that the Comptroller General provide an advisory opinion on the merits of a protest, *TEAC Am. Corp., Inc.*, Comp. Gen. Dec. B-259831, 95-1 CPD ¶ 273; *Test Sys. Assocs.*, Comp. Gen. Dec. B-256813.5, 94-2 CPD ¶ 153; *Florida Professional Review Org., Inc.*, Comp. Gen. Dec. B-253908.2, 94-1 CPD ¶ 17. In such cases, the Comptroller General will rule on the protest even if it would have been untimely if filed with the GAO, *Adelaide Blomfield Management Co.*, Comp. Gen. Dec. B-253128.2, 93-2 CPD ¶ 197. Once the Comptroller General gives a decision to the court, it will not reconsider that decision unless the court requests such action, *Ace Fed. Reporters, Inc.*, Comp. Gen. Dec. B-241309.3, 91-1 CPD ¶ 54.

C. Appeals

Appeals from district court contract award decisions may be taken by either party to the applicable circuit court, in accordance with the usual appeal procedures for civil actions. Court of Federal Claims decisions may also be appealed by either party but must be brought to the Court of Appeals for the Federal Circuit.

There is no specified appeals procedure for Comptroller General decisions because they are not in the nature of judicial decisions. If a protester is dissatisfied with a Comptroller General decision, an action may be brought in either a district court or the Court of Federal Claims, assuming that all requirements for jurisdiction are met, 31 U.S.C. § 3556. Agency reports filed with the Comptroller General are to be considered as part of the agency record by the court hearing the matter. The Court of Federal Claims will not make a de novo review but, rather, will determine whether the Comptroller General's recommendation was rational, *Honeywell, Inc. v. United States*, 870 F.2d 644 (Fed. Cir. 1989). There, the contracting officer held that a competitor's bid was not responsive, but the Comptroller General ruled to the contrary and recommended that the Army award the contract to the competitor. When the Army stated that it would follow that recommendation, Honeywell, Inc., the second low bidder on the contract, filed suit in the Claims Court to enjoin the award. The Claims Court held that the Comptroller General did not have a rational basis for its recommendation and enjoined the award. The Court of Appeals for the Federal Circuit reversed. In its analysis, the federal circuit stated at 647:

> The question before the Claims Court was whether the Army justifiably followed the GAO's recommendation that the bid identified Haz-Tad as the bidder and therefore was responsive to the solicitation. The Claims Court recognized that the controlling inquiry in deciding that question was whether the GAO's decision was a rational one. After paying lip service to that standard, however, the Claims Court impermissibly undertook what can fairly be characterized only as its own independent de novo determination of whether the bid documents identified Haz-Tad as the bidder. Based upon its own weighing and evaluation of those materials, the Claims Court concluded that the GAO had "ignored the blatantly ambiguous wording of the bid, as well as its underlying meaning."

Carothers Constr., Inc. v. United States, 18 Cl. Ct. 745 (1989) further articulated the scope of review at 751, as follows:

> Although Carothers Construction Inc. (Carothers) was not required to file a protest with the GAO, it elected to do so. This election precludes the Claims Court from conducting its own independent de novo determination. *Honeywell*, 870 F.2d at 647.
>
> Even if the court would come to a different conclusion, the procurement agency's decision to follow the Comptroller General's recommendation is proper, unless the Comptroller General's decision itself was irrational. *Honeywell*, 870 F.2d at 648. "If the court finds a reasonable basis for the agency's action, the court should stay its hand even though it might, as an original proposition, have reached a different conclusion as to the proper administration and application of the procurement regulations." *Id.* at 648 (citing *M. Steinthal & Co. v. Seamans*, 147 U.S. App. D.C. 221, 455 F.2d 1289, 1301 (D.C. Cir. 1971).

See also *Logicon, Inc. v. United States*, 22 Cl. Ct. 776 (1991) and *Finley v. United States*, 31 Fed. Cl. 704 (1994), finding the Comptroller General's decision to be reasonable and rational. However, there may be instances where the court will overturn agency actions that were validated by the GAO, *Latecoere Int'l. Inc.*, 19 F.3d 1342 (11th Cir. 1994). Here, the court disagreed with the GAO's finding that the arbitrary rating of a proposal did not prejudice Latecoere. The court stated that the Comptroller General based its conclusion that "Latecoere was not prejudiced by the arbitrary elevation of [the other offeror's] ratings on two assumptions, one of which has no support in the record, and the other of which is flatly contradicted by the record." In *E.W. Bliss Co. v. United States*, 33 Fed. Cl. 123 (1995), the court, while acknowledging that Comptroller General decisions should be given a high degree of deference, stated that "[t]he Court of Claims is not bound by the views of the Comptroller General nor do they operate as a legal or judicial determination of the rights of the parties," quoting *Burroughs Corp. v. United States*, 223 Ct. Cl. 53, 63, 617 F.2d 590, 597 (1980) (citing *Font v. United States*, 219 Ct. Cl. 335, 593 F.2d 388 (1979)). In distinguishing *Honeywell*, the *Bliss* court stated that the federal circuit decision focused on the fact that the Claims Court did not give deference to either the Comptroller General or the contracting officer's decision but rather engaged in an independent de novo analysis. Thus, *Honeywell* should not be read as conferring on the Comptroller General a degree of deference beyond that set forth in *Burroughs*. The court stated at 135:

> The weight of precedent instructs that, although the review is not de novo and the GAO's decision is accorded deference, the court is to answer the question whether the agency's procurement decision or the GAO's decision

> on the protest was reasonable based on the record before the contracting officer or the GAO.

Although the court went to great lengths in analyzing the scope of its review, it in fact agreed with the Comptroller General's decision. Recently, in *Firth Constr. Co. v. United States*, 36 Fed. Cl. 268 (1996), a competitor was the apparent low bidder but had failed to submit a completed SF 1442. After bid opening, the competitor faxed a completed SF 1442 to the agency and was awarded the contract. Following a protest, the Office of Counsel of the agency advised the contracting division that the award was improper because the bid was nonresponsive due to the lack of an original signature on the SF 1442. Given this advice, the contracting officer canceled the award. The competitor protested to the GAO and the Comptroller General sustained the protest. The agency announced its intention to follow the Comptroller General's recommendation and award the contract to the competitor, and Firth Construction filed suit in the Court of Federal Claims. In defining its scope of review, the court reasoned in a circular fashion at 278:

> The precise subject of review in this case is, of course, not the GAO decision. What this court is reviewing is the agency's announced intention to award the contract to Dillard. But whether that determination is arbitrary, capricious, or not in accordance with law, must be considered in light of the GAO recommendation. To the extent that the agency chooses to follow the advice of the GAO, the courts should only intervene if the advice the agency receives is "irrational." *Honeywell Inc. v. United States* [35 CCF ¶ 75,641] 870 F.2d 644, 648 (Fed. Cir. 1989) (stating "a procurement agency's decision to follow the [GAO] recommendation . . . was proper unless the Comptroller General's decision itself was irrational"). Thus, if the GAO's advice is rational, it is not arbitrary or capricious to follow it. This analysis has been applied to the GAO's advice on matters of law, on the theory that the GAO's interpretation of procurement regulations is entitled to deference. See *Shoals Am. Indus., Inc. v. United States* [35 CCF ¶ 75,691], 877 F.2d 883, 888 (11th Cir. 1989).

The court determined that the bid was nonresponsive because it lacked an original signature. Thus, the court held that the Comptroller General's decision was irrational and that the agency would be arbitrary and capricious to follow it.

Like the Court of Federal Claims, a district court will not make a de novo review but rather is limited to the facts contained in the administrative record. If an agency follows a Comptroller General recommendation, the court will look to the rationality of the Comptroller General decision. The district courts generally treat the Comptroller General's decision "as an expert opinion, which [the court] should prudently consider but to which [it] has no obligation to defer," *Delta Data Sys. Corp. v. Webster*, 240 U.S. App. D.C. 182, 744 F.2d 197 (D.D.C. 1984). There is a difference in opinion in the courts as to whether a Comptroller General's decision should be given difference. For instance, in *Qualmed, Inc. v. Office of Civilian Health & Med. Program of the Armed Servs.*, 934 F. Supp. 1227 (D. Col. 1996), Qualmed sought summary judgment in its favor on the grounds that the agency's decision to follow the Comptroller General's recommendation was arbitrary and capricious. The court stated that such a finding would require a showing that the Comptroller General's recommendation itself was irrational. The court held that the Comptroller General's decision was not irrational; therefore, it was not arbitrary and capricious for the agency to follow the Comptroller General's recommendation. The court premised its holding by stating at 1237:

> [T]he GAO's decision is entitled to great deference because it is the decision of a tribunal with longstanding expertise. *Halifax*, 848 F. Supp. at 243. Thus, although the agency must perform an independent analysis of the recommendation, Congress contemplated and intended that procurement agencies normally would follow the Comptroller General's recommendation. Congress viewed an agency's failure to do so as sufficiently unusual as to require the agency to report such noncompliance to the Comptroller General and to require the latter to inform Congress of any instances of noncompliance. In these circumstances, a procurement agency's decision to follow the Comptroller General's recommendation, even though that recommendation differed from the contracting officer's initial decision, was proper unless the Comptroller General's decision itself was irrational.

Even in instances where the court gives great deference to the Comptroller General, it may disagree with the Comptroller General's recommendation, *Mark Dunning Indus., Inc. v. Perry*, 890 F. Supp. 1504 (D. Ala. 1995). In this case, while acknowledging that the Comptroller General should be given deference, the court stated at 1511:

> [W]hile the courts should allow administrative agencies to function with minimum interference by the judiciary, "uncritical deference" to the GAO's decision is inappropriate. *Schoals Am. Indus., Inc.*, 877 F.2d at 899. "[T]here certainly may be instances where the District Court will find procurement illegality that the GAO failed to recognize, or at any event failed

> to correct." *M. Steinthal & Co.*, 455 F.2d at 1305 (quoted in *Latecoere Int'l, Inc. v. United States Dep't of the Navy*, 19 F.3d 1342, 1356 (11th Cir. 1994)). Hence, "[t]he deference owed to an expert tribunal cannot be allowed to slip into a judicial inertia which results in the unauthorized assumption by an agency of major policy decisions properly made by Congress." *American Ship Building Co. v. National Labor Relations Board*, 380 U.S. 300, 318, 85 S. Ct. 955, 967, 13 L.Ed.2d 855 (1965).

Mark Dunning Industries challenged the Navy's termination of its refuse contract and award to another contractor and filed a motion for preliminary injunction in district court. Mark Dunning had previously filed a protest with the GAO which the Comptroller General denied. The court was concerned with whether the terms of the solicitation were so ambiguous as to impede full and open competition, *Mark Dunning Indus., Inc. v. Perry*, 877 F. Supp. 1541 (D. Ala. 1995). The court invited the Comptroller General to address the court's concerns. In a subsequent opinion, 890 F. Supp. 1504 (D. Ala. 1995), the court found the Comptroller General's response to be specious and unpersuasive and granted the preliminary injunction.

A seemingly contrary view is found in *Delta Dental Plan v. Perry*, ___ F. Supp. ___ (N.D. Cal. 1996). Although the court found in favor of the agency, it did not reach its decision by deferring to the Comptroller General's decision. The court reasoned at ___, as follows:

> Although GAO decisions are not technically binding, agencies are strongly encouraged to follow GAO recommendations. *IMS Services, Inc. v. United States*, 33 Fed. Cl. 167, 183-84 (1995) (quoting *Honeywell, Inc. v. United States*, 870 F.2d 644, 648 (Fed. Cir. 1989)). Unless a GAO decision is "irrational," agency reliance upon it is not arbitrary and capricious. *Id.*
>
> This court is aware that there is a difference of opinion regarding the degree of deference or the amount of weight to be given to a GAO decision in an action filed pursuant to the Administrative Procedures Act. Compare *Orbas & Associates*, 863 F. Supp. at 1190 (court "must" defer to GAO decision which is not arbitrary or capricious) with *Delta Data Systems Corp. v. Webster*, 240 U.S. App. D.C. 182, 744 F.2d 197, 201 (D.C. Cir. 1984). This Court is not required to resolve the differing views but will heed the admonition of the District of Columbia Circuit:
>
>> we regard the assessment of the GAO as an expert opinion, which we should prudently consider but to which we have no obligation to defer. We reject [the] contention that every decision of the GAO should be adopted and enforced by the court unless that decision lacks a rational

> basis. On the contrary, it is "the court [that has] the last word and [it] should not shrink from exercising its power."

See also *Strategic Analysis, Inc. v. Department of the Navy*, 939 F. Supp. 18 (D.D.C. 1996), where the protester brought suit in district court as a disappointed bidder following the Comptroller General's denial of its protest. The court stated that the Comptroller General's findings should be treated as an expert opinion but that the court was not required to defer to the Comptroller's recommendation. The court reached an opinion contrary to the Comptroller General's, finding that the Navy violated procurement regulations by conducting discussions with only one of the two offerors in the competitive range.

ACRONYMS AND ABBREVIATIONS

ACO	Administrative Contracting Officer
ADA	Americans with Disabilities Act of 1990
Admin.	Administration
ADPE	Automatic data processing equipment
ADR	Alternative Dispute Resolution
ADRA	Administrative Dispute Resolution Act
A-E	Architect-engineer
AFARS	Army FAR Supplement
AFFARS	Air Force FAR Supplement
aff'd	Affirmed
AFMC	Air Force Materiel Command
AIA	Aerospace Industry Association
AMC	Army Materiel Command
AMS	Administration Management System
APA	Administrative Procedure Act
APM	Acquisition program manager
ARM	Action Request Memorandum
ASPM	Armed Services Pricing Manual
ASPR	Armed Services Procurement Regulation
Ass'n	Association
Assoc.(s)	Associate(s)
BAA	Broad agency announcement
BAFO	Best and final offer
BCA	Board of Contract Appeals Reports (CCH)
BPA	Blanket purchase agreement
CACO	Corporate administrative contracting officer
CASB	Cost Accounting Standards Board
CBD	Commerce Business Daily
CCF	Contract Cases Federal
CCH	Commerce Clearing House (Publisher)
CCR	Central Contractor Registration
CDA	Contract Disputes Act
Cert. denied	Certiorari denied
CFR	Code of Federal Regulations
CICA	Competition in Contracting Act
CID	Commercial item description
Civ. No.	Civil Number (docket number)
Cl. Ct.	U.S. Claims Court
C.O.	Contracting Officer
Co.	Company

COC	Certificate of competency
COFC	U.S.Court of Federal Claims
Comm'n	Commission
Comp. Gen.	Comptroller General (GAO)
Cong. Rec.	Congressional Record
Constr.	Construction
COR	Contracting Officer Representative
Corp.	Corporation
COTR	Contracting Officer Technical Representative
CPAF	Cost-plus-award-fee
CPARS	Contractor performance assessment reporting system
CPD	Comptroller procurement decisions
CPFF	Cost-plus-fixed-fee
CPIF	Cost-plus-incentive-fee
CPM	Critical Path Method
CPPC	Cost-plus-a-percentage-of-cost
CRADA	Cooperative research and development agreement
Ct. Cl.	Court of Claims
Ctr.	Center
D&F	Determination and findings
DAR	Defense Acquisition Regulation
DCAA	Defense Contract Audit Agency
DCAM	Defense Contract Audit Manual
D.C. Cir.	U.S. Court of Appeals for the District of Columbia Circuit
DEA	Drug Enforcement Administration
DEAR	Department of Energy Acquisition Regulation
Dev.	Development
DFARS	Department of Defense FAR Supplement
DFWA	Drug-Free Workplace Act of 1988
DIAR	Department of Interior Regulation
Div.	Division
DLAR	Defense Logistics Agency Regulation
DOD	Department of Defense
DODIG	Department of Defense Inspector General
DOE	Department of Energy
DOI	Department of Interior
DOJ	Department of Justice
DOL	Department of Labor
DOT	Department of Transportation
DRFP	Draft requests for proposals
EAJA	Equal Access to Justice Act
EBB	Electronic bulletin board
ECP	Engineering Change Proposal
EDI	Electronic data interchange
Educ.	Education

Elec.	Electric; electronic
Eng'g	Engineering
Enters.	Enterprises
Envtl.	Environmental
EPA	Environmental Protection Agency
Equip.	Equipment
ESLH	Estimated standard labor hours
Exec. Order	Executive Order
F.2d	Federal Reporter, 2d Series
F.3d	Federal Reporter, 3d Series
FAA	Federal Aviation Administration
FAC	Federal Acquisition Circular
FACNET	Federal Acquisition Computer Network
FAR	Federal Acquisition Regulation
FASA	Federal Acquisition on Streamlining Act of 1994
FECAI	Federal Electronic Commerce Acquisition Registration Instructions
Fed. Cir.	U.S. Court of Appeals for the Federal Circuit
Fed. CL.	Court of Federal Claims
Fed'n	Federation
Fed. Reg.	Federal Register
FERC	Federal Energy Regulatory Commission
FIRMR	Federal Information Resources Management Regulation
FMC	Federal Management Circular
FMS	Foreign military sales
FOIA	Freedom of Information Act
Found.	Foundation
FPASA	Federal Property and Administrative Services Act
FPI	Federal Prison Industries
	Fixed-price incentive
FPMR	Federal Property Management Regulation
FPR	Federal Procurement Regulations
FSS	Federal Supply Service
F. Supp.	Federal Supplement (West Reporter)
FTCA	Federal Tort Claims Act
FTE	Full-time equivalent
FTTA	Federal Technology Transfer Act
G&A	General and administrative
GAO	U.S. General Accounting Office
Gov't	Government
GPO	U.S. Government Printing Office
GSA	General Services Administration
GSAR	General Services Administration Acquisition Regulation

GSBCA	General Services Administration Board of Contract Appeals
GTR	Government technical representative
HCA	Head of Contracting Activity
H.R.	House Report
HUD	Housing and Urban Development
IBCA	Interior Board of Contract Appeals
IDIQ	Indefinite-delivery, indefinity-quantity
IFB	Invitation for bids
Inc.	Incorporated
Indus.	Industry
Info.	Information
Int'l	International
Inv.	Investment
IPT	Integrated product team
IR&D	Independent Research and Development
J&A	Justification and approval
J.V.	Joint Venture
Lab.(s)	Laboratory(ies)
LLC	Life cycle costing
Ltd.	Limited
Mach.	Machinery
MAS	Multiple award schedule
MDE	Major defense equipment
Mfg.	Manufacturing
MIL-STD	Military Standard
Mktg.	Marketing
MOU	Memorandum of Understanding
NAFTA	North American Free Trade Agreement Act
NAIS	NASA Acquisition Internet Service
NAPs	Navy Acquisition Procurement
NASA	National Aeronautics and Space Administration
NDI	Nondevelopmental item
NFS	NASA FAR Supplement
NIST	National Institute of Standards and Technology
OF	Optional Form
OFCCP	Office of Federal Contract Compliance Programs
OFPP	Office of Federal Procurement Policy
OFPPA	Office of Federal Procurement Policy Act
OGD	Office of Grants Debarment
OHA	Office of Hearings and Appeals
OMB	Office of Management and Budget
PCO	Procuring contracting officer
P.L.	Public Law
PRDA	Program Research and Development Announcements

PRM	Price negotiation memorandum
Prods.	Products
Pub. Cont. L.J.	Public Contract Law Journal
QVL	Qualified vendor lists
R&D	Research and development
RCFC	Rules of the United States Court of Federal Claims
Recons. denied	Reconsideration denied
Reh'g denied	Rehearing denied
Rev.	Revised
Rev'd	Reversed
RFI	Requests for information
RFO	Request for offers
RFP	Request for proposals
RFQ	Request for quotations
RFTP	Request for technical proposals
ROA	Research opportunity announcement
SBA	Small Business Administration
SBD	Small Disadvantaged Business
SBIR	Small Business Innovation Research
S. Ct.	Supreme Court
SDD	Suspension and Debarment Division
Serv.(s)	Service(s)
SF	Standard Form
SIR	Screening information request
S. Rep.	Senate Report
SSO	Source selection official
Sys.	System
TINA	Truth in Negotiations Act
TRO	Temporary restraining order
TVA	Tennessee Valley Authority
U.C.C.	Uniform Commercial Code
U.C.F.	Uniform Contract Format
Univ.	University
Unpub.	Unpublished
U.S.C.	United States Code
VAN	Value added network

COURT CASES

BCA DECISIONS

STATUTES

U.S. Code

Executive Orders

Public Laws

REGULATIONS

COMPTROLLER GENERAL DECISIONS

B-NUMBERS

COMPTROLLER GENERAL PROCUREMENT DECISIONS

SUBJECT INDEX

B

D

F

H

I

W